8. Include an SASE that is large enough and contains sufficient postage to return all items

9. Make sure your package is easy to open

10. Use soft plastic cassette cases which are better than hard plastic boxes that tear envelopes and are easily crushed.

11. Address your package to the proper contact person

12. Do not send your package via certified or registered mail unless requested

13. Keep a record of the date, the song titles, and the companies to which you submit

1988 Songwriter's Market

Distributed in Canada by Prentice-Hall of
Canada Ltd., 1870 Birchmount Road,
Scarborough, Ontario M1P 2J7.

Managing Editor, Market Books Department:
Constance J. Achabal

Songwriter's Market. Copyright © 1987.
Writer's Digest Books. Published by
F&W Publications, 1507 Dana Avenue,
Cincinnati, Ohio 45207. Printed and bound
in the United States of America. All rights
reserved. No part of this book may be
reproduced in any manner whatsoever
without written permission from the
publisher, except by reviewers who may
quote brief passages to be printed
in a magazine or newspaper.

International Standard Serial Number
0161-5971
International Standard Book Number
0-89879-276-2

1988
Songwriter's Market

Where to Sell
Your Songs

Edited by
Julie Wesling Whaley

Assisted by
Cynthia Kephart

Writer's Digest Books
Cincinnati, Ohio

Contents

Services & Opportunities

Appendix

1988 Songwriter's Market

From the Editor

The music industry is exciting and glamorous from the outside. We read about big name acts touring the world in their private jets, performing at the best clubs, staying at the nicest hotels, fighting off fans and admirers at every turn. We see the beautiful clothes performers and writers wear as they step out of stretch limousines at the Grammy Awards show. We all hear stories about unbelievably rich songwriters and artists who could retire at a young age, live on a yacht and eat caviar if they chose to do so.

Because of all that glitter, thousands, if not millions, of people are drawn to the music scene and the competition is pretty fierce. But you *know* the entire music industry in its day-by-day routine is not the rich, trouble-free world spotlighted in the media. There are many more people who don't make millions than those who do, and many work very hard to make any profit at all. Most recording artists don't make a fortune on their first album—some don't even break even. Many songwriters, even famous hit writers, have slumps and dry spells; write songs they're not so happy with; and sometimes have a hard time getting someone in the industry to believe in their song.

That shouldn't sound discouraging—it should just be a reminder that you're not alone in your struggles. But at the same time, it should make you realize that you're competing with the very best in the field. Every songwriter and every writer/artist is out there right now, writing songs, making contacts, shopping demos, learning about the industry and doing what it takes to get ahead. So should you be. The bottom line is that the music business is a business. To succeed as a songwriter or writer/artist, the best thing you can do is learn as much about the business as you can. Reading and using *Songwriter's Market* is a crucial step in that learning process. The theme of this edition is Smart Songwriting. Smart songwriters read all they can about the music business, and familiarize themselves with who does what and how things work.

This is *Songwriter's Market*'s tenth anniversary. For ten consecutive years we've been bringing valuable music industry contacts right into your home. We've continually tried to contribute to your music business education, keeping you up-to-date with important trends, and informing you of how the industry functions. You undoubtedly have numerous finished songs or songs-in-progress. If you believe you've written (and re-written and perfected) the best songs you can, songs that can compete in the marketplace, you now have to get them out in public—showcase them and market them—and that's what this book is all about. We continually explore new market possibilities, and this year we've added a section of sheet music publishers to help you further exploit your songs, compositions, and arrangements. Print specialist Ronny Schiff introduces the new section by describing the specialized needs of print publishers, and how you can best approach them with your music projects. This year also features a greatly expanded fine arts section (more than double the number of listings in the section introduced last year), providing contacts for composers wishing to market their classical pieces. All together, there are more than 650 new listings in this edition!

Many songwriters have heard uncomplimentary things about the music industry, and they don't know what to believe or who to trust. So Doug Thiele, Los Angeles songwriter/producer and publisher, has contributed an article on "songsharks," the bad guys of the industry, and how to recognize and avoid them. Writer/producer J. Edward Frawley has written an article on producing demos, emphasizing the songwriter as producer and "boss" of the recording session. It's filled with how-to information, but it also explains when you might want to work with professional arrangers, engineers, musicians and singers, and what they can do for you.

In our Business of Songwriting appendix, Jay Collins, President of the Nashville Association of Musicians, contributes an article on copyright, explaining the need for protecting your material, defining confusing terminology and jargon, and exploring the alternatives and consequences. Bob Leone, National Project Director for The Songwriters Guild of America, has updated his article on contracts, providing advice to help you evaluate any contract offered to you and make smart business deals.

And we've increased the number of Close-ups this year, featuring many tops writers and music industry professionals. Composer Henry Mancini; performer Anne Murray; songwriters Al Kasha and Joel Hirschhorn, Fred Koller, and George Green; Producer Tony Camillo; record industry execs Margie Hunt (CBS) and Tony Prendatt (Polygram); and many others share their knowledge and experience.

There's a lot more to successful songwriting than writing songs. It's up to each songwriter, composer and lyricist to take charge of his own career. If you research and learn about the music industry and its "rules," you're way ahead in terms of smart songwriting. We've tried to provide information to help you toward that end. The next step is up to you!

Julie Wesling Whaley

Using Your Songwriter's Market

Before studying the listings and making your marketing plans, read these suggestions for the most productive use of all the features in *Songwriter's Market*. Especially note the explanations of the information given in the sample listing.

Read the section introductions *first*. Each gives a brief overview of the market area and can help you decide if it's a facet of the music industry appropriate for your style of writing and your personal goals. Keep in mind that the information you are reading came directly from representatives of the companies listed. It is reported exactly as they gave it to us. The Glossary in the back of this book will explain unfamiliar terms you might encounter while reading the listings.

The following information is featured in the listings:

new market	**(1)** *THE CAVE**, Music Publishing and Production, 3121 N.W. 14th St., Gainesville FL 32605. (904)377-0336. **(2)** President: Thomas G. Hubbell.
contact person	Marketing Director: Deborah K. Hubbell. **(3)** Music publisher, record company (Unusual Record Co.) and record producer (The Cave). **(4)** BMI.
size of market	**(5)** Estab. 1986. **(6)** Publishes 0-5 songs/year; publishes 0-5 new songwriters/year. Works with composers and lyricists; teams collaborators.
payment	**(7)** Pays standard royalty.
	Affiliate: (8) Unusual Music Publishing (ASCAP).
submission instructions	**How to Contact: (9)** Prefers cassette or 15 ips reel-to-reel **(10)** (or VHS videocassette) with 1-6 songs and lyric sheet. **(11)** "All material sent with SASE must have correct postage for return. All other material will be filed." **(12)** SASE. **(13)** Reports in 6 weeks.
music needs	**Music: (14)** Mostly rock/pop/top 40, experimental/new music and easy listening; also R&B, folk/ballads and MOR. **(15)** Published "Talk Too
songs recently published	Fast" (by T. Hubbell), recorded by Pure Raisins (rock); "The Date," written and recorded by Cathy Hubbell (ballad); and "Neutral Zone" written and recorded by John Stephens (rock) all on Unusual Records.
comments	**Tips: (16)** "Send exceptional material on a good demo. I am more interested in songs that are unique and marketable, as opposed to sound alikes."

(1) An asterisk appears before the names of companies new to this edition. **(2)** The name of the contact person(s) is supplied by the company listed. Address all submissions to this person unless otherwise indicated in the submission instructions. If no name is given, it's probably best to make contact by mail or phone, asking who the appropriate contact person is, before submitting a tape. **(3)** Each listing provides a description of the company's function(s). The sample listing describes a multi-faceted company and gives the names of the record label and production branches. **(4)** If a company indicated which performing rights societies they are affiliated with, we included this information. ASCAP, BMI and SESAC are the major US societies. PRO CAN, PRS and SACEM are examples of foreign societies. **(5)** The year the company was founded will be given only for companies established in 1986 and after. The risk is sometimes greater when dealing with new companies. So far as we know, all are reputable but some are unable to compete with larger, older companies. Many do survive, however, and become very successful. And most all new companies are wide open to material from new songwriters. **(6)** Figures given (e.g., number of songs published, released or produced per year or number of new songwriters published per year) are approximations to help you determine a market's activity and its openness to material from new songwriters. Some markets list services offered to writers. **(7)** Most companies indicate their payment policy. "Standard" royalty means music publishers split royalties received with the songwriter 50-50. Some markets (advertising agencies, audiovisual firms) pay by the job or per hour rather than by royalty. Some markets (play producers, fine arts) are nonprofit and do not pay at all but offer valuable exposure for songs. The listings in Record Producers and Managers and Booking Agents indicate that they charge a legitimate fee (negotiated in advance) for their services rendered rather than pay money to songwriters. They are still considered "markets" because they are in a position to shop songs to artists and companies for you, and they may be seeking writers/artists to represent. **(8)** If a publisher has affiliated companies, they are listed in this special subhead. The affiliates are usually members of a different performing rights society than the main company listed (in the sample, the main company is a member of BMI, the affiliate is ASCAP) so they can work with writers who are members of either organization. **(9)** The types of music; number of songs you may include in the submission, and the way you should submit your songs are stated in each listing. Failure to follow these instructions could result in your submission being refused or returned. Your close attention to the exact specifications of a particular listing will help assure your success. "Query" means to contact the company by phone or mail *before* submitting anything. "Does not accept unsolicited material" means you should never submit anything before you request and receive permission to submit. **(10)** Some markets may indicate in their listings that you may send for evaluation a video of your act in performance or a group doing your songs in lieu of a standard cassette or reel-to-reel demo. Most have indicated that a videocassette is not required, but told us the format (Beta or VHS) of their VCR should a songwriter/artist want to send one. If no format is stated it is generally safe to assume that either format is acceptable, but it is always a good idea to check with the company *first*. Always be sure to include a lyric and/or lead sheet with your video submission as you would with any other. It's always a good idea to write (or call) first for appropriate video format and television system before sending a videocassette as part of an international submission. Be aware that the television system many foreign countries utilize is different from that of the United States. For example, a Beta or VHS format tape recorded using the US system (called NTSC) will not playback on a standard English VCR (using the PAL system) even if the recorder formats are identical. It is possible to transfer a video demo from one system to another but the expense in both time and money may outweigh its usefulness as opposed to a standard audio demo. Systems for some countries include: NTSC—United States, Canada, and Japan; PAL—United Kingdom (including England), Australia, and West Germany; and SECAM—France. **(11)** Many listings give additional submission instructions. Following these specific requests will increase the chances for your demo to be listened to quickly and favorably. **(12)** All mail should contain a stamped, self-addressed envelope (SASE); submissions to listings in foreign countries should include a self-addressed envelope (SAE) and International Reply Coupons (IRC) available at most major post offices. Some companies will not even answer a query letter unless you include a reply card or an SASE for their response. Those companies with "SASE" printed in their listing have indicated that they will return submissions if a large enough SASE with sufficient postage is included. **(13)** The length of time markets say that they need to report back to songwriters on submissions is approximate. Music professionals go through periods of unbelievably heavy loads of submissions, and sometimes fall behind. Allow extra time for international submissions. If a market doesn't respond within several weeks after the reporting time given in its listing, don't despair. As long as your submission is in the possession of a market there is a chance someone may eventually find the time to review it a second, or even a third time. Every listening your demo gets represents one more chance for it to be picked up. That opportunity ends when your demo is sent back to you. Not receiving your submission back right away doesn't necessarily mean you've been ripped off. If after a reasonable length of time you still haven't received word on your submission, follow up with a *friendly* letter giving detailed information about your submission. Include your name, address and phone number; titles of songs submitted; type of demo submitted; and the date of submission. **(14)** The companies listed indicate which types of music they are most interested in. This is very important—do not bother to send inappropriate material. Some of the terminology is standard (for instance, R&B = rhythm and blues) but some of the descriptions are worded exactly the way the company reported it to us. **(15)** The published works, releases, and productions given within the Music subhead of each listing represent examples of the companies' accomplishments and not a complete list. **(16)** Many listings share additional information to help you further evaluate their needs and goals. Don't overlook this unique information!

Some very important notes:

- *Although every listing in* Songwriter's Market *is updated, verified or researched prior to publication, some changes are bound to occur between publication and the time you contact any listing.*
- *Listings are based on editorial interviews and questionnaires. They are* not *advertisements,* nor *are markets reported here necessarily endorsed by the editor.*
- *Looking for a particular market? Check the Index. If you don't find it there, it is because 1) It's not interested in receiving material at this time. 2) It's no longer in business or has merged with another company. 3) It charges (counter to our criteria for inclusion) for services a songwriter should receive free. 4) It has failed to verify or update its listing annually. 5) It has requested that it not be listed. 6) We have received reports from songwriters about unresolved problems they've had with the company.*
- *A word of warning. Don't pay to have your song published and/or recorded, or to have your lyrics—or a poem—set to music. Read the articles "Swimming Away from Songsharks," by Doug Thiele (in the front of this edition) and "Contracts," by Bob Leone (located in the Business Appendix) to learn how to recognize and protect yourself from the songshark.*
- Songwriter's Market *reserves the right to exclude any listing which does not meet its requirements.*

Swimming Away from Songsharks

by Doug Thiele

Many people have a less-than-attractive opinion of the music business, an opinion they're happy to offer whenever the topic comes up. You've probably heard their uninformed and, in most cases, unsolicited comments before: The music business is sleazy . . . everybody wants his piece of the songwriter pie whether he deserves it or not . . . the only way to succeed as a songwriter is to allow yourself to be ripped off. To more than a few, the whole process of successful songwriting seems like an inherently bogus operation.

This opinion is clearly unjustified. The music industry, in the vast majority of cases, operates in a legitimate manner.

Reputation

Then where do these stories of an industry spiraling into an unethical gutter come from? I think a combination of factors is at work. First of all, the entertainment world has always had a slightly unsavory image: being an actor or musician is akin to being a reformed criminal. The very practice of surviving by one's creative wits never seems like "honest work" to the general population, and so the rewards of songwriting appear to fall in the category of relatively ill-gotten gains. There's the old quote to a songwriter-suitor by the girl's disapproving father: "So, you're a songwriter; what do you do for a *living*?"

Secondly, we've all heard stories about the rock 'n' roll era of the fifties in which artists and songwriters were ripped off with regularity by disreputable personal managers, producers and publishers. The payola scandals of the early sixties further degraded the image of the business.

Lastly, we all hear songs on the radio which we dislike, and it's a natural assumption on our parts that those songs get on the radio through some process other than public approval. Certainly, some songs have bulletted up the charts through payola practices or political circumstances, and some beginning songwriters assume that such behind-the-scenes manipulation of songs is the rule rather than the exception. Some new writers display the "anyone can write that stuff" opinion, and reach the conclusion that songwriters must buy their way into their careers.

Make no mistake: the music business is a dynamic, entrepreneurial and in some ways cutthroat business. Any multi-billion dollar industry will have its share of disreputable fringe elements, and the music corporations will wheel and deal for every contractual point and dollar they can legitimately squeeze from songwriters, artists and others. There *are* scams out there: they may be "legal," but they're wholly unethical. They prey upon the highest of songwriters' aspirations and the lowest of their suspicions. But the limits are well-defined: there are bottom-line industry standards below which no *real* publisher will go. "Real" publishers fall into two general categories: fulltime publishers and "pocket" publishers.

Doug Thiele, *a songwriter and producer, is owner/president of Firelight Publishing (ASCAP) and director of the songwriting program at Groves School of Music. He is also a professor of music business at California State at Northridge, and acts as an independent consultant in Los Angeles. He has written numerous articles for music trade publications, in addition to contributing columns to* Songwriter *Magazine and* Music Connection.

Legitimate music publishers

Fulltime publishers include all the major publishers we've heard of as well as hundreds of other companies which are in business to legitimately exploit songs. They're almost always members of either the NMPA (National Music Publisher's Association) or the AIMP (the Association of Independent Music Publishers), and if they've ever had a song released to the public, they will be a member of at least one of the performing rights societies—ASCAP, BMI and/or SESAC.

Pocket publishers are also legitimate publishers who normally have a career in a related field: producers, personal managers, studio owners, attorneys and others who have an opportunity to deal with songs. This type of company allows them to receive publishing royalties from the songs they deal with in their other businesses.

Of course, music publishers haven't really "published" music for decades. Back when the major exploitation for songs was sheet music, they did publish (release to the public in print form) their songs. But when records became more important than sheet music in the fifties, the job of publishers changed dramatically: they became *agents* for songs. Publishers find appropriate songs and, through their hard work and their own out-of-pocket expenses, hope to exploit a song for financial profit, splitting most resultant royalties 50-50 with the songwriter(s). They acquire the rights to songs through contracts with songwriters, and present the songs to record companies and others for use on records and tapes or in film and television. Publishers want to develop and promote great writers so as to have more great songs to represent. They spend up to $2,000 per song making demonstration tapes to it's easier for producers and others to "hear" a great song.

After they've succeeded in creating a money-maker, they coordinate worldwide sub-publishing efforts to fully exploit that song in foreign markets. They guard the song against unlawful use and prosecute infringement, usually splitting court awards with the writer. After a song has begun earning money, the publisher will recoup songwriter advances and any expenses paid for exploiting that song from the resultant royalties. Songwriters never have to pay back an advance or song costs if the song doesn't make money: that's a part of the publisher's cost of doing business. In fact, in almost all cases, publishers will deduct the expenses of exploiting songs from the gross royalties, not just from the songwriting share of those royalites. This means that publishers and songwriters split those expenses if a song earns money; if it doesn't the entire expense of exploiting a song is borne by the publisher.

Pocket publishers usually don't incur expenses. The typical pocket publisher situation is one in which a producer asks for a "cut-in," or publishing royalties for having his artist record a song acquired directly from a songwriter. But in these cases as well as in the case of full-time publishers, no advance money is required of the songwriter.

There is one important principle to remember here: The supply of very good-to-great songs far outweighs the demand for them. No legitimate publisher ever has to advertise to the public to find songs. Songwriters who know about the music industry procedures common in this country seek out publishers. Even small publishing companies receive many tapes each week. In fact, publishers have always been the first-line screening device for producers, artists and record companies, sifting through mountains of demo tapes for a few musical nuggets.

The sharks

But to the millions of novice songwriters trying to unlock the door to success, anyone offering a way into the "in-crowd" of the music business is worth taking seriously, even if there seems to be an outlay of money involved. It's these new writers who fall prey to a very well-organized array of businesses commonly known as songsharks.

Songsharks are like counterfeit money. They offer the appearance of success without the substance to back it up. Of course, the legitimate industry won't have anything to do with songsharks, but the songsharks never really try to enter that arena. Contrary to their stated purpose, the songsharks aren't interested in exploiting songs but in separating unsuspecting songwriters from their money. Here are some classic songshark approaches. But a word of warning: since these companies play on the fears and suspicions of writers, the variations on these themes can be endless.

Co-writer songsharks

The legitimate industry looks for only completed songs. Probably the most common song-shark operation is designed to help lyricists (writers with words only, or writers with words and a melody line) come up with completed songs. These "song mills" crank out basic "mu-sic" to writers' lyrics for a fee, often using the same music for many lyrics. In the typical situation, a musician with a guitar or at a piano will take five or ten minutes putting a few chords to a lyric and then move on to the next project. The results may be demoed by the company for an additional fee. No attempt is usually made to correct weaknesses in the lyric or to perfect the completed song in any way because that is not the company's function.

Publisher songsharks

Often, the co-writer songsharks offer some publishing services for a fee. They might offer to send the resultant tape of their work to "music industry representatives," or they might promise to get the song on the radio. Remember that most songsharks strive to stay within the law. Making promises through the mail and then not keeping those promises can constitute fraud, so when a songshark promises radio airplay of a writer's song, he must deliver. Of course, these sharks very often buy time on a local radio station at, let's say, 3 a.m. for the song to be played once, and thereby fulfill their obligation.

Record company songsharks

These companies go one step further in their operations, actually recording a writer's song for a fee. Needless to say, legitimate record companies never charge a fee to record a song: They're usually happy to find a great song which fits their artist. Songshark record companies charge over $400 to put songs on their albums. They will fit fifteen songs or more on each of their albums, and will release up to fifty different albums with the same title, each with fifteen or more different writers, making literally hundreds of thousands of dollars in the process. The albums may have patriotic or religious themes (favorite categories for writers) and are poorly recorded. A whole album might be recorded in six hours, with no time for retakes if mistakes are made. Many of these companies have names which sound disturbingly like major record companies so as to add an aura of borrowed legitimacy. These companies promise to promote the albums, but such records rarely appear on the shelves or bins of record stores. Again, record stores know the difference between the real industry and songsharks.

Odds-and-ends songsharks

Songsharks may try to take more than just the money. Some songshark contracts take rights in a song for the work they do (or actually may become co-writers of the finished song in the case of the co-writer songshark), automatically gaining the status of owner of half the rights and royalties of the song, as well as voting privileges on writer decisions about the song. Songsharks will justify taking such rights as evidence of their seriousness about exploiting the song. After all, if they have half the rights and royalties, they have a vested interest in the song's success.

Many songsharks offer a series of services which are in the general scope of the industry. Some will charge a fee to help the writer fill out copyright forms. Others will charge a general administrative fee for other mysterious services. Many songsharks will attempt to keep the songwriter on the string by charging to co-write, then charging more to "publish" the finished song, and more to get airplay on the song. I've even heard of a writer who actually paid money to a songshark on a monthly basis to write exclusively for the songshark. The bad news here is that even though sharks are unethical in their dealings, their contracts are made to be BINDING. If a songwriter signs a songshark contract obligating him to write exclusively for the company, there may not be a way out of the contract. Songsharks offer "services" which, though largely worthless, are legal.

Stalking the prey

In essence, songsharks seek out and target a very specific audience: unschooled songwriters. They present a plausible pitch for services they know the songwriter knows he needs. Assuming the writer is a novice, the idea, even paying the money, seems reasonable.

Songsharks know how to find new songwriters. They put ads into appropriate magazines and periodicals. Remember that magazines may not know or be able to prevent the more sophisticated songshark ads, so we can't assume that the publishers necessarily endorse the products and services advertised in their publications.

Many songsharks go right to the source for writers' names, addresses and number of songs written. They have representatives going through the copyright files at the Library of Congress in Washington D.C. It's public information, after all. If you've registered a song in Washington recently, you probably got a letter from a "record company" telling you that there's a wide, wonderful music industry out there crying for songs, and that your songs have a chance. Normally the first pitch doesn't mention money, but the next ones will eventually. If you've entered song contests, don't be surprised to find the same sort of letter. Song contest officials have been known to sell their mailing lists to anyone with the right amount of money.

Warning signs

Forewarned is forearmed: Songsharks are easy to spot if you know the rules. Here are some ways to recognize sharks:
● Songsharks have to advertise—legitimate companies don't. Legitimate companies won't knowingly refer anybody to a songshark, so the shark has to get the word out, either by ads or by direct mail.
● Songsharks ask for money upfront—or on a time payment plan—and imply that paying such money is the way it's done. (There ARE legitimate services one pays for in advance and some of them will be mentioned later.)
● Songsharks are rarely members of major publishing organizations and associations, nor are they members of performing rights societies like ASCAP, BMI and SESAC unless they've been very sneaky indeed.
● Songshark language almost always has the feel of a pitch. The flavor of the language is normally encouraging, convivial and sales-oriented. There is often a vague implication that theirs is the chosen path to success, or even that *not* taking advantage of their services might be bad in some way.
● Songshark contracts and letters of agreement don't look at all like standard music industry contracts. Instead they look disturbingly like bills of sale.
● Songshark contracts or agreements usually have a disclaimer somewhere in them which says something to the effect that the music business is a changing industry and no one can guarantee success. Obviously, this is for their legal protection.

And more . . .

If anyone wants to give you money to buy your song outright, you should first, run the other way; then, congratulate yourself on having a song that is so marketable others want to pay for it. Better to find a legitimate publisher to represent the song.

The general rule is that if it sounds too good to be true, it usually is. Songsharks succeed not only on the ignorance of some writers, but on their cynicism as well—their belief that everyone in the music industry "takes a cut." If songwriters really could buy their way into the music industry for a few hundred dollars everybody would be tuning up guitars and plugging in synthesizers.

Legitimate charges

There are legitimate costs of doing business which fall on the songwriter's shoulders. A fee negotiated upfront for a legitimate service should not be construed as a rip-off. After all, writers do wind up paying back half the publisher's expenses to shop the song, but only after the song has made money. If the song doesn't earn enough in royalties, there's no publisher repayment from the writer. Songwriters hire studios and players to make demonstration tapes to present to publishers, and the studios charge a fee as do the players. But there's no implication that the studio or player will help the song succeed. There are publicists, record manufacturers, promotion companies and lawyers who may charge a fee for their services, but again, there are no implied promises. Companies will arrange your song for a demo. They'll program synthesizers and they'll do lead sheets, but they won't offer fame and glory—only their good work.

Finding out

If you suspect you've been gnawed by a songshark, it's relatively easy to check it out. Many organizations in the music industry pride themselves on their work protecting songwriters from sharks: The Los Angeles Songwriters Showcase and the National Academy of Songwriters, both Hollywood based, and the Nashville Songwriters Association International in Nashville are such organizations. Legitimate publishers get their performance royalties from either ASCAP, BMI or SESAC, so it's foolish for a publisher *not* to be a member of at least one of these performing rights societies. Sharks, however, are not permitted to join because the societies all have specific clauses in their contracts with publishers which specifically prohibit publishers from charging money upfront. Check with any one of these societies in New York, Nashville or Los Angeles for the credentials of any publisher you do business with. If a company is not a member of any of these organizations, it means that they've never had a song released or they can't qualify as a member in good standing. Your local Better Business Bureau may be of some help, but remember that while sharking is obnoxious and unethical, it is usually legal, and most Bureaus won't specifically name songsharks for fear of being sued for restraint of trade and the like.

Recovery

If you *have* been bitten by a songshark and you're concerned about losing rights or royalties to your lyric or song, you should see an entertainment attorney. There may be a way to recover your rights, and at least you'll be able to assess the damage. DON'T ignore a songshark situation if you plan on reusing any part of a song which a songshark has worked on. For instance, you may not be able to separate a lyric from some songshark music legally. If your song has been recorded and released to the public without the proper copyright notice, there may even be danger of losing the song to the public domain.

Of course, it may be that you've been bitten by the songshark, the wound has healed, and you've moved on to the real music business chalking up your songshark incident to experience. Ultimately, your career probably won't rest on one song, and you'll be healthier for having put the episode aside. Whether you've had a bad experience with sharks, or you've avoided them up to now, I'd advise two courses of action: distance yourself from songsharks and spread the word about them. And remember that *most* of the people you will deal with in the music industry are honest and hard working.

The Songwriter as Producer

by J. Edward Frawley

There has never been a better time for songwriters to step forward and act as their own producers. As consumer-oriented keyboard/drum synthesizers and electronic studio gear become more accessible, songwriters can produce demos at home and control the production from concept to realization. Of course, many songwriters still choose the more traditional method of booking musicians, performers and studio time for their projects. Either way, there are no reasons why talented songwriters should not produce their own demos, and that is what this article is about.

There are many considerations in acting as your own producer, but with some method and organization you can successfully produce your own material. However, if you are more comfortable with someone else handling production, then that is how you should go about it. But if you feel the time is right for you to take charge, read on. You'll find it's not as difficult as it seems.

Many songwriters run into the studio immediately after committing a song to paper, only to find that they are beseiged with problems that could have been avoided in *pre-production* (before going into the studio). Although it may seem tedious, organization is the key to successful session recording and you will save time, money and peace of mind in the end.

Planning ahead

We'll begin the production plan at the point when the song is written and the next step is to record the demo. First, you must decide the genre and mood of your song; that is, the style, tempo, feel, etc. These will be governed largely by your knowledge of the pop music field, inclusive of rock, top 40, R&B "black" music, and country. To achieve the best results, write within the styles of music that you are familiar with. That's not to say that you shouldn't experiment with new ideas. You should always seek to introduce a fresh, unique element in your demo, something that will set it apart from the many demos heard weekly by publishers and artists. But use these ideas in moderation, utilizing only concepts that you understand well enough to easily incorporate into your song.

Next, consider the instrumentation. Most songwriter demos today are *arranged* and recorded basically with keyboard(s), bass and drums, with some *synth* and/or guitar *overdubs* to add dynamics and flavor. Ballads may feature less instrumentation and still be quite effective, depending of course on the arrangement and performance. But if you plan to develop your ballad arrangement from piano intro to big finish, you will most likely want to use some kind of percussion to help move it along.

Before you record, you will need to prepare a written arrangement of your song. This will act as a roadmap for the musicians, telling them basically what to play and where to play it. If you're not comfortable arranging your own material or feel you may not have the expertise— or even if you are just interested in a fresh perspective—don't hesitate to hire a professional. You don't have to hire the hottest arranger in town. There are ways of finding good demo arrangers through ads in the music trades, bulletin boards at local music schools, and even

J. Edward Frawley *has worked as Audio Production Engineer for EMI/America Records, as well as an independent composer/arranger/producer for songwriter/artist and advertising jingle projects. A member of NARAS, he is currently involved in film scoring projects, and has contributed articles to numerous magazines including* Music Connection.

word-of-mouth from local musicians and recording studios. Once you have chosen an arranger, be sure to communicate specifically what you want. This will help to avoid future problems stemming from misunderstanding, and this need for open communication remains true throughout the entire demo production process.

If you're impressed with the synth technology of the 80's, you may very well want to use all-electronic instrumentation, utilizing drum and keyboard synths and perhaps some *outboard mixdown equipment* such as *echo/delay* units, *harmonizers*, and other various *effects*. If such is the case, there are more studios cropping up monthly with an emphasis on recording from completely electronic sources. The equipment itself is becoming easier to use and is improving in quality and becoming more affordable. The synth studios usually charge an hourly rate and most of the good ones advertise in the music trades. (Only the very serious songwriter should consider outfitting a home studio due to the costs of the many necessary components, not to mention the physical logistics involved in setting up the musical instruments and tape recorders. One advantage today is that several manufacturers offer 4-track cassette recorders that are quite compact and most adequate for home demo recording.)

In the case of synth-source recording in a studio, the engineer will most likely also be your programmer, unless you plan on handling that yourself. If so, you should be very experienced in programming various drum and keyboard synthesizers or you'll waste valuable time and money trying to figure things out in the studio. And even in this case, having some kind of written arrangement or simple chord chart will help keep things running smoothly during the session.

Budget considerations

Once you have decided exactly how you want to record your demo, you must establish your budget. You should include costs for the arrangement, musicians and vocalists, recording time and tape, and studio time for the final *mixdown* which is sometimes charged at a rate different from the recording time. Your arrangement and budget will be determining factors in choosing the track format, that is 4-, 8-, 16-, or 24-track. It is more convenient to employ the 24-track format, because you can record twenty-four individual parts without stopping to "bump," or combine, any of the tracks. This style of recording usually produces superior quality, because each "bump" adds a little noise to the demo. But 24-track recording is usually more expensive also. Some studios give discounts for booking *"block" time*, so inquire as to the particulars.

The quality of the recorded product from any studio should be easy to check out. Ask the engineer if you may listen to some work done there recently. Most studios have a few recent examples laying about. Visit more than one studio to hear their finished products. You'll probably notice subtle differences at least, due in large part to the methods of the individual engineers. Naturally, the equipment makes a difference too, and you should be sure to ascertain that the studio you book has all the necessary equipment for your project. Check with the engineer handling your session. Explain your demo in terms of style, instrumentation, and how you'd like it to sound, and listen to his response. If you both seem to be talking along the same lines, you'll be passing the first major hurdle in producing your own material. It is essential to establish a good rapport with your engineer because you will be working closely with him throughout the project. A good engineer will be able to communicate easily with you, make suggestions to help you through the tough spots, and offer some good ideas along the way.

Be sure to check with the engineer regarding the tape supplies you will need for the session.

Editor's Note: This article makes use of technical or specialized words which have been italicizied within the article and defined in a brief glossary. The terms are only in italics the first time they appear. The glossary can be found at the end of this article.

Most studios sell tape on the premises but you may be able to get it cheaper at an electronics supply or audiovisual equipment store. Remember you'll be needing tape for the recording session as well as for the mix session. Tape sizes and brands vary, but the engineer will know what you need.

Hiring musicians and singers

The studio engineer can also be helpful in selecting the right musicians if you don't know any. Although it is tempting to employ friends on sessions in order to save a few bucks, it's a risky business and usually turns out for the worst. Aside from the fact that their attitude may be somewhat less than business-like because they think they are doing you a "favor," you may also be surprised to find that they are less talented than you realized, costing you more time and effort in the long run. Unless you know competent musicians, let someone more experienced suggest players you might call and you can take it from there. Again, be specific when speaking with them in order to determine if they are right for your demo. A good rapport here is immensely helpful too.

You will naturally want to hire the right vocalists as well. Some songwriters prefer to sing their own demos, but this should only be done if you are a professional. There is nothing more distracting than hearing a demo with an amateur vocal track, so take the time to find a singer who will complement your production. As with the studio musicians, the engineer can again be helpful in finding a good vocalist.

As producer, it will be your job to book the sessions and all the necessary personnel. Expect to do a lot of phone calling during this stage. You'll find if you plan far enough in advance (about three or four weeks), everything will be easier to schedule the first time around rather than having to deal with call-backs to postpone or confirm. One suggestion regarding booking: don't try to do everything at once. It is not necessary to complete a demo in one session, although you can if you're eager. An alternative idea would be to record the *basic tracks* and perhaps overdubs at one session, while saving the vocals (and perhaps additional overdubs) for a later session date. This allows you the luxury of "living with the tracks" for a period of time before *laying down* the vocals, giving you the opportunity of making any subtle additions or changes in the parts not yet recorded. It is also handy for those session vocalists who feel they can give a better performance if they have a chance to hear and rehearse with the actual recorded tracks prior to the session date. This allows the singer to concentrate on his performance. Keep in mind that the vocal is the most important aspect of your demo so you want it to be as good as it can be. Anything that helps the singer give a great delivery is recommended.

Needless to say, it is important to establish your relationship as producer during your initial contacts with the performers and studio personnel. It's your money, so you should understandably be concerned with how it will be spent. Don't be afraid to ask questions of anyone, and assure them that they may ask questions of you. Your association with these people will be somewhat intense, over a short period of time, and good communication is essential to a successful production.

The session

Once you get into the studio things can happen fast. Most sessions seem rather chaotic at the outset, what with everyone setting up and all the *pre-roll* formalities (tuning, volume checks, etc.). In order to help the engineer "set up" the board, it's a good idea to provide a *track sheet* for your production. This will act as the engineer's roadmap, telling him the instrumentation involved and how it may be recorded. If you can't write one yourself, discuss it with the engineer sometime prior to the session and he can assist you in making one.

While frustrating things do happen in the studio, it is important that you maintain your composure at all times. As producer, you will be setting the tone by example. When problems arise, it's your job to keep things cool until solutions are found. If the problem is with a musician's equipment, you'll have to allow the musician and/or engineer some time to fix it. You don't have to hover like a mother hen, but you should know what's going on so you can explain the delay to the others. If the problem is caused by faulty studio equipment and results in "down time" during which the studio is inoperable, you should not be charged for that portion of your time. You should check with the individual studios on their charge policies.

Often there will be some problem with the arrangement. This is not unusual and should be seen as an opportunity for improvement. Even the most well-conceived arrangements can benefit from last minute changes at the session. Your demo is not done until it's mixed so you can make practical changes at any point up until then. The good thing about having written charts is that it is easy for the players to notate any last minute changes. Always be ready to explain your song ideas to the musicians, and be open to their input as well. Whether or not they come up with any ideas you employ, they will at least appreciate your consideration in listening politely to what they say.

Time is money in the studio so try to be as focused as possible. While good humor is important, you're not there to party. Stay visibly in control by checking occasionally with the musicians to assure there are no comments or questions. Keep things moving, but don't rush them. A good rule of thumb is to allow about an hour to record the basic tracks for a three or four minute song with a straight-ahead arrangement. Of course you'll need more time for a more involved arrangement. You will also want to allow at least an hour for each lead vocal track. Some vocalists can cut it on the second or third *take*, but others take longer to get the "feel." In any case, it's better to have plenty of time. As for the background vocals and the overdubs, the recording time needed will depend upon how many parts there are and how involved the arrangements are. The arranger can estimate how long it might take.

Overdubs and vocals

Once the basic tracks are recorded, you will add the overdubs, which may consist of various synth parts or even a horn part. If you plan to do this immediately following the basic tracks session, you should leave enough time in between for the basic track musicians to tear down before the overdub musicians have to set up. This is most likely the time you will deal with payment to the musicians, and you should work out the details prior to the session date. While the American Federation of Musician's (musicians' union) technically frowns on nonunion session dates, it tends to look the other way when songwriter demos are involved. (They are mainly concerned about legitimate recording sessions by signed artists for future album release.) It's a fact of life that "scab" sessions happen every day.

Now, back to the overdubs. The best way to handle this phase is one-on-one, so to speak. That is, record one part or musician at a time. Although this may mean other musicians have to wait a bit, there should be no problem if you've explained the circumstances ahead of time. Recording one part at a time will allow you and the engineer to pay special attention to what's happening to insure things go properly.

Unless you have decided to complete your demo in a day, this is a good place to stop. Make a very rough mix of the tracks straight to cassette and take it home with you. Listen to it, live with it, think about it. There's still time to make any last minute changes before adding the vocal. While it's good to be flexible, you can drive yourself crazy with nit-picky changes. Remember that no one expects a demo to sound like a finished product, and your goal is to demonstrate the song, not the production. When you're ready to move on, the next step will be the vocal session.

Here as before, you are in charge. It will be up to you to make the vocalist(s) comfortable so they feel no pressure. Give the engineer time to *mike* the singer and set up the board, and be prepared to run the tracks a few times for the singer to practice. Be open to ideas from the vocalist, but don't be afraid to give constructive criticism about the performance. Offer your comments politely, but don't beat around the bush. A good session vocalist can give you what you want as long as you communicate your desires, and more often than not your guidance is appreciated.

The final steps

Upon completion of the vocals, you're ready to mix. Since this is technically different from recording, the engineer will have to reset the board, which will take a few moments. Consider the mixdown as the final important step in your demo production. It is during this phase that you enhance the positive aspects of your recording, and perhaps even "bury" some of the less pleasant ones (off-color notes, misplayed lines, etc.). It is fantasy to expect a recording session where everything turns out perfect. That is why a good mix is so important, and a good engineer equally so.

Generally, allow about an hour mix time per song. You (and the engineer) will want to run the song down several times to get an idea of how you want the different volume levels adjusted. You will also want to hear each track by itself to set the *equalization*, or tone. This is something the engineer will do automatically, and you should be prepared to discuss any alterations or adjustments you'd like.

If you have any particular effects in mind such as *reverb*, delay, echo, *flanging*, harmonizing, *doubling*, etc., you should also discuss them with the engineer. I've never known one who didn't enjoy tinkering with gadgets, and he may come up with some ideas you like. There are marvelous things possible during mixdown. You can add texture and depth, giving your demo more dimension than you ever thought possible. Have a little fun and try out some different ideas. As producer, it's up to you to explore the potential for a great mix. Take the time to do it right—a lousy mix can spoil any great performance. By now your engineer should have a good idea of the sound you're after, so don't hesitate to seek advice. And don't forget your arranger most likely has some ideas about the final mix, too. Any professional arranger will have taken the final mix into consideration when arranging even the very basic tracks, like painting a masterpiece starting with the background.

The entire demo recording process is a team effort with you as Captain, so let everyone feel they are working with you, not for you. Try always to appear in charge as producer, and always ready to be helpful in a professional manner. Never let your tension (if any) show in the studio as it will breed among the others and ultimately affect their performances in a negative way. Above all, have respect for the professionals you are working with. They will respect you in kind and perform to the best of their abilities, providing you with a quality demo production.

Glossary

Arrange. To prepare a song for a performance or recording, with consideration for the melody, harmony, instrumentation, tempo, style, etc.

Basic tracks. Refers to the recording of the basic instruments in a typical rhythm ensemble (drums, bass, guitar and keyboards), over which the vocals and overdubs are recorded.

Block time. A "block" of time, such as ten hours, which can be rented from a recording studio for a reduced hourly rate if booked in advance.

Delay. An effect that allows for a programmable setting of the rate of echo of a sound.

Doubling. To record the same information on one track and then on another separate track. This may be done by electronically duplicating the original signal or by actually recording the same signal two times.

Echo. The repetition of a signal at regular intervals.

Effects. Refers to signal processing equipment used to enhance recorded sound (or the resulting enhanced sound itself) such as echo, flanging, etc.

Equalization. Refers to the alterations made with regard to the low, middle, and high frequencies of a sound.

Flanging. A signal processing device (effect) used to electronically alter the timbre of an instrument or vocal.

Harmonizer. A type of mixdown equipment (effect) used to electronically alter the pitch of an instrument or vocal.

Laying down. Recording; to "lay down" a vocal or instrumental track is to record that track.

Mike. To adjust the location and volume level of a microphone with respect to the musician/vocalist to be recorded.

Mixdown. The blending of recorded information from a multitrack tape to a single master tape.

Mixdown equipment. Equipment used during the mixdown phase of recording, such as signal processing equipment (and effects).

Outboard. "Extra" signal processing mixdown equipment not included in the original design of the mixing board.

Overdubs. Instrumental or vocal tracks recorded over (in addition to) pre-existing basic tracks.

Pre-production. The time spent readying material before actually going into a studio to record.

Pre-roll. The period of time in the studio before the actual tape recording begins (the time when preparations are made).

Reverb. Refers to an effect in which the "ghost" of a sound lingers after the initial sound has died.

Synth. Synthesizer; refers to electronic drum and keyboard synthesizers in general, and the type of sound created by these instruments (as opposed to acoustic sounds made by acoustic instruments).

Take. Either an attempt to record a vocal or instrumental part, or an acceptable recording of a track (good enough to keep rather than re-record).

Track sheet. The recording engineer's guide to an upcoming session listing the artist, song, instruments, vocals, and where they are to be recorded on the tape (that is, the specific track each is to be recorded on); and any information pertinent to the session like the date, tape speed, personnel involved, etc.

Market conditions are constantly changing! If this is 1989 or later, buy the newest edition of Songwriter's Market at your favorite bookstore or order directly from Writer's Digest Books.

The Markets

Music Publishers

Music publishers don't necessarily "publish" songs the way Writer's Digest Books "publishes" *Songwriter's Market*; that is, in print form. Music publishers are more like agents for songs, making songs/music available to the public in some fixed form. Sometimes that does include printed music, and you can learn more about that in our new Print Music Publishers section at the end of this Music Publishers' "chapter." But more often, music publishers try to get a sound recording cut by a major artist. Other uses for a song include usage in television, motion pictures, videos, ad campaigns, audiovisual presentations, and much more. It's a publisher's duty to find ways of exploiting songs in whatever creative ways he can think of.

When you sign a publishing contract, you are assigning your copyright to the publisher. Ethical publishers don't ask you to "sell" your songs outright, rather you license the rights to the song to the publisher for a specified period of time. The publisher "administers" the copyright during that period. He tries to get the song recorded, printed and used in various ways, and guards it against infringement. Even though the song is your creation, the publisher controls the copyright. He does a lot of the leg work and paperwork for you, and uses his contacts and business savvy to your (and his) advantage. That is why you split the royalties with him, usually 50-50.

Publishers build a reputation within the music industry. Some publishers specialize in certain types of music, others look for crossover potential in songs so they can try to interest many different kinds of artists in the same song. Recording artists, producers, and record company executives all know that publishers are good sources of new material and they go to publishers specifically requesting certain types of songs. So publishers are always in the market for new material. They usually like to establish a relationship with songwriters, help them develop their craft, and then go back to those writers time and time again for new material. Some hire staff writers and pay them a weekly "draw" against future royalties. Because publishers have staff writers and affiliated writers they've already established relationships with, it's sometimes difficult for beginning songwriters to get their material heard. Many publishers are reluctant to accept outside material because of an unfortunate increase in the number of songwriters who claim their copyrighted material was stolen and used in another hit song without giving them proper credit. This is one of the main reasons why it's a good idea to write and ask for permission before submitting your demo. Another advantage of writing first is in letting the publisher know your tape is coming and reinforcing the association of your name with the song title.

Fortunately, all the publishers listed in *Songwriter's Market* have expressed an interest in receiving material from you, our readers, because they believe that if you follow the instructions given in their listings, your submissions will be better than the average tapes they receive.

No one can improve your chances of placing your songs more than you. A professional manner goes a long way in making a good impression. If you submit through the mail, make sure your package is *neat*. Remember that you are competing against songwriters who have written bona fide hits and deal with publishers every day. A tidy package with a typed cover letter and lyric sheet, and a properly labeled tape will get to the top of the stack much faster than a sloppy package put together by an amateur.

If you are able to present your songs in person, you may be able to receive helpful feedback from the publisher you talk with and begin a rapport that could develop into a healthy working relationship. Many people feel it's better to visit as often as you can with a few songs, rather than overstay your welcome on one visit with too many songs. Take several tapes with one song on each—ready to pop into a tape recorder and play. Then the busy publisher won't have to waste time fast-forwarding and rewinding. Give him permission to stop the tape at any time. He'll appreciate your consideration of his demanding schedule.

With so many options, and so much helpful information in the listings in this section, your only problem will be choosing which publishers to contact! Be a smart songwriter and do your homework before sending your materials. Read each listing carefully and learn what types of music each publisher is interested in, what songs he has placed and which artists have recorded them. Be objective in evaluating how your songs stack up against the industry standards—critique them as if you were the person to whom you're submitting.

A Geographic Index is provided at the back of this section to help you plan a trip to Los Angeles, Nashville or New York. Foreign markets are listed in alphabetical order for your information. To keep up week-by-week on which companies are publishing hits, check the charts in *Billboard* and *Cash Box*.

*A STREET MUSIC,Suite 800, 250 W. 54th St., New York NY 10019. (212)580-2688. A&R Director: Terry Selders. Music publisher, record company (A Street Records), record producer (A Street Music). ASCAP. Works with composers, lyricists; teams collaborators. Pays standard royalty.
How to Contact: Prefers cassette. Does not return unsolicited material.
Music: Mostly rock (heavy to pop/radio oriented); also R&B (dance-oriented, radio/pop oriented). Published "Kamikaze", written and recorded by Youth in Asia (heavy rock); "Easy Come, Easy Go", written and recorded by Frank Jordan (oldies-rock style); and "Hot Fire Love", written and recorded by The Remnant (50s rock), all on A Street Records.

ACE ADAMS MUSIC CO., Suite 192, 100-19 Alcott Pl., Bronx NY 10475. (212)379-2593. A&R Department: Adam Puertas. Music publisher. ASCAP, BMI. Publishes 25 songs/year; publishes 10 new songwriters/year. Pays standard royalty.
Affiliate: Adam Puertas Music (ASCAP).
How to Contact: Call first and obtain permission to submit. Prefers cassette (or videocassette) and lyric or lead sheet(s). SASE. Reports in 2 weeks.
Music: Dance, gospel, MOR, pop and blues. Published "Somebody Fool" (by Ace Adams), recorded by Michael Jackson on Epic; "You Make Me Feel Like a Woman" (by Raymon Johns), recorded by Sandra Taylor on Melvern; and "Zoot Zoot Zoot" (by John Colvin), recorded by Tiny Tin on Ro-Jo (all pop).

ACOUSTIC MUSIC, INC., Box 1546, Nashville TN 37202. (615)242-9198. Administrator: Nancy Dunne. Music publisher. BMI. Publishes 35-50 songs/year. Pays standard royalties.
Affiliates: Lawday Music Corp. (BMI), Daydan Music Corp. (ASCAP), and Allmusic Inc. (ASCAP).
How to Contact: Call or write first. Prefers cassette with 2-3 songs. SASE. Reports in 1 month.
Music: Country, folk, MOR and gospel. Published "Come to Me" (by Gene Price), recorded by Aretha Franklin; "Ready to Take My Chances" (by Dewayne Orender and Helen Cornelius), recorded by Oak Ridge Boys on MCA Records; and "Woman, Sensuous Woman," recorded by Ray Charles on CBS Records.

 The asterisk before a listing indicates that the listing is new in this edition. New markets are often the most receptive to freelance submissions.

ACT ONE MUSIC CO./MOONSONG PUBLISHING CO., Box 11565, Atlanta GA 30305. (404)261-6512. President: Jimmy Ginn. Music publisher. BMI, ASCAP. Publishes 20 songs/year; publishes 10 new songwriters/year. Works with composers; teams collaborators. Pays standard royalty.
How to Contact: Call first and obtain permission to submit. Prefers cassette with 3-5 songs and lyric sheet. "Include biography, pictures, clippings or evidence of track record." Does not return unsolicited material. Reports in 3 weeks.
Music: Mostly R&B, bluegrass, pop and gospel. Published "Redd And Hot," written and recorded by Toni Redd (R&B); "I've Come A Long Way Down," written and recorded by Doug Gaddis (country); and "American By Birth," written and recorded by Jeff Bruce (country), all on Wonder Records.
Tips: "Present quality recording with proper information and follow up with phone."

AGENCJA AUTORSKA/AUTHORS' AGENCY, Hipoteczna Street 2, Warsaw 00-950 Poland. 27-58-76. Contact: Music Department. Music publisher and "intermediary on Polish music market." Publishes 300 songs/year.
How to Contact: Submit demo tape by mail. Prefers cassette or records. Does not return unsolicited material.
Music: Mostly pop, rock and background music; also country, blues and serious music.

ALEXIS, Box 532, Malibu CA 90265. (213)858-7282. President: Lee Magid. Music publisher, record company, personal management firm, and record and video producer. ASCAP. Member AIMP. Publishes 50 songs/year; publishes 40 new songwriters/year. Works with composers and lyricists; teams collaborators. Pays standard royalty.
Affiliates: Marvelle (BMI), Lou-Lee (BMI) and D.R. Music (ASCAP).
How to Contact: Prefers cassette (or videocassette of writer/artist) with 1-3 songs and lyric sheet. "Try to make demo as clear as possible—guitar or piano should be sufficient. A full rhythm and vocal demo is always better." SASE. Reports in 1 month "if interested".
Music: Mostly R&B and gospel; also blues, church/religious, country, dance-oriented, folk, jazz and Latin. Published "Jesus Is Just Alright" (by Art Reynolds), recorded by Doobie Brothers on WB Records (rock gospel); "Life's Memories" (by Ron Mack), recorded by Tingle on Grass Roots Records (pop/R&B); and "Alabama" (by Rhys O'Brien/Artie Schiff) recorded by Kim and Sam (R&B/gospel/rock).

ALJONI MUSIC CO., Box 18918, Los Angeles CA 90018. (213)935-7277. General Manager: Al Hall, Jr. Music publisher and record producer. BMI. Publishes 10-12 songs/year; publishes 2-4 new songwriters/year. Pays standard royalty.
Affiliates: Hallmarque Musical Works, Ltd. (ASCAP), Scorpion Tales Music (BMI) and Jacan Jr. Music (ASCAP).
How to Contact: Prefers cassette (or Beta videocassette) with 5-10 songs and lyric sheet. "Songs should have good melody, slick lyrics, nice chord progressions, etc. Rap product welcome." Does not return unsolicited material. Reports in 2 months.
Music: Jazz, R&B, and soul. Published "Future World" (by Hall/King), recorded by Three D. on Westin Town; "Jazzy's Rap" written and recorded by Jazzy D. on Aljoni; "Pictures" (by Hall/King/Hubbard), recorded by various jazz soloists.

AL-KRIS MUSIC, 4322 Mahoning Ave., Youngstown OH 44515. (216)793-7295. Professional Manager: Richard Hahn. Music publisher, record company and record producer. BMI. Publishes 8 songs/year; publishes 4 new songwriters/year. Pays standard royalty.
How to Contact: Query first. Prefers cassette with 3-5 songs and lyric sheet. SASE. Reports in 3 weeks.
Music: Children's, country, folk, gospel, MOR and top 40/pop. Published "Prom Night" (by Don Yalleck), recorded by the B-Minors on Ikon Records; "Teach Me Lovely Lady" (by Hahn); and "Help Me I'm Falling" (by Hahn), recorded by Kirsti Manna on Genuine Records.
Tips: "Submission package must be neat and the demo tape must be of decent quality."

ALL ROCK MUSIC, Box 2296, Rotterdam 3000 CG Holland. (10)4224889. President: Cees Klop. Music publisher, record company (Collector Records) and record producer. Publishes 40-60 songs/year; publishes several new songwriters/year. Pays standard royalty.
Affiliates: All Rock Music (England) and All Rock Music (Belgium).
How to Contact: Submit demo tape by mail. Prefers cassette. SAE and IRC. Reports in 4 weeks.
Music: Mostly 50s rock, rockabilly and country rock; also piano boogie woogie. Published "Loving Wanting You," by R. Scott (country rock) and "Ditch Digger" by D. Mote, (rock), both recorded by Cees Klop on White Label records; and "Bumper Boogie" (by R. Hoeke), recorded by Cees Klop on Downsouth Records (boogie).

ALLDISC, Consultoria e Comercial Fonografica Ltd., Rua Alagoas 159-cj.84, Sao Paulo 01242 Brazil. (011)255-5560. President: Geraldo L. Loewenberg. Music publisher and record company. SICAM. Publishes 50 songs/year; publishes 10-20 new songwriters/year. Works with lyricists and composers. Pays 70% royalty.
How to Contact: Prefers cassette (or VHS NTSC videocassette). "Submit demo (small package, please) via airmail, addressed directly to Geraldo Loewenberg—never to the company. This avoids custom problems." Does not return unsolicited material. Reports in 4 weeks.
Music: Mostly rock, blues and R&B; also film music, reggae and new wave. Published "Bambalalão" (by C. Zamma), (samba); "Xote to Tic Tac" (by P. Afonso), recorded by Marilam Barbosa (xote); and "Jardim do Curumim" (by P. Afonso), recorded by Mininotas (valsa), all on Polyjr. Records.
Tips: "Songs must have a strong musical theme, and be easily assimilated. Since we are a sub-publisher of original songs, we only work with finished recorded music."

*ALMO MUSIC CORP., 1358 N. LaBrea Ave., Hollywood CA 90028. (213)469-2411. Music publisher and record company (A&M Records). ASCAP.
Affiliate: Irving Music Inc. (BMI).
How to Contact: Write and ask for submission policy.

ALPHA-ROBINSON MUSIC, 19992 Stotter, Detroit MI 48234-3142. (313)893-9370. President: Juanita Robinson. Music publisher. ASCAP. Publishes 100 songs/year; publishes 10 new songwriters/year. Pays standard royalty.
How to Contact: Prefers cassette (or videocassette) with 2-4 songs and lyric sheet. SASE. Reports in 1 month.
Music: R&B. Published "I Can't Help Myself," recorded by Silk; "Power," recorded by Sheri Robinson; and "Love Take Me," recorded by Just Us, all written by Eric Parker (all R&B singles).

*ALTERNATIVE DIRECTION MUSIC PUBLISHERS, Box 3278, Station D, Ottawa, Ontario K1P 6H8 Canada. (613)225-6100. President and Director of Publishing: David Stein. Music publisher. PRO-CAN. Publishes 7-10 songs/year; publishes 1-3 new songwriters/year. Pays standard royalty.
How to Contact: Prefers cassette (or Beta videocassette) with 2-4 songs. SASE if sent from within Canada; American songwriters send SAE and $1 for postage and handling. Reports in 6 weeks.
Music: Uptempo rock, uptempo R&B and ballads (rock, R&B and pop). Published "Big Kiss" (by David Ray), recorded by Theresa Bozor on MCA Records (pop/dance).
Tips: "Make certain your vocals are up front in the mix in the demos you submit. Don't waste time showing off your musical chops; get to the chorus in the first 50 seconds and make certain it is strong."

AMALGAMATED TULIP CORP., 117 W. Rockland Rd., Box 615, Libertyville IL 60048. (312)362-4060. President: Perry Johnson. Music publisher, record company and record producer. BMI. Publishes 12 songs/year; publishes 3-6 new songwriters/year. Pays standard royalty.
Affiliate: Mo Fo Music.
How to Contact: Write about your interest. Prefers cassette with 3-5 songs and lyric sheet. SASE. Prefers studio produced demos. Reports in 2 months.
Music: Mostly rock, top 40/pop, dance and R&B; also country, MOR, blues, and easy listening progressive. Published "This Feels Like Love to Me," (by Charles Sermay) recorded by Sacha Distel (pop); "Stop Wastin' Time," (by Tom Gallagher), recorded by Orjan (country); and "In the Middle of the Night," recorded by Oh Boy (pop).
Tips: "We're aggressive and work a song."

*AMALISA,969A Fulham Rd., London SWG 5SS England. (01)731-6373. President: Charles Lucy. Music publisher, record company and record producer. ASCAP. Works with composers and lyricists; teams collaborators. Pays standard royalty.
How to Contact: Prefers cassette with 1-4 songs and lyric or lead sheet. Does not return unsolicited material. Reports in 6 weeks.
Tips: Songwriters should have a "sense of humor."

*AMERICANA SONGS, INC., Box 15 Kasai, Edogawa-Ku, Tokyo 134 Japan. (03)878-6041. President: Terry Kuroda. Music Publisher. JASRAC. Estab. 1986. Publishes 35 songs/year; publishes 5 new songwriters/year. Works with composers.
Affiliates: Alshire Publishing Co., Daval Music, Chesdel Music, Cordoba Music, Brannon, Narada Publishing.
How to Contact: Prefers cassette. Include bio and information about past recordings. Does not return unsolicited material. Reports in 1 month.
Music: Mostly pop, rock and country; also R&B, easy listening and jazz/new age/fusion.

Close-up

Jonathan Haft
Vice President of Business Affairs
Almo/Irving Music

According to Jonathan Haft, publishers are good contacts for songwriters because "they have a mechanism for routinely getting songs in front of the people who are responsible for making music, such as recording artists, A&R executives and producers." As Vice President of Business Affairs at Almo/Irving, Haft makes the contractual deals that bring songwriters and the publishing company together. He believes, "It's difficult for a songwriter to get music in front of the right people without the assistance of a good publisher when major publishers have a whole network of professional people constantly trying to get their own songs 'covered.' "

Perhaps the most realistic option for beginning songwriters is signing a single song contract. This type of agreement gives the publisher rights to one song without making a long-term commitment regarding future songs. Haft draws up many such contracts, and he feels that "at the outset of his career, it may be advantageous for a writer to sell songs one at a time," because in a long-term affiliation, "publishers get a lot of songs of varying quality from prolific writers," some of which are more "coverable" than others. The less coverable songs usually get shelved in favor of new songs with more hit potential. On the other hand, Haft says, "when publishers go out and acquire songs on a single song basis, they've got a pretty good idea that they want to pitch that particular song for a specific project. They wouldn't waste their time, money, and effort documenting and acquiring a song otherwise. Publishers know who's in the studio, they know what those artists are looking for, and when they hear a song they think will work they go after it."

The alternative to a single-song agreement would be some kind of long-term association in which it is agreed that all the songs a writer creates within a negotiated period of time will be published by that publishing company. "When considering a long-term publishing arrangement," Haft says, "songwriters should bear in mind that a good publisher will keep track of what's in their catalog and perhaps years after the songs were delivered, go out and get them recorded. Our company has done just that with great success to the benefit of many current and former writers."

While songwriters should be careful in choosing a publisher they feel they can work with, they shouldn't be overly distrustful of people in the industry, according to Haft. He explains that for their own legal protection, "all publishers that accept unsolicited material have some sort of mechanism set up to make sure that it isn't heard in the office by people who may, consciously or unconsciously, copy it. In songwriting, there's always a possibility that someone's going to hear what you're doing, whether it's at a publishing company or a demo studio or somewhere else. It's a hard line to walk because you want people to hear your music so they'll be interested in doing something with it. At the same time, there's always a risk that somebody somewhere will hear something and copy it. It's just a risk you have to take. This does not mean a writer should abandon his rights in the case of a clear rip-off." Rather, it means that songwriters must use good judgment in setting up publishing and other business relationships.

The bottom line is that songwriters and publishers need to work together to exploit songs to their mutual benefit. "Songwriters should look at the publisher as an ally rather than as an adversary," Haft says. "As a young songwriter, the idea is to work *with* your publisher and listen to him, perhaps not sacrificing your own opinion all the time, but looking at your publisher as an assistant in helping you craft your music and build your career."

—Julie Wesling Whaley

AMERICATONE MUSIC PUBLISHER, 1817 Loch Lomond Way, Las Vegas NV 89102. (702)384-0030. Music publisher, record company, record producer and film production. BMI. Publishes 10 songs/year; publishes 5 new songwriters/year. Pays standard royalty.
How to Contact: Prefers cassette (or videocassette) with 2 songs and lyric sheet. SASE. Reports in 5 weeks.
Music: Bluegrass, children's, country, and top 40/pop. Published "I'm A Luva Luva You," written and recorded by Wally Jemmings (western).

AMERICUS MUSIC, Box 314, Hendersonville TN 37075. (615)824-8308. President: D.L. Riis. Music publisher. ASCAP. Publishes 15-20 songs/year; publishes 4 new songwriters/year. Pays standard royalty.
Affiliates: Stars and Stripes Music (BMI).
How to Contact: Prefers cassette with 1-5 songs. SASE. Reports in 3 weeks.
Music: Mostly country; also bluegrass, easy listening, gospel, R&B and top 40/pop.

AMIRON MUSIC, 20531 Plummer St., Chatsworth CA 91311. (818)998-0443. Manager: A. Sullivan. Music publisher, record company, record producer and manager. ASCAP. Publishes 2-8 songs/year; publishes 2 new songwriters/year. Pays per agreement.
Affiliates: Aztex Productions, and Copan Music (BMI).
How to Contact: Prefers cassette (or Beta or VHS videocassette) with any number songs and lyric sheet. SASE. Reports in 10 weeks.
Music: Country, easy listening, MOR, progressive, R&B, rock and top 40/pop. Published "Lies in Disguise," "Rapid," and "Let's Work It Out," (by F. Cruz), recorded by Gangs Back; and "Try Me," written and recorded by Sana Christian, both on AKO Records (both pop).
Tips: Send songs with "good story-lyrics."

ANDRADE PUBLISHING COMPANY, Drawer 520, Stafford TX 77477. Manager: Daniel Andrade. Music publisher. BMI. Member NSAI. Publishes 24 new songwriters/year. Pays standard royalty.
How to Contact: Write first and obtain permission to submit. Prefers cassette with 2-5 songs and lead sheet. "Include return postage." SASE. Reports in 2 months.
Music: Church/religious, country and top 40/pop. Published "Cheaters Never Win" written and recorded by Daniel Andrade on New England Records (top 40/pop, country); "Hank Williams Is Singing Again," recorded by "Hank the Drifter" on Cattle Records (country); and "A Lonely Stranger," recorded by "Hank the Drifter" on RCA Records (country).

ANGELSONG PUBLISHING CO., 2714 Westwood Dr., Nashville TN 37402. (615)297-2246. President: Mabel Birdsong. BMI, ASCAP. Music publisher and record company (Birdsong Records). Publishes 2 songs/year; publishes 2 new songwriters/year.
How to Contact: Prefers cassette with maximum 4 songs and lyric sheet. Does not return unsolicited material. Reports in 2 weeks, "if requested."
Music: Mostly gospel, country and MOR; also pop.

ANOTHER EAR MUSIC, #V-4, 380 Harding Pl., Nashville TN 37211. (615)834-2682. General Manager: T.J. Kirby. BMI, ASCAP. Music publisher, record company (T.J. Records) and record producer (T.J. Productions). Publishes 4 songs/year; publishes 1 new songwriter/year. Works with composers and lyricists. Pays standard royalty.
Affiliates: Pepermint Rainbow Music/ASCAP.
How to Contact: Write or call first to arrange personal interview. Prefers cassette or 7½ ips reel-to-reel (or VHS videocassette) with 3 songs and lyric sheet. Reports in 2 weeks.
Music: Mostly country/pop and R&B: also gospel, rock and "concept songs." Published "Let it Be Me Tonight" (by Tom Douglas/Bob Lee/T.J. Kirby), recorded by Kathy Ford on Prerie Dust Records; and

"Don't Take a Heart" (by Kirby/Lapp/Smith) and "Faster than a Speeding Bullet" (by Paul Hotchkiss), recorded by Deb Merrit on T.J. Records (all country/pop).
Tips: "Videos are great to help present a writer's concept but don't let the ideas of what you would put in a video stand in the way of writing a great song."

ANTHEM ENTERTAINMENT GROUP, 189 Carlton St., Toronto, Ontario M5A 2K7 Canada. (416)923-5855. A&R Director: Val Azzoli. Music publisher, record company, record producer and management firm. CAPAC, PROCAN. Member CMPA. Publishes 20 songs/year; publishes 1-2 new songwriters/year. Pays standard royalty.
Affiliates: Core Music Publishing, Mark-Cain Music and Brandy Music.
How to Contact: Prefers cassette only with maximum 2 songs and lyric sheet addressed to A&R Department. Prefers studio produced demos. SAE and IRC. Reports in 5 months.
Music: Mostly rock; also progressive and top 40/pop. Published "Bridges Over Borders" (by Deppe/Horne) recorded by Spoons (rock); "The Big Money" (by Lee/Lifeson/Peart), recorded by Rush/Poly-Gram (rock); and "Harmony," written and recorded by Ian Thomas (pop) all on Mercury Records.

*ANTI-CONSCIOUS MUSIC, 822 Roselawn Ave., #607, Toronto, Ontario M6B 1B4 Canada. President: Jaimie Vernon. Music publisher, record company (Bullseye Records), record producer (Simon Truth Productions). CAPAC. Publishes 10-15 songs/year; publishes 2-5 new songwriters/year. Works with teams collaborators. Pays standard royalty.
Affiliates: Ego-A-Gogo Music (PROCAN).
How to Contact: Prefers cassette (or VHS videocassette) with 4 songs and lyric sheet. "Songwriters should be willing to promote their own songs." SAE and IRC.
Music: Mostly new wave, alternative and punk; also top 40, progressive and jazz. Published "Innocents" (by Bouchier/Truth), "Who is God?" (by Truth), "Clever Girl" (by Truth), and "Voices Move Me" (by Bouchier/Schembri), all recorded by Swedish Fish on Bullseye Records (alternative).

APON PUBLISHING CO., Box 3082, Steinway Station, Long Island City, NY 11103. Manager: Don Zemann. Music publisher, record company and record producer. ASCAP. Publishes 250 songs/year. Pays according to special agreements made with individual songwriters.
How to Contact: Call first. Prefers cassette with 1-6 songs and lyric sheet. SASE. Reports in 1 month.
Music: Classical, background music, dance-oriented, easy listening, folk and international. Published "Polka Fever" (by Slawko Kunst), recorded by Czech Brass (polkas); "Russian Gypsy Melodies" (by Sandor Lakatos), recorded by Hungarian Gypsy Orchestra (gypsy tunes); and "Czech Songs" (by Alojz Skolka), recorded by Budvarka Ensemble/Apon Records (folk/pop), all on Apon Records.
Tips: "We are sub-publishers for pop music from overseas."

APPROPRIATE PRODUCTIONS, 1716 Pasadena Glen Rd., Pasadena CA 91107. (213)463-8400. President: Ben Brooks. Music publisher (DGO Music) and record company (Vizion). Publishes 2 songs/year; publishes 2 new songwriters/year. Works with teams collaborators. Pays standard royalty.
How to Contact: Prefers cassette (or VHS videocassette) with 3 songs and lyric sheet or lead sheet. SASE. Reports in 2 weeks.
Music: Pop, rock and R&B. Published "Look What You've Done to Me" (by Billy Purnell) recorded by Oskar (pop). Artists include Tim Kenefick and K.A. Parker.

ARCADE MUSIC CO., Arzee Recording Co., 3010 N. Front St., Philadelphia PA 19133. (215)426-5682. President: Rex Zario. A&R Director: Lucky Taylor. Music publisher, booking agency and record company. ASCAP. Publishes 100-150 songs/year. Pays standard royalty.
Affiliates: Valleybrook (ASCAP), Rex Zario Music (BMI) and Seabreeze Music (BMI).
How to Contact: Prefers cassette with 4-5 songs and lead sheet. SASE. Reports in 5 weeks.
Music: Bluegrass, country, easy listening, folk, gospel, rock (fifties style) and top 40/pop. Published "Why Do I Cry Over You," (by DeKnight and Keefer), recorded by Bill Haley on Arzee Records (country); "Hand Clap For Jesus," (by Rodney Harris), recorded by Gospel Blenders on Arzee Records (gospel); and "I Couldn't See the Tears," (by Miller and Marcin), recorded by Dee Dee Marcin on Arzee Records (country).

*ARS NOVA MANAGEMENT, Box 421268, San Francisco CA 94142-1268. (415)864-2800. Professional Manager: Steven Scott. Music publisher. Publishes 12 songs/year; publishes 3 new songwriters/year. Works with composers and lyricists; teams collaborators. Pays standard royalty.

66 *Never write a bad song. Even if it doesn't get recorded, it'll come back to haunt you.* **99**

—*Al Kasha, songwriter*

Affiliates: Owl and Ars Nova Music, a subsidiary of Ars Nova Music (BMI) and Villa Ars Nova Music (ASCAP).
How to Contact: Prefers cassette with 3 songs. SASE. Reports in 1 month.
Music: Mostly MOR/AC, R&B and jazz/reggae. Published "People on a String" (by K. Wakefield), recorded by Roberta Flack on Columbia/CBS Records (motion picture score); "Voice on a Hotline" (by K. Wakefield), recorded by Don Johnson on Epic Records (rock); and "Best of Friends" (by K. Wakefield), recorded by Jacqui Scott on K-Tel Records (U.K.) (AC).

ART AUDIO PUBLISHING COMPANY/TIGHT HI-FI SOUL MUSIC, 9706 Cameron Ave., Detroit MI 48211. (313)893-3406. President: Albert M. Leigh. Professional Manager: Dolores M. Leigh. Music publisher and record company. BMI, ASCAP. Pays standard royalty.
How to Contact: Prefers cassette with 1-3 songs and lyric or lead sheets. SASE. Reports in 2 weeks.
Music: Mostly MOR, R&B, soul and rock; also disco, easy listening, gospel and top 40/pop. Published "Are You An Angel In Disguise" (by Albert M. Leigh), recorded by Willie Jennings on Echoic Hi-Fi Records (rock); "Jesus Showed Us The Way" (by W. Ayers) on X-Tone Records; and "Twon Special," written and recorded by Jesse Taylor on Echoic Hi-Fi Records (R&B).
Tips: "Basically we are interested only in a new product with a strong title, a love story, or an expressive, emotional sound. Arrange your songs to match a professional recording artist and his or her working style and pattern. Our record company must judge your tape according to the preference and demand of the current market place to decide if your songs are suitable. Keep lyrics up front on demo—make sure words are clearly understandable."

ASSOCIATED ARTISTS INTERNATIONAL (HOLLAND), Maarschalklaan 47, 3417 SE Montfoort, The Netherlands. (0)3484-2860. General Manager: Jochem C.R. Gerrits. Music publisher, record company (Associated Artists Records), record producer (Associated Artists Productions) and radio and TV promotors. BUMA. Publishes 200 songs/year; publishes 50 new songwriters/year. Pays by agreement.
Affiliate: BMC Publishing Holland (BUMA).
How to Contact: Submit demo tape by mail. Prefers compact cassette (or VHS videocassette). SAE and IRC. Reports in 1 month.
Music: Mostly disco, pop and Italian disco; also rock, gospel (evangelic), musicals, MOR and country. Works with "Electra Salsa," who "reached the top 40 in the Benelux countries, and the Disco dance top 50."

ASSOCIATED MUSIC PRODUCTIONS, (formerly Rio Hard Luck Music), Box 198, Grain Valley MO 64029. (816)229-7780. President: Dave Freeman. BMI, ASCAP. Music publisher (Rio Hard Luck Music/BMI), record company (DMI Records), record producer (Associated Music Productions), promotion and distribution company (Pro Music), recording studio and songwriters' organization. Publishes 600 songs/year; publishes 45 new songwriters/year. Works with composers and lyricists; teams collaborators. Pays standard royalty.
Affiliate: Bramble Bush Music.
How to Contact: Prefers cassette or 7½ or 15 ips ½ track reel-to-reel or 7½ ips ¼ track reel-to-reel with 3-4 songs and lyric and lead sheets. SASE. Reports in 6 weeks.
Music: Mostly country, pop and country rock ("all with crossover potential"); also R&B, rock and gospel. Published "How Do You Tell a Lady" (by David Roberts), recorded by Paul Wilson on DMI Records (country/pop); "San Diego" (by Josh Garrett/Dave Freeman), recorded by Sandy Richards (country/MOR crossover); and "My Lord" (by Josh Garrett/Walt Hummel), recorded by Sandra Marsh (gospel).
Tips: "The 'trend' in [writing] a hit song never changes. The production trends do change though, in association with equipment advances for special effects. Hit singles are novelty effects with music and lyrics. Say what you have to say uniquely and differently with a *captivating flair*."

ASTRODISQUE PUBLISHING, Plum Studio, 2 Washington St., Haverhill MA 01830. (617)372-4236. President: Richard Tiegen. Music publisher, record company (Plum Records) and record producer (Magic Sound Productions). BMI. Publishes 12 songs/year; publishes 1 new songwriter/year. Works with composers. Pays standard royalty. "Charges recording and production fees."
How to Contact: Write or call first to obtain permission to submit. Prefers cassette. Does not return unsolicited material. Reports in 3 weeks.
Music: Rock, R&B and country; also New Age and acoustic. Published "Stand by Me Baby" (by Dave Amato), recorded by Quadralaw; and "Let Me Come Home" written and recorded by Larry Milana, both on Plum Records (rock).

ATTIC PUBLISHING GROUP, 624 King St. W., Toronto, Ontario M5V 1M7 Canada. (416)862-0352. President: Al Mair. Professional Manager: Brian Allen. Music publisher and record company. Publishes

50 new songs/year; publishes 15 new songwriters/year. Pays standard royalty.
Affiliates: Pondwater Music (CAPAC) and Abovewater Music (PROCAN).
How to Contact: Prefers cassette with 1-4 songs and lyric sheet. SAE and IRC. Reports in 3 weeks or longer.
Music: Rock and top 40/pop.

AUDIO MUSIC PUBLISHERS, 449 N. Vista St., Los Angeles CA 90036. (213)658-6417. Contact: Ben Weisman. Music publisher, record company and record producer. ASCAP. Publishes 30-50 songs/year; publishes mostly new songwriters. Teams collaborators. Pays standard royalty.
How to Contact: Prefers cassette with 3-10 songs and lyric sheet. "We do not return unsolicited material without SASE." Reports in 1 month.
Music: Mostly pop, R&B, rap, dance and soul; also rock (all types). Published "What Have I Done for You Lately," (by Tolbert/Perry/Quinney), recorded by King MC on Street Talk Records (rap/dance); "Earthquake" written and recorded by Antron (rap); and "Blind Dates" (by Quinney), recorded by 2-counts Ice (rap).

*AUTEUR MUSIC, 705 W. Western, Urbana IL 61801. (217)367-3530. Owner: Michael A. Day. Music publisher. BMI. Publishes 20-40 songs/year; publishes 4 new songwriters/year. Works with composers and lyricists; teams collaborators.
Affiliates: Walkin Music (BMI) and Two Cities Music (BMI).
How to Contact: Prefers cassette with 1-4 songs and lyric sheet. Does not return unsolicited material. Reports in 6 weeks.
Music: Mostly R&B, pop and rock. Published "Right Away" (by M. Day/J. Kipnis/R. Maffit/P. Berry), recorded by Luther Ingram on Profile Records (R&B); "Off & On Love" (by R. Jones, M. Day, R. Maffit), recorded by Champaign on Columbia (R&B); and "Trials of The Heart" (by M. Day/R. Maffit/T. Bishop), recorded by Nancy Shanks on EMI Records (rock).

*AVILO MUSIC, 11112 Griffing Blvd., Biscayne Park FL 33161. (305)759-1405. President: Carlos Oliva. Music publisher, record company and record producer. BMI. Member NARM. Publishes 20 songs/year; publishes 2 new songwriters/year. Works with lyricists and teams collaborators. Pays standard royalty.
Affiliates: Oliva Music (SESAC) and Santa Clara Music (ASCAP).
How to Contact: Prefers cassette with any number of songs and lyric sheet. SASE. Reports in 2 weeks.
Music: Dance-oriented, Spanish and rock. Published "Say That You Love Me," by C. Valencia (pop salsa); "Te Lo Prometo," by M. Palacio (Spanish ballad); and "La Segunda Vuelta," by C. Olivia (pop salsa); all recorded by Los Sobrinos del Juez.
Tips: "Songs should have a strong hook, simple melody and sense-making lyrics."

AXBAR PRODUCTIONS, Box 12353, San Antonio TX 78212. (512)735-3322. Business Manager: Joe Scates. Music publisher, record company, record producer and record distributors. BMI. Member CMA. Publishes 30 songs/year; publishes 10-12 new songwriters/year. Works with composers. Pays standard royalty.
Affiliates: Axbar Productions and Axe Handle Music (ASCAP).
How to Contact: Arrange personal interview. Prefers cassette (or videocassette) with 1-5 songs and lyric sheet. SASE. Reports as soon as possible, but "we hold the better songs for more detailed study."
Music: Mostly country; also country crossover, comedy, blues, MOR and rock (soft). Published "One Bright Day," (by Ron Deming), recorded by Stampede on Axbar Records (country rock); "I Want to Come Back as a Harley," (by Russell Borders), recorded by Rusty Button on Prince Records (comedy); "Rosie Leaves a Ring Around the Tub," (by Ron Knuth), recorded by George Chambers on Axbar Records (country uptempo); and *Versatility* (LP by Kenny Dale), featuring nine songs written and recorded by Kenny Dale and published by Axe Handle Music (country).
Tips: "Polish your material. Don't expect us to rework your lyrics. Bad grammar and poor spelling hurt your chances."

B. SHARP MUSIC, 42 Avenue Clays, Brussels 1030 Belgium. (02)241-41-86. Music publisher, record company (Selection Records) and record producer (Pletinckx). Publishes 50 songs/year.
How to Contact: Submit demo tape by mail. Call first to arrange personal interview. Prefers cassette. Does not return unsolicited material. Reports in 2 weeks.
Music: Jazz and rock. Published "Trainer En Ville," written and recorded by A. Delchambre on Vogue; "Your Precious Love" (by K. Mulligan), and "Palavras" (by Eliane Elias), both recorded by Toots Thielemans on Polydor.

*BABY HUEY MUSIC, Box 121616, Nashville TN 37212. (615)259-2007. Professional Manager: Mark Stephan Hughes. Music publisher. ASCAP. Member NSA, GMA and IMU. Publishes 100 songs/ year; publishes 25 new songwriters/year. Works with composers and lyricists; teams collaborators. Pays standard royalty.
Affiliate: Krimson Hues Music (BMI).
How to Contact: Submit cassette only with 3 songs and typewritten lyric sheet. SASE. Reports in 4 weeks.
Music: Mostly country and R&B; also gospel, MOR, rock, rap, new music and top 40/pop. Published "Anything Worth Knowing,' recorded by Don Rogers on AV Records; "If You Play Your Heart Right," recorded by Jessica James on Trac Records; and "Cold Day in Love" recorded by Kenny Antcliff on Timestar Records.
Tips: "We are looking for commercial material in all styles, and professional songwriters to represent. Submit a good quality demo. We desperately need hit songs! We have producers, artists and labels waiting."

*BAD GRAMMAR MUSIC, 3518 Union-Lake Rd. 107, Mt. Clemens MI 48043. Music Director: Joe Trupiano. Music publisher, record producer (Bad Grammar Ent.) and management company. BMI. Publishes 10-20 songs/year; publishes 5-10 new songwriters/year. Pays standard royalty.
How to Contact: Prefers cassette with 3-4 songs and lyric sheet. Reports in 6 weeks.
Music: Mostly dance-oriented, pop/rock and rock; also easy listening, top 40/ballads and MOR. Published "Car Crazy," by Joey Harlo, (pop/rock); "Feel the Need," by The Detroit Emeralds (dance-oriented); and "Carousel," by Joey Harlo (rock), all recorded by Joey Harlo on Bad Grammar Records.
Tips: "Be commercial and trendy and keep it hooky, but write from your soul. Listen to what's getting airplay, keep music and lyrics simple, and tell a definite story. We need songs that the public can walk away humming. The biggest sellers in our industry today would have to be white R&B, pop/rock and light rock."

BAGATELLE MUSIC PUBLISHING CO., 400 San Jacinto St., Houston TX 77002. (713)225-6654. President: Byron Benton. BMI. Music publisher, record company and record producer. Publishes 40 songs/year; publishes 2 new songwriters/year. Pays standard royalty.
Affiliate: Floyd Tillman Publishing Co.
How to Contact: Prefers cassette (or videocassette) with any number of songs and lyric sheet.
Music: Mostly country; also gospel and blues. Published "Everything You Touch," written and recorded by Johnny Nelmo; "If I Could Do It All Over Again," written and recorded by Floyd Tillman; and "Mona from Daytona," (by Byron Benton), recorded by F. Tillman, all recorded on Bagatelle (country).

BAL & BAL MUSIC PUBLISHING CO., Box 369, LaCanada CA 91011. (213)952-1242. President: Adrian Bal. Music publisher, record company and record producer. ASCAP. Member AGAC and AIMP. Publishes 2-4 songs/year; publishes 2-4 new songwriters/year. Works with composers and lyricists; teams collaborators. Pays standard royalty.
How to Contact: Prefers cassette with 3 songs and lyric sheet. SASE. Reports in 1-3 months.
Music: Mostly MOR, country, rock and gospel; also blues, church/religious, easy listening, jazz, R&B, soul and top 40/pop. Recorded "Tiger Paws," (by Bob Gilbert), recorded by B. Gilbert and Terry Fischer on BAL Records (MOR); "Chilly Bones," written and recorded by Marge Calhoun on BAL Records (country); and "Sunday Service," and "Nicodemus" written and recorded by Jerry Chud on BAL Records (gospel).
Tips: "Songs should be commercial; purchased by 9- to 18-year-old group."

BANJO MAN MUSIC, INC., 3122 Sale St., Dallas TX 75219. (214)522-8900. Vice President Promotion: Ralph Witsell. Music publisher and record company. BMI, ASCAP. Member CMA, TMA. Pays standard royalty.
How to Contact: Prefers cassette with 1-2 songs and lyric sheet. SASE. Reports in 3 weeks.
Music: Strictly country.

BAY TONE MUSIC PUBLISHING, 1218 Hollister Ave., San Francisco CA 94124. (415)467-5157. Owner: Bradbury Taylor. Music publisher. BMI. Pays standard royalty.
Affiliates: Bay-Tone and Soul Set Records.
How to Contact: Write or call first and obtain permission to submit. Prefers cassette, 7½ or 15 ips reel-to-reel (or VHS videocassette) with any number of songs and lyric and lead sheets. Does not return unsolicited material. Reports in 2 months.
Music: Pop, rock and R&B. Published "Just Wasn't Meant to Be," and "Tonight Is Right" (by Elektryk Starr) recorded on Bay Tone Records; "Can You Hang," and "Roller Skate" (by James Tay-

lor), recorded by Frisco on Soul Set Records (R&B); and "Ball & Chain" (by Big Mama Thornton), recorded by Janis Joplin on Columbia Records (blues).
Tips: "Be precise; make sure the story is complete to the music."

BEARSONGS, 190 Monument Rd., Birmingham, B16 8UV England. 44-021-454-7020. Managing Director: Jim Simpson. Music publisher and record company. MCPS, PRS. Publishes 25 songs/year; publishes 15-20 new songwriters/year.
How to Contact: Prefers reel-to-reel or cassette. SAE and IRC. Reports in 2-3 weeks.
Music: Blues, jazz and soul.

BEAUTIFUL DAY MUSIC, % Omnipop Enterprises, Suite 225, 223 Jericho Turnpike, Mineola NY 11501. (516)248-4019. Branch: 22240 Schoenborn St., Canoga Park CA 91304. (818)883-4865. Contact: Tom Ingegno (New York); Mike Frenchik (California). Music publisher and record producer. BMI. Publishes 10-20 songs/year; publishes 4 new songwriters/year. Pays standard royalty.
How to Contact: Prefers cassette with minimum of 3 songs and lyric sheet. SASE. Reports in 3 weeks.
Music: Rock and top 40/pop. Published "Breaking My Heart" (by Ingegno/Monaco/Frenchik); "Tonight" (by Fullerton); and "You Don't Remember Me" (by Ingegno), all recorded by Thrills (all rock).

BECKIE PUBLISHING COMPANY, INC., Box 14671, Memphis TN 38114. (901)272-7039. President: Linda Lucchesi. Music publisher. ASCAP, BMI. Works with artists, producers, record companies, and publishes many new songwriters/year.
Affiliates: Memphis Town Music, Inc. and Simply Grand Music, Inc.
How to Contact: Prefers cassette with 1-3 songs and lyric sheet. SASE. Reports in 1 month.
Music: Mostly pop and soul; also easy listening, MOR, R&B, hard and soft rock.
Tips: "We're the publishing home of 'Wooly Bully'!"

*BEE BOP MUSIC,168 Empress Ave., North York, Ontario M2N 3T8 Canada. (416)221-7445. President: Brian Bell. Music publisher and record producer (B.F.H.B. Audio Inc.). CAPAC. Works with composers and lyricists; teams collaborators. Pays standard royalty.
How to Contact: Write to arrange personal interview. Prefers cassette with 4 songs, and lyric sheet. Does not return unsolicited material. Reports in 1 month.
Music: Mostly pop, new music, and rock; also jazz and MOR. Published "Lucky Ones", "Every Time" and "Feeling Is Love" (all by Black/Ward/Bell), all recorded by Terry and Laurel Black (pop/MOR).

BEE RAY MUSIC, #611, 7046 Hollywood Blvd., Hollywood CA 90028. (213)462-0502. Contact: Harry Gordon. Teams collaborators. Pays standard royalty.
How to Contact: Prefers cassette (or videocassette). SASE.
Music: Mostly country and R&B.

BEECHWOOD MUSIC, 6920 Sunset Blvd., Hollywood CA 90028. (213)469-8371. President: Fred Willms Sr. Vice President: Jack Rosner. Music publisher. BMI and ASCAP. Member NMPA. Publishes several songs/year. Hires staff writers.
Affiliates: Screen Gems/EMI (BMI) and Colgems/EMI (ASCAP).
How to Contact: Call first. Prefers cassette and lyric/lead sheet. Refuses unsolicited material. SASE. Reports in 1 month.
Music: MOR, rock and top 40/pop.

QUINT BENEDETTI MUSIC, Box 2388, Toluca Lake CA 91602. (818)985-8284. Contact: Quint Benedetti. Music publisher, record producer and artist manager. ASCAP. Pays standard royalty.
Affiliate: Mi-Dav-An-Mark Music (BMI).
How to Contact: Prefers cassette with 3 songs and lead sheet. Submit Christmas songs no later than July 15. SASE. Reports in 2 months "or sooner."
Music: Christmas songs only. Published "Christmas Is for Children," "Christmas Presents," and "Put the Loot in the Boot, Santa."
Tips: "Follow instructions to the letter. Be professional and don't bug by phone."

BERANDOL MUSIC LTD., 110A Sackville St., Toronto, Ontario, M5A 3E7 Canada. (416)869-1872. A&R Director: Tony Procewiat. Music publisher, record company, record producer and distributor. BMI. Member CMPA, CIRPA, CRIA. Publishes 25 songs/year; publishes 10 new songwriters/year. Pays standard royalty.
How to Contact: Submit demo tape with 2-5 songs. Reports in 6 weeks.
Music: Hip-hop, funk and R&B; also children's. Published "Love Theme From Canada," recorded by

The Cosmic Orchestra, and "Toy Piano," recorded by Toronto Pops Orchestra, both instrumental pieces written by Ralph Cruickshank.

HAL BERNARD ENTERPRISES, INC., Box 20244, 443 Riddle Rd #1, Cincinnati OH 45220. (513)861-1500. President: Stan Hertzman. Professional Manager: Pepper Bonar. Music publisher, record company and management firm. Pays negotiable royalty.
Affiliates: Sunnyslope Music (ASCAP), Bumpershoot Music (BMI), Apple Butter Music (ASCAP), Barc Music (ASCAP), Saiko Music (ASCAP), TYI Music (ASCAP) and Smorgaschord Music (AS-CAP).
How to Contact: Prefers cassette with 3 songs and lyric sheet. SASE. Reports in 6 weeks.
Music: Rock, R&B and top 40/pop. Published "Twang Bar King" (by Adrian Belew), recorded by Belew on Island Records (progressive); "Fear is Never Boring," "Trust" and "Superboy" recorded by The Bears on PMRC/IRS Records (rock); and "Stupid in Love" (by P. Michael), recorded by The Adults on Strugglebaby Records (rock).
Tips: "Best material should appear first on demo. Cast your demos. If you as the songwriter can't sing it—don't. Get someone who can present your song properly, use a straight rhythm track and keep it as naked as possible. If you think it still needs something else, have a string arranger, etc. help you, but still keep the *voice up* and the *lyrics clear*."

M. BERNSTEIN MUSIC PUBLISHING CO., 2170 S. Parker Rd., Denver CO 80231. (303)755-2613. President: R.J. Bernstein. Music publisher, record company (Finer Arts Records), and record producer (Transworld Records). ASCAP, BMI. Publishes 50 songs/year; publishes 5-10 new songwriters/year.
How to Contact: Prefers cassette and lyric or lead sheet. Does not return unsolicited material. Reports in 1 month.
Music: Rock, country and jazz.

BETH-RIDGE MUSIC PUBLISHING CO., Suite 204, 1508 Harlem, Memphis TN 38114. (901)274-2726. Contact: Professional Manager. Music publisher, record company, record producer and recording studio. BMI. Publishes 40 songs/year; publishes 4-7 new songwriters/year. Pays standard royalty.
Affiliate: Chartbound Music Ltd. (ASCAP).
How to Contact: "Write or call to see what our needs are." Prefers 15 or 7½ ips reel-to-reel or cassette with 3-5 songs and lyric sheet. SASE. Reports in 1 month.
Music: Mostly R&B, top 40, dance and blues; also soul and gospel. Published "Hooked on Love," written and recorded by Eddie Mayberry on Blue Town Records (blues/R&B); "Are You Ready" (by Willie Blair/N. Horn), recorded on GCS Records (gospel); and "Across the Miles," (by Lee Moss) recorded on GCS Records.

BEVERLY HILLS MUSIC PUBLISHING DIVISION, Box 3842, Houston TX 77253-3842. Branch: Box 1659, Beverly Hills CA 90213. Branch: Box 741, Lake Charles LA 70602. President: Dr. Lawrence Herbst. Music publisher. BMI. Publishes 10 songs/year. Pays standard royalty.
Affiliates: Lawrence Herbst Investment Trust Fund, Inc.; K-Larr Broadcasting Network and Larr Computer Corp.
How to Contact: Prefers cassette (or VHS videocassette) and lyric sheet. Does not return unsolicited material. Reports in 3 weeks.
Music: Mostly country, top 40/pop and rock; also bluegrass, blues, easy listening, folk, jazz, progressive, R&B and soul.

*BIG FISH MUSIC, 11927 Magnolia Blvd., North Hollywood CA 91607. (818)984-0377. Professional Manager: Chuck Tennin. Music publisher. BMI. Publishes 30 song/year; publishes 15 new songwriters/year. Works with composers. Pays standard royalty.
Affiliate: California Sun Music (ASCAP).
How to Contact: Write to obtain permission to submit. Prefers cassette with maximum of 1-5 songs and lyric or lead sheet. "All submissions must include a cover letter and SASE with sufficient postage and proper mailing envelope that meets U.S. Postal standards." Reports in 3 weeks.
Music: Mosly pop ballads, rock, and country cross-over; very interested in "instrumental theme and background music for TV (with vocals are OK), novelty songs and some up-tempo gospel and songs in general with a positive uplifting message with lots of feeling." Published "Timewatch" (by B. Pierson) recorded by General Hospital (instumental theme T.V.); "I Can Make It Right Tonight" (by McMeans/Barich), recorded by General Hospital, also on an album project, (pop ballad with vocals); and "I Was Wrong" (by McMeans), recorded by General Hospital, also on an album project. Currently working on album projects with different artists and placing music on various ABC television shows.
Tips: "A clean sounding cassette with clear and understable vocals supplimented with a good musical arrangement. Songs with strong feelings."

*BIG "K" MUSIC INC., Box 9608, Rosedale MD 21237. (301)574-5141. Vice President: Ernest W. Cash. BMI. Music publisher, record company and record producer. Estab. 1986. Publishes 20-30 new songwriters/year. Pays standard royalty.
Affiliates: Guerriero Music, Continental Records and Big "K" Records.
How to Contact: Call first to arrange personal interview. Prefers cassette and lead sheets. Does not return unsolicited material. Reports in 1 month.
Music: Mostly country, gospel and blue grass. Published "Show Me the Way" (by Art Daniels), "Drink Her Memory Down" and "Doctor of Love" all country songs recorded by Ernie Cash on Big "K" Records.

BIG STATE MUSIC PUBLISHING, 1311 Candlelight Ave., Dallas TX 75116. (214)298-9576. President: Paul S. Ketter. Music publisher and record company (Sagittar Records). BMI, ASCAP. Publishes 25 songs/year; publishes 12 new songwriters/year. Pays standard royalty.
Affiliate: Pineapple Music Publishing Co. (ASCAP).
How to Contact: Prefers cassette or 7½ ips reel-to-reel with 1-6 songs and lyric sheet. SASE. Reports in 6 weeks.
Music: Mostly country, folk and blues; also pop and MOR. Published "Someday" (by P.J. Kamel), recorded by Bunnie Mills on Bun Jack Records; "Adam's Rib," written and recorded by Debbie Dierks on Dove Records; and "Lovin' Bound" (by D. Beneteau), recorded by P.J. Kamel on Sagittar Records (all country).
Tips: "Write for today's market—opportunities for new writers have never been better."

BIG WEDGE MUSIC, Box 25329, Nashville TN 37202. (615)754-2950. President: Ralph Johnson. BMI. Music publisher. Publishes 100 new songwriters/year. Works with composers and lyricists; teams collaborators. Pays standard royalty.
Affiliates: Wedge Entertainment Group, Wedge Records, Inc., and Pro-Star Talent, Inc.
How to Contact: Prefers cassette (or videocassette) with maximum of 4 songs and lyric sheet or lead sheet. SASE. Reports in 2 weeks.
Music: Mostly country, pop and rock; also gospel and R&B. Published "Mr. Blue Eyes" (by Jackie Minarik/Chic Bixby/Billy Lee Napier), recorded by Will Beery (country/pop); and "My Dreams Came True" written and recorded by Stella Parton (country/pop), both on Wedge Records.

BILLETDOUX MUSIC PUBLISHING, Box 11960, Chicago IL 60611. (312)561-0027. Production Manager: Nancy Rubin. Music publisher, record company and record producer. BMI. Publishes 10 songs/year; publishes 3 new songwriters/year. Works with lyricists and composers; teams collaborators. Pays standard royalty.
How to Contact: Prefers cassette (or videocassette) with 3-5 songs and lyric sheet. SASE. Reports in 1 month.
Music: Mostly R&B, pop and gospel; also blues, country, MOR, rock (country and hard), soul and top 40/pop. Published "Lie to Me," written and recorded by Mack Simmons on Grandville Records (blues); "Messin' with the Kid," (by Walter Jacob), recorded by M. Simmons on Grandville Records; and "Love You No Matter What," (by C. Rubin), recorded by John Williams on Grandville Records (R&B/pop).

BLACK STALLION COUNTRY PUBLISHING, Box 2250, Culver City CA 90230. (213)419-8142. President: Kenn Kingsbury. Music publisher and book publisher (*Who's Who in Country & Western Music*). BMI. Member ACM, CMA, CMF. Publishes 2 songs/year; publishes 1 new songwriter/year. Pays standard royalty.
How to Contact: Prefers 7½ ips reel-to-reel or cassette with 2-4 songs and lyric sheet. SASE. Reports in 1 month.
Music: Bluegrass, country and top 40/pop.
Tips: "Be professional in attitude and presentation. Submit only the material you think is better than anything being played on the radio."

BLACKHEART MUSIC, Box 15856, St. Louis MO 63114. (314)576-1569. Contact: Robert Schoenfeld. Music publisher, record company and record producer. Publishes 20-30 songs/year; publishes 1-2 new songwriters/year. Pays standard royalty.
How to Contact: Prefers cassette with 4-6 songs and lyric sheet. SASE. Reports in 3 weeks.
Music: Mostly reggae, blues and R&B.
Tips: Looking for "gutsy tunes with character and a message."

MARK BLACKWOOD MUSIC GROUP, Box 172351, Memphis TN 38187. (901)761-5180. President: Mark Blackwood. Music publisher. Publishes 10-25 songs/year; publishes 3-6 new songwriters/

year. Works with composers and lyricists; teams collaborators. Pays standard royalty.
Affiliates: Songs From the Box (BMI), Voice of Paradise (ASCAP).
How To Contact: Write first and obtain permission to submit. Prefers cassette or videocassette with 3 songs and lyric sheet. SASE. Reports in 4 weeks.
Music: Mostly gospel, also rock and pop. Published "The Answer" (by Everette Brown) (gospel); "Show Me Your Way" (by Sparrow Holt) (gospel); and "That's What's Wrong" (by Alan Ladd) all recorded by Blackwood Brothers.

*BLUE CORRAL MUSIC, Box 2469, Havre MT 59501. (406)395-4714. Manager/Editor: Paul F. Russette. Music publisher, record company (KBA Records), and music production company. BMI. "We work primarily with new writers, new material and songs." Works with composers and lyricists; teams collaborators. "We work with writers who need music written for their lyrics, on a 50/50 basis if the writer agrees. We do not charge for this service."
How to Contact: Prefers cassettes with 1-4 songs and lyric sheet. "We do not accept reel-to-reel or 8-track recordings." SASE. Reports in 1 month. "No phone calls, unless we have a signed contract with you."
Music: Country, progressive country and blues. Published "Love You," and "Indian Country," recorded on Kessler Records.

BLUE HILL MUSIC PUBLISHING, 308 Munger Lane, Bethlehem CT 06751. (203)266-7411. Professional Manager: Paul Hotchkiss. Music publisher, record company (Target Records) and record producer (Red Kastle). BMI. Member CMA, CSA. Publishes 10-12 songs/year; publishes 6-7 new songwriters/year. Pays standard royalty.
Affiliate: Tutch Music Publishing (BMI).
How to Contact: Write first. Prefers cassette with 2 songs and lyric sheet. SASE. Reports in 2 weeks.
Music: Mostly country and pop; also MOR/AOR and R&B. Published "Inside Out" (by P. Hotchkiss), recorded by Tina Daniell on Chasta Records (country/pop); "Kadaffy Duck" (by P. Hotchkiss), recorded by Hutchen Brothers on Poole Records (country); and "Texas Honky Tonk's" (by P. Hotchkiss), recorded by Terry Staford on Playback Records (country).
Tips: "Songs should have good solid lyrics with a message; good vocal on the demo."

BLUE ISLAND PUBLISHING, Box 171265, San Diego CA 92117-0975. (619)576-9666. General Manager: Bob Gilbert. Music publisher, record company and record producer. Publishes 50 songs/year. Pays standard royalty.
Affiliates: Bob Fleming Music (BMI), Dahlhouse Publishing (ASCAP), and Bob Gilbert Music (BMI).
How to Contact: Prefers cassette with 3-6 songs and lyric sheets. "Submit only your best single-oriented songs to fit top 40 format. Easy to understand songs with strong hooks and good lyrics make it." SASE. Reports in 3 weeks.
Music: Country, MOR, rock, top 40/pop and disco/dance.

BLUE STANDARD MUSIC, Suite 1502, 6430 Sunset Blvd., Hollywood CA 90028. (213)463-9500. Chairman: Terrence Brown. Music publisher, record company, record producer and video producer. BMI, ASCAP. Member NARAS, NAIRD, NARM, ILA. Publishes 48 songs/year; publishes 12 new songwriters/year. Hires staff writers; pays $600-1,200/month. Pays standard royalty of 50%.
Affiliates: Clear Blue (BMI) and Oz Magical (ASCAP).
How to Contact: Prefers cassette (or videocassette) with "best" songs and lyric sheet. SASE. Reports in 2 months.
Music: Mostly dance/rock and R&B; also dance-oriented, rock, soul and top 40/pop. Published medley with "Please Mr. Postman," and "He Said He Didn't, (by Tom DePiero), recorded by Delia Renee (R&B); and "I Like It" (by Bledsae/Spells/Story/Trummell), recorded by Take One (soul).
Tips: Looking for "new music styles similar to Petshop Boys, Stacey Q, Comunards, Depech Mode, etc."

BLUE UMBRELLA MUSIC PUBLISHING CO./PARASOL MUSIC PUBLISHING CO., 3011 Beach 40th St., Brooklyn NY 11224. (718)372-6436. Contact: Mr. Kadish Millet. Music publisher. ASCAP, BMI. Publishes 10 songs/year; publishes 3 new songwriters/year. Pays standard royalty.
How to Contact: Prefers cassette with 1-10 songs and lead sheet. Prefers studio produced demos. "Wrap cassette well; some cassette boxes have fairly sharp edges and break through envelope. I want a lead sheet (not lyric sheet) and accurate information on who owns the copyright and if it was registered in Washington at the time of submission. Affiliation of writers or non-affiliation needed in order to issue proper contract." SASE "with proper amount of return postage." Reports in 2 weeks.

Music: Country. "I want only country songs with double entendre (sexy, adult type) lyrics such as 'Behind Closed Doors,' 'Almost Persuaded,' 'Here Comes My Weekend Friend,' 'Help Me Make it Through the Night,' 'Sleepin' Single in a Double Bed,' and 'Teach Me to Cheat.' "
Tips: "In this day and age of groups and singer/songwriters (who are fortunate enough to have a recording contract) writing, arranging and recording their own songs, the music business has become virtually impossible. There is no room anymore for just a 'pretty good song'. It has to be a supersong or 'blockbuster'. Even then the odds are against getting a song recorded. Be aware of that fact when sending out material."

*BLUEBIRD MUSIC OY,Henrikintei 5C, Helsinki HK1 37 Finland. (90)557519. Managing Director: Osmo Ruuskanen. Music publisher and record company. TEOSTO. Publishes 100 songs/year. Works with composers and lyricists; teams collaborators. Pays standard royalty.
How to Contact: Prefers cassette. Does not return unsolicited material. Reports in 1 month.
Music: Mostly MOR, pop and rock; also country and R&B.

BOCAGE MUSIC, Box 1061, Willow Grove PA 19090. (215)657-8863. Vice President Marketing: Elena Marino. Music publisher and record company (MusiCrafters). ASCAP. Publishes 50 songs/year; publishes 5 new songwriters/year. Pays standard royalty.
Affiliate: MusiCrafters (BMI).
How to Contact: Submit demo tape by mail. Prefers cassette.
Music: Mostly pop, rock and jazz; also country. Published "Science," by L. Clutterham (rock); "Fresh Start," by L. de Lise and "There and Back," by W. Zaccagni (pop/jazz), all recorded by MusiCrafters Orchestra on MusiCrafters Records.
Tips: "Send instrumentals only. Materials must be copyrighted. Music is published for use as 'Music Library' material only. We prefer to publish finished tracks."

BOGGY DEPOT MUSIC, 10051 Greenleaf, Santa Fe Spring CA 90670. (213)946-3193. President: Overton Lee. Music publisher, record company, record producer and video producer. BMI, ASCAP. Publishes 10 songs/year. Pays standard royalty.
How to Contact: Prefers cassette with 1-3 songs and lyric sheet. Does not return unsolicited material. Reports in 3-4 months.
Music: Mostly country; also bluegrass, blues and gospel. Published "It May Be Tonight," recorded by Gene Davis on O.L. Records (country); "Ordinary Hero," recorded by The Bonner Family on O.L. Records (country); and "I Have a Dream," recorded by Darvy Traylor on O.L. Records (gospel).

BOOGIETUNES MUSIKPRODUKTION GMBH, Hohenzollerndamm 54a, 1000 Berlin 33, West Germany. (030)8237025. Managing Director: Timothy E. Green. Music publisher and record company. Publishes 100 songs/year; publishes 2 new songwriters/year. Pays standard GEMA rate.
How to Contact: Prefers cassette (or VHS videocassette). Does not return unsolicited material.
Music: Mostly disco/dance and electronic. Published "You," (by Peter Sawatzki), recorded by Boytronic on Mercury (disco); and "Geil," (by Bruce Hammond), recorded by Bruce & Bongo on Rush Records (disco/dance).
Tips: "Write good commercial pop."

*BOOTCHUTE MUSIC CO., Suite 360, 12233 West Olympic Blvd., Los Angeles CA 90064. (213)826-3663. Administrator: Warren Wagner. Music Publisher. BMI. Publishes 12 songs/year; publishes 1 new songwriter/year. Pays standard royalty.
Affiliate: Fallin' Arches Music (ASCAP).
How to Contact: Prefers cassette with 1-4 songs and lyric sheet. Reports in 1-2 months "only if interested".
Music: Mostly pop; also bluegrass, blues, classical, country, easy listening, gospel, R&B, rock and soul. Recently published "I Don't Need You" (by R. Christian), recorded by Kenny Rogers on EMI Records (pop/country).

BOP TALK MUSIC, Box 566, Massena NY 13662. (315)769-2448. Vice President: Thomas Gramuglia. Music publisher and record company. Pays standard royalty.
Affiliate: Tom Tom Publishing Co.

66 *If you pay attention for one day, you'll have enough material to write for the rest of your life.* **99**
—Don Schlitz, songwriter, NSAI Symposium

How to Contact: Prefers 7½ ips reel with 1-12 songs. SASE. Reports in 1 month.
Music: Jazz and folk.

*BOTTOM LINE PRODUCTIONS,Box 161358, Memphis TN 38116. (901)332-6540. Chairman: Tommy Boyce. President: Phyllis Presley. Music publisher and record producer (Tommy Boyce Music). Estab. 1986. Publishes 7-47 songs/year; publishes 2-10 new songwriters/year. Works with composers and lyricists; teams collaborators.
How to Contact: Write to obtain permission to submit. Prefers cassette (or VHS videocassette) with maximum of 4 songs and lyric sheet. Does not return unsolicited material. Reports in 2 months.
Music: Mostly rock, pop and country. Published "Roll On Back To You" and "You Can't Break My Heart", both written by Tommy Boyce and recorded by CC Craig and Tommy Boyce (country); and "Johnny B. Lonesome" (by Boyce/Levine), recorded by Tommy Boyce (country).

*BRAINSTORM MUSIC,#20A, 407 Park Ave. S., New York NY 10016. (212)213-9595. Professional Manager: Bernie Mueller. Music publisher and record producer (Amuse America, Inc.). ASCAP.
How to Contact: Write first and obtain permission to submit. Prefers cassette with 3 songs. Does not return unsolicited material. Reports in 6 weeks.
Music: Mostly rock, pop and R&B.

BRANCH INTERNATIONAL MUSIC, Box 31819, Dallas TX 75231. (214)750-0720. A&R Director: Mike Anthony. Music publisher. BMI. Publishes 20 songs/year. Pays standard maximum royalty.
How to Contact: Prefers cassette with 1-4 songs and lead or lyric sheet. SASE. Reports in 1 month.
Music: Country and gospel. Published "Too Many Ladies," by David Denman/Kevin Clark/Bart Barton (country); and "Hide Me," by Jess Hudson/Kenny Serrat (uptempo country) both recorded by D. Denman on Yatahey Records (uptempo country).

BRAVE NEW MUSIC, Box 25695, Los Angeles CA 90025. (213)273-7001. President: Dan Friedman. Music publisher. BMI. Publishes 6 songs/year; publishes 3 new songwriters/year. Pays standard royalty.
Affiliates: Modern Art Music (ASCAP). Administers: Somewhat Urgent Music (BMI), and Millsong Music (ASCAP).
How to Contact: Prefers cassette with 1-4 songs. SASE. Reports in 2 weeks.
Music: Pop/top 40. Published "Moonlight Marvel," (by Craig Donaldson/Tim Schumacher), recorded by WicketyWak on Southside Records-Canada (pop); and "Russian Rock," (compilation), recorded by various artists on Hot Wax Records-Australia.
Tips: "We are primarily involved in international leasing deals and subpublishing, not much song plugging."

BRIGHT & MORNINGSTAR PUBLISHING CO., Box 18A241, Los Angeles CA 90018. (213)512-7823. President: Stan Christopher. Music publisher. ASCAP. Publishes 7 songs/year; publishes 7 new songwriters/year. Pays standard royalty.
How to Contact: Prefers cassette or 15 ips reel-to-reel with 1-3 songs and lyric or lead sheet. SASE. Reports in 3 weeks.
Music: Mostly contemporary Christian, inspirational gospel and gospel/rock; also "message music." Published "Agape Love," "Change Your Life," and "Which Way Are You Going," (by Stan Christopher), recorded by The Messenger on Bright & Morningstar Records (contemporary Christian).
Tips: "Make sure that we can understand the lyrics. Have a strong hook, along with a good story."

BRIGHT EVENING STAR PUBLISHING, Box 125, Kirbyville TX 75956. (409)423-5516. Professional Manager: Robbie Gibson. Music publisher. BMI. Estab. 1985. Publishes 5-10 songs/year; publishes 2-3 new songwriters/year. Pays standard royalty.
How to Contact: Prefers cassette with 1-4 songs and lyric or lead sheet. Reports ASAP.
Music: Gospel. Published "You'd Be Homesick Too" and "Brighter Days" (by Robbie Gibson), recorded by The Gibsons on Gold Street Records (gospel).

BURIED TREASURE MUSIC, 524 Doral Country Dr., Nashville TN 37221. Executive Producer: Scott Turner. Music publisher and record producer. ASCAP. Publishes 75-125 songs/year; publishes 4-6 new songwriters/year. Pays standard royalty.
Affiliates: Captain Kidd Music (BMI) and Aberdeen Productions.
How to Contact: Prefers cassette (or videocassette) with 1-4 songs and lead sheet. Reports in 3 weeks. "Always enclose SASE if answer is expected."
Music: Country, rock, MOR and contemporary. Published "Blue Ridge," (by Rick Malis/Bob Artis), recorded by Jonathan Edwards on Sugar Hill Records (country); "The Hard Times," (by R&J Iantosca), recorded by Billy Joe Royal on Atlantic America Records (pop); and "Any Two Fools," (by George Wurzbach/Dianne Baumgartner), recorded by Jonathan Edwards and Margaret Lester on Custom Records (pop country).

Tips: "*Don't* send songs in envelopes that are 15"x20", or by registered mail. It doesn't help a bit. Say something that's been said a thousand times before . . . only say it differently. A great song doesn't care who sings it. Songs that paint pictures have a better chance of ending up as videos."

BUSH/LEHRMAN MUSIC, 928 Broadway, New York NY 10010. (212)505-7332. Professional Managers: Ted Lehrman, Libby Bush. Music publisher and record producer. ASCAP. Publishes 5 songs/year. Pays standard royalty.
How to Contact: Write or call for permission to submit cassettes only with no more than 3 songs and lyric sheets. Reports in 8 weeks. SASE.
Music: Mostly MOR, rock, R&B/pop and country/pop; also dance and adult contemporary. Published "I Refuse to Lose Your Love Again," (by J.B. White/Ted Lehrman/Libby Bush), recorded by Eleanor Grant on CBS Records (R&B/pop).
Tips: "Send us potential hit singles material only, no album cuts. Strong hooks; positive, intelligent lyrics; medium and up-tempo songs; well-produced demos."

C.T.P., 150 5th Ave., New York NY 10011. (212)691-5630. A&R Director: Bruce E. Colfin. Music publisher. ASCAP. Publishes 10-20 songs/year; publishes 1-2 new songwriters/year.
How to Contact: Prefers cassette (or VHS ¾" videocassette). Does not return unsolicited material.
Music: Mostly pop, rock and pop/rock; also blues, blues/rock and jazz.

*CABRIOLET MUSIC, Box 9, Benton LA 71006. (318)965-0781.Contact: Don Logan. Music publisher. BMI. Pays standard royalty.
How to Contact: Prefers 7½ ips reel-to-reel with 2-4 songs. SASE. Reports as soon as possible.
Music: Country, disco, gospel, soul, and spiritual. Published "That's Alright," recorded by Zion Jubilees (spiritual); "Do You Believe in Disco?", recorded by Sam Benson (disco); and "Hide Behind the Mountain," recorded by Mt. Pleasant Choir (gospel).

CACTUS MUSIC AND GIDGET PUBLISHING, 5 Aldom Circle, West Caldwell NJ 07006. Owner: Tar Heel Pete. Music publisher and record company (Dynamite Records). ASCAP. Publishes 5 songs/year; publishes 3 new songwriters. Works with composers and lyricists. Pays standard royalty.
Affiliate: Jimmy Allison Music (BMI).
How to Contact: Write first and obtain permission to submit. Prefers cassette with 3 songs minimum and lead sheet. Does not return unsolicited material. Reports in 1 month.
Music: Mostly country, rock and gospel; also bluegrass, blues, easy listening, R&B and top 40/pop. Published "One Way Ticket to Love" (by Wellman/Hall), recorded by Wayne Faust (western swing); "Marine Dang Doo" and "Grabbin' at Straws" written and recorded by Jimmy Long (country) all on Dynamite Records.

CALVARY MUSIC GROUP, INC., 142 8th Ave. N., Nashville TN 37203. (615)244-8800. President: Dr. Nelson S. Parkerson. Music publisher (ASCAP, BMI, SESAC) and record company. Publishes 30-40 songs/year; publishes 2-3 new songwriters/year. Pays standard royalty.
Affiliates: Songs of Calvary, Music of Calvary and LifeStream Music, Soldier of the Light, Torchbearer Music.
How to Contact: Prefers cassette with 1-3 songs and lyric sheet. SASE. Reports in 6 weeks.
Music: Church/religious, contemporary Christian, gospel and wedding music.

CAMERICA MUSIC, 535 5th Ave., Penthouse 35th Floor, New York NY 10017. (212)682-8400. Music publisher, record company (Camerica Records/U.S. Records) and record producer (Camerica Productions) . Contact: A&R Dept. ASCAP, BMI. Publishes 40 songs/year; publishes 5 new songwriters/year. Works with composers. Pays standard royalty.
Affiliate: Camex Music.
How to Contact: Prefers cassette with 1-2 songs. "Songs should have great hooks, interesting chord changes, classic melodies and conversational lyrics." Does not return unsolicited material. Reports in 6 weeks. "Include name and address on cassette."
Music: Mostly rock, easy listening, jazz, soul and top 40/pop. Published "Wish We Were Heroes" (by Austin Gravelding), recorded by Kenny Dale on Capitol Records (country/pop); and "Change of Heart" (by Eric Carmen), recorded by Donna Fargo on Warner Bros. Records (pop rock).

CAMPAGNE S.A., 116 Champs Elysées, Paris 75008 France. (4)563-1727. President: Harry Auerhaan. Music publisher and record company. Publishes 20 songs/year. Pays standard royalty.
How to Contact: Prefers cassette. SAE and IRC. Reports in 2 weeks.
Music: Rock, MOR, and reggae. Published "Waikiki Beach" (by Francoeur/Bordello), recorded by Francoeur on Campagne Records (rock); "Jeena" (by J. Detressan), recorded by Detressan on Cam-

pagne/EMT Records (rock); and "A La Fete Du Canton" (by Delanoe/Saferts), recorded by G. Block on Campagne Records.

CANADIAN CUSTOM RECORDS, 749 Warden Ave., Scarborough, Ontario M1L 4A8 Canada. (416)288-1653. President: Barbara L. Kroetsch. Music publisher, record company (Via Records), and record producer (DeBarre Productions). PRO, CAPAC.
How to Contact: Prefers cassette with 6 songs and lead sheet. SAE and IRC. Reports in 4 weeks.
Music: Contemporary, alternative, rock, country, gospel, blues and jazz.

CANADIAN MUSIC PRODUCTIONS, (formerly Mainroads Publishing), 773 Albion Rd., Rexdale, Ontario M9V 1A2 Canada. (416)749-8984. A&R Director: Chris Redner. Music publisher, record company, record producer and distributor. CAPAC, ASCAP, SESAC. Publishes 30-70 songs/year; publishes 3 new songwriters/year. Employs songwriters on a salary basis. Pays standard royalty.
How to Contact: Prefers cassette (or VHS videocassette) with 3 songs and lyric sheet or lead sheet. Does not return unsolicited material. Reports in 2 months.
Music: Mostly gospel; also pop, rock, jazz and country. Published "With My Whole Heart" (by Morley Halsmith), recorded by Diane Alimena (worship); "Rejoice and Be Glad" (by Anne Hilsden), recorded by Diane Alimena (gospel/pop); and "Tears Are So Sweet" (by Lori Dortono), recorded by John and Lori Dortono (ballad/pop).

*CANAM MUSIC, Suite 222, 689 Central Ave., St. Petersburg FL 33701. (813)892-3444. President: Mike Douglas. Music publisher. BMI. Publishes various number of songs and new songwriters/year. Pays standard royalty.
How to Contact: "No phone calls requesting permission to submit. We answer written requests only. When submitting, send a cassette with 3 songs and lyric or lead sheets. Clearly label each item you send with your name and address." Does not return unsolicited material. Reports in 10 days.
Music: Contemporary Christian/gospel.

*CANTUS PUBLISHING CO., INC., 156 Woodburn Ave., Toronto, Ontario M5M 1K7 Canada. (416)484-1728. President: Milan Kymlicka. Music publisher, record company (Firmus Records) and record producer (Cantus Productions Ltd.). CAPAC. Publishes 50 songs/year; publishes 1-2 new songwriters/year. Works with composers and lyricists. Pays standard royalty or 10% retail price.
Affiliate: Firmus Publishing Co. (PRO).
How to Contact: Prefers cassette with 3 songs and lyric sheet. Include a "short resume." Does not return unsolicited material. Reports in 1 month.
Music: Mostly pop and classical. Published "Big Ship" (by Woszak/Dolman), recorded by Dolman on Broadway Records (pop); "Special Love" (by Kymlicka/Tripe), recorded by B. Richardson on Firmus Records (pop); and "Funny" (by Foldy/Shirman), recorded by P. Foldy on Capitol/Polydor Records (pop).

CAPAQUARIUS PUBLISHING & ARTIST MGT., INC., Suite 1106, 4525 Henry Hudson Parkway, Riverdale NY 10463. (212)549-6318 or 222-2933. Europe: Seeburgerstr 87, 100 Berlin 20, West Berlin Germany. (030) 331-4568. President: P. Januari Watts. Music publisher, record producer and artist management firm. ASCAP. Publishes 3-4 songs/year; publishes 1 new songwriter/year. Works with composers and lyricists; teams collaborators. Pays standard royalty.
Affiliate: Yanita Music (BMI).
How to Contact: Prefers cassette (or NTSC/PAL/SECAM videocassette) with 2-3 songs and lead sheet. "Video should be 4-5 minutes in duration, black and white or color." SASE. Reports in 3-4 weeks. "We are also accepting material as listed above at our office in Germany, with return postage."
Music: Mostly rock and gospel rock; also top 40, contemporary gospel, R&B, soul and blues. Published "Being with You" and "Yahna's Blues" (blues), written and recorded by Queen Yahna and co-published with Marie-Marie Musikverlag; and "Doesn't Anybody (Wanna Fall in Love)" (by Q. Yahna/Danny Deutschmark), recorded by Q. Yahna for Another Record Company, GmbH.

CAPITOL STAR ARTIST ENTS., INC., 301 W. Ridge Rd., Rochester NY 14615. (716)266-3252. Director: Don Redanz. Associate Director: Tony Powlowski. Music publisher, record company and record producer. BMI. Publishes 20 songs/year; publishes 5 new songwriters/year. Pays standard royalty.
Music: Country, gospel, and pop. Published "Dust on Mother's Bible," and "Away from Home," (by Anthony Powlowski), recorded by Tony Starr on Capitol Star (country); and "V-8 Detroit," by A. Powlowski.
Tips: "We like country songs with a heartwarming story."

CAPRICORN LTD., Jungstrasse 15A, Zürich CH 8050 Switzerland. (01)302-7401.President: Freddy J. Angstmann. Music publisher, record company and record producer. SUISA, SESAC. Pays standard royalty.
How to Contact: Prefers cassette (or VHS videocassette [PAL]). SAE and IRC.
Music: Mostly gospel, blues and jazz; also country and classical. Published "Who Shall Abide," "Glorious Feeling," and "On My Way To Zion," all by J. Thompson, recorded on Capricorn (gospel).

CARAMBA MUSIC/EDICOES MUSICALS INDEPENDENTS LTD., Rua Rodrigo Da Funseca 95-40, Lisboa 1200 Portugal. (01)684022/659047. President: Fernando de Albuquerque. Music publisher. SPA. Pays standard royalty.
How to Contact: Submit demo tape by mail. Prefers cassette. SAE and IRC. Reports in 1 month.
Music: Disco, pop/rock and international songs. Published "Tango" (by Luis Filipe/Nuno Rodrigues), recorded by Luis Filipe on Transmedia (disco/tango); "Undercover Lover," written and recorded by Manuel Cardoso on Discossete (disco); and "Dancing in the Air" (by Luis Filipe), recorded by Thereza Mayuko on Transmedia (disco).

CA-SONG MUSIC PUBLISHER, Room 1204, 1650 Broadway, New York NY 10019. (212)586-3700/333-3239. Contact: Mike Cassone. Music publisher, record company, record producer and record promoter. BMI, ASCAP, AGAC. Member CMA, AFM. Publishes varying number of songs/year; "many" new songwriters "under negotiation with demos in process." Pays standard royalty.
Affiliates: Glad-Jack Music Publishers (ASCAP) and Comerc Music Publishers (ASCAP).
How to Contact: Submit demo tape and lyric sheet or arrange personal interview. Prefers cassette or records as demo. "Label all cassettes with your name, phone number (address if it fits) and song titles." Does not return unsolicited material. "If demo has an SASE we will return it after review and decisions have been reached, but prefer no returns." Reports "only if we place a song."
Music: Mostly MOR, easy listening and top 40/pop; also country, dance-oriented, gospel, jazz, progressive, R&B, rock, soul, nostalgia, big band and 50s and 60s. Published "Get It Right the First time," written and recorded by Clayton Sinclair on Ca-Song Records; "Tip Toe Dance" (by Cassone/Richards/Reggaguie), recorded by Tiny Tim and Tess Winters; and "I Can't Complain," written and recorded by Marcella Roberts.

CASTLERISING PUBLISHING CO., Box 7084, 10 Michael Dr., Greenville SC 29610. (803)235-1111. President: Christopher Cassels. Music publisher and record producer (Sandcastle Productions). BMI. Publishes 20-30 songs/year; publishes 5-10 new songwriters/year. Pays standard royalty.
How to Contact: Prefers cassette. "Do not expect to receive cassette back."
Music: Mostly pop, country and R&B; also gospel, rock and jazz. Published "The River," by Don Axsom (country); "What Happened To Love," by Barry De Fleron Band (rock); and "Fire In The Night," by David Crossman (rock/pop).

CATERO RECORDS CO., 1301 Chestnut St., San Carlos CA 94070. (415)593-6720. President: Fred Catero. Record company and record producer. Publishes 45 songs/year; publishes 5 new songwriters/year. Pays legal mechanical rate.
How to Contact: Call first and obtain permission to submit. Prefers cassette. "Keep demos short—we'll ask for more if we're interested." Does not return unsolicited material.
Music: Mostly jazz, new age and contemporary pop; also R&B and classical. Published "Moving Day," written and recorded by T. Garthwaite (vocal/pop); "Special to You," written and recorded by R. Vandervort (pop vocal); and "I Like You, You're Nice," (by B. Dearie), recorded by T. Garthwaite (jazz vocal), all on Catero Records.
Tips: "Say something listeners can relate to in a way they wish they had. Target songs to the baby boomer—the 30-40-year-old crowd."

❝ *It takes courage to put your thoughts on paper—to let the world see how your mind works. Because, ultimately, writing means to expose yourself. But to risk exposure is exactly what every first-rate writer has been brave enough to do.* **❞**

—Sheila Davis, from Successful Lyric Writing

*THE CAVE, Music Publishing and Production, 3121 N.W. 14th St., Gainesville FL 32605. (904)377-0336. President: Thomas G. Hubbell. Marketing Director: Deborah K. Hubbell. Music publisher, record company (Unusual Record Co.) and record producer (The Cave). BMI. Estab. 1986. Publishes 0-5 songs/year; publishes 0-5 new songwriters/year. Works with composers and lyricists; teams collaborators. Pays standard royalty.
Affiliate: Unusual Music Publishing (ASCAP).
How to Contact: Prefers cassette or 15 ips reel-to-reel (or VHS videocassette) with 1-6 songs and lyric sheet. "All material sent with SASE must have correct postage for return. All other material will be filed." SASE. Reports in 6 weeks.
Music: Mostly rock/pop/top 40, experimental/new music and easy listening; also R&B, folk/ballads and MOR. Published "Talk Too Fast" (by T. Hubbell), recorded by Pure Raisins (rock); "The Date," written and recorded by Cathy Hubbell (ballad); and "Neutral Zone," written and recorded by John Stephens (rock) all on Unusual Records.
Tips: "Send exceptional material on a good demo. I am more interested in songs that are unique and marketable, as opposed to sound alikes."

*CDW ENTERPRISES, 297 Rehm Rd., Depew NY 14043. (716)684-5323. Contact: Music Department. Music publisher, record company (Da Car Recording), record producer and music distributor. ASCAP. Member Harry Fox Agency, Songwriters Guild. Works with composers and lyricists; teams collaborators. Pays negotiable royalty.
Affiliate: Weyand Music Publishing (ASCAP).
How to Contact: Write or call first and obtain permission to submit. Prefers 7½ ips reel-to-reel. "Only professional material will be considered." Does not return unsolicited material. Reporting time varies.
Music: Mostly classical, easy listening; also pop, country and show tunes. Published "Father for Christmas" (by Janssen/Adair), recorded by C. Weyand (Christmas vocal); "To Seal Our Love" (by Janssen/Lockerbie), recorded by G. Weyand (organ church music); and "Piano Studies," written and recorded by C. Weyand (piano piece), all on DaCar Records.

CEDAR VALLEY PUBLISHING, Rt. 3, Box 243-B, Stephenville TX 76401. (817)965-4132. Contact: Carroll Parham. Music publisher and record company (Scotty Records). Publishes 12 songs/year; publishes 15 new songwriters/year. Pays standard royalty.
Affiliate: Dusty Rose Music.
How to Contact: Prefers cassette. Does not return unsolicited material. Reports in 8 weeks.
Music: Mostly country, gospel and light progressive. Published "Tucumcari," (by Stan Knowles), recorded by Charlotte Brown on Scotty (country); "Growing Older," written and recorded by J.W. Seals on Scotty (gospel); and "Misty Eyes," (by Tony Guess) and "Old Texas Moon," (by Jennings/Mathis), recorded by Joel Mathis.
Tips: "Make sure all material has a good hook and strong lyrics."

FRANK CHACKSFIELD MUSIC/EROS MUSIC, Allegro, Elm Walk, Farnborough Park, Orpington, Kent BR6 8LX England. Farnborough 55509. Contact: Frank Chacksfield. PRS, MCPS, BASCA. Music publisher.
How to Contact: Prefers cassette. SAE and IRC.
Music: Instrumental.

CHAPPELL & CO. (AUST.) PTY LTD., 99 Forbes St., Woolloomooloo, Box KX250 Kings Cross, Sydney, NSW 2011, Australia. 61-02-356-3322. Contact: International Manager or Professional Manager. Music publisher. Member AMCOS, APRA and Australian Music Publishers Association Pty, Ltd. Pays negotiable royalty; royalties paid directly to US songwriters or paid to US songwriters through US publishing affiliate.
How to Contact: Write first. Prefers cassette with 1-5 songs and lyric sheet. SAE and IRC. Reports in approximately 2 weeks.
Music: Blues, children's, country, dance-oriented, easy listening, folk, jazz, MOR, R&B, rock, soul and top 40/pop.
Tips: "Submit good commercial, clear demos."

CHARTBOUND MUSIC PUBLICATIONS, LTD., Suite 204, 1508 Harlem, Memphis TN 38114. (901)274-2726. Contact: Executive Director. Music publisher and recording studio. ASCAP. Member NMPA (pending), BMA, NARAS, MSMA and The Blues Foundation. Publishes 2-4 songs/year; publishes 3 new songwriters/year. Pays standard royalty.
How to Contact: Call or write first. Prefers 15 or 7½ ips reel-to-reel or cassette with 1-5 songs and lyric sheet "or musical tracks without lyrics. Submit only unpublished songs for our consideration. Submit

only your best. Big demo production is not necessary, but it helps." SASE. Reports in 3 weeks.
Music: Dance-oriented, R&B, soul and top 40/pop. Published "Am I Gonna be the One?" (by Thomas, Wade and E.R. Thomas), recorded by Colors on First Take Records (R&B/dance); "Hooked on Love" (by Eddie Mayberry), recorded on Blue Town Records; and "Never Say What You Won't Do" (by Ricky Strickland), recorded by Amnesty on GCS Records.

C. CHASE MUSIC PRODUCTIONS, Division of Chase Dominion Limited, 83 Kneeland Ave., Binghamton NY 13905. (607)797-1190. Director: Dr. Clarence W. Chase. Music publisher and music engraver specializing in hymns; gospel, popular and vocal music; children's songs and lead sheets. ASCAP. Publishes 5 songs/year; publishes 2-3 new songwriters/year. Works with lyricists. Pays minimum standard royalty.
How to Contact: Write first about your interest. Prefers cassette with 1-3 songs and lead sheet. Does not return unsolicited material. Reports "as time allows."
Music: Children's, traditional hymns and country. Published "The Sacred Word and Its Creative Overtones Through Music" by Robert C. Lewis; "For Freedman's Cause" (patriotic) and "Where But in America" (both by C.W. Chase), recorded by Ray Agnew on Ice Records.
Tips: "Hymns must be a marriage of words and music—use words embodying ideas that will stimulate the imagination. Don't just write poetry—make your hymns 'sing.' "

CHEAVORIA MUSIC CO., 1219 Kerlin Ave., Brewton AL 36426. (205)867-2228. Producer: Roy Edwards. Music publisher, record producer and management firm. BMI. Publishes 15 songs/year; publishes 10 new songwriters/year. Works with composers and lyricists; teams collaborators. Pays standard royalty.
Affiliate: Bait String Music (ASCAP).
How to Contact: Query. Prefers cassette with 2 songs and lyric sheet. Reports in 4 weeks. Keeps all tapes on file.
Music: Mostly country, R&B and MOR; also disco, easy listening, progressive, soul and top 40/pop. Published "Heartless Nights", (pop) and "You Make Our Reality" (pop) both written and recorded by Brad Smiley; and "You Made My Life So Wonderful" written and recorded by Roy Edwards (R&B).

CHERIE MUSIC CO., 3621 Heath Ln., Mesquite TX 75150. (214)279-5858. Contact: Jimmy Fields. Music publisher, record company and record producer. BMI. Publishes 30 songs/year; publishes 10-15 new songwriters/year. Pays standard royalty.
How to Contact: Prefers cassette with 5 songs and lyric sheet. Does not return unsolicited material. Reports in 3 months.
Music: Mostly country; also bluegrass and progressive country.
Tips: "Do not over produce—let us hear the melody and lyrics."

*CHERRY LANE MUSIC PUBLISHING COMPANY INC.,Box 430, Port Chester NY 10573. (914)937-8601. Music publisher. ASCAP. Publishes 20 songs/year; publishes 1 new songwriter/year. Works with composers and lyricists; teams collaborators. Pays standard royalty.
Affiliates: First Artists Music Company (ASCAP), Jolly Rogers Publishing Co. (ASCAP), Windstar Music (ASCAP), Cherry River Music Co. (BMI), Management Three Music (BMI) and Windsea Music (BMI) among others.
Music: Mostly adult contemporary, country and classical; also rock. Published "Shy Boy" (by Billy Sheehan), recorded by David Lee Roth on Warner Bros. Records (rock); "Flying For Me" and "Let Us Begin (What are We Making Weapons For)" both written and recorded by John Denver on RCA Records (A/C).

CHEVIS PUBLISHING CORP., 2527 Miami Ave., Nashville TN 37214. (615)889-7305. Manager: Betty Holt. Music publisher. BMI.
Affiliate: Shada Music Inc. (ASCAP).
How to Contact: Query. "No outside material accepted at this time."
Music: Published "Rescue Me," "Higher and Higher," and "I'd Like to Teach the World to Sing."

CHIP 'N' DALE MUSIC PUBLISHERS, INC., 2125 8th Ave. S, Nashville TN 37204. (615)383-6002. President: Gene Kennedy. Vice President: Karen Jeglum. Music publisher. ASCAP. Member NSAI, CMA, NMPA, and ACM. Publishes 200 songs/year; publishes 100 new songwriters/year. Pays standard royalty.
Affiliates: Door Knob Music (BMI) and Lodestar Music (SESAC).
How to Contact: Arrange personal interview. Prefers 7½ ips reel-to-reel or cassette with 1-4 songs and lyric sheet. SASE. Reports in 1-3 weeks.
Music: Country and gospel. Published "Don't Let it Go to Your Heart" (by Bob Stamper), recorded by

Bonnie Nelson; and "Stop and Read My Lips," written and recorded by Stephen Hiles both on Door Knob (country).

*CHRIS MUSIC PUBLISHING, 133 Arbutus Ave., Box 396, Manistique MI 49854-0396. President: Reg B. Christensen. Music publisher and record company (Global Records and Bakersfield Records). BMI. Publishes 30 songs/year; publishes 10-30 new songwriters/year. Teams collaborators. Pays standard royalty.
Affiliate: Saralee Music (BMI).
How to Contact: Query, then submit cassette *only* with 2-5 songs and lyric sheet. "No fancy, big band demo necessary; just one instrument with a clean, clear voice. Copyrighted material only. Send registration number. If not registered with Copyright office, let us know what you've done to protect your material." SASE. Reports in 1 month or ASAP.
Music: Mostly country, MOR and novelty rock; also bluegrass, gospel and soul. Published "Diamonds and Pearls," recorded by the Paradons on K-Tel Records and cassettes (R&B); "Gossip", written and recorded by Bill Woods on Bakersfield Records (country); and "Nashville Nick" (by Ted Tylon), recorded by Bill Woods on Belco Records (country).
Tips: "The writer should indicate if he has a certain singer in mind. Keep songs to 2-2½ minutes. Voice on demo should be clear—if one must strain to listen, interest is lost fast. Give us time—publishers put in a lot of time and money and we have to wait to hear back from managers and record companies, too. Songwriters are cautioned to be careful about writing flippant lettters like 'answer or else,' which most publishers will ignore and deal no further with the writer."

THE CHU YEKO MUSICAL FOUNDATION, Box 10051, Beverly Hills CA 90213. (818)761-2646. Branch: Box 1314, Englewood Cliffs NJ 07632. Producer: Doris Chu. Music publisher, record company, record producer, video and film producer. ASCAP, BMI. Publishes 10-20 songs/year; publishes 2-7 new songwriters/year. Pays negotiable royalty (up to 5-10% of profits).
Affiliates: Broadway/Hollywood International Music Publishers.
How to Contact: Prefers cassette with any number songs and lyric sheet. SASE. Reports in 1 month.
Music: Mostly musicals and film scores; also pop/rock, R&B, country and rock. "Complete musicals or self-contained rock and pop acts already produced in Los Angeles preferred." Published "81 Proof," recorded on CYM Foundation Records; "Here's to L.A." (by Samovitz, Everest, Skyer, etc.), recorded by Paul Wong on CYM Foundation Records (MOR); and "The Gun Control Tango" (by John Everest), recorded by various artists on The CYM Foundation Records (satire).
Tips: Interested in complete musicals, film scores, and top 40/pop, rock, R&B, country, MOR, religious-oriented songs. "Co-publishers welcome."

CIANO PUBLISHING, Box 263, Brigantine NJ 08203-0263. (609)266-2623. President: Ron Luciano. Music publisher, record company and record producer. BMI. Publishes 12 songs/year. Pays standard royalty.
How to Contact: Query. Prefers 7½ ips reel-to-reel, cassette or acetate with 2-6 songs and lead sheet. SASE. Reports in 1 month.
Music: Disco, easy listening, MOR, R&B, rock, soul and top 40/pop. Published "Lucky" (by T. Galloway), recorded by Lucifer/Legz Records (rock); "Fly Away" (by Philip Mitchell and Barron and Susan Sillars), recorded by Lucifer/Tiara Records (folk); and "Love's a Crazy Game" (by Joseph M. Leo and Paul Cannarella), recorded by Voyage on Lucifer Records (top 40/disco).

*CITY PUBLISHING CO., 3966 Standish Ave., Cincinnati OH 45213. (513)793-8191. President: Roosevelt Lee. Music publisher, record company and record producer. BMI. Publishes 8 songs/year. Pays standard royalty.
Affiliate: Carriage Publishing Co. (BMI).
How to Contact: Write first about your interest. Prefers cassette with maximum of 4 songs and lyric sheet. SASE. Reports in 1 month.
Music: Mostly country, R&B and soul. Published "Love City Part 1&2" (by Ronald Lee), recorded by Larry Daley on WES World Records (soul); and "Come Home to Me" (by Mike Ellis), recorded by M. Ellis on Key Records (country).
Tips: "I am looking for finished masters."

CLARUS MUSIC, LTD., 340 Bellevue Ave., Yonkers NY 10703. (914)591-7715. President: Mrs. S. Fass. Music publisher, record company and record producer. ASCAP. Member MENC, NYSSMA, RIAA. "We publish children's records and material." Publishes 2 new songwriters/year. "Royalties paid are based on various reasons (plays, songs, etc.)."
How to Contact: Prefers cassette with 4-10 songs and lyric sheet. SASE. Reports in 1-3 months.
Music: Children's.

CLAYS FERRY MUSIC CO., Box 100743, Nashville TN 37210. (615)833-1955. President: Everett Faulkner. Music publisher, record company and record producer. BMI. Pays standard royalty.
How to Contact: Prefers cassette and lyric or lead sheet. SASE.
Music: Country and bluegrass.

R.D. CLEVERE MUSIKVERLAG, Postfach 2145, D-6078 Neu-Isenburg, West Germany. (6102)52696. Professional Manager: Tony Hermonez. GEMA. Music publisher. Publishes 700-900 songs/year; publishes 40 new songwriters/year. Pays standard royalty.
Affiliates: Big Sound Music, Hot Night Music, Lizzy's Blues Music, Max Banana Music, R.D. Clevére-Cocabana-Music, R.D. Clevére-Far East & Orient-Music, and R.D. Clevére-America-Today-Music.
How to Contact: Prefers cassette or reel-to-reel (or U-matic or VHS [PAL] videocassette) with "no limit" on songs and lyric sheet. SAE and IRC. Reports in 3 weeks.
Music: Mostly pop, disco, rock, R&B, country and folk; also musicals.
Tips: "If the song submitted is already produced/recorded professionally on 16/24-multitrack-tape and available, we can use this for synchronization with artists of the various record companies/record producers."

BRUCE COHN MUSIC, Box 359, Sonoma CA 95476. (707)938-4060. Manager/Owner: Bruce Cohn. Music publisher and management firm. ASCAP, BMI, SESAC. Publishes 10-20 songs/year.
How to Contact: Prefers cassette. SASE. Reports ASAP.
Music: MOR, rock, soul, and top 40/pop.

COLUMN ONE, LTD. MUSIC GROUP, Box 4086, Springfield MO 65808. (417)881-5015. President: Elizabeth Martin. Manager: Lou Whitney. Music publisher, record company (Column One Records, Borrowed Records) and record producer (Column One Productions). ASCAP, BMI. Publishes 20-25 songs/year; publishes 10-12 new songwriters/year. Pays standard royalty.
Affiliates: Column One Music (ASCAP) and Column Two Music (BMI).
How to Contact: Submit demo tape by mail. Write to arrange personal interview. Prefers cassette or 7½ or 15 ips reel-to-reel with 3 songs and lyric sheet. Does not return unsolicited material. Reports in 8 weeks "if interested."
Music: Mostly country and rock. Published "Atomic Bum" (by Ross/Workman), recorded by Boxcar Willie on Castle Records (country); "Trans-AM" (by L. Whitney), recorded by The Skeletons on N.B T. Records (rock); and "Red Georgia Clay" (by B. Emerson), recorded by John Anderson on Warner Bros. Records (country).

*COMET MUSIC CO., 797 Spencer Dr., Palm Springs CA 92262. (619)327-4629. Owner: Max Fidler. Music publisher. BMI. Publishes 10 songs/year; publishes 15 new songwriters/year. Teams collaborators. Pays standard royalty.
How to Contact: Prefers cassette with 2-3 songs and lead sheet. SASE. Reports in 1 month.
Music: Mostly pop and country. Published "Dim Lights" (by Joe Maphis/Max Fidler), recorded by Vern Gusden on Compleat Records (country) and "Heartbreak Ridge" (by Max Fidler), recorded by Gene Autry on Vecca (country).

*COMPUTER MUSIC INTERNATIONAL LTD, 48 Yorkville Ave., Toronto, Ontario M4W 1L4 Canada. (416)964-1885. President: Bradley MacDonald. Music publisher and record producer. PROCAN. Publishes 12 songs/year; publishes 1 new songwriter/year. Works with composers and lyricists; teams collaborators. Pays standard royalty.
How to Contact: Prefers cassette or 15 ips reel-to-reel (or VHS or ¾" videocassette), with 3 songs and lyric sheet. Does not return unsolicited material. Reports in 1 month.
Music: Mostly rock, pop and R&B; also children's records. Published "Party Album" (rock) and "Magic Singing Animal Farm" (children's music), both recorded by The Beastles on Berandol Records.

*CONTINENTAL COMMUNICATIONS CORP., 450 Livingston St., Norwood NJ 07648. (201)767-5551. President: Robert Schwartz. ASCAP, BMI. Music publisher. Publishes 50 songs/year; publishes 20-30 new songwriters/year. Teams collaborators. Pays standard royalty.
Affiliates: 3 Seas Music (ASCAP) and Northvale Music (BMI).
How to Contact: Prefers cassette. SASE. "Submit only a few of the most commercial songs with lead sheets and demo."
Music: Mostly rock.

*COSMOTONE MUSIC, Box 71988, Los Angeles CA 90071-0988. Record Producer: Rafael Brom. Music publisher, record company (Cosmotone Records) and record producer (Cosmotone Studios). AS-CAP. Publishes 10 songs/year; publishes 4 new songwriters/year. Works with composers and lyricists; teams collaborators. Pays standard royalty.
How to Contact: Prefers cassette with any number of songs and lyric sheets. "Include bio and photo." Does not return unsolicited material. Reports only if interested.
Music: Rock, pop, A/C, AOR, soft rock, heavy metal, ballads and gospel. Published "Padre Pio" written and recorded by Lord Hamilton (pop/rock); "O Be the New As Kind" written and recorded by Lord Hamilton and A. Jude (rock); and "A Mockingbird" (by Thomas Dufficy and L. Hamilton) recorded by Lord Hamilton (dance), all on Cosmotone Records.
Tips: "Looking for 'masters' with high tech sound, good melody and original performance."

*COUNTRY BOYS FROM TEXAS MUSIC, 3318-E SSW Loop 323, Tyler TX 75701. (214)581-9945. President: Roy L. Haws. Music publisher, record company (CBT Records) and record producer (Roy L. Haws and CBT Records). BMI. Publishes 15 songs/year; publishes 10 new songwriters/year. Works with composers. Pays standard royalty.
Affiliate: CBT Music (ASCAP).
How to Contact: Prefers cassette. "No lyric sheet necessary. Need professionally prepared demo." Reports in 2 weeks.
Music: Mostly country rock, contemporary rock and modern traditional country. Published "Giddyup Alligators" (by Joe Johnson), recorded by Glenn English (country rock); "Papa's on a Roll" (by Gary Josey), recorded by Steve Campbell (modern tech); and "Honky Tonk Heaven" (by Gary Josey), recorded by Donny Goff (country rock), all on CBT Records.

COUNTRY BREEZE MUSIC, 2911-A Seneca Ave., Kansas City KS 66103-3239. (913)262-0409. President: Ed Morgan. Music publisher and record company (Silverbird Records). BMI, ASCAP. Estab. 1986. Publishes 25-30 songs/year; publishes 20-25 new songwriters/year. Works with composers and lyricists; teams collaborators. Pays standard royalty.
Affiliates: Harmony Street Music (ASCAP) and Walking Hat Music (ASCAP).
How to Contact: Prefers cassette with 4-5 songs and lyric sheet. "Submit in strong mailing envelopes." Reports in 2 weeks.
Music: Mostly country (rock/pop/traditional), gospel (southern/bluegrass and black) and rock. Published "Get Down" (by C. Beth/E. Morgan), recorded by Perfect Harmony on Harmony Street Records (gospel); "The Lonelier She Got" (by Leon Coleman), recorded by Bill Michael Patterson on Skylight Records (country); and "Love and Prayers" (by D. Luz/G. Luz), recorded by Perfect Harmony on Harmony Street Records (gospel).
Tips: "All songs must be original and strong in both lyrics and melody. Have a good clear demo with voice out front. We are also looking for commercial artist for our new Silverbird Label. Videos are very helpful to publishers; it gives us a chance to see and hear the song performed by the writer and sometimes we pick up an artist this way."

COUNTRY CLASSICS MUSIC PUBLISHING CO., Box 15222, Oklahoma City OK 73115. (405)677-6448. General Manager: Sonny Lane. Music publisher and record company. BMI. Publishes 4-6 songs/year; publishes 2 new songwriters/year. Pays standard royalty.
How to Contact: Prefers cassette with 2-4 songs and lyric sheet. SASE. Reports in 3 weeks.
Music: Country, gospel and MOR. Published "Loving' Side of Love" and "Yodel Love" (both written by Yvonne DeVaney), both recorded by Yvonne DeVaney and Wes Onley on Compo Records (country duet); and "Just For a Moment" (by Yvonne DeVaney), recorded by Ragnhild on Tab Records/Sweden (country).

*COUNTRY PARTY MUSIC, Box 192, Pittsboro KS 66702. (316)231-6443. Vice President: Shawn Strasser. Music publisher, record company and record producer. Publishes 40 songs/year; publishes 60 new songwriters/year. Works with composers, lyricists and teams collaborators. Pays standard royalty.
Affiliates: Paint Stallion Music (ASCAP) and Cow Creek Music (SESAC).
How to Contact: Write first and obtain permission to submit. Prefers cassette (or videocassette) and lyric sheet. Does not return unsolicited material. Reports in 3 months.
Music: Mostly country, gospel and novelty; also pop, rock and R&B. Published "Saturn" (by R. Rhuems), recorded by Richard (novelty); "Fire the Governments," by B. Will; and "Diet #110" (by G. Strasser), both recorded by Weird Wilbur (novelty); all on Antique Records.

COUNTRY STAR MUSIC, 439 Wiley Ave., Franklin PA 16323. (814)432-4633. President: Norman Kelly. Music publisher and record company. ASCAP. Publishes 10-15 songs/year; publishes 3-4 new songwriters/year. Pays standard royalty.

Affiliates: Kelly Music Publications (BMI) and Process Music Publications (BMI).
How to Contact: Prefers 7½ ips reel-to-reel or cassette with 1-4 songs and lyric or lead sheet. SASE. Reports in 2 weeks.
Music: Mostly country; also bluegrass, easy listening, folk, rock, gospel, MOR and top 40/pop. Published "Porch Light," (by McHan/Goff/Moon), recorded by J.C. Young on Country Star (country); "Wings (Guarding America)," (by Wright/Struckburg/Hill), recorded by Sal Rainone on Process (MOR); and "Cold Red Georgia Clay" (by McHan/Jones/Goff), recorded by Bob Stamper on Country Star (country).
Tips: "Send only your best songs—ones you feel are equal to or better than current hits."

COUSINS MUSIC, 211 Birchwood Ave., Upper Nyack NY 10960. (914)358-0861. President: Lou Cicchetti. Music publisher, record company (Cousins, Daisy, and Westend) and record producer. BMI, ASCAP. Publishes 2-3 songs/year. Pays standard royalty.
Affiliate: Neems (ASCAP).
How to Contact: Prefers cassette with 3 songs and lyric sheet. SASE. Reports in 2 weeks.
Music: Mostly 50s and 60s rock; also country. Published "The Dancer" (by J.O'Daniel/Sal Pippa), recorded by The Dials (rock); and "One More Heartache" (by T. Percoco), recorded by Coco (country).

COWBOY JUNCTION FLEA MARKET AND PUBLISHING CO., Highway 44 West, Lecanto FL 32661. (904)746-4754. President: Elizabeth Thompson. Music publisher and record producer. BMI. Publishes 24 songs/year. Pays standard royalty.
How to Contact: SASE. Reports as soon as possible.
Music: Country, bluegrass and gospel. Published "The Challenger Tribute to the Crew of 7", "Easter Bunny" and "Easter Day" (all by Boris Max Pastuch), recorded by Buddy Max on Cowboy Junction Records (country).

CREATIVE CORPS., #810, 6253 Hollywood Blvd., Hollywood CA 90028. (213)464-3495. President: Kurt Hunter. Music publisher. BMI, ASCAP. Publishes 40 songs/year; publishes 4 new songwriters/year.
Affiliates: Visual Songs (BMI), and Driving Music (ASCAP).
How to Contact: Write or call first and obtain permission to submit. Prefers cassette (or ½" or ¾" videocassette) with 3 songs and lyric sheet. Does not return unsolicited material. Reports in 10 weeks.
Music: Mostly pop, rock (60s style) and R&B. Published "Doubles" (by Homer Guitarez), recorded by Havana on Day Break (pop); "Come & Love Me" (by Norman Mezey), recorded by Dandy on Curb (country); and "Runaway Train," (by Nicolas-Macias), recorded by Anne Marien on Restless (pop-rock).
Tips: "We are looking for sixties-style, guitar-based rock hits for several artists. Also looking for R&B/soul uptempo or ballads (a la Aretha Franklin, Staple Singers, Jackie Wilson to Eurythmics) for female singer."

CREATIVE ENTERTAINMENT CORPORATION, Suite 1700, 6290 Sunset Blvd., Los Angeles CA 90028. Professional Managers: Mark Savage and Sonia Weisman. Music publisher and management firm. BMI, ASCAP. Member NMPA. Publishes 25 songs/year; publishes 8 new songwriters/year. Pays standard royalty.
Affiliates: Creative Entertainment Music (BMI), Weezy Music (ASCAP).
How to Contact: Prefers cassette (or videocassette) with 1-5 songs and lyric sheet. SASE. Reports in 1 month. "No telephone calls please!"
Music: Mostly R&B, dance, and rock; also pop, and soul. Published "Outside Myself," recorded by Bobby Womack on MCA Records (R&B); "The Last Time," recorded by Eddie Murphy on Epic Records (R&B); and "I Don't Wanna Know," recorded by Earth, Wind and Fire on CBS Records (R&B/pop).

CREATIVE SOURCE MUSIC, Box 2631, Muscle Shoals AL 35662-2631. (205)381-1455. Professional Manager: Billy Lawson. Music publisher and production company (Wishbone, Inc.). BMI. Publishes 100 songs/year; publishes 1-2 new songwriters/year. Employs staff writers; pays standard royalty.
Affiliates: Song Tailors Music Co. (BMI), I've Got The Music Co. (ASCAP) and Terry Woodford Music (ASCAP).
How to Contact: "Submit to the attention of Billy Lawson." Prefers cassette with 2 songs and lyric sheet. SASE. No certified mail accepted. Reports as soon as possible.
Music: Mostly top 40/pop, R&B/pop, country and country/pop; also dance-oriented, rock, MOR, easy listening and new music. Published "One More Try For Love," (by Robert Byrne/Brandon Barnes), recorded by Gary Morris and Crystal Gayle on Warner Brothers Records (country/pop); "I Didn't Hear the Thunder," (by Sue Richards), recorded by Billy "Crash" Craddock on MCA-DOT (country); and "I

Can't Say Goodbye," (by Brandon Barnes/Clayton Ivey), recorded by Marlene on CBS-Sony Japan (Top 40).
Tips: "Be up-to-date with various artists' current style and direction. Submit only top-quality material."

*CREEKSIDE MUSIC, 100 Labon St., Tabor City NC 28463. (919)653-2546. Owner: Elson H. Stevens. Music publisher, record company (Seaside Records) and record producer (Southern Sound Productions). BMI. Publishes 15 songs/year; publishes 5 new songwriters/year. Works with composers, lyricists and teams collaborators. Pays 25-50% royalty.
How to Contact: Write first and obtain permission to submit. Prefers cassette with 3 songs and lead sheets. SASE. Reports in 1 month.
Music: Mostly country, rock and gospel; also "beach music." Published "Nitelife Cafe" (by Debbi Watson), recorded by Debbie Lanier and "Movin On" (by M. Todd), recorded by Silver Star, both on Sea Side Records, and "Miss Teaser" written and recorded by C. Batchelor on JCB Records (all country).

CREOLE MUSIC LTD., 91-93 High St., Harlesden, London NW10 England. 44-01-965-9223. Managing Director: Bruce White. General Manager: Steve Tantum. Music publisher, record company (Creole Records) and record producer. MCPS, PRS, Phonographic Performance Ltd. Member MPA, IFPI. Publishes 100 songs/year; publishes 2 new songwriters/year. Works with composers and lyricists; teams collaborators. Pays 60% royalty; royalties paid directly to US songwriters.
Affiliates: Sheila Music, Revue Music and Cactus Music.
How to Contact: Prefers cassette (or VHS videocassette) with 2-6 songs and lyric sheet. SAE and IRC. Reports in 3 weeks.
Music: Mostly pop, rock, dance and ballads; also country, easy listening, R&B, disco and soul. Published "Caramia" written and recorded by Boris Gardiner (ballad); "All in My Dreams" (by Wallace), recorded by Boris Gardiner (ballad); and "Kool and Deadly" written and recorded by Eastwood and Saint (reggae).
Tips: "It must be brilliant."

CRYSTAL IMAGE MUSIC, 8303 Treasure Ave., Stockton CA 95212. (209)931-3010 or 477-9067. Contact: John Covert. BMI. Music publisher, record company (Berberian/Dream Records Tokay Records, Roll-on Records) and record producer. Publishes 5-10 songs/year; publishes 5 new songwriters/year. Pays standard royalty.
Affiliates: Richard Berberian Music (BMI) and Berberian Publishing (ASCAP).
How to Contact: Prefers cassette with 2 songs and lyric sheet. "We can generally tell from a lyric whether a song will interest us. In fact, we encourage writers to send lyrics with SASE first—it saves them money. If we love the lyric and think it may fit a contact, then we ask to hear tape." SASE. Reports in 10 weeks.
Music: Country/pop, MOR and crossover. Published "Sara Claus" (by Nicholas Amadio, Sr./J. Covert), recorded on Roll-on Records (country); "I'll Take Country Music, Anytime," (by Ann Leisten/Phil Munton/J. Covert), recorded on Roll-on Records (country); and "100 Proof Love" (by R. Berberian), recorded on Berberian (country/rock), all recorded by Crystal Image.
Tips: "We look for positive, uptempo songs. The better a song is cast and the more structured it is (cast to a specific style and attention given to hook, riffs, etc.) the better chance a song has of being cut."

CRYSTAL RAM PUBLISHING, 827 Brazil Pl., El Paso TX 79903. (915)772-7858. President: Harvey Marcus. Music publisher, record company (Crystal Ram) and record producer (April Productions/April Recording Studios). BMI. "Also affiliated with local musicians union 466 in El Paso which includes protection with all major performance organizations." Publishes 6-10 songs/year; publishes 1-3 new songwriters/year. Pays standard royalty.
How to Contact: Prefers cassette or 7½ ips reel-to-reel with 1-3 songs and lyric or lead sheet. "Include current up-dated listing of all available past recording, publishing, and performances of your music." SASE. Reports in 6 weeks.
Music: Mostly jazz, R&B and new wave/rock; also "all ballads plus any material with crossover possibilities such as Mex-Tex, country and instrumental." Published "Amor Amedeas," and "A Donde Vas" (by Ledo), recorded by Jose Jose on CBS/Mexico (Mexican ballad); "Meant to Be," written and recorded by Harvey Marcus on Crystal Ram (Latin/jazz); and "Hold Back," written and recorded by Rubin Castillo and Danny Castellano on Crystal Ram (Latin/jazz).
Tips: "Leave out all the flashy solos if it's not an instrumental. Don't be impatient; we listen and reply to all material, just wait for an answer!"

CSB KAMINSKY GMBH, Wilhelmstrasse 10, 2407 Bad Schwartau, West Germany. (0451)21530. General Manager: Pia Kaminsky. GEMA, PRS. Music publisher and collecting agency. Teams collaborators. Pays 85% royalty.
Affiliates: Copyright Service Bureau, Ltd. and Leosong Copyright Service, Ltd.
How to Contact: Write and submit material. Prefers cassette or videocassette. Does not return unsolicited material. Reports in 4 weeks.
Music: Mostly pop; also rock, country and reggae.

CUDE & PICKENS PUBLISHING, 519 N. Halifax Ave., Daytona Beach FL 32018. (904)252-0381. A&R Director: Bobby Lee Cude. Music publisher, record company and record producer. BMI. Publishes 25-50 songs/year. Pays standard royalty.
How to Contact: Write first. "We are not accepting any new writers at this time." Prefers cassette (or videocassette) with 1-6 songs. SASE. Reports as soon as possible.
Music: Mostly country; also easy listening, gospel, MOR, top 40/pop and Broadway show. Published "Daytona Beach's Sand In My Shoes" and "V-A-C-A-T-I-O-N" recorded by the Hard Hatters on Hard Hat; "Just a Piece of Paper," and "Country Blues," recorded by the Blue Bandanna Country Band on Hard Hat; and "New Generation March" (military march).

D.S.M. PRODUCERS ENT. PUBLISHING CO., 161 W. 54th, New York NY 10019. (212)245-0006. Producer: Suzan Bader. Music publisher and record producer. ASCAP. Publishes 6-20 songs/year; publishes 4-12 new songwriters/year. Works with composers and lyricists; teams collaborators. Pays standard royalty.
How to Contact: Write first and obtain permission to submit. Prefers cassette (or VHS videocassette) and lyric or lead sheet. SASE. Reports in 4 weeks.
Music: Mostly top 40, R&B/dance, CHR and rock; also jazz and country. Published "Easy Kinda Lover" and "Shake Your Body Line" (by E. Mauge), recorded by American Steel (R&B) on Lulu Records; "Miami Cop" written and recorded by P. Brigham (CHR).
Tips: "A neat package with lead sheet, lyric sheet and 1-3 songs per cassette gets the best response."

DAN THE MAN PRODUCTIONS, Box 702, Cleveland OH 44107. President: Daniel L. Bischoff. Music publisher, record company (Dan the Man Records), and record producer (Dan the Man Productions). ASCAP, BMI. Publishes 6 songs/year; publishes 2 new songwriters/year. Pays standard royalty.
Affiliate: Bischoff Music Publishing Co. (BMI).
How to Contact: Write first and obtain permission to submit. Prefers cassette. Does not return unsolicited material. "Include SASE." Reports in 3 weeks.
Music: Mostly country, top 40, love songs and novelty; also easy listening, folk, R&B and soul. Published "Just a Simple Bouquet," (by A. Zanetis and O. Workman), and "King Went on a Journey," (by M. Lambert), recorded by Johnny Wright on Dan the Man Records (country); and "The Michael Jackson Interview," written and recorded by Dan Bischoff on Dan the Man Records (novelty).
Tips: "We like catchy songs and very good love songs."

DANA PUBLISHING CO., 824 83rd St., Miami Beach FL 33141. (305)865-8960. President: Walter Dana. Music publisher, record company and record producer. BMI. Pays standard royalty.
How to Contact: Write first. Prefers 7½ or 15 ips reel-to-reel or cassette. SASE.
Music: Classical and ethnic (Polish).

DARK CLOUD MUSIC, Box 1040, Alpine NJ 07620. (201)567-6855. Vice President: Vincent Castellano. BMI, ASCAP, SESAC. Music publisher and record producer (Silverlining Productions). Publishes 20-30 songs/year; publishes 5-10 new songwriters/year. Pays standard royalty.
Affiliates: We Got Music and D.A.M. Music.
How to Contact: Prefers cassette, 7½ or 15 ips reel-to-reel (or VHS videocassette) with 3 songs and lyric sheet. SASE. Reports in 3 weeks.
Music: Mostly rock (commercial), R&B (contemporary) and AOR; also heavy metal and pop. Published "Who'll Be the First One," and "Breakfast in Bed," written and recorded by Ray Goodman and Brown on Panaramic (R&B).

***DAVID CITY PUBLISHING**, Box 45, David City NE 68632. (402)539-2008. (402)367-3580. Representative: Chuck Parker. Music publisher. Estab. 1986.
How to Contact: Prefers cassette with 2-5 songs. Does not return unsolicited material. Reports in 1 month.
Music: Mostly country, pop and rock. Artists include: Chuck Parker, Pat Boilesen and Bill McKay.

DAVID MUSIC, 1560 Broadway, New York NY 10036. (212)302-5360. President: Morton Wax. Music publisher and record company. BMI. Pays standard royalty.
Affiliates: Felicia Wynne Music (BMI) and Sarah Music (ASCAP).
How to Contact: Prefers cassette and lyric sheet. Does not return unsolicited material. Reports as soon as possible.
Music: All kinds, with strong interest in country/pop.

DAVIKE MUSIC CO., Box 8842, Los Angeles CA 90008. (213)296-2302. Contact: Isaiah Jones. Music publisher. ASCAP. Publishes 4 songs/year. Works with composers and lyricists; teams collaborators. Pays standard royalty.
How to Contact: Query first or arrange personal interview. Prefers 7½ ips reel-to-reel or cassette (or videocassette) and lyric sheet. SASE. Reports in 1 month.
Music: Mostly gospel; also pop, blues, choral, church/religious, disco, easy listening, folk, gospel, MOR, R&B, soul and top 40. Published "God Has Given Us Hope," "Follow Me," and "In the World—Not of the World," (by Jones/Oliver), recorded by Isaiah Jones on Gule Records (gospel).
Tips: "Send lead sheet and lyric sheet with demo."

DE WALDEN MUSIC INTERNATIONAL, INC., #1911, 6255 Sunset Blvd., Hollywood CA 90028. (213)462-1922. Managing Director: Christian de Walden. Music publisher and record producer. ASCAP, BMI. Publishes 75-140 songs/year; publishes 4-5 new songwriters/year. Works with lyricists and composers; teams collaborators. Pays standard royalty.
Affiliates: Chriswald Music, Inc., Father Music, Hopi Sound Music, TSOM Music, Krismik Music and Zoomik Music.
How to Contact: Arrange personal interview if in the area or submit demo tape. Prefers cassette with 1-3 songs and lyric sheet. SASE. Reports in 2 months.
Music: Pop, R&B and dance. Published "100% Chance of Rain" (by A. Roberts/C. Black), recorded by Gary Morris (country); "Strongheart" (by A. Roberts/C. Black/T. Rocco), recorded by T.G. Sheppard (country); and "I'll Still Be Loving You" (by Todd Cerney/P. Bunch/Rose/Kennedy), recorded by Restless Heart (country).

DELEV MUSIC COMPANY, 7231 Mansfield Ave., Philadelphia PA 19138. (215)276-8861. President: W. Lloyd Lucas. Music publisher, record company, record producer and management firm. BMI, ASCAP. Member SG, NAS and CMA. Publishes 10-15 songs/year; publishes 6-10 new songwriters/year. Pays standard royalty.
Affiliates: Sign of the Ram Music (ASCAP) and Surprize Records, Inc.
How to Contact: Write first about your interest. Prefers cassette with 1-3 songs and lyric sheet. SASE. "We will not accept certified mail." Reports in 3 weeks.
Music: Mostly cross-over, pop ballads, R&B, dance-oriented, pop/country, and contemporary gospel and religious; also semi to hard rock. "No heavy metal." Published "Line of Fire," (by W. Guthier/C. Talarico); "Turn of the Key," (by S. McKnight and C. Talarico); "Weakened Heart", "Fallin'", "Unsure of the Night", and "Far Too Long" (by M. Tallarico), all recorded by Valkir (formerly p/k/a/ Valhalla). "Valkir is a rock vocal/instrumental group."
Tips: "Songs submitted must be lyrically and melodically strong with good strong hook lines, and tell a story that will appeal to and be related to by the radio-listening and record-buying public. Most important is that the demo be a clear quality product with understandable vocal and lyrics out front."

THE DEMO FARM, (formerly Mercantile Music), Rt. 4 Box 302, Saundersville Ferry Rd., Mt. Juliet TN 37122. (615)754-2444. President: Kent Fox. Music publisher and record producer. Publishes 12 new songwriters/year. Pays standard royalty.
Affiliates: Blueford Music (ASCAP) and Mercantile Music (BMI).
How to Contact: Query first. Does not accept unsolicited material.
Music: Country.

DENNY MUSIC GROUP, 39 Music Sq. E., Nashville TN 37203. (615)256-3558. Chief Executive Officer: John E. Denny. ASCAP, BMI, SESAC. Music publisher, record company (Dollie Record Co., Jed Record Production) and record producer. Employs songwriters on a salary basis. Pays standard royalty.
How to Contact: Write or call first and obtain permission to submit. Prefers cassette with 3 songs and lyric sheet. Reports in 6 weeks.
Music: Mostly country, gospel and MOR.

DO SOL PUBLISHING, Box 2262, Dorval, Quebec H9S 5J4 Canada. Professional Manager: Robert Salagan. Music publisher and cassette producer. PROCAN. Publishes 40 songs/year; publishes 10 new songwriters/year. Pays standard royalty.

How to Contact: Prefers cassette with 3-7 songs and lyric sheet. "Make purpose of communication clear and fog-free." SAE and IRC. Reports in 1 month.
Music: Country, easy listening, folk, MOR and top 40/pop.

DOC RON PRODUCTIONS, Box 1075, Boca Raton FL 33429. (305)391-0255. Vice President: M. Scott Stander. Music publisher, record company (Soaring Records) and record producer. Publishes 5 songs/year; publishes 4 new songwriters/year. Pays standard royalty.
Affiliates: Doc Ron Publishing (BMI) and Ron Doc Publishing (ASCAP).
How to Contact: Prefers cassette with 2-3 songs and lyric sheet. SASE. Reports in 4 weeks.
Music: Mostly gospel, country and reggae; also blues, Broadway musicals and revues. Published "Rockin Reggae Jam," "Scandal in the Family" and "Feel A Need" (by G. Williams), recorded by Surfside (reggae); and "Know the Feeling" (by Bobby Koster), recorded by Kippi Branon (country gospel); all on Soaring Records.
Tips: "The more polished the product, the better chance you will have for a producer to take the time to listen to your piece of work."

DON-DEL MUSIC/DON-DE MUSIC, 15041 Wabash Ave., South Holland IL 60473. (312)339-0307. President: Donald De Lucia. Music publisher, record producer and record company. BMI and ASCAP. Pays standard royalty.
How to Contact: Prefers 7½ ips reel-to-reel with 4-6 songs and lyric sheet. SASE. Reports in 1 week.
Music: Country, rock and top 40/pop.

DONNA MARIE MUSIC, % International Entertainment Associates, Box 1413, Dept. SM-3, 1701 Pacific Ave., Atlantic City NJ 08401. (609)347-0484. President: Danny Luciano. Associate Producers: Armand Cucinotti and Lew Entin. Music publisher, record company and record producer. ASCAP. Publishes 6 songs/year; publishes 3 new songwriters/year. Pays standard royalty.
How to Contact: Prefers 7½ ips reel-to-reel or cassette with 4-8 songs and lyric sheet. "No 8-tracks." SASE. Reports in 6 weeks.
Music: MOR, R&B, rock, soul and top 40/pop.

DONNA MUSIC PUBLISHING CO., Box 113, Woburn MA 01801. (617)933-1474. General Manager: Frank Paul. Music publisher, record company, record producer, management firm and booking agency. BMI. Publishes 25 songs/year; publishes 15 new songwriters/year. Teams collaborators. Pays standard royalty.
How to Contact: Prefers cassette (or videocassette) with 3-6 songs and lead sheet. "We will listen to tapes but will not return material. If we believe a song has potential, we will contact the songwriter." Reports in 1 month.
Music: Mostly ballads; also country, easy listening, gospel, MOR, R&B, rock, soul and top 40/pop. Published "Happy Happy Birthday Baby," recorded by Mango Sylvia and Gilbert Lopez on Casa Grande Records (R&B); "My Congratulations Baby", recorded by several artists (R&B); and *Gospel Songs* (gospel LP).

*DOWNS PUBLISHING COMPANY, 220-3740 Partage Ave., Winnipeg, Manitoba R3K 0Z9 Canada. Manager: Terry O'Reilly. Music publisher, record company (Downs Record Co. Ltd.) and record producer. Publishes 8-10 songs/year; publishes 3-4 new songwriters/year. Works with composers and teams collaborators. Pays standard royalty.
How to Contact: Prefers cassette with maximum of 4 songs and lyric sheet. Does not return unsolicited material. Reports in 3 weeks.
Music: Mostly country/rock, traditional country and MOR. Published "No Other Love" (by Byron O'Donnell), recorded by Donna and Harvey Henry; "Quit Kickin' My Heart Around" (by R. Booth), recorded by Donna Henry; and "He's All Over You" (by B. O'Donnell), recorded by Jerry Ness, all singles on Downs Records.

DUANE MUSIC, INC., 382 Clarence Ave., Sunnyvale CA 94086. (408)739-6133. President: Garrie Thompson. Music publisher. BMI. Publishes 10-20 songs/year; publishes 1 new songwriter/year. Pays standard royalty.
Affiliate: Morhits Publishing (BMI).
How to Contact: Prefers cassette with 1-2 songs. SASE. Reports in 1 month.
Music: Blues, country, disco, easy listening, rock, soul and top 40/pop. Published "Little Girl," recorded by Ban (rock); "Warm Tender Love," recorded by Percy Sledge (soul); and "My Adorable One," recorded by Joe Simon (blues).

DUPUY RECORDS/PRODUCTIONS/PUBLISHING, INC., Suite 200, 10960 Ventura Blvd., Studio City CA 91604. (818)980-6412). President: Pedro Dupuy. Music publisher, record company and record producer. ASCAP. Member Songwriters Guild. Publishes 50 songs/year; publishes 4 new songwriters/year. Hires staff writers. Pays standard royalty.
How to Contact: Write or call first about your interest or arrange personal interview. Prefers cassette with 2-4 songs and lyric sheet. SASE. Reports in 1 month.
Music: Mostly R&B and pop; also easy listening, jazz, MOR, soul and top 40. Published "Find a Way," "I Don't Wanna Know," and "Precious Love," written and recorded by Gordon Gilman.
Tips: "Songs should have very definitive lyrics with hook."

E.L.J. RECORD CO., 1344 Waldron, St. Louis MO 63130. (314)803-3605. President: Eddie Johnson. Vice President: William Johnson. Music publisher and record company. BMI. Publishes 6 songs/year; publishes 4 new songwriters/year. Pays 5-10% royalty.
How to Contact: Prefers 7½ ips reel-to-reel or cassette with 4 songs and lead sheet. SASE. Reports in 2 weeks.
Music: Mostly top 40, R&B and country; also blues, easy listening, soul and pop. Published "Love Me," written and recorded by Bobby Scott (top 40); "Look at Me," written and recorded by Ann Richardson (blues); and "Who Am I," (by Joe Smith), recorded by Eddie Johnson (blues).

EAGLE ROCK MUSIC CO., 5414 Radford Ave., North Hollywood CA 91607. (213)760-8771. President: Mort Katz. Music publisher. ASCAP. Member Songwriters Guild, ACM, CMA. Publishes 12 songs/year; publishes 3 new songwriters/year. Works with composers and lyricists. Pays standard royalty.
How to Contact: Prefers cassette with 2-3 songs and lyric sheet. SASE. Reports in 3 weeks.
Music: Mostly country; also gospel and MOR. "Would also like to receive more musical show tunes." Published "Chutzpah and the Songwriter," (by Don Borzage/Mort Katz), recorded by Elin Carlson and Joe Montgomery (musical show tunes); "Are We Getting Closer to the End," (by Jacklyn Hopwood/Mort Katz), recorded by John Covert (gospel); and "I'm a Hell Raiser" (by Mort Katz/Jacklyn Hopwood), recorded by Jacklyn Hopwood (country).
Tips: "Be professional and willing to learn and listen. Most writers must learn to re-write when necessary."

EARLY BIRD MUSIC, Waltner Enterprises, 14702 Canterbury, Tustin CA 92680. (714)731-2981. President: Steve Waltner. Music publisher and record company. BMI. Publishes 12 songs/year; publishes 3 new songwriters/year. Works with lyricists. Pays standard royalty on mechanicals.
How to Contact: Prefers cassette with 2-4 songs and lead sheet. SASE. Reports in 3 weeks.
Music: Country, easy listening, MOR and top 40/pop.

*EARTHSCREAM MUSIC PUBLISHING CO., Suite A, 2036 Pasket, Houston TX 77092. (713)688-8067. Contact: Jeff Johnson. Music publisher, record company and record producer. BMI. Publishes 12 songs/year; publishes 6 new songwriters/year. Pays standard royalty.
How to Contact: Prefers cassette (or videocassette) with 2-5 songs and lyric sheet. SASE. Reports in 1 month.
Music: New rock and top 40/pop. Published "Always Happens" (by Pennington/Smith), recorded by Barbara Pennington; "Show Me Reaction" (by Wells), recorded by Rick Bardon; and "New Guy" (by Wells), recorded by Valerie Starr (all pop/rock).

*EB-TIDE, Box 5412, Buena Park CA 90620. (213)513-8120. Contact: Leo J. Eiffert, Jr. Music publisher, record company (Plain Country Records, Young Country Records), and management firm (Leo J. Eiffert, Jr.). BMI. Publishes 30 songs/year; publishes 10 new songwriters/year. Works with composers and lyricists; teams collaborators. "We also work with jingle companies." Pays standard royalty.
Affiliate: Young Country.
How to Contact: Prefers cassette with 3 songs and lyric or lead sheet. SASE. Reports in 6 weeks.
Music: Country. Published "Don't Knock Me Till You've Tried It," and "Ain't Got No Pedigree" (by L.J. Eiffert, Jr.), recorded by Crawfish Band; and "I Got Love," written and recorded by Dulane Austin, all on Plain Country Records (all country).

EDICIONES MUSICALES RELAY S.A., 3930 Pardissien, Buenos Aires 1430 Argentina. 542-8097. Manager: Ana Maria De Visaggio. Music publisher. SADAIC. Publishes 1,000 songs/year. Works with composers and lyricists; teams collaborators.
Affiliates: Baires Export Music S.A. (SADAIC), Gala S.R.L (SADAIC), Roex S.R.L. (SADAIC) and Lalo Fransen Ed. Mus.
How to Contact: Prefers cassette (or videocassette) and lead sheet. Does not return unsolicited material. Reports in 4 weeks.

Music: Mostly blues, jazz and rock; also ballads and pop. Published "Too Late," (by Woolfson/Parsons), recorded by Alan Parsons; "Dedicado," (by Fossati), recorded by Miguel Gallardo; and "Talk to Me," (by P. Fox/F. Gold), record by Chico De Barge, all on RCA Records.

EDIFON S.R.L., Virrey del Pino 2458, 8° "A," 1426 Buenos Aires Argentina. 785-6572/6591. Manager: Elena Suarez de Larrazabal. Music publisher and record company (Microfon Argentina S.A.). SADAIC. Publishes 350 songs/year.
How to Contact: Prefers cassette and lead sheets. Does not return unsolicited material. Reports in 3 weeks.
Music: Melodic, rock and tropical. Published "Yo Pecador te Confieso" (by Londaits/Mochuslke), recorded by Beto Orlando; "Nuestra Bohardilla," written and recorded by Tormenta; and "Vuelve Estoy Arrenpentido" (by Leon/de Mingo), recorded Juan Ramon, all melodic songs on Microfon.

EDITIO MUSICA BUDAPEST, Vörösmarty tér 1., Budapest 1051 Hungary. 184-228. International Promotions Manager: Mr. Gábor Knisch. Music publisher. Publishes 100 songs/year; publishes 10 new songwriters/year. Teams collaborators.
How to Contact: Write first and obtain permission to submit. Prefers cassette with 4 songs and lyric or lead sheet. Does not return unsolicited material. Reports in 12 weeks.
Music: Pop, MOR and easy listening. Published "Midnight Lady," (by Dieter Bohlen), recorded by Superteam (pop); "Johnny and Mary," (by Robert Palmer), recorded by Kati Kovacs (rock); and "Love Me Tender," (by Presley/Matson), recorded by Gyorgy Korda (pop), all on Hungaroton.
Tips: "Editio Musica Budapest has its own printing office and is prepared to print sheet music with amazingly favorable conditions for songwriters."

EDITIONS CARAVAGE, 130 Rue Marius Aufan, Levallois-Perret 92300 France. (1)47 59 94 51. General Manager: Jean-Paul Smets. Music publisher and record company. SACEM. Publishes 50-100 songs/year; publishes 5-10 new songwriters/year. Works with lyricists and teams collaborators. Pays standard royalty.
How to Contact: Prefers cassette. Does not return unsolicited material. Reports in 2 weeks.
Music: "All kinds including instrumental." Published "Soy Apache" (by Agudelo/Besombes/Pascal), recorded by Son Caribe (Spanish disco); "Jonathan" (by G. Vacher/D. Doublet), recorded by Duels (rock); and "Romantic" (by Chretien/Sandra), recorded by Varenne (pop).

EDITORA PRESENCA LTD., C. Postal 2525 Centro, Rio de Janeiro 20001 Brazil. (021)295-9081. President: Wilson F. Felcão. Music publisher and record company (Discos Presença Ltd.). UBC (Uniao Brasileira de Compositores), SOCINPRO (Sociedade Intérpretes e Produtores). Publishes 10 songs/year. Pays 40% royalty.
Affiliates: Editora Brasil Musical Ltd. (UBC), and Edições Musicais Falcão (UBC).
How to Contact: Prefers cassette and lyric or lead sheet. Does not return unsolicited material. Reports ASAP.
Music: Blues, rock and jazz. Published "Superstition," (by W. Falcão Portinho), recorded by Carlos Braga (ballad); "Cala Coração," (by Alvinho), recorded by Neli Miranda (ballad); and "Blusa Roxa," written and recorded by Moacyr MM (samba), all on Discos Presença.

EMANDELL TUNES, 10220 Glade Ave., Chatsworth CA 91311. (818)341-2264. President/Administrator: Leroy C. Lovett Jr. Publishes 6-8 songs/year; publishes 3-4 new songwriters/year. Teams collaborators. Pays standard royalty "twice a year."
Affiliates: Ben-Lee Music (BMI), Birthright Music (ASCAP), Northworth Songs (SESAC), Chinwah Songs (SESAC), Fair Oak Music (ASCAP), Gertrude Music (SESAC), LMS Print/Publishing Co. and Clara Ward Music Group.
How to Contact: Prefers cassette (or videocassette) with 4-5 songs and lead or lyric sheet. Include information about writer, singer or group. SASE. Reports in 3-4 weeks.
Music: Inspirational, contemporary and traditional gospel and chorals. Published "Give Us This Day," written and recorded by Edwin Hawkins (gospel); "Loving You," (by Shiela Mathews), recorded by Lynette (gospel); "The Day Will Come," (by R. Trotter) and "Hold Me Jesus" (by Barbara Hale), both recorded by Brenda Holloway (gospel); all on Birthright Records.
Tips: "Submit high quality demos but keep it simple—no production extras."

EPOCH UNIVERSAL PUBLICATIONS, INC., 10802 N. 23rd Ave., Phoenix AZ 85029. (602)864-1980. Executive Vice President: David Serey. Music publisher, record company and record producer. BMI. Publishes 100-300 songs/year; publishes 20 new songwriters/year. Hires staff writers. "Positions filled at this time, but resumes may be sent to be kept on file." Pays standard royalty.
Affiliates: NALR (BMI), Epoch Music Corp. (ASCAP), Epoch Universal Publications, Ltd. (Canada).

How to Contact: Prefers 7½ ips reel-to-reel or cassette with minimum 3 songs and lyric sheet. SASE. Reports in 1 month.
Music: Children's, choral, church/religious, classical, gospel and liturgical. Published "Here I Am, Lord" (by Dan Schutte), recorded by St. Louis Jesuits on NALR Records (liturgical); "Land of Love" (by Marcy Tigner), recorded by Little Marcy on Sounds of Hope Records (children's); and "The Ones I Love" (by Carey Landry), recorded by C. Landry on NALR Records (liturgical).
Tips: "Songs should be strong but simple enough for congregational singing, preferably in a liturgical setting."

EQUINOX MUSIC, (AVI Music Publishing Group), Suite 1212, 7060 Hollywood Blvd., Hollywood CA 90028. (213)462-7151. Contact: A&R Director. Music publisher, record company, record producer, and artist management. BMI, SESAC. Publishes 90 songs/year; publishes 2 new songwriters/year. Pays standard royalty or as specified in individual contracts.
Affiliates: Bel-Canto Music (ASCAP), Forsythe Music (ASCAP), and Norfolk Music (BMI).
How to Contact: Query first. Prefers cassette with any 1-4 songs and lyric sheet. SASE. Reports in 2 weeks.
Music: Mostly jazz and gospel. Published "Tainted Love" (by Ed Cobb), recorded by Soft Cell on Sire Records (rock/pop); "Take A Look Inside My Heart" (by David Benoit), recorded by D. Benoit on AVI Records (jazz fusion).

ESCHENBACH EDITION, 28 Dalrymple Crescent, Edinburgh EH9 2NX Great Britain. (031)667-3633. A&R Manager: James Douglas. Music publisher, record company (Helios Records), record producer and video producer. PRS, MCPS, PPL. Publishes 70 songs/year; publishes 3 new songwriters/year. Pays negotiable royalty.
How to Contact: Write first and obtain permission to submit or call to arrange personal interview. Prefers cassette, 7½ ips reel-to-reel (or VHS videocassette) with 8 songs and lyric or lead sheet. SAE and IRC. Reports in 6 weeks.
Music: Mostly rock, jazz and gospel; also folk, instrumental and "serious music." Published "Mean City," by A. Bantick, (rock); "Deja Vue," by C. Adams (rock); and "Hebrides," by J. Busby (folk), all on Caritas Label.
Tips: "Aim for an international market."

ETC MUSIC, INC., 1600 Delorimier, 2nd Floor, Montreal, Quebec H2K 3W5 Canada. A&R Director: Jacques Valois. Music publisher and record producer. Pro Canada (BMI), CAPAC (ASCAP). Publishes 25 songs/year; publishes 10 new songwriters/year. Pays negotiable royalty.
Affiliates: Editions Michel Le Francois (CAPAC), St Music (pro Canada), VU Music (CAPAC), Administration: Coup de Foudre (pro Canada), PAD (CAPAC).
How to Contact: Prefers cassette, 15 or 7½ ips reel-to-reel with 4 songs and lyric sheet. SASE. Reports in 3 weeks.
Music: Mostly rock/pop, adult contemporary and jazz; also country, children's music and Latin. Published "Miracles Can Happen" (by Michel Le Francois), recorded by Celine Dion on CBS Records (rock ballad); "Strangers" and "She Had That Look" (both by Michel Le Francois), recorded by Joey Sullivan on Capital Records (rock/pop).

EURO TEC PUBLISHING, Box 3077, Ventura CA 93006. (805)658-2488. Vice President: Bruce Caplin. Music publisher, record company, record producer and management consultants. BMI. Publishes 5 songs/year. Pays standard royalty.
Affiliates: Mikelly Tunes and ETR Publishing.
How to Contact: Write or call first about your interest, or submit demo tape. Prefers cassette with 1-12 songs and lyric sheet. SASE. Reports in 60 days.
Music: Blues, country, dance-oriented, easy listening, MOR, Spanish, R&B, rock and top 40/pop. Published "In My Own Way," (ballad), and "Lucky Break" (adult contemporary), both written and recorded by Michael Bruce.

EURSONG, 6 Heath Close, London W5 England. 44-01-991-0993. Contact: Jan Olofsson. International Music Publishing. Publishes 25-30 songs/year. Pays standard royalty.
Affiliates: Olofsong/Basart (Holland), Blue Eyes/Careere (France), Olofsong Scandinavian Songs (Sweden), and Olofsong Music, Inc. and Crazy Viking Music/BMI (USA).
How to Contact: Prefers cassette (or European VHS videocassette) with 3-12 songs and lyric sheet. SAE and IRC. Reports in 3 weeks.
Music: R&B, rock, black and dance. Published "Carefree Days" written and recorded by Time Gallery; and "Let It Swing" written and recorded by Bobby Sock.
Tips: "Have a complete finished master recording that has hit appeal and can be released in Europe."

EXPRESS MUSIC (LONDON) LTD., Yew Tree Studio, Charing Heath, Kent TN27 OAU England. President: Siggy Jackson. PRS, MRS, MCPS. Music publisher, record company (Spectrum Records) and record producer (Siggy Jackson Productions, Ltd.). Publishes 25 songs/year; publishes 10 new songwriters/year. Pays standard royalty.
Affiliate: Tempo Music Ltd.
How to Contact: Prefers cassette (or videocassette) and lyric and lead sheet. SAE and IRC.
Music: Mostly country, rock, pop; also jazz. Published "Lets Have a Good Time," (by Jackson/Mallot), recorded by Sugarstick on Spectrum (pop).

DOUG FAIELLA PUBLISHING, 16591 County Home Rd., Marysville OH 43040. (513)644-8295. President: Doug Faiella. Music publisher, record company (Studio 7 Records) and record producer (Doug Faiella Productions). BMI. Publishes 25 songs/year; publishes 5 new songwriters/year. Pays standard royalty.
How to Contact: Prefers cassette or 7½ ips reel-to-reel with 1-10 songs and lyric sheet. "Home demo will do. We have professional studio if interested in your songs." SASE. Reports in 8 weeks.
Music: Mostly contemporary country, rock and gospel; also traditional country/bluegrass, jazz and blues.
Tips: "The title, hook, and voice on demo must be strong."

FAME PUBLISHING CO., INC., Box 2527, Muscle Shoals AL 35660. Publishing Manager: Walt Aldridge. Music publisher and record producer. BMI. Publishes 100 songs/year; publishes 5 new songwriters/year. Pays standard royalty.
Affiliate: Rick Hall Music, Inc. (ASCAP).
How to Contact: Prefers cassette with 1-3 songs. "Please include legible lyrics." No tapes returned. Reports in 6 weeks. "No phone calls."
Music: Mostly country/pop and MOR; also R&B and top 40/pop. Published "Once in a Blue Moon," (by Brasfield/Byrne), recorded by Earl Thomas Conley (country); "My Love Is Chemical," (by Aldridge), recorded by Lou Reed (pop); and "One Bad Apple" (by Jackson), recorded by Nolan Thomas (R&B).
Tips: "We appreciate professionalism in presentations."

BOBBY FARRELL MUSIC PUBLISHING COMPANY, Division of Pathfinders, Inc., 1826 Poplar Ln. SW, Albuquerque NM 87105. (505)243-2881. President: Bobby Farrell. Music publisher. BMI, ASCAP, SESAC. Publishes 100 songs/year; publishes 40 new songwriters/year. Works with composers and lyricists; teams collaborators. Pays standard royalty.
Affiliates: Polidori Music Pub. Co. (BMI), Classic Music Pub. Co. (BMI), Farrell Merritt, Ltd. (ASCAP), and Dallastex Music (ASCAP).
How to Contact: Prefers cassette, reel-to-reel (or VHS or Beta videocassette) with "unlimited" songs and lyric or lead sheet. "Print or type name, address and telephone number." Does not return material; maintains permanent file. Reports "upon sale/use."
Music: Mostly pop/R&B/contemporary, gospel, rock and country; also folk, jazz and blues. Published "Perfect Love" (by Greg Seaman), recorded by Cordelia on CBS/Sony (pop/gospel); "Here Today Gone Tomorrow Man," by Colleen Oldham (country); and "In Your Arms," by Robert Cunningham, both recorded by Firedragon on Vandor Records (contemporary/pop).
Tips: "Insert postpaid self-addressed postcard as backup file data."

*****FAZER MUSIC INC.** ,Box 69, Helsinki SF-00381 Finland. (358)0-56011. Professional Manager: Sallamaari Muhonen. Music publisher and record company (Finnlevy). TEOSTO. Publishes 300 songs/year; publishes 5 new songwriters/year. Employs songwriters on a salary basis. Works with composers and lyricists; teams collaborators.
How to Contact: Prefers cassette with 2-6 songs and lyric sheet. Returns unsolicited material with SAE and IRC. Reports in 1 month.
Music: Mostly pop, rock and any kind of ballad; also dance music and R&B.
Tips: "Please send a clear but simple demo—never mind 'the production' as the melody is most important. Country music is out for the Finnish market. Melodic tunes (ballads or not) are essential!"

FIESTA CITY PUBLISHERS, Box 5861, Santa Barbara CA 93150. (805)688-9691. President: Frank E. Cooke. ASCAP. Member Songwriters Guild and SBSA. Publishes 2-4 songs/year; publishes 2 new songwriters/year. Pays standard royalty.
How to Contact: Query first. Prefers cassette with 1-3 songs and lead sheet. "Looking for tight, concise lyrics; memorable melodies; good prosody." SASE.
Music: Mostly MOR, pop and country; also easy listening and gospel. Published "Dinner with Jackie," "Can We Cook?" and "Clearly," (all by F. Cooke), all recorded by Johnny Harris on Homegrown Records (pop/MOR).

Tips: "Submit (after query) clean typewritten double-spaced lyric sheet with lead sheet if available and simple cassette with clearly enunciated lyrics."

FIRELIGHT PUBLISHING, 4706 New York Ave., Glendale CA 91214. (818)249-2416. Owner: Doug Thiele. Music publisher, record producer (Doug Thiele Ents.) and music consultant. ASCAP, BMI. Publishes 5 songs/year. Pays standard royalty.
How to Contact: Write first and obtain permission to submit. Prefers cassette. Does not return unsolicited material. Reports in 6 weeks.
Music: Mostly country/pop, R&B/pop and rock; also political songs. Published "Almost in Love," (by Parks/Thiele), recorded by Dolly Parton on RCA Records; "Heart After Heart" (by Herbstritt/Thiele), recorded by Gary Wolf on Columbia Records; and "Dancin' Like Lovers" (by Herbstritt/Thiele), recorded by Mary MacGregor on RSO Records (all country/pop).

FIRST RELEASE MUSIC PUBLISHING, 6124 Selma Ave., Hollywood CA 90028. (213)469-2296. Creative Director: Danny Howell. Music publisher. BMI, ASCAP, SACEM, GEMA, PRS, MCPS. Publishes 30-50 songs/year; number of new songwriters per year varies. Employs songwriters on a salary basis. Pays standard royalty; co-publishing negotiable.
Affiliates: Fully Conscious Music, Criterion Music, Cadillac Pink, Atlantic Music, Illegeal Songs, I.R.S. Songs and Reggatta Music.
How to Contact: Write first and obtain permission to submit. Prefers cassette with 2 songs and lyric sheet. "We *never* accept unsolicited tapes or phone calls—you must have referral or be requested." Returns all unsolicited material. Reports only if interested.
Music: "We are interested in great songs and great writers. We are currently successful in all areas." Published "One Touch" (by M. Anderson), recorded by Juice Newton on Capitol Records (country/rock); "Private Party" (by Pam Reswick/Alan Rich/Steve Werfel), recorded by Rege Burrell on Epic Records (R&B); and "No Love In You" (by M. Anderson), recorded by John Fogerty on HBO/Warner Bros. Records (rock).
Tips: "Don't always send what you think publishers want to hear—include a song that has personal meaning to you. If you feel very strongly about a song, don't wait. Send a demo of a single instrument and vocals if money or equipment is a problem. Always have vocals on demos at an audible level."

*BOBBY FISCHER MUSIC, 1618 16th Ave., Nashville TN 37212. General Manager: Bobby Fischer. Music publisher, record company and record producer, promoter and distributor. ASCAP. Member CMA, NSAI and FICAP. Publishes 50 songs/year; publishes 1 new songwriter/year. Pays standard royalty.
Affiliates: Tessie's Tunes (BMI), Nashcal Music (BMI) and Bobby's Beat (SESAC).
How to Contact: Prefers cassette with 1 song and lyric sheet. "We review material as time permits and return (with SASE) *if* time permits."
Music: Country (contemporary) and MOR. Published "Not Enough Love To Go Round" (by Bobby Fischer/Rick Giles/Steve Bogard), recorded by Conway Twitty on MCA Records (contemporary country); "Next To You I Like Me" (by B. Fischer/R. Giles/Bill Haynes), recorded by Charlie Pride on 16th Avenue Records (country); and "What in Her World Did I Do" (by B. Fischer/Don Wayne), recorded by Eddy Arnold on RCA Records (country).

*JOHN FISHER & ASSOCIATES, 7 Music Circle N., Nashville TN 37203. (615)256-3616. President: John Fisher. Music publisher, record company and record producer. Works with composers and lyricists; teams collaborators.
How to Contact: Prefers cassette with 1-6 songs and lyric sheets. SASE. Reports in 2 weeks.
Music: Country, 50s rock and R&B.

*FLOW CHART SOUND ENTERPRISES, c/o Pat Davidson, Suite 4, 2777 Lancashire Rd., Cleveland OH 44106. (216)932-9522. Publisher: Pat Davidson. Music publisher. BMI. Estab. 1986. Publishes 5 songs/year; publishes 3 new songwriters/year. Works with composers and lyricists; teams collaborators. Pays standard royalty.
How to Contact: Prefers cassette with 3 songs and lyric sheet. Reports in 3 weeks.
Music: Mostly pop/top 40, rock and techno/pop. Published "Tonight" (by Scott Lockett/Brenda Norman/Pat Davidson), recorded by Brenda Norman on Pac Mac Records (R&B); "Pretty Lady" (by P. Davidson), recorded by Biz Bruckner on Concord Records (rock); and "I'm Missing You" (by Gilbert Zachart), recorded by Lamita Swanson on Concord Records (ballad).
Tips: "We need a writer willing to do rewrites if necessary. Use good recording equipment for demos—midi if possible."

FOCAL POINT MUSIC PUBLISHERS, 920 McArthur Blvd., Warner Robins GA 31093. (912)923-6533. Manager: Ray Melton. Music publisher and record company. BMI. Publishes 6 songs/year; publishes 1 new songwriter/year. Pays standard royalty.
How to Contact: Prefers cassette with 2-4 songs and lead sheet. Prefers studio produced demos. SASE.
Music: Mostly country and gospel; also "old-style pop". Published "Nobody But Jesus," and "We Should Never Give Up," by Wallace Pitts on Pitlaw Records (gospel); "He's Big Enough" written and recorded by C. Dennis on Gospel Voice Records (gospel); and "His Death Was Mine," by L.A. Shepherd on R-M Records.

FRICK MUSIC PUBLISHING CO., 404 Bluegrass Ave., Madison TN 37115. (615)865-6380. Contact: Bob Frick. Music publisher, record company and record producer. BMI. Publishes 50 songs/year; publishes 2 new songwriters/year. Works with lyricists. Pays standard royalty.
How to Contact: Call first. Prefers 7½ ips reel-to-reel or cassette (or videocassette) with 2-10 songs and lyric sheet. SASE. Reports in 1 month.
Music: Mostly gospel; also country, rock and top 40/pop. Published "One Day Closer to Jesus," by Bob Frick; "I'm Headin' for Heaven," and "Precious Jesus," by Bob Frick/Jack Smith; all recorded by Bob Scott Frick (all gospel).

THE FRICON ENTERTAINMENT CO., INC., 1048 S. Ogden Dr., Los Angeles CA 90019. (213)931-7323. Professional Manager: Maxine Harris. BMI, ASCAP. Music publisher. Publishes 50 songs/year; publishes 25 new songwriters/year. Pays standard royalty.
How to Contact: Write first and obtain permission to submit. Prefers cassette with 2-3 songs and lyric sheet. Does not return unsolicited material without SASE. Reports in 6 weeks.
Music: Mostly R&B, rock, pop, dance and country.

FROZEN INCA MUSIC, Suite 201, 450 14th St., Atlanta GA 30318. (404)873-3918. President: Michael Rothschild. Music publisher and record company. BMI. Publishes 10 songs/year; publishes 3 new songwriters/year. Pays standard royalty.
How to Contact: Write or call first. Prefers cassette with 4-10 songs and lyric sheet. SASE. Reports in 1 month.
Music: Mostly blues, dance-oriented and progressive; also jazz, R&B, rock, soul and top 40/pop. Published "Red Dress" (by Tinsley Ellis), recorded by The Heartfixers (blues); "Forever More," written and recorded by Ricky Keller (pop); and "Mr. Bad" (by Peckham/Cancro/Smith), recorded by It (dance).

*FUDGE MUSIC, Box 88, Station H, Montreal, Quebec H3G 2K5 Canada. (514)935-9089. President: Paul Klein. Music publisher, record company and record producer (Money Talks Productions, Inc.). BMI. Publishes 40 songs/year; publishes 20 new songwriters/year. Pays standard royalty "or less."
Affiliates: Urban Contempo (ASCAP), and Mire Music (PROCAN).
How to Contact: Prefers cassette. "Print phone number on tape." Does not return unsolicited material. Reports in 2 months "if material is used."
Music: Mostly dance, R&B and pop; also ballads and rap. Published "Oasis," and "Leaving On My Own," both written and recorded by Mac Thornhill on MWR Records (dance).

FUTURE STEP SIRKLE, Box 2095, Philadelphia PA 19103. (215)844-1947. President: Krun Vallatine. Vice President: S. Deane Henderson. Music publisher, record company and management firm. ASCAP. Publishes 10-15 songs/year; publishes 6 new songwriters/year. Pays standard royalty.
How to Contact: Prefers cassette (or VHS videocassette) with 4-8 songs and lyric sheets. Does not return unsolicited material. Reports in 2 weeks.
Music: Dance-oriented, easy listening, gospel, MOR, R&B, rock, soul, top 40/pop, funk and heavy metal. Published "Hot Number" (by John Fitch), recorded by The Racers (heavy rock); "Delirious" recorded by Molecules of Force (new wave); and "Save Me Jesus" and "In God's Hand" (by Verdell Colbert), recorded by V. Colbert & Off Spring Gospel Singers (gospel), all on Future Step Sirkle Records.

FYDAQ MUSIC, 240 E. Radcliffe Dr., Claremont CA 91711. (714)624-0677. President: Gary Buckley. Music publisher and production company. BMI. Member ACM, CMA, GMA, NARAS, Audio Engineering. Publishes 30-40 songs/year.
Affiliate: Jubilation Music (BMI).
How to Contact: Prefers cassette with 1-4 songs and lead or lyric sheet. SASE. Reports in 3 weeks.
Music: Country, easy listening, MOR, progressive, rock (country) and top 40/pop. Published "She Comes to Me Softly" recorded by Borderline on Quikstar Records (top 40/pop); "Still in the Game" recorded by Michael Noll on Gottabehit Records (top 40/pop); and "It's A Long Lonesome Walk," recorded by Finley Duke on Majega Records.

G.G. MUSIC, INC., Box 374, Fairview NJ 07022. (201)941-3987. President: Irma Proctor. Music publisher and artist management company. BMI. Pays standard royalty.
Affiliate: Wazuri Music.
How to Contact: Prefers cassette with 1-2 songs and lyric sheet. SASE. Reports in 3 weeks.
Music: Dance-oriented, R&B, rock (light), soul and melodies. Published "Strive" (by Linwood Simon/Julius J. Davis Jr.), recorded by Gloria Gaynor on CBS Records (disco rock); "Mack Side" (by L. Simon), recorded by G. Gaynor on Atlantic Records (R&B); and "More Than Enough" (by G. Gaynor), recorded by G. Gaynor on CBS Records (love ballad).
Tips: "The writer should understand that he must recognize all the elements needed to make a hit record: strong lyrics, good hook and an overall progressive and commercial sound the buying public can relate to. Love songs are 90% of records sold."

GALAXIA MUSICAL, Rio Danubio 48-A, D.F. 06500 Mexico. (905)511-6684. Managing Director: Arq. Jose G. Cruz. Music publisher. SACM. Pays standard royalty.
How to Contact: Write first and obtain permission to submit. Prefers cassette (or VHS videocassette) with 1-5 songs. SAE and IRC. Reports in 2 weeks.
Music: Pop ballads and rock.
Tips: "A well-prepared demo signals good craftmanship."

GAMMILL-MURPHY MUSIC, 2913 95th St., Lubbock TX 79423. (806)745-5992. A&R Director: Bill Gammill. Music publisher and record producer. BMI. Publishes 5 songs/year; publishes 1 new songwriter/year. Pays standard royalty.
How to Contact: Prefers cassette with 1-3 songs and lyric sheet. SASE. Reports in 2 months.
Music: Mostly Christian pop and contemporary Christian; also church/religious and gospel. Published "I Pray for You," by Russ Murphy (Christian ballad); and "Let Him In," by Bill Gammill (Christian rock), both recorded by Gammill and Murphy on Easy Chair Records.
Tips: "We are looking for material that is original, fresh and theologically sound, professionally presented."

GANDHARVA MUSIC, 3500 W. Olive Ave. #740, Burbank CA 91505. President: Randy Nite. Music publisher, record company (Nite Records), record producer, pesonal management (Persona Management) and video production company (Maya Video). Publishes 5-20 songs/year; publishes 6 new songwriters/year. Pays standard royalty.
How to Contact: Prefers cassette with 1-3 songs. SASE. Reports in 2 months.
Music: Mostly contemporary country ("uptempo preferred"); also adult contemporary/pop. Published "Blue Light" (by Bobby Blue); "Two Wrongs (Don't Make a Right)" (by Randall Kirk Nite); and "Just for You" (by Bobby Blue/Ann Neiditch), all recorded by Bobby Blue on Nite Records (all contemporary country).

*GEIMSTEINN HF,Skolaveg 12, Keflavik 230 Iceland. (92)2717. Manager: Runar Juliusson. Music publisher, record company and record producer. STEF-FTT-GEMA. Publishes 50-100 songs/year; publishes 1-10 new songwriters/year. Works with composers and lyricists; teams collaborators. Pays standard royalty (Europe standards).
How to Contact: Write or call first to arrange personal interview. Prefers cassette (or VHS videocassette) with 2-3 songs and lyric sheet. Does not return unsolicited material. Reports in 1 month.
Music: Mostly pop, rock and country; also R&B, jazz and gospel. Published: "Hofi," written and recorded by Afris (pop); "Baerinn minnn," written and recorded by Thor Runar (MOR); and "Litla Lina," written and recorded by Bjorn Thoroddsen (jazz); all on Geimsteinn Records.

GENERAL JONES MUSIC, 3550 Sportsway Court, Memphis TN 38118. (901)365-0021. Owner: Danny Jones. Music publisher, record producer and recording engineer. BMI. Publishes 3-4 songs/year; publishes 1-2 new songwriters/year. Pays standard royalty.
Affiliate: Bubshe Shaniel Music (BMI).
How to Contact: Write or call first and obtain permission to submit. Prefers cassette (or VHS videocassette) with 3-6 songs and lyric or lead sheet. SASE. Reports in 4 weeks.
Music: Mostly rock, country and pop; also R&B. Published "King of the Cowboys" by Larry Carney/Roy Rogers, Jr.), recorded by Roy Rogers, Jr. on TeleTex Records (country); "I Need You" (by Scott Snellgrove), recorded by Puppett on Joe Dog Records (pop/rock); and "The Answer" (by Don Mathis/Danny Jones), recorded by Captured on Star Stage Records (pop/rock).

GIBSON DAVIDSONG PUBLISHING, Box X-1150, Buna TX 77612. (409)423-2521. Professional Manager: James Gibson. General Manager: Aline Gibson. Music publisher. ASCAP. Publishes 30-40 songs/year; publishes 2-5 new songwriters/year. Pays standard royalty.

Affiliate: Rushwin Publishing (BMI).
How to Contact: Prefers cassette with 1-4 songs and typed lyric and/or lead sheet. "Clearly label each item sent." SASE. Reports ASAP.
Music: Christian/gospel only. Published "Running Back to You," (by Eva Bonn/Nancy Cyril), recorded by The Harbingers on Gold Street Records; and "I Am the Life," written and recorded by David Bush on Custom Records (both gospel).

*GIFTNESS ENTERPRISE, 3542 Garfield Way SE, Atlanta GA 30354. (404)642-2645. Contact: New Song Department. Music publisher. BMI. Publishes 30 songs/year; publishes 15 new songwriters/year. Employs songwriters on a salary basis. Works with composers and lyricsts; teams collaborators. Pays standard royalty.
Affiliate: Hserf Music (ASCAP).
How to Contact: Prefers cassette with 4 songs and lyric or lead sheet. SASE. Reports in 3 weeks.
Music: Mostly R&B, pop and rock; also country, gospel and jazz. Published "Vicious Rap," written and recorded by Eze T on Northwest Records (dance); "Only in America" (by E. Lyons), recorded by Mojo on Gold Key Records (dance); and "You're So Fine," written and recorded by Cirocco on Geffen Records (R&B).

GIL-GAD MUSIC, 5500 Troost, Kansas City MO 64110. (816)361-8455. General Manager/Publisher: Eugene Gold. ASCAP, BMI. Music publisher and record producer. Publishes 30 or more songs/year; publishes 10 or more new songwriters/year. Pays standard royalty.
Affiliates: 3G's Music Co., Eugene Gold Music.
How to Contact: Prefers cassette (or videocassette) with 4-6 songs and lyric sheet. SASE. Reports in 8 weeks.
Music: Mostly R&B, rock and top 40 pop; also disco/dance, gospel and jazz. Published "Magic," (by Cal-Green, Ronnie & Vicky), recorded by Suspension on 3G's (R&B/top pop); "Bootie Cutie," written and recorded by Robert Newsome on 3G's (R&B); and "Diamond Feather," (by M. Murf), recorded by Bad News Band on NMI (R&B).

*GILLESPIE MUSIC PUBLISHING CO., Box 30562, Oklahoma City OK 73110. President: Jack Gillespie. Music publisher. BMI. Estab. 1987. Publishes 8-10 songs/year; publishes 3 new songwriters/year. Works with composers. Pays standard royalty.
How to Contact: Prefers cassette with 1-3 songs and lyric sheet. "Submit studio produced demo cassette copies only. Videocassettes are not reviewed." Does not return unsolicited material; keeps all submissions on file for future reference. Reports in 2 weeks "only if interested."
Music: Mostly country, pop and R&B; also rock and "all other types."
Tips: "Any type of song can become a hit if it's good enough. All of our publishing contracts are standard, with a one-year reversion clause."

*GLENSONGS, Box 67, Stocksund S-182 71 Sweden. (8)856800. President: Bruno Glenmark. Music publisher, record company (Glendisc) and record producer. STIM/NCB. Publishes 200 songs/year; publishes 10 new songwriters/year. Employs songwriters on a salary basis. Pays standard royalty.
How to Contact: Prefers cassette. Does not return unsolicited material. Reports in 6 weeks.
Music: Mostly pop, rock and country. Published "So Good, So Fine" (by L. Anderson), recorded by Ann-Louise Hanson and Billy Preston on GlenDisc Records (ballad).

GOLD HILL MUSIC, INC., 5032 Lankershim Blvd., N. Hollywood CA 91601. (818)766-7142. Managing Director: Ken Weiss. Music publisher. ASCAP, BMI. Publishes 20-25 songs/year; publishes 2 new songwriters/year. Pays standard and varying royalties.
Affiliates: Kenwon Music, Catpatch Music, and Stephen Stills Music.
How to Contact: Call first and obtain permission to submit. Prefers cassette with 3 songs and lyric sheet. SASE. Reports in 4 weeks.
Music: Mostly rock. Published "Southern Cross," (by M. Curtis), recorded by Crosby, Stills & Nash on Atlantic Records (rock); "Step On Out," (by C. Hillman), recorded by Oak Ridge Boys on MCA Records (country); and "Stranger," written and recorded by Stephen Stills on Atlantic Records (rock).
Tips: Looking for "well constructed, commercial songs with original ideas."

*MANNY GOLD MUSIC PUBLISHER, 895 McDonald Ave., Brooklyn NY 11218. (718)435-1918. President: Manny Gold. Music publisher. ASCAP. Works with composers and lyricists. Pays standard royalty.
How to Contact: Prefers cassette and lyric or lead sheet. SASE. Reports in 1 month.
Music: Mostly easy listening.

*S.M. GOLD MUSIC, INC., % Hippogriff Productions, Inc., Suite 201, 246 Fifth Ave., New York NY 10001. (212)481-9877. President: Steven M. Gold. Music publisher, record producer (Hippogriff Productions, Inc.) and jingle producer. ASCAP. Publishes 10 songs/year; publishes 3 new songwriters/year. Employs songwriters on salary basis; "we employ two staff songwriters who are well-versed in all styles of popular music." Teams collaborators. Pays standard royalty or cash advance (buy-out).
Affiliate: Musical Life Publishing, Inc. (ASCAP).
How to Contact: Prefers cassette with 2-3 songs and lyric sheet. "Submit clear demos with the strongest song first." Does not return unsolicited material. Reports in 2 weeks.
Music: Mostly mainstream pop, R&B, dance/pop; also AOR and dance. Published "The Earth" (by Y. Kehati), recorded by Visa V (dance/pop) and "Let Her Know" (by Dave Prince/S. Gold) recorded by Spy Boy (R&B/pop), both on Hippogriff Records.
Tips: "Submit songs that have top 40 qualities. We're not looking for 'album tracks' or 'B sides.' Hits only!"

*GOLDEN GUITAR MUSIC, Box 40602, Tucson AZ 85717. President: Jeff Johnson. Music publisher. BMI. Publishes 10-15 songs/year. Pays standard royalty.
How to Contact: Prefers 7½ or 15 ips reel-to-reel or cassette with 2-6 songs and lyric sheet. SASE. Reports in 1 month.
Music: Mostly country, MOR and gospel; also bluegrass, church/religious, and light rock. Published "Willy's Boy" (by Jeff Johnson), recorded by Brenda D./Half Moon Records (country); "Wearing a Smile of a Clown" (by Jerry Haymes), recorded by J. Haymes/Umpire Records (country); and "What's This World Coming To?" (by J. Johnson), recorded by Jeff Johnson/Dewl Records (country/religious).
Tips: "Make an effort to submit a good quality demo—not necessarily complicated but clear and clean."

*GOODSOUND SDN. BHD.,66-68 Jln Raja Chulan, Kuala Lumpur 50200 Malaysia. 2300470. Director: NgCheong Hock. Music Publisher. Works with composers and lyricists.
How to Contact: Prefers cassette (or VHS videocassete) with 2 songs and lyric sheet. Does not return unsolicited material.
Music: Mostly pop, rock and disco; also new wave and R&B.
Tips: "Songs must be original in ideas and taste."

GOPAM ENTERPRISES, INC., Suite 13C-W, 11 Riverside Dr., New York NY 10023. (212)724-6120. Managing Director: Laurie Goldstein. Music publisher. BMI. Member NMPA. Pays standard royalties.
Affiliates: Upam Music (BMI), Zawinul Music (BMI), Taggie Music Co. (BMI), Jodax Music Co. (BMI), Semenya Music (BMI), Margenia Music (BMI), Turbine Music (BMI), Appleberry Music (BMI), Kae-Lyn Music (BMI), Jillean Music (BMI), Jowat Music (BMI), John Oscar Music, Inc. (ASCAP), Bi-Circle (BMI), Dillard Music, Pril Music (BMI), Hubtones Music Co. (BMI), Jeruvian Music (ASCAP) and Mulligan Publishing Co., Inc. (ASCAP).
How to Contact: Query; does not accept unsolicied material. "Primarily interested in jazz and jazz related compositions." SASE. Reports ASAP.
Music: Blues, easy listening, jazz, R&B, soul and pop.

*GORDON MUSIC CO., INC., Box 2250, Canoga Park CA 91306. (818)883-8224. President: Jeff Gordon. Music publisher. ASCAP, BMI. Publishes 5-10 songs/year; publishes 2-10 new songwriters/year. Pays standard royalty.
Affiliates: Marlen (ASCAP), JesBy (ASCAP) and Sunshine (BMI).
How to Contact: Call first about your interest and arrange personal interview to play demo or videocassette. Prefers cassette (or VHS videocassette) with 3-4 songs. Does not return unsolicited material. Reports in 1 month.
Music: Mostly pop/rock; also children's, jazz, choral, church/religious and country. Published "Airport," "Big Town," and "Suicide Bridge," (by T. Mockley/T. Lloyd), recorded by Failsafe; and "Hold Me Tight," by Robert White; all released on Paris Records (pop and rock).
Tips: "All material should be recorded on nothing less than a 4-track. The better the quality of sound the better chance of picking up the song."

GOTOWN PUBLISHING COMPANY, 706 Martin Luther King Jr. Dr., Leesville LA 71446-3446. (318)239-7121. President: John E. Kilgore. Music publisher, record company and record producer. BMI. Publishes varying number of songs/year.
How to Contact: Prefers cassette with 4-6 songs and lyric sheet. Reports within 6 months.
Music: Mostly gospel; also church/religious, R&B and soul.

*GRAND MUSIC GROUP, INC., 1708 Grand Ave., Nashville TN 37212. (615)321-5140. Vice-President: Leigh Traughber. Music publisher. Publishes 100 songs/year; publishes 7-10 new songwriters/year. Pays standard royalty.
Affiliates: Southern Grand Alliance Music (ASCAP), Grand Coalition Music (BMI).
How to Contact: Prefers cassette with 2-3 songs and lyric sheet. "Please give phone number on cassette." Does not return unsolicited material. Reports only if interested.
Music: Mostly country and country pop (crossover); also "songs already in a form our pluggers can use." Published "1982" (by Buddy Blackman/Vip Vipperman) and "Messin' With My Mind" (by Joe Allen/Charlie Williams) both recorded by Randy Travis on Warner Brothers Records (country); and "I Always Get It Right With You" recorded by Gene Watson on Epic Records (country).
Tips: "We currently need more country crossover material. If submitting country it must have very strong lyrics."

THE GRAND PASHA PUBLISHER, 5615 Melrose Ave., Hollywood CA 90038. (213)466-3507. Contact: A&R Department. Music publisher, record company and record producer. ASCAP, BMI. Publishes 50-60 songs/year; publishes 3 new songwriters/year.
How to Contact: Write first and obtain permission to submit. Prefers cassette with 3 songs. "No calls or appointments. One submission per 6 months. Professional demos preferred." SASE, "but return not guaranteed." Reports in 6 weeks.
Music: Rock. Published "Stop" (by Jon Butcher), recorded by J. Butcher/Axis; "Dream On" (by Russ Ballard), recorded by King Kobra; and "Iron Eagle," written and recorded by King Kobra (on the *Iron Eagle* soundtrack), all released on Capitol Records (all rock).

BILL GREEN MUSIC, 10452 Sentinel, San Antonio TX 78217. (512)654-8773. Contact: Bill Green. BMI. Music publisher, record company (BGM Records) and record producer. Publishes 5 new songwriters/year. Pays standard royalty.
How to Contact: Prefers cassette with 3 songs and lyric sheet. SASE.
Music: Mostly contemporary country and traditional country. Published "A Texas Songwriter," written and recorded by David Price on BGM Records (country); and "Louisiana Heatwave," written and recorded by Bobby Jenkins on Zone 7 Records (country).

*GROSVENOR PUBLISHING, 16 Grosvenor Rd., Birmingham B20 3NP United Kingdom. (021)356-9636. Contact: John R. Taylor. Music publisher, record company (Grosvenor Records) and record producer (Grosvenor Records). PRS. Publishes 9 songs/year; publishes 3-4 songs/year. Works with composers. Payment varies.
How to Contact: Write or call first to obtain permission to submit.

*NICHOLAS ASTOR GROUF ENTERPRISES, Box 3248, Yale Station, New Haven CT 06520. (212)348-8288. President: Nicholas Astor Grouf. Music publisher, record company (Nick Nack Paddywack Records) and record producer (Yale Undergraduate Productions). Publishes 30 songs/year; publishes 5-10 new songwriters/year. Works with composers and lyricists; teams collaborators. Pays standard royalty. "Charges production fee."
Affiliates: Astor Publishing, No Sweat Records, Chairs for Charity, No Exit Productions, IRS Records, FBI and Warner Bros.
How to Contact: Prefers cassette (or VHS videocassette) with 3-5 songs and lyric sheet. SASE. Reports in 6 weeks.
Music: Mostly new rock, top 40; also folk, jazz and classical. Published "How Civilized Are We," recorded by The Pedestrians (new rock/top 40); "Girl Who Stole My Soul" (by Krantz/Astor/Cooper), recorded by The Lullabye Commando's (top-40/crossover funk); and "Whatev" (by Yale Undergrad Productions), recorded by THE (folk/jazz), all on Nick Nack Paddywack Records.
Tips: "Songs should be both witty and literate, with careful attention to subject matter and motife. We, as an unafilliated Yale Organization, press a number of albums and one double compilation effort which often finds international distribution. We consider all contributions and encourage communication."

FRANK GUBALA MUSIC, Hillside Rd., Cumberland RI 02864. (401)333-6097. Contact: Frank Gubala. Music publisher and booking agency.
How to Contact: Prefers cassette and lead sheet. Does not return unsolicited material. Reports in 3 months.
Music: Blues, disco, easy listening, MOR, top 40/pop, rock and country.

GULE RECORD, 7046 Hollywood Blvd., Hollywood CA 90028. (213)462-0502. Vice President: Harry Gordon. Music publisher, record company and record producer. Pays standard royalty.

How to Contact: Submit demo tape or submit acetate disc. Prefers 7½ ips reel-to-reel tape with 2 songs. SASE.
Music Country, gospel, R&B, rock, soul and top 40/pop.

HALBEN MUSIC PUBLISHING INC., Suite 38, 4824 Cote des Neiges Rd., Montreal, Quebec H3V 1G4, Canada. (514)739-4774. Contact: Professional Manager. Music publisher and record producer. CAPAC. Publishes approximately 100 songs/year; publishes 6-10 new songwriters/year. Pays standard royalty.
Affiliates: Rainy River Music Ltd. (PROCAN), Tranzit Music (CAPAC), In-Tranzit Music (PRO-CAN), Lilbec Music (CAPAC), Angebec Music (PROCAN), Betanne Music (CAPAC), Lapapala Music (PROCAN), Earth Born Music (PROCAN), Eastend Music (CAPAC) and Westend Music (PRO-CAN).
How to Contact: Prefers cassette with 2-3 songs and lyric or lead sheet. SAE and IRC. Reports in approximately 2 months.
Music: Blues, easy listening, MOR, R&B, rock (hard, country), soul and top 40/pop. Published "Montreal," written and recorded by Kenny Karen on Expression Records (contemporary pop ballad); "Elle Est Belle" (by Eddy Marnay/Patrick Lemaitre) recorded by Peter Pringle on A&M Records (ballad); and "On Traverse Un Miroir" (by Isa Minoke/Robert Lafond), recorded by Celine Dion on CBS Records (techno-pop ballad).
Tips: "Songs should have an interesting story line (or catch phrases), and a strong hook in chorus or bridge. Keep song within 2½-3½ minute range and don't over-arrange the idea. Simple guitar/vocal or piano/vocal is acceptable."

HAMMER MUSIK GMBH, Esslinger Strasse 42, 700 Stuttgart, West Germany. (0711)247553 or 242554. Manager: Ingo Kleinhammer. GEMA. Music publisher and record company (Avenue and Boulevard). Publishes 100 songs/year; publishes 5 new songwriters/year. Works with composers and lyricists; teams collaborators. Pays standard royalty.
Affiliates: Belmont, Vertex, Kraut, Hor & Lies, Sound of the Future and Music Avenue.
How to Contact: Prefers cassette. SAE and IRC.
Music: Mostly dance and disco; also jazz, rock and pop.

GEOFFREY HANSEN ENTS., LTD., Box 63, Orinda CA 94563. (415)937-6469. A&R Representative: J. Malcom Baird. BMI. Music publisher, record company (World Artist), record producer and personal management production of TV, concerts and sporting events. Publishes 20 songs/year; publishes varying number of new songwriters/year. Pays standard or negotiable royalty.
How to Contact: Prefers cassette (or ¾ U-matic or ½ VHS videocassette) with lyric and lead sheets. SASE. Reports in 6 weeks.
Music: Mostly top 40, MOR, rock-a-billy, and country-rock; also TV, motion picture and theatrical music, blues, French and Spanish.
Tips: "Send a neat and clear package. We are not interested in form letters or material that is sent to other companies."

*HAPPY DAY MUSIC CO., Box 602, Kennett MO 63857. President: Joe Keene. BMI. Publishes 12-20 songs/year; publishes 3-4 new songwriters/year. Pays standard royalty.
Affiliate: Lincoln Road Music (BMI).
How to Contact: Prefers reel-to-reel or cassette and lead sheet. SASE. Reports in 2 weeks.
Music: Gospel and religious. Published "I'm Going Up," recorded by the Inspirations (gospel); and "Glory Bound," recorded by the Lewis Family (gospel).

*HAPPY NOTE MUSIC,Box 12444, Fresno CA 93777-2444. (209)442-3332. Owners: Robby Roberson and Karla Farrar. Music Publisher. BMI. Estab 1986. Publishes 60 songs/year; publishes 20 new songwriters/year. Employs songwriters on a salary basis. Works with composers. Pays standard royalty.
How to Contact: Prefers cassette with 3 songs and lyric sheet. "Vocals must be clear." SASE. Reports in 6 weeks.
Music: Mostly country, pop and gospel. Published "There" (by A. Sanifar), recorded by Oh Lamour, on Top Secret Records (dance LP); "Angel's Face" (by N. Holley/R. Roberson) and "Walkin" (by Richard Laws/Steve Frye), both recorded by Nick Holley On Lana Records (pop LPs).

HARLEM-HALWILL MUSIC, 1800 Main, Buffalo NY 14208. (716)883-9520. Executive Vice President: Larry Silver. Music publisher and record company (Amherst Records). BMI, ASCAP. Publishes 25-75 songs/year; publishes 25-75 new songwriters/year. Pays standard royalty.
How to Contact: Prefers cassette (or VHS videocassette) with 3-10 songs and lyric sheet. SASE. Reports in 3 weeks.

Music: Mostly R&B, jazz and rock; also blues. Published "Shake Down" (by Jermey Wall), "Alternating Currents" (by Jay Beckenstein), recorded by Spyro Gyra on MCA Records (jazz/fusion); and "Maybe I'm Lonely", written and recorded by Melanie Safka on Amherst Records (pop/top 40); and *Tonight Show Band Vol. I and II* featuring Doc Severinsen.

HARMONY STREET MUSIC, Box 4107, Kansas City KS 66104. (913)299-2881. President: Charlie Beth. ASCAP. Music publisher, record company (Harmony Street Records), and record producer (Harmony Street Productions). Publishes 30 songs/year; publishes 15 new songwriters/year. Works with composers and lyricists; teams collaborators. Pays standard royalty.
Affiliate: Harmony Lane Music.
How to Contact: Prefers cassette (or VHS videocassette) with 1-3 songs and lyric sheet or lead sheet. SASE. Reports in 3 weeks "or as time allows."
Music: Country (all types) and gospel (all types). Published "To Be Worthy" (by Stephen J. Hale), recorded by Sue Drenth on Adoration Records (gospel); "Growing Up" (by Teresa Gravelin), recorded by Terri McClain on Miter Records (country); and "Little Dirt Road," written and recorded by Jimmy Lee on Harmony Street Records (country).
Tips: "Songs must be original, commercial and have a good strong hook. Demo must be clear and clean with voice out front. Submit only your best songs."

JOHN HARVEY PUBLISHING CO., Box 120244, San Antonio TX 78212. President: John Harvey. Music publisher, record company and record producer. BMI. Member Harry Fox Agency. Publishes 24 songs/year; publishes 2 new songwriters/year. Works with composers. Pays standard royalty.
How to Contact: Prefers cassette (or videocassette) with 3-6 songs and lyric sheet. Will accept 7½ reel-to-reel. Will return material with return postage. Include brief resume. No query necessary. Reports as soon as possible.
Music: Country, Latin, polkas, waltzes, New Age music and easy listening. Published "I Took A Gamble" written and recorded by Edward Daniels (country); "Who Could Change" written and recorded by Janet Bishop (country); and "Maybe Someday" written and recorded by John Harvey (easy listening) all on Harvey Records.
Tips: "Make demo as clear-sounding as possible, even if simple. Make all other enclosed material, such as lyric sheets, bios, etc., neat. Send the best material you have. Send photos of yourself if possible. Buy bulk cassettes at low price for demos, and let publishers keep your tape for future reference. This increases chances of your song being reviewed more than once. Needs are changing constantly."

HE ROSE PUBLISHING, 1098 Rose, El Centro CA 92243. (619) 352-5774. Attn: Terry Maston. Music publisher and record company. BMI. Publishes 20 songs/year. Works with composers and lyricists; teams collaborators. Pays standard royalty.
How to Contact: Prefers cassette with 1-3 songs and lyric sheet. SASE.
Music: Gospel and contemporary Christian. Published "Raised Up Again" (by Tom Renard) and "Overcomer" (by Brad Messer), recorded by The New Jerusalem Band; and "He Died That We Might Live" (by Bruce Craw/Tom Horne), recorded by Jonah and the Whalers, all on He Rose Records (all contemporary Christian).
Tips: Looking for music with a "good melody and good doctrine—does it relate to people and minister to a need? Indicate what artist or who's style you think your song would be appropriate for."

HEAVEN SONGS, 14116 E. Whittier Blvd., Whittier CA 90605. (818)288-4332. Contact: Dave Paton. Music publisher, record company and record producer. BMI. Publishes 30-50 songs/year; publishes 10 new songwriters/year. Pays standard royalty.
How to Contact: Prefers 7½ ips reel-to-reel or cassette with 3-6 songs and lyric sheet. SASE. Reports in 2 weeks.
Music: Country, dance-oriented, easy listening, folk, jazz, MOR, progressive, R&B, rock, soul and top 40/pop.
Tips: Looking for "better quality demos."

HEAVY JAMIN' MUSIC, Box 4740, Nashville TN 37216. (615)865-4740. Manager: S.D. Neal. Music publisher. BMI, ASCAP. Publishes 20 songs/year; publishes 6 new songwriters/year. Pays standard royalty.
Affiliates: Sus-Den (ASCAP) and Valynn (BMI).
How to Contact: Prefers 7½ ips reel-to-reel or cassette with 2-6 songs and lyric sheet. SASE. Reports in 3 weeks.
Music: Mostly rock and country; also bluegrass, blues, easy listening, folk, gospel, jazz, MOR, progressive, Spanish, R&B, soul, top 40/pop and rock-a-billy. Published "Bright Lights" (by D. Derwald), recorded by Dixie Dee on Terock Records (rock-a-billy); "Home Again" (by L. Lynde), re-

corded by Linda Lynn on Terock Records (country); and "Lonesome and Blue" (by W. Curtiss), recorded by Wade Curtiss on Lee Records (R&B).

*HELMAR MUSIC,5 Lombard Street East, Dublin, 2 Ireland. (01)791865. Head of A&R: Marcus Connaughton. Music Publisher and record company (Bus Records). Publishes 100 songs/year; publishes 6 new songwriters/year. Works with composers and lyricists. Pays standard royalty.
How to Contact: Prefers cassette with no more than 4 songs and lyric sheet. SAE and IRC.
Music: Mostly country, pop and rock; also R&B. Published "Sweet Bye and Bye" (by Tommy Dooley), recorded by Foster and Allen on Stylus Records/UK (folk); "Jealous Child" (by Robinson/ McCarney), recorded by Quaterdeck on Bus Records (rock); and "Rain On The Wind" by (Don Baker), recorded by Don Baker and Aslan on Bus Records (rock).

JAMES HENDRIX, COMPOSER AND PUBLISHER, Box 90639, Nashville TN 37209. (615)321-3319. Music publisher and record company. Publishes 20 songs/year; publishes 6 new songwriters/year. Pays standard royalty.
Affiliates: Mester Music (BMI), Jimerlean Music (BMI), and Carrie Records Co.
How to Contact: Prefers cassette (or videocassette) with 3-4 songs and lyric sheet. SASE. Reports in one month.
Music: Church/religious, gospel, hymns and anthems. Published "Who Knows" and "Lead You" (by Al and Melita Chew); "You Know What to Do Lord" and "Jesus Will See You Through" by Michael Hunter; "Caravan" by J. Hendrix/M. Hunter (tribute to senior citizens).

HICKY'S MUSIC, 1183 Eastway, Cincinnati OH 45224. (513)681-5436. President: Gordon Hickland. Music publisher, record company (Vibe Records Inc.), and record producer. BMI. Estab. 1986. Publishes 4-8 songs/year; publishes 1-4 new songwriters/year. Works with composers and lyricists; teams collaborators. Pays 25, 33 or 50% royalty, "depending upon input."
How to Contact: Prefers cassette with 1-4 songs and lyric sheet. Reports in 4 weeks.
Music: Mostly pop, R&B (urban contemporary) and dance; also gospel and rap. Published "Heartbeat" (by G. Hickland), recorded by Gordy Clay (dance/R&B); "Stingy" (by G. Hickland/Gwaiver), recorded by Trinia Best (pop); and "Auto Drive" (by G. Hickland/E. Barber/Best), recorded by Trinia Best (urban contemporary), all on Vibe Records.
Tips: "Songs should be well organized, commercial. No pornographic lyrical content."

HIGH-MINDED MOMA PUBLISHING & PRODUCTIONS, Empire Ranch, 2329 Empire Grade, Santa Cruz CA 95060. (408)427-1248. Contact: Kai Moore Snyder. Music publisher and production company. BMI. Pays standard royalty.
How to Contact: Prefers 7½ ips reel-to-reel or cassette with 4-8 songs and lyric sheet. SASE. Reports in 1 month.
Music: Country, MOR, rock (country) and top 40/pop.
Tips: "We have just started to accept outside material."

HILVERSUM HAPPY MUSIC, Maarschalklaan 47, 3417 Montfoort, The Netherlands. (0)3484-2860. International Manager: Joop Gerrits. Music publisher. BUMA. Publishes 100 songs/year; publishes 25 new songwriters/year. Pays by agreement.
How to Contact: Submit demo tape by mail. Prefers compact cassette (or VHS videocassette). SAE and IRC. Reports in 4 weeks.
Music: Mostly pop and Latin American; also country, musicals and gospel. Published "Ruthless Queen," "No Man's Land," and "Keep The Change" (by T. Scherpenzeel), recorded by Kayak on Vertigo Records (Symphonic rock).
Tips: "Demo recording and sheet music required."

HITSBURGH MUSIC CO., Box 1431, 157 Ford Ave., Gallatin TN 37066. (615)452-0324. President/ General Manager: Harold Gilbert. Music publisher. BMI. Publishes 20 songs/year; publishes 10 new songwriters/year. Pays standard royalty.
Affiliate: 7th Day Music (BMI).
How to Contact: Prefers cassette (or quality videocassette) with 2-4 songs and lead sheet. Prefers studio produced demos. Does not return unsolicited material. Reports in 3 weeks.
Music: Country and MOR. Published "Make Me Yours" (by K'leetha Megal), recorded by Kim Gilbert (pop); "I'll Be Hurting" (by Hal Gilbert), recorded by Damon King (pop); and "One Step Away," recorded by Keith Walls (country) all on Southern City Records.

HOLY SPIRIT MUSIC, Box 31, Edmonton KY 42129. (502)432-3183. President: W. Junior Lawson. Music publisher and record company. BMI. Member GMA, International Association of Gospel Music Publishers. Publishes 10 songs/year; publishes 2 new songwriters/year. Pays standard royalty.

How to Contact: Call first. Prefers 7½ ips reel-to-reel or cassette with any number of songs and lyric sheet. SASE. Reports in 3 weeks.
Music: Mostly Southern gospel; also MOR, progressive and top 40/pop. Published "I Went to Jesus," recorded by The Servants; "Excuses," recorded by The Kingsmen; and "Canaanland Is Just in Sight" (by Jeff Gibson), recorded by The Florida Boys (Southern gospel).
Tips: Send "good clear cut tape with typed or printed copy of lyrics."

HOPSACK AND SILK PRODUCTIONS INC., Suite 1A, 254 W. 72nd St., New York NY 10023. (212)873-2272. Associate Director: Ms. Tee Alston. Music publisher (Nick-O-Val Music). Deals with artists and songwriters.
How to Contact: "Not accepting unsolicited material at this time."
Music: R&B.

HOT GOLD MUSIC PUBLISHING CO., Box 25654, Richmond VA 23260. (804)225-7810. President: Joseph J. Carter Jr. Music publisher, booking agency and record company. BMI. Publishes 10 songs/year; publishes 2 new songwriters/year. Pays standard royalty.
How to Contact: Prefers cassette with 1-3 songs. SASE. Reports in 60 days.
Music: Mostly pop and R&B; also rock, soul and top 40. Published "How Long Will I Be a Fool," (by Willis L. Barnet), recorded by the Waller Family on Dynamic Artists Records (pop/soul); "Get Up Everybody," (by Ronnie R. Cokes), recorded by Starfire on Dynamic Artists Records (funk/soul); and "I Believe in You," (by Joseph J. Carter Jr.), recorded by Waller Family on MCA Records (pop/R&B).

HOT KNOBS MUSIC, 607 Piney Point Rd., Yorktown VA 23692. (804)898-8155. Professional Manager: Lana Puckett or Kim Person. BMI. Music publisher, record company (Cimirron/Rainbird Records), record producer (Humdinger Productions) and Wistaria Recording Studio. Publishes 20 songs/year; publishes variable number of new songwriters/year. Pays standard royalty.
How to Contact: Write or call first and obtain permission to submit. Prefers cassette (or videocassette) with 1-5 songs and lyric sheet. SASE. Reports in 5 weeks.
Music: Mostly country, easy listening, children's and top 40; also pop, bluegrass, traditional, rock and gospel. Published "Love Ain't What It Seems" (top 40) and "Hard Habit" (country) (both by L. Puckett/K. Person), recorded by L. Puckett; and "Do Right Woman Lovin' A Do Wrong Man," (by L. Puckett and K. Person), recorded by K. Person (country), all on Cimirron/Rainbird Records.
Tips: "Have good commercially written and well structured lyrics."

HUMANFORM PUBLISHING COMPANY, Box 158486, Nashville TN 37215. (615)373-9312. President: Kevin Nairon. BMI. Music publisher. Pays standard royalty.
How to Contact: Prefers cassette with 4 songs and lyric and lead sheets. SASE. Reports in 4 weeks.
Music: Mostly pop-oriented country and contemporary gospel; also progressive country rock, rock, jazz, blues and progressive rock.
Tips: "Please strive for maximum quality when making your demo."

HUTCHINSON PRODUCTIONS, INC., 56-44 142nd Street, Flushing NY 11355. (718)762-2295. Producer: Clay Hutchinson. Music publisher and record producer. Pays standard royalty.
How to Contact: Prefers cassette and lyric sheet. SASE. Reports in 6 weeks.
Music: Mostly pop/rock and pop/R&B.

I.D. MUSIC/PUBLICATIONS A. PIERSON, 42 Rue du Fer á Moulin, Paris 75005 France. (1)45354425. Manager: P. Ageon. Music publisher. SACEM. Pays standard royalty.
How to Contact: Write first and obtain permission to submit. Prefers cassette. SAE and IRC.
Music: Mostly jazz, blues and rock; also Latin American.

IDEE MUSIK VERLAG, 39 A Boernickerst R., 1000 Berlin 20, West Germany. (030)3619019. Manager: Horst Fuchs. GEMA. Music publisher, record company (Allstar Records) and record producer (Allstar). Publishes 50 songs/year; publishes 2 new songwriters/year. Works with composers and lyricists; teams collaborators. Pays standard royalty.
How to Contact: Prefers cassette (or U-matic videocassette). Does not return unsolicited material. Reports in 4 weeks.

 The asterisk before a listing indicates that the listing is new in this edition. New markets are often the most receptive to freelance submissions.

Music: MOR. Published "Die Schönen Jahre" (by Schurmann), recorded by Peter Parish on All Star Records (MOR); "Ich Schreib Dir Einen Uebesbrie Sar," (by Poldi); and "Didelidei" (by O. Weiizl), recorded by Kelly Family on All Star Records (novelty).

IFFIN PUBLISHING CO., Suite #215, 38 Music Square E., Nashville TN 37203. (615)254-0825. Office Manager: Peggy Bradley. Music publisher. BMI. Publishes 5 songs/year; publishes 2 new songwriters/year. Pays standard royalty.
Affiliates: Sandfiddler (ASCAP); Old Guide Music, Inc. (BMI); First Million Music, Inc. (ASCAP); and Two Bees Music (SESAC).
How to Contact: Write or call first and obtain permission to submit. Prefers cassette and lyric sheet. Prefers studio produced demos. Does not return unsolicited material. Reports in 6 weeks.
Music: Mostly country, pop and MOR; also R&B and rock. Published "Don't Mess Around Mama" (by Michael P. Brown), recorded by Roy Clark on Silver Dollar Records (R&B); "I'm Only Singing Love Songs" (by Brant Miller/Chris Levzinger), recorded by Susan Tyler on Overland Stage Records (country); and "Another Woman's Man" (by Kerry Tolly/Gail Mattis/Michelle Hunt), recorded by Bobbie Lace on GBS Records (country).

THE IMAGE MUSIC GROUP PTY., LTD., 137 Moray St., South Melbourne, Victoria, 3205, Australia. 61-3-699-9999. US: Mason & Sloane, 1299 Ocean Ave., Santa Monica CA 90401. Director: John McDonald. Music publisher, record company and record producer. APRA, AMCOS, Phonographic Performance Co. of Australia Ltd. Member AMPAL. Publishes 30-40 songs/year; publishes 8 new songwriters/year. Pays standard royalty; royalties paid directly to US songwriters ("if signed to our Australian company"), or through US publishing affiliate ("if songwriter is signed to our US company").
Affiliates: Affiliates/Australia: Rainbird Music (APRA) and Haven Music (APRA). Affiliates/US: American Image Music (BMI) and American Rainbird Music (ASCAP).
How to Contact: Prefers cassette with 3-6 songs and lyric sheet. Submit directly to Australian office. "Concentrate on quality rather than quantity: strong melodic hooks (choruses), and meaningful lyrics that tell a story. Forget obvious rhymes. Make good demos—pay attention to playing and singing. We will not return material unless instructed to do so. Foreign submissions will not be returned unless postage is paid in advance." SAE and IRC. Reports in 1 week.
Music: Dance-oriented, MOR, rock (all kinds) and top 40/pop. Published "Oh How She Loves Me" (by Richard Bennett/Larry Williams), recorded by Bluestone on Avenue Records, Australia (top 40/pop); "Thinking of You" (by Lee Conway), recorded by Gary Holton & Casino Steel on Polygram Records, Europe (top 40/pop); and "Coleraine" (by David Hampson), recorded by the Cobbers on Festival Records, Australia and New Zealand (country).

IMAGINARY MUSIC, 239-A E. Thach Ave., Auburn AL 36830. (205)821-JASS. Publisher: Lloyd Townsend, Jr. ASCAP. Music publisher, record company and record producer (Mood Swing Productions). Publishes 5-6 songs/year; publishes 1-2 new songwriters/year. Works with composers and lyricists. Pays standard royalty.
How to Contact: Prefers cassette or 7½ ips reel-to-reel with 4 songs and lyric and lead sheets. "We do not return submissions unless accompanied by proper return envelope and postage." Reports in 2 months.
Music: Mostly rock; also jazz and blues. Published "Hexaphony" (by Somtow Sucharitkul), recorded by Bruce Gaston (improvisational classical fusion); "The Wanderer" (by Les and Mark Lyden), recorded by Nothing Personal (rock); and "Heartbreaker Beware" written and recorded by The Bonnevilles (rock); all on Imaginary Records.

***INSURANCE MUSIC PUBLISHING**, Box 288571, Chicago IL 60628. (312)264-2166. President: Bill Tyson. Music publisher. BMI. Publishes 20 songs/year. Pays standard royalty.
How to Contact: Prefers cassette with 2-4 songs and lyric sheet. Does not return unsolicited material. Reports in 1 month.
Music: Blues, black church/religious/gospel, and R&B.

INTERMEDIA KG, Hindenburgdamm 57, D-1000 Berlin 45, West Germany. (030)834 26 80-93. Music publisher, record company and record producer. GEMA, GVL, DMV. Publishes 50 songs/year; publishes 2-3 new songwriters/year. Pays standard royalty.
Affiliates: Funkturm-Verlage Musikproduktion/Funky Records Produktion.
How to Contact: Prefers cassette or reel-to-reel (or videocassette). SAE and IRC. Reports in 1 month.
Music: Mostly folk and pop; also big band songs, film music and musicals/TV music. Published "Bad Boy," by Syntronic and "For S.," by Stratos-Fear.

INTERNATIONAL ENTERTAINMENT, Box 50727, Washington DC 20004-0727. (703)590-5928. Director: Charles B. Roberts. Music publisher, attorney and record producer. BMI, ASCAP and SESAC. Publishes 10-15 songs/year; publishes 8-13 new songwriters/year. Work with composers and lyricists; teams collaborators. Pays standard royalty.
How to Contact: Prefers cassette with 4-6 songs and lyric sheet. "Place name and telephone number on cassette." Does not return unsolicited material. Reports in 8 weeks.
Music: Mostly rock, pop and R&B; also country. Published "It's You" (by D. Berry), recorded by Anthem on Cynet A-V (pop); and is affiliated with the Ohio Players and Sugarfoot (Warner Brothers Records) and others.
Tips: "Polish, rewrite, prepare quality demos. We prefer up-tempo dance songs a la Pointer Sisters, Bon Jovi, Cameo, Stacy—Q."

*INTERPLANETARY MUSIC, 7901 S. La Salle St., Chicago IL 60620. (312)962-0130. President: James R. Hall III. Vice President: Henry Jackson. Music publisher, booking agency and record company. BMI. Publishes 50 songs/year; publishes 15 new songwriters/year. Works with composers and teams collaborators. Pays standard maximum royalty.
How to Contact: Submit demo tape or arrange personal interview. Prefers cassette. SASE. Reports in 3 weeks.
Music: Disco, soul, R&B and top 40/pop. Published "Girl, Why Do You Want to Take My Heart?", recorded by Magical Connection (pop); and "You Blew My Mind This Time," recorded by Joe Martin (soul/pop/easy listening).

I'VE GOT THE MUSIC COMPANY, Box 2631, Muscle Shoals AL 35662-2631. (205)381-1455. Music publisher, record producer and video production company (Flying Colors Video). ASCAP. Publishes 100 songs/year; publishes 1-2 new songwriters/year. Hires staff writers. Pays standard royalty.
Affiliates: Song Tailors Music Co. (BMI), Terry Woodford Music (ASCAP), Creative Source Music (BMI) and Wishbone, Inc. (production company).
How to Contact: Submit demo tape to the attention of Billy Lawson. Prefers cassette (or videocassette) with 2 songs and lyric sheet. SASE. Reports ASAP. "No certified mail accepted."
Music: Mostly top 40/pop, R&B and country; also dance-oriented, easy listening, MOR, progressive, rock and soul. Published "Old Flame," (by Donny Lowery/Mac McAnally), recorded by Alabama on RCA (country); "Angel In Your Arms," (million—performance song by Terry Woodford/Clayton Ivey/Tom Brasfield), recorded by Barbara Mandrell on MCA (country); "It's A Crazy World," (by Mac McAnally), recorded by Steve Wariner on MCA (country); and "Right Through the Heart," (by Robert Bryne), recorded by Manfred Mann's Earth Band on Arista Records (pop).
Tips: "Be up-to-date on various artists' styles."

IVORY PALACES MUSIC, 3141 Spottswood Ave., Memphis TN 38111. (901)323-3509. President: Jack Abell. Music publisher, record producer (Parable Productions) and sheet music publisher. ASCAP. Publishes 15 songs/year; publishes 1 new songwriter/year. Works with composers and teams collaborators. Pays standard royalty. "Music typesetting and production services require a 50% deposit."
How to Contact: Write first and obtain permission to submit. Prefers cassette with 2-5 songs and lyric sheet. "Submit simple demo with clear vocal." SASE. Reports in 8 weeks.
Music: Mostly religious, educational and classical; also children's, and folk. Published "Little One," written and recorded by T. Starr on Ivory Palaces (Christian); "Larkin's Dulcimer Book," written and recorded by Larkin Bryant on Ivory Palaces (folk); and "Walker of the Way," written and recorded by T. McNabb on Waywalker (Christian).

IZA MUSIC CORP., Box 325, Englewood NJ 07631. (201)567-7538. Contact: Professional Dept. Music publisher. BMI, ASCAP. Publishes 200 songs/year; publishes 4-5 new songwriters/year. Pays standard royalty.
Affiliates: Eden Music Corp (BMI); Prentice Music Inc., and Vanessa Music Corp. (ASCAP).
How to Contact: Prefers cassette with maximum 2 songs and lyric sheet. Prefers studio produced demos. Does not return unsolicited material. Reports in 3 weeks "if time permits."
Music: All kinds; mostly rock, country and R&B. "We have many standards." Published "It's Just a Matter of Time," recorded by Glen Campbell on Atlantic Records.

J.D. MUSIC/FRANKLY MUSIC, Box 8958, Arlington Station, Jacksonville FL 32239. (904)744-7779. Contact: Fred Frank. Music publisher. BMI, ASCAP.
How to Contact: Prefers cassette with 3 songs and lyric sheet. SASE. Reports in 3 weeks.
Music: Mostly R&B and pop; also country, dance-oriented, gospel, rock (country) and top 40/pop.

JACKPOT MUSIC, 133 Walton Ferry, Hendersonville TN 37075. (615)824-2820. President: Clyde Beavers. Music publisher, record producer, record company (Kash Records, JCL Records, New Star Records) and studio. BMI, ASCAP and SESAC. Publishes 40-50 songs/year; publishes 8-10 new songwriters/year. Pays standard royalty.
Affiliates: Eager Beaver Music and His Word Music.
How to Contact: Call first. Prefers 7½ ips reel-to-reel or cassette (or videocassette) with 1-3 songs and lyric sheet. SASE. Reports as soon as possible.
Music: Mostly country, pop and gospel; also bluegrass, children's and folk. Published "The Caller," written and recorded by Lawrence Davis on JCL Records (gospel); "Omaha," written and recorded by Scott Daniels on Kash Records (country); and "Lonely Christmas" written and recorded by Travis Arthur on New Star Records (country).
Tips: "You must have top-grade, professional demos. If you don't have them, we will assist you."

JACLYN MUSIC, 351 Millwood Dr., Nashville TN 37217-1609. (615)366-9999. President: Jack Lynch. Music publisher and record company. BMI. Publishes 1-100 songs/year; publishes 1-100 new songwriters/year. Works with composers and lyricists; teams collaborators. Pays standard royalty.
Affiliates: Nashville Music Sales, Jaclyn Recording Co., Nashville Country Records and Nashville Country Promotions.
How to Contact: Query. Prefers cassette with 1-3 songs and lyric sheet. "We recommend that you send good commercial lyrics on a quality cassette. Send an SASE if you want demos and correspondence returned. Write or call if more information is desired." Reports in 4 weeks.
Music: Country, bluegrass, gospel and MOR. Published "The Bee" and "Adieu False Heart," written and recorded by Curly Ray Cline; "Verdie Let Your Bangs Hang Down," written and recorded by John Wright; and "I Wonder Why" (by Curly Ray Cline), recorded by Ralph Stanley, all on Nashville Country Records (all country).

JAELIUS ENTERPRISES, INC., Box 2874, Van Nuys CA 91401. (818)997-2849. President: James Cornelius. Music publisher. ASCAP, BMI. Publishes 3-5 songs/year; publishes 3 new songwriers/year. Pays standard royalty.
Affiliates: Jaelius Music (ASCAP), Hitzgalore Music (BMI), Magique Toucher Music (ASCAP), and Velvet Touch Music (BMI).
How to Contact: Write first and obtain permission to submit. Prefers cassette. SASE. Reports in 3 weeks.
Music: Mostly pop, country and gospel; also R&B. Published "All Alone on Christmas Eve" (by Elliott Tucker), recorded by The Jets on MCA Records (Christmas); "You're A Perfect Girl," and "L.O.V.E." (both by Greg Penny), performed on Andy William's TV Special by Tina Youthers (pop).

DICK JAMES ORGANIZATION, 63 Music Square E., Nashville TN 37203. (615)320-7870. Branch: #3, 1438 N. Gower St., Los Angeles CA 90028. (213)469-1940. General Manager (U.S. Operation): Arthur Braun. Manager/Nashville Office: Patrick Finch. Professional Manager: Mike Sikkas. Music publisher. ASCAP, BMI. Member NMPA, NMA and CMA. Publishes 60 songs/year: publishes 2 new songwriters/year. Works with composers and lyricists; teams collaborators. Pays standard royalty.
Affiliates: Dejamus Music; Dejamus, Inc. (ASCAP); Dick James Music, Inc.; Theobalds Music, Inc.; Nashlon Music, Inc. (BMI); DeJamus California, Inc.; and Nashlon California, Inc.
How to Contact: Prefers cassette with 1-3 songs and lead sheet. SASE. Reports ASAP.
Music: Mostly rock; also R&B, country, easy listening, MOR, soul and top 40/pop. Published score from NBC's mini-series "Peter The Great"; "Domestic Life," by John Conlee; and "A Face in the Crowd," by Michael Martin Murphy and Holly Dunn.

JAMMY MUSIC PUBLISHERS LTD., The Beeches, 244 Anniesland Rd., Glasgow G13 1XA, Scotland. (041)954-1873. Managing Director: John D. R. MacCalman. PRS. Music publisher and record company. Publishes 50 songs/year; publishes 2 new songwriters/year. Pays royalty "in excess of 50%."
How to Contact: "We are not currently auditioning."
Music: Mostly rock, pop and country; also Scottish. Published "The Wedding Song," (by Bill Padley/ Grant Mitchell), recorded by True Love Orchestra on BBC Records (pop); "Always Argyll," (by Jamieson/McCrone), recorded by Valerie Dunbar on KLUB Records (Scottish); and "We Are the Diamonds," (by Paul Birchard), recorded by Glasgow Diamonds on Scrimmage Sounds Records (pop).

JA/NEIN MUSIKVERLAG GMBH, Hallerstr. 72, D-2000 Hamburg 13, West Germany. (40)4102161. General Manager: Mary Dostal. Music publisher, record company and record producer. GEMA. Publishes 50 songs/year; publishes 10-20 new songwriters/year. Works with composers and lyricists; teams collaborators. Pays 50-60% royalty.

Close-up

Arthur Braun
General Manager
Dejamus, Inc./Nashlon Music, Inc.

If you've written a "my-baby-cheated-on-me-and-now-I-feel-terrible" song, don't send it to Arthur Braun. He doesn't want to hear it. That is, not unless you've found a fresher, more original way to express that idea.

"We get a lot of these cheating songs," says Braun, "but you can't blatantly say, 'Well, my baby was cheating, and now I shot him.' You have to find a different way of saying it.

"Lyrics like that are very trite. That's a major problem we find with the (song) submissions. They lack innovation, which is something we look for very heavily."

Braun says he was delighted to receive a cheating song—one that wasn't trite—from songwriter Taylor Rhodes. "He (Rhodes) had a line in there that I really enjoyed," says Braun. "The line was, 'You flash your eyes to blind me,/Then you do your dance behind me.' That's a different way of saying the same old story."

Braun has been with the Dick James Organization for 13 years. He is currently General Manager for its two American divisions Dejamus, Inc. (ASCAP) and Nashlon Music, Inc. (BMI). "We have developed a strong country AND pop catalog. We consider ourselves a full-service music publishing company; we don't just beg for one type of music," says Braun.

Braun says his upcoming releases will include pop and country songs by Boy George, Loverboy, Jennifer Rush and Anne Murray. He's especially proud that his company's score for "Peter the Great," an NBC-TV mini-series, recently won an Emmy.

Although Dick James employs about 10 staff songwriters, Braun says his organization has an open-door policy for outside material. In fact, he receives hundreds of demo tapes every month. And the company's head of creative operations for Nashville, Patrick Finch, listens to all the songs that come in.

"We like to have the songs on cassette," says Braun. "No more than three songs per cassette, and they must include the typed lyric sheets and a self-addressed, stamped envelope."

Good songs sometimes arrive in the mail, Braun says, from writers he's never met. That was the case with Robert White Johnson. Braun remembers the day he first heard Johnson's songs.

"At the time, I was working in our L.A. office," says Braun. "Johnson mailed me a tape from Nashville. When I was listening to tapes, I found his tape, loved his work, called him up and signed him by mail. I never met him until I actually came to Nashville. And we've had tremendous success with him. He's doing great."

Braun says he would like to get more songs which have the flavor and writing style of the '80s—not the '60s. And he wants more songs which have "great little melodies, those haunting songs like 'Time After Time,' by Cyndi Lauper.

"I pick that one because it's simple, but so well done," says Braun. "Or something like 'Against All Odds.' Great melodies like that—that's what we need."

—Tyler Cox

Affiliates: Pinorrekk Mv., Star-Club Mv., Big Note Mv. (GEMA).
How to Contact: Prefers cassette (or VHS videocassette) and lyric sheet. SAE and IRC. Reports in 6 weeks.
Music: Mostly rock, pop, MOR and blues. Published "Girls," written and recorded by Carl Poland on CBS Records (disco-rock); "You Shine," (by D. Hersee), recorded by Mistral on Vagabond Records (pop); and "Alone," written and recorded by David Baretto on Decca Records (rock).
Tips: "Send Single (A-side) material only or unbelievably great LP concepts."

JAY JAY PUBLISHING, 35 NE 62nd St., Miami FL 33138. (305)758-0000. Contact: Walter Jagiello. Music publisher, record company and record producer. BMI. Member NARAS. Publishes 15-25 songs/year. Pays standard royalty.
How to Contact: Prefers 15 ips reel-to-reel with 2-6 songs and lyric sheet. SASE. Reports in 1 month.
Music: Mostly polkas and waltzes; also country and easy listening.

JEMIAH PUBLISHING, Box 2501, Columbia SC 29202. (803)754-3556. Professional Manager: Myron Alford. Music publisher, record producer and artist management firm. BMI. Publishes 5-10 songs/year; publishes 4 new songwriters/year. Pays standard royalty.
How to Contact: Prefers cassette with 2 songs and lyric sheet. SASE. Reports in 1 month.
Music: Mostly R&B; also gospel, MOR, country, rock (top 40), soul and top 40/pop. Published "Enjoy with Me" (by E. Jackson, M. Alford and R. Hoefer, Jr.), recorded by Midnight Blue on Enjoy Records (R&B); "Wishing" (by M. Alford, D. Bailey, E. Jackson, R. Hoefer, Jr. and D. Hodge, Jr.), and "Feel It and Groove Together" (by D. Hodge, Jr., E. Jackson and M. Alford), both recorded by Midnight Blue on Samarah Records (R&B); and "Reaching Out" and "Filth" (by J. Campbell, G. Parsons, E. Robinson, Jr., J. Duffir, K. Brown, G. Hackett, K. Hubbert), recorded by Private Stash.

JENEANE & JUDE MUSIC, #1103, 150 Fifth Ave., New York NY 10011. (212)691-5630. General Manager: Jude St. George. ASCAP. Music publisher. Publishes 15 songs/year. Pays standard royalty.
How to Contact: Write first and obtain permission to submit. Prefers cassette with 4 songs and lyric sheet. "Typewritten letters preferred." Does not return unsolicited material. Reports in 3-4 weeks.
Music: Mostly progressive; also jazz, blues and New Age. Published: "The Woman in the White Coat," "Tin Shoes," "Angular Be-Bop," and "Now's the Time," (all by Jeneane Claps), all recorded by Freeway Fusion on J&J Musical Enterprises (progressive).
Tips: "Be specific and organized. Songs should be unique."

*JENISCH MUSIKVERLAG, Alberichgasse 8, Wien A-1150 Austria. 92 32 62. Director: Erwin H. Jenisch. Music publisher. Publishes 60-120 songs/year.
How to Contact: Submit "several songs, each on separate cassette. Also looking for lyric manuscripts." SAE and IRC. Reports in 1 month.
Music: Mostly blues, rock and gospel.

JERJOY MUSIC, Box 1264, Peoria IL 61654-1264. (309)673-5755. Professional Manager: Jerry Hanlon. Music publisher. BMI. Publishes 4 songs/year; publishes 3 new songwriters/year. Pays standard royalty.
How to Contact: Prefers cassette with 4-8 songs and lyric sheet. SASE. Reports in 2 weeks.
Music: Country. Published "Love Has Gone Away" (by D. Moody), recorded by Jerry Hanlon (country ballad); "Hey, Little Dan" (by A. Simmons), recorded by J. Hanlon (country); and "Scarlet Woman" (by J. Hanlon and J. Schneider), recorded by J. Hanlon (country).

LITTLE RICHIE JOHNSON MUSIC, 1700 Plunket, Belen NM 87002. (505)864-7441. Managers: Tony Palmer and Doc Danties. Music publisher, record company (LRJ Records) and record producer. BMI. Publishes 25-50 songs/year; publishes 15-25 new songwriters/year. Pays standard royalty.
How to Contact: Prefers cassette with 6-8 songs and lyric sheet. SASE. Reports in 2 weeks.
Music: Country, gospel and Spanish. Published "On My Way to Houston," written and recorded by Sam Wert IV on LRJ Records (country); "Fat Women" (by Larry Britts), recorded by Isleta Poor Boys on Ross Records; and "Take Me Back to Lincoln County" (by Rex White), recorded by Tommy Thompson on Ross Records.

AL JOLSON'S BLACK & WHITE MUSIC, 31 Music Square W., Nashville TN 37203. (615)242-1580. President: Albert Jolson. Music Publisher. BMI.
Affiliate: Jolie House Music, (ASCAP).
How to Contact: Prefers cassette with 3 songs and lyric sheet. Send: Attn. Lollie Teague. SASE. Reports in 6 weeks.
Music: Country and pop.

JON MUSIC, Box 233, 329 N. Main St., Church Point LA 70525. (318)684-2176. Owner: Lee Lavergne. Music publisher and record company. BMI. Publishes 24 songs/year; publishes 6 new song-writers/year. Works with composers and lyricists and teams collaborators. Pays standard royalty.
How to Contact: Prefers cassette with 2-6 songs. SASE. Reports in 2 weeks.
Music: Mostly country; also rock and soul. Published "All Night Man," (by Lee Lavergne), recorded by Classic Ballou on Lanor Records (blues); "Dance With Me," written and recorded by Fred Charlie on Acadiana (Records) country); and "Don't Put Your Hand on That," (by Mike Lachney), recorded by Bad Weather on Lanor Records (zydeco).

JONDI MUSIC, #1106, 130 W. 42nd St., New York NY 10036. (212)819-0920. Contact: President. Music publisher, record company and record producer. BMI. Pays standard royalty.
How to Contact: Prefers cassette (or VHS or ¾" U-matic videocassette) with 3 songs and lyric sheet. Reports in 2 weeks only if SASE is included.
Music: Mostly country, top 40/pop, and gospel.

JUBO MUSIC, Box 4924, Union City NJ 07087. (201)471-3464. Representatives: Julian Hernandez and Bob Allecca. ASCAP. Publishes 6-20 songs/year; publishes 1-3 new songwriters/year. Works with lyricists. Pays standard royalty.
How to Contact: Write first and obtain permission to submit. Prefers cassette with 1 song and lyric sheet. Demos must be professional. SASE. Reports in 8 weeks.
Music: Mostly pop, R&B, dance and ballads; no country music. Published "100 Proof," (by Julian Hernandez), recorded by Toni-Ann on ADS Records (R&B/dance); "Do the Stevie Wonder," (by Julian Hernandez/Michael Roman), recorded by Diamond Z Crew on ADS Records (rap/dance); and "Let the Wall Fall," recorded by Veronica Underwood on Philly World Records (R&B/dance).

JUICY PEEPLE, Anklamer Ring 18, 2000 Hamburg 73, West Germany. (040)647 6280. Contact: Jimmy Pratt. GEMA. Music publisher and record company (Jax Pax). Publishes 50-60 songs/year; publishes 5 new songwriters/year. Pays standard royalty.
How to Contact: Prefers cassette with 2-12 songs. "Send cassette air parcel post with no value on declaration. Send finished product when possible." Does not return unsolicited material. Reports in 2 weeks.
Music: Mostly rock/pop and African influenced; also jazz, electronic and heavy metal. Published "Don't It Make You Feel," (by R. Harper), recorded by The Breathers on Jax Pax (rock/pop); "Doktor! Help Me," (by R&J Zohn), recorded by The Breathers on Jax Pax (rock); and "Red House," (by P. Gillan), recorded by Pauline Gillan & Northern Dancer on Bullet (heavy metal). Other artists include Donkey Kong (jazz/rock/fusion), and Roedelius & Moebius (electronic music).

JUMP MUSIC, Langemunt 71, 9460 Erpe-Mere Belgium. (053)62-73-77. General Manager: Eddy Van Mouffaert. Music publisher, record company (Jump Records) and record producer. Member of SABAM S.V., Brussels. Publishes 20 songs/year; publishes 8 new songwriters/year. Works with composers and lyricists; teams collaborators. Pays via SABAM S.V.
How to Contact: Submit demo tape by mail. Prefers cassette. Does not return unsolicited material. Reports in 2 weeks.
Music: Mostly easy listening, disco and light pop; also instrumentals. Published "Sinds ik Jou Ken" (by Eddy Govert), recorded by Tony Lenders (up-tempo); "Vertrouwen" (by E. Govert), recorded by Eigentijdse Jeugd (ballad); and "Vannacht Blijf ik Bij Jou" (by E. Govert), recorded by Guy Lovely (ballad).
Tips: "Music wanted with easy, catchy melodies (very commercial songs)."

*JUST LYRICS PUBLISHING, 216 Flagler Ave., New Smyrna FL 32069. (904)427-0060. A&R Consultant: Tim Probst. Music Publisher. ASCAP. Estab. 1986. Works with composers and lyricists; teams collaborators. Pays standard royalty.
How to Contact: Prefers cassette with 1-5 songs and lyric or lead sheet. SASE,
Music: Mostly country, pop and gospel; also rock, R&B, and show tunes.

KACK KLICK, INC., Mirror Records, Inc., 645 Titus Ave., Rochester NY 14617. (716)544-3500. Vice President: Armand Schaubroeck. Manager: Kim Simons. Music publisher and record company. BMI. Publishes 20 songs/year; publishes 4-12 new songwriters/year. Pays standard royalty.
How to Contact: Prefers cassette. Include photo. SASE. Reports in 2 months.
Music: MOR, progressive, rock, top 40/pop and new wave. Published "I Cannot Find Her," and "Stop," recorded by Chesterfield Kings; and "I Shot My Guardian Angel," recorded by Armand Schaubroeck Steals.

*JOHANN KAPLAN MUSIC, Bürgergasse 17 19/10/7, 1100 Vienna Austria. (0222) 65 54 104. President: Johann Kaplan, Jr. Music publisher, record company, record producer and artist management firm. Austro Mechana. Publishes 100 songs/year; publishes 15 new songwriters/year. Employs songwriters on a salary basis. Pays standard royalty.
Affiliate: Caplan Music (Austro Mechana).
How to Contact: Write first and obtain permission to submit or write to arrange personal interview. Prefers cassete, reel-to-reel (or VHS videocassette) with 2 songs and lyric or lead sheets. SAE and IRC. Reports in 2 months.
Music: All kinds of music. Published "Dance Dance More" (by Judit), recorded on Sunshine Records (disco); "Goodby My Love" (by Theresa), recorded on Caplan Music (soft rock); and "Guitar Man" (by Sunny), recorded on DCM Records (pop).

KARJAN MUSIC PUBLISHING CO., Box 205, White Lake NY 12786. (914)583-4471. President: Mickey Barnett. Music publisher, record company and record producer. SESAC. Member CMA. Publishes 25 songs/year; publishes 4 new songwriters/year. Pays standard royalty.
How to Contact: Prefers cassette with 1-3 songs and lyric sheet. SASE. Reports in 3 weeks.
Music: Blues, country, easy listening, MOR, R&B and top 40/pop.
Tips: "No ASCAP or BMI, please."

KASPERSIN MUSIC PUBLISHING CO.,2846 Dewey Ave., Rochester NY 14616. (716) 621-6270. President: David R. Kaspersin. BMI. Music publisher and record company (DRC Records). Publishes 10 songs/year; publishes 10 new songwriters/year. Pays standard royalty.
How to Contact: Write or call first and obtain permission to submit. Prefers cassette or 15 ips reel to reel (or ¾" or ½" VHS, Beta or U-matic videocassette) with 4 songs and lyric sheet. Looking for "clean simple demos with no fancy leads or intros. Get right to the hook of the song." SASE. Reports in 6 weeks.
Music: Country/R&B, rock and gospel. Published "Still in the Running," written and recorded by David and Barbara Marek on DRC Records; "Let Go," written and recorded by Richard Schroeder (country); and "Innocent of a Crime," recorded by Prospect Highway (rock).

*KASSNER ASSOCIATED PUBLISHERS LIMITED, 21 Panton St., London SW1Y 4DR England. (01)839-4672. General Manager: David Kassner. Music publisher and record company (President Records Limited). PRS. Publishes 100 songs/year; publishes 10 new songwriters/year. Employs songwriters on a salary basis. Works with composers, lyricists and teams collaborators. Pays standard royalty.
Affiliates: Edward Kassner Music (PRS), Cecil Lennox (PRS), DL Songs (PRS), Pan Musik (PRS), Editions Monica (SESAM), Ame Musikverlag (GEMA), Myers Music (ASCAP), Broadway Music (ASCAP), Tideland Music (BMI), Jayboy Music (BMI).
How to Contact: Prefers cassette (or VHS videocassette) with maximum of 3 songs and lyric or lead sheets. SAE and IRC. Reports in 1 month.
Music: Mostly pop, rock and country; also R&B, jazz and instrumentals. Published "Peace Must Come Again" (by Eddie Hardin), recorded by Iris Williams on President Records (ballad); "Japanese Tears" written and recorded by Denny Laine on President Records (pop); and "Loving on a Shoestring," recorded by Mike D'Abo on President Records (folk rock).

KAYDAY MUSIC, Suite 234, 24285 Sunnymead Blvd., Moreno Valley CA 92388-9971. (714)653-1556. Professional Manager: LaDonna Kay. Music publisher, record company, (Maxima) and record producer (Country Charts). Publishes 20 songs/year; publishes 15 new songwriters/year. Pays standard royalty.
Affiliate: OurWay Music (ASCAP).
How to Contact: Prefers cassette or 7½ ips reel-to-reel (or VHS videocassette) with 1-10 songs and lyric sheet. "Make sure your name and phone number are on the tape. We listen to all tapes submitted. Please specify whether you are affiliated with BMI or ASCAP."
Music: Mostly contemporary country; also all other types. Published "King of Mediocrity," "Living on Love Again" and "Love Struck," all written and recorded by Don Malena on Maxima Records (all contemporary country).

*JOE KEENE MUSIC CO., Box 602, Kennett MO 63857. President: Joe Keene. Music publisher. BMI. Publishes 6-10 songs/year; publishes 3-4 new songwriters/year. Pays standard royalty.
Affiliates: Lincoln Road Music (BMI), Cone Music (BMI), and Smooth Flight Music (BMI).
How to Contact: Prefers reel-to-reel or cassette and lead sheet. SASE. Reports in 2 weeks.
Music: Mostly country, rock and pop; also easy listening. Published "Hobo Wind," written and recorded by G. Blankenship; "Me & Jim & Jack & Johnny" (by Wayne Coonts), recorded by Butch Carter; and "A New Love Affair Every Night" written and recorded by B. Carter all on KSS Records (all country).

KEENY-YORK PUBLISHING, 29 S. Erie, Toledo OH 43602. (419)244-8599. Contact: Michael Drew Shaw. Music publisher, record company, record producer and film producer. BMI. Publishes 50 songs/year; publishes 4 new songwriters/year. Pays standard royalty.
Affiliates: Park J. Tunes (ASCAP) and Newstar International Records.
How to Contact: Prefers cassette with 5-10 songs and lyric sheet. SASE. Reports in 1 month.
Music: Mostly top 40/pop; also country, easy listening and MOR. Published "Oh Them Hens," recorded by Hotlix on MDS Entertainment Records (song and video about the Toledo Mud Hens); "Wherever You Are," recorded by Newstar Studio Band; and "We Are the Future," recorded by Kerry Clark.

KEEP CALM MUSIC LIMITED, Falcon Mews, London SW12 9SJ England. (01)675-5584. Contact: Professional Manager. Music publisher. PRS, MCPS. Publishes 50-75 songs/year; publishes 1-2 new songwriters/year. Pays varying royalty (averages 60%).
Affiliate: Titch Tunes Ltd.
How to Contact: Prefers cassette. Submissions should be "clearly labeled and marked if they are to be returned." Reports in 2 weeks.
Music: Mostly dance oriented material; also black/dance, soul/funk, AOR/rock and pop. Published "Jealousy," written and recorded by David Emmanuel; "Rock Hard," (by Titchener), recorded by Triple Beat Alliance; and "House That Jack Built," (by Titchener/Johnston), recorded by Rush Krush Crew, all on In Recordings.

BUTCH KELLY PRODUCTIONS AND PUBLISHING,11 Shady Oak Trail, Charlotte NC 28210. (704) 554-1611 or 1162. Manager: Butch Kelly. Music publisher, record company, record producer, and songwriter. ASCAP, BMI. Publishes 5 songs/year; publishes 2 new songwriters/year. Pays standard royalty.
How to Contact: Write first and obtain permission to submit. Prefers cassette (or videocassette) with 1-6 songs and lyric or lead sheet."Include photo, if possible." SASE. Reports in 4 months.
Music: Mostly R&B, pop, rap, gospel and rock; also dance oriented, easy listening, jazz, soul, and top 40. Published "MC Perpetrators," (by Tim Greene), recorded by Lady Crush on Executive Records (R&B); "Street Dancin'" and "Miss You," by Fresh Air on Executive Records (R&B); and "Call on Jesus," by Lebo Blackmon on KAM Executive Records (gospel).

KENCO PUBLISHING CO., 3784 Realty, Dallas TX 75244. (214)241-7854. President: K.J. Hughes. Music publisher, record company (Luv Records), record producer and 24 track recording studio. ASCAP. Publishes 50 songs/year; publishes 25 new songwriters/year.
Affiliates: Luvco Music (BMI).
How to Contact: Prefers cassette with 3 songs and lyric sheet. SASE. Reports in 5 weeks.
Music: Mostly country, gospel and novelty; also MOR. Artists include Carlette, Hollie Hughes, Stella Parton, Jacky Ward, Roy Clayton, and Xtra Touch.

GENE KENNEDY ENTERPRISES, INC., 2125 8th Ave. S., Nashville TN 37204. (615)383-6002. President: Gene Kennedy. Vice President: Karen Jeglum. Music publisher, independent producer, distributor and promoter. Publishes 200 songs/year; publishes 100 new songwriters/year. Pays standard royalty.
Affiliates: Chip 'n Dale (ASCAP), Door Knob Music (BMI), Lodestar (SESAC), Bekson (BMI) and Kenwall (ASCAP).
How to Contact: Query or arrange personal interview. Prefers cassette or 7½ ips reel-to-reel with 1-3 songs. "Tape should be accompanied by lyrics." SASE. Reports in 5 weeks.
Music: Country and gospel. Published "New Shade of Blue" (by Fred Horton and Johnette Burton), recorded by Perry LaPointe on Door Knob Records.

KENNING PRODUCTIONS, Box 1084, Newark DE 19715. (302)737-4278. President: Kenneth Mullins. Music publisher and record company (Kenning Records). BMI. Publishes 30-40 songs/year.
How to Contact: Prefers cassette. Does not return unsolicited material.
Music: Mostly rock, new wave and country; also blues, jazz and bluegrass. Published "Crazy Mama," written and recorded by K. Mullins; and "Work Me Over," (by J. Lehane/K. Mullins), recorded by K. Mullins, both on Kenning Records (both rock); and "This Time," (by K. Mullins).

KERISTENE MUSIC, LTD., Suite 602, 523 Pine St., Seattle WA 98101. (206)624-3965. President: Kristine J. Smith. BMI, ASCAP. Music publisher, record company (D-Town Records, Inc.) and record producer (Platinum Sound Productions). Publishes 6-8 songs/year; publishes 3 new songwriters/year. Works with composers and lyricists. Pays standard royalty.
Affiliates: K.H. Smith Music, Coleman, Kestin & Smith, Ltd.
How to Contact: Write or call first and obtain permission to submit. Prefers cassette (or VHS videocassette) with maximum 3 songs and lyric sheet. "Please include SASE for response." Does not return unsolicited material. Reports in 2 months.

Music: Mostly urban contemporary and rock; also heavy metal, gospel, country, R&B and dance. Published "Butterflys" (by Bill Miller), recorded by Bernadette Baslom on Solidarity Records (R&B); and "Double Shot of Loving," written and recorded by Lee Rogers on D-Town Records (R&B).

*KEY-SONG PUBLISHING COMPANY, Box 1573, Rutherford NJ 07070. (201)507-1451. President/Manager: Eddy Malaquias. Music publisher and record company (United Rhythm Records). ASCAP. Publishes 2-4 songs/year; publishes 2 new songwriters/year. Pays standard royalty or "split publishing deals if placed with major label."
How to Contact: Write or call first and obtain permission to submit. Prefers cassette with 1-4 songs and lyric sheet. "SASE must be enclosed for return of material." Reports in 6 weeks.
Music: Mostly easy listening and R&B; also soft rock and country. Published "Saving Lot's of People" (R&B); "Love Cycle" (pop); and "Only In My Dreams" (country), all written and recorded by Eddy Marquis on United Rhythm Records.
Tips: "We prefer a finished demo and a neat package. We also have overseas contacts, so be open minded about overseas publishing and releases."

KICKING MULE PUBLISHING/DESK DRAWER PUBLISHING, Box 158, Alderpoint CA 95411. (707)926-5312. Manager: Ed Denson. Music publisher and record company. BMI and ASCAP. Member NAIRD. Publishes 120 songs/year; publishes 7 new songwriters/year. Pays standard royalties.
How to Contact: Write first. Prefers cassette with 1-3 songs. Does not return unsolicited material. Reports "as soon as possible."
Music: Blues (fingerpicking); and folk (guitar/banjo only). Published "The Sweeper," written and recorded by George Gritzbach on KM Records (folk); "Thunder On The Run" written and recorded Stefan Grossman on KM Records (guitar instrumental); and "Pokerface Smile" (by Robert Force), recorded by Force & D'Ossche (country).
Tips: "We publish only material released on our albums. Since we record virtuoso guitar and banjo players, virtually the only way to get a tune published with us is to be such a player, or to have such a player record your song. We don't publish many 'songs' per se, our entire catalog is devoted 95% to instrumentals and 5% to songs with lyrics. As publishers we are not in the market for new songs. This listing is more of a hope that people will not waste their time and ours sending us blue-sky demos of material that does not relate to our very specialized business."

KIMTRA MUSIC/HATBAND MUSIC, Sound 70 Suite N-101, 210 25th Ave. N, Nashville TN 37203. (615)327-1711. Contact: Douglas Casmus. Music publisher. Publishes 75 songs/year; publishes 5 new songwriters/year. Teams collaborators.
How to Contact: Prefers cassette with 1 "great" song and typed lyric sheet. Will not return any material. "Do not enclose SASE. Will contact only if interested."
Music: Country, rock and top 40/pop. Published "Got My Heart Set on You," (by Dobie Gray), recorded by John Conlee on CBS Records and John Denver on RCA Records (country/pop); "Drinkin' My Baby Goodbye," recorded by Charlie Daniel's Band on Epic Records (country/rock); and "Over and Over," (by D. Gray), recorded by Ray Charles on Epic Records (pop).

KINGSPORT CREEK MUSIC PUBLISHING, Box 6085, Burbank CA 91510. Contact: Vice President. BMI. Music publisher and record company (Cowgirl Records). Employs songwriters on a salary basis.
How to Contact: Prefers cassette (or VHS videocassette) with any number of songs and lyric sheet. Does not return unsolicited material. "Include photos and bio if possible."
Music: Mostly country and gospel; also R&B, and MOR. Published "Tennessee Cowgirl," "Only Life I Know," (country), and "Wash Your Hands," (gospel), written and recorded by Melvene Kaye.
Tips: "Videocassettes are advantageous."

*KITTY MUSIC CORPORATION,Kobayashi Bldg., 1-14-11, Shibuya, Shibuya-ku, Tokyo 150 Japan. (03)499-4711. Manager of International Division: Kazuo Munakata. Music publisher and production company. Publishes 300 songs/year; publishes 40 new songwriters/year. Employs songwriters on a salary basis. Works with composers and lyricists; teams collaborators. Pays standard royalty.
How to Contact: Prefers cassette. Does not return unsolicited material. Reports in 7 weeks.
Music: Mostly rock and pop; also New Age (instrumental). Published "Friend" (by Goro Matsui/Koji Tamaki), recorded by Anzenchitai on Kitty Records (pop); "Surrender" written and recorded by Naoto Nagashima on Kitty Records (pop-rock); and "Hit by a Time Shower" (by Masumi Kawashima/Toshinobu Kubota), recorded by Toshinobu Kubota on CBS Sony (pop/rock).

NEIL A. KJOS MUSIC COMPANY, 4382 Jutland Dr., San Diego CA 92117. (619)483-0501. Editorial Secretaries: Beryl Pagan and Terry White. Educational music publisher. SESAC. Member MPA,

NAMM, RSMDA, ACDA, MENC, MTNA. Publishes 55 choral octavos/year; publishes 3 new composers/year. Pays "standard royalty of 10%."
Affiliates: Kjos West (SESAC), General Words and Music Company (ASCAP), Andrews Publications (SESAC), La Jolla Music (BMI), Loop Music Company (ASCAP), Pallma Music Company (SESAC), Parks Music Corp. (SESAC), Tuskegee Music Press (SESAC), Curtis Music Press (SESAC) and Curtis House of Music (ASCAP).
How to Contact: Write first. Prefers cassette. SASE. "We are an educational publisher, publishing choral music for schools and churches. We do not publish vocal solos. We acknowledge receipt of manuscript in 1 week, make decision in 4 months."
Music: Sacred and secular choral works.
Tips: "We do not publish 'pop' songs."

*JEAN KLUGER,86, Ave. Moliere, 1180 Brussels Belgium. (02) 345 41 29 or 345 42 03. Contact: Jean Kluger or Myriam Dekoster. Music publisher and record producer. SABAM. Works with composers and lyricists.
How to Contact: Prefers cassettes. SAE and IRC. Reports in 2 weeks.
Music: Popular music.

KOCH MUSIKVERLAG, Elbigenalp 91, Tirol A-6652 Austria. 05634/6444, 6445. International Manager: Haakon Brenner. Music publisher, record company (Koch Records International), record producer and manufacturer (Koch Digitaldisc). Member Aûstro Mechana AUME/AKM (Austria). Publishes 1,500 songs/year.
How to Contact: Prefers cassette (or VHS/PAL videocassette) and lyric or lead sheet. Does not return unsolicited material. Reports in 3 weeks.
Music: Mostly pop, rock and MOR; also dance music.

*KOMA PUBLISHING, Box 7309, Vanier, Ontario K1L 8E4 Canada. (613)746-5572. President: Lorenz Eppinger. Music publisher and record company (AMOK Records). CAPAC. Estab. 1986. Publishes 15 songs/year; publishes 6 new songwriters/year. Works with composers and lyricists; teams collaborators.
How to Contact: Prefers cassette and lyric sheet. "Cue the cassette and affix name and address on all submissions. Include photo if possible." SAE and IRC. Reports in 3 weeks.
Music: Mostly "accessible independent," electronic and ethnic; also jazz, original dance and "ambiant." Published "Havana" (by Gilmore/Shawiak), recorded by Condition (jazz/swing); "Fata Morgana" (by Josh/Klein/Mullrich), recorded by Dissidenten (ethnic/dance); and "La Rose" (by Schenkel), recorded by Courage of Lassie (folk/ambiant), all on AMOK Records.

KOMPASS RECORDS, Puistokaari 8, 00200 Helsinki Finland. (90)676445. General Manager: Chris Schwindt. Music publisher and record company. Publishes 25 songs/year.
How to Contact: Submit demo tape by mail.

KOZKEEOZKO MUSIC, Suite 602, 928 Broadway, New York NY 10010. (212)505-7332. Professional Managers: Ted Lehrman and Libby Bush. Music publisher and record producer. ASCAP. Estab. 1986. Publishes 5 songs/year; publishes 2 new songwriters/year. Pays standard royalty.
How to Contact: Call or write first and obtain permission to submit. Cassettes only with 3 songs maximum and typwritten lyric sheet for each song. SASE. Reports in 2 months.
Music: Mostly soul/pop, dance, pop/rock (no heavy metal), adult contemporary. Published "Love Put Some Danger In Me," (muzak, heavy rotation) and "Video! TV-oh!," recorded by Scarlett on Coast-to-Coast Records.
Tips: "Songs with hooky memorable melodies and lyrics that say something in an original way are what we're looking for. Potential hit singles only; no album cuts, please. A well produced demo gives a submitted song an edge."

L&G MUSIC, (formerly Al Gallico Music), Suite 606, 9301 Wilshire Blvd., Beverly Hills CA 90210. (213)274-0165. President: Al Gallico. Music publisher. BMI, ASCAP. Member NMPA. Payment differs from song to song.
Affiliates: Altam (BMI), John Anderson Music (BMI), Galleon (ASCAP) and Mainstay (BMI).
How to Contact: Write or call first and obtain permission to submit. Prefers cassette with 2-4 songs and lyric sheet.
Music: Country, top 40 and R&B. "We're very strong in contemporary country and crossover material." Published "Swingin' " (by John Anderson/Lionel Delmore), recorded by J. Anderson on Warner Bros. Records (country crossover); "The Corvette Song (The One I Loved Back Then)" (by Gary Gentry), recorded by George Jones; and "The Name Game" by Laura Branigan.

Tips: "Be aware of the artists we work with and the artists who record outside material. Study their styles. Study the songs being played on the radio; they're being played because a number of people believed in them and said yes. Come up with fresh ideas and titles; vivid, sincere, relationship-oriented lyrics; catchy melodies; tight structures and contemporary chords and feel. Remember the music industry is based on, and needs, great songs."

LACKEY PUBLISHING CO., Box 269, Caddo OK 74729. (405)367-2798. President: Robert F. Lackey. Music publisher and record producer. BMI. Publishes 6-8 songs/year; publishes 3-4 new songwriters/ year. Pays standard royalty.
How to Contact: Prefers cassette with 1-10 songs. SASE. Reports in 2 weeks.
Music: Mostly country and MOR; also bluegrass, blues, church/religious, easy listening, folk, gospel, progressive, R&B and top 40/pop. Published "The Devil In Tight Blue Jeans," written and recorded by Franklin Lackey (country); "Teenager in Love," written and recorded by Sherry Kenae (pop/country); and "The Rose of Goodbye" (by Franklin Lackey), recorded by Sherry Kenae (progressive country), all on Uptown Records.
Tips: "Have accompaniment of 3 or more musicians."

LARI-JON PUBLISHING CO., 627 Countryview, Columbus NE 68601. (402)564-7034. Owner: Larry J. Good. Music publisher and record company (Lari-Jon Records). BMI. Publishes 25 songs/year; publishes 3 new songwriters/year. Teams collaborators. Pays standard royalty.
How to Contact: Prefers cassette or (or videocassette) with 6 songs and lyric sheet. SASE.Reports in 1 month.
Music: Country and gospel. Published "American Farmer" (by Mick Kovar), recorded by the Kovar Brothers on Rene Records; and "Between the Lies" (by Mick Kovar), recorded by Larry Good on Lari-Jon Records (both country).

LASKO-DELROSE MUSIC, Box 9675, Palm Springs CA 92263. (619)328-8178. President: Dan Laskowitz. Music publisher and record company (Angi Records). Publishes 12 songs/year; publishes 3-4 new songwriters/year. Pays standard royalty.
How to Contact: Prefers cassette (or VHS videocassette) with 1-6 songs and lyric sheet. SASE. Reports in 3 weeks.
Music: Pop, rock and R&B. Published "Lady Liberty Theme," (by Danny Laskowitz), recorded by Ryan Samans; "Criminal," "No Chance," "Obsession for Possession," "Time" and "Breakdown" all by Ron King and Bobby King and "I Can Take It"and "I America" by Danny Laskowitz, all on Angi Records
Tips: "Be innovative, be original. Ask yourself if it is a hit."

*LAUREN-BLICK MUSIC, 723 Lincoln Ave., Carbondale CO 81623. (303)963-3598. Recording Artist and Owner: Patricia Lauren. Music publisher and record company (Track Records). BMI. Publishes 5-10 songs/year; publishes 5-10 new songwriters/year. Pays standard royalty.
How to Contact: Prefers cassette and lyric and lead sheets. Reports in 1 month.
Music: Mostly pop, contemporary country and pop/rock; also ballads, male-female duets and light rock. Published "She's the One," by Larry Wilkins (rock); "Get You Yet," by Patricia Lauren (pop); and "Tears," by Steve McQuarry/Patricia Lauren (ballad), all recorded by Patricia Lauren on Track Records.
Tips: "A great song is a great song and will be heard among the rest. Send songs. Country music is now alive with the sounds of contemporary recording, such as synthesizers, and has created a new market for contemporary country/pop music. We are looking for material currently for Patricia Lauren's second album, on a major label: pop, rock to be marketed on the edge of country."

LE MATT MUSIC, LTD., % Stewart House, Hillbottom Rd., Highwycombe, Bucks, England. 44-0491-36301 or 44-0491-36401. Contact: Ron or Cathrine Lee. Music publisher, record company and record producer. MCPS, PRS. Member MPA, PPL. Publishes 50 songs/year; publishes 15 new songwriters/year. Works with lyricists and composers; teams collaborators. Pays standard royalty; royalties paid directly to US songwriters or through US publishing affiliate.
Affiliates: Lee Music, Ltd., Swoop Records, Grenoville Records, Check Records, Zarg Records, Pogo Records, Ltd., R.T.F.M.
How to Contact: Prefers 7½ or 15 ips reel-to-reel or cassette (or VHS/Beta 625/PAL system videocassette) with 1-3 songs and lyric sheet. "Make sure name and address are on reel or cassette." SAE and IRC. Reports in 3 weeks.
Music: Mostly pop/rock and rock; also bluegrass, blues, country, dance-oriented, easy listening, MOR, progressive, R&B, soul, disco, new wave and top 40/pop. Published *Children of the Night*, by Nightmare; *I'm Only Looking*, by Dawia Boone; *American Girl*, by Hush; and *The Chromatics* (live music), all LPs.

LEMMEL MUSIC LTD., Cray Ave., Orpington, Kent BR5 3QP England. Music Director: Ron Smith. Head of Documents: Miss Sheelagh Gudgeon. Music publisher. PRS. Pays standard royalty.
Affiliates: Rimusic (PRS), and Mason Music Limited (PRS).
How to Contact: Prefers cassette and lead sheet. SAE and IRC.
Music: MOR, instrumental and pop.

LEMON SQUARE MUSIC, Box 31819, Dallas TX 75231. (214)750-0720. A&R Director: Mike Anthony. Music publisher. BMI, ASCAP. Publishes 10 new songwriters/year. Pays standard royalty.
Affiliate: Friends of the General Music (BMI).
How to Contact: Write first and obtain permission to submit. Prefers cassette with 2 songs and lyric sheet. Does not return unsolicited material. Reports in 6 weeks.
Music: Mostly country and gospel. Published "He's My Gentle Man with the Gentle Hands," (by Stan Rattliff), recorded by Audie Henry on CCR Records (country—"on Canadian charts for 18 weeks, number on Cancon, number 4 international).

LEOSONG COPYRIGHT SERVICE PTY. LTD., GPO Box 2089, Sydney, 2001 Australia. (2)29-4972. Contact: Manager. Music publisher. Publishes 50 songs/year; publishes 10 new songwriters/year. Pays standard royalty.
How to Contact: Prefers cassette (or PAL-VHS videocassette). Does not return unsolicited material. Reports in 6 weeks.
Music: Mostly contemporary pop/rock, film soundtracks and country.

LES EDITIONS LA FETE INC., 2306 Sherbrooke E., Montreal, Quebec H2K 1E5 Canada. (514)521-83-03. General Manager: Michel Zgarka. Music publisher. CAPAC, PRO CAN, SODRAC. Publishes 7 songs/year; publishes 5 new songwriters/year. Works with composers and lyricists; team collaborators. Pays standard royalty.
How to Contact: Prefers cassette (or VHS videocasette) with 6 songs and lyric sheet. Does not return unsolicited material. Reports in 6 weeks.
Music: Mostly pop/dance, children's and classical; also French and R&B. Published "Not Ready," (by Howard Forman), recorded by Freddie James (dance music); "Tête De Reveur," (by Guy Trepanier/Marc Desjardins), recorded by Betty Eljarat (ballad—French); and "Take Me There," (by Howard Forman/Michel Rivard), recorded by Fabienne Thibeault (ballad), all on La Fête Records.
Tips: Seeking songs that are "usable in one of our soundtracks (we are a movie production company)."

*LIFE AND DEATH,Box 3654, Hollywood CA 90078. (213)465-9622. President: H. Davis. Music publisher, record company (Life and Death Records) and record producer (Life and Death Productions). BMI. Estab. 1986. Publishes 12 songs/year; publishes 2 new songwriters/year. Works with composers and lyricists; teams collaborators. Pays standard royalty.
How to Contact: Call first to obtain permission to submit. Prefers 7½ ips reel-to-reel (or VHS videocassette) and lyric sheet. SASE. Reports in 3 months.
Music: Hard rock and blues. Published "Blue Christmas," written and recorded by Honey Davis (blues); "Ain't Waitin No More," (by D. Brownfeld), recorded by Hollyrock (hard rock); and "You've Got a Friend," written and recorded by Hollyrock (hard rock), all on Life and Death Records.

LINEAGE PUBLISHING CO., Box 211, East Prairie MO 63845. (314)649-2211. (Nashville branch: 38 Music Sq. E., Nashville TN 37203. (615)255-8005.) Professional Manager: Tommy Loomas. Staff: Mike Clair, Alan Carter and Joe Silver. Music publisher, record producer and record company. BMI. Pays standard royalty.
How to Contact: Query first. Prefers cassette with 2-4 songs and lyric sheet. SASE. Reports in 1 month.
Music: Country, easy listening, MOR, country rock, and top 40/pop. Published "Yesterdays Teardrops," and "Round & Round," (by Phil and Larry Burchett), recorded by the Burchetts on Capstan Records (country).

LINGO MUSIC, 314 W. 53rd St., New York NY 10019. (212)582-8800. Owner/President: Carsten Bohn. Music publisher and record producer. ASCAP, GEMA. Publishes 20-30 songs/year.
Affiliates: Francis Day & Hunter (Hamburg/West Germany), and Screen-Gems (USA).
How to Contact: Prefers cassette (or VHS videocassette) with 3-5 songs and lyric or lead sheet. "Submit photo and resume if possible." SASE. Reports in 2 months.
Music: Mostly contemporary rock/pop and R&B; also jazz and soundtracks. Published "Gimme Your Love" (by George Kochbeck), recorded by Georgie Red on WEA Records (R&B).
Tips: "Be sure you like what you do, or don't bother sending it in. Be tasteful and honest."

LIN'S LINES, #1103, 150 5th Ave., New York NY 10011. (212)691-5630. President: Linda K. Jacobson. Vice President: Jeffrey Jacobson. Music publisher. ASCAP. Publishes 6 songs/year; publishes 3 new songwriters/year. Pays standard royalty.
How to Contact: Prefers cassette (or ½" VHS or NTSC ¾" videocassette). "Send bio and picture." SASE. Reports in 1 month.
Music: Pop and rock; also dance, blues and jazz.

*LISTEN AGAIN MUSIC,165 Beaver St., New Brighton PA 15066. (412)847-4111. Professional Manager: William E. Watson. Music publisher. Estab. 1986. Publishes 5 songs/year; publishes 3 new songwriters/year. Works with composers and lyricists; teams collaborators. Pays standard royalty.
How to Contact: Prefers cassette with 3 songs and lyric sheet. "Must have lyric sheet and SASE. We would also like a brief, biography or resume so we know who we're working with." Reports in 6 weeks.
Music: Mostly country, top-40, rock; also R&B and MOR. Published "One Step Further," (by B. Watson), recorded by C.R. Band on 7 City Records (country).
Tips: "We are a new company with only 1 song actually out on the market at this point. We're building our catalogue and are very receptive to new writers. Submit only your best work; it should have a well conceived title. Concentrate on the lyric—we receive a lot of well produced tapes with weak lyrics."

*LITTLE, BITTY, MIDI CITY MUSIC COMMITTY,Box 897, Hartford CT 06120. (203)522-2371. Director: Silver Sargent. Music publisher, record company (S.O.C.) and record producer (L.U.V. Sound). BMI. Publishes 1-2 songs/year; publishes 1-2 new songwriters/year. Works with composers and lyricists; teams collaborators. Pays standard royalty.
How to Contact: Prefers cassette (or VHS videocassette) with 4-6 songs and lyric or lead sheet. "Include a resume." SASE. Reports in 6 weeks.
Music: Mostly funk, soul and R&B; also gospel, jazz and light rock. Published "Bite It," (by Herb Superb), recorded by Drum (rap); "Shoot Your Best Shot," (by Silver Sargent), recorded by Carol (dance); and "Merci-Ba-Coup," (by Silver Sargent), recorded by Scarph (ballad), all on S.O.C. Records.

LITTLE WIZARD MUSIC PUBLISHER, 116 Wendy Dr., Box 384, Holtsville NY 11742. (516)654-8459. A&R Director: Arthur Christopher. Music publisher, record company and record producer. BMI. Publishes 5-10 songs/year; publishes 1 new songwriter/year. Pays standard royalty.
How to Contact: Write first and obtain permission to submit. Prefers cassette (or videocassette) with 1-3 songs. SASE. Reports in 3 weeks.
Music: MOR, R&B, rock, soul and top 40/pop.

LO PINE MUSIC, Box 444, Taylor MI 48180. (313)722-0616. President: John D. Lollio. BMI. Music publisher. Publishes 10 songs/year; publishes 2 new songwriters/year. Pays standard royalty.
Affiliate: Carrie-Lynn.
How to Contact: Prefers cassette and lyric or lead sheet. SASE. Reports in 2 weeks.
Music: Mostly country and gospel. Published "Sweetest Worlds," written and recorded by Johni Dee on Ace (country); "If That's What Makes You Crazy," written and recorded by Marty Parker on Mystery Train (country); "After the Pain," (by Jim W. Rice), recorded by Johni Dee on Ace (country); and "Jesus, I Love You," by J.D. Lollio on Ace Records (contemporary Christian).

LONG SHADOW MUSIC, Klein Haasdal 87, Schimmert 6333 AJ The Netherlands. 04404-1944. General Manager: John Coenen. Music publisher. BUMA-STEMRA. Publishes 50 songs/year. Pays standard royalty.
How to Contact: Prefers cassette or reel-to-reel (or videocassette). Does not return unsolicited material. Reports in 3 weeks.
Music: Pop, disco and MOR. Published "Misty Islands," "Moonlight Melody," and "Stars Over Napoli," (by K. Hasdal), recorded by Johnny Bee on Sky (MOR).
Tips: Submit "songs with single potential, sing-a-longs, and good coverable songs."

THE LORENZ CORPORATION, 501 E. 3rd St., Dayton OH 45401. Church music publisher. ASCAP, BMI and SESAC. Member NMPA, MPA and CMPA. Publishes approximately 200 songs/year; publishes 10 new songwriters/year. Pays standard royalty or outright purchase.
Affiliates: Lorenz Publishing Company (publishes sacred music for youth and adult choirs as well as for piano and organ); Sacred Music Press (publishes "a more stylized type of sacred music for church"); Heritage Music Press (school music); and Roger Dean Publishing Co. (distributor for Laurel Press, Trune Music, Inc., Sunshine Productions, and American Guild of English Handbell Ringers and Chorister's Guild).
How to Contact: Send manuscripts only—"no demo tapes." SASE. Reports in 1 month.

LOUIE B. PUBLISHING, Box 15117, Kansas City MO 64106. (816)931-5866. General Manager: Marion Brown. BMI. Music publisher, record company (Quinton Productions) and record producer. Publishes varying number of songs and new songwriters/year. Works with composers and lyricists; teams collaborators. Pays standard royalty.
Affiliates: Associated Music Productions, and Rio Hard Luck Music.
How to Contact: Prefers cassette with maximum 3 songs and lyric sheet or lead sheet. SASE. Reports in 2 months.
Music: Top 40, R&B, gospel, country and "crossover." Published "Christmas Came Too Soon," (by L. Brown); "Sing the Love Song" and "I'll Always Be There," (by A. Washington and L. Brown), recorded by Cotton Candy on QP (top-40); "He'll Set You Free," written and recorded by A. Washington on Soulsearch Records (gospel).
Tips: "We are reviewing material for record production so material should be hit single quality with strong hook."

*LOVEFORCE INTERNATIONAL, Box 1648, Los Angeles CA 90024. (213)208-2104. Submissions Manager: T. Wilkins. Music publisher, record company and promotion company. BMI. Publishes 4 songs/year; publishes 1 new songwriter/year. Works with composers and lyricists; teams collaborators. Pays standard royalty.
How to Contact: Write or call first and obtain permission to submit. Prefers cassette (or VHS videocassette) with 2 songs and lyric sheet. SASE. Reports in 6 weeks.
Music: Mostly pop, ballads and R&B; also rock (uptempo), country and gospel. Published "Love Attack," recorded by Mandrill on Arista Records (R&B); "Heart of the City," (by Gray/Karyln/Wilkins), recorded by Decadents on Rococo Records (rock); and "Declare Peace," written and recorded by Bandit on LoveForce International Records (pop/rock).
Tips: "We look for melodic, memorable hooks in music, unique, catchy, personally touching lyrics."

THE LOWERY GROUP, 3051 Clairmont Rd. NE, Atlanta GA 30329. (404)325-0832. Professional Director: Cotton Carrier. Music publisher and record producer. ASCAP, BMI. Member CMA, NARAS and NMPA. Publishes 100-150 songs/year; publishes 6-10 new songwriters/year. Works with composers and lyricists; teams collaborators. Pays standard royalty.
Affiliates: Brother Bill's Music; Low-Sal, Inc.; Eufaula Music; and Low-Twi Inc.
How to Contact: Write or call first and obtain permission to submit. Prefers cassette with 1-4 songs and lyric sheet. Does not return unsolicited material. Reports in 3 weeks.
Music: Contemporary Christian, top 40, rock and country. Published "Desperado Love," (by S. Johns), recorded by Conway Twitty on Warner Bros. Records (country); "Lord of Hearts," (by Carswell/Wells), recorded by Gaither Vocal Band (contemporary Christian); "Old Bridges Burn Slowly" (by Joe South), recorded by Billy Joe Royal on Altantic (country); and "America" (by Sammy Johns), recorded by Waylon Jennings on RCA Records (country).

LUCKY'S KUM-BA-YA PUBLISHING CO., Box 6-9283 Evergreen, Brohman MI 49312. (616)689-1586. Contact: President. Music publisher and record company. ASCAP.
How to Contact: Write first and obtain permission to submit. Prefers cassette.
Music: Country, gospel and pop/light rock. Published "Gospel Jamboree" (gospel/country), "Gooski's Riders" (country), and "All I Want for Christmas" (pop), all written and recorded by Ross Fulton, Sr. on Lucky's Kum-Ba-Ya Records.

HAROLD LUICK & ASSOCIATES MUSIC PUBLISHER, Box B, Carlisle IA 50047. (515)989-3679. President: Harold L. Luick. Music publisher, record company, record producer and music industry consultant. BMI. Publishes 25-30 songs/year; publishes 5-10 new songwriters/year. Pays standard royalty or will negotiate with established writer.
How to Contact: Write or call first about your interest or arrange personal interview. Prefers cassette with 3-5 songs and lyric sheet. SASE. Reports in 3 weeks.
Music: Traditional country and hard core country. Published "It Must Be Love," (by Roger and Sandra Davis), recorded by Bobbie Brown on Footstomper Records; "Cheese and Butter," written and recorded by Darrell C. Thomas on Footstomper Records; and "Waylon Sing To Mama," written and recorded by Darrell C. Thomas on Ozark Opry Records, (all country).
Tips: "Ask yourself these questions: Does my song have simplicity of lyric and melody? Good flow and feeling? A strong story line? Natural dialogue? Hook chorus, lyric hooks, melody hooks? If it doesn't, then why should a publisher or A&R person take the time to listen to it?"

MAGIC MESSAGE MUSIC, Box 2236, Largo FL 33540. (813)595-5115. Contact: Alan Redstone. ASCAP. Music publisher and record company (Sureshot Records). Publishes 3-10 songs/year; publishes 1 new songwriter/year. Pays standard royalty.

How to Contact: Prefers cassette and lyric sheet. SASE. Report in 3 weeks.
Music: Mostly country and rock; also adult contemporary, blues and pop. Published: "This Time Around," Salomé," and "Cars, Girls, Dreams," all written and recorded by Alan Redstone on Sureshot Records.

MAIN TRIPP PUBLISHING INC., 2804 Beechtree Dr., Sanford NC 27330. (919)774-8926. Vice President: Jim Watters. BMI. Music publisher, record company (Main Tripp Record Inc.) and recording studio. Publishes 45-50 songs/year; publishes 30-35 new songwriters/year. Pays standard royalty.
How to Contact: Prefers cassette with "any number of songs and lyric sheet. SASE with sufficient postage or no return." Reports in 6 weeks. "Due to heavy volume received we can no longer guarantee the return of unsolicited material, but we will try."
Music: Mostly country, gospel, and bluegrass; also "some rock." Published "Love Is," written and recorded by Bill Trapp on Attieram Records (country); and "Empty Places," (by Watters/Gordon), recorded by Don Keatley on Main Tripp Records (country/gospel); and "He Delivered Me," (by Stephanie Watters), recorded by Jim Watters and Convenant on Main Tripp Records (gospel).
Tips: "Be sincere. Be patient—we get a lot of material in the mail. Gospel writers should let their pastor look over their lyrics. Country writers—don't send us songs with profanity or x-rated lyrics."

*MANHATTAN COUNTRY, INC.,#18C, 100 W. 57th St., New York NY 10019. (212)757-2495. President: Reginald A. Bowes. Music publisher, and record producer (Manhattan Country Inc.). BMI. Estab. 1987. Publishes 6-12 songs/year; publishes 4 new songwriters/year. Works with compsoers and lyricists; teams collaborators. Pays standard royalty.
How to Contact: Prefers cassette with 2-3 songs and lyric sheet. SASE. Reports in 2 weeks.
Music: Mostly country. Published "Man in the Mirror," (by T.J.White/R. Bowes), recorded by Tommie Joe White and Southern Cookin' (country); "Empty Glasses," (by Cosmo Tillman/R. Bowes), recorded by Cosmo Perry Tillman (country); and "More Than Time," (by Leah Mellman/R. Bowes), recorded by Leah Mellman (pop/ballad), on all Manhattan Country Records.

MARK VIII MUSIC,438 Vallejo, San Francisco CA 94133. Music publisher, record company (Quantum Records) and record producer. BMI. Publishes 30 songs/year; publishes 15 new songwriters/year. Works under co-publishing arrangement.
How to Contact: Prefers cassette, or reel-to-reel (or videocassette) with 1-3 songs and lyric or lead sheet. SASE. Reports in 4 weeks.
Music: Rock, pop, blues, and country; also gospel, jazz and new wave. Published "Searching On," (by Saldate), recorded by Oliver Jicicco on Quantum Records (fusion); "Burning Giants," (by Kim Nomad), recorded by Tom Jones on Fire Brand Records (pop); and "Diamond John," (by Villion), recorded by Dillion on Quantum Records (rock).
Tips: "Put everything together clean and clear."

MARMIK MUSIC, INC., 135 E. Muller Rd., East Peoria IL 61611. (309)699-4000. President: Martin Mitchell. Music publisher and record company. BMI. Publishes 10-12 songs/year; publishes 3-4 new songwriters/year. Works with lyricists and composers; teams collaborators. Pays standard royalty.
How to Contact: Query. Prefers reel-to-reel or cassette with 2-10 songs and lead sheet. "With first submission, include an affidavit of ownership of the material." SASE. Reports in 2 weeks.
Music: Mostly MOR and Christian; also country, church/religious, blues, easy listening and gospel. Published "Happy Anniversary," and "Day After Never," by William Bender (MOR); and "You're the One," by Amos Davis (country), all recorded by Wade Ray.
Tips: "Need songs that are topical and upbeat—too many slow songs on the market."

MARSHALL STREET MELODIES, 8102 Polk St. NE, Minneapolis MN 55432. (612)784-7458. President/General Manager: Michael S.J. Gapinski. Music publisher and record company. BMI. Member MSA. Publishes 15-30 songs/year; publishes 5-8 new songwriters/year. Pays "slightly above" standard royalty.
How to Contact: Write first. Prefers cassette (or videocassette) with 1-3 songs and lyric sheet. "Professional, digital-quality material and MIDI compositions are reviewed first." Does not return material. Reports in 2 weeks.
Music: "Strictly up-tempo material. Mostly looking for modern R&B/pop and country with a rock feel." Published "Ready or Not," "Desire," and Sting-Ray," all written and recorded by Zebop on Marshall Street Melodies Records (all R&B).
Tips: "Almost all successful songs are based on an honest emotion that the lyrics and music form when put together in a unique way. A good recording will help sell a good solid tune and is easier to listen to."

MARULLO MUSIC PUBLISHERS, 1121 Market St., Galveston TX 77550. (409)762-4590. President: A.W. Marullo, Sr. Music publisher, record company and record producer. BMI. Publishes 24 songs/year; publishes 8 new songwriters/year. Pays standard royalty.
How to Contact: Prefers cassette "only" with 4-6 songs and lyric sheet. SASE. Reports in 8 weeks.
Music: Country and country/pop. Published "Travelin' Lover," by Debra Fowler; "Changes & Chances," and "Color This Feelin' of Blue," by Trica Matula (all country/pop).

*ANDY MARVEL MUSIC, Suite N, 226 Springmeadow Dr., Holbrook NY 11741. (516)472-1219. President: Andy Marvel. Music publisher, record company (Alyssa Records), and record producer (Marvel Productions and Ricochet Records). ASCAP. Publishes 30 songs/year; publishes 10 new songwriters/year. Works with composers and lyricists; teams collaborators. Pays standard royalty.
Affiliates: Andysongs (BMI) and Bing, Bing, Bing Music (ASCAP).
How to Contact: Prefers cassette or 7½ ips reel-to-reel (or VHS videocassette) with 3-5 songs and lyric sheet. SASE. Reports in 2 weeks.
Music: Mostly pop, R&B and rock; also country. Published "Learning to Live with a Heartache," (by Andy Marvel/Sheree Sano), recorded by Andy Marvel on Alyssa Records (pop); and "Love Will Never Be the Same Without You," (by Andy Marvel/Don Levy), recorded by John Wesley Shipp on Jamie Records (pop).

MASTER AUDIO, INC./MASTER SOUND, INC./LYRESONG, INC., 1227 Spring St. NW, Atlanta GA 30309. (404)873-6425. Contact: Babs Richardson. Music publisher and recording studio. BMI, ASCAP. Publishes 20 songs/year; publishes 1-2 new songwriters/year. Pays standard royalty.
Affiliates: Paydirt Music (ASCAP), Legal Tender (ASCAP) and Seyah Music (BMI).
How to Contact: Prefers cassette with 2-3 songs. SASE. Reports in 1 month.
Music: Country, disco, gospel, R&B, soul and top 40/pop. Published *Great News*, (by Troy Ramey), recorded by T. Ramey and the Soul Searchers on Nashboro Records (black gospel); "Try Jesus, " recorded by T. Ramey (gospel); "Tea Cups and Doilies," (by Mac Frampton) recorded by M. Frampton on Triumvirate Records (Broadway show type); and "Double Shot (of My Baby's Love)," recorded by Joe Stampley (country).

MASTERLEASE MUSIC PUBLICATIONS, Box 234, St. Louis MO 63166. (314)296-9526. President: Bob Bax. Music publisher and record company. BMI. Publishes 3 songs/year. Pays standard royalty.
How to Contact: Write first about your interest. Prefers cassette with 2-6 songs and lyric sheet. Does not return unsolicited material. Reports in 1 month.
Music: Bluegrass, blues, church/religious, country, gospel, Spanish and R&B.

MASTER'S COLLECTION PUBLISHING & T.M.C. PUBLISHING, Box 362, Station A, Rexdale, Ontario M9W 5L3 Canada. (416)746-1991. President: Paul J. Young. Music publisher and record company. PROCAN, CAPAC. Member CIRPA. Publishes 20 songs/year; publishes 3 new songwriters/year. Pays standard royalty.
How to Contact: Write first. Prefers cassette (or videocassette) with 3-6 songs. Does not return unsolicited material. Reports in 1 month.
Music: Christian/religious. Published "Crown of Glory," (by Ruth Fazal) and "One City Stands," (by Andrew Donaldson), recorded on The Master's Collection Records; and "Christmas Is," (by Frank Hargreaves), recorded by His Ambassadors on The Master's Collection Records (Christmas).

MASTERSOURCE PRODUCTIONS, Division of Tree Publishing (Meadowgreen Music, Nashville), Suite 903, 151 N. Michigan, Chicago IL 60601. (312)819-1515. President: Charles Thomas. Music publisher and record producer. Publishes 2-3 new songwriters/year. Pays standard royalty.
Affiliates: Heart of the Matter Music (ASCAP), and Song du Jour (BMI).
How to Contact: Query, Attn: Stephen Navyac. Prefers cassette with 3 songs and lyric and lead sheets. Does not return unsolicited material. Reports in 3 weeks.
Music: Top 40, AOR, adult contemporary and contemporary Christian. Published "Was It a Morning Like This" (by Jim Croegaert), recorded by Sandi Patti on Word (contemporary Christian).
Tips: "We desire long-term relationships with writers—not individual songs."

MCA MUSIC FRANCE, 1 rue Lamennais, Paris 75008 France. 45-63-38-51, 45-63-66-83. Contact: Artistic Director. Music publisher.
How to Contact: Write first and obtain permission to submit. Prefers cassette. Does not return unsolicited material.
Music: Rock and dance.

JIM McCOY MUSIC, Rt. 2, Box 116 H, Berkeley Springs WV 22601. Owners: Bertha or Jim McCoy. Music publisher, record company (Winchester Records) and record producer (Jim McCoy Productions). BMI. Publishes 25 songs/year; publishes 5 new songwriters/year. Pays standard royalty.
Affiliates: Alear Music, New Edition Music (BMI).
How to Contact: Write or call first and obtain permission to submit. Prefers cassette, 7½ or 15 ips reel-to-reel (or VHS or Beta videocassette) with 6 songs. Does not return unsolicited material. Reports in 4 weeks.
Music: Mostly country, country/rock and rock; also bluegrass and gospel. Published "Outlaw," written and recorded by Jim McCoy on Winchester (country); "Heaven is My Goal," (by Dottie Eyler), recorded by Carroll County Ramblers on Alear (gospel); and "The Greatest," (by Odie Schaeffer/Leroy Eyler), recorded by Carroll County Ramblers on Winchester (country).

MDM PRODUCTIONS, 117 W. 8th, Hays KS 67601. (913)625-9634. President: Mark Meckel. Music publisher, record company and record producer. BMI. Member CASK and SRS. Publishes 8 songs/year; publishes 5 new songwriters/year. Teams collaborators. Pays standard royalty.
How to Contact: Prefers cassette with minimum 3 songs and lyric sheet. SASE.
Music: Mostly country rock, 50s rock, Christian rock, R&B and Christmas; also MOR, gospel, blues and dance-oriented. Published "Christmas Eve Waltz," (by Jack Kavanaugh), recorded by Tommy Harrison (country); "A Friend Like You," written and recorded by Mark Selby (pop/MOR); and "My Heart Keeps Walking (Right Back To You)," (by Paul Hotchkiss/Mike Terry), recorded by Tommy Harrison (country swing), all on M.D.M. Records.
Tips: "Be willing to change and work with a producer."

MEDIA CONCEPTS, INC./MEDIA CONCEPTS MUSIC, 52 N. Evarts Ave., Elmsford NY 10523. (914)347-3545. Professional Manager: Michael Berman. President: Chip Rigo. Music publisher and record producer. BMI, ASCAP. Publishes 15-20 songs/year; publishes 5-10 new songwriters/year. Pays standard royalty; co-publishing deals available for established writers.
Affiliate: Sunsongs Music (BMI).
How to Contact: Prefers cassette with 3-4 songs and lyric sheet. SASE. Reports in 3 weeks.
Music: Dance-oriented, techno-pop, R&B, rock (all styles) and top 40/pop. Published "Big Girl" (by Michael Christian), "What You Get Is What You See," (Etoll/Kalem), and "Nothing But Trouble," (by Robbie Rigo), recorded by Jailbait and performed on Star Search '85 (pop/rock; Jailbait was a finalist and was recently signed to Atlantic Records).

MEGA-STAR MUSIC, 473 Halsey St., Brooklyn NY 11233. (718)574-8067. General Manager: Barry Yearwood. Music publisher and record producer (Barry Yearwood). Publishes 8-12 songs/year; publishes 4 new songwriters/year. Pays standard royalty.
How to Contact: Prefers cassette with 4 songs. Does not return unsolicited material. Reports in 4 weeks.
Music: Mostly dance and R&B; also pop. Published "Dancing to the Beat," written and recorded by Henderson and Whitfield on Park Place Records; "Solar Flight," written and recorded by Richard Bush on Island Records; and "Mind Your Own Business," written and recorded by R. Bush on Laser-7 Records.

MENTO MUSIC GROUP KG, Box 7718, D-2000 Hamburg 20, West Germany. (040) 43-00-339. General Manager: Arno H. v. Vught Jr. Music publisher, record company (Playbones Records) and record producer (Arteg Productions). GEMA. Publishes 200 songs/year; publishes 125 new songwriters/year. Pays standard royalty.
Affiliates: Edition RCP Music, Auteursunie, Edition Kunst and Risiko.
How to Contact: Write or call first to arrange personal interview. Prefers cassette (or VHS videocassette) and lyric sheet or lead sheet. SAE and IRC. Reports in 2 weeks.
Music: Mostly MOR, jazz and country; also background music and film music. Published "Omule," (by Overeem), recorded by Thérèse Steinmetz on CBS (folk); "Agentenfieber," (by Schwarz), recorded by Flagranti on Playbones Records (soft jazz); and "Amore Vieni," (by Di Matteo), recorded by 'Nduccio on Bess Music (MOR).

*MERAK MUSIC PRODUCTION S.R.L., 28, Via De Amicis, Milan 20123 Italy. (02)8050903-8059830. Administrator: Gasparini Roberto. Music publisher, record company, record producer and distributor. Publishes 20 songs/year; publishes 7 new songwriters/year.
How to Contact: Submit demo tape by mail or call to arrange personal interview. Prefers cassette.
Music: Mostly dance, pop and rock; also soul. Published "The Best of My Love" (by M. Tansini/S. Zanini), recorded by John Ryel on Merak Music/EMI Records (pop/dance); "Lancelot" (by M. Tansini/S. Zanini), recorded by Valerie Dore on EMI Records (dance); and "Destination" (by Sangy), recorded by Johnny Parker on Merak Music/EMI Records (dance/funky).

*MERCEY BROTHERS PUBLISHING, 38 Church St. W., Elmira Ontario N3B 1M5 Canada. (519)669-5394. President: Larry Mercey. Music publisher, record company (MBS Records) and record producer (MBS Productions). PRO-CAN. Publishes 25 songs/year; publishes 20 new songwriters/year. Works with composers and teams collaborators. Pays standard royalty.
Affiliate: Elmira Music (CAPAC).
How to Contact: Prefers cassette with 3 songs and lyric sheet. SAE and IRC. Reports in 3 weeks.
Music: Mostly country/pop, country and pop. Published "Take a Little Chance on Love" (by Darrell Scott), recorded by The Mercey Brothers on MBS Records; "Your Eyes Don't Lie" (by Bruce Rawlins/ Terry Carisse), recorded by Bill Anderson on Southern Tracks; and "She's Got a Hold of Me" (by Lee Bach), recorded by Ray Price on Step One Records (all country).

MERTIS MUSIC CO., 8130 Northlawn, Detroit MI 48204. (313)933-6844. Vice President: Olivia John. Music publisher and record company. BMI. Publishes 40 songs/year; publishes 8 new songwriters/year. Works with composers and teams collaborators. Pays standard royalty.
How to Contact: Prefers cassette (or videocassette) with 4-8 songs and lyric and lead sheet. SASE. Reports in 1 month or ASAP.
Music: Mostly gospel, pop and R&B; also country. Published "Jesus Is Mine," and "When I Got Saved," both written and recorded by Leslie Williams (both gospel); and "Why Did You Leave Me," (by M. John), recorded by Chicago Pete (blues) all on Meda Records.

*MIA MIND MUSIC, Suite 4B, 500½ E. 84th St., New York NY 10028. (212)861-8745. General Manager: Steven Bentzel. Music publisher, record producer (Sound Mind Production) and promoter. ASCAP. Publishes 120 songs/year; publishes 6 new songwriters/year. Employs songwriters on a salary basis. Teams collaborators. Pays standard royalty.
How to Contact: Prefers cassette with 3 songs and lyric or lead sheet. SASE. Reports in 1 month.
Music: Mostly dance, pop and rock; also rap and novelty. Published "Cosmic Climb," (by Sargent/ Wernherr), recorded by Madonna on Mindfield/Polydor Records (dance); "Wild Dancing," (by Goodwin/Wernherr), recorded by Madonna on Polydor Records (dance); and "Jingle Yells," (by Bentzel), recorded by Gift Rappers on Mindfield Records (novelty).

*MIC-VIC MUSIC, 77 N. Third St., 3rd Floor, Meriden CT 06450. (203)238-7263. Owner: Steven McVicker. Music publisher and record producer (MIC-VIC Productions). BMI. Publishes 3-6 songs/year; publishes 2 new songwriters/year. Works with composers and lyricists; teams collaborators. Pays standard royalty.
How to Contact: Prefers cassette (or VHS videocassette) with 3 songs and lyric sheet. SASE. Reports in 6 weeks.
Music: Mostly techno-pop, New Age and electronic; also rock, jazz/fusion and MOR/rock. Published "Hold On To Me," (rock) and "Take A Chance," (MOR) both written and recorded by Robert Sullivan on Mic-Vic Productions; and "Give Me Strength," written and recorded by Robert Crossland on Mic-Vic Productions (MOR).
Tips: "Please don't be a format writer. We are interested in hearing artists and writers who are unique and trying to set the trends."

MID AMERICA MUSIC, (a division of Ozark Opry Records, Inc.), Box 242, Osage Beach MO 65065. (314)348-3383. President: Joyce Mace. A&R Agent: Jim Phinney. Music publisher. ASCAP, BMI. Publishes 25 songs/year. Pays standard royalty.
Affiliate: Tall Corn Publishing.
How to Contact: Arrange personal interview. Prefers 7½ ips reel-to-reel or cassette with 1-3 songs and lead sheet. "Tape should be of good quality, and the voice should be louder than the music." SASE. Reports in 3 weeks.
Music: Bluegrass, church/religious, country, disco, easy listening, gospel, MOR and rock. Published "Never Asking for More," (by Rod Johnson), recorded by Graham Fee on Fee-Line Records (MOR); "Losing the Blues" (by Steve and Juli Ann Whiting), recorded by S. Whiting on KRC Records (MOR); and "Iowa a Place to Grow" (by S. Whiting), recorded by S. Whiting on KRC Records (MOR).

THE MIGHTY THREE MUSIC GROUP, 309 S. Broad St., Philadelphia PA 19107. (215)546-3510. Vice President of Publishing Administration: Constance Heigler. Professional Manager: William Lacy. Music publisher. BMI, ASCAP. Member NMPA. Publishes 200 songs/year; publishes 3 new songwriters/year. Pays standard royalty. Sometimes offers advance.
Affiliates: Assorted Music (BMI), Bell Boy Music (BMI), Downstairs Music (BMI), Razor Sharp Music (BMI), Rose Tree Music (ASCAP), World War Three Music (BMI), Piano Music, and Mighty Three Music.

How to Contact: Prefers cassette (or videocassette) with 1-3 songs and lyric sheet. "Must provide large SASE for return." Reports in 8 weeks.
Music: Mostly R&B, pop and MOR; also country, disco, easy listening, folk, gospel, jazz, progressive, rock (hard, country), soul and top 40. Published "Old Friend," (by Bell/Creed), and "Living Alone," (by Gamble/Biggs/Wansel), recorded by Phyliss Hyman; "Jimmy Lee," (by N.M.Walden/P.Glass/J.Cohen/A. Walden), recorded by Aretha Franklin; "Do You Get Enough Love," (by W.Sigler), recorded by Shirley Jones; "Shiver," (by P.Glass/N.Walden/S.Valentine), recorded by George Benson; and "Don't Leave Me This Way," (by Gamble/Huff/Gilbert), recorded by The Communards.

MIGHTY TWINNS MUSIC, 9134 S. Indiana Ave., Chicago IL 60619. (312)737-4348. General Manager: Ron Scott. Music publisher and record producer. BMI. Member NMPA, Midwest Inspirational Writers Association. Publishes 4-10 songs/year; publishes 5 new songwriters/year. Works with lyricists and composers. Pays standard royalty.
How to Contact: Prefers cassette (or Beta videocassette) with 2-4 songs and lyric sheet. SASE "only if you want material returned." Reports in 2 months.
Music: Mostly top 40, R&B, "hot" inspirational and gospel; also children's. Published "I Really Want You," (by E.Z. Kimball), and "Dreams," (by R. Scott), both recorded by Smoke City on Epic Records (top 40/R&B); "Patches," (recorded on Columbia Records); and "I'm gonna Miss You," by the Artistics.
Tips: Looking for "good hot songs with hot hooks."

*MIKALANNA MUSIC,Box 66, Moore SC 29369. (803)574-6104. President: Duane Evans. Music publisher, record company (EBS Records), and record producer. ASCAP. Publishes 12 songs/year; publishes 3 new songwriters/year. Works with composers and lyricists; teams collaborators. Pays standard royalty.
How to Contact: Prefers cassette with 3 songs and lyric sheet. SASE. Reports in 6 weeks.
Music: Mostly pop, rock and country; also R&B, gospel and MOR. Published "Lonely Girls" (by D. Evans/J. Van-Zant), recorded by Van-Zant on Network/Geffen Records (rock); "Lady Luck" (by H. Paul/S. Grisham/D. Evans), recorded by The Outlaws on Pasha Records (rock); and "Tonight" (by B. Mardones/D. Evans), recorded by Benny Mardones and the Hurricanes on BT Records (pop).

BRIAN MILLAN MUSIC CORP.,Suite 1212, 3475 Urbain St., Montreal, Quebec H2X 2N4 Canada. President: Brian Millan. Music publisher and record producer. ASCAP. Publishes 300-350 songs/year; publishes 15-20 new songwriters/year. Pays standard royalty.
Affiliates: Chaverim & Chaverim Music Co. (BMI), Quebissimus Music Co., Ltd, (ASCAP), and E.M.Q. Records.
How to Contact: Submit cassette only with 1-4 songs and lead sheet. Does not return unsolicited material. Reports in 6 weeks.
Music: Country, MOR, top 40, rock, new wave, instrumental, soul, dixieland, classical and children's. Published "If We Never Call It Love," by Ke Rieme on CBS Records (MOR); "Say Something Nice," by Chiarelli-Spilmon on Ariola Records (country); and "Forever More My Love," by Chiarelli-Spilmon on Rediffusion Records, England (MOR).
Tips: "Mail us your best songs. Only the material itself has any weight—not the artist's name. We accept album projects for release in Canada and worldwide."

MIMIC MUSIC, Box 201, Smyrna GA 30081. (404)432-2454. Manager: Tom Hodges. Music publisher, record producer, record company (Trend Records) and management company. BMI, ASCAP. Publishes 20 songs/year. Pays standard royalty.
Affiliates: Skipjack Music (BMI), Stepping Stone (BMI), and British Overseas Airways Music/BOAM (ASCAP).
How to Contact: Prefers cassette with 3-10 songs and lyric sheet. SASE. Reports in 2 weeks.
Music: Bluegrass, blues, church/religious, country, easy listening, gospel, MOR, R&B, rock, soul and top 40/pop. Published "Please Tell Her to Wait" (by Norman Skipper), recorded on Capitol Records (country); and "Good Ole Country Music" (by Helen Humphries), and "Take Away the Roses" (by Burke-Bailey), both recorded on British Overseas Airways Records (country).

*MISS AREAL MUSIC, 2741 N. 29th, Hollywood FL 33020. President: Carl Maduri. Music publisher, record company and record producer. Publishes 5 songs/year; publishes 2 new songwriters/year. Works with composers and teams collaborators. Pays standard royalty.
Affiliate: Miss Sarah Music Co.
How to Contact: Prefers cassette. Does not return unsolicited material.
Music: Mostly R&B and pop.

MISTER SUNSHINE MUSIC, INC., Box 7877, College Park Station, Orlando FL 32854. (305)299-0077. Professional Manager: Kelly Ryder. BMI, ASCAP. Music publisher, record company (Parc Records/CBS) and record producer (Pat Armstrong & Assoc. Inc.). Publishes 40 songs/year; publishes 5 new songwriters/year. Pays standard royalty.
Affiliates: Armco Music, Martik Music, Les Etoiles De La Musique.
How to Contact: Prefers cassette (or VHS videocassette) with lyric sheet. SASE. Reports in 1 month.
Music: Mostly rock/heavy metal and top 40/pop. Published "Flirtin With Disaster," (by D. Hlubek/D. Brown/B. Thomas), recorded by Molly Hatchet on Epic (rock) and approximately 65 additional songs.
Tips: "Listen to AOR, CHR (contemporary hit radio), top 40 and adult contemporary radio and emulate the structure and subject matter."

MISTY RIVER MUSIC LTD., 11 Oxford Circus Ave., 231 Oxford St., London W1R 1AD England. (01)439-2568. General Manager: Joanna Cadman. Music publisher and record company (Mays Records). Publishes 40 songs/year; publishes 4 new songwriters/year. Pays standard royalty.
How to Contact: Prefers cassette. SAE and IRC.

MMA MUSIC, 145 Brougham St., Kings Cross, Sydney, 2011 Australia. Professional Manager: Justin van Stom. Music publisher. APRA. Publishes 300 songs/year; publishes 5-10 new songwriters/year. Pays negotiable royalty.
How to Contact: Prefers cassette (or videocassette of performance if one is available). "Submit photo and biography." Does not return unsolicited material.
Music: Mostly pop, rock and "alternative music"; also new wave. Published "Seven Wonders" (by Sandy Stewart), recorded by Fleetwood Mac on Warner Bros. Records; "Rooms for the Memory" (by Ollie Olsen), recorded by Michael Hutchence of INXS on Atlantic Records; and "The Bottom Line" (by Mick Jones), recorded by Big Audio Dynamite on CBS Records (top 40).
Tips: "Be original. Don't think about writing top 40 songs—just write what comes out naturally. Don't get caught up with technological innovations. Leave that to producers and engineers."

IVAN MOGULL MUSIC CORP., 625 Madison Ave., New York NY 10022. (212)355-5636. Contact: President. Music publisher. ASCAP, BMI and SESAC. Member NMPA. Publishes 10-30 songs/year. Pays standard royalty.
How to Contact: Prefers 7½ ips reel-to-reel or cassette and lyric sheet. SASE. Reports in 2 weeks.
Music: Rock and top 40/pop. Publisher of all Abba hits.

MOMENTS MUSIC LTD., 4 Yarcombe, Adelaide Rd., Subiton Surrey, KT6 4LN United Kingdom. (01)399-7043. Professional Manager: Tracy Ann Dickinson. Music publisher and record producer (Spectrum Music Productions). PRS, MCPS. Publishes 100 songs/year; publishes 5-6 new songwriters/year. Pays standard royalty.
Affiliate: Dickinsong Music (ASCAP).
How to Contact: Prefers cassette or 7½ ips reel-to-reel with "any number" of songs and lyric sheet. SAE and IRC. Reports in 2 weeks.
Music: Mostly pop/rock, country/rock and funk-ballads; also "all types of instrumental material." Published "Hold Me Down," written and recorded by Louis Duncan on G.H. Records (pop/rock); "Touch Me" (by Dave Gold), recorded by Storm on Palm Records (country/rock); and "You & Me & Love," (by Dave Gold), recorded by Dana on Ritz Records (ballad).
Tips: "We like simple well-constructed songs with a hook, and are particularly keen on lyrical and story/theme content. Trends come and go, but songwriters are the cornerstone of music publishing."

MONTINA MUSIC, Box 702, Snowdon Station, Montreal, Quebec H3X 3X8 Canada. Professional General Manager: David P. Leonard. Music publisher. PROCAN. Member MIEA. Pays standard royalty.
Affiliate: Sabre Music (CAPAC).
How to Contact: Prefers 15 or 7½ ips reel-to-reel, cassette, phonograph record (or videocasette) and lyric sheet. Does not return unsolicited material.
Music: Mostly top 40; also bluegrass, blues, country, dance-oriented, easy listening, folk, gospel, jazz, MOR, progressive, R&B, rock and soul.

DOUG MOODY PRODX, Box 1596, San Marcos CA 92069. (619)967-7970. President: Doug Moody. Music publisher, record company (Mystic Records—hardcore rock, teen rock; Ghetto-Way Records—horror, death and dungeon rock; Atmosphear—experimental art label; Solar—sound of Los Angeles rhetoric/spoken word; Thrash Records—"Skateboard"—Rock Music). BMI. Publishes 200 + songs/year; publishes 100 + new songwriter-artists/year. Pays standard royalty.

How to Contact: "Get a local young group to perform your song and send us a cassette of their interpretation."
Music: "All kinds of rock: hardcore, teen, horror, death and 'thrash'."
Tips: "We specialize in teen-age entertainment: records, radio shows, videos. We target 11-year-old to 27-year-old market."

MOON JUNE MUSIC, 4233 SW. Marigold, Portland OR 97219. President: Bob Stoutenburg. Music publisher.
How to Contact: Prefers cassette with 2-10 songs. SASE.

MOON RIDGE MUSIC, 2940 E. Miraloma, Anaheim CA 92806. (714)992-6820. President: Chuck Whittington. ASCAP. Publishes 30 songs/year; publishes 1 new songwriter/year. Pays standard royalty.
How to Contact: Prefers cassette with 2-4 songs and lyric sheet. Does not return unsolicited material. Reports in 1 month.
Music: Country, gospel and top 40/pop. Published *Waltzes & Western Swing* and "Big Tulsa Tillie" (by Donnie Rohrs); and "Building Up to a Letdown" (by Robert Lee Smith), all recorded by Donnie Rohrs on Pacific Challenger Records.

MOTHER BERTHA MUSIC PUBLISHING CO., INC., Back to Mono Music, Inc., Box 69529, Los Angeles CA 90069. (818)846-9900. Administrative Director: Donna Sekulidis. Music publisher, record company (Phil Spector International) and record producer (Phil Spector Productions). BMI. Publishes 10-100 songs/year. Pays on individual basis.
How to Contact: "We are not accepting or reviewing any new material or artists. Any unsolicited correspondence or material will not be returned."

*MOUNTAIN HERITAGE MUSIC CO., Rt. 3, Box 280, Galay VA 24333. (703)236-9079. Owner: Bobby Patterson. Music publisher and record company (Heritage Records). BMI. Publishes 14 songs/year; publishes 2 new songwriters/year. Works with composers. Pays standard royalty.
How to Contact: Prefers cassette with 3 songs and lyric sheet. SASE. Reports in 2 months.
Music: Mostly bluegrass, gospel and Christmas. Published "King of Kings" (by John R. Shaw); "Sing A Song For Jesus" (by Johnny Jackson), and "That's When He Carries You" (by Cullen Galyean) all recorded by The Christian Quartet on Heritage Records (bluegrass/gospel).
Tips: "Words must tell a complete story within 2½-3 minutes."

MR. MORT MUSIC, 44 Music Square E., Nashville TN 37203. (615)255-2175. President: Charles Fields. Music publisher, record company and record producer. ASCAP. Publishes 50 songs/year; publishes 8 new songwriters/year. Pays standard royalty.
Affiliate: Jason Dee Music (BMI).
How to Contact: Prefers cassette with 1-4 songs and lead sheet. SASE. Reports in 2 weeks.
Music: Mostly MOR, easy listening and country; also blues and top 40/pop. Published "Burned Out," recorded by Tina Danielle; and "Seven New Stars," and "Tired of the Same Old Thing" (also a video), both recorded by David Walsh.

MUNICH MUSIC, Albert Schweitzerlaan 9, Bennekom Gelderland 6721 AW Holland. (31)08389-16777. General Manager: Ben Mattyssen. Music publisher. Publishes 24 songs/year. Pays varying royalty.
How to Contact: Prefers cassette (or Beta videocassette) and lyric or lead sheet. Does not return unsolicited material. Reports in 3 weeks.
Music: All types, especially reggae, ethnic and new clasical. Published "Musical Lesson," (by Marley/Livington Tosh), recorded by Tuff Gong (reggae); "Zaterdhgavon," by Scharpenberger/Feltz/Kartner (Dutch pop); and "Breaking Our Hearts," by Jon Strong (pop) all on Munich Records.

MUSIC PUBLISHERS OF HAWAII, Box 25141, Honolulu HI 96825. (808)247-1447. President: Gil M. Tanaka. Music publisher, record company and record producer. BMI. Publishes 24 songs/year; publishes 3 new songwriters/year. Pays standard royalty.
How to Contact: Prefers cassette with 1-6 songs and lyric sheet. SASE. Reports in 1 month.
Music: Mostly top 40/pop; also country, easy listening, jazz and rock. Published *Kevin I.*, written and recorded by Kevin I. on GMT Records (top 40/pop); *Paul Flynn* (by various artists), recorded by Paul Flynn on GMT Records (top 40/pop); and *Music Magic* (by Al Pascua/Fred Schrenders), recorded by Music Magic on GMI Records (jazz).

MUSICRAFTERS, Box 1061, Willow Grove PA 19090. (215)345-TUNE. Vice President Marketing: Elena C. Marino. Music publisher, record producer and producer/distributor of music for advertising,

television, radio, films and other audiovisual applications. BMI, ASCAP. Member AFM, AGAC. Publishes 50 songs/year; publishes 5 new songwriters/year. Payment per sale for production music library.
Affiliate: Bocagé Music.
How to Contact: Prefers cassette. SASE. Reports in 1 month.
Music: Instrumental background music only: bluegrass, classical, country, dance-oriented, easy listening, jazz, MOR, progressive, rock and top 40/pop. Published "Micky's Song," by Kevin Kohn (jazz/pop); "A Children's Piece," by Ron Delseni (jazz/pop); and "Hot Shots," by Lou deLise (rock); all recorded by MusiCrafters.

MUSINFO PUBLISHING GROUP, INC., 2504 Mayfair Ave., Montreal, Quebec H4B 2C8 Canada. (514)484-5419. International office: 30 St. Christophe, Brussels 1000, Belgium. General Manager: Jehan V. Valiquet. Music publisher, record company, record producer, promotion and marketing consultants. PROCAN, CAPAC. Publishes 150 songs/year; publishes 10 new songwriters/year. Works with lyricists and composers; teams collaborators. Pays standard royalty.
How to Contact: Prefers cassette (or videocassette) and lyric sheet. SAE and IRC. Reports in 1 month.
Music: Mostly dance-oriented and top 40/pop in French; also children's, folk, MOR and Spanish. Published "Kanzai," (by Paul Sabu), recorded by Isa Minoke on Impression Records (pop); "Danse de Canards," (by Thomas T. Rendall), recorded by Nathalie Simard on T. Canada Records (novelty); and "Comment Ca Va" (by E. de Heer), recorded by the Shorts on Capitol Records (pop).

*THE MUSIPLEX GROUP, INC., 809 18th Ave. S., Nashville TN 37203. (615)327-0750. Receptionist: Linda Sawyer. Music publisher. Publishes 100 songs/year; publishes 3 new songwriters/year. Works with composers and lyricists; teams collaborators. Pays standard royalty.
Affiliates: Cedarwood Publishing (BMI); Sawgrass Music Publishers (BMI); Sabal Music, Inc. (ASCAP); Guava Music, Inc. (SESAC); all divisions of Musiplex Group, Inc.
How to Contact: Prefers cassette with 3 songs and lyric sheet. "Absolutely no mail-ins—please do not request appointment." Reports in 6 weeks. "Please bring demo tape to address listed."
Music: Mostly country, country rock and pop; also gospel, crossover and rock. Published "Diggin' Up Bones" (by Al Gore/Paul Overstreet), recorded by Randy Travis on Warner Bros. Records (country); "Can't Keep a Good Man Down" (by Bob Corbin), recorded by Alabama on RCA Records (country rock); and "Tobacco Road" (by John Loudermilk), recorded by David Lee Roth on Warner Bros. Records (rock).

MY DEE DEE MUSIC, Box 1255, Gallatin TN 37066-1255. (615)451-3920. General Manager: Dee Mullins. Music publisher, record company (Melodee) and record producer (Dee Mullins Ent.). ASCAP. Member AFM, AFTRA. Publishes 30-40 songs/year; publishes 4-5 new songwriters/year. Pays standard royalty.
Affiliate: Mel-Dee Music (BMI).
How to Contact: Write or call first to arrange personal interview. Prefers cassette (or videocassette) with 1-4 songs and lyric sheet. SASE. Reports in 1 month.
Music: Mostly country and country crossover; also bluegrass, folk. Produced "Stumblin," (by Smokey Colt), and "You'll Never Be Back Anymore," (by Jimmy Faulks), both recorded by Bill Dennis; and "Pamela Brown," written and recorded by Tom Kruser all on Melodee Records (all country crossover).

*MYKO MUSIC,808 S. Pantano Rd., Tucson AZ 85710. (602)885-5931. President: James M. Gasper. Music publisher, record company (Ariana Records) and record producer (Future 1 Productions). BMI. Publishes 6-10 songs/year; publishes 2 new songwriters/year. Works with composers and lyricists; teams collaborators. Pays standard royalty.
How to Contact: Prefers cassette (or ½ " videocassette) with 3 songs and lyric sheet. SASE Reports in 5 weeks.
Music: Mostly dance rock, rock and R&B; also ballads and pop/rock. Published "Take Care of Yourself," by Tom Privett (dance rock); "Life is a Movie," by Ruben Ruiz/Jim Gasper (pop rock); and "Fade to Black," by Jim Gasper/Tom Privett (rock); all recorded by Silent Partners on Ariana Records.

*N.C.L. MUSIC, INC., 7 St. Claire Ave., Old Greenwich CT 06870. (203)637-7975. President: Mark Azoff. Music publisher. BMI. Estab. 1986. Works with composers and lyricists. Pays standard royalty.
How to Contact: Prefers cassette or reel-to-reel (or VHS videocassette) with maximum of 3 songs and lyric or lead sheet. "It would be nice to know if writer is amenable to reworking material if necessary. Flexibility is a plus." SASE. Reports in 3 months.
Music: Country, pop and rock.
Tips: "Lyrics *must* be contemporary without going 'too far'."

NASETAN PUBLISHING, Box 1485, Lake Charles LA 70602. (318)439-8839. Contact: Nasetan Administration. Music publisher. BMI. Publishes 29 songs/year. Pays standard royalty.
Affiliate: Tek Publishing.
How to Contact: Prefers cassette with 4 songs maximum and lyric or lead sheet. Reports in 8 weeks.
Music: Novelty songs and story songs. Published "Take Me As I Am" (by Skip Dowers), recorded by Mayonnaise & Marbles (country/rock); "Bottom Line Baby" (by Mel Pellarin), recorded by Fabulous Thunderbirds on CBS Records ("swamp" pop); and "Don't Sell That Monkey" (by Milton Landry), recorded on Folk-Star Records (zydeco).
Tips: "Song must have strong storyline with broad appeal for us to be interested."

NASHVILLE SOUND MUSIC PUBLISHING CO., Box 728, Peterborough, Ontario K9J 6Z8 Canada. (705)742-2381. President: Andrew Wilson Jr. Music publisher. PRO Canada, CAPAC. Publishes 10 songs/year; publishes 5 new songwriters/year. Pays standard royalty.
Affiliate: Northern Sound Music Publishing Co. (CAPAC).
How to Contact: Write or call first and obtain permission to submit or write or call to arrange a personal interview. Prefers cassette or 7½ ips reel-to-reel with 2-4 songs and lyric sheet. "Please enclose $1 in currency for postage, etc., if you wish material to be returned." Reports in 3 weeks.
Music: Mostly country, country/pop and crossover country; also MOR, top 40, pop/rock and gospel. Published "Leave Me the Memory," by I.M. South/A. Wilson Jr./L. Payne; "I'm Not a Fool" (by L. Payne), recorded by Wendy Tibbits; and "The Devil Made Me Do It Tonight" (by L. Payne), recorded by Bill Michael Patterson on Skylight Records (country).
Tips: "Good demos, strong lyrics and a memorable melody will greatly increase a songwriter's chances."

NEBO RIDGE PUBLISHING, Box 194, New Hope AL 35760. President: Walker Ikard. Manager: Jim Lewis. Music publisher, promotions firm, record producer and record company (Nebo Record Company). ASCAP. Works with composers and lyricists; teams collaborators. Pays standard royalty.
How to Contact: Prefers cassette (or videocassette) with 2 songs and lyric sheet. SASE. Reports in 3 weeks.
Music: Mostly modern country and traditional country; also gospel, pop, MOR and bluegrass. Published "You're the Reason," written and recorded by Walker Ikard; "Mama's Candyman," written and recorded by Osie Ikard; and "Blues, Welcome Home," written and recorded by Charles W. Cooper; all on Nebo Records (all country).
Tips: "Submit in neat form with clear lyrics. Be original; send songs that produce a feeling or effect."

NEPTUNE MUSIC PUBLISHING LIMITED, 31 Old Burlington St., London, W1X 1LB England. (01)437-2066/7. Managing Director: Buzz Carter. Music publisher and record producer. Publishes 45 songs/year; publishes 1-2 new songwriters/year.
How to Contact: Prefers cassette. SASE. Reports in 5 weeks.
Music: Mostly pop, rock and soul; also R&B.
Tips: "It's better to submit one great song than five good ones."

NERVOUS PUBLISHING, 4/36 Dabbs Hill Lane, Northout, Middlesex, London, England. 44-01-422-3462. Managing Director: Roy Williams. Music publisher, record company and record producer. MCPS, PRS and Phonographic Performance Ltd. Publishes 50 songs/year; publishes 10 new songwriters/year. Pays standard royalty; royalties paid directly to US songwriters.
How to Contact: Prefers cassette with 3-10 songs and lyric sheet. "Include letter giving your age and mentioning any previously-published material." SAE and IRC. Reports in 2 weeks.
Music: Mostly rockabilly, psychobilly and rock (impossibly fast music—ex.: Stray Cats but twice as fast); also blues, country, R&B and rock (50s style). Published "Doctor Death" (by P. Connor), recorded by Skitzo (psychobilly); "Rock Strong" (by M. Mansfield), recorded by Torment (rock); and "Edge on You" (by M. Harmon), recorded by Restless (rockabilly) all on Nervous Records.
Tips: We "don't want disco or AOR rock—looking for fast and wild songs to sell to a teen audience."

NEW CLARION MUSIC GROUP, 1013 16th Ave. S., Box 121081, Nashville TN 37212. (615)321-4422. President: Sue K. Patton. Music publisher and record producer (SKP Productions, Inc.). ASCAP, BMI, SESAC. Publishes 250 songs/year; publishes 5 new songwriters/year. Works with composers and lyricists; teams collaborators. Pays standard royalty.
Affiliates: Golden Reed Music, Inc. (ASCAP), Grand Staff Music, Inc. (SESAC), and Triumvirate Music, Inc. (BMI).
How to Contact: Prefers cassette with 3 songs and lyric sheet. Send Attention: Daniel S. Hill, Professional Manager; include SASE. Reports in 8 weeks.

Close-up

Henry Mancini
Composer

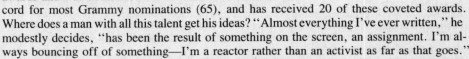

Henry Mancini's mastery of melody writing is obvious when even a fraction of his credits are named. From songs like "Days of Wine and Roses" and "Moon River," to themes like "Pink Panther" and "Baby Elephant Walk," to the music of *Peter Gunn* and the soundtrack from *Victor/ Victoria*, Mancini's music is brilliant. He's won four Oscar awards and was nominated for 13 others. He holds the record for most Grammy nominations (65), and has received 20 of these coveted awards. Where does a man with all this talent get his ideas? "Almost everything I've ever written," he modestly decides, "has been the result of something on the screen, an assignment. I'm always bouncing off of something—I'm a reactor rather than an activist as far as that goes."

Mancini's career in music is rooted in rather simple beginnings—studying flute and piano as a child, playing in a local band as a high school student, and playing and doing arrangements for bands in the service. "I got a lot of good training there," he says, "and it's through connections I made in the service that I was able to get a job right after the war with Tex Beneke and the Glenn Miller Orchestra."

Mancini feels making contacts is a very important step in advancing a career in music, and recommends that songwriters and composers make those types of connections. "If you're trying to get into film music," he says, "I think you have to go where they're making pictures. And then take your chances. Get the best education you can and go where the action is."

Part of that education would include learning about synthesizers and electronics. "They've affected everything," Mancini feels, "commercials, film—the whole scene. They're something the younger people are going to have to study."

For instance, "the demo is very important. Any more, a song is not only a song. It's a *sound*, it's a rhythm. It's been my experience that the better the demo, the better the chance of someone putting it on the tape player and letting it run for more than a few seconds."

It would be tough for beginning composers or songwriters today to follow the path Mancini took. "Fortunately, I got a job with the Universal music department. During my six years there I went through every imaginable kind of picture, both as arranger and composer. And so that's where I learned the trade. There's no mystery about it. If you have a good teacher, you can learn all the technical stuff in pretty short order.

"The staff situation is long gone, but there are a lot of things for a newcomer to do. There are a lot of television projects the new people here have been coming in on, and after that it's all a matter of contacts. That's how it happened to me and that's how it happens to most people. Once I was in the environment here, it was just a matter of how things were going to pan out for me. You just have to give yourself your best shot."

—Julie Wesling Whaley

Music: Mostly country/progressive, pop and MOR; also rock, gospel and New Age. Published "The Loveless Cafe" (by Karen Charlton/Sandy Knox), recorded by Libby Hurley on CBS Records (progessive country); "Bad Paper" and "A Long Way from Lonely" (both by Steve Seskin/Austin Gardner), recorded by Christina Lindberg on Tab Records/Sweden (pop); and "Do You Ever Call My Name" (by Bill Brookshire), recorded by Pake McEntire on RCA Records (country).
Tips: "Stay away from 'stock' melodies and lyrics. Be innovative. We support experimentation."

NEW MUSIC ENTERPRISES, "Meredale," The Dell, Reach Lane, Near Leighton Buzzard Beds, United Kingdom. 052523-7700. Manager: Paul Davis. Music publisher and record company. MCPS, PRS. Publishes 20 songs/year. Pays standard royalty; royalties to US songwriters paid through US affiliate.
Affiliates: Wilhelm Music, Arhelger Music, Silhouette Music, Bridge Music, Eric Anders Music, Sherebiah Music, Clancy Music and Jimmy Payne Music.
How to Contact: Write first. Prefers cassette with any number of songs and lyric sheet. SAE and IRC. Reports in 3 weeks.
Music: All forms of contemporary Christian music (bluegrass, children's, gospel, country, MOR and soul). Published "Breaker Breaker Sweet Jesus" (by Jerry Arhelger), recorded by Thrasher Brothers on Word Records (country gospel); "I'm Going on for Jesus" (by Rick & Rosemary Wilhelm), recorded by Doug Oldham on Benson Records (inspirational); and "God Specializes," written and recorded by Candi Staton, on Berachah Records (black gospel).
Tips: "Songs should have good Christian message and be relevant to everyday living."

NEWCREATURE MUSIC, Box 148296, Nashville TN 37214-8296. (615)868-3407. President: Bill Anderson Jr. Music publisher, record company, record producer and radio and TV syndicator. BMI. Publishes 5 songs/year; publishes 2 new songwriters/year. Pays standard royalty.
How to Contact: Prefers 7½ ips reel-to-reel or cassette (or videocassette) with 4-10 songs and lyric sheet. SASE. Reports in 1 month.
Music: Country, gospel, jazz, R&B, rock and top 40/pop. Published "Cotton, Popcorn, Peanuts and Jesus" (by H. Yates), recorded by Jeanne Cash on Jana Records (gospel); "His Love Is the Reason," written and recorded by Danny Vance on Livingsong Records (gospel); and "Ragged Ole Memory" (by J. Jerigan), recorded by Jim Chute on Cootico Records (country).

NISE PRODUCTIONS INC., Suite 301, 413 Cooper St., Camden NJ 08102. (609)963-3190. President: Michael Nise. Music publisher, record company (Power Up-Sutra), recording studio (Power House) and production company. BMI. Publishes 10 songs/year; publishes 5 new songwriters/year. Pays standard royalty.
Affiliates: Logo III Records, Power Up Records and Wordan Records.
How to Contact: Prefers cassette (or videocassette) with 3 songs. Send Attention: Dan McKeown. SASE. Reports in 1 month.
Music: Mostly dance-oriented, R&B, country and pop, all with pop crossover potential; also children's, church/religious, easy listening, folk, gospel, jazz, rock, soul and top 40.
Tips: "Submit only well-produced demos."

*NISS PRODUCTIONS LTD., 1803 S. 55th Ct., Chicago IL 60650. (312)780-1754. Music publisher (Two Reel Advance) and record producer (Niss Productions). BMI. Publishes 3-8 songs/year; publishes 1-3 new songwriters/year. Employs songwriters on a salary basis. Works with composers.
How to Contact: Write first and obtain permission to submit. Prefers cassette (or VHS videocassette) with 3-4 songs and lyric sheet. SASE. Reports in 6 weeks.
Music: Mostly pop, rock and English pop; also instrumental and jazz. "No heavy metal."
Tips: Send "good material based on tape quality and radio potential."

66 *Exceptional writers are wonderful with words. They just seem to have a sense about how to put words together, and they find topics that are not ordinary.* **99**
—*Tony Camillo, producer and songwriter*

NOCHISTLAN MUSICAL, Box 814, Bryte CA 95605. (916)371-0275. Contact: Pedro V. Reynoso, Jr. ASCAP. Music publisher. Publishes 5 songs/year; publishes 5 new songwriters/year. Pays standard royalty.
How to Contact: Prefers cassette with maximum 4 songs, lyric sheet and brief resume or fact sheet. SASE. Reports in 4-6 weeks. "SASE without proper postage will not be returned."
Music: Mostly contemporary and Latin; also gospel, rock and country. Published "Mas Hermoso" (by Reynoso/Lizarrago), recorded by Raquela Rios on Rocio Records (Mariachi ballad); and "Seran Ideas" and "Esperandote" (by Juan Rodriguez), recorded by Juan Alejandro on Israfel Records (ballads).

*NORTH STAR MUSIC CO., INC., Box 1299, Grapevine TX 76051. (817)481-5658. Contact: Will Johnson or Mark Jaeger. Music publisher, record producer (North Star Records), recording studio and booking agent. ASCAP. Publishes 75-100 songs/year; publishes 10 new songwriters/year. Works with composers, and lyricists; teams collaborators. Pays standard royalty.
How to Contact: Prefers cassette with 1-4 songs and lyric sheet. We "specialize in working with previously unpublished songwriters. Demo can be voice and one instrument, but must be of good quality." SASE. Reports in 1 month.
Music: Mostly country, rockabilly and rock; also crossover (pop/country), new wave, R&B and gospel. Published "Snow (Missing You Now)" (by Dan Seals on EMI Records (country); "Everybody Wants to Dance" (by Tim Williamson/Mike Armstrong), recorded by Sir System on North Star Records (new wave); and "Hard to Find a Love that Lasts," by Teresa Burns (crossover).

*NORTH WOODS PUBLISHING, 6273 Callicott Ave., Woodland Hills CA 91367. (818)992-4481. Owner/President: Diana Weyand. Music publisher. BMI. Estab. 1987. Publishes 10 songs/year; publishes 5 new songwriters/year. Works with composers and lyricists; teams collaborators. Pays standard royalty.
How to Contact: Write first and obtain permission to submit. Prefers cassette with 3-4 songs and lead sheet. "I would like to talk with songwriters first and find out what their interests are. Then we could try to team them up with other writers." SASE. Reports in 2 weeks.
Music: Mostly pop, MOR and children's music; also theme music for film and television.

NOT EVEN MUSIC, Box 2825, Nashville TN 37219-0825. (615)360-3782. Professional Managers: Jim O'Baid, Maggie McGuinness and Liz Cavanaugh. Music publisher and artists manager. ASCAP, BMI. Estab. 1986. Publishes 5-10 songs/year; publishes 3-5 new songwriters/year. Works with composers and lyricists; team collaborators. Pays standard royalty.
Affiliate: Dawn Patrol (ASCAP).
How to Contact: Prefers cassette with 3 songs and lyric sheet. SASE. Reports in 6 weeks.
Music: Mostly country/pop, traditional country and pop/rock; also new wave and jazz. Published "Never Giving Up" (by Matt Caselli), recorded by Ms. Jeannie Cruise on Vega Records (MOR ballad).
Tips: "Listen to the radio. You're competing with what you hear. Your basic demo should be at least— guitar, base and drums, with a good vocal up front."

NOTABLE MUSIC CO. INC., 161 W. 54th St., New York NY 10019. (212)757-9547. General Manager: Eric Colodne. Music publisher. ASCAP. Member NMPA. Publishes 50-75 songs/year. Pays standard royalty.
Affiliates: Portable Music Co., Inc. (BMI).
How to Contact: Call first. Prefers cassette with 3-5 songs. SASE. Reports in 1 month.
Music: R&B, rock, soul and top 40/pop.

NOTEWORTHY PUBLISHING CO., 3-320 Stewardson Way, New Westminster, British Columbia V3M 6C3 Canada. (604)520-3912. Manager: Paul Yaroshuk. Music publisher, record company, record producer and record manufacturer. BMI, PROCAN. Publishes 250 songs/year; publishes 25 new songwriters/year. Pays standard royalty.
How to Contact: Prefers cassette with 10-12 songs and lyric sheet. SAE and IRC. Reports in 1 week.
Music: Church/religious, gospel and gospel rock. Published "I'm Gonna Live" (by Bruce Wright); "In the Spirit of the King" (by Hank Laake); and "Find Your Heart a Home," all gospel/rock songs recorded by Tunesmith on Tunesmith Records.
Tips: "We look for people who can sing their own songs."

NUMBER 9 MUSICAL ENTERPRISES, INC., 498 West End Ave., New York NY 10024. (212)580-6569. Contact: Vicky Germaise. Music publisher and record producer. BMI and ASCAP. Publishes 5 songs/year; publishes 3 new songwriters/year. Pays standard royalty or "we co-publish many tunes, allowing writer to retain publishing income."

Affiliates: Real Zeal Music (ASCAP) and Zoon Tunes Music (BMI).
How to Contact: Prefers cassette with 1-4 songs and lyric sheet. "No tapes returned." Reports in 1 month.
Music: Mostly pop, R&B and rock; also children's songs, soul and top 40. Published "After Love" (by R. Klein/D. Fischel), recorded by Sarah Dash on EMI/Capitol Records (R&B ballad); "When Bad Things Happen," (by R. Klein/R. Rodriquez), recorded by IRT on RCA (R&B); and "A Few Good Men," (by Carole Blake/M. Chase), recorded by Tara Jans on Select (dance).
Tips: "Be specific in style and production. Be interesting lyrically, putting a different slant on the same old emotion. We are looking for melodic, emotional, vocal performance on demo. The performance is the key element of the demo."

NUNLEY PUBLISHING CO., Rt. 7, Box 683W, Canyon Lake, TX 78130. (512)899-7474. Contact: Donald L. Nunley. Music publisher, record producer and management company (Prelude). BMI. Publishes 20-30 songs/year; publishes 2-3 new songwriters/year. Pays standard royalty.
How to Contact: Write or call first and obtain permission to submit. Prefers cassette and lyric sheet or lead sheet. "Make sure cassette is labeled with name, address, phone number and song title." Reports in 10 weeks.
Music: Mostly country, blues and rock.

NU-TRAYL PUBLISHING CO., 10015 W. 8 Mile Rd., Franksville WI 53126. (414)835-4622. Contact: Tommy O'Day. Music publisher, record company and record producer. ASCAP. Publishes 10 songs/year; publishes 3 new songwriters/year. Pays standard royalty.
How to Contact: Prefers 7½ ips reel-to-reel or cassette with 1-3 songs and lyric sheet. SASE. Reports in 1 month.
Music: Country, MOR, rock and top 40/pop. Published "I Heard a Song Today" (by T. O'Day and J. Marvel), "Kiss Your Past Goodbye" (by Peter Richerson), and "Today's Woman" (by T. O'Day and B. Perice), all recorded by T. O'Day on Nu-trayl Records (country).

OCEANS-WIDE MUSIC, Box 20115, Philadelphia PA 19145. (215)467-6617. President: John Potere. Professional Manager/A&R: Nick Travis. ASCAP, BMI, SESAC. Music publisher and record company (Oceans-Wide Records). Publishes 8 songs/year; publishes 6-8 songwriters/year. Pays standard royalty; "for piano copies and sheet music we start at 10% and use a sliding scale."
Affiliates: Elk Music Publishing, Sandy—World Music.
How to Contact: Prefers cassette with 1-5 songs and lyric sheet. SASE. Reports in 2-3 weeks.
Music: Mostly rock, R&B and dance-oriented; also soul, contemporary country and top 40.
Tips: "Spend more time on your songs. Make demos clean, professional sounding."

MICHAEL O'CONNOR MUSIC, Box 1869, Studio City CA 91604. (818)762-7551. Contact: Michael O'Connor. Music publisher. BMI. Member NMPA, AIMP. Publishes 20 songs/year; publishes 2 new songwriters/year. Hires staff writers; pays $175-325/week. Works with composers and lyricists; teams collaborators. Pays standard royalty.
Affiliate: O'Connor Songs (ASCAP).
How to Contact: Prefers cassette (or videocassette) with 1-6 songs and lyric sheet. SASE. Reports in 1 month.
Music: Mostly pop/R&B, pop/rock and pop/country; also easy listening, soul and top 40/pop. Published "Stop and Think," which appeared on Miami Vice; "L-O-V-E, Love You Boy," recorded by Angela on Motown Records; "My Body Keeps Changing My MInd," which appeared on *Body Slammin'* soundtrack; "Manhunt," (by Coulter/Gilbert) which appeared on *Flashdance* soundtrack; and "You Never Gave Up on Me," (by Leslie Pearl), recorded by Crystal Gale on CBS Records.
Tips: "We are looking for songs that have a clever title, hopefully revolving around the subject of love; great lyric images—the kind of lyric you find on a greeting card; and have unique ways of expressing ideas that would strike a responsive chord in the public."

OKISHER MUSIC, Box 20814, Oklahoma City OK 73156. (405)755-0315. President: Mickey Sherman. Music publisher, record company and record producer. BMI. Member OCMA. Publishes 25 songs/year; publishes 5-10 new songwriters/year. Pays standard royalty.
How to Contact: "Enclose press kit or other background information." Prefers 7½ ips reel-to-reel, cassette (or videocassette) with 1-3 songs and lyric sheet. Does not return unsolicited material. Reports in 1 month.
Music: Mostly blues, country and ballads; also easy listening, jazz, MOR, R&B and soul. Published "Hooking," (by Charles Burton), and "Cajun Fiddles," (by Benny Kubiak), both recorded by Janjo on Seed Records; and "Arkansas River Bottom," written and recorded by Charles Shaw on Homa Records (country).

OLD BOSTON PUBLISHING, 180 Pond St., Box 311, Cohasset MA 02025. (617)383-9494. Artist Relations: Rik Tinory. Writer Relations: Claire Babcock. Music publisher, record company and record producer. BMI. Publishes 9 songs/year; publishes 3 new songwriters/year. Pays standard royalty.
How to Contact: Call first. Prefers cassette or 7½ ips reel-to-reel with 2 songs. Does not return unsolicited material.
Music: Published "Scollay Square," (by Rik Tinory), recorded on Old Boston Records (dixie/nostalgia).

OLD GUIDE PUBLISHING INC., Suite 215, 38 Music Square E., Nashville TN 37203. (615)254-0825. Professional Manager: Peggy Bradley. Music publisher. BMI. Publishes 20 songs/year; publishes 8 new songwriters/year. Pays standard royalty.
Affiliates: First Million Music, Inc. (ASCAP) and Two Bees Music (SESAC).
How to Contact: Query first. Prefers cassette with 1-3 songs and lyric sheet. Prefers studio produced demos. Reports in 1 month.
Music: Mostly uptempo MOR; also country and pop. Published "My Best Friend Thinks He's Rambo," written and recorded by Ken Burrows on GBS Records (country comedy); "Gilly, Willie, Waylon and Me," (by P. Hotchkiss/M. Terry), recorded King Mattox on Orbit Records (country ballad); and "Merry Christmas from the Loud Mouse," (by Daniel James), recorded by the Loud Mouse on Nashville American Records (children's Christmas).

O'LYRIC MUSIC, Suite 1, 1837 Eleventh St., Santa Monica CA 90404. (213)452-0815. President: Jim O'Loughlin. Music publisher, manager (O'Lyric Music Management) and production company. BMI. Member California Copyright Conference. Publishes 75-100 songs/year; publishes 10-15 new songwriters/year. Hires staff writers; pays $20,000/year—"only duty expected is songwriting. Writers paid by royalties earned and by advances." Pays standard royalty to outside writers.
Affiliate: O'Lyrical Music (ASCAP).
How to Contact: Prefers cassette with 1-3 songs and lyric sheet. Does not return materials. Reports as soon as possible "if an SASE (or postcard) is provided for reply."
Music: Mostly R&B, rock, top 40, dance and country; also easy listening, MOR, progressive, jazz, soul and Latin. Published "I Live for Your Love" (by P. Reswick/S. Werfil/A. Rich), recorded by Natalie Cole on Manhattan Records (R&B/crossover); "Mr. Right" (by T. Shapiro/M. Garvin), recorded by Smokey Robinson on Motown Records (R&B/crossover); and "I've Still Got the Love We Made" (by Shapiro/Garvin/Waters), recorded by Reba McEntire (country/crossover). Production company works with Max Hitchcock (rock); Jorge Bermudez (Latin), and Califas (Latin).

***OMNI RECORDS**, 33 Rockhill Rd., Bala Cynwynd PA 19003. (215)667-7050. Contact: Alan Rubens. Music publisher and record company. BMI. Publishes 35 songs/year; publishes 3-4 new songwriters/year. Employs songwriters on a salary basis. Teams collaborators.
How to Contact: Prefers cassette. Does not return unsolicited material.
Music: Mostly R&B and dance. Published "Closer than Close" (by Terri Price), recorded by Jean Carne; and "Lonely Road" (by Bryan Williams), recorded by Rose Royce, both on Omni Records (both R&B).

ONE HUNDRED GRAND MUSIC, 11 Norton St., Newburgh NY 12550. (914)561-4483. President: Gregg Bauer. Music publisher, record company and record producer. Publishes 10 songs/year; publishes 2 new songwriters/year. Pays standard royalty.
How to Contact: Call first. Prefers cassette with 3-5 songs and lyric sheet. Submit videocassette "if it has a good story line and good audio." SASE. Reports in 1 month.
Music: Mostly rock, dance and R&B; also choral, dance-oriented, easy listening, folk, jazz, MOR, progressive and soul. Published "Faith," "Special Kind," "Hold On" and "Whitehat," written and recorded by Art Nouveau on 100 Grand (dance rock/Latin rock).

***OPUS**, RECORDS AND PUBLISHING HOUSE, Mlynské nivy 73, Bratislava 827 15 Czechoslovakia. Phone: 222-680. International Manager: Zlatica Môciková. Music publisher, record company and record producer. SOZA (Slovak Copyright Society). Publishes 500 songs/year; publishes 3 new songwriters/year. Works with composers and lyricists. Pays standard royalty.
How to Contact: Prefers cassette. SAE and IRC. Reports in 1 month.
Music: Mostly pop; also classical. Published "Smile" (by J. Lehotsky); "Black Horse" (by R. Grigorov); and "Tiger" (by P. Hammel), all on Opus Records (popular).

ORCHID PUBLISHING, Bouquet-Orchid Enterprises, Box 18284, Shreveport LA 71138. (318)686-7362. President: Bill Bohannon. Music publisher and record company. BMI. Member CMA, AFM. Publishes 10-12 songs/year; publishes 3 new songwriters/year. Pays standard royalty.

How to Contact: Prefers cassette with 3-5 songs and lyric sheet. SASE. Reports in 1 month.
Music: Religious ("Amy Grant, etc., contemporary gospel"); country ("George Strait, The Judds type material"); and top 40/pop ("Peter Cetera & Whitney Houston type material"). Published "Lies," and "All Night," by Lee Haynes; "Those Bitter Tears Can Taste So Sweet," by June Fox; and "My Best Friend's Love," by Randy Gilbert, (all country).

OTIS MUSIC GROUP, 8569 Horner, Los Angeles CA 90035. (213)732-7009. Music publisher and production company. BMI. Publishes 10 songs/year; publishes 5 new songwriters/year. Works with composers and lyricists; teams collaborators. Pays standard royalty.
How to Contact: Prefers 7½ ips reel-to-reel or cassette (or videocassette) with 3-6 songs and lead sheet. SASE. Reports in 1 month.
Music: Mostly pop and gospel; also blues, dance and soul. Published "The Spirit of Christmas" (by P. Davison/J. Webster/M. John) and "Christmas In My Heart" by (D. Fraser), both recorded by Ray Charles on CBS Records (Christmas); and "I Wish You Were Here Tonight" (by Jim Sullens), recorded by S. Easton on Capitol Records (country/pop).
Tips: "Songs should have strong, simple melody and good story. Submit a clear piano/vocal or guitar vocal demo."

OTTO PUBLISHING CO., 7766 NW 44th St., Sunrise FL 33321. (305)741-7766. President: Frank X. Loconto. Music publisher, record company (FXL Records) and record producer (Locanto Productions). ASCAP, BMI, SESAC. Publishes 50 songs/year; publishes 50 new songwriters/year. Pays standard royalty.
Affiliates: Betty Brown Music Co. (BMI), and Clara Church Music Co. (SESAC).
How to Contact: Write first and obtain permission to submit. Prefers cassette with 1-4 songs and lyric sheet. SASE. Reports in 1 month.
Music: Mostly country, MOR and religious. Published "Believe in America" (by Frank X. Loconto), recorded by The Lane Brothers (contemporary country); "Out of the Darkness," by F. Loconto (inspirational); and "Watch It Grow," by Tim Henson (country), all recorded on FXL Records.

PACIFIC CHALLENGER MUSIC, 2940 E. Miraloma, Anaheim CA 92806. (714)992-6820. President: Chuck Whittington. Music publisher, record company and record producer. BMI. Publishes 80 songs/year; publishes 2 new songwriters/year. Pays standard royalty.
How to Contact: Prefers cassette with 2-4 songs and lyric sheet. Does not return unsolicited material. Reports in 1 month.
Music: Mostly country; also gospel and top 40/pop. Published "Someone's Discovery" (by L.B. Garland), recorded by Lula Belle on Pacific Challenger Records; "Legend of Harry and the Mountain" (by L.B. Garland), recorded by Ron Shaw on Pacific Challenger Records; and "Hurtin' Kind of Love" (by R. Shaw), recorded by R. Shaw on Pacific Challenger Records.

PANCHO'S MUSIC CO., 3121 29th Ave., Sacramento CA 95820. (916)455-5278. Contact: Frank Lizarraga. Music publisher and record producer (Israfel Production and Recording Service). BMI. Publishes 5 songs/year; publishes 1 new songwriter/year. Works with composers and lyricists; teams collaborators. Pays standard royalty.
How to Contact: Write first and obtain permission to submit. Prefers cassette (or Beta or VHS videocassette) with 3 songs, lyric sheet and brief resume/fact sheet. SASE. Reports in 2 months.
Music: Mostly Latin, rock and country; also gospel, pop and blues. Published "Hollywood Girl," and "Definition of Love," (by F. Lizarraga), recorded by Suenos (rock and dance rock); "Seran Ideas," (by J. Rodriquez), recorded by Juan Alejando (Latin); and "Sin Tu Amor" (by R. Vargas), recorded by Tony Arana (ballad), all on Israfel Records.
Tips: "We specialize in Latin music and prefer bilingual songwriters."

PARK J. TUNES, 29 S. Erie, Toledo OH 43602. (419)244-8599. Contact: Michael Drew Shaw. Music publisher, record company and record producer. ASCAP. Publishes 25 songs/year; publishes 5 new songwriters/year. Pays standard royalty.
Affiliates: Keeny/York (BMI), Newstar International Records.
How to Contact: Prefers cassette with 3-5 songs and lyric sheet. SASE. Reports in 1 month.
Music: Country and top 40/pop. Published "Wherever You Are," recorded by MDS Studio Band; "We Are the Future," recorded by Kerry Clark; and "Take a Ride," recorded by Mick Payne.

PAYTON PLACE PUBLISHING, Suite 1204, 7000 Fonvilla, Houston TX 77074. (713)776-9219. Contact: President. Music publisher and record producer. BMI. Publishes 10 songs/year; publishes 3 new songwriters/year. BMI.
Affiliates: Clarity Publishing and Split Publishing.

How to Contact: Prefers cassette with 1-2 songs and lyric sheet. SASE.
Music: Mostly cajun and country; also heavy metal, AOR, bluegrass, blues and dance. Published "'Cajun Honey," (by Joe Schiro), recorded by Bob Monroe (cajun); "Joe Bailey Roll," (by S. Bros), recorded by Slim Beaumont (country); and "Rodeo Rider," (by Sheila Lang), recorded by Sundown (country).
Tips: "Include return address and phone number on cassette. Please send country and cajun songs for a promising project. We like good, simple, solid, catchy, earthy songs."

PEER-SOUTHERN ORGANIZATION, Suite 300, 180 Bloor St. W., Toronto, Ontario M5S 2V6 Canada. Music publisher. PROCAN and CAPAC.
How to Contact: Prefers cassette with 1-3 songs. SAE and IRC. Reports in 1 month.
Music: Bluegrass, blues, children's, choral, church/religious, classical, country, dance-oriented, easy listening, folk, gospel, jazz, MOR, progressive, rock, soul and top 40/pop.

PEER-TALBOT MUSIC GROUP, 2 Music Circle S., Nashville TN 37203. (615)244-6200. Director of Nashville Operations: Jana Talbot. Music publisher. BMI, ASCAP. Member NMPA. Publishes 30 songs/year; publishes 2 new songwriters/year. Pays standard royalty.
Affiliates: Charles K. Harris Music (ASCAP), La Salle Music (ASCAP), Melody Lane (BMI), Panther Music (ASCAP), Peer International (BMI), Pera Music (BMI), RFD Music (ASCAP), Southern Music (ASCAP), Talbot Music Publishing Inc. and Saheerdron Music Publishing Inc. (ASCAP).
How to Contact: Query. "We do not generally accept outside material." Prefers cassette with 1-3 songs and lyric sheet. SASE. Reports in 1 month.
Music: Mostly country and pop; also MOR, R&B, rock and top 40/pop. Published "Pass It On," (by D. Dickerson/C. Williams/S. Birins), recorded by Willie Nelson; "Ballad of the Blue Cyclone," (by G. Sutton/L. Cheshier), recorded by Ray Stevens; and "Yankee Don't Go Home," (by B. Keel/B. Stone), recorded by The Forester Sisters.

*PEGASUS MUSIC, 27 Bayside Ave., Te Atatu, Auckland 8, New Zealand. Professional Manager: Errol Peters. Music publisher and record company. Member APRA. Publishes 20-30 songs/year; publishes 2 new songwriters/year. Works with composers and lyricists; teams collaborators. Pays 3-5% to artists on contract and standard royalty to songwriters; royalties paid directly to US songwriters.
How to Contact: Prefers cassette with 3-5 songs and lyric sheet. SAE and IRC. Reports in 1 month.
Music: Mostly country; also bluegrass, easy listening and top 40/pop. Published "Just Bring Some Love," "Music Man," and "I Only See You," all written and recorded by Ginny Peters on RCA Records (country).
Tips: "Be fresh and original. We prefer direct lyrics."

PENNY THOUGHTS MUSIC, 30 Guinaw St., Waltham MA 02154. (617)891-7800. President: John Penny. Music publisher, record company and record producer. Publishes 20-30 songs/year; publishes 6 new songwriters/year. Pays standard royalty.
How to Contact: Write first about your interest. SASE. Reports in 2 weeks. Not accepting material at this time.
Music: Mostly country; also contemporary and rock (country). Published "Give It Away," written and recorded by Stan Anderson Jr. on Belmont Records (country) and "The Hurt That Hurts Me" and "You're the Right Love," by Mike Cummings (country).

*PER PRODUCTIONS, 111 St. Croix Dr., Pittsburgh PA 15235. (412)795-1370. President: Ann L. Strothers. Music publisher. ASCAP. Publishes 3 songs/year; publishes 1 new songwriter/year. Works with composers. Pays standard royalty.
How to Contact: Prefers cassette with 2-4 songs and lyric or lead sheet. SASE. Reports in 2 weeks.
Music: Gospel only. Published "Isn't It Good to Be Here," recorded by Emma White; "Rejoice in Heaven," and "My Life Is In God's Hands," by P.E. Russell.

PERITERRA MUSIC, Box 4386, Long Island City NY 11104. (718)786-2401. President: Franc Peri. Music publisher. BMI.
How to Contact: Prefers cassette and lead sheet. SASE.
Music: Instrumental and dance music.

PHILIPPOPOLIS MUSIC, 12027 Califa St., North Hollywood CA 91607. President: Milcho Leviev. Music publisher. BMI. Member GEMA, NARAS. Publishes 3-5 songs/year; publishes 5 new songwriters/year. Works with compoers and lyricists; teams collaborators. Pays standard royalty.
How to Contact: Query. Prefers cassette with 1-3 songs. Prefers studio produced demos. SASE. Reports in 1 month.

Music: Jazz and classical fusion. Published "A Voyage Again," "Destination," "Isle of Happiness" (all jazz), and "Mediterra," "Nocturne," "Prelude" (all classical), written and recorded by Milcho Leviev on Golden Boy Records.
Tips: "Treat music as an art form."

PINE ISLAND MUSIC, #308, 9430 Live Oak Place, Ft. Lauderdale FL 33324. (305)472-7757. President: Jack P. Bluestein. Music publisher, record company and record producer. BMI, ASCAP. Publishes 10-20 songs/year; publishes 3-4 new songwriters/year. Pays standard royalty.
Affiliates: Lantana Music (ASCAP) and Twister Music (ASCAP).
How to Contact: Prefers cassette or 7½ ips reel-to-reel (or VHS videocassette) with 3 songs and lyric sheet. SASE. Reports in 2-4 months.
Music: Mostly country and pop; also gospel, soft rock and contemporary. Published "The Painted Pony" and "Everybody Listens to the Music" (by Ann Leysten), recorded by Gary Oakes and Lou Garcia on Twister (country/pop); "Please Forgive Me," (by Ronnie Lynn), recorded by Julie Lendon on Twister (country); and "I Made It" (by David Berger/David Lipshutz) on Twisted Records.

*PINEAPPLE MUSIC PUBLISHING CO., 1311 Candlelight Ave., Dallas TX 75116. (214)298-9576. President: Paul Ketter. Music publisher, record producer and record company. ASCAP. Publishes 20-30 songs/year. Pays standard royalty.
Affiliate: Big State Music Pub. Co. (BMI).
How to Contact: Prefers cassette with 1-8 songs and lyric sheet. SASE. Reports in 3 weeks.
Music: Country, folk, country MOR, progressive country and "strong" pop. Published "Bar after Bar" (by F. Feliccia/F. Raffa), recorded by Bunnie Mills (honky tonk country); "Only a Woman" (by D. Baumgartner), recorded by Bunnie Mills (country/ballad); "Theodore" (by D. Gregory/G. Puls), recorded by Dave Gregory (children's Christmas); and "I Wanna Say 'I Do'," recorded by P.J. Kamel, all on Sagittar Records.
Tips: "We only want to hear from writers who have written 100 or more songs. Please do not send us songs that have been already rejected by others."

*PIXIE MUSIC CO. LTD., 10 St. Mary's Hill, Stamford, Lincs., PE9 2DP, England. 44-0780-51736. Managing Director: Ken Cox. Music publisher, record company and record producer. MCPS, PRS and Phonographic Performance Ltd. Publishes 20 songs/year; publishes 3 new songwriters/year. Pays standard royalty; royalties paid directly to US songwriters.
How to Contact: Prefers cassette (or Beta videocassette) with 3-4 songs and lyric sheet. SAE and IRC. Reports in 2 weeks.
Music: Mostly top 40/pop; also country and soul (uptempo).

*PLACER PUBLISHING, Box 11301, Kansas City KS 66111. (913)287-3495. Owner: Steve Vail. Music publisher. ASCAP. Estab. 1986. Publishes 10 songs/year; publishes 10 new songwriters/year. Works with composers and lyricists; teams collaborators.
How to Contact: Prefers cassette (or Beta or ½" VHS videocassette) with 10-12 songs. Does not return unsolicited material. Reports in 6 weeks.
Music: Mostly classical rock, art rock and jazz. Published "Mind's Eye," recorded by Realm on System Records (classical-rock).

PLAYERS PRESS INC., Box 1132, Studio City CA 91604. (818)789-4980. Vice President Editorial: Robert W. Gordon. Music publisher, record company and record producer. Publishes 10 songs/year; publishes 1-2 new songwriters/year. "Contracts are negotiable."
How to Contact: Prefers cassette (or ½" VHS or ¾" U-matic videocassette) and lyric sheet. SASE. Reports in 6 weeks.
Music: Only musical theater. Published "Tune-Line," (by William Lentes); "Machine," (by Jeff Rizzo); and "Wall," (by Joe Sporaco); all recorded by Players Press Inc. on Players Press Records (theatrical).

POCA RIVER MUSIC PUBLISHING CO., Box 667, Fairmont WV 26554. (304)363-3107. President: Kenneth Davidson. Music publisher. BMI. Publishes 10 songs/year; publishes 3 new songwriters/year. Pays standard royalty.
How to Contact: Submit demo tape by mail. Write to arrange personal interview. Prefers cassette (or videocassette) with 6 songs and lyric or lead sheet. SASE. Reports in 3 weeks.
Music: Country, gospel and rock. Published "Beloved" (by Jeret-Ebner), recorded by Troubador (rock); "Dyer Need in Dyersburg," by John Elias (folk rock); and "Sparkling Brown Eyes" (by B. Cox), recorded by W. Jennings on RCA Records (country).

POLKA TOWNE MUSIC, 211 Post Ave., Westbury NY 11590. President: Teresa Zapolska. Music publisher, record company, record producer and booking agency. BMI.
How to Contact: Prefers cassette with 1-3 songs and lead sheet. "Absolutely must send SASE for return of material and/or reply. *No* review or reply without SASE. We review all music once a month." Reports within 6 weeks.
Music: Polkas and "some" waltzes.

*POPULAR MUSIC CO., 49 W. 45th St., 10th Floor, New York NY 10036. President: Mort Browne. Music publisher. ASCAP. Publishes 4-6 songs/year; publishes 4-6 new songwriters/year. Pays standard royalty.
Affiliates: Children's Musical Plays (ASCAP).
How to Contact: Prefers cassette with 2 songs and lead sheet. Does not return unsolicited material. Reports in 2 months.
Music: Mostly R&B, pop and country; also jazz and swing.

PORTAGE MUSIC, 16634 Gannon W., Rosemont MN 55068. (612)432-5737. President: Larry LaPole. Music publisher. BMI. Publishes 5-20 songs/year. Pays standard royalty.
How to Contact: Prefers cassette with 3 songs and lyric sheet. Reports in 4 weeks.
Music: Mostly country and country rock.
Tips: "Keep songs short, simple and upbeat with positive theme."

POST WAR PUBLISHING CO., (formerly Black Watch Publishing), Suite 522, 10 N. Calvert, Baltimore MD 21202. (301)727-7673. President: Patricia Prinster. A&R Department: Ronnie Scruggs. Music publisher, record company (Yellow Rose Records), record producer (Black Watch Productions) and management firm (Yellow Rose). ASCAP. Publishes 100-200 songs/year; publishes 10 new songwriters/year. Works with composers and lyricists; teams collaborators. Pays standard royalty.
Affiliate: Definitely by Friday Publishing Co. (ASCAP).
How to Contact: Prefers cassette with 3-5 songs and lyric sheet. SASE. Reports in 6 weeks.
Music: Mostly top 40/pop and rock; also R&B and MOR. Published "Baby Plays Games" by J. Chance (rock); "Just Say Goodnight" (by J. Chance) recorded by Toy Soldier (rock/ballad); and "Fallen Angel" (by D. Van Landingham); recorded by Mannequin (rock), all on Yellow Rose Records.

PRAISE SOUND PRODUCTIONS LTD., 7802 Express St., Barnaby, British Columbia V5A 1T4 Canada. (604)420-4227. Manager: Metro Yaroshuk. PROCAN, CAPAC. Music publisher, record company and record producer. Publishes 400 songs/year; publishes 100 new songwriters/year.
Affiliates: Noteworthy Publishing Co. and Innovative Publishing Co.
How to Contact: Prefers cassette. SAE and IRC.
Music: Mostly gospel.

PRESCRIPTION COMPANY, 70 Murray Ave., Port Washington NY 11050. (516)767-1929. President: David F. Gasman. Music publisher and record producer. BMI. Pays standard royalty.
How to Contact: Call or write first about your interest. Prefers cassette with any number of songs and lyric sheet. "Send all submissions with SASE (or no returns)." Reports in 1 month.
Music: Bluegrass, blues, children's, country, dance-oriented, easy listening, folk, jazz, MOR, progressive, R&B, rock, soul and top 40/pop. Published "You Came In," "Rock 'n' Roll Blues," and "Seasons," (by D.F. Gasman), all recorded by Medicine Mike on Prescription Records.
Tips: "Songs should be good and written to last. Forget fads—we want songs that'll sound as good in 10 years as they do today. Organization, communication, and exploration of form is as essential as message (and sincerity matters, too)."

PRETTY GIRL MUSIC COMPANY INC., Box 11547, East Station, Memphis TN 38111. (901)525-5414. Professional Manager: Style Wooten. Music publisher. BMI. Publishes 12-24 songs/year; publishes 10 new songwriters/year. Pays standard royalty.
How to Contact: Write or call first. Prefers cassette with 2-4 songs and "typewritten words." SASE. Reports in 1 month.
Music: Mostly country; also bluegrass, R&B and gospel.

JIMMY PRICE MUSIC PUBLISHING, 1662 Wyatt Parkway, Lexington KY 40505. (606)254-7474. President: James T. Price. Music publisher, record company, record producer and music printer. BMI. Publishes 7 new songwriters/year. Pays standard royalty.
How to Contact: Prefers 7½ ips reel-to-reel with 1-6 songs and lyric sheet. SASE. Reports in 1 month.
Music: Bluegrass, blues, church/religious, country, gospel and rock. "Road Block to Your Heart (by James T. Price), and "Angel Just Lost Her Wings" (by Dave Gibson), both recorded by Bud Chowing.

PRITCHETT PUBLICATION (Branch), 171 Pine Haven, Daytona Beach FL 32014. (904)252-4848. Vice President: Charles Vickers. Music publisher and record company. (Main office in California.) BMI. Publishes 14 songs/year; publishes 8 new songwriters/year. Pays standard royalty.
Affiliate: Alison Music (ASCAP).
How to Contact: Write first and obtain permission to submit. Prefers cassette with 6 songs and lyric or lead sheet. SASE.
Music: Gospel, rock-disco and country. Published "Heaven Is Just Over the Hill," (by Leroy Pritchett); "Come Drink This Water", "He's Always Near," and "Sailing Without a Sail (by Charles Vickers), recorded by C. Vickers on King of Kings Records (all gospel).

PROPHECY PUBLISHING, INC., Box 4945, Austin TX 78765. (512)452-9412. President: T. White. Music publisher. ASCAP. Member NMPA. Pays standard royalty, less expenses; "expenses such as tape duplicating, photocopying and long distance phone calls are recouped from the writer's earnings." **Affiliate:** Black Coffee Music (BMI).
How to Contact: "We now only accept songs which are currently on the charts or have a very good chance of entering them in the near future."
Music: Published "Deep in the West" (by Shake Russell), recorded by Waylon Jennings.

PUBLISHING VENTURES, 201 E. 61st St., New York NY 10021. (212)832-2980. Managing Director: John Apostol. Music publisher. ASCAP, BMI. Publishes 15 songs/year; publishes 4 new songwriters/year. Pays standard royalty.
Affiliates: King Kong Music, Gary Bonds Music, Son of Kong Music.
How to Contact: Prefers cassette with 1-3 songs and lyric sheet. Does not return unsolicited material. Reports in 8 weeks.
Music: Rock, top 40/pop and R&B; also ballads, country and MOR. Published "Turn the Music Down" and "Bring Her Back" (by Gary Bonds/Laurie Anderson), recorded by Gary U.S. Bonds on EMI Records (pop/rock).
Tips: Looking for "radio-oriented hit singles with strong hooks and interesting lyrics and titles."

GERARD W. PURCELL ASSOCIATES, 964 Second Ave., New York NY 10022. (212)421-2670, 2674, 2675 and 2676. President: Gerard Purcell. Music publisher. BMI, ASCAP. Member CPM, CMA, NARM. Publishes 50 songs/year; publishes 4 new songwriters/year. Pays standard royalty.
How to Contact: Prefers cassette with maximum 3 songs, lyric sheet and clear lead sheet. SASE. Reports as soon as possible.
Music: Country and MOR.

PURPLE HAZE MUSIC, Box 1243, Beckley WV 25802. (304)252-4836. President: Richard L. Petry. Music publisher. BMI. Publishes 6-12 songs/year; publishes 3-4 new songwriters/year. Teams collaborators. Pays standard royalty.
How to Contact: Prefers cassette with 3-5 songs and lyric sheet. SASE. Reports in 4 weeks.
Music: Country, pop/top 40 and R&B/pop. Published "For a Song," and "Since You've Gone," written and recorded by Steve Willoughby on Country Road (country); and "Video Girl," "Modern Day Woman," and "Challenger," written and recorded by Chris Alaimo (CHR).
Tips: "Songs should be well thought out with clever hooks and lines. We now only accept a professional demo."

PUSTAKA MUZIK EMI (Malaysia) SDN. BHD., No. 8, Jalan Murai Dua, Batu Kompleks, Batu Tiga, Jalan Ipoh, Kuala Lumpur Malaysia. 03-6277511. Contact: A&R Manager. Music publisher and record company. Publishes 50 songs/year; publishes 15 new songwriters/year.
How to Contact: Prefers cassette and lyric or lead sheet. Does not return unsolicited material.
Music: Mostly MOR, country and commercial jazz; also blues and rock. Published "Hati Ku Melekat," (by A. Ryanto), recorded by Sharifah Aini (MOR); "Di Hati Mu Biar," written and recorded by D.J. Dave (slow rock); and "Aku Budak Kampung," (by Adnan Abu Hassan/Sudirman), recorded by Sudirman (commercial rock) all on EMI Records.

QUINTON Q. QUALLS, JR. MUSIC, 39 Music Square E., Nashville TN 37203. (615)256-3558. President: Quinton Q. Qualls, Jr. Music publisher. BMI, ASCAP. Publishes 17 songs/year; publishes 2 new songwriters/year. Employs songwriters on a salary basis. Pays standard royalty.
Affiliates: Tresque Music (BMI) and Golden Biscuits Music (ASCAP).
How to Contact: Prefers cassette with 3 songs and lyric sheet. SASE. Reports in 6 weeks.
Music: Country and country/pop. Published "(I Make the Living) She Makes the Living Worthwhile," (by Pritchard/King Ford), recorded by Sonny James on Dot Records (country); "Sometimes the Blues Are Blonde," by Harlan Sanders/Larry Kingston (country); and "Rebound Baby," by Bobby Keel/Quinton Qualls (country/pop).

QUINONES MUSIC CO., 1344 Waldron, St. Louis MO 63130. President: Eddie Johnson. Music publisher. BMI. Publishes 6 songs/year; publishes 6 new songwriters/year. Teams collaborators. Pays standard royalty.
How to Contact: Prefers cassette with 3 songs and lead sheet. SASE. Reports in 2 weeks.
Music: Mostly blues and top 40; also church/religious, gospel, R&B, soul and pop. Published "Strange Feeling," (by Tab Smith), recorded by Eddie Johnson (top 40); "Tables Are Turned,", written and recorded by Bobby Scott (top 40); and "Strange Love," and "Love Me," written and recorded by Joe Smith (pop), all on E.L.J. Records.

QVQ/LADY J MUSIC, 10 George St., Box 57, Wallingford CT 06492. (203)265-0010. A&R Director: Thomas Cavalier. Music publisher. ASCAP. Publishes 15-20 songs/year. Pays standard royalty.
Affiliate: Rohm Music (BMI) and Trod Nossel Artists (records and management).
How to Contact: Prefers cassette with 1-4 songs. SASE.
Music: Rock. Published "Dreamin' 'Bout Your Love," "I Will Always Love You," and "Is It Just the Night" by Cub Koda.

R. J. MUSIC, 10A Margaret Rd., Barnet, Herts. EN4 9NP England. (01)440-9788. Managing Directors: Roger James and Laura Skuce. Music publisher. PRS. Pays negotiable royalty (up to 75%).
How to Contact: Prefers cassette with 1 song and lyric or lead sheet. SAE and IRC.
Music: Mostly MOR, blues, country and rock; also disco and chart material.

*RADIO TELE MUSIC S.A.., Av. Franklin D. Roosevelt, Brussels 67 1050 Belgium. Phone: (02)640.06.00. Managing Director: Hubert J.M. Terheggen. Music publisher and record company. SABAM.
How to Contact: Write and request submission policy.

RAINBARREL MUSIC COMPANY, 1119½ Leland Ave., Nashville TN 37216. Director: Teresa Parks Bernard. BMI. Music publisher, record company (Paragold Records) and record producer. Publishes 3 songs/year; publishes 1 new songwriter/year. Pays standard royalty.
How to Contact: Prefers cassette with 2 songs and lyric and lead sheets. SASE. Reports in 6 weeks.
Music: Mostly country; also top 40. Published "Ghost of Grand Ol Opry," written and recorded by J. Bernard; "Daddy's Last Letter," (by J. Bernard), recorded by J. Lyne; and "Please Don't Turn Me On," (by Ray Davis), recorded by J. Bernard and Julie Jones, all on Paragold Records (all country).

THE RAINBOW COLLECTION LTD., Box 300, Solebury PA 18963. (215)297-8437. President: Herb Gart. BMI, ASCAP. Music publisher, record company and record producer. Publishes 125 songs/year; publishes 10 new songwriters/year. Occasionally employs songwriters on a salary basis. Pays standard royalty.
Affiliate: Herbert S. Gart Management Inc.
How to Contact: Prefers cassette (or VHS or Beta videocassette) with 1-6 songs. Does not return unsolicited material. Reports in 2 months.
Music: Mostly rock, pop and country; also blues, new wave, reggae, TV and movie scores and jazz. Published "Jenny," (by Nick Holland), recorded by Between the Sheets on Happy Man Records (pop/rock); and "Pretty in Pink," by Mike Hughes (rock/film score).
Tips: "Send me your finest work. If you are original and great and know it—if you believe in yourself and your artistry and are looking for a believer, contact me."

BRIAN RAINES MUSIC CO., Box 1376, Pickens SC 29671. (803)878-2953. President: Brian E. Raines. Music publisher and artist management/booking (Palmetto Productions). ASCAP. Publishes 20 songs/year; publishes 5 new songwriters/year. Pays standard royalty.
Affiliates: Brian Song Music Company (BMI) and Palmetto Records.
How to Contact: Prefers cassette (or VHS videocassette) with 2-3 songs and lyric sheet. "All demos are listened to whether professionally recorded or done at home." SASE. Reports in 2 weeks "or earliest convenience."
Music: Mostly gospel/contemporary Christian, country and pop/adult contemporary; also Christian rock. Published "Since I Met You," written and recorded by Brian Raines on Palmetto Records (country); "No More Heartaches" (by Chet Johnson), recorded by The Greenes on Riversong Records (gospel); and "It Makes Me Glad" (by Jim Hubbard), recorded by Joe Russell on White Line Records (gospel).
Tips: "Send good chart material, we also like a biography of writer with a photo if possible. Try to send material that has been recorded by 'local' artists, or that is currently being performed on a local level. SASE required!"

*RASHONE MUSIC, Rt. 3, Box 57, Troy AL 36081. (205)566-7932. Contact: Eddie Toney. Music publisher, record company (Earth Records) and record producer. BMI. Publishes 5 songs/year; publishes 4 new songwriters/year. Works with composers and lyricists.
How to Contact: Write or call first and obtain permission to submit or to arrange personal interview. Prefers cassette and lead sheet. SASE. Reports in 3 weeks.
Music: Published "Cheese Line," by Ed Mally (easy listening); "Starking Hard," by Never Thoms (disco); and "Don't Give Up," by Never Thoms (MOR) all on Earth Records.

RAY MACK MUSIC, Box 120675, Nashville TN 37212. (615)255-1068. Owner: Ray McGinnis. Music publisher, record company (Orbit Records) and record producer (Ray Mack Productions). ASCAP, BMI. Publishes 10-20 songs/year; publishes 4-5 new songwriters/year. Teams collaborators. Pays standard royalty.
Affiliate: Nautical Music Co. (BMI).
How to Contact: Prefers cassette with 4 songs and lead sheet. SASE. Reports in 6 weeks.
Music: Country, country rock and rock. Published "So Many Memories" (by Peggy Wilson), recorded by Kenny Wilson; "I'm Gonna Quit It" (by S. Laurene), recorded by Sonny Martin; and "Dancin," written and recorded by Teddy Hale, all on Orbit Records (all country).
Tips: "Keep your songs short and simple with strong hook lines."

RAYBIRD MUSIC, Suite 303, 457 W. 57th St., New York NY 10019. (212)245-2299. President: Ray Passman. General Manager: Teddy Charles. Music publisher. BMI. Publishes 6-7 songs/year; publishes 2 new songwriters/year. Pays standard royalty.
Affiliates: Kips Bay Music (ASCAP), TaJah Music (BMI).
How to Contact: Write first. Prefers cassette with 3-5 songs. SASE. Reports in 2 weeks.
Music: Jazz. Published "The Cove" (by Barbara Dzuro); "Cross Me Off Your List" (by Al Coifin/H. Wasserman/J. Garcock); and "Unusual For April" (by Mark Murphy/Dick Dallas), all recorded by Meredith D'Ambrosio on Sunnyside Records (jazz ballads).
Tips: "Study new, important writers like Dave Frishberg, Rupert Holmes and Bob Dorough. Listen to great old and new jazz singers and the material they record."

READY TO ROCK MUSIC, Box 46445, Hollywood CA 90046. (213)656-8845. President: P.J. Birosik. Music publisher. BMI. Publishes 50-75 songs/year; publishes 2-3 new songwriters/year. Pays standard royalty.
How to Contact: Prefers cassette (or VHS videocassette) with 4-6 songs and lyric sheet. SASE.
Music: Mostly rock, pop and New Age; also soundtrack material. Published "Going Backwards," (by Joe Ramirez), recorded by Rayonics; "Under the Trees," and "I'm Gonna Make You Love Me," (by A. Alm/J. Ramirez), recorded by Art of Persuasion, all on Ready to Rock Records (all pop).

RED BUS MUSIC INTERNATIONAL, LTD., 48 Broadley Terrace, London NW1, England. 44-01-258-0324. Telex: 25873 Red Bus G. Director: Eliot M. Cohen. Music publisher and record company. PRS, ASCAP, BMI. Member MPA. Publishes 120 songs/year; publishes 6 new songwriters/year. Pays standard royalty; royalties paid to songwriter through US publishing affiliate.
Affiliates: Our Music Ltd., Chibell Music Ltd., Grade One Music Ltd. and Mother Goose Music Ltd.
How to Contact: Prefers cassette and lyric sheet. SAE and IRC. Reports in 1 month.
Music: Dance-oriented, MOR, rock and top 40/pop. Published "Cruel Summer" (by Jolley/Swain), recorded by Bananarana on London Records (pop); "Thank You My Love," and "Found My Love" (by John/Ingram), recorded by Imagination on Elektra Records (R&B); and "Soul Street," (by Jolley/Swain), written and recorded by Jolley and Swain on London Records (R&B).

> **66** *It's really important for a writer to not play it safe. Go somewhere that might seem a little odd or phrase it in a strange way.* **99**
> —**Diane Warren, songwriter,**
>   **in LASS Musepaper**

REN MAUR MUSIC CORP., 521 5th Ave., New York NY 10175. (212)757-3638. President: Rena L. Feeney. Music publisher and record company. BMI. Member AGAC and NARAS. Publishes 6-8 songs/year. Pays 4-8% royalty.
Affiliate: R.R. Music (ASCAP).
How to Contact: Prefers cassette with 2-4 songs and lead sheet. SASE. Reports in 1 month.
Music: R&B, rock, soul and top 40/pop. Published "Same Language," "Do It to Me and I'll Do It to You," and "Once You Fall in Love," (by Billy Nichols), recorded by Rena; and "Lead Me to Love," (by Brad Smiley), recorded by Carmen John (ballad/dance) all on Factory Beat Records.
Tips: "Send lead sheets and a good, almost finished cassette ready for producing or remixing."

LEON RENE PUBLICATIONS/RECORDO MUSIC PUBLISHERS, 2124 W. 24th St., Los Angeles CA 90018. (213)737-5125. Manager: Rafael Rene. Music publisher. BMI, ASCAP and AGAC. Publishes 1 song/year. Pays standard royalty.
Music: Mostly R&B and popular; also religious, jazz, and film music. Published "When the Swallows Come Back to Capistrano" (by Leon Rene), official song of Capistrano; and "When It's Sleepytime Down South" (by Leon Rene), recorded by many outstanding orchestras.

GARY REVEL MUSIC/JONGLEUR MUSIC, #5, 5341 Lona Linda Ave., Los Angeles CA 90027. (213)464-5574. President: Linda Revel. Music publisher. ASCAP. Publishes 20 songs/year; publishes 4 new songwriters/year. Works with composers and lyricists; teams collaborators. Pays standard royalty.
How to Contact: Prefers cassette (or videocassette) with 1-12 songs and lyric sheet. SASE. Reports in 1 month "usually, but does not guarantee return of material."
Music: Mostly pop/rock; also blues, children's, church/religious, country, rock, rockabilly and top 40. Published "Treat America Like a Lady" (by Jerry Guthrie/Gary Revel), recorded by Czar Tuck, Hal Jon Norman, John Barrymore, and Melvena Kaye; "Pac Man on Her Mind," (by G. Revel/Joe Yore), recorded by Gary Revel on Top's Records (rockabilly); "Wouldn't It Be Nice," written and recorded by G. Revel on Top's Records (pop/country); and "River Bottom Road," (by Mary Head/G. Revel), recorded by G. Revel on Top's Records (country rock).
Tips: "Don't predict future song trends; but express true inner feelings."

RHYTHMS PRODUCTIONS, Whitney Bldg., Box 34485, Los Angeles CA 90034. President: Ruth White. Music publisher and record company. ASCAP. Member NARAS. Publishes 10 cassettes/year. Pays negotiable royalty.
Affiliate: Tom Thumb Music.
How to Contact: Submit lead sheet with letter outlining background in educational children's music. SASE. Reports in 1 month.
Music: "We're only interested in children's songs that have educational value. Our materials are sold in schools and homes, so artists/writers with a teaching background would be most likely to understand our requirements." Published "Watch Me Grow," (cassette series for children).

RIC RAC MUSIC, Ric Rac Inc., Box 712, Nashville IN 47448. (812)837-9569. Professional Manager: Sue Hanson. Music publisher. ASCAP. Publishes 5-10 songs/year; publishes 2 songwriters/year. Works with composers and lyricists; teams collaborators. Pays standard royalty.
Affiliate: Rick Hanson Music (BMI).
How to Contact: Write first and obtain permission to submit. Prefers cassette with 1-4 songs and lyric sheet. SASE. Reports in 8 weeks.
Music: Mostly country; also rock, gospel, folk, pop, jazz, R&B and easy listening. Published "Stay Away" (by Greg Washel) and "Morning Light" (by David Billey), both recorded by X-it (both rock); and "Life's Not Worth The Ride," written and recorded by Rick Hanson (country) all on Ric Rac Records.
Tips: "Be as professional as possible."

RIDGE MUSIC CORP., Suite 1100, 1650 Broadway, New York NY 10019. (212)582-1667. President/General Manager: Paul Tannen. Music publisher and manager. BMI, ASCAP. Member CMA. Pays standard royalty.
Affiliates: Natson Music Corp. and Tannen Music Inc.
How to Contact: Prefers cassette with 3-5 songs and lyric sheet. SASE. Reports in 1 month.
Music: Country, dance-oriented, rock and top 40/pop.

RMS TRIAD PUBLISHING, 6267 Potomac Circle, West Bloomfield MI 48033. (313)661-5167. Contact: Bob Szajner. Music publisher, record company, and record producer. ASCAP. Publishes 9 songs/year; publishes 1 new songwriter/year. Pays negotiable royalty.

How to Contact: Write first about your interest. Prefers cassette with 3 songs and lead sheet. Does not return unsolicited material. Reports in 3 weeks.
Music: Jazz. Published "Meeting Competition," "That's Pretty," and "Royal Outhouse Blues," (all by Bob Szajner), recorded by Triad/RMS Records (jazz).

FREDDIE ROBERTS MUSIC, Box 99, Rougemont NC 27572. (919)477-4077. Manager: Freddie Roberts. Music publisher, record company, record producer, and management and booking agency. BMI. Publishes 35 songs/year; publishes 15 new songwriters/year. Works with lyricists; teams collaborators. Pays standard royalty.
How to Contact: Write first about your interest or arrange personal interview. Prefers 7½ ips reel-to-reel or cassette with 1-5 songs and lyric sheet. SASE.
Music: Mostly country, MOR and top 40/pop; also bluegrass, church/religious, gospel and southern rock (country). Published "Jilted" (by Doug McElroy), recorded by Susie Sharp on Sugar Mountain Records (southern rock); "Going Over" (by Freddie Roberts), recorded by Robert Reunion on Bull City Records (gospel); and "Why Not" (by David Laws), recorded by Billy McKeller on Bull City Records (country).
Tips: "Write songs, whatever type, to fit today's market. Send good, clear demos, no matter how simple."

ROB-LEE MUSIC, Box 1338, Merchantville NJ 08109. (609)962-6000. Vice Presidents: Rodney Russen, Eric Russen, Janice Russo, Bob Francis. Music publisher, record company, record producer, and manager. ASCAP. Publishes 15-20 songs/year; publishes 6-10 new songwriters/year. Works with composers and lyricists; teams collaborators. Pays standard royalty.
Affiliates: Rock Island (BMI) and Heavy Weather Music (ASCAP).
How to Contact: Prefers cassette (or VHS videocassette) with 4-8 songs and lyric sheet. Does not return unsolicited material. Reports in 2 weeks.
Music: Dance-oriented, easy listening, MOR, R&B, rock, soul, top 40/pop and funk. Published "Sign of the Times" (by Mark Prater), recorded by Phoenix on Castle Records (dance); "Dream Lovers" (by Rob Russen), recorded by Millionaires on Jade Records (ballad); and "Rock Monster" (by Eric Russen), recorded by Flaming White Caucasions on Ricl Island Records (rock).
Tips: "Send demos on good quality cassettes in order that we may properly hear your material."

ROCKEN RYTHMN PUBLISHING, Box 34813, Memphis TN 38134. (901)358-5006. A&R Director: Don Von Maurer. Music publisher, record company and record producer. BMI. Member Memphis Music Association, Blues Foundation. Publishes 50 songs/year; publishes 2 new songwriters/year. Pays standard royalty.
How to Contact: Prefers cassette with 1-4 songs and lyric sheet. "Specify number of songs on the tape." SASE, but "we keep tape on file." Reports if interested.
Music: Mostly blues, R&B, pop, rock, top 40 and soul. Published "Where You Want Me," and "Straight and Narrow Line," (by B. Lusk/T. Fosko), recorded by B. Lusk on Rocken Rhythm Records (R&B).

ROCKER MUSIC/HAPPY MAN MUSIC, #806, 50 Music Sq. W, Nashville TN 37203. (615)320-1177. Executive Producer: Dick O'Bitts. BMI, ASCAP. Music publisher and record producer (Rainbow Collections Ltd.). Publishes 50 songs/year; publishes 10 new songwriters/year. Pays standard royalty.
Affiliate: Happy Man Music.
How to Contact: Prefers cassette with 4 songs and lyric sheet or lead sheet. SASE.
Music: "All types."

ROCKFORD MUSIC CO., Suite 6-D, 150 West End Ave., New York NY 10023. (212)873-5968. Manager: Danny Darrow. Music publisher, record company, record and video tape producer. BMI, ASCAP. Publishes 2-4 songs/year; publishes 1-2 new songwriters/year. Works with composers and lyricists; teams collaborators. Pays standard royalty.
Affiliates: Corporate Music Publishing Company (ASCAP), Stateside Music Company (BMI), and Rockford Music Company (BMI).
How to Contact: Prefers cassette with any number songs and lyric sheet. SASE. Reports in 2 weeks.
Music: Mostly blues, MOR and top 40/pop; also country, dance-oriented, easy listening, folk and jazz. Published "Falling in Love," (by Brian Downen), "A Part of You," (by B. Downen/Randy Lakeman), and "Into the Night," (by Nicole Robinette), all recorded by D. Darrow on Mighty Records (rock ballads).
Tips: "Listen to top 40 and write current lyrics and music."

ROCKLAND MUSIC, INC., 117 W. Rockland, Libertyville IL 60048. (312)362-4060. Contact: Perry or Rick Johnson. Music publisher, record company and record producer. BMI. Publishes 5 songs/year. Pays standard royalty.
How to Contact: Prefers cassette with 5 songs and lyric sheet. Reports in 8 weeks.
Music: Mostly rock/pop, dance/R&B and country; also blues. Published "This Feels Like Love to Me," (by C. Sermay), recorded by S. Distel (pop).

ROCKMORE MUSIC, 1733 Carmona Ave., Los Angeles CA 90019. (213)933-6521. Contact: Willie H. Rocquemore. Music publisher and record company. BMI. Publishes 5 songs/year; publishes 5 new songwriters/year. Pays 10% royalties USA; 50% foreign countries.
How to Contact: Prefers cassette with maximum 4 songs and lyric sheet. "We request photo of writers." SASE. Reports in 2 months.
Music: Mostly ballads, pop, rock and blues; also dance-oriented, R&B, soul and top 40. Published "Crumb-Jumpers," and "Cry Any More," recorded by Pam Baity on Rockin' Records; and "Any Thing He Can Do," by Jimmy Holiday on Rockin' Records.

*ROCKOKO MUSIC GMBH, Nordendstr. 30, Frankfurt/Main 6000 West Germany. Phone: (69)55 26 32. Managing Director: Peter Hauke. Music publisher and record producer (Rockoko Production). GEMA. Publishes 80 songs/year; publishes 2 new songwriters/year. Works with composers and lyricists; teams collaborators. Pays standard royalty.
How to Contact: Prefers cassette and lyric sheet. Does not return unsolicited material. Reports in 1 month.
Music: Mostly rock and pop. Published "Live Wire" (by T. Carey), recorded by Jennifer Rush on CBS Records (rock); "I Wanna Look in Your Eyes (by Craaft/Carey), recorded by Craaft on Epic Records (rock); and "We Wanna Live," written and recorded by Tony Carey on MCA Records (rock).

ROCKSONG, 152 Goldthorn Hill, Penn., Wolverhampton WV2 3JA England. (902)345345. A&R Manager: David Roberts. Music publisher, record company (FM-Revolver Records and labels in United Kingdom, Japan, Canada and Europe) and record producer. PRS, MCPS, MRS, MPA. Publishes 200 songs/year; publishes 3 new songwriters/year. Pays negotiable royalty.
Affiliates: Heavy Metal Music, Andersong Music.
How to Contact: Prefers cassette (or VHS/Beta PAL System videocassette) with 3 songs. "Send photos and bios if also an artist." Does not return unsolicited material. Reports in 1 month.
Music: Hard rock, "chart-oriented material" and AOR. Published "Call It Democracy," written and recorded by Bruce Cockburn on Revolver Records (pop/rock); "Metal Queen," written and recorded by Lee Aaron on Virgin 10 Records (hard rock); and "Hellbound" (by Pesch), recorded by Warlock on Phonogram Records (heavy metal).
Tips: Submit "solid, killer songs that have international chart potential."

ROMAR MUSIC PUBLISHING CO., (Div. of Ronin Music Records, Inc.), 445 Grand Blvd., Massapequa Park NY 11762. (516)541-7870. General Manager: Robert Giorgi. Music publisher and record company (Ronin Music Records Inc.). BMI. Publishes 12 songs/year; publishes 6 new songwriters/year. Pays standard royalty.
How to Contact: Prefers cassette and lyric or lead sheets. Does not return unsolicited material. Reports in 8 weeks.
Music: Mostly contemporary, country and rock; also blues. Published "Someday," "Only a Fool," and "I Must Remember" recorded by Don Masi on Ronin Records (contemporary/country).

ROOTS MUSIC, Box 111, Sea Bright NJ 07760. President: Robert Bowden. Music publisher. BMI. Publishes 4 songs/year; publishes 1 new songwriter/year. Works with composers and lyricists; teams collaborators. Pays standard royalty.
How to Contact: Prefers cassette (or videocassette) with any number songs and lyric sheet. "I only want inspired songs written by talented writers." SASE. Reports in 1 month.
Music: Mostly country and pop; also church/religious, classical, folk, MOR, progressive, rock (soft, mellow) and top 40. Published "Always," and "Make Believe," (by Toy), recorded by Marco/Sision (pop); and "Henry C," written and recorded by Robert Bowden (pop).

ROPERRY MUSIC, 645 Madison Ave., New York NY 10022. (212)836-4437. General Manager: Jane Lowy. Music publisher, record company, record producer and personal management firm. BMI. Publishes varying number of songs/year; publishes 2 new songwriters/year. Pays standard royalty and uses standard publishing contract.
How to Contact: Call first about your interest. Prefers cassette with 1-3 songs. "Tell a little about yourself and include lyric sheets." SASE. Reports in 3 weeks.

Music: Mostly top 40/pop, MOR and easy listening; also children's and dance-oriented. Published "Just A Little Imagination," (by Patsy Maharam), recorded by Patsy (pop and adult contemporary); "Single Again," (by P. Maharam), recorded by Joey Latini (pop); and "You Are the Sun (Keep On Shining)," by Joey Latini.

Tips: "Song should be a complete tune—not just a beat or rhythm. It's not necessary to have a full-blown production; a simple piano/vocal, guitar/vocal is fine."

ROSE HILL GROUP, 1326 Midland Ave., Syracuse NY 13205. (315)475-2936. A&R Director: Vincent Taft. Music publisher and record producer. BMI and ASCAP. Publishes 12 songs/year; publishes 2 new songwriters/year. Works with composers and lyricists; teams collaborators. Pays standard royalty.

Affiliates: Katch Nazar Music (ASCAP) and Bleecker Street Music (BMI).

How to Contact: Prefers cassette with 1-5 songs and lyric sheet. SASE. Reports in 2 weeks.

Music: Mostly top 40/pop, rock, dance; also MOR and jazz. Published "Hot Button" (by D. Chen), recorded by Prowlers on Star City Records (dance R&B); "Free World" (by A. George), recorded by Z-Team on Garage Records (dance pop); and "So What?" (by E. Danielian), recorded by Io on D.O.A. Records (dance rock).

Tips: Submit "simple, memorable, melodic songs with convincing lyrics. No long songs or instrumental breaks."

ROSETTE MUSIC LTD., 5/6 Lombard St., Dublin 2 Ireland. (01)779046/779244. General Manager: Michael O'Riordan. Music publisher, record company (Ritz Records) and record producer. PRS (London), MCDS. Publishes 20 songs/year; publishes 7-10 new songwriters/year. Pays standard royalty.

Affiliate: Emma Music Ltd. (PRS/MCPS).

How to Contact: Prefers cassette and lyric sheet. "No more than 4 songs at one time." Does not return unsolicited material. Reports in 4 weeks.

Music: Mostly MOR/commercial, country and pop; also "standards." Published "She Sang the Melody" (by Sheerin), recorded by Ray Lynam (country); "Unconditional Surrender," written and recorded by FastLane (pop); and "On My Own," written and recorded by Luv Bug (pop) all on Ritz Records.

BRIAN ROSS MUSIC, Box 2950, Hollywood CA 90078. President/Professional Manager: Brian Ross. Music publisher, record company (Starborn Records), record producer and worldwide music representatives and administrators. BMI; also member of all foreign performance societies. Member CCC, AIMP, NARAS. Publishes 250-300 songs/year; publishes 90% new songwriters/year. Sometimes hires staff writers. Works with composers and lyricists; teams collaborators. Pays standard royalty, cash bonuses and advances.

Affiliates: Thrush (BMI), New High (ASCAP) and IMC (ASCAP), and Record, Video and Film Music (ASCAP).

How to Contact: Prefers cassette (or videocassette) with 1-6 songs and lyric sheet. Print your name on both cassette and cassette box. SASE. "Please send champion clasp envelope with all SASEs. A video makes the presentation personal—very simple and inexpensive is best." Does not assume responsibility for materials lost or damaged in the mail. Reports ASAP.

Music: Mostly dance music, techno-pop and top 40; also contemporary, MOR, disco and new wave. Published "I'm on Fire" (by Robert Jason), recorded by Barry White on CBS Records (ballad); "Talk Talk" (by Bonniwell), recorded by Music Machine on Rhino Records (pop); and "I'm Waiting for You," written and recorded by Lance Powers on Starborn Records (rock).

Tips: "Have a good hook and send up-tempo dance music only! No ballads!"

ROUND SOUND MUSIC, 1918 Wise Dr., Dothan AL 36303. (205)794-9067. President: Jerry Wise. Music publisher. BMI. Member CMA, GMA. Publishes 10-20 songs/year, publishes 5-10 new songwriters/year. Pays standard royalty.

How to Contact: Write first about your interest. Prefers 7½ ips reel-to-reel or cassette with 1-6 songs and lyric sheet. SASE. Reports in 1 month.

Music: Mostly country; also easy listening, MOR, rock, soul and top 40/pop. Published "Cheatin Side of Town," written and recorded by Richard Hoover on Raven Records (country).

Tips: "Songs must be commercial."

ROYAL FLAIR PUBLISHING, 106 Navajo, Council Bluffs IA 51501. (712)366-1136. President: Bob Everhart. Music publisher and record producer. BMI. Publishes 5-10 songs/year; publishes 1-2 new songwriters/year. Pays standard royalty.

How to Contact: Query. Prefers cassette with 2-6 songs. SASE. Reports in 6 weeks.

Music: Traditional country, bluegrass and folk. Published "Hero of Gringo Trail," "Time After Time," and "None Come Near," written and recorded by R. Everhart on Folkways; and "Smoky Mountain Heartbreak," written and recorded by Bonnie Sanford on Folkways (all country).

Tips: "Song definitely has to have old-time country flavor with all the traditional values of country music. No sex, outlandish swearing, or drugs-booze type songs accepted. We have an annual Hank Williams Songwriting Contest and winners are granted publishing."

S.M.C.L. PRODUCTIONS, INC., Box 84, Boucherville, Quebec J4B 5E6 Canada. (514)641-2266. President: Christian Lefort. Music publisher and record company. CAPAC. Publishes 100 songs/year.
Affiliates: A.Q.E.M. Ltee (CAPAC), Bag Enrg. (CAPAC), C.F. Music (CAPAC), Big Bazaar Music (CAPAC), Sunrise Music (CAPAC), Stage One Music (CAPAC), L.M.S. Ltee (CAPAC), ITT Music (CAPAC), Machine Music (CAPAC), Dynamite Music (CAPAC), Danava Music (PRO/SDE), Coincidence Music (PRO/SDE), and Music and Music (CAPAC).
How to Contact: Prefers 7½ ips reel-to-reel with 4-12 songs and lead sheet. SAE and IRC. Reports in 1 month.
Music: Dance, easy listening, MOR, top 40/pop and TV and movie soundtracks. Published "Where Is My Man," recorded by the Eartha Kitt on Able Records (dance); and "Sex Over the Phone," recorded by Village People on Celsius Records (dance).

LARRY SABISTON MUSIC, 1419 S. 25th St., Terre Haute IN 47803. (812)238-9841. President: Larry Sabiston. BMI. Music publisher, record company and record producer. Publishes 26 songs/year; publishes 15 new songwriters/year. Pays standard royalty.
How to Contact: Prefers cassette with 1-3 songs and lyric or lead sheet. Copyrighted material only. "An SASE with proper postage is a must or material will not be reviewed." Reports in 8 weeks.
Music: Mostly humorous, Latin pop and Christmas. Published "Songs That'll Make 'Em Laugh!" (by various artists) on Airit Records; "Love Songs and Guitars," written and recorded by Stephen Michael Portugal on Airit International Records; and "When My Baby Says It's Alright" (by Helen Poe and Phil Coley), recorded by Phil Coley on Airit International Records.
Tips: "We look for 'belly-laugh', humorous songs—anything that'll make 'em laugh! We like songs with good hooks, catchy melodies and tight, polished lyrics."

SABRE MUSIC, Box 702, Snowdon Station, Montreal, Quebec H3X 3X8 Canada. Professional General Manager: D. Leonard. Music publisher. CAPAC. Member MIEA. Pays standard royalty.
Affiliate: Montina Music (CAPAC).
How to Contact: Prefers 7½ or 15 ips reel-to-reel, cassette or record and lyric sheet. Does not return unsolicited material.
Music: Mostly top 40; also blues, country, dance-oriented, easy listening, folk, gospel, jazz, MOR, progressive, R&B, rock, soul and pop.

SALMO MUSIC, 331 E. 9th St., New York NY 10003. (212)473-7833. President: S.J. Mollica. ASCAP. Music publisher. Publishes 10 songs/year; publishes 1-2 new songwriters/year. Pays standard royalty.
How to Contact: Write first and obtain permission to submit. Include SASE.

*TRACY SANDS MUSIC SALES, Suite 119, 2170 W. Broadway, Anaheim CA 92804. (714)491-8546. Artist Relations: Leonard Horowitz. Music publisher, record company (Torchlight Records) and record producer (Gee Productions). BMI. Publishes 24 songs/year; publishes 4 new songwriters/year. Works with composers and lyricists; teams collaborators. Pays standard royalty or negotiates contract.
Affiliates: Bastion Music (BMI), Robert Wahlsteen Music (ASCAP) and Gee Music, Ltd. (PRS).
How to Contact: Prefers cassette with 3-4 songs and lyric sheet. SASE. Reports in 6 weeks.
Music: Mostly love songs, novelty and seasonal; also instrumental and gospel. Published "The Comet" (by Robert Wahlsteen), recorded by Wahlsteen and Sands on Torchlite Records (New Age); "Black Will Be the Color" and "Warriors of the Night" (both by Tom Harris), recorded by Manhunter on Torchlite Records (country).
Tips: "A sense of humor is essential."

SASHA SONGS, UNLTD. & THE GRAND PASHA PUBLISHER, Division of The Pasha Music Org., Inc., 5615 Melrose, Hollywood CA 90038. (213)466-3507. President: Spencer D. Proffer. General Manager: Carol Peters. Music publisher, record production company and independent label distributed by CBS. BMI. Publishes 100 songs/year; publishes 3-4 new songwriters/year. Pays standard royalty.

 The asterisk before a listing indicates that the listing is new in this edition. New markets are often the most receptive to freelance submissions.

How to Contact: Write first. Include SASE for submission policy. Send material to A&R Director. Prefers cassette with 2-3 songs. Reports in 3 weeks.
Music: Mostly rock; also progressive. Published "Hot Cherie" (by Randy Bishop et al), recorded by Danny Spanos (rock); "Up the Creek" (by R. Nielsen and R. Bishop), recorded by Cheap Trick (rock); and "The Heat" (by R. Bishop), recorded by Heart (rock).
Tips: "Song needs strong conceptual lyrics; get a great industry attorney."

SATRIL MUSIC, 444 Finchley Rd., London, NW2 2HY, England. (01)435-8063. Professional Manager: Beverley King. PRS, MCPS. Music publisher, record company (Satril Records, Big Red Records, Crash Records), and record producer (Henry Hadaway Organization). Publishes 20 songs/year; publishes 2-3 new songwriters/year. Pays standard royalty.
Affiliates: Torill Music, Casino Music, Sava Music.
How to Contact: Prefers cassette. SASE.
Music: Mostly pop, rock, soul, disco and "chart material of all kinds."

SCORE PRODUCTIONS, INC., 1790 Century Blvd. NE., Atlanta GA 30345. (404)636-1211. President: Bob May. A&R Director: Darrel Evans. Music publisher and record company (Perfect Pitch). Publishes 50 songs/year; publishes 5 new songwriters/year. Pays standard royalty.
Affiliates: Deaf Monkey, Ape's Hit.
How to Contact: Prefers cassette with 3 songs and lyric sheet.
Music: "All styles except gospel."

SCOTTI BROTHERS MUSIC PUBLISHING, 2114 Pico Blvd., Santa Monica CA 90405. (213)450-4143. Professional Manager: Richie Wise. Music publisher and record company. BMI, ASCAP. Member NMPA, AIMP, RIAA and CMA. Publishes 40 songs/year; publishes 2 new songwriters/year. Pays standard royalty.
Affiliates: Flowering Stone and Holy Moley.
How to Contact: Prefers cassette with 1-2 songs and lyric sheet. Does not return unsolicited material; "we report only if we're interested."
Music: Mostly top 40/pop and country; also easy listening, MOR and rock. Published "Eye of the Tiger" (by J. Peterick/F. Sullivan), recorded by Survivor on Scotti Bros.-CBS Records (rock); "How Do You Fall Out of Love," recorded by Janie Fricke on CBS Records (country-pop); and "Them Good Ol' Boys Are Bad" (J. Harrington/J. Pennig), recorded by John Schneider on Scotti Bros.-CBS Records (country).

SCRAMROCK MUSIC CO., 139 E. Harding Rd., Springfield OH 45504. (513)399-6708. Professional Manager: Robert T. "Dusty" Jones. Music publisher. BMI. Publishes 4-5 songs/year; publishes 3-4 new songwriters/year. Works with composers and lyricists; teams collaborators. Pays standard royalty.
How to Contact: Prefers cassette (or videocassette). "Include photo of artist or group." SASE. Reports in less than 1 week.
Music: Mostly heavy metal, thrash metal and hard rock; also commercial rock and melodic ballads. Published "Out of the Ashes," and "We Rock to Rock," (by S. Wallace/B. Bodine/C. Weiser); and "With You All Along" (by Chris Weiser), all recorded by War Minister (all heavy metal).
Tips: Submit "hard driving, high energy tunes with good catchy hooks and melodies."

SCREEN GEMS/EMI MUSIC, INC., 6920 Sunset, Hollywood CA 90028. (213)469-8371. Professional Department: Lisa Wells. Music publisher.
How to Contact: Write or call first and obtain permission to submit. Prefers cassette with 3-4 songs and lyric sheet. SASE. Reports in 6 weeks.
Music: Mostly pop/top 40, rock and R&B; also country.
Tips: "We get our songs recorded by all kinds of artists. Good quality demos help!"

SCULLY MUSIC CO., 800 S. 4th St., Philadelphia PA 19147. (215)755-7000. President: Walter Kahn. Music publisher and record production company. Member AGAC. Publishes 50 songs/year; publishes 20 new songwriters/year. ASCAP, BMI. Works with composers and lyricists; teams collaborators. Pays standard royalty.
Affiliate: Orange Bear Music (BMI).
How to Contact: Prefers 7½ ips reel-to-reel, or cassette (or VHS or ¾" videocassette) with 1-4 songs and lyric sheet or lead sheet. Prefers studio produced demos. SASE. Reports in 1 month.
Music: Mostly dance, pop, R&B; also MOR, top 40 and rock. Published "Love Stimulation," (by Monahan/Stokes/George), recorded by David St. George on Malaco Records (R&B); "Do You Have a Car," (by L. Williams), recorded by Kid Seville on Salsoul Records (R&B); and "Deetour," (by A. Cohen), recorded by Karen Young on Atlantic Records (pop).
Tips: Need songs that "suit the styles of the artists on the roster of affiliated Sunshine Records."

SEA DREAM MUSIC, 236 Sebert Rd., Forest Gate, London E7 0NP England. (01)534-8500. Senior Partner: Simon Law. PRS. Music publisher and record company (Plankton Records). Publishes 50 songs/year; publishes 2 new songwriters/year. Pays 66²/₃% royalty.
Affiliates: Scarf Music Publishing, Really Free Music, Ernvik Musik (Sweden) and Light Factory Productions.
How to Contact: Prefers cassette with 3 songs and lyric sheet. "Technical information about the recording is useful, as are the songwriter's expectations of the company—i.e., what they want us to do for them." SAE and IRC. Reports in 6 weeks.
Music: Mostly funk/rock, rock and blues; also gospel. Published "Shameful Secret," and "Distance Grows," written and recorded by Pete Ward; and "Anti-Anti" (by Rue Randall), recorded by Solid Air (pop rock), all on Plankton Records.
Tips: "We are specifically interested in material with a Christian bias to the lyrics."

AUGUST SEITH MUSIKVERLAGE, Haydnstrasse 2, D-8000 Munich Germany. (089)53 09 331. Music publisher. Publishes 150 songs/year.
Affiliates: Edition Riva, Palma Musikverlag, Florida Muskverlag.
How to Contact: Prefers cassette. Does not return unsolicited material.
Music: Published "Du Schönes Europa," (by Rudi Redl), recorded by Andreas Hauff on Koch (pop).

SEIXAS MUSIC, Box 1732, Murray Hill Station, New York NY 10156. (718)528-1760. Contact: Ron Seixas. Music publisher. BMI. Publishes variable number of songs/year; publishes 2 new songwriters/year. Pays standard royalty.
How to Contact: Prefers cassette (or Beta videocassette) with 2 songs and lyric sheet. SASE. Reports in 3 week.
Music: Mostly "rock music with top 40 appeal and new music." Published "Even Exchange" (by R. Seixas), recorded by Cynthia (dance rock); "Hours" (by R. Seixas), recorded by Megabite (instrumental/new wave); and "Bright Light" (by R. Seixas), recorded by Seixas (dance rock), all on Cargo Records.

SELLWOOD PUBLISHING, 170 N. Maple, Fresno CA 93702. (209)255-1717. Owner: Stan Anderson. Music publisher and record company (Trac Record Co.). BMI. Publishes 10 songs/year; publishes 5 new songwriters/year. Pays standard royalty.
How to Contact: Prefers cassette (or VHS videocassette) with 2-4 songs and lyric sheet. Reports in 2 months.
Music: Country, top 40 and rock. Published "Consider It Sold," and "Polish Up My Buckle," (by Thomas Richard Lewis), recorded by Buddy T. Lewis; and "Rodeo Man" (by Jerry Hobbs), recorded by Jessica James, all on Trac Records (all country).

SEYCHELLES MUSIC, Box 13 01 44, Cologne 1 D-5000 West Germany. (0221)72 01 79. Managing Director: Walther Kahl. Music publisher. GEMA. Publishes 40-50 songs/year; publishes 2-3 new songwriters/year. Pays standard royalty.
How to Contact: Prefers cassette and lyric sheet. Reports in 3 weeks.
Music: MOR, rock and country.

LARRY SHAYNE ENTERPRISES, Suite 120, 1334 Lincoln Blvd., Santa Monica CA 90401. (213)395-6680. Music publisher. ASCAP. Member SGA. Publishes 50 songs/year; publishes 20 new songwriters/year. Works with composers and lyricists. Pays standard royalty.
Affiliate: Workers Union Music (BMI).
How to Contact: Prefers cassette (or videocassette) and lyric sheet. "I will not return cassettes unless SASE is enclosed." Reports in 2 weeks.
Music: Mostly pop, R&B and country; also easy listening, top 40 and MOR. Published "A House Is Not a Home" (by Bacharach/David), recorded by Luther Vandross on Epic Records (MOR/R&B); "Think Again" (by Chris Boardman), recorded by Wishful Thinking on Pausa Records (jazz); and "What I Did for Love" (by Hamlisch/Kleban), recorded by Johnny Mathis on CBS records (MOR).
Tips: "Be very critical about your own material and try to find the flaws in the song before you submit it to us. We are only interested in 'great' songs not good ones."

*SHOTGUN MUSIC CORP., 1242 Colborne St. E., Brantford, Ontario N3T 5L4 Canada. (519)752-0839. President: Len Wilde. Music publisher, record company (Shotgun/Empire/Listen/Gator), record producer and recording studio. PRO CAN, CAPAC, SESAC. Publishes 50 new songwriters/year. Works with composers and lyricists. Pays standard royalty.
Affiliates: Like Always Music (PRO CAN), West Star Music (CAPAC), Wild Beach Music (SESAC).

How to Contact: Prefers cassette with 3 songs and lyric or lead sheet. SAE and IRC. Reports in 1 month.
Music: Mostly pop, country and rock; also gospel.

SIEBENPUNKT VERLAGS GMBH, Habsburger Platz 1, D-8000 München 40 West Germany. (89)33 1808. General Manager: Mr. Schmidt. Music publisher. GEMA. Publishes 250 songs/year; publishes 7 new songwriters/year. Pays standard royalty or by contract.
How to Contact: Prefers cassette (or VHS videocassette) with 1-2 songs. SAE and IRC. Reports in 3 weeks.
Music: Rock, dance and pop; also fusion-jazz. Published "On the Air Tonight," (by Peter Bardens), recorded by Willy Finlayson; and "Solo" (by Peter Bardens), recorded by Leo Sayer.
Tips: "Get in contact with us as quickly as possible."

SIEGAL MUSIC COMPANIES, 2 Hochlstr, 80 Munich 8000 West Germany. 089-984926. Managing Director: Joachim Neubauer. Music publisher, record company, (Jupiter Records) and record producer. GEMA. Publishes 5,000 songs/year; publishes 20-30 new songwriters/year. Employs songwriters on a salary basis.
Affiliates: Many affiliates, including E. Meridian, Step One (Holland), Step Two (Austria), Step Four (France) and Yellowbird (Switzerland).
How to Contact: Prefers cassette. SAE and IRC. Reports in 8 weeks.
Music: Mostly pop, disco and MOR; also country and soul. Published "Fly Robin Fly" (by Levay), recorded by Silver Convention on Jupiter (disco); "A Little Peace" (by Siegel), recorded by Nicole on Jupiter (ballad); and "Mania Magdalena" (by Cretu), recorded by Sandra on Virgin (pop).

SILICON MUSIC PUBLISHING CO., Ridgewood Park Estates, 222 Tulane St., Garland TX 75043. President: Gene Summers. Vice President: Deanna L. Summers. Public Relations: Steve Summers. Music publisher. BMI. Publishes 10-20 songs/year; publishes 2-3 new songwriters/year. Pays standard royalty.
How to Contact: Prefers cassette with 1-2 songs. Does not return unsolicited material. "We are usually slow in answering due to overseas tours."
Music: Mostly rockabilly and 50s material; also country and MOR. Published "Ready to Ride/Ode to a Stuntman" (from the HBO presentation "Backlot"), written and recorded by Pat Minter on Domino Records; "Loco Cat," (by Eddie Hill/Tom Toms), recorded by Gene Summers on White Label; and "Love Me Til I Do," written and recorded by Joe Hardin Brown on Domino Records.
Tips: "We are very interested in 50s rock and rockabilly *original masters* for release through overseas affiliates. If you are the owner of any 50s masters, contact us first! We have releases in Holland, Switzerland, England, Belgium, France, Sweden, Norway and Australia. We have the market if you have the tapes!"

SILVERFOOT PUBLISHING, 4225 Palm St., Baton Rouge LA 70808. (504)383-7885. President: Barrie Edgar. BMI. Music publisher, record company (Gulfstream Records) and record producer (Hogar Musical Productions). Publishes 10-30 songs/year; publishes 1-5 new songwriters/year. Pays standard royalty.
How to Contact: Prefers cassette with maximum 4 songs and lyric sheet. "Patience required on reporting time."
Music: Mostly rock, blues ("not soul") and country. Published "You," (by Liscomb/Ratzlaff); "Leave You Girl," (by R. Liscomb); and "Picture on Page Ten," (by G. Ratzlaff); all recorded by B. Edgar on Cicadelic Records (rock).

SIVATT MUSIC PUBLISHING CO., Box 7172, Greenville SC 29610. (803) 269-3961. President: Jesse B. Evatte. Music publisher. BMI. Publishes 20 songs/year; publishes 5 new songwriters/year. Pays standard royalty.
How to Contact: Prefers cassette with 3-4 songs and lyric sheet. SASE. Reports in 6 weeks.
Music: Gospel. Published "Sittin' On Ready" (by Larry Orr) and "He Leads Me Higher" (by Mae Jernigan), both recorded by Jesse Evatte on Mark Five Records (gospel); and "I Believe the Promise" (by Mike Lyle), recorded by Dixieland Quartet on Dixieland Records (gospel).

SLATER PICHINSON MUSIC, INC., Box 1042, Studio City CA 91604-0042. (818)980-6800. President; Martin Pichinson. BMI, ASCAP and all foreign societies. Music publisher. Publishes varying number of songs/year; publishes varying number of songwriters/year. Employs songwriters on a salary basis. Pays standard royalty.
Affiliates: Songs of Cash, SlaPich Music, Black Cabinet Music, Lifeboat Music, Veridian Music and Family of Man.

How to Contact: Prefers cassette with 2-5 songs and lyric and lead sheets. Does not return unsolicited material.
Music: Mostly country, pop and rock; also gospel, children's and hard rock. Published "Be Bop on the Beach," (by Mike Love), recorded by The Flirts on Polydor for *Karate Kid* (pop); "Goin' Down Hill," (by Y. Lincoln), recorded by John Anderson (country); and "Heaven Sounding Sweeter," (by The Deweys), recorded by Jimmy Swaggert on Jim Records (gospel).
Tips: "We also purchase established music catalogs."

*SNOWTOWN MUSIC, 312 Washington Ave. N., Minneapolis MN 55401. (612)339-4741. President: Owen Husney. Music publisher, record company (American Artists/CBS Records/A&M Records), record producer (American Artists Productions) and management firm (American Artists Management). ASCAP. Estab. 1986. Publishes 10-20 songs/year; publishes 3 new songwriters/year. Employs songwriters on a salary basis. Works with composers and lyricists; teams collaborators. "Each royalty is different."
Affilite: Almo Irving Publishing.
How to Contact: Prefers cassette (or VHS videocassette) with 3 songs. SASE. Reports in 2 months.
Music: Mostly R&B, pop and rock; also music for soundtracks (film).
Tips: "In the beginning it is a good idea to pay attention to universal meaning in your songs as well as song structure."

SNUGGLEBUSH MUSIC COMPANY, Suite 12C, 124 W. 60th St., New York NY 10025. Assistant to President: Karen Koster. Music publisher and record producer. BMI, ASCAP. Publishes 50 songs/year; publishes 2 new songwriters/year. Pays standard royalty or negotiates payment.
Affiliates: Snugglebug (ASCAP) and Iren Koster Music (BMI).
How to Contact: Prefers cassette (or videocassette) with 2 songs and lyric sheet. "SASE if it's to be returned." Reports in 2 weeks.
Music: Dance, easy listening, MOR, R&B and top 40/pop. Published "Rainbows," (by I. Koster), recorded by Jack Jones (pop); "I Won't Forget . . .," (by I. Koster), recorded by Stylistics (R&B); and "Superwoman," (by I. Koster), recorded by Dells (R&B).

SOCIETE D'EDITIONS MUSICALES ET ARTISTIQUES "ESPERANCE", 85 Rue Fondary, Paris 75015 France. (1) 45 77 30 34. Manager: Michel David. Music publisher and record company. SACEM/SDRM. Publishes 200 songs/year. Pays standard royalty.
How to Contact: Prefers cassette. SAE and IRC. Reports in 4 weeks.
Music: African, West Indian and salsa music. Published "Chefo Mae Mae," written and recorded by Kaba Mane; "Ne Nde," written and recorded by Ngalle Jojo; and "Mboa Su," written and recorded by Kossas, all on Esperance Records (all African).
Tips: "Only interested in songwriters/singers."

SONG FARM MUSIC, Box 24561, Nashville TN 37202. (615)321-4875. President: Tom Pallardy. Music publisher and record producer. BMI. Member NSAI. Publishes 2-3 songs/year; publishes 1-2 new songwriters/year. Pays standard royalty.
How to Contact: Prefers cassette with maximum 2 songs and lyric or lead sheet. SASE required. Reports in 1 month.
Music: Mostly country, R&B and pop; also crossover and top 40. Published "Another Heartache" (by Annette Lumsden), recorded by Carl Finney (country); "When I Close My Eyes," by Stephen Younger (country/MOR); and "I'm Squealin'," by Joyce Tamburine/Donna Battistone (country).
Tips: "Material should be submitted neatly and professionally with as good quality demo as possible. Songs need not be elaborately produced (voice and guitar/piano are fine) but they should be clear. Songs must be well constructed, lyrically tight, good strong hook, interesting melody, easily remembered; i.e., commercial!"

SONG TAILORS MUSIC CO., Box 2631, Muscle Shoals AL 35662-2631. (205)381-1455. Contact: Billy Lawson. Music publisher. BMI. Publishes 100 songs/year; publishes 1-2 new songwriters/year. Pays standard royalty.
Affiliates: I've Got the Music (ASCAP), Terry Woodford Music (ASCAP), and Creative Source Music (BMI).
How to Contact: Prefers cassette with 2 songs and lyric sheet. SASE. Reports "as soon as possible. No certified mail accepted."
Music: Mostly country, top 40/pop, country pop and R&B; also dance, easy listening, MOR, progressive, rock and soul. Published "Angel In Your Arms," (a million-performance song by Terry Woodford/Clayton Ivey/Tom Brasfield), recorded by Barbara Mandrell on MCA Records (country/pop); "End of the Lyin'," (by Robert Byrne/Alan Schulman), recorded by Alabama on RCA Records (coun-

try/pop); and "I Didn't Hear the Thunder," by Sue Richards recorded by Billy "Crash" Craddock on MCA/DOT Records (country).
Tips: "Be up-to-date with current artists' styles."

SON-TON MUSIC, 11 N. Perry St., New Riegel OH 44853. (419)435-6525 or 595-2677. Professional Manager: Rex H. Felton. Music publisher, record company and record producer. ASCAP. Publishes 12 songs/year; publishes 4 new songwriters/year. Pays standard royalty.
Affiliate: Fresh Air Music.
How to Contact: Prefers cassette with 2-8 songs and lyric sheet. SASE. Reports in 1 month.
Music: Mostly rock; also bluegrass, church/religious, country, dance-oriented, MOR, soul and top 40/pop. Published "Bottom of the Bottle" (by Fred Blackstone), recorded by Buzz Coady (country); and (rock); and "Boffo" (by G. McGladdfry), recorded by Other Half (rock).
Tips: "Try to contact me personally. Find a group to record your song."

*SOUND CEREMONY RECORDS, 28 South, Villas, London NW1 9BT England. Phone: (01)486-2240 or 405-9883. Director: R.W. Ganderton. Music publisher and record producer (Celestial Sound Productions). PRS. Publishes various number of songs and new songwriters/year. Works with composers and lyricists; teams collaborators. Pays standard or negotiable royalty.
Affiliate: Centridge Publishing.
How to Contact: Prefers cassette (or videocassette) and lyric sheet. SAE and IRC. Reports in 3 weeks.
Music: Mostly rock, pop and country; also jazz and soul. Published "Giggle Amidst the Teary" on Centridge Records (rock); "Your Breaking My Heart" on Celestial Sound Records (rock); and "Dream Girl" on Sound Ceremony Records (pop), all by R.W. Ganderton and recorded by Sound Ceremony.

SOUND COLUMN COMPANIES, 160 Westgate Fine Arts Center, 342 W. Second South, Salt Lake City UT 84101. (801)355-5327. Professional Manager: Clive Romney. Music publisher. BMI, ASCAP, SESAC. Member CMA. Publishes 50 songs/year; publishes 2 new songwriters/year. Hires staff writers. Works with composers and lyricists; teams collaborators. Pays standard royalty.
Affiliates: Ronarte Publications (ASCAP), Mountain Green Music (BMI), Macanudo Music (SESAC), Sound Column Productions and SCP Records.
How to Contact: Query first. Prefers cassette with 1-3 songs and lyric sheet. SASE. Reports as time permits.
Music: Mostly pop, country and A/C; also all other styles. Published "Someone's Watching You" (by Simpson/Romney/Simpson), recorded by Dave Beckstrand on SCP Records (contemporary gospel); "Talk to Me" (by Clive Romney), recorded by Jenny Reece on Breeze Records (pop); and "That's You and That's Me" (by Simpson/Romney), recorded by Cody Hale on SCP Records (pop).
Tips: "We very rarely accept outside submissions so be careful about song form and quality of demo."

SOUND IMAGE PUBLISHING, 6556 Wilkinson, North Hollywood CA 91606. (818)762-8881. President: Martin John Eberhardt. Vice President: David Chatfield. Music publisher, record company, record producer and video company. BMI. Member NARAS. Publishes 60 songs/year; publishes 10 new songwriters/year. Pays standard royalty.
How to Contact: Prefers cassette (or VHS or Beta videocassette) with 2-6 songs and lyric sheet. Does not return unsolicited material. Reports in 2 months.
Music: Mostly rock; also dance, R&B and top 40/pop. Published "Good Woman's Love," written and recorded by Mark Steed on Sound Image Records (country); and "Oh Marie," and "Rush In The Night" (by Jack Conrad), recorded by Alp on Sound Image Records (rock).
Tips: "Demos should be professionally recorded. We suggest 16-24 track recording on cassette submissions."

*SOURWOOD MUSIC, 773 Hoop Pole Rd., Guilford CT 06437. (203)457-0881. President: Phil Rosenthal. Music publisher. BMI. Publishes 6 songs/year; publishes 2 new songwriters/year. Works with composers and lyricists; teams collaborators. Pays standard royalty.
How to Contact: Prefers cassette and lyric sheet. SASE. Reports in 3 weeks.
Music: Mostly children's music, folk and country; also bluegrass. Published "Muddy Water" (by P. Rosenthal), recorded Johnny Cash on Columbia Records (country); "Snowy Day," written and recorded by P. Rosenthal on American Melody Records (children's); and "Open Up the Window" (by P. Rosenthal), recorded by the Seldom Scene on Sugar Hill Records (bluegrass).

SOUTHERN MOST PUBLISHING CO., Box 40276, Overland Park KS 66204. (913)362-2242. President: Dann E. Haworth. Music publisher. BMI. Publishes 10 songs/year; publishes 5 new songwriters/year. Pays standard royalty.

How to Contact: Prefers cassette or 7½ or 15 ips reel-to-reel with 5-6 songs and lyric or lead sheets. SASE. Reports in 1 month.
Music: Mostly rock (no heavy metal), country and gospel; also blues, jazz and folk. Published "Give Them a Chance," "Walking Real Slowly," "Really Like to Hold You," and "People Are Changing," all by Monty Dale Luke (country); "Good Love," by John Rivetti (rock); and "I Should Have Gone and Stayed in Love," by Lloyd Conn (bluegrass).

SPECTRUM ONE MUSIC,(A division of Spectrum 1 Network Inc.,) Box 7464, Burbank CA 91510. A&R Director: Richard De A'Morelli. Music publisher and record company (Reliance Records). BMI, ASCAP. Publishes 10-12 songs/year; publishes 2-5 new songwriters/year. Pays standard royalty.
Affiliates: Shadow Three Music and Seven Palms Music.
How to Contact: Submit demo tape by mail; cassette only. SASE. Reports in 3 months.
Music: Funk/dance, and disco. Published "You're My Fantasy," (by K. McGettigan), recorded by Marisa on Reliance Records (dance).
Tips: "No unsolicited phone calls. Material cannot be returned without SASE. Submit in our main areas of interest only. We have seen country bluegrass, waltzes, ballads and other material that has nothing at all to do with the dance, which is our one and only interest at this time."

SPHEMUSATIONS, 12 Northfield Rd., Onehouse, Stowmarket Suffolk 1P14 3HF England. General Manager: James Butt. Music publisher. Publishes 200 songs/year; publishes 6 new songwriters/year. Pays by arrangement.
How to Contact: Submit demo tape by mail. Prefers cassette. SAE and IRC. Reports in 12 weeks.
Music: Mostly country, blues and jazz, also "serious modern music." Published "Map of Hebrides," "Paths on Scarp," and "Rainbow Plantation," (by A. Adams), recorded by Andree Back S. Schlomowitz on Sphemusations (serious modern).

***STANG MUSIC PUBLISHING**, 168 Buckingham St., Hartford CT 06106. (203)524-5656. Producer: Jack Stang. Music publisher, record company and record producer. BMI. Publishes 20 songs/year; publishes 8 new songwriters/year. Works with composes and lyricists; teams collaborators. Pays standard royalty.
How to Contact: Prefers cassette with 1-3 songs and lyric sheet. SASE. Reports in 3 weeks.
Music: Dance-oriented, easy listening, MOR, R&B, rock and top 40/pop. Published "Girls Like You" written and recorded by B. Chapin (top 40); "Smokin" (by B. Chapin), recorded by Joe Frazier (R&B); and "Good Night Song" written and recorded by Alpha Sonas (ballad), all recorded on Nickel Records.

***STARBOUND PUBLISHING CO.**, 9717 Jensen, Houston TX 77093. (713)695-3648. President: Buz Hart. Music publisher and record producer. BMI. Publishes 10 songs/year; publishes 3 new songwriters/year. Works with composers and lyricists; teams collaborators. Pays standard royalty.
How to Contact: Prefers cassette with 3 songs and lyric sheet. Does not return unsolicited material.
Music: Mostly country, R&B and gospel. Published "Plugged and Abandoned," written and recorded by R. Kizziar; "Mama's Home," written and recorded by J. Tyson; and "You're the Girl" (by Hart/ Watson), recorded by J. Watson; all on Juke Box Records (all country).

STARCAP MUSIC, 9265 Dorrington Place, Arleta CA 91331. (818)891-1273. President: Valerie Starr. Music publisher. ASCAP. Publishes 10 songs/year. Pays variable royalty.
How to Contact: Submit demo tape by mail. Prefers cassette. SASE.
Music: Pop and rock. Published "Hot Pursuit" (by Starr/Jandrositz), "Trial Basis" (by Valerie Starr), and "Work Or Play" (by Starr/Jandrositz), all recorded by JJ Starr on Damp Silk Records.

STARTIME MUSIC, Box 643, LaQuinta CA 92253. (619)564-4823. President: Fred Rice. Music publisher, record company (Startime Records) and record producer (Fred Rice Productions, Inc.; Rob Carter Enterprises). Publishes 1-6 songs/year; publishes 2-4 new songwriters/year. Works with composers and lyricists; teams collaborators. Pays standard royalty.
Affiliate: Yo Yo Music (BMI).
How to Contact: Prefers cassette (or VHS videocassette) with 1-2 songs and lyric sheet. SASE. Reports in 6 weeks.
Music: Mostly top 40/pop, country and novelties; also rock. Published "Tender Love" (by Carl Whitener/Tim Schwanke); "Straight From The Heart" (by Tim Schwanke/Carl Whitener); and "Let Your Body Speak to Me" (by Carl Whitener/Andre J. Baptiste), all recorded by Johnny Porsche on Yo-Yo Music Records (pop/R&B singles).
Tips: "Like songs that have 'short story' endings, novelty twists or provocative subjects. Please consider the visual potential of your song—it should lend itself to a storyboard for future video production."

STARWEST MUSIC, 1335 14th, Longview WA 98632. (206)423-9085. Contact: Michael Poe. Music publisher and record company. BMI. Publishes 6 songs/year; publishes 2 new songwriters/year.
How to Contact: Submit demo tape by mail. Prefers cassette. SASE.
Music: Rock, blues and country. Published "Love You So Much," "Rough Cut," and "Drivin Hard."

STEADY ARM MUSIC, Box 2277, Gainesville FL 32602. (904)378-8156. General Manager: Charles V. Steadham Jr. Professional Manager: Allen R. McCollum. Music publisher. BMI. Pays standard royalty.
How to Contact: Write first; is not currently accepting unsolicited material. Prefers cassette with 2-3 songs. Reports "as soon as possible.".
Music: Bluegrass, country, dance, folk, MOR, rock (country), soul, top 40/pop, R&B, and comedy. Published "Micah" and "Enoch Ludford," written and recorded by Don Dunaway on Milltop Records (folk); "Kennesaw Line" (by Dunaway) recorded by Gamble Rogers on Flying Fish Records (folk); and "Airstream Trailer Orgy," and "The Bible Salesman," written and recorded by G. Rogers on Flying Fish Records.

STORZ GROUP OF COMPANIES, Box 1670, Hauptstr. 114, 3360 Osterode West Germany. (05522)7041. Music publisher and record company (Catena Vision, Arminia).
Affiliates: Musikverlag Storz KG, Edition Catena.
How to Contact: Prefers cassette or reel-to-reel (or VHS videocassette).

STREET CITY MUSIC, Suite 1006, 9000 Sunset Blvd., Los Angeles CA 90069. Personal Manager: Bambi Bryens. Music publisher and record producer. BMI. Publishes 35 songs/year; publishes 3 new songwriters/year. Pays standard royalty.
How to Contact: Query first. Prefers cassette with 1-4 songs and lyric sheet. SASE. Reports in 3 weeks.
Music: Commercial rock and pop.

STREET SINGER MUSIC, 117 W. 8th, Hays KS 67601. (913)625-9634. President: Mark Meckel. BMI. Music publisher, record company (MDM Records) and record producer (MDM productions). Publishes 15 songs/year; publishes 4 new songwriters/year. Teams collaborators. Pays standard royalty.
How to Contact: Prefers cassette with 2-4 songs and lyric or lead sheet.
Music: Mostly country swing, country rock, 50s rock and Christmas; also R&B, country, gospel and country R&B. Published "Get Into That Christmas Feeling," (by Robert Hayes), recorded by Kim Hager (pop); "A Friend Like You," by Mark Selby; "My Heart Keeps Walking (Right Back to You)," (by Paul Hotchkiss/Mike Terry), recorded by Tommy Harrison (country swing); and "Christmas Eve Waltz," (by Jack Kavanagh), recorded by Kim Hager, all on M.D.M. Records.
Tips: "Be willing to make changes and work with a producer."

STRIKING RESEMBLANCE MUSIC, Route 1, Box 197, Killen AL 35645. (205)757-2880. President: Mark Narmore. Music publisher. BMI. Estab. 1986. Publishes 20 songs/year; publishes 3 new songwriters/year. Pays standard royalty.
How to Contact: Prefers cassette with 1-5 songs and lyric sheet. Prefers studio produced demos. "A polished demo sells the song." SASE. Reports in 2 weeks.
Music: Mostly contemporary country and traditional country; also adult contemporary, contemporary gospel, traditional gospel, commercial pop and rock. Published "What Will I Do" and "Old Piano" written and recorded by Mark Narmore on Lamp Records (pop).

JEB STUART MUSIC CO., Box 6032, Station B, Miami FL 33123. (305)547-1424. President: Jeb Stuart. Music publisher, record producer and management firm. BMI. Publishes 4 songs/year. Pays standard royalty.
How to Contact: Query. Prefers cassette or disc with 2-4 songs and lead sheet. SASE. Reports in 1 month.
Music: Mostly gospel, jazz/rock, pop and R&B; also blues, church/religious, country, disco, and soul. Published "Saucy Music," "Somebody's Got to Win," and "You're So Right for Me," written and recorded by Jeboria Stuart on Esquire (jazz/pop/R&B).

*SUBAR MUSIC PUBLISHING CO. LTD., 21, Any Ma'amin St., Ramat-Hasharon 47212 Israel. Phone: (03)471323. Manager: Dr. Ophira Bar-Elan. Music publisher. ACUM Ltd. Publishes 5-10 songs/year; publishes 3-5 new songwriters/year. Works composers and lyricists.
Affiliates: Sharon Music Publishing (ACUM Ltd.), Pa'amonim Music Publishers (ACUM Ltd.).
How to Contact: Prefers cassette and lyric or lead sheet. Does not return unsolicited material. Reports in 1 month.
Music: Mostly pop, rock and country.

*SUGAR MAMA MUSIC, #805, 4545 Connecticut Ave. NW, Washington DC 20008. (202)362-2286. President: Jonathan Strong. Music publisher, record company (Ripsaw Records) and record producer (Ripsaw Productions). BMI. Publishes 3-5 songs/year; publishes 2 new songwriters/year. Works with composers and lyricists. Pays standard royalty.
Affiliates: Neck Bone Music (BMI), Southern Crescent Publishing (BMI).
How to Contact: Prefers cassette and lyric sheet. SASE. Reports in 1 month.
Music: Mostly rockabilly and traditional rock. Published "Tough Girls," "What Do I Hafta Do," and "I Wanna Be With You," all written and recorded by Bobby Smith on Ripsaw Records (popabilly).

*PRESTON SULLIVAN MUSIC, 1217 16th Ave. S., Nashville TN 37212. (615)372-8129. President: Preston Sullivan. Music publisher. ASCAP. Publishes 150 songs/year; publishes 10 new songwriters/year. Works with composers and lyricists; teams collaborators. Pays standard royalty.
Affiliate: Surespin Songs (BMI).
How to Contact: Prefers cassette and lyric sheet. "Please have clearly written lyrics and understandable vocals." Does not return unsolicited material. Reports in 2 weeks.
Music: Mostly pop, rock, R&B and country; also gospel.

SULTAN MUSIC PUBLISHING,Box 461892, Garland TX 75046. (214)271-8098. President: Don Ferguson. Music publisher. BMI. Publishes 15 songs/year including some new songwriters. Works with composers and lyricists; teams collaborators. Pays standard royalty.
Affiliates: HRS Publishing (ASCAP), Puzzle Records.
How to Contact: Prefers cassette with 3 songs and lyric sheet. SASE. Reports in 3 weeks.
Music: Mostly country; also MOR. Published "Slow Song" (by Paul Hotchkiss/Mike Terry), recorded by Benji Wilholte on Playback Records; and "One More Time," written and recorded by Cheryl Killman, and "Holdin Back the Tears" (by June Fox), recorded by Mary Craig, both on Puzzle Records.
Tips: "The best quality demo makes the listener more receptive."

SULTRY LADY MUSIC, Suite 205, 380 Lafayette Rd., St. Paul MN 55107. (612)228-0719. Professional Manager: Thomas A. Del Vecchio. Music publisher. Publishes 1-2 songs/year; publishes 1 new songwriter/year. Pays standard royalty.
How to Contact: Prefers cassette with 3-5 songs "and a lyric sheet for each song. No submissions will be returned without SASE." Reports in 8 weeks.
Music: Mostly rock, MOR and jazz; also pop, top 40 and blues.

*SUMWARASHU PRODUCTIONS, Box 234, Somerville MA 02143. (617)623-1066. Contact: Stephen J. Seltzer. Music publisher and record producer. BMI.
How to Contact: Prefers cassette with 3-5 songs and lyric sheet. SASE. Reports in 3 weeks.
Music: Mostly dance pop and fringe rock.

*SWAIM PUBLISHING, Box 2154, Carolina Beach NC 28428. (919)458-8651. Owner: Lanny Swaim. Music publisher. ASCAP. Publishes 10 songs/year; publishes 2 new songwriters/year. Works with composers and lyricists. Pays standard royalty.
How to Contact: Write first and obtain permission to submit. Prefers cassette (or VHS videocassette) with 3-4 songs and lead sheet. Does not return unsolicited material. Reports in 6 weeks.
Music: Contemporary Christian, pop and country. Published "A Child Is Born" and "For You" (by L. Swaim), recorded by Latter Rain (contemporary Christian); and "Pete's Place" (by D. Page/G. Dixon/L. Swaim), recorded by Gary Dixon (nostalgia 50s), all on Sand Dollar Records.
Tips: "Send good quality, studio cassette; and self addressed, stamped envelope for reply."

SWEET JUNE MUSIC PUBLISHING, 10125-227th Ave. Ct. E., Buckley WA 98321. (206)862-1877. Contact; Tom Thrasher. Music publisher. BMI. Publishes 12 songs/year; publishes 3 new songwriters/year. Pays standard royalty.
How to Contact: Prefers cassette (or videocassette) with 2-5 songs and lyric sheet. SASE. Reports in 1 month.
Music: Mostly gospel, country and country/rock; also bluegrass, easy listening, folk. Published "I'm Satisfied," (by Tom Thrasher), recorded by Tom Stopp (country/rock); "Easy to Love," (by Tom Thrasher), recorded by Nashville Rebels (country); and "For You—For Me," written and recorded by Tom Thrasher (gospel), all on CMI Records.

SWEET SINGER MUSIC, The Mathes Company, Box 22653, Nashville TN 37202. President: Dave Mathes. BMI. Member CMA, GMA, NMPA, NARAS and AFM. Publishes 30-100 songs/year; publishes 10-30 new songwriters/year. Pays standard royalty.
Affiliates: Star of David (SESAC) and Sing Sweeter Music (ASCAP).

How to Contact: Accepts "any tape configuration, including videos. Full music videos are unnecessary, but we would like material to be well-performed and extremely well-written." Prefers cassette with 1-3 songs and lyric sheet. SASE.

Music: Mostly country and gospel; also contemporary Christian and MOR. Published "My Love For You" (by David and Deanna Mathes), recorded by Warner Mack on Sapphire Records (country/MOR); "Dreamer" (by Glen Bates), recorded by Jimmy Gateley on Sapphire Records (country); and "Baby You Know (How I Love You)" (by Larry Coen, Jr./Helen Cornelius), recorded by Jim Ed Brown and Helen Cornelius on RCA Records (country).

Tips: Needs "well-thought out lyrics, resulting from rewriting until satisfied that the song is as good as the top ten songs on the chart. We avoid controversial, political or demoralizing songs. Traditional country songs are making a comeback. Positive songs are 'in' once again. Duets and group songs are in demand. We will comment on material and we listen to every song submitted. It is useless in today's market to send simple guitar or piano demos—we cannot get producers to listen to them. Get a quality demo no matter where you submit it."

SWEET SWAMP MUSIC, Red Kill Road, Fleischmanns NY 12430. (914)254-4565. President/General Manager: Barry Drake. Music publisher, booking agency, record company and management firm. BMI. Publishes 25 songs/year. Pays standard royalty.

How to Contact: Prefers cassette with 3-5 songs and lead sheet. SASE. Reports in 1 month.

Music: Bluegrass, blues, country, easy listening, folk, MOR, progressive, rock (hard or country) and top 40/pop. Published "Grandma's Old Piano," "The King of the Sidewalk," and "The Saint of South Poughkeepsie," written and recorded by Barry Drake on Catskill Mountain Records; and "America is Dancin' Again," by Larry Mangum.

SWEET TOOTH MUSIC PUBLISHING, 2716 Springlake Ct., Irving TX 75060. (214)790-5172. General Manager: Kenny Wayne Hagler. Music publisher, record company, record producer, recording artist and traveling musician and vocalist. BMI. Publishes 10-20 songs/year; publishes 5 new songwriters/year. Works with composers and lyricists; teams collaborators. Pays standard royalty.

How to Contact: Prefers cassette with 1-4 songs and lyric sheet. "Be sure to include sufficient return envelope and sufficient postage. No replies without SASE." Reports in 1 month.

Music: Mostly rock, country and R&B; also new rock, blues, MOR, soul and top 40/pop. Published "I Hope You Don't Lose," (by Michael Jeffrey), recorded by Kenny Wayne on Ace Records; "You've Got Those Eyes," (by William Blacker), and "8 Days Inn," (by Mark Roman), both recorded by Billy Blast Band on Candy Records (new rock).

Tips: "Compare all songs with the hits of today. Make sure the song has a good hook and is commercially appealing. I don't need B sides or LP filler. I need top 10 commercial hits! All styles!"

SWING & TEMPO MUSIC PUBLISHING INC., 1995 Broadway, New York NY 10023. (212)787-1222. Vice President: Bill Titone. Music publisher and record producer. BMI. Publishes 50 songs/year. Pays standard royalty.

How to Contact: Prefers 7½ ips reel-to-reel with 2-4 songs and lyric sheet. SASE. Reports in 1 month.

Music: Jazz and R&B.

TABITHA MUSIC, LTD., 39 Cordery Rd., St. Thomas, Exeter, Devon EX2 9DJ England. Managing Director: Graham Sclater. Music publisher and record producer. MCPS, PRS. Member MPA. Publishes 25 songs/year; publishes 6 new songwriters/year. Pays standard royalty; royalties paid directly to US songwriters.

Affiliate: Dice Music.

How to Contact: Prefers cassette with 1-4 songs and lyric sheet. SAE and IRC. Reports in 2 weeks.

Music: Mostly MOR and pop; also country, dance-oriented, Spanish, rock, soul and top 40. Published "Conscience" (by Norman Graveney), recorded by Montellas on Sign Records (R&B); and "Video Boys" (by Goode/Partineton), recorded by Circuit on Micro Records (electro pop).

TANDEM TUNES, INC., Suite 204, 1300 Division St., Nashville TN 37203. President: Beverly Beard. Music publisher. ASCAP, BMI. Publishes 2-6 songs/year. Pays standard royalty.

Affiliates: CoPenCo Music (ASCAP), and Leacom Music (BMI).

How to Contact: Prefers cassette with 3 songs and lyric sheet. "Clear cassette recording and typed lyric sheet appreciated." Does not return unsolicited material. Reports only if "we feel we can get it recorded. Then we will ask for a contract."

Music: Country. Published "Ain't It Too Bad (It Was too Good to Be True)" (by Jerry McBee/Tom C. Armstrong/Beverly Beard), recorded by Bill Phillips on NSD Records; "Love Gets Expensive When It's Free," (by Vernis Pratt/Tom C. Armstrong), recorded by Joe Anthony on Player Records; and "Just Like the Night Before," written and recorded by Marty Martel on Ridgetop Records (all country).

Close-up

Steve Wariner
Singer/Songwriter

When country singer/songwriter Steve Wariner writes a song, he says he always asks himself a question: "When I sing this song, what are those people sitting out in the audience, watching my live show or listening to the radio at home going to think? Are they gonna say, 'Gosh, that's me. That's my life'?

"Honest truth," he says. "You can't beat it. That's what's great about *country* music—you can hear that truth real clearly."

Wariner says fans at concerts always see a bit of truth in his hit song "What I Didn't Do," co-written by Mike Noble and Wood Newton. One particular line in the song, he says, always stirs an emotional reaction. "I love the line that says, 'Now it's easy to see why her love died./ She was planning her nights by the *TV Guide*.' "

Another one of Wariner's songs, "Some Fools Never Learn," was a hit, he feels, because it deals with the truth and the experiences of everyday life which the average person can relate to.

Wariner, who records for MCA Records, says he's been writing songs since he was 16. When he was only 17, Dottie West discovered him at an Indiana club and gave him a job playing bass and singing background vocals in her band. A few years later, he met his boyhood idol, Chet Atkins, who signed Wariner to a singles deal at RCA Records and produced his first #1 single, "All Roads Lead to You."

Since then, Wariner has signed with MCA Records, and has five #1 singles (four in the last year alone) and eight Top-10 hits to his credit. He also sings the theme song on ABC-TV's hit comedy series, "Who's the Boss?".

What advice does Wariner have for songwriters? The most important thing, he says, is to learn the virtue of patience.

"Just keep on writing," he says, "because obviously the more you do something, the better you're going to get. It's honing your craft. You just don't start out being good."

Wariner says too many songwriters take the wrong approach in pitching their songs to artists. Speaking from experience, he feels it's rude to stick a handful of your tapes in an artist's face as soon as he steps off the tour bus.

"There's a couth way of doing it [pitching songs] and a wrong way of doing it," says Wariner. "And the best way of doing it is through a reputable publisher.

"And I say this not to criticize people. The best way to do it is to get in with a publisher and let *him* pitch your songs because you're more valid that way. And the statistics show the hit songs that I record are not handed to me by some guy just publishing this stuff out of his house. I get a very, very high percentage of songs through reputable publishers and writers and virtually none hand-to-hand."

—Tyler Cox

TANNEN MUSIC COMPANIES, 1650 Broadway, New York NY 10019. (212)582-1667. Contact: Paul Tannen. BMI. Music publisher and manager.
How to Contact: Prefers cassette. SASE.
Music: Mostly rock, country and dance.

DALE TEDESCO MUSIC CO., 17043 Romar St., Northridge CA 91325. (818)885-0775. President: Dale T. Tedesco. General Manager: Betty Lou Tedesco. Music publisher. BMI. Publishes 20-50 songs/year; publishes 10-35 new songwriters/year. Works with composers and lyricists; teams collaborators. Pays standard royalty.
Affiliate: Tedesco Tunes (ASCAP).
How to Contact: Prefers cassette with 1-2 songs and lyric sheet. SASE. Reports in 3 weeks.
Music: Mostly pop, R&B and AC; also dance-oriented, R&B, instrumentals, jazz, MOR, rock and soul.
Tips: "We want a very commerical vehicle with excellent lyrics and melodies."

DJ TEMPLETON MUSIC, Box 95841, Seattle WA 98145. (206)282-7860. Owner: David Templeton. Music publisher. ASCAP. Publishes 20 songs/year; publishes 3 new songwriters/year. Pays negotiable royalty.
How to Contact: Prefers cassette or 15 ips reel-to-reel with 3 songs. Reports in 1 week.
Music: Adult contemporary, ballads and light jazz. Published "Short but Sweet," "Home," and "Memory Flash," all written and recorded by David Templeton on Mason Ridge Records (all solo piano).
Tips: "Local Seattle area artists preferred. Easy listening is what we like, stuff you listen to in front of a warm fire."

*TENALINA MUSIC, 1609 Congress, Eastover SC 29044. (803)776-2328. President: Howard A. Knight, Jr. Music publisher, record company (Pegasus Records) and record producer (Howard Knight Ent.). Publishes 50 songs/year; publishes 10 new songwriters/year. Works with composers and lyricists; teams collaborators. Pays standard royalty.
Affiliate: Howard Knight Music (SESAC).
How to Contact: Prefers cassette with 3 songs and lyric sheet. Does not return unsolicited material. Reports only if interested.
Music: Mostly country, pop and rock. Published "Wadda You Done With My Heart" (by Lance Middlebrook), recorded by Mark Alan and "Still Missing You" (by Jessie Blevins), and "Airwaves of Love" (by John Joslin), both recorded by Bandit Band, all on Pegasus Records.

TEXAS CRUDE PUBLISHING INC., 5536 N. Lamar, Austin TX 78751. (512)440-1976. Manager: Jane Quisenberry. Music publisher and record company. BMI, ASCAP. Publishes 100-200 songs/year; publishes 8-10 new songwriters/year. Pays standard royalty.
Affiliate: Texas Lady Jane Music (ASCAP). ·
How to Contact: Submit demo tape by mail. Write or call first to arrange personal interview. Prefers cassette with 3 songs and lyric sheet. SASE. Reports in 4 weeks.
Music: Mostly country, rock and gospel; also jazz, swing and pop/dance. Published "Honky Tonk Parking Lot," written and recorded by Mark Luke Daniels on Luke Juke Records; "Everything's Right," written and recorded by C.J. Parker and Jane Quisenberry on Countie Mountie Records; and "Terri Shaw," written and recorded by Terri Shaw (all country).

TIKI ENTERPRISES, INC., 195 S. 26th St., San Jose CA 95116. (408)286-9840. President: Gradie O'Neal. Music publisher and record company (Rowena Records). BMI, ASCAP. Publishes 40 songs/year; publishes 12 new songwriters/year. Pays standard royalty.
Affiliates: Tooter Scooter Music (BMI), Rememberance Music (ASCAP), and Janell Music (BMI).
How to Contact: Prefers cassette with 3 songs and lyric or lead sheets. SASE. Reports in 3 weeks.
Music: Mostly rock/pop, country and gospel; also international and jazz/fusion. Published "Get Your Reindeer Off My Roof" (by Saxafraz), recorded by Jeannine O'Neal; "How Ya Do That Santa Claus" (by Dave Conway); and "Baby On Board" (by Demian Perry).

TIMBERTREE PUBLISHING, Rt. 8, 425 Orebank Rd., Kingsport TN 37664. (615)323-3152. Manager: J.W. Hutchins. Music publisher. BMI. Member AFTRA. Publishes 6-12 songs/year; publishes 1 new songwriter/year. Pays standard royalty.
How to Contact: Write or call first about your interest. Prefers cassette with 1-2 songs and lyric sheet. Does not return unsolicited material . Reports "if it's found favorable."
Music: Country, country rock and country gospel. Published "Memories of Loving You," "Writing on the Wall," and "Country on Tap," written and recorded by J.W. Hutchins on Tandem Records (country).

TIME MINSTREL MUSIC, Box 241, Cameron MO 64429. (816)632-6039. Director: E.K. Bruhn. BMI. Music publisher and record company (Crusader) and record producer (Crusader Records & Tapes). Publishes 20 songs/year; publishes 5 new songwriters/year. Works with composers and lyricists; teams collaborators. Pays standard royalty.
How to Contact: Prefers cassette or 7½ ips reel-to-reel with 1-3 songs and "optional" lyric sheet or lead sheet. "Include short write-up about your interests." SASE. Reports in 6 weeks.
Music: Mostly pop/country, novelty and gospel; also "clean" comedy show material. Published "Night Tracks," by Filley/Dodson/Kopperfield (pop/country); "Go It Alone," by Jim Haefs/Kopperfield (rock); and "Heartland Hotel," by Sabastian Sanchez (rock/pop), all recorded by Kopperfield on Crusader Records.
Tips: "Complete your song idea—finish the story."

TOMPAUL MUSIC CO., 628 South St., Mount Airy NC 27030. (919)786-2865. Owner: Paul E. Johnson. Music publisher, record company, record producer and record and tape distributor. BMI. Publishes 175 songs/year; publishes 80 new songwriters/year. Works with composers and teams collaborators. Pays standard royalty.
How to Contact: Prefers 7½ ips reel-to-reel with 3-6 songs and lyric or lead sheet. SASE. Reports in 1 month.
Music: Mostly country, bluegrass and gospel; also church/religious, easy listening, folk, MOR, rock, soul and top 40. Published "Nobody's Promised Tomorrow," written and recorded by Roger H. Bell on Stark (country); "Forever and a Day," written and recorded by Bobby Lee Atkins on Webco (bluegrass); and "I'm Satisfied," written and recorded by Early Upchurch on Stark (country).
Tips: "Try to write good, commercial songs. The lyrics should match the music. Use new ideas; don't try to make alterations in a song that is already established."

TOPOMIC MUSIC, 105 Rue de Normandie, Courbevoie 92400 France. (1)4333 6515. President: Pierre Jaubert. Music publisher and record producer. SACEM, ASCAP. Publishes 100 songs/year; publishes 50 new songwriters/year. Works with composers and lyricists; teams collaborators.
Music: "We're looking for new songs for movie soundtrack, and top 40 style singers for movie soundtracks and dance records productions." Published "Monday Woman," written and recorded by Willie Mabon (blues); "Not Made for Me," written and recorded by Richard Sanderson (pop); and "Que Mundo e Este," written and recorded by Alice Canelas (Portugese).

TOSHIBA-EMI MUSIC PUBLISHING CO., LTD., 5-21 Toranomon 2-Chome, Minato-ku, Tokyo 105 Japan. Phone: (03) 593 1731. International Division: Toshi Hosokawa. JASRAC. Music publisher. Publishes 200 domestic songs/year; publishes 5-20 new songwriters/year. Works with lyricists and teams collaborators. Pays 50-60% royalty, "we sometimes pay 30% to author and 30% to composer."
How to Contact: Prefers cassette (or Beta or VHS videocassette) and lyric sheet. Does not return unsolicited material. Reports in "a few" weeks.
Music: Mostly pop, rock and R&B; also country. Published "Ginza no Biyoushi Monogatari" (by Y. Mizushima), recorded by Yaya (pop); "Ai no Monologue" (by T. Ohnuki), recorded by Jennifer Connelly (ballad); and "Ai Soshite Anata" (by T. Fujiwara), recorded by Ruika Kurahashi (ballad), all on Toshiba/EMI.

TOULOUSE MUSIC PUBLISHING CO., INC., Box 96, El Cerrito CA 94530. Executive Vice President: James Bronson, Jr. Music publisher, record company and record producer. BMI. Member AIMP. Publishes 1 new songwriter/year. Hires staff writers. Pays standard royalty.
How to Contact: Prefers cassette with 2-4 songs and lyric sheet. SASE. Reports in 1 month.
Music: Bluegrass, gospel, jazz, R&B and soul.

*TOWNSWAY MUSIC, Box 69180, Los Angeles CA 90069. Vice President: Eric Borenstein. Music publisher. BMI. Publishes 25 songs/year; publishes 1-2 new songwriters/year. Works with composers and lyricists; teams collaborators. Pays standard royalty.
Affiliates: Kamakazi Music (BMI), Manilow Music (BMI), Cityscape Music (ASCAP).
How to Contact: Prefers cassete with 1-2 songs. SASE. Reports in 3 months.
Music: Mostly pop, R&B and rock; also country.

TRAGREY MUSIC PUBLISHING, 17 Ponca Trail, St. Louis MO 63122. (314)821-2741. Producer: Greg Trampe. Music publisher, record producer and recording studio. BMI. Member NARAS. Publishes 50 songs/year. Pays standard royalty.
How to Contact: Write about your interest or arrange personal interview. Prefers 7½ ips reel-to-reel, cassette (or videocassette) with 1-4 songs and lyric sheet. Does not return unsolicited material. Reports in 1 month.

Music: Mostly top 40/pop, progressive and rock; also blues, church/religious, country, dance-oriented, easy listening, gospel, jazz, MOR, R&B and background library.

TREE PUBLISHING CO., INC., 8 Music Square W., Nashville TN 37203. (615)327-3162. President: Buddy Killen. Vice President: Donna Hilley. Director of Creative Services: Bob Montgomery. Professional Managers/Song Pluggers: Dan Wilson and Walter Campbell. Music publisher. BMI, ASCAP. Member NMPA.
Affiliates: Cross Keys Publishing, Twittybird Music Publishing, Uncanny Music, Warhawk Music, Tree/Harlan Howard Songs, Kentree Music, Stairway Music and Meadowgreen Music.
How to Contact: Call first "to see if we're currently accepting material," then submit demo tape. Prefers cassette with 1-3 songs. "Voice and guitar or piano accompaniment is sufficient. There is no need to have full orchestra or band on track. We just need to hear the words and melody clearly." SASE. Reports in 10-12 weeks. "We will not return material unless proper postage is on SASE."
Music: Country, MOR, rock (hard or country), soul, top 40/pop and contemporary Christian.

TREEHOUSE MUSIC, Box 12151, Nashville TN 37212. (615)321-4030. Contact: Theo A. French. Music publisher and record producer. ASCAP. Publishes 12 songs/year; publishes 2 new songwriters/year. Works with composers and lyricists. Pays standard royalty.
How to Contact: Prefers cassette with 1-3 songs and lyric sheet. SASE. Reports in 3 weeks.
Music: Mostly gospel and rock; also easy rock and top 40/pop. Published "White Robe," and "Following You," written and recorded by Patricia White; and "Only You Can See," recorded by Dilion on Word Records, Inc. (all contemporary gospel).

TROUBLE BOY MUSIC, Box 256277, Chicago IL 60625. (312)764-1144. President: Tom Petreli. Music publisher. BMI. Publishes 5-15 songs/year; publishes 4 new songwriters/year. Pays standard royalty.
How to Contact: Prefers cassette (or videocassette) with 2-4 songs and lyric sheet. SASE. Reports in 1 month.
Music: Mostly new wave; also all other types. Published "Arizona," by Arizona; and "Angels on Horseback," by Broken Toys.

TRUSTY PUBLICATIONS, Rt. 1, Box 100, Nebo KY 42441. (502)249-3194. President: Elsie Childers. Music publisher and record company. BMI. Member CMA and NSAI. Publishes 3-5 songs/year; publishes 3-5 new songwriters/year. Pays standard royalty.
How to Contact: Prefers 7½ ips reel-to-reel or cassette with 2-4 songs and lead sheet. SASE. Reports in 1 month.
Music: Mostly country and country/pop; also blues, church/religious, disco, easy listening, folk, gospel, MOR, soul and top 40. Published "Goodbye," and "This World's Too Big," written and recorded by Randy Hudson.
Tips: "Performing artists get the best shot with us."

TUMAC MUSIC PUBLISHING, Box 384, Senoia GA 30276. (404)599-6935. Professional Manager: Phil McDaniel. General Manager: Joe McTamney. Music publisher, record producer and record company (2-mac Records). ASCAP, BMI. Publishes 2-3 songs/year; publishes 1-2 new songwriters/year. Works with composers and teams collaborators. Pays standard royalty.
Affiliate: Shandy Gaff (BMI).
How to Contact: Prefers cassette with 1-2 songs and lyric or lead sheet. SASE. Reports in 4 weeks.
Music: Mostly pop, ballads and R&B; also dance, easy listening, jazz (country), MOR, rock (adult/country), top 40/pop and country. Published "Garden for a Special Friend," (by Holloway/McTammy), recorded by Cristy Lane on LS Records; and "She's the Only Miss America for Me," (by Holloway/McTammy), recorded by Chris Holloway on Raindawn Records.
Tips: "Prefer studio demos, and songs that can be performed by the top names in the business. Be professional in your approach to songwriting—it's a business."

THE TWL PUBLISHING GROUP, Box 372, Flint MI 48501-0372. (313)695-3790. Attention: A&R Department. ASCAP, BMI, SESAC. Music publisher. Publishes 10-20 songs/year; publishes 1-2 new songwriters/year. Teams collaborators. Pays standard royalty; negotiates foreign subpublishing..
Affiliates: Lady Marion, Isle Cay Music, Sunscape.
How to Contact: "Solicited submissions only!" Write and obtain permission to submit. Prefers cassette with 2-3 songs and typed lyric sheet. SASE. Reports in 16 weeks.
Music: "Highly commercial" pop/dance, pop/rock, country and easy listening. Published "Don't Stop," (by M. Grabowski), recorded by Cerberus on Starstream (rock); *Champion*, and "What a Friend," written and recorded by Ron Moore on Morada (pop); and "Crazy in Your Ways," written and recorded by R.R. Jackson on Windguest Records (pop).

Tips: "The writer must be flexible and have the (obvious) potential to write not just one commercial success but many. The writer must also have a great amount of persistance, patience, and perseverance."

UBM, Mommsenst. 61, 5000 Koln 41 West Germany. Phone: 43 13 13. President: Uwe Buschkotter. Music publisher, record company and record producer. Gema (West Germany), BMI (USA). Pays standard royalty.
How to Contact: Prefers cassette (or Beta videocassette) and lead sheets. Does not return unsolicited material. Reports in 4 weeks.
Music: Mostly jazz, pop and MOR; also classical.

UNITED ENTERTAINMENT MUSIC, 4024 State Line, Kansas City KS 66103. (913)262-3555. Director of Publishing: Michael T. Harvey. Music publisher, record company (United Entertainment Productions) and record producer. BMI. Publishes 30-40 songs/year; publishes 30-40 new songwriters/year. Pays negotiable royalty. "If we do not sign the writer, we could still do a mailing to appropriate radio stations and try to promote the artist for a fee."
How to Contact: Prefers cassette or 15/30 ips reel-to-reel and lyric sheet. Does not return unsolicited material.
Music: Mostly rock, R&B/blues and jazz; also country and pop. Published "Steal Away," and "Moon Is Risin'," (by R. Lucente), recorded by Bon Ton Band on Graphic Records (R&B); and "Meanstreak" (by M. Collins), recorded by The Bentleys on Leslie Records (pop).
Tips: "We are looking for tunes that suit our artists and have a message that is positive and current."

UNIVERSAL STARS MUSIC, INC., HC-80, Box 5B, Leerville LA 71446. National Representative: Sherree Stephens. Music publisher. BMI. Publishes 12-24 songs/year; publishes 1 new songwriter/year. Pays standard royalty.
Affiliate: Headliner Music.
How to Contact: Prefers cassette with 1-6 songs and lyric or lead sheets. Does not return unsolicited material. Reports in 1 month, if interested.
Music: Mostly religious; also bluegrass, church, country, folk, gospel and top 40/pop. Published "Jesus, You're Everywhere," "I Can Depend On You," and "I Just Came to Thank You Lord," (all by Sherree Stephens), all recorded by J.J. and S. Stephens (religious).

UNREGULATED MUSIC, Box 81485, Fairbanks AK 99708. (907) 456-3419. President: Michael States. Music publisher, record company and record producer. BMI. Publishes 25 songs/year; publishes 8 new songwriters/year. Pays standard royalty.
How to Contact: Prefers cassette with 2-5 songs and lyric sheet. "Include a statement of your goals." SASE. Reports in 1 month.
Music: Gospel, black gospel, and new wave gospel. Published "Swimming the Straits of Hormuz," recorded by Mike Wedgwood (new wave); "The Faith Of the Little Ones," by John Lentine (gospel); "Slow Elvis," recorded by Randy Reaves (country rock); and "Balance of Power," by Robyn Hood (new wave gospel).

*UP TREND MUSIC, 1-C, 207 Madison St., Eden NC 27288. (919)623-9394. President/Founder: J.W. Rice. Music publisher. BMI. Works with composers and lyricists. Pays standard royalty.
How to Contact: Write or call first and obtain permission to submit. Prefers cassette with 4-7 songs and lyric sheet. SASE. Reports in 2 weeks.
Music: Gospel only.

URSULA MUSIC, Suite 1, 621 Park City Center, Lancaster PA 17601. President/Professional Manager: Joey Welz. Music publisher, record company (Music City, Canadian American, Caprice, American Radio) and booking agency. BMI. Member AFM. Publishes 12-18 songs/year; publishes 8 new songwriters/year. Works with composers and lyricists. Pays standard royalty.
Affiliates: Welz Music (ASCAP), Comet Tale Music (ASCAP), Florentine Music (BMI) and Wynwood Music (BMI).
How to Contact: Prefers cassette with 4-8 songs and lead sheet. Does not return unsolicited material. "We hold until we need material for a session, then we search our files."
Music: Mostly rock; also top 40, country, dance, MOR, and pop. Published "In My Car" (by Gerry Granahan/Joey Welz), "I Love the Radio" (by Smith/Lovi), "No More Nightmares" (by Jerry Durand), and "I Remember Rock and Roll" (by Gary Conahan/Joey Welz), all recorded by J. Welz on American Radio Records/Fraternity Records.

VAAM MUSIC, Suite C-114, 3740 Evans St., Los Angeles CA 90027. (213)664-7765. President: Pete Martin. Music publisher and record producer. ASCAP, BMI. Publishes 8 new songwriters/year. Pays standard royalty.
Affiliate: Pete Martin Music.
How to Contact: Prefers cassette with maximum 2 songs and lyric sheet. SASE. Reports in 1 month.
Music: Top 40/pop, country and R&B. "Submitted material must have potential of reaching top 5 on charts."

TOMMY VALANDO PUBLISHING GROUP, Suite 2110, 1270 Avenue of the Americas, New York NY 10020. (212)489-9696. President: Tommy Valando. General Manager: Arthur Valando. Director of Publications: Paul McKibbins. Music publisher. BMI, ASCAP. Member NMPA. Publishes varying number of songs/year. Pays standard royalty. Printed material percentage—rate varies.
Affiliates: Revelation Music Publishing Corp. (ASCAP) and Fiddleback Music Publishing Co., Inc. (BMI).
How to Contact: Call first. Prefers cassette with 1-3 "clear" songs. SASE. Reports "as quickly as possible."
Music: Musical theater scores exclusively.
Tips: "We prefer writer to perform own song to give a true idea of what he or she is trying to convey. Demo does not have to be elaborate."

VALCO MUSIC CO., 1327 Cobb St., Kalamazoo MI 49007. (616)342-5328. Contact: Victor Taylor. Music publisher, record company and record producer. BMI. Pays standard royalty.
How to Contact: Prefers reel-to-reel or cassette with 2-10 songs and lyric sheet. SASE. Reports in 3 weeks.
Music: Mostly country; "some" R&B.

VALENTINE MUSIKVERLAG, Box 7718, D-2000 Hamburg 20 West Germany. Phone: (040) 43.00.339. General Manager: Arno H.V. Vught Jr. GEMA. Music publisher, record company (Bandleader Records, Range Records) and record producer. Publishes 350 songs/year; publishes 235 new songwriters/year. Pays standard royalty.
How to Contact: Write or call first to arrange personal interview. Prefers cassette (or VHS videocassette) and lyric sheet or lead sheet. SAE and IRC. Reports in 2 weeks.
Music: Mostly country, jazz, big band, background music and MOR; also film music. Published "Song In a Seashell" (by Hall), recorded by Tom T. Hall on Mercury (country); "Mother I Love You," (by Smith), recorded by Sydney Devine on Scotdisc (folk); and "If You Don't Like" (by Kristofferson), recorded by H. Williams on Warner Bros. (country).
Tips: "Send full lead sheet and information about the writer(s)."

VIC-RAY PUBLISHING, Box 2277, Gainesville FL 32602. (904)378-8156. General Manager: Charles V. Steadham, Jr. Professional Manager: Allen R. McCollum. Music publisher. ASCAP.
How to Contact: Write first; is not currently accepting unsolicited material. Prefers cassette with 2-3 songs and lyric sheet. Reports "as soon as possible."
Music: Bluegrass, country, dance, folk, MOR, soul, top 40/pop, R&B and comedy. Released *Live and Kickin'* featuring "Whiskey 'fore Breakfast," " The Scotsman," "Bounty Hunter," " Elma Turl," and "Kentucky Song" (by Mike Cross), recorded live by Mike Cross on Sugar Hill Records (country/rock); placed "Leon McDuff" (by Mike Cross) recorded by The Nitty Gritty Dirt Band on Warner Bros. Records.

VIDEO—DIDEO PUBLISHING, 156 Freda Jane Ln., Birmingham AL 35215. (205)854-7177. General Manager: Dannie Warren. Music publisher, record producer (Psychophonic Records) and musical consulting firm. BMI. Publishes 15 songs/year; publishes 6 new songwriters/year. Pays standard royalty.
Affiliate: Revolver Publishing (BMI).
How to Contact: Submit demo tape by mail. Write or call first to arrange personal interview. Prefers cassette, or 15 ips reel-to-reel (or VHS videocassette). with 4 songs and lyric sheet. Does not return unsolicited material. Reports in 1 month.
Music: Mostly new wave, punk rock and rock; also jazz, fusion and heavy metal. Published "My Little Girl," written and recorded by Revolver (rock); "Involuntary Emotion" by A. Park/D. Thompson/S. Bonds), recorded by Revolver (new wave); and "Hell On Earth" (by R. Redwine), recorded by Toney Tuff (new wave), all on Rubber Records.

VIN-JOY MUSIC, 872 Morris Park Ave., Bronx NY 10462. (212)792-2198. Contact: Vice President. Music publisher, record company (Dragon Records) and record producer. BMI, ASCAP. Pays standard royalty.

How to Contact: "We accept material by recommendation only."
Music: Easy listening, MOR and top 40/pop.
Tips: "Material has to be exceptional—not amateurish."

VOKES MUSIC PUBLISHING, Box 12, New Kensington PA 15068-0012. (412)335-2775. President: Howard Vokes. Music publisher, record company, booking agency and promotion company. BMI.
How to Contact: Submit cassette and lead sheet. SASE. Reports "a few days after receiving."
Music: Bluegrass, country and gospel. Published "Blue, Blue, Blue," "My Heart Needs an Overhaul Job," "If All the Other Girls Were Like You," "I'm Going Out of Your Arms," "Honky Tonk Row," "The Sycamore Tree," "It Takes Six Men to Carry a Man to His Grave (But Only One Woman to Put Him There)," "Break the News, But Break It Gently," "Empty Victory," "West of the Yukon," "I'm Falling in Love Again," "City of Strangers," "Back When You Loved Me," and "Saddest Man That Walks Upon Two Feet."

WALK ON WATER MUSIC, Rt. 2, Box 566-H, New Braunfels TX 78130. (512)629-4396. Producer/Manager: Kenneth D. Brazle. ASCAP, BMI. Music publisher, record company, record producer and recording studio. Publishes 6 songs/year; publishes 1 new songwriter/year. Pays standard royalty.
How to Contact: Write first and obtain permission to submit. Prefers cassette or 7½ ips reel-to-reel (or VHS videocassette) with 2-3 songs and lyric sheet. SASE. Does not return unsolicited material. Reports in 6 weeks.
Music: Mostly AOR-pop/rock, new music and country.

*WARNER BROS. MUSIC, 9000 Sunset Blvd., Los Angeles CA 90069. Music publisher. Deals with artists and songwriters.
How to Contact: "We do not consider unsolicited submissions." Write or call first and obtain permission to submit. SASE.

WEB IV MUSIC PUBLISHING, 2107 Faulkner Rd. NE, Atlanta GA 30324. (404)321-5993. Contact: Ilene Berns. Music publisher. Pays standard royalty.
How to Contact: Submit demo tape by mail. "Please don't call." Prefers cassette with 3-4 songs and lyric sheet. SASE. Reports in 1 month.
Music: R&B, rock and top 40/pop.

WEEDHOPPER MUSIC, #811, 225 Oxmoor Circle, Birmingham AL 35209. (205)942-3222. President: Michael Panepento. BMI. Music publisher and record company (Pandem Records, Inc.). Publishes 5-10 songs/year; publishes 3 new songwriters/year. Pays standard royalty.
Affiliate: Panepentunes (ASCAP).
How to Contact: Write or call first and obtain permission to submit. Prefers cassette or 15 ips reel-to-reel with 3 songs. SASE. Reports in 3 weeks.
Music: Mostly AOR, R&B/jazz and rock; also all others. Published "Kings of Steel," (by J. Batton/D. White), recorded by Assault (heavy metal); "Dancin in the Wrong Shoes," (by S. McDavid), recorded Ian Hunter (AOR); and "Who's Been Sleeping in My Bed," (by S. McDavid), recorded by Scotti (AOR), all on Polymusic Records.

RON WEISER PUBLISHING, 6918 Peach Ave., Van Nuys CA 91406. Contact: Ron Weiser. Music publisher, record company and record producer. BMI. Publishes 30-50 songs/year; publishes 6 new songwriters/year. Pays standard royalty.
How to Contact: Prefers cassette (or videocassette) and lyric sheet. Does not return unsolicited material.
Music: Mostly rockabilly, 50s, R&B and "roots R&B"; also country. Published "Marie, Marie" and "American Music," (by D. Alvin), recorded by the Blasters on Warner Bros. Records (rockabilly); and "Tennessee and Texas," written and recorded by the Magnetics on Rollin' Rock Records (rockabilly).

*WELTKLANG-VERLAG, Mouson Str. 12, Frankfurt, Hessen 6000 West Germany. (69)445092. President: Horst Lelald. Music publisher. Publishes 30 songs/year; publishes 3-4 new songwriters/year. Pays "more than standard royalty."
How to Contact: Prefers cassette with 8-10 songs. SAE and IRC. Reports in 1 month.
Music: Mostly rock, jazz-rock and pop/funk/disco; also "all other kinds of fresh, good music." Published *Percussion/Right Back* (by P. Tjernberg), recorded by A. Lind/P. Tjernberg on Fog Records (LP); *Cleaners from Venus*, written and recorded by Martia Newell on Modell Records (LP); and *Johnny the Moondog*, written and recorded by Clive Stevens on Frog Records (LP).

BERTHOLD WENGERT (MUSIKVERLAG), Hauptstrasse 100, D-7507 Pfinztal-Soellingen, West Germany. Contact: Berthold Wengert. Music publisher. Teams collaborators. Pays standard GEMA royalty.
How to Contact: Prefers cassette and complete score for piano. SAE and IRC. Reports in 4 weeks.
Music: Mostly light music and pop.

BOBE WES MUSIC, Box 28609, Dallas TX 75228. (214)681-0345. President: Bobe Wes. Music publisher. BMI. Publishes 20 songs/year. Pays standard royalty.
How to Contact: Prefers cassette. "State if songs have been copyrighted and if you have previously assigned songs to someone else. Include titles, readable lyrics and your full name and address. Give the same information for your co-writer(s) if you have one. State if you are a member of BMI, ASCAP or SESAC. Lead sheets are not required. Comments will follow only if interested." SASE.
Music: Blues, country, disco, gospel, MOR, progressive, rock (hard or soft), soul, top 40/pop, polka, and Latin dance. Published "It Won't Seem like Christmas (without You)," recorded by Elvis Presley (pop/country); "Blue Memories," and "I Don't Know What I'm Doing," recorded by Dean Martin; "Our Last Rendezvous," recorded by Stu Phillips; "A Railroad Bum," and "You're Slipping Away from Me," recorded by Jim Reeves.

WESCO MUSIC GROUP, Box 24281, Nashville TN 37202-4281. (615)242-5588. Professional Manager: Jerry West. Music publisher and record company (Electric Records). BMI, ASCAP.
Affiliates: Wanted Music (BMI) and Grahams Tree Top Songs (ASCAP).
How to Contact: Prefers cassette with 3 songs and lyric sheet. SASE.
Music: Country, pop and gospel. Published "Muddy Missippi," (by Julie Jones/J. Coleman), recorded by Reba McEntire on Mercury Records; and "Black & White Rainbow" recorded by Jacky Ward on Elektra/WEA Records, (both country).

WESJAC MUSIC, 129 W. Main St., Box 743, Lake City SC 29560. (803)394-3597. General Manager: W.R. Bragdton Jr. Music publisher and record company. BMI. Publishes 3 songs/year; publishes 1 new songwriter/year. Pays standard royalty.
How to Contact: Prefers 7½ or 15 ips reel-to-reel with 2 songs and lyric or lead sheets. Does not return unsolicited material. Reports in 1 month.
Music: Gospel. Published "One More Time" (by W.J. Sanders), recorded by Royal Travelers; and "If Jesus Can't Fix It" (by Billy M. Graham) and "Jesus Is My Only Friend" (by Barney Dozier), both recorded by Gospel Creators, all on Wes Jac Records (all gospel).
Tips: "We are interested in old-fashioned gospel music with a strong message and good rhythm." Likes "good material and good cooperation in the matter."

WESTBURY MUSIC LTD.,56 Wigmore St., London W1H 9DG England. (01)935 5133. Directors: Caroline Robertson and Francis Pettican. Music publisher. PRS. "We operate principally as a music publishing consultant/administrator. Our relationships within the music business allow us the opportunity to place good songs. Our clients include Ultravox, Dead or Alive and Cat Stevens.
Affiliates: Riff-Raff Music, Bosco Music and Escape Music Ltd.
How to Contact: Prefers cassette and lyric sheet. Does not return unsolicited material. Reports in 2 weeks.
Music: "Music should be commercial soul or funk based songs with good melodic structure. No guitar rock."
Tips: "Regardless of the style of song, it must have a good basic melody."

*WESTRAX PUBLISHING, 484 W. 43 St., New York NY 10036. Contact: Peter Link. Music publisher. ASCAP. Publishes 3 songs/year; publishes 1 new songwriter/year. Works with composers and lyricists; teams collaborators. Pays standard royalty.
How to Contact: Prefers cassette with 3 songs and lyric sheet. SASE. Reports in 6 weeks.
Music: Pop, R&B and dance. Published "Call Me Anytime," by Link/Lowe (dance); "Don't It Feel Good," by Link (dance); and "The River," by Link (R&B), all recorded by Jenny Burton on Atlantic Records).

WESTUNES MUSIC PUBLISHING CO., Box 754, Edison NJ 08818-0754. (201)548-6700. President: Victor Kaplij. Music publisher. ASCAP. Estab. 1986. Publishes 15 songs/year; publishes 5 new songwriters/year. Pays standard royalty.
How to Contact: Prefers cassette with 3 songs and lyric sheet. SASE. Reports in 6 weeks.
Music: Rock, pop and country. Published "Open Your Eyes," written and recorded by Aerrage on WDHA (rock); "Nightmare," written and recorded by Aerrage on New Renaissance (Rock); and "Kimberly Row," written and recorded by Kevin McCabe on Rockbeat (pop).
Tips: Submit a "neat promotional package; attach biography of the songwriter."

WHEATLEY MUSIC PTY. LTD., #4.5 Illoura Bldg., 424 St. Kilda Rd., Melbourne, Victoria 3004 Australia. (03)267-8811. Professional Manager: Doris Tyler. Music publisher, record company (Wheatley Records) and record producer (Ross Fraser).
How to Contact: Submit demo tape by mail. SAE and IRC.
Music: Rock. Published "Time For Us," (by Goble/Nelson), recorded by Little River Band on EMI/Capitol Records; "Love an Adventure," (by Canham), recorded by Psuedo Echo on EMI Records; and "Flame," (by Sterry Zatorski), recorded by Real Life on Wheatley Records.

WHITE CAT MUSIC, Box 3247, Shawnee KS 66203. (913)631-6060. Professional Manager: Frank Fara. Producer: Patty Parker. Music publisher. Member CMA, GMA-CARAS, ACME, BCCMA and BBB. Publishes 60 songs/year; "50% of our published songs are from non-charted and developing writers." Pays standard royalty.
Affiliate: Rocky Bell Music (BMI).
How to Contact: Prefers cassette with 1-4 songs and lyric or lead sheet. SASE. Reports in 2 weeks.
Music: Mostly adult contemporary, traditional country and contemporary country; also contemporary gospel. Published "When Two Hearts Speak," written and recorded by R.J. McClintock; "Woman (You Make Me Feel So Good)," written and recorded by Charlie Rundlett; and "Catch A Tiny Teardrop," written and recorded by R.J. McClintock, all on Comstock Records (all traditional country).
Tips: "Urgently need adult contemporary/pop songs for new Paylode division servicing US and Canada. Also in need of European and Canadian songwriters to balance our writer roster."

*WHITE CROW MUSIC, INC., 19 Marble Ave., Burlington VT 05401. Director: Douglas G. Jaffe. Music publisher and recording studio (White Crow Audio). BMI. Pays standard royalty.
How to Contact: Prefers cassette with 3 songs maximum and lyric sheet. SASE. Reports in 3 weeks.
Music: "Heart and Soul in any genre."
Tips: "We are more likely to take interest in a submission that is imaginative and sincere."

*WILD WEST MUSIC OF CANADA LTD., Box 1500, Edmonton, Alberta T5J 2M7 Canada. (403)486-1386. Director of Songwriters: Rita Miller. Music publisher and record company (Disc Records). CAPAC. Publishes 10-20 songs/year; publishes 2-3 new songwriters/year. Works with composers and lyricists; teams collaborators. Pays standard royalty.
Affiliate: Wilder Yet Music (PRO).
How to Contact: Prefers cassette with maximum of 3 songs and lyric or lead sheet. "We would also appreciate biographical material and photos if available." SAE and IRC. Reports in 2 months.
Music: Mostly top 40, rock and pop; also MOR (easy listening), country and R&B/jazz. Published "Love in the Big City" (by G. Sinclair), recorded by Kim Kastle on Disc Records (pop); "Need to Feel," written and recorded by Thunderfoot on Boiler Records (rock); and "You & I," written and recorded by R. Miller on Theta Records (pop).

SHANE WILDER MUSIC, Box 3503, Hollywood CA 90078. (818)896-5506. President: Shane Wilder. Music publisher and record producer. BMI. Publishes 30 songs/year; publishes 12 new songwriters/year. Pays standard royalty.
How to Contact: Prefers cassette (or videocassette) with 3-10 songs and lyric sheet. "Include SASE if you wish tape returned. Photo and resume should be sent if you're looking for a producer." Reports in 1 month.
Music: Country, soft and country rock. Published "We Graduate This Summer," and "The Joker," (by Craig Reynolds), recorded by Teresa O'Dell (country).

LUTHER WILSON MUSIC CO., 312 S. Mill St., Kansas City KS 66101. (913)621-1676. Contact: Luther Wilson Jr. Music publisher, record producer, recording studio, music copying and record company (LW Records). ASCAP. Publishes 15-20 songs/year; publishes 2 new songwriters/year. Works with composers. Pays standard royalty.
How to Contact: Prefers cassette with minimum 4 songs and lyric sheet. "If songwriter has videocassette, call for submission instructions." SASE. Reports in 2 weeks.
Music: Mostly top 40 and R&B; also bluegrass, blues, country, dance-oriented, easy listening, folk, gospel, jazz, MOR, rock and soul. Published "Crying in the Rain," by Greenfield/King (easy listening); and "Give Me the Right," by Wise/Blayman (top 40), both recorded by Jared Howe on LW Records.
Tips: "Use good quality tapes and get voice out front. We openly encourage songwriters to send us material. Send only the songs with strong catchy hooks and lyrics. Listen to the radio for ideas."

WISHBONE, INC., Box 2631, Muscle Shoals AL 35662-2631. (205)381-1455. President: Terry Woodford. Music publisher, record producer, studio and video production company (Flying Colors Vid-

eo). BMI, ASCAP. Publishes 100 songs/year; publishes 1-2 new songwriters/year. Hires staff writers. Pays standard royalty.
Affiliates: Song Tailors Music Co. (BMI), Terry Woodford Music (ASCAP), I've Got the Music Co. (ASCAP) and Creative Source Music (BMI).
How to Contact: Prefers cassette with 2 songs and lyric sheet. SASE. Reports as soon as possible. Submit to the attention of Billy Lawson.
Music: Mostly top 40/pop, country, country/pop, R&B and rock; also dance-oriented, easy listening, MOR, progressive, and soul. Published "Angel In Your Arms," (a million performance song by Terry Woodford/Clayton Ivey/Tom Brasfield), recorded by Barbara Mandrell on MCA Records (country); "If I Knew Then What I Know Now," (by Robert Byrne/Richard Butler), recorded by Gary Morris on Warner Bros. Records (country); and "She's Going Out Of My Mind," (by Mac McAnnally) recorded by John Anderson on Warner Bros. Records (country).
Tips: "Be up-to-date with various artists' styles."

WOODRICH PUBLISHING CO., Box 38, Lexington AL 35648. (205)247-3983. President: Woody Richardson. Music publisher and record company. BMI. Publishes 25 songs/year; publishes 5 new songwriters/year. Teams collaborators. Pays 50% royalty less expenses.
Affiliates: Mernee Music (ASCAP).
How to Contact: Prefers 7½ ips reel-to-reel, or cassette (or ¾" videocassette) with 2-4 songs. Prefers studio produced demos. SASE. Reports in 1 month.
Music: Mostly country and gospel; also bluegrass, blues, choral, church/religious, easy listening, folk, jazz, MOR, progressive, rock, soul and top 40/pop. Published "Still Small Voice" (by Roger Johnson), recorded by Heaven's Mountain Band (gospel); "Homecoming Tennessee," written and recorded by Wayne Yocom (country); and "Thanking the Lord" (by Ivory Ellison), recorded by Ellison Family (black gospel), all on Woodrich Records.
Tips: "Use a studio demo if possible. If not, be sure the lyrics are extremely clear."

WORD MUSIC, Division of Word, Inc., Box 1790, Waco TX 76796. (817)772-7650. Creative Director: Debbie Atkins, Word Records: Suite 110, 33 Music Square W., Nashville TN 37203. Music publisher and record company. ASCAP. Member GMA. Publishes 25 songs/year; publishes 1-3 new songwriters/year.
Affiliates: Rodeheaver (ASCAP), Dayspring (BMI) and The Norman Clayton Publishing Co. (SESAC).
How to Contact: Prefers cassette with 1-3 songs and lead sheet. SASE. "Please send a demonstration tape of a choir singing your anthem to Ken Barker, Print Director." Reports in 10 weeks.
Music: Choral anthems and octavos; also children's, choral, church/religious.
Tips: "Lead sheets, or final form—anything submitted—should be legible and understandable. The care that a writer extends in the works he submits reflects the work he'll submit if a working relationship is started. First impressions are important."

YAMAHA MUSIC FOUNDATION, 3-24-22 Shimomeguro, Meguro-ku Tokyo 153 Japan. (03)719-3101. Secretary General, Festival Committee: Hiro Murakami (Mr.). Music publisher, record producer, and organizer and sponsor of World Popular Song Festival in Tokyo. JASRAC. Publishers 1,100 songs/year; publishes 700 new songwriters/year. Pays standard royalty.
How to Contact: Prefers cassette or 7½ ips reel-to-reel with any number of songs and lyric or lead sheets. "Enclose singer's picture and biography." Does not return unsolicited material.
Music: "Any type of music including European, Latin and Oriental."

*ZABAVNE MELODIJE-DSH, Berislaviceva 9, 41000 Zagreb, Yugoslavia. (041)423-443. Music publisher. Publishes 150-200 songs/year; publishes 20-30 new songwriters/year. Pays 10-25% royalty.
How to Contact: Write or call first and obtain permission to submit. Does not return unsolicited material. Reports in 3 weeks.
Music: Mostly blues, country and jazz. Published "great hits and melodies of Yugoslavia (pop and dance music) not much known in USA. We have subpublished some European songs."

REX ZARIO MUSIC, 3010 N. Front St., Philadelphia PA 19133. (215)426-5682. Production Manager: Lucky Taylor. Music publisher, record company and record producer. BMI. Publishes 15-25 songs/year. Pays standard royalty.
Affiliates: Jack Howard Publishing (BMI), Seabreeze Music (BMI), Valley Brook Publishing (ASCAP), Arcade Music Co. (ASCAP).
How to Contact: Prefers 7½ ips reel-to-reel or cassette with 4-6 songs and lyric sheet. SASE. Reports in 1 month.

Music: Country, MOR, rock and bluegrass. Published "Night Wind," (by Lucky Taylor/Doris Frye/ Rex Zario/Jesse Rogers), recorded by J.Rogers on Arcade Records (MOR); "Go Man Go, Get Gone," (by L. Taylor/D. Frye/R. Zario), recorded by R. Zario on Rollercoaster Records in England (country); and "Worlds Apart," (by Ray Whitley/R. Zario), recorded by R. Whitley on Arzee (country).

*ZEBRA DISCORDE MUSIC GROUP, INC., 1040 N. Las Palmas, Los Angeles CA 90038. (213)461-8631. Chairman: Carlo Nasi. Music publisher, record company (Striped Horse Records, Inc.) and record producer (Zebra Discorde Music Group). BMI. Publishes 10-20 songs/year; publishes 2-3 new songwriters/year.
Affiliate: Striped Horse Music, Inc. (ASCAP).
How to Contact: Write first and obtain permission to submit. Prefers cassette with 3-4 songs and lyric sheet. Does not return unsolicited material. Reports in 1 month.
Music: Mostly pop, R&B and dance; also rock. BMI. Published "Red Light" (by Veitch/Winding), recorded by Patty Brard (dance); "Room 999" (by Veitch/Donaggio/Brard/Steffan), recorded by P. Brard (pop); and "Golden Empire" (by Ike Turner), recorded by Ike and Tina Turner (pop), all on Striped Horse Records.

*ZIP KID PUBLISHING, Suite 2-2, 400 Hwy. 34, Aberdeen NJ 07747. (201)583-5578. Contact: Jacques Battel. Music publisher and record company (Entertainment Network Service). BMI. Pays standard royalty.
How to Contact: Prefers cassette (or VHS videocassette) with lyric or lead sheet. SASE. Reports in 1 month.
Music: Mostly rock and country; also pop and R&B. Published "Teenage Dilemma" (by Lee Wiggins), recorded by Person to Person (rock); "Too Much" (by Jeff Cornad), recorded by Romance (rock); and "Half a Bottle" (by Lee Wiggins), recorded by ENS (country), all on Zip Kid Records.

Geographic Index

The U.S. section of this handy geographic index will quickly give you the names of publishers located in the music centers of Los Angeles, Nashville and New York. While there are many valuable contacts to be made in other cities, you will probably want to plan a trip to one of these established music centers at some point in your career, and try to see as many of these publishers as you think appropriate. The International section lists, geographically, markets for your songs in foreign countries.

Find the names of companies in this index, and then check listings within the Music Publishers section for addresses, phone numbers and submission details.

Nashville

Acoustic Music, Inc.
Angelsong Publishing Co.
Another Ear Music
Baby Huey Music
Big Wedge Music
Buried Treasure Music
Calvary Music Group Inc.
Chevis Publishing Corp.
Clays Ferry Music Co.
Denny Music Group
Bobby Fischer Music
John Fisher & Associates
Grand Music Group, Inc.
Heavy Jamin' Music
James Hendrix, Composer and
    Publisher
Humanform Publishing Compa-
    ny
Iffin Publishing Co.
Jaclyn Music
Dick James Organization
Al Jolson's Black & White Mu-
    sic
Gene Kennedy Enterprises, Inc.
Kimtra Music/Hatband Music
Mr. Mort Music
Musiplex Group, Inc.
New Clarion Music Group
Newcreature Music
Not Even Music
Old Guide Publishing Inc.
Peer-Talbot Music Group
Quinton Q. Qualls, Jr. Music
Rainbarrel Music Company
Ray Mack Music
Rocker Music/Happy Man Mu-
    sic
Song Farm Music
Preston Sullivan Music
Sweet Singer Music
Tandem Tunes, Inc.
Tree Publishing Co., Inc.
Treehouse Music
Wesco Music Group

New York

A Street Music
Brainstorm Music
Bush/Lehrman Music
C.T.P.
Camerica Music
Ca-Song Music Publisher
D.S.M. Producers
David Music
S.M. Gold Music, Inc.
Gopam Enterprises, Inc.
Hopsack and Silk Productions
    Inc.
Jeneane & Jude Music
Jondi Music
KozKeeOzKo Music
Lingo Music
Lin's Lines
Manhattan Country, Inc.
Mia Mind Music

Ivan Mogull Music Corp.
Notable Music Co. Inc.
Number 9 Musical Enterprises,
    Inc.
Popular Music Co.
Publishing Ventures
Gerald W. Purcell Associates
Raybird Music
Ren Maur Music Corp.
Ridge Music Corp.
Rockford Music Co.
Roperry Music
Salmo Music
Seixas Music
Snugglebush Music Company
Swing & Tempo Music Publish-
    ing Inc.
Tannen Music Companies
Tommy Valando Publishing
    Group
Westrax Publishing

International
ARGENTINA

Ediciones Musicales Relay S.A.
Edifon S.R.L.

AUSTRALIA

Chappell & Co. (Aust.) Pty.,
    Ltd.
Image Music Group Pty., Ltd.
Leosong Copyright Service Pty.,
    Ltd.
MMA Music
Wheatley Music Pty., Ltd.

AUSTRIA

Jenisch Musikverlag
Johann Kaplan Music
Koch Musikverlag

BELGIUM

B. Sharp Music
Jump Music
Jean Kluger
Radio Tele Music S.A.

BRAZIL

Alldisc
Editora Presenca Ltd.

CANADA

Alternative Direction Music
    Publishers
Anthem Entertainment Group
Anti-Conscious Music
Attic Publishing Group
Bee Bop Music
Berandol Music Ltd.
Canadian Custom Records
Canadian Music Productions
Cantus Publishing Co., Inc.
Computer Music International
    Ltd.
Do Sol Publishing
Downs Publishing Company

Etc. Music Inc.
Fudge Music
Halben Music Publishing, Inc.
Koma Publishing
Les Editions La Fete Inc.
Master's Collection Publishing
    & T.M.C. Publishing
Mercey Brothers Publishing
Brian Millan Music Corp.
Montina Music
Musinfo Publishing Group, Inc.
Nashville Sound Music Publish-
    ing Co.
Noteworthy Publishing Co.
Peer-Southern Organization
Praise Sound Productions Ltd.
S.M.C.L. Productions, Inc. '
Sabre Music
Shotgun Music Corp.
Wild West Music of Canada
    Ltd.

CZECHOSLOVAKIA

Opus, Records and Publishing
    House

FINLAND

Bluebird Music OY
Fazer Music Inc.
Kompass Records

FRANCE

Campagne S.A.
Editions Caravage
I.D. Music/Publications A. Pier-
    son
MCA Music France
Societe D'Editions Musicales et
    Artistiques "Esperance"
Topomic Music

HUNGARY

Editio Musica Budapest

ICELAND

Geimsteinn HF

ISRAEL

Subar Music Publishing Co.
    Ltd.

ITALY

Merak Music Production S.R.L.

JAPAN

Americana Songs, Inc.
Kitty Music Corporation
Toshiba-EMI Music Publishing
    Co., Ltd.
Yamaha Music Foundation

66 *Unless your song is so strong that your dog could bark it out, get as good a singer as you can afford to do the demo. If you have a strong singer, the demo can be really simple, but it still has to be played in tune and it has to sound professional.* **99**

—*Fred Koller, songwriter*

Music Print Publishers

Sheet Music Means Extra Revenue

by Ronny S. Schiff

Music is the only medium where _published_ does not necessarily mean _printed_. The companies who produce printed music are called "music print publishers." They license the rights to print, package and distribute music from the copyright owners or administrators (music publishers).

Printed music falls into two categories: popular and educational. Popular includes sheet music; mixed books (folios), which are collections of tunes around a theme; matching books, those that match a specific record album; and personality books, collections of a specific artist's or group's songs. Educational music encompasses choral, band, orchestral and instrumental ensemble arrangements; and method (how-to) books.

There are a few companies who print both pop and educational music, a few who produce just pop music, and many who fall into various areas of educational print. There are also several religious print publishers who publish sheet music, books and choral music, and distribute primarily to churches and religious bookstores. [Each of the listings in this section indicates the specific type(s) of music it is interested in.]

Pop music

For popular music, a print deal can come into play when a song reaches the upper portion of the singles charts, or if it's on a Top 100 LP. [Many of the companies listed indicate the lowest chart position held by a song they printed sheet music for, or say they will print music for songs not yet on the charts.] If you have movement on the charts with many tunes, you can negotiate a catalog deal with a print publisher, giving them your entire group of songs to print. (You can negotiate for different degrees of exclusivity and nonexclusivity for each song.) Or, you can shop each tune as it hits the charts and take the deal that offers the best features for you.

You've probably been through some school music programs and may think your pop tune is suitable for a marching or jazz band, or a choir arrangement. Get to know your print publisher and tell them your ideas. But be realistic. If the tune's in 3/4 time, it's not "marchable." If it has a racy lyric, it's not suitable for a school chorus.

Let the print publisher know if there have been any other covers on your tune with different types of arrangements, or if it's going to be featured on television or in a movie, so the tune can be placed in more than one category of mixed folios. If the recording of your tune features some outstanding guitar playing, the print company may want to include it in a book of guitar arrangements (especially heavy metal). Push for an easy piano arrangement—these sell well, especially if the theme of the song is a "youngish" concept. This very basic form of communication with the print company will bring more print usages and more revenue.

Print royalties

Print royalties for songs used in books range from 10-15% of the retail selling price, pro rated to the number of songs in the book. Educational royalties also range from 10-15% of the retail selling price. Sheet music is paid on a flat rate per sheet, which usually works out to be

Ronny S. Schiff has worked as production manager for several major print companies including Hansen Publications, Warner Bros. Music, Almo Publications and Cherry Lane Music. She also served as Vice President of Dick Grove Publications, and has had her own company for ten years, producing and packaging music books and books about music for most of the major music print publishers in the U.S. She also does licensing for educational music and music software, and acts as an agent for music-based books.

one-fifth of the retail selling price. Artists also receive a small name and likeness royalty for personality books, and give this right exclusively to one print company. The royalties from print music are usually split between the music publisher and the songwriter 50-50, but here deals vary. With a catalog deal, the music publisher and print company communicate often, and there may be an advance (for the overall catalog) the print company must work off by utilizing that catalog.

If your songs are not on the charts, there are other ways to bring in print income. One rural music teacher wrote a charming children's piece and arranged it for school choirs. She then sold it to an educational print company. The arrangement was so successful that her first royalty check almost equaled her yearly teaching income.

Educational and religious music

Educational and religious print companies accept original songs suitable for choral arrangement (some companies do stipulate that the songs be in 2-, 3-, or 4-part harmony). Others look for original jazz band, concert band, marching band or instrumental ensemble pieces. With these, as well as with chorals, you must be familiar with the capabilities of school age performers or church musicians.

How-to-play books can be financial life insurance for you. Just ask Mel Bay, the man who wrote the first successful guitar method book (even Elvis learned from it), which has sold millions of copies (unusual in the print business). Watch the trends. Special guitar and keyboard styles, and electronic music technology are especially popular now, but a unique harmonica or drum method can be just as successful.

You may even aspire to become a part of the print industry. There's always a need for good print arrangers for sheet music, band or choral pieces, instrumental or guitar solos (knowing tablature helps here), especially if you have perfect pitch and can transcribe off a record. There are also calls for people knowledgeable in instruments as varied as autoharp to zither.

For names and addresses (but no marketing information) of other print publishers, check the National Music Publishers Association's list, Billboard's *International Buyer's Guide*, or the annual *Musical America Directory*.

*ANOTHER EAR MUSIC, #V-4, 380 Harding Pl., Nashville TN 37211. Owner/President: T.J. Kirby. Prints 4 songs/year, mostly individual songs. Has published uncharted songs. Pays 9% royalty.
How to Contact: Prefers cassette and lyric sheet. SASE. Reports in 1 month.
Music: Mostly country/pop and R&B; also MOR and gospel. Published "Believing In Your Love" (by T.J. Kirby/Lanny Smith), recorded by Cristy Lane (gospel); "Let It Be Me Tonight" (by T.J. Kirby/Bob Lee/Tom Douglas), recorded by Kathy Ford (country/pop, #80 on charts when music was printed); and "Don't Take a Heart" (by T.J. Kirby/L. Smith), recorded by Deb Merritt (country/pop).

BIRCH TREE GROUP LTD., Box 2072, Princeton NJ 08540. (609)683-0073. Contact: Editorial Department. Music publisher. ASCAP, SESAC, Harry Fox Agency. Prints 25 pieces/year, mostly method books.
How to Contact: "We are interested in manuscripts for educational music material only." SASE. Reports in 1 month.
Music: Mostly educational and school performance. Published Frances Clark Library and The Suzuki Method.
Tips: "We are interested in Suzuki-related material and early childhood music education."

*BLUE UMBRELLA/PARASOL MUSIC, (ASCAP/BMI), 3011 Beach 40th St., Brooklyn NY 11224. (718)372-6436. President: Kadish Millet. Prints 10 songs/year, mostly individual songs. Pays .06¢/song to songwriter for each sheet sold.
How to Contact: Prefers cassette and lead sheet (lyric sheet if lead sheet is not available). SASE. Reports in 2 weeks.
Music: Country ("double entendre").

*BOSTON MUSIC CO., 116-122 Boylston, Boston MA 02116. (617)426-5100. Contact: Editorial Department. Prints 100 pieces/year, both individual pieces and music books. Pays standard royalty.

How to Contact: Submit "legible manuscript." Do not send tapes. Reports in 6 months.
Music: Choral pieces, instrumental solo pieces, methods books, and "piano instructional materials that piano teachers would be interested in."

*BOURNE COMPANY, 5 W. 37th St., New York NY 10018. (212)391-4300. Contact: Editorial Department. Prints 75 pieces/year, mostly individual pieces. Pays varying royalty.
How to Contact: Query "to see if we're scheduling that type of music. We'll write as soon as possible."
Music: Band pieces, choral pieces, and handbell pieces.

*CHERRY LANE MUSIC CO., INC., 110 Midland Ave., Port Chester NY 10573. (914)937-8601. General Manager of Print Division: Michael Lefferts. Prints 50 songs/year, both individual songs and folios. Lowest chart position held by a song published in sheet form was "at least in the Hot 100." Pays standard royalty.
How to Contact: Prefers "distributed record" or cassette. Returns material with SASE "only if there's time to do so." Reports "if interested, according to time limitations."
Music: Pop, rock, heavy metal, and A/C. Publishes songs by Lionel Richie, Huey Lewis, Bruce Hornsby, Boston, John Denver, and "other top-name artists. Educational materials published are based on the pop songs—the artist/songwriter would agree to have the song exploited in both ways. If a song were suitable for a choral arrangement, etc., we would pursue that."

*COLUMN ONE, LTD., MUSIC GROUP, Box 4086, Springfield MO 65808. (417)881-5015. Manager: Lou Whitney. Prints 20-25 songs/year, mostly individual songs. Pays standard royalty.
How to Contact: Prefers cassette and lyric sheet. "No returns! We'll contact within 60 days only if interested. We listen to everything."
Music: Mostly CHR, country and rock; also "esoteric roots," rockabilly, blues and folk. Published "Atomic Bum" (by Ross/Workman), recorded by Boxcar Willie (country); "Trans Am" (by L. Whitney), recorded by The Skeletons (roots rock); and "Red Georgia Clay" (by B. Emerson), recorded by John Anderson (country).

*CREOLE MUSIC, 91/93 High St., Harlesden, London NW10, England. Phone: (01)965-9223. Director: Bruce White. General Manager: Steve Tantum. Prints 100 songs/year, mostly folios. Lowest chart position held by song published in print form is 74.
How to Contact: Prefers cassette and lyric sheet. SAE and IRC. Reports in 1 month.
Music: "Any good songs."

*DAVIKE MUSIC CO., Box 8842, Los Angeles CA 90008. (213)296-2302. Owner: Isaiah Jones, Jr., Prints 4 songs/year, mostly individual songs. Pays 50% royalty.
How to Contact: Prefers cassette and lead and lyric sheets or complete score. SASE. Reports in 1 month.
Music: Mostly gospel, pop, R&B and inspirational; also folk and country. Published "Great and Wondrous," by I. Jones Jr. (gospel); "Never Be the Same Again," by I. Jones/G. McKinnie (gospel); and "Loving, Caring," by I. Jones (pop).

*DOC RON PUBLISHING/RON DOC PUBLISHING, ((BMI/ASCAP), Box 1075, Boca Raton FL 33439. (305)391-0255. Vice President: M. Scott Stander. Prints 5 songs/year, mostly individual songs. Lowest chart position held by a song published in sheet form is 52. Pays 50% royalty.
How to Contact: Prefers cassette. Does not return unsolicited material. Reports in 6 weeks.
Music: Pop, reggae, gospel, Broadway and country. Published "Rockin Reggae Jam" and "Feel a Need" (by G. Williams), recorded by Surfside (reggae folios); and "Know the Feeling" (by Bobby Koster), recorded by Kippi Brown.

*EDICIONES MUSICALES RELAY SA, 3930 Pardissien, Buenos Aires 1430, Argentina. Manager: Ana Maria de Visaggio. Prints 1,000 songs/year, both individual songs and folios. Pays 10% royalty.
How to Contact: Prefers cassette and lead or lyric sheets or complete score. SAE and IRC. Reports in 1 month.
Music: Mostly ballads, pop and MOR; also rock, jazz and blues. Published "Too Late" (by Woolfson/Parsons), recorded by Alan Parsons; "Dedicado" (by I. Fossati), recorded by M. Gallardo; and "Talk to Me" (by P. Fox/F. Gold); recorded by Chico de Barge.

*EDITIONS CARAVAGE, 130 Rue Marius Aufan, Levallois-Perret, 92300 France. Phone: (1)47-59-94-51. General Manager: Jean-Paul Smets. Prints 50-100 songs/year, mostly individual songs. Pays 10% royalty.

How to Contact: Prefers cassette. Does not return unsolicited material. Reports in 1 month.
Music: Published "Soy Apache" (by Agudelo/Besombes/Pascal), recorded by Son Caribe (Spanish/disco); "Jonathan" (by G. Vacher/D. Doublet), recorded by Duels (rock), and "Romantic" (by Chretien/Sandra), recorded by Varenne (pop).

*EMANDELL TUNES/BIRTHRIGHT MUSIC, % 10220 Glade Ave., Chatsworth CA 91311. (818)341-2264 or 405-0356. Administrator: Leroy C. Lovett Jr. Prints 15-20 songs/year, both individual songs and folios. Lowest chart position held by song published in sheet form is 36. Pays statutory royalty or 15¢/song to songwriter for each sheet sold.
How to Contact: Write or call first and obtain permission to submit. Prefers cassette and lyric sheet. SASE. Reports in 6 weeks.
Music: Inspirational, contemporary and traditional gospel, and chorals. Published "Give Us This Day," written and recorded by Edwin Hawkins; "Loving You" (by Shiela Mathews), recorded by Lynnette; "The Day Will Come" (by R. Trotter), recorded by Brenda Holloway; and "Help Me Jesus" (by Barbara Hale), recorded by Brenda Holloway (all gospel).

GENEVOX MUSIC GROUP, (formerly Broadman Press), 127 9th Ave. N., Nashville TN 37234. (615)251-3770. Music Production Manager: David Danner. Music publisher. SESAC, ASCAP and BMI. Publishes 100 songs/year; publishes 10 new songwriters/year.
How to Contact: Submit demo tape and choral arrangement or lead sheet. Prefers reel-to-reel or cassette with 1-15 songs on demo. SASE. Reports in 2 months.
Music: Choral, church/religious and gospel. "We publish all forms of sacred music including solo/choral for all ages, and instrumental for handbell, organ, piano and orchestra." Published "All That I Was" (by Wes Forbis/Mark Hayes), recorded by Kelly Nelson Thompson (contemporary Christian); "Gloria," by Bob Burroughs (childrens' anthem); and "And Then There Is Peace," by Terry York/David Danner (SATB choral anthem).
Tips: "Most of what we publish is designed for use by church choirs and instrumentalists, therefore music that is already in that format is preferred."

GWYNN PUBLISHING CO., Penygroes, Caernarfon, Gwynedd, Wales 44-0286-881-797. Leading publishers of Welsh folk songs and dances in printed form. Publishes 12 songs/year. "We specialize in songs and arrangements for choirs (male, female and SATB) as well as Welsh classical solos and children's songs." Pays 25-50% "of trade discount."
How to Contact: "Send for more information to the above address."
Music: Choral works. Published "Christmas Star," by Mansel Thomas (S.S./piano); "There Is a River," by Daniel Protheroe (SATB/piano); and "Beautiful Dreamer," by Mansel Thomas (TTBB/piano).

*HAMMER MUSIK GMBH, Esslinger Str. 42, Stuttgart 7000, West Germany. Phone: (711)247553/4. Contact: Ingo Kleinhammer. Prints mostly individual songs. Pays 10% royalty.
How to Contact: Prefers cassette. SAE and IRC. Reports in 2 weeks.
Music: Mostly dance, disco and pop; also rock and jazz.

*HANSEN HOUSE, 1870 West Ave., Miami Beach FL 33139. (305)532-5461, or (800)327-8202. TV Marketing Director: Anthony Brimhall. Prints 200-300 pieces/year, mostly music books (educational books of text and music); and 100-200 songs/year, both individual songs and folios. Has printed music for uncharted songs. Pays negotiable royalty to composer or songwriter per sheet or book sold.
How to Contact: Submit complete manuscript (and tape if applicable) for educational material; cassette and lyric or lead sheet of popular songs. Send Attention: Anthony Brimhall, New Product Department. "Send a letter; a concise, clear tape; and be sure to label things properly." SASE. Reports in 1 month.
Music: All styles; mostly pop, jazz, rock and country. Catalog includes pieces by Buddy Greco, Liberace, Roy Clark, Pat Boone and Claude Bolling (music books).
Tips: "We have over 2,700 titles in our catalog. We publish all kinds of music—once we obtain licenses we will print sheet music if it's appropriate, and the song may be included in a number of folios. We also have contacts in the music industry and we sometimes recommend songwriter/artists to them. It has happened that songwriters submitted original songs to us and landed recording contracts after we recommended them to major labels."

*IVORY PALACES MUSIC, 3141 Spottswood Ave., Memphis TN 38111. (901)323-3509. President: Jack Abell. Prints 15 songs/year, mostly book/tape combinations. Pays 10% retail price or 50% license income.
How to Contact: Write first and obtain permission to submit. Prefers cassette and lyric sheet. SASE. Reports in 2 months.

Music: Mostly classical; also religious. Published "Larkin's Dulcimer Book," written and recorded by Larkin Bryant (folk).

*JA/NEIN MUSIKVERLAG GMBH, Hallerstr. 72, D-2000 Hamburg 13, West Germany. Phone: (40)410-21-61. General Manager: Mary Dostal. Prints 50 songs/year, both individual songs and folios. Has printed music for uncharted songs.
How to Contact: Prefers cassette. SAE and IRC. Reports in 3 weeks.
Music: Rock, pop, MOR and blues. Published "April Mood," "Make Me Call California," and "Boogie Du Printemps," all written and recorded by Axel Zwingenberger (all boogie woogie), all members of folios, and all songs that had not charted.

JENSON PUBLICATIONS INC., 2770 S. 171 St., New Berlin WI 53151. (414)784-4620. Publications Director: Roberta Davies Dorgan. Prints 300 pieces/year, both individual pieces and music books. Pays 10% royalty for "original material."
How to Contact: Query with complete score and tape of piece. Prefers cassette. SASE. Reports in 1 month.
Music: Choral pieces and "elementary material."

*JUMP MUSIC, Langemunt 71, 9460 Erpe-Mere, Belgium. Phone: (053)62-73-77. General Manager: Eddy Van Mouffaert. Prints 20 songs/year, mostly individual songs. Pays 10% royalty.
How to Contact: Prefers cassette and lead sheet or complete score. Does not return unsolicited material. Reports in 2 weeks.
Music: Pop, ballads and instrumental. Published "Vertrouwen," recorded by Eigentijdse Jeugd (ballad); "Sinds Ik Jou Ken," recorded by Tony Lenders (uptempo); and "Vannacht Blijf Ik Bij Jou," recorded by Guy Lovely (ballad), all written by Eddy Govert.

*LEMATT MUSIC LTD./LEE MUSIC LTD./POGO RECORDS LTD., % Stewart House, Hillbottom Rd., Highwycombe Buckinghamshire, England. Phone: (0494) 36301 or 36401. A&R: Xavier Lee. Prints 50 songs/year, mostly individual songs. Lowest chart position held by a song published in sheet form is 41. Pays negotiable royalty.
How to Contact: Prefers cassette or 7½ or 15 ips reel-to-reel and lyric and lead sheets or complete score. SAE and IRC. Reports in 6 weeks.
Music: All types, Published "Hit Man" (by M.J. Lawson), recorded by Emmit Till (rock); "Rock 'n' Roll Revival" (by M. Tyer), recorded by Elmer Goodbody Jr. (rock); and "Mood Music" (by R.C. Bowman), recorded by R.K. Band (MOR).

*LES EDITIONS LA FETE INC., 2306 Sherbrooke St. E. Montreal, Quebec H2K 1E5 Canada. (514)521-8303. General Manager: Michel Zgarka. Prints 7 songs/year, both individual songs and folios. Lowest chart position held by a song published in sheet form is 18. Pays 50% royalty.
How to Contact: Prefers cassette. Does not return unsolicited material. Reports in 2 months.
Music: Mostly "songs to be used in film scores;" also uptempo dance music. Published "Not Ready," (dance) and "When We're Together," (ballad), (both by C. Debski/H. Forman), both recorded by Freddie James; and Tête de Rêveur" (by C. Debski/G. Trepanier/M. Desjardins), recorded by Betty Eljarat (ballad), all parts of movie soundtracks.

LILLENAS PUBLISHING CO., Box 419527, Kansas City MO 64141. (816)931-1900. Music Editor: Lyndell Leatherman. Music publisher and record company. SESAC. Publishes 300 songs/year; publishes 5 new songwriters/year. Pays 10% royalty.
How to Contact: "Submit manuscript—demo tape optional." Prefers cassette with 1-6 songs and lead sheet. SASE. Reports in 10 weeks.
Music: Sacred, traditional gospel and contemporary religious.

*HAROLD LUICK & ASSOCIATES , (BMI), Box B, Carlisle IA 50047. (515)989-3679. President: Harold Luick. Prints 4-5 songs/year, mostly individual songs. Lowest chart position held by a song published in sheet form is 98. Pays 4% royalty.
How to Contact: Write and obtain permisison to submit or submit through publisher or attorney. Prefers cassette or reel-to-reel and lyric sheet. SASE. Reports in 3 weeks.
Music: Mostly traditional country; also novelty songs. Published "Waylon Sing to Mama," written and recorded by Darrell C. Thomas (country, #78 on charts when music was printed).

*MARSHALL STREET MELODIES, 8102 Polk St. NE, Minneapolis MN 55432. (612)784-7458. President/General Manager: Mike Gapinski. Prints 15-30 songs/year, mostly individual songs. Has printed music for uncharted songs. Pays 50-60% royalty.

How to Contact: Write first and obtain permission to submit. Prefers cassette and lyric sheet. Does not return unsolicited material. Reports in 2 weeks.
Music: Mostly R&B/funk; also country/pop. Published "Ready or Not" (by T. Graham), "Desire" (by R. Heyne/G. Ford/J. Kuczek), and "Stingray" (by J. Kuczek), all recorded by Zebop (all R&B), all members of folios, and all new releases that had not charted.

*MASTERSOURCE PRODUCTIONS, Suite 903, 151 N. Michigan, Chicago, IL 60601. (312)819-1515. Office Manager: Stephen Navyac. Contracts print deals for 2-12 songs/year, mostly individual songs.
How to Contact: Write first and obtain permission to submit. Prefers cassette or lyric sheet. Does not return unsolicited material. Reports in 5 weeks.
Music: Mostly top 40 and contemporary Christian; "We are also interested in jingle writers and arrangers." Published "Was It a Morning Like This" (by Jim Croegaert), recorded by Sandi Patti (contemporary Christian, nominated for song of the year).

*MMA MUSIC AUSTRALIA, 145 Brougham St., Kings Cross, Syndney 2024 N.S.W. Australia. Phone: (02)356-4944. Professional Manager: Justin Van Stom. Prints 10 songs/year, mostly individual songs. Lowest chart position held by a song published in print is 40. Pays negotiable royalty.
How to Contact: Prefers cassette and lyric sheet. Does not return unsolicited material. Reports in 1 month.
Music: Rock, pop and new music. Published "The Bottom Line" (by Mick Jones), recorded by Big Audio Dynamite (#38 on charts when music was printed); "Great Wall," written and recorded by Boom Crash Opera (#26 on charts); and "Rooms for the Memory" (by Ollie Olsen), recorded by Michael Hutchence (#11 on charts).

*MUSIC SALES CORP., 5 Bellvale Rd., Chester NY 10918. (914)469-2271. Telemarketing Manager: Robert Morris. Prints 100-200 pieces/year, mostly music books; and 50-100 songs/year, mostly folios. Lowest chart position held by a song published in sheet form was "at least in the Hot 100."
How to Contact: Query with complete manuscript and cassette for instructional pieces; write first and obtain permission to submit cassette and lead sheet of popular songs. SASE. Reports in 2 months.
Music: Instrumental solo books and methods books; and rock. Published *Joy of First Classics*, and *Learning to Play Piano*, by Dennis Agay (piano methods books); and *Rock Riffs for Guitar, Book II*, by Steve Tarshis. Also handles the catalogs of AC/DC, Pink Floyd and Black Sabbath. "We are a diverse company. We distribute picture books of artists like Peter Gabriel and David Bowie."

*PLYMOUTH MUSIC CO., INC., 170 NE 33rd St., Ft. Lauderdale FL 33334. (305)563-1844. General Manager: Bernard Fisher. Prints 40 pieces/year: 35 individual pieces and 5 music books. Pays 10% of list price to composer per sheet or book sold.
How to Contact: Prefers cassette. SASE. Reports in 1 month.
Music: Choral pieces.

THEODORE PRESSER COMPANY Presser Place, Bryn Mawr PA 19010. (215)525-3636. Publications Manager: Laurence Broido. Music publisher. ASCAP, BMI and SESAC. Member MPA. Publishes 50 "mostly choral" songs/year. Payment by contracted royalty.
How to Contact: Prefers cassette and lyric sheet. Reports as soon as possible.
Music: Mostly choral; also children's church/religious, classical and gospel. "No popular songs."
Tips: "We primarily publish serious music by emerging and established composers, and vocal/choral music which is likely to be accepted in the church and educational markets, as well as gospel chorals of high musical quality. We are *not* primarily a publisher of song sheets or pop songs."

*QUEBISSIMUS MUSIC CO., LTD., #121, 3475 St. Urbain St., Montreal, Quebec, H2X 2N4 Canada. (514)288-3550. Prints 300-350 songs/year, mostly folios and "classics." Lowest chart position held by song published in sheet form is 100. Pays 50% gross.
How to Contact: Submit cassette and lead sheet or complete score. Does not return material, "All unaccepted tapes are disposed of." Reports in 6 weeks.
Music: "All types of commercially-oriented music, classical music for piano, and chamber music." Published *La Solution* (LP concept), "a top 10 charted work in the US and distributed worldwide."
Tips: "We also have an international record label, E.M.Q. Records, and a subsidiary company in the state of New York that handles our ASCAP and BMI affiliates."

*BRAIN RAINES MUSIC CO., Box 1376, Pickens SC 29671. (803)878-2953. President: Brian E. Raines. Prints 2-3 songs/year, mostly individual songs. Lowest chart position held by a song published in sheet form is 40. Pays 10% royalty or 10-20¢/song to songwriter for each sheet sold.

How to Contact: Prefers cassette and lyric sheet. SASE. Reports in 3 weeks.
Music: Mostly southern gospel; also contemporary Christian and country.

*SEA DREAM MUSIC, 236 Sebert Rd., London E7 ONP England. Phone: (01)534-8500. Senior Partner: Simon Law. Prints 20 songs/year, mostly individual songs. Has printed sheet music for uncharted songs. Pays 66⅔% royalty.
How to Contact: Prefers cassette and lyric sheet. SAE and IRC. Reports in 6 weeks.
Music: Mostly funk/rock, rock, blues and gospel; also "music with a Christian bias to the lyrics." Published "Rich Man," by Simon Law/Graham Claydon (modern hymn, not recorded and not charted); "Living In the Love" (by Ruth Turner/Cheryl Mead), recorded by the Limpsfield Choir on Plankton Records (anthem folio); and "I Have Called You," written and recorded by Ruth Turner on Plankton Records (solo and folio).

SHAWNEE PRESS, INC., Delaware Water Gap PA 18327. (717)476-0550. Director of Publications: Lewis M. Kirby Jr. Music publisher and record company. ASCAP. Member NMPA, MPA, CMPA. Publishes 150-200 songs/year; publishes 25 new songwriters/year. Pays royalty negotiated at the time of purchase.
How to Contact: Prefers cassette and lead sheet. SASE. Reports in 2 months.
Music: Children's, choral, church/religious, classical, easy listening, folk, gospel, MOR and top 40/pop. "Shawnee Press is primarily a publisher of choral and instrumental music for educational or religious use." Published "Sing to the Lord," (by Robert Sterling), recorded by Sandi Patti on Impact Records (MOR gospel); "There's a Turning," written and recorded by Ken Medema; and "Black & White," (by Robinson and Arkin), recorded by Three Dog Night on ABC-Dunkill (top 40).
Tips: "Send material for review suitable for use in schools or churches or for publication/recording for gospel market. Primarily interested in choral music."

*LARRY SHAYNE ENTERPRISES, #120, 1334 Lincoln Blvd., Santa Monica CA 90401. (213)395-6680. Professional Manager: Dennis Poore. Prints 50 songs/year, mostly individual songs and film scores. Pays standard royalty.
How to Contact: Prefers cassette and lyric sheet, SASE. Reports in 2 weeks.
Music: Mostly pop, R&B and country; also MOR and jazz. Published "A House Is Not a Home;; (by Bacharach/David), recorded by Mel Torme (MOR/jazz, #20 on charts when music was printed); "Take Me Home (by J. Mandell/Alan and Marilyn Bergman), recorded by Sue Raney (MOR); and "A Shot in the Dark" (by Barry DeVorzon), recorded by Patty Weaver (pop/rock); "A Chorus Line" (by Hamlisch/Kleban), stage and motion picture (pop).

*3 SEAS MUSIC/NORTHVALE MUSIC, 450 Livingston St., Norwood NJ 07648. (201)767-5551. Vice President: Gene Schwartz. Prints mostly individual songs. Lowest chart position held by a song published in sheet form is 20. Pays .14¢/song to songwriter for each sheet sold.
How to Contact: Prefers cassette and lead sheet or complete score. SASE. Reports in 1 month.
Music: Rock.

*TOPOMIC MUSIC 105, Rue de Normandie, Courbevoie 92400, France. Phone: (1)43-33-65-15. President: Pierre Jaubert. Prints 150 songs/year, mostly individual songs. Has printed music for uncharted songs. Pays "SACEM rate—50/50" (French performing rights society).
How to Contact: Prefers cassette and lead sheet. Does not return unsolicited material. Reports in 2 weeks.
Music: Mostly top 40 and film soundtracks; also dance music. Published "Every Lover Can See" (by Beriat/Stive), recorded by Carol (ballad, #5 on charts in Norway when music was printed); *Roll Them Slim*, written and recorded by Memphis Slim (complete LP); and "Junie Rug" (by R. Bell/R. Sanderson), recorded by R. Sanderson (dance, #2 on charts).

WEYAND MUSIC PUBLISHING, 297 Rehm Rd., Depew NY 14043. (716)684-5323. Proprietor: C.D. Weyand. Music publisher. ASCAP. Member NMPA, AGAC and Harry Fox Agency. Works with composers. Pays negotiable royalty.
How to Contact: "Only fully written piano and orchestral arrangements will be considered. Please—no *lead* sheets. SASE a must. All material submitted must be complete and copyrighted by the person(s) making submission. Write first—important!"
Music: Classical and instrumentals. "Submissions must be fully scored. We accept only press-ready proofs." Published the collected piano works of Carlton Davis and C.D. Weyand, recorded by Weyand on Da Car Records (classical).
Tips: "Instrumental and orchestral works must be of a professional nature when recorded on tape or on cassette and must include a full 'conductor' score for proper review. During the course of the year, we

are reviewing many submittals. Therefore, write us first, setting forth, in detail, your background and description of proposed compositions to be considered. We have, at the moment, quite a background of material still under consideration. This fact oftentimes constitutes a prolonged delay in returning manuscripts. Manuscripts with adequate return postage *will* be returned after due review and consideration.''

THE WILLIS MUSIC COMPANY, 7380 Industrial Rd., Florence KY 41042. (606)283-2050. Editor: David B. Engle. Music publisher. Member SESAC. Publishes 2-3 songs/year; "no charted songs in our catalog." Pays 10% of retail price or outright purchase.
How to Contact: Prefers fully notated score. SASE. Reports in 12 weeks.
Music: Mostly early level piano teaching material; also instrumental solo pieces, methods books and "supplementary materials." Published "Spending Christmas with You," by Offutt (pop); "Jesus, I Love You So," by Galyean (religious); and "Psalm 67," by Edwards (sacred solo).

66 *You have to be aggressive. There are those who want and there are those who are hungry. Those who are hungry will usually get what they're after. Those who want will keep on wanting* **99**

—*Tony Prendatt, A&R, Polygram Records*

Record Companies

Having a song recorded by a nationally-known artist probably represents the greatest potential income for songwriters. Record company executives, particularly those in the A&R (Artist and Repertoire) departments are in a position to recommend songs for the artists on their labels. Evaluating tapes from outside writers is an every-day part of A&R people's jobs. But keep in mind that each artist can only release so many albums, each album can only contain so many songs, and many artists write their own material.

Still, the record companies listed here have expressed an interest in receiving demos from outside writers. Many record company people recommend that writers keep their demos simple. Your song should have a definite "feel" without being overproduced. You should give the company's producer room to work with the song—a finished demo will tend to pigeonhole your song. However, if you're contacting them as a songwriter/artist looking for a record deal, your demo should be more complex; A&R people want to know how a finished album will sound. Read the listings to see just what type of demos the companies prefer.

Along with your tape, include a letter explaining whether the songs are being submitted for consideration as material for another artist, or if you're seeking a recording contract. Many companies also like to know something about your background, so include the additional materials they request in their listings. These may include a resume, a list of previous credits for a writer; and reviews, press clippings and photos of a self-contained act. If you are submitting songs for another artist, you should be specific and mention by name the artist you think the songs are appropriate for and why. The song will have a better chance of being used if you "cast" it for an artist who *doesn't* write his own material.

Record companies are responsible for recording and releasing records—the *product* of the music industry. They sign artists to recording contracts, decide what songs those artists are going to record and then decide which of their songs to release. They are responsible for providing facilities; securing producers and musicians; and the manufacturing, distributing, and promoting of new releases. This translates to an investment of thousands of dollars on each song.

Because such a great financial investment is required of the record companies, they are extremely selective in choosing songs for their artists, and even more particular in signing new acts to their label. They have one goal in mind, and that is to sell records. This "bottom line" attitude makes record companies pick only what they consider to be the best available songs to record. But this need for the best can work to the advantage of unknown songwriters. Even though record companies count on publishers for most of their songs—and many even have their own publishing branch—they don't care where the song comes from as long as it's what they're looking for!

There are two situations you should be aware of when submitting songs for specific artists through their record companies. First, artists sometimes agree to record a song only if they can make certain changes. Maybe they want a slightly different wording in the lyric, a change in the melody to show off their vocal range, or an instrumental bridge to display their virtuosity. They may request to receive credit as co-writer, even if the changes are minor. That means that the artist would share in all of the writer's royalties, even if a different artist records the song in the future. Some songwriters feel it's worth sacrificing a portion of the royalties just to get national exposure for their song (depending, of course, on who the artist is). Others feel the artist doesn't deserve credit as co-writer and turn down such an offer. If an artist refuses to record one of your songs unless he receives credit as a co-writer, it's something you'll have to think about.

Second, there is an increasing trend for record companies to offer contracts to artists only on the condition that they agree to a "controlled composition" clause. It occurs most frequently in offers made to self-contained acts or writer/artists, and it means that the record company won't give a contract unless the writer(s) agree to accept a mechanical royalty rate of ¼ off the standard rate. It's not really fair from the writer's point of view, but record companies can do it because they control the financial aspects of their artists' recording careers. Outside songwriters sometimes refuse to settle for a ¾ rate, so if an artist under a controlled composition clause wanted to include outside material, he'd have to make up the ¼ of the rate out of his own pocket. Not many artists are willing to do that. What happens is that songwriters have an even harder time getting cuts of their songs, and the quality of albums suffers as the artist fills it up with mediocre material he had to write himself.

Most of the record companies in this section indicate in their listings that they pay "compulsory" or "statutory" rate to publishers per song on record, per record sold. This means they pay the maximum royalty allowed by law, which is then split between the publisher and the songwriter. Songwriters receive mechanical royalties from the sales of records, tapes, and CDs themselves, plus performance royalties for radio airplay, jukebox use and live performances. (See the Business of Songwriting appendix for more information about royalties.)

The companies listed here have indicated exactly what types of songs they are looking for, what artists they work with and how they want to be contacted. Read through these listings and choose the companies interested in the styles of music you write or work with the types of artists you think may be appropriate to perform/record your songs.

A Geographic Index is provided at the end of this section to help you plan a trip to Los Angeles, Nashville, or New York. Foreign markets are listed in alphabetical order for your information. Check *Billboard* and *Cashbox* charts for the names of top recording artists currently releasing hits and the labels on which they record.

*A STREET RECORDS,Suite 800, 250 W. 54th St., New York NY 10019. (212)580-2688. A&R Director: Terry Selders. Record company, music publisher (A Street Music) and record producer (A Street Music). Works with musicians/artists and songwriters on contract. Pays compulsory rate to publishers.
How to Contact: Prefers cassette. Does not return unsolicited material
Music: Mostly rock, heavy to pop/radio-oriented; also R&B, dance to pop/radio-oriented. Released "Kamikaze," written and recorded by Youth In Asia; "Easy Come, Easy Go," written and recorded by Frank Jordan; and "Hot Fire Love," written and recorded by The Remnant, all singles on A Street Records.

A&M RECORDS, INC., 1416 N. La Brea, Hollywood CA 90028. (213)469-2411. Record company and music publisher (Almo Irving Music). Releases 100 singles and 50-60 LPs/year. Works with artists and songwriters on contract.
How to Contact: "Direct all material through a publisher." Prefers studio produced demos. SASE.
Music: R&B, AOR and top 40. Released "Somebody," by Bryan Adams (pop/rock single); "Be Your Man," by Jesse Johnson (R&B/dance single); and "Oh Girl," by Boy Meets Girl (pop/rock single).
Tips: Looking for "female pop vocalists and male and female R&B artists. The more commercial and 'coverable,' the better."

A&M RECORDS OF CANADA, LTD., 939 Warden Ave., Scarborough Ontario M1L 4C5 Canada. (416)752-7191. Administrative Assistant: Mary Ann Burgess. Record company and music publisher (Almo/Irving/Rondor). Professional Manager: John David Redmond. Member CRIA. Releases 20 singles and 6 LPs/year. Works with musicians/artists and songwriters on contract. Pays statutory rate to publishers for each record sold.
How to Contact: Write or call first and obtain permission to submit. Prefers cassette (or VHS or Beta videocassette) with 3 songs and lyric sheet. SAE and IRC. Reports in 6 weeks.
Music: Pop/rock and pop. Released albums and singles recorded by The Arrows, Veronique Believeau, Paul Janz, Johnnie Lovesin, Stan Meissner, Kim Richardson and Erroll Starr, all on A&M Records.
Tips: "Listen to the current hits being released regularly and be aware of what you are competing with for radio airplay, sales, concerts, video, etc.

ABACUS, Box 186, Cedarburg WI 53012. (414)375-1482. Producer: Bob Wiegert. Record company, record producer and music publisher (RobJen Music). Works with musicians/artists on contract and mu-

sicians on salary for in-house studio work. Pays negotiable royalty to artists on contract; compulsory rate to publishers for each record sold.
How to Contact: Write first about your interest. Submit cassette only with 1-3 songs and lyric sheet. Does not return unsolicited material. Reports in 1 month.
Music: New Age, soundtrack productions and fine arts.
Tips: "We are always on the lookout for a talented composer, but would advise all to write first. Unsolicited material will not be sent back."

ACTS INTERNATIONAL, 36 Kneesworth St., Royston, Herts. SG8 5AB England. (0763)48991. Musical Director: J. Harwood-Bee. Labels include Folly Island Records, Gaza and Dodgy Records. Record company and record producer (Flying Ducks Productions and Dodgy Productions). Releases 5-10 singles and 5 LPs/year. Works with musicians/artists and songwriters on contract.
How to Contact: Prefers cassette (or VHS videocassette) with 4 songs and lyric sheet. SAE and IRC. Reports in 6 weeks.
Music: Mostly pop, disco and rock; also soul and jazz. Released "Extra Special," and "Betcha," written and recorded by Jerome on PRT Records (singles); and "I'm the One Who Said He Really Loves You," (by Stock/Aitkin/Waterman), recorded by Austin Howard on PWL Records (single). Other artists include June De Cruze, AKA and "The Late Gary Holton."

AIRIT INTERNATIONAL RECORDS, % Larry Sabiston Music, 1419 S. 25th St., Terre Haute IN 47803. (812)238-9841. A&R Director: Larry Sabiston. Record company, record producer and music publisher. Number of releases per year varies. Works with artists and songwriters on contract; pays compulsory rate to publishers for each record sold.
How to Contact: Prefers cassette with 1-3 songs. Copyrighted material only. Reports in 2 months. "Will not review material from writers who fail to enclose a SASE with proper return postage."
Music: Humorous, Christmas and Latin-beat pop. Released "When Someone Cares" (by Stephen Michael Portugal), recorded by Phil Coley and Ruth Beamon (single); "When My Baby Says It's Alright," (by Helen Poe/Phil Coley), recorded by Phil Coley (single); and "Love Songs and Guitars," written and recorded by Stephen Michael Portugal (cassette album), all recorded on Airit International Records.
Tips: "Best chances are for belly-laugh humorous songs and great Christmas songs with classic potential."

AIRWAVE RECORDS, #1502, 6430 Sunset Blvd., Hollywood CA 90028. (213)463-9500. Labels include Airwave, Zebra, Oz Magical. Copyright Director: Terrence M. Brown. Record company, record producer, music publisher (Blue Standard/ASCAP, Clear Blue/BMI, Oz Magical/ASCAP and OZCO/BMI) and video producer. Member NARAS, RIAA, NAIRD, ILA. Releases 40 singles and 6 LPs/year. Works with artists and songwriters on contract. Pays 5-10% royalty to artists on contract; compulsory rate to publishers for each record sold.
How to Contact: Prefers cassette (or videocassette) with maximum 3 songs and lyric sheet. SASE. Reports in 2 months.
Music: Mostly dance and R&B; also soul, progressive, rock, and top 40/pop. Released "The Calling," (by Tam Tam), recorded by Ken Heaven; "Johnny is a Male Dancer," written and recorded by Seduction; and "I Don't Want Your Love," written and recorded by Eleven Bells, all 12-inch singles on Airwave Records. Other artists include Marthe Reeves, Delia Renee, Take One and Freddy Gee.

AKO RECORDS, 20531 Plummer, Chatsworth CA 91311. (818)998-0443. President: A.E. Sullivan. Labels include Dorn Records and Aztec Records. Record company, music publisher (Amiron Music) and record producer (AKO Productions). Releases 2 singles and 2 LPs/year. Works with musicians/artists and songwriters on contract. Pays negotiable royalty to artists on contract.
How to Contact: Write first and obtain permission to submit. Prefers cassette (or Beta or VHS videocassette) and lyric sheet. SASE. Reports in 2 months.
Music: Top 40/pop, rock and pop/country. Released *Touch of Fire*, by Touch of Fire (LP); *Gang Back*, by F. Cruz (LP); and "Sana Christian," by Sana Christian (single), all on AKO Records.

ALEAR RECORDS, Box 574, Sounds of Winchester, Winchester VA 22601. (703)667-9379. Labels include Master Records, Winchester Records and Real McCoy Records. Record company, music publisher (Jim McCoy Music, Clear Music, New Edition Music/BMI), record producer and recording studio. Releases 20 singles and 10 LPs/year. Works with artists and songwriters on contract; musicians on salary. Pays 2% minimum royalty to artists; statutory rate to publishers for each record sold.
How to Contact: Prefers 7½ ips reel-to-reel or cassette with 5-10 songs and lead sheet. SASE. Reports in 1 month.
Music: Bluegrass, church/religious, country, folk, gospel, progressive and rock. Released "Like Always," by Al Hogan (country single); and *Mr. Bluegrass Here's to You*, by Carroll County Ramblers

(bluegrass LP). Other artists include Alvin Kesner, Jubilee Travelers, Jim McCoy, and Middleburg Harmonizers.

*ALLAGASH COUNTRY RECORDS, 45 7th St., Auburn ME 04210. (207)784-7975. President/A&R Director: Richard E. Gowell. Labels include Allagash Country Records and Gowell Records. Record company, music publisher (Richard E. Gowell Music, BMI) and record producer. Estab. 1986. Releases 2 singles and 1 LP/year. Works with musicians/artists and songwriters on contract. Pays 3-50% royalty to artist on contract; compulsory rate to publisher per song on record.
How to Contact: Prefers cassette with 2-10 songs and lyric or lead sheet. Does not return unsolicited material. Reports in 3 months "only if accepted."
Music: Mostly country, pop/country and country rock; also gospel. Released "Workin' Overtime," and "Take Me Back to Georgie" (by R.E. Gowell), recorded by Phil Coley on Allagash Country Records (pop/country single); and "Pretty Sinorita" written and recorded by Rich Gowell on Gowell Records (country single). Other artists include Wendy Violette, Karla Mitchell, Sandy Gowell and "Heavenly Flight" (gospel trio).
Tips: "We prefer to work with self-contained groups and songwriters in New England area. Our label is newly formed and we're currently seeking high quality finished masters with publishing open. Submit chrome cassette, copyrighted and ready for record pressing. Never send original master—copies only."

ALLDISC, Consultoria e Comercial Fonografica Ltd., Rua Alagoas 159, cj.84, Sao Paulo 01242 Brazil. (011)255-5560. President: Geraldo L. Loewenberg. Record distributor. Releases 12-24 LPs/year. Works with musicians/artists and songwriters on contract. Pays 5-15% royalty to artists on contract.
How to Contact: Prefers cassette (or VHS NSTC videocassette). Does not return unsolicited material. Reports in 1 month. "Ship demo via airmail (small package), addressed directly to Geraldo L. Lowenberg—never to the company."
Music: Mostly rock, blues and heavy metal; also film music, reggae and new age new wave. Released albums by Trini Lopez, Ray Charles, Black Sabbath, Smurfs and others.
Tips: "We only release albums on license basis. We would appreciate receiving any finished recorded product from any songwriter to be released by us."

ALLEGIANCE RECORDS, 1419 N. La Brea, Hollywood CA 90028. (213)851-8852. Director, Artist Development: Michael Dion. Labels incude Allegiance Records, Treasury of Recorded Classics and Takoma Records. Record company. Releases 12 singles and 12 LPs/year. Works with musicians/artists on contract.
How to Contact: Write first and obtain permission to submit. Prefers cassette "or finished product (master)." Does not return unsolicited material. Reports in 6 weeks.
Music: Dance, R&B, pop and jazz. Artists include John Fahey, Leo Kottke, and the Run Aways.

*ALYSSA RECORDS, Suite N, 226 Springmeadow Dr., Holbrook NY 11741. (516)472-1219. President: Andy Marvel. Labels include Ricochet Records. Record company, music publisher (Andy Marvel Music), and record producer (Marvel Productions and Andysongs). Releases 12-15 singles and 4-6 LPs/year. Works with musicians/artists and songwriters on contract; musicians on salary for in-house studio work.
How to Contact: Prefers cassette or 7½ IPS reel-to-reel (or VHS videocassette) with 3-5 sngs and lyric sheet. SASE. Reports in 2 weeks.
Music: Mostly pop, R&B, and rock; also country. Released "You Can't Hide Your Fantasies," by Andy Marvel, Steve Perri and Tom Siegel; "Express (10 Items Or Less)," by Andy Marvel; and "Meant To Be," by Andy Marvel and Don Levy, all recorded by Andy Marvel on Alyssa records.

AMALGAMATED TULIP CORP., 117 W. Rockland Rd., Libertyville IL 60048. (312)362-4060. Labels include Dharma Records. Director of Publishing and Administration: P. Johnson. Record company and music publisher. Works with musicians on salary; artists and songwriters on contract. Pays royalty to artists and songwriters on contract.
How to Contact: Prefers cassette with 2-5 songs. SASE. Reports in 1-3 months.
Music: Rock (progressive and easy listening), dance/R&B and top 40/pop. Released *Songs by the Group Milwaukee*, by Milwaukee; "Sunday Meetin' In the Morning," by Ken Little and the Band; and "This Feels Like Love to Me," by Mirrors.

*AMERICAN ARTISTS/CBS RECORDS/A&M RECORDS, 312 Washington Ave.N., Minneapolis MN 55401. (612)339-4741. President: Owen Husney. Record company, music publisher (SnowTown Music), and record producer (American Artists Productions and American Artists Management). Estab. 1986. Releases 3-6 singles and 2-3 LPs/year. Works with musicians/artists and songwriters on contract; musicians on salary for in-house studio work. Pays 11% to publisher per song on record.

How to Contact: Prefers cassette with 3 songs. SASE. Reports in 2 months.
Music: Mostly R&B, pop and rock. Artists include Brian McDonald and Craig Holliman.
Tips: "Pay attention to song structure and universal themes."

AMERICAN COMMUNICATIONS ENTERPRISES (A.C.E.), Box 444, Taylor MI 48180. (313)722-0616. President: John D. Lollio. Labels include A.C.E. Records, Mystery Train. Record company and record producer. Releases 5 singles and 2 LPs/year. Works with musicians/artists and songwriters on contract. Pays 6% royalty to artists on contract.
How to Contact: Prefers cassette and lyric sheet or lead sheet. SASE. Reports in 2 weeks.
Music: Mostly country and gospel. Released "Jesus, I Love You," by J.D. Lollio (contemporary Christian); "I'm Still Around," (by Carnes/Parson), recorded by W.P. Carnes on ACE Records (contemporary single); and *It Keeps Right on a Hurtin*, (by Tillotson), recorded by Johni Dee on ACE Records (country single and LP). Other artists include Marty Parker, David Atkins and Le Moine.

*AMERICAN MELODY RECORDS,773 Hoop Pole Rd., Guilford CT 06437. (203)457-0881. President: Phil Rosenthal. Record company, music publisher (Sourwood Music) and record producer. Releases 5 LPs/year. Works with musicians/artists and songwriters on contract. Pays 8-10% royalty to artists on contract; compulsory rate to publisher per song on record.
How to Contact: Prefers cassette wtih 1-6 songs. SASE. Reports in 3 weeks.
Music: Mostly children's music, folk and country. Released "Little Hands," written and recorded by Jonathan Edwards; "Grandma's Patchwork Quilt," written and recorded by Larry Penn; and "Snowy Day," written and recorded by Phil Rosenthal, all LPs on American Melody Records. Other artists include John McCutcheon, Cathy Fink, Mike Stein and Ann Vaughn.

AMERICAN MUSIC NETWORK INC./SCARAMOUCHE RECORDS, Drawer 1967, Warner Robins GA 31099. (912)953-2800. President: Robert R. Kovach. Record company and record producer. Releases 4 singles and 1 LP/year. Works with artists and songwriters on contract. Works with composers and lyricists; teams collaborators. Pays 5% royalty to artists on contract; pays statutory rate to publishers for each record sold.
How to Contact: Prefers cassette with 3-5 songs and lyric sheet. SASE. Reports in 1 month.
Music: Blues, country, easy listening, R&B, rock, gospel and pop. Released "Real Country Livin'," by Little Rudy (country single); and "When Your Light Comes On," by Theresa Justus (pop single). Other artists include Napoleon Starke.
Tips: "Submit it! We listen to each and every tape we receive. We are looking for new publishers, producers, artists, songwriters, musicians and lyricists. We are also interested in old established acts, artists and songwriters who are not signed to a label."

AMERICATONE RECORDS, 1817 Loch Lomond Way, Las Vegas NV 89102. (702)384-0030. President: Joe Jan Jaros. Record company, record producer and music publisher. Releases 5 singles and 2 LPs/year. Works with artists and songwriters on contract; musicians on salary for in-house studio work. Pays 6% minimum royalty to artists on contract.
How to Contact: Prefers cassette (or videocassette) with 2 songs and lyric sheet. SASE. Reports in 5 weeks.
Music: Mostly pop; also bluegrass, children's, country, easy listening, rock and Spanish.

AMHERST RECORDS, 1800 Main St., Buffalo NY 14208. (716)883-9520. President: Leonard Silver. General Manager and Vice President: David E. Parker. Record company and music publisher (Harlem Halwill). Releases 20 singles and 15 LPs/year. Works with musicians/artists and songwriters on contract.
How to Contact: Prefers cassette (or VHS videocassette) with 3-10 songs and lyric sheet. SASE. Reports in 3 weeks.
Music: Mostly jazz, rock and R&B; also children's and novelty. Artists include Paul Butterfield, Anthony Watson, Jeff Tyzik, Val Young, Glenn Medeiros and Doc Severenson.

AMIRON MUSIC/AZTEC PRODUCTIONS, 20531 Plummer St., Chatsworth CA 91311. (213)998-0443. General Manager: A. Sullivan. Labels include Dorn Records and Aztec Records. Record company, booking agency and music publisher (Amiron Music). Releases 2 singles/year. Works with artists and songwriters on contract. Pays 10% maximum royalty to artists on contract; standard royalty to songwriters on contract. Pays statutory rate to publishers.
How to Contact: Prefers 7½ ips reel-to-reel or cassette and lead sheet. SASE. Reports in 3 weeks.
Music: Bluegrass, blues, country, dance, easy listening, folk, gospel, jazz, MOR, rock ("no heavy metal") and top 40/pop. Released "Look In Your Eyes," by Newstreet; and "Midnight Flight," recorded by Papillon.

Tips: "Be sure the material has a hook; it should make people want to make love or fight. Write something that will give a talented new artist that edge on current competition."

*AMOK RECORDS, Box 7309, Vanier, Ontario K1L 8E4 Canada. (613)746-5572. President: Lorenz Eppinger. Record company, music publisher (KOMA Publishing) and distributor agent. Releases 3 singles and 5 LPs/year. Works with musicians/artists and songwriters on contract.
How to Contact: Prefers cassette and lyric sheet. SAE and IRC. Reports in 3 weeks.
Music: Mostly "accessible independent," electronic and ethnic; also jazz, dance and "ambiant." Released *Red Hot and Blue* (by Gilmore/Strawiak), recorded by Condition; *The Temptation to Exist* (by Schenke/Nelson), recorded by Courage Of Lassie; and *Life at the Pyramids* (by Josch/Mullrich/Klein), recorded by Dissidenten, all LPs on AMOK Records. Other artists include Tupac Amaru, Look People, Dario Domingues, Fluid Waffle, Ultima Thule and Singing Fools.

ANGI RECORDS, Box 9675, Palm Springs CA 92263. (619)328-8178. President: Larry Delrose. Record company and music publisher (Lasko-Delrose Music). Releases 4 singles and 1 LP/year. Works with musicians/artists and songwriters on contract. Pays 4-12% royalty to artists on contract.
How to Contact: Prefers cassette (or VHS videocassette) with 3-6 songs and lyric sheet. SASE. Reports in 3 weeks.
Music: Pop/top 40 and rock. Released "I Can Take It," (by Danny Laskowitz), and "Time," and "Breakdown," (by Ron King), all recorded by the King Orchestra on Angi Records (all LPs).
Tips: "We like lyrics that tell a story with an original idea. Be innovative—be up-to-date."

*ANTIQUE RECORDS, Box 192, Pittsboro KS 66762. (316)231-6443. Owner: Shawn Strasser or Eugene (Geno) Strasser. Labels include Catfish, Big Brutus. Record company, music publisher (Country Party Music) and record producer. Releases 6 singles and 2 LPs/year. Works with musicians/artists and songwriters on contract.
How to Contact: Write first and obtain permission to submit. Prefers cassette (or videocassette) with 5 songs and lyric sheet. Does not return unsolicited material. Reports in 3 months.
Music: Mostly country, gospel and novelty; also pop and rock. Released "Fire the Government," written and recorded by Weird Wilbur (single); "In the Spirit of America," written and recorded by Rich Rhuems (single); *Dewayne Bowman*, recorded by Dewayne Bowman (LP); all on Antique Records. Other artists include Tony Tubo, Dewayne Bowman and Gene Strasser.

APON RECORD COMPANY, INC., Box 3082, 44-16 Broadway, Long Island City, NY 11103. (718)721-5599. Contact: Don Zemann. Labels include Apon, Dicapon and Auraoleo. Record company, record producer and music publisher (Apon Publishing Company and Discapon Publishing Company). Releases 30 LPs/year. Works with artists and songwriters on contract. Pays according to special agreements made with individual songwriters; statutory rate to publishers for each record sold.
How to Contact: Call first. Prefers 15 ips reel-to-reel or cassette with 1-12 songs and lyric sheet. SASE. Reports in 1 month.
Music: Church/religious, classical, dance-oriented, easy listening, folk and international. Released *Polka Fever*, by Slawko Kunst (polka LP); *Russian Gypsy Melodies*, by Sandor Lakatos (gypsy music LP); and *Budvarka*, by Alojz Skolka Ensemble (folk/pop LP).

ARIANA RECORDS, 808 S. Pantano Rd., Tucson AZ 85710. (602)885-5931. President: James M. Gasper. Vice President: Thomas M. Dukes. Record company, record producer and music publisher (Myko Music). Releases 2 singles and 1 LP/year. Works with artists and songwriters on contract; musicians on salary.
How to Contact: Prefers cassette with 3-5 songs and lyric sheet. Does not return unsolicited material. Reports in 1 month.
Music: Mostly R&B, rock, dance rock, top 40/pop and AOR. Released "How Do You Feel," (by J. Gasper/P. Murphy), recorded by Fellowship (MOR rock); "Take care of Yourself," by T. Privett, (dance rock), and "Life is a Movie," (by J. Gasper/R. Ruiz) both recorded by Silent Partners; all on Ariana Records. Others artists include The El Caminos and 4 Walls.
Tips: "Be professional; first impressions are very important."

ARIOLA-EURODISC GMBH, Steinhauser Strasse 3, D-8000 Munich 80, West Germany. (089)4136-442. Contact: A&R Managers. Labels include Ariola, Arista, Hansa. Distributes Chrysalis, Island, Bronze, Towerbell and CGD. Record company. Releases 270 singles/year and 250 LPs/year. Works with musicians/artists on contract; musicians on salary for in-house studio work.
How to Contact: Prefers cassette. SAE and IRC. Reports in 2 weeks.
Music: Mostly pop, MOR and rock.

ARK RECORD CO., Box 100743, Nashville TN 37210. (615)833-1955. President: Everett Faulkner. Record company, music publisher (Clays Ferry Music Co./BMI) and record producer. Works with musicians/artists and songwriters on contract.
How to Contact: Prefers cassette and lyric sheet.
Music: Bluegrass and country.

ARMINIA MUSIKPRODUKTION ERICH STORZ, Box 1670, Hauptstr. 114, 3360 Osterode, West Germany. (05522) 7 30 41. Contact: Juditha Storz. Record company, music publisher and record producer. Works with musicians/artists and songwriters on contract.
How to Contact: Prefers cassette and lyric or lead sheets. SAE and IRC. Reports in 2 weeks.
Music: Mostly German folk music; also pop and rock.

ART ATTACK RECORDS, INC./CARTE BLANCHE RECORDS, Box 31475, Ft. Lowell Station, Tucson AZ 85751. (602)881-1212. Contact: William Cashman. Record company, music publisher (Cardio Music) and record producer. Member RIAA. Releases 2 singles and 2 LP's/year. Works with artists on contract; mechanical rate negotiable.
How to Contact: Prefers cassette (or videocassette) with 3-10 songs and lyric sheet. "We are interested in the artist's performance abilities and would need to see photos and biographical materials as well as to hear the music." Does not return unsolicited material. Reports in 1 month.
Music: Rock, jazz and progressive.

*ARZEE RECORD COMPANY, 3010 N. Front St., Philadelphia PA 19133. (215)426-5682. President: Rex Zario. Labels include Arcade Records and Arzee Records. Record company, music publisher and record producer.
How to Contact: Prefers cassette with 4-5 songs and lead sheet. SASE. Reports in 5 weeks.
Music: MOR, rock and country.

ASSOCIATED ARTISTS RECORDS INTERNATIONAL, Maarschalklaan 47, 3417 SE Montfoort, The Netherlands. (0)3484-2860. Release Manager: Jochem C.R. Gerrits. Labels include Associated Artists, Disco-Dance Records and Italo. Record company, music publisher (Associated Artists International), record producer (Associated Artists Productions) and TV promotions. Releases 12 singles and 4 LPs/year. Works with musicians/artists on contract and licensed material. Pays by agreement.
How to Contact: Prefers compact cassette or 19 cm/sec reel-to-reel (or VHS videocassette) with any number of songs and lyric or lead sheets. Records also accepted. SAE and IRC. Reports in 5 weeks.
Music: Mostly disco, Italian disco and pop; also easy listening, gospel/evangelic and music for film scores. Released "You Are" (by Jones), recorded by Hot Eyes; "Your Revolution" (by Causo), recorded by Platimon; and "Today" (by H. Jansen), recorded by Realists, all on Associated Artists Records (all singles and LPs).

ASTAN RECORDS, (formerly Echo Records), 824 83rd St., Miami Beach FL 33141. (305)865-8960. Record company, record producer and music publisher (Dana). Releases 2 singles and 1 LP/year. Pays statutory rate to publishers for each record sold.
How to Contact: Write first. Prefers 7½ or 15 ips reel-to-reel or cassette as demo. SASE. Reports in 1 week.
Music: Classical and ethnic (Polish).

ATTIC RECORDS LTD., 624 King St. W., Toronto, Ontario M5V 1M7 Canada. (416)862-0352. Contact: President. Labels include Attic and Viper. Record company and music publisher (Attic Publishing Group). Member CARAS, CRIA. Releases 25 singles and 30 LPs/year. Works with artists and songwriters on contract. Pays statutory rate to publishers for each record sold.
How to Contact: Prefers cassette with 3-5 songs and lyric sheet. SAE and IRC. Reports in 3 weeks or more.
Music: Blues, MOR, rock and top 40/pop. Artists include Nylons, Lee Aaron, Haywire and Terry Jacks

AVALON RECORDS, TAPES, COMPACT DISCS, INC., Box 3237, Pasadena CA 91030. (818)441-0887. President/Director A&R: David Evans. Record company and music publisher (Blackberry River Music Publishing/BMI). Releases 5 LP's/year. Works with musicians/artists on contract.
How to Contact: Prefers cassette (or VHS or Beta videocassette) with 2-5 songs. Does not return unsolicited material. Reports in 3 weeks. Include "photo, bio, press kit, plans for future, goals."
Music: "Jazz, no straight ahead." Released *The Fifth Season*, written and recorded by Timothy Donahue on Avalon (LP).
Tips: "Enclose with submission, why the material is marketable, why Avalon should become involved, why this material will sell. We operate on a national basis, and look to see if material will appeal to an au-

dience at the national level. Will it receive airplay on 250 radio stations in the top 25 markets simultaneously? Will retailers give the product floor space? Are the media interested in material and the artist(s)? Is it interesting, creative, individualistic material? If the answers to these questions are 'Yes,' then please, send in your demo."

AXBAR RECORDS, Box 12353, San Antonio TX 78212. (512)735-3322. Producer: Joe Scates. Labels include Axbar, JATO, Prince, and Charro. Record company, record producer, music publisher (Axbar Productions/BMI and Axe Handle Music/ASCAP) and distributors of country music products. Member CMA and Academy of Country Music. Releases 15-18 singles and 3-6 LP's/year. Works with artists and songwriters on contract; musicians on salary. Works with composers. Pays 8% maximum royalty to artists on contract; statutory rate to publishers for each record sold.
How to Contact: Prefers cassette (or videocassette) with 1-5 songs and lyric sheet. "Send us only your best shots." SASE. Reports ASAP, "but don't rush us."
Music: Mostly country; also MOR crossover, comedy, blues, western, and soft rock. "No hard rock or reggae." Released *Versatility*, by Kenny Dale (country LP); "Country Girl Going to Town," by Terrah Sloane (country single); "Rodeo Cowboy," by Mark Chesnutt (country single); and *Our Way*, by Carla Neet and Jerry Blanton (country pop LP).
Tips: "We like interesting titles with good hook lines."

AZRA RECORDS, Box 411, Maywood CA 90270. (213)560-4223. Artist Development: D. T. Richards. Labels include Azra, Metal Storm, Iron Works, Not So Famous David's Records, T.A.S.S. and Condor Classics. Record company. Releases 10 EPs/year. Works with artists on contract. "Artists usually carry their own publishing." Pays 10% royalty to artists on contract; compulsory rate to publishers for each record sold.
How to Contact: Prefers cassette (or VHS videocassette) with 3-5 songs and lyric sheet. Include bio and photo. SASE. Reports in 2 weeks.
Music: Heavy metal, hard rock and novelty. Released *Salute The Flag*, (by Brent Turner), recorded by Mad Reign (EP) and *Forgotten Shadows*, (by Bruce Cythe), recorded by Ninja (LP), both on Iron Works Records; and *Fortress*, by Fortress on Azra Records (LP). Other artists include Ripper, Mad Man Matt, Spyder, Mersinery, Ruby Topaz and Anaconda.
Tips: "We prefer groups that have been together a minimum of 6 months and solo artists who can write for specific projects."

*B.C. ENTERPRISES OF MEMPHIS INC., 726 E. McLemore, Memphis TN 38106. (901)947-2553. President: Bob Catron, Jr. Labels include Brian Manor Records and Katron Records. Record company, music publisher (Epitone Music Co.), and record producer. Releases 2 singles and 1 LP/year. Works with musicians/artists and songwriters on contract. Pays 10% royalty to artists on contract; compulsory rate to publisher per song on record.
How to Contact: Prefers cassette. Does not return unsolicited material.
Music: Mostly R&B and gospel. Released "My Friend Alfred" (by Brandan Renaldo), recorded by Sis Gennyslay (single); and *Is This Not the Carpenter's Son* (by Ernst Dotson), recorded by Ann Milan (LP), both on Epitome Records.

BAGATELLE RECORD COMPANY, 400 San Jacinto St., Houston TX 77002. (713)225-6654. President: Byron Benton. Record company, record producer and music publisher (Floyd Tillman Music Co.). Releases 20 singles and 10 LPs/year. Works with songwriters on contract; musicians on salary for in-house studio work. Pays negotiable royalty to artists on contract.
How to Contact: Prefers cassette and lyric sheet. SASE. Reports in 2 weeks.
Music: Mostly country; also gospel. Released "This is Real," by Floyd Tillman (country single); "Lucille," by Sherri Jerrico (country single); and "Everything You Touch," by Johnny Nelms (country single). Other artists include Jerry Irby, Bobby Beason, Bobby Burton, Donna Hazard, Danny Brown and Sonny Hall.

BAL RECORDS, Box 369, La Canada CA 91011. (818)952-1242. President: Adrian Bal. Record company, record producer and music publisher (Bal & Bal Music). Releases 2-4 singles/year. Works with artists and songwriters on contract; musicians on salary for in-house studio work. Works with composers and lyricists; teams collaborators. Pays standard royalty to artists on contract; statutory rate to publishers for each record sold.
How to Contact: Prefers cassette (or videocassette) with 1-3 songs and lyric or lead sheet. SASE. Reports in 15-20 weeks.
Music: Mostly ballads, AC/rock, gospel and jazz; also blues, church/religious, R&B, soul and top 40/pop. Released "Chilly Bones," and "Love on Law," both written and recorded by Marge Calhoun; and "Nicodemus," and "Sunday Service," both written and recorded by Jerry Chud, all on Bal Records (all singles).
Tips: "Send what you feel is your most commercial material."

BAM-CARUSO RECORDS, 9 Ridgmont Rd., St. Albans, Herts., England. 44-0727-32109. General Manager: Phil Smee. Labels include Waldo's Records. Record company and music publisher (Waldo's Music). Releases 10 singles and 15 LPs/year. Works with musicians on salary for in-house studio work. Pays 2-16% royalty to artists on contract; pays statutory rate to publishers for each record sold. Royalties paid directly to US songwriters and artists.

How to Contact: Prefers cassette with minimum 2 songs plus photos if possible. Does not return unsolicited material. Reports in 1 month.

Music: Mostly 60's music-new psychedelic bands, "beat groups" and R&B; also folk. Released *Danse Mcabre*, written and recorded by Paul Roland; *The Great Indoors*, written and recorded by Nick Haeffner; and *Beginning Here*, written and recorded by Palace of Light, all on Bam-Caruso Records (all LPs). Other artists include The Black Atlas, Bran Is Sex, The Patriots, The Chicayns, Fortunate Sons, Carolyn Dee, Tortilla Flats and The Time Machine.

Tips: "We specialize in compilations of small bands. We will consider any good song or band that shows promise. No synthetic instruments."

BAY-TONE & SOUL SET RECORDS, 1218 Hollister Ave., San Francisco CA 94124. (415)467-5157. Owner: Bradbury Taylor. Record company, music publisher and record producer. Releases 2 singles/year. Works with songwriters on contract. Pays variable royalty.

How to Contact: Write or call first and obtain permission to submit. Prefers cassette, 7½ or 15 ips reel-to-reel (or VHS videocassette) with any number of songs and lyric and lead sheets. Does not return unsolicited material. Reports in 2 months.

Music: Rock, pop and R&B. Released "Party Hardy," by Cold Fire (R&B single), "Badder than Bad," by Reese/Rillera (jazz single), and "Dancing," by Reese/Rillera (dance single), all recorded by Cold Fire; and "My Nose to the Grindstone" (by Brad Taylor), recorded by Little Joe Blue (blues single), all on Soul Set Records.

BEAU-JIM RECORDS INC., Box 2149, Alvin TX 77512-2149. President: Buddy Hooper. Record company, music publisher (Beau-Jim Music, Inc./ASCAP and Beau-Di Music, Inc./BMI), record producer and management firm. Member CMA, NSAI, NMA, AGAC. Releases 4 singles and 1 LP/year. Works with artists and songwriters on contract.

How to Contact: Prefers cassette (or videocassette) with 3-5 songs on demo. SASE. Reports in 3 weeks.

Music: Country. Artists include Debbie Kay and Joe Neddo.

BEE HIVE JAZZ RECORDS, 1130 Colfax, Evanston IL 60201. (312)328-5593. Producer: Susan L. Neumann. Record company, music publisher and record producer. Works with musicians on salary; artists and songwriters on contract. Pays 50% royalty to artists on contract; standard royalty to songwriters on contract.

How to Contact: Write or call first. SASE. Reports in 1 month.

Music: Jazz only. Released *Baritone Madness* by Nick Brignola, *Fire & Filibree* by Curtis Fuller, and *Neo/Nistico* by Sal Nistico, (all jazz Lps).

BELLA MUSICA TONTRAEGER GMBH, Albert-Schneble-Str. 2, D-7582 Buehlertal, West Germany. (07223) 7014. Labels include Emston. Record company, music publisher and record producer. Releases 10 singles and 10 LPs/year. Works with musicians/artists and songwriters on contract. Pays 10% royalty to artist on contract.

How to Contact: Prefers cassette. SAE and IRC. Reports in 2 weeks.

Music: Mostly German pop/rock and country (German); also jazz and instrumentals for background. Released "Nur Wir Beide Allein," (by Peter Dorr), recorded by Severine; "Die Feierwehr," (by Helmut Walter Theobald), recorded by Die Mainzer Hofsanger; and "Mallorca," (by Achim Danner/Roland Haring), recorded by Achim Danner, all on Bella Musica, (all singles). Other artists include Franco Cordi, Martina, Big Ben, Peter Patrick, Miki Reo, Andreas and Bernd, Theo Ansy, Andreas Fon, Manni Daum, Baboon, Herbert Ferstl, Billy White, Hans Volkl, Schwarz-Ferdl and Hans Van Der Sys Und Die St. Adelheimer Gagtime Band.

BELMONT RECORDS, 30 Guinan St., Waltham MA 02154. (617)891-7800. Labels include Waverley Records. President: John Penny. Record company, record producer and music publisher (Penny Thoughts Music/BMI). Releases 8 singles and 2 LPs/year. Pays statutory rate to publishers for each record sold.

How to Contact: Write first. Prefers cassette. SASE. Reports in 2 weeks. "We are not accepting at this time."

Music: Mostly country and contemporary; also country rock. Released "I'm Ready," (by Edward Rieck), recorded by Midnight Traveler (country rock single); "Nights Out AT The Days Inn," (by J. Fox/L. Wilson/R. Ball), recorded by Jimmy Allen (country single); and "Feels Like Love," (by G. Shepherd/Karen Harrs/Vicci Bixby), recorded by Liz Baordo (country single), all on Belmont Records.

BERANDOL RECORDS, 110A Sackville St., Toronto, Ontario M5A 3E7 Canada. (416)869-1872. A&R Director: Tony Procewiat. Labels include Plumtree. Record company. Releases 5 singles and 5 LPs/year. Works with musicians/artists on contract. Pays negotiable royalty to artists on contract.
How to Contact: Prefers cassette with 2-5 songs. SAE and IRC.
Music: Mostly children's; also "ultra-contemporary dance music (hip-hop/funk)." Released *Music Builders Kindergarten*, by Music Builders (children's triple LP); and "Love Theme from Canada," by Cosmic Orchestra (instrumental single). Other artists include Sandy Offenheim, Toronto Pops Orchestra and The Beastles.

BEVERLY HILLS MUSIC PUBLISHING,(formerly Lawrence Herbst Investment Trust Fund, Inc.), Box 3842, Houston TX 77253-3842. Branch: Box 1659, Beverly Hills CA 90213. Branch: Box 741, Lake Charles LA 70602. President: Dr. Lawrence Herbst. Produces 1-5 singles and 1 LP/year. Labels include Total Sound, Lawrence Herbst, Best Way and Larr. Record company. Works with artists and songwriters on contract: musicians on salary for in-house studio work. Pays 50% royalty to artists on contract; pays compulsory rate to publisher per song on record.
How to Contact: Prefers cassette, 7½ ips reel-to-reel (or videocassette) and lyric sheet. Does not return unsolicited material. Reports in 3 weeks.
Music: Mostly top 40/pop, country and rock; also bluegrass, blues, easy listening, folk, gospel, jazz, progressive, R&B, and soul.

BGM RECORDS, 10452 Sentinel, San Antonio TX 78217-3824. (512)654-8773. Contact: Bill Green. Labels include Zone 7, BGM and Rainforest Records. Record company, music publisher (Bill Green Music) and record producer. Releases 10 singles and 1-2 LPs/year. Works with songwriters on contract.
How to Contact: Prefers cassette. SASE. Reports in 2 months.
Music: Mostly contemporary country and traditional country. Released *Texas Songwriter*, written and recorded by David Price on BGM Records (country LP); "Louisiana Heatwave," and "Me & Margarita," written and recorded by Bobby Jenkins on Zone 7 Records (country single). Other artists include Kenny Dale, Easy Money, and Billy Mata.

BIG BEAR RECORDS, 190 Monument Rd., Birmingham, B16 8UU, England. 44-021-454-7020. A&R Director: Jim Simpson. Labels include Big Bear, Truckers Delight and Grandstand Records. Record company, record producer and music publisher (Bearsongs). Releases 12 singles and 6 LPs/year. Works with artists and songwriters on contract. Teams collaborators. Pays 8-10% royalty to artists on contract; 6¼% to publishers for each record sold. Royalties paid directly to the songwriters and artists or through US publishing or recording affiliate.
How to Contact: Prefers 7½ or 15 ips reel-to-reel, cassette (or videocassette) and lyric sheet. SAE and IRC. Reports in 2 weeks.
Music: Blues, jazz, R&B and soul. Artists include Roy Ree & Energee, The Gangsters, Muscles and jazz and blues artists.

BLIND PIG RECORDS, Box 2344, San Francisco CA 94126. (415)526-0373. Contact: Edward Chmelewski. Record company, record producer and music publisher (Viper Music/BMI). Member NAIRD. Releases 3-6 LPs/year. Works with artists on contract. Pays negotiable royalty to artists on contract; negotiable rate to publishers for each record sold.
How to Contact: "Looking for finished master tapes of LP length by performing artists only. Send cassette with promo/press material. SASE a must." Reports in 3 months.
Music: Blues, R&B (40s, 50s) and rock (rockabilly). Released *Everybody Needs It*, by Ellen McIlwaine and Jack Bruce (rock/rhythm LP); *It's All Rock & Roll*, by Steve Nardella (rock/rockabilly LP); and "Drinking TNT and Smoking Dynamite," by Buddy Guy and Jr. Wells.

BLUE GEM RECORDS, C-114, 3740 Evans St., Los Angeles CA 90027. (213)664-7765. President: Pete Martin. Record company, music publisher (Vaam Music/BMI, Pete Martin/ASCAP) and record producer (Pete Martin Productions). Releases 12 singles and 5 LPs/year. Works with musicians/artists and songwriters on contract. Pays varying royalty to artists on contract.
How to Contact: Prefers cassette with 2 songs and lyric sheet. SASE. Reports in 1 month.
Music: Mostly pop/top 40, rock and country; also R&B. Released "Feeling Love," (by Ray Hepinstal), recorded by Ray & Annie on Blue Gem Records (top 40 single); "Do It," (by Reynolds Ohai), recorded by Reynolds Inc. on Hi-Lite Records (country single); and *Stoned Cold Heart*, (by Sherry Campbell and Robbie Campbell), recorded by Night Vision on Blue Gem Records (rock LP). Other artists include Kamie Redell, P.S. Lambert, Hot Flash, Cosme, Meza and Victoria Limon.

BLUE ISLAND RECORDS, Box 171265, San Diego CA 92117-0975. (619)576-9666. Contact: Bob Gilbert. Labels include BOB. Record company, record producer and music publisher (Blue Island Publishing and Bob Gilbert Music). Releases 5 singles/year. Works with artists and songwriters on contract. Pays 12% royalty to artists on contract; statutory rate to publishers for each record sold.

How to Contact: Prefers cassette with 3 songs and lyric sheet. SASE. Reports in 3 weeks.
Music: Country, MOR, rock, top 40/pop and disco/dance.
Tips: "I review *every* song presented. So many in this industry only listen to selected songs per tape. I listen to all songs because you never can tell who will present the next hit song."

*BLUEBIRD MUSIC OY,Henriuintie 5C, Helsinki C0370 Finland. Managing Director: Osmo Ruuskanen. Labels include Lebaron and Hit-Ear. Record company and music publisher. Releases 20 singles and 10 LPs/year. Works with musicians/artists and songwriters on contract. Pays 4-10% royalty to artists on contract; pays compulsory rate to publisher per song on record.
How to Contact: Prefers cassette. Does not return unsolicited material. Reports in 1 month.
Music: Mostly MOR, pop and rock; also country and R&B.

BOLIVIA RECORDS, 1219 Kerlin Ave., Brewton AL 36426. (205)867-2228. Labels include Known Artist. President: Roy Edwards. Record company, record producer and music publisher (Cheavoria Music Co.). Releases 8 singles and 4 LPs/year. Works with artists and songwriters on contract; musicians on salary for in-house studio work. Pays royalty to artists on contract; statutory rate to publishers for each record sold.
How to Contact: Write first. Prefers cassette with 3 songs and lyric sheet. All tapes will be kept on file. Reports in 1 month.
Music: Country, easy listening, MOR, R&B and soul. Released "Make Me Forget," by Bobbie Roberson (country/MOR single); "Always and Forever," by Jim Portwood (country single); and "Music Inside," by Ray Edwards (MOR single).

BOOT RECORDS, LTD., Unit 25, 5730 Coopers Avenue, Mississauga, Ontario L4Z 2E9 Canada. (416)890-5678. General Manager: Peter Krytiuk. President: Jury Krytiuk. Labels include Boot, Cynda, Generation, Boot Master Concert Series and Boot International Records. Record company and music publisher (Morning Music Ltd./CAPAC). Releases 10 singles and 5 LPs/year. Pays 9-12% royalty; pays statutory rate to publishers for each record sold. "We operate on a lease basis, with a 3-year renewable term."
How to Contact: Prefers 7½ or 15 ips reel-to-reel or cassette with 3-6 songs. SAE and IRC. Reports in 1 week.
Music: Mostly folk; also classical, polka, bluegrass, mood music, country, dance, MOR and rock. Released *Man From Snowy River*, by Bruce Rowlands (soundtrack LP); *My Toot Toot*, by Walter Ostanek (polka/country LP); and "It's Almost Over," by Kelita Haverland (country single).
Tips: "Enough material should be recorded so that we would be considering an LP, not just a 45."

BOUQUET RECORDS, Bouquet-Orchid Enterprises, Box 18284, Shreveport LA 71138. (318)686-7362. President: Bill Bohannon. Record company and music publisher (Orchid Publishing/BMI). Releases 3-4 singles and 2 LPs/year. Works with artists and songwriters on contract. Pays 5% maximum royalty to artists on contract; pays statutory rate to publishers for each record sold.
How to Contact: Prefers cassette with 3-5 songs and lead sheet. SASE. Reports in 1 month.
Music: Religious (contemporary or country-gospel, Amy Grant, etc.), country ("the type suitable for George Strait, John Schneider, Crystal Gayle, etc.") and top 50 ("the type suitable for Peter Cetera, The Georgia Satellites, Whitney Houston, etc."). Released "Lies," by Teresa Gilbert (country single); and "The Reason is Love," by Adam Day (top 50 single).
Tips: "Submit material that relates to what is currently being charted. A strong story line will help."

*BOVINE INTERNATIONAL RECORD COMPANY, 593 Kildare Rd., London, Ontario N6H 3H8 Canada. A&R Director: J.A. Moorhouse. Labels include Bovine and Solid Ivory. Record company. Releases 1-10 singles and 1-5 LPs/year. Works with musicians/artists on contract and musicians on salary for in-house studio work. Pays 30-50% royalty to artists on contract; compulsory rate to publisher per song on record.
How to Contact: Cassette only with 2-3 songs and lyric and lead sheets. SAE and IRC. Reports in 2 weeks.
Music: Mostly country, pop and R&B: also children's records, blues and jazz. Released "It's Time to Go," by J. Moorhouse (single); "I Love How You Love Me," by Kilber/Mann (single); *Original Hits*, by J. Moorhouse (LP/cassete); all recorded by J. Moorhouse on Bovine Records. Other artists include Solid Ivory, Bros Band and Merle Morgan.

BREAD 'N HONEY RECORDS, Box 3391, Ventura CA 93006. (805)644-1821. Contact: Mark Craig. Record company, record producer and music publisher (Bread 'N Honey/ASCAP, and Honeybread/BMI). Releases 5-6 LPs/year. Member GMA. Pays statutory rate to publishers for each record sold.
How to Contact: Prefers cassette and lyric sheet. SASE. Reports in 3 weeks.

Music: Gospel. Released "Silver And Gold," by Johnny Hall; "Walk On The Clouds," by Karen Kelley; and "The Very Best In Me," by Kathie Sullivan.

BRIDGES RECORDS, 9701 Taylorsville Rd., Louisville KY 40299. (502)267-9658. Administrator: J.D. Miller. Labels include Rondo. Record company and record producer (Falls City Music Co.). Releases 10 singles and 5 LPs/year. Works with artists and songwriters on contract; musicians on salary for in-house studio work. Pays statutory rate to publishers for each record sold.
How to Contact: Prefers cassette (or videocassette) with 1-4 songs and lyric sheet. SASE. Reports in 2 weeks.
Music: Mostly gospel and country; also church/religious and top 40/pop. Released "One Love," by Perry Hines (R&B); and "Please Don't Change the Taste," by Doc & Smitty Band (country), both on Bridges Records.

BRIGHT & MORNINGSTAR RECORDS, Box 18A241, Los Angeles CA 90018. (213)512-7823. President: Stan Christopher. Record company. Releases 2 singles/year and 2 LPs/year. Works with musicians/artists and songwriters on contract; musicians on salary for in-house studio work. Pays 3% royalty to artists on contract.
How to Contact: Prefers cassette or 15 ips reel-to-reel with 1-3 songs and lyric and lead sheet. SASE. Reports in 3 weeks.
Music: Mostly contemporary Christian, inspirational gospel and gospel rock; also "message music." Released "Agape Love," "Change Your Life," and "Which Way Are You Going," (all by Stan Christopher), all recorded by The Messenger on Bright & Morningstar Records (singles).

BROADWAY/HOLLYWOOD PRODUCTIONS, Box 10051, Beverly Hills CA 90213-3051. (818)761-2646. Producer: Doris Chu. Labels include Take Home Tunes!, Original Cast, Broadway Baby, Disco and The C.Y. Musical Foundation. Record company, music publisher, record producer, video and film producer. Releases 2 LPs/year.
How to Contact: Prefers cassette (or VHS videocassette) with any number of songs. SASE. Reports in 20 weeks."Film score writers needed. Send final mix. Memorable melodies, great lyrics only."
Music: Mostly rock/pop, music videos and films. Released "Dracula Goes to London," and "Mean City," (by Fred Grat), recorded by Sweet Chariot (music videos).

BRYDEN RECORD PRODUCTIONS, 526 N. 24th, Portland OR 97210. Contact: A&R Director. Record company, music publisher and record producer. Releases 30 singles and 3 LPs/year. Works with musicians/artists on contract. Pays 50% royalty.
How to Contact: Prefers cassette (or VHS videocassette) with 2-3 songs and lead sheet. SASE. Reports in 2 months.
Music: Mostly new wave, funk and heavy metal; also reggae, blues and rock.

BUDDAH RECORDS, INC., 18th Floor, 1790 Broadway, New York NY 10019. Labels include Sutra and Beckett Records.
How to Contact: Prefers cassette with 1-3 songs and lyric sheet. SASE. Reports in 1 month.
Music: Blues, choral, country, dance, easy listening, folk, jazz, MOR, progressive, R&B, rock, soul and top 40/pop.

BULL CITY RECORDS, Box 99, Rougemont NC 27572. (919)477-4077. Manager: Freddie Roberts. Record company, record producer and music publisher (Freddie Roberts Music). Releases 20 singles and 6 LPs/year. Works with artists and songwriters on contract; musicians on salary for in-house studio work. Pays standard royalty to artists on contract; compulsory rate to publishers for each record sold.
How to Contact: Write or call first about your interest or to arrange personal interview. Prefers 7 1/2 ips reel-to-reel, cassette (or videocassette) with 1-5 songs and lyric sheet. "Submit a clear, up-to-date, demo." SASE. Reports in 3 weeks.
Music: Mostly country, MOR, southern rock, top 40/pop; also bluegrass, church/religious, gospel and rock country. Released *"Heartthrob,"* written and recorded by Rodney Hutchins (LP); "Going Over," (by Freddie Roberts), recorded by The Roberts Reunion, (single); and "What's In It For Me," (by Anita Kearney), recorded by Brenda Owens (single), all on Bull City Records. Other artists include Sittin Tall, The Kimbroughs, David Laws, Billy McKellar and Doug McElroy.

BULLDOG RECORDS, 8 Mark Ln., New City NY 10956. Head of A&R: Howard Kruger. President: J.S. Kruger. Labels include Ember and Bulldog Records. Record company. Works with artists and songwriters on contract. Pays 5-8% royalty to artists on contract; standard royalty to songwriters on contract.
How to Contact: Prefers cassette with 2-6 songs and lead sheet. SASE. Reports in 1 month.
Music: Dance, soul and top 40/pop. Released "Fabulous Babe," by Kenny Williams (European pop

single); *Glen Campbell Live in Concert*; "How Can You Tell You Got It," by David Soul; and "Monies Too Tight To Mention," by Valentine Brothers.
Tips: "We operate more in Europe than in the US, so allow time for material to flow overseas."

*BULLSEYE RECORDS, #607, 822 Roselawn Ave., Toronto, Ontario M6B 1B4 Canada. (416)781-4158. President: Jaimie Vernon. Labels include Swindled Music Stuff, Inc. Record company, music publisher (Anti-Conscious Music/CAPAC and EGO-A-GOGO/PROCAN) and record producer (Simon Truth Prod.). Releases 5-10 singles and 3-5 LPs/year. Works with musicians/artists and songwriters on contract. Pays 50% royalty to artists on contract.
How to Contact: Prefers cassette (or VHS videocassette) with 4 songs. SAE and IRC. Reports in 1 month.
Music: Mostly new wave, alternative and punk; also top 40, progressive and jazz. Released *Sam The Transcentdental Man*, Allison Went Walking, and *Knife Fight With Grandma*, all written and recorded by Daughaus on Bullseye Records (all cassette LPs). Other artists include Moving Targetz, Vic Saed and the Dark and Swindled.
Tips: "Due to our northern location in Canada, a Canadian or at least northern US act with self supporting budgets are preferred."

*BUS RECORDS,5 Lombard Street East, Dublin, 2 Ireland. (01)791865. Head of A&R: Marcus Connaughton. Record company and music publisher (Helmar Music). Releases 12 singles and 3 LPs/year. Pays compulsory rate to publisher per song on record.
How to Contact: Prefers cassette with no more than 4 songs and lyric sheet. SAE and IRC.
Music: Mostly country, rock and R&B; also pop. Released "People Are Telling Me," (by Charlie McGettigan), recorded by Apache Lightening (pop single); "Millionaire," written and recorded by Barry Ronan (rock single); and *Jealous Child*, (by Robinson/McCarney), recorded by Quarterdeck (rock LP), all on Bus Records. Other artists inlcude Tommy Dooley and Frame of Mind.

*CADENCE JAZZ RECORDS, LTD., Cadence Bldg., Redwood NY 13679. (315)287-7852. Producer: Bob Rusch. Labels include Cadence Blues Records. Record company and record producer. Releases 5-10 LPs/year. Works with artists on contract. Pays negotiable royalty to artists on contract; statutory rate to publishers for each record sold.
How to Contact: Prefers cassette (or videocassette). SASE. Reports in 1 week.
Music: Blues and jazz. Released *Nightwork*, by Rory Stuart; *The Improvisor*, by Chet Baker; and *An Engineer of Sound*, by Jimmy Stewart (all jazz LPs).

THE CALVARY MUSIC GROUP, 142 8th Ave. N., Nashville TN 37203. (615)244-8800. Artist Development: Nelson S. Parkerson, Jr. Labels include Calvary, Lifestream, Frontline, Heart Song and Wedding Song. Record company, record producer, music publisher and distribution company. Member GMA. Releases 10 singles and 12 LPs/year. Works with artists and songwriters on contract. Pays statutory rate or negotiates rate to publishers for each record sold.
How to Contact: Prefers cassette with 1-3 songs, typed lyric sheet and cover letter. SASE. Reports in 1 month.
Music: Mostly gospel; also wedding music. Released "Soul Fillin' Station," by the Hinsons (southern gospel single/LP); "Always," by the Freemans (southern gospel single/LP); "Keep Your Eyes on Him," by The Singing Echoes (old-time gospel single/LP); and "The Answer," by the Blackwood Brothers (gospel).

CAMBRIA RECORDS & PUBLISHING, Box 374, Lomita CA 90717. (213)427-1494. Director of Recording Operations: Lance Bowling. Labels include Charade. Record company and music publisher. Releases 4 LPs/year. Works with artists on contract; musicians on salary for in-house studio work. Pays negotiable royalty to artists on contract; compulsory rate to publisher for each record sold.

66 *It's like climbing Everest every time to get a song recorded and so you have to believe in what you are writing.* **99**

—*Randy Goodrum, songwriter, NSAI Symposium*

How to Contact: Write first. Prefers cassette. SASE. Reports in 1 month.
Music: Mostly classical; also jazz, nostalgia and crossover. Released *Songs of Elinor*, by Remick Warren on Cambria Records (LP). Other artists include Marie Gibson (soprano), Mischa Leftkowitz (violin), Leigh Kaplan (piano) and North Wind Quintet.

CAMERICA RECORDS, 535 5th Ave., Penthouse 35th Fl., New York NY 10017. (212)682-8400. Contact: A&R Department. Record company, music publisher (Camex Music, Inc.), record producer (Camerica Productions) and video producer. Works with musicians/artists and songwriters on contract; musicians on salary for in-house studio work.
How to Contact: Prefers cassette (or VHS videocassette) with 2 songs maximum. Does not return unsolicited material. Reports in 6 weeks.
Music: Mostly rock, R&B and country; also film music.

*CANAM RECORDS, Suite 222, 689 Central Ave., St. Petersburg FL 33701. (813)892-3444. President: Mike Douglas. Record company and music publisher (Canam Music/BMI). Releases various number of singles and LPs/year.
How to Contact: "No phone calls requesting permission to submit. We answer written requests only. When submitting, send a cassette with 3 songs and lyric or lead sheets. Clearly label each item you send with your name and address." Does not return material. Reports in 10 days.
Music: Contemporary Christian/gospel.

CANDY RECORDS, 2716 Springlake Ct., Irving TX 75060. (214)790-5172. General Manager: Kenny Wayne Hagler. Labels include Sweet Tooth, Lil' Possum and Holli Records. Record company, record producer and music publisher (Sweet Tooth Music/BMI). Releases approximately 4 singles and 5 LPs/year. Works with artists on contract. Pays 5% royalty to artists on contract; statutory rate to publishers for each record sold.
How to Contact: Prefers cassette with 3-4 songs and lyric sheet. "Send only quality material." SASE. Reports in 1 month. "No replies without SASE."
Music: Mostly country and rock; also soul, blues and top 40/pop. Released "Green Eyes", by Reign (country rock single); *In Motion*, by Kenny Wayne & The Komotions (top 40 LP); *Born with the Blues and Raised on Rock and Roll*, by Kenny Wayne & His Very Specal Guest (rock/blues LP); and "You've Got Those Eyes," by The Billy Blast Band (new music single). Others artists include Carter Holcomb and Michael Jeffrey.

CANYON CREEK RECORDS, Box 31351, Dallas TX 75231. (214)750-0720. Chief Executive Officer: Bart Barton. A&R: Mike Anthony. Record company, music publisher (Eagle Nest and Lemon Square) and record producer. Works with musicians/artists and songwriters on contract. Pays 50% royalty to writers on contract.
How to Contact: Write first and obtain permission to submit. Prefers cassette (or VHS videocassette) with 2 songs and lyric sheet. Reports in 10 weeks.
Music: Country and gospel. Artists include Audie Henry, Rosemary Sharp, and Dana Presley.

CAPRICE RECORDS/AMERICAN RADIO RECORDS, Suite 1, 621 Park City Center, Lancaster PA 17601. A&R Vice President: Joey Welz. Labels include Canadian American Recordings and Music City Records. Record company. Releases 6 singles and 4 LPs/year. Workw with musicians/artists and songwriters on contract. Pays 5% royalty to artists on contract.
How to Contact: Prefers cassette with 4 songs and lyric sheet. Does not return unsolicited material. Prefers to "hold material and search files."
Music: Rock, MOR and country. Released "Return of Haley's Comet," (by Bob McCormick/Joey Welz); "Rock and Roll Hall of Fame," (by Welz/Bannister); and "Old Fashioned Rock and Roll," (by Duane McCaskin/Joey Welz), all recorded by Joey Welz on Caprice Records (all rock). Other artists include Gerry Granahan, Santo and The Great Train Robbery.

CAPRICORN LTD., Jungstrasse 15A, Zürich CH 8050 Switzerland. President: Freddy J. Angstmann. Record company, music publisher and record producer. Releases 12 LPs/year. Works with musicians/artists and songwriters on contract. Pays 3-6% royalty to artists on contract.
How to Contact: Prefers cassette (or VHS/PAL videocassette). SAE and IRC.
Music: Mostly gospel, blues and jazz; also classical. Released *Christmas Album*; and *Who Shall Abide* (by Johnny Thompson), and *Gospel at the Opera* (by Radio Zürich singers) both LPs on Capricorn Records. Other artists include Mickey Baker, Erich Lauer, Errol Dixon and Anne Morrëe.

CAPSTAN RECORD PRODUCTION, Box 211, East Prairie MO 63845. (314)649-2211. Nashville Branch: 38 Music Sq. E., Nashville TN 37203. (613)255-8005. Contact: Joe Silver or Tommy Loomas.

Record company, music publisher and record producer. Works with artists on contract. Pays 3-5% royalty to artists on contract.
How to Contact: Write first about your interest. Prefers cassette with 2-4 songs and lyric sheet. SASE. Reports in 1 month.
Music: Country, easy listening, MOR, country rock and top 40/pop. Released "Dry Away the Pain," by Julia Brown (easy listening single); "Country Boy," by Alden Lambert (country single); "Yesterday's Teardrops," by The Burchetts (country single); and "Round & Round," by The Burchetts. Other artists include Shuri Castle, Skidrow Joe and Fleming.

*CAR PRODUCTION AND MANAGEMENT, 3122 Sale St., Dallas TX 75219. (214)522-8874. President: Chuck Robinson. Record company, music publisher (Carpad Music, BMI) and management firm. Estab. 1987. Works with musicians/artists and songwriters on contract. Pays statutory rate to publisher per song on record.
How to Contact: Prefers cassette with 1-2 songs and lyric sheet. SASE. Reports in 1 month.
Music: Country. Artists include Mark Nesler (country recording artist).

CARAVAGE, 130 rue Marius Aufan, 92300 Levallois-Perret 92300 France. (1)47 59 94 51. General Manager: Jean-Paul Smets. Labels include Caravage, Axis, Chloe and Pochette Surprise. Record company, music publisher (Editions Caravage) and record producer (Productions Caravage). Releases 5-10 singles and 5-10 LPs/year. Works with musicians/artists on contract. Pays 5-10% royalty to artists on contract.
How to Contact: Prefers cassette. SAE and IRC. Reports in 2 weeks.
Music: Mostly instrumental. Released "Neige," (by D. Doublet), recorded by Duels; "Soy Apache," (by Agudelo/Besombes/Pascal), recorded by Son Caribe; and "Captain Cook," (by Sandra), recorded by Florida's Band, all on Caravage Records (all singles). Other artists include Lou Bennett, Georges Schmitt, Marcia Maria, Angelo Petisi, Harry Kalapana, Varenne, and Gregory.

CARGO RECORDS, Box 1732, Murry Hill Station, New York NY 10156. (718)528-1760. Contact: Ron Seixas. Record company and record producer. Member AFMSC. Releases 5 singles and 3 LPs/year. Works with artists on contract. Pays variable royalty to artists on contract; statutory rate to publishers for each record sold.
How to Contact: Prefers cassette (or Beta videocassette) with minimum 2 songs and lyric sheet. SASE. Include photograph. Reports in 3 weeks.
Music: Rock music with top 40 appeal and new wave. Released *Even Exchange*, by Cynthia (dance rock LP/single); *Sensation*, by Seixas (rock/variety LP); and *Killo Beat*, by Megabite (new wave LP).
Tips: "Songwriters promoted as the recording artist should send a photograph or videocassette."

*CARLYLE RECORDS, INC.,1217 16th Ave. South, Nashville TN 37212. (615)327-8129. President: Laura Fraser. Record company. Releases 2 singles and 1 LP/year. Works with musicians and artists on contract. Pays compulsory rate to publisher per song on record.
How to Contact: Prefers cassette (or VHS videocassette). Does not return unsolicited material. Reports in 2 weeks.
Music: Mostly pop, rock, country and R&B. Released "Feelin' Lucky" and "I'll Take It Lying Down," (both by Burke/Black/Morrison/Phelps/Palmer), recorded by Preston Sullivan on Carlyle Records (singles).

CAROUSEL RECORDS, INC., 1273½ N. Crescent Hts. Blvd., Los Angeles CA 90046. (213)650-6500. A&R: Stuart Lanis. Record company, music publisher and record producer. Works with musicians on contract.
How to Contact: Prefers cassette with 3-6 songs and lyric sheet. SASE. Reports in 3 weeks.
Music: Children's, country, church/religious, classical, easy listening, gospel, MOR, and top 40/pop.

CARRIE RECORDS CO., Box 90639, 902-42nd Ave. N., Nashville TN 37209. (615)321-3319. President: James Hendrix. Record company and music publisher (Mester Music/BMI). Releases 12 singles and 4 LPs/year. Works with songwriters on contract. Pays 5% royalty to artists on contract; compulsory rate to publishers for each record sold.
How to Contact: Prefers cassette with 3-4 songs and lyric sheet. SASE. Reports in 1 month.
Music: Mostly pop and traditional gospel; also R&B. Released *Sounds of The Fabulous Sixties*, featuring Clifford Binns, Edward Hamilton and the Arabians, Mitch Rider, Cornell Blakely, and The Valentines (R&B LP); and "Something to Do With Love," (by Andy Cato), recorded by James Hendrix (gospel single), both on Carrie Records.

CASA GRANDE RECORDS, Box 113, Woburn MA 01801. (617)933-1474. Manager: Frank Paul. Labels include Don-Mar Records and Shawmut Records. Record company, record producer and music

Close-up

Margie Hunt
Manager of A&R
CBS Records

Songwriters have unusual ways of approaching Margie
Hunt, Manager of A&R (Artists & Repertoire) for CBS
Records. She has received tapes in balloon arrangements,
flower arrangements and even had one cassette taped to the
windshield of her car. Once while dining out, her waiter
realized who she was and immediately broke into song—
hoping it was his big chance to break into the music business.

Hunt agrees that A&R people are among the best contacts for songwriters. In her position,
she is involved in all facets of the creative process of recording, including finding a producer
and selecting songs for artists. Asked what her job duties are, Hunt responds, "40-50% of my
time is devoted to listening to songs and selecting material for the 40 artists on our label. At
one time or another, I have found songs for all of them." Casting the right songs for the right
artists is a big part of her job. For example, "a song that just doesn't sound right for Willie
Nelson might be perfect for John Conlee."

Due to a policy change, CBS has not accepted unsolicited material for quite a few years
(unless it comes from a publisher), but they still receive 75-100 solicited tapes each week.
Hunt says, "I listen to all the tapes we receive, and it takes awhile. I have a cassette player in
my car and I listen to tapes to and from work so I'm not disturbed by phones, etc." She attends
a lot of showcases and tries to "keep a constant finger on the pulse of the songwriting community." Sometimes she gets a "gut feeling" about a song and she tries to listen to her instincts—they're usually right. "This may sound corny, but sometimes I'll listen to a song and
it gives me chills and makes the hair on the back of my neck stand up and I know it's a hit."

Hunt does listen to tapes from songwriters who don't have a track record. She says, "There
is so much potential there, and that is one of the main ways I get songs." She develops ongoing relationships with songwriters and if she thinks someone with potential has a particular
song that isn't great, she may suggest the songwriter find a co-writer or try to rewrite.

Her advice to beginning songwriters is "develop your craft before submitting your songs.
Go with your best shot and make sure you've done your homework [research appropriate art-
ists] before going to a record company."

Hunt has been at CBS for 11 years and loves her work. She likes other people to have a positive attitude about their work as well. She says, "You can't make it in the music business unless you really love it."

—*Cynthia Kephart*

66 *Hits don't care who sing them.* **99**

—*Margie Hunt*

publisher (Donna Music Publishing Company and Antone Music Publishers). Number of releases/year varies. Works with artists and songwriters on contract. Pays 3% minimum royalty to artists on contract.
How to Contact: Prefers cassette with 3-6 songs and lyric sheet. SASE. Reports as soon as possible.
Music: Mostly ballads; also children's, country, easy listening, folk, gospel, MOR, Spanish, R&B, rock, soul and top 40/pop. Released *My Congratulations Baby*, recorded by several artists (R&B); and *Gospel Songs*.

CA-SONG RECORDS, Room 307A, 1650 Broadway, New York NY 10019. (212)586-3700. Contact: Mike Cassone. Labels included Rialto, Como and Rollins Records. Record company, record producer, music publisher (Glad-Jack Music Publishing/ASCAP, Ca-Song Music Publishing/BMI) and record promoter. Releases varying number of singles and LPs/year. Works with artists and songwriters on contract; musicians on salary for in-house studio work. Pays 2-5¢/record sold to artists on contract; statutory rate to publishers for each record sold.
How to Contact: Submit demo tapes and lyric sheet, or arrange personal interview. Prefers cassette with "as many songs as you want to submit. Put name and phone number (address if possible) and titles of song on tape. If there is no SASE, we report only if we place the material with an artist."
Music: Mostly MOR, easy listening and top 40/pop; also country, dance, gospel, jazz, progressive, R&B, rock, soul, nostalgia, big band and 50s and 60s. Artists include Sandra Toder Dancer, Carole Ann, Cathi Tully, Cullen Elliott, The Ink Spots, Scott Ferris, Carl Richards, Tiny Tim, Carol Meyers, Louie Prima, Susan Alfaro, Coleman Hawkins, The M&M Singers, Ultra Violet, Tess Winters, Clayton Sinclair, and Vicki Darnell.

*CASTLE RECORDS, Box 1338, Merchantville NJ 08109. (609)962-6000. Vice President: Rodney Russen. Labels include Castle Rock Island, Jade, Heavy Weather, Phoenix and Camden Soul. Record company, record producer and music publisher (Rob-Lee Music). Member RIAA. Releases 6-10 singles and 3-6 LPs/year. Works with artists and songwriters on contract. Pays 4-8% royalty to artists on contract; statutory rate to publishers for each record sold.
How to Contact: Prefers cassette (or VHS videocassette) with 4-8 songs and lyric sheet. Reports in 2 weeks.
Music: Mostly R&B, funk, dance-oriented and rock; also easy listening, MOR, soul and top 40/pop. Released "Gotcha!," by Sheldon Price (dance single); *Forbidden Fruit*, by Snow (rock single and LP); and *Hot Record*, by The Racers (rock 12" EP). Others artists include Phoenix, Heavy Weather, David Lawrence, Roman, Negative Space, Dirty Martha, The Coasters, The Orlowe, Necca, Big El and TCB Band.

CATSKILL MOUNTAIN RECORDS, Red Kill Rd., Fleischmanns NY 12430. (914)254-4565. President: Barry Drake. Record company, record producer, music publisher (Sweet Swamp Music/BMI), talent and management firm. Releases 1-2 singles and 1-2 LPs/year. Works with artists and songwriters on contract.
How to Contact: Prefers cassette with 1-3 songs and lyric sheet. SASE. Reports in 1 month.
Music: Bluegrass, blues, country, folk, MOR, rock (soft, country) and top 40/pop. Released "Solo Survivor," by Barry Drake.

*CBS RECORDS, 34 Music Square E., Nashville TN 37203. (615)742-4321. Labels include CBS, CBS Masterworks, Columbia, Epic, Odyssey, and Portrait/Lorimar. Record company.
How to Contact: Write and ask for submission policy.

*CBT RECORDS, 3318-E SSW Loop 323, Tyler TX 75701. (214)581-9945. President: Roy L. Haws. Record company, music publisher (Country Boys from Texas Music) and record producer (Roy L. Haws, CBT Records). Releases 10 singles and 2 LPs/year. Works with artists and songwriters on contract. Pays negotiable royalty to artists on contract; compulsory rate.
How to Contact: Prefers cassette. SASE.
Music: Mostly country rock, contemporary country and modern traditional country. Released "Giddy Up Alligator" (by Joe Johnson), recorded by Glenn English; "Papa's on a Roll" (by Gary Johnson), recorded by Steve Campbell; and "Honky Tonk Heaven" (by Gary Josey), recorded by Donny Goff, all on CBT Records. Other artists include David Houston, Patty Covert, Teresa Gilbert, Michael Knight, Deborah Meadows and Mayf Nutter.

CENTURY RECORDS, INC., 1429 Hawthorne St., Pittsburgh PA 15201. (412)781-4557. President: Edward J. Moschetti. Labels include Star Records. Record company. Works with songwriters on contract.
How to Contact: Prefers cassette. SASE.
Music: Country.

CHA-CHA RECORDS, 15041 Wabash Ave., South Holland IL 60473. (312)339-0307. President: Donald L. De Lucia. Labels include Cha-Cha (rock) and Cap (country). Record company, record producer, and music publisher (Don-Del Music/BMI and Don-De/ASCAP). Releases 2 singles and 2 LPs/year. Works with artists on contract. Pays 3%/record to artists on contract; statutory rate to publishers for each record sold.
How to Contact: Prefers 7½ ips reel-to-reel with 4-6 songs and lyric sheet. SASE. Reports in 1 week.
Music: Country, rock, and top 40/pop. Released *99 Chicks*, by Ron Haydock and the Boppers (rock LP). Other artists include Don Glasser and Lois Castello.

CHAMELEON MUSIC GROUP, (formerly Suite Beat Music), 3355 W. El Segundo, Hawthorne CA 90250. (213)973-8800. President: Bob Marin. Labels include Epitaph, MMC, Vee-Jay, American Arcade and Suite Beat. Record company. Releases 3-5 LPs, cassettes and CDs/month. Works with musicians/artists on contract. Pays negotiable royalty to artists on contract.
How to Contact: Prefers cassette (or ½" VHS videocassette) with maximum 3 songs and lyric sheet. SASE. Reports in 6 weeks.
Music: Mostly rock/pop and modern new punk; also psychedelic and jazz.

CHARTA RECORDS, 44 Music Sq. E., Nashville TN 37203. (615)255-2175. President: Charlie Fields. Labels include Delux. Record company, music publisher and record producer. Releases 10 singles/year and 6-8 LPs/year. Works with musicians/artists on contract; musicians on salary for in-house studio work. Pays standard royalty to artists on contract.
How to Contact: Call first to arrange personal interview. Prefers cassette or reel-to-reel with 2-3 songs and lyric sheet and lead sheet. Does not return unsolicited material. Reports in 3 weeks.
Music: Mostly MOR, blues and country. Released "Burned Out," by Tina Danielle; and "Tired of the Same Old Thing," by David Walsch.

CHATTAHOOCHEE RECORDS, 5300 Sepulveda Blvd., Van Nuys CA 91411. (213)788-6865. Contact: Chris Yardum. Record company and music publisher (Etnoc/Conte). Member NARAS. Releases 4 singles/year. Works with artists and songwriters on contract.
How to Contact: Prefers cassette with 2-6 songs and lyric sheet. SASE. Reports in 6 weeks.
Music: Top 40/pop.

THE CHU YEKO MUSICAL FOUNDATION, Box 10051, Beverly Hills CA 90213. (818)761-2646. Branch: Box 1314, Englewood Cliffs NJ 07632. Messages: (201)567-5524. Producer: Doris Chu. Labels include The Chu Yeko Musical Foundation, Take Home Tunes! Record Co., Original Cast Records and Broadway Baby Records. Record company and music publisher (Broadway/Hollywood International Music Publishers/ASCAP). Releases 5-10 LPs/year. Works with songwriters on contract. Teams collaborators. Pays 1-10% royalty to artists on contract; statutory rate or less to publishers for each record sold.
How to Contact: Prefers cassette (or VHS videocassette) with any number of songs and lyric sheet. "Final mix, top professional quality only." SASE. Reports in 1 month.
Music: Pop, rock, R&B and musicals in entirety.
Tips: "Need female singer or rock/pop/group touring L.A./CA area. Also need final mix songs for film scores. Only highly professional tapes are accepted. Include phone, address, SASE and cassette tape."

CIMIRRON/RAINBIRD RECORDS INC., 607 Piney Point Rd., Yorktown VA 23692. (804)898-8155. Professional Managers: Lana Puckett and Kim Person. Record company, music publisher (Hot Knobs Music), record producer (Humdinger Productions) and Wistaria Recording Studio. Releases 5 singles and 2 LPs/year. Works with musicians/artists and songwriters on contract.
How to Contact: Write or call first and obtain permission to submit. Prefers cassette (or Beta videocassette) with 1-5 songs and lyric sheet. SASE. Reports in 1 month. Also submit bio, credits and glossy photograph.
Music: Mostly country, easy listening and pop; also gospel, bluegrass and children's music. Released "Even Cowgirls Get The Blues," (by L. Puckett/K. Person), recorded by Kim Person; and "You Can't Take The Country From The Man," by Mike Glass. Other artists include Rich Follett.

CLARUS MUSIC, LTD., 340 Bellevue Ave., Yonkers NY 10703. (914)591-7715. President: S. Fass. Records company, record producer and music publisher. Member MENC, NYSSMA, RIAA. Releases 1-2 LPs/year. Works with artists and songwriters on contract. Pays current royalty rate to artists on contract; statutory rate to publishers for each record sold.
How to Contact: Prefers cassette with 4-10 songs and typed lyric sheet. SASE. Reports in 3 months.
Music: Children's plays.

CLAY PIGEON RECORDS, Box 20346, Chicago IL 60620. Contact: President or A&R Director. Labels include Clay Pigeon International and Patefonas Records. Record company. Releases 3-5 singles and 2-5 LPs/year. Works with musicians on salary; artists and songwriters on contract. "Royalties on records start at 2% of retail. All acts negotiate with us individually. Four percent is common. Royalties paid to publishers are often at 2¢ per selection, per record sold."
How to Contact: "Inquire by mail first (do not phone), describing yourself and your material in some depth. We cannot consider any material without a written query. Cover letter should explain songwriter's background, type of songs written and why songs are unique enough to be listened to." Prefers 7½ ips reel-to-reel, cassette or disc with 1-5 songs. SASE. Reports in 2 months.
Music: Avant-garde, new wave, MOR, progressive, rock and top 40/pop. Released "Tribe of Dolls," by Vyto B (modern rock single); "Band That Never Made It," by Bena Neva Mada (modern rock single); and "I'm Sure Now," by Seetz Executive (MOR ballad).

CLOUDBURST RECORDS, Box 31, Edmonton KY 42129. (502)432-3183. President: Rev. Junior Lawson. Record company and music publisher (Holy Spirit Music). Releases 3 singles and 4 LPs/year. Works with songwriters on contract. Pays 4¢ royalty to artists on contract.
How to Contact: Call first. Prefers 7½ ips reel-to-reel or cassette and lyric sheet. SASE. Reports in 3 weeks.
Music: Mostly southern gospel; also country, gospel, MOR and progressive. Released *Introducing the Cornerstones* and *Extra! Extra!*, by The Cornerstones (southern gospel LPs); and *Old-Fashioned Ways*, by the Sounds of Joy (southern gospel LP). Other artists include The New Apostles.

COAST TO COAST RECORDS, Box 8958, Arlington Station, Jacksonville FL 32239. Record company and music publisher (Frankly Music/BMI, J.D. Music/ASCAP). Releases 2 LPs/year. Works with musicians and songwriters on contract.
How to Contact: Prefers cassette with 2-3 songs and lyric sheet. Does not return unsolicited material. Reports in 2 weeks.
Music: Disco, MOR and R&B.

*COLLECTOR RECORDS, Box 2296, Rotterdam 3000 CG Holland. (10)4224889. Research: Cees Klop. Labels include All Rock, Downsouth, Unknown, Pro Forma and White Label. Record company, music publisher (All Rock Music Pub.) and record producer (Cees Klop). Releases 10 singles and 30 LPs/year. Works with musicians/artists and songwriters on contract. Pays standard royalty to artists on contract.
How to Contact: Prefers cassette. SAE and IRC. Reports in 1 month.
Music: Mostly 50's rock, rockabilly and country/rock; also piano boogie woogie. Released *Eddie Bond* (by Bond), recorded by Bond/Klop on White Label Records (rock LP); *Louis Gittens*, written and recorded by Gittens on White Labels Records (rock LP); and *Rob Hoeke* (by Hoeke), recorded by Cees Klop on Downsouth Records (boogie LP).

COMMA RECORDS & TAPES, Postbox 2148, 6078 Neu-Isenburg, West Germany (6102)5640. General Manager: Roland Bauer. Labels include: Big Sound, Comma Int'l, Max-Banana-Tunes. Record company. Releases 50-70 singles and 20 LPs/year. Works with musicians/artists and songwriters on contract. Pays 7-10% royalty to artists on contract.
How to Contact: Prefers cassette, reel-to-reel (or U-matic or VHS [PAL] videocassette) and lyric sheet. Reports in 3 weeks.
Music: Mostly pop, disco, rock, R&B and country; also musicals.

COMPO RECORD AND PUBLISHING CO., Box 15222, Oklahoma City OK 73115. (405)677-6448. President: Yvonne De Vaney. General Manager: Sonny Lane. Record company and music publisher (Country Classics Music/BMI). Releases 4-6 singles and 1-2 LPs/year. Works with artists and songwriters on contract. Pays standard royalty to artists and songwriters on contract; statutory rate to publishers for each record sold.
How to Contact: Prefers cassette with 2-4 songs and lead sheet. SASE. Reports in 3 weeks.
Music: Country, gospel and MOR. Released "Lovin Side of Love," "Yodel Waltz" and "Yodel Love," (all by Y. DeVaney), recorded by Yvonne DeVaney and Wes Onley (country duet singles).
Tips: "We like simple melodies with strong lyrics."

COMSTOCK RECORDS LTD., Box 3247, Shawnee KS 66203. (913)631-6060. Canadian, United States and European distribution on Paylode & Comstock Records. Production Manager/Producer: Patty Parker. President: Frank Fara. Record company, music publisher (White Cat Music/ASCAP, Rocky Bell Music/BMI), Nashville Record Production, and International Record Promotions. Member CMA, GMA, ACME, MACE, BCCMA, BBB, British & French C&W Associations, and CARAS. "Comstock Records, Ltd. has three primary divisions: Production, Promotion and Publishing. We distribute and promote both our self-produced recordings and outside master product." Releases 24-30 singles and 2-4 LPs/year. Works with artists and songwriters on contract; musicians on salary. Pays 7% royalty to artists on contract; statutory rate to publishers for each record sold.

How to Contact: Prefers cassette (or VHS videocassette) with 1-4 songs "plus word sheet. Enclose stamped return envelope if cassette is to be returned." Reports in 2 weeks.

Music: Adult contemporary and country; also contemporary gospel. Released "It Only Hurts When I Cry,"(by Dave Richardson/Max Troy Barnes), recorded by Alibi; and "I'll Never Get Over You," (by Roger and Anne Lord), recorded by Anne Lord, both on Comstock Records. Other artists include R.J. McClintock, Doug Peters, Marty Gillan, Alibi, Ray Dean James and Ray St. Germain.

Tips: "We have an immediate need for adult contemporary material for our new USA/Canada division, Paylode Records. Our international division consists of master distribution and promotion to the following nations: England, France, Germany, Belgium, Ireland, Luxembourg, The Netherlands, Scotland, Switzerland, Norway and Canada."

*COSMOTONE RECORDS, Box 71988, Los Angeles CA 90071-0988. Record Producer: Rafael Brom. Record company, music publisher (Cosmotone Music ASCAP) and record producer (Cosmotone Studios). Releases 1 single and 1 LP/year. Works with musicians/artists and songwriters on contract and musicians on salary for in-house studio work. Pays standard royalty; compulsory rate to publisher per song on contract.

How to Contact: Prefers cassette with any number of songs and lyric sheet. "Include bio with photo." Does not return unsolicited material. "Contact is made only if interested."

Music: Rock, pop, R&B, gospel, soul, adult contemporary, progressive (all types) and country. Released *Padre Pio*, recorded by Lord Hamilton (LP); *No. 1*, written and recorded by R.B. (LP); and "A Mockingbird" (by Thomas Dufficy/Lord Hamilton), recorded by Lord Hamilton (single), all on Cosmotone Records. Other artists include Adrian Romero, Oliver Hamilton, A. Jude and Johnny Cheesecake.

Tips: "Looking for hot masters with high tech sound, good melody and original performance. Publishing must be open."

*COUNTERPART CREATIVE STUDIOS, 3744 Applegate Ave., Cincinnati OH 45211. (513)661-8810. President: Shad O'Shea. Record company, music publisher (Hurdy Gurdy Music Co., Counterpart Music/BMI) and jingle company. Member RIAA. Releases 24 singles and 6 LPs/year. Works with musicians on salary.

How to Contact: Write first. Prefers 7½ ips reel-to-reel with 1-2 songs. Does not return unsolicited material. Reports in 1 week.

Music: Bluegrass, blues, children's, choral, church/religious, classical, country, dance, easy listening, folk, gospel, jazz, MOR, progressive, rock, funk, soul and top 40/pop. Released "McLove Story," by Shad O'Shea on Plantation Records; "Hot Fun in the Summertime," by Dayton on Capitol Records; "Freakazoid" and "Wet My Whistle," by Midnight Star on Warner Bros. Records.

COUNTRY INTERNATIONAL, 23 Music Circle E., Nashville TN 37203. (615)327-4656. President: Sherman Ford. Vice President, Promotion: Jake Payne. Record company. Works with artists and songwriters on contract; musicians on salary for in-house studio work. Pays statutory rate to publishers for each record sold.

How to Contact: Prefers cassette with 1-4 songs and lyric sheet. SASE. Reports in 2 weeks.

Music: Country.

COUNTRY SHOWCASE AMERICA, 14134 Brighton Dam Rd., Clarksville MD 21029-1327. (301)937-2328. President: Francis Gosman. Record company. Releases 2 singles/year. Works with musicians/artists and songwriters on contract. Pays 3% royalty to artists on contract; compulsory rate to publishers for each record sold.

How to Contact: Prefers cassette and lyric sheet. SASE.

Music: Country. Released "Christmas Flower," (by Gosman/O'Leary), recorded by O'Leary; "Sweet Yesterdays," (by Marrino/Gellspie), recorded by Country Cavalier on CSA; and "Heavens Bed," and "Mountain Man," recorded by J. Anthony (all country singles).

COUNTRY STAR INTERNATIONALS, 439 Wiley Ave., Franklin PA 16323. (814)432-4633. Contact: Norman Kelly. Labels include CSI, Country Star, Process and Mersey Records. Record company and music publisher (Country Star/ASCAP, Process and Kelly/BMI). Releases 10-15 singles and 3-5 LPs/year. Member AFM and AFTRA. Works with artists and songwriters on contract; musicians on salary for in-house studio work. Works with lyricists and composers. Pays 6% royalty to artists on contract; statutory rate to publishers for each record sold.

How to Contact: Write first. Prefers 7½ ips reel-to-reel or cassette with 1-4 songs. SASE. Reports in 2 weeks.
Music: Mostly country; also bluegrass, easy listening, folk, MOR, rock and top 40/pop. Released "Porch Light," by J.C. Young; "It's Pickle Time Again," by Bonnie Baldwin; "A Step from Your Heart," by Denver Bill; and "Cold Red Georgia Clay," by Bob Stamper (all country singles).
Tips: "Send only your best efforts."

COURRIER RECORDS, 1560 Broadway, New York NY 10036. (212)302-5360. President: Morton Wax. Labels include Overseas Wax. Record company, record producer and music publisher (David Music, Inc./BMI). Works with artists and songwriters on contract. Pays standard royalty to artists on contract; statutory rate to publishers for each record sold.
How to Contact: Prefers cassette and lyric or lead sheet. Does not return unsolicited material. Reports ASAP.
Music: Mostly country and rock; also "all kinds."
Tips: "Have patience."

COWBOY JUNCTION FLEA MARKET AND PUBLISHING CO., Highway 44 W., Lecanto FL 32661. (904)746-4754. Contact: Elizabeth Thompson. Record company, record producer and music publisher. Releases 3 singles and 1-2 LPs/year. Works with musicians/artists and songwriters on contract. Pays 50% royalty to artists on contract.
How to Contact: Prefers cassette with 1-4 songs and lyric sheet. SASE. Reports ASAP.
Music: Country, gospel and bluegrass. Released "The Challenger and Crew of 7," "Easter Bunny," and "Easter Day," (all by Boris Max Pastuch), all recorded by Buddy Max on Cowboy Junction Records (all singles). Other artists include Wally Jones, Dusty Handson, Lloyd Stone, Leo Vargason and Johnny Pastoch.

COWGIRL RECORDS, Box 6085, Burbank CA 91510. Contact: Vice President. Record company and music publisher (Kingsport Creek). Works with musicians/artists and songwriters on contract; musicians on salary for in-house studio work. Pays statutory rate to publishers for each record sold.
How to Contact: Prefers cassette (or VHS videocassette) with any number of songs and lyric sheet or lead sheet. Does not return unsolicited material. "Include a photo and bio if possible."
Music: Mostly country, R&B, MOR and gospel. Released "Never Gonna End," "I Do," and "Cryin" recorded by Melvena Kaye.

CREOLE RECORDS LTD., 91/93 High St., Harlesden, London NW10, England. 44-01-965-9223. Managing Director (record demos): Bruce White. Publishing Manager (publishing demos): Steve Tantum. Labels (England): Creole, Ecstacy, Dynamic, 909, Cactus, Replay, Blast from the Past. Labels (US): Creole Music, Inc. Record company, record producer and music publisher. Member BPI, PPL and IFPI. Releases 40 singles and 12-15 LP's/year. Works with artists and songwriters on contract. Works with composers and lyricists; teams collaborators. Pays 8-16% royalty to artists on contract; 6¼% to publishers for each record sold.
How to Contact: "Do not write to ask if you may submit—just send tapes." Prefers cassette (or VHS videocassette) with 3 songs and lyric and lead sheet. SAE and IRC. Reports in 3 weeks.
Music: Pop, soul and dance. Released "White Horse," by Laid Back (pop/dance single); and "That Feeling," by Zoot Alors (pop/dance single). Other artists include Pete McDonald, Ellie Hope, Adrian Baker, Bob Puzey (writer), Terry Hanton, Enigma, Ricky Anderson, Peter Green, Ocean and Boris Gardiner.

CRITIQUE RECORDS INC., 400 Main St., Reading MA 01867. (617)944-0423. Contact: Professional Manager. Record company, record producer and music publisher (Solid Smash). Releases 10 singles and 2 LPs/year. Works with artists on contract.
How to Contact: Prefers cassette (or videocassette) with 1-3 songs and lyric sheet. SASE. Reports in 1 month.
Music: Mostly R&B and dance; also country, rock, soul and top 40/pop. Released "Dear Michael," by Kim Fields (pop/R&B single); and "Breaking Up Is Hard on You," by American Comedy Network (pop single).

 The asterisk before a listing indicates that the listing is new in this edition. New markets are often the most receptive to freelance submissions.

CSB RECORDS, 5180 Park Ave., Memphis TN 38187. (901)795-5354. A&R Director: Mark Blackwood. Record company. Estab. 1986. Releases 3 singles/year and 3 LPs/year. Works with musicians/artists and songwriters on contract; musicians on salary for in-house studio work. Pays 5% of suggested list price of record.
How to Contact: Prefers cassette with 3 songs and lyric sheet. SASE. Reports in 1 month.
Music: Gospel, rock and pop. Released *Crucible of Love* (by Tony Pilcher), recorded by Mylon LeFevre on Myrrh Records (LP and cassette); *Blessed Be Thy Name* (by Sparrow Holt), recorded by Blackwood Brothers on Benson Records (LP and cassette); and *The One For Me* (by Sparrow Holt), recorded by Jeff Stice on CSB Records (LP and cassette). Other artists include Andy Childs.

CURTISS RECORDS, Box 4740, Nashville TN 37216. (615)865-4740. President: Wade Curtiss. Record company and producer. Works with artists and songwriters on contract. Pays 8¢/record royalty to artists on contract; 2½¢/record royalty to songwriters on contract.
How to Contact: Prefers 7½ ips reel-to-reel with 2-8 songs and lead sheet. SASE. Reports in 3 weeks.
Music: Bluegrass, blues, country, disco, folk, gospel, jazz, rock, soul and top 40/pop. Released "Book of Matches," by Gary White; and "Rompin' " and "Punsky," by the Rhythm Rockers.

DA CAR RECORDING, 297 Rehm Rd., Depew NY 14043. (716)684-5323. Proprietor and Producer: C.D. Weyand. Record company and music publisher (Weyand Music Publishing/ASCAP). Member NMPA, Songwriter's Guild and Harry Fox Agency. Works with composers. Works with artists and songwriters on contract as negotiated. Pays negotiatiable rate to artists on contract; compulsory rate to publishers.
How to Contact: Write first, then submit professional, studio produced demo tape. Prefers cassette or 7½ ips reel-to-reel on 5-inch reel with 1-5 songs and leader tape between songs. "Full piano arrangement *must* be included with tape or cassette. With orchestral or instrumental works—full score is requested for proper review of material. Only copyrighted material will be listened to; all other will be returned." SASE.
Music: Mostly classical (piano, strings and symphonic pieces); also dance, easy-listening and jazz. Released *A Father for Christmas* (by Werner Janssen/Hazel Adair), recorded by C. and G. Weyand; *To Seal Our Love*, by Janssen and Lockerbie; and *Piano Selections*, written and recorded by C.D. Weyand, all on Da-Car Records (all LPs).
Tips: "Keep vocal distinct and out front. Full band required. We prefer arrangements featuring strings. We require fully written out piano and/or orchestral scores. SASE a must! Write first. Material submitted must be of 'master tape' quality."

DAN THE MAN PRODUCTION/WESTBURY RECORDS, Box 702, Cleveland OH 44107. (216)251-1618. President: Daniel L. Bischoff. Record company, record producer and music publisher (Dan The Man Music Publishing Co./ASCAP). Releases 3-6 singles and 0-1 LP/year. Works with artists and songwriters on contract. Pays 5-15¢ per record sold to artists on contract; statutory rate to publishers for each record sold.
How to Contact: Write first and obtain permission to submit. Prefers cassette (or videocassette) with 2-4 songs and lyric sheet. Does not return unsolicited material. SASE for reply. Reports in 3 weeks.
Music: Mostly country, R&B, soul, top 40 and rock; also novelty, easy listening and folk. Released "The Michael Jackson Interview," and "E.T. Interview," by Dan the Man (novelty singles); and "Telephone Gossip," by Johnny Wright (country single).
Tips: Looking for "novelty records, catchy tunes."

*DB RECORDS,Box 589, Charlotte Hall MD 20622. Labels include Sleeping Dog. Record company and music publisher (Glotab Rose Music, ASCAP). Releases 10 singles and 2-3 LPs/year. Works with musicians/artists on contract. Pays 5-10% royalty to artists on contract. Pays compulsory rate to publisher per song on record.
How to Contact: Prefers cassette and lyric sheet. Does not return unsolicited material Reports in 6 weeks.
Music: Mostly country, pop and rock. Released "Southern Comfort," (by W. Bricker), recorded by The Brickers; "Little Boy," (by Tommy Dodson), recorded by T.C. Roberts; and "Moon Song," (by Lathan), recorded by Mercedes, all on db Records (all singles). Other artists include Sam Neely, Lowell Shyette, Tabby Crabb and Sam Toder.

DESTINY RECORDS, 31 Nassau Ave., Wilmington MA 01887. (617)658-8391. Owner: Larry Feeney. Record company, record producer and music publisher (Seismic Music). Releases 4 singles and 2 LP's/year. Works with artists and songwriters on contract; musicians on salary for in-house studio work. Pays 50% rate to artists on contract; statutory rate to publishers for each record sold.
How to Contact: Write first. Prefers cassette with 2 songs maximum.

Music: Mostly blues; also bluegrass, church/religious, country, dance, easy listening, folk, jazz, MOR, progressive, R&B, soul and top 40/pop. Released "Decisions," by Rude Awakening (rock single); "Prisoners," by Tinted Glass (rock single); and "Ritzi Anna," by Myron Skav (rock single).

DHARMA RECORDS,117 W. Rockland Rd., Box 615, Libertyville IL 60048. (312)362-4060. Vice President: Rick Johnson. Labels include Future and Homexercise. Record company, record producer and music publisher (Amalgamated Tulip Corp.). Releases 3 singles and 2 LPs/year. Works with artists and songwriters on contract. Pays negotiable royalty to artists on contract; negotiable rate to publishers for each record sold.
How to Contact: Prefers cassette with 3-5 songs and lyric sheet. Prefers studio produced demos. SASE. Reports in 1 month.
Music: Rock, top 40/pop, country, dance/R&B, MOR and progressive rock. Released *Active Music for Children*, by Bill Hooper (education LP); "Oh Boy," by Oh Boy (pop rock single); and *Not Marmosets Yet*, by Conrad Black (rock LP).

DISCOS PRESENCA LTD., C. Postal 2525 Centro, Rio de Janeiro 20001 Brazil. (021)295-9081. President: Wilson F. Falcão. Labels include Campeão and Falcão. Record company and music publisher. Releases 5 singles and 1 LP/year. Works with musicians on salary for in-house studio work. Pays varying royalty to artists on contract.
How to Contact: Call first and obtain permission to submit. Call to arrange personal interview. Prefers cassette. Does not return unsolicited material. Reports ASAP.
Music: Blues, rock and jazz. Released "Superstition" (by W. Falcão/Portinho), recorded by Carlos Braga (ballad single); "Cala Coração" (by Alvinho), recorded by Nelí Miranda (ballad single); and "Blusa Roxa," written and recorded by Moacyrmm (samba single), all on Discos Presenca. Other artists include Marion Duarte, Flavio Miranda, Grupo Familia, Ilka Brito, Rosilene and Wilson Madrugada.

DISCOS VICTORIA, S.A., 20 O'Donnell, Madrid 28009 Spain. (91)435-50-84. General Manager: Gorhard Haltermann. Labels include Victoria, Diana, Stiff and Statik. Record company and music publisher (Victoria Ediciones Musicales, S.A.). Releases 30 singles and 50 LPs/year. Works with musicians/artists and songwriters on contract.
How to Contact: Prefers cassette. Reports in 2 weeks.
Music: Rock, punk and disco/dance. Released "Girlie Girlie" (by A. Davis), recorded by Sophia George on Winner (reggae single); *In the Hothouse* (by A. Borland), recorded by The Sound on Statik (pop LP); and *Blackhearts* (by Boulton/Wright), recorded by Tokyo Blade on Victoria (heavy LP).

DOMINO RECORDS, LTD., Ridgewood Park Estates, 222 Tulane St., Garland TX 75043. Contact: Gene or Dea Summers. Public Relations/Artist and Fan Club Coordinator: Steve Summers. Labels include Front Row Records. Record company and music publisher (Silicon Music/BMI). Releases 5-6 singles and 2-3 LPs/year. Works with artists and songwriters on contract. Pays negotiable royalties to artists on contract; standard royalty to songwriters on contract.
How to Contact: Prefers cassette (or VHS videocassette) with 1-3 songs. Does not return unsolicited material. SASE. Reports ASAP.
Music: Mostly 50's rock/rockabilly; also country and R&B. Released "The Music of Jerry Lee," by Joe Hardin Brown (country single); "Ready to Ride," (from the HBO Presentation *Backlot*), by Pat Minter (country single); and *Texas Rock and Roll* and *Gene Summers Live In Scandinavia*, by Gene Summers (50's LPs).
Tips: "If you own masters of 1950s rock and rock-a-billy, contact us first! We will work with you on a percentage basis for overseas release. We have active releases in Holland, Switzerland, Belgium, Australia, England, France, Sweden, Norway and the US at the present. We need original masters. You must be able to prove ownership of tapes before we can accept a deal. We're looking for little-known, obscure recordings. We have the market if you have the tapes!"

DORE RECORDS, 1608 Argyle, Hollywood CA 90028. (213)462-6614. President: Lew Bedell. Record company and music publisher (Hillary/BMI and Meadowlark/ASCAP). Releases 10 singles and 3 LPs/year. Works with musicians/artists and songwriters on contract. Pays 6% royalty to artists on contract.
How to Contact: Prefers cassette and lyric sheet. Does not return unsolicited material. Reports in 2 weeks.
Music: Mostly rock, R&B and novelty; also comedy and country.

*DORN RECORDS, 20531 Plummer St., Chatsworth CA 91311. (213)998-0443. Manager: A. Sullivan. Labels include DORN, AKO and ATEC Records. Record company, record producer and music

publisher (AMIRON Music/ASCAP). Releases 4 singles and 1 LP/year. Works with songwriters on contract. Pays 5-10% royalty to artists on contract; statutory rate to publishers for each record sold.
How to Contact: Prefers 7½ips reel-to-reel or cassette and lyric sheet. SASE. Reports in 3 weeks.
Music: Blues, country, dance-oriented, easy listening, MOR, progressive, Spanish, R&B, rock and top 40/pop. Released *Newstreet* (rock LP and single); and "Better Run" (pop/rock single), by Newstreet. Other artists include Lista Brown, El Chicano, Zell Black, Zaral, AKO, Johnny Forever, One Flite Up, Debbie Rockwell, Pyramid, Monica Lewis, The Stauntons and Touch of Fire.

*DOWNS RECORD COMPANY LIMITED, 220-3740 Portage Ave., Winnipeg, Manitoba R3K 0Z9 Canada. (204)889-9371. President: Terry O'Reilly. Record company, music publisher (Downs Publishing Co.) and booking agency (West-Can Entertainment Services). Releases 8-10 singles and 2-3 LPs/year. Works with musicians/artists on contract and musicians on salary for in-house studio work. Pays negotiable rate to publisher per song on record.
How to Contact: Prefers cassette with maximum of 4 songs and lyric sheet. Does not return unsolicited material. Reports in 3 weeks.
Music: Mostly country/rock, traditional country and MOR. Released "No Other Love" (by Bryon O'Donnell), recorded by Donna and Harvey Henry; "Quit Kickin' My Heart Around" (by R. Booth), recorded by Donna Henry; and "He's All Over You" (by B. O'Donnell), recorded by Jerry Ness, all singles on Downs Records.
Tips: "As we are a Canadian label publishing must be open to negotiation either worldwide or specific territory."

*DOWNTOWN RECORD COMPANY, Stenenmolenstraat 7, B-2580 St., Katelyne-Waver Belgium. (15) 41 13 31. Managing Director: Piroux Ghislain. Record company and record producer (Piroux G.C.J.). Releases 20-25 singles and 3-5 LPs/year. Works with musicians/artists and songwriters on contract. Pays negotiable royalty to artists on contract.
How to Contact: Prefers cassette or reel-to-reel (or videocassette) with 2-6 songs and lyric sheet. "Always addressed to Mr. Piroux Ghislain." SAE and IRC. Reports in 6 weeks.
Music: Mostly pop, mainstream rock, funk (disco/funk); also new wave, R&B, golden oldies. "No pop/rock or heavy metal." Released "Never In A Million Years," recorded by Linda Scott; "Jungle Drums," recorded by Clyde Otis; and "Happy Together," recorded by The Turtles, all on Downtown Records (all singles). Other artists include Guenaelle (new female singer), and Kokomo (female singer).
Tips: We are an independent company which is an enormous advantage in a small country like Belgium. We can easily distribute items ourselves. If it's a hit in Belgium, Europe is watching."

DRAGON RECORDS, INC., 872 Morris Park Ave., Bronx NY 10462. (212)792-2198. Contact: President. Labels include Agon Records. Record company and record producer. Works with artists and songwriters on contract. Pays statutory rate to publishers for each record sold.
How to Contact: Write first.
Music: Easy listening, MOR and top 40/pop.

DRG RECORDS, INC., Suite 1403, 157 W. 57th St., New York NY 10019. (212)582-3040. A&R Director: Van-John Sfiridis. Labels include DRG Records, DRG Archive, Disques Swing (Swing Records) and Stet Records. Record company. Releases 20-30 LPs/year. Works with musicians/artists on contract.
How to Contact: Prefers cassette (or VHS videocassette). Does not return unsolicited material.
Music: Pop/jazz, film scores and cast recordings. Released *A Room With A View* (by Richard Robbins), recorded by FilmTrax; *Nuances*, (by Claude Bolling); and *Tony Bennett, The McPartlands and Friends*, all LPs on DRG Records.

D-TOWN RECORDS, Suite 601, 523 Pine St., Seattle WA 98101. (206)624-3965. President: Kenneth H. Smith. Labels include Platinum Sound, KHS/Futura and DROC. Record company, music publisher (Keristene Music, Ltd.) and record producer (Platinum Sound Productions). Releases 3 singles and 6 LPs/year. Works with musicians and artists on contract. Pays 7½ to 33⅓% royalty to artists on contract. Pays compulsory rate to publisher per song on record.
How to Contact: Write or call first and obtain permission to submit. Prefers cassette (or VHS, Beta or ¾" videocassette) with maximum 3 songs. Does not return unsolicited material. Reports in 2 months. "Our current policy is to review only finished product. The exception is outstanding demos."
Music: Mostly urban dance, rock and R&B; also heavy metal and country. Released *Connie*, written and recorded by Connie Butler; and *Venus*, written and recorded by Merrell Fankhauser (both LPs, D-Town Records). Other artists include Bernadette Bascom, City Chyld, Tie Pantys and Lee Rogers.

*DUM DUM RECORDS, Opernring #1, A-1010 Vienna, Austria. (022)56 86 01. Managing Director: Wolfgang Strobl. Record company and record producer. Works with musicians/artists on contract; musicians on salary for in-house studio work.
How to Contact: Prefers cassette (or VHS videocassette) and lyric sheet. Does not return unsolicited material. Reports in 6 weeks.
Music: Mostly disco dance, rock dance and wave dance; also jazz dance.

DUPUY RECORDS/PRODUCTIONS/PUBLISHING, INC., Suite 200, 10960 Ventura Blvd., Studio City CA 91604. (818)980-6412. President: Pedro Dupuy. Record company, record producer and music publisher (Dupuy Publishing, Inc./ASCAP). Releases 5 singles and 5 LPs/year. Works with artists and songwriters on contract; musicians on salary for in-house studio work. Pays negotiable rate to publishers for each record sold.
How to Contact: Write or call first or arrange personal interview. Prefers cassette with 2-4 songs and lyric sheet. SASE. Reports in 1 month.
Music: Easy listening, jazz, MOR, R&B, soul and top 40/pop. Artists include Gordon Gilman, Michael Gruwell, Jack D. Colombo, Krisanthi Pappas, Michael R. Iannatuoni and Amy Nuzum.
Tips: Needs "very definite lyrics with hook."

DYNAMIC ARTISTS RECORDS, Box 25654, Richmond VA 23260. (804)225-7810. President: Joseph J. Carter Jr. Record company, music publisher (Hot Gold Music Publishing Co./BMI), booking agency, management firm and production firm. Releases 6 singles and 2 LPs/year. Works with musicians on salary; artists and songwriters on contract; statutory rate to publishers for each record sold. Pays 9-12% royalty to artists on contract.
How to Contact: Prefers cassette (or VHS videocassette) with 1-3 songs. SASE. Reports in 60 days.
Music: Mostly R&B and pop; also dance and rock. Released "Without You Tonight," by Waller Family (ballad single); *Love Moods*, by Waller Family (soul and pop LP); and "I Want to Sing This Song for You," by Starfire (pop/R&B single).

DYNAMIC RECORDING COMPANY, 2846 Dewey Ave., Rochester NY 14616. President: David R. Kaspersin. Record company and music publisher (Kaspersin Music Publishing Co.). Releases 10 singles and 10 LPs/year. Works with artists and songwriters on contract; musicians on salary for in-house studio work. Pays negotiable royalty to artists on contract; statutory rate to publishers for each record sold.
How to Contact: Write or call first and obtain permission to submit. Prefers cassette or reel-to-reel (or ¾ or ½" Beta or ½" VHS videocassette with digital sound) with 4 songs and lyric sheet. Reports in 6 weeks.
Music: Mostly country, R&B and gospel; also rock and straight country. Released "I Still Do," by Prospect Highway (rock single); *Still in the Runnin*, by David and Barbara Marek (country LP); "Tennessee Man," by Nancy Park (country single); and *Saidi Wind*, by Ibrahim Turmen (dance LP).
Tips: "Submit clean simple demos, no fancy leads or introductions. Get right to the hook of the song."

DYNAMITE, 5 Aldom Circle, West Caldwell NJ 07006. Contact: Gidget Starr (gospel music) or Jim Hall (other music). Labels include Dynamite, Deadwood, Tar Heel, True Love, Cactus, Peek Records and Deadwood-Dynamite cassette tapes. Record company, record producer and music publisher. Releases 3 singles/year. Works with artists and songwriters on contract. Pays 5% royalty to artists on contract; statutory rate to publishers for each record sold.
How to Contact: Write first about your interest. Prefers 7½ ips reel-to-reel or cassette with 5 songs and lyric or lead sheet. Does not return unsolicited material. Reports in 1 month.
Music: Bluegrass, blues, country, gospel and rock. Released "Back to North Carolina," written and recorded by Bill Price on Tar Heel Records; "Christmas Tree By The Window," (by Eugene Welkman/Jim Hall), recorded by J. Hall on Dynamite Records; and "Hello Blues" (by Rod Morris), recorded by J. Hall on Dynamite Records (all singles). Other artists include Doc Hopkins and Tune Twisters, Sal Franco, Gidget Starr, Dusty Rhodes, J.C. Davis and Charlie Bailey.

E.L.J. RECORD CO., 1344 Waldron, St. Louis MO 63130. President: Eddie Johnson. Record company, record producer and music publisher (Quinones/BMI). Works with musicians on salary; artists and songwriters on contract. Releases 6 singles and 3 LPs/year. Pays 3% minimum royalty to artists on contract; statutory rate to publishers for each record sold.
How to Contact: Prefers 7½ ips reel-to-reel or cassette with 4 songs and lead sheet. SASE. Reports in 2 weeks.
Music: Mostly top 40; also easy listening, blues, church/religious, R&B, soul and pop. Released "Strange Feeling," by Eddie Johnson (top 40 single); "Tables Are Turned," by Bobby Scott (top 40 single); and "Hold Me," by Ann Richardson (soul single).

*E.M.O. RECORDS, LTD., #211, 1811 W. Katella Ave., Anaheim CA 92804. (714)896-0588. A&R Director: Emile LeBlanc. Record company. Releases 50 singles and 4 LPs/year. Works with musicians/artists and songwriters on contract and musicians on salary for in-house studio work.
How to Contact: Prefers Beta videocassette. SASE. Reports in 10 weeks.
Music: Mostly gospel/Christian, rock/pop and country; also music videos and Christian music.

EARTH RECORDS CO., Rt. 3, Box 57, Troy AL 36081. (205)566-7932. Record company, record and video producer and music publisher. Releases 4 singles and 3 LPs/year. Works with artists and songwriters on contract. Pays statutory rate to publishers for each record sold.
How to Contact: Write or call first to arrange personal interview to play demo tape. Prefers cassette (or videocassette) with 2-9 songs. SASE. Reports in 2 weeks.
Music: Children's, country, easy listening, gospel and top 40/pop. Released "Cheese Line," and "Express Line," by E. Toney (easy listening singles); and "Ready for Love," by Kim (soul single).

EAST COAST RECORDS INC., 604 Glover Dr., Runnemede NJ 08078. (609)931-8389. President: Anthony J. Messina. Record company and music publisher. Releases 10 singles and 3 LPs/year. Works with artists and songwriters on contract. Pays 4-7% royalty to artists on contract; standard royalty to songwriters on contract.
How to Contact: Prefers 7½ ips reel-to-reel or cassette with 3-12 songs and lyric sheet. SASE. Reports in 3 weeks.
Music: Classical, MOR, rock, and top 40/pop. Released "Remembering," by Lana Cantrell (MOR single); "Drifting Away," by Uproar (rock single); and *England Made Me* (soundtrack from the motion picture), by London Philharmonic (classical LP). Other artists include Lynn Redgrave, Harold Melvin & The Bluenotes, Dakota, Aviator and X-Dream.

*ELECTRIC RECORDS, Suite 300, 54 Music Sq. E., Nashville TN 37203. (615)242-5588. Owner: Jerry West. Labels include Police and Maze. Record company, music publisher and record producer. Works with musicians/artists and songwriters on contract and musicians on salary for in-house studio work.
How to Contact: Prefers cassette (or videocassttte). SASE. Reports in 1 week.
Music: Country and southern gospel. Released *Greatest Hits*, recorded by Jack Ward on Electric Records (country LP).

EMI AMERICA RECORDS, 1370 Avenue of the Americas, New York NY 10019. (212)757-7470. Contact: A&R Director. (Los Angeles office: 6920 Sunset Blvd., Los Angeles CA 90028. A&R Directors: Jeff Forman (R&B) and John Guarnieri.) Record company and music publisher (Screen Gems). Releases several singles and LPs/month.
How to Contact: Prefers reel-to-reel or cassette and lyric sheet. "Mail in no more than 3 songs on a cassette at a time. Include an SASE that will support all the materials sent as we keep nothing on file." Reports in 3 weeks.
Music: All types of music. Released "West End Girls," by Pet Shop Boys (pop single); "Do It to Me Good Tonight," by Michael Henderson (R&B single); and "The Knife Feels Like Justice," by Brian Setzer ("multi-format" single). Other artists include Peter Tosh, Corey Hart, Talk Talk, Sheena Easton, David Bowie, Kate Bush and Kim Carnes.

EMI (MALAYSIA) SDN. BHD., 8 Jalan Murai Dua, Kompleks Batu, Batu 3, Jalan Ipoh, Kuala Lumpur 51000 Malaysia. (03)6277511/6277612. Contact: A&R Manager, Malay Division. Record company. Releases 12-14 LPs year. Works with musicians/artists on contract.
How to Contact: Prefers cassette or 7½ ips reel-to-reel (or VHS PAL videocassette) with 5-10 songs and lyric sheet or lead sheet. Does not return unsolicited material. Reports in 2 weeks. "We only record in Malay language, therefore please send materials only with vocal guide or melody lines together with basic rhythm."
Music: Mostly country, commercial jazz and R&B; also rock. Released *Sudirman*, recorded by Adnan Abu Hassan; *Sweet September*, recorded by Razzi M.; and *Sharifah Aini*, recorded by Fauzi Marzuki, all LPs on EMI Records.

EURO TEC RECORDS AND TAPES, Box 3077, Ventura CA 93006. (805)658-2488. Vice President: Bruce Caplin. Labels include ETR. Record company, record producer, music publisher and management consultants. Releases 3-5 singles and 1-3 LPs/year. Works with artists and songwriters on contract. Pays 12-15% royalty to artists on contract; statutory or variable rate to publishers for each record sold.
How to Contact: Write or call first. Prefers 15 ips reel-to-reel or cassette (or videocassette) with 1-12 songs. SASE. Reports in 60 days.
Music: Dance, rock, top 40, pop, Latin rock, AOR, MOR and CHR (Contemporary Hit Radio). Re-

leased *Rock Rolls On*, by Michael Bruce (AOR/CHR LP); "Too Young," by M. Bruce (rock-AOR single); and *Vintage Cooper Wildness*, recorded by M. Bruce and Alice Cooper (rock/AOR LP).

EXECUTIVE RECORDS, 11 Shady Oak Trail, Charlotte NC 28210-7409. (704)554-1162. Executive Producer: Butch Kelly Montgomery. Record company, record producer, music publisher (Butch Kelly Production) and songwriter. Member AGAC. Releases 4 singles/year and 2 LPs/year. Works with artists on contract; musicians on salary for in-house studio work. Pays 50% to artists on contract; statutory rate to publishers for each record sold.
How to Contact: Prefers cassette (or videocassette) with 3 songs and lyric sheet and pictures. SASE. Submit pictures with demo. Reports in 2 months.
Music: Mostly R&B and pop; also dance, soul and top 40. Released "Oh Happy Days," by Stanley Alexander (gospel single); *M.C. Perpetrators*, by Lady Crush (rap LP); "Dr. Feelgood," by Lindia Straite (R&B single); and "Street Dancin" (R&B) and "Miss You" (ballad) both by Fresh Air.

FACTORY BEAT RECORDS, INC., 521 5th Ave., New York NY 10175. (212)757-3638. President: Rena L. Feeney. Labels include R&R, Ren Rome and Can Scor Productions, Inc. Record company, record producer and music publisher (Ren-Maur Music Corp.). Member NARAS, BMI and Songwriters Guild. Releases 4 singles and 2 LPs/year. Works with musicians/artists and songwriters on contract; musicians on salary for in-house studio work. Pays 4-12% royalty to artists on contract; statutory rate to publishers for each record sold. Pays 8% royalty to artists on contract.
How to Contact: Submit cassette and lyric sheet only. SASE. Reports in 3 weeks. "Do not phone— we will return material."
Music: Mostly R&B, contemporary and rap; also rock, soul and top 40/pop. Released "Human Beat Box," recorded by P.C. Crew; "Saturday Night," recorded by Fantasy Force; and "Same Language Once You Fall in Love," recorded by Rena, all written by B. Nichols, (all singles, Factory Beat Records).

FAMOUS DOOR RECORDS, Box 92, Station A, Flushing NY 11358. (718)463-6281. Contact: Harry Lim. Record company. Member NARAS. Releases 6 LPs/year. Works with artists on contract. Pays 5% in royalty to artists on contract; statutory rate to publishers for each record sold.
How to Contact: Write first. Prefers cassette with minimum 3 songs. Prefers studio produced demos. SASE. Reports in 1 month.
Music: Jazz. Released *L.A. After Dark*, by Ross Tomkins Quartet; *More Miles and More Standards*, by the Butch Miles Sextet; and *Buenos Aires New York Swing Connections*, by George Anders Sextet.
Tips: Looking for "good instrumentals."

FARR RECORDS, Box 1098, Somerville NJ 08876. (201)725-3850. Contact: Candace Campbell. Record company and record producer. Member RIAA. Releases 30 singles and 30 LPs/year. Works with musicians/artists on contract. Pays negotiable royalty to artists on contract; compulsory rate to publishers for each record sold.
How to Contact: Prefers cassette with 4 songs and lyric sheet. SASE. Reports in 2 weeks.
Music: Mostly pop and folk; also country, dance-oriented, easy listening, MOR, rock, soul and top 40.

50 STATES RECORDS & TAPES, Box 314, Hendersonville TN 37075. (615)824-8308. A&R Director: Johnny Howard. Record company, record producer and music publisher (Chap's Music). Releases 12 singles and 6 LPs/year. Works with artists and songwriters on contract. Pays negotiable royalty to artists on contract; statutory rate to publishers for each record sold.
How to Contact: Prefers cassette with 1-5 songs and lyric sheet. SASE. Reports in 3 weeks.
Music: Mostly country and top 40; also bluegrass and gospel. Released "England, America Loves You," by Fabulous Fryers (country/pop single); *You Lay So Easy On My Mind*, by Jack Paris (country/pop LP); and "Wake Up America" by J.T. Lampman Singers (country/pop single).

FINER ARTS RECORDS/TRANSWORLD RECORDS, 2170 S. Parker Rd., Denver CO 80231. (303)755-2613. President: R.J. Bernstein. Record company, music publisher (M. Bernstein Music Publishing Co.) and record producer. Releases 5 singles and 2 LPs/year. Works with musicians/artists and songwriters on contract; musicians on salary for in-house studio work.
How to Contact: Write first and obtain permission to submit. Prefers cassette (or VHS videocassette) and lyric sheet or lead sheet. Reports in 3 weeks.
Music: Rock, jazz and country.

*FIRMUS RECORDS, 156 Woburn Ave., Toronto, Ontario M5M 1K7 Canada. (416)484-1728. President: Milan Kymlicka. Record company, music publisher (Cantus/Firmus Publishing) and record producer (Cantus Publishing Ltd.). Releases 2 singles and 1 LP/year. Works with musicians/artists and

songwriters on contract. Pays 7-14% royalty to artists on contract; compulsory rate to publisher per song on record.
How to Contact: Prefers cassette with 3-4 songs and lyric sheet. Does not return unsolicited material. Reports in 5 weeks.
Music: Mostly pop and classical. Released "Farewell," written and recorded by M. Kymlicka (single); "This is a Man" (by Woszak/Dolman), recorded by B. Richardson (single); and *Pulsbeat* (by M. Kymlicka/Tripe) (LP), all on Firmus and A&M Records.

*FIRST STRING RECORDS, 2741 N. 29th Ave., Hollywood FL 33020. (305)921-5998. President: Carl Manuri. Record company, music publisher (Miss Sarah Music Co./Miss Areal Music) and record producer (Calr Maduri). Releases 5 singles and 2 LPs/year. Works with musicians/artists and songwriters on contract. Pay compulsory rate to publisher per song on record.
How to Contact: Prefers cassette and lyric sheet. Does not return unsolicited material.
Music: Mostly R&B and pop. Artists include Betty Wright, Marita, Steve Gordon and Cynthia Hinds.

*JOHN FISHER & ASSOCIATES, 7 Music Circle N., Nashville TN 37203. (615)256-3616. President: John Fisher. Labels include Player International, Crusader, Gold Country and Pulsation. Record company, music publisher and record producer. Releases 2 singles and 1 LP/year. Works with musicians/artists on contract.
How to Contact: Prefers cassette with up to 6 songs and lyric or lead sheets. SASE. Reports in 2 weeks.
Music: Mostly country, 50s rock and blues; also rock-a-billy. Artists include Terry Stafford, Steve Ricks, Henson Cargill, Ray Peterson and Webb Pierce.

415 RECORDS, Box 14563, San Francisco CA 94114. (415)621-3415 or 522-9828. President: Howie Klein. Record company and music publisher (Very Safe Music/BMI and Even Safer Music/ASCAP). Releases 4 singles and 4 LPs/year. Works with artists on contract. Pays statutory rate to publishers for each record sold.
How to Contact: Prefers cassette (or Beta or VHS videocassette) with 1-5 songs. SASE.
Music: Rock and new wave. Released *I'll Do You*, by Wire Train; *Un-Alone*, by Translator; *China*, by Red Rockers (all rock singles and LPs).

*4-QUARTET SONGS, Box 344, Wimbledon, London SW19 1EY England. (01)543-6504. Record company, music publisher and management representation. Estab. 1986. Releases 6 singles and 2 LPs/year. Works with musicians/artists and songwriters on contract. Pays 9-12% royalty to artists on contract. " We are a specialist publisher covering Europe, signing writers with multi-facetted potential for cover versions/musical scores/media, etc."
How to Contact: Prefers cassette or 15 ips reel-to-reel. "Tapes returned only in SAE and IRC are included."
Music: Mostly soul, R&B and fusion; also adult contemporary "with soul bias." Artists include 2 Brave (Norwegian group licenses via MCA), and Andy Holmes and Dave Leming (writers).

FOUR WINDS RECORD PRODUCTIONS INC., Box 11547, East Station, Memphis TN 38111. (901)525-5414. Contact: A&R Department. Record company. Works with artists on contract; musicians on salary for in-house studio work. Pays 10-20% royalty to artists on contract; statutory rate to publishers for each record sold.
How to Contact: Write or call first. Prefers cassette with 2-4 songs. SASE. Reports in 1 month.
Music: Mostly country; also R&B, bluegrass and "gut bucket blues."

FRANNE RECORDS, Box 8135, Chicago IL 60680. (312)224-5612. A&R Director/Executive Producer: R.C. Hillsman. Labels include Superbe Records. Record company, music publisher and producer. Works with artists and songwriters on contract. Pays 3½% royalty to artists and songwriters on contract.
How to Contact: Write or call to arrange personal interview. Prefers 7½ or 15 ips ¼" reel-to-reel or cassette with 4-6 songs and lyric sheet. Send material "by registered mail only." SASE. Reports in 3 weeks.
Music: Church/religious, country, disco, gospel, jazz, MOR, rock and top 40/pop. Released "He's Love" and "You Better Get Right," by Allen Duo (gospel singles).

*FRESH ENTERTAINMENT, 3542 Garfield Way SE, Atlanta GA 30354. (404)642-2645. Vice President, Marketing/A&R: Willie Hunter. Record company and music publisher (Hserf Music/ASCAP). Estab. 1986. Releases 5 singles and 2 LPs/year. Works with musicians/artists and songwriters on contract. Pays standard royalty to artists on contract.
How to Contact: Prefers cassette (or VHS videocassette) with at least 3 songs and lyric sheet. SASE. Reports in 2 weeks.

Music: Mostly R&B, rock and pop; also jazz, gospel and rap. Released "Girls with Me," written and recorded by Ede' (pop single); "Tell the Story" (by W. Gates), recorded by J. Gates (dance 12" single); and "Love to Live" (by F. McKinney/B. James), recorded by Heart to Heart (R&B 12" single), all on Fresh Records. Other artists include Sir Anthony with Rare Quality, and Larion.
Tips: "We're a new label looking for new ideas and acts."

FUTURE STEP SIRKLE, Box 2095, Philadelphia PA 19103. (215)844-1947. A&R Director: S. Deane Henderson. Labels include Molecules of Force Records. Record company, record producer, music publisher (Communciation Concept) and management firm. Releases 6-10 singles and 3-6 LPs/year. Works with artists and songwriters on contract. Pays 4-10% royalty to artists on contract; statutory rate to publishers for each record sold.
How to Contact: Prefers cassette (or VHS videocassette) with 4-8 songs and lyric sheet. "Lyrics only are returned." Reports in 2 weeks.
Music: Mostly R&B, funk, rock and heavy metal; also dance-oriented, easy listening, gospel, MOR, soul and top 40/pop. Released *Hot Number*, by Racers (rock LP); *Save Me Jesus*, by Offspring Gospel (gospel LP); and "Exercise," by M.D.F. (dance single). Other artists include Dean Morrow, Shonee, 4 Way Ping and Nasty Rumors.

FXL RECORDS, 7766 NW 44th St., Sunrise FL 33351. (305)741-7766. President: Frank Loconto. Record company, music publisher and record producer. Releases 10 singles and 10 LPs/year. Works with musicians/artists and songwriters on contract; musicians on salary for in-house studio work. Pays 5% royalty to artists on contract.
How to Contact: Write first and obtain permission to submit. Prefers cassette. SASE.
Music: Released *Seminole Man*, by Frank Loconto), recorded by James Billie on Bird Clan Records (LP); *Several*, written and recorded by Marie Alicata; and *Adele*, written and recorded by Frank Loconto, both on FXL Records (both LPs). Other artists include Lisa Heart, June/Jr Battiest, Wayne Carson, Obediah Colebrook, and Marie Alicata.

*GALLERY II RECORDS, 2301 W. 59th St., Los Angeles CA 90043. (213)294-7286. President: Johno Waller. Labels inlcude Jumpin' Jack Records. Record company, music publisher (Best Songs in the Universe, Shofars Publishing), and record producer. Releases 6 singles and 2 LPs/year. Works with musicians/artists and songwriters on contract. Pays 4% royalty to artists on contract. Pays negotiated rate to publisher per song on record.
How to Contact: Submit demo tape by mail or write to arrange personal interview. Prefers cassette, 15 ips reel-to-reel (or VHS or Beta videocassette) with 2 songs and lyric sheet. "All cassettes must be accompanied by either photos or a video." Reports "only if interested."
Music: Mostly R&B, gospel and rap; also rock, pop and jazz. Released "Idiot" (by Tyrone Von Trapper), recorded by Tee Trap; "Check It Out" (by Andre Wilmore), recorded by Big Time Fresh; and "Pimpin" (by Stacy Lett/Andre Willmore), recorded by Ms. Frostie. Other artists/writers include Wallace Rayford, Rodney Conner, Brandy Robinson, Marsha Stewart, Precision, and the Mighty Voices of Faith.

GCS RECORDS, Suite 206, 1508 Harlem, Memphis TN 38114. (901)274-2726. A&R Directors: Daniel Boga and Willie Blair. Labels include Del-A-Ron Records, Great-Day Records and Blue-Town Records. Record company and music publisher. Releases 40 singles and 7 LPs/year. Works with artists on record contract and musicians on salary for in-house studio work. Also works with composers and teams collaborators. Pays 3-7% royalty to artists on contract; statutory rate to publishers for each record sold.
How to Contact: Write or call about your interest or arrange personal interview. Prefers 7½ or 15 ips reel-to-reel or cassette (or VHS videocassette) with 3-5 songs and lyric sheet. SASE. Reports in 1 month.
Music: Mostly R&B; also gospel, blues and dance. Released "The Beat is Fresh," by First Class Crew (rap); "Are You Ready," by Victory (gospel); and "Love Song," by Music Man (R&B).

*GEIMSTEINN HF, Skolaveg 12, Keflavik 230 Iceland. (92)1717. President/Manager: Runar Juliusson. Labels include Hljomar. Record company, music publisher and record producer. Releases 5-10 LPs/year. Works with musicians/artists and songwriters on contract; musicians on salary for in-house studio work.
How to Contact: Write first and obtain permission to submit or to arrange personal interview. Prefers cassette (or VHS videocassette) with 2-3 songs and lyric sheet. Does not return unsolicited material. Reports in 6 weeks.
Music: Mostly pop, rock and country; also jazz, R&B and gospel. Released *Rustir*, (by Stefan), recorded by Gammar; *Stalio*, written and recorded by Afris; and *Hvar?*, (by Thor Baldursson), recorded by Thor and Runar, all LPs on Geimsteinn Records. Other artists include Runar Juliusson and Bjorn Thoroddsen.

GENESEE RECORDS, INC., 7931 Genesee, Litchfield MI 49252. (517)542-3051. President: Junior A. Cole. Record company, music publisher (J.A. Cole Publishing) and record producer. Releases 3 singles/ year. Works with musicians/artists on contract.
How to Contact: Prefers cassette. SASE. Reports in 6 weeks.
Music: Country. Released *In the Name Freedom*, by J. Cole (LP); and "Sleepless Blue," by D. Pack (single), both recorded by Country Express on Genesse Records.

GLAD-HAMP RECORDS INC., 1995 Broadway, New York NY 10023. (212)787-1223. A&R: Charlie Mack. Record company. Works with artists and songwriters on contract. Pays 5-15% royalty to artists on contract; standard royalty to songwriters on contract.
How to Contact: Prefers 7½ ips reel-to-reel or cassette with 2-4 songs and lyric sheet. SASE. Reports in 1 month.
Music: Jazz, R&B and soul. Released "School Daze," by Brothers Unique (12" rap); *Hamp in Japan* and *Ambassador at Large*, by Lionel Hampton (jazz LPs); and "Vibramatic," (breakdance).

*GLENDISC, Box 67, Stocksund, Sweden S-182 71. (8)856800. President: Bruno Glenmark. Record company, music publisher (GlenSongs) and record producer (Glenprod AB). Releases 20 singles and 5 LPs/year. Works with musicians/artists and songwriters on contract; musicians on salary for in-house studio work. Pays 5-10% royalty to artist on contract.
How to Contact: Prefers cassette. SAE and IRC. Reports in 6 weeks.
Music: Pop, rock and country. Released "So Good, So Fine" (by L. Anderson), recorded by Billy Preston and Ann-Louise Hanson on Glen Disc (single).

GLO RECORDS, 98 Hamilton Park, Columbus OH 43203. (614)461-9555. Contact: President. Record company.
How to Contact: Prefers cassette with minimum of 3 songs and lead sheet. SASE. Reports in 1 month.
Music: Jazz, R&B and pop.

GLOBAL RECORD CO., Box 396, Manistique MI 49854. President: Reg B. Christensen. Labels include Bakersfield Record Company. Record company and music publisher (Chris Music/BMI and Sara Lee Music/BMI). Releases 5-10 singles and 3-5 LPs/year. Works with artists and songwriters on contract. Pays 10-20% royalty to artists on contract; statutory rate to publishers for each record sold.
How to Contact: Prefers cassette with 3 songs and lyric sheet. SASE. Reports in 1 month.
Music: Mostly top 40, R&B, country, MOR, rock, and novelty types. Released *Diamonds & Pearls*, by Paradons on K-Tel Records and Cassettes; "Nashville Nut," (by Jay James), recorded by Ron Roy on Global Records (single); and "Ask Me No Questions," written and recorded by Bill Wood on Bakersfield Records (single). Other artists include Louie Moore.

*GOLD GUITAR RECORDS, Rt. 8, Box 3, Beaumont TX 77705. (409)842-2884. President: Don Gilbert. Record company, record producer and music publisher (Don Gilbert Music/BMI). Releases 10 singles/year. Works with songwriters on contract; musicians on salary for in-house studio work. Pays 8-15% royalty to artists on contract; statutory rate to publishers for each record sold.
How to Contact: Prefers 7½ ips reel-to-reel or cassette with 2-10 songs and lyric sheet. SASE. Reports in 3 months.
Music: Religious music only. Released "Five Rooms of Memories" and "The Other One," by Don Gilbert (country singles). Other artists include Sherry Black, George Lee and Scottie.

*GOLDBAND RECORDS, Box 1485, Lake Charles LA 70602. President: Eddie Shuler. Labels include Folk-Star, Tek, Tic-Toc, Anla, Jador and Luffcin Records. Record company and record producer. Works with artists and songwriters on contract; musicians on salary for in-house studio work. Pays 3-5% royalty to artists on contract; standard royalty to songwriters on contract.
How to Contact: Prefers cassette with 2-6 songs and lyric sheet. SASE. Reports in 2 months.
Music: Blues, country, easy listening, folk, R&B, rock and top 40/pop. Released *Katie Webster Has the Blues* (blues LP), and "Things I Used to Do" (blues single), by Katie Webster; "Waiting For My Child," by Milford Scott (spiritual single); "Gabriel and Madaline," by Johnny Jano (cajun country single); and "Cajun Disco," by the La Salle Sisters (disco single). Other artists incude Jimmy House, John Henry III, Gary Paul Jackson, Junior Booth, Rockin Sidney, Ralph Young, Tedd Dupin, R. Sims, Mike Young and Everett Brady.

GOLDEN BOY RECORDS, 3929 Kentucky Dr., Los Angeles CA 90068. (818)980-7501. A&R Director: Billy Johnson. Labels include Golden Boy and Alva. Record company. Releases 6 singles and 2 LPs/year. Works with artists on contract.

How to Contact: Prefers cassette (or videocassette) with maximum 3 songs and lyric sheet. Reports in 3 weeks.
Music: Mostly R&B and soul; also jazz.

GOLDEN RULE RECORD PRODUCTION CO., INC., Box 18018 Holiday City Station, Memphis TN 38181-0018. (901)525-5414. Contact: A&R Department. Record company. Releases 25 singles and 6 LPs/year. Works with artists on contract; musicians on salary for in-house studio work. Pays 4-10% royalty to artists on contract; statutory rate to publishers for each record sold.
How to Contact: Write first. Prefers cassette with 2-4 songs. SASE. Reports in 1 month.
Music: Gospel, country gospel, balck gospel and choir gospel.

GRANDVILLE RECORD CORP., Box 11960, Chicago IL 60611-0960. (312)561-0027. Executive Producer/President: Clifford Rubin. Record company, record producer and music publisher (Billetdoux Music/BMI). Releases 5 singles and 2 LPs/year. Works with artists and songwriters on contract; musicians on salary for in-house studio work. Pays 3-5% royalty to artists on contract; statutory rate to publishers for each record sold.
How to Contact: Prefers cassette with 3-5 songs and typewritten lyric sheet. SASE. Reports in 2 months.
Music: Mostly R&B, gospel, funk-soul and pop; also blues, country, rock and top 40. Released "All I Can Do to Think of You," "Tonight," and "Our Special Hour," by John Williams.
Tips: "We want commercial hooks with lyrics that are to the point as well as universal. Tapes should not be too long. An edited version of a whole performance is best. We are more interested in originals, of course."

GRASS ROOTS RECORD & TAPE/LMI RECORDS, Box 532, Malibu CA 90265. (213)858-7282. President: Lee Magid. Labels include LMI Records. Record company, record producer and music publisher (Alexis/ASCAP, Marvelle/BMI). Member AIMP, NARAC. Releases 6 singles and 6 LPs/year. Works with artists and songwriters on contract. Pays 2½-5% royalty to artists on contract; negotiable royalty to publishers for each record sold.
How to Contact: Prefers cassette with 3 songs and lyric sheet. "Please, no 45s." SASE. Reports in 1 month minimum.
Music: Mostly pop/rock, R&B, country, gospel, jazz/rock and blues; also bluegrass, children's and Latin. Released "Jack Be Quick," (by Rose Dulin), recorded by Tingle; "Cornbread," (by Wes Greene), recorded by Kim and Sam; and "Everyday," (by D. Goodin), recorded by Marva Josie, all on Grass Roots Records. Other artists include Gloria Lynne, L.A. Jazz Choir, Tom Vaughn, Tingle, Papa John Creach, Marva Josie, and Kim and Sam.

GRAVACOES ELETRICAS S. A., 4667 Av. Do Estado, São Paulo 01515 Brazil. 279-6811. Contact: International Label Manager. Labels include Continental, Chantecler and Phonodisc. Record company. Releases 3,600 singles/year and 300 LPs/year. Works with musicians/artists and songwriters on contract. Pays 7% royalty to artists on contract.
How to Contact: Prefers cassette or 15 ips reel-to-reel with 10 songs. Does not return unsolicited material. Reports in 4 weeks.
Music: Mostly Caribbean, rock and country; also blues and spirituals. Released *Sossega Leão*, recorded by Sossega Leão (Latin LP); *Degradèe*, recorded by Degradèe (rock LP); and *Fissura*, recorded by Chiclete C/Banana (carnaval music LP), all on Continental Records. Other artists include Belchior, Jorginho Do Império, Jamelão, Luiz Bordon and Millonário E Zé Rico.

*GROSVENOR RECORDING STUDIOS, 16 Grosvenor Rd., Birmingham B20 3NP United Kingdom. Managing Director: John R. Taylor. Labels include Grosvenor Records, Hollick and Taylor. Record company, music publisher (Grosvenor Publishing) and record producer. Releases 3 singles/year and 20 LPs/year. Works with musicians/artists and songwriters on contract; musicians on salary for in-house studio work. Pays variable royalty to artists on contract; variable rate to publishers per song on record.
How to Contact: Write or call first to obtain permission to submit.

GULE RECORDS INC., #611, 7046 Hollywood Blvd., Hollywood CA 90028. (213)462-0502. A&R: Harry Gordon. Record company, music publisher (Bee Ray Music) and record producer (Harry Edward Co.). Works with songwriters on contract.
How to Contact: Prefers cassette. SASE. Reports in 2 weeks.
Music: Mostly country and R&B.

GULFSTREAM RECORDS, 4225 Palm St., Baton Rouge LA 70808. (504)383-7885. President: Barrie Edgar. Record company, music publisher (Silverfoot) and record producer (Hogar). Works with musi-

cians/artists and songwriters on contract; musicians on salary for in-house studio work. Pays 3-10% royalty to artists on contract.
How to Contact: Prefers cassette with 4 songs and lyric sheet. SASE. "Patience required on reports."
Music: Mostly rock, blues (not soul) and country. Released "Louisiana's Basin Child," by Top Secret on Gulfstream (rock single). Other artists include Joe Costa.

HACIENDA RECORDS, 1236 S. Staples, Corpus Christi TX 78404. (512)882-7066. Producer: Rick Garcia. Labels include: Las Brisas. Record company, music publisher (Dark Heart Music, El Palacio Music, Roland Garcia Music) and record producer. Releases 20-100 singles/year and 5-20 LPs/year. Works with artists and songwriters on contract; musicians on salary for in-house studio work. Pays royalties or per LP to artists on contract.
How to Contact: Prefers cassette. Does not return unsolicited material. Reporting time varies.
Music: Rock, Spanish and country, pop, MOR, international and gospel. Released "Ready as Hell," (by Jim D./Ricky R./Johnny C.), recorded by Jim Dandy's Black Oak Arkansas on Hacienda (rock single & LP), "It's Majic," (by Pio Trevino), recorded by Majic on Hacienda (English single from Spanish LP); and "Ran Kan Kan," (by Tito Puente), recorded by Steve Jordan on Hacienda (Spanish single). Other artists include Freddy Fender, Romance, Gary Hobbs, Fuego, Janie C., Steve Borth and Rowdy Friends.

*HALPERN SOUNDS, Box 2644, San Anselm CA 94960. (415)485-5321. President: Steven Halpern. Labels include Halpern Sounds and Hear & Now Records. Record company and record producer. Releases 2 LPs/year. Works with musicians/artists on contract; musicians on salary for in-house studio work. Pays 2% royalty to artists on contrct.
How to Contact: Prefers cassette. SASE. Reports in 2 months.
Music: New age and adult contemporary. Released "Shared Visions" recorded by Freesen; "Lifetide" recorded by Mazer & Smith; and "Connections," recorded by Horn, (all by Halpern) all on Halpern Sounds. Other artists include Steven Halpern.
Tips: "Music should be uplifting but not a repeat of everybody else. No drum boxes. Must be in tune!"

HAPPY BEAT RECORDS, Box 266775, Houston TX 77207. (713)645-5391. President: Roger L. Cummings. Labels include MSB Records. Record company, music publisher (Sirloin Music Publishing/BMI), promotion and distribution firm. Releases 5 singles and 3 LPs/year. Works with artists and songwriters on contract; musicians on salary for in-house studio work. Pays negotiable royalty to artists on contract; negotiable rate to publishers for each record sold.
How to Contact: Prefers cassette with 3-6 songs and lyric sheet. "Don't send your master and state speed on videocassette box. Artists should include photo." SASE. Reports in 1 month.
Music: Mostly rock, soul and dance; also blues, jazz, R&B and top 40/pop. Released "Let the Music in Your Mind," by Chance (dance single); and *Drum Licks*, by Friction (drum songs EP). Other artists include Carl Adams, Steve Cummings, Carl Stewart and Invasion.

HARD HAT RECORDS AND CASSETTES, 519 N. Halifax Ave., Daytona Beach FL 32018. (904)252-0381. President: Bobby Lee Cude. Labels include Hard Hat, Maricao, Blue Bandana and Indian Head. Record company, record producer and music publisher (Cude & Pickens Publishing/BMI). Releases 6 singles and 12 LPs/year.
How to Contact: Write first. Does not use outside material.
Music: Mostly country; also easy listening, gospel, MOR, top 40/pop and Broadway show. Released "Sand in My Shoes," and "V-A-C-A-T-I-O-N," recorded by the Hard Hatters; "Just a Piece of Paper," "Can't Get Over Lovin' You," and "Only Lies," recorded by Blue Bandana Country Band; and "New Generation March," and "Los Angeles Town" (marching band arrangements).

*HARMONY STREET RECORDS, Box 4107, Kansas City, KS 66104. (913)299-2881. President: Charlie Beth. Record company, music publisher (Harmony Street Music, ASCAP and Harmony Lane Music, BMI), and record producer (Harmony Street Productions). Releases 10-20 singles and 4-6 LPs/year. Works with musicians/artists and songwriters on contract; musicians on salary for in-house studio work. Pays 5-10% royalty to artists on contract; pays statutory rate to publishers per song on record.
How to Contact: Prefers cassette (or VHS videocassette) with no more than 3 songs and lyric or lead sheet. SASE. Reports in 3 weeks.
Music: Mostly country (all types) and gospel (all types). Released "Little Dirt Road," written and recorded by Jimmy Lee (country single); "I Want To Thank You," (by Sue G. Mahurin/Terry Allen), recorded by Terry Allen (country single); and "Get Down," (by Ed Morgan/Chalrie Beth), recorded by Perfect Harmony (gospel single), all on Harmony Street Records. Other artists include Michael G and Terri McClain.
Tips: "Songs submitted to us must be original, commercial and have a good strong hook. Demos should

be clear and clean with voice out front. We are interested in working with commercial artists with professional attitudes and career goals."

HE ROSE RECORDS, 1098 Rose Ave., El Centro CA 92243. (619)352-5774. A&R Department: Danny Berg. Record company and music publisher. Member GMA. Releases 2 singles and 2 LPs/year. Works with artists and songwriters on contract. Pays 7% of $8.98 list; statutory rate to publishers for each record sold.
How to Contact: Prefers cassette with 1-3 songs and lyric sheet. SASE. Reports in 6 months.
Music: Gospel/contemporary Christian, choral and church/religious. Released *Raised Up Again*, and *Overcomer*, by The New Jerusalem Band; and *Reasons*, by Chronicles (all contemporary Christian LPs).

HEAVY METAL RECORDS, 152 Goldthorn Hill, Penn, Wolverhampton, WV2 3VA England. 44-(0902)-345345. A&R Manager: David Roberts. Labels include Heavy Metal Records, Revolver Records, Heavy Metal America, Heavy Metal Worldwide and FM. Record company, record producer and music publisher. Releases 20 singles and 50 LPs/year. Works with musicians/artists and songwriters on contract. Pays negotiable royalty to artists on contract; compulsory rate to publishers per song on record.
How to Contact: Prefers cassette (or VHS PAL videocassette) with 2-4 songs. "Send photos and bios." Does not return unsolicited material. Reports in 1 month.
Music: Mostly heavy metal/hard rock, AOR/FM rock and "alternative" guitar-based rock. Released *Fashion by Passion* (by Churchill/Dries), recorded by White Sister on FM Records (AOR LP); "American Fool" (by John Mellencamp), recorded by Jack Green on Revolver Records (rock/pop single); and "Home Sweet Home," written and recorded by King Kobra on FM Records (rock/dance single). Other artists include Bruce Cockburn, Geisha, The Stone Roses, Dream, Dansworks, Tyler Kahn, The Vibrators, Francis X and The Bushmen, and James "Jy" Young.

HELIOS RECORDS, 28 Dalrymple Crescent, Edinburgh EH9 2NX Great Britain. (031)667-3633. A&R Manager: J. Douglas. Labels include Caritas. Record company, music publisher (Eschenbach Edition) and record producer. Releases 50 singles and 20 LPs/year. Works with musicians/artists and songwriters on contract; musicians on salary for in-house studio work. Pays 4½-6¼% royalty to artists on contract.
How to Contact: Prefers cassette, 7½ ips reel-to-reel (or VHS videocassette) with 8 songs and lyric sheet or lead sheet. SAE and IRC. Reports in 6 weeks.
Music: Mostly rock, jazz and gospel; also folk/vocal, folk/instrumental and "serious music." Released *Mean City* (by C. Adams); *Hebrides* (by J. Busby); and *Emblems* (by J. Douglas) all LPs produced by Helios on Caritas. Other artists include Philip Shevchuk and Catherine Nicholson.

HOLLYROCK RECORDS, Suite 170, 14116 E. Whittier Blvd., Whittier CA 90605. (213)945-5449. A&R Director: Dave Paton. Record company, record producer and music publisher (Heaven Songs/BMI). Releases 4 singles and 6 LPs/year. Works with artists and songwriters on contract; musicians on salary for in-house studio work. Pays negotiable royalty to artists on contract; statutory rate to publishers for each record sold.
How to Contact: Prefers 7½ ips reel-to-reel or cassette with 3-6 songs and lyric sheet. SASE. Reports in 2 weeks.
Music: Progressive, top 40/pop, country, easy listening, folk, jazz, MOR and rock. Released *Everything* (movie soundtrack).

HOMESTEAD RECORDS, Box 256577, Chicago IL 60625. (312)764-1144. President: Tom Petreli. Record company and record producer. Releases 8-15 singles and 2-5 LPs/year. Works with artists on contract; musicians on salary for in-house studio work.
How to Contact: Prefers cassette (or videocassette) with 2-4 songs and lyric sheet. SASE. Reports in 1 month.
Music: Mostly country; also bluegrass, church/religious and Spanish. Released *Arizona*, by Arizona Country (country LP). Other artists include Tom Petreli, Sweetwater, Tempe and Messa.

HOTTRAX RECORDS, 1957 Kilburn Dr., Atlanta GA 30324. (404)662-6661. Vice President, A&R: Oliver Cooper. Labels include: Dance-A-Thon, Hardkor. Record company and music publisher (Starfox Publishing). Releases 12 singles and 3-4 LPs/year. Works with musicians/artists and songwriters on contract. Pays 5-7% royalty to artists on contract.
How to Contact: Prefers cassette with 3 songs and lyric sheet. SASE. "We will not return tapes without adequate postage." Reports in 2 months.
Music: Mostly top 40/pop, rock and country; also hard core punk and jazz-fusion. Released *P Is For Pig*, written and recorded by The Pigs (top 40/pop LP); "The World May Not Like Me," (by Mike

Fitzgerald), recorded by Mike Angelo (rock single); and *Introducing The Feel*, written and recorded by The Feel (new rock LP) all on Hottrax Records. Other artists include Burl Compton (country), Michael Rozakis & Yorgos (pop), Starfoxx (rock), The Night Shadows (rock), The Bop (new wave), and Secret Lover.

HULA RECORDS INC., Box 2135, Honolulu HI 96805. (808)847-4608. President: Donald P. McDiarmid III. Labels include Hawaii Calls, Inc. and Surfside Records, Inc. Record company, record producer and music publisher (Kona-Kai Distribution Co.). Releases 2 singles and 5-10 LPs/year. Works with musicians/artists and songwriters on contract; musicians on salary for in-house studio work. Pays 10% of wholesale to artists on contract; statutory rate to publishers for each record sold.
How to Contact: Prefers cassette with 5 songs and lyric or lead sheet. SASE. Reports in 1 month.
Music: Hawaiian.

HYBRID RECORDS, Box 333, Evanston IL 60204. (312)328-0400. President: Graham Carlton. Record company, record producer and music publisher (Graham Carlton Music Co.). Releases 130 singles and 40 LPs/year. Works with artists and songwriters on contract; musicians on salary for in-house studio work. Pays maximum 14% royalty to artists on contract; statutory rate to publishers for each record sold.
How to Contact: Prefers cassette (or videocassette) with 1-5 songs and lyric sheet. SASE. Reports ASAP.
Music: Mostly country and soul; also bluegrass, blues, dance-oriented, easy listening, folk, jazz, MOR, progressive, R&B, rock, top 40/pop and humorous. Released "Al Capone Clone," by Hustlers, Inc. (dance single); and "More & More," by Annie Wynne (country single).

*ICE RECORDS, Suite 210, Nypenn Trade Center, Johnson City NY 13790. (607)729-2291. President/Producer: Larry Lupole. Vice President/Sales: David J. Monahan. Record producer, music publisher (Larry Gene Music/BMI) and record prducer. Releases 3-5 singles and 2-3 LPs/year. Works with musicians/artists and songwriters on contract; musicians on salary for in-house studio work. Pays negotiable royalty to artists on contract; compulsory rate to publisher per song on record.
How to Contact: Query first. Prefers cassette or 7½ ips reel-to-reel with 2-6 songs and lyric or lead sheet. Does not return unsolicited material. Reports in 2 months.
Music: Mostly pop, country and rock; also R&B and gospel. Released "Where But in America," (by Dr. C.W. Chase/Carolyn Houck), recorded by Raymond Agnew (country single); "Leave it Alone," (by Bob Domiano), recorded by The Neos (pop single); and "Catskill Mountain Home," written and recorded by Raymond Agnew, (country single), all on Ice Records. Other artists include The Neals (pop).
Tips: "We can't stress enough to the beginner artist/songwriter that when creating compositions stick to one basic idea. Too many lyrics we recieve are too vague."

IMAGINARY RECORDS, 239-A E. Thach Ave., Auburn AL 36830. (205)821-JASS. Proprietor: Lloyd Townsend, Jr. Record company, music publisher (Imaginary Music), record producer (Mood Swing Productions) and distribution firm (Imaginary Distribution). Releases 2-3 singles and 2-3 LPs/year. Works with musicians/artists on contract. Pays 10-12% royalty to artists on contract; compulsory rate to publisher per song on record.
How to Contact: Prefers cassette or 7½ ips reel-to-reel with 4 songs and lyric or lead sheet. SASE. Reports in 2 months.
Music: Mostly jazz, blues and rock; also classical, folk and spoken word. Released *Surfin' Aliens*, (by Tom Smeltzer), recorded by Ebb Arnold and the Friction Pigs; *The Situation*, (by Paul Presley), recorded by Paul the Quest; and *The Wanderer*, (by Les and Mark Lyden), recorded by Nothing Personal, all LPs on Imaginary Records. Other artists include Mr. Resistor, The Bonnevilles, Slow Natives, Kidd Blue, Streetwise, Somtow Sucharitkul, The Moderns and Malibu Barbie.

INTERMODAL PRODUCTIONS, LTD., Box 2199, Vancouver, British Columbia V6B 3V7 Canada. President: John Rodney. Record company and management firm. Releases 12-24 singles and 4-8 LPs/year. Works with artists and songwriters on contract. Pays 4-14% royalty to artists on contract. Charges for some services: "depends on the type of contract the artist is comfortable with, and how much independence he wishes in the creative area."
How to Contact: Prefers 7½ ips reel-to-reel with 1-6 songs. SAE and IRC. Reports in 1 month.
Music: Classical, country, MOR and top 40/pop. Released "Can't Hear for Listening," by Elmer Gill and Lockjaw Davis; "Moonlight Sonata," by Robert Silverman; "Hawaii's Golden Voice," by Eddie Kekaula; and "Matter of Time," by The Biz.

*INTREPID RECORD & FILMWORKS, Box 2803, Grand Rapids MI 49501. (616)454-5851. Director of Operations: Rick Eyk. Record company. Releases 3 singles and 2 LPs/year. Works with musicians/artists and songwriters on contract. Pays "equitable" royalty to artists on contract; compulsory rate to publisher per song on record.

How to Contact: Prefers cassette (or VHS videocassette) or 7½ ips reel-to-reel with maximum of 7 songs and lyric sheet. SASE. Reports in 1 month.

Music: Mostly rock, new music and country; also jazz, classical and blues. Released *How Do You Like It So Far*, by various writers (LP), and "Sometimes You Have to Steal" and "Oh Baby You Know I Really Love You," both by Rick Eyk (both singles), all recorded by Little Edward and the G-Men on Intrepid Records.

*IVORY TOWER RECORDS, Tusveld Ag, Bornerbroek, 7627 NW Holland. 05408-718. A&R Manager: Bobby Rootveld. Labels include NL Grammofoonplaten, SR Records and Power Tower. Record company and record producer (Distribution Company Recording Studios). Releases 100 singles and 50 LPs/year. Works with musicians/artists on contract.

How to Contact: Prefers cassette with 4-5 songs and lyric or lead sheet. Does not return unsolicited material. Reports in 2 weeks.

Music: Mostly MOR, country and gospel. Released "Ouwe Gabber" (by Iglesias), recorded by Han Wellerdiek (single); *Hollandse Toppers* (by Rootveld), recorded by various artists (LP/MC); and *Hollywood Star*, written and recorded by GG (LP), all on Ivory Tower Records. Other artists include Jantje Koopmans, Jeffrey Hall and Friends, Apollo Trio, Blackburry Accident and Drenthe Plat.

J&J MUSICAL ENTERPRISES, Box 575, Kings Park NY 11754. (516)265-5584. President: Jude St. George. Labels include JAJ Records. Record company, music publisher (Jeneane & Jude Music) and record producer. Releases 1-2 LPs/year. Works with musicians/artists on contract and musicians on salary for in-house studio work. Pays variable royalty to artists on contract.

How to Contact: Write first and obtain permission to submit. Prefers cassette with 4 songs and lyric sheet. Does not return unsolicited material. Reports in 1 month. "Typed letters preferred."

Music: Mostly progressive, jazz and blues; also New Age. Released *Overtime, As We Speak* and *It's All In A Day* (all by Jeneane Claps), recorded by Freeway Fusion on JAJ Records (EPs).

JALYN RECORDING CO.,351 Millwood Dr., Nashville TN 37217. (615)366-9999. President: Jack Lynch. Record company, music publisher (Jaclyn Music) and distributor. Releases 1-10 singles and 1-10 LPs/year. Works with musicians/artists and songwriters on contract. Pays 5-10% royalty to artists on contract; compulsory rate to publishers for each record sold.

How to Contact: Write or call first. Prefers cassette with 1-3 songs and lyric sheet. SASE. Reports in 1 month.

Music: Country, bluegrass, church/religious and gospel. Released *I Wonder Why* (by Ray Cline), recorded by Ralph Stanley; *Adieu False Heart*, written and recorded by Ray Cline; and *Verdie Let Your Bangs Hang Down*, written and recorded by John Wright, all on Nashville Country Records (all LPs). Other artists include Jack Lynch and the Nashville Travelers, and Miguel Adkins.

Tips: "We prefer songs with good lyrics that tell a story with a certain amount of rhyming, a good melody sung by a good singer, and as good a production as is feasible. Our biggest need is good, commercial country songs."

JAMAKA RECORD CO., 3621 Heath Ln., Mesquite TX 75150. (214)279-5858. Contact: Jimmy Fields. Labels include Felco, and Space View Records. Record company, record producer and music publisher (Cherie Music/BMI). Works with artists and songwriters on contract. Pays royalty to artists on contract; statutory rate to publishers for each record sold.

How to Contact: Prefers cassette with songs and lyric sheet. "A new singer should send a good tape with at least 4 strong songs, presumably recorded in a professional studio." Does not return unsolicited material. Reports ASAP.

Music: Bluegrass, country, easy listening and progressive country.

Tips: "Songs should have strong lyrics with a good story, whether country or pop."

JAY JAY PUBLISHING, 35 NE 62nd St., Miami FL 33138. (305)758-0000. Contact: Walter Jagiello. Record company, record producer and music publisher (BMI). Releases 6 singles and 6 LPs/year. Works with composers and lyricists; teams collaborators. Pays standard royalty.

How to Contact: Prefers cassette with 2-6 songs and lyric sheet. SASE. Reports in 1 month.

Music: Mostly polkas and waltzes; also country, novelty and easy listening. Released "God Bless Our Polish Pope," "Jelly Bean Polka" and "Polish Feelings," by Li'l Wally (polka singles); "I'd Rather Have a Hooker Than a Wife," by J. Rowland/Bonfire (country); and "There's A Full Moon Out Tonight," by D. Rowland.

Tips: "Send your demos by registered mail to ensure that they aren't lost."

JENERO RECORD CO., 300 Court St., Soda Springs ID 83276. President: Ronald Watts. Record company and music publisher. Works with artists and songwriters on contract. Pays 2-7% royalty to artists

on contract; standard royalty to songwriters on contract. Charges for some services: "If recording done for purposes of submitting to another record company."
How to Contact: Prefers cassette with 2-6 songs and lyric sheet. Does not return unsolicited material. Reports in 3 weeks.
Music: Country, easy listening, MOR, rock (soft or country) and top 40/pop. Released *Mem'rys* and *Yesterday and Today*, by Bill Corbett (easy listening LPs); "You'll Feel Better When I Hold You in My Arms," by Rocky Watson (country single); and "I Believe in You," by Eugene Sibbett (easy listening single).

JENIFER RECORDS & TAPES, Box 6253, Arlington VA 22206. (703)671-4551. A&R Director: Ted Macaluso. Record company, record producer and music publisher (Macaluso Music Company). Releases 1-2 singles and 1-3 LPs/year. Works with musicians/artists and songwriters on contract. Pays 5-10% royalty to artists on contract.
How to Contact: Prefers cassette with 1-3 songs and lyric sheet. BETA format videocassette for artists optional; not necessary for songwriters. Artists include bio. SASE. Reports in 6 weeks.
Music: Mostly folk/acoustic and rock; also country, contemporary: zydeco, African and New Age. Released *The Moon Is Rising*, recorded by Steppin' Out on Jenifer Records (folk LP); "Lend Me Your Comb," by Ace Smith (rock single); and *Blue Light*, by Stars and Bars (country/traditional LP).

*JIMBOCO RECORDS, Box 203, Ansonia Station, New York NY 10023. Owner: James Reynolds. Record company, record producer, music publisher (Jimboco Music), and distributor. Releases 2 LPs/year. Works with musicians/artists on contract. Pays variable royalty; "every deal is different."
How to Contact: Prefers cassette (or videocassette) with 2-6 songs and lyric sheet. "Enclose photo."
Music: Mostly rock, "hardcore," and psychedelic; also folk, and top 40/pop. Released *Hotel for Women*, by Nails (rock EP); and *Hi Sheriffs of Blue*, by Hi Sheriffs of Blue (reggae/blues EP). Other artists include TMA, the Rousers and Dizzy & The Romilars.

JRM RECORDS, Box 993, Salem VA 24153. (703)387-0208. President: Jack Mullins. Labels include Dominion. Record company and music publisher (Powhatan Music and Double Jack Publishing). Releases 4-6 singles and 2-4 LPs/year. Works with artists and songwriters on contract. Teams collaborators. Pays 5-15% to artists on contract; statutory rate to publishers for each record sold.
How to Contact: Prefers cassette (or videocassette) with 1-3 songs and lyric sheet. Does not return material. Reports if interested.
Music: Mostly country rock, R&B and rock; also crossover country, bluegrass and country. Released "All this Way" and "One More Shot" (pop/country singles) and *Classic Country* (pop/country LP), recorded by Donna Dean; "Dark Side of Love," recorded by Stairwell (country/rock single); *and Vietnam—The Soldiers' Story*, recorded by Bobby and Virginia Lee (with sounds and back-ups by VietNam veterans).

*JUKE BOX RECORDS,3318-E SSW, Loop 323, Tyler TX 75701. (214)581-9945. President: Lonnie W. Wright. Labels include Quazar and Eden. Record company, music publisher (Starbound Publishing Co.) and record producer (Lonnie Wright). Releases 5 singles and 1 LP/year. Works with musicians/artists and songwriters on contract. Pays standard 5% royalty to artists on contract.
How to Contact: Prefers cassette with 3 songs and lyric sheet. Does not return unsolicited material.
Music: Mostly country. Released "Mama's Home," written and recorded by J. Tyson on Juke Box Records (country single); "Snap Your Fingers," recorded by Oscar Perry on Quazar Records (R&B single); and "Plugged and Abandoned," written and recorded by Ron Kizziar on Juke Box Records (country single). Other artists include Bonnie Miller, Gene Thomas and James Watson.

JUMP RECORDS & MUSIC, Langemunt 71, Erpe-Mere 9460 Belgium. (053)62-73-77. General Manager: Eddy Van Mouffaert. Labels include Jump, Yeah Songs and Flower. Record company, music publisher (Jump Music) and record producer. Releases 20 singles and 3 LPs/year. Works with musicians/artists and songwriters on contract. Pays 5% royalty to artists on contract; compulsory rate to publisher per song on record.
How to Contact: Prefers cassette. Does not return unsolicited material. Reports in 2 weeks.
Music: Mostly easy listening, disco and light pop; also instrumentals. Released "Laat Je Hart Toch Even Spreken," and "Summer Holiday," written and recorded by Eddy Govert; "First Day of Spring" (by Eddy Govert), recorded by Franky Francis, all on Scorpion Records (all singles). Other artists include Rocky, Le Grand Julot, Eigentijdse Jeugd, Marijn Van Duin, Connie-Linda, Guy Lovely, Tom Davys, Laurie, Cindy, Patrik, Allan David and Peggy Christy.

(KAM) EXECUTIVE RECORDS, 11 Shady Oak Trail, Charlotte NC 28210. (704)554-1162. Executive Director: Butch Kelly. Vice President/Producer: Tim Greene. Labels include Executive (R&B), Heaven

Sent (gospel), Newtown (R&B/pop) and Jazz (jazz). Record company. Releases 3-4 singles and 2-3 LPs/year. Works with musicians/artists and songwriters on contract; musicians on salary for in-house studio work. Pays 9% royalty to artists on contract.

How to Contact: Prefers cassette (or any format videocassette) with 1-6 songs and lyric sheet or lead sheet. Does not return unsolicited material. Reports in 3 months. Writer/artist should include photo. SASE for response.

Music: Mostly R&B, pop and rap; also jazz, rock, gospel and country. Released *M.C. Perpetrators*, (by Tim Greene), recorded by Lady Crush, On KAM Executive Records (rap LP); *Street Dancin'* , and *Miss You*, (by Gregory Johnson), recorded by Fresh Air, on Fresh Ave Records (R&B LPs); and *What's Your Decision*, written and recorded by L.A. Stars on KAM Executive Records (R&B LP). Other artists include Melisa Kelly Montgomery, Dean Mancuso, Willie Hill and Fresh Air.

KANSA RECORDS CORP., Box 1014, Lebanon TN 37088. (615)444-3865. (Nashville address: Suite 106, 1300 Division St., Nashville TN 37203. (615)255-0303.) General Manager: Kit Johnson. Labels include Sunflower. Record company, music publisher (Great Leawood Music, Inc./ASCAP and Twinsong Music/BMI), record producer and promotion. Releases 5 singles/year and 2 LPs/year. Works with musicians/artists and songwriters on contract. Pays 6¢ per copy royalty to artists on contract.

How to Contact: Prefers cassette with 4 songs and lead sheet. SASE. Reports in 6 weeks "if we like it."

Music: Country, progressive country and country/rock. Released "I Remember Mama's Arms," recorded by Steffin Sisters; and "Memory Remover" (by Al Green), recorded by Geary Hanley. Other artists include Lea Ann Cox, Dan Davis and P.J. Allman.

*JOHANN KAPLAN MUSIC, Burgerasse 17 19/10/2/7, 1100 Vienna Austria. (0222)64 54 104. Send mail to: O.G.F.K.T., Box 233, 1014 Vienna Austria. President: Johann Kaplan. Labels include Sunshine Records, China Music, Caplan Music, Vienna Music and Record Company of Austria. Record company, music publisher, record producer and artists management firm. Releases 60 singles and 40 LPs/year. Works musicians/artists and songwriters on contract; musicians on salary for in-house studio work. Pays 10-15% royalty to artists on contract.

How to Contact: Write to obtain permission to submit or write to arrange personal interview. Prefers cassette (or VHS videocassette) or reel-to-reel with 2 songs and lyric or lead sheet. SAE and IRC. Reports in 2 months.

Music: Mostly all kinds of music. Released "Double Dealing Dude" (by Gloria Balck), recorded on Jody Records (disco single); "Lady's Man" (by Music Row), recorded by DeBut Records (country single); and *I'm Somebody* (by Adler Alexander), recorded on Jody Records (disco EP). Other artists include Ron Seagram, Tony Graye, Dan Davis, Inn The Mirror, Dania, Ray Rivera, The Commercials, Eddy Hailey and The Vise.

KENNING RECORDS, Box 1084, Newark DE 19715. (302)737-4278. President: Kenny Mullins. Record company and music publisher (Kenning Productions). Releases 14 singles and 3 LPs/year. Works with musicians/artists on contract.

How to Contact: Write first and obtain permission to submit. Prefers cassette. Does not return unsolicited material. Reports in 2 months.

Music: Mostly rock, country and new wave; also jazz, blues and bluegrass. Released *This Time*, and *Crazy Mama*, by K. Mullins; and *Work Me Over*, by K. Mullins and Jerry Lahouz, all recorded on Kenning Records (tapes).

KEYNOTE RECORDS, 4322 Mahoning Ave., Youngstown OH 44515. (216)793-7295. Executive Producer: Richard M. Hahn. Record company, record producer and music publisher (Al-Kris Music/BMI). Releases 5 singles and 2 LPs/year. Works with artists and songwriters on contract. Pays 3-5% royalty to artists on contract; statutory rate to publishers for each record sold.

How to Contact: Query by letter first. Prefers cassette with 3-5 songs and lyric sheet. "Must have decent quality tape and clear lead or lyric sheet." SASE. Reports in 3 weeks.

Music: Children's, country, folk, gospel, MOR and top 40/pop. Released "Here Come the Browns," by Kardiak Kids (MOR singles); "Jubilee" and "His Lovin'," by Cycles (top 40 singles); "Help Me I'm Falling," by Kirsti Manna (MOR ballad single). Other artists include Phil Hickman, Jim Stack, The B-Minors, Ken Crosslin, Leigh Fisher, and Gary Kekel.

KICKING MULE RECORDS, INC., Box 158, Alderpoint CA 95411. (707)926-5312. Head of A&R: Ed Denson. Record company and music publisher (Kicking Mule Publishing/BMI, Desk Drawer Publishing/ASCAP). Member NAIRD. Releases 12 LPs/year. Works with artists on contract. Pays 10-16% royalty to artists on contract; standard royalty to songwriters on contract.

How to Contact: Prefers reel-to-reel or cassette with 3-5 songs. SASE. Reports in 1 month.

Music: Bluegrass, blues and folk. Released *Mooncoin*, by Mickie Zekley (Irish traditional LP); *New York Banjo Ensemble Plays Gershwin* (pop music LP); *Blue Hula Stomp*, by Bob Brozman (pop/blues LP). Other artists include Michael Rugg, Neal Hellman, Bert Jansch, John Renbourn, Stefan Grossman, John James, Happy Traum, Fred Sokolow, Bob Stanton, Bob Hadley, Leo Wijnkamp, Jr., Mark Nelson, Lea Nicholson and Hank Sapoznik.
Tips: "We are a label mostly for instrumentalists. The songs are brought to us by the artists but we contact the artists because of their playing, not their songs. First, listen to what we have released and don't send material that is outside our interests. Secondly, learn to play your instrument well. We have little interest in songs or songwriters, but we are quite interested in people who play guitar, banjo, or dulcimer well."

KILGORE RECORDS, INC., 706 Martin Luther King Dr., Leesville LA 71446-3446. (318)239-7121. President: John E. Kilgore. Labels include Gotown Records and Masie Records. Record company, record producer and music publisher (Gotown Publishing Company/BMI). Releases 3 singles/year. Works with artists and songwriters on contract. Pays minimum 3% royalty to artists on contract; 5¢ to publishers for each record sold.
How to Contact: Prefers cassette with 4-6 songs and lead sheets. SASE. Reports in 6 months.
Music: Mostly soul and gospel; also church/religious, R&B and soul. Released "Change in My Life," by Sensation (gospel single); "Pass Me Not," by Golden Links (gospel single); and "Little" by Samuel Wallace. Other artists include Echoes of Heaven, Sister Alfredia Allen Jones, Rev. Harrison Fields, The Gospelerettes, The Gospel Harmonettes and Midnight Love Affair.

KING OF KINGS RECORD CO., 38603 Sage Tree St., Palmdale CA 93550. (805)947-4657. (Branch office: 171 Pine Haven, Daytona Beach FL 32014. (904)252-4849.) President: Leroy Pritchett. A&R Director: Charles Vickers. Labels include King of Kings, L.A. International and Tropical of California. Record company and music publisher. Releases 1-2 singles and 1-5 LPs/year. Works with songwriters on contract. Pays 5-15% royalty to artists on contract; statutory rate to publishers for each record sold.
How to Contact: Prefers cassette and lyric or lead sheet. SASE. Reports in 1 month.
Music: Mostly gospel; also country. Released *The Magic of Gospel* (LP), "Let Your Light Shine" (single), and "Sailing Without a Sail" (single), all written and recorded by Charles Vickers on King of Kings Records.

*KITTY RECORDS, INC.,Kobayashi Bldg., 1-14-11, Shibuya, Shibuya-ku, Tokyo 150 Japan. (03)499-4711. Manager of International Division: Kazuo Munakata. Record company. Releases 30-35 singles and 20-25 LPs/year. Works with musicians/artists on contract.
How to Contact: Prefers cassette. Does not return unsolicited material. Reports in 7 weeks.
Music: Mostly rock, pop and New Age (instrumental); also jazz (with classical music flavor), and soul (pop-soul). Released *Anzenchitai V*, (by Matsui/Tamaki, etc), recorded by Anzenchitai (pop LP); *Rhapsody in Blue*, recorded by Yosuke Yamashita (jazz LP); and *Memoire D'un Touriste*, recorded by Mark Goldenberg (jazz LP), all on Kitty Records. Other artists include Takoa Kisugi, Shoko Minami, Cindy Yamamoto, Naoto Nagashima and Date of Birth Band.

SID KLEINER MUSIC ENTERPRISES, 3701 25th Ave. SW, Naples FL 33964. (813)455-2696. Contact: Sid Kleiner. Labels include Musi-Poe, Top-Star, This Is It, Token, and Country-King Records. Record company and consulting firm to music industry. Releases 10 LPs/year. Works with musicians and songwriters on contract. Charges for some services: "We may, at our option, charge *actual* production expense. We are not get-rich-quickers or rip-off artists. But we are too small to pay all of these bills!"
How to Contact: Prefers cassette (or VHS videocassette) and lead sheet. SASE, "otherwise materials aren't returned." Reports in 3 weeks.
Music: Bluegrass, country, easy listening, folk, jazz, and "banjo and guitar soloists and features." Released *Burd Boys on Stage* and *Chartbusters and Other Hits* (country LPs), by the Burd Boys; and *Find a Simple Life*, by Dave Kleiner (folk/rock LP). Other artists include Sid Kleiner.

*KLW INTERNATIONAL, INC., 408 Kathleen Ave., Cinnaminson NJ 08077. (609)786-8486. Executive Producer: Kevin L. Weakland. Record company, music publisher and record producer. Releases 2-3 singles and 1-2 LPs/year. Works with musicians/artists and songwriters on contract and musicians on salary for in-house studio work. Pays 5% royalty to artists on contract; compulsary rate to publisher per song on record.
How to Contact: Prefers cassette (or Beta videocassette). SASE. Reports in 2 weeks.
Music: Mostly pop, gospel and R&B: also rock and country.

KOCH RECORDS INTERNATIONAL, Elbigenalp 91, Tirol A-6652 Austria. 05634/6444, 6445. A&R International Manager: Haakon Brenner. Labels include Koch Records Special, Roko, Koch Records,

Fantastik, Five Star, and Micki. Record company, music publisher (Koch Musikverlag), record producer and manufacturer/distributor. Releases 200 singles/year and 200 LPs/year. Works with musicians/artists and songwriters on contract. Pays varying royalty to artists on contract.
How to Contact: Prefers cassette (or VHS/PAL videocassette) and lyric sheet or lead sheet. Does not return unsolicited material. Reports in 3 weeks.
Music: Mostly pop, rock and MOR; also dance music—no heavy metal.

KOMPASS RECORDS, Puistokaarl 8, Helsinki 00200 Finland. General Manager: Chris Schwindt. Record company and music publisher. Releases 6 LPs/year. Pays 4-8% royalty to artists on contract.
How to Contact: Submit demo tape by mail. Prefers cassette.

LA LOUISIANNE RECORDS, 711 Stevenson St., Lafayette LA 70501. (318)234-5577. Labels include Tamm and Belle. President: (Mr.) Carol J. Rachou, Sr. Record company, record producer, recording studio and music publisher (La Lou Music/BMI). Releases 10-20 singles and 4-6 LPs/year. Works with artists and songwriters on contract. "We also deal with promoters, managers, agents, etc." Pays statutory rate to publishers for each record sold.
How to Contact: Prefers 7½ ips reel-to-reel or cassette with 1-6 songs and lyric sheet. "If possible, submit different musical variations of songs (tempos, styles, keys, etc.)." SASE.
Music: Mostly Cajun/French; also blues, church/religious, classical, country, folk, gospel, jazz, MOR, progressive, R&B, rock, top 40/pop, comedy, French comedy and instrumental. Released *Lache Pas La Patate*, by Jimmy C. Newman (French Cajun LP—Gold record in Canada); *A Cajun Tradition Vol. 2*, by Nathan Abshire (French Cajun LP); *Cajun Fiddle*, by Rufus Thibodeaux (Cajun/country LP); *That Cajun Country Sound*, by Eddy Raven (French and English Cajun/country LP); and *Authentic French Music*, by Ambrose Thibodeaux (traditional Cajun LP). Other artists include Vin Bruce, Aldus Roger, Merlin Fontenot, L.J. Foret, Blackie Forestier, The Dusenbery Family, Alex Broussard and Bud Fletcher.

LAMON RECORDS, Box 25371, Charlotte NC 28212. (704)537-0133. Contact: Dwight or Carlton Moody. Labels include Panhandel Records. Record company, record producer and music publisher (Laymond Publicity Co./BMI and CDT Products/ASCAP). Releases 25 singles and 12 LPs/year. Works with artists and songwriters on contract; musicians on salary for in-house studio work. Pays statutory rate to publishers for each record sold.
How to Contact: Write first and obtain permission to submit. Prefers cassette with minimum of 2 songs. Prefers studio produced demos. SASE. Reports in 1 month.
Music: Mostly beach, country and R&B. Released "Back by My Side," (by William James), recorded by A.J. McBride; "Midnight Flyer," by Cathy Moody; "Only A Fool," by Vanessa Parker; "On A Night Like This," by Hutchins Brothers; and "Lost Without A Trace," by Dale Upton.

*LANA RECORDS, Box 12444, Fresno CA 93777-2444. (209)442-3332. Executive Producer: Robby Roberson. Labels include Lana Records, Country Roots Records, GGT Records and El Country Records. Record company, music publisher (Happy Note Music), and record producer. Releases 3 singles and 2 LPs/year. Works with musicians/artists and songwriters on contract; musicians on salary for in-house studio work. Pays 7-10% royalty to artists on contract; compulsory rate to publisher per song on record.
How to Contact: Prefers cassette with 3 songs and lyric sheet. SASE. Reports in 1 month.
Music: Mostly country, gospel and pop. Released *There*, (by A. Sanifar), recorded by Oh Lamour on Top Secret Records (dance LP); *Has It All Ended*, (by R. Garabedian), recorded by Nick Holley on Lana Records (pop LP); and *High Sierra*, (by Ronnie Reno/Wayne Walker), recorded by Robby Roberson on Lana Records (country LP). Other artists include Hud Rose and Sharon Riley.

LANDMARK (AUDIO OF NASHVILLE), Box 148296, Nashville TN 37214. (615)868-3407. Producers: Bill Anderson, Jr. and D.D. Morris. Labels include Looking Glass, Smokehouse. Record company, record producer and music publisher (Newcreature Music/BMI). Releases 4 singles and 4 LPs/year. Works with artists and songwriters on contract; musicians on salary for in-house studio work. Teams collaborators. Pays 5-7% royalty to artists on contract; statutory rate to publishers for each record sold.
How to Contact: Prefers 7½ ips reel-to-reel or cassette with 4-10 songs and lyric sheet. SASE. Reports in 1 month.
Music: Country/crossover, gospel, jazz, R&B, rock and top 40/pop. Released *Battle Hymn of the Republic*, by Joanne Cash (gospel LP); "Here We Are," by Dottie Lee Snow (gospel single); and *One*, by Vernon Oxford (country LP).

LANDSLIDE RECORDS, 450 14th St. NW, Atlanta GA 30318. (404)873-3918. President: Michael Rothschild. Record company and music publisher (Frozen Inca/BMI). Member NARAS. Releases 2 singles and 5 LPs/year. Works with artists and songwriters on contract. Pays 5-15% royalty to artists on contract; statutory rate to publishers for each record sold.

How to Contact: Write or call first. Prefers cassette with 4-10 songs and lyric sheet. SASE. Reports in 1 month.

Music: Mostly progressive and dance-oriented; also blues, jazz, R&B, rock and soul. Released *Isles of Langerham*, by The Late Bronze Age (progressive LP); *Tore Up*, by Nappy Brown (R&B); and *Middle of the Night*, by Bruce Baxter (pop/new music LP). Other artists include David Earle Johnson, Defuser, The Heartfixers, Curlew and Dan Wall.

Tips: "Don't be afraid to go to extremes in presenting your work."

LANOR RECORDS, 329 N. Main St., Box 233, Church Point LA 70525. (318)684-2176. Contact: Lee Lavergne. Labels include Lanor and Joker Records. Record company and music publisher. Releases 12-18 singles and 1-3 LPs/year. Works with artists and songwriters on contract. Pays 3-5% royalty to artists on contract; statutory rate to writers for each record sold.

How to Contact: Prefers cassette with 2-6 songs. SASE. Reports in 2 weeks.

Music: Mostly country; also rock, and soul. Released "Good Hearted Man" and "Rockin' Zydeco," by Rockin' Sidney and Jim Olivier.

Tips: Submit "good material with potential in today's market. Use good quality cassettes—I don't listen to poor quality demos that I can't understand."

LAURIE RECORDS/3C RECORDS, % Continental Communication Corp., 450 Livingston St., Norwood NJ 07648. (201)767-5551. Vice President: Gene Schwartz. Labels include Rust Records. Record company. Releases 10 singles and 7 LPs/year. Works with musicians/artists and songwriters on contract; musicians on salary for in-house studio work. Pays varying royalty to artists on contract.

How to Contact: Prefers cassette and lyric sheet. SASE.

Music: Mostly rock and "some" MOR.

LAVAL RECORDS, 1327 Cobb St., Kalamazoo MI 49007. (616)342-5328. Contact: Vic Laval. Record company, record producer and music publisher (Valco Music/BMI). Releases 15 LPs/year. Works with artists and songwriters on contract. Pays 3-5¢/single sold and 60-80¢/album sold to artists on contract; statutory rate to publishers for each record sold.

How to Contact: Prefers 7½ ips reel-to-reel or cassette with 4-8 songs and lyric sheet. SASE. Reports in 1 month.

Music: Blues, church/religious, country, gospel, R&B, rock and soul. Released *Don't Tax Me In*, by Joe Blue (blues LP); *Stoop Down Baby*, by Chick Willis (blues LP); and *The Best of Jimmy Lynch*, by Jimmy Lynch (soul LP). Other artists include Eddie Vespa, Frisco, Ben Stafford, John Brown, Tommy Brown and The Terry's.

*LE DISQUE HOLLAND B.V.,'S-Gravelandseweg 62, Hilversum 1217 ET Holland. (35)234622. General Manager: Michael C. Lambrechtsen. Record company and music publisher (Le Disque Music Publishing).

How to Contact: Prefers cassette (or VHS videocassette) with minimum of 5 songs and lead sheet. SAE and IRC. Reports in 6 weeks.

Music: Mostly pop, rock and R&B; also soul and country. Artists include Bolland and Bolland, Play it Again Sam, and Numero Uno.

Tips: "Never stop working and be patient."

LE MATT MUSIC LTD., % Stewart House, Hill Bottom Rd., Highwycombe, Buckinghamshire, England. 0494-36301/36401. Contact: Ron or Cathrine Lee. Labels include Swoop, Zarg Records, Genouille, Pogo and Check Records. Record company, record producer and music publisher (Le Matt Music, Ltd., Lee Music, Ltd., R.T.F.M. and Pogo Records, Ltd.). Member MPA, PPL, PRS, MCPS. Releases 25 singles and 20 LPs/year. Pays negotiable royalty to artists on contract; compulsory rate to publishers for each record sold. Royalties paid to US songwriters and artists through US publishing or recording affiliate.

How to Contact: Prefers 7½ or 15 ips reel-to-reel, cassette (or videocassette) with 1-3 songs and lyric sheet. Include bio and photo. SAE and IRC. Reports in 3 weeks.

Music: Bluegrass, blues, country, dance-oriented, easy listening, MOR, progressive, R&B, 50s rock, disco, new wave, rock, soul and top 40/pop. Released *Mood Music* (by R.C. Bowman), recorded by R.C. Band on R.T.F.M. Records; *Rock 'n' Roll Revival* (by M. Shereden), recorded by Elmer Goodbody Jr. on Swoop Records; and *Swoop's Greatest Hits*, written and recorded by various artists on Swoop Records (all Lps). Other artists include Emmitt Till, Touche, Orphan, Jonny Moon, Ian "Sludge" Lees and Kyro Groucho.

LEVIATHAN RECORDS, Box 399063, Cincinnati OH 45239. President: David T. Chastain. Labels include Starbound Records. Record company, music publisher (McChas Music/BMI) and record producer. Releases 3-5 LPs/year. Works with musicians/artists on contract. Pays 8% royalty to artists on contract; compulsory rate to publisher per song on record.
How to Contact: Prefers cassette (or Beta videocassette) with 9 songs and lyric sheet. Does not return unsolicited material. Reports in 6 weeks.
Music: Heavy metal, rock and jazz (instrumental). Released *World Gone Mad*, written and recorded by CJSS; *The 7th of Never*, written and recorded by Chastain; and *Praise The Loud*, written and recorded by CJSS, all on Leviathan Records (all LPs). Other artists include Leather Leone.

LIAISON RECORDS, Suite 303, 11330 Cherry Hill Rd., Beltsville MD 20705. (301)937-6161. A&R Director: Rebecca Marcus. Record company and distributor. Releases 3-5 singles/year. Works with musicians/artists on contract. Pays negotiable royalty to artists on contract.
How to Contact: Call first and obtain permission to submit. Prefers cassette. Reports in 2 weeks. "If artists request return of cassettes, we will do so, otherwise we keep them on file."
Music: Mostly R&B, rock and jazz/fusion; also country and gospel. Released *Beyond Words* on Speechless Records (mini LP); "Transport," by London Loop (12" single); and *Darker Days*, recorded by the Connells on Black Park Records (LP).

*LIFETIME RECORDINGS, 170 Sylvan Rd., Rochester NY 14618. (716)244-7526. Contact: Lester W. Osband. Labels include Lifetime, Joker and Lindell Records. Record company.

LIGHT RECORDS, Box 2222, Newbury Park CA 91320. (805)499-5881. Vice President, Director of A&R: Allan Abrahams. Record company and music publisher (Lexicon Music). Releases 25 singles/year and 25 LPs/year. Works with musicians/artists and songwriters on contract.
How to Contact: Call first. Not accepting unsolicited material. Prefers cassette with 2-3 songs and lyric sheet. SASE. Reports in 1 month. "Check out who is recording prior to submitting 'blind' material."
Music: Gospel only. Released "Look Up and Live," by the New Jersey Mass Choir; "Go Tell Somebody," by Commission; and "Unspeakable Joy," by Douglas Miller. Other artists include Allies, Bryan Duncan, Sandra Crouch, and Walter Hawkins.

*LIPHONE RECORDS, Box 51, S-451 15 Uddevalla Sweden. Phone: 4652262081. Owner: Borge Lindquist. Record company and music publisher (LiTUNE Music). Releases 3-5 singles and 15-20 LPs/year. Works with musicians/artists and songwriters on contract. Pays compulsory rate to publisher.
How to Contact: Prefers cassette and lyric sheet. Does not return unsolicited material. Reports in 5 weeks.
Music: Mostly country, pop and rock; also folk, R&B and gospel. Released *The Thumb* by Lars Larholm, *On My Way* by Arne Janson, and *Swedish Folksongs* by Gosta Enar, all on Liphone Records (all LPs). Other artists include "about 40 artists from the Scandinavian countries."

LITTLE GIANT RECORDS, Box 205, White Lake NY 12786. (914)583-4471. A&R Director: Mike Pell. Labels include Killer Records. Record company, record producer and music publisher (Karjan Music Publishing Co./SESAC). Releases 6 singles and 6 LPs/year. Works with artists and songwriters on contract. Pays standard royalty to artists on contract; statutory rate to publishers for each record sold.
How to Contact: Prefers cassette with 1-3 songs and lyric sheet. SASE. Reports in 3 weeks.
Music: Country, easy listening, MOR, R&B and top 40/pop. Released *Self Styled*, by Terry Gorka (country LP); and *You Requested This*, by Mickey Barnett (MOR LP). Other artists incude Bobby Gold, The Third Edition, Chuck Wilson, Kenny Adams and T. Barry Kaminski.

LITTLE RICHIE RECORDS, 1700 Plunket, Box 3, Belen NM 87002. (505)864-7441. Manager: Tony Palmer. Owner: Little Richie Johnson. Labels include LRJ and Chuckie Records. Record company, record producer and music publisher (Little Richie Johnson Music/BMI, Little Cowboy/ASCAP). Releases 10 singles and 2-4 LPs/year. Works with artists on contract.
How to Contact: Call first. Prefers cassette with 4-6 songs and lyric sheet. SASE. Reports in 1 month.
Music: Country. Released "Houston," written and recorded by Sam West IV; "Shade of Blue" (by Albert), recorded by Vic Chavez; and "Honey" (by Russell), recorded by Carlos Quinto, all on LRJ Records. Other artists include Ron Urban, Albert Young Eagle, Jimmy Snyder, Barbie Phillips, Isleta Poor Boys and Al Smith.

LONGHORN RECORDS, Box 93457, Hollywood CA 90093. (213)850-0986. Contact: Harvey Appell or Lillian Rodell. Record company and music publisher (Udder Publications/BMI and Golden Gelt/ASCAP). Releases singles and albums "depending on commitments to artists." Works with artists on an individual basis; "songwriters are generally given statutory rate unless other arrangements are made. Musicians are paid union scale on all sessions."

How to Contact: Arrange personal interview by mail or phone. Prefers cassette "on good quality tape" and lyric and lead sheet. Does not return unsolicited material. Reports back ASAP.

Music: All types of country. Released "It Was Love What It Was," (by W. Shafer/S. Throckmorton), recorded by Bobby Borchers; "When I Thought Whiskey Was A River," written and recorded by Bobby Borchers; and "Houston Bounce," (by C. Brewer), recorded by River Road Boys, all singles on Longhorn Records. Other artists include The Mulligans and Bill Nash.

Tips: "A well prepared cassette with good songs is the only requirement for having a song recorded at Longhorn."

LUCIFER RECORDS, INC., Box 263, Brigantine NJ 08203-0263. President: Ron Luciano. Record company, booking agency and music publisher. Works with artists and songwriters on salary and contract.

How to Contact: Arrange personal interview. Prefers cassette with 4-8 songs. SASE. Reports in 3 weeks.

Music: Dance, easy listening, MOR, rock, soul and top 40/pop. Released "I Who Have Nothing," by Spit-N-Image (rock single); "Lucky," and "Smoke Ya," by Legz (rock singles); and "Loves a Crazy Game," by Voyage (disco/ballad single).

LUNA RECORDS CORP., 434 Center St., Healdsburg CA 95448. (707)433-4138. Labels include Luna, Lugar, Yuriko and Sony Records. President: Abel De Luna. Record company, booking agency and music publisher (Yema Publishing/ASCAP and De Luna Publishing/BMI). Releases 30 singles and 20 LPs/year. Works with artists and songwriters on contract. Pays 8% royalty to artists on contract; statutory rate.

How to Contact: Prefers cassette with 5-10 songs and lead sheet. Does not return unsolicited material. Reports in 3 weeks.

Music: Children's and Latin. Released "El Solitario," by Los Pasteles Verdes; "Que Me Entierren Cantando," by Los Huracanes Del Norte; and "Te Vas O Quedar Liorando," by La Banda Int'de Ray Camacho, (all Spanish singles and LPs). Other artists include Los Luceritos de Michoacan, Los Astros, Los Buhos, Tany Ponce, Grupo Santa Maria, Los Flamantes Del Norte, and Los Errantes Del Norte.

LUV RECORDS, 3784 Realty, Dallas TX 75244. (214)241-7854. President: K.J. Hughes. Labels include Pinecrest Records. Record company, record producer, music publisher (Luvco Music/BMI and Kenco Publishing Co./ASCAP) and 24-track recording studio. Member CMA, TMA. Releases 20-40 singles and 10-15 LPs/year. Works with artists and songwriters on contract; musicians on salary for in-house studio work. Pays 3¢/song royalty to artists on contract; statutory rate to publishers for each record sold.

How to Contact: Prefers cassette with 1-3 songs and lyric sheet. SASE. Label tape with address and phone number. Reports in 1 month.

Music: Mostly country and novelty; also bluegrass, R&B and top 40/pop. Artists include Carlette, Hollie Hughes, Jacky Ward, Stella Parton, Roy Clayton, Xtra Touch, Birch Denney and J. Andrew Cody.

M.R.C. RECORDS, Box 2072, Waynesboro VA 22980. (703)949-0106. Contact: John Major. Labels include MRC, Lark and Echo Records. Record company, music publisher and recording studio. Releases 10 singles and 20 LPs/year. Pays 5-7% royalty to artists on contract; statutory rate to publishers for each record sold.

How to Contact: Prefers cassette and lyric sheet. SASE. Reports in 2 weeks.

Music: Bluegrass, gospel, country, easy listening, dance, MOR, rock (country, hard), soul and top 40/pop. Released "Honky Tonk Angel," by Joey Davis (country single).

Tips: "Don't submit songs with tunes purchased from advertisements. Don't submit songs that have been rejected by other publishers."

M RECORDS, INC., Suite 463, 263A W. 19th St., New York NY 10011. (212)741-0470. A&R Director: Sharon White. Record company. Releases 7-10 singles and 2 LPs/year. Works with musicians/artists and songwriters on contract; musicians on salary for in-house studio work. Pays 3% royalty to artist on contract; statutory rate to publisher per song on record.

How to Contact: Prefers cassette with 3 songs and lyric sheet. SASE. Reports in 2 weeks.

Music: Dance music (commercial), rock and R&B. Released "Lovelight" (by Van Hemert), recorded by Jerney (pop/adult contemporary); "Running" (by G. Pressley/C. Boyd), recorded by Gwen Pressley (R&B), both on M Records (12" singles); and "The Way of Love" recorded by Cheryl Alexander (hi-energy disco 12" single). Other artists include Patsi Gitelle.

Tips: "Demo tapes should be recorded well so that *all* tracks can be heard. High-bias/metal-tape should be used."

MAIN TRIPP RECORDS INC., 2804 Beechtree Dr., Sanford NC 27330. (919)774-8926. Vice President: Jim Watters. Record company and music publisher. Releases 6-10 singles and 12-20 LPs/year. Works with musicians/artists and songwriters on contract; musicians on salary for in-house studio work. Pays 3-10% royalty to artists on contract; compulsory or negotiated rate to publishers for each record sold.
How to Contact: Prefers cassette with any number of songs and lyric sheet. SASE. Reports in 6 weeks. "Due to volume of material received we can no longer guarantee return of unsolicited material, but we will try. No return if postage is insufficient."
Music: Country, gospel and bluegrass. Released "Love is," written and recorded by Bill Tripp on Atteiram Records (country single); "Empty Places" (by Jim Watters/Robert Gordon), recorded by Don Keatley on MTR Records (gospel single); and "He Delivered Me (Because He Delights in Me)" (by Stephanie Watters), recorded by Jim Watters and Covenant on Main Tripp Records (gospel cassette, *Songs We Have Lived*). Other artists include Backwoods Bluegrass, the Noblemen, The Travelers, Beechville Bluegrass, Bobby Pender and Light, and Tommy Green.
Tips: "Send clean, positive songs. Be patient. Good projects take a lot of time."

MAINROADS PRODUCTIONS, #14, 310 Judson St., Toronto, Ontario M8Z 1V3 Canada. (416)961-8001. A&R Director: Stephen Nicolle. Record company, music publisher and record distributor. Releases 25 LPs/year. Works with musicians/artists on contract. Pays 10% royalty to artists on contract; compulsory rate to publisher per song on record.
How to Contact: Prefers cassette (or VHS videocassette) with 3 songs and lyric sheet or lead sheet. Does not return unsolicited material. Reports in 6 weeks.
Music: Mostly light contemporary; also gospel, pop, rock, jazz and country. Released *Way Back Home*, written and recorded by Phil Keaggy on Pan Pacific Records; *John Starnes Live*, recorded by John Starnes on Shiloh Records; and *Lines Are Falling*, recorded by September on Sugar Records. Other artists distributed include Tim and LaDonna Johnson, Power Alley, Jimmy Swaggart, Tim Miner, Janet Paschal, Lisa Whelchel, Cindy Cruse, Karen Kelly and Bruce Stacey.

MAJEGA RECORDS, 240 E. Radcliffe Dr., Claremont CA 91711. (714)624-0677. President: Gary K. Buckley. Record company. Works with artists and songwriters on contract; musicians on salary for in-house studio work. Pays negotiable royalty to artists on contract; standard royalty to songwriters on contract; statutory rate to publishers for each record sold.
How to Contact: Prefers cassette with 1-4 songs and lyric or lead sheet. SASE. Reports in 3 weeks.
Music: Country, easy listening, MOR, rock (country or pop) and top 40/pop. Released *To God, with Love* and *Country Love*, recorded by Jerry Roark (gospel/country LPs); "Songwriter," (pop single) and *Buche*, (top 40 LP) by Rick Buche; *Steppin' Out*, by The Gospelmen (gospel LP); "Our America," by June Wade and the Country Congregation (country/gospel single); "Is It Right," "Touch Me Now," "It's Alright," and "What You Doin' to Me," by Borderline (top 40 singles); and *Sky's the Limit* by Michael Noll (top 40 LP).

MALACO RECORDS, Box 9287, Jackson MS 39206. (601)982-4522. Producers: Wolf Stephenson, Tommy Couch. Labels include Malaco and Muscle Shoals Sound Records. Record company, music publisher and record producer. Works with artists and songwriters on contract and salary. Pays standard royalty.
How to Contact: Prefers cassette with 1-5 songs and lyric sheet. SASE. Reports in 1 month.
Music: R&B music only.

***MANHATTAN COUNTRY, INC.**, #18C, 100 W. 57th St., New York NY 10019. (212)757-2495. President: Reginald A. Bowes. Music publisher and record producer. Estab. 1987. Releases 3 singles and 2 LPs/year. Works with musicians/artists and songwriters on contract. Pays standard royalty to artists on contract.
How to Contact: Write or call first and obtain permission to submit or to arrange personal interview. Prefers cassette with 2-3 songs and lyric sheet. SASE. Reports in 2 weeks.
Music: Country. Released *The Legendary Album*, by Asst., (LP); and "Legend/Beer Is My Salvation" (by Tom Stuart/Jim Glasgow), both recorded by Tommie Joe White and Southern Cookin' on Manhattan Country Records; and "Read the Signs/The Drifter," written and recorded by Steve Zoyes and Gabe Johnson on Star Lips Records (single). Other artists include Cosmo Perry Tillman and Leah Bowes.

MANQUIN, Box 2388, Toluca Lake CA 91602. (818)985-8284. Contact: Manny Rodriquez. Record company, music publisher, record producer, management firm and public relations firm. Works with artists and songwriters on spec only. Pays standard royalty to artists and songwriters on contract.
How to Contact: Prefers cassette with 2-3 songs and lead sheet. SASE. Reports in 2 months.
Music: Country and Latin only.

MARMIK, 135 E. Muller Rd., East Peoria IL 61611. (309)699-4000. President: Martin Mitchell. Record company and music publisher. Releases 10-12 singles and 3-4 LPs/year. Works with musicians and songwriters. Pays negotiable royalty; statutory rate to publishers for each record sold. Sometimes buys material from songwriters outright; payment negotiable.
How to Contact: Query first. Prefers reel-to-reel or cassette with 2-10 songs. "With first submission include an affidavit of ownership of material." SASE. Reports in 2 weeks.
Music: Mostly Christian, MOR and country; also blues, children's, choral, church/religious, easy listening, and gospel. Released "Happy Anniversary" (MOR single), "Day After Never" (MOR single), and "You're the One" (country single), by Wade Ray.
Tips: "The country seems to be going into a happier time now. Keep songs up-tempo and positive."

MASON RIDGE RECORDS, Box 95841, Seattle WA 98145. (206)282-7860. Executive Director: David Templeton. Record company and music publisher (DJTempleton Music/ASCAP). Releases 8 singles and 2 LPs/year. Works with musicians on salary for in-house studio work. Pays negotiable royalty to artists on contract.
How to Contact: Prefers cassette or 15 ips reel-to-reel with 3 songs. SASE. Reports in 1 week.
Music: New Age acoustical, female vocal contemporary and pop ballads. Released *Time Alone*, written and recorded by David Templeton on Mason Ridge (solo piano LP).

MASTER-TRAK ENTERPRISES, 413 N. Parkerson, Crowley LA 70526. (318)788-0773. General Manager and Chief Engineer: Mark Miller. Assistant Manager and Producer: R.P. Harrell. Labels include Master-Trak, Showtime, Kajun, Blues Unlimited and Par T. Recording studio and record companies. Releases 20 singles and 6-8 LPs/year. Works with musicians/artists on contract. Pays 4-6% artist royalty. (No studio charges to contract artists.) Studio available on an hourly basis to the public. Charges for some services: "We charge for making audition tapes of any material that we do not publish."
How to Contact: Prefers cassette and lead sheet. SASE. Reports in 1 month.
Music: Mostly country, rock, R&B, cajun and Zydeco. Released "The Flame Is Out" (by R. Lagneaux), recorded by S. Kershaw; "Diggy Liggy Lo" (by J. Miller), recorded by Sammy & Tammy; "I Wish I had a Job" (by P. Marx), recorded by Paul Marx, all singles on Master-Trak Records. Other artists include Freddie Pate, Tammy Lynn, Al Ferrier, Fernest & The Thunders, Wayne Toups.
Tips: "The song is the key. If we judge it to be a good song, we record it and it sells, we are happy. If we mis-judge the song and/or the artist and it does not sell, we must go back to the drawing board."

THE MASTER'S COLLECTION LIMITED, Box 362, Station A, Rexdale, Toronto, Ontario M9W 5L3 Canada. (416)746-1991. President: Paul J. Young. Labels include Sharon, T.M.C., The Master's Collection, Pilgrim and Little Pilgrim. Record company and music publisher (T.M.C. Publishing/CAPAC and Master's Collection Publishing/PROCAN). Member CIRPA. Releases 3 singles and 10 LPs/year. Works with artists and songwriters on contract. Pays 5-12½% royalty to artists on contract; statutory rate to publishers for each record sold.
How to Contact: Write first. Prefers cassette with 3-6 songs. Does not return unsolicited material. Reports in 1 month.
Music: Mostly Christian gospel ("any style"); also church/religious. Released *He Will Carry You*, by Ruth Fazel (gospel LP); *Count the Raindrops*, by Nigel Hasthorne (children's LP); and *RU486*, by Straight & Narrow (gospel LP). Other artists include Rick Piche, Mark Moore, Wiz Bryant, Gene MacLellan and Cathy Rempel.

*MASTERS RECORDS, Dreilinden Str. 42, St. Gallen 9011 Switzerland. Phone: (071)255 666. Owner/Producer: Victor Waldburger. A&R Manager: Carlos Peron. Record company and music publisher (Master Publishing).
How to Contact: Write or call first and obtain permission to submit. Prefers cassette (or Beta videocassette) and lyric or lead sheet. SASE. Reports in 5 weeks.
Music: Mostly new techno, speed metal, R&B, pop, country and rock; also avant garde, commercial songs and film music. Artists include Carlos Perón, Taboo and Tomes Beluga.

*MAUI RECORDS, Box 335, Haweva New Zealand. A&R: Dalvanius. Record company, music publisher (Maui Music) and record producer (Maui Productions). Releases 20 singles and EPs, and 3 LPs/ year. Works with musicians/artists and songwriters on contract. Pays 10% or negotiable royalty to artists on contract.
How to Contact: Prefers cassette (or VHS videocassette) and lyric or lead sheet. Does not return unsolicited material. Reports in 1 month. "Must send 8x10 b&w photo and biography."
Music: Mostly rock, R&B/soul and jazz; also gospel, country and ethnic. Released "E Papa," by Tawhare (single and EP); and *Raukura*, by Dalvanius and Ngoi Pewhaivangi (LP), all recorded by Patea Maori Club on Maui Records. Other artists include Fascinations, Taste of Bounty and Tama Band.

MAVERICK RECORDINGS, Box 11361, Washington DC 20008. (202)462-6172. A&R: Robert Wardrick. Record company and music publisher (BMI/ASCAP). Releases 10-12 singles and 6-8 LPs/year. Works with musicians/artists and songwriters on contract; musicians on salary for in-house studio work. Pays 5-10% royalty to artists on contract; compulsory rate to publishers for each record sold.
How to Contact: "Query us first."
Music: Mostly R&B and pop, top 40, dance and progressive. Released "Go For It," written and recorded by Yvonne Moore (single); "Choose Another," written and recorded by David Silver (single); and *Borders* (by S&W Walter), recorded by Suburban Sprawl, all on Maverick Records (LP). Other artists include Gumbo and David Parson.

MAXIMA RECORDS, Suite 234, 24285 Sunnymead Blvd., Moreno Valley, CA 92388-9971. (714)653-1556. Professional Manager: LaDonna Kay. Record company, music publisher (KayDay Music) and record producer (Country Charts and OurWay Music). Releases 4-5 singles and 1-2 LPs/year. Works with musicians/artists and songwriters on contract. Pays standard royalty to artists on contract; compulsory rate to publisher per song on record.
How to Contact: Prefers cassette (or VHS videocassette) with 1-10 songs and lyric sheet. Reports in 1 month.
Music: Mostly contemporary country; also MOR and pop. Released "Livin' on Love Again," "You Showed Me How to Love," and "Ready or Not," all written and recorded by Don Malena on Maxima Records (all singles).

MAYS RECORDS, 11 Oxford Circus Ave., 231 Oxford St., London W1R 1AD England. (01)439-2568. General Manager: Joanna Cadman. Record company and music publisher (Misty River Music). Releases 2 singles/year. Works with musicians/artists and songwriters on contract.
How to Contact: Prefers cassette. SAE and IRC.
Music: Released "Let's Dance," recorded by Balham Alligators; and "Winner's Song," written and recorded by Ralph McTell, both singles on Mays Records.

MAZINGO'S, INC., 4317 Rounding Run Road, Matthews NC 28105. (704)542-7000. President: Ben W. McCoy. Record company. Payment negotiable.
How to Contact: Prefers cassette or 8-track (cartridge) with 2-8 songs and lead sheet. SASE. Reports in 1 month.
Music: Bluegrass, blues, children's, choral, church/religious, classical, country, folk, gospel, jazz, polka, progressive, soul, and top 40/pop.

*MCA RECORDS, 445 Park Ave., New York NY 10022. (212)605-0670. East Coast A&R Director: Kate Hyman. Labels include Camel, Costellation, Cranberry, Curb, IRS, Motown, London, Stiff, Virgin, Zebra and Philly World. Record company and music publisher (MCA Music). Works with musicians/artists on contract.
How to Contact: Call first and obtain permission to submit. Prefers cassete (or VHS videocassette) and lyric or lead sheet. SASE.
Music: Mostly top 40, pop/R&B, dance and rock. Released "Right on Track" (by Stephen Bray/Gilroy), recorded by Michael Verdick on MCA Records (on *Breakfast Club* LP); *Andy White*, written and recorded by Andy White on MCA Records. Other artists include Billy and Lisa, The Belle Stars, The Fixx, Charlie Sexton, Untouchables and Rushman Bamboo.

*MCJAMES MUSIC, Box 34, East Irvine CA 92650. (714)891-0868. Owner: Steve McClintock. President: Tim James. Record company (37 Records), music publisher (More Baroque Music, McClintock Music/BMI), and record producer (Headway Productions). Releases 10 singles and 5 LPs/year.
How to Contact: Write first and obtain permission to submit. Prefers cassette with 1 song and lyric sheet. Does not return unsolicited material. Reports in 10 weeks.
Music: Mostly pop, R&B and country; also New Age and folk. Released *Talk to Me* (by Garm Beall/Rob Lawrence), recorded by Rickie Schroeder (pop single and LP); *Deadly Prey*, by Tim Heintz/Tim James/Steve McClintock (film score); and *Christmas Needs Love to Be Christmas* (by S. McClintock/T. James), recorded by Pat Boone (traditional single and LP).

MEDA RECORDS INC., 8130 Northlawn, Detroit MI 48204. (313)862-5139. West Coast: 8569 Horner, Los Angeles CA 90035. (213)732-7009. A&R Director: Joe Hunter. Vice President/Marketing & Promotion: Mable John. Record company, record producer and music publisher (Mertis Music Company). Releases 4 singles and 4 LPs/year. Works with artists and songwriters on contract. Pays 4-12% royalty to artists on contract; statutory rate to publishers for each record sold.
How to Contact: Prefers cassette with 4-8 songs and lead sheet. SASE. Reports in 1 month or ASAP.
Music: Mostly R&B and pop; also gospel, jazz and top 40. Released "Christmas Comes Once a Year,"

by The Lamp Sisters (pop single); *A New Day*, by Mertis John (pop LP); *Heaven Bound*, by Mable John (gospel LP); and *For Thee Lord I Sing*, by Lorine Thompson (gospel LP).

*MEL VERN RECORDS, Box 412, Bronx NY 10462. (212)829-7033. President: Vernon Wilson. Record company and record producer (Wilson Productions). Releases 2 singles and 2 LPs/year. Works with musicians/artists on contract. Pays 3-6% royalty to artists on contract.
How to Contact: Write or call first to arrange personal interview. Prefers cassette with 3 songs. Does not return unsolicited material. Reports in 1 month.
Music: Mostly top 40, love ballads and dance (commercial). Released "You Make Me Feel Like A Woman" (by Raymond Johnson/Vernon Wilson) and "Rock Me Well" (by Farley Herndon), both recorded by Sandra Taylor on Mel Vern Pearl Records (both singles). Other artists include Lisa Williamson.
Tips: "Be determined to work hard, as hard as we do. Most important, know the business."

MELODEE RECORDS, Box 1255, Gallatin TN 37066-1255. (615)451-3920. General Manager: Dee Mullins. Record company, record producer, music publisher (My Dee Dee Music/ASCAP, Mel-Dee Music/BMI), and promotion and distribution firm. Member NARM, Music Expo, MIDEM. Releases 10-20 singles and 20-30 LPs/year. Works with artists and songwriters on contract; musicians on salary for in-house studio work. Pays 8% royalty to artists on contract; compulsory rate to publishers for each record sold.
How to Contact: Write or call first about your interest, or arrange personal interview to play demo tape. Prefers cassette with 1-4 songs and lyric sheet. Prefers studio produced demos. SASE. Reports in 1 month.
Music: Mostly country, country crossover and country rock. Released "Stumblin" (by Smokey Colt) and "You'll Never Be Back Anymore" (by Jimmy Faulks), both recorded by Bill Dennis; and "Pamela Brown," written and recorded by Tom Kruger, all singles on Melodee Records.
Tips: "When submitting, make clear if we are listening to artist or material or both."

MICROFON ARGENTINA S.A., Virrey Del Pino 2458, 7th Floor, Buenos Aires 1426 Argentina. 785-6584/86. President: Mario Ruben Kaminsky. Record company. Releases 100 singles ("only promotional copies, because there is no market for singles in Argentina") and 100 LPs/year. Works with musicians/artists on contract. Pays 2-5% royalty to artists on contract.
How to Contact: Submit demo tape by mail. Prefers cassette. Does not return unsolicited material.
Music: Mostly adult contemporary, rock and pop; also jazz/blues. Released *El Idolo*, recorded by Juan Ramon; *Bailando Con La Coneja*, recorded by La Barra De La Coneja, and *Lo Mejor Del Conjunto Ivoti*, recorded by Conjunto Ivoti, all LPs on Microfon Records. Other artists include Tormenta, Beto Orlando, Los Hermanos Cuestas, Barbara and Yuli Y Los Girasoles.

*MINDFIELD RECORDS, Suite 304, 750 8th Ave., New York NY 10036. President: O. Wernherr. Vice President: Steve Bentzel. Record company, music publisher (Mia Mind Music) and record producer (Sound Mind Production). Releases 12 singles and 12 LPs/year. Pays 4-6% royalty to artists on contract.
How to Contact: Prefers cassette with lyric or lead sheet. SASE.
Music: Novelty, dance and rap. Released "Jingle Yells" (by Bentzel/Pierport), recorded by The Gift Rappers on Mindfield Records (novelty); "Wild Dancing" (by Bentzel/Goodwin/Wernherr), recorded by Madonna/Otto Von Wernherr on Polydor Records (dance) and "Right to Remain Silent" (by Bentzel/Rosenman/Wernherr), recorded by Slyclone, all on Mindfield Records (dance). Other artists include Dr. Otto & His Patients, The Christopher Street Gay Children's Choir and The VPs.

MIRROR RECORDS, INC., 645 Titus Ave., Rochester NY 14617. (716)544-3500. Vice President: Armand Schaubroeck. Labels include Mirror and House of Guitars Records. Record company and music publisher. Works with artists and songwriters on contract; musicians on salary for in-house studio work. Pays 33% royalty to artists on contract; negotiable royalty to songwriters on contract.
How to Contact: Prefers 7½ ips reel-to-reel or cassette. Include photo with submission. SASE. Reports in 2 months.
Music: Folk, progressive, rock, punk and heavy metal. Released "I Shot My Guardian Angel," by Armand Schaubroeck Steals; "She Told Me Lies," "Don't Open 'Till Doomsday," "Stop," and "The 99th Floor," by the Chesterfield Kings; "In Your Face," by Dirty Looks.

*MONEY-TALKS PRODUCTIONS, INC., Box 88, Station H, Montreal, Quebec H3G 2K5 Canada. President: Paul Klein. Labels include Musicworks Records, Street Level Records, and AM-FM Records. Record company, music publisher (Fudgemusic/BMI), and record producer and distributor. Releases 12 singles and 2 LPs/year. Works with musicians/artists and songwriters on contract. Pays 6% royalty to artists on contract; 50% "or less" to publisher per song on record.

How to Contact: Prefers cassette. Does not return unsolicited material. Reports in 2 months "if material is used."
Music: Mostly dance, R&B and pop; also ballads. Released "So Shy," written and recorded by Mac Thornhill on MWR Records (dance 12" single); "Don't Break My Heart," written and recorded by Jacqui on MWR Records (dance 12" single); and "Ronnie's Rap" (by Ron Soraic), recorded by Ron & DJ on Profile Records (rap 12" single). Other artists include Ty Benskia and Suzanne Riches.

*MONOTONE RECORDS, 281 E. Kingsbridge Rd., Bronx NY 10458. (212)733-5342. President: Murray Fuller. Record company, record producer and music publisher (Sun Island Music Publishing Co.). Releases 1 single/year. Works with artists and songwriters on contract. Pays 3-5% royalty to artists on contract; statutory rate to publishers for each record sold.
How to Contact: Prefers cassette with 3-5 songs and lyric sheet. SASE. Reports in 6 weeks.
Music: Blues, dance-oriented, easy listening, jazz, R&B, soul and top 40/pop.

MONTICANA RECORDS, Box 702, Snowdon Station, Montreal, Quebec H3X 3X8 Canada. (514)345-4142. General Manager: David P. Leonard. Labels include Dynacom and Monticana Records. Record company, record producer, and music publisher (Montina Music/BMI). Member MIEA. Works with artists and songwriters on contract. Pays negotiable royalty to artists on contract; statutory rate to publishers for each record sold.
How to Contact: Prefers 7½ or 15 ips reel-to-reel, phonograph record (or VHS videocassette) and lyric sheet. Does not return unsolicited material.
Music: Mostly top 40, blues, country, dance-oriented, easy listening, folk, gospel, jazz, MOR, progressive, R&B, rock and soul.

MOPRO RECORDS, INC., 2959 Kling Ave., Cincinnati OH 45211. (513)661-0500. President: Helen Y. Morr. Record company and record producer. Member IAJRC, NAIRD, NARAS. Releases 3-4 singles and various number of LPs/year. Works with artists on contract. Pays statutory rate to publishers for each record sold.
How to Contact: Write first and obtain permission to submit. Prefers cassette (or videocassette) with 2-3 songs. Does not return unsolicited material. Reports in 2 weeks.
Music: Jazz and big band. "No fusion, only straight-ahead jazz." Released *Rollin' with Von Ohlen*, by Blue Wisp Band (jazz/big band LP); *Crack'd Rib*, by Cal Collins and the Steve Schmidt Trio (jazz LP); and *Round Midnight*, by Bobby Shew and the Steve Schmidt Trio (jazz LP). Other artists include Marshall Vente/Project Nine (jazz) and Ron Boustead (jazz singer).

MOR RECORDS, 17596 Corbel Court, San Diego CA 92128. (619)485-1550. President: Stuart L. Glassman. Record company and record producer. Releases 6 singles/year. Works with musicians on salary for in-house studio work.
How to Contact: Prefers cassette (or VHS videocassette). Does not return unsolicited material. Reports in 2 months.
Music: Mostly pop instrumental/vocal MOR; also novelty songs. Released "Symphony," (pop/instrumental single); and "What a Difference a Day Makes," by Rosa/Wincher (English-Spanish single).

*MORDISCO, Diag. Norte 570, 5-5th Piso, Buenos Aires 1035 Argentina. A&R Director: Oscar Sayavedra. Labels include Mordisco, RPM, Abraxas, Almendra and Raton Finta. Record company, record producer and management. Releases 5 LPs/year. Works with musicians/artists on contract and musicians on salary for in-house studio work. Pays 4-10 % royalty to artists on contract.
How to Contact: Prefers cassette (or VHS videocassette). SAE and IRC. Reports in 2 weeks. "Send biographies, photos and other information about each artist."
Music: Mostly rock, pop and folk; also country, soul/funky and R&B. Released *Cuando Pase El Temblor* and *Nada Personal* (by G. Cerati), recorded Soda Stero; and *El Regalao* (by Piero-Jose), recorded by Piero, on CBS Argentina (all LPs). Other artists include David Lebon (rock artist for CBS), Los Enanitos Verdes (rock and pop group for CBS), Friccion (new rock act for interdisc), Raul Porchetto (rock and ballads artists for RCA Argentina).

*MOSEKA RECORDS, 11 N. Perry St., New Riegel OH 44853. (419)435-6525 or 595-2677. Producer: Ron Hanson. Record company, record producer and music publisher (Son-Ton Music/ASCAP). Releases 15-18 singles and 2-5 LPs/year. Works with artists and songwriters on contract. Pays statutory rate to publishers for each record sold.
How to Contact: Prefers cassette with 2-8 songs and lyric sheet. SASE. Reports in 1 month.
Music: Mostly rock; also bluegrass, church/religious, country, dance, MOR, soul and top 40/pop. Released "Bottom of the Bottle" (by Fred Blackstone), recorded by Buzz Coady (country single); and "Boffo" (by G. McGladdfry), recorded by The Other Half (rock single), both on Moseka Records.

MTM MUSIC GROUP, 21 Music Square E., Nashville TN 37203. (615)242-1931. Administrative A&R: Vicki Hicks. Record company, music publisher and record producer. Releases 25 singles/year and 8 LPs/year. Works with musicians/artists and songwriters on contract.
How to Contact: "Not accepting outside material unless requested specifically."
Music: Released "Until I Met You" (by Hank Riddle), recorded by Judy Rodman on MTM (country/pop single). Other artists include The Girls Next Door, Holly Dunn, In Pursuit.

MUNICH RECORDS B.V., Albert Schweitzerlaan 9, Bennekom 6721 AW Holland. (31)8389 16777 & 19377. General Manager: Ben Mattijssen. Labels include Munich, MR, Oldie Blues and Stoof. Record company and music publisher (Munich Music). Releases 20 singles and 200 LPs/year. Works with musicians/artists and songwriters on contract; musicians on salary for in-house studio work. Pays "high" royalty to artists on contract.
How to Contact: Prefers cassette (or Beta videocassette) and lyric sheet or lead sheet. Reports in 3 weeks.
Music: Mostly reggae, blues and jazz; also folk, classical and ethnic. Released "Musical Lesson," (by Bob Marley/N.O. Livingston/Peter McIntosh), recorded by Tuff Gong on MR/TG Records; *Reggae Showcase Vol. One*, written and recorded by various artists on Munich Records (LP); and "Breaking Our Hearts," (by Melanie Harrold), recorded on Munich/MR Records (single).

MUSICRAFTERS, Box 1061, Willow Grove PA 19090. (215)657-TUNE. Vice President/Marketing: Elena Marino. Record company and music publisher (Bocage Music). Releases 6 LPs/year. Works with musicians/artists and songwriters on contract; musicians on salary for in-house studio work. Pays varying royalty to artists on contract.
How to Contact: Prefers cassette. SASE. Reports in 3 months.
Music: Mostly pop, jazz and rock; also country. "Music must be instrumental only for use in internationally distributed music library." Released *Soft Touch*, *Dynamo*, and *Hot Shots*, written by various artists and recorded by Musicrafters Orchestra on Musicrafters.

MYSTIC OAK RECORDS, 1727 Elm St., Bethlehem PA 18017. (215)865-1083. Talent Coordinator: Bill Byron. Record company and record producer. Releases 12-20 singles and 6-10 LPs/year. Works with artists on contract. Pays variable royalty to artists on contract; compulsory rate to publishers for each record sold.
How to Contact: Write first and obtain permission to submit. Prefers 15 ips reel-to-reel or cassette (or videocassette) with 3-6 songs. Include bio and performance information. SASE. Reports in 1 month if interested.
Music: Mostly synth-pop and dance-oriented rock; also folk and top 40/pop. Released "Weekend Watchers" (by Byron), recorded by The Videttes (single); "Trendsetter," written and recorded by Trendsetters (single); and *Scorched* (by Byron), recorded by The Irons (LP), all on Mystic Oak Records. Other artists include EGO, Psychic Warriors, Steve Brosky and the BBC, and the Polygraphs.
Tips: "Be professional in all respects and work toward being able to formulate 'hit' songs. Also, send videos. Videos allow us to evaluate an act's entire image and presentation."

NEAT RECORDS, 71 High St. E, Wallsend, Tyne & Wear NE 28 7RJ England. (091)2624999. Managing Director: David Wood. Record company, music publisher and record producer (Keith Nichol). Releases 8 singles and 10-12 LPs/year. Works with musicians/artists and songwriters on contract; musicians on salary for in-house studio work. Pays negotiable royalty to artists on contract. Pays compulsory rate to publisher.
How to Contact: Prefers cassette (or VHS videocassette) with lyric and lead sheets. SAE and IRC.
Music: Mostly heavy metal; also rock. Released "Only Time (Can Heal)" (by Alan Blevins), recorded by Garbo on Floating World (single); *Nightmare* (by C. Lant/J. Dunn), recorded by Venom on Neat Records (LP); and "Restless," written and recorded by Shotgun Brides on Neat Records (single). Other artists include Black Rose, Artillery, Atomkraft, J.S.R., Peer Günt and War Machine.
Tips: "Send only what you consider your best song(s) and no more than 3 songs total. We will contact you if we want to hear more. Good videos are selling songs and we expect the market to expand. However, we do not expect songwriters to go to the expenses of video production."

*NERVOUS RECORDS, 4/36 Dabbs Hill Lane, Northholt, Middlesex, England. 44-01-422-3462. Managing Director: R. Williams. Record company, record producer and music publisher (Nervous Publishing and Zorch Music). Member MCPS, PRS, PPL. Releases 2 singles and 6 LPs/year. Works with musicians/artists and songwriters on contract. Pays 3-10% royalty to artists on contract; 6½% to publishers for each record sold. Royalties paid directly to US songwriters and artists or through US publishing or recording affiliate.
How to Contact: Submit demo tape with 4-15 songs and lyric sheet. SAE and IRC. Reports in 2 weeks.

Music: Mostly rock 'n' roll and rockabilly; also R&B. "No heavy rock, disco or pop." Released *Psyclops Carnival* (by S. Brand), recorded by Torment; *Early years 1981-83* (by Harman/Cooper), recorded by Restless; *Get Smart* (by Philips), recorded by Get Smart, all LPs on Nervous Records. Others artists include Skitzo, Pharaohs and Wigsville Spliffs.

Tips: "Want wild and fast music—really demented rockabilly not punk."

*NETTWERK PRODUCTIONS, Box 330, 1755 Robson St., Vancouver, British Columbia V6G 1C9 Canada. (604)687-8649. Director: Mark Journett. Record company and music publisher (Nettoverboard Publishing/Nettwerk Publishing). Releases 12 singles and 14 LPs/year. Works with musicians/artists on contract. Pays 10-14% royalty to artists on contract.

How to Contact: Prefers cassette and lyric sheet. SAE and IRC. Reports in 1 month.

Music: Mostly progressive music; also folk and modern classical. Released *Mind: Perpetual Intercourse* (by Dave Ogilve), recorded by Skinny Puppy; *September Bowl of Green* (by Greg Ruby), recorded by Grapes of Wrath; and *Come Visit Big Bigot* (by Tom Ellerd), recorded by Severed Heads, all on Nettwerk Records (all LPs). Other artits include Chris & Cosey, Moev, SPK, Pretty Green, Waterwalk and Front 242.

Tips: "Be unique/experimentive—production is the least important thing on songs that count."

NEW MUSIC ENTERPRISES, "Meredale," The Dell, Reach Lane, Near Leighton Buzzard Beds. United Kingdom. 052523-7700. Manager: Paul Davis. Labels/England: New Music, Herald, Pilot and Fig Tree. Labels/US: Herald. Record company and music publisher (New Music Enterprises). Member PRS, MCPS. Releases 20 LPs/year. Works with artists on contract; also licenses foreign LPs. Pays negotiable royalty to artists on contract; statutory rate to publishers for each record sold. Royalties paid to US songwriters and artists through US publishing or recording affiliate.

How to Contact: Write first. Prefers cassette with 2-4 songs. SAE and IRC.

Music: Mostly "Christian music of all styles if contemporary (i.e., non-classical);" also bluegrass, country, easy listening, MOR and rock. Released *Travelin' On*, by Jerry Arhelger (country LP); and *Personally* by The Samuelsons (gospel LP). Other artists include Linda Hargrove Bartholomew, Erv Lewis, Judy Herring, Rosemary Wilhelm, Roland Friday and Eric Anders.

NEW WORLD RECORDS, Suite 11, 2309 N. 36th St., Milwaukee WI 53210. (414)445-4872. President: Marvell Love. Labels include New World and More-Love Records. Record company, music publisher (Jero Limited/BMI) and record producer. Releases 2-3 singles and 1 LP/year. Works with artists and songwriters on contract; musicians on salary for in-house studio work. Pays 3½-5% royalty to artists on contract; standard royalties to songwriters on contract; compulsory rate to publishers for each record sold.

How to Contact: Prefers cassette with 3-5 songs and lyric sheet. SASE. Reports in 3 weeks.

Music: R&B, pop and gospel. Released "You're My Lady" (by Raynaldo Norton) and "Let Me Do" (by Lee Hightire/Jim Busy), recorded by Russell Dancy on New World Records (singles); and *I Can Tell the World*, written and recorded by Harris Crusaders on More-Love Records (gospel LP). Other artists include Tony Washington and Marvell Love.

NEWSTAR INTERNATIONAL RECORDS, 29 S. Erie, Toledo OH 43602. (419)244-8599. Assistant to the President: Deborah Christian. Labels include MDS, Northcoast, Heritage, Jamestune, Newstar and Toledo. Record company, record producer and music publisher (Keeny-York, Park J. Tunes). Releases 12 singles and 8 LPs/year. Works with artists and songwriters on contract. Pays negotiable royalty to artists; statutory rate to publishers for each record sold.

How to Contact: Prefers cassette with 5-10 songs and lyric sheet. SASE. Reports in 1 month.

Music: Mostly pop; also country, easy listening and MOR. "We're beginning to review jazz."

*NICK NACK PADDYWACK RECORDS, Box 3248 Yale Station, New Haven CT 06520. (212)348-8288. President: Nicholas Astor Grouf. Labels include IRS Records, Warner Bros., No Sweat Records, Chairs for Charity. Record company, music publisher (Nicholas Astor Enterprises) and record producer (Nicholas Astor). Works with musicians/artists and songwriters on contract. Pays compulsary rate to publisher per song on record.

How to Contact: Prefers cassette (or VHS videocassette) with 3-5 songs and lyric sheet. SASE. Reports in 6 weeks.

Music: Mostly new rock and top 40; also folk, jazz and classical. Released *How Civilized Are We?* recorded by The Pedestrians (new rock/top 40 LP); "Girl Who Stole My Soul" (by Krantz/Astor/Cooper), recorded by The Lullabye Commandos (top 40/crossover funk single); and "WHATEV" (by Yale Undergrad), recorded by The Commandos (folk/jazz single), all on Nick Nack Records. Other artists include The Lift, The Glance and The Society of Orpheus & Bacchus.

Tips: "Songs shoud be both witty and literate, with careful attention to subject matter and motif. We as an unaffiliated Yale Organization, press a number of albums and compilations which often find international distribution. We consider all contributions and encourage communication."

NICKEL RECORDS, 168 Buckingham St., Hartford CT 06106. (203)524-5656. Producer: Jack Stang. Record company, record producer and music publisher (Stang Music Publishing). Releases 3 singles and 3 LPs/year. Works with musicians/artists and songwriters on contract; musicians on salary for in-house studio work. Pays 4-7% royalty to artists on contract; compulsory rate to publishers for each record sold.
How to Contact: Prefers cassette with 1-3 songs and lyric sheet. SASE. Reports in 3 weeks.
Music: Mostly dance and top 40/pop; also easy listening, MOR, R&B and rock. Released *Girls Like You*, written and recorded by Bill Chapin; *Thunder Road* (by B. McDonald); *Smokin* (by Joe Frazier), all LPs on Nickel Records. Other artists include Ken Hamber, Michael Kelly, Perfect Tommy, Diane Howe and Alpha Sonas.

NIGHTHAWK RECORDS, Box 15856, St. Louis MO 63114. (314)576-1569. Managing Director: Robert Schoenfeld. Record company, music publisher (Blackheart Music/BMI) and record producer (NH Records). Releases 2-4 singles and 3-5 LPs/year. Works with musicians/artists and songwriters on contract. Pays negotiable royalty to artists on contract.
How to Contact: Prefers cassette with 4-6 songs and lyric sheet. SASE. Reports in 3 weeks.
Music: Mostly reggae, blues and R&B. Released *Serious Thing*, (by A. Griffiths), recorded by Gladiators on Nighthawk Records (reggae LP); *Give Me Power*, (by A. Porter), recorded by Itals on Nighthawk Records (reggae LP); and *Travel With Love*, (by Justin Hinds), recorded by J.H. Dominoes on Night Records (reggae LP).

NITE RECORDS, #740, 3500 Olive Ave., Burbank CA 91505-4628. (213)273-6001. President: Randy Nite. Record company, music publisher (Gandharva Music), record producer, video production company (Maya Video), and personal management (Persona Management). Releases 6 singles and 3 LPs/year. Works with musicians/artists and songwriters on contract. Pays 3-7% royalty to artists on contract.
How to Contact: Prefers cassette with 1-3 songs. SASE. Reports in 4 weeks.
Music: Contemporary country. Released "Once Upon a Time," (by Gary Tanner), and "Blue Light," (by Bobby Blue), both recorded by Bobby Blue on Nite Records (singles); and *Turn on the Blue Light* (by Bobby Blue/Randall Kirk Nite/Ann Neiditch), recorded on Nite Records (LP).

NORTH AMERICAN LITURGY RESOURCES, 10802 N. 23rd Ave., Phoenix AZ 85029. (602)864-1980. Music Editor: Henry Papale. Labels include NALR and Livingsong. Record company, record producer and music publisher (NALR/BMI). Releases 5-8 LPs/year. Works with artists on contract; musicians on salary for in-house studio work. Pays statutory rate to publishers for each record sold.
How to Contact: Prefers cassette with 5-12 songs and lyric sheet. SASE. Reports in 1 month.
Music: Children's, choral, church/religious, liturgical and Christian rock and inspirational. Released *Companions on the Journey*, by Rev. Carey Landry (Christian LP); *Here In Our Midst*, by Michael Joncas (Catholic LP); and *The Message Goes Forth*, by Daniel Consiglio. Other artists include St. Louis Jesuits, The Dameans, Tutti Camarata, Ellis and Lynch.
Tips: "Be familiar with our recordings. Free catalogs and brochures supplied on request."

NORTHCOAST ENTERTAINMENT, 29 S. Erie, Toledo OH 43602. (419)244-8599. Manager, A&R: Reen Shaw. Labels include Toledo Records, My Reen Records, Park J. Tunes, Jamestune Records and Newstar International Records. Record company, music publisher (Keeny/York Publishing) and record producer (MDS Productions). Releases 10 singles and 3 LPs/year. Works with musicians/artists and songwriters on contract. Pays standard royalty to artists on contract.
How to Contact: Prefers cassette with 3 songs and lyric sheet. Does not return unsolicited material. Reports in 6 weeks.
Music: Country, jazz, rock and MOR. Released "Rich Man," "Jesse," and "Oh Them Hens," (by Michael Drew Shaw), all recorded by Hotlix on Reen Records (rock singles). Other artists include Suzy Rice, Mark Kieswetter, Lori Lefevre, Dan Faehnle, Kerry Clark, Woody Brubaker, Polyphony, Mick Payne and Patti Whack.
Tips: "Currently seeking new artists for Newstar International Records."

NUCLEUS RECORDS, Box 111, Sea Bright NJ 07760. President: Robert Bowden. Record company and music publisher (Roots Music/BMI). Member AFM (US and Canada). Releases 2 singles/year. Works with songwriters on contract. Pays up to 10% royalty for each record sold; statutory rate to publishers for each record sold.
How to Contact: Prefers cassette (or videocassette) with any number songs and lyric sheet. Prefers studio produced demos. SASE. Reports in 1 month.

Music: Mostly country and pop; also church/religious, classical, folk, MOR, progressive, rock (soft, mellow) and top 40. Released "Always," and "Make Believe," by Marco Sison (pop singles); and "Henery C," by Robert Bowden (pop single).

O.L. RECORDS, INC., 10051 Greenleaf, Santa Fe Springs CA 90670. (213)946-1524. President: Overton Lee. Record company, record producer, video production and music publisher (Boggy Depot, Overton Lee Music). Releases 6 singles and 2 LPs/year. Works with artists and songwriters on contract. Pays statutory rate to publishers for each record sold.
How to Contact: Prefers cassette with 1-3 songs and lyric sheet. Reports in 4 months.
Music: Mostly country and bluegrass; also blues and gospel.

OATWILLIE PRODUCTIONS,10-03 48th Ave., Long Island City NY 11101. President: Debra Chiusano. Vice President: Jim Carney. Record company, music publisher and record producer. Works with artists on contract; musicians on salary for in-house studio work. Pays 4½%-8% royalty to artists on contract; statutory rate to publishers for each record sold.
How to Contact: Prefers cassette (or VHS videocassette) with 1-3 songs and lyric sheet. Does not return unsolicited material.
Music: Mostly top 40/pop, dance, R&B and rock (all types).

ON TIME RECORDS, INC., Box 314, New York NY 10037. Contact: Director of A&R. Record company. Releases 12 singles and 6 LPs/year. Works with musicians/artists and songwriters on contract; musicians on salary for in-house studio work.
How to Contact: Prefers cassette, reel-to-reel (or videocassette) with 3 songs and lyric or lead sheet. SASE. Reports in 2 months.
Music: Mostly urban dance, R&B dance and R&B/funk. Released "Spicey (You're So Shady)," recorded by Cherokee (urban dance single); and "Pushin' the Nation," recorded by The Majestic MC's (rap dance single), both on On Time Records.

100 GRAND RECORDS, A Division of One Hundred Grand Music, 11 Norton St., Newburgh NY 12550. (914)561-4483. President: Gregg Bauer. Record company, record producer and music publisher. Releases 5 singles and 2 LPs/year. Works with artists and songwriters on contract. Pays 3-8% royalty to artists on contract; statutory rate to publishers for each record sold.
How to Contact: Prefers cassette (or videocassette) with 3-5 songs and lyric sheet. SASE. Reports in 1 month.
Music: Mostly rock, dance/rock and MOR; also choral, easy listening, folk, jazz, progressive, soul and top 40/pop. Released "Hold On," "Whitehat," "Faith," and "Special Kind," all on the LP *Color Coded* by Art Noaveau (dance rock). Other artists include John Mulligan.
Tips: "Song must have good dance appeal. Strong hook."

*OPUS—RECORDS AND PUBLISHING HOUSE, Mlynské nivy 73, Bratislava 827 15 Czechoslovakia. Phone: 222-680. International Manager: Ing. Rudolf Homér. Record company, music publisher and record producer. Releases 100 LPs/year. Works with musicians/artists and songwriters on contract. Pays 8% royalty to artist on contract.
How to Contact: Prefers cassette. SAE and IRC. Reports in 1 month.
Music: Mostly pop; also classical. Released *Jockey* (by P. Nagy); *Cajhouskij* (by Fifth Symphony); and *Atelier of Soul* (by Gombitoua), all LPs on Opus Records.

ORANGE RECORDS, % Jacobson & Colfin, Suite 1103, 150 5th Ave., New York NY 10011. (212)691-5630. President: Dave Peel. Labels include Praise, Fraser, Ariga, and Auravox. Record company.
How to Contact: Prefers cassette with 1-4 songs and lyric sheet. SASE. Reports in 1 week.
Music: Mostly progressive; also blues, classical, country, R&B, rock and soul.

*ORBIT RECORDS, Box 120675, Nashville TN 37212. (615)255-1068. Owner: Ray McGinnis. Record company, music publisher (Nautical Music Co.) and record producer (Ray Mack Productions). Releases 6 singles and 4 LPs/year. Works with musicians/artists and songwriters on contract. Pays 10-20% royalty to artists on contract; compulsory rate to publisher per song on record.
How to Contact: Prefers cassette with 4 songs and lead sheet. Does not return unsolicited material. Reports in 1 month.
Music: Country, rock and R&B. Released "I'm Gonna Quit It" (by S. Smith), recorded by Sonny Martin (country single); *Southern Living* (by S. McGregory), recorded by Sonny Martin (country LP); and "It's So Easy," written and recorded by Billy Burnett (country single), all on Orbit Records. Other arists include Kenny Wilson, Moetta, "Ky" King, Wayne Pierce, Jan Marie and Sonja.

Tips: "We like songs that are simple and tell a story, within no more than 3 verses and bridge; strong hook lines. Remember to keep it simple.

OUTLET RECORDING CO. LTD., Outlet House, H8 Smithfield Square W., Belfast BT1 1JE, Nothern Ireland. (0232)222826. Managing Director: William McBurney. Labels include: Top Spin, Homespun, Praise. Record company and music publisher (Outlet-Ulster Music). Releases 20 singles and 30 LPs/year. Works with musicians/artists and songwriters on contract. Pays 5% royalty to artists on contract.
How to Contact: Prefers cassette and lyric sheet ("required"). Does not return unsolicited material. Reports in 1 month.
Music: Mostly country and gospel. Released *Belfast*, (by Alex Quinn), recorded by Barn Brack (single and LP); and *Rathlin Island*, (by B. Conner), recorded by Pat Woods (single and LP) both on Homespun Records. Other artists include Susan McCann, Ann Breen, and Gene Fitzpatrick.

LEE MACE'S OZARK OPRY RECORDS, INC., Box 242, Osage Beach MO 65065. (314)348-3383. President: Joyce Mace. Labels include Ozark Opry, Kajac, Ven Jence, Vision, KRC and Red Rock Records. Record company, music publisher and record producer. Works with artists and songwriters on contract; musicians on salary for in-house studio work. Pays standard royalty to songwriters on contract.
How to Contact: Arrange personal interview. Prefers 7½ ips reel-to-reel or cassette with 2-4 songs and lead sheet. SASE. Reports in 2 weeks.
Music: Bluegrass, blues, church/religious, country, gospel and R&B. Released "Waylon Sing to Mama," by Darrell Thomas (country single); *Lee Mace 25 Years*, by the Ozark Opry (country LP); and *Songs Like We Sing*, by Lee Mace and the Ozark Opry (country LP).

P.M. RECORDS, INC., 20 Martha St., Woodcliff Lake NJ 07675. (201)391-2486. President: Gene A. Perla. Record company, music publisher (Perla Music/ASCAP) and record producer. Works with artists on contract.
How to Contact: Prefers cassette and lead sheet. SASE.
Music: All types. Released *Secret Places*, by Nina Sheldon (jazz vocal LP); *Pharoah's Gold*, by Bob Ackerman and Claude Johnson (jazz LP); *Con Brio*, by Con Brio (jazz LP); and *Day Dream*, by Pam Purvis (jazz vocal LP).

PACIFIC CHALLENGER RECORDS, 2940 E. Miraloma Ave., Anaheim CA 92806. (714)992-6820. Labels include Moonridge. Record company, record producer and music publisher (Pacific Challenger Music/Moonridge Music). Releases 8 singles and 4 LPs/year. Works with artists and songwriters on contract. Pays statutory rate to publishers for each record sold.
How to Contact: Prefers cassette with 2-4 songs and lyric sheet. Does not return unsolicited material. Reports in 1 month.
Music: Mostly country; also gospel, country rock and top 40/pop. Released "Waltzes & Western Swing," by Donnie Rohrs (country single); *Social Errors*, by Don Hinson (comedy LP); and "Hurtin' Kind of Love," by Ron Shaw (country single).

***PALACE RECORDS INC.**, #40, 2464 El Camino Real, Santa Clara CA 95051. (408)980-7257. Vice President: Lance Gasich. Labels include Palace and Piranha. Record company, music publisher (Passion Play Music Productions) and record producer (Michael Lindsay). Estab. 1986. Releases 5 singles and 3 LPs/year. Works with musicians/artists and songwriters on contract. Pays 9-13% royalty to artists on contract; compulsory rate to publisher.
How to Contact: Prefers cassette (or VHS videocassette). Does not return unsolicited material. Reports in 2 weeks.
Music: Rock and pop. Released *Shining Knight* (pop/rock LP) and "Follow Me Follow You" (pop/rock single), both written and recorded by Graham Grace on Palace Records. Other artists include Sato and Carousel.

PARADE, 88 St. Francis St., Newark NJ 07105. (201)344-4214. Vice President, Product Development/A&R Director: Joey Porello. Labels include Peter Pan, Power, Connection and Jammo. Record company. Releases 10-20 singles and 5-10 LPs/year. Works with artists and songwriters on record contract. Pays varying royalty to artists on contract; statutory rate to publishers for each record sold.
How to Contact: Prefers cassette with 1-3 songs and lyric sheet. SASE. Reports in 1 month.
Music: Mostly dance, children's and MOR; also country, R&B and rock. Released *Aerobics*, by Joanie Greggains (exercise LP); and "Can't Judge a Book," by Cookie (dance single).

PARAGOLD RECORDS & TAPES, 1119½ Leland Ave., Nashville TN 37216. Director: Teresa Bernard. Record company, music publisher (Rainbarrel Music Co./BMI) and record producer. Releases 2 singles and 1 LP/year. Works with musicians/artists and songwriters on contract; musicians on salary

for in-house studio work.
How to Contact: Prefers cassette (or VHS videocassette) with 2 songs and lyric or lead sheets. SASE. "Unpublished songs are welcome." Reports in 6 weeks.
Music: Country and top 40. Released "Ghost of Grand Ol Opry," written and recorded by Johnny Bernard; "Daddy's Last Letter," (by J. Bernard), recorded by J. Lyne; and "Don't Turn Me On Today," (by Ray Davis), recorded by J. Bernard, all on Paragold Records (all country singles). Other artists include Justin Christie, 7th Heaven Band, and Sunset Cowboys.

PARC RECORDS, Box 547877, Orlando FL 32854-7877. (305)299-0077. A&R: Andy Deganahl. Record company and music publisher (Mister Sunshine Music, Inc.). Releases 8 singles and 4-5 LPs/year. Works with musicians/artists and songwriters on contract.
How to Contact: Prefers cassette (or videocassette) with 3-5 songs and lyric sheet. SASE. Reports in 1 month. "Picture and write-ups are appreciated."
Music: Mostly contemporary hit music/top 40 and rock/pop. Artists released in 1986-87 include Molly Hatchett, Ona (debut album), Tuesday Night (debut album), and Stranger.

PARHAM SOUND STUDIO, Rt. 3, Box 243-B, Stephenville TX 76401. (817)965-4132. Contact: Carroll Parham. Labels include Scotty Records of Texas and Cedar Valley Records. Record company, music publisher (Cedar Valley Publishing) and record producer. Releases 9 singles and 4 LPs/year. Works with musicians/artists and songwriters on contract. Pays standard royalty to artists on contract.
How to Contact: Prefers cassette. Does not return unsolicited material. "Please make sure demo is clean and presentable."
Music: Mostly country and gospel. Released "Misty Eyes" (by Tony Guess) and "Old Texas Moon" (by Mathis Jennings), both recorded by Joel Mathis (singles); and *Across Rio Grand* (by Green), recorded by Tommy Horton (LP), all recorded on Scotty Records. Other artists include Gene Williams, Tommy Kent, Delores Ayres, Joe Bass & Double Mountain Boys, Curtis Lovejoy and Lana Newman.

PARIS RECORDS, Box 2250, Canoga Park CA 91306. (818)883-8224. President: Jeff Gordon. Record company, music publisher (Gordon Music Co. Inc.) and management firm. Releases 2-4 singles and 1-2 LPs/year. Works with artists and songwriters on contract. Pays statutory rate to publishers for each record sold.
How to Contact: Call first and obtain permission to submit. Prefers cassette (or VHS videocassette) with 2-4 songs and lyric or lead sheet. Does not return unsolicited material. Reports in 1 month.
Music: Pop rock, jazz, and children's. Released *Bravados* and *Suicide Bridge*, by Failsafe (rock LPs); *Greg Chapman*, by G. Chapman (rock/top 40 EP); "Hold Me Tight," by Robert White; and "Mr. D.J.," by Concept.

*PARSIFAL PVBA, Gulden Vlieslaan, 67, Brugge 8000 Belgium. Phone: (050)339516. Contact: Nico Mertens. Labels include Parsifal, Sundown, Moonshine, Blue Sting and Discus. Record company, music publisher and record producer. Releases 2 singles and 10 LPs/year. Works with musicians/artists on contract; musicians on salary for in-house studio work.
How to Contact: Prefers cassette. Does not return unsolicited material. Reports in 1 month.
Music: R&B and blues. Other artists include St. James (Belgium), Avalanche (Netherlands), Zora Young (USA), Tip On In (Netherlands), and The Zoots (Belgium).

THE PASHA MUSIC HOUSE, 5615 Melrose Ave., Hollywood CA 90038. (213)466-3507. Contact: A&R Department. Subsidiary of CBS/Epic and Capitol Records. Record company, music publisher (The Grand Pasha Publisher) and record producer. Releases 5 singles and 12 LPs/year. Works with musicians/artists and songwriters on contract.
How to Contact: Write first ("enclose SASE") and obtain permission to submit. Prefers cassette with 3 songs. SASE. "Return of unsolicited material is not guaranteed." Reports in 6 weeks. "No phone calls, no personal appointments. One submission every 6 months by individuals or groups; one per month by an agency."
Music: Rock. Released *Along the Axis*, written and recorded by Jon Butcher on Capitol Records (LP and single); *Thrill of a Lifetime*, written and recorded by King Kobra on Capitol Records (LP); and *Isle of Man*, written and recorded by Isle of Man on Epic Records (LP and single). Other artists include Quiet Riot, Kick Axe, W.A.S.P., Ava Cherry, Zuma II and The Outlaws.

FRANK PAUL ENTERPRISES, Box 113, Woburn MA 01801. (617)933-1474. General Manager: Frank Paul. Labels include Casa Grande, Don-Mar and Shawmut Records. Record company, booking agency and music publisher. Works with artists and songwriters on contract. Pays 3% minimum royalty to artists and songwriters on contract.
How to Contact: Prefers cassette with 3-6 songs and lead sheet. SASE. Reports in 1 month.

Music: Blues, children's, choral, church/religious, classical, country, dance, easy listening, folk, gospel, MOR, rock, soul and top 40/pop. Released "Happy, Happy Birthday Baby," by the Timeweavers (R&B single); and "God Said He Would Fight My Battle," by the Fabulous Bullock Brothers (gospel single).

*PEGASUS RECORDS, 1609 Congress, Eastover SC 29044. (803)776-2328. President: Howard A. Knight, Jr. Labels include Wago and Boss. Record company, music publisher (Tenallina Music) and record producer (Howard Knight Ent.). Releases 6 singles and 2 LPs/year. Works with musicians/artists and songwriters on contract; musicians on salary for in-house studio work. Pays compulsory rate to publisher per song on record.
How to Contact: Prefers cassette with 3 songs and lyric sheet. Does not return unsolicited material. Reports only if interested.
Music: Mostly country, pop and rock. Released "Do You Wanna Fall in Love" (by K. Bell, R. Cox), recorded by Bandit Band; "Give In" (by J.P. McMeens), recorded by Randy Chapman; and "The Man in My Life" (by M. Hutson), recorded by Candy Hutson, all country singles on Pegasus Records.

PENTAGRAMM RECORDS, Box 384, 116 Wendy Dr., Holtsville NY 11742. (516)654-8459. President/A&R Director: Art Poppe. Record company, record producer and music publisher (Little Wizard Music). Releases 5 singles and 1 LP/year. Works with artists and songwriters on record contract. Pays statutory rate to publishers for each record sold.
How to Contact: Write first. Prefers cassette (or videocassette) with 3 songs. SASE. Reports in 3 weeks.
Music: MOR, R&B, rock, soul and top 40/pop.

PENTHOUSE RECORDS, 6728 Eton Ave., Canoga Park CA 91303. (213)872-1780. Director: Toni Biggs. Record company and music publisher (Tonina Music Publishing). Releases 5 singles and 5 LPs/year. Works with artists and songwriters on contract. Pays 5-8% royalty to artists on contract; statutory rate to publishers for each record sold.
How to Contact: Prefers cassette (or videocassette) with lyric sheet and photographs of artist. SASE. Reports in 2 months.
Music: Mostly rock, R&B and dance; also easy listening, progressive, soul, top 40/pop and "space wave/mod hot." Released *Caligula*, by various artists (soundtrack LP); *Threshold*, by Threshold (disco LP and single); and *Carlin on Campus*, by George Carlin (comedy LP).

PERFECT PITCH RECORDS, 1790 Century Blvd. NE, Atlanta GA 30345. (404)636-1211. A&R Director: Darrell Evans. Record company, music publisher and record producer (Score Productions, Inc.). Releases 10 singles and 50 LPs/year. Works with musicians/artists and songwriters on contract. Pays negotiable royalty to artists on contract.
How to Contact: Call first and obtain permission to submit. Prefers cassette with 1 song and lyric sheet. SASE. Reports in 1 month.
Music: Country, MOR and pop. Released "Tone Up," "In Concert," and "Silver Anniversary Tribute to the Beatles," all on Perfect Pitch Records.

PILOT RECORDS AND TAPE COMPANY, 628 S. South St., Mount Airy NC 27030. (919)786-2865. President and Owner: Paul E. Johnson. Labels include Stork, Stark, Pilot, Hello, Kay, Sugarbear, Southcoast, Songcraft and Blue Jay. Record company, music publisher (Tompaul Music Company/BMI) and record producer. Releases 30 singles and 25 LPs/year. Works with musicians/artists and songwriters on contract; musicians on salary for in-house studio work. Pays 30% royalty to artists on contract.
How to Contact: Prefers cassette or 7 ½ ips reel-to-reel with 6 songs and lyric sheet. SASE. Reports in 1 month. "The songwriters should give their date of birth with submissions. This information will be used when copyrighting a songwriter's song."
Music: Mostly country, gospel and bluegrass; also rock, folk and blues. Released "Nobody's Promised Tomorrow," written and recorded by R.H. Bell on Stark Records (country single); *Forever and a Day*, written and recorded by B.L. Atkins on Webco Records (bluegrass LP); and "I Can't Wait" (by K.L. Combs), recorded by B.L. Combs on Pilot Records (country single). Other artists include Paul Edgar Johnson, The Blue Ridge Mountain Boys, Kathy UpChurch, Early UpChurch, Don Sawers, The Carolina Gospel Singers, The Stanley Brothers, The Deep River Boys and Ellen Fielder.

*PLAIN COUNTRY RECORDS, Box 5412, Buena Park CA 90620. (213)513-8120. Contact: Leo J. Eiffert, Jr. Labels include Plain Country and Young Country. Record company, music publisher (Eb-Tide/BMI) and management firm (Leo J. Eiffert, Jr.). Releases 11 singles and 2 LPs/year. Works with musicians/artists on contract. Pays statutory rate to publisher per song on record.

How to Contact: Prefers cassette with 3 songs and lyric or lead sheet. SASE. Reports in 6 weeks.
Music: Country. Released "Don't Knock Me Till You've Tried It," and "Ain't Got No Pedigree" (by L. Eiffert, Jr.), recorded by Crawfish; and "I Got Love," written and recorded by Delane Austin, all on Plain Country Records (all country singles).

PLAIN TRUTH RECORDS CORP., Box 0290, Baldwin NY 11510. (516)593-7343. A&R Director: Steve Sola. Labels include High Caliber Records. Record company and music publisher (Plain Truth Publishing). Releases 1-3 singles and 1-3 LPs/year. Works with musicians/artists on contract. Pays 5-33% royalty to artists on contract.
How to Contact: Prefers cassette or 7½ or 15 ips reel-to-reel (or ½" videocassette) with 1-5 songs. SASE. Reports in 1 month.
Music: Mostly dance/metal, rock and new music; also pop, disco/punk/jazz/metal and go-go/metal. Released "Don't Go Disco," and "Don't Antagonize the Cat," (by Crispy/Fabio), recorded by Kyoto (singles); and *Sugar Daddy*, and *Disco Boys* (by Cropanese/Sola), recorded by Holy Terror (EPs), all on Plain Truth Records.

*PLANKTON RECORDS, 236 Sebert Rd., Forest Gate, London E7 0NP England. (01)534-8500. Senior Partner: Simon Law. Labels include Plankton, Sea Dream, Embryo Arts (licensed, Belgium), Gutta (licensed, Sweden), and Radio (licensed, United Kingdom). Record company and music publisher (Sea Dream Music). Releases 1 single and 2 LPs/year. Works with musicians/artists and songwriters on contract. Pays 10% royalty to artists on contract; compulsory rate to publishers.
How to Contact: Prefers cassette with 3 songs and lyric sheet. SAE and IRC. Reports in 6 weeks.
Music: Mostly funk/rock, R&B and gospel; also blues. Released *Living in the Love* (by Turner/Mead), recorded by Choir (contemporary gospel LP); *Never Surrender* (by Cliff Bergdahl), recorded by Really Free (rock LP); and *Distance Grows*, written and recorded by Pete Ward (modern rock LP), all on Plankton Records. Other artists include Fresh Claim, Solid Air, Light Factory, and Marc Catley.
Tips: "We specialize in bands with a Christian bias, regardless of their musical style."

PLAYBONES RECORDS, Box 7718, 2000 Hamburg 20, West Germany. (040) 4300339. Producer: Arno v. Vught. Labels include Rondo Records. Record company, music publisher (Mento Music Group KG.) and record producer (Arteg Productions). Releases 12 singles and 10 LPs/year. Works with musicians/artists and songwriters on contract. Pays 8-16% royalty to artists on contract.
How to Contact: Write or call first to arrange personal interview. Prefers cassette (or VHS videocassette) and lyric or lead sheet. SASE. Reports in 2 weeks.
Music: Mostly instrumentals, country and jazz; also background music, rock and gospel. Released *Einfach So*, by Flagranti (soft jazz LP); *Wolfgang Lackerschmid Connection*, (jazz LP); and *Last Chance*, by Plugpoint (MOR LP). Other artists include H.J. Knipphals, Gaby Knies, Jack Hals, H. Hausmann, Crabmeat and M. Frommhold.

POLKA TOWNE RECORDS, 211 Post Ave., Westbury NY 11590. President: Teresa Zapolska. Record company, music publisher, record producer and booking agency. Works with artists and songwriters on contract.
How to Contact: Prefers cassette with 1-3 songs. SASE for report and SASE for return of cassette. "We review music once a month. No review or reply without SASE."
Music: Mostly polkas; also "some" waltzes.

POLYGRAM RECORDS, 810 7th Ave., New York NY 10019. (212)333-8000. Contact: A&R Assistant. Record company. Works with artists on contract.
How to Contact: "We review songs submitted by established publishers. Not accepting unsolicited material, but welcome queries when accompanied by press and/or chart clippings and SASE. Do *not* send recordings or lyrics until requested." Recommends referral from a reputable industry source.
Music: Rock, top 40/pop, R&B and dance/urban. Current roster includes Bon Jovi, John Mellencamp, Cinderella, Robert Cray, The Rainmakers, Tom Kimmel, Billy Branigan, Kiss, The Everly Brothers, Kool and the Gang, Cameo, Commodores, Fat Boys, Gwenn Guthrie, Rush, Moody Blues, ELP and Scorpions.
Tips: "Be patient—you will be contacted if there's interest. Keep in mind that most of the artists write their own material. We're most open to female-oriented and pop acts to balance out heavy-hitting hard rock and R&B roster."

*POLYGRAM RECORDS PTY. LTD., 122 McEvoy St., Alexandria, Sydney NSW 2015 Australia. A&R Director-Australia: Clive Hodson. Labels include Mercury, Polydor, Vertigo. Record company. Releases 250 singles and 200 LPs/year. Works with musicians/artists on contract. Pays 8-14% royalty to artists on contract.

Close-up

Tony Prendatt
Director of A&R
Polygram Records

As Director of A&R (Artists and Repertoire) in Polygram's
urban contemporary music department, Tony Prendatt
works with established acts like the Commodores and Irene
Cara, and new artists Doc Powell (currently with Luther
Vandross) and Cindy Valentine (a Canadian artist). To prepare himself for an executive position in the music industry, he studied both music (education and composition) and
business (music business and general accounting). He strongly recommends that aspiring
songwriters and musicians do the same today. "Unfortunately, most creative people go
through a phase where they think they're above learning about business," he says. Yet it takes
a thorough knowledge of business to develop a strategy for success. "There's a reality to
earning six figures a year. Someone who studied woodwinds in a classical program at a university may sit third chair in a symphonic orchestra, but he may be able to make hundreds of
thousands of dollars if he also becomes known as the best woodwind player in jingle sessions."

Specifically, songwriters would do well to learn more about how A&R works because
A&R executives, along with music publishers, are songwriters' best contacts in the music
business. These professionals seek new material for artists to record. "There are some bad
executives out there," Prendatt admits, "but mostly A&R people are misunderstood. People
hate you because you don't sign their act or their song. You have to understand that an unsolicited song is subject to an audition." Songs are rigorously judged for quality and suitability,
regardless of who submits them. "The bottom line is that it's our job to find hits. The artists I
choose and the songs I choose must continue to generate a profit for the company.

"Let's say we receive 100 demo tapes each week. Ninety-eight percent of them are going
to contain good material. We do try to help people and we do give people breaks, but you
can't sign everyone. So you look for the five percent that's a cut above the rest. I would say
everyone trying to break in should do whatever they have to do to *be* a cut above the rest."

In listening to demos, Prendatt finds that the most common error is "sloppy presentation.
Some of the material that accompanies the tapes is handwritten and in bad English. It needs to
be more professional, both the audio tape and the written material. We receive so much unsolicited material that there is naturally an automatic process of elimination. If we see something that is sloppy, it is eliminated right away. If you only have a half-page bio, that's okay,
but make it neat."

Prendatt insists that songwriters without a track record can succeed if they have the right
"approach—by having strong aspirations and ambition." He says, "The best advice I could
give to any creative person is *don't stop trying*. Remember that for every person who's trying
to accomplish something there are probably 1,000 other people trying to accomplish the same
thing. So you have to be aggressive, but you also have to be courteous and patient. Just don't
stop trying. Even after 100 doors are slammed in your face, one door will be opened for you."

—Julie Wesling Whaley

How to Contact: Prefers cassette. Does not return unsolicited material. Reports in 2 weeks.
Music: Rock, pop, R&B and jazz. *Dreams of Ordinary Men* (by A. Mansfield/T. Hunter/D. Parry/M. Hunter/T. Rundgeson), recorded by Dragon on Polydor Records (LP); "Primitive Love Rites" (by R. Wilson/JJ Hackett), recorded by Mondo Rock; and "Dreaming" (by B. Callinan), recorded by Radiators. Other artists include GANGgajang, Rockmelons, Mondo Rock, Koo De Tah, Peter Blakeley, Go-Betweens, Ed Keupper, That's That and Marching Girls, and Hunter.

POWDERWORKS RECORDS AND TAPES PTY. LTD.,28 Cross St., Brookvale 2100, Australia. (02) 938-2200. Managing Director: J. Evans. A&R Manager: J. Kenneth. Record company.
How to Contact: Prefers cassette. Does not return unsolicited material.
Music: Contemporary, MOR, country, chidlren's, jazz and dance.

POWER UP, Suite 101, 413 Cooper St., Camden NJ 08102. (609)963-3190. President: Michael Nise. Labels include Power House Recording. Record company, music publisher and record producer. Releases 6 singles and 4 LPs/year. Works with artists and songwriters on contract, musicians on salary for in-house studio work. Payment negotiable.
How to Contact: Prefers cassette (or VHS videocassette) with 1-3 songs. SASE. Reports in 1 month.
Music: Mostly R&B and pop/crossover; also children's, church/religious, country, dance, easy listening, folk, gospel, jazz, rock, soul and top 40/pop.

PRAISE, % Jacobson & Colfin, 150 5th Ave., New York NY 10011. (212)691-5630. Contact: Jeffrey E. Jacobson. Record company. Works with musicians/artists and songwriters on contract.
How to Contact: Prefers cassette (or ½" VHS videocassette). SASE. Reports in 1 month.
Music: Gospel, R&B and country.

*PRESIDENT RECORDS LIMITED, 21 Panton St., London SW1Y 4DR England. (01)839-4672. Labels include President, Joy, Rhapsody Seville, Spiral and Jayboy. Record company and music publisher (Kassner Associated Publishers). Releases 15-20 singles and 30 LPs/year. Works with musicians/artists and songwriters on contract. Pays 10% royalty to artists on contract; compulsory rate to publisher per song on record.
How to Contact: Prefers cassette (or VHS videocassette) with maximum of 3 songs and lyric or lead sheet. SAE and IRC. Reports in 1 month.
Music: Mostly pop, rock and country; also R&B, jazz and instrumental. Released *Indestructable*, written and recorded by Mike D'Abo on President Records (folk rock LP); "Everlasting Love," recorded by Maggie Bell on President Records (pop single); and *Wild Cat Blues* recorded by Clarence Williams/Blue Five on Rhapsody Records (jazz blues LP). Other artists include Denny Laine, Mars-Fenwick Band, Jack Bruce, Iris Williams, Eddie Hardin and Maria Morgan.

PRIME CUT RECORDS, Box 1387, Lyndonville VT 05851. (802)626-3317. President A&R: Bruce James. Record company and record producer. Releases 4-12 singles and 4 LPs/year. Works with musicians/artists and songwriters on contract. Pays compulsory rate to publisher for each record sold.
How to Contact: Prefers cassette (or VHS videocassette) with 1-5 songs and lyric sheet. "Songs should be hit material telling compelling story." SASE. Reports only if interested.
Music: Country and top 40/pop. Released *Old Nights*, written and recorded by Jackie O; *In Throughout*, written and recorded by Champlain; and *Dance Dance*, recorded by Dance Dance, all LPs on Prime Cut Records. Other artists include Contagious and Littlewing.
Tips: "We need songs with strong, compelling storylines that will rivet listener throughout song to see how the story ends."

QUINTO PRODUCTIONS/RECORDS, Box 2388, Toluca Lake CA 91602. (818)985-8284. Contact: Quint Benedetti. Labels include Quinto, Suzi, Fun, Top 'n' Bottom and Clovermint Records. Record company, music publisher (Quint Benedetti Music) and demo producer. Releases 2 singles and 1 LP/year. Works with songwriters on contract. Pays standard royalty.
How to Contact: Prefers cassette with 2-3 songs and lead sheet. SASE. Reports in 10 weeks.
Music: Christmas songs only. Released *Topsy or Sorry about that Harriett*, recorded by the original cast (LP); and "Christmas Presents," recorded by children's chorus (single), both on Quinto.

R.E.F. RECORDS, 404 Bluegrass Ave., Madison TN 37115. (615)865-6380. Contact: Bob Frick. Record company, record producer and music publisher (Frick Music Publishing Co./BMI). Releases 10 LPs/year. Works with artists and songwriters on contract. Pays 3-5¢ royalty to artists on contract; statutory rate to publishers for each record sold.
How to Contact: Call first. Prefers 7½ ips reel-to-reel or cassette with 2-10 songs and lyric sheet. SASE. Reports in 1 month.

Music: Country, gospel, rock and top 40/pop. Released "I Love You In Jesus," "Warm Family Feeling," and "Our Favorites," all by Bob Scott Frick. Other artists include Larry Ahlborn, Francisco Morales, Candy Coleman, and Peggy Beard.

RA-JO INTERNATIONAL, Suite 19L, 100-19 Alcott Pl., Bronx, NY 10475. (212)379-2593. A&R Producer: Joe Adams. Labels include Abbco. Record company. Releases 10 singles and 3 LPs/year. Works with musicians/artists and songwriters on contract. Pays 10% royalty to artists on contract.
How to Contact: Call first and obtain permission to submit. Prefers cassette and lyric sheet. SASE. Reports in 2 weeks.
Music: Mostly rock, blues and pop. Released "Honky Tonk," (by Doggett), recorded by Beach Boys on Capitol Records (pop); "Everybody's Somebody's Fool," (by A. Adams), recorded by Michael Jackson on Motown Records (pop); and "No More in Life," (by A. Adams), recorded by Arthur Prysock on Bloor Records (pop).

RAREFACTION RECORDS, Box 390331, Mountain View CA 94039. (415)346-7537. Owner: Paul Korntheuer. Labels include Blue Cloud Records. Record company. Releases 3 LPs/year. Works with musicians/artists on contract. Pays 15% royalty.
How to Contact: Prefers cassette. SASE.
Music: "Avant-garde," post-punk/industrial and jazz. Released *Tomorrow's Rein* (by King/Wilkins), recorded by Amongst; *Urdu* (by Rick Davies), recorded by URDU; and *Nite of . . .* (by King/Cross), recorded by The Calm, all on Rarefaction cassettes. Other artists include Palmetto State and Orange Curtain.

RAVEN RECORDS, 1918 Wise Dr., Dothan AL 36303. (205)793-1329. President: Jerry Wise. Labels include Studio Four Records. Record company and music publisher (Round Sound Music/BMI). Member CMA and GMA. Releases 3-6 singles and 5-10 LPs/year. Works with artists and songwriters on contract. Pays 2-20% royalty to artists on contract; standard royalty to songwriters on contract; pays statutory rate to publishers for each record sold.
How to Contact: Write first. Prefers 7½ ips reel-to-reel or cassette with 1-6 songs and lyric sheet. SASE. Reports in 1 month.
Music: Country, easy listening, MOR, rock, soul, top 40/pop and gospel.

RCA RECORDS, 6363 Sunset Blvd., Los Angeles CA 90028. (213)468-4039. Talent Manager: Teri Muench. Record company. Works with artists and songwriters on contract.
How to Contact: Query. Not accepting unsolicited material.
Music: Top 40/pop only.

READY TO ROCK RECORDS, Box 46445, Hollywood CA 90046. (213)656-8845. President: P.J. Birosik. Record company, music publisher (Ready to Rock Music/BMI), record producer (P.J. Birosik) and talent agency (Vox). Releases 12 LPs/year. Works with musicians/artists on contract. Pays varying royalty to artists on contract.
How to Contact: Prefers cassette (or VHS videocassette) with 4 songs and lyric sheet. SASE. Reports in 1 month. "Include current bio, clips and upcoming performance dates, if any."
Music: Rock, pop and New Age. Released *Invasion*, by Greg Leon on Ready to Rock Records (LP); *The Fun Sessions*, by Levi Dexter on PVC Records (LP); and "Going Backward," by Rayonics on Ready to Rock Records (dance single). Other artists include Invaders, Secret Agent and Commando.

REALITY RECORDS PRODUCTIONS, 19 Roxborough Place, Willingboro NJ 08046. (609)877-7653. Producer: "Hank" Strasser. Record company and record producer (Reality Productions).
How to Contact: Prefers cassette; bios appreciated. SASE. Reports ASAP.
Music: Jazz and electronic music.
Tips: "We're looking for commercially viable jazz. We believe the future is in electronic music, but product choices probably won't stray too far from mainstream jazz."

RECORD COMPANY OF THE SOUTH (RCS), 5220 Essen Lane, Baton Rouge LA 70809. (504)766-3233. President: Cyril E. Vetter. Record company, music publisher and record producer. Works with musicians on salary; artists and songwriters on contract. Pays 3-7% royalty to artists on contract; standard royalty to songwriters on contract.
How to Contact: Write first. Prefers cassette (7½ ips reel-to-reel OK) with 1-10 songs and lyric sheet. SASE. Reports in 1 month.
Music: Country, MOR, R&B, rock (hard and country), soul, top 40/pop and new music. Released "Suddenly Single," by Butch Hornsby (country single); *Don't Take It Out on the Dog*, by Butch Hornsby (country LP); and *Safe with Me*, by Irma Thomas (pop single and LP). Other artists include Luther Kent, Gregg Wright and Floyd Brown.

RED BUD RECORDS, A Division of CAE, Inc., 611 Empire Mill Rd., Bloomington IN 47401. (812)824-2400. General Manager: Pam Land. Labels include Sirius Music. Record company and record producer. Member NARAS. Releases 1 single and 4 LPs/year. Works with musicians and artists on contract. Pays statutory rate to publishers for each record sold.
How to Contact: Call or write first and obtain permission to submit. Prefers cassette with 2-5 songs. SASE. "Include bio and gig list." Reports in 1 month.
Music: Mostly jazz and folk; also bluegrass, rock and "some" classical. "We'll listen to anything." Released *Solo Guitar*, by Royce Campbell (jazz LP); *Buffalo Gal*, by Leftwich and Higginbotham (folk LP) and "Josef Gingold: Seventy-five," by Josef Gingold (classical). Other artists include Bill Wilson, Eric Rosser, Jan Henshaw, High Ground, Eclectricity and Kiethe-Lowrie Duet.

RED DOT RECORDS-MARULLO PRODUCTIONS, 1121 Market, Galveston TX 77550. (409)762-4590. President: A.W. Marullo Sr. Labels include Red Dot, Rotab, Graffiti. Record company, record producer and music publisher (A.W. Marullo Music/BMI). "We also lease masters from artists." Releases 7 singles and 1 LP/year. Works with artists and songwriters on contract; musicians on salary for in-house studio work. Pays 10-12% royalty to artists on contract; statutory rate to publishers for each record sold.
How to Contact: Prefers cassette with 4-7 songs and lyric sheet. SASE. Reports in 2 months.
Music: Country and country pop. Released "Travel'n Lover," by Debra Fowler; "Changes & Chances," and "Color This Feelin of Blue," by Tricia Matula (all country/pop).

RELIANCE RECORDS, A division of Spectrum 1 Network Inc., Box 7464, Burbank CA 91510. A&R Director: Richard De A'morelli. Labels include Reliance Records and Lynné Records. Record company and music publisher. Releases 3-8 12" singles/year. Works with musicans/artists and songwriters on contract. Pays negotiable royalty to artists on contract; statutory rate to publishers for each record sold.
How to Contact: Prefers cassette (or videocassette). SASE. "Absolutely no phone inquiries on unsolicited material." Reports in 3 months.
Music: Funk, dance, romantic new wave and disco. Released "You're My Fantasy," written and recorded by Kevin McGettigan on Reliance Records (dance).

REVONAH RECORDS, Box 217, Ferndale NY 12734. (914)292-5965. Contact: Paul Gerry. Record company and booking agency. Releases 2-4 LPs/year. Works with artists and songwriters on contract. Teams collaborators. Pays negotiable royalty to artists on contract. Pays statutory rate to publishers for each record sold.
How to Contact: Arrange personal interview. Prefers reel-to-reel, cassette, 8-track cartridge (or videocassette) and lead sheet. SASE. Reports in 1 month.
Music: Bluegrass, country, folk and gospel. Released *The Fiddler & His Lady*, by Tater Tate (bluegrass LP); *Back Home in Madison County*, by Red Rector (bluegrass LP); *Saturday Night*, by Bristol Mountain Bluegrass (bluegrass LP); and *Before the Fire Comes Down*, by Northern Lights (bluegrass LP). Other artists include Mac Martin, the Shenandoah Cutups, Stacy Phillips, Simon St. Pierre, Gene Elders, Fred Pike, Roger Bellow, Del McCoury, The Stuart Family, Mountain Grass, Walter Hensley, Clinton King, Jerry Oland and The Gospelites.

RIC RAC RECORDS, % Ric Rac, Inc., Box 712, Nashville IN 47448. (812)837-9569. President: R.L. Hanson. Labels include Country Bump. Record company, music publisher, record production and promotion firm. Releases 4-6 singles/year. Works with musicians/artists and songwriters on contract. Pays 3-6% royalty to artists on contract; compulsory rate to publishers for each record sold.
How to Contact: Write first and obtain permission to submit. Prefers cassette with 1-4 songs and lyric or lead sheet. SASE. Reports in 2 months. "Do not make phone inquiries as to status of material submitted. Material submitted to A&R must be represented by publisher. We are only interested in videos of live performances."
Music: Mostly country; also rock, gospel, folk and easy listening (MOR). Released "Stay Away" (by Greg Washel) and "Morning Light" (by David Biller), both recorded by X-It on Ric Rac Records (rock singles); and "Life's Not Worth The Ride," written and recorded by Rick Hanson on Ric Rac (country single). Other artists include Jack Lawles and Glori McFall.

*RICHIE RECORDS, 5630 N. Elston Ave., Chicago IL 60646. (312)763-3090. President: Richard Milucky. Record company. Estab. 1986. Releases 4-6 singles, 10-12 dance 12" singles and 2 LPs/year. Works with songwriters on contract.
How to Contact: Prefers cassette (or VHS videocassette) with maximum of 3 songs and lyric or lead sheets. SASE. Reports in 6 weeks.
Music: Pop. "Currently seek material for female vocalists (trio).
Tips: "We work one project at a time, we *are* a custom label; place product with majors. Will listen to

masters of pop group for placement as long as it's pop—no heavy metal, anti-anything material."

*RICOCHET RECORDS, Suite N., 226 Springmeadow Dr., Holbrook NY 11741. (516)472-1219. President: Andy Marvel. Labels include Alyssa Records. Record company, music publisher (Andy Marvel Music), record producer (Marvel Productions) and Alyssa Records. Releases 4-6 singles and 2-4 LPs/year. Works with musicians/artists and songwriters on contract.
How to Contact: Prefers cassette or 7½ ips reel-to-reel (or VHS videocassette) with 3-5 songs and lyric sheet. SASE. Reports in 2 weeks.
Music: Mostly pop, R&B and rock; also country.

RIDDLE RECORDS, 603 W. MacArthur, Bloomington IL 61701. (309)829-7023. President/General Manager: Don L. Riddle. Record company. Releases 1 single/year. Works with musicians/artists and songwriters on contract. Pays standard royalty to artists on contract.
How to Contact: Prefers cassette with 1-3 songs. SASE. Reports in 2 weeks. "Songs with hooks and original concepts count, and can make the difference between good and bad."
Music: Country and contemporary. Released "Dream Lover" (by D.L. Riddle), recorded by Susie Brading on Riddle Records (country single).

RIPSAW RECORD CO., Suite 805, 4545 Connecticut Ave. NW, Washington DC 20008. (202)362-2286. President: Jonathan Strong. Record company, record producer, and music publisher (Southern Crescent Publishing/BMI and Sugar Mama Music/BMI). Releases 1-5 singles and 1-2 LPs/year. Works with musicians/artists and songwriters on contract. Payment negotiable with artists on contract; standard royalty to songwriters on contract; compulsory rate to publishers for each record sold.
How to Contact: Prefers cassette and lyric sheet. SASE. "Invite us to a club date to listen." Reports as soon as possible.
Music: Rockabilly and "traditional" rock 'n' roll. Released "Tough Girls," by Bobby Smith (rock); and "I Wanna Be With You," and "What Do I Hafta Do," by B. Smith (rockabilly).
Tips: "Keep it rockabilly."

*RISER RECORDS, 5045 Sidely St., Burnaby, British Columbia V5J 1T6 Canada. (604)430-5664. A&R Manager: Alison A. Medd. Labels include Riser Records and Colly Records. Record company. Releases 5-6 singles, 4 EPs and 1-2 LPs/year. Works with musicians/artists on contract and musicians on salary for in-house studio work.
How to Contact: Prefers cassette (or VHS videocassette) with 4-10 songs and lyric sheet. "Include photo and bio." SAE and IRC. Reports in 1 month.
Music: Mostly pop, pop/rock and rock; also avant garde/psychedelic, alternative new music, MOR and new wave-punk. Released "Automaton/Soft Touch" (by D. Medd/J. Nichols), recorded by Dorian Gray (single); "He's a Tease/Lover Lover" (by D. Medd & J. Nichols), recorded by Menage A. Trois (single); and *Brock & Friends Music Society Presents* (by D. Medd & B. Shaw), recorded by Medd & Shaw (LP), all on Riser Records. Other artists include Mike Usual.

RITZ RECORDS LTD., 5/6 Larbard St., 1 Dublin Ireland. 779046/779244. Managing Director: Michael Clerkin. General Manager: M. O'Riordan. Labels include Ritz Records (UK) and Roxy Records (UK). Record company and music publisher. Releases 15 singles and 6 LPs/year. Works with songwriters on contract; musicians on salary for in-house studio work. Pays varying royalty to artists on contract.
How to Contact: Submit demo tape by mail. Prefers cassette. Does not return unsolicited material. Reports in 6 weeks. "Enclose all relevant details."
Music: MOR, country and pop. Artists include Furey Brothers, Foster & Allen, Ray Lynam, Philomania Beeley, Billie Jo Spears, Ricky Skaggs, Daniel O'Donnell, Luv Bug, Bagatelle and Tequila Sunrise.

RMS TRIAD RECORDS, 6267 Potomac Circle, West Bloomfield MI 48033. (313)661-5167. Contact: Bob Szajner. Record company, record producer and music publisher. Releases 3 LPs/year. Works with artists on contract. Pays negotiable royalty to artist on contract; statutory rate to publishers for each record sold.
How to Contact: Write first about your interest. Prefers cassette with 2-4 songs. SASE. Reports in 3 weeks.
Music: Jazz. Released *Sound Ideas*, and *Afterthoughts*, by Triad (jazz instrumental LPs).

ROBBINS RECORDS, INC., HC80, Box 5B, Leesville LA 71446. National Representative: Sherree Scott. Labels include Headliner Stars Records. Record company and music publisher (Headliner Stars Music and Universal Stars Music/BMI). Releases 12-14 singles and 1-3 LPs/year. Works with artists and songwriters on contract. Pays standard royalty to artists on contract; statutory rate to publishers for each record sold.

How to Contact: Prefers cassette with 1-6 songs and lyric sheet. Does not return unsolicited material. Reports only if interested.
Music: Mostly church/religious; also bluegrass, country, folk, gospel, and top 40/pop. Released "Jesus, You're Everywhere," "I Can Depend on You," and "I Just Came to Thank You Lord," by J.J. and Sherree Stephens (religious singles). Other artists include Renee Wills and Melodee McCanless.

*ROB-LEE MUSIC, Box 1338, Merchantville NJ 08109. (609)962-6000. Vice President/A&R: Bob Francis. Labels include Castle, TCB, Jade, Rock Island and Camden Soul Records. Record company and record producer. Member RIAA. Releases 15-20 singles and 4-6 LPs/year. Works with artists and songwriters on contract. Pays 4-8% royalty to artists on contract; standard royalty to songwriters on contract; pays 5¢/song or 1¢/minute to music publishers for each record sold.
How to Contact: Prefers 7½ ips reel-to-reel or cassette (or videocassette) with 2-8 songs and lyric sheet. "Include biography and photos if possible." SASE. Reports in 2 weeks.
Music: Mostly funk; also dance, jazz, progressive, rock and top 40/pop. Released "My Lady Friend," by James "Grumpy" Brogsdale (R&B ballad single); "Luscious," by Heavy Weather (funk single); and *Greatest Hits*, by the Orlons (compilation LP). Other artists include Full House, Big El, TCB Band, Snow, Phoenix and Adrienne Wett.

ROCKIN! RECORDS, 1733 Carmona Ave., Los Angeles CA 90019. (213)933-6521. Labels include Rockmore Records. Manager: Perry Rocquemore. A&R Director: Willie H. Rocquemore. Record company, music publisher and record producer. Member RIAA. Releases 2 singles and 1 LP/year. Works with artists and songwriters on contract. Teams collaborators. Pays 5-10% royalty to artists on contract, pays statutory rate to publishers for each record sold.
How to Contact: Prefers cassette with 4 songs maximum and photo and lyric sheet. SASE. Reports in 1 month.
Music: Pop rock, blues, rock, ballad and soul. Released "Crumb Jumpers" and "Cry Any More," by Pam Baity; and "Anything He Can Do," by Jimmy Holiday. Other artists include Jennifer Well.
Tips: "Listen to top 40 hits on radio."

ROLLIN' ROCK RECORDS, 6918 Peach Ave., Van Nuys CA 91406. Contact: Ron Weiser. Labels include Rockabilly Rebel, Rockabilly Uprising. Record company, record producer and music publisher (Ron Weiser Publishing, Rockin' Ronny Music). Releases 2-3 singles and 2 LPs/year. Works with artists and songwriters on contract; musicians on salary for in-house studio work. Pays 5-7% royalty to artists on contract; statutory rate to publishers for each record sold.
How to Contact: Prefers cassette and lyric sheet. Does not return unsolicited material.
Music: Mostly rockabilly and 50s R&B and rock; also country and R&B. Released *Hollywood Cats*, by Ray Campi; and *American Music*, and *Marie Marie*, by Blasters (all rockabilly LPs). Other artists include American Music.

ROPER RECORD CO. INC., 45-15 21st St., Long Island City NY 11101. (718)786-2401. President: Franc Peri. Record company. Works with musicians/artists on contract.
How to Contact: Prefers cassette and lead sheet. SASE.
Music: Instrumental and dance music.

ROPERRY RECORDS, 645 Madison Ave., New York NY 10022. (212)836-4437. General Manager: Jane Lowy. Record company, record producer, music publisher and personal management firm. Releases approximately 3 singles and 1-2 LPs/year. Works with artists and songwriters on contract. Rates paid to artists and publishers "dependent on contract."
How to Contact: Call first about your interest. Prefers cassette with 1-3 songs and lyric sheet. SASE. "Include picture and biography." Reports in 3 weeks.
Music: Mostly top 40/pop, MOR and easy listening; also children's. Released "Joggin'" (pop/dance/ MOR single), "Just a Little Imagination," (adult/contemporary single), and "Kid Santa Claus," (a Prose Production) all by Patsy; and "Single Again," by Joey Latini.

ROSEBUD RECORDS, % Jacobson & Colfin, Suite 1103, 150 5th Ave., New York NY 10011. President: Joel Kohn. Record company. Releases 3 singles/year. Works with musicians/artists on contract.
How to Contact: Prefers cassette (or ½" videocassette). SASE. Reports in 1 month.
Music: Comedy and technopop. Released "Songs for Micro Kids," and "Chip Shtick," written and recorded by J. Kohn on Rosebud Records.

 The asterisk before a listing indicates that the listing is new in this edition. New markets are often the most receptive to freelance submissions.

*ROTO-NOTO RECORDS, 148 Erin Ave., Hamilton, Ontario L8H 3Z3 Canada. (416)549-5275. President: Randall Cousins. Record company (Roto-Noto) and music publisher (Alleged Iguana-PROCAN and Secret Agency (CAPAC).
How to Contact: Prefers cassette with 2 songs and lyric sheet. SAE and IRC. Reports in 6 weeks.
Music: Mostly pop, country and rock; also R&B. Other artists include Bobby McGee, Frank Rondell and Steve Middleton.

RSO RECORDS, 1775 Broadway, New York NY 10019. (212)975-0700. Director of A&R: James Dayley. Record company, music publisher and record producer. Releases 5 singles/year and 2 LPs/year. Works with musicians/artists and songwriters on contract. Pays 5-8½% royalty to artists on contract; statutory rate to publishers for each record sold.
How to Contact: Prefers cassette (or VHS or ¾" videocassette) with 1-3 songs. SASE. Reports in 1 month. Include photo, bio, press clippings, etc. with submission.
Music: Mostly rock and pop; also video music.

RTP INTERNATIONAL, Box 311, 180 Pond St., Cohasset MA 02025. (617)383-9494. President: Rik Tinory. Artist Relations: Claire Babcock. Labels include Sequel and Old Boston. Record company, record producer and music publisher (Old Boston Publishing). Releases 10 singles and 8-12 LPs/year. Works with musicians/artists and songwriters on contract; musicians on salary for in-house studio work.
How to Contact: Call first. Prefers cassette with 1-3 songs and lead sheet. Does not return unsolicited material. "All material submitted must be copyrighted."

SAGITTAR RECORDS, 1311 Candlelight Ave., Dallas TX 75116. (214)298-9576. President: Paul Ketter. Record company and music publisher (Big State Music/BMI). Releases 6 singles/year and 3 LPs/year. Works with musicians/artists and songwriters on contract; musicians on salary for in-house studio work. Pays 100% royalty to artists on contract.
How to Contact: Prefers cassette or 7½ ips reel-to-reel with 3-6 songs and lyric sheet. SASE. Reports in 6 weeks.
Music: Country, folk and pop/MOR. Released *Only a Woman* (by Diane Baumgartner), recorded by Bunnie Mills (country LP); "Lovin Bound" (by R. Beneteau), recorded by P.J. Kamel (country single); and "Theodore" (by Grace Puls), recorded by Dave Gregory (country single), all on Sagittar Records. Other artists include Jody Witt, Reece Free and Patty Stewart.
Tips: "We are interested in leasing album masters for release in overseas markets."

*SAM RECORDS, GL. Kongevej 148, Copenhagen F., Denmark 1850. (01)24 4700. Managing Director: Ole Dreyer. Record company and music publisher (Sam Music). Releases 10 singles and 10 LPs/year. Prefers cassette (or U-Matic videocassette). Does not return unsolicited material. Reports in 3 weeks.
Music: "New rock and punk." Released *Cutting Through* written and recorded by Martin Hall; *McMLXXXVI*, written and recorded by Die Kapelle; and *Strange Fruit*, written and recorded by Buoyant Blue, all on Sam Records (LPs). Other artists include Under For, Corps Diplomatique and The Galley of How Do I.

*SAND DOLLAR RECORDS, Box 2154, Carolina Beach NC 28428. (919)458-8651. Owner, A&R: Lanny Swaim. Record company, music publisher (Swaim Publishing), record producer (Sand Dollar Records), booking agent and concert promotion. Releases 3 singles and 1 LP/year. Works with musicians/artists and songwriters on contract; musicians on contract for in-house studio work. Pays 5-7% royalty to artists on contract. Pays compulsory rate to publisher per song on record.
How to Contact: Write first to obtain permission to submit. Prefers cassette (or VHS videocassette) with 3-4 songs and lead sheet. "Send good quality studio cassette." Does not return unsolicited material. Reports in 6 weeks.
Music: Contemporary Christian, pop and country. Released "Just A Young Man" and "A Child is Born" (both by Lanny C. Swaim), recorded by Latter Rain; and "Pete's Place" (by D. Page/G. Dixon/L. Swaim), recorded by Gary Dixon, all singles on Sand Dollar Records.

SCENE PRODUCTIONS, Box 1243, Beckley WV 25802. (304)252-4836. President/Producer: Richard L. Petry; Marketing Director: Mac Thompson. Labels include Rising Sun and Country Road Records. Record company, record producer and music publisher (Purple Haze Music/BMI). Member of AFM. Releases 1-2 singles and 1-2 LPs/year. Works with musicians/artists and songwriters on contract. Pays 4-5% minimum royalty to artists on contract; standard royalty to songwriters on contract; compulsory rate to publishers for each record sold. Charges "initial costs, which are conditionally paid back to artist."
How to Contact: Write first about your interest (recording only). Prefers cassette with 2-5 songs and

lyric sheet. Prefers studio produced demos. SASE. Reports in 1 month.
Music: Mostly country, top 40, R&B/crossover and pop/rock; also MOR, light and commercial rock. Released "For a Song," and "Since You've Gone," by Steve Willoughby (contemporary country singles); and "Modern Day Woman," by Chris Alaimo (hi-tech pop singles). Other artist includes Dave Runion.
Tips: "Songs should be well thought-out and well constructed with good demo."

SCP RECORDS, Division of the Sound Column Companies, 160 Westgate Fine Arts Center, 342 W. 2nd South, Salt Lake City UT 84101. (801)355-5327. A&R Professional Manager: Clive Romney. Labels include Big Sky Records. Record company, record producer and music publisher (Ronarte Publications/ASCAP, Mountain Green Music/BMI and Macanudo Music/SESAC). Member CMA. Releases 3 singles and 4 LPs/year. Works with artists and songwriters on contract; musicians on salary for in-house studio work. Pays negotiable royalty to artists on contract; statutory rate to publishers for each record sold.
How to Contact: Write first. Prefers cassette with 1-3 songs. SASE. "Demand varies—we favor our staff writers, and most artists have their own material. Query first as to demand." Reports as soon as possible. "Once in awhile we get seriously behind—but you'll eventually be heard. These days we pay increasing attention to the quality of the demo, including production values."
Music: Mostly top 40/pop and country; also adult contemporary. Released *Someone's Watching You*, by Dave Beckstrand (cassette pop album); *Songs for Mother*, by The Robinsons (gospel cassette); and *The Best is Yet to Be*, by Dan Clark (pop cassette).

*****SEASIDE RECORDS**, 100 Labon St., Tabor City NC 28463. (919)653-2546. Owner: Elson H. Stevens. Labels include SeaSide and JCB. Record company, music publisher and record producer. Releases 10 singles and 5 LPs/year. Works with musicians/artists and songwriters on contract; musicians on salary for in-house studio work. Pays 3-5% royalty to artists on contract; compulsory rate to publisher per song on record.
How to Contact: Write or call first to obtain permission to submit. Prefers cassette with 3 songs and lyric or lead sheet. SASE. Reports in 1 month.
Music: Mostly country, rock and gospel; also "beach music." Released "Midnight Cafe" (by Debbie Watson), recorded by Debbie Lanier; and "Moving On" (by M. Todd), recorded by Silver Stor, both on Sea Side Records; and "Miss Teaser", written and recorded by J.C. Batchelor on JCB Records (all singles). Other artists include Glen Todd, Sehila Gore and Gayle Mathies.

SEEDS RECORDS, Box 20814, Oklahoma City, OK 73156. (405)755-0315. Labels include Homa. Record company, record producer and music publisher (Okisher Publishing/BMI). Releases 8-12 singles and 4-6 LPs/year. Works with artists and songwriters on contract. Pays 10% royalty to artists on contract; statutory rate to publishers for each record sold.
How to Contact: Prefers cassette (or videocassette) with 1-3 songs and lyric sheet. Does not return unsolicited material. Reports in 1 month.
Music: Mostly blues, country and ballads; also easy listening, jazz, MOR, R&B and soul. Released *Hooking*, by Burton Band (disco LP); *New Connection*, by Janjo (rock LP); and *Arkansas River Bottom Woman*, by Charley Shaw (country LP).

SELECTION-B SHARP, 42 Avenue Clays, Brussels 1030 Belgium. 02/241-41-86. Director: P. Pletinckx. Record company and music publisher (B. Sharp Selection). Releases 3 LPs/year. Works with musicians/artists and songwriters on contract; musicians on salary for in-house studio work. Pays varying royalty to artists on contract.
How to Contact: Prefers cassette. Does not return unsolicited material. Reports in 2 weeks.
Music: Jazz, rock and instrumental. Released *Jo Carlier*, *Stephane Martini*, and *Toots Thielemans* (all instrumental LPs) on Selection Records. Other artists include Guy Cabay, Jacques Siroul and Albert Delchambre.

*****SHANACHIE RECORDS**, Dalebrook Park, Hohokus NJ 19144. (201)445-5561. Labels include Greensleeves—USA, Message, Ogham and Meadow Lark. Releases 5 singles and 25 LPs/year. Works with musicians/artists on contract. Pays compulsory rate to publisher per song on record.
How to Contact: Prefers cassette. SASE. Reports in 1 month.
Music: R&B, reggae and pop. Released *Music for Silences to Come* written and recorded by Dan Ar Bras on Shanachie (LP); *We've Come a Long Way*, written and recorded by Makem and Clancy on Shanachie Records (LP); and *Until* (by Willie Lindo), recorded by Nadine Sutherland on Meadowlark Records (LP). Other artists incude Rita Marley, Judy Mowatt, Steeleye Span, Yellowan, Augusons Pablo and The Chieftains.

SHEPERD RECORDS, 2307 N. Washington Ave., Scranton PA 18509. (717)347-7395. A&R: Fran Grogan. Record company. Releases 1-3 singles/year and 1 LP year. Works with musicians/artists and songwriters on contract; musicians on salary for in-house studio work. Works with composers and lyricists; teams collaborators.
How to Contact: Prefers cassette with 1-2 songs. Does not return unsolicited material. Reports in 6 weeks.
Music: Mostly rock and pop. Released "Talkin' Bout Love," by Monroe (pop single); and *Encounter*, by McGlynn (pop LP).

*SHOTGUN MUSIC CORP., 1242 Colborne St. E., Brantford, Ontario N3T 5L4 Canada. President: Len Wilde. Labels include Shotgun Records, Empire Records, Listen Records and Gator Records. Record company, music publisher (Like Always/West Star Music), record producer and recording studio. Releases 25 singles and 12 LPs/year. Works with musicians/artists on contract. Pays compulsory rate to publisher per song on record.
How to Contact: Prefers cassette with 3 songs and lyric or lead sheet. SAE and IRC. Reports in 1 month.
Music: Mostly pop, country and gospel; also rock. Released "Mendin' My Heart" written and recorded by Eric McMillan on Shotgun Records (country single); *One Dreamer, One Redeemer*, written and recorded by Don Sommerville on Listen Records (gospel LP); and "Total Love Devotion" (by Charles Cozens), recorded by Barbara Redpath Empire Records (pop single). Other artists include Danny Thompson, Linda Lee, Dale Page, Ron Martin, Albi and Whisky Hollow.

SIRR RODD RECORD & PUBLISHING CO., Box 58116, Philadelphia PA 19102-8116. President: Rodney J. Keitt. Record company, music publisher and record producer. Works with artist on contract. Pays 5-10% royalty to artists on contract; statutory rate to publishers for each record sold.
How to Contact: Prefers cassette (or videocassette) with 3-5 songs and lyric sheet. SASE. Reports in 1 month.
Music: Top 40/pop, gospel and jazz. Released "The Essence of Love," "West Oak Lane Jam," and "Ghetto Jazz," all by R.J. Keitt.

*SKIFAN H/F, Borgartun 24, Reykjavik 105 Iceland. (354)-1-29544. Managing Director: Jon Olafsson. Record company. Releases 10 LPs/year. Works with musicians/artists on contract.
How to Contact: Prefers cassette. SAE and IRC. Reports in 2 weeks.
Music: Pop and rock. Released *STRAX*, recorded by Strax and *Bo Halldors*, recorded by Bo Halldors both LPs on Skifan Records.

SLASH RECORDS, Box 48888, Los Angeles CA 90048. (213)937-4660. Contact: A&R Director. Labels include Slash and Warner. Record company and music publisher. Releases 5 singles and 6-10 LPs/year. Works with artists on contract. Pays negotiable royalty to artists on contract; statutory rate to publishers for each record sold.
How to Contact: Write first and obtain permission to submit. Prefers cassette with 3-5 songs. Does not return unsolicited material. Reports in 1 month.
Music: Alternative rock. Released "Hallowed Ground," by The Violent Femmes; and "Long Gone Dead," by Rank & File.

SOCIETE SONODISC, 85 Rue Fondary, Paris 75015 France. (1)45 77 30 34. Manager: Mr. Michael David. Labels include Africa Oumba, Alegre, Ararad, Cotique, Debs International, Egrem/Areito, Esperance, Fania, GD Productions, Gema, Genidia, Kouma, LYS Records, Oceane Productions, Ozileka, Piros, Royal, Seeco, SLD, Sonafric, Songhoi Records, Tico, Tropical, Vacances, Vaya, Voice of Stars and WS Latino. Record company. Releases 50 LPs/year.
How to Contact: Prefers cassette. SAE and IRC. Reports in 1 month.
Music: African, West Indian and Salsa Music. Released *Chefo Mae Mae*, written and recorded by Kaba Mane on Esperance Records (LP); *Hafi Deo*, written and recorded by Tabu Ley on Genidia Records (LP); and *Keyna* written and recorded by M'bila Bel on Genidia Records (LP). Other artists include Toto Guillaume, Kassav and Ngalle Jojo.

SONIC WAVE RECORDS, Box 256577, Chicago IL 60625. (312)764-1144. President: Tom Petreli. Record company. Releases 5-10 singles and 2-5 LPs/year. Works with artists on contract. Pays statutory rate.
How to Contact: Prefers cassette (or videocassette) with 2-4 songs and lyric sheet. SASE. Reports in 1 month.
Music: New wave. Released "80's," by Understrain (new wave single and LP).

*SOUND CEREMONY, 28 South Villas NW, London NW1 9BT England. (01)405-9883 or (01)485-2240. Director: Ron Warren Ganderton. Labels include Celestial Sound, QRecords and Centridge. Record company, music publisher and record producer. Works with musicians/artists and songwriters on contract; musicians on salary for in-house studio work.
How to Contact: Prefers cassette and lryic sheet. Reports in 3 weeks. Does not return unsolicited material.
Music: Mostly rock, pop and country; also jazz and soul. Released "Giggle Amidst the Tears" (by RW Ganderton), recorded by Sound Ceremony on Centridge Records (single); *Precious as England* and *Guitar Star* (both by RW Ganderton), recorded by Sound Ceremony, both LPs on Sound Ceremony Records. Other artists include Quasar, Carole Boyce and Popinjays.

SOUND IMAGE RECORDS, 6556 Wilkinson, North Hollywood CA 91606. (818)762-8881. President: Martin J. Eberhardt. Vice President Sales & Studio Manager: Chuck Kopp. Vice President and General Manager: David Chatfield. Labels include Sound Image and Harmony. Record company, record producer, music publisher (Sound Image Publishing), 24 track recording studio and video company. Member NARAS. Releases 8 singles and 4 LPs/year. Works with artists and songwriters on contract; musicians on salary for in-house studio work. Pays 5-12% royalty to artists; statutory rate to publishers for each record sold.
How to Contact: Prefers cassette with 3-6 songs and lyric sheet. Include photo and bio. SASE. Prefers studio produced demos. Reports in 60 days.
Music: Mostly rock/top 40, AOR and R&B; also dance oriented, and techno-pop. Released "Good Woman's Love," by Mark Steed (country LP/single); "Oh Marie," and "Rush in the Night," by Alp (rock LPs/singles).

*SOUND MASTERS, 9717 Jensen Dr., Houston TX 77093. (713)695-3648. Producer: A.V. Mittelstedt. Labels include Cherry Record and A.V. Records. Record company, music publisher (Publicare) and record producer. Releases 100 singles and 20 LPs/year. Works with musicians/artists and songwriters on contract; musicians on salary for in-house studio work.
How to Contact: Prefers cassette. SASE. Reports in 2 months.
Music: Mostly country, gospel and crossover; also MOR and rock.

*SOUNDS OF CONNECTICUT, Box 897, Hartford CT 06120. (203)522-2371. A&R Head: Ms. "Bottles" Polite. Labels include S.O.C., Blue Wave and L.U.V. Record company. Releases 4-12 singles and 13 LPs/year. Works with musicians/artists and songwriters on contract. Pays 5-12% royalty to artists on contract. Pays compulsory rate to publisher per song on record.
How to Contact: Prefers cassette (or VHS videocassette) with 4-6 songs and lyric or lead sheet. SASE. Reports in 6 weeks.
Music: Mostly funk, R&B and soul; also gospel, jazz and light rock. Released "Bite It" (by Herb Superb), recorded by Drum (Rap); "Shoot Your Best Shot" (by Silver Sargent), recorded by Carol (dance); and "Merci-Ba-Coup" (by Silver Sargent), recorded by Scarph (ballad), all on S.O.C. Records. Other artists include Native American, Red Rappen Hood, Barbara Fowler, Angie Champaigne, Toni Harrington and Kimberlee.

SOUNDS OF WINCHESTER, Rt. 2, Box 116-H, Berkeley Springs, WV 25411. Contact: Jim or Bertha McCoy. Labels include Alear, Winchester and Real McCoy Records. Record company, music publisher (Jim McCoy Music, Alear Music and New Edition Music/BMI) and recording studio. Releases 20 singles and 10 LPs/year. Works with artists and songwriters on contract; musicians on salary for in-house studio work. Pays 2% royalty to artists and songwriters on contract; statutory rate to publishers for each record sold.
How to Contact: Arrange personal interview. Prefers 7½ ips reel-to-reel with 4-12 songs. Does not return unsolicited material. Reports in 1 month.
Music: Bluegrass, country, country rock, gospel, and top 40/pop. Released "One More Time," by Earl Howard (country single); *Thank You Jesus*, by Jubilee Travelers (gospel LP); and "String Along," by Dave Elliott (country single). Other artists include Jim McCoy, Carroll County Ramblers and Alvin Kesner.

THE SOURCE UNLTD., 331 E. 9th St., New York NY 10003. (312)473-7833. Vice-President: S. Mollica. Record company. Releases 2 EPs/year. Works with musicians on salary for in-house studio work.
How to Contact: Submit demo tape. SASE.
Music: Acoustic-oriented, modern folk music. Released "The American Way," and *Music from the Street*, written and recorded by Santo (ep).

*SOUTHERN TRACKS RECORDS, 3051 Clairmont Rd. NE, Atlanta GA 30329. (404)325-0832. Record company and record producer. Releases 15 singles and 2 LPs/year. Works with musicians/artists

and songwriters on contract. Pays average of 5% royalty to artists on contract.
How to Contact: Prefers cassette with 3 unpublished songs and lyric sheet. Does not return unsolicited material.
Music: Interested in all types of music. Released "Burns Like a Rocket," recorded by Billy Joe Royal; "We Always Agree on Love," recorded by Atlanta; and "Sheet Music," recorded by Bill Anderson, all on Southern Tracks Records. Other artists include Bertie Higgins, Sammy Johns and Jimmy Ellis.

PHIL SPECTOR INTERNATIONAL AND WARNER/SPECTOR RECORDS INC., Box 69529, Los Angeles CA 90069. (818)846-9900. Labels include Philles Records Inc. Record company, music publisher (Mother Bertha Music Inc. and Back to Mono Music Inc.) and record producer (Phil Spector Productions). Releases varying number of singles/year. Pays varying royalty to artists on contract.
How to Contact: "Company is not accepting or reviewing any new material or artists. Any unsolicited material or correspondence will not be returned."

SPHEMUSATIONS, 12 Northfield Rd., Onehouse, Stowmarket Suffolk 1P14 3HF England. Contact: General Manager. Record company and music publisher. Releases 12 LPs/year. Works with musicians/artists and songwriters on contract. Pays 10% royalty to artists on contract.
How to Contact: Write first and obtain permission to submit; write to arrange personal interview. Prefers cassette. SAE and IRC. Reports in 3 months.
Music: Mostly country, blues and jazz; also "serious modern." Released *Music For Mime*, recorded by Phoenix Ensemble Duo Cantare, B.B.C. Symphony Orchestra on Sphemusations; *Little Boy Dances*, recorded by James Butt on Sphemusical; and *Magic of Harp & Voice*, all LPs. Other artists include Dartington Quartet, Woodbridge Quartet and Andreé Back.

SPRING RECORDS, 161 W. 54th St., New York NY 10019. (212)581-5398. A&R Director: Jules Rifkind. Record company. Works with artists and songwriters on contract; musicians on salary for in-house studio work.
How to Contact: Prefers master demo and lyric sheet.
Music: Dance and R&B. Released "He's Number One," by Fantasy (R&B/dance); and "You Needed Me," by Millie Jackson and Isaac Hayes (R&B/ballad).

STARBORN RECORDS, Box 2950, Hollywood CA 90078. Producer: Brian Ross. Record company; record producer; music publisher (Brian Ross Music/BMI, Thrush Music/BMI, IMC Music/ASCAP, Ian Anothony Ross Music, and New High Music /ASCAP); and worldwide record promotion, distribution, marketing and merchandising firm. Member AFM, AFTRA, AIMP, CCC, NARAS and NARM. Releases 35 singles and 25 LPs/year. Works with musican/artists and songwriters on contract; musicians on salary for in-house studio work. Pays 50% "of all money earned by Starborn Records to artists and songwriters on contract"; compulsory rate to publishers for each record sold.
How to Contact: Prefers cassette (or ½" VHS videocassette) with 2-4 songs and lyric sheet. "Print your name and address clearly on tape box *and* cassette. Include photo and short biography." SASE. Does not assume responsibility for materials damaged or lost in the mail. Reports in 1 week.
Music: Mostly new wave, technopop and top 40/pop contemporary "with great hooks and good melodies and chord changes;" also all other types. Released "We are the World" (by Michael Jackson/Lionel Richie), recorded by Children of the World; "I'm Waiting For You," recorded by Lane Powers; and "Talk, Talk" (by Bonni Well), recorded by Kongress, all singles on Starborn Records. Other artists include Invisible Ink, The Music Machine, Matter, Will Teague, Joey G., Didi Anthony, Barbara Smith Reed and Jamtrack.
Tips: "This international record label specializes in releasing masters from foreign countries. Currently accepting finished masters for consideration as well as new song material. Starborn Records maintains licensing operations in over 35 countries outside of North America. Will give feedback as soon as possible, no calls please. Submit your product in 'easy-open' envelopes, do not use staples on your packages. Please enclose photo and short biography of yourself, your musical background, education, credits (if any) and be clear as to what you are looking for, i.e., a publishing deal, a record contract, both, or work as a writer in television and motion pictures."

STARCREST PRODUCTIONS, INC., 209 Circle Hills Dr., Grand Forks ND 58201. (701)772-6831. President: George J. Hastings. Labels include Meadowlark and Minn-Dak Records. Record company, management firm and booking agency. Releases 2-6 singles and 1-2 LPs/year. Works with artists and songwriters on contract. Payment negotiable to artists on contract; statutory rate to publishers for each record sold.
How to Contact: Write first. Prefers cassette with 1-6 songs and lead sheet. SASE. Reports in 1 month.
Music: Country and top 40/pop. Released "A Good Yellow Rose," by Gene Wylos (country single);

and "Holding Back Teardrops" and "Gypsy I Am," by Mary Joyce (country singles).

STARGARD RECORDS, Box 138, Boston MA 02101. (617)296-3327. Artist Relations: Anthony Greenaway. Labels include Oak Groove Records. Record company. Releases 12 singles and 2 LPs/year. Works with songwriters on contract; musicians on salary for in-house studio work. Pays 6-8% royalty to artists on contract; compulsory rate to publisher per song on record..
How to Contact: Write first to arrange personal interview. Prefers cassette (or VHS videocassette) and lyric and lead sheet. SASE. Reports in 2 months. "Sending bio along with picture or glossies is appreciated but not necessary."
Music: Mostly R&B, dance/disco and pop; also reggae and jazz. Released "Pipe Dreaming," and "Separate," (by Troy DeVoe), recorded by Tow Zone on Stargard Records (singles); and "Run Me Down," (by Joseph Williams), recorded by Tiger Brown on Stargard Records (single). Other artists include Down Time and Al Wright.

STARGEM RECORDS, INC., 43 Music Square E., Nashville TN 37203. (615)244-1025. President and A&R Director: Wayne Hodge. Record company, record producer and music publisher (Newwriters Music/BMI, Timestar Music/ASCAP and Kristal International/SESAC). Works with artists and songwriters on contract; musicians on salary for in-house studio work.
How to Contact: Write first. Prefers cassette with 1-4 songs and lyric sheet. "Have clear recording and use new tape." SASE.
Music: Mostly gospel (all styles); also country, contemporary and MOR.

*STARLITE RECORDS, 3 Taloma Ave., Lurnea NSW 2170 Australia. (02)607-7088. Vice President: Suzanne Aufderheide. Labels include Starlite, Spotlite and Leedon. Record company, music publisher (Starlite, Leepro), record producer (Spotlite Promotions), and record promoter (US and Australia). Releases 2-20 singles and 4-10 LPs/year. Works with musicians/artists and songwriters on contract; musicians on salary for in-house studio work. Pays negotiable royalty to artists on contract. Pays negotiable rate to publisher per song on record.
How to Contact: Prefers cassette (or Beta videocassette). SAE and IRC. Reports in 3 months.
Music: Mostly pop, rock and country; also gospel and contemporary Christian. Released *Dreamin'* (by Michael Turner), recorded by MDLT (LP); *Dream In You Life*, written and recorded by Tony Vogliano (LP); and "I'm Holding" (byDavid Rix), recorded by Lonnie Lee (single), all on Starlite Records.

STARTIME MUSIC, Box 643, LaQuinta CA 92253. (619)564-4823. President: Fred Rice. Labels include Hook, Yo-Yo, Nova, Western Americana (documentary). Record company and music publisher. ASCAP. Releases "as many potential hits as we can find." Pays 5-10% royalty. Pays compulsory rate to publisher per song on record.
How to Contact: Prefers cassette with 1-2 songs and lyric sheet. SASE. Reports in 6 weeks.
Music: Mostly novelty, country and top 40/pop; also soul and comedy. Released "Tender Love" and "Straight from the Heart" (by Carl Whitener/Jim Schwanke) and "Lay it on Me" (by Carl Whitener) all recorded by Johnny Porche on Yo-Yo Records (all singles). Other artists include Rob Carter.
Tips: "Don't write a song, write a record! Think of the complete record title—intro, the hook, tempo, beat, words, music, arrangement, base track,and lastly the market timing."

STARWEST RECORDS, 1335 14th, Longview WA 98632. (206)423-9085. Owner: Michael Poe. Record company and music publisher. Releases 6 singles and 2 LPs/year. Works with musicians/artists and songwriters on contract.
How to Contact: Prefers cassette. SASE.
Music: Mostly rock, blues and country. Released *Love You So Much*, written and recorded by Dreamer (LP and single); "Rough Cut" (by F. Harris), recorded by Rough Cut (single); and "Drivin Hard" (by S. Jasen), recorded by Poker (single), all on Starwest Records.

STATUE RECORDS, 2810 McBain St., Redondo Beach CA 90278. A&R Director: Lincoln M. Damerst. Record company. Releases 5-10 singles and 5-10 LPs/year. Works with musicians/artists and songwriters on contract. Pays 1-10% or negotiable royalty to artists on contract.
How to Contact: Prefers (in order of preference) "high quality" cassette or 7 or 15 ips reel-to-reel with 3-5 songs and lyric sheet. Accepts unsolicited material. Reports in 1 month. "Please include glossy photo(s) if you are a group looking for a recording deal."
Music: Mostly "up-tempo rock, with *strong* hooks and new wave." Released *Last Chance*, by England (rock LP); *Parity Error*, by Blue Network (new wave LP); and "Big Mac Attack," by Krakatoa (metal single).

STERLING SILVER ENT., GRP., INC., (formerly Success Records Int. Inc.), Box 601473, N. Miami Beach FL 33160. (305)949-4277. President: Steven A. Silvers. Labels include T'Som and Success Records Int., Inc. Record company and music publisher (Silver Touch Publishing Co./BMI and Who Wrote That Music/BMI). Releases 3-5 singles and 1-2 LPs/year. Works with artists and songwriters. "Prefers self contained acts." Pays 6-10% royalty to artists on contract. Pays compulsory rate to publisher per song on record.

How to Contact: Prefers cassette (or VHS videocassette) with 3-5 songs. SASE. Reports in 6 weeks. Songs "must be on high quality tapes and be produced with as high of a professional quality as possible."

Music: Mostly R&B and crossover; also top 40 pop. Released *The Artist* (R&B LP), "The Girl is Cheating While She's Wearing My Ring" (R&B/pop rock single) and "You" (R&B funk dance single) all written and recorded by Michael Sterling on New Records. Other artists include Formula VI and Cool Love Brothers.

STINSON RECORDS, Box 3415, Granada Hills CA 91344. (818)709-3640. President: Jack M. Kall. Record company (JMK/ASCAP). Releases 4 LPs/year. Works with artists and songwriters on contract. Pays negotiable royalty to artists on contract; statutory rate to publishers for each record sold.

How to Contact: Prefers reel-to-reel or cassette with 1-3 songs. Does not return unsolicited material. Reports in 1 month.

Music: Bluegrass, folk, and jazz.

*STRIPED HORSE RECORDS, INC., 1040 N. Las Palmas, Los Angeles CA 90038. (213)461-8631. Chairman: Carlo Nasi. President: Barney Ales. Record company, music publisher (Striped Horse Music, Inc.) and record producer (Zebra Discorde Music). Releases 3-5 singles and 3-5 LPs/year.

How to Contact: Write first and obtain permission to submit. Prefers cassette with 3-4 songs and lyric sheet. Does not return unsolicited material. Reports in 1 month.

Music: Mostly pop, R&B and dance; also rock. Released *Red Light* (by Veitch/Winding), recorded by Patty Brard (dance LP); "Living for the City" (by S. Wonder), recorded by Ike & Tina Turner (pop single); and "Golden Empire" (by Ike Turner), recorded by Ike & Tina Turner (R&B pop LP) all on Striped Horse Records. Other artist includes De Barge.

STUDIO 7 RECORDS, 16591 County Home Rd., Marysville OH 43040. (513)644-8295. President: Doug Faiella. Labels include Seven O'Clock Rock and Seventh Heaven. Record company, music publisher (Doug Faiella Publishing/BMI), record producer (Doug Faiella Productions) and recording studio. Releases 15 singles and 6 LPs/year. Works with musicians/artists and songwriters on contract; musicians on salary for in-house studio work. Pays 10% royalty to artists on contract.

How to Contact: Prefers cassette or 7½ ips reel-to-reel with 1-10 songs and lyric sheet. Reports in 2 months. "Send along with the demo a list of bookings and an 8x10 glossy photo."

Music: Mostly contemporary country, rock and gospel; also traditional country/bluegrass, jazz and blues.

STUDIOEAST RECORDING, INC., 5457 Monroe St., Charlotte NC 28212. (704)536-0424. Co-Owners: Tim Eaton and Don Lawrence. Labels include Pyramid Records, Metro Records, Sandblast Records, Sandman, East Coast Records and Peach. Record company, music publisher (Eastwood Publishing) and record producer. Estab. 1985. Releases 50 singles and 20 LPs/year. Works with musicians/artists and songwriters on contract; musicians on salary for in-house studio work. Pays standard royalty to artists on contract.

How to Contact: Prefers cassette 15 ips reel-to-reel (or VHS videocassette) with any number of songs. Does not return unsolicited material. Reports in 2 months. "If we feel material is unusable we will not contact artist. We will, however, keep material on file for possible future use."

Music: Mostly top 40/rock, country and jazz; also blues and gospel. Released "Behind Your Lies" (by Rick Sanders), recorded by Entertainers on RCA Records (single/LP); "I'll Always Love You" (by G. Smith/B. Smith), recorded by Poor Souls on Surfside Records (single); and "Alway Be My Girl" (by Chris Keaton), recorded by Band of Oz on Band of Oz Records (single). Other artists include Montuno Jazz, Barry Duke, Fat Jack Band, John Thompson, Breeze Band and Tim Smith.

SUGAR HILL RECORDS, 96 West St., Englewood NJ 07631. (201)569-5170. Contact: A&R Department. Record company. Works with musicians/artists and songwriters on contract; musicians on salary for in-house studio work.

How to Contact: Prefers cassette. SASE. Reports in 1 month.

Music: Mostly R&B, pop and jazz; also gospel, rock and rap. Released "Funk it up 85," recorded by Sequence; "Ain't That Much Love in the World," recorded by The Giding; and "I Can Make You Feel It," recorded by Sugar Hill Gang, all on Sugar Hill Records.

SUN INTERNATIONAL CORP., 3106 Belmont Blvd., Nashville TN 37212. (615)385-1960. Professional Manager: Shelby Singleton. Labels include Plantation Records and SSS International Records.

Record company, record producer and music publisher (Shelby Singleton Music, Prize Music). Member RIAA and NARAS. Releases 30 singles and 25 LPs/year. Works with artists and songwriters on contract. Pays 8-15% royalty to artists on contract; statutory rate to publishers for each record sold.
How to Contact: Prefers cassette with 1-3 songs and lyric sheet. SASE. Reports in 1 month.
Music: Country, easy listening, MOR, easy rock and top 40/pop. Artists include Rita Remington, Patti Page, Charlie Walker, Dave Dudley and Jimmy C. Newman.
Tips: "Present professional demo along with lyrics and explanation of career-goals. Artists should have a working band."

SUNNY DAY PRODUCTIONS, 1931 SE Morrison, Portland OR 97214. (800)547-5547 or (503)238-4525 in Oregon. President: Russell E. Gorsline. Labels include Cricket, New Day and Rexius. Record company, record producer and music publisher (Klickitat Music). Releases 4-8 singles and 2-5 LPs/year. Works with artists and songwriters on contract. Pays negotiable royalty to artists on contract; statutory rate to publishers for each record sold.
How to Contact: Write or call first. Prefers cassette with 2-5 songs and lyric sheet. SASE. Reports in 2 weeks.
Music: Mostly contemporary Christian, pop, MOR and jazz; also choral, church/religious and gospel.

SUN-RAY RECORDS, 1662 Wyatt Pkwy., Lexington KY 40505. (606)254-7474. President: James T. Price. Labels include Sun-Ray and Sky-Vue Records. Record company and music publisher (Jimmy Price Music Publisher/BMI). Releases 9 singles/year. Works with songwriters on contract; musicians on salary for in-house studio work. Pays statutory rate to publishers for each record sold.
How to Contact: Prefers 7½ ips reel-to-reel with 2-6 songs and lead sheet. SASE. Reports in 3 weeks.
Music: Bluegrass (sacred or country), church/religious, country and gospel. Released "I Don't Want to Fool Around," (by Dave Gibson), recorded by Bud Chowning; "Roadblock," by Bud Chowning; "Steel Guitar Man," by Don Bowman; and "Hey Nashville," by Shirley Drovin.
Tips: "We need songs with a good story along with rhyme and meter."

*SUNRISE RECORDS, LTD., 77-4 Chungshan North Rd., Sec, 2, Taipei 10419 Taiwan. (02)551-8085. Managing Director: Mrs. Pearl Lin. Record company, licensee, record importer and recording studio. Releases 12 LPs/year. Works with musicians/artists on contract; musicians on salary for in-house studio work. Pays 5-10% royalty to artists on contract. Pays compulsory rate to publisher per song on record.
How to Contact: Write or call first and obtain permission to submit. Prefers cassette and lyric sheet. Does not return unsolicited material. Reports in 3 weeks.
Music: Mostly pop, easy listening and light classical; also folk music. Released "Shoreless Port" (by Hsie Ming-chuan), recorded by Johnny Yin; "Love Games (by Lin Hsio-yuan), recorded by Johnny Yi; and "Inseparable Friends" (by Mai Tz), recorded by Debbie Huang, all on Sunrise Records. Other artist includes Lu Chen.

SUNSET RECORDS INC., 1577 Redwood Dr., Harvey LA 70058. (504)367-8501. President: George Leger. Labels include Sunburst Records. Record company, record producer, and music publisher (Country Legs Music and Golden Sunburst Music). Member CMA. Releases 5 singles/year. Works with artists and songwriters on contract. Works with lyricists and teams collaborators. Pays 7% royalty to artists on contract.
How to Contact: Prefers clean, good quality cassette with 3-5 songs and lyric and lead sheets. "Artists—send tape showing vocal abilities." SASE. Reports in 2 months.
Music: Mostly country; also gospel, progressive country, R&B, and seasonal (Christmas, Mother's Day, etc.). Released "Broken Homes," by Sonny Tears (country single); and "I Don't Care," by Larry Maynard (country single).
Tips: "Write one good, smoothly flowing song rather than 10 songs that aren't."

SUNSHINE RECORDS, 800 S. 4th St., Philadelphia PA 19147. (215)755-7000. Director of A&R: Walter Kahn. Labels include Sunshine, Moonshine and Lattitude. Record company and music publisher (Scully/Orange Bear Music Co.). Releases 15 singles and 3 LPs/year. Works with musicians/artists on contract. Pays statutory rate to publishers for each record sold.
How to Contact: Prefers cassette (or VHS videocassette) with 3-4 songs and lyric sheet. SASE. "Include an 8x10 photo, if available."
Music: Mostly R&B/dance and pop; also rap and new wave. Released "I Saw Him Standing There," by Juliet (pop/dance single); and "I'm Rappin'," by David St. George (rap single).

SURESHOT RECORDS, Box 2236, Largo FL 33540. (813)595-5115. Contact: Alan Redstone. Record company and music publisher (Magic Message Music). Releases 1 single and 1 LP/year. Pays standard royalty. Works with songwriters on contract; musicians on salary for in-house studio work.

How to Contact: Prefers cassette and lyric sheet. SASE. Reports in 3 weeks.
Music: Mostly rock, country and adult contemporary; also pop and blues. Released "Cold Hands and Wet Feet," (country rock single), "Magic Message," (adult contemporary single), "I Didn't Mind," "This Time Around," and "Cars, Girls, Dreams" (rock/pop singles), all written and recorded by Alan Redstone on Sureshot Records.
Tips: "It's got to be good and it's got to be real."

SURPRIZE RECORDS, INC., 421 W. Ellet St., Philadelphia PA 19119. (215)276-8861 or 247-4317. President: Gilda C. Woods. Vice President: W. Lloyd Lucas. Record company, record producer and music publisher (In the Woods). Member ASCAP, BMI and SRS. Releases 6 singles and 3 LPs/year. Works with musicians/artists and songwriters on contract; musicians on salary for in-house studio work. Pays standard royalty to artists on contract; compulsory rate to publishers for each record sold.
How to Contact: Write first and obtain permission to submit. Prefers cassette with maximum of 3 songs and lyric or lead sheet. SASE. "Do not send certified mail." Reports in 1 month.
Music: Mostly ballads, R&B, dance-oriented and gospel and/or contemporary Christian; also pop rock and country pop—no rockabilly. Released "This Could Be the Night," by Karla Garrison (dance single); "Pledging My Love," by Bill Lucas (single); and "Shadow People," by Dave James (single). Other artists include Valkir, Tiujuana Rose, Encore, Mimi Lopez, Darryl Lucas and Richie Merritt.
Tips: "The artist should be upfront with company executives and other roster acts and also be dedicated to the business of making top quality commercial products."

SURVIVOR RECORDS, #323, 349 S. Lafayette Pk. Pl., Los Angeles CA 90057. (213)650-6800. Contact: A&R Director. Labels include Rough Diamond and Revelation. Record company, music publisher (Ten of Diamonds Music), record producer and talent development company. Works with musicians/artists and songwriters on contract; musicians on salary for in-house studio work.
How to Contact: Prefers cassette (or VHS videocassette) with maximum 3 songs and lyric sheet or lead sheet. SASE. Reports in 10 weeks.

SUSAN RECORDS, Box 4740, Nashville TN 37216. (615)865-4740. A&R Director: Russ Edwards. Labels include Denco Records. Record company and music publisher. Releases 2-20 singles and 1-5 LPs/year. Works with artists and songwriters on contract. Pays 6¢/record to artists on contract. Buys some material outright; payment varies.
How to Contact: Prefers 7½ ips reel-to-reel with 1-6 songs and lead sheet. SASE. Reports in 2 weeks.
Music: Blues, country, dance, easy listening, folk, gospel, jazz, MOR, rock, soul and top 40/pop.

*SUZY RECORDS, Gruska lo, Zagreb 41000 Yugoslavia. Phone: 0038-041-519-955. A&R: Ranko Antonic. Labels include Favorite. Record company and music publisher (Favorite Music). Releases 50 singles and 120 LPs/year. Works with musicians/artists and songwriters on contract. Pays 10-12% royalty to artists on contract. Pays compulsory rate to publisher per song on record.
How to Contact: Call first to arrange personal interview. Prefers cassette and lyric sheet. Does not return unsolicited material. Reports in 3 weeks.
Music: Mostly rock and pop; also country and instrumental. Released *Sonja* and *Gradske Cure* (by M. Drljaca), and *Jasmina* (byD. Novkovic), all on Suzy Records (all pop LPs). Other artists include ITD Band, Tuti Fruiti, Balkan Band, Senad and Limeni Bubanj.

T.C. RECORDS, 121 Meadowbrook Dr., Somerville NJ 08876. (201)359-5110. Vice President: Cynthia Rustia. Record company. Releases 24 singles and 6-8 LPs/year. Works with artists and songwriters on contract. Pays 5½-8½% royalty to artists on contract; compulsory rate to publishers for each record sold.
How to Contact: Write first and obtain permision to submit. Prefers cassette with maximum 2-5 songs and lead sheet. SASE. Reports in 1 month.
Music: Dance, soul, MOR and top 40/pop. Artist include Barry Miles (keyboardist/conductor for Robert Flack), G-Men, and Valerie Ford.

*TARGET RECORDS, Box 163, West Redding CT 06896. (203)438-5366. President: Paul Hotchkiss. Labels include Kastle Records. Record company, music publisher (Tutch Music/Blue Hill Music) and record producer (Red Kastle Prod.). Releases 5 singles and 2 LPs/year. Works with musicians/artists and songwriters on contract. Pays standard royalty to artists on contract; compulsory rate to publisher per song on record.
How to Contact: Write first and obtain permission to submit. Prefers cassette with 2 songs and lyric sheet. SASE. Reports in 3 weeks.
Music: Country and crossover. Released "Gilley Willie Waylon & Me" (by P. Hotchkiss), recorded by Ky King on Target Records (single); "Ease the Pain" written and recorded by F. Taylor on Kastel Re-

cords (single); and "Wrong Seems Right," written and recorded by W. Carter on Axbar Records (single). Other artists include Hutcher Bros., Fran Taylor, Malone & Hotch and Jimmy Hartley.

*TAURO, Koekoekstraat 62, Schelle 2621 Belgium. (03)888 43 67. Managing Director: Livia Verbrugge. Labels include Tauro, Livia, Proms and Diamond. Record company and music publisher. Releases 20 singles and 10 LPs/year. Works with musicians/artists and songwriters on contract; musicians on salary for in-house studio work.
How to Contact: Submit demo by mail. Prefers cassette and lyric sheet. Does not return unsolicited material. Reports in 1 month.
Music: MOR, classical and pop. Released "The Waltz" (by Van Echelpoel), recorded by Van Lucas on Polygram Records (single); *Night of the Proms*, recorded by various artists on Proms Records (LP); and "Letkiss," recorded by G. Jankins (single).

TELESON-AMERICA, 62 Fairfax St., Somerville MA 02144. (617)776-2146. Labels include Grand Orgue, Motette-Ursina and Solist. Record company. Releases 20-30 LPs/year. Works with artists on contract.
How to Contact: Write first. Prefers 7½ or 15 ips reel-to-reel. SASE. Reports in 4 months.
Music: Pipe organ and religious choral (classical). Artists include Pierre Labric, Marie-Andree Morisset-Balier, Heinz Bernhard Orlinski, Jean Langlais, Almut Rossler, Michel Morisset, Gunther Kaunzinger, Marie-Louise Jacquet-Langlais, Gaston Litaize, Hermann Harrassowitz, Johannes Ricken, Rosalinde Haas, Daniel Roth, Jean-Jacques Grunenwald and Paul Wisskirchen.

TEROCK RECORDS, Box 4740, Nashville TN 37216. (615)865-4740. Manager: S.D. Neal. Labels include Terock, Susan, Denco, Rock-A-Nash-A-Billy. Record company, record producer, and music publisher (Heavy Jamin' Music/ASCAP). "We also lease masters." Member ASCAP, BMI. Releases 4 singles and 3 LPs/year. Works with artists and songwriters on contract. Pays 5-8% royalty to artists on contract; standard royalty to songwriters on contract.
How to Contact: Prefers 7½ ips reel-to-reel or cassette with 3-6 songs and lyric sheet. SASE. Reports in 3 weeks.
Music: Mostly country and rockabilly; also bluegrass, blues, easy listening, folk, gospel, jazz, MOR, progressive, Spanish, R&B, rock, soul and top 40/pop. Released "That's Why I Love You," by Dixie Dee (country); "Born to Bum Around," by Curt Flemons (country); and "Big Heavy," by the Rhythm Rockers (rock).

TEXAS CRUDE, 5536 N. Lamar, Austin TX 78751. (512)440-1976. Manager: Jane Quisenberry. Labels include Harvest and Texas Crude. Record company (Texas Crude Publishing Inc.). Works with musicians on salary for in-house studio work. Pays varying royalty to artists on contract.
How to Contact: Submit demo tape by mail. Write or call first to arrange a personal interview. Prefers cassette with 1-3 songs and lyric sheet. SASE. Reports in 1 month.
Music: Mostly country, rock and gospel; also jazz, swing and pop/dance. Released *Living For a Song*, recorded by Roy Head on Texas Crude Records (LP); "Everythings Right," written and recorded by C.J. Parker and Jane Quisenberry on County Mounty Records (single); and "What About Tonight" (by Jane Quisenberry/Jamie Lee Bradford), recorded by Jane Quisenberry and Tommy Hill on Harvest Records (single). Other artists include Jimmy Mac, Lance Roberts, Tom Holden.

3 G'S INDUSTRIES, 5500 Troost, Kansas City MO 64110. (816)361-8455. General Manager: Eugene Gold. Labels include NMI, Cory, 3 G's and Chris C's Records. Record company, record producer and music publisher (Eugene Gold Music and Gid-Gad Music). Releases 8 singles and 6 LPs/year. Works with artists and songwriters on contract; musicians on salary for in-house studio work. Pays 4-6% royalty to artists on contract; statutory rate to publishers for each record sold.
How to Contact: Prefers cassette (or videocassette) with 4-8 songs and lyric sheet. SASE. Reports in 1 month.
Music: Mostly R&B and jazz; also church/religious, gospel and soul. Released *Baby We Can Make It* and *You Left Me at a Bad, Bad Time*, by Ronnie and Vicky (R&B EPs); and "Diamond Feather," by Bad News Band (R&B single). Other artists include Suspension, L. Washington, Thrust's, Jeff Lucas, James "Fuzzy" West, Cal Green and L.S. Movement Band.

TITAN INTERNATIONAL PRODUCTIONS, LTD., 185A, Newmarket Rd., Norwich, Norfolk, NR4 6AP, England. 44-0603-51139. Director: Peter Newbrook. Labels include Esquire, Starlite and Titan. Record company and music publisher (Esquire Music Co.). Releases 12 LPs/year. Works with artists on contract. Pays negotiable royalty to artists on contract; 6¼% to publishers for each record sold. Royalties paid to US songwriters and artists through US publishing or recording affiliate.
How to Contact: Write first. Prefers cassette. SAE and IRC. Reports in 1 month.

Music: Mostly jazz; also MOR. Artists include Cleo Laine, Teddy Wilson, John Dankworth, Mary Lou Williams, Stan Getz and Zoot Sims.

TNA RECORDS, Box 57, 10 George St., Wallingford CT 06492. (203)269-4465. A&R Director: Thomas Cavalier. Record company, record producer, music publisher (Rohm Music, QVQ Music, Linesider Music, BIG Music) and personal management. Releases 1-3 singles and 2-5 LPs/year. Works with artists and songwriters on contract. Pays 12-15% royalty to artists on contract; statutory rate to publishers for each record sold.
How to Contact: Prefers cassette (or videocassette) with 1-3 songs and lyric sheet. Include statement of goals and purposes. SASE. Reports in 2 months.
Music: Mostly rock, R&B and top 40/pop; also blues and dance.
Tips: "Artists and songwriters should have high code of ethics coupled with enthusiasm. Being in Northeast, NY area helps with communication in management and direction."

TOMMY BOY, 1747 1st Ave., New York NY 10128. (212)722-2211. A&R/Promotion Manager: Joseph Gardner. Labels include Body Rock. Record company, music publisher (T-Boy/T-Girl) and record producer. Releases 20-25 singles and 5-7 LPs/year. Works with musicians/artists on contract; musicians on salary for in-house studio work. Pays varying royalty to artists on contract.
How to Contact: Call first and obtain permission to submit. Prefers cassette with 1-3 songs and lyric sheet. SASE. "When submitting a demo, please do not call to see if we are going to use it. If we are going to, you will be the first to know. We accept calls on Wednesdays after 3:00 only."
Music: Mostly R&B/rap, soul and R&B/dance. "No pop." Released "Tender Love," by The Force M.D.'s (R&B); "One Way Love," by TKA (R&B/dance); and "Running," by Information Society (dance).

*TOP RECORDS, Gall. del Corso, 4 Milano 20122 Italy. (02)791141. Manager/Director: Guido Palma. Labels include United Colors Productions, Dingo Music, Telex Music and Record, KIWI Record, Smoking Record and Tapes. Record company and music publisher. Releases 10 singles and 7 LPs/year. Works with musicans/artists and songwriters on contract.
How to Contact: Prefers cassette (or videocassette) with 5 songs and lyric sheet. Does not return unsolicited material.
Music: Mostly pop and dance; also soundtracks. Released *Contrabbandieri di Musica* (by Goran Kuzminac); *Space Vampires* (by Henry Mancini); *Le Mie Follie* (by Sandro Speechia) recorded by Magnelli; and *Pipes and Strings of Scotland* (by Tommy Scott); all LPs on TOP Records. Other artists include Massimo Magnelli, Vanna Brosio, Lello, Stendardo, Francoise Hardy, Azzurra Disabato, Shirley Bassey and Fausto Billy.

*TORCHLITE RECORDS, Suite 119, 2170 W. Broadway, Anaheim CA 92804. (714)491-8546. Vice President, A&R: Harold Shmoduquet. Labels include Orange Records, Palace Hi-Fi Records and Beet Records. Record company, music publisher (Tracy Sands Music) and record producer (Gee Productions). Releases 7-12 singles and 2 LPs/year. Works with musicians/artists on contract. Pays 1-9% royalty to artists on contract; compulsory rate to publisher per song on record.
How to Contact: Prefers cassette with 3-4 songs and lyric sheet. Does not return unsolicited material. Reports in 6 weeks.
Music: Mostly "small, self-contained, guitar oriented trios, quartets, quintets that do love songs"; also ethnic music, especially East Indian. Released "The Comet" (by Robert Wahlsteen), recorded by Wahlsteen and Sands (New Age); "Pataki," written and recorded by Scarlett (New Age); and "Warriors of the Night" (by Tom Harris), recorded by Manhunter (country), all singles on Torchlite Records. Other artists include Vance Tucker, The Chills, Bob Chance, No Sweat, Jubal's Children and Cub Hayden.

TOTAL EXPERIENCE RECORDS, 6226 Yucca St., Hollywood CA 90028. (213)462-6585. Director of A&R: Maggie Williams. Record company. Releases 15-20 singles and 10-15 LPs/year. Works with musicians/artists and songwriters on contract; musicians on salary for in-house studio work. Pays standard royalty to songwriters; statuatory rate to publishers.
How to Contact: Prefers cassette with lyric and lead sheet. SASE. Reports ASAP. "Include phone number for faster reply."
Music: Mostly R&B, jazz and pop. Released "Guilty," written and recorded by Yarbrough & Peoples; "Going In Circles," written and recorded by GAP Band; and "Best Friends," written and recorded by ET all on Total. Other artists include Gabriella, Dorian, Mini Curry, Prime Time, Joe Stonestreet, and Pattie Howard.

TOUCHE RECORDS, Box 96, El Cerrito CA 94530. Executive Vice President: James Bronson, Jr. Record company, record producer (Mom and Pop Productions, Inc.) and music publisher (Toulouse Music

Co./BMI). Member AIMP. Releases 2 LPs/year. Works with artists and songwriters on contract; musicians on salary for in-house studio work. Pays compulsory rate to publishers per song on record.
How to Contact: Prefers cassette with 2-4 songs and lyric sheet. SASE. Reports in 1 month.
Music: Mostly jazz; also bluegrass, gospel, jazz, R&B and soul. Released *Bronson Blues* (by James Bronson), *Nigger Music* and *Touché Smiles* (by Smiley Winters), all recorded by Les Oublies du Jazz Ensemble on Touché Records (all LPs). Other artists include Hi Tide Harris.

TRAC RECORD CO., 170 N. Maple, Fresno CA 93702. (209)255-1717. Owner: Stan Anderson. Record company and music publisher (Sellwood Publishing/BMI). Releases 10-20 singles and 5 LPs/year. Works with musicians/artists and songwriters on contract. Pays negotiable royalty. Pays compulsory rate to publisher per song on record.
How to Contact: Prefers cassette (or VHS videocassette) with 2-4 songs and lyric sheet. SASE. Reports in 2 months.
Music: Country, top 40 and rock. Released "Consider it Sold" and "Polish Up My Buckle" (both by Thomas Richard Lewis), recorded by Buddy T. Lewis; and "Rodeo Man" (by Jerry Hobbs), recorded by Jessica James, all singles on Trac Records. Other artists include Gil Thomas and Jim Smith.

*TRACK RECORDS, 723 Lincoln Ave., Carbondale CO 81623. (303)963-3598. A&R Director: Patricia Lauren. Record company, music publisher (Lauren-Blick Music/BMI) and record producer (Producer: Kenneth Thomas). Releases 2 singles and 2 LPs/year. Works with songwriters on contract. Pays negotiable royalty.
How to Contact: Prefers cassette with 3-5 songs and lyric and lead sheet. SASE. Reports in 1 month.
Music: Contemporary rock, crossover country/pop, ballads and duets. Released *Patricia Lauren* and *Patricia Lauren II*, by Patricia Lauren, both on Track Records (both LPs).

TREND RECORDS, Box 201, Smyrna GA 30081. (404)432-2454. President: Tom Hodges. Labels include Trendsetter, Atlanta and Stepping Stone Records. Record company, music publisher, record producer and management firm. Releases 6-10 singles and 2-8 LPs/year. Works with artists on contract. Pays 5-7% royalty to artists on contract: standard royalty to songwriters on contract.
How to Contact: Prefers cassette with 3-6 songs and lead sheet. SASE. Reports in 3 weeks.
Music: Bluegrass, country, gospel, MOR, rock and soul. Released *Feet*, "I Stole the Flowers from Your Garden," and "All That Glitters Is Not Gold," by Jim Single (country); "Sugar Daddy," by Frank Brannon (country single); and "Kennesaw Get Your Guns," by Jim Moore. Other artists include Jo Anne Johnson.

TRIX RECORDS, INC., Drawer AB, Rosendale NY 12472. (914)687-9573. Contact: Peter B. Lowry. Labels include: Ghetto Farms Records. Record company, music publisher (Baby Tate Music Corp.) and record producer (Katward Ho Productions). Releases 1-2 LPs/year. Works with musicians/artists on contract. Pays standard royalty to artists on contract.
How to Contact: Prefers cassette. Does not return unsolicited material.
Music: Mostly blues and jazz; also folk. Released *Does 12*, by Robert Jr. Lockwood (blues LP); *Get Outta Town Man*, by Maurice Reedus-El (jazz LP); and *I've Been Around*, by David "Honeyboy" Edwards (blues LP) all on Trix Records. Other artists include Roy Dunn, Dan Del Santo, Frank Edwards, Eddie Kirkland, Homesick James, and John Cephas.

TRUE NORTH RECORDS, The Finkelstein Management Co. Ltd., Suite 302, 151 John St., Toronto, Ontario M5V 2T2 Canada. (416)596-8696. Contact: Jehanne Languedoc. Record company, management company, record producer, music publisher (Mummy Dust Music) and production company. Member CIRPA, CMPA, PROCAN, CAPAC. Releases approximately 18 singles and 6 LPs/year. Works with artists on contract. Pays negotiable royalty to artists on contract; negotiable rate to publishers for each record sold.
How to Contact: Call first and obtain permission to submit. Prefers cassette with 2-4 songs. Prefers studio produced demos. Include bio. Does not return unsolicited material. Reports in 1 month but tape will not be returned.
Music: Top 40/pop and CHR/AOR. Released "If I Had a Rocket Launcher," and "Lovers in a Dangerous Time," by Bruce Cockburn (pop singles); and "Never Did Like That Train," by Murray McLauchlan (country single). Other artists includes Rough Trade, Doug Cameron, Tony Kosinec, Johnny MacLead and Barney Bentall.

TRUSTY RECORDS, Rt. 1, Box 100, Nebo KY 42441. (502)249-3194. President: Elsie Childers. Record company and music publisher (Trusty Publications/BMI). Member NSAI, CMA. Releases 2-3 singles and 1 LP/year. Works with artists and songwriters on contract. Pays 2% royalty to artists on contract; statutory rate to publishers for each record sold.

Close-up

George Green
Songwriter

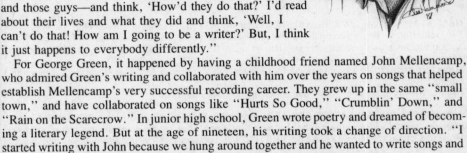

"I don't think you'll ever find a formula for becoming a writer. I searched for one in vain when I was young. I used to read about other writers—Fitzgerald, Hemingway and those guys—and think, 'How'd they do that?' I'd read about their lives and what they did and think, 'Well, I can't do that! How am I going to be a writer?' But, I think it just happens to everybody differently."

For George Green, it happened by having a childhood friend named John Mellencamp, who admired Green's writing and collaborated with him over the years on songs that helped establish Mellencamp's very successful recording career. They grew up in the same "small town," and have collaborated on songs like "Hurts So Good," "Crumblin' Down," and "Rain on the Scarecrow." In junior high school, Green wrote poetry and dreamed of becoming a literary legend. But at the age of nineteen, his writing took a change of direction. "I started writing with John because we hung around together and he wanted to write songs and he knew I wrote poems and stuff—so we kind of put the two together."

Even now Green takes a very literary approach to songwriting. "I read a lot," he says. "I love literature. I like to write songs that are real interesting short stories that rhyme. I try to tell a complete story with a beginning, a middle, and an end. I try to put myself in that person's place [the character in the song] and try to project how I would feel.

"Most of the things I write about are things I've gone through myself or ideas I get from people I know and the things they tell me. I kind of compose a little scenario in my head and try to make a lyric out of it. There's something ambiguous about telling stories, it's hard to describe that. Mostly I like to write about people who work, who have goals and dreams, and what happens to them."

"Rain on the Scarecrow" is an especially meaningful song because it describes a situation very close to home. "We felt we had to write a song about the farm situation because it affects a lot of people around here where we live. That song wasn't hard to write, because the truth was right there in front of me. All I had to do was tell the story. I talked to a lot of people in that situation [losing their farms]; I didn't have to make anything up."

Writing honestly about subjects that people can relate to is something Green recommends to other songwriters. "Just write the truth as well as you can and try to think up new ways to say things."

Green's situation is unusual in that one of his best friends is a recording artist who enjoys collaborating and including Green's songs on his albums. But while Mellencamp was Green's main contact when he first started, he now collaborates with other writers, and has had songs recorded by Lacy J. Dalton, Gary Morris, Willie Nelson, and The Oak Ridge Boys. He is also in the process of writing his second novel. "I enjoy writing. That's what I've always wanted to do. John only does so many albums—I write more than he could ever use." So collaborating with other songwriters and networking new contacts "gives me an opportunity to write for other people."

—*Julie Wesling Whaley*

How to Contact: Prefers 7½ ips reel-to-reel or cassette with 2-4 songs and lead sheet. SASE. Reports in 1 month.
Music: Mostly country; also blues, church/religious, dance, easy listening, folk, gospel, MOR, soul and top 40/pop.
Tips: "Writer-artists and people with road tours are given top consideration."

TYSCOT RECORDS, 3532 N. Keystone Ave., Indianapolis IN 46218. (317)923-3343. Contact: A&R Director. Record company, record producer and music publisher (Tyscot, Inc./ASCAP, Scott Residence Distributors/BMI). Releases 2 singles and 4-8 LPs/year. Works with artists and songwriters on contract. Pays 3-12% royalty to artists on contract; compulsory rate to publisher per song on record.
How to Contact: Prefers cassette (or ½" VHS videocassette) with 4 songs and lyric sheet. SASE. Reports in 1 month.
Music: Gospel and church/religious. Released *You Can Count On Me*, by The Fords; *Say You Believe*, by Deliverance; *Glorious Day*, by Derrick Brinkley; and *Gospel of Yesterday and Today*, by Rev. Bill Sawyer (all gospel LPs). Other artists include Tetrec Choir, John Kee, Gospel Shepherds, Witness, Laura Lee, Al Hobbs and Eternal Light.

UBM, 61 Mommsenst., 5000 Koln 41, West Germany. 43 13 13. President: Buschkotter. Labels include Largo and Button. Record company, music publisher and record producer. Releases 12 LPs/year. Works with musicians/artists on contract; musicians on salary for in-house studio work. Pays 12-15% royalty to artists on contract.
How to Contact: Prefers cassette and lead sheet. Does not return unsolicited material. Reports in 1 month.
Music: Mostly jazz, pop, MOR and instrumentals; also classical.

*UMBRELLA ORGANISATION PTY. LTD., Box 2089, Sydney 2001, Australia. (2)294-972. Contact: Manager. Works with songwriters on contract. Music publisher, record company and record producer.
How to Contact: Prefers cassette (or VHS [PAL] videocassette). Does not return unsolicited material. Reports in 6 weeks.
Music: Mostly contemporary pop/rock, film soundtracks and country.

UNIVERSAL-ATHENA RECORDS, Box 1264, Peoria IL 61654-1264. (309)673-5755. A&R Director: Jerry Hanlon. Record company and music publisher (Jerjoy Music/BMI). Works with artists and songwriters on contract; musicians on salary for in-house studio work. Pays statutory rate to publishers for each record sold.
How to Contact: Prefers cassette with 4-8 songs and lyric sheet. SASE. Reports in 2 weeks.
Music: Country. Released *Memories* and *Everybody Wants To Be A Cowboy*, by Jerry Hanlon and the Midwest Playboys (country LPs).

UNREGULATED RECORD CO., INC., Box 81485, Fairbanks AK 99708. (907)456-3419. President: Michael States. Labels include Lift Records. Record company, record producer and music publisher (Unregulated Music/BMI). Releases 3 singles and 3 LPs/year. Works with artists and songwriters on contract. Pays negotiable royalty to artists on contract; statutory rate to publishers for each record sold.
How to Contact: Prefers cassette with 2-5 songs and lyric sheet.
Music: Gospel (avant garde, soul, reggae). Released *Beat the Cynics*, by Cynics (new wave gospel LP); and *Christmas with Jesus*, by Lily of the Valley Choir (new wave/black gospel LP).

*UNUSUAL RECORD CO., 3121 N.W. 14th St., Gainesville FL 32605. (904)377-0336. Producer: Thomas G. Hubbell. Labels include Cave Songs. Record company, music publisher (Unusual Music Publishing) and record producer (The Cave). Estab. 1986. Releases 0-5 singles and 0-3 LPs/year. Works with musicians/artists and songwriters on contract. Pays negotiable royalty to artists on contract; pays compulsory rate to publisher per song on record.
How to Contact: Write first and obtain permission to submit. Prefers cassette or 15 ips reel-to-reel (or VHS videocassete) with 3-6 songs and lyric sheet. SASE. Reports in 6 weeks.
Music: Mostly rock/pop/top 40, experimental/new music and easy listening; also R&B, folk/ballads and MOR. Released "Talk Too Fast" (by T. Hubbell), recorded by Pure Rasins on Unusual Records (rock/single); "The Date," written and recorded by Cathy Hubbell on Unusual Records (ballad/single); and "Neutral Zone," written and recorded by John Stephens (rock/single). Other artists include Larry Newcomb, Jory Ziggelboim, Aaron Brask, Bozo Berrilli, Chris Kazimier, and Debbi Norton.
Tips: "Be unique and marketable."

URBAN ROCK RECORDS, Suite 3W, 40 W. 56th St., New York NY 10019. (212)315-0540. Record company, record producer and music publisher (Cousin Ice). Releases 8 singles and 2 LPs/year. Works with artists on contract. Pays negotiable royalty to artists on contract; statutory rate to publishers for each record sold.

How to Contact: Prefers cassette with 3-4 songs and lyric sheet. Prefers studio produced demos. "Submit a feeling, not just a formula. Use high quality cassettes." SASE. Reports in 1 month.

Music: Mostly soul; also dance, R&B/soul and rap. Released "So Smooth," by Krystal Davis (R&B single); "Bust It," by D.B.L. Crew (rap single); "Do You Like Me?" by TDC M.C.'s (rap single); and *Treacherous*, by Cousin Ice (contemporary LP).

VANDOR MOTION PICTURE AND PHONORECORDS GROUP, 1826 Poplar Ln. SW, Albuquerque NM 87105. (505)243-2881. Director of Productions: Louis Temby Beach. Labels include Vandor, Nemus, Nightstar, Juke Records of Tennessee, FMC Ltd., Classic, BFI, QRZ, Lang, Mesa and Icefire. Record company, music publisher (Bobby Farrell Intl. Music), record producer, distributor and licensor. Releases 35 singles and 50 LPs/year. Works with musicians/artists and songwriters on contract; musicians on salary for in-house studio work. Pays "scale/flat rate" to artists on contract.

How to Contact: Prefers cassette or reel-to-reel (or Beta or VHS videocassette) with any number of songs and lyric or lead sheet. Does not return material; maintains permanent file. "Print or type identification: titles, names, addresses and phone numbers."

Music: Pop/rock/R&B, contemporary/jazz, gospel, classical and bluegrass, "anything new and different." Released "Carolina Blue" (by R. L. Rowley), recorded by Ron Aaron on Juke Records (country single); "In Your Arms" (by R. Cunningham), recorded by Firedragon on Vandor Records (pop single); and "A Million Miles Away" (by R. Cunningham), recorded by Strange Brew on Juke Records (contemporary LP). Other artists include Earlene Vernon, Seltzerbelch, Carman Lehoy and Smokey Robinson.

VELVET PRODUCTIONS, 517 W. 57th St., Los Angeles CA 90037. (213)753-7893. Manager: Aaron Johnson. Labels include Velvet, Kenya, Normar and Stoop Down Records. Record company, booking agency and promoter. BMI. Releases 3 singles and 1 LP/year. Works with artists and songwriters on contract. Pays 5% royalty to artists on contract.

How to Contact: Submit demo and/or lead sheet by mail. Arrange personal interview. Prefers cassette with 3-5 songs and lead sheet. SASE. Reports in 2 months.

Music: Blues, gospel, rock, soul and top 40/pop. Released *There's Two Sides to Every Coin*, by Arlene Bell.

VIBE RECORDS INC., 1183 Eastway, Cincinnati OH 45224. (513)681-5436. President: Gordon Hickland. Record company, music publisher (Hicky's Music) and record producer. Releases 1-4 singles/year and 2 LPs/year. Works with musicians/artists and songwriters on contract. Pays 7-9% royalty to artists on contract.

How to Contact: Prefers cassette with 1-4 songs and lyric sheet. SASE. Reports in 1 month.

Music: Mostly pop, R&B (urban contemporary) and dance; also gospel and rap. Released "Heartbeat" (by G. Hickland), recorded by Gordy Clay (12" single); "Stingy" (by G. Waiver/G. Hickland) and "Auto-Drive" (by E. Barber/T. Best/G. Hickland), recorded by Trinia Best (singles), all on Vibe Records. Other artists include Tim Napier, Belva Childress and Irell Wallace.

VIC RECORDS, 1327 Cobb St., Kalamazoo MI 49007. (616)342-5328. Contact: Vic LaVal. Record company and record producer. Releases 50 singles and 20 LPs/year. Pays statutory rate to publishers for each record sold.

How to Contact: Prefers reel-to-reel or cassette with 2-10 songs and lyric sheet. SASE. Reports in 1 month.

Music: Country and country rock. Released *Letter to My Ex Wife*, by Eddie Vispa (country LP); and *Stoop Down Baby*, by Chick Willis (R&B LP). Other artists include Val Vegas, Cold Fire, Kathleen Hill, Frisco, Hot Nuts, The R.A.R.S. and Ben Stafford.

VOKES MUSIC PUBLISHING & RECORD CO., Box 12, New Kensington PA 15068. (412)335-2775. President: Howard Vokes. Labels include Vokes and Country Boy Records. Record company, booking agency and music publisher. Releases 8 singles and 5 LPs/year. Works with artists and songwriters on contract. Pays 2½-4½¢/song royalty to artists and songwriters on contract.

How to Contact: Submit cassette only and lead sheet. SASE. Reports in 2 weeks.

Music: Bluegrass, country and gospel. Released *Songs of Broken Love Affairs* and *Tears at the Grand Ole Op'ry*, by Howard Vokes; *Hank Williams Isn't Dead*, by Denver Duke and Jeffery Null; *Ballad of Johnny Horton*, by Hank King, Jimmy Parker, Larry Dale and Rudy Thacker; and *Billy Wallace Sings His Hits*, by Billy Wallace.

WALK ON WATER RECORDS, Rt. 2 Box 566-H, New Braunfels TX 78130. (512)629-4396. Producer/Manager: Kenneth D. Brazle. Record company, music publisher, record producer and recording stu-

dio. Releases 2 singles and 1 LP/year. Works with musicians/artists and songwriters on contract. Pays 7-11% royalty to artists on contract.
How to Contact: Write first and obtain permission to submit. "Include SASE for reply." Prefers cassette, 7½ ips reel-to-reel (or VHS videocassette) with 2-3 songs and lyric sheet. Does not return unsolicited material. Reports in 6 weeks.
Music: Mostly AOR-pop/rock, new music and country.

WALTNER ENTERPRISES, 14702 Canterbury, Tustin CA 92680. (714)731-2981. President: Steve Waltner. Labels include Calico. Record company and music publisher (Early Bird Music/BMI). Releases 2-5 singles and 1 LP/year. Works with musicians and songwriters on contract. Pays 5-10% royalty to artists on contract; standard royalty to songwriters on contract; pays statutory rate to publishers for each record sold.
How to Contact: Prefers cassette (or videocassette) with 2-4 songs and lead sheet. SASE. Reports in 3 weeks.
Music: Country, easy listening, MOR and top 40/pop. Released "Will You Be Here in the Morning," by Jason Chase (country/pop single); "Country's Here to Stay," by Steve Shelby (country single); and "Slim & Lefty," by Lester Cash (country novelty single).

WAM RECORDS LTD., 901 Kenilworth Rd., Montreal, Quebec H3R 2R5 Canada. (514)341-6721. President: Leon Aronson. Record company, music publisher (Think Big Music) and record producer. Works with artists and songwriters on contract. Pays 5% minimum royalty to artists on contract; standard royalty to songwriters on contract.
How to Contact: Query or submit demo. Prefers cassette with 1-4 songs and lead sheet. SAE and IRC. Reports in 6 weeks.
Music: Dance, MOR, rock and top 40/pop. Released "Savin' It Up," by Marty Butler (MOR single); *Larry Patten*, written and recorded by L. Patten on CTL Records (pop LP); and *Entre Nous*, by Diane Tell (pop LP). Other artists include Basic Black and Pearl and 1945.

WATERHOUSE RECORDS, 526 Nicollet, Minneapolis MN 55402. (612)332-6575. Vice President: Rand Levy. Record company, music publisher and management firm. Releases 2 LPs/year. Works with musicians/artists and songwriters on contract. Pays negotiable royalty to artists on contract.
How to Contact: Prefers cassette (or VHS videocassette). Does not return unsolicited material.
Music: Rock and country. Artists include Roy Buchanen, Lamont Cranston Band and Micheal Bloomfield.

WEA MUSIC OF CANADA, LTD., 1810 Birchmount Rd., Scarborough, Ontario M1P 2J1, Canada. (416)291-2515. A&R Manager: Bob Roper. Labels include Warner Bros., Elektra, Atlantic, Reprise, Sire, Geffen, Qwest, Asylum, Nonesuch, Atco, Alligator, Swan Song and WEA. Record company and music publisher (Don Valley Music, Home Cooked Music). Member CRIA, CARAS. Releases 250 singles and 300 LPs/year. Works with artists on contract. Pays negotiable royalty to artists on contract; statutory rate to publishers for each record sold.
How to Contact: Currently interested in Canadian artists only. Prefers cassette with 4-6 songs and lyric sheet. Include photos, bio and any other pertinent information. SASE. Reports in 1 month.
Music: Mostly rock and top 40/pop; also classical, country, dance-oriented, easy listening, folk, jazz, MOR, progressive, R&B and soul. Released *The Big Prize* (rock LP), and "Feel It Again" (rock single), by Honeymoon Suite; and *Brighton Rock*, by Brighton Rock (rock EP).

*WEDGE RECORDS, 114 Catalpa Dr., Mt. Juliet TN 37122. (615)754-2950. President: Ralph D. Johnson. Labels include Dome Records and Fleet Records. Record company, music publisher (Bid Wedge Music), record producer (Ralph D. Johnson) and Pro-Star Talent Agency. Releases 3 singles/year. Works with musicians/artists and songwriters on contract. Pays 10¢ royalty to artists on contract; 5% to publisher per song on record.
How to Contact: Write or call first to arrange personal interview. Prefers cassette and lyric or lead sheet. SASE.
Music: Mostly country, rock, gospel and pop; also R&B. Released "Body Language," written and recorded by Randy Jack Wiggins; "Legs," written and recorded by Stella Parton; and "Another Little Piece of Her Love," written and recorded by Kenny Pierce all on Wedge Records (all singles). Other artists include Little Dave Farmer, T.J. Christian and Judy Rivers.

WESJAC RECORD ENTERPRISES, 129 W. Main St., Box 743, Lake City SC 29560. (803)394-3597. A&R Director: W.R. Bragdton Jr. Record company, music publisher (Wesjac Music/BMI) and record producer. Releases 3 singles/year. Works with musicians/artists and songwriters on contract; musicians on salary for in-house studio work. Pays 5% royalty to artists and songwriters on contract; pays statutory rate to publishers for each record sold.

How to Contact: Prefers cassette or 7½ or 15 ips reel-to-reel with 2 songs and lead or lyric sheet. SASE. Reports in 1 month.

Music: Gospel. Released "One More Time" (by W.J. Sanders), recorded by Royal Travelers; and "If Jesus Can't Fix It" (by Billy M. Graham) and "Jesus Is My Only Friend" (by Barney Dozier), both recorded by Gospel Creators, (all gospel) all on WesJac Records (all singles).

W/G PUBLISHING AND RECORD CO., 991 Oak St., West Barnstable MA 02668. (617)362-4908. President: Mike Welch. Labels include Welchy Grape Records. Record company, record producer and music publisher (WelchyGrape Publishing). Releases 2 singles and 1 LP/year.

How to Contact: Write first. Prefers cassette of records (LP or single) with 5 songs. SASE. Reports in 3 months.

Music: Country, easy listening, folk/rock, MOR, rock (country and hard rock) and top 40/pop. Released *Renovations*, by Mike Welch (MOR LP); *Resurgence*, (MOR/rock LP); "Everybody Knows," (MOR single); and "Turning Point," (rock single) all by Mike Welch and Renovations Band.

Tips: "Looking for more established artists."

WHEATLEY RECORDS PTY LTD., #4.5 Illoura Bldg., 424 St. Kilda Rd., Melbourne, Victoria 3004 Australia. A&R Director: Ross Fraser. Record company, music publisher (Wheatley Music) and record producer (Ross Fraser). Releases 15-20 singles and 12 LPs/year. Works with musicians/artists and songwriters on contract; musicians on salary for in-house studio work.

How to Contact: Prefers cassette. SAE and IRC. Reports in 6 weeks.

Music: Rock. Released "Only You" (by Ottewell/Harrison), recorded by FX; "Heart of Warrior" (by D. McDonald), recorded by Kaha; and "One Blind Love" (by Sterry/Zatorski), recorded by Real Life, all on Wheatley Records (all singles).

MARTY WILSON PRODUCTIONS, INC., 185 West End Ave., New York NY 10023. (212)580-0255. Labels include D&M Sound and Cyma Records. Record company and music publisher. Works with songwriters on contract; musicians on salary for in-house work. Payment varies for artists on contract; pays standard royalty to songwriters on contract.

How to Contact: Prefers 7½ or 15 ips reel-to-reel or cassette with 1-3 songs and lead sheet. SASE. Reports in 1 month.

Music: Easy listening, jazz, MOR and top 40/pop.

WINCHESTER RECORDS, Rt. 2, Box 116H, Berkeley Springs WV 25411. Owners: Bertha or Jim McCoy. Labels include Master, Mountain Top and Winchester. Record company, music publisher and record producer (Jim McCoy Productions). Releases 12 singles and 6 LPs/year. Works with musicians/artists and songwriters on contract; musicians on salary for in-house studio work. Pays standard royalty to artists on contract.

How to Contact: Write or call first and obtain permission to submit. Prefers cassette, or 7½ or 15 ips reel-to-reel (VHS or Beta videocassette) with 6 songs and lyric or lead sheet. SASE. Reports in 1 month.

Music: Mostly country, rock and gospel; also country/rock and bluegrass. Released "Tryin to Quit," written and recorded by Jim McCoy on Winchester Records (single); and *Carroll County Ramblers Sing Bluegrass Gospel*, written and recorded by Carroll County Ramblers on Alear Records (LP).

WISHBONE RECORDS, Weiherstr. 21, 4630 Bochum 1, West Germany. (0234)37031, 37032. Contact: Ferdinand Kother. Labels include: Backbone Records and Wishbone Records. Record company, record producer and distributor. Releases 0-5 singles and 5-10 LPs/year. Works with musicians/artists and songwriters on contract. Pays 10-40% royalty to artists on contract.

How to Contact: Prefers cassette (or VHS/PAL videocassette) with 5-10 songs. Does not return unsolicited material. Reports in 2 months.

Music: Mostly heavy metal, new wave/psychobilly and punk; also mainstream rock and oldies (re-releases). Released "Black Dream," written and recorded by Mainstreet; "Future Sound Spectacular," written and recorded by Europe-X-Post; and "Holding On," written and recorded by Darxon, all on Wishbone Records (all singles). Other artists include Metal Sword and Der Riss.

Tips: "Sound quality is not as important as good performance. Songs should have good hook-lines and arrangement, even if aimed at specialist's market. Must give exclusive right for Europe (EEC)."

WONDER RECORD CO., Box 11565, Atlanta GA 30305. (404)261-6512. President: Jimmy Ginn. Record company and music publisher (Act One Music Co.). Works with musicians/artists and songwriters on contract. Pays 8-15% royalty to artists on contract. Pays negotiable rate to publisher per song on record.

How to Contact: Prefers cassette (or VHS videocassette) with 4-6 songs and lyric sheet. Does not re-

turn unsolicited material. Reports in 5 weeks. "Submit quality recordings in neat form; include pictures and biography of group and track record."
Music: Mostly gospel, R&B and bluegrass; also blues, country, rock, pop and jazz. Released "Redd & Hot" (by Walker/Houser), recorded by Toni Redd; "I've Come a Long Way Down," written and recorded by Doug Gaddis; and "American By Birth," written and recorded by Jeff Bruce, all singles on Wonder Records. Other artists include Red, White and Bluegrass; Dorthy Norwood; John Edwards; and Sammy Johns.

WOODRICH RECORDS, Box 38, Lexington AL 35648. (205)247-3983. President: Woody Richardson. Record company and music publisher (Woodrich Publishing Co.) and record producer (Woody Richardson). Releases 3 singles and 6 LPs/year. Works with songwriters on contract. Pays 50% royalty to artists on contract.
How to Contact: Prefers cassette with 4 songs and lyric sheet. SASE. Reports in 2 weeks. "We prefer a good studio demo."
Music: Mostly country, gospel and bluegrass; also rock and jazz. Released *Still Small Voice* (by Roger Johnson), recorded by Heaven's Mountain Band (gospel LP); "Homecoming Tennessee," written and recorded by Wayne Yocom (country); and "Thanking the Lord" (by Ivory Ellison), recorded by Ellison Family (black gospel), all on Woodrich Records.

WORLD ARTIST, Box 63, Orinda CA 94563. (415)937-6469. A&R Representative: J. Malcom Baird. Record company, music publisher (Hansen Music Company), record producer (Geoffrey Hansen Enterprises) and personal management firm. Releases varying number of singles and LPs/year. Works with musicians/artists and songwriters on contract; musicians on salary for in-house studio work. Pays negotiable royalty to artists on contract.
How to Contact: Prefers cassette (or videocassette) and lyric sheet or lead sheet. SASE. Reports in 6 weeks. "We do not want the same material that you are sending to other companies. We are looking for the 50s and 60s style rock and doo-wop vocal harmony plus artists with star quality."
Music: Mostly top 40/MOR, rock-a-billy and country-rock; also blues, French and Spanish. Released "This is Hilo, Hawaii" (by B. Friel), *Surf Rock Guitar* (by C. Trouten), and *Hawaii Rock 85* (by B. Friel), all recorded by Bert Friel on World Artist Records (Hawaiian LPs). Other artists include various Hawaiian artists, and artists in Japan, Philippines, Korea and Latin America.

WOULD'N SHOE/L'ORIENT, Suite 7, 124 W. 81st St., New York NY 10024. (212)787-8103. Contact: A&R Coordinator. Labels include Would'n Shoe, L'Orient and Hatch. Record company, record producer (It's A Hit Productions) and management firm (Bullet Management). Releases 2-5 singles and 2-3 LPs/year. Works with artists and songwriters on contract. Pays minimum of 2% royalty to artists on contract; statutory rate to publishers for each record sold.
How to Contact: Write first. Prefers 7½ ips reel-to-reel or cassette with 3-8 songs and lyric sheet. Does not return unsolicited material. Reports in 1 month.
Music: Mostly pop rock and country rock; also country and MOR. Released "Are You Afraid of Falling?," by Estes Boys; "Lovers in Trouble," by the Secrets; and "Keep on Singing," by Dean Adrien.
Tips: Looking for "professionalism, hook, structure and presentation."

*YELLOW JACKET RECORDS, 10303 Hickory Valley, Ft. Wayne IN 46835. President: Allan Straten. Record company. Releases 3-4 singles and 1 LP/year. Works with musicians/artists and songwriters on contract and musicians on salary for in-house studio work. Pays standard royalty to artists on contract.
How to Contact: Prefers cassette with 3-4 songs and lyric sheet. SASE. Reports in 1 month.
Music: Country and MOR. Released "Countin' Down to Love," "Call Me Each Evening" and "One of a Kind" (by Grogg/Straten), recorded by April on YJR Records (single).

YELLOW ROSE RECORDS, INC., Suite 522, 10 N. Calver St., Baltimore MD 21202-1820. (301)727-7673. A&R Departmen: Ronnie Scruggs. Record company, record producer (Black Watch Productions), music publisher (Post War Publishing Co./ASCAP) and management firm (Yellow Rose Talent Management). Releases 5-6 singles and 2-3 LPs/year. Works with artists and songwriters on contract. Pays 12% royalty to artists on contract. Pays compulsory rate to publisher per song on record.
How to Contact: Prefers cassette with 3-5 songs. SASE. Reports in 2 months.
Music: Dance-oriented, rock, top 40/pop, R&B and MOR. Released "Never My Love" (by Adrissi); "Don't Go" (by Chance); and "Street Angel" (by Weiss), all recorded by Toy Sholdier on Yellow Rose Records (all singles). Other artists include Mannekin, TNA and Crystal Ball.
Tips: "Must want to work and cooperate—have good solid originals which are commercially viable."

ZONE RECORD CO., 2674 Steele, Memphis TN 38127. (901)357-0064. Owner: Marshall E. Ellis. Record company, music publisher and record producer. Works with songwriters on contract. Pays 4¢/re-

cord royalty to artists on contract; statutory royalties to songwriters on contract.
How to Contact: Prefers cassette with 4 songs. "Be sure the words are clear. Don't try to make a master—just a good clean tape." SASE. Reports in 2 weeks.
Music: Country and country/pop. Released "You're the Best," by Bobby Dave; "I Never Liked to Waltz Anyway," by Richard Patterrow; and "The Way You Shake It," by Eddie Bond, all on Zone Records (all country).

Geographic Index

The U.S. section of this handy geographic index will quickly give you the names of record companies located in the music centers of Los Angeles, Nashville and New York. While there are many valuable contacts to be made in other cities, you will probably want to plan a trip to one of these established music centers at some point in your career, and try to visit as many of these companies as you think appropriate. The International section lists, geographically, markets for your songs in foreign countries.

Find the names of companies in this index, and then check listings within the Record Companies section for addresses, phone numbers and submission details.

United States
Los Angeles
Blue Gem Records
Bright & Morningstar Records
Carousel Records, Inc.
Cosmotone Records
Gallery II Records
Golden Boy Records
RCA Records
Rockin! Records
Slash Records
Phil Spector International and
    Warner/Spector Records Inc.
Striped Horse Records, Inc.
Survivor Records
Velvet Productions

Nashville
Ark Record Co.
The Calvary Music Group
Capstan Record Production
Carlyle Records, Inc.
Carrie Records Co.
CBS Records
Charta Records
Country International
Curtiss Records
Electric Records
John Fisher & Associates

Jalyn Recording Co.
Landmark (Audio of Nashville)
MTM Music Group
Orbit Records
Paragold Records & Tapes
Stargem Records, Inc.
Sun International Corp.
Susan Records
Terock Records

New York
A Street Records
Buddah Records, Inc.
Bulldog Records
Camerica Records
Cargo Records
Ca-song Records
Courrier Records
DRG Records, Inc.
EMI America Records
Factory Beat Records, Inc.
Glad-Hamp Records Inc.
Jimboco Records
M Records, Inc.
Manhattan Country, Inc.
MCA Records
Mindfield Records
On Time Records, Inc.
Orange Records

PolyGram Records
Praise
Roperry Records
Rosebud Records
RSO Records
The Source Unltd.
Spring Records
Tommy Boy
Urban Rock Records
Marty Wilson Productions, Inc.
Would'n Shoe/L'Orient

International
ARGENTINA
Microfon Argentina S.A.
Mordisco

AUSTRALIA
Polygram Records Pty.
Powderworks Records and Tapes
    Pty. Ltd.
Starlite Records
Umbrella Organisation Pty. Ltd.
Wheatley Records Pty. Ltd.

AUSTRIA
Dum Dum Records

Johann Kaplan Music
Koch Records International

BELGIUM
Downtown Record Company
Jump Records & Music
Parsifal PVBA
Selection-B Sharp
Tauro

BRAZIL
Alldisc
Discos Presenca Ltd.
Gravacoes Eletricas S.A.

CANADA
A&M Records of Canada, Ltd.
AMOK Records
Attic Records Ltd.
Berandol Records
Boot Records, Ltd.
Boyine International Record
    Company
Bullseye Records
Downs Record Company Limit-
    ed
Firmus Records
Intermodal Productions, Ltd.
Mainroads Records
The Master's Collection Limited
Money-Talks Productions, Inc.
Monticana Records
Nettwerk
Riser Records
Roto-Noto Records
Shotgun Music Corp.
True North Records
WAM Records Ltd.
WEA Music of Canada, Ltd.

CZECHOSLOVAKIA
Opus-Records and Publishing
    House

DENMARK
Sam Records

FINLAND
Bluebird Music OY
Kompass Records

FRANCE
Caravage
Societe Sonodisc

ICELAND
Geimsteinn HF
Skifan H/F

ITALY
Top Records

JAPAN
Kitty Records, Inc.

MALAYSIA
EMI (Malaysia) SDN. BHD.

THE NETHERLANDS
Associated Artists Records In-
    ternational
Collector Records
Ivory Tower Records
Le Disque Holland B.V.
Munich Records B.V.

NEW ZEALAND
Maui Records

SPAIN
Discos Victoria, S.A.

SWEDEN
Glendisc
Liphone Records

SWITZERLAND
Capricorn Ltd.
Masters Records

TAIWAN
Sunrise Records, Ltd.

UNITED KINGDOM
ACTS International
Bam-Caruso Records
Big Bear Records
Bus Records
Creole Records Ltd.
4-Quartet Songs
Grosvenor Recording Studios
Heavy Metal Records
Helios Records
Le Matt Music Ltd.
Mays Records
Neat Records
Nervous Records
New Music Enterprises
Outlet Recording Co. Ltd.
Plankton Records
President Records Limited
Ritz Records Ltd.
Sound Ceremony
Sphemusations
Titan International Productions,
    Ltd.

WEST GERMANY
Ariola-Eurodisc GMBH
Arminia Musikproduktion Erich
    Storz
Bella Musica Tontraeger GMBH
Comma Records & Tapes
Playbones Records
UBM
Wishbone Records

YUGOSLAVIA
Suzy Records

66 *If a dumb kid from Indiana can come from nowhere
and have a hit record it can happen to anybody.* **99**
—*John Cougar Mellencamp in* Newsweek

Record producers can be valuable contacts for songwriters because they work so closely with the artists whose records they produce. They are extremely creative and artistic people, typically with a lot more freedom than people in executive positions, and they are known for having good "ears," or being able to "hear" hit potential in a song or artist. Some producers work on the staff of a record company, and they often find new talent for executives who may be less creative. They are especially good contacts for songwriter/artists looking for a record deal with that specific label.

Other producers are independent, not affiliated with any one record label, but free to "shop" around for the best deal they can negotiate. Independent producers can be excellent contacts for songwriters, because they record new acts with new material and try to sell the finished masters to various record companies. They may also go directly to record companies seeking contracts to produce specific acts already signed to that label (sometimes major recording artists). Either way, the producer needs material. Since independent producers are well-acquainted with record company executives and artists, they can often get your material through doors not open to you.

The fact that an independent producer works for himself means he can be open to a variety of musical styles. Many of the producers listed here are also publishers. This can work to your advantage. Producers who act as publishers will always be looking for good songs (whether they need them for a current recording project or not) because they can always "shop" the songs to another producer or record company.

Because of their creativity and flexibility, record producers often make good business partners for those songwriters and artists whose material is thought of as being outside the popular music mainstream. They are usually more receptive to innovative and experimental use of musical instruments and recording techniques. Many producers will work with songwriters and make suggestions they think will improve the songs and help songwriters develop their craft. A lot of producers are songwriters themselves, and if you can find a producer you are comfortable collaborating with, the songs you create together may have an even better chance of being picked up. The producer will naturally use his connections to try to get a song recorded if he co-wrote it himself.

The listings that follow outline which aspects of the music industry each producer is involved in, what type of music he is looking for, what records and artists he's recently produced and what other artists he produces on a regular basis. Study the listings carefully, noting the names of artists each is working with, and consider if any of your songs might fit a particular artist's style. For a weekly update on who's producing what and whom, refer to the charts in *Billboard* and *Cash Box*.

*A STREET MUSIC, Suite 800, 250 W. 54th St., New York NY 10019. (212)580-2688. A&R Director: Terry Selders. Record producer and music publisher (A Street Music). Deals with artists and songwriters. Fee derived from outright fee from recording artist.
How to Contact: Prefers cassette. Does not return unsolicited material.
Music: Mostly rock, heavy metal and pop/rock; also R&B, R&B/pop and dance. Produced "Kamikaze," written and recorded by Youth In Asia (rock single); "Easy Come, Easy Go," written and recorded by Frank Jordan (oldies rock single); and "Hot Fire Love," written and recorded by The Remnant (50s rock single) all on A Street Records. Other artists include Hybrid Ice and PapDaddy.

ABERDEEN PRODUCTIONS, (A.K.A. Scott Turner Productions), 524 Doral Country Dr., Nashville TN 37221. (615)646-9750. President: Scott Turner. Record producer and music publisher (Buried Trea-

sure/ASCAP, Captain Kidd/BMI). Deals with artists and songwriters. Works with 30 new songwriters/year. Produces 15-30 singles and 10 LPs/year. Fee derived from sales royalty and production fee.
How to Contact: Prefers cassette with maximum 4 songs and lead sheet. SASE. Reports in 3 weeks.
Music: Mostly country, MOR and rock; also top 40/pop. Produced "Appalachian Blue" (by S.C. Rose), recorded by Shauna Lee (single, A.R.C. Records); "Phanton Cadillac (by S.C. Rose), recorded by Jim Cartwright (single, Fame & Fortune Records); and "When the Wind Blows in Chicago" (by Audie Murphy/Scott Turner), recorded by Robert & Bouchard (single, Clearwood Records). Other artists include Slim Whitman, Jonathan Edwards, Hal Goodson, Jimmy Clanton and Bobby Lewis.
Tips: "Be unique. A great song doesn't care who sings it."

ABRAXAS/A.B.R. S.A., 875 Av. Callao, Buenos Aires, Argentina. 42-8254 or 41-2832. President: Carlos Ynurrigarro. Vice President A&R: Bernardo Bergeret. Record producer, music publisher (Abraxas RPM) and concert management. Produces 15 LPs/year. Deals with artists and songwriters. Fee derived from sales royalty and outright fee from recording artist.
How to Contact: Prefers cassette or 15 ips reel-to-reel (or VHS videocassette) with 4 songs and lyric sheet. Does not return unsolicited material. Reports in 3 weeks.
Music: Mostly rock, pop and jazz; also ballads. Produced *De Cama En Cama* (by K. Johansen), recorded by Instruccion Civica and *No Vayas a Selir* (by E. Alvarez), recorded by Eva Y Los Peccadores, both on CBS Records; and *Cola De Amor*, written and recorded by Leon Gieco on MH Records. Other artists include Sachet, Besame Cataline, Los Estomagos, L.A. Spinetta and Fen 8 Lili Rossi.

ACCENT RECORDS, 71906 Highway 111, Rancho Mirage CA 92270. (619)346-0075. President: Scott Seely. Record producer and music publisher (S&R Music). Deals with artists. Produces 10 singles and 5 LPs/year. Fee derived from sales royalty.
How to Contact: Prefers cassette with any number of songs and lyric sheet. SASE.
Music: Mostly A/C, country and MOR; also all other types. Produced *Armendares*, by J. Armendares (contemporary gospel, JRA Records); *Along the Line*, by Richard Christopher (pop, Accent Records); and *Classics in Rythmn*, by Buddy Merrill. Other artists include Chante, Kirby Hamilton, Eddie Rose, Don Malena, The Last Live Band, Jeri Sullivan and Jeffer.

ACE ADAMS PRODUCTIONS CO., 100-19 Alcott Pl., Bronx NY 10475. (212)379-2593. Producer: Joe Adams. Record producer. Deals with artists and songwriters. Produces 10 singles/year and 3 LPs/year. Fee derived from sales royalty.
How to Contact: Call first and obtain permission to submit. Prefers cassette. SASE. Reports in 2 weeks.
Music: Mostly pop and blues.

AKO PRODUCTION, 20531 Plummer, Chatsworth CA 91311. (818)998-0443. President: A. Sullivan. Record producer and music publisher (Amiron). Deals with artists and songwriters. Produces 2-6 singles/year and 2-3 LPs/year. Fee derived from sales royalty.
How to Contact: Write first and obtain permission to submit. Prefers cassette (or Beta or VHS videocassette) and lyric sheet. SASE.
Music: Pop/rock and modern country. Produced *Lies in Disguise*, by Gang Back (pop LP, AKO Records); *Touch of Fire* LP; and "Try Me," by Sana Christian (pop single, AKO Records).

ALHART MUSIC PUBLISHING CO., Box 1593, Lakeside CA 92040. (619)443-2170. A&R: RueAnna Boland. Record producer, music publisher, record company and promoter. Deals with artists, songwriters and producers. Works with 18-25 new songwriters/year. Produces 1-4 singles/year. Fee derived from sales royalty.
How to Contact: Prefers cassette with 1-3 songs and lyric sheet. Prefers studio produced demos. Reports "if a song is placed."
Music: Mostly country and MOR; also bluegrass. Produced "You'll Be My Baby Tonight" and "Party For One," by Dani Michaels (country singles, Alhart Records); and "Don't Turn My Gold to Blue," by D. Michaels (MOR single, Oak Records). Other artists include John Malazzo.

ALLEN & MARTIN PRODUCTIONS, 9701 Taylorsville Rd., Louisville KY 40299. (502)267-9658. Producer: J.D. Miller. Major productions include national and regional jingles and exclusive song demo production for Falls City Music. Deals with artists, songwriters and singers. Fee derived from sales royalty or by outright fee from songwriter/artist or record company.
How to Contact: Prefers 7½ ips reel-to-reel or cassette with 3-5 songs and lyric sheet. Does not return unsolicited material. Reports in 2 weeks.
Music: Pop and country. Produced "One Love" (by J.D. Miller), recorded by Perry Hines (pop, Bridges Records); and "The Boy Had Nashville Written All Over His Face" (by Gary Doc Dockery)

and "Please Don't Change the Taste of Coke" (by Ron Orwick), recorded by Doc and Smitty Band (country, Bridges Records).

*AMALISA,969A Fulham Rd., London SW6 5JJ England. (01)731-6373. President Charles Lucy. Record producer, music publisher and Instrument designers. Deals with artists and songwriters. Fee derived from sales royalty and performances.
How to Contact: Prefers cassette (or VHS [PAL] videocassette) with lyric sheet. Does not return unsolicited material. Reports in 6 weeks.
Music: Artists include Paradoxe Paradis.
Tips: Songwriter should have a "sense of humour."

AMERICAN ARTISTS PRODUCTIONS, 312 Washington Ave. N., Minneapolis MN 55401. (612)339-4741. Contact: Alison Cummings. Record producer, music publisher (SnowTown Music) and management firm (American Artists). Deals with artists and songwriters. Fee derived from sales royalty or outright fee from record company.
How to Contact: Prefers cassette (or VHS videocassette) with 3 songs only and lyric sheet. SASE. Reports in 10 weeks.
Music: Mostly R&B, pop, rock and metal; also music for film soundtracks. Artists include Brian McDonald and Craig Holliman.

AMERICAN COMMUNICATION ENTERPRISES, Box 444, Taylor MI 48180-0444. (313)722-0616. Producer: John D. Lollio. Record producer and music publisher (Lo Pine Music). Deals with artists and songwriters. Produces 10 singles and 2 LPs/year. Fee derived from sales royalty.
How to Contact: Prefers cassette and lyric sheet or lead sheet. SASE. Reports in 2 weeks.
Music: Mostly country and gospel. Produced *Sweetest Words*, *Change in Love*, and *After the Pain*, by Johni Dee (country LPs and singles on ACE Records). Other artists include Marty Damler, David Atkins and Le Moine.

*AMERICANA RECORDS, INC., Box 15 Kasai, Edogawa-Ku, Tokyo 134, Japan. (03)878-6041. Telex: J29400 Tokin BTH. President: Tom Kawai. Record producer and record company. Deals with artists and songwriters. Fee derived from sales royalty.
How to Contact: Prefers cassette. "We like to receive promo sample of record if it has been isused in the US." Does not return unsolicited material. Reports in 1 month.
Music: Mostly pop, rock and R&B; also easy listening and country.
Tips: "Teenage female singer and heavy metal or rock group will be accepted in Japanese market. Most of our clients are in advertising, so we are looking for good music writer who is interested in writing songs for TV and radio commercials."

*ANAND MAHARJH, Box 88, Station H, Montreal Quebec H3G 2K5 Canada. (514)935-9089. President: Paul Klein. Record producer and music publisher (Fudgemusic/BMI). Deals with artists and songwriters. Produces 12 singles and 2 LPs/year. Fee derived from sales royalty.
How to Contact: Prefers cassette. "Print phone number on cassettes." Does not return unsolicited material. Reports in 1 month "if we are using the material."
Music: Mostly dance, R&B and pop; also ballads and rap. Produced *Don't Break My Heart*, written and recorded by Jacqui on MWR Records; *So Shy*, written and recorded by Mac Thornhill on MWR Records; and *Ronnie's Rap* (by Ron Soraice), recorded by Ronnie & DJ on Profile Records (all dance EPs). Other artists include Ty Benskin and Suzanne Riches.

APON RECORD COMPANY, INC., Box 3082, Steinway Station, Long Island City NY 11103. (718)721-5599. Manager: Don Zemann. Record producer and music publisher (Apon Publishing). Deals with artists and songwriters. Produces 20 LPs/year. Fee derived from outright fee from record company.
How to Contact: Prefers cassette with 2-6 songs and lyric sheet. SASE. Reports in 1 month.
Music: Classical, folk, Spanish, Slavic, polkas, and Hungarian gypsy. Produced *Czech Polka Festival* and *Polka Fever*, by Kunst (polka LPs, Apon Records); and *Holiday in Spain*, by Yavaloyas Orchestra (songs and dances LP, Apon Records).

APPROPRIATE PRODUCTIONS, 1716 Pasadena Glen Rd., Pasadena CA 91107. Producer: Ben Brooks. Record producer, music publisher (DGO/ASCAP and DudGor/BMI), and promoter. Deals with artists and songwriters. Produces 2 singles/year. Fee derived from sales royalty or outright fee from record company.
How to Contact: Prefers cassette with 1-3 songs and lyric sheet. Prefers studio produced demos. SASE. Reports in 3 weeks.

Music: Rock, R&B and pop; also country and MOR. Produced "Look What You've done to Me" (by Billy Purnell), recorded by Oskar Scotti (single, Vizion Records) and "Hard to Kick" written and recorded by Gary Riley. Other songwriters include K.A. Parker and T.M. Kenefick.
Tips: "Be professional. Learn the business and music well enough to create for the market place."

APRIL RECORDING STUDIOS/PRODUCTIONS, 827 Brazil Pl., El Paso TX 79903. (915)772-7858/565-4692. President: Harvey Marcus. Record producer, music publisher (Crystal Ram Publishing/BMI) and recording studio. Deals with artists and songwriters. Produces 1-3 singles/year and 1-2 LPs/year. Fee derived from sales royalty and/or outright fee from record company.
How to Contact: Prefers cassette or 7½ ips reel-to-reel (or VHS videocassette) with 1-3 songs and lyric or lead sheets. "Include current up-dated listing of all available past recordings, publishing, and performances of your material." SASE. Reports in 2 months.
Music: Mostly jazz, R&B and new wave/rock; also "all ballads, and material with crossover possibilities such as Mex/Tex, country and instrumental." Produced *Amor Amedeas*, and *A Donde Vas*, by Jose Jose (Mexican ballad LPs, CBS/Mexico Records); "Meant to Be," by Harvey Marcus (Latin/jazz single, Crystal Ram); and *Hold Back*, by Danny Castillio and Ruben Castellano (Latin/jazz LP). Other artists include The Street Boys and The Code.
Tips: "Please be patient! We answer and listen to all material. Also, leave out all the flashy solos unless the song is an instrumental."

*ARTASIA MUSIC PRODUCTIONS, Suite A-440, 410 West Coast Hwy., Newport Beach CA 92663. (714)722-0797. Producer: Rande Isabella. Record producer. Deals with artists and songwriters. Produces 8-10 singles and 3-4 LPs/year. Fee derived from sales royalty or outright fee from record company.
How to Contact: Prefers cassette (or VHS videocassette) with 1-5 songs and lyric sheet. "Songwriters may submit demo tape by mail, unsolicited. Artists must write before sending tapes. Registered mail will not be accepted." Does not return unsolicited material. Reports in 2 months.
Music: Mostly pop/top 40, dance/R&B and Christian/gospel; also rock, new wave and sports songs. Produced "Countdown" (by Robert Sorita), recorded by Roxy on Accent Records (dance/top 40 single); "Hurricane Rap" (by Rande Isabella/David Pugh/Henry Vales), recorded by Terence Clayton & Friends on Artasia Records (single—official University of Miami Fiesta Bowl fight song); and "Baseball, We Love It," produced for NBC Sports/AT&T Celebrity Baseball Challenge. Other artists include Joy Angelyn (Dutch artist), Jon Kodi, Bordeaux, and Emmanuel.
Tips: "Songwriters should spend their time on *rewrites* rather than on fancy production. The song is 80% of the record. We spend 80% of our energies looking for and working with the song and the songwriter. We have noticed a resurgence of 'classic' rock 'n' roll and Motown-style songs, and we are actively seeking these songs in addition to 'modern' hits."

ARZEE, ARCADE AND CLYMAX RECORDS, 3010 N. Front St., Philadelphia PA 19133. (215)426-5682. Production Manager: Lucky Taylor. Record producer and music publisher (Rex Zario Music/BMI, Seabreeze Music/BMI, Jack Howard Publishing/BMI, Arcarde Music Co./ASCAP, Valley Brook Publishing/ASCAP). Deals with artists and songwriters. Produces 8-12 singles and 1-3 LPs/year. Fee derived from sales royalty.
How to Contact: Prefers 7½ ips reel-to-reel or cassette with 4-6 songs and lyric sheet. SASE. Reports in 1 month.
Music: Mostly country; also bluegrass, MOR and rock. Produced "Ten Gallon Stetson," by Bill Haley (country, Arzee Records); "This World of Mine," by Shorty Long (country, Arzee Records); and "Blues on the Block," by Charlie Stone (MOR, Arzee Records). Other artists include Dick Thomas, Rusty Wellington, Al Taber, Ben Taber, Willis Meyers, James E. Myers, Al Rex, Frank Marshall, Ray Coleman, Ray Hatcher, Bob Saver, Tex Carson, Eddie Thompson, Dallas Turner, Tommy Carr, Bob Dean, Jimmy Collett and Rex Zario.

ASTAN RECORDS, (formerly Echo Records), 824 83rd St., Miami Beach FL 33141. (305)865-8960. President: Walter Dana. Record producer and music publisher (Dana Publishing). Deals with artists. Produces 2 singles and 1 LP/year.
How to Contact: Write first about your interest. Prefers 7½ or 15 ips reel-to-reel or cassette. SASE.
Music: Classical and Polish. Produced "Senoritas Y Caballeros," "September Song," and "Bandoneon Arabello," by Walter Dana.

*TOM ATOM PRODUCTIONS, 28B Howden Rd., Toronto, Ontario M1R 3E4 Canada. (416)757-8775. Producer: Tom Atom. Record producer, music publisher and record company. Deals with artists and songwriters. Produces 2 singles and 2 LPs/year. Works with 4 new songwriters/year. Also works with lyricists and composers and teams collaborators. Fee derived from sales royalty or outright fee from

artist/songwriter or record company.
How to Contact: Prefers cassette with 1-5 songs and lyric sheet. SASE. Reports in 3 weeks.
Music: Mostly pop; also MOR, rock (heavy metal) and top 40. Produced "Eve of Rock," by Rapid Tears (heavy pop single, Chameleon Records); and "Baby Took a Train," by Paladins (rockabilly single, Star Records). Other artists include Young Lions.

*AZURE RECORDS, Rt. 8, Box 3, Beaumont TX 77705. (409)842-2884. President: Don Gilbert. Record producer and music publisher (Don Gilbert Music/BMI) and record company. Deals with artists and songwriters. Produces 10 singles and 2 LPs/year. Fee derived from sales royalty.
How to Contact: Prefers cassette with 2-10 songs and lyric sheet. SASE. Reports in 3 months.
Music: Religious music only. Produced "Sweet and Simple," by Randy McClain (country MOR single, Azure Records); "Take Your Memories Too," by Sherry Black (country MOR single, Gold Guitar Records); and "Cajun Lullaby," by Jesse Stuart (country MOR single, Gold Guitar Records). Other artists include Silver Strings and Don Gilbert.

*B.F.H.B. AUDIO INC.,168 Empress Ave., North York, Ontario M2N 3T8 Canada. (416)221-7445. President: Brian Bell. Record producer and music publisher. Deals with artists and songwriters. Produces 5 singles and 1 LP/year. Fee is derived from sales royalty or outright fee from record company.
How to Contact: Write first to arrange personal interview. Prefers cassette with 4 songs and lyric sheet. Does not rturn unsolicited material. Reports in 1 month.
Music: Mostly pop, new music and rock; also jazz and MOR. Produced *Shades Of '45*, *Angel Please*, *Watching You* and *Amorasian Dreams*, all written and recorded by Gary O'Connor on RCA Records (all LPs). Other artists include Terry and Laurel Black, Sailcats, Whales and Jordana.

B.G. PRODUCTIONS, (formerly MTI Records), Box 39268, Redford MI 48239. (313)531-5353. President: Nick Canzano. Record producer and music publisher (No-Town Productions). Deals with artists and songwriters. Produces 12 singles and 4 LPs/year. Fee is negotiable.
How to Contact: Write or call first and obtain permission to submit. Prefers 7½ or 15 ips reel-to-reel with 4-5 songs and lyric and lead sheet. Does not return unsolicited material. Reports in 1 month.
Music: Pop, contemporary/top 40 and dance. Produced "Stay the Night," by Rick Canzano (top 40 single); and "This Is Music," by Denise McCullen (pop single). Other artists include Nucleus.

*BAD GRAMMAR ENTERPRISES, Box 248, Roseville MI 48066. (313)294-0797. Production Engineer: Joe Trupiano. Record producer, music publisher (Bad Grammar Music) and management company. Deals with artists and songwriters. Produces 2 singles and 2 LPs/year. Fee derived from sales royalty.
How to Contact: Prefers cassette (or videocassette) with 3-4 songs and lyric sheet. SASE. Reports in 6 weeks.
Music: Mostly pop/rock, mainstream rock and heavy metal; also easy listening, ballads and MOR. Produced "Car Crazy" (rock), "Feel the Need (In Me)" (pop/rock); and "Carousel" (heavy metal), all by Joey Harlo, all singles on Bad Grammar Records. Other artists include Tuff Kids and The Sirens.

BAL RECORDS, Box 369, LaCanada CA 91011. (818)952-1242. President: Adrian Bal. Record producer and music publisher (Bal & Bal Music). Deals with artists and songwriters. Produces 3-4 singles/year. Fee derived from sales royalty.
How to Contact: Prefers cassette with 3 songs and lyric sheet. SASE. Reports in 1 month.
Music: Mostly MOR, country, jazz, R&B, rock and top 40/pop; also blues, church/religious, easy listening and soul. Produced "Chilly Bones," written and recorded by Marge Calhoun (country single); "Sunday Service" and "Nicodemus" both written and recorded by Jerry Chud (singles) all on Bal Records.

JOHN BAUERS MUSIC PRODUCTIONS, 1200 Park Ave., Hoboken NJ 07030. Creative Department: John Bauers and Tim Dobel. Record producer and music publisher. Deals with artists and songwriters. Produces 2-8 singles and 1-2 LPs/year. Fee derived from sales royalty.
How to Contact: Prefers cassette with 1-3 songs and lyric sheet. SASE. Reports in 1 month.
Music: Mostly R&B, dance and top 40/pop. New releases include "Reach Out Your Hand," and "Your Love Is All I Need" (by Hahn/Bauers/Sullivan), recorded by Carol Hahn on Dice Records (dance); and "I Need A Lover Tonight," (by Dobel/Bauers), recorded by Karen Cole on Power Records. Other artists include Joy Rose, Kerl Harris and Moore Soule.

*THE BEAU-JIM AGENCY, INC., Box 2149, Alvin TX 77512-2149. President: Buddy Hooper. Record producer and music publisher (Beau-Jim Music, Inc., ASCAP; Beau-Di Music, Inc., BMI). Deals

with artists and songwriters. Produces 4 singles and 1 LP/year.
How to Contact: Prefers cassette (or videocassette) with 3-5 songs and lyric sheet. SASE. Reports in 3 weeks.
Music: Mostly country.

HAL BERNARD ENTERPRISES, INC., 2181 Victory Parkway, Cincinnati OH 45206. (513)861-1500. President: Stan Hertzmann. Record producer and music publisher (Sunnyslope Music Inc., Bumpershoot Music Inc.). Deals with artists and songwriters. Produces 5 singles and 3-4 LPs/year. Fee derived from sales royalty.
How to Contact: Prefers cassette with 1-3 songs and lyric sheet. SASE. Reports in 1 month.
Music: Produced *Lone Rhino* and *Desire Caught By The Tail*, by Adrian Belew (rock LPs, Island Records); *The Bears*, by The Bears (rock LP, PMRC/MCA Records); and *Ladies and Gentlemen . . .*, by The Adults (rock LP, Strugglebaby Records). Other artists include The Young Invaders and Charlie Fletcher.

RICHARD BERNSTEIN, 2170 S. Parkla Rd., Denver CO 80231. (303)755-2613. Contact: Richard Bernstein. Record producer, music publisher (M. Bernstein Music Publishing Co.) and record label. Deals with artists and songwriters. Produces 5-10 singles/year and 2-5 LPs/year. Fee derived from sales royalty, outright fee from songwriter/artist and/or outright fee from record company.
How to Contact: Prefers cassette and lyric or lead sheets. Does not return unsolicited material. Reports in 3 weeks.
Music: Rock, jazz and country.

BIG BEAR, 190 Monument Rd., Birmingham, B16 8UU, England. 44-021-454-7020. Managing Director: Jim Simpson. Record producer, music publisher (Bearsongs) and record company (Big Bear Records). Works with lyricists and composers and teams collaborators. Produces 15 singles and 10 LPs/year. Fee derived from sales royalty.
How to Contact: Write first about your interest, then submit demo tape and lyric sheet. Reports in 2 weeks.
Music: Blues, jazz, R&B and soul.

P.J. BIROSIK/READY TO ROCK PRODUCTIONS, Box 46445, Hollywood CA 90046. (213)656-8845. President: P.J. Birosik. Record producer, music publisher (Ready to Rock Music/BMI) and record label (Ready to Rock Records). Deals with artists and songwriters. Produces 10-15 LPs/year. Fee derived from sales royalty, outright fee from record company (master licensing) and various other sources.
How to Contact: Prefers cassette (or VHS videocassette) with 4 songs and lyric sheet. SASE. Reports in 1 month.
Music: New age and hard rock only. Produced *Invasion*, by Greg Leon (hard rock LP, Ready to Rock/AZRA); "Going Backward," by Rayonics (dance pop single, Ready to Rock); and *Levi Dexter*, by Levi Dexter (rockabilly LP). Other artists include Invaders, Secret Agent and Art of Persuasion.

BLACK DIAMOND MUSIC PUBLISHING & PRODUCTION GROUP, Box 467, Yeadon PA 19050-3505. (215)477-5003. President: Allen Gabriel. Record producer and publisher. Deals with artists, songwriters, producers, record companies and musicians. Fee derived from product sales. Administrative service charge to contractor.
How to Contact: Write first about your interest. Prefers cassette (or VHS or Beta videocassette) with 2 songs and lyric sheet. "All demos must be of good quality and all lyric sheets must be clearly printed." Does not return unsolicited material, but include SASE for reply. Reports in 6 weeks.
Music: Mostly children's, gospel, jazz, R&B, soft rock, reggae and commercial jingles ("various, product oriented"); also dance, Hispanic, progressive, soul, rock and top 40/pop.

*BLACK WATCH PRODUCTIONS, Suite 522, 10 N. Calvert, Baltimore MD 21202. (301)727-7673. A&R Department: Ronnie Scruggs. Record producer, music publisher (Post War Publishing), and sound/lighting company. Deals with artists and songwriters. Produces 5-6 singles and 2-3 LPs/year. Fee derived from sales royalty.
How to Contact: Prefers cassette with 3-5 songs and lyric sheet. "Must send SASE for return of material." Reports in 6 weeks.
Music: Mostly rock, top 40 and R&B; also country, gospel and metal. Produced *Forward March*, by Chance (rock LP); "Street Angel," by Weiss (rock single); and *Stand Up and Fight*, by Mannekin (rock LP), all on Yellow Rose Records. Other artists include Toy Soldier, TNA, and Crystal Ball.
Tips: Looks for "good, solid, original songs that are commercially viable, and a willingness to work and cooperate."

MARK BLACKWOOD MUSIC GROUP, 5180 Park Ave., Memphis TN 38119. (901)761-5180. President: Mark Blackwood. Executive Secretary: Leigh Chandler. Record producer and music publisher (Songs From The Box/BMI, Voice Of Paradise/ASCAP). Deals with artists and songwriters. Produces 3-4 singles and 3-5 LPs/year. Fee derived from sales royalty.
How to Contact: Prefers cassette with 3 songs and lyric sheet. Does not return unsolicited material. Reports in 1 month.
Music: Mostly gospel; also rock and pop. "We are primarily interested in Christian MOR songs and artists." Produced *The Answer*, recorded by The Blackwood Brothers on Calvary Records (gospel LP), featuring "Man of Sorrow," (by Chuck Bianchi); "Show Me Your Way," (by Sparrow Holt); and "The Answer," (by Everette Brown). Other artists include Jeff Stice and Jimmy Blackwood.

THE BLUE GROUP, Box 2970, Hollywood CA 90078-2975. (213)463-9500. Executive Producer: Terrence Brown. Record producer, music publisher (Clear Blue/BMI, Blue Standard/ASCAP and Oz Magical/ASCAP and record company. Deals with artists, songwriters and producers. Produces 48 singles and 4 LPs/year. Fee derived from sales royalty.
How to Contact: Prefers cassette (or videocassette) with maximum 3 songs and lyric sheet. SASE. Reports in 2 months.
Music: Mostly R&B; also top 40/pop, dance and pop/rock. Produced "Please Mr. Postman," by Delia Renee (R&B single, Airwave Records); and "Get Up Off the Funk," by Freddy Gee (R&B single, Airwave Records). Other artists include Billy Ocean, Den Harrow, Pleasure and the Beast and Xcursion.

BLUEBIRD MUSIC, Henrikintie 5C, Helsinki 37 Finland. (90)552519. General Manager: Osmo A. Ruuskanen. Record producer and music publisher. Deals with artists and songwriters. Produces 20 singles and 15 LPs/year. Fee derived from sales royalty.
How to Contact: Prefers cassette with 2-6 songs and lead sheet. Does not return unsolicited material. Reports in 3 weeks.
Music: MOR and rock. Produced *Romantic Moods*, by Francis Goya; *Magic Pan Flute*, by D. Luca; and *Only Love*, by Lea Laven (all LPs on Bluebird).

DAVID BLUEFIELD, Box 726, Hollywood CA 90028. (213)463-SONG (7664). Contact: President. Record producer, music publisher and recording studio. Deals with artists and songwriters. Produces 5 singles and 3 LPs/year. Fee derived from outright fee from songwriter/artist or studio rental.
How to Contact: Write or call first to arrange personal interview. Prefers cassette (or VHS videocassette) with 5 songs. Does not return unsolicited material. Reports in 4 weeks.
Music: Mostly pop, rock and R&B. Produced "Kick It In," by Virg L. Beckham (country crossover single, Dblue); and "Everybody Likes Rock 'n' Roll, by Pop Signal (pop R&B single, Dblue).

BOUQUET-ORCHID ENTERPRISES, Box 18284, Shreveport LA 71138. (318)686-7362. President: Bill Bohannon. Record producer and music publisher (Orchid Publishing). Deals with artists and songwriters. Produces 5 singles/year. Fee derived from sales royalty.
How to Contact: Prefers cassette with 3-5 songs and lyric sheet. "Include brief background information. Make lyrics clear and the demos as strong as possible." SASE. Reports in 1 month.
Music: Country, contemporary gospel and top 40/pop. Produced "Lies," by Theresa Gilbert; and "Two Steps Away," by the Bandoleers, both on Bouquet Records (both country singles).

*TOMMY BOYCE MUSIC, Box 161358, Memphis TN 38116. (901)332-6540. Chairman: Tommy Boyce. President: Phyllis Presley. Record producer and music publisher (Bottom Line Time Productions). Estab. 1986. Deals with artists and sogwriters.
How to Contact: Write first and obtain permission to submit. Prefers cassette (or VHS videocassette) with 4 songs maximum and lyric or lead sheets. Does not return unsolicited material. Reports in 2 months.
Music: Mostly rock, pop and country. Produced "Roll On Back To You," "You Can't Break My Heart," and "Johnny B. Lonesome," all written and recorded by T. Boyce (all singles).

BOBBY BOYD PRODUCTIONS, 2609 NW. 36th St., Oklahoma City OK 73112. (405)942-0462. Producer: Bobby Boyd. Record producer (Boyd Records) and music publisher (Watonga Publishing/ASCAP and Catalpa Publishing/BMI). Deals with artists and songwriters. Produces 10-12 singles/year.
How to Contact: Prefers cassette or record with 3-12 songs and lyric sheet. Does not return unsolicited material. Reports in 2 weeks "if interested."
Music: Country, R&B, rock, soul and top 40/pop. Produced *Trucking Truth*, by Marvin Ray (country LP, Boyd Records). Artists include Dale Greear.

WILLIAM R. BRAGDTON, JR., Box 743, 324 Scott, Lake City SC 29560. (803)394-3597. General Manager/Owner: William R. Bragdton, Jr. Record producer and music publisher (WesJac Music). Deals

with artists and songwriters. Produces 3 singles/year and 1 LP/year.
How to Contact: Submit demo tape by mail. Write first to arrange personal interview. Prefers cassette or 7½ or 15 ips reel to reel with 2 songs and lyric or lead sheets. Does not return unsolicited material. Reports in 1 month.
Music: Gospel. Produced "One More Time," by Royal Travelers; and "Jesus Is My Only Friend," and "If Jesus Can't Fix It," by Gospel Creators (all gospel singles, WesJac Records).

*BREAKFAST COMMUNICATIONS,Box 42139, Philadelphia PA 19101. Creative Director: Rick Aster. Record producer and record company. Deals with artists only. Produces 1 single and 3 LPs/year. Fee derived from sales royalty or outright fee from recording artist.
How to Contact: Write first and obtain permission to submit. Prefers cassette and lyric or lead sheet. Does not return unsolicited material. Reports in 2 weeks.
Music: Mostly rock.
Tips: "We work only with well-rounded artists who are strong in singing, playing and songwriting."

BRIGHT AND MORNINGSTAR PRODUCTIONS, Box 18A241, Los Angeles CA 90018. (213)512-7823. President: Stan Christopher. Record producer. Deals with artists and songwriters. Produces 2 singles and 2 LPs/year. Fee derived from outright fee from record company.
How to Contact: Prefers cassette or reel-to-reel with 1-3 songs and lyric or lead sheets. SASE. Reports in 3 weeks.
Music: Mostly contemporary Christian, inspirational gospel and gospel/rock; also "message music." Produced "Agape Love," "Change Your Life," and "Which Way Are You Going," all by The Messenger (contemporary Christian singles, Bright & Morning Star Records).
Tips: "Make sure that we can understand the lyrics on the vocal. Have a strong hook along with a good story."

BROADWAY PRODUCTIONS, INC., 1307 Broadway St., Box 551, Sheffield AL 35660. (205)381-1833. President: David Johnson. Vice President of Publishing and Production: Cal Freeman. Record producer and music publisher (Love House Music/ASCAP, Tired Iron Publishing/BMI and Gold of the Shoals Music/BMI). Deals with artists and songwriters. Produces 10 singles and 2-4 LP's/year. Works with 5-6 new songwriters/year. Teams collaborators. Fee derived from sales royalty.
How to Contact: Prefers 7½ ips reel-to-reel or cassette with 1-3 songs and lyric sheet. SASE. Reports in 2 weeks.
Music: Mostly pop and country; also rock, R&B, soul and top 40/pop. Produced "It's So Nice to Be With You," by Jim Gold (pop single); "Perfect Match," by Lynne Wilson (country single); and "Help Myself Start Gettin Over You," by Kenny Price (country single). Other artists include James Govan, Jack Denton, Gus Hardin and Percy Sledge.

*RAFAEL BROM, Box 71988, Los Angeles CA 90071-0988. Record Producer: Rafael Brom. Record producer, music publisher (Cosmotone Music/ASCAP), record company (Cosmotone Records) and recording studio. Deals with artists and songwriters. Produces 1 single and 1 LP/year. Fee derived from sales royalty.
How to Contact: Prefers cassette with any number of songs and lyric sheet. Does not return unsolicited material. "Contact is made only if interested."
Music: Rock, pop, gospel, R&B, dance, adult contemporary, soul, progressive and country. Produced *Padre Pio* recorded by Lord Hamilton (LP); *No. 1*, written and recorded by R.B. (LP); and "A Mockingbird" (by Thomas Dufficy/Lord Hamilton), recorded by Lord Hamilton (single), all on Cosmotone Records. Other artists include Adrian Romero, A. Jude, Oliver Hamilton and Johnny Cheesecake.

*RON BROWN MANAGEMENT, Box 15375, Pittsburgh PA 15237. (412)486-7740. Producer: Ron Brown. Record producer, music publisher (Etna Music/BMI) and record company (Brown Bear Records). Deals with artists and songwriters. Produces 5-15 singles and 3 LPs/year. Fee derived from sales royalty or outright fee from record company.
How to Contact: "Submit only cassette tapes and lead sheet. Reel-to-reel and 8 track tapes will not be accepted." SASE. Reports in 2 weeks.
Music: Mostly R&B, dance and soul; also blues, dance, easy listening, MOR, progressive, rock and top 40/pop. Produced "Funky Fun for Everyone," and *It's Rocker Time*, written and recorded by Rocker Band on Brown Bear Records (dance); and "Its My Heart," (by Terry Guadagni), recorded by Shaker on Brown Bear Records. Other artists include Hytek, Fresh and Herb Fame.

BENNIE BROWN PRODUCTIONS, 3011 Woodway Lane, Box 5702, Columbia SC 29206. (803)788-5734. Contact: Bennie Brown Jr. Deals with artists, songwriters and music publishers. Produces 6 singles and 3 LPs/year. Works with composers and lyricists; teams collaborators. Fee derived from sales royalty.

How to Contact: Query. Prefers cassette with 2-4 songs and lead sheet. SASE. Reports in 3 weeks.
Music: Mostly contemporary gospel; also dance, pop country, MOR, soul, and top 40/pop. Produced "Holding On" (by Willie T. Jones), recorded by The Five Singing Stars (gospel); "This Man Call Jesus" (by Morgan Hill), recorded by Freestyle (contemporary gospel); and "One More River" (by Bennie Brown), recorded by Willie Pinson, all on Nu-Tone Records.

NATHAN BRYDEN MUSIC, Box 1508, Clackamas OR 97015. (503)656-9603. Contact: A&R Department. Record producer and music publisher. Deals with artists and songwriters. Produces 20 singles and 2 LPs/year. Fee derived from sales royalty.
How to Contact: Write first and obtain permission to submit. Prefers cassette (or VHS videocassette) with 2 songs and lead sheets. SASE. Reports in 8 weeks.
Music: Mostly new wave, funk and heavy metal; also reggae, blues and rock.

BULLDOG RECORDS, 8 Mark Lane, New City NY 10956. (914)634-8282. Vice President: Howard Kruger. Record producer and music publisher (Songs for Today, Inc./SESAC). Deals with artists, songwriters and foreign publishers. Produces 10 singles and 20-30 LPs/year. Fee derived from sales royalty.
How to Contact: Prefers cassette with 1-4 songs and lyric sheet. Does not return unsolicited material. Reports in 2 weeks.
Music: MOR, R&B and soul. Produced *Live, In Concert*, by Glen Campbell (MOR LP, RCA Records); and *Me and My Friends*, by David Soul (MOR LP, Energy Records). Other artists include Going Straight, Simon Spiro, Diane Solomon and Dave Martin.

BILL BYRON PRODUCTIONS, 1727 Elm St., Bethlehem PA 18017. (215)865-1083. Project Coordinator: Heather Lynne. Record producer and record company (Mystic Oak Records). Deals with artists. Produces 12 singles and 6-8 LPs/year. Works with 4-6 new songwriters/year. Fee derived from sales royalty.
How to Contact: Write first and obtain permission to submit. Prefers cassette (or videocassette) with 3-9 songs. SASE. Reports in 2 months.
Music: Mostly synthesized rock; also new wave and experimentals. Produced *Weebeard Walkers* (by Byron) recorded by The Videttes (LP); "Trendsetter" and "Sonic Bop," both written and recorded by The Trendsetters (singles), all on Mystic Date Records. Other artists include Even Stephen, Ego, Trendsetter, Psychic Warriors, the BBC, Steve Brosky and Wall to Wall.
Tips: "We are looking for artists with both good studio ability and a good live show. Inform us of any performance dates you might have in the northeast region."

*CALIFORNIA'S BLUE ROSE©, 629 W. Milwaukee St., Jefferson WI 53549. (414)674-5199. Contact: Felix Kubik. Record producer and music publisher.
How to Contact: Write first. Does not return unsolicited material. Reports in 1 month.
Music: Mostly "moderate" rock; also country rock.

THE CALVARY MUSIC GROUP, 142 8th Ave. N, Nashville TN 37203. (615)244-8800. Artist Development: Nelson S. Parkerson Jr. Record producer and music publisher. Deals with artists and songwriters. Produces 10 singles and 12 LPs/year. Fee derived from sales royalty or outright fee from songwriter/artist.
How to Contact: Prefers cassette (or videocassette) with 1-3 songs and lyric sheet. Reports in 1 month "if SASE is included."
Music: Mostly gospel; also choral, church/religious and wedding music. Produced "The Lighthouse," by The Hinson (southern gospel); and "He Is Here," by David Baroni (contemporary gospel).

CAMERICA PRODUCTIONS, 535 5th Ave., Penthouse 35th Floor, New York NY 10017-3610. (212)682-8400. Contact: A&R Department. Record producer and music publisher. Deals with artists

66 *If you do something well, it doesn't have to be lost even if it doesn't find its audience the first time. Things are resurrected—they come back.* **99**

—*Joel Hirschhorn and Al Kasha, songwriters*

and songwriters. Produces 10 singles/year and 5 LP's/year.
How to Contact: Prefers cassette (or VHS videocassette) with 2 songs. Reports only if interested.
Music: "Hits."

*CANTUS PRODUCTIONS LIMITED, 156 Woburn Ave., Toronto, Ontario M5M 1K7 Canada. (416)484-1728. President: Milan Kymlicka. Record producer and music publisher (Cantus/Firmus). Deals with artists and songwriters. Produces 2 singles and 1 LP/year. Fee derived from sales royalty.
How to Contact: Prefers cassette with 3-5 songs and lyric sheet. Does not return unsolicited material. Reports in 5 weeks.
Music: Pop and classical. Produced "Someone" (by Hararlton), recorded by Tara on Doremi Records (single); "Farewell" written and recorded by M. Kymlikca on Firmus A&M Records (single); and "Comedy" (by Waczek/Dolman), recorded by Dolman on Broadway Records (single).

CARLSON-ATLANTA, 1014 Shadowood Pkwy., Atlanta GA 30339. (404)952-8459. President: Kevin Carlson. Record producer, music publisher (Shadow Mountain Music), and record company. Deals with artists and songwriters. Produces 10 singles and 5 LPs/year. Fee derived from sales royalty or outright fee from record company.
How to Contact: Prefers cassette (or VHS videocassette) with 3 songs and lyric or lead sheets. "Clearly label each item that is sent." Does not return unsolicited material. Reports in 1 month.
Music: Mostly rock, pop and contemporary jazz; also New Age and contemporary Christian. Produced *The Electronic Minstrel* written and recorded by Jeff Blanks on Greenleaf Records (contemporary jazz LP); and *Wonderful Days*, written and recorded by Bill Giakas on CPI Records (rock LP). Other artists include Time Zone, Henry Lee Roberts, Vendetta and Freewill.
Tips: "Send lyric sheets! Also, include phone number on all correspondence. Send bio and photo when available."

CAROLINA PRIDE PRODUCTIONS, Box 99, Rougemont NC 27572. (919)477-4077. Manager: Freddie Roberts. Record producer, music publisher (Freddie Roberts Music/BMI) and management firm and booking agency. Deals with artists, songwriters and session musicians. Produces 7 singles and 2 LPs/year. Fee derived from sales royalty.
How to Contact: Call or write first. Prefers 7½ ips reel-to-reel or cassette with 1-5 songs and lyric sheet. SASE. Reports in 3 weeks.
Music: Mostly country, MOR and top 40/pop; also bluegrass, church/religious, gospel and country rock. Produced "Together" (by Brenda Owens), recorded by Roberts Reunion on Bull City Records (single); *Instrumental Favorites*, recorded by Doug McElroy on Sugar Mountain Records (LP); and "I'll Be Gone," written and recorded by Bill McKellar on Bull City Records (single). Other artists include Sleepy Creek, Rodney Hutchins, Gene Thomas and David Laws.

DON CASALE MUSIC, INC., 377 Plainfield St., Westbury NY 11590. (516)333-7898. President: Don Casale. Operations Officer: Andrew B. Krieger. Record producer, music publisher, management firm and studio engineering. Produces 20 singles/year. Deals with artists and songwriters. Fee derived from sales royalty.
How to Contact: Call or write (include SASE) *before* submitting.
Music: Rock, pop, country, black/R&B and new wave. Produced "One For the Money" (by Ahrend/Burke), recorded by Sleeque on Easy Street Records (single); and "Some Country Music" written and recorded by Buffalo T. Jones on Country Records (single). Other artists include Ricky Lane, Suzanne Scott, Carrell Ziti, Genie Swinson and James D'Angelo.
Tips: "Submitted songs should have a 'special' nature about them; a different quality and lyric. Melodies should be particularly 'catchy'."

CATERO PRODUCTIONS, 1301 Chestnut St., San Carlos CA 94070. (415)592-2072. Producer/Engineer: Fred Catero. Record producer and record company. Deals with artists. Produces 2 singles/year and 10 LPs/year. Fee derived from sales royalty or outright fee from songwriter/artist or record company; "depends on the deal."
How to Contact: Call first and obtain permission to submit. Prefers cassette and lyric sheet. "Keep demo clean and short with lyrics up front." Does not return unsolicited material.
Music: Mostly jazz, New Age and contemporary pop; also R&B and classical. Produced *Sweet & Lovely*, by Di Hindman (jazz trio LP); *Messenger of the Son*, by C. Verdeaux (New Age LP), and *Sarah's Samba*, by Mel Martin (jazz LP), all on Catero Records.

*THE CAVE, MUSIC PUBLISHING AND PRODUCTION,3121 N.W. 14th St., Gainesville FL 32605. (904)377-0336. Producer: Thomas G. Hubbell. Record producer, music publisher (The Cave) and record company (Unusual Records). Estab. 1986. Deals with artists and songwriters. Produces 0-5

singles and 0-3 LPs/year. Fee derived from sales royalty.
How to Contact: Write first and obtain permission to submit. Prefers cassette or 15 ips reel-to-reel (or VHS videocassette) with 3-6 songs and lyric sheet. "Make sure there is enough postage on SASE." Reports in 6 weeks.
Music: Mostly rock, experimental/new music and easy listening; also R&B, folk/ballads and MOR. Produced "Don't Talk Too Fast," (by T. Hubbell), recorded by Pure Raisins (rock/single); "The Date," written and recorded by Cathy Hubbell (ballad/single); and "Neutral Zone," written and recorded by John Stephens (rock/single), all on Unusual Records. Others artists include Aaron Brask, Debbi Norton and Larry Newcomb (P.T.).
Tips: "Send marketable material that is unique."

*CBT RECORDS, 3318-E SSW Loop 323, Tyler TX 75701. (214)581-9945. President: Roy L. Haws. Record producer and music publisher. Deals with artists and songwriters. Produces 10 singles and 2 LPs/year.
How to Contact: Prefers cassette with 3 or less songs. "No lyric sheets necessary. Need professionally prepared demo." Reports in 2 weeks.
Music: Country rock, contemporary country and modern traditional country. Produced "Giddy Up Alligator" (by Joe Johnson), recorded by Glen English; "Papa's On a Roll" (by Gary Josey), recorded by Steve Campbell; and "Honky Tonk Heaven" (by Gary Josey), recorded by Donny Goff, all on CBT Records. Other artists include David Houston, Teresa Gilbert, Deborah Meadows, Patty Covert, Michael Knight and Mayf Nutter.

*CHA CHA RECORDS, 15041 Wabash Ave., South Holland IL 60473. (312)339-0307. President: Donald DeLucia. Record producer and music publisher (Don-Del Music/BMI and Don-De Music/ASCAP). Deals with artists. Produces 3 singles and 2 LPs/year. Fee derived from sales royalty.
How to Contact: Prefers cassette with 4-6 songs and lyric sheet. SASE. Reports in 1 week.
Music: Country, rock and top 40/pop.

LOU CICCHETTI, 211 Birchwood Ave., Upper Nyack NY 10960. (914)358-0861. Contact: Lou Cicchetti. Record producer and music publisher (Cousins Music). Deals with artists and songwriters. Produces 2-3 singles/year. Works with 3-4 new songwriters/year. Works with composers. Fee derived from sales royalty.
How to Contact: Prefers 7½ or 15 ips reel-to-reel or cassette with any number songs and lyric sheet. SASE. Reports in 3 weeks.
Music: 50s and 60s country and rock. Produced "The Dancer" (by S. Corrente/J.O'Daniel), recorded by The Dials (rock single); and "One More Heartache," (by T. Percoco), recorded by Coco and Squirt Band, (country single), both on Cousins Records.
Tips: "Melody is disappearing, but I am totally interested in melody. In my opinion, rhythm alone does not make a song. We must do something soon to revitalize the singles market or some viable replacement."

*CISUM PRODUCTIONS, Box 192, Pittsburg KS 66762. (316)231-6443. Vice President: Shawn Strasser. Record producer and music publisher (Country Party Music). Deals with artists and songwriters. Fee derived from sales royalty.
How to Contact: Write first and obtain permission to submit. Prefers cassette (or videocassette) with 5 songs and lyric sheet. Does not return unsolicited material. Reports in 3 months if interested.
Music: Mostly country, novelty and country gospel-rock; also rock, pop and R&B. Produced "Fire the Governments" (by B. Witt), recorded by Weird Wilbur (single); Diet #110 (by G. Strasser), recorded by Wierd Wilbur (single); and *Dewayne Bowman*, by various artists (LP), all on Antique Records. Other artists include Gene Strasser, Dale Anderson and Rich Rhuems.

CLOUDBURST RECORDS, Box 31, Edmonton KY 42129. (502)432-3183. President: W. Junior Lawson. Record producer, music publisher (Holy Spirit Music) and record company. Deals with artists and songwriters. Produces 3 singles and 4 LPs/year. Fee derived from sales royalty.
How to Contact: Prefers 7½ ips reel-to-reel or cassette and lyric sheet. SASE. Reports in 3 weeks.
Music: Mostly southern gospel; also MOR. Produced "I Went to Jesus," by the Servants; "Don't Let the Ship Sail Without You," by the New Apostles; and "When I See the Great King," by the Helmsmen (all southern gospel singles, Cloudburst Records).
Tips: "Be honest. Submit material with less volume on instruments and more volume on voices."

*COLLECTOR RECORDS, Box 2296, Rotterdam Holland 3000 CG The Netherlands. (10)4224889. Research: Cees Klop. Record producer and music publisher (All Rock Music). Deals with artists and songwriters. Produces 10 singles and 30 LPs/year. Fee derived from sales royalty.

How to Contact: Prefers cassette. SAE and IRC. Reports in 1 month.
Music: Mostly 50s rock, rockabilly and country rock; also piano boogie woogie. Produced *Eddie Bond* (by Bond), recorded by Bond/Klop on White Label Records (rock LP); *Louis Gittens*, written and recorded by Gittens on White Label Records (rock LP); and *Rob Hoeke* (by Hoeke), recorded by Cees Klop on Downsouth Records (boogie LP). Other artists include Teddy Redell, Gene Summers and Benny Joy.

*MICHAEL COLLINS/FRANTIC RECORDS,2105 Maryland Ave., Baltimore MD 21218. (301)685-8500. Vice President: Michael Collins. Record producer and promoter. Deals wtih artists and songwriters. Produces 2 LPs/year. Fee derived from outright fee from recording artist.
How to Contact: Prefers cassette or 7½ ips reel-to-reel (or VHS, Beta or ¾" videocassette) with at least 4 songs. Does not return unsolicited material. Reports in 1 month.
Music: Mostly rock, "hard core" and heavy metal. Produced *Eyes of the Wolf*, *When Thunder Comes*, (by Mission) and *8 Essential Attitudes*, all on Frantic Records (all LPs).

CONTINENTAL, Suite 212, 450 Livingston St., Norwood NJ 07648. (201)767-5551. Vice President: Gene Schwartz. Record producer and music publisher (3 Seas Music/ASCAP and Northvale Music/BMI). Deals with artists and songwriters. Produces 12 singles and 5 LPs/year. Fee derived from sales royalty.
How to Contact: Prefers cassette and lyric sheet. SASE. Reports in 2 weeks.
Music: Dance-oriented and top 40/pop.

COUNTRY CHARTS, Suite 234, 24285 Sunnymead Blvd., Moreno Valley CA 92388-9971. (714)653-1556. Professional Manager: LaDonna Kay. Record producer, music publisher (KayDay/BMI, OurWay/ASCAP) and record company (Maxima Records). Deals with artists and songwriters. Produces 5-10 singles and 3 LPs/year. Fee derived from sales royalty and production fee.
How to Contact: Prefers cassette or 7½ ips reel-to-reel (or VHS videocassette) with 1-10 songs and lyric sheet. "Make sure your name and phone number are on the tape." SASE. Reports in 1 month.
Music: Mostly contemporary country; also all other types. Produced "King of Mediocrity," "Livin' On Love Again," and "Love Struck," all written and recorded by Don Malena on Maxima Records (all contemporary country).

COUNTRY STAR PRODUCTIONS, 439 Wiley Ave., Franklin PA 16323. (814)432-4633. President: Norman Kelly. Record producer and music publisher (Country Star Music/ASCAP, Kelly Music/BMI and Process Music/BMI). Deals with artists and songwriters. Produces 8-10 singles and 2-3 LPs/year. Works with 3-4 new songwriters/year. Works with composers and lyricists; teams collaborators. Fee derived from outright fee from artist/songwriter or record company.
How to Contact: Prefers 7½ ips reel-to-reel or cassette with 2-4 songs and lyric sheet. SASE. Reports in 2 weeks.
Music: Mostly country; also bluegrass, easy listening, folk, gospel, MOR, rock and top 40/pop. Produced "Climbing Mountains" (by Ora DeLamar), recorded by Lady Sugar Belle; "The Old Train Station" (by Daniel Travis), recorded by John York on Country Star Records; and "Every Now and Then" (by Don McHan/Ernie Goff/Billy Ready), recorded by Ruthie Phillips on Process Records. Other artists include Bonnie Baldwin, Denver Bill, Virge Brown and Bob Stamper.
Tips: "Submit only your best efforts."

*COVERT RECORD PRODUCTIONS INC., 7 Pratt Blvd., Glen Cove NY 11542. (516)759-4290. Producers: Ric Wake, Clay Hutchinson and Richie Cannata. Record producer and music publisher. Deals with artists and songwriters. Produces 15 singles and 2 LPs/year. Fee derived from sales royalty.
How to Contact: Prefers cassette and lyric sheet ("and picture if artist").
Music: Dance only. Produced *Tell It to My Heart* (by Sewersky), recorded by Taylor Dane on Artista Records (dance EP); and *I Will* (by Wake/Forbes/Tancredi), recorded by Lori Zee on Covert Records (dance EP). Other artists include Cheryl Patrick.

COWBOY JUNCTION FLEA MARKET AND PUBLISHING CO., Hwy. 44 W., Lecanto FL 32661. (904)746-4754. Contact: Elizabeth Thomson. Record producer and music publisher (Cowboy Junction). Deals with artists and songwriters. Produces 3 singles and 2 LPs/year. Works with 6 new songwriters/year. Works with lyricists and composers and teams collaborators. Fee derived from sales royalty.
How to Contact: Prefers 7½ ips reel-to-reel or cassette with 1-4 songs and lyric sheet. SASE. Reports ASAP.
Music: Mostly country, gospel and bluegrass. Produced "The Challenger—Tribute to Crew of Seven," and "Easter Bunny," (by Boris Max Pastuch), and "Easter Day," recorded by Buddy Max (country

singles, Cowboy Junction Records). Other artists include Wally Jones, Leo Voyason, Johnny Pastuck, Ruth Handson, Charlie Floyd and Lloyd Stevens.

CRUSADER RECORDS AND TAPES, Box 241, Cameron MO 64429. (816)632-6039. President: E.K. Bruhn. Record producer, music publisher (Time Minstrel Music) and record company (Crusader Records). Deals with artists, songwriters and other producers. Produces 3-6 singles and 2-5 LPs/year. Fee is derived from sales royalty or outright fee from artist/songwriter or record company.
How to Contact: "Write or call about your interest." Submit cassette, reel-to-reel or record with 2 songs." SASE. Reports in 10 weeks.
Music: Country/rock and top 40/pop. Produced *Kopperfield Christmas* (by various writers), recorded by Kopperfield (Christmas/pop LP and cassette); "I Can't Let My Heart" (by Linscombe/Parvin/Kopperfield), recorded by Allen Parvin (country single); and *Nighttracks* (by Filley/Dodson/Kopperfield), recorded by Kopperfield (pop LP and cassette), all on Crusader Records. Other artists include Terry Alden and Edna Graham.
Tips: "We like working with energetic artists who like promoting their material."

D.S.M. PRODUCERS, Suite 1204, 161 W. 54th St., New York NY 10019. (212) 245-0006. Contact: Dominie Celanio. Producer/A&R: Suzan Bader. Record producer, music publisher (D.S.M. Producers Enterprises Publishing Co./ASCAP), and personal management and merchandising firm. Deals with artists and songwriters. Produces 6-12 singles and 2-4 LPs/year. Fee derived from sales royalty, outright fee from songwriter/artist or record company. Requires 50% deposit for studio time 10 days prior to start of session, unless a major label contract.
How to Contact: Write or call first to arrange personal interview. Prefers cassette (or VHS videocassette) with 1-3 songs and lyric or lead sheets. SASE. Reports in 6 weeks.
Music: Mostly top 40, R&B/dance and rock; also country and jazz. Produced "Shake Your Body Line," and "Spend Some Time," by American Steel (R&B singles); "Dancin' On Air," by Tommy Goode (rock/dance single); "Easy Kinda Love," by E. Mauge on LuLu Records; and "Last Train to Clarksville," recorded by Fonda Rae on Urban Rock Records (single). Other artists include Tommy Goode, Lovette, Roxxara, and Oswald and the Herring Bones.
Tips: Have a great tune with lyric or lead sheet."

***DALVANIUS**, 87 Wilson St., Haweva, New Zealand 87272. A&R: Dalvanius. Record producer, music publisher (Maiu Music) and record company. Deals with artists and songwriters. Produces 20 singles and 3 LPs/year. Fee derived from sales royalty.
How to Contact: Prefers cassette (or VHS videocassette) and lyric or lead sheet. "Include an 8x10 b&w photo and biography." Does not return unsolicited material. Reports in 1 month.
Music: Mostly rock, soul and blues; also jazz, country and gospel. Produced "Poi E," "Aku Raukura," and "Hei Konei Ra" all by Patea Maoviclub (all rock singles on Maui Records). Other artists include Tama Band and Taste of Bounty.

DAN THE MAN PRODUCTIONS, Box 702, Cleveland OH 44107. President: Daniel L. Bischoff. Record producer, music publisher (Dan the Man Music Publishing Co./ASCAP and Bischoff Music Publishing/BMI) and record company. Deals with artists, songwriters and producers. Produces 4 singles/year. Works with 4-6 new songwriters/year. Works with lyricists and teams composers. Fee derived from sales royalty.
How to Contact: Prefers cassette with 2-4 songs and lyric sheet. SASE. Reports in 2-3 weeks.
Music: Mostly country, R&B and top 40; also novelty, rock and soul. Published "E.T. Interview," and "The Michael Jackson Interview," (by Dan Bischoff), recorded by Dan the Man on Dan the Man Records (novelty); and "Telephone Gossip," (by M. Lambert), recorded by Johnny Wright on Dan the Man Records (country).

MAL DAVIS, 730 S. Harvey, Oak Park IL 60304. (312)386-7355 or 653-1919. Producer: Mal Davis. Record producer and engineer. Deals with artists and songwriters. Produces 4 singles and 8 LPs/year. Fee derived from sales royalty or outright fee from songwriter/artist or record company.
How to Contact: Prefers cassette, 7½ or 15 ips reel-to-reel (or VHS videocassette) with 2-6 songs and lyric sheet or lead sheet. Does not return unsolicited material; SASE for reply. Reports in 6 weeks.
Music: Mostly contemporary gospel, MOR rock and progressive rock and jazz; also country. Produced "Time To Fly," written and recorded by Chris Christensen (contemporary Christian); "Random Factor," (instrumental), and "Jugular," (MOR), written and recorded by Dennis Osterman, all on Custom Records.

DAWN PRODUCTIONS, Suite 1, 621 Park City Center, Lancaster PA 17601. President: Joey Welz. Record producer, music publisher and record company. Deals with artists, songwriters and producers.

Produces 6 singles and 3 LPs/year. Works with 2-4 new songwriters/year. Teams collaborators. Fee derived from sales royalty.
How to Contact: Prefers cassette with 3-6 songs and lyric sheet. Does not return unsolicited material. "We hold submissions for consideration."
Music: Mostly pop, rock and country; also dance, easy listening, folk, MOR and top 40/pop. Produced "Old Fashion Rock and Roll," (by Duane McCaskin/Joey Welz); "There Will Always Be Rock and Roll," (by James Myers/Alan Freed); "Bring Back the Music," (by Frankie Beecher/Joey Welz, all recorded by Joey Welz on Caprice Records (all 45s). Others artists include Gerry Granahan, Santo and The Great Train Robbery.
Tips: "Write commercial music and try to have a demo that would be good enough to be pressed."

*DAWN PROMOTIONS AND AGENCY, LTD., 10 St. Mary's Hill, Stamford, Lincs., PE9 2DP, England. 44-0780-51736. Managing Director: Ken Cox. Record producer, music publisher (Pixie Music Co. Ltd.) and record company (Soul Stop, Buffalo and Weasel). Works with artists and songwriters. Produces 20 singles and 2 LPs/year. Fee derived from sales royalty.
How to Contact: Submit demo tape and lyric sheet. Prefers cassette with 2-6 songs on demo. SAE and IRC. Reports in 1 month.
Music: Mostly country and up-tempo soul; also top 40/pop.

*AL DELORY AND MUSIC MAKERS, #11, 3000 Hillsboro Rd., Nashville TN 37215. (615)292-2140. President: Al DeLory. Record producer, music publisher (DeLory Music) and career consultant. Deals with artists and songwriters. Produces 20 singles and 10 LPs/year. Fee derived from sales royalty, outright fee from recording artists or record company, and consultation fees. Charges for "consultation and critique of material."
How to Contact: Write or call first and obtain permission to submit or to arrange personal interview. Prefers cassette (or VHS videocassette) with 2 songs and lyric or lead sheet. Does not return unsolicited material. Reports in 6 weeks.
Music: Mostly pop, R&B and country; also rock. Produced "Gentle On My Mind," "By the Time I Get to Phoenix," and "Wichita Lineman," recorded by Glen Campbell; "Put Your Head on My Shoulder," and "Hurt So Bad," recorded by Lettermen; and "Go Where You Wanna Go," recorded by Mamas & Papas.

THE DEMO FARM, (formerly Mercantile Music), Rt. 4 Box 302, Saundersville Ferry Rd., Mt. Juliet TN 37122. (615)754-2444. President: Kent Fox. Record producer and music publisher (Mercantile Music/BMI and Blueford Music/ASCAP). Deals with artists and songwriters. Fee derived from sales royalty.
How to Contact: Query first. Does not accept unsolicited material.
Music: Country.

DESTINY PRODUCTIONS, INC., 117 W. Rockland Rd., Box 615, Libertyville IL 60048. (312)362-4060. Vice President: Rick Johnson. Record producer and music publisher (Amalgamated Tulip Corp.). Deals with artists and songwriters. Produces 4 singles and 2 LPs/year. Works with 5 new songwriters/year. Fee derived from sales royalty.
How to Contact: Prefers cassette with 3-5 songs and lyric sheet. SASE. Reports in 2 months.
Music: Mostly rock, top 40 and country; also pop, MOR, hard rock, dance, R&B and blues. Published *Conrad Black*, by Conrad Black (rock/R&B LP, Dharma Records); *Dancexercise*, by Johnson & Poole (exercise LP, Homexercise Records); and "Walkin In a Straight Line," by Nouvea Riche (pop rock).

DMI PRODUCTIONS, #1911, 6255 Sunset Blvd., Hollywood CA 90026. (213)462-1922. Managing Director: Christian de Walden. Record producer and music publisher (De Walden Music International, Inc./BMI, ASCAP). Deals with artists and songwriters. Produces 8-9 singles and 3-4 LPs/year. Fee derived from sales royalty.
How to Contact: Arrange personal interview if in the area or write or call and obtain permission to submit. Prefers cassette with 2-3 songs and lyric sheet. Does not return unsolicited materials. Reports in 5 weeks or ASAP.
Music: Dance, R&B, MOR and top 40/pop. Produced *Just Me*, by Bonnie Bianco (pop/rock LP); and *Secret Passions* by Amanda Lear (dance LP). Published "I'll Still Be Loving You," recorded by Restless Heart (country). Other artists include B.J. Thomas.

DODGY PRODUCTIONS, 1 Prince of Wales Passage, London NW1 3EE England. (01)388-8635. Managing Director: Safta Jaffery. Record producer and manager. Deals with artists and songwriters. Produces 20 singles and 5 LPs/year. Fee derived from sales royalty and/or outright fee from record company.

How to Contact: Prefers cassette (or VHS videocassette) with 4 songs and lyric sheet. Include bio and photo. SAE and IRC. Reports in 6 weeks.
Music: Mostly rock, soul and disco; also pop and heavy metal. Produced *The Dark*, written and recorded by Metal Church on Elektra Records (heavy rock LP); *Mania*, written and recorded by Lucy Show, on Big Time Records (rock LP); and *Never Say Die*, written and recorded by Steve Jerome on PRT Records (soul LP). Other artists include Accept, Austin Howard, XTC, Roger Waters, Wa Wa Nee, The Wooden Tops and The Stage.

*DOUGH PRODUCTIONS AND MANAGEMENT,1111 Warren Ave., Cherry Hill NJ 08002-3260. (609)795-3471. Producer/Owner: Alexander Esposito. Record producer and music publisher (Radio Vienna/Dough Music). Deals with artists and songwriters. Fee derived from outright fee from recording artist or record company.
How to Contact: Write or call first and obtain permission to submit. Prefers cassette with 2-3 songs and lyric or lead sheets. Does not return unsolicited material. Reports in 7 weeks.
Music: Mostly R&B/pop, R&B, pop/rock and jazz; also 20th century string music and baroque contrapuntle compositional style. Produced "The Pictures," written and recorded by The Pictures; and "John Dough," written and recorded by John Dough.

*DOWNTOWN RECORD PRODUCTIONS,Steenmolenstraat, 7, St. Katelijne Waver 2800 Belgium. (15)42 38 39. Managing Director: Piroux Ghislain. Record producer and record company. Deals with artists and songwriters. Produces 20-25 singles and 3-5 LPs/year. Fee derived from sales royalty.
How to Contact: Prefers cassette or reel-to-reel (or videocassette) with 2-6 songs and lyric sheet. SAE and IRC. Reports in 6 weeks.
Music: Mostly pop, mainstream rock, funk (and disco/funk); also new wave, R&B and "golden oldies" (no heavy metal). Produced "Never In A Million Years," recorded by Linda Scott; "Jungle Drums," recorded by Johnny Otis; and "Happy Together," recorded by The Turtles all on Downtown Records (all singles). Other artists include Kokomo and Guenaelle.
Tips: "We are an independent company which is an enormous advantage in a small country like Belgium. We can easily distribute product ourselves. If it's a hit in Belgium—the other countries of Europe are all watching. In our country a product stands much more chance of becoming a hit if it is danceable."

DRAGON RECORDS, INC., 872 Morris Park Ave., Bronx NY 10462. (212)792-2198. Vice President: Mr. "G". Record producer and music publisher (Vin-Joy Publishing). Deals with artists and songwriters. Produces 20 singles and 5 LPs/year. Fee derived from sales royalty.
How to Contact: "We accept material by recommendation only."
Music: Easy listening, country, MOR and top 40/pop. Produced "Promise Me," (by J. Heath), recorded by Smokey Heath; "A Letter to D.J.," (by V. Gagliano), and "One Prayer," (by Gagliano and Heath), both recorded by Joyce Heath, all on Dragon Records, (all singles).

*DUANE MUSIC, INC., 382 Clarence Ave., Sunnyvale CA 94086. (408)739-6133. President: Garrie Thompson. Record producer and music publisher. Deals with artists and songwriters. Fee derived from sales royalty.
How to Contact: Prefers cassette with 1-2 songs. SASE. Reports in 1 month.
Music: Blues, country, rock, soul, and top 40/pop. Produced "Wichita," (country single, Hush Records); and "Syndicate of Sound," (rock single, Buddah Records).

*DUM DUM RECORDS, Opernring #1, 1010 Vienna, Austria Europe. (0222)568601. Managing Director: Wolfgang Strobl. Record producer. Deals with artists and songwriters. Fee derived from sales royalty. Prefers cassette (or VHS videocassette) and lyric sheet. Does not return unsolicited material. Reports in 6 weeks.
Music: Mostly disco dance, rock dance and wave dance; also jazz dance.

DUPUY RECORDS/PRODUCTIONS/PUBLISHING, INC., Suite 200, 10960 Ventura Blvd., Studio City CA 91604. (818)980-6412). President: Pedro Dupuy. Record producer and music publisher (Dupuy Publishing, Inc./ASCAP). Deals with artists, songwriters, music arrangers, copyists, musicians, background vocalists, singers and recording engineers. Produces 5 singles and 5 LPs/year. Fee derived from sales royalty; differs with each artist.
How to Contact: Write or call first or arrange personal interview. Prefers cassette with 2-4 songs and lyric sheet. SASE. Reports in 1 month.
Music: Easy listening, jazz, MOR, R&B, soul and top 40/pop. Artists include Gordon Gilman, Michael Gruwell, Jack D. Colombo, Krisanthi Pappas, Michael R. Iannantuoni and Amy Nuzum.
Tips: "Artists and songwriters should have strong songs, versatility, and open minds."

DYNAMIC ARTISTS PRODUCTION COMPANY, Box 25654, Richmond VA 23260. (804)288-3939. Producer: Joe Carter. Record producer, music publisher (Hot Gold Music Publishing Co.) and record company (Dynamic Artists Records). Deals with artists and songwriters. Produces 20 singles and 2 LPs/year. Fee derived from sales royalty.
How to Contact: Prefers cassette with 3-5 songs and lyric sheet. Does not return unsolicited material. Reports in 1 month.
Music: Mostly top 40/pop, R&B and soul; also gospel and jazz. Produced "Without You Tonight," by Waller Family (ballad single, Dynamic Artists Records); "I Believe in You," by Waller Family (ballad single, MCA Records); and "Let Me Lay My Funk on You," by Poison (dance/funk single, Roulette Records).

EARTH RECORDS CO., Rt. 3, Box 57, Troy AL 36081. (205)566-7932. Producer: Eddie Toney. Record producer and music publisher (Rashone Music/BMI). Deals with artists and songwriters. Produces 4 singles/year. Fee derived from sales royalty or outright fee from record company.
How to Contact: Call first about your interest. Prefers cassette with 2-4 songs. SASE. Reports in 3 weeks.
Music: Blues, children's, country, gospel, progressive, R&B, rock and soul. Produced "Need Your Loving," by Tim Toney (soul single, Earth Records).

*EBONY STAR PRODUCTIONS, 1612 Marlbrook Dr., Atlanta GA 30307. (404)371-8583. A&R: Rob Easterday. Record producer and management firm (Briefcase of Talent). Deals with artists and songwriters. Produces "several" singles and LPs/year. Fee derived from outright fee from recording artist.
How to Contact: Write or call first and obtain permission to submit. Prefers cassette (or VHS videocassette) with 3-4 songs and lyric sheet. Does not return unsolicited material. Reports in 2 weeks.
Music: Mostly progressive, new wave and punk; also rock, funk and R&B. Produced "Yuppie Alcoholic," (by Stan Hodgen), recorded by Rob Easterday on ESR Records; "Another Funk," (by Stan Hodgen), recorded by Robert Howell on ESR Records; and "Faerchild," (by Scott Faerchild), recorded by Robert Howell, (all EPs). Other artists include Max Density, Georgia Vidiots and Charley Knunks.
Tips: "Professionalism is the absolute key to everything. A quality demo is essential for any submission—always the best product should be sent."

GEOFFREY ENGLAND, 2810 McBain, Redondo Beach CA 90278. (213)371-5793. Contact: Geoffrey England. Record producer. Deals with artists and songwriters. Produces 10 singles and 2 LPs/year. Fee derived from sales royalty and/or outright fee from record company.
How to Contact: Prefers cassette and lyric sheet. SASE. Reports in 2 months.
Music: Mainstream melodic rock. Produced *England 402*, by England (rock LP, Statue Records); *The 1st*, by The Asteroids (rock LP, Statue Records); and *Black*, by Blood Rock (rock LP, EMI Records).

EPOCH UNIVERSAL PUBLICATIONS, INC., 10802 N. 23rd Ave., Phoenix AZ 85029. (602)864-1980. President/Executive Producer: Raymond P. Bruno. Music Editor: Henry Papale. Record producer and music publisher. Affiliate: North American Liturgy Resources (NALR). Deals with artists, songwriters and authors. Produces 12 LPs/year. Fee derived from sales royalty or outright fee from artist/songwriter or record company.
How to Contact: Prefers 15 or 30 ips reel-to-reel, cassette (or videocassette) with minimum 6 songs and lyric sheet. SASE. Reports in 1 month.
Music: Mostly liturgical; also children's, choral, church/religious, and gospel. Produced *The Message Goes Forth*, written and recorded by Daniel Consiglio (liturgical LP, Epoch/NALR Records); *Do Not Fear to Hope*, written and recorded by Rory Cooney (liturgical LP, Epoch/NALR Records) and *The Steadfast Love*, written and recorded by The St. Louis Jesuits (liturgical LP, Epoch/NALR Records). Other artists include Carey Landry, Fr. Lucien Deiss, Michael Joncas and Grayson Brown.
Tips: "Songs should be written to be sung by congregation."

ESQUIRE INTERNATIONAL, Box 6032, Station B, Miami FL 33123. (305)547-1424. President: Jeb Stuart. Record producer, music publisher and management firm. Deals with artists and songwriters. Produces 6 singles and 2 LPs/year. Fee derived from sales royalty or independent leasing of masters and placing songs.
How to Contact: Write or call first. Prefers cassette or disc with 2-4 songs and lead sheet. SASE. Reports in 1 month.
Music: Blues, church/religious, country, dance, gospel, jazz, rock, soul and top 40/pop. Produced "Can't Count the Days," (R&B single, Kent Records); "Sitba," (R&B single, King Records); and "You're So Right For Me," (disco single, Esquire Records), all by Jeb Stuart. Other artists include Valerie and Stone Foxx.
Tips: "When sending out material make sure it is well organized and put together as neatly as possible and it is of good sound quality."

ETC MUSIC INC., 1600 Delorimier, Second Floor, Montréal Québec H2K 3W5 Canada. Vice President, Production: Michel Le Francois. Record producer and music publisher. Deals with artists and songwriters. Produces 10 singles and 12 LPs/year. Fee derived from sales royalty, outright fee from songwriter/artist and/or outright fee from record company.
How to Contact: Prefers cassette or 15 or 7½ ips reel-to-reel with 4 songs and lyric sheet. "For artists, biography and photo required." SAE and IRC. Reports in 3 weeks.
Music: Mostly pop/rock, adult contemporary and Latin; also jazz, children's and country. Produced *Jean Vanasse/Miroslav Vitous*, by J. Vanasse on Justin Records; *Nuance*, by Nuance on Time ISBA Records; and *Dorais*, by J. Dorais on CBS Records (all LPs). Other artists include Jean Beaudet, Anne Renee, Manuel Tadros, Max, Martin Savoria and Jano Bergeron.

JACK EUBANKS PRODUCTIONS, Box 390, Hendersonville TN 37077-0390. (615)824-1219. Secretary: Helen Strahan. Record producer and music publisher (House of Manor Music). Deals with artists and songwriters. Produces 10-12 singles and 8-10 LPs/year. Fee is derived from sales royalty or outright fee from songwriter/artist or record company.
How to Contact: Call *first* and obtain permission to submit. Prefers cassette (or VHS videocassette) with 3 songs and lyric sheet. SASE. Reports in 1 month.
Music: Country, MOR and gospel. Produced *Golden Legacy*, by Chuck Wagon Gang (gospel LP, Copperfield Records); "Dixie U.S.A.," by Craig Southern (MOR single, Royal Master Records); and "Red, White, Blue and Gray," by the Chuck Wagon Gang ("American" single, Copperfield Records). Other artists include: Sierra, Ronna Reeves, Fred Smothers, and The Northains.
Tips: "I only deal with people who have potential."

EURO TEC RECORDS AND PRODUCTIONS, Box 3077, Ventura CA 93006. (805)658-2488. Vice President: Bruce Caplin. Record producer, music publisher (Mikelly Tunes); and record label. Deals with artists and songwriters. Produces 5 singles and 1 LP/year. Fee derived from sales royalty.
How to Contact: Write or call about your interest. Prefers cassette (or Beta 2 or VHS videocassette) with 1-12 songs and lyric sheet. SASE. Reports in 2 months.
Music: Mostly top 40/pop, rock, dance oriented, hard rock, easy listening and Spanish rock; also blues, country, MOR and R&B.

JESSE EVATTE, Box 7172, Greenville SC 29610. (803)269-3961. Owner/Producer: Jesse Evatte. Record producer and music publisher (Sivatt Music Publisher). Produces 4 singles and 6 LPs/year. Deals with artists and songwriters. Fee derived from outright fee from artist and/or record company.
How to Contact: Prefers cassette with 3-4 songs and lyric sheet. SASE. Reports in 6 weeks.
Music: Gospel and inspirational. Produced *Sittin' on Ready*, (by Larry Orr), recorded by Jesse Evatte on Mark Five Records (LP and single); "A Brand New Me," (by Randy Buxton), recorded by The Buxtons on Mark Five Records (single); and *No More Heartaches*, (by Chet Johnson), recorded by Kenny Barnes on SOS Records (LP).

FACTORY BEAT RECORDS, INC., 521 5th Ave., New York NY 10175. (212)757-3638. Producer/President: Rena L. Feeney. Record producer and music publisher (Ren-Maur Music/BMI). Produces 4-6 singles and 2 LPs/year. Fee derived from sales royalty.
How to Contact: Prefers cassette with 2-4 songs and lyric sheet only. SASE. Reports in 3 weeks.
Music: R&B, rock, soul and top 40/pop. Produced "Do It To Me and I'll Do It To You," "Once You Fall In Love," and "Same Language" by Rena Romano; and "Champagne and Caviar" and "Saturday Night" by Fantasy Force (rap).
Tips: "Have a finished product, ready to master and press for commercial use."

BOBBY FARRELL PHONORECORD PRODUCTIONS, 1826 Poplar Lane SW, Albuquerque NM 87105. (505)243-2881. A&R Director: Robert F. Cunningham. Record producer, music publisher (Bobby Farrell, International), distributor and foreign licensor. Deals with artists, songwriters and independent producers. Produces 35 singles and 50 LPs/year. Fee derived from outright fee from record company (custom production fees for services).
How to Contact: Prefers cassette (or Beta or VHS videocassette) with any number of songs and lyric or lead sheets. "Home productions are fine with typewritten lyric sheets and cassette. Include name, address, telephone and copyright claim on all sheets. Name and telephone on tapes. Insert postpaid postcard with submitted materials. We'll send it back to verify receipt. Limit running time to three minutes or less until established, for everything except classical works. Artists send home production of your singing. Don't waste money on studio production we can't use. No advance permission required." Does not return material; "we maintain submissions on a permanent file for future use." Reports when material is sold/used.
Music: Mostly R&B, country, rock, gospel and contemporary. Produced "Long Month of Sundays"

(by J. Edison), recorded by Dynamite Jim on FMC Records (country single); "A Love I Used to Know" (by L. Beach), recorded by Kwani Kwan on Juke Records (pop single); and "Morning Memories, Nighttime Nightmares" (by D. Lewis), recorded by Tristy Hall on Vandor Records (rock LP). Other artists include Polidori, Lorraine Moore, Warchylde, Goldhue, Concrete Candy, Inspiration, Merry Bells, Shorty Howard, Hank Marshal, and Shiprock.

CHARLIE FIELDS, 44 Music Sq. E., Nashville TN 37203. (615)255-2175. President: Charlie Fields. Record producer and music publisher (Charta Records). Deals with artists and songwriters. Produces 10 singles/year and 6-8 LPs/year. Fee derived from sales royalty or outright fee from songwriter/artist.
How to Contact: Prefers cassette or reel-to-reel with 2-3 songs and lyric sheet. SASE. Reports in 3 weeks.
Music: Mostly MOR, blues and country; also gospel. Produced "Seven New Stars," by David Walsh (MOR/country); "Sweet Loves Bandit," by John Walter Morrison (MOR/country); and "Boogie Woogie Baby," by Mike Arnett (MOR/country). Other artists include Marge & Debby Rhoads, David Walsh and Donna, Darlene and Jack Elliott.

*JOHN FISHER & ASSOCIATES, 7 Music Circle N., Nashville TN 37203. (615)256-3616. President: John Fisher. Record producer and music publisher. Deals with artists and songwriters. Fee derived from outright fee from recording artist or record company.
How to Contact: Prefers cassette with 1-6 songs and lyric sheet. SASE. Reports in 2 weeks.
Music: Country, 50s rock and R&B. Artists include Terry Stafford and Steve Ricks.

FM-REVOLVER RECORDS LTD., 152 Goldthorn Hill, Penn, Wolverhampton, WV2 3VA, England. 44-(0902)345345. Contact: Managing Director. Record producer, music publisher (Rocksong Music Publishing Co.) and record company (Heavy Metal America, Heavy Metal Records and Heavy Metal Worldwide). Works with artists, songwriters and label producers. Produces 15-20 singles and 20 LPs/year.
How to Contact: Prefers cassette (or VHS/PAL videocassette) with 1-3 songs. Does not return unsolicited material. Reports in 1 month.
Music: Pop, rock, AOR, dance and alternative. Artists include White Sister, Jack Green and King Kobra.
Tips: "Send good photographs, short bio (50-100 words maximum); and *relevant* press clippings, i.e., charts, etc."

*FROG RECORDS/EFA DISTRIBUTION, Mouson St. 12, Frankfurt, Hessen 6000 West Germany. (69)445092. Creative Producers: Ulrich Vortiehr and Horst Lehand. Record producer and music publisher. Deals with artists only. Produces 4 singles and 6-8 LPs/year.
How to Contact: Prefers cassette with 8-10 songs. SAE and IRC. Reports in 1 month.
Music: Rock, jazz and disco/funk. Produced *Raining Heart*, written and recorded by P. Heckmann/US (pop 12"); *Romantic Warrior*, written and recorded by C. Kuhlmann/US (jazz rock LP); and "Strangers" (by M. Brycz), recorded by P. Heckmann/US (disco 12"), all on Frog Records. Other artists include Japotage, Etranger, Romantic Warrior, and Andreas Facke.

FUTURE 1 PRODUCTIONS, 808 S. Pantamo Rd., Tucson AZ 85710. (602)885-5931. Producers: James M. Gasper and Thomas M. Dukes. Record producer and music publisher (Myko Music/BMI). Deals with artists and songwriters. Produces 2 singles and 1 LP/year. Fee derived from sales royalty.
How to Contact: Write first. Submit cassette (or videocassette) with 2-4 songs and lyric sheet. Does not return unsolicited material. SASE. Reports in 6 weeks.
Music: Rock, dance rock and AOR. Produced "How Do You Feel," (by J. Gasper/P. Murphy), recorded by Fellowship (rock); "Life Is A Movie," (by J. Gasper and R. Ruiz), recorded by Silent Partners (pop/rock); and "Take Care of Yourself," (by Tom Privett), recorded by Silent Partners (dance rock), all on Ariana Records. Other artists include 4 Walls, The Rakeheads and the El Caminos.

FUTURE STEP SIRKLE, Box 2095, Philadelphia PA 19103. (215)844-1947. Vice President: S. Deane Henderson. Record producer, music publisher and promoter (Communication Concept). Deals with artists and songwriters. Produces 3 LPs/year. Fee derived from sales royalty.
How to Contact: Prefers cassette (or VHS videocassette) with 4 songs and lyric sheet. Does not return unsolicited material. Reports in 3 weeks.
Music: Mostly heavy metal; also church/religious, gospel, hard rock and top 40/pop. Produced "Delirious," by Molecules of Force, (Future Step Sirkle Records); "Live by Faith," by Verdell Colbert and Off Spring Gospel Singers (gospel single, Future Step Sirkle Records); and "Just Hurry On Up," by Molecules of Force (new wave/R&B single, Future Step Sirkle Records). Others artists include Dean Morrow, The Racers, Krun Vallatine, Shonee, and Voronica Johnson.

FYDAQ PRODUCTIONS, 240 E. Radcliffe Dr., Claremont CA 91711. (714)624-0677. President: Gary K. Buckley. Record producer. Deals with artists, songwriters and record companies. Produces 2-5 singles and 4-5 LPs/year. Fee derived from sales royalty, outright fee from record company, or outright fee from songwriter/artist.
How to Contact: Write first. Prefers cassette with 1-4 songs and lead sheet. SASE. Reports in 3 weeks.
Music: Country, easy listening, folk, MOR, rock, soul and top 40/pop. Produced "Touch Me Now," by Borderline (top 40/single, Majega Records); *Sky's the Limit*, by Michael Noll (top 40/pop LP, Gottabehit Records); and *My Simple Song*, by Debbie Norheim (gospel LP, DNC Records).

MICHAEL GALE ENTERTAINMENT, 29 S. Erie, Toledo OH 43602. (419)244-8599. President: Michael Drew Shaw. Record producer and music publisher. Deals with artists and songwriters. Produces 5-10 singles and 1-5 LPs/year. Fee derived from sales royalty.
How to Contact: Prefers cassette with 3 songs and lyric sheet. Does not return unsolicited material. Reports in 6 weeks.
Music: Country, MOR, jazz and rock. Produced "Ring-a-Ding," and "Helluva Nite," by Hotlix (MOR singles, MDS Records); and "A Place to Hide," by Mikki Walsh (MOR single, Jamestune Records). Other artists include Lori Le Fevre, Nevada Flatts, Mick Payne, Polyphony, Woody Brubaker, Kerry Clark and Ebenezr.
Tips: "Actively seeking acts for new record label (Newstar Internatioal Records) during next two years. Interested in self-contained acts ready to tour. Will review any type act regardless of music style."

TERRY GARTHWAITE, Box 14, San Geronimo CA 94963. (415)488-4778. Producer: Terry Garthwaite. Record producer. Deals with artists and songwriters. Produces 3 LPs/year. Fee derived from sales royalty or outright fee from artist.
How to Contact: Prefers cassette. SASE.
Music: Mostly New Age, light rock and jazz; also women's music, blues/folk, R&B and pop. Produced *Power of My Love*, by Susan Savell (New Age LP, Heartlight Records); *Harmony*, by Hunter Davis (folk rock LP, Redwood Records); and *Wild Strings* by Jasmine (rock LP, Kebergg Records). Other artists include Nicholas/Glover/Wray and Terry Garthwaite.
Tips: "I don't need highly produced demos to understand a song. A clear vocal with simple accompaniment to guide the feel is fine. Most of my artists are writers looking for someone else's way of saying something they didn't, but the words are important. I produce albums for writers/artists with or without bands, and work with them from selecting songs for an album through production of the master tape. There are more independent labels now than ever before and more independent artists striking out on their own. A song on any label has more chance of being heard than if it stays in your head. Spread your ideas/songs around (even pop artists record inspirational songs)."

GCS PRODUCTIONS, Suite 206, 1508 Harlem, Memphis TN 38114. (901)274-2726. Producer: Reginald Eskridge. Record producer. Deals with artists and songwriters. Produces 20 singles and 7 LPs/year. Fee derived from sales royalty or outright fee from record company.
How to Contact: Prefers 7½ or 15 ips reel-to-reel with 3-7 songs and lyric sheet. SASE. Reports in 6 weeks.
Music: Mostly top 40/pop, R&B and gospel; also blues and soul. Produced "Early Morning Man," by Cheryl Fox (top 40/pop single, GCS Records); "The Beat is Fresh," by First Class Crew (rap single, GCS Records); and "Hooked on Love," by Eddy Mayberry (R&B single, Blue Town Records).

*GEIMSTEINN, THOR BALDURSSON, RUNAR JULIUSSON,Skolaveg 12, Keflavik 230 Iceland. (92) 2717. Manager: Runar Juliusson. Record producer, music publisher and Artists Arrangers Record Company. Deals with artists and songwriters. Produces 5-10 LPs/year. Fee derived from sales royalty, or outright fee from recording artist or record company.
How to Contact: Write first and obtain permission to submit or to arrange personal interview. Prefers cassette (or VHS videocassette) with 2-3 songs and lyric sheet. Does not return unsolicited material. Reports in 6 weeks.
Music: Mostly pop, rock and country; also jazz, R&B and gospel. Produced *All I Wanna Do*, written and recorded by Runar Juliusson; *Hvar*, written and recorded by Thor; and *Gammar*, (by Thor), recorded by Gammar, all LPs on Geimsteinn Records.

*GELSIE RECORDING, PRODUCTION & MANAGEMENT, Box 728, Valley Cottage NY 10989. (914)268-5966. President/Producer: Dolores M. Gelsomine. Record producer and music publisher (Nasty Rumors Publishing). Deals with artists and songwriters. Produces 4 singles and 2 LPs/year. Fee derived from sales royalty.
How to Contact: Prefers cassette with 3-5 songs and lyric or lead sheet. Send bio or press release if

available. SASE. Reports in 6 weeks.
Music: Mostly pop/rock, R&B and "DOR"; also "theme music." Produced "Another World Now" by Roger Monaco, and "So Right" and "Pretty Girls" by N. Delaney/C. Hammond, all recorded by Cathy Hammond on NRP Records (all singles). Other artists include Jamey Andreas.

PAUL GERRY ENTERPRISES, Box 217, Ferndale NY 12734. (914)292-5965. Owner: Paul Gerry. Record and video producer. Deals with artists and songwriters. Produces 4 LPs/year. Fee derived from outright fee from songwriter/artist.
How to Contact: Write or call first and obtain permission to submit. Prefers cassette (or any format videocassette). SASE. Reports in 1 month.
Music: Mostly bluegrass, country and gospel; also jazz and contemporary. Produced *When the Fire Comes Down*, by Northern Lites (bluegrass LP, Revonah Records); *Memories of Marty*, by Bev King (country LP, Revonah Records); and *Cindy & Rob*, by Cindy & Rob (standards LP, Soap Records). Other artists include "Tater" Tate, Bristol Mountain Bluegrass, Damian, Watchers, Red Rector, Willie May's Band, and Track Works.

GMT PRODUCTIONS, Box 25141, Honolulu HI 96825. (808)247-1447. President: Gil M. Tanaka. Record producer and music publisher (Music Publishers of Hawaii). Deals with artists and songwriters. Produces 6 singles and 6 LPs/year. Fee derived from sales royalty.
How to Contact: Prefers cassette and lyric sheet. SASE. Reports in 1 month.
Music: Mostly top 40/pop; also country, easy listening, jazz, R&B, rock and soul. Produced *Kevin I.*, by Kevin I. (top 40/pop LP, GMT Records); *Morning Light*, by Paul Flynn (top 40/pop LP, GMT Records); and *Music Magic*, by Music Magic (jazz LP, GMT Records).

MORRIS D. GOLODNER, 8946 Ellis Ave., Los Angeles CA 90034. (213)836-4028. Executive Producer: Morris D. Golodner. Record producer and music publisher (Super Sound Productions). Deals with artists and songwriters. Produces 7-12 singles and 4-6 LPs/year. Fee derived from sales royalty or outright fee from recording artist or record company.
How to Contact: Prefers cassette, 7½ ips reel-to-reel (or videocassette) with maximum 10 songs. SASE. Reports in 3 months.
Music: Mostly pop/rock, metal, country, jazz, gospel, folk, R&B and jingles; also novelty songs. Produced "Apartheid," (by Ed Malik), recorded by Morris Golodner on Nightown Records (single); *Shoulder To Shoulder*, (by M. Golodner), recorded by Raashmeen on Supersound Records (LP); and *Only One Love*, written and recorded by Digital Synthesis on ABTCO Records (LP). Other artists include "Adeem and Raashmeen"—India's famous duo, L.A.'s own "Mambo-Rambo-Jackson", Nashville's "Lee T. Porter".
Tips: "Good songs and concepts are always welcome. All prospective talent, let me hear from you. We audition for our numerous video productions."

GOPHER BAROQUE PRODUCTION, 7560 Garden Grove Blvd., Westminster CA 92683. (714)893-3457. Contact: Michael Mikulka. Record producer, music publisher (More Baroque Music/BMI) and recording studio. Deals with artists and songwriters. Produces 8-10 singles and 4-5 LPs/year. Fee negotiable.
How to Contact: Prefers cassette with no more than 3 songs. Artists should include 8x10 b&w photo. Reports in 1 month.
Music: Commercial pop/rock, dance new music and country.
Tips: "See what's selling out there . . . be commercial!"

GRASSROOTS PROJECTS UNLIMITED, Box 4689, San Francisco CA 94101. Contact: James L. Heisterkamp. Record producer and music publisher (Grassroots Projects Unlimited/BMI). Fee derived from sales royalty.
How to Contact: Write first. "We are really not looking for new talent at this time. We have an in-house operation and use San Francisco talent when needed." SASE.
Music: "Ragtime, songs about San Francisco by San Francisco writers, and gospel by Bay Area talent." Latest musical publications include *San Francisco Souvenirs* and *Lyric Suite For Piano*, both a collection of piano compositions about San Francisco by in-house composer Frank Levin; *Inspiration Back to Back*, with "Let's Give Thanks," by Frank Levin and "He Loves Me So," by Baron Von Heisterkampf; and *Three Rainbow Lullabies*, by Toby Lynn and Frank Levin.
Tips: "Believe in yourself and your material. Be prepared to invest in your own projects should that become necessary. No one would give me a chance to have my songs published or recorded, so I did it myself. That is how I got started in the business. I now try to help set up that first rung on the ladder of success to those with whom I have personal contact."

BILL GREEN, 10452 Sentinel, San Antonio TX 78217-3824. (512)654-8773. Contact: Bill Green. Record producer and music publisher. Deals with artists and songwriters. Produces 20 singles/year and 3 LPs/year. Fee derived from outright fee from songwriter/artists or record company.
How to Contact: Prefers cassette with 1-4 songs and lyric sheet. SASE. Reports in 2 months.
Music: Mostly contemporary country and traditional country. Produced "Blackjack Whiskey," by Bobby Jenkins (country single, Zone 7); "Getting to the Heart of You," by Jay Eric; and "Me & Margarita," by Bobby Jenkins (country single, Zone 7). Other artists include Diana Hart and David Price.

*GROSVENOR RECORDS, 16 Grosvenor Rd., Birmingham B20 3NP United Kingdom. (021)356-9636. Managing Director: John R. Taylor. Record producer and music publisher (Grosvenor Publishing). Deals with artists and songwriters. Produces 3 singles and 20 LPs/year. Fee derived from sales royalty or outright fee from recording artist.
How to Contact: Write or call first and obtain permission to submit. Prefers cassette with 3-4 songs and lyric or lead sheet.

GST MUSIC PRODUCTIONS, 17 Ponca Trail, St. Louis MO 63122. (314)821-2741. Producer: Gregory Trampe. Record producer and music publisher (Tragrey Music Publishing/BMI). Deals with artists and songwriters. Produces 8-12 singles and 2 LPs/year. Works with 6-10 new songwriters/year. Works with lyricists and teams collaborators. Fee derived from sales royalty or outright fee from record company.
How to Contact: Write or call first or arrange personal interview. Prefers 7½ ips reel-to-reel or cassette with 2-4 songs and lyric sheet. SASE. Reports in 1 month.
Music: Mostly top 40, rock, country and contemporary gospel.

HALLWAYS TO FAME PRODUCTIONS, Box 18918, Los Angeles CA 90018. (213)935-7277. General Manager: Al Hall, Jr. Record producer and music publisher (Aljoni Music Co./BMI, Hallmarque Musical Works, Ltd./ASCAP). Deals with artists and songwriters. Produces 6 singles and 8 LPs/year. Fee derived from sales royalty.
How to Contact: Prefers cassette (or Beta videocassette) with 5-10 songs and lyric sheet. Does not return unsolicited material. Reports in 2 months.
Music: Rap, jazz, R&B and dance-oriented R&B, and soul. Produced "Future World," by Louis King (rap, AlJoni/Jazzy's Rap-Jazzy D.).
Tips: "We seek artists with strong direction and positive attitude; songs with good melodies, slick lyrics (hooks) and nice chord progressions. Rap Product welcome."

R L HAMMEL ASSOCIATES, Box 531, Alexandria IN 46001-0531. Contact: Randal L. Hammel. Record producer, music publisher (Ladnar Music/ASCAP) and consultants. Deals with artists and songwriters. Produces 1-2 singles and 3-4 LPs/year. Fee derived from sales royalty, outright fee from artist/songwriter or record company, or negotiable fee per project.
How to Contact: Write first and obtain permission to submit, include brief resume (including experience, age, goal). Prefers cassette with 3 songs maximum. "Lyrics (preferably typed) *must* accompany tapes!" SASE. Reports as soon as possible.
Music: Blues, church/religious, country, easy listening, gospel, MOR, progressive, R&B, rock (usually country), soul and top 40/pop. Produced *Still Got Room to Grow*, by Shannon (contemporary Christian LP, Master Touch Records); and "Painted Ladies," by Crossroads (country single). Other artists include Overeasy, Heigh-Liters, Morris Chapman, Jeff Steinberg, Carlton-Taylor Band and Carey Landry.
Tips: "Though there are certain stigmas that go along with being from the Midwest, we still maintain that quality work can be done, and our good reputation with the 'biggies' in Chicago, Los Angeles, Nashville, etc. will bear us out. Only those who have a full knowledge of the sacrifice involved with this industry (or those willing to hear it) should consider contacting this office. We will shoot straight, and it is *always* explained that our observations are just that—'ours', and another company/production team/etc., will present a different opinion. Always get a second opinion (or more)."

HAM-SEM RECORDS, INC., 727 S. Spring St., Los Angeles CA 90014. (213)627-0557. A&R Director: Dianna Green. Record producer (Four Buddies/ASCAP). Deals with artists and songwriters. Produces 4 singles and 1 LP/year. Fee derived from sales royalty or outright fee from artist/songwriter.
How to Contact: Call first about your interest. Prefers cassette with 4-10 songs. Does not return unso-

The asterisk before a listing indicates that the listing is new in this edition. New markets are often the most receptive to freelance submissions.

licited material. Reports in 1 month.
Music: Church/religious, gospel (contemporary), MOR, rap, R&B and top 40/pop. Produced *Secret Love*, by Charles Scott (disco LP, Ham-Sem Records); "Share Your Love," by C. Scott (ballad single, Ham-Sem Records); and "Two of Hearths," by VITU.

GEOFFREY HANSEN ENTS. LTD., Box 63, Orinda CA 94563. (415)937-6469. A&R Representative: J. Malcom Baird. Record producer, music publisher, record company, personal management, and production firm. Produces varying number of singles and LPs/year. Fee derived from sales royalty, outright fee from songwriter/artist or record company or contract.
How to Contact: "Do not call in advance. It's a waste of time to call prior to hearing material." Prefers cassette, (¾" or VHS videocassette) and lyric or lead sheet. "Send a neat and clean package. We are looking for talent with star quality." SASE. Reports in 6 weeks.
Music: Mostly top 40/MOR, rock-a-billy, jazz (big-band) and country rock; also blues, French and Spanish. "We are looking for 50s and 60s style rock 'n' roll and do-wop vocal harmony tunes plus TV motion pictures and theatrical music."
Tips: "We do not read form letters. Do not send the same thing to us that you send to other companies."

R. MARK HANSEN, #3, 3685 W. 6200 S., Kearns UT 84118. (801)969-8174. Producer: R. Mark Hansen. Record producer. Deals with artists and songwriters. Fee derived from sales royalty, outright fee from songwriter/artist and/or outright fee from record company.
How to Contact: Prefers cassette with "any number of" songs and lyric sheet. SASE. Reports in 3 weeks.
Music: Mostly hard rock, new wave and progressive rock; also classical, jazz and blues. Produced "Who's Lies Are Right?" by Johnny Sleeze and the Dead Preps (new wave single); and "Promises, Promises" by Covenant (hard rock single). Other artists include WolfBane and Enticers.
Tips: "I prefer to work on projects with a message. You should believe what you're singing, writing, etc."

RICK HANSON PRODUCTIONS, %Ric Rac Inc., Box 712, Nashville IN 47448. (812)837-9569. Executive Producer: Rick Hanson. Record producer and music publisher. Deals with artists and songwriters. Produces 4-6 singles/year. Works with 2 new songwriters/year. Fee derived from sales royalty, outright fee from record company, or fees from spec and custom clients.
How to Contact: Write first and obtain permission to submit. Prefers cassette with 3 songs and lyric sheet. "Do not make phone inquiries as to status of material submitted." SASE. Reports in 2 months.
Music: Mostly country, pop and rock; also gospel , R&B and classical. Produced "Stay Away," (by Greg Washel), recorded by X-IT, (rock single); "Life's Not Worth the Ride," written and recorded by Rick Hanson (country single); and "The Other Way Around," (by William Schleicher), recorded by Rick Hanson (country single), all on Ric Rac Records. Other artists include Jack Lawles and Glori McFall.
Tips: "Have a good understanding of the music business overall. Be as professional as possible."

HARD HAT PRODUCTIONS, 519 N. Halifax Ave., Daytona Beach FL 32018. (904)252-0381. President/producer: Bobby Lee Cude. Record producer and music publisher (Cude & Pickens Publishing). Produces 12 singles and 6 LPs/year.
How to Contact: Produces "only in-house material."
Music: Mostly country; also easy listening, gospel, MOR, top 40/pop and Broadway show. Produced "Sand in My Shoes" and "V-A-C-A-T-I-O-N" by the Hard Hatters; "Just a Piece of Paper," by the Blue Bandana Country Band; "Blue Pacific Calls" and "Hawaii Goodbye" (song performance contest for the State of Hawaii); and "Los Angeles Town" and "New Generation March," (band performance contest for the National High School Band Directors Hall of Fame). Other artists include Cityfolks Country Band and Carribean Knights.

JOHN HARVEY ENTERPRISES, Box 120244, San Antonio TX 78212. President: John Harvey. Record producer, record company and music publisher (John Harvey Publishing Co./BMI). Deals with artists and songwriters. Produces 6 singles and 6 LPs/year. Works with 2 new songwriters/year. Fee derived from sales royalty.
How to Contact: Prefers cassette with 3-6 songs and lyric sheets. Will accept 7½ ips reel-to-reel. "Include letter giving brief resume of artist/songwriter with submission and photos if possible." Reports ASAP.
Music: Mostly country; also New Age, polka, Latin, easy listening and folk. Produced *Maybe Someday*, written and recorded by John Harvey; *I Took A Gamble*, written and recorded by Edward Daniels; and *Who Could Change*, written and recorded by Janet Bishop, all LPs on Harvey Records. Other artists include Johnny Gonzalez and Holland Geneva.

Tips: "Have fun with your music. While seriously and persistently working at it, don't take rejection seriously. Do the best you can with what you have and continuously try to improve your songwriting, singing and instrument-playing ability. All the electronic instruments (keyboards and recording equipment) are allowing the artist more room in which to express his/her creativity."

HAWORTH PRODUCTIONS, 3580 Rainbow,#816, Kansas City KS 66204. Send correspondence to Southern Most Publishing Company, Box 40276, Overland Park KS 66204. (913)381-8378. Owner: Dann E. Haworth. Record producer, recording engineer and music publisher (Southern Most Publishing Co.). Deals with artists and songwriters. Fee derived from sales royalty, outright fee from songwriter/artist and/or outright fee from record company.
How to Contact: Prefers cassette, 7½ or 15 ips reel-to-reel (or VHS videocassette) with 6 songs and lyric or lead sheets. SASE. Reports in 1 month.
Music: Mostly country, rock and gospel; also blues, jazz and folk.

GENE HEIMLICH/MASADA MUSIC INC./SAVAGE ANGEL, 888 8th Ave., New York NY 10019. (212)757-1953. President: Gene Heimlich. Record producer. Deals with artists and songwriters. Produces 1-5 singles/year and 8-12 LPs/year. Fee derived from sales royalty, outright fee from songwriter/artist and/or outright fee from record company.
How to Contact: Call first and obtain permission to submit and to arrange personal interview. Prefers cassette or 7½ ips reel-to-reel (or VHS or Beta videocassette) with 6-8 songs and lyric or lead sheets. "Film music acceptable as well as completed LPs." Does not return unsolicited material. Reports in 5 weeks.
Music: Mostly New Age, pop/folk and jazz; also film music, classical and ethnic. Produced "Concerto for Astronauts," by Emile Sichkin (pop/classical); "Music to Disappear In," by Raphael (New Age LP, Savage Angel); "Totem," by Gabriell Roth and The Mirrors (urban dance, Moving Center); and "Thomas Cameron Pope" (pop/folk, Amitabha Records). Other artists include Richard Shulman, Pete Castillo, Don Conraux, Sela, Christina Poor and Rachel Faro.
Tips: "Focus on your market and make clear, concise demos."

JAY HENRY/VISUAL MUSIC, 3D, 235 E., 13th St. New York NY 10003. (212)505-9281. Artist Relations: Theresa Hunter. Record producer, music publisher (Visual Music), recording services and image styling. Deals with artists and songwriters. Produces 6 singles/year and 2-3 LPs/year. Fee derived from sales royalty, outright fee from songwriter/artist and/or outright fee from record company.
How to Contact: Prefers cassette (or VHS videocassette) with 3-4 songs and lyric sheet. "Artist or songwriter must follow up by phone in two weeks for response." Does not return unsolicited material.
Music: Mostly rock, dance-oriented rock pop, adult-oriented rock and R&B. Produced "Lavender Lane" (by Steve Bennett) and "Guilty" (by S. Reno/S. Bennett) both recorded by Design For Living; and "Cruise Control" (by Daina Shukis), recorded by Daina and the Tribe, all rock singles. Other artists include Streetchild, Dough Boys and Duncan-Brown.
Tips: "Never give up!!!"

GORDON HICKLAND, 1183 Eastway, Cincinnati OH 45224. (513)681-5436. Producer: Gordon Hickland. Record producer, music publisher (Hickey's Music) and record company (Vibe Records). Deals with artists and songwriters. Produces 7-9 singles and 2 LPs/year. Fee derived from sales royalty or outright fee from songwriter/artist or record company.
How to Contact: Prefers cassette with 1-4 songs and lyric sheet. Reports in 1 month.
Music: Mostly pop/R&B; also dance and urban contemporary. Produced "Heartbeat," (by G. Hickland), recorded by Gordy Clay on Vibe Records (dance); "Stingy," (by G. Waiver/G. Hickland), recorded by Trinia Best on Vibe Records (pop/R&B); and "You," written and recorded by E. Morgan on Strength Records (pop/R&B). Other artist include Velocity (group).

*JOHN HILL MUSIC, INC., 116 E. 37th St., New York NY 10016. (212)683-2448. President: John Hill. Record producer and music publisher (Salami Music/ASCAP). Deals with artists and songwriters. Produces 3 singles and 1 LP/year. Fee derived from sales royalty or by outright fee from record company.
How to Contact: Prefers cassette with 3 songs and lyric sheet. SASE. Reports in 1 month.
Music: Mosty pop; also dance-oriented and rock (punk, new wave). Produced *City Kids*, by Sterling (top 40/new wave LP, A&M Records); *Pacific Gas & Electric*, by Pacific Gas & Electric (pop/R&B LP, ABC Records); and *I'm Gonna' Getcha*, by Jimmy Maelen (disco LP, Epic Records).

*HIPPOGRIFF PRODUCTIONS, INC.,Suite 201, 246 Fifth Ave., New York NY 10001. (212)481-9877. Producers: Steve Gold and John Alters. Record producer and jingle producer. Deals with artists and songwriters. Produces 4 singles/year. Fee derived from sales royalty or outright fee from record company.

How to Contact: Prefers cassette with 3-4 songs and lyric sheet. "Submit clear demos with the strongest song first. If you are an artist/songwriter, please send a photo." Does not return unsolicited material. Reports in 2 weeks.

Music: Mostly mainstream pop, R&B/pop and dance/pop; also AOR and dance. Produced "Let Her Know" (by David Prince/Steve Gold), recorded by Spy Boy; and "The Earth," (by Y. Kehati), recorded by Visa V both on HPI Records (both singles); and jingles for Kraft, Acutrim and Cadillac.

Tips: "Artists/songwriters: package yourself correctly, establish image ideas that best suit your individual musical and vocal style. Songwriters: Submit songs that have top-40 qualities. We're not looking for 'album tracks' or 'B-sides.' Hits only!"

HIT AND RUN STUDIOS INC., 18704 Muncaster Rd., Rockville MD 20855. (301)948-6715. Owner/Producer: Steve Carr. Record producer and recording studio. Deals with artists and songwriters. Produces 12 singles/year and 8 LPs/year. Fee derived from outright fee from songwriter/artist and/or outright fee from record company.

How to Contact: Call first and obtain permission to submit. Prefers cassette. Does not return unsolicited material. Reports in 2 weeks.

Music: Mostly rock, rockabilly and funk; also reggae, country and blues. Produced "Faith in Love," by Tommy Keene (rock single, Geffin Records); and *There is No God*, by 9353 (new psychedelic LP, Fountain of Youth Records). Other artists include Crippled Pilgrims, Hyaai, Bomb Squad and May Day.

*CLIVE HODSON, % PolyGram Records, Sydney NSW Australia. (02)699 1399. Local A&R Manager/In-House Producer: Clive Hodson. Record producer. Deals with artists and songwriters. Fee derived from sales royalty.

How to Contact: Write to arrange personal interview. Prefers cassette. SASE. Reports in 2 weeks.

Music: Rock, blues and jazz. Artists include "guitar oriented bands."

HOGAR MUSICAL PRODUCTIONS, 4225 Palm St., Baton Rouge LA 70808. (504)383-7885. President: Barrie Edgar. Record producer and music publisher (Silverfoot). Deals with artists and songwriters. Produces 0-5 singles and 0-2 LPs/year. Fee derived from outright fee from record company.

How to Contact: Prefers cassette with maximum 4 songs and lyric sheet. SASE.

Music: Mostly rock, blues ("not soul") and country. Produced "Louisiana's Basin Child," by Top Secret (rock single, Gulfstream Records).

HOMESTEAD PRODUCTIONS, Box 256577, Chicago IL 60625. (312)399-5535. President: Tom Petreli. Record producer. Deals with artists and songwriters. Produces 8-15 singles and 2-5 LPs/year. Fee derived from sales royalty.

How to Contact: Prefers cassette (or videocassette) with 2-4 songs and lyric sheet. SASE. Reports in 1 month.

Music: Mostly country; also bluegrass, church/religious, gospel and Spanish. Produced "Arizonia," by Arizonia Country (country single). Other artists include Tom Petrei, Sweetwater, Tempe and Messa.

*ASHLEY HOWE,1123 Northern Blvd., Baldwin NY 11510. (516)379-5664. Producer: Ashley Howe. Director: Heli Noormae. Record producer (Howzat Productions) and engineer. Deals with artists and songwriters. Produced 4 singles and 2 LPs/year. Fee derived from sales royalty and outright fee from record company.

How to Contact: Prefers cassette with lyric sheet and lead sheet. "Include address and telephone number." Does not return unsolicited material. Reports in 1 month.

Music: Mostly rock, pop and top-40; also ballads and heavy metal. Produced *Mannekins*, (by Mannekin/Bryan Adams/Robert Fleischman), recorded by Mannekins on Yellow Rose Records (rock); *Two Minute Warning*, written and recorded by Angle City on MCA Records (rock); and *Penetrator* (by Ted Nugent/Bryan Adams/Robin George), recorded by Ted Nugent on Atlantic Records (rock).

Tips: "Send legible lyric and lead sheets, contact address and phone; send follow-ups."

HUMDINGER PRODUCTIONS, 607 Piney Point Rd., Yorktown VA 23692. (804)898-8155/595-4191. Professional Managers: Lana Puckett and Kim Person. Record producer, music publisher (Hot Knobs Music) and recording studio. Produces 10 singles/year and 4 LPs/year. Fee derived from outright fee from songwriter/artist or record company.

How to Contact: Write first and obtain permission to submit. Prefers cassette (or Beta videocassette) with 1-5 songs and lyric sheet. "Material must be presented on a decent demo—whatever it takes to get song across." SASE. Reports in 3 weeks.

Music: Mostly country and easy listening; also pop, bluegrass, gospel and children's music. Produced

Modern Day Minstrel, by Rich Follett (contemporary LP, Unicorn Records); "You Bring Out the Woman in Me," by Lana Puckett (pop single, Cimirron/Rainbird Records); and "Do Right Woman, Do Wrong Man," recorded by Kim Person (contemporary country single, Cimirron/Rainbird Records).
Tips: "Artist must have a professional attitude and be willing to work hard."

*HUP HUP SDN. BHD.,66-68 Jln Raja Chulan, Kuala Lumpur 50200 Malaysia. 2307904. Managing Director: Ng Cheong Hock. Record producer. Deals with artists and songwriters. Produced 15-20 LPs/year. Fee derived from sales of albums.
How to Contact: Prefers cassette (or VHS videocassette) with 2 songs and lyric sheet. Does not return unsolicited material. Reports in 1 month.
Music: Mostly pop, rock and R&B.

IEA/INTERNATIONAL ENTERTAINMENT ASSOCIATES, 1701 Pacific Ave., Box 1413, Dept. SM-1, Atlantic City NJ 08401. (609)347-0484. President: Danny Luciano. Associate Producer: Armand Cucinotti. Record producer and music publisher (Donna Marie Music/ASCAP). Deals with artists and songwriters. Produces 2 singles and 1 LP/year. Fee derived from sales royalty.
How to Contact: Prefers cassette with 4-8 songs and lyric sheet. "No 8 track." SASE. Reports in 6 weeks.
Music: MOR, R&B, rock (all types), soul and top 40/pop. Produced "Ting-A-Ling Doubleplay," by Larry Bowa and Dave Cash of the Philadelphia Phillies (top 40 single, Molly Records).

IF PRODUCTIONS, % Omnipop Enterprises, Suite 225, 223 Jericho Tpke., Mineola NY 11501. (516)248-4019. (Branch: 22240 Schoenborn St., Canoga Park CA 91304. (213)883-4865). New York Contact: Tom Ingegno. California Contact: Mike Frenchik. Record producer and music publisher (Beautiful Day Music). Works with artists. Producers 3-5 singles and 2 LPs/year. Fee derived from sales royalty or outright fee from record company.
How to Contact: Prefers cassette with minumum 3 songs and lyric sheet. SASE. Reports in 3 weeks.
Music: R&R and top 40/pop. Produced "First Thrills," "Front Page News," and "Thrills Three," by Thrills (rock singles, G&P Records).

INNOCENT LUST PRODUCTIONS, Box 333, Evanston IL 60204. (312)328-0400. President: Graham Carlton. Record producer, music publisher (Graham Carlton Music Co.) and record company. Deals with artists and songwriters. Produces 130 singles and 40 LPs/year. Fee negotiated.
How to Contact: Prefers cassette (or videocassette) with 1-5 songs and lyric sheet. SASE. Also send biographical material and photos. Reports as soon as possible.
Music: Bluegrass, blues, country, dance-oriented, easy listening, folk, jazz, MOR, progressive, R&B, rock, soul, top 40/pop and humorous. Produced *Mr. Love*, by Shackle (punk LP, Hybrid Records); *Quitting Time*, by Dawn Martin (country LP, Hybrid Records); and *Tomorrow*, by Sue Stassen (R&B LP, Hybrid Records). Other artists include Down Home Band, Eddie Wilson and Bob Barton.

INSIGHTOUT PRODUCTIONS, Box 5509, Mill Valley CA 94942. (415)388-8107. President/C.E.O./Producer: Jay A. Leibovitz. Record producer and recording production and distribution company. Deals with artists and songwriters. Produces 2-4 LPs/year. Fee derived from sales royalty or outright fee from recording artist. "We seek collaborative ventures with other book, video and record/tape publishing companies. Interested in developing thematic radio programs of music and stories."
How to Contact: Prefers cassette (or VHS videocassette) "preferably of performance" with 1-10 songs and lyric sheet and lead sheet "if available. We produce primarily acoustic music for children, 'nature lovers,' and storytellers. Other submissions will be accepted. Contact by mail or phone before submitting, if desired." SASE. Reports in 4 weeks.
Music: Mostly music appropriate for children's audiences (all ages), storytellers and folk/traditional; also music for relaxation/stress reduction, folk/contemporary and "nature/environmental" music. Produced *For the Child in Us All*, by Jay Leibovitz (children's LP, InsightOut Productions); *We're Goin' to the Zoo*, an anthology (children's LP, InsightOut Productions); and 1987 Bay Area Storytelling Festival tape (live). Other artists include Redmond O'Connell and Cindy Barnett (storyteller).
Tips: "We will consider re-release of previously published materials, and include material in anthologies. Submit 1 song, even if you feel it's the only one ready at the time. Regardless of whether you submit music and/or stories, we look for content which promotes positive relationships to ourselves, others and to our landscapes."

INTERNATIONAL ENTERTAINMENT, Box 50727, Washington DC 20004. (703)590-5928. Director: Charles B. Roberts. Record producer and music publisher. Deals with artists and songwriters. Produces 2-4 singles/year and 2 LPs/year. Fee derived from sales royalty.
How to Contact: Prefers cassette with 4-6 songs. SASE. Reports in 2 months.

Music: Mostly rock, pop and R&B; also country. Produced *New Evidence*, by Anthem (mainstream pop LP and single, Cynet A-V). Other artists include the Ohio Players, Sugarfoot (Warner Bros. Records), and "other major label artists."
Tips: "Polish, rewrite, prepare quality demos and submit press/promotional package. We prefer uptempo dance songs a la Springsteen, Pointer Sisters."

*ISRAFEL PRODUCTIONS, (and Recording Services), 3121 29th Ave., Sacramento CA 95820. (916)455-5278. Producer: John Frank Lizarraga. Record producer and music publisher (Pancho's Music Co.). Deals with artists and songwriters. Produces 3 singles and 2 LPs/year. Fee derived from sales royalty.
How to Contact: Write or call first and obtain permission to submit. Prefers cassette (or VHS or Beta videocassette) with 3 songs and lyric or lead sheets. SASE. Reports in 2 months.
Music: Mostly Latin; also rock, pop, blues, country and gospel. Produced "Hollywood Girl" (by F. Lizarraga), recorded by Suenos (ballad single); "Sin Tu Amor" (by Ralph Vargas), recorded by Tony Arana (ballad single); and *00:30/A.D.* (by A.D. Lizarraga), recorded by A.D. (rock LP), all on Israfel Records. Other artist include Juan Alejandro, Los Hermanos Figueroa, Fernando Quiroz, Jim Rich, J.J. Zuniga and Lew Fratis.
Tips: "We specialize in Latin music and prefer bilingual artists and songwriters."

ITS A HIT PRODUCTIONS, Suite 7, 124 W. 81st St., New York NY 10024. (212)787-8103. Chief Executive Officer: Stephen Bond Garvan. Record producer, record company (Wouldn Shoe, L'Orient, Hatch Records) and management firm (Bullet Management). Deals with artists and songwriters. Produces 2-5 singles/year and 1-2 LPs/year. Fee derived from sales royalty or outright fee from songwriter/artist or record company.
How to Contact: Prefers cassette. SASE.
Music: Mostly rock, pop and country. Produced *Lovers in Trouble*, by the Secrets; "Hearts Overflowing," by AMA (pop single, Wouldn Shoe Records); and "Once They're Gone," by Allen Estes (pop rock single, Greenpeace Records). Other artists include Secrets.

*IVORY TOWER STUDIOS, Tusveld Ag, Bornerbroek 7627 NW Holland. (05408)795. A&R Manager: Bobby Rootveld. Record producer and recording studios. Deals with artists and songwriters. Produces 100 singles and 50 LPs/year. Fee derived from sales royalty.
How to Contact: Prefers cassette with 4 songs and lyric or lead sheet. Does not return unsolicited material. Reports in 2 weeks.
Music: MOR, country and gospel. Produced "De Bajesklant" (by Rootveld), recorded by Reinhart Hack (single); *Pirate-Disco* recorded by The Pirates (LP/MC); and *Top '66 Pop Festival* recorded by various artists (LP), all on Ivory Records. Other artists include Medler Trio, Jantje Koopmans and Stickey Fridge.

J & J MUSICAL ENTERPRISES, Suite 1103, 150 Fifth Ave., New York NY 10011. (212)691-5630. General Manager: Jude St. George. Record producer and music publisher (Jeneane & Jude Music/ASCAP). Deals with artists. Fee derived from outright fee from songwriter/artist.
How to Contact: Write first and obtain permission to submit. Prefers cassette with 4 songs and lyric sheet. "Typewritten letters preferred." Does not return unsolicited material. Reports in 1 month.
Music: Mostly progressive; also jazz, New Age and blues. Produced *Duo*, by Freeway Fusion (progressive LP, JAJ Records).
Tips: "Be neat, organized and original."

J.C.W. MUSIC ENTERPRISES, INC., Box 22805, Highland Heights Station, Memphis TN 38122. Contact: Music Consultant. Record producer. Deals with artists and songwriters. Produces 30 singles and 10 LPs/year. Works with 15-30 new songwriters/year. Fee derived from sales royalty or outright fee from artist/songwriter or record company.
How to Contact: Prefers cassette with minimum 4 songs and lyric sheet. SASE. Reports in 1 month.
Music: Mostly country, gospel and R&B; also soul.

J.P. PRODUCTIONS, 414 Vanderbilt Ave., Brooklyn NY 11238. (718)622-7524. Contact: John A. Pergamo. Record producer, recording studio and record company (ACE Records). Deals with artists and songwriters. Produces 5 singles and 3 LPs/year. Fee derived from sales royalty, or outright fee from songwriter/artist or record company; "depending on negotiations."
How to Contact: Write first to arrange a personal interview. Prefers cassette, 15 ips reel-to-reel (or VHS videocassette) with 3-5 songs and lyric sheet or lead sheet. SAE. Reports in 1 week.
Music: Mostly heavy metal, dance, rap, pop/funk and reggae; also blues, 50s, country and new wave. Produced "Four Ways to Rock" (by Tony Dunney/John Pergamo), recorded by Nuclear Energy (heavy

metal); "Skips a Beat" (by Keith Jackson/John Pergamo/Diana Jackson), recorded by Diana Jackson (club dance); and "You're My Number One" (by Willie Martinez/John Pergano/Tiny), recorded by Derek (club dance) all singles on Ace Records. Other artists include Omari Gaia, Superdude, Buddy Bowzer, King Bee, Jackie Blue and David Sage.
Tips: "Send clear quality sound recording and cover letter explaining exactly what you want to do."

*ALEXANDER JANOULIS PRODUCTIONS,1957 Kilburn Dr., Atlanta GA 30324. (404)662-6661. President: Alex Janoulis. Record producer. Deals with artists and songwriters. Produces 6 singles and 2 LPs/year. Fee derived from sales royalty, or outright fee from recording artist or record company.
How to Contact: Write first and obtain permission to submit. Prefers cassette with 1-3 songs. "Tapes will not be returned with SASE." Reports in 2 months.
Music: Mostly top-40, rock, pop; also black and disco. Produced "He's A Rebel," (by Gene Pitney), recorded by Secret Lover on HotTrax Records (pop single); *Stop!*, written and recorded by the Chesterfield Kings on Mirror Records (rock LP); and *P is For Pig*, written and recorded by The Pigs on HotTrax Records (pop LP). Other artists include Night Shadows, Starfoxx and Splatter.
Tips: "Letters should be short requesting submission permission."

PIERRE JAUBERT, 105 Rue De Normandie, Courbevoie 92 400 France. (1)4333-6515. Contact: President. Casting agent for singers to perform songs in movie soundtracks. Deals with singers and songwriters. Produces 10 LPs/year. Fee derived from sales royalty.
How to Contact: Submit demo tape by mail. Prefers cassette with one song only.
Music: Pop/top 40. Produced *Diva* (by Vladimir Cosma), recorded by Chet Baker (LP on Carrere Records). Other artists include Richard Sanderson and Cook da Books.

LITTLE RICHIE JOHNSON PRODUCTIONS, Box 3, 1700 Plunket, Belen NM 87002. (505)864-7441. President: Little Richie Johnson. Record producer and music publisher (Little Richie Johnson Music/ BMI and Little Cowboy Music/ASCAP). Deals with artists and songwriters. Produces 10-15 singles and 4-5 LPs/year. Works with new songwriters, lyricists and composers. Fee derived from sales royalty or outright fee from recording artist.
How to Contact: Call first. Prefers cassette or 7½ ips reel-to-reel with 4-8 songs. SASE. Reports in 2 weeks.
Music: Country, gospel and Spanish. Produced "Tennessee Bird Walk," by Jack and Misty; "Take Me Back Lincoln County," (by Rex White), recorded by Tommy Tomson on Ross Records; and "On My Way To Houston," written and recorded by Sam West IV on LRJ Records. Other artists include Vic Chaney, Carlos Quintos and Ron Urban.

*RALPH D. JOHNSON, 114 Catalpa Dr., Mt. Juliet TN 37122. (615)754-2950. President: Ralph D. Johnson. Record producer, music publisher (Big Wedge Music) and record company. Deals with artists and songwriters. Produces 3 singles/year. Fee derived from sales royalty.
How to Contact: Write or call first to arrange personal interview. Prefers cassette with maximum of 4 songs and lyric or lead sheet. SASE. Reports in 2 weeks.
Music: Mostly country, rock and gospel; also pop and R&B.

STEVE V. JOHNSON, (Elegance Productions/Search'n Rescue Remixes), 861 Elizabeth St., San Francisco CA 94114-3117. (217)379-3164. Producer: Steve V. Johnson. Record producer, recording and preproduction consultant. Deals with artists and songwriters. Produces 6 singles/year and 2 LPs/year. Fee derived from sales royalty, outright fee from songwriter/artist and/or outright fee from record company.
How to Contact: Prefers cassette with 3-5 songs and lyric or lead sheets. "Please include basic as well as arranged versions of songs and all relevant and current business data: manager, agent, resume, work currently released, etc." Does not return unsolicited material. Reports in 6 weeks.
Music: Mostly rock/high tech, funk and international.

DANNY JONES PRODUCTIONS, Star Stage Inc., 37 E. Carolina Ave., Memphis TN 38103. (901)526-7827. Producer: Danny Jones. Record producer, music publisher (General Jones Music/BMI) and recording engineer. Deals with artists and songwriters. Produces 10 singles/year and 4 LPs/year. Fee derived from sales royalty, outright fee from artist and/or outright fee from record company.
How to Contact: Write or call first and obtain permission to submit. Prefers cassette (or VHS videocassette) with 3-6 songs and lyric sheet. "Please enclose name, address and phone number. Cassettes will not be returned." Reports in 1 month.
Music: Mostly rock, country and pop; also R&B. Produced "Don't Ya'll Know," by Gold Rush (country single, LA Records); "Believe It," by Creed (rock EP); and "Shine On America," by Dan Carey (MOR single, Tidal Wave).
Tips: "Send potential hit songs in a neat, professional manner."

JUMP PRODUCTIONS, 71 Langemunt, Erpe-Mere 9460 Belgium. (053)62-73-77. General Manager: Eddy Van Mouffaert. Record producer and music publisher (Jump Music). Deals with artists and songwriters. Produces 25 singles and 3 LPs/year. Fee derived from sales royalty.
How to Contact: Prefers cassette. Does not return unsolicited material. Reports in 2 weeks.
Music: Mostly ballads, up-tempo, easy listening, disco and light pop; also instrumentals. Produced "Laat Je Hart Toch Even Spreken," by Eddy Govert (ballad); "Ik Wil Bij Jou Zijn," by Rocky (ballad); and "First Day of Spring," by Frankie Francis (intrumental), all singles on Scorpion. Other artists include Eigentijdse Jeugd, Marijn Van Duin, Connie-Linda, Le Grand Julot, Peggy Christy, Allan David and Guy Lovely.
Tips: Submit "easy catching melodies (very commercial songs)."

JUNE PRODUCTIONS LTD., Toftrees Church Rd., Weldingham, Surrey CR3 7JH England. Managing Director: David Mackay. Record producer. Produces 12 singles and 6 LPs/year. Deals with artists and songwriters. Fee derived from sales royalty.
How to Contact: Prefers cassette with 1-2 songs and lyric sheet. SAE and IRC. Reports in 2 weeks.
Music: MOR, rock and top 40/pop. Produced "We're the Bunburies" (by Barry Gibb), recorded by The Bunburies on Island Records (single); *Up With People*, recorded by Up With People on UWP Records (LP); and "The Way Love Is" (by Marvin Gaye), recorded by Jimmy Wail on Virgin Records (single). Other artists include Joe Fagin, Max Boyce and No Hat Moon.

*JOHANN KAPLAN MUSIC, Bürgergasse 17 19/10/2/7, 1100 Vienna Austria. (0222)64 54 104. President: Johann Kaplan Jr. Record producer, music publisher and artist management firm. Deals with artists and songwriters. Produces 20 singles and 10-15 LPs/year. Fee derived from sales royalty, outright fee from songwriter/artist or record company.
How to Contact: Write first and obtain permission to submit or to arrange personal interview. Prefers cassette or reel-to-reel (or VHS videocassette) with 2 songs and lyric or lead sheet. SAE and IRC. Reports in 2 months.
Music: All kinds of music. Produced "Dance Dance More," recorded by Judith on Sunshine Records (disco single); and *Goodby My Love*, recorded by Theresa on Caplan Music (soft rock single and LP). Other artists include Locomotive.

DAVID R. KASPERSIN, 2846 Dewey Ave., Rochester NY 14616. (716)621-6270. Studio Manager: Phyllis Bishop. Record producer and music publisher (Kaspersin Publishing). Deals with artists and songwriters. Produces 10 singles and 10 LPs/year. Fee derived from sales royalty and/or outright fee from songwriter/artist.
How to Contact: Prefers cassette or 15 ips reel-to-reel (or VHS or Beta videocassette) with 4 songs and lyric sheet. SASE. Reports in 5 weeks.
Music: Country/R&B, top 40, rock and "straight country." Produced "DWI Blues," by Fred DeCarr (country); "Innocent of a Crime," by Prospect Highway (rock); and "Tennessee Man," by Nancy Park (country), all singles on DRC Records. Other artists include Lou Sweigman, Peg Dolan and Jeff Elliott.

BUTCH KELLY PRODUCTION, 11 Shady Oak Trail, Charlotte NC 28210. (704)554-1162. Executive Director: Butch Kelly. Record producer and music publisher. Deals with artists and songwriters. Produces 4 singles and 4 LPs/year. Fee derived from sales royalty.
How to Contact: Write first and obtain permission to submit. Prefers cassette (or videocassette) with 1-6 songs and picture and lyric or lead sheet. SASE. Reports in 4 months.
Music: Mostly pop and R&B; also dance, jazz, gospel, soul and top 40. Produced "What's Your Decision," (by Dennis Jones), recorded by L.A. Stars on KAM Executive Records (R&B single); "Street Dancin'," and "Miss You," (both written by Greg Johnson), both recorded by Fresh Air on Fresh Ave. Records, (both R&B singles). Other artists include L.A. Stars, Dean Mancuso and Melissa Kelly.
Tips: "Send your best songs."

KENCO PRODUCTIONS, INC., 3784 Realty, Dallas TX 75244. (214)241-7854. President: K.J. Hughes. Record producer, music publisher (Luvco Music/BMI and Kenco Publishing/ASCAP), record company (Love Records) and 24-track recording studio. Deals with artists and songwriters. Produces 20-30 singles and 8-12 LPs/year. Fee derived from sales royalty.
How to Contact: Prefers cassette with 1-3 songs and lyric sheet. SASE. Reports in 1 month.
Music: Most country and novelty; also bluegrass, R&B and top 40/pop. Produced "Waltzing With Daddy," by Carlette; "Sixty-Seven Miles to Cow Town," by Hollie Hughes; and "Cross My Heart," by Stella Parton. Other artists include Butch Denny, and Xtra Touch (rock band).

Close-up

Fred Koller
Songwriter

Fred Koller believes in novelty songs. "What do you remember Tiny Tim for? Or Ray Stevens? Or Sheb
Wooley?" To name a few. Koller has written or co-written
numerous novelty songs, including "Lord, I Want My Rib
Back," "Let's Talk Dirty in Hawaiian," and "Little Green
Buttons," a clever song describing how a woman recap-
tured the passion of her husband of ten years by having
buttons tattoed on "her birthday suit." While most music professionals say novelty songs are
too risky, Koller has been successful at getting his recorded. How? "By writing them as well
as I would write a normal song. By not telling the same joke twice. The key is to have a lot of
action in a novelty song—where a whole funny movie is being played out. To me those songs
work the best. They're riskier, but there are fewer novelty songs than there are pop ballads.
And if an artist is trying to fill out an album, he'll be more likely to include a good, funny song
because everyone loves a good, funny song." And many performers like singing funny songs
on stage as well.

While he enjoys dealing with funny subjects in his songs, Koller takes the subject of
songwriting very seriously. An avid reader and prolific writer, Koller knows the importance
of good writing skills *and* marketing skills. About the writing of songs, he says, "I really
think it is a craft. It has to come from the same things as any other kind of writing—you have
to love the words, you have to love the music, you have to know what you're trying to create.
Write songs for the love of writing rather than trying to get the songs recorded or to get rich
quick. Songs that are written from the heart will eventually see the light of day. Other people
will recognize that quality and will want to do them."

As to the marketing of songs, Koller recommends researching appropriate artists. "Beginning writers should focus on entertainers who do outside material, whose philosophy (as
shown through their previous songs) and style agree with the writer's." A songwriter can tell
if an artist is likely to be receptive to his work "generally by listening to and reading the album. If you look at an album you can usually tell if the artist wrote all the songs or if he
published all the songs. Ask yourself, 'Would this lyric fit other types of lyrics he's recorded?
Is the melody in his range?' All artists have a trademark, or else they would have nothing to
make them stand out. You can go through their albums and find out what key they like to sing
in. If every album is all acoustic guitars, you don't pitch a demo that's all trumpets and piano."

To a professional like Fred Koller, songwriting not only must be taken seriously, it must be
considered an art form. "I really feel that songwriting is right up there with writing poems or
short stories. Songwriters everywhere really owe it to themselves to try to write better songs,
and they need to work at getting better recognition. I'd like to see more songwriters on talk
shows and performing their own songs in public. I'd like to see more music awards based on
craft instead of sales. Writing songs is not like writing copy for a cereal box—you're putting
your name on these. Write songs that you yourself can perform with pride."

—*Julie Wesling Whaley*

GENE KENNEDY ENTERPRISES, INC., 2125 8th Ave. S., Nashville TN 37204. (615)383-6002. President: Gene Kennedy. Vice President: Karen Jeglum. Record producer, independent distribution and promotion firm and music publisher (Chip 'N' Dale Music Publishers, Inc./ASCAP, Door Knob Music Publishing, Inc./BMI and Lodestar Music/SESAC). Deals with artists and songwriters. Produces 40-50 singles and 3-5 LPs/year. Fee derived from outright fee from artist or record company.
How to Contact: Arrange for personal interview. Prefers 7½ ips reel-to-reel or cassette with up to 3 songs and lyric sheet. SASE. Reports in 3 weeks.
Music: Country or gospel. Produced "New Shade of Blue," (by Johnette Burton/Fred Horton), recorded by Perry LaPointe (single); *Early Morning Love* (LP), and *The First Time*, (LP),(both by John Love), recorded by Gail O'Doski, all on Door Knob Records. Other artists include Bobby G. Rice, Stephen Hiles, Bonnie Nelson, Suthern Comfort and B.B. Secrist.
Tips: "We are looking for hit songs and good talent."

KEYNOTE PRODUCTIONS, 4322 Mahoning Ave., Youngstown OH 44515. (216)793-7295. Executive Producer: Richard Hahn. Record producer and music publisher (Al-Kris Music/BMI). Deals with artists and songwriters. Produces 5 singles and 2 LPs/year. Fee derived from sales royalty or outright fee from songwriter/artist.
How to Contact: Query by mail first. Prefers cassette with 3-5 songs and "neat" lyric sheet. SASE. Reports in 3 weeks.
Music: Country, gospel, MOR and top 40/pop. Produced "Here Come the Browns," by Kardiak Kids (MOR single, Keynote Records); "Help Me I'm Falling," by Kirsti Manna (MOR single, Genuine Records); "Teach Me Lovely Lady," by Jim Stack (country single, Peppermint Records); and "The San Francisco 49er's Fight Song" and "Prom Night," by the B-Minors (MOR singles). Other artists include Leigh Fisher and Gary Kekel.
Tips: "The artist or writer should be willing to compromise on creative decisions by the producer to achieve the best possible product."

KINGSPORT CREEK MUSIC, Box 6085, Burbank CA 91510. Contact: Vice President. Record producer and music publisher. Deals with artists and songwriters.
How to Contact: Prefers cassette (or VHS videocassette). Does not return unsolicited material. "Include photo and bio if possible."
Music: Mostly country, MOR, R&B, pop and gospel. Produced "Never Gonna End" (R&B), "I Do" (MOR), and "Cryin'," (country), by Melvena Kaye (all singles on Cowgirl Records).

PAUL KITCHEN/THE INSYNC ASYLUM, Box 62, Burtonsville MD 20866. (301)384-8480. Producer: Paul Kitchen. Record producer, and recording studio. Deals with artists and songwriters. Produces 10 singles and 5 LPs/year. Fee derived from sales royalty or outright fee from record company.
How to Contact: Write first and obtain permission to submit. Prefers cassette (or Beta videocassette) with 4 songs and lyric and lead sheets. SASE. Reports in 6 weeks.
Music: Progressive rock, pop and top 40. Produced *Dress to the Left*, recorded by Cartel (AOR); *Vital Sines*, recorded by Paul Kitchen (progressive rock); and *Holding Patterns*, recorded by Petty Tyrant (AOR), all LPs on Insync Asylum. Other artists include Marcos Green and Frankie Kelly.
Tips: "Artists must be creative and professional in attitude. Demo must be listenable and undistorted; lyrics must be typed."

***JIM KLEIN/MISTER GUY MUSIC**,360 Eighth St., Brooklyn NY 11215. (718)768 6725. Contact: Jim Klein. Record producer. Deals with artists and songwriters. Produces 2 singles and 2 LPs/year. Fee derived from sales royalty, or outright fee from recording artist or record company.
How to Contact: Prefers cassette with lyric sheet. "No phone calls please." Does not return unsolicted material Reports in 1 month.
Music: Mostly R&B, pop and rock. Produced *Rock De La Stet*, (by Daddy-O), recorded by Stetasonic on Warner Bros./Tommy Boy Records; and *Whap-A-Dang*, (by Daddy-O), recorded by Ranch Hands on Relativity Records (both LPs).

***JEAN KLUGER**,86 Ave Moliere, Brussels 1180 Belgium. (02)345 41 29 or 345 42 03. Contact: Jean Kluger or Myriam Dekoster. Record producer and music publisher. Deals with artists and songwriters.
How to Contact: Prefers cassette. SAE and IRC. Reports in 2 weeks.
Music: Mostly popular music.

***KLW INTERNATIONAL, INC.**, 408 Kathleen Ave., Cinnaminson NJ 08077. (609)786-8486. Executive Producer: Kevin L. Weakland. Record producer and music publisher. Deals with artists and songwriters. Produces 2-3 singles and 1-2 LPs/year. Fee derived from sales royalty.
How to Contact: Write first and obtain permission to submit. Prefers cassette (or Beta videocassette).

SASE. Reports in 2 weeks.
Music: Mostly pop, gospel and R&B; also rock and country.

*HOWARD KNIGHT ENTERPRISES,1609 Congress, Eastover SC 29044. (803)776-2328. President: Howard A. Knight, Jr. Record producer, music publisher (Tenalina Music and Pegasus Records). Deals with artists and songwriters. Producers 6 singles and 2 LPs/year. Fee derived from sales royalty.
How to Contact: Prefers cassette with 3 songs and lyric sheet. Does not return unsolicited material. Reports only if interested.
Music: Mostly country, pop and rock. Produced "Do You Wanna Fall In Love," (by K. Bell/R. Cox), recorded by Bandit Band; "Give In," (by John P. McMeens), recorded by Randy Chapman; "Wadda Ya Done With My Heart" (by Lance Middlebrook, recorded by Mark Alan; and "The Man In My Life," (by M. Hutson), recorded by Candy Hutson, all singles on Pegasus Records.

KNOWN ARTIST PRODUCTIONS, 1219 Kerlin Ave., Brewton AL 36426. (205)867-2228. President: Roy Edwards. Record producer and music publisher (Cheavoria Music Co./BMI and Baitstring Music/ASCAP). Deals with artists and songwriters. Produces 12 singles and 3 LPs/year. Fee derived from sales royalty or outright fee from record company.
How to Contact: Write first about your interest. Prefers cassette with 3 songs and lyric sheet. Reports in 1 month. "All tapes will be kept on file."
Music: Country, easy listening, MOR, R&B and soul. Produced "Music Inside," by Roy Edwards (MOR single, Bolivia Records); "Make Me Forget," by Bobby Roberson; and "Always and Forever," by Jim Portwood (country singles, Bolivia Records).
Tips: "Write a good song that tells a good story."

KOCH RECORDS INTERNATIONAL GMBH, Elbigenalp 91, Tirol A-6652 Austria. 05634/6444, 05634/6445. A&R International Manager: Haakon Brenner. Record producer, music publisher (Koch Musikverlag), record manufacturer and record distributor. Deals with artists and songwriters. Produces 200 singles/year and 200 LPs/year.
How to Contact: Prefers cassette (or VHS/PAL videocassette) with "as many songs as you have artists" and lyric sheet. Does not return unsolicited material. Reports in 3 weeks.
Music: Mostly pop, rock and MOR; also dance music.
Tips: "We are a musical enterprise that can offer all services to the artist who has final productions available for the territory of Europe. Our international department works superbly when it comes to licensing musical programs worldwide with clients in Hong Kong, Venezuela, Spain, Italy, France, Benelux and Scandinavia."

ROBERT R. KOVACH, Drawer 1967, Warner Robins GA 31099. (912)953-2800. Producer: Robert R. Kovach. Record producer. Deals with artists and songwriters. Produces 2 singles/year. Works with composers and lyricists; teams collaborators. Fee derived from sales royalty.
How to Contact: Prefers cassette with 3 songs and lyric sheet. SASE. Reports in 1 month.
Music: Mostly country and pop; also easy listening, R&B, rock and gospel. Produced "Real Country Livin," by Little Rudy (country single, Scaramouche Records). Other artists include Justice with Theresa Queen of the Drums and Napoleon Starke.
Tips: "Be simple and sincere in what you write."

GARY LAMB PRODUCTIONS, Box 24396, Nashville TN 37202. (615)383-0438. President: Gary Lamb. Record producer, music publisher and entertainment consultant. Deals with artists and songwriters. Produces 24 singles/year and 5 LPs/year. Fee derived from sales royalty, outright fee from songwriter/artist and/or outright fee from record company. Songwriters/artists are charged for consultation.
How to Contact: Write or call first and obtain permission to submit. Prefers cassette with 3 songs and lyric sheet. Does not return unsolicited material. Reports in 3 weeks.
Music: Mostly country/pop, rock and gospel; also TV or motion picture themes and scores. Produced "Blue All Over You," by Cheryl Gatlin (country); "Easy," by Bobby Hood (country single, Chute Records); and "Charity," by Steve Gorman (pop single, Blossom Gap Records). Other artists include Basin Brothers Band, Bill Dixon, Bill Nash, Karen Brooks, Dickie Bates, Ann Marie Glennon, Rootie Tootie Band, Malo and Sheena.

LAMON RECORDS/PANHANDEL RECORDS, Box 25371, Charlotte NC 28212. (704)537-0133. President: Dwight Moody. A&R: Carlton Moody. Record producer and music publisher (Laymond Publishing Co. and CDT Productions). Deals with artists, songwriters and publishers. Produces 30 singles and 15 LPs/year. Fee derived from sales royalty.
How to Contact: Write first and obtain permission to submit. Prefers cassette (or VHS videocassette) with minimum 2 songs. Does not return unsolicited material. Reports in 1 month.

Music: All types. Produced "Cotton Eyed Joe," recorded by Carlton Moody and the Moody Brothers (country single, Lamon Records); "Merry Christmas," recorded by Billy Scott (beach single, Lamon Records); and "Love Is Free," recorded by C. Moody (gospel single, Lamon Records). Other artists include Vanessa Parker, Allen Ray, Hutchins Brothers, Routabouts and Nelson Young.

LANDMARK AUDIO OF NASHVILLE, Box 148296, Nashville TN 37214-8296. (615)868-3407. Producers: Bill Anderson, Jr. or D.D. Morris. Record producer, music publisher (Newcreature Music/BMI) and TV/radio syndication. Deals with artists and songwriters. Produces 4 singles and 4 LPs/year. Works with 1 new songwriter/year. Works with composers and lyricists; teams collaborators. Fee derived from sales royalty.
How to Contact: Prefers 7½ ips reel-to-reel, cassette (or videocassette) with 4-10 songs and lyric sheet. SASE. Reports in 1 month.
Music: Mostly country crossover; also blues, country, gospel, jazz, rock and top 40/pop. Produced *Sincerely, Rhonda*, by Rhonda Ingle (MOR LP, Phonorama Records); and *The Traditional Continues*, by Vernon Oxford (country LP, Audiograph Records). Other artists include De Fox and Wayne Oldham.

*LARKSPUR RECORDS, Box 1001, Soquel CA 95073. Owner/Manager: Jon Hutchings. Record producer and music publisher (Larkspur Music/BMI). Deals with artists and songwriters. Produces 5-9 singles and 4 LPs/year. Fee derived from outright fee from recording artist.
How to Contact: Prefers cassette and lyric sheet. SASE. Reports in 6 weeks.
Music: Rock and top 40. Produced *Heat From* (by Mars), recorded by Larkspur and *A Distant Fire* (by Wildfire).

OVERTON LEE, 10051 Green Leaf, Santa Fe Spring CA 90670. (213)946-1524. President: Overton Lee. Record producer and music publisher (Boggy Depot, Overton Lee Music). Deals with artists and songwriters. Produces 6 singles and 2 LPs/year. Fee derived from sales royalty.
How to Contact: Prefers cassette with 1-3 songs and lyric sheet. SASE. Reports in 4 months.
Music: Mostly country; also bluegrass, blues, country and gospel. Produced *Hard On the Heart* and *Some Where in Houston*, both by Johnny Blankenship (Overton Lee Records); and *May You Never Be Alone*, by Overton Lee (Overton Lee Records). Other artists include Alan Lee Blackwell, Gene Davis, Eddie Marie, The Bonner Family, Carmen Wilder and Darvy Traylor.

ROOSEVELT LEE INTERNATIONAL RECORDS, 3966 Standish Ave., Cincinnati OH 45213. (513)793-8191. President: Roosevelt Lee. Record producer and music publisher (Carriage Music). Deals with artists and songwriters. Produces 4 singles and 2 LPs/year. Fee derived from sales royalty.
How to Contact: Prefers cassette with 4 songs and lyric sheet. SASE. Reports in 1 month.
Music: Country, R&B and soul. Produced "Love City," by Larry Daby (soul single, Wes World Records); and "Come Home to Me," by Mike Ellis (country single, Wes World Records).

LES EDITIONS LA FÊTE, % Michel Zgarka, 2306 Sherbrooke E., Montreal Quebec H2K 1E5 Canada. (514)521-8303. Record producer, music publisher (Simone Publishing/CAPAC, Meka Publishing/PROCAN) and international music consultant. Deals with artists, songwriters, managers and independent producers in finding them international releases. Produces 5 singles and 1 LP/year. Works with 10-15 new songwriters/year. Works with lyricists and teams collaborators. Fee derived from sales royalty and publishing advances.
How to Contact: Prefers 7½ ips reel-to-reel, cassette (or videocassette) with 2-8 songs and lyric sheet. Include bio and photo. SAE and IRC. Reports in 5 weeks.
Music: Mostly up-tempo instrumental, dance-oriented and R&B; also soul, top 40/pop and French. Produced the music score from the movies *The Dog Who Stopped the War (La Guerre des Tuques)*, *The Peanut Butter Solution (Opération Beurre de Pinottes)*, *Bach et Bottine (Bach and Broccoli)*, *The Young Magician (Le Jeune Magicien)* and *The Great Land of Small*.

*LIFE AND DEATH PRODUCTIONS, Box 3654, Hollywood CA 90078. (213)465-9622. President: H. Davis. Record producer, music publisher (Life & Death) and record company. Estab. 1986. Deals with artists and songwriters. Produces 3 singles and 3 LPs/year. Fee derived from sales royalty or outright fee from recording artist or record company.
How to Contact: Write or call first and obtain permission to submit. Prefers 7½ ips reel-to-reel (or VHS videocassette if available) with 3 songs.

LIFETIME RECORDINGS, 170 Sylvan Rd., Rochester NY 14618-1339. (716)244-7526. Contact: Lester W. Osband. Record producer.
How to Contact: Prefers cassette and lyric sheet. SASE. Reports in 1 month.
Music: "Any kind."

LITTLE GIANT ENTERPRISES, Box 205, White Lake NY 12786. (914)583-4471. President: Mickey Barnett. Record producer and music publisher (Karjan Music Publishing Co./SESAC). Deals with artists and songwriters. Produces 3 singles and 5 LPs/year. Fee derived from outright fee from artist/songwriter.
How to Contact: Prefers cassette with 1-3 songs and lyric sheet. SASE. Reports in 3 weeks.
Music: Blues, country, easy listening, MOR, R&B and top 40/pop. Produced *Self Styled*, by Terry Gorka (country LP, Killer Records); and *Songs by Request*, by Mickey Barnett (LP). Other artists include Chuck Wilson, The Third Edition, Mickey Barnett, The Little Giants and T. Berry Kaminski.

LOCONTO PRODUCTIONS, 7766 NW 44th St., Sunrise FL 33321. (305)741-7766. President: Frank X. Loconto. Record producer and music publisher. Deals with artists and songwriters. Produces 50 singles and 50 LPs/year. Fee derived from sales royalty, outright fee from songwriter/artist and/or outright fee from record company.
How to Contact: Write first and obtain permission to submit. Prefers cassette. SASE.
Music: Produced "Makin Waves," by Tim Henson (bluegrass LP/single); "Out of the Darkness," by June/Jr. Battiest (inspirational LP/single); and "Marie," by Marie Alicatal (top 40 LP/single), all on FXL Records. Other artists include Bruce Mullin and Obediah Colebrook.

HAROLD LUICK & ASSOCIATES, Box B, 110 Garfield St., Carlisle IA 50047. (515)989-3679. Record producer, music industry consultant and music publisher. Deals with artists and songwriters. Produces 20 singles and 6 LPs/year. Fee derived from sales royalty, outright fee from artist/songwriter or record company, and from consulting fees for information or services.
How to Contact: Call or write first. Prefers cassette with 3-5 songs and lyric sheet. SASE. Reports in 3 weeks.
Music: Traditional country, gospel, contemporary country and MOR. Produced "It Must Be Love," (by Roger Davis/Sandy Davis), recorded by Lee Mace on Foot Stomper Records (country single); "For A Little While/Before I Go," (by T. Neil Smith); and "She Is America (by Tony E. Palmer), recorded by Trade Mark. "Over a 12 year period, Harold Luick has produced and recorded 412 singles and 478 albums, seven of which charted and some of which have enjoyed independent sales in excess of 30,000 units."
Tips: "We are interested in helping the new artist/songwriter make it 'the independent way.' This is the wave of the future. As music industry consultants, our company sells ideas, information and results. Songwriters can increase their chances by understanding that recording and songwriting is a business. 80% of the people who travel to large recording/publishing areas of our nation arrive there totally unprepared as to what the industry wants or needs from them. Do yourself a favor. Prepare, investigate and only listen to people who are qualified to give you advice. Do not implement anything until you understand the rules and pitfalls."

LUST ENTERPRISES, 8769 Sharmead Way, Fair Oaks CA 95628. (916)966-1437. Executive Producer: Gary Koekoek. Record producer and promoter. Deals with artists and songwriters. Produces 2-3 LPs/year plus movie soundtracks. Fee derived from sales royalty or outright fee from record company.
How to Contact: Prefers cassette 15 ips reel-to-reel (or VHS videocassette) with 1-5 songs and lyric sheet. "Lyric sheets, basic rhythm track and vocals encouraged." SASE. Reports in 1 month.
Music: Heavy metal, high energy rock, glamour rock, melodic rock and unusual music. Produced *Livin' in Sin* and *Guillotine*, by Vincent Michael (rock LP, Lust Records); and "Windsong," by V. Michael (MOR single, 4-Star International Records).
Tips: "We would like to keep tapes and cassettes on file—might use some performers in one of our groups. Artists should also submit bios and photos if possible. Currently, we have a backlog and tapes to be returned will be whenever we get there. All submitted material will be listened to."

***MACDONALD—DALLER PRODUCTIONS**, 48 Yorkville Ave., Toronto Ontario M4W IL4 Canada. (416)964-1885. Contact: Brad MacDonald. Record producer. Works with artists and songwriters. Produces 2 singles and 2 LPs/year. Fee derived from sales royalty or outright fee from record company.
How to Contact: Prefers cassette or 15 ips reel-to-reel (or VHS or ¾" videocassette) with 3 songs and lyric sheet. Does not return unsolicited material. Reports in 1 month.
Music: Mostly pop, rock and R&B; also children's music. Produced *Party Album*, (rock) and *Magic Singing Animal Farm*, (children's music), both LPs, recorded by The Beastles on Berandol Records.

DON MACK, 6951 Ranchito Ave., Van Nuys CA 91405. (818)988-3271. Producer/Engineer: Don Mack. Record producer and engineer/arranger. Deals with artists only. Produces 5-6 singles and 2-3 LPs/year. Fee derived from sales royalty, outright fee from record company or "fee from songwriter/artist if not signed by record company."
How to Contact: Prefers cassette. "The order of songs and titles with times of each song should be in-

cluded." SASE "or cassette mailer if return needed."

Music: Mostly rock, hard rock and progressive rock; also new wave, new music and "synth-based music." Produced *12 O'Clock High*, written and recorded by Odin on RCA Japan Records (LP); "One Day/We Believe," (by Bryan and Tim Kelly), recorded by Allegiance on DEMO Records (single); and *Back to Me*, written and recorded by Syren on Independent Records (LP). "Other artists I have worked with include Y&T, Huey Lewis and the News, Brian End/David Byrne, Hellion, Letchen Grey, Alliance and Walt Disney Productions."

Tips: "Present yourself as professionally as possible."

*CARL MADURI PRODUCTIONS, 2741 N. 29th Ave., Hollywood FL 33020. (305)921-5998. President: Carl Maduri. Record producer and music publisher (First String Records). Deals with artists and songwriters. Fee derived from sales royalty.

How to Contact: Prefers cassette. Does not return unsolicited material.

Music: R&B and pop.

LEE MAGID PRODUCTIONS, Box 532, Malibu CA 90265. (213)858-7282. President: Lee Magid. Record producer and music publisher (Alexis Music, Inc./ASCAP, Marvelle Music Co./BMI) and management firm. Deals with artists, songwriters and producers. Produces 10 singles and 10-12 LPs/year. Publishes 10-15 new songwriters/year. Works with composers and lyricists; teams collaborators. Fee derived from sales royalty and "advance fee against royalties"; sometimes pays a flat outright sum.

How to Contact: "Send cassette giving address and phone number; include SASE." Prefers cassette (or videocassette) with 3-6 songs and lyric sheet. Reports only if interested, "as soon as we can after listening."

Music: Mostly R&B, rock, jazz, and pop; also bluegrass, church/religious, easy listening, folk, blues, MOR, progressive, soul, instrumental and top 40. Produced *Jack Be Quick*, written and recorded by Tingle (LP/single); *I Can't Trust Myself Alone* (by Earl Himes), recorded by Marva Josie (LP); and "Alabama" (by A. Schiff), recorded by Kim and Sam (single). Other artists include Papa John Creach, Four Freshman, Ralph Young and Dino and Charles.

Tips: "The visual effect is just as important as the audio. An act should have theatrical as well as musical ability."

MAINROADS PRODUCTIONS, INC., Unit 14, 310 Judson St., Toronto, Ontario, Canada M8Z 1V3. (416)254-9146. Vice President of Sales: Jim Sturgeon. Vice President: Paul Kelly. Record producer, music publisher (Mainroads Publishing/CAPAC, 100 Huntley St. Publishing/PRO). Deals with artists and songwriters. Produces 5 LPs/year. Fee derived from sales royalty.

How to Contact: Write first about your interest. Prefers cassette (or VHS videocassette) with 3 songs and lyric or lead sheet. Does not return unsolicited material. Reports in 6 weeks.

Music: Pop, rock, country, jazz and children's. Produced *The Scroll* (contemporary musical LP, Mainroads/Light Records); *Music Is a Language* (children's LP, Mainroads Records); and *Reyn Rutledge*, by Reyn Rutledge (inspirational/MOR LP, Mainroads Records).

*MANHATTAN COUNTRY, INC.,100 W. 57th St., #18C, New York NY 10019. (212)757-2495. President: Reginald A. Bowes. Record producer and music publisher (Manhattan Country, Inc.). Estab. 1987. Deals with artists and songwriters. Produces 3 singles and 2 LPs/year. Fee derived from sales royalty.

How to Contact: Write first and obtain permission to submit or to arrange personal interview. Prefers cassette with 2-3 songs and lyric sheet. SASE. Reports in 2 weeks.

Music: Mostly country. Produced *The Legendary Album*, (LP) and "Legend/Beer Is My Salvation," by Tom Stuart/Jim Glasgow, (single), both recorded by Tommie Joe White and Southern Cookin' on Manhattan Country Records; and "Read The Signs/The Drifter," written and recorded by Steve Zoyes and Gabe Johnson on Starlips Records (single).

MARIER MUSIC, 9 Walnut Rd., Glen Ellyn IL 60137-4727. (312)951-0246. Contact: Donn Marier. Record producer and music publisher (Denture Whistle Music/BMI and Substantial Music/ASCAP). Deals with artists, songwriters and lyricists; teams collaborators. Produces 6 singles and 3-4 LPs/year. Fee derived from sales royalty or outright fee from record company.

How to Contact: Write or call first about your interest. Prefers 7½ ips reel-to-reel or cassette with 3-6 songs and lyric sheet. SASE. Reports in 3 weeks.

Music: Pop/rock, children's, classical, country, jazz, MOR, progressive, R&B and soul. Produced "Don't Hold Back," (by Buscemi/Marier), recorded by Joe Contaffio on RCA Records (pop/rock); "I'll Love You For Eternity," (by Marier), recorded by Citizen (pop/rock ballad); and "Hello My Friend," written and recorded by Lisa Steele (pop ballad). Other artists include Shotzie (RCA Records, new wave classic) and Dominic Buscemi (Island Records).

PETE MARTIN/VAAM MUSIC PRODUCTIONS, Suite C-114, 3740 Evans St., Los Angeles CA 90027. (213)664-7765. President: Pete Martin. Record producer and music publisher (Vaam Music/ BMI, Pete Martin Music/ASCAP). Deals with artists and songwriters. Produces 5-10 singles and 2-8 LPs/year. Fee derived from sales royalty.
How to Contact: Prefers cassette with 2 songs and lyric sheet. SASE. Reports in 1 month.
Music: Mostly top 40/pop, country and R&B. Artists include Night Vision, Victoria Limon, Reynolds Inc. and The Music Company.

*MARVEL PRODUCTIONS,Suite N, 226 Springmeadow Drive, Holbrook NY 11741. (516)472-1219. Producer: Andy Marvel. Record producer, music publisher (Andy Marvel Music and Ricochet Records). Deals with artists and songwriters. Produces 12 singles and 3 LPs/year. Fee derived from sales royalty.
How to Contact: Prefers cassette or 7½ ips reel-to-reel (or VHS videocassette) with 3-5 songs and lyric sheet. SASE. Reports in 2 weeks,
Music: Mostly pop, R&B and rock; also country. Produced: *You Can't Hide Your Fantasies*, (by Andy Marvel/Steve Perri/Tom Siegel); *Express (10 Items or Less)*, and *Meant to Be*, (by Andy Marvel), all recorded by Andy Marvel on Alyssa Records (all LPs).

MASTERSOURCE PRODUCTIONS, Suite 903, 151 N. Michigan, Chicago IL 60601. (312)819-1515. Executive Producer: Charles Thomas. Commercial producer and music publisher. Deals with artists and songwriters. Produces 8-10 singles/year. Fee derived from sales royalty. "We desire long-term artist relationships."
How to Contact: Query, Attn: Stephen Navyac. Prefers cassette with 3 songs and lyric and lead sheets. Does not return unsolicited material. Reports in 3 weeks.
Music: Top 40, AOR, adult contemporary and contemporary Christian. Produced *Gift of Gladness*, by Chris Christensen (contemporary Christian LP, World Christen Records); *Sold*, by Jim Miller (contemporary Christian LP, World Christen Records); and "Modern Motion," by Stan Hickerson (top 40 single, Mega Media Records).

MASTERVIEW MUSIC PUBLISHING CORP., Ridge Rd. and Butler Ln., Perkasie PA 18944. (215)257-9616. General Manager: Thomas Fausto. President: John Wolf. Record producer, music publisher (Masterview Music/BMI), record company and management firm. Deals with artists and songwriters. Produces 12 singles and 3-4 LPs/year. Fee derived from sales royalty.
How to Contact: Arrange personal interview. Prefers 7½ or 15 ips reel-to-reel with 2-6 songs and lead sheet. SASE. Reports in 2 weeks.
Music: Only gospel. Produced "Up North to Bluegrass," by Country Boys (bluegrass); "I Am Happen," by El Botteon (Rheta Records); and "Footprints," by Charles Newman (religious single, Masterview Records). Other artists include Sugarcane.

DAVID MATHES PRODUCTIONS, Box 22653, Nashville TN 37202. (615)822-6119. President: David W. Mathes. Record producer. Deals with artists and songwriters. Produces 6-10 singles and 4-6 LPs/year. Fee derived from sales royalty.
How to Contact: Prefers 7½ or 15 ips reel-to-reel or cassette (or videocassette) with 2-4 songs and lyric sheet. "Enclose correctly stamped envelope for demo return." Reports as soon as possible.
Music: Mostly country and gospel; also bluegrass, R&B and top 40/pop. Produced "Simple Love Song" (by Bass/Mathes/Pelleteri), recorded by DeAnna (MOR/country, Rising Star/Sapphire Records); "Changes" written and recorded by Don Frost on NRS Records (MOR); and "I Found Jesus In Nashville" (by Lin Butler), recorded by DeAnna (country/gospel, Nashville Gold Records). Other artists include Johnny Newman, Nashville Sidemen and Singers and Silver Eagle Band.
Tips: "We look for professional material and presentations."

JIM McCOY PRODUCTIONS, Rt. 2, Box 116 H, Berkeley Springs WV 25411. President: Jim McCoy. Record producer and music publisher (Jim McCoy Music/BMI). Deals with artists and songwriters. Produces 12 singles and 6 LPs/year. Fee derived from sales royalty.
How to Contact: Write or call first and obtain permission to submit. Prefers cassette or 7½ or 15 ips reel-to-reel (or BETA or VHS videocassette) with 6 songs and lyric or lead sheets. Does not return unsolicited material. Reports in 1 month.
Music: Mostly country, rock and gospel; also country/rock and bluegrass. Produced *Carroll Country Ramblers Sing Gospel*, by Carroll County Ramblers (country LP, Alear Records); "Tryin To Quit," by Jim McCoy (country single, Winchester Records); and *Gospel All the Way*, by Gospel Descenders (gospel LP, Master Records). Other artists include Ernie Hedrick and Alvin Kessner.

*McJAMES MUSIC, Box 34, East Irvine CA 92650. (714)891-0868. Owner: Steve McClintock. President: Tim James. Record producer (Headway Production), record company (37 Records), and music

publisher (More Baroque Music, McClintock Music/BMI). Produces 10 singles and 5 LPs/year. Fee derived from sales royalty and/or outright fee from recording artist or record company.
How to Contact: Write first and obtain permission to submit. Prefers casette with 1 song and lyric sheet. Does not return unsolicited material. Reports in 10 weeks.
Music: Mostly pop, R&B and country; also New Age and folk. Produced *Talk to Me* (by Garm Beall/ Rob Lawrence), recorded by Rickie Schroeder (pop single and LP); *Deadly Prey*, by Tim Heintz/Tim James/Steve McClintock (film score); and *Christmas Needs Love to Be Christmas (by S. McClintock/T. James), recorded by Pat Boone (traditional single and LP)*.

*DORIAN MEDD, 5045 Sidley St., Burnaby, British Columbia V5J 1T6 Canada. (604)430-5664. Independent Producer: Dorian Medd. Record producer (in-house independent producer for Riser Records). Deals with artists. Produces 3-4 singles and 1-2 LPs/year. Fee derived from sales royalty or outright fee from recording artist or record company.
How to Contact: Prefers cassette (or VHS videocassette) with any number of songs and lyric sheet. SAE and IRC. Reports in 3 weeks.
Music: Mostly pop, new wave/punk and rock; also "esoteric," MOR and reggae. Produced "Automaton" (by D. Medd/J. Nichols), recorded by Dorian Gray; "Movie Love Affair" (by D. Medd), recorded by Medd & Shaw; "He's a Tease" (by D. Medd/J. Nichols), recorded by Menage A Trois, all singles on Riser Records.

*MERAK MUSIC PRODUCTION/SRC, Via De Amicis 28, Milano Italy. (02)8050803-8059830. Producer: Roberto Gasparini. Record producer and music publisher. Deals with artists and songwriters. Produces 20 singles and 2 LPs/year. Fee derived from sales royalty.
How to Contact: Write or call first to arrange personal interview.
Music: Mostly dance, pop and rock; also soul. Produced "The Best of My Love" (pop single) on Merak Music/EMI; *Lancelot* by SaPerie Dore (dance single and LP/EMI); and "Destination" by Johnny Parker (funk-dance single) Merak Music/EMI. Other artists include Alba, Diana Barton, Steve Martin and Valerie Allington.

*MIC—VIC PRODUCTIONS,77 N. Third St., 3rd Floor, Meriden CT 06450. (203)238-7263. Owner/ Producer: Steven McVicker. Record producer and music publisher (Mic-Vic Music, BMI). Deals with artists and songwriters. Fee derived from sales royalty or outright fee from recording artist or record company.
How to Contact: Prefers cassette (or VHS videocassette) with 3 songs and lyric sheet. "Please submit photo and letter relating personal music history." SASE. Reports in 6 weeks.
Music: Mostly techno-pop, New Age, electronic; also rock, jazz-fusion and MOR rock. Artist include Robert Sullivan, Robert Crossland, Jim Murtaugh, Steven McVicker, Ron Rockett and The Tuners
Tips: "Don't write for a market! Write what you love and create a market."

*MIKALANNA MUSIC, Box 66, Moore SC 29369. (803)574-6104. President: Duane Evans. Record producer, music publisher (Mikalanna Music) and recording studio. Deals with artists and songwriters. Produces 6 singles and 3 LPs/year. Fee derived from recording studio fee.
How to Contact: Write or call first and obtain permission to submit. Prefers cassette with 5 songs and lyric sheet. Does not return unsolicited material. Reports in 6 weeks.
Music: Mostly pop, rock and country; also R&B, gospel and MOR. Produced *American Dreams* (by B. Mardones/D. Evans), recorded by Benny Mardones and the Hurricanes on BT Records (rock LP); "Dreaming Dreams," written and recorded by Butch Bowen on EBS Records (country single); and *Mainiax*, written and recorded by Mainiax on EBS Records (heavy metal LP). Other artists include Henry Paul, Billy Scott, Swinging Medallions, Reds, and Tony Joe Younger.

JAY MILLER PRODUCTIONS, 413 N. Parkerson Ave., Crowley LA 70526. (318)783-1601 or 788-0773. Contact: Jay Miller. Manager: Mark Miller. Record producer and music publisher. Deals with artists and songwriters. Produces 50 singles and 15 LPs/year. Fee derived from sales royalty.
How to Contact: Arrange personal interview. Inquiries are invited. Prefers 7½ ips reel-to-reel or cassette for audition. SASE.
Music: Mostly country; also blues, Cajun, disco, folk, gospel, MOR, rock, top 40/pop, and comedy. Produced *Zydecajun*, by Wayne Toups (LP); "I Wish I Had A Job," by Paul Marx (single); and "The Likes Of Texas," by Sammy Kershaw, (single). Other artists inlcude Little Willie Davis and His Zydeco Hitchhikers, Tammy Lynn, and Camey Doucet.
Tips: "Inquiries are invited."

MISSILE RECORDS, Box 5330 Kreole Station, Moss Point MS 39563. (601)474-1171. President: Joe F. Mitchell. Record producer and music publisher (Bay Ridge Publishing Co.). Deals with artists and

songwriters. Fee derived from sales royalty.
How to Contact: Call or write first and obtain permission to submit. Prefers cassette and lead sheet. SASE. Reports in 2 months.
Music: Mostly country, blues and rock; also MOR and religious. Produced "Grandma Can I Read to You," and "Crying Melody," by Sam Frazier Jr.; and " You Mean So Much To Me," and "Hoop-A-Hoop-A-Loo," by Jerry Wright all on Missile Records (all country).
Tips: "A good cassette tape recording of your song can make the difference in acceptance and rejection. Always write and ask what type of songs we are looking for and always enclose sufficient return postage."

*A.V. MITTELSTEDT, 9717 Jensen Dr., Houston TX 77093. (713)695-3648. Producer: A.V. Mittelstedt. Record producer and music publisher (Sound Masters). Works with artists and songwriters. Produces 100 singles and 20 LPs/year. Fee derived from sales royalty and outright fee from recording artist.
How to Contact: Prefers cassette. SASE. Reports in 2 months.
Music: Mostly country, gospel, crossover; also MOR and rock.

*MJD PRODUCTIONS, INC.,Box 153, Sea Isle City NJ 08243. (609)263-1777. President: Mark J. Dicciani. Record producer, music publisher (Allora Music Publishing) and producer of audio for video, film, commercial. Deals with artists and songwriters. Produces 20 singles and 4 LPs/year. Fee derived from sales royalty or outright fee from recording artist or record company.
How to Contact: Prefers cassette (or VHS videocassette) with 2-3 songs and lyric sheet. SASE. Reports in 3 weeks.
Music: Mostly rock, pop and R&B; also jazz. Produced "It's Alright," (by Tony Ventura), recorded by Ant on Allora Records (single); "Dance On Air," (by Bob Pruitt), recorded by Ben Vereen on Manhattan Records (single); and "You're the First Thing," (by Mary Welch), recorded by Bobby Rydell on Applause Records (single).
Tips: "Keep song and artist demos uncluttered with the vocals out front."

MO FO MUSIC, 117 W. Rockland, Libertyville IL 60048. (312)362-4060. Contact: Perry or Rick Johnson. Record producer and music publisher. Deals with artists and songwriters. Produces 12 singles and 2 LPs/year. Fee derived from sales royalty.
How to Contact: Prefers cassette with 5 songs and lyric sheet.

S.J. MOLLICA, 331 E. 9th St., New York NY 10003. (212)473-7833. Producer: S.J. Mollica. Record producer. Deals with songwriters. Produces 2 singles/year. Works with 2 new songwriters/year. Outright fee from record company.
How to Contact: Write first about your interest. Prefers cassette or 15 ips reel-to-reel (or VHS videocassette) with 3-6 songs and lyric sheet. SASE. Reports in 1 month.
Music: Folk, gospel, jazz, progressive, R&B and rock. Produced *Music from the Street*, "Son of a Working Man" and "Never to Deliver," by Santo (Source Unlimited Records).

MOM AND POP PRODUCTIONS, INC., Box 96, El Cerrito CA 94530. Executive Vice President: James Bronson, Jr. Record producer, record company and music publisher (Toulouse Music/BMI). Deals with artists, songwriters and music publishers. Fee derived from sales royalty.
How to Contact: Prefers cassette with 2-4 songs and lyric sheet. SASE. Reports in 1 month.
Music: Bluegrass, gospel, jazz, R&B and soul. Artists include Les Oublies du Jazz Ensemble.

LEN MONAHAN PRODUCTIONS, 9967-US-A20, Delta OH 43515. Producer: Len Monahan. Record producer and music publisher (World Airwave Music). Deals with artists. Produces 4 singles and 2 LPs/year. Fee derived from sales royalty.
How to Contact: Write first and obtain permission to submit. Does not return unsolicited material. Reports in 1 month. "Not currently looking for new material."
Music: All types. Produced *Sending You My Thoughts* (LP), "Another Road," and "Tapping at Your Window," (singles), all by Len Francis Monahan (all on World Airwave Music).

*MONOTONE RECORDS, 281 E. Kingsbridge Rd., Bronx NY 10458. (212)733-5342. President: Murray Fuller. Record producer and music publisher (Sun Island Music Publishing Co.). Deals with artists and songwriters. Produces 1 single/year. Fee derived from sales royalty.
How to Contact: Prefers cassette with 3-5 songs and lyric sheet. SASE. Reports in 6 weeks.
Music: Blues, dance-oriented, easy listening, jazz, R&B, soul and top 40/pop.

MONTICANA PRODUCTIONS, Box 702, Snowdon Station, Montreal, Quebec H3X 3X8 Canada. Executive Producer: David Leonard. Record producer. Deals with artists, songwriters and artists' man-

agers. Fee derived from sales royalty.
How to Contact: Prefers 7½ or 15 ips reel-to-reel, cassette, phonograph record (or VHS videocassette) with maximum 10 songs and lyric sheet. "Demos should be as tightly produced as a master." Does not return unsolicited material.
Music: Mostly top 40; also bluegrass, blues, country, dance-oriented, easy listening, folk, gospel, jazz, MOR, progressive, R&B, rock and soul.

MOOD SWING PRODUCTIONS, 239-A E. Thach Ave., Auburn AL 36830. (205)821-JASS. Contact: Lloyd Townsend, Jr. Record producer and music publisher (Imaginary Music). Deals with artists and songwriters. Produces 2-3 singles and 2-3 LPs/year. Works with 3-4 new songwriters/year. Fee derived from sales royalty.
How to Contact: Prefers cassette or 7½ ips reel-to-reel with 4 songs and lyric sheet or lead sheet. SASE. Reports in 2 months.
Music: Mostly jazz; also blues and rock. Produced "Hexaphony," written and recorded by Somtow Sucharitkul (avant garde, Imaginary Records); "Tons of Art," by Mr. Resistor and the Incapacitators (R&B/rock); and "Sonic Defense Initiative," by various artists (rock, Imaginary). Other artists include Nothing Personal, Bonnevilles, Streetwise, Kidd Blue and Ebb Arnold and the Friction Pigs.

DOUG MOODY PRODX, Box 1596, San Marcos CA 92069. (619)967-7970. President: Doug Moody. Record producer, music publisher and music library. Deals with artists, songwriters and record producers. Produces 20 singles and 30 LP's/year. Fee derived from sales royalty as negotiated by individual contract.
How to Contact: "Get a local young group to perform your song and send us a cassette of their interpretation."
Music: "All kinds of rock: hardcore, teen, horror, death and thrash. We specialize in teen-age entertainment."

*MORDISCO, (Alberto Ohanian), Diag. Norte 570, 5th Piso, Buenos Aires 1035 Argentina. (01)33-3338 or 30-1905 or 30-9764. A&R Director: Oscar Sayavedra. Record producer and management company (Ohanian Productions). Deals with artists and songwriters. Produces 5 LPs/year. Fee derived from sales royalty or outright fee from songwriter/artist or record company.
How to Contact: Prefers cassette (or VHS videocassette). "Please send us samples of your work from previous years." Does not return unsolicited material. Reports in 2 weeks.
Music: Mostly rock, pop and folk; also country, soul/funk and R&B. Produced *Nada Personal*, by Soda Stereo (rock/pop); *El Regalao*, by Piero (folk); and *7 x 7*, by David Lebon (rock), all LPs and singles on CBS Argentina. Other artists include Los Enanitos Verdes (rock/pop act for CBS), Friccion (new rock act for Interdisc), Raul Porchetto (rock/ballad artist for RCA Argentina) and Charly Garcia (rock artist for CBS).
Tips: "We're the most important management company in rock music in this country. We work only with *top* artists."

MORE RONG NOTES PRODUCTIONS, Box 150951, Nashville TN 32215. (615)352-6134. President: Ron Oates. Production company and music publisher (Jesfine Music/BMI, Rong Songs/ASCAP). Reviews material for acts.
How to Contact: Prefers cassette with 4 songs and lyric and lead sheets. Reports in 2 weeks.
Music: Mostly country, adult contemporary and top 40. Works primarily with vocalists. Current acts include Engelbert Humperdinck and Adam Baker.

MR. WONDERFUL PRODUCTIONS, INC., 1730 Kennedy Rd., Lousiville KY 40216. (502)774-4118. President: Ronald C. Lewis. Record producer and music publisher (Ron "MisterWonderful" Music/BMI, and 1730 Music/ASCAP). Deals with artists and songwriters. Produces 3 singles and 4 LPs/year. Fee is derived from outright fee from recording artist.
How to Contact: Prefers cassette and lyric sheet. SASE. Reports in 3 weeks.
Music: R&B, crossover pop and gospel. Produced "Connect," (by Harold Johnson), recorded by Jerry Green on BroFeel Records; and "First on the Dance Floor," written and recorded by Jerry Green on Wonderful Records (both singles). Other artists include Margaret Beaumont, Maxx Franklin, Nocomo and Golden Crowns (gospel).

MUNCHKIN VALLEY PRODUCTIONS, Box 5110, Sherman Oaks CA 91413. (213)973-8800. Director: Scott Bergstein. Record producer, music publisher (Crunchy Frog Music) and international consultant. Estab. 1986. Deals with artists. Produces 6 LPs/year. Fee derived from sales royalty; outright fee from songwriter/artist and/or outright fee from record company.
How to Contact: Submit finished masters (or VHS videocassette) and lyric sheet. SASE.

Music: Rock, contemporary, jazz and New Age. Produced *Is It Safe*, by Windows (fusion LP, Intima/Enigma Records); *New England Theatre*, by Edwin Cohn (New Age LP, Catero Records); and *Vibrate*, by Spencer Davis Group (rock LP, Munchkin Valley Records); and *Poems of the Five Mountains*, by Timmermans and Skipper Wise. Other artists include Kindness of Strangers.

*MUSICON,375 N. Melrose, Vista CA 92083. (619)945-0939. President Bill Berry. Record producer, duplication services, recording and arranging. Estab. 1986. Deals with artists and songwriters. Produces 50 singles and 4 LPs/year. Fee derived from outright fee from recording artist.
How to Contact: Prefers cassette and lead sheet. SASE. Reports in 2 weeks.
Music: Mostly pop, R&B and rock; also gospel. "If You Don't Know," written and recorded by Bob Lapietra on Art Records (single); "Rolling Down," (by Chris Delpit), recorded by Chris and The Knights on Horizon Records (single); and "Come Let Us Sing," written and recorded by Debby Smith on Heart Records (single). Other artists include John Achord and Nancy Caldwell.
Tips: "Be creative don't be afraid to break the mold. Use strange rhythms, chords, melody lines to give your song flavor then work on making it flow smoothly so people think, 'that was nice, what did they do there?' "

NARADA PRODUCTIONS, 1845 N. Farwell, Milwaukee WI 53202. (414)272-6700. Creative Director: Eric Lindert. Record producer and music publisher. Deals with artists and songwriters. Produces 30 LPs/year. Fee derived from sales royalties.
How to Contact: Prefers cassette. Does not return unsolicited material. Reports in 1 month.
Music: "We specialize in New Age and accoustic music." Produced *Quiet Fire*, By Ancient Future, and *Indian Summer*, by Friedemann, (both New Age LPs).

NASHVILLE INTERNATIONAL MUSIC GROUP, 116 17th Ave. S,. Nashville TN 37203. (615)254-3464. President: Reggie M. Churchwell. Vice President: Mark Churchwell. General Manager, Music Group: Ben Haynes. Record producer and music publisher. Labels include Phoenix Records and Nashville International Records. Deals with artists and songwriters. Produces 6 singles and 2 LPs/year. Fee derived from sales royalty and outright fee from record company.
How to Contact: Write first about your interest. Prefers cassette with 1-4 songs and lyric sheet. Does not return unsolicited material "unless prior contact has been made."
Music: Country, MOR, R&B (crossover), rock (country, pop, power pop), soul (crossover), and top 40/pop. Produced "Letter in Red," written and recorded by Kenny Durham (pop/gospel); and "Mother Trucker," written and recorded by Kymberlee Knight (country), both on Phoenix Records.

*CARLO NASI,1040 N. Las Palmas, Los Angelos CA 90038. (213)461-8631. Chairman: Carlo Nasi. Record producer and music publisher (Zebra Discorde Music Group, Inc.). Deals with artists and songwriters. Produces 4-6 singles and 3-5 LPs/year.
How to Contact: Write first and obtain permission to submit. Prefers cassette with 3-4 songs and lyric sheet. Does not return unsolicited material. Reports in 1 month.
Music: Mostly pop, R&B and dance; also rock. Produced *Red Light*, (by Veitch/Winding), recorded by Patty Brard on Striped Horse Records (dance LP). Other artists include Maurizio Colonna.

NERVOUS MUSIC, 4/36 Dabbs Hill Lane, Northolt, Middlesex, London England. 44-01-422-3462. Managing Director: Roy Williams. Record producer, music publishing (Nervous Publishing) and record company (Nervous Records). Produces 5 singles and 10 LPs/year. Deals with artists and songwriters. Fee derived from sales royalty.
How to Contact: Prefers cassette with 3-10 songs and lyric sheet. "Include photo and a letter giving your age and career goals." SAE and IRC. Reports in 2 weeks.
Music: Mostly rock 'n' roll, psychobilly and rockabilly; also blues, country and R&B. Produced "Skitzomania," (by Connor), recorded by Skitzo on Nervous Records (LP); "Rumble in the Jungle," (by Glazebrook), recorded by Rochee and the Sarnos on Anagram Records (LP); and *Rattlin Boogie* (by Peck), recorded by The Rattlers on Lost Moment Records (LP). Other artists include The Pharoahs, Get Smart and Torment.

NEW HORIZON RECORDS, 3398 Nahatan Way, Las Vegas NV 89109. (702)732-2576. President: Mike Corda. Record producer and music publisher. Deals with artists and songwriters. Fee derived by sales royalty.
How to Contact: Prefers cassette with 1-3 songs and lyric sheet. SASE.
Music: Blues, country, easy listening, jazz and MOR. Artists include Mickey Rooney, Bob Anderson, Jan Rooney, Joe Williams and Robert Goulet.

NEW WORLD RECORDS, Suite 11, 2309 N. 36th St., Milwaukee WI 53210. (414)445-4872. President: Marvell Love. Record producer and music publisher (Jero Limited Music/BMI). Deals with artists

and songwriters. Produces 8 singles and 2 LPs/year. Fee derived from sales royalty.
How to Contact: Prefers cassette with 3-5 songs and lyric sheet. SASE. Reports in 3 weeks.
Music: Mostly R&B and soul ballads; also church/religious, gospel, soul and top 40/pop. Produced "You're My Lady," by Russell Yancy (ballad); "Thought I Wasn't Gonna Make It Back," by the Viceroys (love ballad single, Castalia Records); "I'll Miss You," by Jim Spencer (easy listening single, New World Records); "Red Tape," by Tony Dawkins and "Oh, What a Friend," by Phebe and Darrell Hines. Other artists include the Majestics and Danny Finckley.

KEITH NICHOL, 71 High St. E, Wallsend, Tyne and Wear NE28 7RJ England. Producer/Engineer: Keith Nichol. Record producer and music publisher (Impulse Studios). Deals with artists and songwriters. Produces 10 singles and 12 LPs/year. Fee derived from sales royalty, outright fee from songwriter/artist and/or outright fee from record company.
How to Contact: Prefers cassette (or VHS videocassette) and lyric or lead sheets. SAE and IRC.
Music: Pop and rock. Produced *Eine Kleine Nachtmusik*, by Venom on Neat Records (heavy metal LP); *Prelude*, by Irene Hume on Filmtrax Records (New Age LP); and "Jambo Johnny," by Alan Blevins on Floating World Records (single).

NIGHTHAWK RECORDS PRODUCTIONS, Box 15856, St. Louis MO 63114. (314)576-1569. Contact: Robert Schoenfeld. Record producer and music publisher (Blackheart Music). Deals with artists and songwriters. Produces 2-4 singles/year and 3-5 LPs/year. Fee negotiable.
How to Contact: Prefers cassette with 4-6 songs and lyric sheet. SASE. Reports in 3 weeks.
Music: Mostly reggae, blues and R&B. Produced *Serious Thing*, by Gladiators; *Give Me Power*, by Itals; and *Travel with Love*, by J.H. & Dominoes (all reggae LPs on Nighthawk Records).
Tips: Looking for "gutsy original tunes with character and a message."

NIGHTWORK RECORDS, 355 W. Potter Dr., Anchorage AK 99502. (907)562-3754. Contact: Kurt Riemann. Record producer and music licensor (electronic). Deals with artists. Produces 10 LPs/year. Fee derived from outright fee from record company.
How to Contact: Prefers cassette or 15 ips reel-to-reel with 1-3 songs. "Send jingles and songs on separate reels." Does not return unsolicited material. Reports in 1 month.
Music: Mostly electronic and electronic jingles. Produced *Gaia*, By K. Riemann; *Aurora*, by Eelshake; and *Denali*, by Boxer, all LPs on Nightworks Records. Other artists include "most Alaskan artists and independent producers."

*NISS PRODUCTIONS, LTD,1803 S. 55th Court, Chicago IL 60650. (312)780-1754. Producer Michael Niss. Record producer and music publisher (Two Reel Advance). Deals with artists and songwriters. Produces 2-6 singles and 1-2 LPs/year. Fee derived from sales royalty or outright fee from record company.
How to Contact: Write first and obtain permission to submit. Prefers cassette (or VHS videocassette) with 3-4 songs and lyric or lead sheet. SASE. Reports in 1 month.
Music: Mostly pop, rock and English pop; also instrumental and jazz.

RANDY NITE, #740, 3500 W. Olive Ave., Burbank CA 91505. President: Randy Nite. Record producer, music publisher (Gandharva Music), record company (Nite Records), personal management firm and video production company (Maya Video). Deals with artists and songwriters. Produces 6 singles/year and 3 LPs/year. Fee derived from sales royalty.
How to Contact: Prefers cassette with 1-3 songs. SASE. Reports in 2 months.
Music: Contemporary country. Produced "Once Upon a Time," (single); *Turn on the Blue Light* (LP), "Just For You" (single), and "Blue Light," (single), all by Bobby Blue (contemporary country, Nite Records).

*NITE-LIFE PRODUCTION, INC., 120 8 Alcott Pl., Bronx NY 10475. (212)671-6842. President: Rocky Bucano. Record producer, music publisher (Milt-Just Music/ASCAP) and record company (M-Low Records, Strong City Records). Deals with artists and songwriters. Produces 10 singles and 2 LPs/year. Fee derived from sales royalty and outright fee from record company.
How to Contact: Prefers cassette and lyric or lead sheet. SASE. Reports in 2 weeks.
Music: Mostly pop/dance, R&B/funk and ballads; also rap. Produced "No Favors" by Temper on MCA Records (dance single); and "Crime" by MCS on M-Low Records (rap single).

NMI RECORDS, 5500 Troost, Kansas City MO 64110. (816)361-8455. President: Eugene Gold. Record producer and music publisher (Eugene Gold Music/BMI). Deals with artists and songwriters. Produces 6 singles and 2 LPs/year. Fee derived from sales royalty.
How to Contact: Call first and obtain permission to submit. Prefers cassette with 4-6 songs. SASE.

Reports in 1 month.
Music: Church/religious, gospel, jazz, R&B and soul. Produced "Diamond Feather," by Bad New Band (R&B single, NMI Records); "Give Into the Power of Love," by the Committee (R&B single); and *He's Worthy to Be Praised*, by Mt. Vernon Inspirational Choir (gospel LP). Other artists include LaVerne Washington, Ronnie and Vicky, Paula Lucas, Jeff Lucas, Supension, Bump and the Soul Stomper, and Barbara White and the Wing of Grace.

DAVID NORMAN PRODUCTIONS, (formerly His Head is Wedged Productions), Box 5342, Macon GA 31208. President: David Norman. Record producer and recording studio. Deals with artists. Produces 4 singles and 2 LPs/year. Fee derived from outright fee from record company or artist.
How to Contact: Prefers cassette with 3-5 songs. SASE. Reports in 2 weeks.
Music: Mostly funk; also R&B. Produced "Money" (by A. Waters), recorded by AC Black and the Mean Katz (LP), "Rich Girls" (by J. Westley), recorded by The Society (single); and "Covergirls," (by D. Norman), recorded by Charmaine (LP). Other artists include Page Boy and K.I.T.T.E.N.
Tips: "Songwriter/performer must have very open attitude. He/she must be constantly thinking of their future. Patience will be the key in making or breaking you. Financial backing to a small degree at the beginning of the recording session will help. It also helps if you have some form of image."

100 GRAND RECORDS, 11 Norton St., Newburgh NY 12550. (914)561-4483. President: Gregg Bauer. Record producer and music publisher. Deals with artists and songwriters. Produces 5 singles and 2 LPs/year. Works with 3 new songwriters/year. Fee derived from sales royalty or outright fee from record company.
How to Contact: Prefers cassette (or videocassette) with 3-5 songs and lyric sheet. SASE. Reports in 1 month.
Music: Mostly rock, dance and jazz; also choral, easy listening, folk, soul and top 40/pop. Produced "White Hat," and "Hold On," (by G. Bauer/P. Otero) and "Faith," written and recorded by Art Nouveau (dance rock singles, 100 Grand Records).

JEANNINE O'NEAL, 195 S. 26th St., San Jose CA 95116. (408)286-9840. Producer: Jeannine O'Neal. Record producer and arranger. Deals with artists and songwriters. Produces 10 singles and 5 LPs/year. Fee derived from sales royalty, outright fee from songwriter/artist and/or outright fee from record company.
How to Contact: Prefers cassette with 3 songs and lyric or lead sheets. SASE.
Music: Mostly rock/pop, country and gospel; also jazz and international. Produced *I Know I Know*, written and recorded by Jim Garewal (LP); "Wondering," recorded by Johnny Gi-tar (single) and 'Try Again," written and recorded by Ed Brown (single) all on Rowena Records. Other artists include Fabrizio.

FRANCIS O'NEILL ORGANIZATION (FONO), 71 Rue de Provence, Paris 75009 France. (33-1)48 74 11 12. President: Francis F. O'Neill. Record producer and music publisher (FONO). Deals with songwriters. Fee derived from sales royalty.
How to Contact: Submit demo by mail. Call first to arrange personal interview. Prefers cassette (or VHS videocassette "when available") with 3-4 songs and lyric sheet. Does not return unsolicited material. Reports in 2 weeks.
Music: Mostly top 40, dance and rock; also "background music library." Produced (or published) "Paradise Me Amor," by Lune de Miel (pop single, W.E.A. Records); "Lover Why," by Century (pop/dance single/LP, Clever Records); and "I Feel Love," by Bronsky Beat (pop single, London Records). Other artists include Paul Ives and Christian Ardissono.
Tips: "1) Write better songs than the best professional writers; 2) try to be different and original; 3) better to write a good song than have to rely on an outstanding arrangement!"

***OPUS**,Mlynske nivy 73; Bratislava 827-15 Czechoslovakia. 222-680. International Manager: Rudolf Homer. Record producer and music publisher. Deals with artists and songwriters. Produces 30 singles and 100 LPs/year. Fee derived from outright fee from record company.
How to Contact: Prefers cassette. SAE and IRC. Reports in 1 month.
Music: Mostly pop; also classical. Produced Tchaikovsky's *Fifth Symphony*, (classical), *Concerto for Handolive*, by J.N. Hummel (classical), and *Jockey*, by P. Nagy (pop), all LPs on Opus Records.

***ORIGINAL PROJECTS UNLIMITED**,7926 So. Alder Way, Littleton CO 80123. (303)972-3679. President: Lauri Day-Workman. Record producer and management company. Estab. 1986. Deals with artists and songwriters. Fee derived from outright fee from recording artist or record company.
How to Contact: Prefers cassette (or VHS videocassette) with 3-4 songs and lyric sheet. "We require a letter from the artist or songwriter explaining what services or help they are looking for." Does not return

unsolicited material. Reports in 6 weeks.
Music: Mostly rock, pop and progressive rock; also new music (art rock) and R&B. Produced Tails From the Big Green, recorded by The Original Rabbits on Rabbit Trax Records; and *Knight of Crime*, by Private Eye on Air Castle Records (both LPs).
Tips: "Looking for bands who are serious about their musical careers with strong songwriting ability and marketability."

OUTLOOK PRODUCTIONS, Box 180, Star Route, Bethel ME 04217. (207)824-3246. Record producer. Deals with artists and songwriters. Produces 12 singles and 6 LPs/year. Fee derived from sales royalty and/or outright fee from record company.
How to Contact: Prefers cassette or 15 ips reel-to-reel (or VHS videocassette) with 1 song and lyric sheet. "Please include your name and phone number on the tape." Does not return unsolicited material.
Music: Mostly rock, pop and country; also new wave, heavy metal and avant-garde. Produced *Hills & Valleys*, by Jay Roy (country LP, Outlook Records); *Private WA I&II*, by Willie Alexander (rock/avant garde EPs, Outlook Records); and *War Paint*, by Connie St. Pierre (rock LP).

OZARK OPRY RECORDS INC., Box 242, Osage Beach MO 65065. (314)348-3383. A&R/Producer: Jim Phinney. Record, jingle and commercial producer. Deals with artists and songwriters. Fee "quoted by individual project."
How to Contact: Prefers 7½ ips reel-to-reel or cassette with 1-3 songs and lyric sheet. "Please include cover letter, explaining general information about material." SASE. Reports in 1 month.
Music: Bluegrass, blues, children's, church/religious, country, dance, easy listening, gospel, jazz, MOR, progressive, R&B, rock, soul and top 40/pop. Produced "Waylon, Sing to Mama," by Darrell Thomas (country single, Ozark Opry Records); "Untanglin' My Mind," by Larry Heaberlin (country single, Hoedown U.S.A. Records); and "Don't Say No to Me Tonight," by Mark Sexton (pop/country single, Son De Mar Records). Other artists include Robbie Wittkowski and Lee Mace's Ozark Opry.

PACIFIC CHALLENGER PRODUCTIONS, 2940 E. Miraloma Ave., Anaheim CA 92806. (714)992-6820. President: Chuck Whittington. Record producer and music publisher (Moonridge). Deals with artists and songwriters. Produces 8 singles and 4 LPs/year. Fee derived from sales royalty.
How to Contact: Prefers cassette with 1-4 songs and lyric sheet. Does not return unsolicited material. Reports in 1 month.
Music: Mostly country; also gospel and top 40/pop. Recently published *Waltzes & Western Swing* and "Big Tulsa Tillie," (by Donnie Rohrs); and "Building Up to a Letdown," (by Robert Lee Smith), all recorded by Donnie Rohrs.

***PAD RECORDS AND DEMO STUDIO**, Rt #2, Box 219, Myrtle MS 38650. Publisher: Glenn Summers. Record producer. Deals with artists, songwriters and "people who want to make tapes for demo purposes." Produces 2 singles/year. Fee derived from sales and airplay royalties.
How to Contact: Write first. Prefers cassette or 8-track with 1-2 songs. SASE. Reports in 1 month.
Music: Mostly country; also bluegrass, blues, gospel, jazz and R&B. Produced "Actions Speak Louder Than Words" and "Let Freedom Ring," (by Glenn Summers), recorded by Tommy Warren on PAD Records (singles).
Tips: "There have been constant changes in the music field, country music is not true country music anymore, it is a mixture of rock and blues."

PANDEM RECORDS, (formerly Michael Panepento), #811, 225 Oxmoor Circle, Birmingham AL 35209. (205)942-3222. President: Michael Panepento. Record producer, music publisher (Weedhopper Music) and recording studio/record label. Deals with artists and songwriters. Produces 5 singles and 5 LPs/year. Fee derived from sales royalty or outright fee from record company.
How to Contact: Write first and obtain permission to submit or arrange personal interview. Prefers cassette or 15 ips reel-to-reel with 3 songs and lyric sheet. SASE. Reports in 3 weeks.
Music: Mostly MOR, pop, rock, AOR and jazz/R&B; also country, jazz/straight and classical. Produced *Listen To Me*, (by Randy Hunter), recorded by Hunter/Panepento (LP); and "Photo Finish," (by Ben Trexel), recorded by Daughter Judy (single), both on Pandem Records.

PANIO BROTHERS LABEL, Box 99, Montmartre, Saskatchewan S0G 3M0 Canada. Executive Director: John Panio, Jr. Record producer. Deals with artists and songwriters. Produces 1 single and 1 LP/year. Works with lyricists and composers and teams collaborators. Fee derived from sales royalty or outright fee from artist/songwriter or record company.
How to Contact: Prefers cassette with any number of songs and lyric sheet. Does not return unsolicited material. Reports in 1 month.
Music: Country, dance, easy listening and Ukrainian. Produced "Christmas Is Near," by the Panio

Brothers Band (Christmas single); and "Celebrate Saskatchewan," by Panio Brothers (Ukrainian).

THE PASHA MUSIC ORG., INC., 5615 Melrose Ave., Hollywood CA 90038. (213)466-3507. General Manager: Carol Peters. Record production and music publisher. Custom label distributed by CBS. Deals with artists and songwriters. Fee derived by sales royalty.
How to Contact: "Write first for submission policy. Address letters to A&R Department. No phone calls please." Prefers cassette with 1-3 original songs. SASE. Reports in 6 weeks.
Music: Progressive, rock and top 40/pop.

DAVE PATON, Suite 170, 14116 E. Whittier, Whittier CA 90605. Contact: Dave Paton. Record producer and music publisher (Heaven Songs/BMI). Deals with artists and songwriters. Produces 20 singles and 3-5 LPs/year. Fee negotiable.
How to Contact: Write first. Prefers 7½ ips reel-to-reel or cassette with 3-6 songs and lyric sheet. SASE. Reports in 2 weeks.
Music: Country, dance, easy listening, jazz, MOR, progressive, R&B, rock, top 40/pop and comedy.

PENTAGRAMM PRODUCTIONS, Box 384, 116 Wendy Dr., Holtsville NY 11742. President: Arthur Poppe. Record producer and music publisher (Little Wizard). Deals with artists and songwriters. Produces 5 singles and 2 LPs/year. Fee derived from sales royalty.
How to Contact: Write first about your interest. "Don't phone." Prefers cassette (or videocassette) with 1-3 songs. SASE. Reports in 3 weeks.
Music: MOR, R&B, rock, soul and top 40/pop.

PAUL PETERSON CREATIVE MANAGEMENT, 4611 Vesper Ave., Sherman Oaks CA 91403-2834. (818)906-1131. Contact: Paul Peterson. Record producer, music publisher and personal management firm. Deals with artists and songwriters. Produces 2 LPs/year. Fee derived from sales royalty or outright fee from songwriter/artist or record company.
How to Contact: Prefers cassette and lyric sheet. SASE. Reports in 1 month.
Music: Mostly rock, pop and jazz; also country. Produced *Lost Cabin Sessions*, (by Steve Cash), recorded by Ozark Mountain Daredevils on Legend Records (country/rock LP); "Love At First Sight," (by Conrad Stolze), recorded by Dogs? on Dogs? Records (rock EP); and *Everything's Alright*, written and recorded by Priscilla Bowman on Legend Records (blues/rock LP).

MICHAEL ROBERT PHILLIPS/CYNTHIA PRODUCTIONS, c/o Orinda Records, Suite 200, 111 Deerwood Place, San Ramon CA 94583. (415)254-2000. Producer: Michael Robert Phillips. Record producer and video producer. Deals with artists and songwriters. Produces 10-20 LPs/year. Fee derived from sales royalty or outright fee from record company and advance.
How to Contact: Prefers cassette (or ½" videocassette) and lyric sheet or lead sheet. Does not return unsolicited material. Reports in 2 months.
Music: Mostly rock, pop rock and pop.

PLATINUM SOUND PRODUCTIONS, Suite 602, 523 Pine St., Seattle WA 98101. (206)624-3965. President: Kenneth H. Smith. Record producer, music publisher (Keristene Music, Ltd.) and video production firm. Deals with artists. Produces 3 singles and 6 LPs/year. Fee derived from sales or outright fee from record company.
How to Contact: Write or call first and obtain permission to submit. Prefers cassette (or VHS videocassette) with maximum 3 songs and lyric sheet. Does not return unsolicited material. Reports in 2 months.
Music: Mostly R&B; also urban dance, punk, rock, heavy metal and country. Produced *Connie*, written and recorded by Connie Butler; *Venus*, by Merrell Fankhauser; and *Contents Under Pressure*, (by K.H. Smith), recorded by Tie Pantys (all LPs on D-Town Records). Other artists include Lee Rogers and Bernadette Bascom.
Tips: "We are looking for finished product and polished acts."

P. PLETINCKX, 42 Avenue Clays, Brussels 1030 Belgium. (02)241-41-86. Record producer. Produces 3 LPs/year. Fee derived from sales royalty and/or outright fee from record company.
How to Contact: Prefers cassette. Does not return unsolicited material. Reports in 2 weeks.
Music: Jazz, rock and instrumental music.

PLUM STUDIO LTD. (Magic Sound Productions), 2 Washington St., Haverhill MA 01830. (617)372-4236. President: Richard Tiegen. Record producer and music publisher (Astrodisque/BMI). Deals with artists and songwriters. Produces 4 singles/year and 2 LPs/year. Fee derived from outright fee from songwriter/artist and/or record company.

How to Contact: Write first to arrange personal interview. Prefers cassette (or VHS videocassette) with 3 songs. Does not return unsolicited material. Reports in 2 weeks.
Music: Rock, blues and New Age. Produced *Nude*, by Yu Yu Hop (punk LP); "Seventeen", by Vic Scionti (novelty single); and *Break*, by Starflash (R&B EP), all on Plum Records. Other artists include End of the Line Band.
Tips: "Must be professional—no drugs, no booze; must have promo package—pictures, bio, etc."

PRAISE SOUND PRODUCTIONS LTD., 7802 Express St., Burnaby, British Columbia V5A 1T4, Canada. (604)420-4227. Manager: Metro Yaroshuk. Record producer. Deals with artists. Produces 25 singles and 50 LPs/year. Fee derived from sales royalty.
How to Contact: Prefers cassette with 1-12 songs and lyric sheet. SAE and IRC. Reports in 2 weeks.
Music: Bluegrass, children's, choral, church/religious, country, folk, gospel and gospel/rock.

PRELUDE MANAGEMENT CO., Rt 7, Box 683W, Canyon Lake TX 78130. (512)899-7474. Contact: Donald L. Nunley. Record producer, music publisher (Nunley Publishing Co.) and management firm. Deals with artists and songwriters. Fee derived from sales royalty or percentage for management.
How to Contact: Write or call first and obtain permission to submit. Prefers cassette and lyric sheet or lead sheet. "Make sure cassette is labeled with name, address, song title and phone number." SASE. Reports in 10 weeks.
Music: Mostly country, blues and rock. Produced "Hey Little Girl," and "Sink or Swim," by Gayle Smith (MOR singles, Tama).

THE PRESCRIPTION CO., 70 Murray Ave., Port Washington NY 10050. (516)767-1929. President: David F. Gasman. Vice President A&R: Kirk Nordstrom. Tour Coordinator/Shipping: Bill Fearn. Secretary: Debbie Fearn. Record producer and music publisher (Prescription Co./BMI). Deals with artists and songwriters. Fee derived from sales royalty or outright fee from record company.
How to Contact: Write or call first about your interest then submit demo. Prefers cassette with any number songs and lyric sheet. Does not return unsolicited material. Reports in 1 month. "Send all submissions with SASE or no returns."
Music: Bluegrass, blues, children's, country, dance, easy listening, jazz, MOR, progressive, R&B, rock, soul and top 40/pop. Produced "You Came In" and "Rock 'n' Roll Blues," by Medicine Mike (pop singles, Prescription Records); and *Just What the Doctor Ordered*, by Medicine Mike (LP, not yet released).
Tips: "We want quality—fads mean nothing to us. Familiarity with the artist's material helps too."

*QUEST MUSIC,3078 Florida Blvd., Lake Park FL 33410. Producer: Scott Brown. Record producer and recording engineer. Estab. 1986. Deals with artists and songwriters. Produces 3 singles and 1 LP/year. Fee derived from sales royalty or outright fee from recording artist.
How to Contact: Write first and obtain permission to submit. Prefes cassette and lead sheet. Does not return unsolicited material. Reports in 1 month.
Music: Mostly rock, rock/jazz fusion and country/rock; also contemporary ballads.

QUINTO PRODUCTIONS/RECORDS, Box 2388, Toluca Lake CA 91602. (818)985-8284. Producer: Quint Benedetti. Record producer, music publisher (Quint Benedetti Music/ASCAP) and artist manager. Deals with artists and songwriters on speculation only. Produces 1-2 singles and 1-2 LPs/year. Fee derived from sales royalty.
How to Contact: Prefers cassette with 2-3 songs and lead sheet. "SASE or no return of material." Reports in 10 weeks.
Music: Seasonal and Christmas songs only. Produced "Christmas Is for Children" and "Christmas Presents" (Quinto Records).

*QUINTON PRODUCTIONS,Box 15511, Kansas City MO 64106. Manager/Producer: Marion Sheyke. Music publisher (Louie B. Publishing BMI), Releases varied number of singles/year. Labels include QP, Kaytown, Soulsearch. Works with artists and songwriters on contract. "May consider producing artists with exceptional talent."
How to Contact: Prefers cassette (or VHS videocassette) with 3-4 songs and lyric or lead sheet. Include 8x10 photo if available. SASE.
Music: Top 40 (dance), R&B crossover, R&B, blues and gospel; also country. Produced "Sing The Love Song" (top 40 ballad), and "I'll Always Be there," (top 40 dance) both by Cotton Candy.
Tips: "We are looking for hit single material with strong hook. Songs relating to everyday life are great. Send the best quality tape you can afford."

R.E.F. RECORDS, 404 Bluegrass Ave., Madison TN 37115. (615)865-6380. President: Bob Frick. Manager: Shawn Frick. A&R Director: Scott Frick. Record producer and music publisher (Frick Music Publishing Co./BMI). Deals with artists, songwriters and producers. Produces 2 singles and 10 LPs/year. Fee derived from sales royalty.
How to Contact: Write or call first and obtain permission to submit, then submit 7 ½ ips reel-to-reel or cassette with 2-10 songs and lyric sheet. SASE. Reports in 1 month.
Music: Mostly gospel; also country, rock and top 40/pop. Produced "Unworthy," recorded by Bob Myers; and "One Day Closer to Jesus," and "Heading for Heaven," recorded by Bob Scott Frick (all gospel singles, R.E.F. Records). Other artists include Larry Ahlborn.

RAINBOW COLLECTION LTD., #806, 50 Music Sq. W, Nashville TN 37203. (615)320-1177. Executive Producer: Richard O'Bitts. Record producer, music publisher (Rocker Music, Happy Man Music) and management firm. Deals with artists and songwriters. Produces 10 singles and 4 LPs/year.
How to Contact: Prefers cassette with 4 songs and lyric sheet. SASE.
Music: All types. Artists include Don McLean, Janis Ian and Tony Bryd.

*ROBERT RAINES/LITTLE RED HEN PRODUCTIONS,261 W. 19th St., New York NY 10011. (212)989-3954. Producer: Robert Raines. Record producer, demo studio and pre-production facility. Deals with artists and songwriters. Produced 5 singles and 2 LPs/year. Fee derived from outright fee from record company. "Charges for demos and production only."
How to Contact: Prefers cassette (or VHS videocassette) with 3-5 songs and lyric sheet. SASE. Reports in 1 month.
Music: Mostly rock, pop and R&B; also country. Produced "Anything You Want (by Basi/Warren), recorded by Chickletts on RBI Records; "Don't Want To Stop," (by Steele/Jewler), recorded by Reve Time on LRH Records; and "Network,' (by Folsom), recorded by Pass Players on Venture Records (all singles). Other artists inlcude William Oborn, Mary Boze and The Hardhats.

RANDALL PRODUCTIONS, Box 11960, Chicago IL 60611-0960. (312)561-0027. President: Drusilla O'Conner. Record producer, video producer, and musical services to artists/songwriters.. Produces 5 singles, 2 LPs and 2 music videos/year. Fee derived from sales royalty.
How to Contact: Prefers cassette with 3-5 songs and lyric sheet. SASE. Reports in 2 months.
Music: Mostly R&B, pop and gospel; also MOR, rock, jazz and soul. Produced "Lie to Me," by Mack Simmons, and "Messin' with the Kid," by Walter Jacob (blues singles); and *Love You No Matter What*, by C. Rubin and John Williams (R&B/pop LP), Grandville Records.

RAWLS BROTHERS PRODUCTIONS CO., % Fun City Record Co., 281 W. 6th St., Mansfield OH 44903. Executive Producer: L.A. Rawls. A&R Director: M. "Tub" Sharp. Record producer. Deals with artists. Produces 5 singles and 3 LPs/year. Fee derived from sales royalty.
How to Contact: Write first and obtain permission to submit. Prefers cassette with 3-4 songs and lyric sheet. Does not return unsolicited material. Reports in 6 weeks.
Music: Ballads, R&B and top 40/pop. Produced "You're Gonna Need Me" (by C. Rawls/L. Rawls), recorded by Larry Rawls; "Headline My Show" (by C. Rawls), recorded by Rawls Brothers; and "Tonite" (by L. Rawls), recorded by New Groove Band, all singles on Fun City Records. Other artists include Jeff Jones.

RAY MACK PRODUCTIONS, Box 120675, Nashville TN 37212. (615)255-1068. President: Ray McGinnis. Record producer and music publisher (Nautical Music/BMI and Ray Mack Music/ASCAP). Deals with artists and songwriters. Produces 5 singles and 1-3 LPs/year. Fee derived from sales royalty, outright fee from recording artist and/or outright fee from record company.
How to Contact: Prefers cassette with 4 songs and lyric or lead sheet. SASE. Reports in 6 weeks.
Music: Mostly country, country rock and rock. Produced "Rock-A-Bye Baby," by Sonny Martin (single); "It's So Easy," by Billy Burnett (single); "The Lady," by B.J. Morgan (single); *I've Always Been Country*, by Sonny Martin (LP), all on Orbit Records. Other artists include Johnny Martinez, Kenny Wilson, "Ky" King, and Moetta.

*RED KASTLE PRODUCTIONS, Box 163, West Redding CT 06896. (203)438-5366. Manager: Ri Kidd. Record producer and music publisher (Blue Hill Music/Tutch Music). Deals with artists and songwriters. Produces 5 singles and 2 LPs/year. Fee derived from sales royalty.
How to Contact: Write or call first and obtain permission to submit. Prefers cassette with 2 songs and lyric sheet. SASE. Reports in 3 weeks.
Music: Country and country pop/crossover. Produced "Heart Keeps Walking" (by P. Hotchkiss), recorded by Tom Hanson on MOM Records (country single); "Rest of Your Love," written and recorded by Patty Terry on Target Records (pop single) and "Reindeer Don't Run Over Grandmas" (by J. Rickes-

ing, Jr.), recorded by Charlie Shemer on Puzzle Records (single). Other artists include Kristin Bivona and Hutcher Brothers.

REDBUD RECORDS, A Division of CAE Inc., 611 Empire Mill Rd., Bloomington IN 47401. (812)824-2400. General Manager: Pam Land. Record producer. Deals with artists, songwriters and bands. Produces 1 single and 4 LPs/year. Payment negotiated.
How to Contact: Call first about your interest. Prefers cassette with 2-10 songs. SASE. Reports in 1 month.
Music: Mostly folk and jazz; also bluegrass, choral, church/religious, classical, and easy listening. "We'll listen to anything!" Produced *Chicago Style*, by Friedlander and Hall (swing LP, RedBud Records); *Solo Guitar*, by Royce Campbell (jazz LP, RedBud Records); and *Buffalo Gal*, by Leftwich and Higginbotham (folk LP, RedBud Records). Other artists include Eric Rosser, Jan Henshaw, High Ground, Kiethe-Lowrie Duet and Bill Wilson.
Tips: "Perform a lot and be willing to sell records at your gigs. Have a professional approach to the business end of things. Play your music well—with taste and humor."

*FRED RICE PRODUCTIONS, INC., Box 643, La Quinta CA 92253. (619)564-4823. President: Fred Rice. Record producer and music publisher (Yo-Yo Music/BMI). Deals with artists and songwriters. Produces 1-6 singles/year. Fee derived from sales royalty.
How to Contact: Prefers cassette with two songs and lyric sheet. SASE.
Music: Mostly novelty, pop/MOR and country; also soul and comedy. Produces "How Many More Last Times," "Let's Take a Chance on Love Again," and "When Love Is at an End," (all by Sandra Storm/Rick Rueda), all recorded by R. C. Cole on Yo-Yo Music (all singles). Other artists include Rob Carter and Kenny King.

*RIPSAW PRODUCTIONS, #805, 4545 Connecticut Ave. NW, Washington DC 20008. (202)362-2286. President: Jonathan Strong. Record producer, music publisher (Sugar Mama Music/BMI) and record company (Ripsaw Records). Deals with artists and songwriters. Produces 0-4 singles and 0-3 LPs/year.
How to Contact: Prefers cassette and lyric sheet. SASE.
Music: Rockabilly and roots rock. Produced *Two Sides*, written and recorded by Bobby Smith (EP); and *Wanted: True R&R*, written and recorded by Billy Hancock (EP); both recorded on Ripsaw Records.

RMS TRIAD PRODUCTIONS, 6267 Potomac Circle, West Bloomfield MI 48033. (313)585-2552. Contact: Bob Szajner. A&R Manager: Laura Holiday. Record producer, record company and music publisher (RMS Triad Publishing/ASCAP). Deals with artists and composers (instrumental). Produces 3 LPs/year. Fee derived from outright fee from artist/composer or record company.
How to Contact: Write first about your interest. Prefers cassette with 1-3 songs. SASE. Reports in 3 weeks.
Music: Jazz instrumental. Produced *Jazz Opus 20/40*, *Detroit Jazz Center* and *1981 Montreaux/Detroit Live*, by Triad (jazz instrumental LPs, RMS Records); *Are You Glad to Be in America*, by James "Blood" Ulmer; and *Where Flamingos Fly*, by Gil Evans (jazz instrumental LPs, Artist's House Records). Other artists include Frank Isola and Roy Brooks.

*ROBBY ROBERSON PRODUCTIONS, Box 12444, Fresno CA 93777. (209)442-3332. Owner: Robby Roberson. Record producer, music publisher (Three Kings Music/BMI) and television and record production. Produces 3 singles and 3 LPs/year. Deals with artists only. Fee derived from sales royalty.
How to Contact: Prefers cassette with 3 songs and lyric sheet. SASE.
Music: Country, gospel and crossover. Produced *Angel's Face* written and recorded by Nick Holley on LANA Records (pop LP); *There* and *It's Over Now* (by Alli Sanifar), recorded by Oh La mour on Top Secret Records (dance LPs). Other artists include Hud Rose, Sharon Riley and Robby Roberson.
Tips: "Get educated as to what is really happening in the business, before you make application."

ROCKLAND MUSIC, INC., 117 W. Rockland Rd., Libertyville IL 60048. (312)362-4060. President: Perry Johnson. Record producer and music publisher (Rockland Music). Deals with artists and songwriters. Produces 5 singles and 2 LPs/year. Fee derived from sales royalty.
How to Contact: Prefers cassette with 1-5 songs and lyric sheet. SASE. Reports in 2 months.
Music: Dance/R&B, top 40/pop, rock and country. Produced *Animation*, by Animation (pop/rock LP); *Taxi*, by Taxi (hard rock LP); and *Nightbeat*, by Oh Boy (pop LP on Rockland Records). Other artists include Madelyn Brown, McCormick Sinclair, Linda Quick, and Slim Huston.
Tips: "Send single commercial songs, not album cuts."

*ROCKOKO PRODUCTION, Nordendstr. 30, Frankfurt/Main 6000 West Germany. (69) 55 26 32. Producer: Peter Hauke. Record producer and music publisher (Rockoko Music, GmbH). Deals with art-

ists and songwriters. Produces 6 LPs/year. Fee derived from sales royalty or outright fee from record company.
How to Contact: Prefers cassette and lyric sheet. Does not return unsolicited material. Reports in 1 month.
Music: Mostly rock and pop. Produced *I Wanna' Look In Your Eyes* (by Craaft/Carey), recorded by Craaft on Epic Records (LP); *Blue Highway*, written and recorded by Tony Carey on MCA Records (LP); and *Viel Zu Heiss*, written and recorded by Jocco Abendroth on Metronome Records (LP). Others artists include Saga, Planet P, Karo and White Lion.

*ROCKY MOUNTAIN HEARTLAND PRODUCTIONS, Box 6904, Denver CO 80206. (303)690-6904. Executive Producer: Steve Dyer. Record and video producer and advertising firm. Deals with artists and songwriters. Fee derived from sales royalty or outright fee from songwriter/artist or record company.
How to Contact: Write or call first and obtain permission to submit. Prefers cassette (or videocassette) with 3-5 songs and lyric sheet or lead sheet. Does not return unsolicited material. Reports in 1 month.
Music: Mostly gospel, top 40 and rock; also jazz and country. "Music open and not limited to these types." Produced *The Best Is Yet to Come*, by Kent Parry (big band and orchestra gospel LP on Record Harvest); *From Here to Kingdom Come*j, by Heart Song (mild gospel/top 40 LP on Record Harvest); and *Going, Going, Gone*, by Heart Song (gospel rock LP on Record Harvest).
Tips: "We are investing in new, up and coming artists."

ANGELO ROMAN, Box 65134, Los Angeles CA 90065. (213)465-9626. Producer: Angelo Roman. Record producer and management/consultant. Also administrates the Los Angeles Vocal Register, "a network for professional vocalists." Primarily deals with singer-songwriters. Works with 5-10 new songwriters/year. Works with composers and lyricists; teams collaborators. Fee derived from "various arrangements with artists and production companies. Always negotiable."
How to Contact: Write first; does not accept unsolicited material. Prefers cassette with 1-3 songs. SASE. Reports in 1 month.
Music: Mostly R&B/pop; also top 40/rock, jazz, MOR and soul. Produced "You Win," and "I Believe in Love," by Vennette Gloud (R&B pop single). Other artists include John and Baba Elefante.

ROOSTER PRODUCTIONS, LTD., 1234 W. 6th Ave., Vancouver, British Columbia V6H 1A5 Canada. (609)734-1217. Contact: Rolf Hennemann. Record producer. Deals with artists and songwriters. Fee derived from sales royalty, outright fee from songwriter/artist and/or outright fee from record company.
How to Contact: Prefers cassette. Does not return unsolicited material.
Music: Rock, pop and blues. Produced *Perennial*, by Perennial on Jet City Records (rock LP); and *Clocks*, by Clocks (rock LP) on Boulevard/CBS Records; and "Without You," by Steven Drake on MCA Canada Records (rock single).

ROPERRY, 645 Madison Ave., New York NY 10022. (212)836-4437. General Manager: Jane Lowy. Record producer, music publisher and record company. Deals with artists and songwriters. Produces approximately 3 singles and 1-2 LPs/year. Fee depends on contract.
How to Contact: Call first. Prefers cassette with 1-3 songs and lyric sheet. "Send a picture, bio, lead sheets and SASE." Reports in 3 weeks.
Music: Mostly top 40/pop; also children's, dance-oriented, easy listening and MOR. Produced *Patsy*, by Patsy (pop LP, Roperry Records); "Single Again," by Joey Latini (pop single, Roperry Records); "Just a Little Imagination," by Patsy (adult contemporary single, Roperry Records); and "Kid Santa Claus", by Patsy Maharam (a Prose production).
Tips: "Try to be professional—don't send lyrics we can't read or distorted tapes. Roperry is looking for growing talents."

ROSE HILL GROUP, 1326 Midland Ave., Syracuse NY 13205. (315)475-2936. A&R Director: Vincent Taft. Record producer and music publisher (Katch Nazar Music/ASCAP, Bleecker Street Music/BMI). Produces 5 singles and 2 LPs/year. Fee derived from sales royalty or outright fee from artist/songwriter or record company.
How to Contact: Prefers cassette with 3 songs maximum. SASE. Reports in 2 weeks.
Music: Mostly top 40/pop, rock, dance; also jazz and MOR. Produced "Hot Button," by Prowlers (dance/R&B single); "Free World," by Z Team (dance/pop single); and "So What," by IO (dance/rock single).

ROSEMARY MELODY LINE CO., Box 1078, E. Landis Ave., Vineland NJ 08360. (609)696-0943. Producer: Dennis Link. Record producer and recording studios. Deals with artists and songwriters. Produces 3-5 LPs and videos/year. Works with composers and lyricists; teams collaborators. Fee derived from sales royalty or outright fee from artist/songwriter.

How to Contact: Write first. Prefers cassette (or Beta hi-fi or 8mm videocassette) with 3 songs. SASE. Reports in 2 months.

Music: Christian rock and experimental. Produced Rosary Video by United World Entertainment; and "Talk to You," by Windrose (RMC Records).

ROSEWOOD PRODUCTIONS, 3½ Fern St., New Castle PA 16101. (412)654-3023. Contact: Lee Ayres. Record producer. Deals with songwriters. Produces 4 LPs/year. Fee derived from sales royalty.

How to Contact: Prefers cassette and lyric sheet. Does not return unsolicited material. Reports in 3 weeks.

Music: Bluegrass/gospel and oldtime music. *From the Heart*, written and recorded by Wes Homner on Rosewood Records (gospel); *Basic Blue*, written and recorded by Mac Martin on Old Homestead Records (bluegrass); and *Therapy Session*, written and recorded by Mountain Therapy on Rosewood Records (bluegrass), all LPs. Other artists include Ron Mesing, M&M Express and Dixie Travelers.

Tips: "Please send only the type of music requested."

BRIAN ROSS PRODUCTIONS, Box 2950, Hollywood CA 90078. A&R Producer: Brian Ross. Record producer and music publisher (Brian Ross Music/BMI); also international music representation in all foreign countries. Deals with artists, songwriters, attorneys, agents and managers. Produces 25 singles and 15 LPs/year. Fee derived from sales royalty.

How to Contact: Prefers cassette (or ½" videocassette) with 1-4 songs; also include photo and bio (if artist) "giving details about management, performances, etc. Be professional. Pick your 2-4 best songs, enclose SASE, and label clearly. Send all submissions care of Ian Ross, Director of A&R." Reports in 1 week, "24 hours if good." Does not assume responsibility for materials damaged or lost in the mail.

Music: Mostly dance-oriented, top 40/pop, ballads, contemporary and MOR; also all types of music including techno-pop and new wave. Produced *Best of the Music Machine* (by Bonniwell), recorded by the Music Machine on Rhino Records (LP). "I'm Waiting For You," written and recorded by Lance Powers and "Body Contact" (by Mike Grant), recorded by Didi Anthony, both singles on Starborn Records. Other artists include Ian Ross.

Tips: "Foreign releases are our specialty. For a copy of our free brochure, write to us with 'brochure' on the outside of the envelope. Please send SASE." Affiliated with International Music Commission USA.

RSD PRODUCTIONS, 7459 Arroyo Vista Ave., Cucamonga CA 91730. (714)980-4242. Contact: Robert S. Dire. Record producer and 24-track recording studio. Deals with artists and songwriters. Produces 25 singles and 3-5 LPs/year. Fee derived from outright fee from record company.

How to Contact: Prefers cassette (or VHS videocassette) with 3 songs and lyric sheet or lead sheet. "Also send resume and picture. Cassettes will not be returned—will be kept on file." Reports in 2 months.

Music: Top 40/crossover, rock and country. "No heavy metal." Produced "I'm Too Young To Go Steady," (by Ransom Turner), recorded by Raven Williams (dance/single); *One Summer In Heaven*, by Paul Carson (LP); and "Can Stay," (by Ransom Turner), recorded by Twice as Nice, all on Wax to Watch Records. Other artists include Gina Schock (formerly of the Go-Go's), Harold Brown (WAR) and Wally George.

*RUF-MIX PRODUCTIONS, 12966 La Maeda St., Sherman Oaks CA 91423. (818)760-0269. President: Taari Mote. Record producer. Estab. 1986. Deals with artists and songwriters. Produces "many" singles and LPs/year. Fee derived from sales royalty, outright fee from recording artist and/or outright fee from record company.

How to Contact: Prefers cassette with maximum of 4 songs and lyric sheet. SASE. Reports in 1 month.

Music: Mostly rock, R&B and pop; also gospel and dance. Produced "Love and Hate" (by Andre Cymone), recorded by Pebbles on Paramount Records for *Beverly Hills Cop II*; and "Still a Thrill," and "Hasta La Vista," recorded by Jody Watley on MCA Records (LPs and singles). Other artists include Klymaxx, New Edition, Ready for the World, Madonna, The Untouchables, and Natalie Cole.

RUSHWIN PRODUCTIONS, (formerly James L. Gibson), Box 1150, Buna TX 77612. (409)423-2521. Producer: James L. Gibson. Record producer and music publisher (Rushwin Publishing and Gibson Davidson Publishing) and record company (Fountain Records), and record mailing service (Gospel Record Service). Deals with artists and songwriters. Produces 5-10 singles and 3-4 LPs/year. Fee derived from sales royalty, outright fee from songwriter/artist and/or outright fee from record company, depending on the project.

How to Contact: Prefers cassette with 1-4 songs and "typed lyric sheet. Lead sheets optional. Clearly label each item you send. Include photo and bio if possible. SASE (6x9 or larger)." Reports ASAP, "usually in 1 month."

Music: Gospel/Christian only. Produced "My Sheep," (by Robbie Gibson), recorded by The Gibsons (on Gold Street Records (gospel single); *The Third Day*, (by Stephen Mattox), recorded by Third Day on New Breeze Records (gospel LP); "Reachin' Thru The Thorns" (by James Gibson), recorded by the Gibsons on Gold Street Records (gospel single).

Tips: "We only consider sincere, hard working artists who are willing to grow with us. We are a small independent operation on the grow with a bright future. It would be most helpful to us if an artist would include a press package with their submission to familiarize us with their ministry/music (past, present and future plans). We have an open door policy for songwriters."

*SAGITTAR RECORDS, 1311 Candlelight Ave., Dallas TX 75116. (214)298-9576. President: Paul Ketter. Record producer, record company and music publisher. Deals with artists and songwriters. Produces 12 singles and 3 LPs/year. Works with 3 new songwriters/year. Works with composers and lyricists; teams collaborators.

How to Contact: Prefers cassette with 3-12 songs and lead sheet. SASE. Reports in 1 month.

Music: Mostly country; also folk, MOR (country), and progressive (country). Produced "Stay Till I Don't Love You Anymore," "I Wanna Say 'I Do'," and "Lovin' Bound," by P.J. Kamel (country singles), "Theodore Csanta's Right-Hand-Man," by Dave Gregory (country single, and *Only A Woman* by Bunnie Mills (country LP), all on Sagittar Records. Other artists include Jay Douglas, Sandra Storm, Jackie Rosser, Buddy Howard, Joe Johnson and Jodi Witt.

Tips: "Be familiar with the top 10 songs on country charts." We are now looking for album masters for export to overseas markets.

SAMARAH PRODUCTIONS, INC., Box 2501, Columbia SC 29202. (803)754-3556. President: Daniel Hodge, Jr. Record producer, music publisher (Jemiah Publishing/BMI) and artist management. Deals with artists, songwriters and record companies. Produces minimum of 4 singles/year. Fee derived from sales royalty or outright fee from record company.

How to Contact: Prefers cassette with 1-3 songs, lyric sheet "and lead sheet if possible." SASE. Reports in 1 month.

Music: Country, MOR, R&B, rock (top 40), soul and top 40/pop. Produced "I Who Have Nothing," by Midnight Blue (R&B/pop single, Motown Records); and "Wishing" and "Feel It and Groove Together," by Midnight Blue (both R&B singles, Samarah Records).

Tips: "Rhythm tracks and vocals on tape must be tight. Before sending tape compare the *feel* of your song to the *feel* of a successful artist's song in the same market."

RICK SANDIDGE, 10 Michael Drive, Greenville SC 29610. (803)235-1111. Producer: Rick Sandidge. Record producer and music publisher (Castlerising and Adonikam/BMI). Deals with artists and songwriters. Produces 10 singles/year and 4 LPs/year. Fee derived from outright fee from record company.

How to Contact: Prefers cassette. Does not return unsolicited material. Reports in 6 weeks.

Music: Mostly country, rock and R&B; also gospel, soul and jazz. Produced "The River," by Don Axsom (country); "Whatever Happened to Love," by Barry De Fleron Band (rock); and "Fire in the Night," by Cindy Orr (pop rock). Other artists include J.D. Wilson and Rob Cassels Band.

*SILVER J. SARGENT, Box 897, Hartford CT 06120. (203)522-2371. Producer: Silver J. Sargent. Record producer, music publisher (LUV Sound/BMI) and recording label (Sounds of Connecticut— S.O.C.). Deals with artists and songwriters. Produces 4 singles and 2 LPs/year. Fee derived from sales royalty or outright fee from record company.

How to Contact: Prefers cassette (or VHS videocassette) with 4-5 songs and lyric or lead sheet. SASE. Reports in 6 weeks.

Music: Mostly funk, soul and R&B; also gospel, light rock and jazz. Produced "Bite It," (by Herb Superb), recorded by Drum (rap); "Shoot Your Best Shot," (by Silver Sargent), recorded by Carol (dance); and "Merci-ba-coup," (by Silver Sargent), recorded by Scarph (ballad), all singles on S.O.C. Records. Other artists include X.Y. Eli, Kimberlee, Barbara Fowler, Native American, Angie Champaigne.

Tips: "Send only your best, make sure your vocals are understood."

STEVE SCHARF, Steven Scharf Productions, Suite 4N, 61 Jane St., New York NY 10014. (212)929-2068. Contact: Steve Scharf. Record producer, music publisher (Weeze Music Co./BMI) and independent record producer. Produces 8 singles and 4 LPs/year. Deals with artists and songwriters. Fee derived from sales royalty or outright fee from artist/songwriter or record company. Production fees charged for demos and records.

How to Contact: Call first. Prefers cassette with maximum 4 songs and lyric sheet. SASE.

Music: Mostly rock and pop. Produced "Dancing on the Ice," "We Might Fall in Love," and "Only

You," all by Duke Jupiter (Motown Records). Other artists include Bob Halligan, Jr. Produces "local rock and pop bands developing in New York City, as well as out of state."
Tips: "Songwriters and artists must have great attitudes as people, then original hit material."

SECOND SUN PRODUCTIONS, Rt. 4, Box 428, Vashon Island WA 98070. (206)463-2850. Producer: Robert Krinsky. Record producer and music publisher (Ferry Boat Music/ASCAP, Thea Music/BMI). Record labels include Second Sun and Pinup. Deals with artists and songwriters. Produces 2 singles and 3 LPs/year. Fee derived from sales royalty.
How to Contact: Prefers cassette with 1-4 songs and lyric sheet. "Include cover letter stating whether you are submitting for artist or publishing consideration. Artists should be regionally located." Does not return unsolicited material.
Music: Blues, jazz, rock and top 40/pop. Produced *Lonesome City Kings*, by the Lonesome City Kings (rock LP, First American Records); *Big Time Blues Man*, by Isaac Scott (blues LP, Music Is Medicine Records); and *Diane Schuur I and II*, by Diane Schuur (jazz vocal LPs, First American Records).

SEIXAS MUSIC PRODUCTIONS, Box 1732, Murry Hill Station, New York NY 10156. (718)528-1760. President: Ron Seixas. Record producer and record company (Cargo Records). Deals with artists and songwriters. Produces 5 singles/year and 3 LPs/year. Fee derived from sales royalty.
How to Contact: Prefers cassette (or Beta videocassette) with 2 songs and lyric sheet. Include photograph. SASE. Reports in 3 weeks.
Music: Mostly dance rock or rock music with top-40 appeal; also new wave. Produced *Even Exchange*, by Cynthia (dance rock LP and single); *Sensation*, by Seixas (rock/variety LP); and *Locked On*, by Megabite (new wave LP), all recorded on Cargo Records.

*STEPHEN J. SELTZER,Box 234, Somerville MA 02143. (617)623-1066. Record producer and music publisher (Sumwarashu Productions). Deals with artists and songwriters. Fee derived from sales royalty or outright fee from recording artist.
How to Contact: Prefers cassette with 3-5 songs and lyric sheet. SASE. Reports in 3 weeks.
Music: Mostly dance pop and fringe rock.

*SHOTGUN MUSIC CORP., 1242 Colborne St. E., Brantford, Ontario N3T 5L4 Canada. (519)752-0839. President: Len Wilde. Record producer, music publisher (Like Always/West Star Music) and record company/recording studio. Deals with artists and songwriters. Produces 25 singles and 12 LPs/year. Fee derived from outright fee from recording artist.
How to Contact: Prefers cassette with 3 songs and lyric or lead sheet. SAE and IRC. Reports in 1 month.
Music: Mostly pop, country and rock; also gospel.

SIGHT AND SOUND ENTERTAINMENT MARKETING, Box 34183, Memphis TN 38134. (901)358-5006. A&R Director: Don Von Maurer. Vice President/Entertainment: Gary Drassin. Record producer and music publisher (Rocken Rythmn Publishing). Deals with artists, songwriters, producers and promoters. Fee derived from sales royalty or outright fee from artist/songwriter or record company.
How to Contact: Prefers cassette with 1-4 songs and lyric sheet. Specify the number of songs on the tape. SASE, but "we keep the tape on file and contact writer if interested."
Music: Mostly blues, top 40 and pop/R&B. Produced "Only a Moment," and "Say Yes," by Dotz (rock). Artists include Blues Rambles.

SILVERLINING PRODUCTIONS, Box 1040, Alpine NJ 07620. (201)767-5715. Producer: Vince Castellano. Record prducer, music publisher and management firm (Know Talent Management). Deals with artists and songwriters. Produces 8-10 singles and 4 LPs/year. Fee derived from sales royalty.
How to Contact: Prefers cassette, 7½ or 15 ips reel-to-reel (or VHS videocassette) with 3 songs and lyric sheet. SASE. Reports in 6 weeks.
Music: Mostly rock (commercial), R&B (contemporary) and AOR; also heavy metal and pop. Artists include Ray Goodman & Brown (R&B), Connie Francis (pop), Lonnie Young Blood (R&B), and Grand Master and Flash (rap).

SILVER-LOOMAS PRODUCTIONS, 38 Music Square E., Nashville TN 37203. (615)255-8005. Production Manager: Tommy Loomas. Executive Director: Joe Silver. Record producer, music publisher (Lineage Publishing Co.) and record company (Capstan Records). Deals with artists and songwriters. Produces 10 singles and 4 LPs/year. Fee derived from sales royalty, outright fee from songwriter/artist and/or outright fee from record company.
How to Contact: Write or call first and obtain permission to submit to arrange personal interview. Prefers cassette (or VHS videocassette) with 4 songs and lyric or lead sheets. "Submissions must be profes-

sional." Reports in 6 weeks.

Music: Mostly country, easy listening and bluegrass; also rock. Produced "Angel," by Rock Candy (rock single, Capstan Records). Other artists include Fleming McWilliams and Skidrow Joe.

DONOVAN "SOUND" SMITH, 1327 Cabrillo, Torrance CA 90501. (213)533-9531. President: Donovan Smith. Record producer. Deals with artists and songwriters. Produces 96 singles and 8 LPs/year. Fee is derived from outright fee from songwriter/artist and/or outright fee from record company.
How to Contact: Prefers cassette or 15 ips reel-to-reel (or VHS videocassette) with 4 songs and lyric sheet or lead sheets. SASE. Reports in 6 weeks.
Music: Mostly AOR/pop MOR and R&B/pop; also rock, youth rock and rap. Co-produced "The Fly," by World Class and "He's Bionic," by Wreckin Cru/World Class (both rap singles, CBS/Epic Records); and *World Class*, by Wreckin Cru (rap LP, CBS/Epic Records). Other clients include Donny Dean, Toyota Motor Sales and Mattel Toys.
Tips: "A good demo never hurts—not a master production, just a good representation of the song."

*SONGWRITERS' NETWORK, Box 190446, Dallas TX 75219. (214)823-1113. President: Phil Ayliffe. Record producer, music publisher (Songwriters' Network Music Publishing/ASCAP), and record company (Meridian Records, Songwriters' Network Records). Deals with artists and songwriters. Produces 2 singles and 1 LP/year. Fee derived from sales royalty and "publication subscription, and promotion."
How to Contact: Prefers cassette (or videocassette) with 5 songs and lyric sheet. "Five songs should include an uptempo opener; an uptempo, positive song; a ballad; a hand-clapping rouser; and a dramatic, personal philosophy song as a closer. Vocal must be mixed up-front. Any straining to hear the lyric and the tape is immediately rejected. Material is returned only if accompanied by an SASE." Reports in 6 weeks.
Music: Mostly adult contemporary, pop and MOR; also country crossover, "new acoustic," and show tunes/musical theatre.
Tips: "We are most interested in working with the singer/songwriter/producer entrepreneur, so we would like the best produced material possible, though vocal and instrument demo is OK. You must sing on pitch with your instrument in tune, otherwise don't bother."

*SOUND ARTS RECORDING STUDIO, 2036 Pasket, Houston TX 77092. (713)688-8067. President: Jeff Wells. Record producer and music publisher (Earthscream Music). Deals with artists and songwriters. Produces 12 singles and 3 LPs/year. Fee derived from outright fee from recording artist.
How to Contact: Prefers cassette with 2-5 songs and lyric sheet. SASE. Reports in 1 month.
Music: Mostly pop/rock and dance. Produced "Always Happens," written and recorded by Barbara Pennington; "Show Me Reaction" (by Wells), recorded by Rick Bardon; and "New Guy" (by Wells), recorded by Valerie Starr, all on Earth Records.

*SOUND CEREMONY PRODUCTIONS, 28 South Villas NW1, London NW1 9BT England. (01)4059883 or 4852240. Managing Director: Ron Warren Ganderton. Record producer. Deals with artists and songwriters.
How to Contact: Prefers cassette (or videocassette) and lyric sheet. SAE and IRC. Reports in 3 weeks.
Music: Mostly rock, pop, country, R&B and gospel; also soul and jazz. Produced *Sound Ceremony*, by Ron Ganderton on Sound Ceremony Records (rock LP); "Giggle Amidst the Tears," by Sound Ceremony on Centerage Records (rock single); and *Erotic Rock*, by Ron Ganderton on Sound Ceremony Records (LP). Other artists include Carole Boyce, Quasar, Goya, Monika Wint and Popin Jays.

SOUND COLUMN PRODUCTIONS, Division of Sound Column Companies, 160 Westgate Fine Arts Center, 342 W. Second South, Salt Lake City UT 84101. (801)355-5327. General Manager: Clive Romney. Record producer, music publisher (Ronarte Publications/ASCAP, Mountain Green Music/BMI and Macanudo Music/SESAC). Deals with artists. Produces 4 singles and 8 LPs/year. Fee derived from sales royalty.
How to Contact: Write first. Prefers cassette with 1-3 songs. SASE. "We work mainly with staff writers at our affiliated publishing companies and other established publishers. Our demand fluctuates according to projects we're doing." Reports as soon as possible—"honestly we do get backed up, but you'll eventually be heard."
Music: Mostly pop and country crossover; also easy listening, gospel, MOR and top 40. Produced *Out of the Blues*, (by Steve Eaton), recorded by Jenni Michels on Breaz Records; *Who Do You Know*, (by Romney/Simpson), recorded by Dave Beckstrand on SCP Records; and *Free To Choose*, (by Simpson/Romney), recorded by Cody Hale on LDS Records (all LPs). Other artists inlcude Dave Compton, Janine Lindsay and The Jensens.
Tips: "Send only good quality demos and lyric sheets. Remember the artist usually has plenty of album cuts—we're looking for singles."

SOUND IMAGE PRODUCTIONS, 6556 Wilkinson, North Hollywood CA 91606. (818)762-8881. Vice President: David Chatfield. President: Martin John Eberhardt. Vice President Sales/Studio Manager: Chuck Kopp. Record producer, music publisher (Sound Image Publishing), record company and 24-track recording studio. Deals with artists, songwriters and producers. Produces 8 singles and 4 LPs/year. Fee derived from sales royalty, outright fee from artist/songwriter and/or record company.
How to Contact: Submit finished masters. Prefers cassette (or VHS stereo hi-fi or ¾" videocassette) with 2-6 songs and lyric sheet. Does not return unsolicited material. Reports in 2 months.
Music: Mostly rock and top 40; also dance and R&B. Produced "Good Woman's Love," written and recorded by Mark Steed (country single, Sound Image Records); and "Oh Marie," and "Rush in the Night," (both by Jack Conrad), both recorded by Alp (rock singles, Sound Image Records).

SOUNDS OF WINCHESTER, Rt. 2 Box 116 H, Berkley Springs WV 25411. Contact: Jim McCoy. Record producer and music publisher (New Edition Music, Jim McCoy Music and Alear Music/BMI). Deals with artists and songwriters. Produces 20 singles and 10 LPs/year. Fee derived from sales royalty.
How to Contact: Prefers 7½ ips reel-to-reel or cassette with 4-10 songs and lead sheet. SASE. Reports in 1 month.
Music: Bluegrass, country, gospel, MOR and rock. Produced "One More Time," by Earl Howard (country single, Alear Records); and *Thank-You Jesus*, by Jubilee Travelers (gospel LP, Faith Records). Other artists include Dave Elliott, Alvin Kesner, Carroll County Ramblers, Jim McCoy, Al Hogan and Jimmie Rogers.

SOUTHERN SOUND PRODUCTIONS, 100 Labon St., Tabor City NC 28463. (919)653-2546. President: Elson H. Stevens. Record producer, music publisher (Creekside Music/BMI) and record company. Deals with artists, songwriters and radio stations. Produces 10 singles and 4-5 LPs/year. Fee derived from sales royalty or outright fee from recording artist.
How to Contact: Write first about your interest. Prefers cassette or 8-track tape with 1-3 songs and lyric or lead sheets. SASE. Reports in 1 month.
Music: Mostly country; also bluegrass, gospel, rock (country and hard) and beach music. Produced "I'm Ready," and "Rock Forever," by Fred Rodgers and Crossroads (southern rock singles); and "It's My Life" (rock), and "I'm a Dream" (R&B), by Celestee Kelly. Other artists include Mitch Todd, Copper Creek, The Entertainers, Glin Todd, Sheila Gore, and Gayle Mathies.
Tips: "Please make sure that all songs submitted have a very strong hook. Limit of 3 songs per submission."

PHIL SPECTOR PRODUCTIONS INC., Box 69529, Los Angeles CA 90069. (818)846-9900. Administrative Director: Donna Sekulidis. Record producer and music publisher (Mother Bertha Music Inc. and Back to Mono Music Inc.). Deals with artists and songwriters.
How to Contact: "Company is not accepting or reviewing any new material or artists. Any unsolicited material or correspondence will be returned."

SPECTRUM MUSIC PRODUCTIONS, 4 Yarcombe Adelaide Rd., Surbiton, Surrey KT6 4LN Great Britain. (01)399-7043. A&R Director: Al Dickinson. Record producer and music publisher (Spectrum Music, Moments Music Ltd. and Dickinsong Music/ASCAP). Deals with artists and songwriters. Produces 10 singles and 10 LPs/year. Fee derived from sales royalty, performance royalty and mechanical royalties.
How to Contact: Prefers cassette or 7½ ips reel-to-reel with "any number of" songs and lyric sheet. "Tapes sent from overseas should include correct amount of International Reply Coupons for tape returns." Reports in 2 weeks.
Music: Mostly pop/rock, country/rock and funk-ballads; also all types of instrumental music. Produced "Hold Me Down," by Louis Duncan (pop/rock single, G.H. Records); "One Life," by Ozzie Vox (pop/rock single, Paro Records); and "I Will," by Dr. Heavy (pop/rock single, Switch Records). Other artists include Rhythm Shop and Artwork.
Tips: "Our keyword is *entertainment*. If it's not that, forget it."

SPRING/POSSE RECORDS, 161 W. 54 St., New York NY 10019. (212)581-5398. President: Julie Rifkind. Vice President: Roy Rifkind. Treasurer: Steve Rifkind. Record producer and music publisher (Guacho Music Corp./BMI and Sandbox Music/ASCAP). Deals with artists and songwriters. Produces 12 singles and 2-3 LPs/year. Fee derived by sales royalty or outright fee from record company.
How to Contact: Prefers cassette with 2-4 songs and lyric sheet. "Masters only." SASE. Reports in 3 weeks.
Music: Mostly R&B; also gospel. Produced *Joe Simon's Greatest Hits*, by Joe Simon (R&B LP, Posse

Records); *Hard Times*, by Millie Jackson (R&B LP, Spring Records); *Is This the Future?*, by Fatback Band (R&B LP, Spring Records); and *Lay My Burden Down*, by Jackie Verdell (gospel LP). Other artists include Fonda Rae and Joe Simon.

SSS INTERNATIONAL, 3106 Belmont Blvd., Nashville TN 37212. (615)385-1960. Producer: Billy Self. Record producer. Deals with artists and songwriters. Produces 8 singles and 6 LPs/year. Fee derived from sales royalty or outright fee from songwriter/artist or record company.
How to Contact: Call about your interest. Prefers cassette with 1-3 songs and lyric sheet. Does not return unsolicited material. Reports in 1 month.
Music: Mostly country and MOR; also easy listening, gospel and top 40/pop. Produced "Bogalusa," by Jim Owen (country single, Sun Records); "Barbara's Daughter," by Patti Page (MOR/country single, Plantation Records); and *Double Winners*, by Ken Lowery (country LP, Plantation Records). Other artists include Paul Martin, Norris Treat, Rita Remington and Dave Dudley.
Tips: "We (the act and myself) must be in total agreement in our direction and have the utmost mutual trust in our abilities."

STAIRCASE PROMOTION, Box 211, E. Prairie MO 63845. (314)649-2211. Managers: Tommy Loomas and Alan Carter. Record producer and music publisher. Deals with artists and songwriters.
How to Contact: Prefers cassette with 2-4 songs and lyric sheet. SASE. Reports in 1 month.
Music: Country, easy listening, MOR, country rock and top 40/pop. Produced "Yesterdays Teardrops," and "Round & Round," by The Burchetts (country singles, Capstan Records).

STAR RECORD CO. PRODUCTIONS, INC., 521 5th Ave., New York NY 10017. (212)682-5844. Record producer and music publisher (McRon Music Co.). Produces 10-12 singles and 3-9 LPs/year. Deals with artists and songwriters.
How to Contact: Call first about your interest. Prefers 15 ips reel-to-reel or cassette with 3 songs. Does not return unsolicited material. Reports in 3 weeks, "if solicited."
Music: Mostly church/religious, easy listening, MOR, R&B, rock and Jewish Klezmer Cantorial music; also children's, choral and folk. Produced *Silent No More*, by Theodore Bikel (ethnic LP, Star Records); and *The Art of Klezmer*, by Giora Fridman (Jewish Klezmer LP, Star Records).

STARK RECORDS AND TAPE CO., 628 S. South St., Mount Airy NC 27030. (919)786-2865. Contact: Paul E. Johnson. Record producer and music publisher (TomPaul Music Company/BMI). Deals with artists, songwriters, publishers and recording companies. Produces 25 singles and 30 LPs/year. Works with 80 new songwriters/year. Fee derived from outright fee from record company.
How to Contact: Prefers 7½ ips reel-to-reel or cassette with 4-6 songs and lyric sheet. SASE. "My return address should be on the SASE." Reports in 1 month.
Music: Country, bluegrass, pop and gospel. Produced "Nobody's Promised Tomorrow," written and recorded by Roger H. Bell (country single, Star Records); "Forever And A Day," written and recorded by Bobby Lee Atkins (bluegrass single, Webco Records); "I'm Satisfied," written and recorded by Early UpChurch (country single, Stark Records); and "I Can't Wait," written and recorded by Kathy L. Combs (country single, Stark Records). Other artists include Paul Edgar Johnson, The Blue Ridge Mountain Boys, Kathy Upchurch, Don Sawyers, The Carolina Gospel Singers, The Stanley Brothers, The Deep Valley Boys, Ellen Fielder, Sanford Teague and Ella Mae Crabtree.

A. STEWART PRODUCTIONS, 22146 Lanark St., Canoga Park CA 91304. (818)704-0629. President: Art Stewart. Record producer and music publisher (Famosonda Music/BMI and Sonada/ASCAP). Deals with artists and songwriters. Produces 4 singles and 2 LPs/year. Fee determined by sales royalty.
How to Contact: Prefers 7½ ips reel-to-reel or cassette with 1-4 songs and lyric sheet. SASE. Reports in 1 month.
Music: All types. Produced "Eboni Band," by Eboni Band (Afro/American, Eboni Records); *Cherry*, by Platypus (soul LP, Casablanca Records); "Same Old Story," by Sai Whatt (soul single, Stache Records); "Got to Give It Up," by Marvin Gaye; "You and I," by Rich James; and "Lil' Suzy," by Ozone. Other artists include Charades and Randie Coulter.

STRAIGHT ARROW RECORDINGS, 3½ Kent St., Montpelier VT 05602. (802)223-2551. Producer: Mike Billingsley. Record producer. Produces 4 singles and 10 LPs/year. Deals with artists only. Fee derived from combination of fees and royalties.
How to Contact: Write or call first and obtain permission to submit. Prefers cassette or 7½ or 15 ips reel-to-reel (or Beta videocassette—digital or hi-fi) with 1-4 songs. "We assist with demos and produce live perfomance recordings. We release recordings on our own label." SASE. Reports in 3 weeks.
Music: Mostly acoustic "folk"/ethnic/blues and contemporary experimental; also classically-derived, ethnically-derived and native Third World compositions. Produced "The Wind" (by Jim Bell), recorded

by The Fiddlehead Society on Moonglow Records (single); *One More Time*, recorded by Nicht Geferlach Klezmer Band on Straight Arrow Records (LP); and *Classic Piano*, recorded by Michael Arnowitt on Crescendo Records (LP). Other artist include African Djole, Michael Arnowitt, Woods Tea Company, Grupo Aymara, Selesshe Demassae, Fran Cerulli and Vermont Philharmonic Orchestra.
Tips: "All new projects are recorded direct-to-digital. We appreciate artists who are prepared to reap the rewards of tight musical productions, without overdubs, in natural acoustic spaces. Musical style is not a primary, or even secondary, consideration. Rather, we are looking for interesting, tight, heartfelt music that can exploit the dynamic range and airiness of digital."

STUDIOEAST, 5457 Monroe Rd., Charlotte NC 28212. (704)536-0424. Co-owners: Tim Eaton and Don Lawrence. Record producer and music publisher (Eastwood Publishing). Deals with artists and songwriters. Produces 50 singles/year and 20 LPs/year. Fee derived from sales royalty.
How to Contact: Prefers cassette or 15 ips reel-to-reel (or VHS videocassette) with any number of songs. Does not return unsolicited material. Reports in 2 months.
Music: Mostly top 40/rock, country and jazz; also blues and gospel. Produced "Behind Your Lies," by Entertainers (R&B single, RCA Records); "I'll Always Love You," by Poor Souls (R&B single, Surfside Records); and "Always Be My Girl," by Band of Oz (R&B single, Band of Oz Records). Other artists include Montuno Jazz, Barry Duke, Fat Jack Band, John Thompson, Breeze Band and Tim Smith.

*PRESTON SULLIVAN ENTERPRISES,1217 16th Ave. S., Nashville TN 37212. (615)327-8129. President: Preston Sullivan. Record producer. Deals with artists and songwriters. Produces 10 singles/year.
How to Contact: Prefers cassette (or videocassette) and lyric sheet. Does not return unsolicited material. Reports in 2 weeks.
Music: Mostly pop, rock, R&B and country; also gospel.

SUNNY DAY PRODUCTIONS, 1931 SE Morrison, Portland OR 97214. (503)238-4525. Executive Producer: Russell E. Gorsline. Record producer and music publisher (Klickitat Music). Deals with artists and songwriters. Produces 3-5 singles and 3-5 LPs/year. Fee derived from sales royalty.
How to Contact: Prefers cassette with 2-3 songs and lyric sheet. SASE. Reports in 1 month.
Music: Mostly pop/top 40 and rock. Produced "It's So Easy," by Tom Miles (Country EP, Cricket Records); and "Alone in the City," by P. Cansler (pop single, Cricket Records).
Tips: Songwriter "must have tremendous potential as an artist or writer. Must be open to changes in material and very versatile."

SUNSET PRODUCTIONS, (formerly M.D.M. Productions), 117 W. 8th, Hays KS 67601. (913)625-9634. President: Mark Meckel. Record producer, music publisher (Street Singer Music, BMI) and record company. Deals with artists and songwriters. Produces 8 singles and 6 LPs/year. Fee derived from sales royalty.
How to Contact: Prefers cassette with 3 songs and lyric or lead sheet. SASE. Reports in 1 month.
Music: Mostly country, country rock, Christmas and 50s rock; also gospel, rock/Christian and country R&B. Produced "My Heart Keeps Walking (Right Back To You)" (by P. Hotchkiss/M. Terry), recorded by Tommy Harrison (country single); *A Friend Like You*, written and recorded by Mark Selby (pop LP); and "Christmas Eve Waltz" (by Jack Kavanagh), recorded by Tommy Harrison (Christmas single), all on M.D.M. Records. Other artists include Terry Sharman and Rusty Bush.
Tips: "Be willing to make changes and work with a producer."

SUNSET PRODUCTIONS, 15 Albert Crescent, Penarth, South Glamorgan, South Wales, United Kingdom. 44-0222-704279. Director: Paul Barrett. Record producer. Deals with artists and songwriters. Fee derived from sales royalty. Royalties paid directly to US songwriters and artists.
How to Contact: Prefers cassette and lyric sheet. SAE and IRC. Reports in 3 weeks.
Music: 50s rock only. Produced *Good Times and Some Mighty Fine Rock 'n' Roll*, by Ben Hewitt on Bear Family Records (rock LP); *Tiger*, by Shakin' Stevens and Sunsets (rock LP); *Unleashed*, by Blue Caps (rock LP); and "Down on the Farm" by "Big" Al Downing on Rollercoaster Records. Other artists include Wee Willie Harris, Rockin' Louie, The Class of '58, The Red Hot Pokers, Jackie Lee Cochran and Ray Campi.

THE SUNSHINE GROUP, 800 S. 4th St., Philadelphia PA 19147. (215)755-7000. President: Walter Kahn. Record producer (Sunshine Records) and music publisher (Scully Music/ASCAP and Orange Bear Music/BMI). Works with artists and songwriters on contract. Produces 30 singles and 5 LPs/year. Pays standard royalty.
How to Contact: Prefers 7½ ips reel-to-reel, or cassette (or VHS or ¾" videocassette) with 1-4 songs

and lyric sheet. SASE. Reports in 1 month.
Music: Mostly pop, R&B and dance; also top 40 and rock. Produced "Takin' Me Out Tonite," by Juliet Kandar (pop single); "Mirror Mirror," by Special Guess (R&B single); and "The Flute," by Pipedream (CBS/Epic Records).

SURPRIZE RECORDS, INC., Box 42707, Philadelphia PA 19101-2707. (215)276-8861. President: Gilda C. Woods. Vice President: W. Lloyd Lucas. Record producer, music publisher (Delev Music Co./ BMI, Sign of the Ram Music/ASCAP and In the Woods Music/BMI) and management firm. Deals with artists, songwriters and publishers. Produces 3-6 singles and 1-3 LPs/year. Fee derived from sales royalty.
How to Contact: Write or call first and obtain permission to submit. Prefers cassette with 1-3 songs and lyric or lead sheet. SASE. Reports in 1 month.
Music: R&B, soul, top 40/pop, dance-oriented and MOR; also rock and country. Produced *Weakened Heart* and *Far Too Long* (by Marco Talarico), and *Line of Fire* (by C. Talarico/Guthier), all recorded by Valkir (rock EP projects).
Tips: "We are impressed with very positive lyrics and great hooklines and near finished demo 'masters'. It does not matter if the artist has or has not had extensive experience working in front of an audience, but it does matter if his or her attitude is in a positive posture. Determination and the ability to take constructive criticism most important. We have no time for ego trippers."

*LANNY SWAIM, Box 2154, Carolina Beach NC 28428. (919)458-8651. Producer: Lanny Swaim. Record producer, music publisher (Sand Dollar Records, Swaim Publishing/ASCAP) record company, booking agent and concert promotor. Deals with artists and songwriters. Produces 3 singles and 1 LP/ year.
How to Contact: Write first and obtain permission to submit. Prefers cassette (or VHS videocassette) with 3-4 songs and lead sheet. Does not return unsolicited material. Reports in 6 weeks.
Music: Mostly contemporary Christian, pop and country. Produced "Just a Young Man" and "A Child is Born," (by Lanny C. Swaim), recorded by Latter Rain on Sand Dollar Records (singles); and "Pete's Place," (by D. Page/G. Dixon/L. Swain), recorded by Gary Dixon on Sand Dollar Records (single).
Tips: "Contemporary Christian should spend less time copying pop chart sound and more time being creative."

SWORD & SHIELD RECORDS, Box 211, Arlington TX 76010. (817)572-1414. Contact: Calvin Wills. Record producer. Deals with artists. Produces 6 singles and 20 LPs/year. Fee derived from sales royalty.
How to Contact: Call first about your interest. Prefers cassette with 2-6 songs. Does not return unsolicited material. Reports in 1 month.
Music: Mostly southern gospel and contemporary Christian music. Produced "Daybreak," by Taynia Meyers (contemporary Christian single). Other artists include Joe Atkinson.

SYSTEM, Box 11301, Kansas City KS 66111. (913)287-3495. Executive Producer: Steve Vail. Record producer, management, booking and film company. Deals with artists and songwriters. Produces 1-3 LPs/year. Fee derived from outright fee from songwriter/artist or record company.
How to Contact: Prefers cassette or 7½ ips reel-to-reel (or ½" or ¾" VHS or ½" Beta videocassette) with 1-10 songs and lyric sheet. Does not return unsolicited material. Reports in 6 weeks.
Music: "Classical rock, jazz fusion and art rock." Produced *Time Tales*, recorded by Realm (art rock LP); *Outlines*, recorded by Navigator (dance rock LP) and *Rituals*, written and recorded by Vail, all on System Records.

T.C. RECORDS AND PROMOTIONS, (formerly Venture Sound Studio Productions), 121 Meadowbrook Dr., Somerville NJ 08876. (201)359-5110. Producer: Tony Camillo. Record producer, music publisher and production company. Deals with artists and songwriters. Produces 21-25 singles and 5-8 LPs/year. Fee derived from sales royalty or outright fee from record company.
How to Contact: Query. Prefers cassette with 2-5 songs and lead sheet. "Send as complete a package as possible." SASE. Reports in "1 month or longer depending on schedule."
Music: Dance, soul, MOR and top 40/pop; "excellent material only." Produced "Midnight Train to Georgia" (by Jim Weatherly), recorded by Gladys Knight and the Pips on Buddah Records.

TABITHA PRODUCTIONS, 39 Cordery Road, St. Thomas, Exeter, Devon EX2 9DJ England. 44-0392-7991X. Producer: Graham Sclater. Record producer, music publisher (Tabitha Music, Ltd.) and record company (Tabitha/Willow Records). Works with artists and songwriters. Produces 6 singles and 2 LPs/year. Works with 6 new songwriters/year and works with composers. Fee derived from sales royalty.

Close-up

Tony Camillo
Producer

As a songwriter, arranger and producer with credits such as "Dynamite Bazooka"; "Love Can't Turn Around," by Philly Cream; "Midnight Train to Georgia," by Gladys Knight; and "Band of Gold," by Freda Payne, Tony Camillo believes "the song is always the key to a successful record. The production obviously is important, but matching up the right song to the artist is very important."

Camillo began his career producing for Motown and other record companies, but eventually established T.C. Records and Promotions. A major part of his job has always been choosing songs for the recording projects he's involved in. He says he currently receives hundreds of demos each week, and he does find good songs that way. His advice to aspiring songwriters is, "make sure all the material you send is in tune with the kinds of things you're hearing on the airwaves. Your songs have to be competitive in the sense that they are as strong lyrically and melodically as anything else that's out there.

"The biggest problem we have with accepting material is that what people write about is so common. The hardest thing [about writing a song] is to find a topic—or a twist on a topic—that captures your attention. You don't have a lot of time to get to somebody's imagination so you have to choose words and string them together in a way that is captivating. That's the whole idea of hooks and hit songs—they have an appeal based on words that are right to the point and somehow imaginative."

Another problem Camillo cites with demos he receives is that "we get material for an act that is completely wrong, and presented so completely wrong. It's important to be in tune to the artist that you're trying to get a song to. I'm not saying copy their style to a 'T,' I'm just saying it's not a good idea to present the song in a way so totally removed that an artist has difficulty imagining himself singing it."

Camillo explains it's extremely important for songwriters to submit appropriate material in a professional manner. Artists who review outside material receive many submissions and the competition is great. "If songwriters shop their own material, they should read tip sheets or other publications and find where the material is to be submitted and when an artist is going into the studio. The reality of that, though, is that producers or record companies (or whoever lists the fact that they're looking for material) are deluged."

Because major record labels have so many projects going on and so many artists to represent, Camillo feels smaller companies like his are more accessible to songwriters, but they represent a different kind of opportunity. He explains, "Because we're small, we can only put out so much product. We can't put out 10, 20, 50 singles/month as the major record companies do. Major record companies release *hundreds* of albums each year. And on each album you have anywhere between 8 and 10 songs. On a small label like ours, we may do 5, 6, 8 albums/year and 2 singles/month, because that's all we can realistically follow up.

"But big companies operate under a different principle. They throw out 25 albums and the one that takes hold is the one they'll pursue and the others go down the tubes." So while a small label doesn't present the number of opportunities for songwriters that a major label does, it can promise more attention and commitment to the songs released.

Tony Camillo feels, "The music business is a very challenging and exciting field. People should have an awareness about the challenges, the expectations, and the competition before they go into the field full-fledged. I find the biggest problem most people have is they don't really understand their limitations or their capabilities. They should really open their eyes and do some research and find out where they fit in and what they're really good at."

—Julie Wesling Whaley

———

How to Contact: Prefers cassette with 2-6 songs and lyric sheet. SAE and IRC. Reports in 3 weeks. **Music:** Mostly AOR, MOR and pop; also country, dance, soul and rock. Produced "I'm Your Man," written and recorded by Tony Carey on Tabitha Records (pop); "Groovy Kind of Love" (by Bayer-Sager), recorded by Andy Lord (pop/reggae); and "Summer Love Affair" (by Bradbury/Artes), recorded by Beat the Heat (pop). Other artists include Shoot to Kill, Montellas and Colin Wilson.

TAKE HOME TUNES! RECORD CO., Box 10051, Beverly Hills CA 90213. (818)761-2646. Branch: Box 1314, Englewood Cliffs NJ 07632. Messages: (201)567-5524. Producer: Doris Chu. Record producer and music publisher (The Chu Yeko Musical Foundation/BMI and Broadway/Hollywood International Music/ASCAP). Deals with artists and songwriters. Produces 8 LPs/year and film scores. Fee derived from sales royalty.
How to Contact: Call first. Prefers cassette with any number songs and lyric sheet. SASE. Reports in 1 month. "For film score records, submit a final mix of only the most professional, highest quality. Address to Department FS 2001."
Music: Children's, classical, country, easy listening, jazz, MOR, musicals, R&B and top 40/pop. Produced *King of Hearts*, by Millicent Martin and Don Scardino; *Lovesong*, by the original cast; and *Christy (Playboy of the Western World)*, by the original cast (musical LPs, Original Cast Records); and *KaBoom!* and *Fly with Me*, by the original cast (musical LPs, Chu Yeko Musical Foundation Records).
Tips: "We're interested in the 'top 10' pop types of songs with memorable melodies and great lyrics; original cast musicals that had a production somewhere (preferably Los Angeles); and R&B songs sung by new singers, groups, etc. touring the Los Angeles area. Co-production possible."

***TAR HEEL ENTERPRISES**, 5 Aldom Circle, W. Caldwell NJ 07006. Owner: Tar Heel Pete. Record producer. Deals with artists and songwriters. Fee derived from sales royalty.
How to Contact: Write first and obtain permission to submit. Prefers cassette with 3 songs and lead sheet. Does not return unsolicited material. Reports in 1 month.
Music: Blues, rock and pop. Produced "Back to North Carolina," written and recorded by Bill Price on Tar Heel Records; "Christmas Tree by the Window" (by Eugene Wellman/Jim Hall), recorded by Jim Hall on Dynamite Records; and "Hello Blues" (by Rod Morris), recorded by Jim Hall on Dynamite Records (all singles). Other artists include Sal Franco, Gidget Starr, Dusty Rhodes, J.C. Davis and Doc Hopkins.

TARGET COMMUNICATIONS INTERNATIONAL, 1123 Rosewood, Inglewood CA 90301. (213)419-4017. Managing Director: Tony Thomas. Record producer and advertising music production company. Deals with artists and songwriters. Produces varying number of singles and LPs/year. Fee depends on project.
How to Contact: Submit demo tape by mail. Write or call first to arrange personal interview. Prefers cassette or 7½ ips reel-to-reel (or Beta videocassette) and lyric sheet. "Please label submissions." Does not return unsolicited material. Reports in 6 weeks.
Music: Mostly pop, jazz/fusion instrumentals and R&B; also jingles, "stingers/music beds and bumpers."
Tips: "Develop your own style and make sure that style shines through on your demo."

***TCR PRODUCTIONS**,Box 589, Charlotte Hall MD 20622. Director: R.T. Crabb. Record producer. Deals with artists and songwriters. Produces 10 singles and 2-3 LPs/year. Fee derived from sales royalty or outright fee from recording artist or record company.
How to Contact: Prefers cassette with 3-4 songs and lyric sheet. Does not return unsolicited material. Reports in 6 weeks.
Music: Mostly pop, rock and country; also contemporary Christian. Produced "Southern Comfort,"

(by W. Bricker), recorded by The Brickers; "Little Boy," (by T. Dodson), recorded by T.C. Roberts; and "Moon Song," (by Lathan), recorded by Mercedes, all on db Records (all top 100 singles). Other artist include Sam Neely.

TEROCK RECORDS, Box 4740, Nashville TN 37216. President: Wade Curtiss. Record producer and music publisher. Deals with artists and songwriters. Fee derived from sales royalty.
How to Contact: Prefers 7½ ips reel-to-reel with 2-6 songs and lyric sheet. SASE. Reports in 3 weeks.
Music: Bluegrass, blues, country, dance, easy listening, folk, gospel, progressive, R&B, hard rock, soul and top 40/pop.

DOUG THIELE ENTERPRISES, 4706 New York Ave., Glendale CA 91214. (818)249-2416. Producer: Doug Thiele. Record producer, music publisher (Firelight Publishing/Retro Music) and music consultant. Deals with artists and songwriters. Produces 8 singles and 1 LP/year. Fee derived from sales royalty and/or outright fee from songwriter/artist.
How to Contact: Write first and obtain permission to submit. Prefers cassette. Does not return unsolicited material. Reports in 6 weeks.
Music: All commercial styles. Produced "No Light," by Terri Stockwell (female power pop single); "Happy Hour," by Mike Stanton (country single); and "Blue-Blue Heart," by Rich Rudolph (R&B/pop single).

THIRD FLOOR PRODUCTIONS/STEVE R. PINKSTON, Box 40784, Nashville TN 37204. (615)383-0586. Record producer and music publisher. Produces 4-6 LPs/year. Deals with artists and songwriters. Fee derived from sales royalty, outright fee from songwriter/artist and/or outright fee from record company.
How to Contact: Write first and obtain permission to submit. Prefers cassette (or VHS videocassette) with 3-4 songs or 15 ips reel-to-reel with 1-4 songs and lyric sheet. Does not return unsolicited material. Reports in 6 weeks.
Music: Mostly pop/top 40, rock, Christian contemporary and blues—"no country." Produced *Knock Me Out*, by Buddy Hyatt (pop); *Nashville Blues*, by Mac Gayden (pop/blues); and *White Shoes*, by White Shoes (rock/pop), all LPs on Audigram Records; and *L.E.D.*, by the EQ's on Barefoot Records. Other artists include J.J. Cale, Paul Craft, Geoff Moore, Buddy Hyatt and The Face.
Tips: "It's the song that sells!! Don't spend needless money on promos, pictures fancy stationery. You can't sell me a lemon with a sugar coating."

*KENNETH C. THOMAS, 723 Lincoln Ave., Carbondale CO 81623. (303)923-5995. Producer: Kenneth Thomas. Record producer, music publisher (Lauren-Blick Music, BMI) and record company (Track Records). Deals with artists and songwriters. Produced 5-10 singles and 2-3 LPs/year.
How to Contact: Prefers cassette with 3-5 songs and lyric and lead sheets. SASE. Reports in 1 month.
Music: Mostly contemporary pop, rock; also contemporary country, duets and ballads. Produced *Patricial Lauren II*, (by Lauren/Thomas), recorded by Patricia Lauren on Track Records (pop/LP); *Aspen Flyers* and *Aspen Flyers I* by Steve Saylor, Ken Thomas and Mark Ross both on Criminol Records (rock LPs). Other artists include "local area artists."
Tips: " We are always looking for great songs for our own projects as well as for other artists. We listen to and review all submitted material. Send your best songs, a great song will be heard above the rest."

THREE G'S INDUSTRIES INC., 5500 Troost, Kansas MO 64110. (816)361-8455. A&R Directors: Eugene Gold and Chris King. Record producer and music publisher (Eugene Gold Music/BMI and Gil-Gad Music/ASCAP). Deals with artists and songwriters. Produces 6 singles and 5 LPs/year. Fee derived from sales royalty.
How to Contact: Prefers cassette with 4-6 songs and lyric sheet. SASE. Reports in 1 month.
Music: Gospel, jazz, MOR, R&B and soul. Produced *There Must Be Something God Wants You To Do*, by Lucille Harris on 3 G's Records; *He Has Not Given Us the Spirit Of Fear*, by Michael Charles on C.M.C. Records, both gospel LPs.
Tips: "I like songs with a good beat, and a good storyline."

*RICHARD TIEGEN/MAGIC SOUND PRODUCTIONS, 2 Washington St., Haverhill MA 01830. (617)372-4236. Producer: Richard Tiegen. Record producer and music publisher (Astrodisque Music). Deals with artists and songwriters. Produces 12 singles and 6 LPs/year. Fee derived from outright fee from recording artist or record company. "Charges for production/recording/mechanicals."
How to Contact: Write or call first and obtain permission to submit. Prefers cassettes. Does not return unsolicited material. Reports in 3 weeks.
Music: Mostly rock, R&B and country; also New Age and acoustic. Produced "Stand By Me Baby,"

(by Dave Amato), recorded by Quadralaw on Plum Records (rock single); *New Moon*, written and recorded by Patricia McKernon on Sound Mind Records (New Age LP); and "Let Me Come Home," written and recorded by Larry Milano on Plum Records (rock single). Other artists include Louis Heffernan.

RIK TINORY PRODUCTIONS, 180 Pond St., Box 311, Cohasset MA 02025. (617)383-9494. Artist Relations: Richard Tinory, Jr. Record producer and music publisher (Old Boston Publishing). Deals with artists and songwriters. Produces 5-10 singles and 3-12 LPs/year. Works with 1-2 new songwriters/year. Fee derived from sales royalty.
How to Contact: Call first and obtain permission to submit. Call to arrange personal interview. Prefers cassette or 7½ ips reel-to-reel with 2 songs and lyric or lead sheets. Does not return unsolicited material.
Music: Produced "Here's to You, L.A.," by Rik Tinory (swing single on RTP Records).
Tips: "We are looking for master recordings with strong material ready for release."

TMC PRODUCTIONS, 3800 San Pedro Ave., San Antonio TX 78212. (512)735-3322. Producer: Joe Scates. Record producer, music publisher (Axbar Productions/BMI, Axe Handle Music/ASCAP) and record distributor. Deals with artists and songwriters. Produces 12-15 singles and 3-6 LPs/year. Fee derived from sales royalty.
How to Contact: Prefers cassette with 1-5 songs and lyric sheet. SASE. Reports "as soon as possible, but don't rush us."
Music: Blues, country, comedy and rock (soft). Produced "When I Be Five" (from the LP *Versatility*) by Kenny Dale (country single); "One Bright Day" (by Ronald Deming), recorded by Stampede; "This Darn Pen" (by Ernie Lobello), recorded by Billy D. Hunter (single, Axbar Records); and "Country Girl Going to Town," written and recorded by Terrah Sloane on Arbar Records. Other artists include Juni Moon, Rusty Button, Ray Sanders, and Wayne Carter.
Tips: "Send only your best shots. Average songs just don't make it anymore."

GEORGE TOBIN PRODUCTIONS, 11337 Burbank, N. Hollywood CA 91601. (818)506-4487/980-0880. Artistic Development: Brad Schmidt. Record producer and music publisher (George Tobin Music). Produces 5-8 singles/year and 1-3 LPs/year. Deals with artists and songwriters.
How to Contact: Prefers cassette (or VHS videocassette) with 3-4 songs. SASE. Reports in 6 weeks. "We prefer not to send tapes back as it takes time, but we do if a letter is included requesting it."
Music: R&B/pop, pop/rock and country. Produced various songs by Mark Paul and John Duarte, recorded by Jennifer Holliday on Geffen Records. Other artists include New Edition and Tiffany.

*TORCHLITE/GEE PRODUCTIONS, Suite 119, 2170 W. Broadway, Anaheim CA 92804. (714)491-8546. Producer: Robert Wahlsteen. Record producer and music publisher (Off the Wall Music). Deals with artists and songwriters. Produces 6 singles and 2 LPs/year. Fee derived from sales royalty or outright fee from songwriter/artist.
How to Contact: Prefers cassette with 3-4 songs and lyric sheet. Does not return unsolicited material. Reports in 6 weeks.
Music: Love songs and novelty songs. Produced "In God We Trust," by Wahlsteen & Sands (pop), "Angel Eyes," by Mary Hart (pop), and "Lovesick," by Wayne Copeland (blues), all singles on Torchlite Records. Other artists include Bob Chance, Los Amigos and Wayne Gabriel.
Tips: "Most demos received at our office tend to sound like just about anything you'll find on contemporary hit radio at that time. Our company is not in competition with today's top 40, however, most songwriters are. We are looking for visionary composers who are not intimidated by the current state of pop music."

TREEHOUSE PRODUCTIONS, Box 3294 Miami FL 33013. (305)940-9197. Contact: Ted French. Record producer and music publisher. Deals with artists and songwriters. Produces 2 singles and 2 LPs/year. Fee derived from sales royalty and outright fee from record company.
How to Contact: Prefers cassette with 1-6 songs and lyric sheet. "Include bio." SASE. Reports in 3 weeks.
Music: Mostly contemporary gospel and pop; also children's and top 40/pop. Produced *In Touch Again*, written and recorded by Suncast on Word Records (gospel LP); *The Prodigal*, written and recorded by Jerry Shoemaker on Zapatero Records (gospel LP); and *White Robe*, by Patricia White (contemporary gospel LP). Also produced "numerous jingles for various clients."

TREND PRODUCTIONS, Box 201, Smyrna GA 30081. (404)432-2454. Manager: Tom Hodges. Record producer, music publisher and artist manager. Deals with artists, songwriters and musicians. Fee derived from sales royalty.
How to Contact: Prefers cassette with 3-10 songs and lyric sheet. SASE. Reports in 3 weeks.

Music: Bluegrass, blues, country, gospel, MOR, R&B, rock, soul and top 40/pop. Produced "Sugar Daddy Man," by Frank Brannon (country single); "To See the Kids," by Jo Ann Johnson (country single); "Be Bop A Lula," by Dempsey (country single); and "Kennesaw Get Your Guns," by Jimmy Moore. Other artists include Terry Brand.

TRIBAL RECORDS, Box 6495, Buena Park CA 90620. (714)554-0851. Contact: Jerry Wood. Record producer. Deals with artists and songwriters. Fee derived from sales royalty or outright fee from record company.
How to Contact: Prefers 7½ ips reel-to-reel or cassette with 3 songs and lyric sheet. SASE. Reports in 2 weeks.
Music: Country, easy listening and MOR. Produced "Many Are the Colors," by Roy Dee; "99 Years," by Ron Hayden; and "Gold Plated Boy Scout Knife," by Jeanne Taylor, all on Tribal Records (all country singles).

TRIPLE T/AFTER FIVE and Associated Labels,(formerly ARPCO Productions Ltd./Burnt Out Music), 1552 W. Madison, Chicago IL 60607. (312)829-6116. CEO: Donald Burnside. Chairman: Milton Crump. Record company, record producer and music publisher (Buillion Music, Burnt Out Music). Deals with artists and songwriters. Produces 10 singles and 5 LPs/year. Fee derived from sales royalty.
How to Contact: Prefers cassette with 4-6 songs. Prefers studio produced demos. SASE. Reports in 3 weeks.
Music: Mostly urban/CHR; also dance, R&B, soul and top 40/pop. Produced "You Bring Me Up," (by D. Cameron/H. Wayne), recorded by Captain Sky on Triple T Records (urban single); "Comin' Ta Getcha," (by F. Smith), recorded by Essence on Narcis Records (urban single); and "Until I Saw You," (by E. Records), recorded by Chi-Lites on After Five Records (urban/ballad single). Other artists include Donell Pitman, Gene Chandler, Jerry Butler, Otis Clay, Handsome Wayne, Velia Thompson, Johnny P., Romeo and Master Tyree.

TROD NOSSEL ARTISTS, 10 George St., Box 57, Wallingford CT 06492. (203)269-4465. Executive Director: Thomas 'Doc' Cavalier. Record producer, music publisher (Rohm Music, Linesider Music, BIG Music) and record company manager. Produces 3-5 singles and 2-5 LPs/year. Fee derived from sales royalty.
How to Contact: Prefers cassette with 2-3 songs and lyric sheet. "Include statement of goals and purposes." Prefers well recorded demos. Does not return unsolicited material. Reports in 10 weeks.
Music: Rock, R&B and pop. Artist include Cub Koda, Bob Mel and Rebel Montez.

TUMAC MUSIC, 2097 Vistadale Ct., Tucker GA 30084. (404)938-1210. Professional Manager: Phil McDaniel. Record company, music publisher and record producer. Produces 1 single/year. Deals with artists and songwriters on contract. Fee derived from sales royalty.
How to Contact: Prefers cassette with 1 song and lyric sheet. SASE. Reports in 3 weeks.
Music: Mostly country and MOR; also blues, country jazz, R&B, soft rock and top 40/pop.

TUTCH PRODUCTIONS, Box 163, West Redding CT 06896. (203)438-5366. President: Paul Hotchkiss. Record producer and music publisher. Deals with artists and songwriters. Produces 5 singles and 1 LP/year. Fee derived from sales royalty.
How to Contact: Prefers cassette with 2 songs and lyric sheet. Include bio. SASE. Reports in 3 weeks.
Music: Mostly country and country/pop. Produced "Wrong Seems Right," by Wayne Carter (Axbar Records); "Wheeler Dealer," by Mary Craig (Puzzle Records); and "Gilley, Willie, Waylon and Me," by King Maddox (Orbit Records). Other artists include Gerry Malone, Hutcher Brothers, and T-Bone Stankus.

TWO STAR PRODUCTIONS, 250 Cosburn Ave., Toronto, Ontario M4J 2H1 Canada. (416)423-3845. Producer: Bob Johnston. Record producer. Deals with artists and songwriters. Produces 5 singles and 1 LP/year. Works with 3-4 new songwriters/year. Works with composers and lyricists. Fee derived from outright fee from songwriter/artist.
How to Contact: Call or write first. Prefers cassette with 2-4 songs. Does not return unsolicited material.
Music: Mostly country and country crossover; also easy listening, MOR and rock (commercial). Produced "For Loving You," (by Bob Johnston/Brett McNaul), recorded by B. McNaul (country crossover single, Young St. Records); "Nothing More We Can Do," (by Bob Johnston/Lili Zlamal), recorded by Donny Jerrett & Lilianne (country single, Young St. Records); and "I'm Holding Memories Tonight," (by B. McNaul/Bob Johnston/ Doug Virgin), recorded by B. McNaul (country crossover single, Young St. Records).

UPSWING PRODUCTIONS, % Jacobson & Colfin, Suite 1103, 150 5th Ave., New York NY 10011. (212)691-5630. Vice President: Bruce Colfin. Record producer. Deals with artists and songwriters. Fee derived from sales royalty, outright fee from songwriter/artist and/or outright fee from record company.
How to Contact: Prefers cassette (or ½" videocassette). SASE. Reports in 3 weeks.
Music: Mostly rock, blues and country; also jazz and dance. Produced "Blues Alive," by John Mayell's Bluebreakers, with Mick Taylor, John McVie, et. al (blues VHS and videodisc, RCA/Columbia Pictures Home Video).

CHARLES VICKERS MUSIC ASSOCIATION, 171 Pine Haven, Daytona Beach FL 32014. (904)252-4849. President/Producer: Dr. Charles H. Vickers D.M. Record producer and music publisher (Pritchett Publication/BMI). Deals with artists and songwriters. Produces 3 singles and 6 LPs/year. Works with 1 new songwriter/year. Teams collaborators. Fee derived from sales royalty.
How to Contact: Write first. Prefers 7½ ips reel-to-reel or cassette with 1-6 songs. SASE. Reports in 1 week.
Music: Mostly church/religious, gospel and hymns; also bluegrass, blues, classical, country, easy listening, jazz, MOR, progressive, reggae (pop), R&B, rock, soul and top 40/pop. Produced "Let Your Light Shine" and "The Other Side of the Rainbow," by Charles Vickers (gospel singles, King of Kings Records); *If God Is for You Who Can Be Against You*, and *Heaven Is Just Over the Hill*, by King of Kings (gospel LPs, L.A. International Records); "Sailing Without A Sail" and "He's Always Near," by Charles Vickers, (gospel singles, L.A. International Records).

WILLIAM F. WAGNER, Suite 218, 14343 Addison St., Sherman Oaks CA 91423. (818)905-1033. Contact: Bill Wagner. Record producer. Deals with artists and songwriters. Produces 6-8 singles and 4-8 LPs/year. Works with 25 new songwriters/year. Fee derived from sales royalty or outright fee from record company.
How to Contact: Prefers cassette with 1-5 songs and lead sheets "no lyric sheets; material should be copyrighted." SASE. Reports in 1 month.
Music: Mostly top 40, pop, gospel and jazz; also blues, choral, country, easy listening, MOR, progressive, rock, soul and pop. Produced *Billy May For President*, by Pat Longo (jazz/dance-oriented album, Town Hall Records); "Suspicion," by Burn With Passion (rock/jazz single); and "Hearts Aflame," written and recorded by Vicki McClure (top 40 single, VMC Records). Other artists include Dewey Erney, Mikie Bellamy and Frank Sinatra, Jr.
Tips: "Please tune up the music and instruments. Get a decent singer to do the demo."

WALK ON WATER PRODUCTIONS, Rt. 2, Box 566-H, New Braunfels TX 78130. (512)629-4396. Producer/Manager: Kenneth D. Brazle. Record producer, music publisher and recording studio. Deals with artists and songwriters. Produces 2 singles/year and 1 LP/year. Fee derived from sales royalty or specific contract negotiation.
How to Contact: Write first and obtain permission to submit; "Include SASE for reply." Prefers cassette or 7½ ips reel-to-reel (or VHS videocassette) with 2-3 songs and lyric sheet. SASE. Does not return unsolicited material. Reports in 6 weeks.
Music: Mostly AOR pop/rock, new music and country.

MATTHEW WALLACE/DANGEROUS RHYTHM PRODUCTIONS, Suite 1-H, 2321 Russell St., Berkeley CA 94705. (415)843-3923. Producer/Enginer: Matthew Wallace. Record producer and engineer. Deals with artists and songwriters. Produces 5 singles and 12 LPs/year. Fee derived from sales royalty, outright fee from songwriter/artist and/or outright fee from record company.
How to Contact: Prefers cassette. Does not return unsolicited material unless requested.
Music: Mostly "modern post punk/pop funk," rock and pop; also country, "esoteric and ambient." Produced *Blue Moon*, by Yo (folk/rock LP, Enigma Records); *Introduce Yourself*, by Faith No More (heavy rock LP, Slash/Warner Bros. Records); and *This Must Be the Place*, by Monkey Rhythm (post punk/progressive rock LP, 415/Columbia Records). Other artists include Necropolis of Love, All Fell Down (CBS Records), Castle Blak, Naked Into and Glorious Din.
Tips: "Call or write anytime."

*****JOHNO WALLER**, 2301 W. 59th St., Los Angeles CA 90043. (213)294-7286. President: Johno Waller. Record producer, music publisher (Best Songs in the Universe), and record company (Gellery II Records, Jumpin' Jack Records). Deals with artists and songwriters. Produces 6 singles and 2 LPs/year. Fee derived from sales royalty.

 The asterisk before a listing indicates that the listing is new in this edition. New markets are often the most receptive to freelance submissions.

How to Contact: Write first and obtain permission to submit. Prefers cassette or 15 ips reel-to-reel (or 3/4" or 1/2" VHS or Beta videocassette) with 2 songs and lyric sheet. Send pictures and resume if available. SASE. Reports in 1 month.
Music: Mostly R&B, gospel and rock; also rap, pop and jazz. Produced "I'm Always Losing You" (by Spike Marlin), recorded by Marsha Stewart; "Sexy Little Treat," written and recorded by Percision; and "I've Overcome," written and recorded by The Mighty Voices of Faith, all on Gallery II Records (all singles). Other artists include Martha Dudley and The Guitar Queen.

WAM RECORDS, LTD., 901 Kenilworth Rd., Montreal, Quebec H3R 2R5 Canada. (514)341-6721. President: Leon Aronson. Record producer and music publisher (Think Big Music). Deals with artists and songwriters. Produces 10 singles and 6 LPs/year. Fee derived from sales royalty.
How to Contact: Prefers cassette with 6 songs and lyric sheet. SAE and IRC. Reports in 1 month.
Music: Mostly pop/rock; also dance. Produced *Marty Butler*, by Marty Butler (pop/rock LP, RCA Records); *Good Girl Gone Bad*, by Terry Crawford (rock LP, RCA Records); and *Larry Patten*, by Larry Patten (pop/rock LP, WAM Records).

WARD MUSIC, 438 Vallejo St., San Francisco CA 94133. Record producer, music publisher (Mark VIII Music) and record company (Quantum Records). Deals with artists and songwriters. Produces 10 singles/year and 5 LPs/year. Works with 10 new songwriters/year. Fee derived from sales royalty.
How to Contact: Prefers cassette (or videocassette) with 1-3 songs and lyric sheet. "A chorded song is acceptable." SASE. Reports in 1 month.
Music: Mostly rock; also pop, new wave, blues, country, gospel and jazz. Produced "Black Hawk," written and recorded by Saladate (rock, Quantum Records); "Dollar Signs," (by P.J. Jones), recorded by R. West (new wave); and "Outrage," (by Villion), recorded by Oberheim (folk rock, Quantum Records).
Tips: "Be as professional as possible. Think out a good plan and do it! Simplicity is vital."

THE WEISMAN PRODUCTION GROUP, 449 N. Vista St., Los Angeles CA 90036. (213)658-6417. Contact: Ben Weisman. Record producer and music publisher (Audio Music Publishers). Deals with artists and songwriters. Produces 30 singles and 4 LPs/year. Fee derived from sales royalty.
How to Contact: Prefers cassette with 3-10 songs and lyric sheet. SASE. "Mention *Songwriter's Market*. Please make return envelope the same size as the envelopes you send material in, otherwise we cannot send everything back." Reports in 1 month.
Music: Mostly R&B, soul, dance and top 40/pop; also all types of rock. Produced "The Beast," by Freddie Starr (rap single); and "Oak Tree Rapp," by Star Crew (rap/dance single); and "What Have I Done For You Lately?," by King M.C. (rap/dance), both on Street Talk Records. Other artists include Bennie Harris, Carman Perez, Serada Johnson and Ed Tate.

WEST ALDEN PRODUCTIONS, 4637 Verdugo Rd., Los Angeles CA 90065. (818)846-6675. Producer: Mick Thompson. Record producer, music publisher (Town Line Music) and manager. Deals with artists. Produces 6 singles and 2 LPs/year. Fee derived from sales royalty or outright fee from artist/songwriter.
How to Contact: Write first about your interest. Prefers cassette with maximum 4 songs and lyric sheet. SASE. Reports in 1 month.
Music: Mostly rock, top 40/pop, R&B and new wave.
Tips: "Send your best hit material that is competitive with what is on the charts. We're mostly interested in new music groups."

*WEST & CO. PRODUCTIONS, #300, 54 Music Sq. E., Nashville TN 37203. (615)242-5588. Contact: Jerry West. Record producer, music publisher (Wesco Music Group), record label and management firm. Deals with artists and songwriters. Produces 12 singles and 4 LPs/year.
How to Contact: Prefers cassette (or videocassette). SASE. Reports in 1 week.
Music: Country and southern gospel. Produced *Greatest Hits*, by Jacky Ward (country LP on Electric Records); and *Heart Break Blues*, by Randy Parton (country/rock LP on Compleat Records). Other artists include Coy Ray and Montgomery Meece Band.

SHANE WILDER PRODUCTIONS, Box 3503, Hollywood CA 90078. (818)896-5506. President: Shane Wilder. Record producer and music publisher. Deals with artists and songwriters. Produces 25-30 singles and 10-15 LPs/year. Fee derived from sales royalty plus production fee.
How to Contact: Prefers cassette with 6-8 songs and lyric sheet. SASE. Reports in 4 weeks.
Music: Country. Produced "We Graduate This Summer," by Teresa O'Dell (country single); "Part Time Love," by Crystal Blue (disco single); and "Old Liars, Umpires and a Woman Who Knows," by Mike Franklin (country single, N.S.D. Records). Other artists include Priscilla Emerson, Laurie Loman

(MCA recording artist) and Terry Brooks (rock artist, Jet Records).
Tips: "Looking for top country acts for record contract and management—acts must be highly commercial."

*WILSON PRODUCTIONS,Box 412, New York NY 10462. (212)829-7033. President: Vernon Wilson. Record producer. Deals with artists only. Produces 2 singles and 2 LPs/year.
How to Contact: Write first to arrange personal interview. Prefers cassette with 3 songs. Does not return unsolicited material. Reports in 1 month.
Music: Mostly pop. Produced "You Make Me Feel Like A Woman," (by Vernon Wilson/Raymond Johnson), recorded by Sandra Taylor on MelVern Records (single).
Tips: "Be prepared to do shows, concerts as well as perform."

WISHBONE, INC., Box 2631, Muscle Shoals AL 35662. (205)381-1455. President: Terry Woodford. Record producer, music publisher (I've Got The Music Co./ASCAP, Song Tailors Music Co./BMI, Terry Woodford Music/ASCAP and Creative Source Music/BMI) and video producer. Deals with artists and songwriters.
How to Contact: Prefers cassette with 2 songs and lyric sheet. SASE. Reports ASAP.
Music: Mostly top 40/pop and country; also dance-oriented, easy listening, MOR, progressive, R&B, rock and soul. Produced *Nothing But the Truth*, by Mac McAnally (top 40/pop/easy listening/rock LP, Geffen Records).

*LONNIE WRIGHT,Rt. 16 Box 675, Tyler TX 75701-9744. (214)581-9945. President: Lonnie W. Wright. Record producer. Deals with artists and songwriters. Produces 10 singles and 2 LPs/year. Fee derived from sales royalty or outright fee from recording artist or record company.
How to Contact: Prefers cassette with 3 songs and lyric sheet. Does not return unsolicited material.
Music: Mostly country, R&B and gospel. Produced "Mama's Home," written and recorded by J. Tyson on Juke Box Records (country single); "Snap Your Fingers," written and recorded by O. Perry on Quazar Records (R&B single); and "Sometimes," written and recorded by Gene Thomas on Banka Records (pop single). Other artist include Ron Kizziar.

YELLOW ROSE, Box 1255, Gallatin TN 37066-1255. (615)451-3920. General Manager: Dee Mullins. Record producer and music publisher (My Dee Dee Music, Mel Dee Music/BMI). Deals with artists and songwriters. Produces 10-20 singles and 20-30 LPs/year. Works with 2-5 new songwriters/year. Fee derived from sales royalty.
How to Contact: Write or call first and obtain permission to submit, or arrange personal interview. Prefers cassette with 1-4 songs. Prefers studio produced demos. SASE. Reports in 1 month.
Music: Country and country crossover. Produced "Stumblin'," (by Smokey Colt), and "You'll Never Be Back Anymore (by Jimmy Faulks), both recorded by Bill Dennis on Melodee records (both singles); and "Pamela Brown," written and recorded by Tom Kruger on Melodee Records (single). Other artists include Dee Mullins.
Tips: "Tell us in writing if your desire is to be a recording artist or a songwriter or both."

*JOHN YOUNG/MODE MUSIC PRODUCTIONS,130 S. Bonsall St., Philadelphia PA 19103. (215)561-3108. Record producer, music publisher (W.W.T. Music), and CMI programmer. Deals with artists and songwriters. Produces 5 singles and 3 LPs/year. Fee derived form sales royalty or outright fee from songwriter/artists or record company.
How to Contact: Prefers cassette (or VHS videocassette) and lyric sheet. "Send only your strongest material." SASE. "No phone calls please."
Music: Heavy dance oriented, "supersonic" disco, heavy metal, rap and "dub. We're looking for anything that has a fresh edge and will scorch the dance floor." Produced *Fire & Ice*, recorded by Executive Slacks and *Bloodlust Mayhem*, recorded by The Church Burners, both LPs.
Tips: "Be outrageous and work to achieve some notoriety. Take a few chances. The world can live without mediocrity."

ZALESKI AND ASSOCIATES, (formerly Paul Zaleski), Box 34032, Bartlett TN 38134. (901)794-6923. Contact: Paul Zaleski. Record producer and music publisher (Apache's Rhythm/ASCAP). Deals with artists and songwriters. Produces 10 singles and 15 LPs/year. Fee derived from sales royalty or outright fee from record company or record artist.
How to Contact: Prefers cassette with 4-10 songs and lyric sheet. SASE. Reports in 2-3 weeks.
Music: Mostly contemporary Christian; also country, easy listening and R&B. Produced "Jesus Will Fix It," written and recorded by Al Green on A&M Records (single); *Soul Survivor*, recorded by Al Green on A&M Records (LP); and "Loving Her Way Across Texas," (by Alan O'Day), recorded by Don Christian on Stairway Records (single). Other artists include Cybil Sheperd, Picture This, Bill Pershak, Masqueraders, and Terri & Tonya.
Tips: "Submit good songs with structure and good easy hook."

Managers and Booking Agents

Managers and booking agents are important members of recording artists' careers. A personal manager juggles the complicated, day-to-day business affairs of his clients while providing guidance and encouragement to further their careers. Part of that guidance includes selecting appropriate material for the artists to perform and record, and most managers in this section indicate that they do review material for their acts. Managers earn the trust of their clients. They tend to limit the number of acts they represent in order to have time to build relationships with each. When they recommend a song to one of their artists, you can bet it's a song they believe in totally. They are often the closest contact to the artists that new songwriters are able to reach.

If you are a songwriter submitting songs to managers for their artists, notice the names of the acts they represent and the types of music they need. Managers of nationally-known artists and groups are located mostly in Los Angeles, New York or Nashville and approaching them is often nearly as difficult as approaching the artists themselves. But you need go no farther than your town, or a short radius thereof, to find talent needing songs. Managers of local acts will have more to say in the choice of material than those located in music centers (where the producer often makes the final decision about which songs an artist should record). Local acts work hard to make a reputation for themselves in hope of going on to stardom. It certainly doesn't hurt to become a favorite songwriter of a talented local entertainer. If the artist or group goes on to bigger things, you could go with them. If a manager or booking agent works only with local or regional acts, it will be indicated in the listing. Otherwise, you can figure that the firm works with acts from anywhere.

The listings in this section also include booking agencies. The booking agent is a coordinator actively finding work for his clients: club engagements, concerts or other performance opportunities. He is an employment agency of sorts. A booking agent tends to represent many more clients and may review material for them, but probably doesn't get to know each one as well as the personal manager. The booking agent finds the jobs; the manager guides career development. Each listing specifies whether the company is a booking agency, management firm, or both.

Managers and booking agents are particularly good contacts for performing writers/artists. Managers and agents provide many services for their clients, and they take a percentage of the artist's income (usually around 20%). So the more acts they can successfully represent, the more their potential earnings. If you want to perform your songs regularly in a concert situation—and possibly tour regionally, nationally, or even internationally—then you may want to consider contacting a manager or booking agent not just to submit songs for the other artists they represent but to consider you as an artist/client.

You may want to send a query letter asking a firm what their current needs are. Always follow the submission instructions given in the listings. If you are a songwriter/artist looking for a manager, you should also include a glossy photo, a list of songs you perform (both covers and originals), a current itinerary, and any relevant press clippings. You may want to submit a live demo recording or a videocassette to show off your performing abilities. If you are an entertainer or if a local group is performing your songs, make arrangements for managers and/or agents to see your work live. Always be specific in contacting them as to your intentions: whether you are a nonperforming songwriter wishing to have your material reviewed for other artists, or a writer/artist wishing to hire a manager or agent to handle your own career.

ACADEMY AWARD ENTERTAINMENT, 11 Shady Oak Trail, Charlotte NC 28210. (704)554-1162. Agent: Butch Kelly. Represents national acts and comedians. Currently handles 10 acts. Receives 20-25% commission. Reviews material for acts.
How to Contact: Prefers cassette, demo records or videocassette with 5-10 songs and pictures. "Send bio information if possible." SASE. Reports in 2 months.
Music: Rock, pop, R&B, rap, beach, soul, gospel, country and comedy. Works primarily with artists for show and dance groups and concerts. Current acts include Fresh Air (R&B), Lady Crush (rapper), Dean Mancuso (country), Melisa Kelly (R&B/pop); L.A. Stars (R&B), and Hill (soul, R&B, pop).
Tips: "Be professional and want to work. Include 8x10 photo, bio, good press kit or news clips."

*ACE PRODUCTIONS, 3407 Green Ridge Dr., Nashville TN 37214. (615)883-2875. Contact: Jim Case. Management firm and booking agency. Represents artists, groups and songwriters; currently handles 12 acts. Receives 15-20% commission. Reviews material for acts.
How to Contact: Prefers cassette (or VHS videocassette) with 2-4 songs and lead sheet or lyric sheets. Reports in 1 month. Does not return unsolicited material.
Music: Mostly country; also rock (hard and country) and bluegrass. Works primarily with show, dance and bar bands. Current acts include the Parrotts (B.J. and Kim), Garland Frady (country and country/rock), Cissie Lynn (country) and Roni Stoneman (country and comedy).
Tips: "We are looking for material, not bands. On demos, keep intros short and just do turnarounds between verses."

ACT "1" ENTERTAINMENT, Box 1079, New Haven CT 06504. (203)785-8338. President: Johnny Parris. Management firm and booking agency. Represents individual artists and groups; currently handles 40 acts. Reviews material for acts. Receives 10-20% commission.
How to Contact: Query by mail, arrange personal interview or submit demo and lead sheet. Prefers cassette (or VHS videocassette) with 5-10 songs. "Material will not be returned without sufficient SASE". Reports in 2 weeks.
Music: Mostly top 40, pop, soul, R&B and dance; also, easy listening, jazz, MOR and rock. Current acts include Bob Mel (top 40/pop), Splash (rock/top 40), Thin Ice (rock/top 40), Ricky Marz (top 40), Carl Barone (rock/top 40), Nick Fradiani (top 40/pop), Star (top 40), Juicy (top 40/pop), Karen and Lobo (top 40/rock), Just Friends (top 40, pop and soul), Bill Rowen (rock, top 40), Jam Machine (jazz), Double Play (top 40), Tony Biello (top 40/jazz), Bill Burton (top 40), T-N-T (top 40) and Cheers (top 40)..
Tips: "I'm looking for people with a professional attitude and drive and determination—people who are ethical and not into drugs. If you are ethical and stay completely away from drugs, you will make a lot of friends who will help you in your career, whether it's song writing, performing or managing."

ADORATION, INC., (aka Spirit III Music), Suite 2-A, 6750 W. 75th St., Overland Park KS 66204. (913)384-1050. Vice President: Betty Tatom. Management firm, booking agency, publishing and public relations company. Represents artists, groups and songwriters—"all are nationally known." Currently handles 9 acts. Receives 25-30% commission.
How to Contact: Write first and obtain permission to submit. Prefers cassette and lead sheet. Does not return unsolicited material. Reports "when various artists need material to record."
Music: Mostly contemporary gospel and MOR gospel; also country/pop gospel. Works primarily with gospel solos, trios, quartets and groups. Current acts include Kathie Sullivan (gospel singer), The Lads (gospel quartet), Eternity (gospel group of 15), Johnny Hall (gospel singer), Bobby Jones & New Life (gospel group of 9), Jessy Dixon (gospel singer), and Rock City Boys (gospel trio).
Tips: "All material sent must be gospel."

*AFTERSCHOOL PUBLISHING COMPANY, Box 14157, Detroit MI 48214. (313)822-7590. President: Herman Kelly. Management firm, booking agency, record company (Afterschool Co.) and music publisher (Afterschool Pub. Co.). Represents individual artists, songwriters, producer, arrangers and musicians. Currently handles 1 act. Reviews material for acts.
How to Contact: Prefers cassete with 3 songs and lyric or lead sheet. SASE. Reports in 1 month.
Music: Mostly pop, R&B and country; also gospel, soul and rap. Current acts include Herman Kelly.

AJAYE ENTERTAINMENT CORP., #1, 443 Riddle Rd., Box 20244, Cincinnati OH 45220. (513)221-2626. Artist Relations: Elaine Furlong. Booking agency. Represents artists and groups; currently represents 33 acts. Receives 10-20% commission.
How to Contact: Submit demo tape and write or call to explain the purpose of submission. Prefers cassette with 3-6 songs, song list, equipment list, photo and bio. SASE. Reports in 1 week.
Music: Progressive, rock, soul and top 40/pop. Current acts include Bell Jar, Brian Lovely and the Secret, The Cruise, CJSS, Prizoner, Elaine and the Biscaynes, Painter, Caliber, The Twist, Danny Morgan, Free Rein, Suspect, The Daybreakers, The Tritones, Larry and Gary, The Lusters, The Pack, No Brakes, Minx, Cinti Slim and Headhunters.

ALAMO TALENT AND PRODUCTIONS, 217 Arden Grove, San Antonio TX 78215. (512)225-6294. President: Carl Mertens. Management firm and booking agency. Represents artists and groups; currently handles 32 acts. Receives 15-25% commission. Reviews material for acts.
How to Contact: Query by mail. Prefers 7½ ips reel-to-reel or cassette with 3-5 songs. Does not return unsolicited material.
Music: Mostly country; also folk, MOR and Spanish. Works primarily with dance and club bands. Current acts include Lisa Lopez (Spanish artist), Janie C. Ramirez & Cactus Country, and American Express (C&W group).

ALIVE ENTERPRISES, 8271 Melrose Ave., Los Angeles CA 90046. (213)852-1100. President: Shep Gordon. Management firm. Represents artists, groups and songwriters; currently represents 7 acts. Receives 20% minimum commission.
How to Contact: Prefers cassette with 2-4 songs and lead sheet. SASE. Reports in 3-5 weeks.
Music: Rock (all types), soul and top 40/pop. Works with "major record company signed artists." Current acts include Alice Cooper (rock), and Luther Vandross (R&B).

*ALL NIGHT ENTERTAINMENT, 1461 S. Sherbourne Dr., Los Angeles CA 90035. (213)657-6221. President: Scott Hurowitz. Management firm (All Night Management), record company (All Night Productions) and music publisher (All Night Music). Represents individual artists, groups and songwriters; currently handles 2 acts. Receives 15-20% commission. Reviews material for acts.
How to Contact: Prefers cassete (or VHS videocassette) with 1-6 songs and lyric sheet. Does not return unsolicited material. Reports in 6 weeks.
Music: Mostly rock, pop and country. Works primarily with vocalists and rock bands. Current acts include Jef Scott and Rick Ryan.
Tips: "If you are strictly a songwriter, and not a performing artist, please indicate who *you* feel the song is right for. Also, for any submission please make us aware of any industry affiliations, such as management, past label or publishing deals, etc."

*ALL STAR TALENT, Box 1338, Merchantville NJ 08109. (609)962-6000. President: Rob Russen. Management firm, booking agency and music publisher. Represents artists, groups, songwriters and producers; currently handles 24 acts. Receives 4-10% commission. Reviews material for acts.
How to Contact: Prefers 7½ ips reel-to-reel or cassette (or videocassette) with 2-6 songs and lyric sheet. Does not return unsolicited material. Reports in 1 month.
Music: Dance-oriented, easy listening, jazz, MOR, progressive, R&B, rock, soul and top 40/pop. Works primarily with self-contained bands. Current acts include Phoenix (funk group), Philly Cream (R&B group), and The Kidd Band (rock).
Tips: "Have good hooks, catchy melody and effective lyrics."

ALL STAR TALENT AGENCY, Box 82, Greenbrier TN 37073. (615)643-4208. Agent: Joyce Brown. Booking agency. Represents professional individuals, groups and songwriters; currently handles 5 acts. Receives 10-15% commission. Reviews material for acts.
How to Contact: Prefers reel-to-reel or cassette with 1-4 songs and lead sheet. SASE. Reports ASAP.
Music: Mostly country; also bluegrass, gospel, MOR, rock (country) and top 40/pop. Works primarily with dance, show and bar bands, vocalists, club acts and concerts. Current acts include Bill Carlisle and the Carlisles (country group), Ronnie Dove (MOR/country artist), Randy Parton (pop artist), Charlie McCoy (instrumentalist), Tommy Overstreet (country artist), and Del Wood (Grand Ole Opry star).

*ALLEGIANCE ENTERTAINMENT CORP., INC., Box 370386, Atlanta GA 30037. (404)373-7000. Contact: Creative Department. Management agency, record company (Major Label Records) and music publisher (Bohdisattva). Represents individual artists, groups and songwriters; currently handles 3 acts. Receives 20% commission. Reviews material for acts.
How to Contact: Prefers cassette (or videocassette) with lyric or lead sheet. Does not return unsolicited material. Reports in 4 weeks.
Music: Mostly R&B, pop and jazz fusion; also experimental acoustic. Works primarily with "any self-contained artist or act that is commercially marketable." Current acts include Dale Sanders, Earl Johnson and First Reaction.
Tips: "We prefer to work with those who are actively involved in the music industry on a professional level."

RAMON ALSINA, ARTIST REPRESENTATIVE, 228 E. 80th, New York NY 10021. (212)988-2542. President: Ramon Alsina. Management agency. Represents individual artists and groups; currently handles 15 acts. Receives 10-30% commission. Reviews material for acts.

How to Contact: Write first and obtain permission to submit. Prefers cassette. Does not return unsolicited material.
Music: Mostly art songs and classical music. Works primarily with vocalists. Current acts include Priscilla Gordon, Alberto Figols and The Figols Family.

AMIRON MUSIC, 20531 Plummer St., Chatsworth CA 91311. (818)998-0443. Manager: A. Sullivan. Management firm. Represents artists and groups in local area only; currently handles 6 acts. Receives 10-25% commission. Reviews material for acts.
How to Contact: Prefers cassette and lyric sheet. SASE. Reports in 1 month.
Music: Top 40/pop and rock. Works primarily with self contained groups. Current acts include Sunset (show group), Chozen Few (show group), and Paris (pop rock).

AND MORE ENTERTAINMENT CORPORATION, (formerly T.D.I. Direction & Management Division), 14352 SW 142nd Ave., Miami, FL 33186. (305)662-1135. Manager: Larry Brahms. Management firm, publishing and production company. Represents artists, groups, songwriters and record producers; currently handles 6 acts. Receives 15% commission. Reviews material for acts.
How to Contact: Query or submit demo tape and lyric sheet. Prefers cassette (or videocassette) with 3-4 songs. SASE. Reports in 2 weeks.
Music: Mostly dance-oriented; also country, country rock, MOR, rock, R&B, soul and top 40/pop. Works primarily with studio musicians, local musicians and major recording artists. Looking for additional artists. Current acts include Celi Bee (vocalist), Sleight Touch, and Olga (dance recording artist).
Tips: "Any background information (e.g., press kit) is always helpful but not essential. Make sure material is copyrighted."

DON ANDERSON PRODUCTIONS, INC., Suite 170, 840 Malcolm Rd., Burlingame CA 94010. (415)692-9444 or (800)334-6777. President: Donald Anderson.
How to Contact: Prefers cassette with 3-5 songs and lead sheet.

*ANJOLI PRODUCTIONS, 24 Center Square Rd., Leola PA 17540. (717)656-8215. President: Terry Gehman. Management firm, booking agency and music publisher (Younger Bros. Music). Represents individual artists, groups and songwriters; currently handles 25 acts. Receives 15% commission. Reviews material for acts.
How to Contact: Prefers cassette (or VHS videocassette) with 3-6 songs and lyric sheet. Does not return unsolicited material.
Music: Country, pop and R&B. Works primarily with vocalists and show groups. Current acts include Shucks, Pat Garrett and The Hollanders.

*MICHAEL ANTHONY AGENCY, #220, 165 S. Union Blvd., Lakewood CO 80228. Office Manager: Linda S. Smith. Management firm and booking agency. Represents artists and groups; currently handles 14 acts. Receives 15% commission. Reviews material for acts.
How to Contact: Prefers cassette (or VHS videocassette), song list and 8x10 photo. SASE.
Music: "Hot 100," dance and R&B. Works primarily with nightclub dance groups and concert-oriented show bands. Current acts include No Doubt About It (showy dance/top 40 band), A Million Rumors (5-piece hot 100 cover act), Vis-A-Vis (6 piece top 40/R&B cover act).

ARISTO MUSIC ASSOCIATES, INC., Box 22765, Nashville TN 37202. (615)320-5491. President: Jeff Walker. Publishing Coordinator: Terri Walker. Public relations and media consulting firm. Represents artists, groups and songwriters. "We deal with artists on a national and international level." Currently handles 8 clients. Receives negotiable commission for public relations services "based on estimated time and services involved." Reviews material for acts.
How to Contact: Query by mail. "At present we are only interested in artists with national distribution." Prefers cassette with 2-4 songs or videocassette if available. Prefers a "low-key, patient approach." SASE. Reports in 1 month.
Music: Country, easy listening, MOR and top 40/pop. Works primarily with country groups and artists. Current acts include Karen Taylor-Good (Mesa Records), the Nashville Roster of the Entertainment Artists Agency, Robin Lee (female country solo artist), Andie Henry (Canadian recording artist), and Mason Dixon (country vocal group).
Tips: Songwriters "need to be professional in their approach to the music business. Presently establishing affiliated publishing companies."

PAT ARMSTRONG & ASSOCIATES, INC., Suite 202, 1500 Lee Rd., Lee Square Bldg., Orlando FL 32810. (305)299-0077. President: Pat Armstrong. Vice President: Jack Armstrong. Management firm, production company and music publisher. Represents artists, groups and songwriters; currently handles

8 acts. Receives 20% commission. Reviews material for acts.
How to Contact: Query by phone. Prefers cassette with 4-6 songs and lead sheet. SASE. Reports in 2 weeks.
Music: Progressive, rock (hard, country, heavy), top 40/pop and modern music. Works primarily with developing artists and bands. Current acts include Molly Hatchet (Southern rock group/Parc Records CBS), Pat Travers (rock/PolyGram Records), Stranger (rock group/Epic Records), and Four In Legion (modern music/CBS Assoc. Label/CBS Records).

ARTISTS'/HELLER AGENCY, #N, 21430 Strathern, Caioga Park CA 91304-4153. (818)702-9276. President: Jerry Heller. Management firm. Represents artists, groups and songwriters; currently handles 15 acts. Reviews material for acts. Receives 15-25% commission.
How to Contact: Query by mail. Prefers cassette with 4-7 songs. SASE. Reports in 1 month.
Music: Mostly R&B, rap and jazz; also rock, soul and progressive. Works primarily with concert groups. Current acts include Rose Royce (R&B), Rodney Franklin (jazz/R&B), L.A. Dream Team, The Egyptian Lover, Bobby Jimmy & The Critters, Russ Parr, Keith Patrick, World Class Wreckin' Cru, C.I.A., Family Dream and Yours Truly.

*ATTRACTIONS INTERNATIONAL, 1019 17th Ave. S., Nashville TN 37212. (615)320-5600. Agent: Nola Brown. Management firm and booking agency. Represents individual artists and groups; currently handles 6 acts. Receives 15% commission. Reviews material for acts.
How to Contact: Prefers cassete (or videocassette) with 6-8 songs. "Send promo package—color picture, song and equipment lists." Reports in 3 weeks.
Music: Mostly pop, rock and country; also R&B. Works primarily with dance bands. Current acts include The Revue, Phyllis Horne and Lifeguards.
Tips: "Currently 60's music is the 'big thing' everyone wants."

AZTEC PRODUCTIONS, 20531 Plummer St., Chatsworth CA 91311. (818)998-0443. General Manager: A. Sullivan. Management firm and booking agency. Represents individuals, groups and songwriters; currently handles 7 acts. Receives 10-25% commission.
How to Contact: Prefers 7½ ips reel-to-reel or cassette and lead sheet. SASE. Reports in 3 weeks.
Music: Disco, MOR, rock, soul and top 40/pop. Works primarily with club bands, show groups and concert groups. Current acts include El Chicano (Latin/rock), Abraxas (MOR), Storm (show group), Tribe (soul/R&B), New Street, Kelly Lynn, Ako, Zaral and Debbie Rockwell.

*BACKSTAGE PRODUCTIONS INTERNATIONAL, 1-3015 Kennedy Rd., Scarborough, Ontario M1V 1E7 Canada. (416)291-4913. President: Steve Thomson. Management firm, booking agency, record company (Triology Records), music publisher (Melmar Publishing) and Star-Satelite). Represents individual artists, groups and songwriters. Currently handles 5 acts. Reviews material for acts.
How to Contact: Prefers cassette (or Beta or VHS videocassette). SAE and IRC. Reports in 6 weeks.
Music: Rock, pop and country. Works primarily with pop vocalists and rock bands; rock and country vocals. Current acts include Ronnie Hawkins, Patti Jannetta and David Sereda.

GARY BAILEY ENTERTAINMENT AGENCY, 207 Queen St., Port Stanley, Ontario, Canada. (519)782-3570. President: Gary Bailey. Booking agency. Represents artists and groups in Ontario; currently handles 20 acts. Receives 15-20% commission. Reviews material for acts.
How to Contact: Query by mail. Prefers cassette or videocassette with 3-5 songs. Does not return unsolicited material. Reports in 2 weeks.
Music: Mostly MOR, 60s and top 40; also dance, easy listening and rock. Works primarily with dance bands and bar bands. Current acts include Rudy Davis (MOR), Player (MOR); and Bustin Loose (60s).
Tips: "Be honest, hard working and have a clean appearance."

BARNARD MANAGEMENT SERVICES (BMS), 2219 Main St., Santa Monica CA 90405.(213)396-1440. Agent: Russell Barnard. Management firm. Represents artists, groups and songwriters; currently handles 2 acts. Receives 10-20% commission. Reviews material for acts.
How to Contact: Write first and obtain permission to submit cassette with 3-10 songs and lead sheet. Artists may submit VHS videocassette. SASE. Reports in 1 month.
Music: Mostly country crossover; also blues, country, R&B, rock and soul. Works primarily with country crossover singers/songwriters. Current acts include Helen Hudson (singer/songwriter), and Mark Shipper (songwriter/author).

*BILL BATZKALL PRODUCTIONS, INC., Box 1541, Elk Grove IL 60009-1541. (312)981-0198. President: Bill Batzkall. Management firm, record company (Lake Effect Records, Inc.) and music publisher (Lake Effect Publishing, Inc.). Represents local individual artists, groups and songwriters;

currently handles 3 acts. Receives 15-20% commission. Reviews material for acts.
How to Contact: Prefers cassette or 7½ ips reel-to-reel (or VHS videocassette) with 4 songs and lead sheet. SASE. Reports in 2 weeks.
Music: Jazz, rock and R&B. Works primarily with artists of original material "hit oriented." Current acts include Michael Mason (jazz flutist), Pursuit (rock) and Mark Colby/Frank Caruso (jazz act).

*WILLIE BELL MANAGEMENT, 29 Castlehill Rd., Bearsden, Glasgow G61-4DD Scotland. 011-44-41-357-0658. Owner/Proprietor: Willie Bell. Management firm. Represents individual artists and groups; currently handles 10 acts. Receives 15-20% commission. Reviews material for acts.
How to Contact: Prefers cassette with lyric sheet. Reports in 2 weeks.
Music: Mostly pop, country and rock; also R&B. Works primarily with vocalists. Current acts include Jim Crown, High Street and Penny Simons.

HARVEY BELLOVIN, 410 E. 64th St., New York NY 10021. (212)752-5181. Contact: Harvey Bellovin. Personal manager. Represents artists, groups and lyricist/composers in New York area. Receives 10-20% commission. Reviews material for acts.
How to Contact: Write first or submit cassette and lyric sheet. SASE. Reports in 3 weeks.
Music: MOR, rock, top 40/pop and musical scores. Works primarily with rock bands; composer/singer (MOR, rock, top 40/pop); lyricist and/or composer (musicals).

BGM RECORDS, 10452 Sentinel, San Antonio TX 78217. (512)654-8773. President/General Manager: Bill Green. Booking agency, record company and publishing company. Represents artists, groups and songwriters; currently handles 7 acts. Receives 15% commisson. Reviews material for acts.
How to Contact: Prefers cassette with 1-4 songs and lyric sheet. SASE. Reports in 1 month.
Music: Mostly contemporary and traditional country. Works primarily with vocalists and vocal groups. Current acts include Bobby Jenkins, Dianna Hart, Kenny Dale, and Jay Eric (all country).

J. BIRD BOOKING AGENCY, 4905 S. Atlantic Ave., Daytona Beach FL 32029. (904)767-4707. Contact: John Bird. Booking agency. Represents artists and groups; currently handles 125 acts. Receives 15-25% commission. Reviews material for acts.
How to Contact: Prefers cassette (or videocassette) with 3-4 songs. "Initial interview is usually by phone; after demo material is received we usually ask person to contact us again in 1 week-10 days." Does not return unsolicited material.
Music: Bluegrass, blues, church/religious, country, dance-oriented, easy listening, folk, jazz, R&B, soul, country rock and top 40/pop. Works primarily with "top 40 dance and show bands, rock bands (dance and concert), and concert groups (major label touring bands). Particularly active in national college concerts. Most of our demand is for dance bands since we generally work with high schools and universities." Current acts include The Original Drifters (nostaliga), Jimmy Buffett (concert), Cloudburst (convention-show-dance), Tommy Cashwell and Old Gold (50's dance) and Sound Society (top 40 dance).
Tips: "We solicit established professional acts interested in touring full time. The groups should have or be willing to prepare a promotional package containing audio and/or videotape, photos, song, personnel, and equipment lists. Since we are the largest 'one nighter' agency in the Southeast, providing entertainment to colleges nationwide, artists submitting materials should be geared for that market."

BLADE AGENCY, Box 1556, Gainesville FL 32602. (904)372-8158 and 377-8158. General Manager: Charles V. Steadham Jr. Management firm and booking agency. Represents professional individuals and groups; currently handles 36 acts. Receives 15-20% commission. Reviews material for acts.
How to Contact: Query. Prefers cassette (or videocassette) with 2-3 songs, publicity materials and itinerary. Does not return unsolicited material. Reports as soon as possible.
Music: Bluegrass, blues, country, show and dance-oriented, easy listening, folk, MOR, soul and top 40/pop. Current acts include Gamble Rogers (country/folk artist), Tom Parks (comedian), Mike Cross (country/folk artist), Mike Reid (MOR/pop), Zeal (R&B/pop), George Hamilton IV (country/gospel), The Fall Guys and A Gal (musical variety), Andy Andrews (comedy), Barbara Bailey Hutchison (folk/pop), Sinbad (comedy), Franklyn Ajaye (comedy), and The Malones (country/pop).

*BLANK & BLANK, 1530 Chestnut St., Philadelphia PA 19102. (215)568-4310. Treasurer, Manager: E. Robert Blank. Management firm. Represents individual artists and groups.
How to Contact: Write or call first to obtain permission to submit.

*BLUE OX TALENT AGENCY, 1268 Main St. E., Hamilton, Ontario L8K 1A7 Canada. (416)544-5705. General Manager: David S. Bach. Management firm, booking agency, record company (Blue Ox Records) and music publisher (Blue Ox Music). Represents individual artists, groups, songwriters, variety acts and actors/actresses; currently handles over 200 acts. Receives 10-15% commission. Reviews material for acts.

How to Contact: Prefers cassette or 7½ ips reel-to-reel (or VHS videocassette of 20 minutes maximum) with 3-4 songs and lyric or lead sheet. Does not return unsolicited material. Reports in 6 weeks.

Music: Mostly pop/top 40, adult contemporary, country, rock and R&B; also classical and jazz. Works primarily with dance bands, club bands, show bands and vocalists. Current acts incude Larry Mac-Donald (singer/songwriter), David Sebastian Bach (singer/songwriter) and Chooz (group/songwriters).

WILLIS BLUME AGENCY, Box 509, Orangeburg SC 29116. (803)536-2951. President: Willis Blume. Management firm and booking agency. Represents artists and groups in the southeast; currently handles 35 acts. Receives minimum 15-20% commission. Reviews material for acts.

How to Contact: Query by mail. Prefers cassette with 4 songs maximum. Artists may submit videocassette. SASE.

Music: Mostly adult contemporary, R&B, dance; also easy listening, MOR, soul and top 40/pop. Works primarily with show and dance bands. Current acts include Shagtime, The Swingin' Medalions, and The Catalinas (all show and dance bands/recording acts), the Tams (beach/top 40/pop artists) and Archie Bell.

Tips: "Only interested in adult contemporary songs and artists."

BONNIE LOU ENTERPRISES, RD 3, Box 323, Seaford DE 19973. (302)629-6441. Manager: Bonnie L. Carver. Management firm and booking agency. Represents individual artists and groups. Currently handles 3 acts. Receives 20% commission. Reviews material for acts.

How to Contact: Prefers cassette (or videocassette) with 1-3 songs and lyric sheet. SASE. Reports in 6 weeks.

Music: Country and top 40/pop. Works primarily with vocalists and dance bands. Acts include Kim Marie (contemporary country vocalist), Loose Change (dance/show band), Stevie Taylor (top 40 vocalist) and Beverly Austin (country vocalist).

Tips: "Make sure your songs have good hooks and are original and commercial."

*BORZOI MUSIC ARTISTS, 222 Duncan, San Francisco CA 94131. (415)641-7333. Manager: Tim McKenna. Management firm. Represents individual artists; currently handles 2 acts. Reviews material for acts.

How to Contact: Prefers cassette and lyric sheet. SASE.

Music: Mostly R&B, pop and "radio." Current acts include Sylvester and Jeanie Tracy.

BOUQUET-ORCHID ENTERPRISES, Box 18284, Shreveport LA 71138. (318)686-7362. President: Bill Bohannon. Management firm. Represents individuals and groups; currently handles 3 acts. Receives 15% minimum commission. Reviews material for acts.

How to Contact: Prefers cassette with 2-5 songs, song list and lyric sheet. Include brief resume. SASE. Reports in 1 month.

Music: Country, rock (country), and top 40/pop. Works primarily with solo artists and small combos. Current acts include Teresa Gilbert, Adam Day and the Bandoleers (top 40/pop group).

*BRANCHING-OUT PRODUCTION, 281 E. Kingsbridge Rd., Bronx NY 10458. (212)733-5342. President: Murray Fuller. Management firm. Represents artists, groups and songwriters; currently handles 5 acts. Receives 10-20% commission. Reviews material for acts.

How to Contact: Prefers cassette (or videocassette) with 3-6 songs and lyric or lead sheets. SASE. Reports in 1 month.

Music: Dance-oriented, easy listening, jazz, R&B, rock and soul. Works primarily with dance and bar bands, and bands for concert support. Current acts include Ray Rivera (jazz artist), Boncellia Lewis (contemporary vocalist), and Tony Graye (jazz artist).

BROTHERS MANAGEMENT ASSOCIATES, 141 Dunbar Ave., Fords NJ 08863. (201)738-0880 or 738-0883. President: Al Faucera. Management firm and booking agency. Represents artists, groups and songwriters; currently handles 30-70 acts. Receives variable commission. Reviews material for acts.

How to Contact: Query by mail, arrange personal interview. Prefers cassette with 3-6 songs and lyric sheet. Include photographs. SASE. Reports as soon as possible.

Music: Mostly top 40/pop, dance and R&B; also blues, classical, country, show, easy listening, jazz, rock and soul. Works primarily with top 40 groups, preferably female; dance bands, show groups and 50s and 60s acts. Current acts include Waterfront (top 40/show), Chelsea (top 40/rock), and Benny Troy and Company (top 40/show).

Tips: "We need very commercial, chart oriented material."

BENNIE BROWN PRODUCTION, 3011 Woodway Ln., Columbia SC 29223. (803)788-5734. President: Bennie Brown, Jr. Management agency, record company (Nu-Tone) and music publisher (Ben-Brown/BMI). Represents individual artists, groups and songwriters; currently handles 2 acts. Receives 20% commission. Reviews material for acts.
How to Contact: Prefers cassette with 3-4 songs and lyric sheet or lead sheet. SASE. Reports in 3 weeks.
Music: Mostly contemporary gospel, easy listening/top 40 and country; also soul. Works primarily with vocalists and groups. Current acts include Willie Penson, Linda Martell and Free Style.

*JIM BRUMMETT ENTERPRISES, Box 2498, Hendersonville TN 37077. (615)822-8747. Owner: Jim Brummett. Management firm, booking agency, music publisher (Jimbo Music) and concert promoter. Represnets individual artists, groups and songwriters; currently handles 3 acts. Receives 20-33⅓% commission. Reviews material for acts.
How to Contact: Prefers cassette with lyric or lead sheets. Does not return unsolicited material.
Music: Country and gospel. Works primarily with vocalists and vocal groups; duets, trios, and quartets. Current acts include The Blazer Brothers, The Bibb Sisters and Ava Barber.
Tips: "Only interested in traditional country artists and material. Currently looking for a traditional female quartet."

*BULLETT MANAGEMENT, Suite 7, 124 W. 81st St., New York NY 10024. (212)787-8103. Contact: Stephen Bond Garvan. Management firm, record company (Would'n Shoe Records, L'Orient Records, Hatch Records) and record producer (It's a Hit Productions).
How to Contact: Write first about your interest. Submit 7½ ips reel-to-reel or cassette (or videocassette) after initial response, with 3 songs and lyric sheet. Does not return unsolicited material.
Music: Mostly rock, pop/rock and country/rock; also country. Current acts include Secret (country/rock).

AL BUNETTA MANAGEMENT, INC., Suite 215, 4121 Wilshire Blvd, Los Angeles CA 90010. (213)385-0882. President: Al Bunetta. Management firm. Represents producers, artists and songwriters. Receives variable commission. Reviews material for acts and films.
How to Contact: Prefers cassette with 1-3 songs and lead sheet. SASE. Reports in 1 month.
Music: R&B, rock, new music, top 40/pop and adult contemporary. Works primarily with national recording artists. Current acts include John Prine (singer/songwriter/recording artist), and Rave-Ups (pop).

C.M. MANAGEMENT, 7957 Nita, Canoga Park CA 91304-4706. (818)704-7800. President: Craig Miller. Management firm and music publisher. Represents artists, groups, producers and publishers; currently handles 4 acts. Receives 15-20% commission—"occasional flat fee."
How to Contact: Query by mail, then submit demo tape and lead sheet. Prefers cassette with 3-5 songs. Submit material "with the best package, (i.e., representation) possible." SASE. Reports in 1 month.
Music: Jazz, rock and fusion. Works primarily with acoustic musicians and composers. Current acts include David Grisman (MCA Records recording act), and Mark O'Connor (WB Records recording act).
Tips: "Send an interesting and complete package. If a song works with just a vocal and accompaniment of just one instrument, then it should be a good song."

CACTUS INDUSTRIES MUSIC INC., 870 Woodland Rd., Ingomar PA 15127. (412)364-5095. President: Chuck Surman. Management firm, publisher and record producer. Represents artists, musical groups and songwriters from anywhere; currently handles 30 acts. Receives publishing administration fee plus percentage of artist's earnings. Reviews material for acts.
How to Contact: Prefers 7½ ips reel-to-reel or cassette with 3-15 songs. Writers should include a short bio. SASE. Reports ASAP.
Music: Mostly pop, rock, R&B and dance; also country, MOR and top 40/pop. Works primarily with rock/top 40/pop bands and black dance and R&B groups. Current acts include the X-15 (hard rock group, Precision Records), Silencers (hard rock group, Precision Records); Jeff Mills (pop/rock, RCA Records), and Wilson Pickett (R&B/dance, Precision Records).

CANDY RECORDS, 2716 Springlake Ct., Irving TX 75060. (214)790-5172. Owner/General Manager: Kenny Wayne. Management firm, booking agency, record company (Candy Records) and music publisher (Sweet Tooth Music). Represents individual artists, groups and songwriters; currently handles 5 acts. Receives "standard new artist" commission. Reviews material for acts.
How to Contact: Prefers cassette with 3-4 unpublished songs and lyric sheet. Reports in 1 month. "I do not answer any mail or return tapes, lyrics, etc. without appropriate SASE, no matter how good!"

Music: Mostly commercial rock, country and blues; also R&B, gospel and pop/MOR. Works primarily with "vocalists and bands with commercial appeal." Current acts include Billy Blast Band, Kenny Wayne & His Rockin' Rhythm & Blues Revue, and Reign.
Tips: "Compare your material to the hits on the charts and radio now. It gets more competitive each day, therefore if your act and songs are unprofessional, then you're wasting both our time and reputations."

CAN'T STOP PRODUCTIONS, INC., Suite 428, 420 Lexington Ave., New York NY 10170. (212)818-0640. International Manager: Henri Belolo. General Manager: Max Dahaot-Lavelle. Management firm, production company and music publisher. Represents artists, groups and songwriters. Receives variable commission. Reviews material for acts.
How to Contact: Prefers cassette with 1-3 songs and lead sheet. SASE. Reports in 2 months.
Music: Dance-oriented, MOR, progressive, R&B, rock (no hard or country) and top 40/pop. Current acts include Ritchie Family, Village People, Break Machine (pop and R&B), and Eartha Kitt (dance/pop).

CAPITOL BOOKING SERVICE, INC., 11844 Market St., North Lima OH 44452. (216)549-2155. President: David Musselman. Booking agency. Represents all types of entertainment; currently handles 7 acts. Reviews material for acts "on occasion.".
How to Contact: Query. Prefers cassette with minimum 3 songs. "We would like references. We also have video equipment, and if artist has videotape, we would like to see this." SASE. Reports ASAP.
Music: Mostly MOR; also country, dance-oriented, easy listening, folk, gospel, patriotic and top 40/pop. Works primarily with "self-contained musical groups that play all-around music for mixed audiences; young American or Las Vegas-type show reviews, some country and the New Seekers who are, of course, a name act from the '70s." Current acts include Life, Sunshine Express, Higher Power (show groups), Seekers (name act); Alann & Hays Show; Bobby Mercer Road Show (show and dance group); Eddie Jaye (ventriloquist and comedy M.C.); and JoAnn Castle (formerly of Lawrence Welk Show).
Tips: "Acts should have good literature, well choreographed and produced show."

*CARCO PRODUCTIONS, INC., Suite 3, 3129 Trussel Way, Sacramento CA 95825. (916)481-2029 and 485-1736. President: Charles Rovenstine. Management firm, record company (Carco Recording Ltd.) and music publisher. Represents individual artists, groups and songwriters; currently handles 5 acts. Receives 10-15% commission. Reviews material for acts.
How to Contact: Prefers cassette with 1-5 songs and lyric sheet. SASE. Reports in 2 weeks.
Music: Mostly country, comedy story ballads and bluegrass; also ballads. Works primarily with vocalists and variety acts. Current acts include Charlie Red, Hal Slawson and The Gary Snell Puppetts.
Tips: "We are actively looking for new material for Charlie Red's new album—primarily, story ballads and more traditional sounding country songs. No 'divorce tunes' please."

CARMAN PRODUCTIONS, INC., 15456 Cabrito Rd., Van Nuys CA 91406. (213)873-7370. Contacts: Joe Gottfried or Tom Skeeter. Management firm and music publisher. Represents individual artists, groups and songwriters.
How to Contact: Prefers cassette and lyric or lead sheet. SASE.
Music: Pop, rock and country. Works primarily with pop/rock vocalists, bands or individuals.

*DICK CHARLES, 130 W. 42nd St., New York NY 10036. (212)819-0920. President: Dick Charles. Management firm and music publisher (Jondi Music). Represents individual artists and songwiters; currently handles 2 acts. Reviews material for acts.
How to Contact: Prefers cassette with no more than 3 songs.
Music: Country and pop. Works primarily with vocalist/recording artists. Current acts include Jon Soleather.

CHRISTIAN IMAGE AGENCY, Box 91337, Mobile AL 36691. (205)473-4327. Management firm and booking agency. Represents individual artists and groups; currently handles 9 acts. Receives 20% commission.
How to Contact: Prefers cassette (or videocassette) with 3 songs maximum and lyric sheet. SASE.
Music: Gospel or contemporary Christian. Works primarily with solo artists and groups. Current acts include Wayne Watson, Paul Smith, Steve and Annie Chapman, Karla Worley, Luke Garrett, Michael James Murphy, Steve Adams, Lula Roman and Morris Chapman (all gospel/contemporary Christian acts).
Tips: All material submitted must be copyrighted prior to submitting.

*CIRCUIT RIDER TALENT & MANAGEMENT CO., 123 Walton Ferry Rd., 2nd Floor, Hendersonville TN 37075. (615)824-1947. President: Linda S. Dotson. Management firm, booking agency and

music publisher (Channel Music, Cordial Music). Represents individual artists, songwriters and actors; currently handles 4 acts. Commission varies. Reviews material for acts.
How to Contact: Write or call first and obtain permission to submit. Prefers cassette with 3 songs and lyric sheet. Videocassettes required of artists only. SASE. Reports in 6 weeks.
Music: Mostly pop, country and R&B; also gospel and comedy. Works primarily with vocalists. Current acts include Sheb Wooley, Buck Trent, Ben Colder and Benji Wilhoite.
Tips: "Artists have your act together. Have a full press kit, videos, and be professional."

CLOCKWORK ENTERTAINMENT MANAGEMENT AGENCY, Box 1600, Haverhill MA 01831. (617)373-6010. President: Bill Macek. Management firm and booking agency. Represents groups and songwriters throughout New England; currently handles 6 acts. Receives 15% commission. Reviews material for acts.
How to Contact: Query or submit demo tape. Prefers cassette with 3-12 songs. "Also submit promotion and cover letter with interesting facts about yourself." Does not return unsolicited material unless accompanied by SASE. Reports in 1 month.
Music: Rock (all types) and top 40/pop. Works primarily with bar bands and original acts. Current acts include "Kneworld" (5-piece high energy top 40), The Gail Savage Band (5-piece FM rocker), Quartet (4-piece high energy top 40/rock), and Code 5 (5-piece top 40).

C-M-I RECORDS/TTA MANAGEMENT, 10125 227th Ave., Buckley WA 98321. (206)862-1877. Contact: Tom Thrasher. Management firm and record company. Represents artists, groups and songwriters in the Northwest; currently handles 3 acts. Receives 10-50% commission. Reviews material for acts.
How to Contact: Prefers cassette (or videocassette) with 3-10 songs and lyric sheet. Songwriters and artists may submit videocassette. SASE. Reports in 1 month.
Music: Mostly gospel, country and country/rock; also bluegrass, blues, easy listening, and folk. Works primarily with vocalists, show bands and concert groups. Current acts include The Nashville Rebels (country), Tom Stopp (country/rock) and Tom Thrasher (gospel).
Tips: "Keep tape simple—clean vocal track with guitar/keyboard."

*COAST LINE EVENTS/SHORELINE MANAGEMENT, Box 2472, Norfolk VA 23501. (804)625-4100. General Manager: Oscar Jai-Tee. Management firm and booking agency. Estab. 1986. Represents individual artists and groups from the Mid-Atlantic region; currently handles 7 acts. Receives 15-25% commission. Reviews material for acts.
How To Contact: Prefers cassette with 3 or more songs and lyric sheet. SASE. Reports in 5 weeks.
Music: Mostly R&B, pop and rock; also jazz, dance and gospel. Works primarily with concert acts and dance bands. Current acts include Phase 7, Phree Phlyte, and Nite Cruise.

COMMUNICATION CONCEPT, Box 2095, Philadelphia PA 19103. (215)844-1947. President: S. Deane Henderson. Management firm and promotion and talent scout handling copyrights and trademarks. Represents artists, groups and songwriters; currently handles 13 acts. Receives 10-15% commission. Reviews material for acts.
How to Contact: Prefers cassette (or VHS videocassette) with 4-8 songs and lyric sheet. Does not return unsolicited material.
Music: Mostly rock, top 40 and gospel; also dance-oriented, easy listening, jazz, MOR, soul, top 40/pop and funk. Works primarily with dance bands and recording acts. Current acts include Verdell Colbert and Offspring (gospel), The Racers (rock), Sparkles (top 40/R&B), and Veronica Johnson (vocalist).
Tips: "Please submit your best tape or VHS video."

BURT COMPTON AGENCY, Box 160373, Miami FL 33116. (305)238-7312. Contact: Burt Compton. Booking agency. Represents groups; currently handles 36 acts. Receives 10-20% commission. Reviews material for acts.
How to Contact: Query by mail, then submit demo tape. Prefers cassette with 3-6 songs. "Include complete repertoire, 8x10 photo and resume." Does not return unsolicited material. Reports in 1 month.
Music: Mostly top 40/pop; also rock (hard/dance). Works primarily with dance and bar bands. Current acts include Heroes (dance band), Fantasy (recording/concert group), and Wildlife (recording/concert group).
Tips: "Have your promotional materials professionally packaged. We don't like having to decipher handwritten resumes with misspelled words and incomplete sentences."

CONTEMPORARY ARTIST MANAGEMENT, Box 250, Fern Park FL 32730. (305)834-6677. Artist Management: Monte Taylor, Terrie Miner and Fred Weiss. Management firm. Represents musical groups; currently handles 17 acts. Receives 10-15% commission. Reviews material for acts.

How to Contact: Query by mail. Prefers cassette (or videocassette "with artists attired the way they would be in front of a live audience") with 4-6 songs and lyric sheet. SASE. Reports in 3 weeks.

Music: Mostly dance and contemporary top 40/pop; also MOR, R&B, rock and soul. Works primarily with high-energy show acts, including dance acts. Current acts include Coast to Coast, Special Effect, the Right Touch, and Franco and Mary Jane (show groups).

ROBB COOPER TALENT AGENCY, Box 93965, Los Angeles CA 90093. (818)710-7515. Talent Agent: Jim Roberts. Booking agency. Represents individual artists, groups and songwriters; currently handles 70 acts. Receives 10% commission. Reviews material for acts.

How to Contact: Write first and obtain permission to submit. Prefers cassette (or VHS videocassette of 30 minutes maximum) with lyric sheet, lead sheet and photos. SASE. Reports in 6 weeks.

Music: Mostly R&B, rock and MOR; also comedy. "We prefer non-synthesized songs." Works primarily with R&B/MOR opening acts for major recording artists, vocalists, show bands and comedians. Current acts include Stephanie Mills (R&B), Chaka Khan (R&B), The Weather Girls (R&B duo), and Sylvester.

Tips: "Absolutely no phone calls or personal deliveries. Unsolicited material will be refused and returned. After obtaining permission, submit a professional-quality tape with no more than three songs (2 up-beat and 1 ballad preferred) and a brief cover letter, bio and lead sheets/charts. Patience is a major asset when submitting."

COUNTRY MUSIC SHOWCASE INTERNATIONAL, INC., Box 368, Carlisle IA 50047. (515)989-3679. President: Harold L. Luick. Management agency and booking agency. Represents individual artists, groups and songwriters; currently handles 18 acts. Receives 5-20% commission. Reviews material for acts.

How to Contact: Prefers cassette (or VHS videocassette) with 3 songs and lyric sheet. SASE. Reports in 3 weeks.

Music: Mostly contemporary, hard core country and traditional country; also bluegrass, western swing and comedy. Works primarily with "single acts and group acts that are self contained and uniformed." Current acts include Mr. Elmer Bird (banjo virtuoso), Granny ("sitdown" comedian), and Country Classics USA (12 piece stage show).

Tips: "We want artists who are willing to work hard to achieve success and songwriters that are skilled in their craft."

COUNTRY STAR ATTRACTIONS, 439 Wiley Ave., Franklin PA 16323. (814)432-4633. Contact: Norman Kelly. Booking agency. Represents artists and musical groups; currently handles 10 acts. Receives 10-15% commission. Reviews material for acts.

How to Contact: Prefers 7½ ips reel-to-reel and cassette with 1-4 songs and lyric sheet; include photo. SASE. Reports in 2 weeks.

Music: Mostly country; also bluegrass, gospel, rock or top 40/pop. Works primarily with vocalists, self-contained country shows and bar bands. Current acts include Junie Lou (country), Bob Stamper (country singer), Lady Brown Sugar (rock singer with band), and Woodsmoke (country dance band).

CRASH PRODUCTIONS, Box 40, Bangor ME 04401-0040. (207)794-6686. Manager: Jim Moreau. Booking agency. Represents individuals and groups; currently handles 9 acts. Receives 10-25% commission.

How to Contact: Query. Prefers cassette (or videocassette) with 4-8 songs. Include resume and photos. "We prefer to hear groups at an actual performance." SASE. Reports in 2 weeks.

Music: Mostly 50s-60s and country rock; also country. Works primarily with groups who perform at night clubs (with an average of 150-200 patrons) and outdoor events (festivals and fairs). Current acts include Tim Ferrell & Cabin Country Band (bluegrass), Mainly Country (country), Bushwhack (50s and 60s), Air Fare (top 40), Boot Leg (country rock), Sea Breeze (country rock), and Fox Run (country rock).

CROSBY MUSIC AGENCY, 7730 Herschel Ave., La Jolla CA 92037. (619)454-0383. Agent: Rhonda Gill. Booking agency. Deals primarily with San Diego artists. Represents artists and groups; currently handles 120 acts. Receives 10-15% commission.

How to Contact: Submit demo tape, photo and song list. Songwriters and artists may submit videocassette. "Evaluation usually within 2 weeks. SASE for return of material."

Music: Mostly contemporary and MOR; also jazz, rock (hard rock and country rock), top 40 and new wave. Works with wide variety of performers: show bands, dance bands, bar bands and duos. Current acts include Magic (5 piece bar/dance band), Ray Lipson (solo pianist), and Forcast (5-piece jazz band).

Tips: "Send a complete promotional package including a good photo, complete song list, and clear demo tape. At the present time, we are not interested in original material. However, we do have plenty of casual work for contemporary groups."

*CROSSCURRENTS MANAGEMENT GROUP, 3523 Old Petersburg Rd., Martinez GA 30907. (404)863-2694. President: Edward U. Huguenin. Management firm, booking agency and music publisher. Represents individual artists, groups and songwriters; currently handles 4 acts. Receives 10-20% commission. Reviews material for acts.
How to Contact: Prefers cassette (or VHS videocassette) with 2-5 songs. Reports in 2 weeks.
Music: Mostly country, rock and blues; also pop and R&B. Works primarily with singers/songwriters, vocalist and composers. Also works with "synthesist and numerous musicians playing music other than MOR." Current acts include Wallace Thomas, P.J. Blake and Lee Gilbert.
Tips: "Take time to carefully prepare your submitted tape. Try to make your presentation as professional as possible."

*CSK MANAGEMENT, 345 California Dr., Box 770-165, Burlingame CA 94011. (415)343-2262. Director: Christine Kradjian. Management and booking agency. Represents individual artists and groups; currently handles 18 acts. Receives 10-20% commission. Reviews material for acts.
How to Contact: Write or call first and obtain permission to submit. Prefers cassette (or VHS videocassette). "Include photo, resume, professional lead sheet, reviews, recommendations, list of previous successes, and goals." SASE. Reports in 6 weeks.
Music: Mostly classical, jazz and pop. Works primarily with pops/jazz and classical vocalists and ensembles. Current acts include Cesar Cancino (pops composer/pianist/arranger with Joan Baez), and Rudolf Haken (classical composer).

*DAS COMMUNICATIONS, LTD., 83 Riverside Dr., New York NY 10024. (212)877-0400. President: David Sonenberg. Management firm and music publisher. Represents individual artists, groups and songwriters; currently handles 10 acts. Reviews material for acts.
How to Contact: Prefers cassette (or ¾" or VHS videocassette) with 1-5 songs. SASE. Reports in 2 months.
Music: Pop/rock. Current acts include Southside Johnny & The Jukes, Jim Steinman and Bill Branigan.

DAWN PRODUCTIONS/INTERNATIONAL TALENT, Suite 1, 621 Parr City Center, Lancaster PA 17601. President: Joey Welz. Management firm, booking agency and record company (Caprice Records). Represents artists, groups and songwriters; currently handles 8 acts. Receives 5-50% commission. Reviews material for acts.
How to Contact: Prefers cassette with 4-8 songs. Does not return unsolicited material. Reports in 1 month "if we can use material."
Music: Mostly rock, country and top 40/pop; also easy listening and R&B. Works primarily with "commercial recording artists who sell records." Current acts include Joey Welz of Bill Haley's Comets (rock), Santo of Santo & Johnny, Gerry Granahan, and The Great Train Robbery Band (country/rock).
Tips: "Send commercial material good enough to be pressed on our label."

*THE EDWARD DE MILES COMPANY, Exchange Park, Box 45566, Dallas TX 75245. (214)954-8481. President & CEO: Edward De Miles. Vice President: J. Parrish Smith. Management firm, booking agency, entertainment promoter, and TV/radio broadcast productions. Represents film, television, radio and musical artists; currently handles 15 acts. Receives 10-20% commission.
How to Contact: Write first about your interest. Prefers cassette (or videocassette) with 3-5 songs, 8x10 photo and lyric sheet. "Copyright all material before submitting." SASE. Reports in 1 month.
Music: Dance-oriented, easy listening, gospel, R&B, soul and top 40/pop. Current acts include Stanley Williams (R&B/soul artists, Hotline Records); Kilo (dance-oriented, Artista Records); Crystal (dance-oriented, Artista Records); Klas (dance band); and Mike Clive (radio announcer).
Tips: "Performers need to be well prepared with their presentations (equipment, showmanship a must.)"

LARRY DELROSE MANAGEMENT, Box 9675, Palm Springs CA 92263. (619)320-6335. President: Larry Delrose. Management firm, booking agency, record company (Angi) and music publisher (Lasko Delrose Music). Represents individual artists, groups and songwriters; currently handles 3 acts. Receives 10-25% commission. Reviews material for acts.
How to Contact: Prefers cassette (or VHS videocassette) with 2-6 songs and lyric sheet. SASE. Reports in 3 weeks.
Music: Pop, rock and R&B. Works primarily with vocalists and show bands. Current acts include The Kings, Danny Laskowitz, King Orchestra, Ron King and Bobby King.
Tips: "Have a gimmick. Be prepared, be professional."

MARV DENNIS & ASSOCIATES, INC., 1002 18th Ave. S, Nashville TN 37212. (615)320-7022. Management firm, booking agency and music publisher (Denwright). Represents artists, groups and songwriters; currently handles 30 acts. Receives 10-20% commission. Reviews material for acts.
How to Contact: Prefers cassette (or videocassette) with 3-5 songs and lyric sheet. "Include b&w or color photo of artist. Mark package Attn: Brian Kovach." Does not return unsolicited material. Reports in 1 month "only if used.".
Music: Mostly country and top 40/pop; also dance-oriented and all types of rock. Works primarily with dance and bar bands. Current acts include Wright Bros. (country), Longrider (country pop) and Kathy Lee (country).

*DEW PRODUCTIONS LTD., #102, 1011 First St. SW, Calgary, Alberta T2R 1J2 Canada. (403)269-3632. Consultant: Karry Conway. Booking agency. Represents individual artists and groups. Receives 10-20% commission.
How to Contact: Prefers cassette (or videocassette). SAE and IRC.
Music: Mostly top 40 and country rock; also MOR, R&B and rock. Works primarily with dance bands and show groups. Current acts include Gene Williams, Dodge Brothers, and The Walkers.
Tips: "We require complete promo materials, song lists, pricing and references."

*DIRECTION FOUR MANAGEMENT, 200-70 Albert St., Winnipeg, Manitoba R3B 1E9 Canada. (204)947-9200. Vice President: Kerry B. Renaud. Management firm and music publisher (Direction Four Music). Represents individual artists, groups and songwriters from Canada; currently handles 4 acts. Reviews material for acts.
How to Contact: Prefers cassette (or VHS videocassette) with 4 songs and lyric or lead sheet. SAE and IRC. Reports in 5 weeks.
Music: Mostly country/pop, pop and children's. Current acts include Double Eagle, Danny Kramer and Fred Penner.
Tips: "Actively looking for contemporary country material with strong vocal potential and crossover potential."

*DIRTY POOL ARTISTES, Box 146, Rushcutters Bay 2011, Sydney, Australia. Phone: (03)360-2755. Manager: Rod Willis, John Woodruff and Keith Welsh. Management firm and booking agency. Represents individual artists and groups; currently handles 4 acts. Reviews material for acts.
How to Contact: Write first and obtain permission to submit. Prefers cassette (or videocassette). Does not return unsolicited material. Reports in 1 month.
Music: Mostly rock and pop. Works primarily with rock bands. Current acts include Icehouse, Angel City, DoReMi, and Boom Crash Opera.

DMR AGENCY, Box 401, Fayetteville NY 13066-0401. (315)637-4471. Contact: David M. Rezak. Booking agency. Represents individuals and groups; currently handles 25 acts. Receives 10-15% commission.
How to Contact: Submit cassette (or videocassette) with 1-4 songs and press kit. SASE.
Music: Mostly rock (all styles); also jazz, R&B and progressive. Works primarily with bar and concert bands; all kinds of rock for schools, clubs, concerts, etc. Current acts include Kingsnakes (blues), Screentest (pop) and Zoid (rock).
Tips: "We strictly do booking and have no involvement in artists repetoire."

*COL. BUSTER DOSS PRESENTS, Box 7181, Tyler TX 75711. (214)561-1484. Producer: Col. Buster Doss. Management firm, booking agency, record company (Stardust) and music publisher (Buster Doss Music/BMI). Represents individual artists, groups, songwriters and shows; currently handles 15 acts. Receives 15% commission. Reviews material for acts.
How to Contact: Prefers cassette with 2-4 songs and lyric sheet. SASE. Reports in 2 weeks.
Music: Country, gospel and progressive. Works primarily with show and dance bands and single acts. Current acts include Rooster Quantrell, Shawn Lee and Keith Sewell.

BARRY DRAKE ENTERPRISES, Red Kill Rd., Fleischmanns NY 12430. (914)254-4565. Contact: Barry Drake, Patricia Padla. Management firm and booking agency. Represents individuals, groups and songwriters; currently handles 2 acts. Receives 10-20% commission. Reviews material for acts.
How to Contact: Query or submit demo tape. Prefers cassette with 1-3 songs and lyric sheet. SASE. Reports in 1 month.
Music: Bluegrass, blues, country, folk, MOR, progressive, rock and top 40/pop. Works primarily with solo singer/songwriters. Current acts include Barry Drake and Larry Mangum.

*DUET ARTISTS' MANAGEMENT, Box 2144, Kankakee IL 60901. (815)933-1958. Owner: Patricia M. Hudson. Management firm. Represents local and regional individual artists, groups and songwrit-

ers; currently handles 5 acts. Receives 10-20% commission. Reviews material for acts.
How to Contact: Prefers cassette (or VHS videocassette) with lyric sheet. SASE. Reports in 1 month.
Music: Mostly R&B, top 40 and country; also gospel. Works primarily with R&B dance band/top 40.
Current acts include Grand Staff, West Phillips and Vital Signs.
Tips: "We will listen to all material submitted but want only artists that have their 'act together'."

*LEO J. EIFFERT, JR., Box 5412, Buena Park CA 90620. (213)513-8120. Owner: Leo J. Eiffert, Jr.
Management firm, record company (Young Country/Plain Country) and music publisher (Young Country/Eb-Tide BMI). Represents individual artists, groups and songwriters; currently handles 3 acts. Receives 15% commission. Reviews material for acts.
How to Contact: Prefers cassette with 3 songs and lyric or lead sheet. SASE. Reports in 6 weeks.
Music: Mostly country and country/rock. Works primarily with songwriters. Current acts include
Crawfish Band, Teeci Clark and Leo J. Eiffert, Jr.

*GINO EMPRY PUBLIC RELATIONS & PERSONAL MANAGEMENT SERVICES, INC., Suite 104,
25 Wood St., The Maples, Toronto, Ontario M4Y 2P9 Canada. (416)977-1153. President: Gino Empry.
Management firm, booking agency and public relations firm. Represents artists, groups and songwriters; currently handles 25 acts. Receives 10-15% commission. Reviews material for acts.
How to Contact: Write first. Prefers cassette (or videocassette) with "3 selections or 10 minutes long
maximum." SAE and IRC. Reports in 1 month.
Music: Mostly MOR; also dance-oriented, and jazz. Works primarily with vocalists and dance bands.
Current acts include Spitfire, Michael Danso and Peggy Lee (night club artist).
Tips: "Send full background and current photos with demo."

ENCORE ENTERTAINMENT, Box 1259, Lake Dallas TX 75065. (214)484-2664. President: John S.
Milam. Management firm (Milam Music Group), booking agency (Encore Entertainment) and music
publisher (Bayou Songbook). Represents groups, songwriters and country artists with label deals. Deals
with regional artists (Texas/Louisiana) or artists from anywhere; currently handles 6 acts. Receives 10%
commission. Reviews material for acts.
How to Contact: Will accept unsolicited submissions as long as material is copyrighted. Prefers cassette and lyric sheet. Does not return unsolicited material. Reports in 2 weeks.
Music: Contemporary country music. Works only with country artists. Acts include Canyon, Bayou,
Natalie & Heartbreak, "Southern Reigh," and White Oak. "We are only interested in material to be cut
by our artists."

ENCORE TALENT, INC., 2137 Zercher Rd., San Antonio TX 78209-1194. (512)822-2655. President:
Ronnie Spillman. Management firm and booking agency. Represents individual artists and groups.
Deals with local and "name" artists; currently handles 5 acts. Receives 15% commission.
How to Contact: Call first and obtain permission to submit. Prefers cassette. Does not return unsolicited material. "We will contact ASAP only if material is selected and can be used."
Music: Country. Works primarily with country vocalists and dance bands. Current acts include Moe
Bandy, Johnny Bush and Johnny Duncan.

*ENTERTAINMENT EXPRESS MANAGEMENT AND PRODUCTIONS, Suite 200, 7870 Olentangy
Valley Centre, Worthington OH 43085. (614)885-2245. President: Dan Silveous. Management firm
and booking agency. Represents individual artists and groups from the Midwest; currently handles 2
acts. Receives 14-18% commission. Reviews material for acts.
How to Contact: Prefers cassette (or videocassette of 15 minutes maximum) with 3-6 songs and lyric
sheet. "Please include a cover letter stating the availability of your group and how much you wish to
work. Also include a schedule of previous gigs and average income." SASE. Reports in 3 weeks.
Music: Commercial rock, top 40 and lounge rock. Works primarily with "commercial rock, high energy shows with 50% original material." Current acts include Hollywood, Bran Silveous, and John Castetter.

*ENTERTAINMENT INTERNATIONAL—COBRA, Box 7148, Station A, Canton OH 44705-0148.
(216)454-4843. National President: Don Bennafield. Management firm, booking agency, music publisher (Trident Enterprises) and member of Global Trade Association of Entertainment Industry. Represents individual artists, groups and songwriters; currently handles 3 acts. Receives 10-20% commission. Reviews material for acts.
How to Contact: Write first and obtain permission to submit. Prefers cassette (or VHS videocassette)
with 4-5 songs and lryic or lead sheet. SASE. Reports in 3 weeks.
Music: R&B, country and rock. Current acts include Unique, Sirene and Chico.

Tips: "Put together a good portfolio. All materials are scrutinized carefully by Paul Riser, well-renowned songwriter and composer."

ENTERTAINMENT MANAGEMENT ENTERPRISES, 454 Alps Rd., Wayne NJ 07470. (201)694-3333. President: Richard Zielinski. Management firm. Represents artists and musical groups; currently handles 2 acts. Receives minimum of 20% commission. Reviews material for acts.
How to Contact: Prefers cassette (or VHS or ¾" videocassette) with 4-6 songs and lyric sheet. Include 8x10 glossy and bio. "Let us know, by mail or phone, about any New York area performances so we can attend." SASE. Reports in 2 weeks.
Music: Mostly rock. Works primarily with rock groups with vocals, synthesized rock and contemporary singers. Current acts include Voyager (progressive rock) and Sinful (metal).
Tips: "A good press kit is important."

*EVENTS UNLIMITED, INC., Box 22333, Cleveland OH 44122. (216)974-9100. President: John S. Latimer, Jr. Management firm, booking agency, record company (Play Records), music publisher (Latitunes Publishing) and television show (Good Rockin' Tonight). Represents individual artists, groups and lecturers; currently handles 12 acts. Receives 10-15% commission. Reviews material for acts.
How to Contact: Prefers cassette (or VHS or ¾" videocassette) with 4-5 songs and lyric sheet. Does not return unsolicited material. Reports in 1 month.
Music: Mostly rock, new wave and metal. Works primarily with rock groups and dance bands. Current acts include Pete Best.
Tips: "Be professional and persistent but not bothersome; correspond by mail."

*FALCON PRODUCTIONS, 3080 Lenworth Dr., Mississaugo, Ontario L4X 2G1 Canada. (416)625-3865. Publicist: Rod Albrecht. Management firm and music publisher (Peregrine). Represents individual artists, groups and songwriters; currently handles 3 acts. Reviews material for acts.
How to Contact: Prefers cassette (or VHS videocassette) with 3 songs and lyric sheet. Does not return unsolicited material. Reports in 2 weeks.
Music: Rock, pop and R&B. Works primarily with rock bands. Current acts include Refugee, Siam, and Kelly & The Shadow.

*FANTASMA PRODUCTIONS, INC., 2000 S. Dixie Hwy., West Palm Beach FL 33401. (305)832-6397. Agent: Henry Rosquete. Management firm and booking agency. Represents groups; currently handles 12 acts. Receives 10-20% commission. Reviews material for acts.
How to Contact: Submit demo tape by mail.

FILM ARTISTS ASSOCIATES, Suite 104, 470 S. San Vicente Blvd., Los Angeles CA 90048. (213)651-1700. Music Department Head: Martha Henard. Management firm and booking agency. Represents individual artists, groups and songwriters. Receives 10-20% commission "depending upon artist and deal made." Reviews material for acts.
How to Contact: "Do not call!" Prefers cassette, pictures, resumes, and lyric or lead sheet. SASE.
Music: Mostly MOR/rock, hard rock and blues/country; also gospel and jazz. Works with solo and group artists. Current acts include Syzygy, U.S. Network, and Beverly Hills Unlisted Jazz Band.
Tips: Submit "good quality tapes and pictures, have a desire to work, and be available."

FIREBALL MANAGEMENT, Box 588, Freeport NY 11520. (516)223-1244. President: Joel Peskin. Management firm. Receives 20-25% commission. Reviews material for acts. "We also book nationwide tours."
How to Contact: Query by mail. Prefers cassette with 2-5 songs and lead sheet. SASE. Reports in 2 weeks.
Music: Rock (hard). Works primarily with hard rock concert groups.
Tips: "Be dedicated and hardworking."

FISHER & ASSOCIATES ENTERTAINMENT, INC., 2238 Park Rd., Charlotte NC 28203. (704)332-9090. President: Dave Fisher. Management firm and booking agency. Represents musical groups in the Southeastern states including North Carolina, South Carolina, Virginia, Georgia, Tennessee, Alabama, Mississippi and Florida; currently handles 40 groups. Receives 10-20% commission. Reviews material for acts.
How to Contact: Prefers cassette (or videocassette) with 6-8 songs. "Include resume, bio, references and publicity photos." SASE. Reports in 1 month.
Music: Dance-oriented, funk, rock (commercial and danceable) and top 40/pop. Works primarily with club and lounge groups (4 to 8 pieces), and dance groups suitable for the young adult market (ages 16-40). Current acts include The Creek (rock), Top Secret (top 40/variety), Dreamerz (top 40/rock), The

Spontanes (top 40/show/variety), Panama (rock), The Ticket (top 40), Nuthin' Fancy (pop country), East Coast (top 40/variety), Special Delivery (top 40/variety), and Gaston (funk).

*FIVE STAR ENTERTAINMENT, 3701 25th Ave. SW, Naples FL 33964. (813)455-2963 or 455-2696. Assistant Manager: Sid Kleiner. Management firm, booking agency and record company (Top-Star). Represents individual artists and groups; currently handles over 50 acts. Receives 10-25% commission. Reviews material for acts.
How to Contact: Prefers cassette (or VHS videocassette) with 4-8 songs and lyric sheet. SASE. Reports in 1 month.
Music: Mostly top 40, MOR and country; also ethnic, pop and rock. Works primarily with organized dance bands and self-contained singles. Current acts include Sid Kleiner ("Gents of Jazz"), Ron Hart ("Upbeat"), and Johnny Dee ("All Stars").
Tips: "Furnish as much information as possible: glossies, VHS video demo tapes, song lists, equipment lists, availability, price per single engagement, price per on-going weekly engagement, costuming, etc."

FLASH ATTRACTIONS AGENCY, 38 Prospect St., Warrensburg NY 12885. (518)623-9313. Agent: Wally Chester. Management firm and booking agency. Represents artists and groups; currently handles 106 acts. Receives 15-20% commission. Reviews material for acts. "We are celebrating 35 years in business, and are fully licensed by the American Federation of Musicians and the state of New York."
How to Contact: Query by mail. Prefers cassette with 1-6 songs and lead and lyric sheet. Songwriters and artists may submit "professionally done" videocassettes. SASE. Reports in 1 month.
Music: Mostly country, calypso, Hawaiian and MOR; also blues, dance, easy listening, gospel, jazz, top 40, Spanish and country rock. Works primarily with vocalists, dance bands, bar bands, floor show groups and lounge acts. Current acts include Prince Pablo's Caribbean Extravaganza (steel band and floor show), "Mirinda" and the American Gentlemen (country music show), The Country Belles (all girl variety band), The Ronnie Prophet Country Music Show (Canada's #1 country music TV star), North Country Preservation Dixieland Jazz Band, "Kaena" and her Polynesian Paradise Revue, and Wally Chester's Chordsmen Trio (lounge act).

THE FRANKLYN AGENCY, #312, 1010 Hammond St., West Hollywood CA 90069. (213)272-6080. President: Audrey P. Franklyn. Management firm, public relations firm, SRS/Hollywood judge and American Song Festival judge. Represents artists, musical groups and businesses; currently handles 7 acts. Receives 5-15% commission. Reviews material for acts.
How to Contact: Query by mail, arrange personal interview, or submit demo. Prefers cassette or videocassette with 4 songs and lead sheet. SASE. Reports in 1 month.
Music: Mosly rock, country and pop; also blues, easy listening, gospel, jazz,.MOR, progressive and R&B. Works primarily with rock bands and single soloist singers. Current acts include Marilyn Johnson (pop singer), Marco Valenti (pop and semi-classical), and Lennart Flindt (jazz pianist).
Tips: "No amateurs—be funded for promotional efforts."

FREADE SOUNDS ENTERTAINMENT & RECORDING STUDIO, Rt. 1, Box 231, Chattaroy WA 99003. (509)292-2201. Agent/Engineer: Tom Lapansky. Booking agency and recording studio. Represents groups; currently handles 25 acts. Receives 10-15% commission. Reviews material for acts.
How to Contact: Query by mail or submit demo. Prefers cassette with 4-6 songs and pictures/song list. SASE. Reports in 2 weeks.
Music: Mostly rock 'n' roll and production rock; also R&B and top 40/pop. Works primarily with dance/concert groups. Current acts include Warning (top 40 production rock); Nasty Habit (top 40 production rock group); D.V.B. (top 40 production rock group); Justin Sayne (top 40 production rock); and Fanatic (top 40 production rock).

FREDDIE CEE ATTRACTIONS, 193 Konhaus Rd., Mechanicsburg PA 17055. (717)766-7644. Contact: Fred Clousher. Booking agency. Represents groups and comedy and novelty acts in Pennsylvania, Maryland, Virginia, West Virginia, New York, New Jersey and Ohio; currently handles approximately 75 acts. Receives 10-25% commission.
How to Contact: "Performers submit cassette or VHS videocassette with 5-10 songs, 8x10 glossies, credits or current routing schedule, instrumentation of group, partial song list, and approximate fee expected." Bands should submit tape in VHS format, preferably recorded before a live audience and at least 20 minutes in length." Does not return materials. Reports in 3 weeks.
Music: Mostly country, ethnic/novelty and top 40; also bluegrass, gospel, easy listening, Hawaiian and German. Works primarily with "marketable groups in country, country rock, bluegrass, gospel, variety show groups, etc." Current acts include the Hawaiian Revue '88 (floor show and dance act), Michael Lee Clayton (comedy and variety dance music), Little Jimmy Dickens (country), and Jay Kirk (comic).

*PETER FREEDMAN ENTERTAINMENT, Suite 22, 238 E. 58th St., New York NY 10022. (212)832-1733. President: Peter Freedman. Management firm and booking agency. Estab. 1986. Represents individual artists and groups; currently handles 2 acts. Receives 10-20% commission. Reviews material for acts.
How to Contact: Prefers cassette (or VHS videocassette) with 3 songs. Does not return unsolicited material. Reports in 3 weeks.
Music: Mostly rock/pop, new music, MOR and variety; also rock songwriters and comedians. Works primarily with pop/rock original acts. Current acts include The Sharks and The Ocean Blue.
Tips: "Have a very serious and realistic attitude. Aspiring acts must be dedicated and motivated."

FREEDOM PRODUCTIONS, INC., Box 20005, Westland Station, Jackson MS 39209. (601)366-9450. Manager: Jesse Thompson, Jr. Management firm, booking agency and production company. Represents artists, groups and songwriters; currently handles 3 acts. Receives 15-20% commission. Reviews material for acts.
How to Contact: Query by mail. Prefers cassette (or videocassette) with 3-7 songs. SASE. Reports in 3 weeks.
Music: R&B and pop. Works primarily with dance, show groups and single performers. Current acts include Freedom (R&B show group), Unity One (R&B show band), and Dwight Ross (R&B artist).

FROST & FROST ENTERTAINMENT, 3985 W. Taft Dr., Spokane WA 99208. (509)325-1777. Agent: Dick Frost. Booking agency. Represents individuals and groups; currently handles 15 acts. Receives 10-15% commission.
How to Contact: Query. Prefers cassette with 5 songs and lyric sheet. Include information on past appearances, as well as list of references. SASE. Reports in 2 weeks.
Music: Country and MOR, dance-oriented, easy listening, modern country, rock (country and 50s) and top 40/pop (no heavy metal). Works primarily with dance bands, show bands and individual artists. Current acts include Big Tiny Little, Kay Austin (C&W/MOR act), and Stagecoach West.
Tips: "Send promo package, glossy and performing locations."

GAIL AND RICE PRODUCTIONS, 11845 Mayfield, Livonia MI 48150. (313)427-9300. Vice President: Chris Nordman. Booking agency. Represents individuals and groups; currently handles 25 acts. Receives 10-20% commission.
How to Contact: Prefers cassette with 3-6 songs and lead sheet. Does not return unsolicited material. Reports in 3 weeks.
Music: Bluegrass, children's, country, dance-oriented, jazz and top 40/pop. Works primarily with "self-contained groups (1-8 people), show and dance music, listening groups, and individual name or semi-name attractions." Current acts include Dream Dance (vocal/dance act), Glenn Haywood (comedian/ventriloquist), and Tim Rowlands (comedy/juggling).

GALLIN-MOREY ASSOCIATES, 8730 Sunset Blvd., Los Angeles CA 90069. (213)659-5593. Manager: Barry Josephson. Management firm. Represents individual artists, groups and established recording stars; currently handles 6 acts. Reviews material for acts.
How to Contact: Write first and obtain permission to submit. Prefers cassette. "Contact must be made first before we can accept submissions." Does not return unsolicited material. Reports in 4 weeks.
Music: Pop, R&B and country. Works primarily with "self contained groups and solo artists who are also songwriters." Current acts include Dolly Parton, Pointer Sisters and Patti LaBelle.
Tips: "Submit only finished demos. Rough cassettes are very hard to listen to."

BOB GALLION PRODUCTIONS, Box 78, Fairview OH 43736. (614)758-5812. President: R.H. Gallion. Management firm and booking agency. Represents individuals, groups and songwriters; currently handles 44 acts.
How to Contact: Write first or submit demo tape. Prefers cassette. Does not return unsolicited material. Reports in 2 months.
Music: Mostly country; also bluegrass, folk, gospel, MOR and top 40/pop. Works primarily with country and gospel artists and groups. Current acts include Bob Gallion (country), Patti Powell (country), The Younger Brothers Band, and Susquehanna River Band.

*GANGLAND ARTISTS, 707-810 W. Broadway, Vancouver, British Columbia V5Z 1J8 Canada. (604)872-0052. Contact: Allen Moy. Management firm, production house and music publisher. Represents artists and songwriters.
How to Contact: Prefers cassette (or VHS videocassette) and lyric sheet. SAE and IRC. Reports in 1 month.
Music: Rock, pop and R&B.

*G.V. GARRETT PRODUCTIONS, INC., 6938 Kimkris Ct., Indianapolis IN 46278. (317)872-9955. President: George V. Garrett. Management firm and booking agency. Represents individual artists and groups; currently handles 3 acts. Receives 20% commission. Reviews material for acts.
How to Contact: Call first and obtain permission to submit. Prefers cassette with 4-6 songs. Does not return unsolicited material. Reports in 2 weeks.
Music: Mostly "Bluegrass that lends itself to be more progressive than the 'die hard' traditionalist style"; also country and country-rock. Works primarily with "Bluegrass bands that are proven winners (all of our bands have superior vocals and instrumentalists)." Current acts include Pine Mountain, Classified Grass and Union Station.

GLO MANAGEMENT CORP., 98 Hamilton Park, Columbus OH 43203. (614)461-9555. President: Pablo Davis. Management firm. Represents artists, groups and songwriters; currently handles 3 acts. Negotiates fees and royalties. Reviews material for acts.
How to Contact: Prefers cassette with minimum of 3 songs and lead sheet. SASE. Reports in 2 weeks.
Music: Jazz, R&B and pop. Current acts include Dwain Mitchell, Victor Burks, Stick, Griffin, Twala Jones, Allen Burney, Eclypse, and Ayrforce.

DAVID GOLIATH AGENCY, Box 11960, Chicago IL 60611. (312)561-0027. Booking Manager: Howard Hagler. Management firm and booking agency. Represents artists and groups; currently handles 25 acts. Receives 15-20% commission. Reviews material for acts.
How to Contact: Write first and obtain permission to submit. Prefers cassette (or VHS videocassette) with 3-5 songs. "Send 8x10 glossy and promotional material. Include songlist, previous engagements, recording experience, etc." SASE. Reports in 2 months.
Music: Mostly R&B/funk, soul/top 40 and pop; also blues, church/religious, dance-oriented disco funk, gospel and soul. Works primarily with dance bands and show bands that "entertain and appeal to broad audiences." Current acts include "Lovers" (R&B/soul), Stutz (progressive rock), Malcolm Simmons (blues/R&B), Centerfold (R&B/pop), Jadu (Urban contemporary), Image (R&B/soul), and Henry Lee Lincoln (blues).

GARY GOOD MANAGEMENT, 2500 NW 39th St., Oklahoma OK 73112. (405)947-1503. Contact: Gary Good. Management firm. Represents artists, groups and songwriters mainly from Oklahoma; currently handles 12 acts. Receives 15-20% commission. Reviews material for acts.
How to Contact: Prefers cassette with 1-5 songs and lyric sheet. Songwriters and artists may submit videocassete of 10-15 minutes maximum. SASE. Reports ASAP.
Music: Mostly country; also pop country, MOR, dance, easy listening and top 40/pop. Works primarily with solo vocalists and variety club bands. Current acts include The Tim Sullvian Band, Julie Grafa (vocalist), Christi Dannemiller (vocalist/songwriter), Andrea Vaughn (vocalist), Colleen Sheppard (vocalist), Sailor Band, Focus (band), and Rusty Aldridge & Susan Wright (duo).

BILL GRAHAM MANAGEMENT, Box 1994, San Francisco CA 94101. (415)864-0815. Creative Development: Mick Brigden. Management firm. Represents artists and groups; currently handles 6 acts. Reviews material for acts.
How to Contact: Prefers cassette and lead sheet. SASE. Reports as soon as possible.
Music: Mostly rock and pop ballads; also progressive, R&B, and top 40/pop. Works primarily with original songwriters and vocalists; current acts include Santana, Marc Anthony Thompson, John Hiatt, Charlie Peacock, and Bob Dylan.
Tips: "Rather than emphasize commercial sound, emphasize originality."

GREAT PLAINS ASSOCIATES, INC., Suite 208, 706 Massachusetts, Lawrence KS 66044. (913)841-4444. Contact: Mark Swanson or Stuart Doores. Booking agency. Represents groups in Midwest; currently handles 45 acts. Receives 15-20% commission. Reviews material for acts.
How to Contact: Prefers cassette with 3-5 songs. Artists may submit videocassette. SASE.
Music: Mostly rock; also country, R&B and soul. Works primarily with dance bands "for college mini-concerts to bar band dances." Current acts include Valentine and the Very Wealthy (dance band), Homestead Grays (dance band), Unidos (soul), and Blue Wave (beach band).
Tips: "We are constantly looking for and expect our artists to have a *definite* idea of what they want and where they are going."

GREIF-GARRIS MANAGEMENT, Mezzanine Suite 6, 368 N. LaCienga Blvd., Los Angeles CA 90048. (213)653-4780. Vice President: Sid Garris. Management firm. Represents artists, groups and songwriters; currently handles 3 acts. Receives minimum 15% commission. Reviews material for acts.
How to Contact: Write first and obtain permission to submit. Prefers cassette with 3-5 songs. SASE. Reports ASAP.

Music: All types of "good music." Current acts include The New Christy Minstrels (folk), The Crusaders (jazz fusion), and Nelson Riddle Orchestra (MOR).
Tips: "Artists and writers should be critical enough to ensure that what is being sent is the *best* of their ability."

GREIL-HOOPER MANAGEMENT, (formerly Vision Management), 59 Music Square W., Nashville TN 37203. (615)726-0777. Personal Managers: Kathy Hooper and Steven Greil. Management firm. Represents individual artists and groups; currently handles 4 acts. Reviews material for acts.
How to Contact: Call first and obtain permission to submit. Prefers cassette and lyric sheet. SASE. Reports in 1 month.
Music: Country. Works primarily with vocalists. Current acts include Helen Cornelius, Con Hunley, The O'Kanes, and Pam Tillis.
Tips: "Artists must have label deal and songwriters' music must be published."

BOB HALE TALENT/LJ PRODUCTIONS, 227 Prospectors, Billings MT 59105-1662. (406)245-2174. President: Laurie Jensen. Management firm and booking agency. Represents artists, groups and songwriters; currently handles 15 acts. Receives 12-15% commission (booking) to 20% (management). Reviews material for acts.
How to Contact: Prefers 7½ ips reel-to-reel or cassette (or "natural," unedited videocassette) with maximum 5 songs. "Demo should emphasize vocal with minimum amount of production." SASE. Reports in 2 weeks.
Music: Country, show and dance-oriented, rock (50s and 60s), and top 40/pop. Works primarily with bar and dance bands, and show and dance bands. Current acts include Prairie Fire (country/country rock), Boot Hill and Mirror Image (50s/60s country/rock and top 40/pop acts).

BILL HALL ENTERTAINMENT & EVENTS, 138 Frog Hollow Rd., Churchville PA 18966. (215)357-5189. Contact: William B. Hall III. Booking agency and production company. Represents individuals and groups; currently handles 30 acts. Receives 15% commission. Reviews material for acts, depending on engagement and type of attraction.
How to Contact: "Letter of inquiry preferred as initial contact." Prefers cassette with 2-3 songs "and photos, promo material, and record or tape." Does not return unsolicited material. Reports in 1 month.
Music: Marching band, circus and novelty ethnic. Works primarily with "unusual or novelty attractions in musical line, preferably those that appeal to family groups." Current acts include Fralinger and Polish-American Philadelphia Championship Mummers String Bands (marching and concert group); Erwin Chandler Orchestra (show band); and "Mr. Polynesian" Show Band and Hawaiian Revue (ethnic group).

GEOFFREY HANSEN ENTERPRISES, LTD., Box 63, Orinda CA 94563. (415)937-6469. Artist Relations: J. Malcom Baird. Management firm. Represents artists, groups and songwriters. Receives 15-25% commission. Also paid on a contract basis. Reviews material for acts.
How to Contact: Submit demo tape, lead sheet, photograph and cover letter. Prefers cassette. SASE.
Music: Top 40/country, R&B and MOR in English, Spanish, French and Japanese. Works with top 40 and country artists; recording acts and overseas international stars. Current acts include Bert Friel (MOR/Hawaiian artist),Pilita Corrales (top 40 Spanish/English MOR).
Tips: "We are always looking for new talent. Anyone who has a demo and is interested in the international scope of the entertainment industry, contact us. We are ready to listen. We are looking for female vocalists, girl groups and show bands to tour overseas in Bermuda, Jamaica, Bahamas, Hawaii, Japan and various foreign markets. Send photos, bio, song list, demo tape and SASE. All styles of music wanted."

HARMONY ARTISTS, INC., Penthouse, 8833 Sunset Blvd., Los Angeles CA 90069. (213)659-9644. President: Michael Dixon. Vice President: J.D. Ross. Booking agency. Represents groups; currently handles 60 acts. Receives 10-15% commission. Reviews material for acts.
How to Contact: Prefers cassette with 3-5 songs and lyric sheet, photo and promotional material. Reports in 2 weeks.
Music: Easy listening, MOR, progressive, rock and top 40/pop. Current acts include Ice, Bank, City Lights, Midwest Coast, Taxi, and Mick Smiley.

GEORGE HARNESS ASSOCIATES, 1 Timberline Dr., Springfield IL 62707. (217)529-8550. President: George Harness. Management firm and booking agency. Represents artists and groups. Receives 10-20% commission. Reviews material for acts.
How to Contact: Query by mail. Prefers cassette or videocassette with 6-8 songs and lyric sheet. SASE. Reports in 2 weeks.

Close-up

Anne Murray
Recording Artist

"I've never written a song in my life," says Anne Murray, one of Canada's most successful recording artists. When she began her singing career some 17 years ago, she "didn't have any burning desire to write. The songs were all there. And now it would just be hard work. A lot of people think you just sit down and are inspired. Or all of a sudden in the middle of the night you wake up and write a song. Well, that doesn't happen. It's very time-consuming."

Naturally for an artist who doesn't write songs, it's crucial to find the right material from outside writers, and while Murray doesn't have time to compose, she does spend a lot of time choosing her own material. She explains that she gets most of her songs from "reputable publishers, publishers we've dealt with in the past, and songwriters I know personally or whose songs I've sung before." Murray says she records some songs by Canadian songwriters and others by American songwriters—it doesn't really matter as long as it's good material.

It's clear from her long career of releasing hits like "Snowbird" and "You Needed Me," that Murray can hear potential in demos and is able to choose material that not only suits her, but will also be received well by her audience. But there's no formula in selecting songs, she says. "All it is, really, is I listen to the song, I like it and I do it. It's so basic I can't even pinpoint it. I go very much by instinct and gut reaction. There's no checklist or anything, it's just a matter of personal taste."

One song she liked but had a hard time convincing others it was a hit, was "You Needed Me," one of her biggest successes. "I listened to it after I'd listened to about 500 songs, and I didn't hear anything but I did put it aside, just casually. Then I went back and listened to it about two weeks later, and I actually had to sit down. I couldn't believe how good it was and that I hadn't reacted the first time. But you understand why, when your ears are tired you just don't really care any more."

After recording the song for an album, she found out "they weren't even going to release 'You Needed Me' as a single. I had to go to the president of Capitol Records and say, 'Will you please go with me on this one. We have to put this song out!' And he went along with it."

That song was, as many of Anne Murray's hits were, a country/pop crossover. With her last two albums she has tried to appeal once again to a more pop-oriented audience. "I *was* established as a pop artist at one time," Murray explains. "And then the dance music started to happen, and no one was listening to lyrics any more. Some of that music was wonderful, but I kind of got lost in the shuffle. So now it's just a matter of trying to get back on top 40 radio. People are listening again."

Murray has always had control over her own career, from choosing her own songs (and stylistic direction) to dictating her own touring schedule (she refuses to be away from her family for more than twelve days at a time). She has also insisted that she live and record in Toronto rather than move to a U.S. music center. She claims, "It's not difficult at all. The studios here are as good as any in the world. And I can fly directly from Toronto to any place. You'd be surprised the number of musicians who live and record here. Loverboy, Rush, Bryan Adams,

Corey Hart, Gordon Lightfoot—most of them now can do that. In the old days, Paul Anka, Joni Mitchell, Neil Young—they had to move. No one was paying attention to them. That's not necessary any more. You can live anywhere now."

Julie Wesling Whaley

———

Music: Mostly MOR and top 40/pop; also dance. Current acts include Oliver, Earl Turner & Earl Turner Group, and Moses & Highbrows (all show & dance acts).

*ARNIE HARRIS PRODUCTIONS, 26011 Red Bluff Dr., Calabasas CA 91302. (818)880-5540. President: Peggy March. Management firm and music publisher (Peg Leg Music). Represents local individual artists, songwriters and many European soloists. Currently handles 3 acts. Receives 15% commission. Reviews material for acts.
How to Contact: Prefers cassette with 3 songs and lyric sheet. SASE. Reports in 10 days.
Music: Mostly pop, rock and country; also "melodies needing lyrics." Works primarily with "vocalists with recording potential . . . writers of own material." Current acts include Peggy March, Ed Lojeski, and Jurgen Marcus (West Germany).
Tips: "Demos do not have to be 'major productions'. Clarity of melody line and a legible lyric sheet is important."

HAT BAND MUSIC, 210 25th Ave. N., Nashville TN 37203. Professional Manager: Douglas Casmus. Management firm and publishing company (Hat Band Music/BMI, Kimtra Music/ASCAP). Represents artists and songwriters; currently handles 3 acts. Reviews material for acts.
How to Contact: Cassettes only with 1-2 songs and typed lyric sheet. Does not return any material. "No SASE. No phone calls please." Reports only if interested.
Music: Country, rock and novelty. Works primarily with major recording artists. Current acts include Charlie Daniels Band (country rock), Dobie Gray (country), and Dickey Betts (country).
Tips: "Be honest and very critical of your own work. It must be as good or better than what's on the radio or in the record stores. If it's not, keep improving until it is."

*HAUTE ROCK MANAGEMENT, 220 12A St. NE, Calgary, Alberta T2E 4R7 Canada. (403)269-8526. President: Stephan T. Poulos. Management firm, booking agency, record company (Haute Rock Records) and music publisher (Haute Rock Music). Represents individual artists, groups and songwriters; currently handles 5 acts. Receives variable commission. Reviews material for acts.
How to Contact: Prefers cassette (or VHS videocassette) with 3-4 songs and lyric or lead sheet. SAE and IRC.
Music: Mostly rock, pop and country; also R&B. Works primarily with vocalists, rock bands, R&B bands and country bands. Current acts include Ted Moore & The Border, Derek and Cindy Warren.

*HEADQUARTERS ENTERTAINMENT CORP., #436, 366 Adelaide St. E., Toronto, Ontario M5A 3X9 Canada. (416)363-7363. President: Wayne Thompson. Mangement firm.. Represents individual artists and groups; currently handles 1 act. Reviews material for acts.
How to Contact: Prefers cassette and lyric or lead sheet. SAE and IRC. Report in 2 weeks.
Music: Pop and R&B. Works with vocal group The Nylons.

RON HERBERT MANAGEMENT, 618 Terrace Ave., Virginia Beach VA 23451-4743. (804)428-5021. President: Ron Herbert. Management firm. Represents individual artists and groups; currently handles 3 acts. Receives 20% commission. Reviews material for acts.
How To Contact: Prefers cassette with 2 songs and lead sheet. Does not return unsolicited material. Reports in 2 weeks.
Music: Pop/rock and country. Works primarily with "recording acts—original music only." Current acts include Snuff and Kingdom.

HITCH-A-RIDE MANAGEMENT, 278 Merrevay Dr., Florence KY 41042. (606)371-5469. Manager: J.H. Reno. Management firm, booking agency and publishing company. Represents professional individuals, groups and songwriters; currently handles 4 acts. Receives 15% commission. Reviews material for acts.
How to Contact: Write first and obtain permission to submit. Prefers cassette with 1-4 songs and lyric sheet. SASE. Reports in 1 month.
Music: Bluegrass, country and MOR. Works primarily with vocalists. Current acts include Sheila Reno, Pam Hanna, and Jack Reno (country vocalists).

HOEKSTRA AGENCY, INC., Box 1360, Altamonte Springs FL 32715-1360. (305)327-3000. President: Bob Hoekstra. Vice President: Scott Hoekstra. Booking agency. Represents artists and groups; currently handles approximately 95 acts. Receives 15-20% commission. Reviews material for acts.
How to Contact: Query by mail or submit demo tape. Prefers cassette with 3-5 songs and lyric sheet. SASE. Reports in 1 month.
Music: Country, MOR, bluegrass, dance, easy listening and top 40/pop. Works primarily with lounge acts. Current acts include David Duncan & Printers Alley and Doug Robinson (country), Scott Berry (rock and easy listening), Levi John (80s reggae), Ray Peterson (50s and 60s recording artist), Rob Labby (comedy), and Big Mama (MOR).
Tips: "Have good vocal, wide variety of music, friendly attitude and be easy to get along with. You must have a professional package, including pictures, and you must have a good approach."

*HORRICK TALENT AGENCY,RR #15, Onion Lake Rd., Thunder Bay, Ontario P7B 5N1, Canada. (807)345-0101. Owner: Tom Horrick. Management firm, booking agency, record company (Covered Wagon Records), and music publisher (Earthshine Music and Bird Dance Music). Represents groups and songwriters; currently handles 12 acts. Reviews material for acts.
How to Contact: Prefers cassette and lyric sheet. Does not return unsolicited material. Reports "if interested."
Music: Mostly top 40 and commercial country. Works primarily with vocalists, dance and bar bands. Current acts include Boardwalk, Rival and Bulletz.

*JEFF HUBBARD MANAGEMENT, Box 68045, Indianapolis IN 46268. (317)291-9314. Contact: Jeff Hubbard. Management firm. Represents individual artists and groups; currently handles 3 acts.
How to Contact: Prefers cassette with "any number of songs" and lyric sheet. Does not return unsolicited material. Reports only if interested.
Music: Pop, rock and R&B. Current acts include Gary Lewis & The Playboys, Dennis Yost of the Classics IV and Sonny Geraci.

DAVID J. HULL MUSIC ENTERPRISES, 16325 Addison, Southfield MI 48075. (313)559-4871. President: David J. Hull. Management and accounting firm. Represents artists, groups and songwriters in the Michigan area; currently handles 21 acts. Receives 10-15% commission. Reviews material for acts.
How to Contact: Write first and obtain permission to submit. Prefers cassette (or videocassette) with 3-6 songs. Include pictures. SASE. Reports in 3 weeks.
Music: Mostly blues and jazz; also R&B. Works primarily with instrumental groups that do original material and covers. Current acts include Debit Productions (studio), Blues Buzz Band (blues), and Rockett 88's (R&B).

IEA/INTERNATIONAL ENTERTAINMENT ASSOCIATES, 1701 Pacific Ave., Box 1413, Dept. SM-2, Atlantic City NJ 08404-1413. (609)347-0484. President: Danny Luciano. Booking agency and record producer. Represents artists, groups and songwriters. Receives 10-25% commission. Reviews material for acts.
How to Contact: Prefers cassette with 4-8 songs and lead sheet. "No 8-tracks. Include picture and promotion package if self-contained performing artist." SASE. Reports in 6 weeks.
Music: Country, MOR, R&B, soft country rock and top 40/pop. Works primarily with dance bands, show groups and recording artists. Current acts include Atlantic City III, Mixx, Carousel, Lorraine Allison, and Rock & Roll Revival Showcase.

*INSIDE MUSIC, INC., Suite A, 28405 Sand Canyon Rd., Canyon Country CA 91351. (805)298-0164. President: Judy A. Gossett. Management firm, music publisher and production company. Represents individual artists and songwriters; currently handles 4 acts. Receives 15% commission for management. Reviews material for acts.
How to Contact: Prefers cassette with 3-4 songs and lyric or lead sheet. Does not return unsolicited material. Reports in 1 month.
Music: Mostly rock, pop and R&B; also gospel and country. Works primarily with vocalists, songwriters and some bands. Current acts include Sandra Crouch, Pattie Howard and Jean Johnson.
Tips: "We are interested especially in strong writers who are serious about doing business with integrity and character. Looking for strong lyrical content in songs with groove."

*INTER-ARTS ENTERPRISES, % Barbara Rocco, 115 E. Montgomery Ave., Ardmore PA 19003. (215)259-7015. Branch: c/o Bobbie Christopher, # 201, 1800 Garrett Rd., Lansdowne PA 19050. Owner: Bobbie Christopher. Management firm, booking agency, record company and music publisher. Represents individual artists, groups, songwriters, background musicians and entertainers. Receives various commissions.

How to Contact: Call first and obtain permission to submit. Prefers cassette and lyric or lead sheet. Does not return unsolicited material.
Music: Mostly country, pop and R&B; also MOR, top 40/disco and rock. Current acts include Bobbie Christopher, Terry Seurratt and Chris Capehart.
Tips: "All artists and songwriters are included in entertainment and music packages built around Bobbie Christopher. Publicity credits and compensation provided."

INTERMOUNTAIN TALENT, Box 942, Rapid City SD 57709. (605)348-7777. Owner: Ron Kohn. Management firm, booking agency and music publisher (Big BL music). Represents invididual artists, groups and songwriters; currently handles 8 acts. Receives 10-20% commission. Reviews material for acts.
How to Contact: Query. Prefers cassette with 3 songs and lyric sheet. Artist may submit videocassette. SASE. Reports in 3 weeks.
Music: Mostly rock; also top country/rock. Current acts include Hod Rod Dee Luxx, Doctor K and the Shantays (rock bands), Midwest Express (country band), Bold Lightning (rock), Innocent Mischief (rock) and Dan Asnicar.

INTERNATIONAL ENTERTAINMENT, Box 50727, Washington DC 20004-0727. (703)590-5928. Director: Charles B. Roberts. Management firm, publisher and producer. Represents artists and songwriters; currently handles 2 acts and 5 songwriters. Receives 15-25% commission. Reviews, produces and shops material for acts and writers .
How to Contact: "Call us to determine our needs or submit demo with 1-4 songs and lyric sheets. Also, include video, 8x10 photo, bio and credits if available." Returns materials after they are reviewed. Reports in 2 months.
Music: Mostly rock, R&B, pop and new music (hardcore, Go-Go, etc.); also country, gospel and jazz. Works primarily with dance and show bands. "We base selection of projects primarily on the needs of major and independent labels and producers with whom we are associated." Current acts include Ohio Players, SugarFoot (on Warner Bros. Records) and "other major label artists."

*INTERNATIONAL MUSIC MANAGEMENT, 6525 Sunset Blvd., Hollywood CA 90028. (213)464-1800. Executive Assistant: Frances Sheen. Management firm. Represents individual artists, groups and songwriters; currently handles 2 acts. Receives 15% commission. Reviews material for acts.
How to Contact: Prefers cassette with 2-3 songs. Does not return unsolicited material. Reports in 1 month.
Music: Pop and rock. Works primarily with vocal and musical recording artists. Current acts include Jose Feliciano and Porter Hansen.

*J AND L SERVICES, 216 Flagler Ave., New Smyrna FL 32069. (904)427-0060. Personal Manager: Bob Wright. Management firm, booking agency and music publisher (Just Lyrics). Estab. 1986. Represents individual artists, groups and songwriters in Southeastern US; currently handles 10 acts. Receives 15-50% commission. Reviews material for acts.
How to Contact: Prefers cassette (or VHS videocassette) with 1-5 songs and lyric or lead sheet. SASE.
Music: Mostly country, pop and gospel; also R&B, rock and jazz. Works primarily with vocalists and dance bands. Current acts include The Hardly Legal Band, Tim Probst and Justin Innamorato.

J.D. PRODUCTIONS, LTD., Box 444, Taylor MI 48180. (313)722-0616. President: John D. Lollio. Management firm, booking agency, music publisher and record company. Represents artists, groups and songwriters; currently handles 6 acts. Receives 10-15% commission. Reviews material for acts.
How to Contact: Query by phone first. Prefers cassette with minimum 2 songs. SASE. Reports in 1 week.
Music: Country and gospel; also MOR and top 40/pop. Works primarily with country and country rock groups. Current acts include Johni Dee (country), W.P. Carnes (contemporary), and LeMoine (A/C).
Tips: "We are always interested in new material."

*J.F. IMAGES, INC., #100, 5251 DTC Pwky., Englewood CO 80111-2702. (303)779-8888. Entertainment Director: Susan Pobrislo. Booking agency. Represents artists and groups; currently handles 32 acts. Receives 10-20% commission. Reviews material for acts.
How to Contact: Query by mail, arrange personal interview, or submit demo tape and lyric sheet. Prefers cassette or ½" or ¾" videos with 3 songs on demo. "If the band is a cover band, I prefer 50-60 second spots of approximately 10 songs showing a good variety." Include bio, picture and song list. SASE. Reports in 4 weeks.
Music: Mostly jazz, easy listening and top 40/pop; also bluegrass, classical, country, dance-oriented,

commercial rock, soul and dixieland. Works primarily with singles and duos, branching into groups of all kinds.

*J. T. MANAGEMENT, Suite 101, 153 Ranleigh Ave., Toronto, Ontario M4N 1X2 Canada. (416)482-1092. Manager: Jeff Thrasher. Management firm. Represents individual artists, groups and songwriters; currently handles 2 acts. Receives 20-25% commission. Reviews material for acts.
How to Contact: Prefers cassette (or Beta videocassette) with 3-5 songs and lyric and lead sheets. "Include photo and bio."
Music: Pop, dance and rock. Works primarily with pop/dance/rock acts and bands. Current acts include Only Human (pop band) and Allen Booth (songwriter). Other projects include "Demo Cates," saxophone/vocalist dance recording project.
Tips: "Listen to the radio! Have a realistic attitude and know what you want to accomplish."

JACKSON ARTISTS CORP., Suite 200, 7251 Lowell Dr., Shawnee Mission KS 66204. (913)384-6688. President: Dave Jackson. Management firm, booking agency and music publisher. Represents artists, groups and songwriters; currently handles 32 acts. Receives 10-20% commission from individual artists and groups; 10% from songwriters. Reviews material for acts.
How to Contact: Query, arrange personal interview or submit demo. Prefers cassette (or VHS videocassette) with 2-4 songs and lead sheet. "Mark names of tunes on cassettes. May send up to 4 tapes. We do most of our business by phone." Will return material if requested with SASE. Reporting time varies.
Music: Mostly pop, country and gospel; also bluegrass, blues, easy listening, disco, MOR, progressive, rock (soft), soul and top 40/pop. Works with dance, bar and show bands and vocalists; lounge acts primarily. Current acts include "Ragtime Bob" Darch (songwriter/entertainer), Eddie Tobin (piano), The Country Rockets (country trio), Sunny & Mel (duo), Jim Knapp (organ-single), Doug & Darla (duo), Butlerfields (country band), and The Five Scamps (jazz).
Tips: "Although it's not necessary, we prefer lead sheets with the tapes—send 2 or 3 that you are proud of. Also note what 'name' artist you'd like to see do the song."

*JOE JACKSON PRODUCTIONS, INC., Suite 716, 6255 Sunset Blvd., Hollywood CA 90028. (213)466-7315. Publicist: Charles J. Butler. Management firm, record company (Jackson Records) and music publisher (Jokay Music Publishing). Represents individual artists, groups, songwriters and theatrical artists; currently handles 50 acts. Receives 20% commission. Reviews material for acts.
How to Contact: Write or call first and obtain permission to submit. Prefers cassette (or ½" VHS videocassette) with 3 songs and lyric or lead sheet (and picture and bio if applicable). Does not return unsolicited material. Reports in 6 weeks.
Music: Mostly R&B, pop and rock; also country. Works primarily with vocalists. Current acts include Janet Jackson, La Toya Jackson and Loretta Chandler/FAME.
Tips: "Tapes must have piano and drum track with vocals. Include cover letter and typed lyric sheets."

*JAM JAM TALENT BOOKING, 2108 Queen St. E., Toronto, Ontario M4E 1E2 Canada. (416)698-2498. President: J.A. Meer. Booking agency. "We are affiliated with JAM JAM Concert Productions and JAM JAM Artist Management." Represents individual artists, groups and songwriters. Receives 10-15% commission.
How to Contact: Write or call first and obtain permission to submit. Prefers cassette (or VHS videocassette) with lyric sheet. Does not return unsolicited material. Reports in 1 month.
Music: Mostly rock/new wave, reggae and punk/hardcore; also country, R&B and funk/soul.

*JANC MANAGEMENT, Box 5563, Rockford IL 61125. (815)398-6895. President: Nancy Lee. Management firm, booking agency and record company. Represents individual artists, groups and songwriters; currently handles 2 acts. Reviews material for acts.
How to Contact: Prefers cassette (or VHS videocassette) with 4 songs and lyric sheet. SASE. Reports in 2 weeks.
Music: Mostly country (contemporary) and pop; also up-tempo songs, ballads and novelty. Works primarily with vocalists, dance bands and show bands. Current acts include George James and the Mood Express.
Tips: "Be very neat and professional with your submissions."

JVS PRODUCTIONS, Box 113, Hays KS 67601. (913)625-6215. Manager: Vern Staab. Management firm, booking agency and performers. Represents local and regional groups from Kansas, Colorado, Nebraska, New Mexico, South Dakota and Iowa; currently handles 2 acts. Receives 15-20% commission. Reviews material for acts.
How to Contact: Prefers cassette with 3-5 songs and lyric sheet or lead sheet. SASE. Reports in 4 weeks.

Music: Mostly country, story songs and gospel; also country/rock. Works primarily with "duos and trios or four-pieces in the country field, performing in clubs, the college circuit and coffeehouses, and as opening acts for national mid-level acts." Currently acts include Kristyl, and June and Vern.

Tips: "We are not currently looking for acts or artists to represent. We are looking for original material to use in performing opening acts and on the college circuit."

*ROSSI KANE MANAGEMENT, Box 46, Newton Centre MA 02159. (617)332-2791. Manager: Rossi Kane. Independent manager. Represents groups and songwriters; currently handles 1 act. Reviews material for acts.

How to Contact: Prefers cassette with 1-4 songs and lyric sheet. Does not return unsolicited material. Reports in 5 weeks.

Music: Pop-rock and hard rock. Works with rock group Sunlending.

BEN KAYE INTERNATIONAL, Suite 38, 4824 Cote des Neiges Rd., Montreal, Quebec H3V 1G4 Canada. (514)739-4774. President: Ben Kaye. Management firm and record producer. Represents artists, groups and songwriters; currently handles 4 acts. Receives variable commission "depending on the name value of the talent." Reviews material for acts.

How to Contact: Prefers cassette with 1-3 songs, lyric sheet and resume. Reports in 1 month.

Music: Mostly top 40/pop, hard rock and dance; also easy listening, MOR ballads and country rock. Works primarily with pop artists ("both English and French, because of our location"), hard rock groups and dance-oriented groups; "most write their own material but we are constantly on the look-out for strong writers." Current acts include Ted Tevan (radio personality-narrator "The Ballad of America"); Roberto Aspri-Georges Tremblay (instrumentalists, released *Visions* LP); Kenny Karen (pop artist/jingle writer/songwriter); and A-N-S [Assorted Nuts and Sounds] (pop-rock group).

*KINDOG PRODUCTIONS, 614 Moorewood Ct., Nashville TN 37207. (615)227-3922. Managing Director: Chris S. Buchanan. Management firm, booking agency and music publisher (Mo-Wood). Represents individual artists in Southeastern US; currently handles 3 acts. Receives 7.5% commission. Reviews material for acts.

How to Contact: Prefers cassette (or VHS standard videocassette) with 3 songs and lead sheet. Reports in 6 weeks.

Music: Mostly R&B, pop and jazz. "No country please." Current acts include Leo's Trio, Zipbusters and Market Place.

HOWARD KING AGENCY, INC., #104, 9060 Santa Monica Blvd., Los Angeles CA 90069. (213)858-8048. President: Howard King. Management firm and booking agency. Represents artists, groups and songwriters. Receives 10-15% commission. Reviews material for acts.

How to Contact: Prefers cassette with maximum 3 songs, photo, publicity material and lyric sheet. SASE. Reporting time varies.

Music: Mostly top 40; also country, dance-oriented, easy listening, jazz, MOR, rock and pop. Works primarily with top 40 artist singles, duos and groups.

*MICHAEL KONOPKA, 120 Duane St., New York NY 10007. (212)693-0261. Contact: Michael Konopka, Esq. Management and law firm. Represents individual artists, groups and songwriters; currently handles 4 acts. Receives 15-20% commission. Reviews material for acts.

How to Contact: Prefers cassette and lyric sheet. SASE. Reports in 2 weeks.

Music: Mostly New Age, rock and jazz; also rap-rock. Works with "a wide range of artists, from individuals to groups." Current acts include Sharon K. Janda, Tough Love and Michael Dinwiddie.

Tips: A songwriter should "concentrate initially on the creative aspects of his or her career. The business and legal aspects will fall in place at the appropriate time, with the help of proper management and legal advice."

KOPPERFIELD ENTERPRISES, Box 241, Cameron MO 64429. (816)632-6039. Manager: E.K. Bruhn. Management firm and booking agency, record company (Crusader) and music publisher (Time Minstrel Music). Represents individual artists, groups and songwriters. Deals mainly with local artists. Currently handles 3 acts. Receives 10-25% commission. Reviews material for acts.

How to Contact: Write or call first and obtain permission to submit. Prefers cassette or 7½ ips reel-to-reel with 3-5 songs and "optional" lyric sheet or lead sheet. "Include resume and write up of intentions." We prefer a video of a live show to look at and listen to for total show presentation and audience response. SASE. Reports in 10 weeks.

Music: Mostly country; also gospel and pop/top 40. Works primarily with vocalists and groups for county fairs and family shows. Acts include Elaine Sanders (country), Terry Alden (gospel) and Kopperfield (variety).

BOB KUBAN, 5 Biritz Court, St. Louis MO 63137. (314)869-6056. Contact: Bob Kuban. Represents artists and groups; currently handles 10 acts. Receives minimum 15% commission.
How to Contact: Query by mail. Prefers cassette with maximum 5 songs and lyric sheet. SASE. Reports in 2 weeks.
Music: Mostly top 40; also soul and pop. Works primarily with top 40 and big band dance bands. Current acts include Bob Kuban Brass (top 40, soul and big band), Everyday People (top 40 and soul), and Collage (top 40, jazz, standards). "All are very dance-oriented."
Tips: "I need good top 40 dance material."

L.D.F. PRODUCTIONS, Box 406, Old Chelsea Station, New York NY 10011. (212)925-8925. President: Mr. Dowell. Management firm and booking agency. Represents artists and choirs in the New York area. Receives 15-25% commission.
How to Contact: Write first and obtain permission to submit. Prefers cassette with 2-8 songs and lyric sheet. SASE. Reports in 1 month.
Music: Mostly black gospel; also choral and church/religious. Works primarily with vocalists and choirs. Current acts include L.D. Frazier (gospel artist/lecturer); and Frazier's (gospel workshop choir).
Tips: "Those interested in working with us must be original, enthusiastic and persistent."

L 2 MANAGEMENT, Box 372, Flint MI 48501-0372. (313)695-3790. Contact: A&R Department. Management firm. Represents individual artists and groups; currently handles 3 acts. "We actively seek artists for and from the foreign marketplace." Receives 10-25% commission. Reviews material for acts.
How to Contact: Write and obtain permission to submit. Prefers cassette (or VHS, NTSC or PAL videocassette) with maximum 3 songs and typed lyric sheet. "Include photo and bio if possible." SASE. Reports in 3 months.
Music: "Only highly commercial" pop/rock, country and dance. Works primarily with vocalists, bar bands, pop-rock acts and self-contained dance bands. Acts include Tera Daven (rock), Renee Roya Jackson (pop), and Ron Moore (pop).
Tips: "New artists/songwriters must be ready to commit themselves 110%. Established artists/songwriters must continue to be better than the previous product released!"

*LA LA LA PRODUCTIONS, Krukmakargatan 29, Stockholm S-11651 Sweden. (46)8-844720. Managing Director: Alexander Bard. Management firm and booking agency. Represents individual artists, groups and songwriters; currently handles 3 acts. Reviews material for acts.
How to Contact: Call first and obtain permission to submit. Prefers cassette (or VHS videocassette) with 1-4 songs and lyric sheet. Does not return unsolicited material. Reports in 5 weeks.
Music: Mostly dance-oriented contemporary music; also "hip-hop, hi-energy disco and avant garde disco." Works primarily with "artists, groups, songwriters with a repertoire of dance-oriented contemporary music aimed for the international market." Current acts include Barbie, Baton Rouge and Pop Talk.
Tips: We look for "a flashy visual image, a contemporary production with lots of programming and sampling, hip-hop, hi-energy, avantgarde dance music, crusscultural ambition."

LANDSLIDE MANAGEMENT, 928 Broadway, New York NY 10010. (212)505-7300. Principals: Ted Lehrman and Libby Bush. Management firm. Represents singers, groups and singer/songwriters; currently handles 5 acts. Receives 15% commission. Reviews material for acts.
How to Contact: Submit demo tape and lyric sheet "of potential hit singles only—not interested in album cuts." SASE. "Include picture, resume and (if available) ½" videocassette if you're submitting yourself as an act." Reports in 2 months.
Music: Dance-oriented, MOR, rock (soft, pop), soul, top 40/pop and country/pop. Works primarily with vocalists and soul groups. Current acts include Susan Hartley (MOR), Kevin Cort, Touch of Class (soul group), Laura Pearson, and Deborah Free and Leslie Bisno (soul/pop/cabaret).

THE CHARLES LANT AGENCY, 569 Lynwood Dr., Box 1085, Cornwall, Ontario K6H 5V2 Canada. (613)938-1532. Contact: Charles W. B. Lant. Booking agency. Represents individuals and groups. Receives 10-20% commission.
How to Contact: Query or phone. Prefers cassette with 3-10 songs. SAE and IRC. Reports ASAP.
Music: Country and big bands. Works primarily with country groups. Current acts include The Stardusters Orchestra (17-piece band), the Robbie Lee Show (country), and The Jimmy Lee Huff Show (country).

*STAN LAWRENCE PRODUCTIONS, 191 Presidential Blvd., Bala Cynwyd PA 19004. (215)664-6666. Artist Development: Robyn Adler. Management firm and booking agency. Represents individual artists and groups. Receives 10-20% commission. Reviews material for acts.

How to Contact: Write to arrange personal interview. Prefers cassette (or VHS videocassette) with 2-5 songs and lead sheet. SASE. Reports in 3 weeks.
Music: Pop and adult contemporary. Works primarily with vocalists and dance bands.

GARY LAZAR MANAGEMENT, 3222 Belinda Dr., Sterling Heights MI 48310. (313)977-0645. Contact: Gary Lazar. Management firm, booking agency and music publisher. Represents artists, groups and songwriters; currently handles 4 acts. Receives 10-20% commission. Reviews material for acts.
How to Contact: Prefers cassette (or ¾" or VHS videocassette) with maximum 3 songs and lead sheet. Does not return unsolicited material. Reports in 1 month.
Music: Mostly rock; also children's and top 40/pop. Works primarily with recording artists and songwriters/lyricists. Current acts include Mark Lindsay (former lead singer with with Paul Revere & The Raiders) and Eric Burdon (rock act/songwriter).

BUDDY LEE ATTRACTIONS, INC., Suite 300, 38 Music Square E., Nashville TN 37203. (615)244-4336. Artists and Groups Contact: Tony Conway. Songwriters Contact: Nancy Dunn. Management firm and booking agency. Represents individuals and groups; currently handles 60 acts. "Principally, we deal with established name acts who have recording contracts with major labels." Receives 10-15% commission. Reviews material for acts.
How to Contact: Prefers cassette with minimum 4 songs and lead sheet. Does not return unsolicited material. Reports as soon as possible on solicited material.
Music: Bluegrass, country, MOR, rock, soul and top 40/pop. Works primarily with concert attractions. Current acts include Danny Davis and the Nashville Brass (country/MOR instrumental), Willie Nelson and Family, Waylon Jennings (country/pop), Johnny Rivers (pop/rock), Vern Gosdin, Neil Young, David Allan Coe, Kris Kristofferson, Emmylou Harris, George Jones, John Conlee, John Anderson, Bill Monroe and Porter Wagoner (all country artists).

OVERTON LEE MANAGEMENT, Box 2686, Cypress CA 90630-1386. (213)946-3193. Owner: Overton Lee. Management firm. Represents individual artists and groups; currently handles 5 acts. Receives 20% commission. Reviews material for acts.
How to Contact: Prefers cassette with 2-3 songs and lyric sheet. SASE. Reports in 4 months.
Music: Country and rock. Works primarily with "artists that we can record and put on TV." Current acts include The Bonner Family, Randy Zane Gray and Touch of Country.

LEGION ARTISTS, 38 Music Sq. E., Nashville TN 37203. (615)255-8005. President: Tommy Loomas. Vice President: Michael Clair. Agents: Joe Silver, Alan Carter, Glen Horsley. Management firm and booking agency. Estab. 1986. Represents individual artists and groups; currently handles 23 acts. Receives 15-25% commission. Reviews material for acts.
How to Contact: Write or call first and obtain permission to submit or to arrange personal interview. Prefers cassette (or VHS videocassette) with 4 songs and lyric or lead sheet. SASE. Reports in 6 weeks.
Music: Mostly country, easy listening and bluegrass; also rock. Works primarily with vocalists. Current artists include Lane Brody, Thom Bresh, Georgi Baker, Rebecca Holden, Bobby Lee Morgan, and Dennis Loccorie.
Tips: "Be professional. We deal only with artists who are committed and serious about performing."

LEMON SQUARE MUSIC, Box 31819, Dallas TX 75231. (214)750-0720. Contact: Bart Barton. Production company. Represents artists, groups and songwriters; currently handles 7 acts. Reviews material for acts.
How to Contact: Query by mail, then submit demo tape. Prefers 7½ ips reel-to-reel or cassette with 2-4 songs. SASE. Reports in 1 month.
Music: Country and gospel. Works primarily with show bands. Current acts include Dania Presley (country), Glen Bailey (progressive country artist), Steve Reed (songwriter), Denman & Clark Band (country band/show band), Craig Solieau (comedy act);,Christy Hedges (country singer), and Audie Henry (progressive country singer).

*LES PRODUCTIONS HOT STUFF/HOT STUFF PRODUCTIONS, 6741 St-Hubert, Montreal, Quebec Canada. (514)495-3473. Director: Frank Farkas. Management firm and booking agency. Represents individual artists, groups and songwriters; currently handles 20 acts. Receives 10-20% commission. Reviews material for acts.
How to Contact: Write first and obtain permission to submit. Prefers cassette (or VHS videocassette) with 3 songs and lyric sheet. Does not return unsolicited material. Reports in 6 weeks.
Music: Commercial rock, pop and new music. Works primarily with top 40 cover bands, original bands, recording bands, bar and show bands. Current acts include Dorion and the Freeriders (rock band), Romance at Eleven (rock band), Kinky Foxx, and De Pluss (new music band).
Tips: "Have a professional attitude; submit professional material."

*LESTER PRODUCTIONS, Box 225, Rockaway NJ 07866. (201)627-0690. Theatrical Agent: Sylvia Stevens. Booking agency. Represents artists, groups and lecture demonstrators; currently handles 15-20 acts. Receives 10-25% commission. Reviews material for acts.
How to Contact: Prefers cassette (or videocassette) with 5-10 songs and lyric sheet. Send complete promotional package. SASE. Reports in 2 weeks.
Music: Mostly rock, country rock and country; also bluegrass, blues, church/religious, classical, dance-oriented, easy listening, folk, gospel, jazz, R&B and soul. Works primarily with dance bands (rock and country), vocalists (all types), and single musicians (one-man bands). Current acts include Saturday Nite Special (tribute to Lynyrd Skynyrd), Mantis (progressve rock band), and Gangbusters (rockabilly show band).

*LETTERMEN PRODUCTIONS, 10010 Shoshone, Northridge CA 91325. Company Manager: Carole Tosti. Management firm, record company (Alpha Omega) and music publisher (Grey Fox Inc.). Represents groups and songwriters; currently handles 1 act.
How to Contact: Prefers cassette. Does not return unsolicited material. Reports in 1 month.
Music: Pop and country. Current acts include The Lettermen.

LEVINSON ENTERTAINMENT VENTURES INTERNATIONAL, INC., Suite 250, 650 N. Bronson Ave., Los Angeles CA 90004. (213)460-4545. President: Bob Levinson. Management firm. Represents national individual artists, groups and songwriters; currently handles 5 acts. Receives 15-20% commission.
How to Contact: Write first and obtain permission to submit or to arrange personal interview. Prefers cassette (or VHS videocassette) with 6 songs and lead sheet. Does not return unsolicited material. Reports in 1 month.
Music: Rock, MOR, R&B and country. Works primarily with rock bands and vocalists.

*LINE-UP PROMOTIONS, INC., 9A, Tankerville Place, Newcastle-Upon-Tyne NE2 3AT United Kingdom. Phone: (091)2816449. Director: C.A. Murtagh. Management firm, booking agency, record company (On-Line) and music publisher (Line-Up). Represents individual artists, groups and songwriters; currently handles 4 acts. Receives 15-20% commission. Reviews material for acts.
How to Contact: Prefers cassette (or videocassette) and lyric sheet. "Send press kit." Does not return unsolicited material. Reports in 1 month.
Music: Mostly pop and rock; also reggae, African and blues. Works primarily with songwriters and groups. Current acts include "T.R. 28-20," "Swimming Pool," "Fan Heater," "Royal Family," "Leg Theory," "Seize the Infidels" and "Paper Walls."

LOCONTO PRODUCTIONS, 7766 NW 44th St., Sunrise FL 33321. (305)741-7766 or (305)940-2626 (Miami). Contact: Phyllis Finney Loconto. Management firm. Represents artists and groups. Receives 10-25% commission. Reviews material for acts.
How to Contact: Prefers cassette with maximum 3 songs. "We are looking primarily for country artists and songs with strong hooks and crossover potential." SASE. Reports in 1 month.
Music: Mostly country; also bluegrass, children's, church/religious, country, easy listening, folk, gospel, MOR, and top 40/pop. Works primarily with country vocalists, country bands, MOR vocalists and bluegrass artists. Current acts include Donna Perito, Jeanne Cia, and Dick Contino.

*LORD/AXILTREE MANAGEMENT, Suite 8C, 222 W. 15th St., New York NY 10011. (212)255-2565. Managers: Sandra Lord and George Axiltree. Management firm and entertainment columnists/writers. Estab. 1986. Represents individual artists and groups; currently handles 4 acts. Receives 20% commission. Constantly reviews material for acts.
How to Contact: Write or call first and obtain permission to submit. Prefers cassette (or VHS videocassette) with 3-5 songs and lyric sheet. SASE. Reports in 6 weeks.
Music: Mostly R&B/dance, rock and pop; also jazz, rap, and country. Works primarily with vocalists (performing and recording), show and dance bands and lounge performers. Current acts include Hot Lips, Donny B., R.C. Tass and Michaelangelo.
Tips: "Please be professional in your presentation. We are interested in honest, hardworking and dedicated artists."

RON LUCIANO MUSIC CO., Box 263, Brigantine NJ 08203-0263. (609)266-2623. President: Ron Luciano. Management firm and booking agency. Represents artists, groups and recording/specialty acts; currently handles 10 acts. Receives 10-25% commission. Reviews material for artists.
How to Contact: Query or submit picture and biography. Prefers 7½ ips reel-to-reel or cassette (or VHS videocassette) with 4-8 songs. "Can also approach by sending a copy of their record release." SASE. Reports in 6 weeks.

Music: Mostly MOR and "redone oldies"; also disco, rock, soul and top 40/pop. Works with 4- or 5-piece, self-contained groups "that play in Holiday Inns, Sheratons, etc. We also book a lot of oldie groups like the Belmonts, Flamingos and Duprees." Current acts include Voyage (top 40/disco), Legz (rock), Spit-N-Image (rock group), Lee Estrada (tribute to Elvis show), and Charles Lamont (Hypnotist), Dawn (female singer), Tony Vallo (male artist/comedian), Tom Arico (male artist/songwriter), Danger Zone (rock group—formerly Vanilla Fudge), and The Duprees (oldie group).

RICHARD LUTZ ENTERTAINMENT AGENCY, 5625 0 St., Lincoln NE 68510. (402)483-2241. General Manager: Cherie Worley. Management firm and booking agency. Represents individuals and groups; currently handles 200 acts. Receives 15-20% minimum commission. Reviews material for acts.
How to Contact: Query by phone. Prefers cassette (or videocassette) with 5-10 songs "to show style and versatility" and lead sheet. "Send photo, resume, tape, partial song list and include references. Add comedy, conversation, etc., to your videocassette." SASE. Reports in 1 week.
Music: Mostly top 40 and country; also dance-oriented and MOR. Works primarily with show and dance bands for lounge circuit. "Acts must be uniformed." Current acts include Sharlyn & C.P.R. (variety), Rainbow Express (country group), Great Imposters (50s dance band), and The Edge (top 40 group).

M & M TALENT AGENCY INC., 958 Sibley Tower Bldg., Rochester NY 14604. (716)325-2930. Contact: Carl Labate. Management firm and booking agency. Represents artists and groups; currently handles 15 acts. Receives 15-25% commission. Reviews material for acts.
How to Contact: Prefers cassette with minimum 3 songs and lyric sheet. May send video if available; "a still photo would be good enough to see the type of performance." SASE. Reports in 3 weeks.
Music: Mostly top 40; also dance, rock and R&B. Works primarily with vocalists, dance groups and recording artists. Current acts include Resurrection (original rock), Margaret Wilson (R&B), Chesterfield Kings (new music/rock) and J.B. Strut Band (R&B).
Tips: "We seek serious people willing to work and accept criticism."

*M.T.A., 1026 W. Colorado Ave., Colorado Springs CO 80904-4328. (303)577-4704 or 577-4705. Agent: Lucy Mattas. Management firm and booking agency. Represents artists, groups and songwriters; currently handles 74 acts. Receives 12-15% commission. Reviews material for acts.
How to Contact: Prefers cassette (or videocassette) with 3-8 songs and lyric sheet. SASE. Reports in 3 weeks.
Music: Mostly top 40, rock/pop and top 40 country; also easy listening, MOR and country rock. No hard rock. Works primarily with club bands and vocalists. Current acts include Andy Elliott (songwriter/artist), Kathy Wolfe (Wild Honey group), and Randy Louden (songwriter/artist).
Tips: "Make sure all songs are copyrighted, or we will help you do so. Be willing to change any part of any song a company wants you to."

*KEVIN MABRY ENTERPRIZES, 8 E. State, Milford Center OH 43045. (513)349-2971. Owner/Artist: Kevin Mabry. Management firm and booking agency. Represents local and regional artists, groups and songwriters; currently handles 2 acts. Receives 10-15% commission. Reviews material for acts.
How to Contact: Prefers cassette or 7½ ips reel-to-reel with 4 songs and lyric sheet. Does not return unsolicited material.
Music: "Positive" country, contemporary Christian and MOR/pop. Works primarily with vocalists, country groups and contemporary Christian acts. Current acts include Kevin Mabry, and Kevin Mabry & Liberty Street.
Tips: "I'm looking for positive country songs with good message—mostly up-tempo. Also great contemporary Christian songs. Positive material is in demand."

*MAINSTAGE MANAGEMENT INTERNATIONAL, INC., 22 Sprindrift Way, Annapolis MD 21403. (301)268-5596. Executive Vice President: Paul Bartz. Management firm and booking agency. Represents individual artists and groups; currently handles 24 acts. Receives 20% commission. Reviews material for acts.
How to Contact: Prefers cassette (or VHS videocassette) and lyric sheet. SASE. Reports in 1 month.
Music: Pop and MOR. Works primarily with vocalists. Current acts include Petula Clark.
Tips: "Please do not continually call to assess status of tapes."

ED MALHOIT AGENCY, Box 2001, Claremont NH 03743. (603)542-8777. Agents: Ed Malhoit and Kathy Shull. Management firm and booking agency. Represents groups in eastern US; currently handles 20 acts. Receives 10-20% commission. Reviews material for acts.
How to Contact: Write first. Prefers cassette with minimum 5 songs. SASE. Reports in 1 month.
Music: Rock. Current acts include Downpour, Double Cross, Fox, and 8084 (all rock concert/club acts.)

*MANAGEMENT PLUS, 112 21st Ave. S., Nashville TN 37203. (615)329-9933. Manager: Georgeann Galante. Management firm. Represents individual artists, songwriters and musicians; currently handles 4 acts. Receives 15% commission. Reviews material for acts.
How to Contact: Call to arrange personal interview. Prefers cassette. SASE.
Music: Pop, rock and contemporary country. Works primarily with vocalists. Current acts include Bellamy Brothers, Teddy Heard and Keith Christopher.

MANAGEMENT VII, 1811 NE. 53rd St., Ft. Lauderdale FL 33308. (305)776-1004. Contact: Vic and Romona Beri. Management firm. Represents artists, groups and songwriters; currently handles 5 acts. Receives 10-20% commission. Reviews material for acts.
How to Contact: Prefers cassette with 3-10 songs and lyric sheet. SASE. Reports in 1 month.
Music: Country, crossover, and top 40/pop. Current acts include Greg Bonham (top 40 trumpet/vocals); 2EZ (top 40 duo), and Richard Williams (piano, country crossover).

*LOUIS MAREK MUSIC INC., 3928 Shrine Park, Leavenworth KS 66048. (913)682-8065. President: Lou Marek. Booking agency and record company (Rainbow Records). Represents individual artists, groups and songwriters; currently handles 10 acts. Receives 15-20% commission. Reviews material for acts.
How to Contact: Prefers cassette (or VHS videocassette). SASE.
Music: Mostly pop, country and rock; also comedy and dancers. Works primarily with vocalists, dance bands and individual musicians. Current acts include Carla Christy, Private Stock and Johny Stuart.

MARS TALENT AGENCY, 168 Orchid Dr., Pearl River NY 10965. (914)735-4569. Contact: Arnie Kay. Management firm and booking agency. Represents artists and groups; currently handles 7 acts. Receives 10-20% commission. Reviews material for acts.
How to Contact: Write first and obtain permission to submit. Prefers cassette and lead sheet. SASE. Reports in 3 weeks.
Music: Easy listening, MOR and R&B. Works primarily with artists and groups from the 50s and 60s era. Current acts include Crystals, Duprees, Earls, Regents, Cleftones, and Reparata and the Delrons.

RICK MARTIN PRODUCTIONS, 125 Fieldpoint Road, Greenwich CT 06830. (203)661-1615. President: Rick Martin. Personal manager and independent producer. "Office of Secretary of the Conference of Personal Managers, East." Represents groups, artists/songwriters, actresses/vocalists, and comedians/vocalists; currently handles 5 acts. Receives 15-25% commission. "Occasionally, we are hired as consultants, production assistants or producers of recording projects." Reviews material for acts.
How to Contact: Prefers cassette with 2-4 songs. SASE. "We prefer serious individuals who represent themselves professionally. Call for report 10 days after submission."
Music: Mostly top 40, rock and dance; also easy listening and pop. Produces rock dance groups, female vocalists, songwriters and actress/vocalists (pop). Current acts include Babe (all female revue—top 40), Eddie and Ruth Ayres (comedy/vocalists), Marisa Mercedes (vocalist/pianist/songwriter), Sabel (vocalist/songwriter), and Jo Ann Latham (vocalist/actress).
Tips: "Don't spend a lot of money on recordings, but be prepared to have some financial backing if attempting to be an artist. Depend on yourself for everything including, most importantly, creativity. Present material in the simplest way."

MASADA MUSIC, INC., 888 8th Ave., New York NY 10019. (212)757-1953. President: Gene Heimlich. Management consultant firm and production/engineering house. Deals with artists in East Coast region only. Represents artists, groups and songwriters; currently handles 10 acts. Receives 10-25% commission or salary against commission. Reviews material for acts.
How to Contact: Write or call first to obtain permission to submit or to arrange personal interview. Prefers 7½ ips reel-to-reel or cassette with 2-5 songs. SASE. Reports in 3 weeks.
Music: Mostly New Age, new music, contemporary and film scores; also dance, progressive and pop. Works with singers/songwriters, vocalists and composers. Also works with "composers, synthesists and numerous musicians playing other than pop (i.e., Indian, Latin, African, etc.)." Current acts include Raphael (New Age); Gabriell Roth and the Mirrors (contemporary); Tom Pope, Jim Scott (contemporary); and Emile Sichkin/Concerto for Astronauts (New Age).
Tips: "Present clean, simple demos and focus on your market."

*MCFADDEN ARTIST CORPORATION, 818 18th Ave. S., Nashville TN 37203. (615)242-1500. Chairman: Jack McFadden. Management firm and music publisher (Music General Corp.). Represents individual artists and groups; currently handles 12 acts. Reviews material for acts.
How to Contact: Prefers cassette with 3-4 songs and lyric sheet. Does not return unsolicited material. Reports as soon as possible.

Music: Mostly country, country rock and pop/black. Current acts include Buck Owens, Keith Whitley, Lynn Anderson, Shelly West and Johnny Lee.

MEADOWLARK MUSIC, Box 7218, Missoula MT 59807. (406)728-2180. Contact: Chris Roberts. Management firm and booking agency. Represents groups in the western US; currently handles 70 acts. Receives 15-20% commission.
How to Contact: Write first for permission to submit or arrange personal interview. Prefers cassette (or videocassette) with 3-7 songs. SASE. Reports in 2 weeks.
Music: Mostly rock; also MOR, R&B and top 40/pop. Works primarily with bands. Current acts include Prophecy (top 40 rock), Kinroq (rock), and Pressure (top 40 rock).
Tips: "Follow through. Be organized. Have promotional material."

JOHN MEDLAND PRODUCTIONS, 334 Dufferin St., Toronto, Ontario M6K 1Z6 Canada. (416)536-4882. President: John Medland. Represents local artists and musical groups; currently handles 3 acts. Receives 10-20% commission. Reviews material for acts.
How to Contact: Prefers cassette with 1-5 songs. Groups should include bios, photo, repertoire, personnel and equipment list. SAE and IRC. Reports in 1 month.
Music: Mostly top 40/pop; also rock and dance. Works primarily with full time traveling bands (bars, colleges, etc.). Current acts include S.X.S. (top 40/pop), Idle Threat (tribute to Billy Idol), and Firedance Overture (tribute to U2).

MENES LAW CORP., Suite 1240, 1901 Avenue of the Stars, Los Angeles CA 90067. (213)277-4895. Directors: Barry Menes and Paul I. Menes. Law firm handling business affairs and some limited management. Represents companies, artists, groups, songwriters, video companies, agencies, personal managers and some publishing companies; currently handles "several" acts. "Mostly paid by the hour, but on rare occasion we'll accept contingency over guarantee." Reviews materials for acts.
How to Contact: Prefers cassette (or short videocassette). Include bio. SASE. Reports in 1 month.
Music: All types. Works primarily with individuals and bands with original materials. Current clients include Lee Ritenour (jazz/pop band); Four Tops (R&B/pop band), Victor Musical Industries, and Hit and Run Music and Music Publishing.

GREG MENZA ARTIST MANAGEMENT, Box 723591, Atlanta GA 30339. (404)262-6444. Director: Greg Menza. Management firm, booking agency and concert producers. Represents artists, groups and songwriters; currently handles 8 acts. Receives 10-20% commission. Reviews material for acts.
How to Contact: Query by mail. Prefers cassette (or VHS videocassette) with 3-6 songs. Reports in at least 1 month. "Include SASE if you wish material returned. Send only high quality finished demos."
Music: Gospel, rock and country, "contemporary Christian rock bands and clean cut positive secular acts." Works primarily with contemporary Christian rock artists. Current acts include Mylon Lefevre and Broken Heart, Sacred Fire, David Teems and the Calling, Bash-N-the Code (all Christian contemporary music); Look Up (secular), Vision (featuring Billy Powell, formerly of Lynyrd Skynyrd), The Innocence Mission (all rock); and Bailey and the Boys (country).

MERCEY BROTHERS LTD., 38 Church St., Elmira, Ontario N3B 1M5 Canada. (519)669-5394 or 669-5428. President: Larry Mercey. Booking agency, record company (MBS Records) and music publisher (Mercey Brothers Publishing and Elmira Music). Represents individual artists and songwriters; currently handles various acts. Receives 10-15% commission. Reviews material for acts.
How to Contact: Prefers cassette with 3 songs and lyric sheet. SAE and IRC. Reports in 3 weeks.
Music: Country and pop/country. Works primarily with vocalists. Current acts include The Mercey Brothers, Eddie Eastman and Joan Kennedy.
Tips: "We are interested in publishing and sub-publishing for Canada."

JOSEPH C. MESSINA, 699 Weaver St., Larchmont NY 10538. (914)834-5676. Attorney/manager. Represents artists, groups, songwriters, movie directors and screenwriters; currently handles 2 acts. Receives negotiable commission.
How to Contact: Prefers cassette with 1-2 songs and lead sheet. Does not return unsolicited material.
Music: Top 40. Works primarily with male and female vocal/dance. Current acts include Spyder Turner (R&B/top 40) and Andrea & Hot Mink (top 40).

MID-EAST ENTERTAINMENT INC., Suite 200, 553 S. Limestone, Lexington KY 40508. (606)254-3327. Agent: Robert Moser. Represents artists and groups; currently handles over 200 acts. Receives 10-20% commission. Reviews material for acts.
How to Contact: Prefers cassette, photo and songlist with 3-6 songs. SASE. Reports in 1 month.
Music: Mostly top 40 and R&B; also country, dance-oriented, easy listening, jazz, rock, soul and pop.

Works primarily with dance bands. Current acts include Good Nuff (R&B/top 40); Perfect Stranger (top 40/rock); and Paradox (top 40/rock).

*MIDNIGHT LIFE ASSOCIATES, Garden Suite, 187 Prospect Place, Brooklyn NY 11238. (718)622-6166. General Partner: Christopher R. Owens. Management firm, record company (Cromusica) and music publisher. Estab. 1986. Represents individual artists and groups; currently handles 4 acts. Receives negotiable commission. Reviews material for acts.
How to Contact: Prefers cassette (or VHS videocassette) and lyric sheet. SASE. Reports in 3 months.
Music: Mostly R&B, pop and rock; also upbeat country and innovative blues. Works primarily with original-oriented groups with "danceable" material; pop vocalists with innovative styles. Current acts include Midnight Landing, Jody Gorman-Jacobs and Chris Ownes.
Tips: "We are open-minded about original material *with a positive theme* (do not send us material with "super-sex" drippy lyrics. We need good material for male-tenor and female soprano and second soprano voices (alto oriented material is also OK). We will work with you if you want us to, on material that we are intrested in. We are new—but we are fair!"

*MILAM MUSIC GROUP, Box 807, Lake Dallas TX 75065. President: John S. Milam. Management firm, booking agency, music publisher (Canyon Songbook/ASCAP, and Bayou Songbook/ASCAP). Represents country groups; currently handles 5 acts. Receives 10% commission. Reviews material for acts.
How to Contact: Prefers cassette (or VHS videocassette) and lyric sheet. SASE. Reports in 2 weeks.
Music: Contemporary country only. Works primarily with high energy contemporary country groups—at least 3 lead vocals. Current acts include Canyon, Bayou, and Natalie & Heartbreak.
Tips: "Good solid high energy country groups are in demand, but they must be professional in both appearance and attitude. They can get anywhere from $2,500 to $4,000 including accomodations, per week. If the groups are less than 100%, their value drops considerably. It's very simple, good acts work: bad acts don't."

THE GILBERT MILLER AGENCY, Suite 243, 21243 Ventura Blvd., Woodland Hills CA 91364. (818)888-6363. Agent: Jeff Miller. Booking agency. Represents musical and variety/novelty groups; currently handles 12 acts. Receives 15% commission. Reviews material for acts.
How to Contact: Write to obtain permission to submit. Prefers cassette with 3-6 songs, 8x10 photo and lyric sheet. SASE. Reports in 2 weeks.
Music: Mostly rock. Works primarily with heavy metal/commercial hard rock groups. Current acts include Terriff with Frank Dimino of Angel (heavy metal), Scarlet with Andy Parker of U.F.O (hard rock), and Perfect Stranger (new wave).

*ROBERT MONTGOMERY AND ASSOCIATES, 9170 Yellowhead Trail, Edmonton, Alberta T5B 1G2 Canada. (403)477-1286. President: Robert Montgomery. Management firm and music publisher (San Paku Music). Represents individual artists and groups; currently handles 3 acts. Receives 15-20% commission. Reviews material for acts.
How to Contact: Prefers cassette with no more than 3 songs and lyric sheet. Does not return unsolicited material. Reports in 1 month.
Music: Rock and pop. Current acts include Darkroom, Absolute 9 and Mike Wiskar.

*MOONSHOT MANAGEMENT, 3730 N. Clark, Chicago IL 60613. (312)935-1295. President: Peter Katsis. Management firm, booking agency and music publisher (Badoads music). Represents individual artists, groups and songwriters; currently handles 3 acts. Receives 20% commission. Reviews material for acts.
How to Contact: Prefers cassette with 4 songs. Does not return unsolicited material. Reports in 3 weeks.
Music: Rock, pop and R&B. Works primarily with songwriters who are strong performers. Current acts include Nicholas Tremulis, Chac Mool, and Last Gentleman.

*DALE MORRIS AND ASSOCIATES, 818 19th St. S., Nashville TN 37203. (615)327-3400. Booking Agent: Barbara Hardin. Booking agency. Represents "Alabama."
How to Contact: Write first for submission policy.

*MUSIC COMPANY, 14 Harvey Place SW, Calgary, Alberta T2V 3A5 Canada. (403)259-5282. Manager: Fred Thoutenhoofd. Booking agency. Represents individual artists and groups; currently handles 120 acts. Receives 10-20% commission. Reviews material for acts.
How to Contact: Write or call first and obtain permission to submit. Prefers cassette (or Beta videocassette) with 5 songs minimum and photo. Does not return unsolicited material. Reports in 1 week.

Music: Mostly commercial pop, country and variety material. Works primarily with dance bands, one night stands, pop and crossover singles and bands. Current acts include 20/20, Mark Koenig and Anne Sitter.
Tips: "We are looking for people who are performance oriented in live clubs. We need to know booking status (schedule), songlist and equipment."

MUSKRAT PRODUCTIONS, INC., 44 N. Central Ave., Elmsford NY 10523. (914)592-3144. Contact: Bruce McNichols. Represents individuals and groups; currently represents 23 acts. Deals with artists in the New York City area. Reviews material for acts.
How to Contact: Write first. Prefers cassette (or short videocassette) with 3 songs minimum. SASE. Reports "only if interested."
Music: "We specialize in old-time jazz, dixieland and banjo music and shows;" also old time, nostalgia, country and jazz. Works primarily with dixieland, banjo/sing-along groups to play parties, Mexican mariachi bands and specialty acts for theme parties, dances, shows and conventions. Current acts include Smith Street Society Jazz Band (dixieland jazz), Your Father's Mustache (banjo sing-along), Roaring 20s Revue (show and dance band), and Harry Hepcat and the Boogie Woogie Band (50s rock revival).

FRANK NANOIA MANAGEMENT, 1999 N. Sycamore Ave., Los Angeles CA 90068. (213)874-8725. President: Frank Nanoia. Management firm. Represents artists, groups and songwriters; currently handles 15 acts. Receives 15-25% commission. Reviews material for acts.
How to Contact: Prefers 7½, 15 ips reel-to-reel or cassette (or videocassette) with 3-5 songs and lyric and lead sheets. Does not return unsolicited material. Reports "only if material is above average. No phone calls please."
Music: Mostly R&B and dance, also top 40/pop, jazz fusion, country, easy listening, MOR, gospel and soul. Works primarily with vocalists and show and bar groups. Current acts include Marc Allen Trujillo (vocalist/songwriter); Paramour (R&B show group), and Richard Yniguez (vocalist).

*NASHVILLE INTERNATIONAL MUSIC GROUP, 116 17th Ave. S., Nashville TN 37203. (615)254-3464. President: Reggie M. Churchwell. Management firm (Reggie M. Churchwell Artist Management), record company (Phoenix Records, Inc.) and music publisher (Four Seasons Music/ASCAP, Sir Winston Music/BMI). Represents individual artists and groups; currently handles 5 acts. Receives 15% commission. Reviews material for acts.
How to Contact: Write first and obtain permission to submit. Prefers cassette with 2-3 songs and lyric or lead sheets. SASE. Reports in 3 weeks.
Music: Mostly country, pop and gospel. Works primarily with vocalists. Current acts include Bruce Bright, Hotline, Charlie McCoy, Donna Fargo and Dennis Weaver.

NATIONAL BOOKING AGENCY OF DALLAS, 2605 Northridge Drive, Garland TX 75043. (214)240-2222. Executive Producer: Robert Morgan. Management firm, booking agency and recording company. Represents artists, groups and songwriters; currently handles 25 acts. Receives 15-20% commission. Reviews material for acts.
How to Contact: Prefers cassette (or videocassette) with 3-12 songs and lyric sheet. Does not return unsolicited material. Reports in 3 weeks.
Music: Mostly top 40/pop and 50s and 60s nostalgia rock; also country, MOR and rock. Works primarily with dance and show bands. Current acts include Dash Riprock (50s-60s show band), Custom Made (50s/soul/top 40 show band), Starfire (50s-60s/top 40s/country), and Rendezvous (top 40/pop/MOR/50s-60s).

NATIONAL TALENT ASSOCIATES, INC., 715 Florida Ave. S., Minneapolis MN 55426. (612)545-8211. President: Mark Alan. Management firm. Represents individual artists, groups and songwriters; currently handles 10 acts. Receives 20% commission. Reviews material for acts.
How to Contact: Prefers cassette (or VHS videocassette). Does not return unsolicited material. Reports in 90 days.
Music: Pop, R&B (black) and rock. Works primarily with groups and solo artists. Current acts include Andre Cymone, Airkraft, Peggi Blu, Riopelle and Zwarté.

NEVADA TALENT AND BOOKING, % Ward Johns and Sabian Simpson, Suite 101, 550 E. Plumb Lane, Reno NV 89502. (702)827-3648. Management firm and booking agency. Represents artists,

 The asterisk before a listing indicates that the listing is new in this edition. New markets are often the most receptive to freelance submissions.

groups and songwriters; currently handles 15-25 acts. "We represent all types of music to record labels and booking/management firms throughout the world." Receives 7½-15% commission. Reviews material for acts.

How to Contact: Query by mail, arrange personal interview or submit demo tape. Prefers cassette (or VHS or Beta videocassette) or VHS or Beta video cassette with 4-10 songs and lyric sheet. "It's important to have VHS or Beta tape and a professional 16-24 track demo. Also send pictures and printed resume."

Music: Mostly pop/rock and new wave; also country and all other types. Works primarily with rock groups, original jazz artists and original rock/pop/soul/R&B artists. Current acts include Michael De Jong (blues); Phil Delta and the Delta band (country), Gary Henley (country), Ron Shirrel (country), Robin Baxter (rock), Jessica Hart (rock), Larry Elliott (MOR/rock), Michael Stosic (pop), Melvin Lee (country), and Bobby Wrenn (pop).

NEW ARTIST'S PRODUCTIONS, 131 Connecticut Ave., N. Bay Shore NY 11706. (516)666-1876. Professional Department: Jeannie G. Walker. Management firm, record company and music publisher. Represents individual artists, groups and songwriters; currently handles 35-50 acts. Receives 20% commission. Reviews material for acts.

How to Contact: Prefers cassette (or videocassette) and lyric sheet. SASE. Reports in 6 weeks.

Music: Mostly pop, country and easy listening; also rock, gospel and blues. Works primarily with vocalists and dance bands. Current acts include Rory Bennett (night club act), Cherokee (vocalist & dance band), and Mindset (dance band).

Tips: "New Artist's Productions will listen to all newcomers in the music field. We will evaluate and give an honest opinion of their songs and help them produce, arrange or market the songs we feel show potential."

THE NEW MUSIC TIMES, INC., Box 8573, Albany NY 12208. (518)438-4815. President: Jeri Goldstein. Management firm and music publisher. Represents individual artists and songwriters; currently handles 3 acts. Receives 15-25% commission. Reviews material for acts.

How to Contact: Write first and obtain permission to submit. Prefers cassette with no more than 4 songs and lyric or lead sheets. SASE. Reports in 6 weeks.

Music: Mostly country, blues and gospel; also rock-a-billy and country-rock. Works primarily with country/folk vocalists and country bands with national touring experience. Current writers include Robin and Linda Williams and Jerome Clark.

Tips: "Looking for individual songs, not artists, at this time."

NIGHTSTREAM MUSIC, 670 Lindsay Rd., Carnegie PA 15106. A&R Director: Tom Balistreri. Management firm, recording company and music publisher. Works with artists, groups and songwriters; currently handles 6 acts. Receives 10-25% commission. Reviews material for acts.

How to Contact: Submit cassette (or videocassette) with 1-5 songs and lead sheet. SASE. Reports in 1 month.

Music: Mostly top 40/pop; also dance-oriented, easy listening, MOR, R&B and R&R. Works primarily with top 40 and country bands. Current acts include Nightstream (pop band), Tom Balistreri (singer/songwriter), Gary Gallagher (singer/songwriter); and the Gas House Band (country rock).

*CRAIG NOWAG'S NATIONAL ATTRACTIONS,6037 Haddington Dr., Memphis TN 38119. (901)767-1990. President: Craig Nowag. Management firm, booking agency and music publisher (Getwell Music, Nowag International). Represents indidvidual artists and groups; currently handles over 50 acts. Recieves 20-25% commissions. Reviews material for acts.

How to Contact: Prefers cassette with 5-7 songs. SASE. Reports in 1 month.

Music: Mostly R&B, pop and soft rock; also hard rock and dance tunes. Works primarily with dance bands, rock acts, duos and singles.

N2D/BREEZEWAY PUBLISHING COMPANIES, Box 23684, Nashville TN 37202. Contact: Douglas Casmus. Management firm and publisher. Represents artists, groups, songwriters and comedians; currently handles 2 acts. Reviews material for acts.

How to Contact: Prefers cassette with 2 songs and lyric sheet. Does not return material. Reports only if interested.

Music: Country, rock and comedy. Current acts include David Lee Murphy and Johnny Cobb (country). "We've had songs recorded by Ray Charles, John Denver, John Conlee, Maines Brothers Band, Dobie Gray and more."

Tips: "Looking for great songs—any format! Also open to crazy and novelty material."

*OFF THE TRAIL PRODUCTIONS, 72 Park Ave., Wakefield MA 01880. (617)246-0009. Management Director: Bobby Heart. Management firm, music publisher (Off The Trail) and record company (Big Records). Represents individual artists, groups, songwriters and video artists; currently handles 3 acts. Receives 20% commission. Reviews material for acts.
How to Contact: Prefers cassette (or VHS videocassette) with 3 songs. SASE. Reports in 6 weeks.
Music: Mostly pop, country and rock; also R&B. Works primarily with pop and country groups and artists. Current acts include Sunny Cowboys, Doug Heart, and Bobby Heart.

OPERATION MUSIC ENTERPRISES, 233 W. Woodland Ave., Ottumwa IA 52501. (515)682-8283. President: Nada C. Jones. Management firm and booking agency. Represents artists, groups and songwriters; currently handles 4 acts. Receives 15-25% commission. Reviews material for acts.
How to Contact: Prefers cassette and lyric sheet. Artists should include references and may submit videocassette. SASE. Reports in 2 months.
Music: Mostly country; also blues. Works primarily with vocalists, and show and dance groups. Current acts include Reesa Kay Jones (country vocalist and recording artist), John Richards Show, Country Class, Prairie Fire and Larry Gillaspie and the Rocky Mountain White Water Band.

ORBISON TOURS INC., 5414 Blackwell Rd., Memphis TN 38134. (901)386-0614. Manager: Terry Elam. Management firm and booking agency. Represents local artists, groups and songwriters; currently handles 3 acts. Receives 10-15% commission. Reviews material for acts.
How to Contact: Write first and obtain permission to submit. Prefers cassette (or VHS videocassette) and lyric or lead sheet. Does not return unsolicited material. Reports in 1 month.
Music: Mostly pop ballads, rock and country; also R&B and gospel. Works primarily with vocalists, show bands and groups as recording artists. Current acts include Roy Orbison, Small Talk and Nicholas Wall.
Tips: "Make your presentation brief and get directly to the point."

OREGON MUSICAL ARTISTS, Rt. 2, Box 411, Yamhill OR 97148-9601. (503)662-3309. Contact: Michael D. LeClair. Management firm and production agency. Represents artists, groups and songwriters; currently handles 5 acts. Receives 10-25% commission. Reviews material for acts.
How to Contact: Prefers cassette (or videocassette) with 3-10 songs and lyric sheet. Does not return unsolicited material. Reports in 1 month.
Music: Mostly top 40/pop and R&B; also blues, church/religous, country, dance, easy listening, gospel, jazz, MOR, progressive, hard and mellow rock and soul. Works primarily with dance bands "with excellent vocalists." Current acts include The Hoyt Brothers (easy country ballads), David Gaylord (top 40/pop), and Danny Wilson (funk/R&B).

ORPHEUS ENTERTAINMENT, Box 647, Orange NJ 07051. (201)375-5671. Contact: A&R Department. Management firm and production company. Represents music and variety artists, producers and songwriters; currently handles 10 acts. Receives 10-35% commission. Reviews material for acts.
How to Contact: Query by mail. Prefers cassette with 2-6 songs and lead sheet. Does not return material.
Music: Mostly pop; also jazz, comedy, MOR, progressive, R&B, rock, soul, top 40 and fusion. Works primarily with original recording and concert artists. Current acts include Jimmy Ponder (guitar jazz), Where We Live (fusion/progressive rock), Mack Goldbury and the Jazz Explosion (jazz), Willie Asbury (comedy), Albert Owens (comedy), Whyte Lyte (progressive rock), Grover Kemble and Blow Daddyo (vocal blues/jazz), Instant Instant (pop), Project 19 (progressive rock), Suburban Dog (rock), Elaine Silver (folk), The Left (new wave), The Metropolis Theatre Co., and Teruo Nakamura and the Rising Sun Band (pop).

*OVATION ENTERTAINMENT, LTD., Box 252, Roslyn NY 11576. (212)938-5572 [or (516)621-8604 (Talent Review Dept)]. President: Al Friedman. Vice President: Stuart Greenfield. Management firm. Estab. 1986. Represents individual artists, groups and songwriters; currently handles 3 acts. Receives 15-20% commission. Reviews material for acts.
How to Contact: "We will accept unsolicited submissions, but we prefer prospective artists/songwriters to write or call first for permission. We review *solicited* material first." Prefers quality cassette (16-24 track) and lyric or lead sheets. "If videocassette is not available, submit professional photos."). SASE. Reports in 6 weeks.
Music: Mostly R&B/blues, pop and rock; also country. Works primarily with R&B dance bands, pop/rock bands and vocalists or vocal groups. Current acts include Nitestarr, Little Buster and Chapter Two.
Tips: "The best tip I can give any artist, songwriter or artist/songwriter is to demonstrate a professional approach and demeanor towards your work. Show a willingness and ability to take professional advice regarding the future course of your career."

P. D. Q. DIRECTIONS, INC., 528 26th St., Santa Monica CA 90402. (213)394-8442. President: Leo Leichter. Management firm and production company. Represents artists and musical groups; currently handles 5 acts. Receives 15-25% commission. Reviews material for acts.
How to Contact: Prefers cassette (or videocassette) with 4-6 songs and lead sheet. Does not return unsolicited material. Reports in 1 month.
Music: Country, rock (country), top 40/pop and MOR. Current acts include Peter McCann (award winning songwriter), Johnny Guitar Watson (R&B), Herman Brood (rock), Society of Seven (MOR), The Limeliters (contemporary), and The Diamonds (50s rock).
Tips: "Artists should be earning at least $100,000/year and have strong work experience and professional stage presence."

*PAINTER ASSOCIATES, 1432 Ivyton St., Lancaster CA 93534. (805)942-7108. President: Richard Allan Painter. Management firm, booking agency and music publisher (R.A.P. Music). Represents individual artists, groups and songwriters; currently handles 3 acts. Receives 15-20% commission. Reviews material for acts.
How to Contact: Write or call first and obtain permission to submit. Prefers cassette (or VHS ½" videocassette) with 4 songs and lyric or lead sheets. SASE. Reports in 1 month.
Music: Mostly pop, rock and R&B; also adult contemporary, jazz/New Age. Current acts include Zion, Bob Book and Trace Balin.
Tips: "Must possess songs that have hit potential for radio airplay. Must also possess stage appearance/presence/performance visually conducive to video/TV recording exposure."

*PAPER CLIP PRODUCTIONS, INC., % Orion Pictures, 1888 Century Park E., Los Angeles CA 90067. (213)282-2754. Vice President; Kathy Lymberopoulos. Management firm and production company. Represents individual artists and groups; currently handles 7 acts. Receives 15% commission. Reviews material for acts.
How to Contact: Write or call first and obtain permission to submit. Prefers cassette (or VHS or Beta videocassette) with minimum of 3 songs and lyric sheet. SASE. Reports in 2 weeks.
Music: Mostly pop, rock and R&B; also jazz, New Age and country. Works primarily with vocalists and dance bands.

PARADISE PRODUCTIONS, Box 8721, Honolulu HI 96815. (808)942-8564. General Manager: Kathy Koran. Management firm and booking agency. Represents artists, groups and songwriters. Receives minimum 15% commission. Reviews material for acts.
How to Contact: Prefers cassette (or VHS videocassette) with minimum 4 songs and lyric sheet. SASE. Reports in 1 week.
Music: Mostly rock, top 40/pop, soul, easy listening and Las Vegas style show groups; also dance-oriented, jazz, MOR, progressive, R&B and light rock. Works primarily with Las Vegas show groups, dance bands, vocalists and high energy rock concert groups. Current acts include Rod Young (Las Vegas show band), Triple X (concert rock group), and Bobby Hutton (soul/pop show group).
Tips: "Polished songs and show are most desirable."

*PARKESONS INC., 170 Cameron Dr., Holland PA 18966. (215)355-3079. President: William J. Parkes. Management firm. Represents groups; currently handles 1 act. Receives 15% commission.
How to Submit: Prefers cassette. SASE. Reports in 1 month.
Music: Mostly Irish folk; also traditional Irish. Current acts include Ireland's Barley Bree (all Irish quartet/show band).

*PAT PATTON AND ASSOCIATES, 8622 Corbin Ave., Northridge, Los Angeles CA 91324. (818)772-0220. President: Pat Patton. Vice President: Alan Harris. Management firm. Represents individual artists, groups and songwriters; currently handles 4 acts. Receives 20% commission. Reviews material for acts.
How to Contact: Prefers cassette (or VHS videocassette) with 2-4 songs and lyric sheet. SASE. Reports in 3 weeks.
Music: Rock, country rock and pop. Works only with original recording acts and songwriters. Current acts include Richard Ferreira, Hunter Brucks, Dust Poets and Labor of Love.

PAUL PETERSON CREATIVE MANAGEMENT, 4611 Vesper Ave., Sherman Oaks CA 91403-2834. (818)906-1131. Contact: Paul Peterson. Management firm. Represents artists and groups from the Midwest and West Coast; currently handles 3 acts. Receives 15-20% commission. Reviews material for acts.
How to Contact: Prefers cassette (or ¾" or VHS videocassette) with 2-4 songs and lyric sheet. SASE. Reports in 3 weeks.

Music: Mostly pop/rock and rock; also jazz and top 40/pop. Works with rock bands doing original material. Current acts include Cinema (pop/rock band), Man About Town (pop/rock band), and Priscilla Bowman (jazz/blues).

*PHIL'S ENTERTAINMENT AGENCY LIMITED, 889 Smyth Rd., Ottawa Ontario K1G 1P4 Canada. (613)731-8983. Booking agency. Represents artists and groups; currently handles 25 acts. Receives 10-15% commission. Reviews material for acts "occasionally."
How to Contact: Query by mail. Prefers cassette with 4-7 songs. Does not return unsolicited material.
Music: Country, country/rock, MOR and "old rock 'n' roll." Works primarily with recording artists, groups and bar bands. Current acts include Gerry Allard (songwriter/recording artist), and Midnite Sun and Northern Express (country/rock bar bands).
Tips: "Be professional and business-like. Keep agency supplied with up-to-date promo material and develop entertainment ability. Videotape your live performance, then give yourself an honest review."

*PIETRO TALENT U.S.A., Box 1082, Hurst TX 76053. (817)589-7116. Owner/Manager: Vin Pietro. Management firm and booking agency. Represents individual artists and groups; currently handles 55 acts. Receives 10-20% commission. Reviews material for acts.
How to Contact: Prefers cassette (or videocassette) and lyric sheet or lead sheet. Does not return unsolicited material. Reports in 3 weeks.
Music: Mostly rock and pop; also country. Works primarily with vocalists, rock bands, top 40 and pop bands. Current acts include The Fanatix, Affirmation and Cesar & Sandy.
Tips: "We are always looking for pop tunes that can be incorporated into a zany, wild and crazy show for *The Fanatix*. Novelty songs are also welcomed. The songs are always recorded first. Duets are sought for Cesar and Sandy that are 'middle of the road' and give a romantic message."

BRIAN POMBIERE PRODUCTIONS, INC., 202 Villeneuve St. W., Montreal, Quebec H2T 2R7 Canada. (514)849-5252. Booking agency. Represents groups; currently handles 20 acts. Receives 10-15% commission. Reviews material for acts.
How to Contact: Prefers cassette with minimum 4 songs and lyric sheet. "Label all material with band name and telephone number. Label packages as promotional material." SAE and IRC. Reports in 3 weeks.
Music: Top 40, commercial rock and heavy rock. Works primarily with bar bands and show bands. Current acts include Avenue Road, The Beasties (Beatle's clone band), The Cast, The Device (new music bar band), The Edge, Frankly Scarlett (top 40 bar band), and Robin Trip.

*PPK AG, Wiesliacher 21, Zurich CH-8053 Switzerland. (01) 55 47 55. Director: Fritz Portner. Management firm and music publisher (PPK-Publishing). Represents individual artists, songwriters and producers; currently handles 3 acts. Receives variable commission. Reviews material for acts.
How to Contact: Prefers cassette with 1-5 songs and lyric sheet. SAE and IRC. Reports in 5 weeks.
Music: Mostly country and R&B. Works primarily with vocalists and country bands. Current acts include John Brack, Angelika Milster and Che & Ray.

PREFERRED ARTIST MANAGEMENT, INC., 9701 Taylorsville Rd., Louisville KY 40299. (502)267-5466. President: Dan Green. Secretary: David H. Snowden. Management firm. Deals with artists in Eastern US and Midwest states. Represents artists and groups; currently handles 6 acts. Receives 10-20% commission. Reviews material for acts.
How to Contact: Query. Prefers cassette (or video of performance) with 3-5 songs. SASE. Reports in 1 month.
Music: Dance, rock (funk, medium) and country. Works with artists ranging from bar bands to single and group concert acts. Current acts include Fine Line (top 40/original artists), Gresham (country), Lee Bradley Band (country), The Rizzuto Sisters (country), NYX (top 40/original), and Herma Lee (country).

*PREMIER ARTISTS, 9 Dundas Ln., Albert Park, Victoria 3206 Australia. (03)699-9555. Booking agency. Represents groups; currently handles 100 acts. Receives 10% commission.
How to Contact: Prefers cassette (or VHS videocassette) with any number of songs. Does not return unsolicited material. Reports in 2 weeks.
Music: Mostly rock and pop. Works primarily with rock bands. Current acts include John Farnham, Painters and Dockers, and Paul Kelly and the Coloured Girls.

*PRICELE$$ PRODUCTIONS—THE BOOKIE ENTERTAINMENT AGENCY, Box 474, Welland, Ontario L3B 5R2 Canada. (416)788-0055. President: Gary Price. Booking agency, record company (Pricele$$ Records), music publisher (Pricele$$ Music Publishing) and concert promoter. Represents

local, regional and selected individual artists, groups, songwriters and novelty acts; currently handles 15 acts. Receives 15-25% commission. Reviews material for acts.
How to Contact: Write first and obtain permission to submit. Prefers cassette (or VHS videocassette) with 3 songs and lead sheet. Does not return unsolicited material. Reports in 5 weeks.
Music: Mostly novelty and other music acts; also magic acts, puppeteer, clown. Works primarily with specialty acts; "unusual acts of all types." Current acts include Muddington A. Pearl III (country/bluegrass/novelty), The Quest (teenage trio), and Swamp Gas (country rock/novelty).
Tips: "To succeed you must be totally, full-time, enthusiastically committed to your chosen profession. Better quality acts get booked faster for more money, particularly show, novelty and variety acts. Video demos are slowly becoming more important to buyers."

PRISM PRODUCTIONS, INC., Box 8125, Ann Arbor MI 48107. (313)665-4755. Contact: Tom Stachler, Lee Berry. Management firm, booking agency and concert promoter. Represents artists, groups and songwriters; currently handles 5 acts. Receives 10-20% commission. Reviews material for acts.
How to Contact: Prefers cassette and lyric sheet. Does not return unsolicited material. Reports in 2 weeks.
Music: Mostly rock; also blues, reggae, dance-oriented, progressive and top 40/pop. Works primarily with progressive dance groups. Current acts include SLK (rock/ska group), Buzztones (pop-dance group), and Dick Siegel (blues/folk songwriter).

PROCESS TALENT MANAGEMENT, 439 Wiley Ave., Franklin PA 16323. (814)432-4633. Contact: Norman Kelly. Management firm. Represents artists and groups; currently handles 15 acts. Receives 10-15% commission. Reviews material for acts.
How to Contact: Write or call first and obtain permission to submit. Prefers 7½ ips reel-to-reel, cassette or 8-track cartridge with 2-6 songs. SASE. Reports in 2 weeks.
Music: Mostly country; also bluegrass, country, gospel, jazz and rock. Works primarily with vocalists, self-contained country shows and bar bands. Current acts include Junie Lou (country), Lady Brown Sugar (rock), Woodsmoke (bar band), and Bob Stamper (country singer).

QUADRANGLE MANAGEMENT, and Open Door Management, Suite 365, 845 Via de la Paz, Pacific Palisades CA 90272. (213)459-2559. President: Bill Traut. Associate: Rev Moore. Management firm and production company. Represents artists, groups and songwriters; currently handles 8 acts. Receives 15-20% commission. "We are sometimes paid $150/hour as consultants, and we also package with the artist on a 50/50 basis from time to time." Reviews material for acts.
How to Contact: Prefers cassette with 1-4 songs (or videocassette with 2-3 songs). SASE "with enough postage." Reports in 6 weeks.
Music: Hard rock, pop rock, jazz and New Age. Works primarily with New Age artists, hard rock bands and singer/songwriters. Artists include Y&T (pop metal rock); Osamu Kitajima (New Age composer and instrumentalist, CBS Masterworks Records); Eliza Gilkyson (pop/rock singer/songwriter); Steve Kujala (classical/jazz/fusion flute, CBS Masterworks Records); Paul McCandless (jazz/New Age oboe and reeds, Windham Hill Records); and Ian Matthews (New Age singer, has recorded 21 albums on various labels).
Tips: "Quality is important to us, both of the music and of the presentation. Send a current photo and your credits along with your demos."

QUINTO PRODUCTIONS/RECORDS, Box 2388, Toluca Lake CA 91602. Owner: Quint Benedetti. Management firm, booking agency, record company (Quinto Records) and music publisher (Quint Benedetti Music). Represents individual artists; currently handles 2 acts.
How to Contact: Prefers cassette with 3 songs and lead sheet. "Follow instructions exactly: enclose SASE, submit cassette demo and lead sheets. No phone calls please." Reports in 10 weeks.
Music: Commercial Christmas songs only.

R&J ENTERPRISES, 2 Hawkes Ave., Ossining NY 10562. (914)762-2867 or 739-0937. President: Red Brigham. Vice President: Jennifer Dreaper. Booking agency. Represents individual artists and groups; currently handles 3 acts. Receives 10-20% commission. Reviews material for acts.
How to Contact: Prefers cassette with 4-6 songs.
Music: Traditional country only. Current acts include Red Brigham (country guitarist/vocalist), Jennifer Dreaper (country vocalist/bassist), and Appalachian Jubilee Acts (traditional country show).
Tips: "Songs should be in good taste. Acts should be family-oriented and neatly dressed; music should be traditional country."

THE RAINBOW COLLECTION, LTD., Box 300, Solebury PA 18963. (215)297-8437. A&R Director: Herb Gart. Management, production and publishing firm. Represents artists, groups and songwriters;

currently handles 6 acts. Receives 20% commission. Reviews material for acts.
How to Contact: Prefers cassette (or VHS or Beta videocassette) with 3 songs. Does not return unsolicited material. Reports in 6 weeks.
Music: Rock, pop, heavy metal, country and dance-oriented. Works "almost exclusively with strong songwriters whether they are solo artists or bands." Current acts include Lorne Elliott, Ashley Cleveland, Between the Sheets, and Funhouse.
Tips: "Don't necessarily worry about current trends in music. Just do what you do to the best of your ability. With our company the song is the thing even if production-wise it's in its infant stages. If you feel you have a great and unique talent, contact us."

*RAINBOW COLLECTION LTD., Suite 806, 50 Music Square W., Nashville TN 37203. (615)320-1177. Executive Producer: Richard (Dick) O'Bitts. Management firm, record company (Happy Man Records) and music publisher (Rocker Music and Happy Man Music). Represents individual artists, groups, songwriters and producers; currently handles 4 acts. Reviews material for acts.
How to Contact: Prefers cassette (or VHS videocassette) with 4 songs and lyric sheet. SASE. Reports in 1 month.
Music: All types. Works primarily with writer/artists and groups of all kinds. Current acts include Ashley Cleveland, Tommy Cash, and Miracle 7.

RAINBOW PRODUCTIONS AND PROMOTIONS, 11704 Ventura Blvd., Studio City CA 91604. (818)766-3538. President: Victor Perrotti. Management firm, music publisher (Vision Qwest Publishing) and promotion and production firm. Represents individual artists, groups, songwriters and other record companies; currently handles 3 acts. Receives 20% commission. Reviews material for acts.
How to Contact: Submit demo tape by mail. Write first to arrange personal interview. Prefers cassette and lyric sheet. Does not return unsolicited material.
Music: Mostly rock, R&B and gospel. Works primarily with "Christian artists in the rock/R&B and gospel areas." Current acts include Darrell Mansfield, Noel Paul Stookey (of Peter, Paul and Mary), and Shout.
Tips: "We are a full-line production and promotion company. We get our records played."

THE RECORD COMPANY OF THE SOUTH (RCS), 5220 Essen Ln., Baton Rouge LA 70809. (504)766-3233. President: Cyril E. Vetter. Vice President: Andrew Vetter. Management firm, music publisher and record company. Represents artists, groups and songwriters; currently handles 5 acts. Receives 20-25% commission. Reviews material for acts.
How to Contact: Prefers cassette with 2-6 songs and lyric sheet. SASE. Reports in 6 weeks.
Music: Country, R&B, rock, soul and top 40/pop. Works primarily with artists, bands and songwriters. Current acts include Irma Thomas (top 40/pop and R&B), Luther Kent (top 40/pop and R&B), and Butch Hornsby (country).

RECORD MUSIC, INC., Box 182, Middle Village, New York NY 11379. (212)898-3027. President: Peter Paul. Management firm, music publisher and record producer. Represents artists, groups and songwriters worldwide.
How to Contact: Prefers cassette. SASE. Reporting time "varies."
Music: Bluegrass, blues, dance-oriented, easy listening, jazz, MOR, progressive, R&B, soul and top 40/pop.

RODGERS REDDING & ASSOCIATES, Box 4603, Macon GA 31208. (912)742-8771. President: Rodgers Redding. Booking agency. Represents artists and groups; currently handles 10 acts. Receives 10-15% commission. Reviews material for acts.
How to Contact: Query by mail, then submit demo tape. Prefers cassette with 4-12 songs. SASE. Reports in 1 month.
Music: Mostly R&B; also soul, blues and top 40/pop. Works primarily with dance and bar bands. Current acts include Clarence Carter (male vocalist/musician), Tyrone Davis (male vocalist), Brick (5-piece self-contained R&B group), Denise La Salle, Latimore, Johnny Taylor, The Reddings (R&B group), Betty Wright (R&B vocalist), Formula Five, and Joe Simon.
Tips: "Be yourself."

REED SOUND RECORDS, INC., 120 Mikel Dr., Summerville SC 29483. (803)873-3324. Contact: Haden Reed. Management firm. Represents artists and groups; currently handles 3 acts. Receives 2-4% commission. Reviews material for acts.
How to Contact: Query by mail. Prefers cassette with 1-4 songs. SASE. Reports in 1 month.
Music: Mostly country; also church/religious, easy listening and gospel. Current acts include Becky Knowles and The Country Blues, Haden Reed (country songwriter), Vocalettes (gospel), and Country Blues (show band).

*JOEY RICCA, JR.'S ENTERTAINMENT AGENCY, 408 S. Main St., Milltown NJ 08850. (201)287-1230. Owner/President: Joseph Frank Ricca, Jr. Management firm and booking agency. Represents individual artists, groups and songwriters; currently handles 75-100 acts. Receives 10-15% commission. Reviews material for acts.
How to Contact: Write or call to arrange personal interview. "We prefer that all material be copyrighted and that a letter be sent right before submitting material, but neither of these is essential." Prefers cassette or reel-to-reel (or videocassette) with 3-4 songs and lyric or lead sheets. Does not return unsolicited material. Reports in 6 weeks.
Music: Mostly love songs/ballads, songs for big band vocalists, and soft jazz/Latin; also good commercial material. Current acts include Maria Angela, Donny "Z," and Anthony Paccone.
Tips: "Good lyrics and strong musical arrangements are essential if one of our vocalists are to select a song they would like to sing."

JOANNE RILE MANAGEMENT, INC., Box 27539, Philadelphia PA 19118. (215)233-2333. President: Joanne Rile. Management firm, booking agency, promotion firm and consultant. Represents artists, groups, novelty acts (magic show) and dance and theater presentations; currently handles 50 acts. Receives 20% commission; "fees are used for preparation of promotional work." Reviews material for acts.
How to Contact: Query by mail. "Send reviews and brochures with letter of inquiry." Prefers cassette with 6-10 songs. SASE. Reports between June and August.
Music: Mostly classical; also bluegrass, choral, folk, gospel and jazz. Works primarily with classical, soft rock and folk soloists and brass ensembles (quartets, trios, quintets). Current acts include Chestnut Brass Co. (classical brass ensemble), Ed McDade (soft rock/folk singer/songwriter), and Leon Bates (classical pianist).
Tips: "We deal with experienced artists who have been performing and have reviews, brochures, glossy photos, records or tapes (or some professional bio material)."

*RIOHCAT MUSIC, 104 Walnut Trace, Hendersonville TN 37075. (615)824-1435. Contact: Robert Kayne. Management firm, booking agency, record company (Avita) and music publisher (Riohcat Music). Represents individual artists and groups; currently handles 3 acts. Receives 15% commission. Reviews material for acts.
How to Contact: Prefers cassette and lead sheet. Does not return unsolicited material. Reports in 6 weeks.
Music: Mostly contemporary jazz and fusion. Works primarily with jazz ensembles. Current acts include Jerry Tachoir Quartet, Marlene Tachoir, and Jerry Tachoir/Van Manakas Duo.
Tips: "Be organized, neat and professional."

RMS TRIAD PRODUCTIONS, 6267 Potomac Circle, West Bloomfield MI 48033. (313)585-2552. Owner: Bob Zaner. Entertainment producer/consultant. "We are an entertainment production/consultation firm which deals with national organizaton convention needs." Represents individual artists and groups; currently handles numerous acts. Receives flat fee. Reviews material for acts.
How to Contact: Write first and obtain permission to submit. Prefers cassette with 3 songs. Does not return unsolicited material. Reports in 3 weeks.
Music: Jazz/instrumental.

*RNJ PRODUCTIONS, INC., 11514 Calvert St., North Hollywood CA 91606. (818)762-6105. President: Rein Neggo, Jr. Management firm. Represents individual artists; currently handles 3 acts. Receives 10-25% commission. Reviews material for acts.
How to Contact: Prefers cassette (or videocassette) with 3 songs and lead sheet. SASE. Reports in 1 month.
Music: Mostly country, pop and folk. Works primarily with vocalists. Current acts include Glenn Yarbrough, Arizona Smoke Review and Peggy Moyer.

*ROB-LEE MUSIC, Box 1338, Merchantville NJ 08109. (609)962-6000. President: Rob Russen. Management firm, booking agency, publishing company and record company. Represents artists, groups and songwriters; currently handles 30 acts. Receives 4-6% commission. Reviews material for acts.
How to Contact: Prefers cassette (or videocassette) with 2-6 songs and lyric sheet. Does not return unsolicited material. Reports in 1 month.
Music: Mostly dance-oriented, R&B and rock; also easy listening, jazz, MOR, soul and top 40/pop. Current acts include The All Stars (R&B/blues), Sheldon Price (R&B), Snow (rock), Big El (top 40), Thriller (Michael Jackson show act), and Phoenix (funk), Bill Haley's Comets (rock), The Castnos (rock), The Dovells (rock), and Rainbow Bridge (rock).

ROCHESTER TALENT UNLIMITED, INC., 346 Ridge Rd. E, Rochester NY 14621. (716)342-4650. President: Thomas DiPoala. Management firm and booking agency. Represents groups in New York state; currently handles 40-50 acts. Receives 15-30% commission. Reviews material for acts.
How to Contact: Query by mail or submit demo tape. Prefers cassette with 3-6 songs. "We need promotional material, photos, song lists, letters of recommendation and news clippings." SASE. Reports in 2 weeks.
Music: Mostly top 40/pop, funk and country; also dance, MOR, R&B, rock and soul. Works primarily with dance bands (high energy to MOR) and vocalists. Current acts include Incognito (showy dance band), Brother to Brother (lounge duo), Labella (lounge duo—show/dance), and Perfect Stranger (top 40/rock/show).
Tips: "We need a good cassette and professional photos. We are always on the lookout for good quality acts that we might manage."

ROCK-A-BILLY ARTIST AGENCY, Box 4740, Nashville TN 37216. (615)865-4740. A&R Director: S.D. Neal. Management firm, booking agency and record company. Represents artists and groups; currently handles 6 acts. Receives 15% commission. Reviews material for acts.
How to Contact: Prefers cassette with 2-6 songs and lyric sheet. SASE. Reports in 3 weeks.
Music: Mostly rock and country; also all other types including rockabilly. Works primarily with vocalists. Current acts include Dixie Dee, Rhythm Rockers, and Rufus Thomas.

RODANCA MUSIC, 3627 Park Ave., Memphis TN 38111. (901)454-0300. Music publisher and consultant. Represents songwriters; currently handles 7 acts. Receives 15-25% commission. Reviews material for acts.
How to Contact: Prefers 7½ ips reel-to-reel or cassette (or ½" home or ¾-1" professional videocassette) with 4 songs and lead sheet. Does not return unsolicited material. Reports in 2 weeks.
Music: Mostly gospel; also R&B and pop-country. Works primarily with groups and solo vocalists. Current acts include Donald Watkins (gospel vocalist), Lisa Boxx, and Thomas V. Murphy (Christian contemporary).

***ROLLING THUNDER PRODUCTIONS**, Box 144, Holmes PA 19043. President: Lori Gallagher. Management firm and concert promoter. Represents individual artists and groups; currently handles 24 acts. Receives 15% commission. Reviews material for acts.
How to Contact: Prefers cassette with 3 songs. "Submit photo and bio." Does not return unsolicited material. Reports in 3 weeks.
Music: Mostly hard rock, progressive hard rock and heavy metal. Works primarily with hard rock bands and individual artists. Clients include Cinderella (heavy metal, Polygram Records), Anvil Bitch, and Britny Fox.
Tips: "Currently seeking catchy hard rock talent for concerts and possible management."

RUSCH PRODUCTIONS INC., ENTERTAINMENT AGENCY, 3588 N. Thomas Rd., Freeland MI 48623. (517)781-1553. President: Dean A. Rusch. Booking agency. Represents groups in Michigan; currently handles over 300 acts. Receives variable commission. Reviews material for acts.
How to Contact: Write first and obtain permission to submit. Prefers cassette (or VHS videocassette) with 3-10 songs and lyric sheet. SASE. Reports in 2 weeks.
Music: Mostly top 40/pop; also country, dance-oriented, easy listening and rock. Works primarily with dance bands. Current acts include Ceyx, Dedication, Harmony, Loose Change, Evergreen and Infinity (all dance bands).

***S.R.P. SOUND PRODUCTIONS**, 159 New St., New Brunswick NJ 08901. (201)246-4701. President: James Bratton. Management firm, record company (S.R.P. Sound), music publisher (Bratton and White Publishing/ASCAP) and music production company. Deals with artists from east coast; currently handles 5 acts. Receives 20% commission. Reviews material for acts.
How to Contact: Prefers cassette with 3 songs and lyric sheet. SASE
Music: R&B, pop and rock. Works primarily with vocalists. Current acts include Sybil, Jason Smith and Kelly Charles.
Tips: "We are geared toward the dance music and some top 40. Our company primarily caters to solo artists who show potential of being an entertainer. More importantly, we look toward those artists who possess the ability to handle a music career on a professional business level with a sharp mind."

SALT WORKS MUSIC, INC., 21 Fleetwood Ave., Jackson OH 45640-1806. (614)286-3420. (Branch: 39 Music Square E., Nashville TN 37203.) President: R.J. Elliot. Vice President: M.A. Morgan. Management firm and music publisher (Sojourner Music/BMI and Salt Creek Music/ASCAP). Estab. 1986. Represents individual artists, groups and songwriters (Nashville talent and regional artists; Ohio, West

Virginia and Kentucky); currently handles 5 acts. Reviews material for acts.
How to Contact: "Requests and tapes should be sent to our Jackson, Ohio office." Prefers cassette or 7½ ips reel-to-reel with 3-4 songs and demo and lyric sheet. "We will not return tape unless postage paid envelope is provided." Reports in 3 weeks.
Music: Mostly country, country rock and gospel; also pop and MOR. Works primarily with vocalists and country bands, also some gospel acts.

SAMARAH PRODUCTIONS, INC., Box 2501, Columbia SC 29202. (803)754-3556. President: Daniel Hodge Jr. Vice President: Myron Alford. Management firm, booking agency, music publisher and record production company. Represents artists, groups and songwriters primarily from the southeast; currently handles 5 acts. Receives 20-25% commission. Reviews material for acts.
How to Contact: Query by mail, then submit demo tape. Prefers 7½ ips reel-to-reel or cassette with 4-8 songs. "Will only negotiate with serious and dedicated people." SASE. Reports in 3 weeks.
Music: R&B, top 40/pop, country, soul and rock. Works primarily with "self-contained dance/show bands; solo, duet, trio, or quartet performers." Current acts include Remmel Young (show band), Midnight Blue (R&B self-contained band), Joannie Dickens (country artist), Distance, Saffire (R&B bands), and Tony Howard (top 40).
Tips: "Have patience, dedication and of course, *talent*."

SCOTT-DEAN AGENCY, 428 Hill St., Reno NV 89501. (702)322-9426. Contact: Steve Cox. Booking agency. Represents artists, groups and songwriters; currently handles 150 acts. Receives 10-15% commission. Reviews material for acts.
How to Contact: Write first and obtain permission to submit or arrange personal interview. Prefers cassette and lyric sheet. Artists may submit videocassette. SASE. Reports in 2 weeks.
Music: Mostly top 40, country/rock and R&B; also country, dance-oriented, MOR, rock, soul and pop. Works primarily with dance and show bands. Current acts include Tommy Bell (country/rock/blues), The Wrays (country/rock), Starfire (show band), St. Romain (top 40 show/dance), and Command Performance (show/dance).

SEEDS, INC., Box 220601, Charlotte NC 28222. (704)376-4388. President: Bob Ferster. Management firm. Represents artists, groups and speakers from the southeast; currently handles 3 acts. Receives 15-25% commission. Reviews material for acts.
How to Contact: Query by mail. Prefers cassette with 3-6 songs and lyric sheet. SASE. Reports in 1 month.
Music: Mostly contemporary Christian; also bluegrass, easy listening, gospel, MOR, rock (hard and pop) and top 40/pop. Works primarily with 4-7 member Christian rock bands. Current acts include Don Hall (MOR), Deliverance (gospel), and Heir Express (rock).

*SEGUE MANAGEMENT, Box 3612, New York NY 10185. (212)614-0565. President: Steven E. Grill. Management firm. Represents individual artists, groups and songwriters; currently handles 3 acts. Receives 10-50% commission. Reviews material for acts.
How to Contact: Prefers cassette (or VHS videocassette) and lyric sheet. Does not return unsolicited material. Reports in 1 month.
Music: Mostly rock, folk/rock and pop. Works primarily with folk/rock oriented singer/songwriters. Current acts include Kim Parent, Barry Richman and Donna Christy.

*SEIDSADDLE PRODUCTIONS, 112 16th Ave. S., Nashville TN 37203. (615)794-4156 or 225-6565. President: Michael A. Seidel. Management firm, booking agency, record company (NEO Records), music publisher (Fountain of Songs Music) and concession management. Represents individual artists, groups and songwriters; currently handles 9 acts. Receives variable commission. Reviews material for acts.
How to Contact: Write or call first and obtain permission to submit. Prefers cassette or 15 ips reel-to-reel (or videocassette) with 2 songs. SASE. Reports in 1 month.
Music: Mostly country, pop and gospel; also bluegrass, adult contemporary and R&B. Works primarily with vocalists. Current acts include The White's, Leroy Van Dyke and Connie M. Kurtz.
Tips: "We are also interested in original bands who write original music."

WILLIAM SEIP MANAGEMENT, INC., 104 King St. S, Waterloo, Ontario, N2J 1P5 Canada. (519)885-6570. President: William Seip. Management firm. Represents musical groups from the Ontario region (at present); currently handles 11 groups. Receives 10-25% commission. Reviews material for acts.
How to Contact: Query by mail or phone, then arrange personal interview. Prefers cassette (or videocassette) with 1-3 songs. SAE and IRC. Reporting time varies.

Music: Mostly commercial rock; also rock (heavy) and top 40/pop. Works with bar bands and concert acts. Current acts include Helix (heavy R&R), Kickaxe (heavy R&R), Vigilants (commercial to heavy R&R) and Lone Bony (commercial rock).

*SELECT ARTISTS ASSOCIATES, 7300 E. Camelback Rd., Scottsdale AZ 85251. (602)994-0471. Owner/Operator: Charles T. Johnston. Booking agency. Represents individual artists and groups; currently handles 25 acts. Receives 15% commission. Reviews material for acts.
How to Contact: Prefers cassette (or videocassette). SASE. Reports in 1 month.
Music: Mostly rock (top 40), pop and R&B. Works primarily with dance bands. Current acts include Corte, Unity and The Enrico Brothers.

*SHADOWFACTS MANAGEMENT, 2108A Westmont Rd. NW, Calgary, Alberta T2N 3N2 Canada. (403)247-1166. General Manger: Dan Cloutier. Management firm and publicity company. Represents local and regional individual artists, groups and songwriters; currently handles 3 acts. Receives negotiable commission. Reviews material for acts.
How to Contact: Prefers cassette (or VHS videocassette) with 3-5 songs and lyric sheet. SAE and IRC. Reports in 1 month.
Music: Mostly pop and rock. Works primarily with recording artists and bar bands. Current acts include Aaron James, Theme and 20-20.
Tips: "Must be highly motivated and commercial."

*SHOE STRING BOOKING AGENCY, 696 The Queensway, Toronto Ontario M8Y 1K9 Canada. (416)255-5166. Contact: Armin Darmstadt. Management firm and booking agency. Represents local artists; currently handles 10 acts. Receives 15% commission. Reviews material for acts.
How to Contact: Write first and obtain permission to submit. Prefers cassette (or VHS videocassette) with 2-4 songs and lyric sheet. Does not return unsolicited material. Reports in 3 weeks.
Music: Mostly rock, R&B/pop and country/rock. Works primarily with vocalists and dance bands. Current acts include SAB, Gigalo and Pulsations.

SHORE MANAGEMENT CO., 12409 Ventura Ct., Studio City CA 91604. (818)509-0316. A&R Directors: Steve Shore and Mark Anderson. Management firm. Represents artists, groups and songwriters; currently handles 20 acts. Receives 10-25% commission. Reviews material for acts.
How to Contact: Query by mail, then submit demo tape. Prefers cassette with 3-5 songs and lyric sheet. Does not return unsolicited material. Reports in 1 month.
Music: Metal to pop. Works primarily with original rock acts seeking recording contracts. "We are active in the international rock market, and can arrange production/distribution deals." Current acts include Agent Steel (heavy metal), Club Adobe, and Four Eyes (original rock acts).
Tips: "We look for a unique, identifiable sound that's consistent from song to song."

*SHOWCASE PRODUCTIONS, Suite 2, 2585 Portage Ave., Winnipeg, Manitoba R3J 0P5 Canada. (204)889-5567. Owner & President: Doug Mac Farlane. Management firm, booking agency and record company (Down Recording Company). Represents individual artists, groups and specialty acts; currently handles 45 acts. Receives 5-15% commission. Reviews material for acts.
How to Contact: Write first and obtain permission to submit or to arrange personal interview. Prefers cassette (or Beta or VHS videocassette) with 6-8 songs and lyric sheet. Does not return unsolicited material. Reports in 1 week.
Music: Mostly country rock, top 40 and old rock 'n' roll; also blues and specialty acts. Works primarily with dance bands, rock bands and blues bands. Current acts include Buddy Knox, Larry Laker Trio, Whiskey Bent Band and Gateway Band.

*SHOWTIME PRODUCTIONS, 120 North St., Bolivar MO 65613. (417)326-3244. Manager: Charley Ealy. Management firm. Represents individual artists. Currently handles 1 act. Reviews material for acts.
How to Contact: Prefers cassette. Does not return unsolicited material.
Music: Mostly country. Works primarily with vocalists.

SIDARTHA ENTERPRISES, LTD., Box 1414, East Lansing, MI 48823. (517)351-6780. President: Thomas R. Brunner. Management firm and booking agency. Represents artists and groups; currently handles 14 acts. Receives 15-20% commission. Reviews material for acts.
How to Contact: "Always make phone contact first." Prefers cassette with at least 4 songs and lyric sheet. SASE. Reports in 1 month.
Music: Rock and top 40/pop. Works primarily with bar bands and recording acts. Current acts include Normandy (rock), Savage Grace (rock), and Blitz.

Close-up

Al Kasha and Joel Hirschhorn

Songwriters, Authors
Beverly Hills, California

Al Kasha

Joel Hirschhorn

Rejection—*that terrifying word. All frightened people dread it, equate it with emotional death. . . .*

As a person who has fought and survived the rejections of show business, I can say that rejection is largely a matter of what we perceive in advance. When someone—a publisher, a producer—says no, you swallow hard, stand up straight, and go on. The anticipation of it is what overwhelms you.

—Al Kasha and Joel Hirschhorn from Reaching the Morning After

It seems odd that after twenty years of successful collaboration, Al Kasha and Joel Hirschhorn have written a book dealing with rejection. Titled *Reaching the Morning After*, their book is actually about many different things. As Kasha explains, "it's both our life stories. It's how to overcome struggles and how to maintain some kind of balance. It tells about the pitfalls of creativity."

The songwriting team stresses that success in the music industry, at least for them, has not been simply one glorious accomplishment after another—there have been ups and downs. Even as they were winning Oscars and collecting gold records, Kasha was terrified of leaving his home. He and his brother had been abused as children; their mother was a battered wife. Al hoped that through achieving success he could rescue his mother from that terrible situation. Basing his whole life on accomplishment, he became over responsible and developed agoraphobia—the fear of open places. "When you're a phobic," Kasha says, "you imprison a lot of people. I imprisoned Joel—I had to write in my home. And then I would tell fibs all the time to get other people to my home."

"What sustained Al," Hirschhorn feels, "was this strong creative drive. The love of writing kept him focused when he thought the world was falling apart. It was like an anchor." They both feel that tenacity has been a key ingredient in their successful careers.

All songwriters can learn from the experience of these two men, as they have tackled various projects. In addition to three books on songwriting and the music industry, they've written Oscar-winning pop songs ("The Morning After," "We May Never Love Like This Again"), Tony-nominated Broadway scores (*Seven Brides for Seven Brothers*, *Copperfield*), and the Oscar-winning film musical (*Pete's Dragon*). They both feel that this diversification was necessary to keep their careers moving forward. As Kasha says, "I think the reason Joel and I have stayed partners for all these years is that we have never gotten stale. If you're talented, you should be able to move [onto different styles of music and different types of projects]. When you get cold, you've got to think of a different avenue to turn you on. A great artist is one who will stretch his creative muscles and challenge himself."

Hirschhorn agrees. "An actor plays different roles. The fun of acting is to get into a different character completely. Trying all these different things, we're trying out different characters. We're playing roles, too."

"Everyone tries to put everyone in little boxes, and it's not the truth," Kasha continues. "Everyone says Burt Bacharach writes songs that have jazz syncopations. But he wrote 'Magic Moments' for Perry Como which is the squarest song you could possibly think of. Cole Porter—everyone thinks he was a sophisticated Broadway writer, but he wrote 'Don't Fence Me In.' No writer really likes to be put into a pigeonhole."

"Great writers," Hirschhorn concludes, "who have really lasted, have written for *everybody*."

Kasha and Hirschhorn rely on outside stimulation for ideas and that is something they recommend to other songwriters. Kasha advises, "Find out what's happening in the news. To relate to your times is terribly important. Another thing we do to keep that creativity flowing is to listen to a lot of other people's music."

The team also suggests songwriters carefully evaluate each writing project. Kasha and Hirschhorn critique their own work, as well as ask for outside opinions. Kasha says, "You've got to be tough on yourself as well as applaud yourself." Or as Hirschhorn puts it, "You've got to ask yourself, 'Is this the best it can be? We've gone ninety percent—is there *anything* that can be improved?' "

If it's not your best effort, Kasha suggests, "it'll only come back to haunt you later. I always ask for two opinions from people I respect but who don't know each other. Then we'll see if there's a consistency in their comments. If someone we really respect says something about our work, we will listen to them. But I always tell writers to get two confirmations."

"And if someone criticizes your work," Hirschhorn adds, "you have to think to yourself, 'Maybe there's some validity there—they had an emotional response to it.' I mean, you can say they're crazy and so forth, but then you don't grow. When you're listening to and studying records you might want to say, 'Oh, how did that get to number one, that's just trash.' That, again, is a mistake because there's a *reason* why every single thing succeeds, whether it happens to be to your taste or not."

"Most people can't deal with rejection," Kasha feels. "The minute they're rejected once, they're gone. But I think the only way you get better at your craft is through rejection."

Kasha and Hirschhorn have certainly developed a way to deal with rejection and learn from criticism. The absolute love of writing and an intense desire to be successful writers have been and continue to be the things that get them over some very tough hurdles. And it is this spirit they wish to share with other songwriters. "I think passion is everything, not winning is everything," Kasha says. "You have to love what you do. When my life was falling apart in many other ways, the love of writing was the thing that got me through."

" 'The Morning After,' " Hirschorn explains, "aside from a song, has been our creed. There's got to be a morning after. We wrote of our feelings, our optimism, our hope, our determination."

Kasha agrees. "What we'd like to leave behind is a positive message that there's love and hope for all people. We always wrote very positive songs, even when I was going through my hell of child abuse and agoraphobia. That's what we felt would be our stamp, you know, to leave very positive songs behind."

—Julie Wesling Whaley

SILVER/LOOMAS PRODUCTIONS, 38 Music Square E., Nashville TN 37203. (615)255-8008. Contact: Vice President. Management agency, record company (Capstan Records), and music publisher (Lineage/BMI). Represents individual artists, groups and songwriters; currently handles 3 acts. Receives negotiable commission. Reviews material for acts.
How to Contact: Prefers cassette with no more than 3 songs and lyric sheet. "Songs should be no longer than three minutes." SASE. Reports in 3 weeks.
Music: Country and country/rock. Works primarily with vocalists.
Tips: "Cooperative attitude most important."

SIMMONS MANAGEMENT CO., Suite 1004, 5 W. Hargett St., Raleigh NC 27601. (919)828-1277. President: Harry Simmons. Vice President: Debbie Cecil. Management firm. Represents producers, artists, groups and songwriters; currently handles 5 acts. Receives 15-20% commission. Reviews material for acts.
How to Contact: Prefers cassette (or ¾" or VHS videocassette) with 3-6 songs and lyric sheet; also submit promotional material, photos and clippings. SASE. Reports in 6 weeks.
Music: Mostly modern pop; also modern rock, new wave, dance-oriented, MOR, R&B and top 40/pop. Works primarily with "original music recording acts or those that aspire to be." Current acts include Don Dixon (producer, songwriter and performer), and Marti Jones (recording artist).
Tips: "We are interested in strong songs; style is not so important."

BRAD SIMON ORGANIZATION, INC., 445 E. 80th St., New York NY 10021. (212)988-4962. President: Brad Simon. Represents individual artists, record producers, musical groups and songwriters; currently handles 12 acts. Receives 20% commission. Reviews material for acts.
How to Contact: Prefers cassette (or VHS videocassette) with minimum 3 songs. SASE. Reports in 2 months.
Music: R&B/pop, easy listening, jazz, MOR, progressive, rock (all types) and top 40/pop. Works with artists, groups and songwriters in contemporary rock, pop, jazz with strong commercial appeal and crossover potential, vocal and instrumental artists with strong performing and writing skills. Current acts include John Blake (jazz/R&B), Tom Grant (pop/jazz), Harvie Swartz (jazz), and Max Roach (jazz).
Tips: "Songwriters and artists must have original and distinctive material with strong commercial appeal."

*MICHAEL SKINNER PRODUCTIONS, 101 McDuffie St., Manchester NH 03102. (603)669-6353. President: Michael Skinner. Management firm and booking agency. Represents individual artists and groups. Currently handles 10 acts. Receives 10-15% commission. Reviews material for acts.
How to Contact: Prefers cassette with 3 songs. SASE. Reports in 3 weeks.
Music: Mostly rock and pop. Works primarily with rock groups. Current acts include Toiz, Section 8 and Peer Pressure.
Tips: "Send complete promo package along with a resume."

T. SKORMAN PRODUCTIONS, INC., 2362 Barbados Dr., Winter Park FL 32792. (305)677-9399. Management firm. Represents groups; currently handles 25 acts. Receives 10-25% commission. Reviews material for acts.
How to Contact: "Phone for permission to send tape." Prefers cassette with 3 songs (or videocassette of no more than 15 minutes). Does not return unsolicited material. Reports in 1 month.
Music: Mostly top 40 and dance; also rock, MOR and pop. Works primarily with high-energy dance acts, recording acts, and top 40 bands. Current acts include Bonalyn (recording act), Frontrunner (dance), Rain (dance), No Ones Ark (dance), and Joe Keys (show group).
Tips: "We have many pop recording acts, and are looking for commercial material for their next albums."

*SKYLINE MUSIC CORP., 85 Fairhaven Ln., Marstans Mills MA 02648. (617)420-2225. President: Bruce Houghton. Management firm, booking agency and record company (Adventure Records). Represents individual artists and groups. Currently handles 12 acts. Receives 10-20% commission. Reviews material for acts.
How to Contact: Prefers cassette with 3 songs. Does not return unsolicited material.
Music: Mostly rock and pop. Works primarily with concert rock attractions and dance bands. Current acts include Foghat, Wishbone Ash and Black Oak Arkansas.

JOANNE SMALE PRODUCTIONS, Suite 2, 466 Spadina Ave., Toronto, Ontario M5T 2G8 Canada. (416)961-3424. Contact: Joanne Smale. Public relations firm. Represents artists, groups and songwriters. Receives negotiable commission. Reviews material for acts.

How to Contact: Query by mail or submit demo. Prefers cassette (or videocassette) and lyric sheet. SASE. Reporting time varies.
Music: Mostly rock; also blues, folk, MOR, progressive, R&B, soul and top 40/pop. Current acts include Bruce Cockburn (folk/rock), Murray McLavehlan (country/folk/rock), and Johnny MacLeod (rock/folk).

DAN SMITH AGENCY, Box 3634, Shawnee Mission KS 66203. (913)648-3906. Contact: Dan Smith. Management firm and booking agency. Represents artists, groups and songwriters in the Midwest. Receives 10-20% commission. Reviews material for acts.
How to Contact: Prefers cassette with 3-5 songs and lyric sheet. SASE. Reports in 1 month.
Music: Mostly country rock, top 40, progressive and R&B; also bluegrass, blues, country, dance-oriented, folk, jazz, MOR and soul. Works primarily with dance and concert bands. Current acts include Riverrock (country rock), Glow (progressive rock), Bob Smith (folk single), and Crossroads (country rock).
Tips: "Have complete promo—bio, photo (glossy), song list, credits, etc."

*SONRISE INTERNATIONAL, #208, 3761 Stocker St., Los Angeles CA 90008. (213)295-4371. Agent: Carol Houston. Booking agency. Represents individual artists, groups and songwriters. Currently handles 16 acts. Receives 10-15% commission. Reviews material for acts.
How to Contact: Call first and obtain permission to submit. Prefers cassette. Does not return unsolicited material.
Music: Gospel only. Works primarily with Christian vocalists. Current acts include Sandra Crouch, Daryl Coley and Shirley Miller.
Tips: Songwriter must have "commitment to the ministry of the gospel of Christ through song."

SOPRO, INC., Box 227, Chicago Ridge IL 60415. (312)425-0174. Contact: Bud Monaco or Red Rose. Management firm and artist development firm. Represents artists and groups in the local region; currently handles 7 acts. Receives maximum 20% commission. Reviews material for acts.
How to Contact: Write first and obtain permission to submit. Prefers cassette with 3-6 songs and lead sheet. Does not return unsolicited material. Reports in 2 weeks if interested.
Music: Mostly rock, dance-oriented and top 40; also R&B, MOR and progressive rock. Works primarily with concert rock and dance-oriented bands. Current acts include John Hunter (rock/dance), Don Griffin and The Griff Band (rock/R&B), Tony Wilson (top 40/rock), The Midwest Expedition (rock), Bottoms Up (rock), Trytan (rock), and Jody Noa & The Sho'Nuff Blues Band (blues).

SOUND '86 TALENT MANAGEMENT, Box 222, Black Hawk SD 57718. (605)343-3941. Management firm. Represents artists and groups. Receives 5-10% commission. Reviews material for acts.
How to Contact: Query by mail or submit demo tape. Prefers cassette with 3-8 songs and lyric sheet. SASE. Reports in 1 month.
Music: Mostly rock (all types); also bluegrass, country, dance, easy listening and top 40/pop. Works primarily with bands.

SOUTHERN CONCERTS, 7050 the Ridge Cove, Memphis TN 38115. (901)755-9920. President: Buddy Swords. Management firm and record company (SCR Records). Represents artists; currently handles 4 acts. Receives 15-20% commission. Reviews material for acts.
How to Contact: Prefers cassette with maximum 4 songs. Does not return unsolicited material. Reports in 1 week.
Music: Country, country/rock and top 40/pop. Current acts include Jerry Lee Lewis, Wendel Adkins, Tony Joe White (all country/rock artists); and Dennis James (bar band).

SOUTHERN TALENT INTERNATIONAL, 2925 Fallowridge Ct., Snellville GA 30278. (404)979-0847. President: John M. Titak. Management firm and booking agency. Represents groups and songwriters; currently handles 45 acts. Receives 10-15% commission. Reviews material for acts.
How to Contact: Call first and obtain permission to submit. Prefers cassette (or videocassette) with 3 songs and lead sheet. SASE. Reports in 1 month.
Music: Mostly rock, heavy metal and top 40; also bluegrass, dance, easy listening, R&B and soul. Works primarily with bar bands and recording artists. Current acts include Stalker, Bad Influence, Ruby Starr, Black Oak Arkansas, Warchylde, Strange Angle, Bad Finger, Arson, Jack Secret , No Control, Van Zant, Cub Koda, Head East, Pat Traverse and Dead Boys.

SPIDER ENTERTAINMENT CO., 5 Portsmouth Towne, Southfield MI 48075. President: Arnie Tencer. Vice President: Joel Zuckerman. Management firm. Represents artists, groups and songwriters; currently handles 1 act. Receives minimum 20% commission. Reviews material for acts.

How to Contact: Prefers cassette with 3-6 songs. Does not return unsolicited material. Reports only if interested.
Music: Mostly contemporary pop; also rock (hard) and top 40/pop. Works primarily with "rock bands with good songs and great live shows." Current acts include The Romantics (rock band).
Tips: Artists "must have commercially viable material."

STAR ARTIST MANAGEMENT INC., Box 114, Fraser MI 48026. (313)979-5115. President: Ron Geddish. Executive Vice President: Mike Quillin. Director of Canadian Operations: Brian Courtis. Director of West Coast Operations: Greg McCutcheon. Director of East Coast Operations: Nat Weiss. Management firm and record company (Track Records). Represents solo rock performers and rock groups; currently handles 4 acts. Receives 10-20% commission. Reviews material for acts.
How to Contact: Prefers cassette with 2 songs. SASE. Reports ASAP.
Music: Rock. Works primarily with new music and rock groups. Current acts include Toby Redd (rock, RCA Records); Bitter Sweet Alley (rock, Orient/RCA Records), Infra-Red (rock, Track Records); and Beldren (rock, Track Records).

STARBOUND MANAGEMENT, INC., Suite 915, Three Rivers N, Ft. Wayne IN 46802. (219)426-7827. Entertainment consultant: Ryan Aldrich. Management firm and booking agency. Represents artists and groups; currently handles 18 acts. Receives 15-20% commission.
How to Contact: Query by mail or submit demo. Prefers cassette (or live "full set" VHS videocassette) with 4-8 songs. "All submissions should include one 8x10 photo, song list and equipment list." Does not return unsolicited material unless SASE is provided. Reports in 2 weeks.
Music: Mostly contemporary (dance-oriented) MOR; also easy listening, rock and top 40/pop. Works primarily with road-units working clubs and lounges. Current acts include Ketch-II (MOR lounge duo), Flashfire (rock/top 40), The Do-Whop Kings (show band) and Makin Change (MOR lounge duo).
Tips: "Our clubs are booked 2-3 months in advance, so we have no immediate gigs. Also we do not book country rooms."

*STARCREST PRODUCTIONS, INC., 209 Circle Hills Dr., Grand Forks ND 58201. (701)772-6831. President: George J. Hastings. Management firm and booking agency. Represents artists, groups and songwriters; currently handles 6 acts. Receives 10-20% commission. Reviews material for acts.
How to Contact: Query by mail. Prefers 7½ ips reel-to-reel or cassette with 2-10 songs and lyric sheet. SASE. Reports in 1 month.
Music: Mostly country/gospel; also country, gospel and top 40/pop. Works primarily with vocalists and dance bands. Current acts include Mary Joyce (country/gospel), Swinging Doors (country/country rock), The Pioneers (country/country rock), and Bob Angel (country songwriter).

*STARLITE ENTERPRISES INC., 9731 Pickett Ln., Manassas VA 22110. (703)361-1033. President: Terence C. Burton, Esq. Management firm, booking agency and cabaret/variety show production company. Represents individual artists; currently handles 8 acts. Receives 10% commission. Reviews material for acts.
How to Contact: Prefers cassette (or VHS videocassette) with lyric or lead sheet. "Always send fullest information including cassette, 8x10 pictures, list of past and future venues, credits and videocassette, if available." SASE. Reports in 5 weeks.
Music: Mostly pop, ballads and standards. Works primarily with vocalists, variety/cabaret entertainers, musicians and dance bands. Current acts include Terry Calvar, The Excitement Show (cabaret revue) and The Cockney Pride Band.

STARTIME MUSIC, Box 643, LaQuinta CA 92253. (619)564-4873. President: Fred Rice. Management firm, music publisher and record company. Currently handles 7 acts. Receives 15-25% commission.
How to Contact: Prefers cassette (or VHS videocassette) with 1-2 songs and lead sheet. SASE. Reports in 6 weeks.
Music: Mostly novelty; also country, rock and top 40/pop, "short (2:30) pop single material." Current acts include Rob Carter (singer/composer), Neo (avant-garde actor/composer), R.C. Cole (country singer), Rockenstein (rock singer), and Johnny Porsche (R&B singer/composer).

BILL STEIN ASSOCIATES INC., Box 1516, Champaign IL 61820. Artists Manager: Bill Stein. Management firm. Represents artists and groups; currently handles 8 acts. Receives 10-15% commission. Reviews material for acts.
How to Contact: Prefers cassette (or Beta videocassette) with 3-6 songs and promotional material. "Send complete promo package including video and audio tapes, pictures, references, song and equipment lists." SASE. Reports in 1 month.

Music: Mostly pop rock, country and country rock; also dance, R&B, progressive, and soul. Works primarily with bar bands, dance bands, show bands and concert groups. Current acts include Duke Tomatoe (R&B), H20 (pop), Gator Alley (country), Kick in the Pants (nostalgia), French Quarter (R&B, funk), and High Sierra (country rock).

*STILETTO, LTD., Box 69180, Los Angeles CA 90069. Vice President: Eric Borenstein. Management firm and music publisher. Represents individual artists, groups and songwriters; currently handles 10 acts. Reviews material for acts.
How to Contact: Prefers cassette. SASE. Reports in 10 weeks.
Music: Mostly R&B/pop, pop/rock and hard rock; also country/pop. Current acts include Barry Manilow, Brenda Russell, John McVie, The Heaters, A Taste of Honey, Suzette Charles, Howie Rice, Skin Deep, Hans Naughty, and Jill Hollier.

STINNETTE ENTERTAINMENT AGENCY, Box 06404, Portland OR 97206. (503)235-5988. President: Tom Stinnette. Booking agency. Represents artists and groups in Northwest, Alaska and Canada; currently handles over 300 acts. Receives 10-15% commission.
How to Contact: Write first and obtain permission to submit. Prefers cassette with 5-10 songs. Does not return unsolicited material. Give references from appearances. Reports in 2 weeks.
Music: Mostly top 40/rock; also country, dance-oriented, MOR, 50s and country rock and pop. Works primarily with singles, duos, "on up to 6-piece groups." Current acts include Front Page (top 40/rock group), Room Service (top 40 rock group), and Sh-Boom (50s rock show).
Tips: "Be well rehearsed, and have good press kit, including 8x10 pictures."

STUDIO 7, 16591 County Home Rd., Marysville OH 43040. (513)644-8295. President: Doug Faiella. Management firm, record company, music publisher (Doug Faiella Pub.) and recording studio. Represents local individual artists, groups and songwriters. Receives 10-50% commission. Reviews material for acts.
How to Contact: Prefers cassette or 7½ ips reel-to-reel with 1-10 songs and lyric sheet. "Vocals must be strong. Send list of bookings and 8x10 glossy." SASE. Reports in 2 months.
Music: Mostly contemporary country, rock and gospel; also traditional country/bluegrass, jazz and blues. Works primarily with "musicians who are songwriters and performers."
Tips: "We are looking for a musician/songwriter/performer combination, either group or individual."

*SUPERSTAR PRODUCTIONS, LTD., 6863 Fremlin St., Vancouver, British Columbia V6P 3W3 Canada. Personal Manager: Lyvia Smith. Managment firm and booking agency. Represents individual artists and groups; currently handles 12 acts. Receives 10-15% commission. Reviews material for acts.
How to Contact: Prefers cassette (or Beta videocassette) and lyric or lead sheet. Does not return unsolicited material. Reports in 1 month.
Music: Mostly ballads, pop and MOR; also jazz, blues and rock ballads. Works primarily with vocalists. Current acts include Sheryl Rae (pop/MOR vocalist), Marc Belliveau (jazz/blues vocalist), and Ray Carroll (pop/MOR vocalist).
Tips: "Be reliable, honest, talented, hard-working and a nice person to work with on and off stage."

SURVIVOR ENTERTAINMENT INDUSTRIES, INC., Suite 323, 349 S. Lafayette Park Place, Los Angeles CA 90057-1646. (213)650-6800. Promotion: Greta Warren. Publishing: Billy Rogers. Management firm, record company (Survivor Records) and music publisher (Ten of Diamonds). Represents individual artists, groups and songwriters; currently handles 37 acts. Receives 15-75% commission. Reviews material for acts.
How to Contact: Prefers cassette (or VHS videocassette) and lyric or lead sheets. "Submit only 3 songs at a time; only your best." SASE. Reports in 1 month.
Music: Mostly pop, country and rock/R&B; international, MOR and gospel. Current acts include Shilo Gamboa/Spear (rock/new wave/reggae) and Sally Ride (country).
Tips: "Survivor Entertainment is dedicated to artist development of professional and semi-professional candidates."

THE T.S.J. PRODUCTIONS INC., 6640 14th Ave. S, Richfield MN 55423. (612)869-1779. Vice President/Artist Manager: Katherine J. Lange. Management firm and booking agency. Represents artists, groups and songwriters; currently handles 1 act. Receives 10-15% commission. Reviews material for acts.
How to Contact: Query by mail or submit demo. Prefers "any reel or cassette—inquire before sending video—with 2-6 songs and lyric sheet." SASE. Reports in 2 weeks.
Music: Mostly country rock, symphonic rock, easy listening and MOR; also blues, country, folk, jazz, progressive, R&B and top 40/pop. Works with Thomas St. James (vocalist).

TALENT ATTRACTIONS, Box 8542, Asheville NC 28814. (704)253-4161. President: Larry Phillips. Management firm and booking agency. Represents artists, groups and songwriters; currently handles 4 acts. Receives 10-20% commission. Reviews material for acts.
How to Contact: Prefers cassette (or videocassette) with 1-5 songs and lyric or lead sheet. SASE. Reports in 30-50 days.
Music: Country, rock and top 40/pop. Works primarily with 4-6 piece groups and single vocal artists. Current acts include Natalie Nugent (vocalist and actress), Joe Berry (country, top 40/pop vocalist), Johnny Weathers (MOR and classic country), and Justice (top 40/pop, country band).
Tips: "At present I am only interested in original copyrighted songs. An inexpensive cassette is sufficient. If I like the songs, I will ask for a studio demo."

TALENT MASTER, Box 158558, Nashville TN 37215. (615)646-1511. President: Steve Bess. Vice President: Charli McMillan. Booking agency. Represents artists and musical groups from Tennessee and surrounding states; currently handles 14 acts. Receives 15-20% commission.
How to Contact: Prefers personal interview (artist/group only) or submit demo with good promo kit. Prefers live cassette (or videocassette) with 1-3 songs. Does not return unsolicited material. Reports in 3 weeks.
Music: Country, dance, easy listening, MOR and rock (top 40, country). Works primarily with recording artists and dance and show bands. Current acts include Larry G. Hudson, Charlie McCoy, Barbara Fairchild, and Bill Baldwin (all recording artists).

*TALENT NETWORK INTERNATIONAL/JACKSON ENTERPRISES, Suite 807, 9000 Sunset Blvd., West Hollywood CA 90069. (213)271-8048. General Manager: Alice M. Jackson. Booking agency and music publisher. Represents artists, groups and songwriters; currently handles 40 acts. "We book acts in foreign markets." Receives 15% commission. Reviews material for acts.
How to Contact: Prefers cassette ("copy only—do not send original") with 2-4 songs and lead sheet. SASE. Reports in 2 months.
Music: Blues, country, dance-oriented, MOR, R&B, rock, soul, jazz and top 40/pop. Works primarily with "dance bands, keyboardist/singers, combos, lounge groups, concert and jazz artists and singles."
Tips: "Be different. Present something unique in sound. Have good lyrics that tell a story. Music should be up-tempo and not too laid back."

TAS MUSIC CO./DAVE TASSE ENTERTAINMENT, Route 4, Box 641, Lake Geneva WI 53147-9731. Contact: David Tasse. Booking agency, record company and music publisher. Represents artists, groups and songwriters; currently handles 100 acts. Receives 10-20% commission. Reviews material for acts.
How to Contact: Prefers cassette (or videocassete) with 2-4 songs and lyric sheet. SASE. Reports in 3 weeks.
Music: Mostly funk/jazz; also dance, MOR, rock, soul and top 40/pop. Works primarily with show and dance bands. Current acts include David Hulburt (pop), Donald Austin (country), and Major Hamberlin (jazz).

*WILLIAM TENN MANAGEMENT, Suite 502, 25 Bay Mills Blvd., Agincourt, Toronto Ontario M1T 3P4 Canada. (416)292-3510. President: William Tenn. Management firm and music publisher (Saskasongs Music). Represents individual artists, groups, songwriters and recording artists; currently handles 6 acts. Receives 10-20% commission. Reviews material for acts.
How to Contact: Prefers cassette (or VHS videocassette) with 3-4 songs and lyric sheet. SAE and IRC. Reports in 2 weeks.
Music: Rock, pop and new music. Works primarily with "Canadian recording artists seeking international success." Current acts include Brian Plummer, Midnite Ramblers, Andrew Cash, Eugene Ripper, Head First and Ron Sexsmith.
Tips: "Present your tunes on high quality tape, with lyric sheets and a brief background (no hype required . . . music speaks for itself). Let the listener tell *you* how much he likes the material as opposed to attempting to tell him how much he *should* like it."

THRUST (INTERNATIONAL), Box 850, Pt. Dover, Ontario N0A 1N0 Canada. (519)426-3799. President: Wayne Elliot. Management, promotion, and marketing firm. Represents artists, groups, comedians, models and actors; currently handles 3 acts. Receives 5-15% commission, "depending on services requested." Reviews material for acts.
How to Contact: Prefers cassette (or videocassete) and promotion package. Does not return unsolicited material. Reports in 1 week.
Music: Mostly top 40/pop and comedy; also rock. Works primarily with top 40 female bands, models,

comedians and novelty-type acts. Current acts include Kirby Ellis, Minx (all girl band), and Bill Cayley and Friends.

Tips: "You have to look like a winner to be a winner. Gimmicks help a good manager—and talent."

*TOP BANANA INC., 1864 McLeary Ave., Santurce Puerto Rico 00911. (809)726-1762 or 727-6973. Manager: Liesa Dileo. Management firm, booking agency, record company (Top Banana Records), and music publisher (QB Music). Represents individual artists, groups and songwriters; currently handles 4 acts. Receives 15-20% commission. Reviews material for acts.

How to Contact: Prefers cassette (or VHS videocassette) with 3-4 songs and lyric or lead sheets. SASE. Reports in 1 month.

Music: Mostly pop, rock, R&B; also jazz and Latin. Works primarily with original pop/rock bands. Current acts include Top Banana; Quito Blanco and Ramon Gonzalez.

Tips: "Be explicit in exactly what you wish to achieve and have information in good order."

A TOTAL ACTING EXPERIENCE, Suite 300-A, 6736 Laurel Canyon, N. Hollywood CA 91606. (818)765-7244. Agent: Dan A. Bellacicco. Talent agency. Represents vocalists, lyricists, composers, groups; currently handles 24 acts. Uses the services of in-house talent for scoring of motion pictures, television, musicals, jingles and TV commercials. Receives 10% commission.

How to Contact: Prefers cassette (or VHS videocassette) with 3-5 songs and lyric or lead sheets. "Singers and groups who write their own material should also submit photo and resume." SASE. Reports in 10 weeks.

Music: Mostly "theme songs for new films, TV shows and special projects"; also top 40/pop, jazz, blues, country, R&B, dance and MOR. Current acts include Aida (vocalist/actress/lyricist), Merri Schaffer (vocalist/composer/lyricist) and Morris Rossenfeld (lyricist).

Tips: "No calls please. We will respond via your SASE. Please use a new tape and keep vocals up front. We welcome young, sincere talent who can give total commitment. We are seeking female vocalists a la Streisand or Whitney Houston, who can write their own material. All material must have a freshness to it—perhaps topical and unpredictable—with substance, and of course, market value. Your business skills must be strong. In return, you will receive tender loving care."

TRIANGLE TALENT, INC., 9701 Taylorsville Rd., Louisville KY 40299. (502)267-5466. President: David H. Snowden. Booking agency. Represents artists and groups; currently handles 60 acts. Receives 10-20% commission. Reviews material for acts.

How to Contact: Query. Prefers cassette (or VHS videocassette) with 2-4 songs and lyric sheet. SASE. Reports in 2 weeks.

Music: Mostly rock/top 40 country and R&B; also bluegrass and pop. Current acts include The Score (top 40), Gresham (country), and Bonnie Nelson (contemporary country).

UMBRELLA ARTISTS MANAGEMENT, INC., Box 20244, 443 Riddle Rd., #1, Cincinnati OH 45220. (513)861-1500. President: Stan Hertzman. Management firm. Represents artists, groups and songwriters; currently handles 4 acts.

How to Contact: Prefers cassette with 3 songs and lyric sheet. SASE. Reports in 1 month.

Music: Progressive, rock and top 40/pop. Works with contemporary/progressive pop/rock artists and writers. Current acts include The Young Invaders (AOR rock group); The Bears (modern band); Charlie Fletcher (pop rock, artist-songwriter); and Adrian Belew (engineer/producer/songwriter/arranger) whose credits include Frank Zappa, David Bowie, Talking Heads, Tom Tom Club, Cyndi Lauper, Laurie Anderson and Paul Simon.

*UMPIRE ENTERPRIZES, 2403 Stardust, Longview TX 75604. (214)297-3692. Owner/Manager: Jerry Haymes. Management firm, music publisher (Enterprize and Golden Guitar) and record company (Enterprize Records). Represents individual artists, groups and songwriters; currently handles 4 acts.

How to Contact: Prefers cassette with lyric or lead sheet. SASE. Reports in 2 weeks.

Music: Country, pop and gospel. Works primarily with vocalists and bands. Current acts include Jerry Haymes, Over the Hill Gang and Debra Green.

UNITED ARTIST MANAGEMENT, Box 06906, Portland OR 97206. (503)236-0590. President: Gary W. Perman. Management firm. Represents recording artists and groups. Receives 10-20% commission. Reviews material for acts.

How to Contact: Prefers cassette with 2-4 songs, photo and biography. SASE. Reports in 1 month.

Music: Rock (all types), R&B, top 40/pop and country-rock. Works primarily with "nightclub bands who aspire national recognition and opening acts for major recording artists."

UNITED ENTERTAINMENT PRODUCTIONS, 4024 State Line, Kansas City KS 66103. (913)262-3555. Director of Publishing: Michael T. Harvey. Management firm, booking agency, record company

(Graphic Records) and music publisher (United Entertainment Music). Represents individual artists, groups and songwriters (national and international record acts). Receives 15-20% commission. Reviews material for acts.
How to Contact: Prefers cassette and lyric sheet. Does not return unsolicited material.
Music: Mostly pop/rock, R&B and jazz; also country. Current acts include The Bon Ton Band, The Clique and The Verandas.
Tips: "It's been my experience that following a trend keeps you behind in the music business. I look for original material and original artists."

*UNIVERSAL MANAGEMENT, Box 17272, Memphis TN 38187-0272. Director: Ron Clark. Management firm, music publisher, booking agency and record company. Represents individual artists, groups and songwriters; currently handles 10 acts. Reviews material for acts.
How to Contact: Prefers cassette (or videocassette) with 3 songs and lyric sheet. Does not return unsolicited material. Reports in 10 weeks "if used."
Music: Mostly country, gospel and MOR. Works primarily with vocalists and quartets.

VALEX TALENT AGENCY, and Pyramid Sound Records, Box 241, Ithaca NY 14851. (607)273-3931. Publishing President: John Perialas. Booking Vice President: Tom McNerney. Management firm, booking agency and publishing house. Represents artists, groups and songwriters in northeast US; currently handles 20-30 acts. Receives 15-25% commission. Reviews material for acts.
How to Contact: Prefers 7½ ips reel-to-reel or cassette with 3-6 songs and lead sheet. SASE. Reports in 1 month. "Songwriters please send cassettes or 7½ ips reel-to-reel in care of John Perialas, Copper John Music. After sending material allow appropriate time for material to be reviewed (2 weeks); then follow with call."
Music: Mostly top 40, rock and new wave; also country pop, dance, easy listening, MOR, R&B, rock, and pop. Works with vocalists, show, dance and bar bands. Current acts include Atlas (contemporary funk/rock), Charlie Starr (country rock), Bernie Milton (soul/R&B) and Raven (heavy metal).

*RICHARD VARRASSO MANAGEMENT, Box 387, Fremont CA 94537. (415)792-8910. Talent Coordinator: Denise M. Varrasso. Management firm. Represents individual artists, groups and songwriters; currently handles 2 acts. Receives 15-25% commission. Reviews material for acts.
How to Contact: Prefers cassette and lyric sheet. Does not return unsolicited material.
Music: Mostly rock, pop and R&B; also country and classical. Works primarily with major headliner, recording artists. Current acts include Greg Kihn and Jimmy Lyon.

VELVETT RECORDING COMPANY, 517 W. 57th St., Los Angeles CA 90037. (213)753-7893. Manager: Aaron Johnson. Management firm and record company. Represents artists, groups and songwriters; currently handles 5 acts. Reviews material for acts.
How to Contact: Prefers cassette with 2-3 songs and lead sheet. SASE.
Music: Mostly blues and gospel; also church/religious, R&B, rock, soul and top 40/pop. Works primarily with show and dance bands and vocalists. Current acts include Arlene Bell (soul/top 40/pop artist), Chick Willis (blues artist), and Jay Harmon (top 40 singer).

VOKES BOOKING AGENCY, Box 12, New Kensington PA 15068. (412)335-2775. President: Howard Vokes. Booking agency. Represents individuals, groups and songwriters; currently handles 25 acts. Receives 10-20% commission.
How to Contact: Query. Accepts cassette only with 3-6 songs and lead sheet. SASE. Reports in 2 weeks.
Music: Bluegrass, country and gospel. "We work with bluegrass and hard country bands who generally play bars, hotels and clubs. However, we also book in ole-time artists as singles. We want nothing to do with hard rock or country rock." Current acts include Country Boys (country), 100% Proof Country (country), and Mel Anderson (country).

VON KLEIST TALENT MANAGEMENT, Box 310, Carmichael CA 95609-0310. (916)485-9092. Contact: Mari Minke. Management firm. Represents local artists; currently handles 1 act. Receives 10% commission. Reviews material for acts.
How to Contact: Prefers cassette and lyric and lead sheets. SASE. Reports in 3 weeks.
Music: Mostly contemporary crossover country and contemporary Christian; also blues and jazz. Works with Rachel Minke (recording artist and stage act).
Tips: "We are looking for original music for recording projects."

*WAILING WALL PRODUCTIONS, 281 E. Kingsbridge Road, Bronx NY 10458. (212)733-5342. President: Murray Fuller. Booking agency. Currently handles 6 acts. Recieves 10-25% commission. Reviews material for acts.

How to Contact: Prefers cassette (or videocassette) with 3-5 songs and lyric or lead sheet. SASE. Reports in 6 weeks.

Music: Mostly soul; also jazz and R&B. Works primarily with vocalists. Current acts include The Essence of Sound (R&B), Boncellia Lewis (R&B/contemporary), and Opus and Personal Touch (R&B).

WESTWOOD ASSOCIATES, Box 754, Edison NJ 08818-0754. (201)548-6700. President: Victor Kaplij. Artist management agency. Represents local individual artists and groups. Receives 15% commission. Reviews material for acts.

How to Contact: Prefers cassette with 3 songs and lyric sheet. SASE. Reports in 6 weeks.

Music: Mostly rock, pop and country. Works primarily with singer/songwriters and rock groups. Current acts include Aerrage and Kevin McCabe.

*THOMAS WIGGINS & ASSOCIATES, Box 21118, Castro Valley CA 94546. (415)490-2015 or 355-0282. Agency office: Golden Pen Management, 335 Waterford St., Pacifica CA 94044. President: Tom Wiggins. Management firm, booking agency, record company (Great Ethnic Records, Co. and No-Bull Records) and music publisher ("we negotiate deals and are an affiliate of GIL Music of San Francisco, Los Angeles, Nashville, New York, London"). Represents individual artists, groups, songwriters and "international artists and shows"; currently handles 5-10 acts. Receives 20-25% commission. Reviews material for acts.

How to Contact: Submit demo by mail or write to arrange personal interview. Prefers cassette (or VHS videocassette) with 3-6 songs and lyric or lead sheet. Reports in 6 weeks.

Music: Mostly country; also pop, blues/ethnic music, R&B and jazz. Works primarily with artists who write and perform original material. Current acts include Bobby Enriquez (jazz), Charlie Musselwhite (jazz/blues) and Rosie Gaines (R&B/pop, Epic Records).

Tips: "Do your homework and be very professional. Don't waste our time and we won't waste yours. Artists who try to play with more than one manager or booking agency at a time are simply cutting their own throats. Go with one company or person and stick with it. Be realistic in your work and attitude. Be patientMDdon't expect miracles overnight becuase they just don't happen that way. Most 'overnight' successes take about fifteen years."

SHANE WILDER ARTISTS' MANAGEMENT, Box 3503, Hollywood CA 90078. (818)896-5506. President: Shane Wilder. Management firm. Represents artists and groups; currently handles 10 acts. Receives 15-25% commission. Reviews material for acts.

How to Contact: Prefers cassette with 4-10 songs and lyric sheet. SASE. Reports in 1 month.

Music: Country. Works primarily with single artists and groups. Current acts include Mike Franklin (country recording artist), Laurie Loman (singer), Honey Wilder (actress), Teresa O'Dell (country artist), Denise Myatt, Craig Reynolds (songwriter), and Greta Goehle (recording artist).

Tips: "Make sure your work is highly commercial. We are looking for strong female country songs for major artists. Material should be available for publishing with Shane Wilder Music, BMI."

RICHARD WOOD ARTIST MANAGEMENT, 42 Clinton Ave., Staten Island NY 10301. (718)981-0641. Contact: Richard Wood. Management firm. Represents musical groups; currently handles 1 act. Receives 10-15% commission. Reviews material for acts.

How to Contact: Prefers cassette and lead sheet. SASE.

Music: Mostly R&B and top 40/pop; also MOR. Works primarily with "high energy" show bands.

Tips: "Please be versatile and able to make changes in material to suit the type of acts I book."

WORLD WIDE MANAGEMENT, 1500 Front St., Yorktown Heights NY 10598. (914)962-2727. A&R Director: Mr. Stevens. Management firm and booking agency. Represents artists, groups, songwriters and actors; currently handles 4 acts. Receives 15-25% commission. Reviews material for acts.

How to Contact: Write first and obtain permission to submit or to arrange personal interview. Prefers cassette (or videocassette) with 3-5 songs. SASE. Reports in 1 month.

Music: Mostly folk, folk/rock and New Age; also pop, rock, jazz, bluegrass, blues, country and R&B. Works primarily with self-contained bands and vocalists. Current acts include Marie Menna (singer/songwriter), Aztec Two-Step (folk/rock duo), Devonsquare (folk/pop trio), and Reynolds & Cowan (traditional folk/country duo).

*YELLOW BALLOON PRODUCTIONS LTD., Micadam, 21 Fairmile Ave., Cobham Surrey KT11 2JA England. (0932-67211/68144). Managing Director: Mike Smith. Public Affairs: Debbie Hanson. Management firm, booking agency, record company (Yellow Balloon Records), and music publisher (Mike Music). Represents individual artists, groups and songwriters; currently handles 6 acts. Receives 15-20% commission. Reviews material for acts.

How to Contact: Prefers cassette (or VHS videocassette) with no more than 5 songs and lyric or lead sheets. SAE and IRC. "Always enclose envelope and postage. If promoting act as well as material, enclose photos and biography; gig sheet if working. Do not phone—always write in to submit artists/material." Reports in 2 weeks.
Music: Mostly pop, rock and instrumentals; also film/TV theme material, comedy songs and lyrics. Works primarily with solo artists, musicians, TV and film people and groups. Current acts include Bobby Dauro, Hazel O'Connor and Bruce Foxton.

ZANE MANAGEMENT, INC., 700 Three Penn Center, Philadelphia PA 19102. (215)563-1100. President: Lloyd Zane Remick. Entertainment/sports consultants and managers. Represents artists, songwriters, producers and athletes; currently handles 5 acts. Receives variable commission.
How to Contact: Prefers cassette and lyric sheet. SASE. Reports in 4 weeks.
Music: Dance, easy listening, folk, gospel, jazz (fusion), MOR, rock (hard and country), soul and top 40/pop. Current acts include Phil Hurtt, Bunny Sigler (disco/funk), Pieces of a Dream (consultant), Grover Washington, Jr. (management), and Phyllis Nelson (management).

*ZARATT EXPRESS, INC., 2821 Ch. Des Mesanges, Gloucester, Ontario K1T 2C7 Canada. (613)526-2233. President: Doug Wigney. Management firm, record company (Zaradisc) and music publisher (Editions Zaratt Express). Represents groups and songwriters; currently handles 2 acts. Receives negotiable commission. Reviews material for acts.
How to Contact: Prefers cassette with 3-4 songs and lyric sheet. SAE and IRC. Reports in 3 weeks.
Music: Mostly new music and pop. Works primarily with "dance oriented bands doing original music." Current acts include Social Rhythms, and Demars.

*ZEE TALENT AGENCY, 3095 Sinclair St., Winnipeg, Manitoba R2P 1Y6 Canada. (204)338-7094. President/Agent: Linda Zagozewski. Agent: Duncan Wilson. Booking agency. Represents groups; currently handles 17 acts. Receives 10-15% commission. Reviews material for acts.
How to Contact: Write first and obtain permission to submit. Prefers cassette. SAE and IRC. Reports in 2 weeks.
Music: Mostly rock, top 40 and country/rock; also variety and show music. Current acts include Kickaxe, MacLean & MacLean, and New Alliance.

66 *Of course videos are affecting the music business, but motion pictures are also having a tremendous effect on contemporary music. I can see a time, in the not too distant future, when these two separate entities will be interdependent of each other.* **99**
—*Dorian W.W. Medd, independent producer*

Writing jingles and music for commercials is very different from writing songs. Songwriters and composers must be prepared to write on assignment, about specific aspects of a particular product or service (sometimes even the words or slogans are pre-determined), and must be able to turn a project around quickly. Many songwriters enjoy that fast pace, and like the challenge it presents. Advertising agencies are willing to pay well for innovative music that meets their demands and pleases their clients.

Advertising agencies, unlike record companies or music publishers, work on assignment as their clients' needs arise. They work closely with their clients on broadcast campaigns. Through consultation and input from the creative staff, agencies establish a "feel" they believe commercials should project for a client's product. They seek jingles and music to stimulate the consumer to identify with a product and hum the commercial in his head—while paying the cashier. When listening to a demo, agencies are not looking for a finished product so much as for an indication of creativity and diversity.

When contacting ad agencies, keep in mind that they are looking for music that can capture and hold an audience's attention in a very short time span (sometimes within 10 or 15 seconds). When submitting a demo, include samples of any previously aired work you may have. Your musical selections should fade in and fade out and include a variety of music styles. You should type on the label and/or indicate in your cover letter that you are the composer, to differentiate your tape from those of singers and musicians looking for jingle work.

Jingle writing is not a simple task. It's an extremely demanding, highly competitive field. Some agencies will expect strings, horns, and background vocals, and you will be expected to produce that sound, sometimes on short notice, at the lowest cost possible. Show that you can be creative in advertising by being creative in "selling" yourself as a jingle writer. You can make a good impression on advertising agency executives by finding an inventive way of calling attention to your demo package.

For additional names and addresses of advertising agencies (but no marketing information), refer to the _Standard Directory of Advertising Agencies_ (National Register Publishing Co.).

ADELANTE ADVERTISING, INC., 386 Park Ave. S, New York NY 10016. (212)696-0855. President: Sy Davis. Advertising agency. "Clients interested in marketing to Hispanic and black consumer markets." Uses independent songwriters, lyricists and music houses for background music for commercials and jingles. Commissions 2 songwriters and 2 lyricists/year. Pays by the job. Buys all rights or one-time rights; "agency observes all union regulations where applicable."
How to Contact: Write first to obtain permission to submit. Prefers cassette (or Beta videocassette). SASE, but prefers to keep material on file. Reports in 2 weeks.
Music: Latin tempo, blues, pop and rock—"current with preferences of blacks and Hispanics" for "original jingles and music beds for radio and TV commercials for blacks and Hispanics."
Tips: "Must be familiar with current black and Hispanic music tempos and instrumentation. Learn recording studio operation regarding commercial—trend is leaning toward computerized music. Send cassette for agency to keep on file. Not necessary to contact agency. We'll make contact if interested."

ALPINE ADVERTISING, INC., 2639 St. Johns Ave., Box 30895, Billings MT 59107. (406)652-1630. (Also 1550 E. 79th St., Bloomington MN 55420. (612)854-2180.) President: James F. Preste. Advertising agency. Serves financial, automotive and food clients. Uses jingles. Commissions 20 pieces/year. Pays $2,500-7,500/job. Buys all rights.
How to Contact: Submit demo tape of previously aired work. Prefers 7½ ips reel-to-reel with 5-12 pieces. Does not return unsolicited material. Reports in 1 month.

*ANDERSON COMMUNICATIONS, 1465 Westwood, Atlanta GA 30310. (404)752-9353. President: Al Anderson. Producer: Vanessa Vaughn. Advertising agency and syndication operation. Uses the services of independent songwriters for jingles and background music for commercials. Pays by the job. Buys all rights.
How to Contact: Call first and obtain permission to submit. Prefers cassette. SASE, but prefers to keep material on file. Reports in 2 weeks.
Music: Uses a variety of music for music beds for commercials and jingles for nationally syndicated radio programs.

ARKS ADVERTISING AND MARKETING, Harcourt Centre, 50/53 Harcourt St., Dublin 2 Ireland. 757981. Creative Director: Eamonn O'Flaherty. Advertising agency. Clients include Guinness, Pan Am, Chesebrough Ponds and Anadin. Uses independent songwriters, lyricists and music houses for background music for commercials and jingles. Commissions 15 songwriters and 12 lyricists/year. Buys all rights or one-time rights.
How to Contact: Submit demo tape of previously aired work. Prefers cassette (or videocassette). SAE and IRC, but prefers to keep material on file. Reports in 3 weeks.
Music: All styles of music for jingles, music beds and background music for TV, radio, etc.

N. ARMSTRONG ADVERTISING AGENCY, Suite 223, 3610 Avenue Q, Lubbock TX 79412. (806)765-6283. Contact: Nelda Armstrong. Advertising agency. Uses services of songwriters, music libraries and jingle companies for jingles and background music for commercials. Commissions 1 songwriter and 1 lyricist/year. Pays by the job. Buys all rights.
How to Contact: Arrange personal interview or query with resume of credits. Prefers cassette with 2-4 songs. SASE.
Music: Uses country and contemporary music for 60- and 30-second jingles and music beds. "Present lyrics (without music) that could be produced using various types of music formats."

*ARTEL VIDEOGRAPHICS CORPORATION, 4424 Carver Woods Dr., Cincinnati OH 45242. (513)791-9005. Vice President: Joe Rosenberger. Advertising agency. Uses services of music houses for jingles and background music for commercials. Commissions 3-8 songwriters/year. Pays $1,000-8,000/job. Buys all rights.
How to Contact: Submit demo tape of previously aired work. Prefers cassette. SASE, but prefers to keep material on file. Reports in 2 weeks.
Music: Uses easy listening and up-tempo music for jingles, music beds and A/V tracks.

*TED BARKUS COMPANY, INC., 1512 Spruce St., Philadelphia PA 19102. (215)545-0616. Executive Vice President: Allen E. Barkus. Advertising agency. Uses the services of independent songwriters and music houses for jingles and background music for commercials. Commissions 1-3 songwriters/year. Pays by the job. Buys all rights.
How to Contact: Call to arrange personal interview or write to obtain permission to submit. Prefers cassette (or VHS videocassette) with 3-5 pieces. SASE, but prefers to keep material on file "when the style matches our objectives."
Music: Uses various styles of music depending upon client needs for "positioning concepts with musical beds, doughnut for inserted copy."
Tips: "Learn as much as possible about the product and who the consumer will be before starting a project. Understand that the commercial also has to work with the print and television media in terms of everything else the client is doing."

*BCP STRATEGY CREATIVITY, 1000 Sherbrooke West, Montreal, Quebec H3A 3G9 Canada. (514)285-1414. Vice President, Creative: Pierre Audet. Advertising agency. Uses services of independent songwriters and music houses for jingles and background music for commercials. Pays $2,000-5,000 (Canadian) for original music or song. Buys all rights or "in a campaigning situation, rearrangement fees for each new execution."
How to Contact: Write or call to arrange personal interview or submit demo tape of previously aired work. Prefers cassete. Does not return unsolicited material; prefers to keep on file. Reports in 3 weeks.
Music: "Music must fit creative objectives." Uses "all advertising genres."

*BEALS ADVERTISING AGENCY, 5005 Pennsylvania, Oklahoma City OK 73112. (405)848-8513. Copy Director/Creative: Dawna Robertson. Advertising agency. Serves primarily business to business accounts. Uses the services of independent songwriters and music houses for jingles and background music for commercials. Pays by the job. Buys one-time rights.
How to Contact: Submit demo tape of previously aired work. Prefers cassette (or ¾" videocassette). SASE, but prefers to keep material on file.
Music: Uses various styles of music for music beds and background for TV and radio.

RON BERNS & ASSOCIATES, 520 N. Michigan Ave., Chicago IL 60611. (312)527-2800. President: Ron Berns. Advertising agency. Uses services of independent songwriters for jingles. Pays by the job. Buys all rights.
How to Contact: Submit demo tape of previous work. Prefers cassette. Prefers studio produced demo. Does not return unsolicited material; prefers to keep on file. Reports when needed.

BERNSTEIN REIN, Suite 1500, 4600 Madison, Kansas City MO 64112. (816)756-0640. Creative Director: Jeff Bremser. Ad agency. Uses services of songwriters for jingles and background music in commercials. Commissions 10-20 pieces/year from 3-5 songwriters. Pays $25,000 maximum/job. "We buy complete production, not just songs."
How to Contact: Submit demo tape of previously aired work. Prefers cassette with 5 songs minimum on tape. SASE. "We keep tapes on file; we do not report."
Music: "All styles for use as jingles and commercial scores."

RALPH BING ADVERTISING CO., 16109 Selva Dr., San Diego CA 92128. (619)487-7444. President: Ralph S. Bing. Advertising agency. Uses the services of music houses for jingles. Commissions 1-2 songwriters/year. Pays by the job as determined by the producer. Buys all rights.
How to Contact: Write first and obtain permission to submit. Prefers cassette with 3-6 songs. SASE, but prefers to keep material on file. Reports "when and if needed."
Music: Easy listening.
Tips: "Go with current trends as they occur."

BLAIR ADVERTISING, INC., a member of the Omnicom Group, 96 College Ave., Rochester NY 14607. (716)473-0440. Senior Vice President/Creative Director: John R. Brown. Advertising agency. Member of AFTRA, SAG, ASCAP. Serves consumer, financial and packaged good clients. Uses staff writers and independent songwriters for jingles. Commissions 15 songwriters and 2 lyricists/year. Pays $500-5,000/job.
How to Contact: Query. Prefers cassette with 3-5 songs. Does not return unsolicited material.
Music: "We're seriously interested in hearing from good production sources. We have some of the world's best lyricists and songwriters working for us, but we're always ready to listen to fresh, new ideas."

*GEORGE BLAKE & ASSOC., 473 Magellan Dr., Sarasota FL 34243. President: George Blake. Advertising agency. Uses the services of songwriters for jingles. Pays by the job. Buys all rights.
How to Contact: Query first. Prefers cassette with 3-6 songs on demo. Does not return unsolicited material; prefers to keep on file. Reports in 1 month-3 years.
Music: Various types.

*BOZELL & JACOBS/PACIFIC, Suite 1300, 12121 Wilshire Blvd., Los Angeles CA 90025. (213)879-1800. Producer: Jan Rosenthal. Advertising agency and public relations firm. Serves financial, food and realty clients. Uses individual songwriters and music houses for jingles and background music for commercials. Commissions 1 songwriter/year. Pays $500 and up/job. Buys all rights.
How to Contact: Submit demo tape of previously aired work ("if no previously aired work, samples OK"). Prefers reel-to-reel. "We want a representative amount of songs. If songwriter has 10 award-winning commercials, we want to hear them all. If only one has been sold, send that one and then some other work, too." SASE; but prefers to keep on file. Reports "as needed only."
Music: All types.
Tips: "Be diverse and easy-going."

DICK BRONSON, INC., 31 Central St., Bangor ME 04401. (207)947-7376. Sales Manager: Tammie Breen. Advertising agency. Clients include auto dealerships, bookstore chain, automotive parts chain, convenience store chain, bank chain, beer and wine area wholesaler, recreation vehicle dealership, paint store chain, meat packer, state fairs, racetracks and others. Uses the services of independent songwriters and lyricists for backround music for commercials and jingles. Commissions 10 songwriters/year and 10 lyricists/year. Pays $2,500-4,000 job. Buys all rights.
How to Contact: Submit demo tape of previously aired work. Prefers cassette. SASE. Reports in 2 weeks.
Music: Needs country, MOR and pop for jingles and soundbeds for radio and TV.
Tips: "In addition to writing 60- and 30-second spots, write also for :10's and :15's. At time of commissioning a work, we will outline requirements."

JOE BUSER & ASSOCIATES, Suite 400, 2800 Texas Ave., Bryan TX 77802. (409)775-0400. Producer: J.R. Buser. Advertising agency. Clients include financial institutions, automobile dealers, real estate developers, restaurants, manufacturing companies, newspapers and insurance agencies. Uses the services of independent songwriters and music houses for background music for commercials, jingles and original scores for AV shows. Commissions 1-2 songwriters/year. Pays $500-2,000/job. Buys all rights.
How to Contact: Submit demo tape of previously aired work. Prefers 15 ips reel-to-reel with 5-10 pieces. Does not return unsolicited material; prefers to keep on file. Reports in 2 weeks.
Music: Country, pop, specialty music for video projects and identity jingles; some background music (AV music beds).
Tips: "Don't get discouraged. Some projects take months or years to develop while others pop up today and are due yesterday!"

*CARAVETTA ALLEN KIMBROUGH/BBDO, Suite 60, 7200 Corporate Center Dr., Miami FL 33126. (305)448-4741. Senior Vice President/Creative Director: Lane Atkins. Advertising agency. Uses the services of songwriters for jingles and background music. Commissions 3-4 songwriters/year. Pays flat fee, negotiated by project. Buys all rights.
How to Contact: Submit demo tape of previous work. Prefers cassette with 3-15 songs on demo. Does not return unsolicited material; prefers to keep on file. "We respond by telephone, but only if we are requesting a bid on a project."
Music: Background music for TV commercials, post-scored to picture; and occasional jingles for TV and radio.

THE CARSON GROUP, 1708 Hwy. 6 S., Houston TX 77077. (713)496-2600. Broadcast Producer: Brent Smith. Advertising agency. Serves retail clients. Uses the services of music houses for jingles. Pays $5,000-7,000 for produced package. Buys all rights.
How to Contact: Submit demo tape of previously aired work. Prefers cassette (or VHS videocassette). Does not return unsolicited material; prefers to keep on file. Reports when a need arises.
Music: MOR, country and pop for radio and TV jingles.
Tips: "Have a good reel with at least 5-8 pieces on it. Your product has to break through the clutter to get noticed, and your work has to get noticed before it's purchased."

CARTER ADVERTISING INC., 800 American Tower, 401 Market St., Shreveport LA 71101-3248. (318)227-1920. Production Manager: Kristi M. Webb. Advertising agency. Clients include "banks, hospitals, restaurants/food chains, industrial, dairy, bakeries." Uses the services of independent songwriters and music houses for background music for commercials and jingles. Commissions 1-5 songwriters/year. Pays by the job. Buys all rights or one-time rights.
How to Contact: Submit demo tape of previously aired work. Prefers cassette or 7½ ips reel-to-reel (or VHS videocassette) with 6-8 pieces and lyric or lead sheets. "Please label spots, telling how many and an average cost of production." SASE, but prefers to keep material on file. Reports in 12 weeks.
Music: "Blues, pop, jazz, classical, some rock and contemporary for bank jingles, industrial background music, etc. (Radio in particular for banks and other financial institutions.)"
Tips: "Please state how you heard of our agency; and please allow us to keep tapes on file, as we catalog all demos and pull from these. Thank you."

*CHENOWETH & FAULKNER, INC., 5201 W. Kennedy, Tampa FL 33609. (813)870-3427. Creative Director: James Barr. Advertising agency. Uses music houses for jingles and background music for commercials. Commissions 2 songwriters/year. Pays by the job. Buys all rights.
How to Contact: Write to arrange personal interview or submit demo tape of previously aired work or tape demonstrating composition skills. Prefers cassette (or ¾" videocassette). Does not return unsolicited material; prefers to keep on file.
Music: Uses all styles of music for jingles and music beds.

CHIAT/DAY ADVERTISING, 517 S. Olive, Los Angeles CA 90013. (213)622-7454. President/Creative Director: Lee Clow. Creative Secretaries: Dana Miller and Georgia Nelson. Serves health care, entertainment, packaged food, home loan, automotive, fast food and motorcycle clients. Uses background music in commercials. Commissions 1 piece/year. Pays by the job.
How to Contact: Submit demo tape of previously aired work. Prefers 7½ ips reel-to-reel. SASE. Reports "as soon as possible."

COAKLEY HEAGERTY, 122 Saratoga, Santa Clara CA 95051. (408)249-6242. Traffic Manager: Laura Wilde. Advertising agency. Clients include consumer, business to business and high tech. Uses the services of independent songwriters, lyricists and music houses for background music for commercials and jingles. Commissions 15 songwriters and 10 lyricists/year. Pays $3,000-20,000/job. Buys all rights or one-time rights.

How to Contact: Submit demo tape of previously aired work. Prefers cassette or 7½ ips reel-to-reel with 8-10 pieces. Does not return unsolicited material; prefers to keep material on file. Reports in 2 weeks.

Music: All kinds of music for jingles and music beds.

COONS, CORKER & ASSOCIATES, Penthouse, W. 6th, 21 Mallon, Spokane WA 99201. Ad agency, marketing and public relations firm. Creative Director: Danita Petek. Serves industrial, retail, media, financial, public utility, real estate and automotive clients. Uses songwriters, lyricists, pre-marketed music and production houses for jingles and background music for commercials; uses lyricists for jingles—individual radio and TV spots. Commissions 2 songwriters and 2 lyricists/year. "Pay variable on project-by-project basis." Buys all rights.

How to Contact: Submit demo tape of previously aired work or tape showing jingle/composition skills and styles. Prefers cassette with 7-15 songs. *The cost of submitted productions would be helpful.*" Does not return unsolicited material. Reports "immediately, if we have a need."

Tips: "We're not interested in hearing from songwriters *per se*. We usually deal with music houses that are in the business of selling music for radio and TV commercials."

CREATIVE HOUSE ADVERTISING, INC., Suite 301, 30777 Northwestern Hwy., Farmington Hills MI 48018. (313)353-3344. Executive Vice President/Creative Director: Robert G. Washburn. Ad agency and graphics studio. Serves commercial, retail, consumer, industrial, medical and financial clients. Uses the services of songwriters and lyricists for jingles, background music for radio and TV commercials and corporate sales meetings films and videos. Commissions 3/4 songwriters/year. Pays $50-100/hour or $1,500-5,000/job depending on job involvement. Buys all rights.

How to Contact: Query with resume of credits or submit tape demo showing jingle/composition skills. Submit cassette (or ¾ inch videocassette) with 6-12 songs. SASE, but would prefer to keep material on file. "When an appropriate job comes up associated with the talents/ability of the songwriters/musicians then they will be contacted."

Music: "The type of music we need depends on clients. The range is multi, from contemporary, disco, rock, MOR and traditional."

CRESWELL, MUNSELL, FULTZ & ZIRBEL, INC., Box 2879, Cedar Rapids IA 52406. (319)395-6500. Executive Producer: Terry Taylor. Ad agency. Serves agricultural, consumer and industrial clients. Uses songwriters and music houses for jingles and background music in commercials and multi-image soundtracks. Commissions 7-8 songwriters for 15 pieces/year. Pays by the job. Buys rights on talent residuals.

How to Contact: Submit demo tape of previously aired work. Prefers 7½ or 15 ips reel-to-reel or cassette with 7-8 songs maximum. Does not return unsolicited material. Reports "when we want figures on a job."

Music: All types. Likes to hear a good range of music material. Will listen to anything from "small groups to full orchestration."

Tips: "Create unique, recognizable melodies."

*DAVIS ADVERTISING, INC., Suite 3, 600 Azalea Dr., Surfside Beach SC 29577. (803)238-2288. Creative Director: James S. Carver. Advertising agency. Uses music houses for jingles. Pays $2,500-6,000/job. Buys all rights.

How to Contact: Write first to arrange personal interview. Prefers cassette and lyric sheet. Does not return unsolicited material; prefers to keep on file. Reports "when necessary."

Music: Up-tempo and pop for jingles and music beds.

*DE LEEUW FERGUSON BASHAW, 26555 Evergreen, Southfield MI 48026. (313)352-1300. Creative Director: Greg Bashaw. Advertising agency. Uses the services of music houses for jingles and background music for commercials. Commissions 20 songwriters/year. Pays by the job. Rights negotiable.

How to Contact: Write or call to arrange personal interview. Prefers cassette. Does not return unsolicited material; prefers to keep on file. Reports in 1 week.

Music: Rock and pop for jingles, music beds and background music.

DELTA DESIGN GROUP, INC., 518 Central, Greenville MS 38701. (601)335-6148. President: Noel Workman. Advertising agency. Serves industrial, financial, agricultural and retail commercial clients. Uses the services of songwriters for jingles. Commissions 3-6 pieces/year. Pays $500-2,500/job. Buys "rights which vary geographically according to client. Some are all rights; others are rights for a specified market only. Buy out only. No annual licensing."

How to Contact: Submit demo tape showing jingle/composition skills. Prefers 7½ ips reel-to-reel

with 3-6 songs. "Include typed sequence of cuts on tape on the outside of the reel box." SASE. Reports "when services are needed."
Music: Needs "30- and 60-second jingles for banks, agricultural, health care, auto dealers and chambers of commerce."

DALLAS C. DORT & COMPANY, 900 Northbank Center, Flint MI 48502. (313)238-4677. Production Manager: Yvonne M. Penberthy. Advertising agency. Clients include auto parts, health maintenance organizations, hospitals, insurance companies, banks and vacation resorts. Uses music houses for background music for commercials and jingles. Buys all rights or one-time rights.
How to Contact: Prefers cassette (or ¾" U-matic videocassette). Does not return unsolicited material; prefers to keep on file. Reports in 2 weeks.

*CHARLES EDELSTEIN ADVERTISING, INC., 92 Austin Dr., Holland PA 18966. (215)355-5015. President: Charles Edelstein. Advertising agency. Pays $500-5,000/job. Buys all rights.
How to Contact: Write first and obtain permission to submit. Prefers cassette. Does not return unsolicited material.
Music: Uses all styles of music for various kinds of assignment.

EHRLICH-MANES & ASSOCIATES, 4901 Fairmont Ave., Bethesda MD 20814. (301)657-1800. Vice President, Creative Services: Lee Blom. Advertising agency. Serves a wide variety of local, regional and national accounts. Uses jingles and background music for commercials. Commissions 5-10 pieces/year. Pays by the job. Rights purchased vary.
How to Contact: Query with resume, tape of previously aired work or submit demo tape showing jingle/composition skills. Prefers cassette. Does not return unsolicited material.

ESTEY-HOOVER, INC., Suite 225, 3300 Irvine Ave, Newport Beach CA 92660. (714)756-8501. Creative Director: Art Silver. Ad agency. Uses the services of songwriters for jingles and background music. Commissions 2 songwriters and 1 lyricist/year. Pays by the job. Buys all rights.
How to Contact: Query first; submit demo tape of previous work. Prefers cassette with 5-7 songs. SASE, but prefers to keep on file. Responds as need arises.
Music: "Depends upon the specific assignment. We have used, for example, heavy romantic schmaltz and also upbeat middle-of-the-road."
Tips: "Get samples on your reel ASAP. Sell yourself as a bargain when you're starting out just to build a reel. In time you'll make plenty of money if you're good."

EVANS BARTHOLOMEW POLLACK NORMAN, INC., 2128 15th St., Denver CO 80202. (303)534-2343. Advertising agency. Serves consumer, public service and financial clients. Uses music houses for jingles and background music for commercials and radio. Commissions 6 pieces/year. Pays $2,000 minimum/job. Buys all rights or "one year buyout."
How to Contact: Submit demo tape of previously aired work. Prefers cassette. Does not return tape; prefers to keep on file.
Music: All types.

EVANS/CICCARONE, INC., 420 NW 42 Ave., Miami FL 33126. (305)445-1433. President: Peter Evans. Ad agency. Uses the services of songwriters and lyricists for jingles and background music. Commissions 3 songwriters and 1 lyricist/year. Payment negotiated. Buys all rights.
How to Contact: Query with resume of credits or submit demo tape of previous work. Prefers cassette with 3-6 songs. SASE, but prefers to keep on file. Responds as needs arise.
Music: All kinds.

EXCLAMATION POINT ADVERTISING, Suite 424, 424 Hart-Albin Bldg., Billings MT 59101. (406)245-6341. Media Director: Barbara Diekhans. President: Janet Cox. Advertising agency. Serves financial, real estate, retail clothing and lumber clients. Uses jingles. Pays on a per-job basis. Buys all rights.
How to Contact: Submit demo tape of previously aired work or tape showing jingle/composition skills. Prefers reel-to-reel or cassette. SASE. Reports in 1 month.
Music: 30-second jingles.

FALLIS COMMUNICATIONS, INC., (formerly Falls/Garrett Enterprises), 3665 Cascade Rd. SW, Atlanta GA 30331. (404)691-3988. Contact: Maynard Eaton. President: Carolyn Fallis. Advertising agency. Uses the services of songwriters for jingles, background music and video; lyricists for writing jingles. Commissions 1 songwriter and 1 lyricist/year. Pays $2,000-6,000/job. Buys all rights.
How to Contact: Query with resume of credits or submit demo tape of previous work. Prefers cassette (or ¾" or ½" videocassette) with 3 songs. SASE.

FERGUSON & ASSOCIATES ADVERTISING, 76 W. Main St., Rexburg ID 83440. (208)356-9381. Producer/Director: Brad Shaw. Advertising agency. Clients include Diet Center, Inc. (in-house agency). Uses independent songwriters, lyricists and music houses for background music for commercials, jingles and motivational, promotional and training audiovisual presentations. Commissions 3 songwriters and 3 lyricists/year. Pays by the job. Buys all rights.
How to Contact: Submit demo tape of previously aired work. Prefers cassette (or ¾'' videocassette). Does not return unsolicited material; prefers to keep on file. Reports "as jobs occur."
Music: Easy listening, country, pop and rock for jingles, music beds, TV, promotional films and exercise music.

GALLAGHER GROUP, INC., 885 Third Ave., 14th Floor, New York NY 10002. (212)836-0616. Vice President/Creative Director: Bill Murtha. Advertising agency. Clients include automotive, car dealers, outdoor advertising and TV stations. Uses independent songwriters, lyricists and music houses for background music for commercials, jingles and radio spots. Commissions 3-7 songwriters/year. Pays by the job. Buys all rights or one-time rights.
How to Contact: Submit demo tape of previously aired work. Prefers 7½ ips reel-to-reel. Does not return unsolicited material, prefers to keep material on file.
Music: Pop, rock and MOR for jingles, music beds, radio and TV.

GARDINER—A MARKETING COMPANY, Box 30, Salt Lake City UT 84110. (801)364-5600. Vice President/Creative Director: Gordon A. Johnson. Advertising agency. Clients include: "financial institutions, automotive, fast foods and utility." Uses music houses for background music for commercials and jingles. Commissions 3-6 songwriters/year. Pays $1,000-5,000/job. Buys all rights; "unlimited buyout per market."
How to Contact: Accepts "demo tapes of established music houses only." Prefers cassette or 7½ ips reel-to-reel (or ¾'' or VHS videocassette) with 5 or more pieces. SASE, but prefers to keep material on file. Reports in 2 weeks.
Music: All styles of music for jingles and scoring for TV commercials.
Tips: "We prefer full cuts of music. Don't think of it as a 'jingle' but more as a 'song'."

JAN GARDNER AND ASSOCIATES, Suite 229, 3340 Poplar, Memphis TN 38111. (901)452-7328. Production Director: Mark Thompson. Ad agency. Uses services of songwriters and lyricists for jingles. Commissions 2 songwriters and 2 lyricists/year. Pays by the job. Buys all rights.
How to Contact: Submit demo tape of previous work. Prefers 7½ ips reel-to-reel or cassette with 3-12 songs. SASE, but prefers to keep material on file.
Music: "We have a wide range of clients and needs."

GARNER & ASSOCIATES, INC., Suite 350, 3705 Latrobe Dr., Charlotte NC 28211. (704)365-3455. President: John Garner. Creative Director: Morris Phifer. Ad agency. Serves a wide range of clients; client list available upon request. Uses the services of songwriters for jingles. Pays by the job. Buys all rights.
How to Contact: Write first to arrange personal interview or submit demo tape of previous work. Prefers 7½ ips reel-to-reel "with enough songs to showcase your best work." Prefers studio produced demos. Does not return unsolicited material; prefers to keep on file for possible future use.
Music: All types.
Tips: "Be flexible when it comes to price."

GILBERT, WHITNEY & JOHNS, INC., 110 S. Jefferson Blvd., Whippany NJ 07981. (201)386-1776. Creative Administrative Assistant: John Mimnaugh. Ad agency. Clients include consumer package goods, service and industrial firms. Uses music houses and songwriters for background music for commercials and jingles. Pays by the job. Buys all rights or one-time rights.
How to Contact: Write or call first to obtain permission to submit. Prefers cassette (or ¾'' videocassette. SASE.
Music: Various styles.

GILLHAM ADVERTISING, 5th Floor, Desert Plaza, 15 E. First S., Salt Lake City UT 84111. (801)328-0281. Producer: Gene Yates. Advertising agency. Serves financial, real estate, fast food, mall and automobile dealer clients. Uses services of songwriters, composers and local production companies for jingles and background music for radio and TV commercials. Commissions 6 composers/year. Pays by the job.
How to Contact: Submit demo tape of previously aired work. Prefers cassette with 6-12 songs. Pre-

fers studio produced demo. Does not return unsolicited material. Responds as needs arise.
Music: "Identity jingles for a variety of clients in a local market."
Tips: "Keep us up-to-date on your work with occasional demo tapes and inquiries about our needs. We may be looking for economical, quick turnaround on music for short term use."

GRAVES & ASSOCIATES, 109 Tacoma Ave. N, Tacoma WA 98403. (206)627-9128. Associate Creative Director: Charlee Parker Glock. Advertising agency. Clients include car dealer, bank, health insurance, electric utility and construction materials. Uses independent songwriters and music houses for background music for commercials, jingles, industrial films and slide shows. Commissions 5-10 songwriters/year. Pays by the job. Buys all rights.
How to Contact: Submit demo tape of previously aired work. Prefers cassette, (or ½" VHS videocassette). SASE, but prefers to keep material on file. "Please contact us within 2 weeks to verify our receipt of your material and to receive our comments."
Music: "Just about all styles of music, except heavy metal, used for jingles, music beds and TV scores."
Tips: "Be *unique*! Don't sound like everyone else. Dull and predictable is deadly! If you use synthesizers, use them creatively and differently."

*GREEN ADVERTECTS, INC., 1500 Forest Ave., Richmond VA 23229. (804)282-4622. President: Francis Green. Advertising agency. Uses the services of independent songwriters, lyricists and music houses for jingles. Buys local rights only.
How to Contact: Submit demo tape of previously aired work. Prefers cassette. Does not return unsolicited material; prefers to keep on file.
Music: Up-tempo and classical for jingles.
Tips: "We are currently looking for a car care or carwash jingle. We can use something previously produced for others."

GREY ADVERTISING, 777 Third Ave., New York NY 10017. (212)546-2000. Creative Director: Richard Karp. Serves retail department store, tape and audio manufacturer, television, media, business, machine and airline clients. Uses songwriters and music houses for jingles, background music in commercials and sound effects.
How to Contact: Submit demo tape of previous work or tape showing jingle/composition skills. Prefers cassette with 5-10 songs. SASE, prefers to keep on file.
Music: All types.

HERB GROSS & CO., 84 Edgerton St., Rochester NY 14607. (716)244-3711. President: Herb Gross. Consumer advertising specialist. Uses services of songwriters for jingles and movies. Commissions 3 songwriters/year. Pays $1,500-8,000/job; "depending on total authorized budget."
How to Contact: Submit demo tape of previous work. Prefers cassette with 3-6 songs. SASE, but prefers to keep material on file.
Music: Needs "60-second radio spots, 30- and 10-second TV spots. Uptempo, contemporary styles. Long form industrial videos."

GROUP TWO ADVERTISING, 2002 Ludlow St., Philadelphia PA 19103. (215)561-2200. Senior Producer: Bobbi Helms. Ad agency. Serves industrial, real estate, hotel/motel and retail clients. Uses services of songwriters for jingles and background music for commercials. Commissions 1 songwriter/year. Pays $2,500-6,000/job. Buys one-time rights.
How to Contact: Submit demo tape of previously aired work. Prefers cassette with 5 songs minimum. Prefers studio produced demos. Does not return unsolicited material. "We prefer to keep material on file for future reference. We'll contact the person when a job comes up. A price list (no matter how general) is also helpful for us to keep on file."
Music: "Due to the variety of clients we handle, with various budgets, assignments can be of any nature."
Tips: "Be willing to do free demos and work within specified time frame."

HANNA/WHEELER & ASSOCIATES, Box 2025, Coeur d'Alene ID 83814. (208)667-2428. Media Coordinator: Cindy Yocum. Advertising agency. Uses independent songwriters, lyricists and music houses for background music for commercials and jingles. Pays by the job. Buys all rights or one-time rights.
How to Contact: Submit demo tape of previously aired work. Prefers cassette. Does not return unsolicited material; prefers to keep material on file.
Music: "Styles of music and kinds of assignments are dependent on client need."

HBM/CREAMER-ALBERT JAY ROSENTHAL, 400 N. Michigan Ave., Chicago IL 606ll. (312)337-8070. Contact: Executive Creative Director. Advertising agency. Serves fashion, consumer foods, kitchen utensils, financial services, automotive products and cosmetic clients. Uses the services of independent songwriters and music houses for jingles, background music and post-scoring for commercials, films and slide shows. Commissions 8-10 music houses/year. (Provides own lyrics.) Pays by the job. Buys all rights.
How to Contact: Submit demo tape of previously-aired work. Prefers cassette 3-5 minutes long. Does not return unsolicited material.
Music: Uses all types.
Tips: "We do not use aspiring songwriters trying to break into the business. Applicants must show convincing proof they have produced actual advertising assignments."

HEALY-SCHUTTE & COMPANY ADVERTISING, 1207 Delaware Ave., Buffalo NY 14209. (716)884-2120. Broadcast Production Manager: Len Tobin. Advertising agency. Uses the services of jingle producers for jingles, background music and AV presentations. Commissions 3 songwriters and 3 lyricists/year. Pays $1,500-4,000/job. Buys all rights.
How to Contact: Submit demo tape of previous work. Prefers cassette with 6-12 songs, with log enclosed. Prefers studio produced demos. Does not return unsolicited material; prefers to keep on file.

HEPWORTH ADVERTISING CO., 3403 McKinney Ave., Dallas TX 75204. (214)526-7785. President: S.W. Hepworth. Advertising agency. Serves financial, industrial and food clients. Uses services of songwriters for jingles. Pays by the job. Buys all rights.
How to Contact: Call first and obtain permission to submit or submit demo tape of previously aired work. Prefers cassette. SASE. Reports as need arises.

JANUARY & ASSOCIATES, INC., 5560 Franklin Pike Circle, Box 2017, Brentwood TN 37027. (615)377-9111. Corporate Secretary: Sylvia January. Serves industrial, entertainment, food, movies, shoes, insurance and political clients. Uses jingles and background music in commercials. Commissions 6 pieces/year. Payment depends on pre-determined budget.
How to Contact: Query first by mail. Prefers 7½ ips reel-to-reel or cassette with minimum 3 songs. SASE. Reports in 2 weeks.
Music: All types.

THE JAYME ORGANIZATION, 23200 Chagrin Blvd., Cleveland OH 44122. (216)831-0110. Creative Supervisor: Merritt Johnquest. Advertising agency. Uses the services of songwriters and lyricists for jingles and background music. Pays by the job. Buys all rights.
How to Contact: Query first; submit demo tape of previous work. Prefers cassette with 4-8 songs. SASE. Reponds by phone as needs arise.
Music: Jingles.

KELLER RUBINSTEIN & JACOBS ADVERTISING, 56 Central Ave., East Farmingdale NY 11735. (516)293-9595. Director of Productions: Glenn Beers. Advertising agency and broadcast production (radio/TV). Clients include retail and business-to-business. Uses independent songwriters, lyricists and music houses for background music for commercials, jingles, training films and presentations. Commissions 12 songwriters/year and 12 lyricists/year. Pays $1,000-5,000/job. Buys all rights.
How to Contact: Submit demo tape of previously aired work. Prefers cassette. Does not return unsolicited material.
Music: All styles for various assignments.

KETCHUM ADVERTISING, 6 PPG Place, Pittsburgh PA 15222-5488. (412)456-3500. Vice President/Director of Broadcast Services: Dick Sleeman. Ad agency. Serves consumer and business clients. Uses services of production houses for jingles, background music for commercials and "sometimes" films. Supplies lyricists with "basic strategic directions and background and often excellent lyrics as well." Commissions 10-15 songwriters and 10-15 lyricists for 15-20 pieces/year. Pays $500 minimum/job, "depends on markets." Buys all rights.
How to Contact: Query with resume of credits or submit demo showing jingle/composition skills. Prefers cassette with 7-15 songs. Does not return unsolicited material. "Material is kept on file in our creative department. Will respond only if writer calls."
Music: "We use a wide range of styles with memorable melodies and excellent production. Assignments are generally original, specific and with excellent lyrics supplied as a direction."
Tips: "Be simple. Be original. Be around."

KETCHUM/MANDABACH & SIMMS, INC., (formerly Mandabach & Simms, Inc.), 111 North Canal, Chicago IL 60606. (312)902-1300. Creative Director: Burt Bentkover. Vice President of Creative

Design: Linda Masterson. Ad agency. Serves industrial, financial and consumer clients. Uses jingles and background music for commercials. Commissions 5-10 songwriters/year. Pays union scale. "We normally work with complete production houses, not individuals." Rights purchased dependent upon client's needs.

How to Contact: Submit demo tape of previously aired work. Prefers cassette with minimum 6 songs. Does not return unsolicited material.

Music: All types for TV, radio and audiovisual presentations.

Tips: "Make sure tapes are labeled and dated. We normally don't acknowledge or comment on unsolicited material. We contact only if needed."

LA GRAVE KLIPFEL CLARKSON, INC., ADVERTISING, PUBLIC RELATIONS, MARKETING, Suite 300, 2700 Grand, Des Moines IA 50312. (515)283-2297. Copywriter/Producer: Bob Harbert. Serves wide range of clients including financial, industrial and retail; client list available on request. Uses services of songwriters and music libraries for jingles; uses lyricists for lyrics. Commissions 0-5 songwriters and 3-5 lyricists/year. Pays $2,400-10,000/job. Rights negotiable.

How to Contact: "Telephone first then follow up with mailed information." Prefers reel-to-reel or cassette with any number songs. Does not return unsolicited material; prefers to keep material on file.

Music: Primarily interested in jingles.

Tips: "Don't rely on mailing demo—follow up. Have a good product; have a good track record; do free piano demos. Send a variety of finished pieces."

LD&A ADVERTISING CORP., 717 W. Main St., Batavia IL 60510. (312)879-2000. President: Leo Denz. Ad agency, public relations firm and audiovisual company. Serves consumer and industrial clients. Uses jingles and background music for commercials and audiovisual shows. Payment depends on use. Buys one-time rights or all rights.

How to Contact: Query with resume of credits or submit demo tape of previously aired work. Prefers cassettes. "Don't mix 'types' on a single cassette; for example, don't put jingles on the same tape as background music." SASE. "We'll keep material on file for client review. We like to let our clients have a hand in choosing talent for their commercials and films. Usually we select 3 and let them make the final choice."

Music: "Jingles: We will furnish the points to cover and their relative importance. Background: We will furnish the edited film with a description sheet of what the music is to accomplish."

S.R. LEON COMPANY, INC., 111 Great Neck Rd., Great Neck NY 11021. (516)487-0500. Creative Director: Max Firetog. Ad agency. Serves industrial, drug, automotive and dairy product clients. Uses jingles and background music for commercials. Commissions vary. Rights purchased are limited to use of music for commercials.

How to Contact: Submit demo tape of previously aired work. Prefers cassette. No length restrictions on demo.

Music: Uses all types.

LEWIS, GILMAN & KYNETTE, INC., 1700 Market St., Philadelphia PA 19103. (215)568-3775. Broadcast Business Manager: Valencia Tursi. Ad agency. Serves industrial and consumer clients. Uses music houses for jingles and background music in commercials. Commissions 4 pieces/year. Pays creative fee asked by music houses.

How to Contact: Submit demo tape of previously aired work. Prefers cassette. Will return with SASE if requested, but prefers to keep on file.

Music: All types.

*AL MAESCHER ADVERTISING, INC., 11433 Olde Cabin Rd., Creve Coeur MO 63141. (314)727-6981. President: Al Maescher. Advertising agency. Serves industrial, retail and financial clients. Uses the services of songwriters for jingles. Pays by the job. Buys one-time rights, for exclusive use in service area.

How to Contact: Submit demo tape of previously aired work. Prefers 7½ ips reel-to-reel or cassette. SASE, but prefers to keep material on file. Responds as needs arise.

*MAISH ADVERTISING, 280 N. Main, Marion OH 43302. (614)382-1191. Contact: Creative Director. Advertising agency. Serves industrial, financial and home building products clients. Uses jingles. Payment negotiable for complete packages, including production. Buys all rights.

How to Contact: Submit demo tape of previously aired work. Prefers 7½ ips reel-to-reel.

MALLOF, ABRUZINO & NASH MARKETING, 477 E. Butterfield Rd., Lombard IL 60148. (312)964-7722. President: Ed Mallof. Advertising agency. Works primarily with auto dealer jingles.

Uses music houses for jingles. Commissions 5 songwriters/year. Pays $600-3,500/job. Buys all rights.
How to Contact: Submit demo tape of previous work. Prefers cassette with 4-12 songs. SASE; but prefers to keep material on file. Reports "when we feel a need for their style."
Tips: "Submit good driving music with clever lyrics."

MARKETING GROUP INC., 312 E. Buffalo, Milwaukee WI 53202. (414)347-4150. Creative Director: Dave Belling. Advertising agency. Serves marine, lawn and garden, industrial and consumer clients. Uses the services of independent songwriters for jingles. Commissions 2-3 songwriters/year. Pays $5,000/job. Buys all rights.
How to Contact: Write or call first to obtain permission to submit or submit demo tape of previously aired work. Prefers cassette. "Interested in original jingles written and produced for recognized national clients, or local work that has received award recognition within the advertising community." Does not return unsolicited material; prefers to keep material on file. Reports in 8 weeks.
Tips: "We are not looking for rearrangements of national jingles. There is a trend toward using old popular songs for national ad campaign jingles. We prefer to use original music."

*MAXWELL ADVERTISING INC., 444 W. Michigan, Kalamazoo MI 49007. (616)382-4060. Creative Director: Jess Maxwell. Advertising agency. Uses the services of lyricists and music houses for jingles and background music for commercials. Commissions 6-8 lyricists/year. Pays $4,000-20,000/job. Buys all rights or one-time rights.
How to Contact: Submit demo tape of previously aired work or tape demonstrating composition skills. Prefers cassette (or VHS videocassette). SASE, but prefers to keep material on file. Reports in 2 weeks.
Music: Uses various styles of music for jingles and music beds.

McCANN-ERICKSON LOUISVILLE, 1469 S. 4th St., Louisville KY 40208. (502)636-0441. Contact: Russ Cashon. Advertising agency. Serves packaged goods, fast food, industrial and service clients. Uses jingles and background music in commercials. Commissions about 12 pieces broadcast music/year. Buys rights on "13 week or yearly cycles according to AFM codes, etc."
How to Contact: Write first, then submit reel-to-reel or cassette with 6-8 songs. Reports in 1 week.

*McCANN-ERICKSON WORLDWIDE, Briar Hollow Bldg., 520 S. Post Oak Rd., Houston TX 77056. (713)965-0303. Creative Director: Jesse Caesar. Advertising agency. Serves all types of clients. Uses services of songwriters for jingles and background music in commercials. Commissions 10 songwriters/year. Pays production cost and registrated creative fee. Arrangement fee and creative fee depend on size of client and size of market. "If song is for a big market, a big fee is paid; if for a small market, a small fee is paid." Buys all rights.
How to Contact: Submit demo tape of previously aired work. Prefers 7½ ips reel-to-reel. "There is no minimum or maximum length for tapes. Tapes may be of a variety of work or a specialization. We are very open on tape content; agency does own lyrics." SASE, but prefers to keep material on file. Responds by phone when need arises.
Music: All types.

*McDONALD DAVIS & ASSOC., 250 W. Coventry Ct., Milwaukee WI 53217. (414)228-1990. Associate Creative Director Group Head: Jim Orgill. Advertising agency. Uses music houses for background music for commercials. Commissions 15 composers and producers/year. Pays $1,000-3,000/job. Buys all rights.
How to Contact: Write to arrange personal interview or submit demo tape of previously aired work or tape demonstrating composition skills. Prefers cassette (or ¾" videocassette) with 10 pieces and resume of credits. Does not return unsolicited material; prefers to keep on file. "We report in 1 week on solicited material.
Music: Uses all styles of music for post-scoring television commercials.

MITCHELL & ASSOCIATES, 6917 Arlington Rd., Bethesda MD 20814. (301)986-1772. President: Ronald Mitchell. Advertising agency. Serves food, high-tech, transportation, financial, real estate, automotive and retail clients. Uses independent songwriters, lyricists and music houses for background music for commercials, jingles and post TV scores for commercials. Commissions 3-5 songwriters and 3-5 lyricists/year. Pays $3,000-10,000/job. Buys all rights.
How to Contact: Submit demo tape of previously aired work. Prefers cassette or 7½ ips reel-to-reel. Does not return unsolicited material; prefers to keep on file.
Music: "Depends upon client, audience, etc."

MYERS & ASSOCIATES, 951 Colorado Ave., Stuart FL 33497. (305)287-1990. Vice President: Doris McLaughlin. Advertising agency. Serves financial, real estate and hotel clients. Uses music houses for background music for commercials and jingles. Commission 2-3 songwriters/year and 2-3 lyricists/year. Pays by the job. Buys all rights.

How to Contact: Submit demo tape of previously aired work. Prefers cassette. Does not return unsolicited material; prefers to keep material on file.

Music: Uses "various style of music for jingles, music beds and complete packages depending on clients' needs."

FRANK C. NAHSER, INC., 18th Floor, 10 S. Riverside Plaza, Chicago IL 60606. (312)845-5000. Contact: Alan Schulman. Advertising agency. Uses the services of independent songwriters, lyricists and music houses for jingles, background music for commercials and industrial/sales presentations. Commissions 6-10 songwriters and 4 lyricists/year. Pays $5,000-15,000 for finished production.

How to Contact: Submit demo tape of previous work. Prefers cassette. Does not return unsolicited material; prefers to keep on file. "No phone calls, please. When a cassette is submitted I listen to it for reference when a project comes up. I ignore most cassettes that lack sensitivity toward string and woodwind arrangements unless I know it's from a lyricist."

Music: "We mostly use scores not jingles. Young songwriters should be aware of the difference and have the expertise to score, not just write songs."

Tips: "The writing speaks for itself. If you know composition, theory and management it quickly becomes evident. Electronic submissions are great tools; however, they are no substitute for total musicianship. Learn to read, write, arrange and produce music and, with this book's help market your music. Be flexible enough to work along with agency on a score or jingle. We like to write and produce as much as you do."

*NEW YORK COMMUNICATIONS, 207 S. State Rd., Upper Darby PA 19082. (215)352-5505. Contact: Paul Greeley. Advertising agency. Uses services of independent songwriters, lyricists and music houses for jingles and background music for commercials. Pays by the job. Buys all rights.

How to Contact: Submit demo tape of previously aired work; or tape demonstrating composition skills. Prefers cassette with 6 pieces. SASE.

Music: Uses easy listening, up-tempo and pop for music campaigns for local news promotions and music beds.

*NEWTON ASSOCIATES, INC., Box 50, St. Davids PA 19087. (215)964-9300. Creative Director: Jon Newton. Advertising agency. Uses music houses for jingles; some background music for corporate film work. Commissions 3-5 songwriters/year. Pays by the job. Buys all rights or negotiates rights.

How to Contact: Write or call first and obtain permission to submit. Prefers cassette. SASE, but prefers to keep material on file.

Music: Uses jingles for radio and TV.

OGILVY & MATHER INC., 2 E. 48th St., New York NY 10017. (212)907-3400. Director of Music: Faith Norwick. Ad agency. Serves all types of clients. Uses services of songwriters for jingles and background music for commercials. Commissions 20-30 songwriters for about 50 pieces/year. Pays by the job. "A nationally used jingle pays $5,000-10,000."

How to Contact: Send tape of previously aired work or tape showing jingle/composition skills to Director of Music. Do not include unsolicited jingles relating to clients because of possible legal implications. Prefers cassette with "bits of songs, 2 minutes is enough. 10 pieces on a jingle demo is sufficient." Likes to file tapes for later review. Does not return unsolicited material. Reports "when something comes up."

Music: Uses all types.

PEARSON, THOMAS, LEVY, KING & WHITE, Suite 800, 6200 Courtney Campbell Causeway, Tampa FL 33607. (813)874-2511. Creative Director: Pete Tiisler. Associate Creative Director: Elena Bonsignori. Advertising agency and public relations firm. Serves industrial, financial, fast food, shelter and packaged goods clients. Uses services of songwriters for jingles. Payment varies. Rights negotiated.

How to Contact: Submit demo tape of previously aired work. SASE, but prefers to keep material on file. Reports by phone or mail as needs arise.

PHOENIX ADVERTISING CO., (formerly Mohawk Advertising Co.), 1307 6th St. SW, Mason City IA 50401. (515)423-1354. President: Jim Clark. Advertising agency. Serves financial and industrial clients, agricultural industries, fast food restaurants and insurance companies. Uses services of independent songwriters for jingles and background music in commercials, films and slide shows. Commissions 3-5 songwriters/year. Pays by the job. Prefers to buy one-time rights.

How to Contact: Submit demo tape of previously aired work or submit demo tape showing jingles/compositions for a particular client. Prefers 7½ ips reel-to-reel or cassette with 5-10 songs. Material

kept on file for reference.
Tips: "Follow up your demos with occasional notes/phone calls. But be good first."

PRINGLE DIXON PRINGLE, Suite 1500, 245 Peachtree Center Ave., Atlanta GA 30303. (404)688-6720. Creative Director: Perry Mitchel. Ad agency. Serves fashion, financial, fast food and industrial clients; client list available on request. Uses services of songwriters for jingles and background music. Pays by the job. Rights vary, depending on job.
How to Contact: Submit tape of previous work. Prefers cassette. SASE.
Music: All types.

PRO/CREATIVES, 25 W. Burda Place, Spring Valley NY 10977. President: David Rapp. Advertising and promotion agency. Serves consumer products and services, sports and miscellaneous clients. Uses background music in TV and radio commercials. Payment negotiable.
How to Contact: Query with resume of credits. SASE.

***PUBLICITE IMAGE ADE**, 3855 Decarie Blvd., Montreal, Quebec H3A 3J6 Canada. (514)481-0291. General Manager/Production: Reg Weiswall. Advertising agency. Clients include automobile leasing, office furniture and highway transport firms. Uses independnet songwriters, lyricists and music houses for background music for commercials and jingles. Pays by the job. Buys all rights or one-time rights.
How to Contact: Prefers cassette. Does not return unsolicited material; prefers to keep on file. Reports in 2 weeks.
Music: MOR for jingles, music beds or background music.

RAMEY COMMUNICATIONS, 3008 Wilshire Blvd., Los Angeles CA 90010. (213)384-2700. Producer: Adrienne Lowe. Ad agency. Uses services of songwriters for jingles and background music. "We have copywriters on staff." Commissions 5 songwriters/year. Pays by the job. Buys all rights.
How to Contact: Submit demo tape of previous work. Prefers reel to reel or cassette with 5-10 songs. Does not return unsolicited material, prefers to keep on file. Reports "when the need arises."
Music: "We have many broadcast accounts—each project has its own qualifications."

RAPP & COLLINS, INC., 475 Park Ave. S., New York NY 10016. (212)725-8100. Associate Creative Director: Jerry Genova. Advertising agency. Serves various clients. Uses the services of independent songwriters and music houses for background music for commercials. Pays by the job. Buys all rights.
How to Contact: Write first to obtain permission to submit. Prefers cassette or reel-to-reel. SASE.
Music: Uses music beds and background music.
Tips: Writers need "willingness to do work on speculation."

***RICHARDSON & ASSOCIATES**,Suite 315, Fifth Street Center, Covington KY 41011. Contact: Steve Deiters. Clients include small to medium size retailers, and political candidates. Uses the services of songwriters for jingles.
How to Contact: Submit demo tape of previously aired work or tape showing composition skills. SASE. Reports in 3 months.
Music: All styles.

RUHR/PARAGON, INC., (formerly Chuck Ruhr Advertising, Inc.), 1221 Nicollett Mall, Minneapolis MN 55403. (612)332-4565. Creative Director: Doug Lew. Advertising agency. Serves consumer and industrial clients; client list available on request. Uses the services of songwriters and music houses for jingles and background music. Commissions 4-5 songwriters and 1-2 lyricists/year. Pays by the job. Initial fee negotiated, after that pays union scales. Pays residuals for subsequent use of material. Rights purchased are negotiable.
How to Contact: Submit demo tape of previous work. Prefers cassette. Reports "when needed."
Music: Uses background music and "originals befitting the message."
Tips: "Be original and be flexible. Study the best examples."

THE SAVAN COMPANY, INC., 6528 Clayton Rd., St. Louis MO 63117. (314)647-7777. President: Sidney Savan. Advertising agency. Uses the services of songwriters for jingles and background music. Pays by the job. Buys all rights.
How to Contact: Query first; submit demo tape of previous work. Prefers cassette with 2 songs. Does not return unsolicited material; prefers to keep on file.

***SCHOENBACK ADVERTISING, INC.**, 1111 Park Ave., Baltimore MD 21201. (301)728-5566. Executive Vice President: Jim O'Reilly. Advertising agency. Uses music houses for jingles and background music for commercials. Pays by the job. Buys all rights or one-time rights.

How to Contact: Submit demo tape of previously aired work. Prefers cassette or reel-to-reel (or ¾" VHS videocassete). Does not return unsolicited material.

SHAFFER SHAFFER SHAFFER, INC., 226 Hanna Bldg., Cleveland OH 44115. (216)566-1188. President: Harry Gard Shaffer, Jr. Advertising agency. Uses services of songwriters, lyricists and music houses for jingles and background music. Commissions 4-5 songwriters/year. Pays $2,000-15,000/job. Buys all rights.
How to Contact: Query with resume of credits. Prefers 7½ ips reel-to-reel with 6-12 songs. SASE, but prefers to keep on file. Responds as needs arise.

*SHEEHY & KNOPF INC., 10400 Linn Station Rd., Louisville KY 40223.(502)426-1314. Vice President/Associate Creative Director: Rosyln Hosier. Advertising agency. Uses music houses for jingles and background music for commercials. Pays by the job or per hour. Buys all rights.
How to Contact: Write to arrange personal interview or submit demo tape of previously aired work. Prefers cassette (or ¾" videocassete). SASE, but prefers to keep material on file.
Music: "Mostly jingles, some music beds."

*SHIMER VON COUNTRY, Bousse Bldg., Philadelphia PA 19106. (215)627-3535. Creative Director: Rick DeDonato. Advertising agency. Uses the services of independent songwriters and music houses for jingles, background music for commercials and corporate videos. Commissions 2 songwriters/year. Pays $500-8,000/job. Buys all rights.
How to Contact: Submit demo tape of previously aired work. Prefers cassette. "Put name and phone number on tape and indicate cost of production." SASE, but prefers to keep material on file. Reports "if the submitted demo seems appropriate to a job."
Music: "Mostly up-tempo music for jingles."

SNYDER-READE & WOODRUFF, Suite 890, 1380 Lawrence St., Denver CO 80204. (303)893-0606. Associate Producer: Sheri Kazmierski. Advertising agency. Clients include McDonalds, Front Range Buick Dealers, Deep Rock Water and Boyer Coffee. Uses independent songwriters, lyricists and music houses for background music for commercials and jingles. Commissions 6 songwriters/year and 6 lyricists/year. Pays by the job. Buys all rights or one-time rights.
How To Contact: Write first to obtain permission to submit. Prefers cassette (or ¾ or ½ videocassette). SASE, but prefers to keep material on file.
Music: MOR, rock and pop for jingles and background music.
Tips: "Send tapes and follow up with phone calls. Timing is critical—depending on upcoming projects."

ROBERT SOLOMON AND ASSOCIATES ADVERTISING, Suite 1000, 505 N. Woodward, Bloomfield Hills MI 48013. (313)540-0660. Copywriter/Producer: Richard Wochoski. Advertising agency. Clients include "food service accounts, convenience stores, retail accounts and small service businesses." Uses independent songwriters, lyricists and music houses for jingles and special presentations. Commissions 1-10 songwriters and 1-10 lyricists/year. Pays by the job. Buys all rights.
How to Contact: Submit demo tape of previously aired work. Prefers cassette or 7½ ips reel-to-reel with 1-5 pieces and lyric or lead sheets. "Submissions must be up-to-date and up to industry standards." Does not return unsolicited material; prefers to keep on file.
Music: "MOR, pop or rock jingles describing specific products or services."
Tips: "Please make sure all information presented is CURRENT!"

EDGAR S. SPIZEL ADVERTISING, INC., 1782 Pacific Ave., San Francisco CA 94109. (415)474-5735. President: Edgar S. Spizel. Advertising agency, public relations firm and TV/radio production firm. Serves consumer clients "from jeans to symphony orchestras, from new products to political." Uses background music in commercials. Pays $1,500 minimum/job. Buys all rights.
How to Contact: Query. Prefers cassette with 3-5 songs. Does not return unsolicited material.

STERN/MONROE ADVERTISING, 2905 Maple, Dallas TX 75201. (214)871-7171. Producer: Paula Jarrell. Advertising agency. Clients include fast foods, hotels, banks and package goods. Uses the services of independent songwriters and music houses for background music for commercials and jingles. Pays by the job. Buys all rights.
How to Contact: Submit demo tape of previously aired work. Call first to arrange personal interview. Prefers cassette. Does not return unsolicited material; prefers to keep material on file. Reports in 4 weeks.
Music: "Possibility of using all styles depending on creativity and who we're trying to reach." Uses jingles, music beds and background music for TV and radio.
Tips: "Just keep trying. Be flexible."

*STOLZ ADVERTISING COMPANY, 7701 Forsyth, St. Louis MO 63144. (314)863-0005. Director of Creative Services: Sallie Ervin. Advertising agency. Uses music houses for jingles and background music for commercials. Commissions 10-20 songwriters/year. Pays $1,000-15,000/job. Buys all rights or one-time rights.
How to Contact: Submit demo tape of previously aired work. Prefers cassette. "Cassette must have log of contents and name, address and phone number on it." Does not return unsolicited material; prefers to keep on file. Reports in 1-2 weeks or less on requested material. Does not report on unsolicited material.
Music: Uses pop jingles. "Good ones with cut-through. No vanilla stuff. Many of our clients are entertainment-oriented."
Tips: "Produce mock commercials. Take a product and write thirty or sixty seconds piece of music for it. Bringing in full-length songs doesn't give us an idea of what you can accomplish in thirty seconds. Don't send us bland jingles that could fit anything from a bank to a bordello."

STONE & ADLER, INC., #1800, 1 S. Wacker Dr., Chicago IL 60606-4614. Vice President/Creative Director: David Moore. Advertising agency and direct marketing firm. Serves industrial, consumer, entertainment and financial clients. Uses music houses for background music in commercials. Commissions 3-4 pieces/year. Pays according to budget. Usually buys one-time rights.
How to Contact: Submit demo tape of previously aired work. Prefers reel-to-reel or cassette. Returns material if requested with SASE; but prefers to keep tape on file.
Music: All types.

*SULLIVAN & FINDSEN ADVERTISING, INC., 2165 Gilbert Ave., Cincinnati OH 45206. (513)281-2700. Broadcast Producer: Gary Stephenson. Advertising agency. Uses the services of independent songwriters, lyricists and music houses for jingles, background music for commercials and music for sales films. Commissions 4 songwriters/year. Pays by the job. Buys all rights.
How to Contact: Submit demo tape of previously published aired work.

TAL, INC., 3645 W. Lake Rd., Erie PA 16505. (814)838-4505. Audiovisual, Broadcast Production: Jane Chitester. Ad agency. Uses services of songwriters and jingle houses for jingles and background music. "Lyrics usually are part of jingle package." Commissions 3-4 songwriters/year. Pays $1,500-7,500/job. Buys all rights.
How to Contact: Submit demo tape of previous work. Prefers 7½ ips reel-to-reel with 6-12 songs. Prefers studio produced demos. Does not return unsolicited material; prefers to keep material on file. Reports by phone when a project comes up.
Music: Needs stand-alone jingles for both TV and radio; also background music for TV, radio and AV shows.
Tips: "Be patient! Be persistent! Be productive! Show me something new. We tend to shy away from music that is too commercial. We need fresh, new approaches that fit the particular demographic profile and mood of our campaigns."

*TALLANT/YATES ADVERTISING, Suite 400, 5200 DTC Parkway, Englewood CO 80111. (303)771-0960. Copy Chief: Joel R. Cooper. Advertising agency. Uses the services of independent songwriters and music houses for jingles, background music for commercials, videotapes (industrial) and slide shows. Number of songwriters and lyricists commissioned per year varies. Pay ranges anywhere from $500-3,000 or more/job, depending on budget. Buys all rights or one-time rights.
How to Contact: Submit demo tape of previously aired work or tape demonstrating composition skills. "No phone calls, please." Prefers cassette and lyric sheet or resume of credits. "Keep demos short—three or four of your best selections will do nicely." Does not return unsolicited material; prefers to keep on file. Reports "only when interested."
Music: Uses all styles, mostly pop and up-tempo for jingles, music for radio and TV spots and soundtracks for videotape.
Tips: "Be patient. We'll contact you if we like what we hear and need you. To rise above the noise level in the marketplace, music must be more than well-produced garbage. Slick production values cannot disguise music lacking 'guts' and an original concept."

TOWELL, INC. ADVERTISING AND MARKETING, 5201 Old Middleton Rd., Madison WI 53705. (608)231-3471. Broadcast Producer: Michael S. Mahnke. Advertising agency. Serves "both consumer and industrial clients." Uses music houses for background music for commercials and jingles. Pays $2,000-3,000/job. Buys all rights.
How to Contact: Submit demo tape of previously aired work. Prefers cassette or 7½ ips reel-to-reel

(or VHS videocassette) with 5 or more pieces. Does not return unsolicited material; prefers to keep material on file. Reports in 6 weeks.
Music: "MOR, pop and rock for jingles and background music for TV."
Tips: "Be flexible and open to change."

TRAVIS/WALZ & ASSOC., ADVERTISING, 8417 Santa Fe Dr., Overland Park KS 66212. (913)341-5022. Associate Creative Director: Bev Bellinger. Ad agency. Uses services of songwriters and music production companies for jingles, background music and post scoring. Commissions 2-3 songwriters/year. Pays by the job. Buys all rights.
How to Contact: Submit demo tape of previous work. Prefers cassette with 3-10 songs. Prefers studio produced demos. SASE, but prefers to keep material on file. Reports "when a project suited to a specific songwriter's style comes along."
Music: Needs "jingle package (10-, 30- and 60-second versions with and without vocals) composing a pre-established theme line to music." Prefers experienced songwriters.
Tips: "Learn to create music that edits cleanly into 10 seconds segments to keep music versatile for ad use. Basically your demo sells you—make it as professional (and original, of course) as possible."

*TUCKER WAYNE & CO., Suite 2700, 230 Peachtree St. NW, Atlanta GA 30043. (404)522-2383. Contact: Mr. McNulty or Markay Wiley. Serves financial, industrial, software, textile, food and tobacco clients. Uses the services of independent songwriters, lyricists and music houses for jingles and background music in commercials. Commissions 5-50 pieces/year. Pays by the job. Buys all rights.
How to Contact: Call for appointment to listen to demo. Prefers 7½ ips reel-to-reel; tape should be no longer than 7-8 minutes. Prefers to keep tape on file.
Music: All types.

TULLY-MENARD, INC., 2207 S. Dale Mabry, Tampa FL 33629. (813)253-0447. Copy Chief: Robert A. Ackroyd. Advertising agency. Uses the services of songwriters and music houses for jingles, background music and film and AV soundtracks. Commissions 2-3 songwriters/year. Payment negotiable, "dependent on project, budget and needs." Buys all rights.
How to Contact: Submit demo tape of previous work. Prefers 7½ ips reel-to-reel with 7-15 songs. SASE, but prefers to keep material on file. "We research our file at the onset of need to determine candidates and parameters, then obtain bids and demos."
Music: "Broadcast and off-line; jingles and music tracks. Institutional jingles for a wide variety of clients."
Tips: "Stay current with today's sound, but be different—give it your own personality. Listen carefully to the parameters we give you, and if you don't quite grasp what we're looking for, ask!"

*USI ADVERTISING, INC., 2311 Fairmount Ave., Philadelphia PA 19130. President: Allan Keyne. Advertising agency. Serves retail and consumer clients. Commissions 12 pieces/year. Pays $500 minimum/job. Buys all rights.
How to Contact: Query with resume of credits. Submit demo tape of previously aired work. Prefers cassette with 8 songs minimum. SASE. Reports in 2 weeks.
Music: Uses jingles.

CALDWELL VAN RIPER, 1314 N. Meridian, Indianapolis IN 46202. (317)632-6501. Executive Creative Director: Jeffrey Leiendecker. Advertising agency and public relations firm. Serves industrial, financial and consumer/trade clients. Uses jingles and background music for commercials. Commissions 25 pieces/year.
How to Contact: Submit demo tape of previously aired work or submit tape showing jingle/composition skills. Prefers 7½ ips reel-to-reel. SASE. Reports "as soon as possible."

WALKER ASSOCIATES, 1100 Morgan Keegan Tower, 50 Front St., Memphis TN 38103. (901)522-1100. Creative Director: Randy Hartzog. Copywriter: Dave Rohrer. Ad agency. Uses the services of songwriters, lyricists and music production houses for jingles and background music. Commissions 1-3 songwriters and 1-3 lyricists/year. Pays $2,500-10,000/job. Buys all rights (30% of the time) or one-time rights (70% of the time).
How to Contact: Query first; submit demo tape of previous work and arrange a personal interview. Prefers cassette or 7½ ips reel-to-reel with 3-6 songs. Prefers studio produced demos. Does not return unsolicited material; prefers to keep on file. Responds "when the writer's product suits our needs."
Music: Suitable work for financial institutions (to project an image), fast food restaurants, retail merchants and health care institutions.
Tips: "Know your target market; be creative, but don't obscure your message with too much flash and dash. Also, be patient, be flexible, and keep prices realistic. Be honest about your musical opinions and

respect the budget limitations of small agencies. If you can't produce a decent job for the money, say so. Buy-outs are preferable."

WEBER, COHN & RILEY, 444 N. Michigan Ave., Chicago IL 60611. (312)527-4260. Executive Creative Director: C. Welch. Advertising agency. Serves real estate, financial and food clients. Uses music houses for jingles and background music for commercials. Commissions 6 songwriters and 6 lyricists/year. Pays $500 minimum/job. Buys all rights or one-time rights, "open to negotiation."
How to Contact: Write a letter of introduction to creative director. SASE. "We listen to and keep a file of all submissions, but generally do not reply unless we have a specific job in mind." Songwriters may follow up with a phone call for response.
Music: "We use music for a variety of products and services. We expect highly original, tight arrangements that contribute to the overall concept of the commercial. We do not work with songwriters who have little or no previous experience scoring and recording commercials."
Tips: "Don't aim too high to start. Establish credentials and get experience on small local work, then go after bigger accounts. Don't oversell when making contacts or claim the ability to produce any kind of 'sound.' Producers only believe what they hear on sample reels. Produce a sample reel that's professional and responsive to today's needs. Present a work that is creative and meets our strategies and budget requirements."

WEITZMAN, DYM & ASSOCIATES, Suite 1100, 7474 Greenway Center Dr., Greenbelt MD 20770. Chairman: Alan Weitzman. Ad agency. Clients include national, regional and local advertisers. Uses independent songwriters for jingles and background music. Commission 12 songwriters/year. Pays $2,000-40,000/job. Buys all rights.
How to Contact: Write first to obtain permission to submit. Prefers cassette. Does not return unsolicited material; prefers to keep material on file. Reports in 4 weeks.
Music: MOR, pop, rock for jingles, music beds or background music for TV, radio, etc.

ARTHUR E. WILK, INC., 875 N. Michigan, John Hancock Center, Chicago IL 60611. (312)280-2800. Director of Broadcast Production: Mr. Clair Callihan. Advertising agency. Uses music houses for background music in commercials and longer films/filmstrips. Commissions 2-4 songwriters for 3-4 pieces/year. Pays by the job. Buys all rights.
How to Contact: Query by mail or phone, then submit tape of previous work with cover letter. Prefers cassette. Prefers studio produced demos. Will also review videocassettes and 16mm film but *call* before submitting. Does not return unsolicited material. Reports "only if interested in specific material."
Music: All types.

WOLKCAS ADVERTISING, 435 New Karner Rd., Albany NY 12205. (518)869-4846. Creative Director: Stewart Sacklow. Ad agency. Uses the services of songwriters and lyricists for jingles, background music and slide shows. Commissions 4 songwriters and 6-8 lyricists/year. Pays by the job and buy out. Buys all rights.
How to Contact: Submit demo tape of previous work. Prefers 7½ ips reel-to-reel with 3-5 songs. Prefers studio produced demos. Does not return unsolicited material; prefers to keep on file. Responds when needs arise.
Music: Various types depending on client—"from full string orchestra to hard rock and synthesizers."
Tips: "Keep submitting updated work; we are always looking for something new and fresh for our clients. Also, we need more short music to accompany IDs for TV."

WOMACK/CLAYPOOLE/GRIFFIN, Suite 501 N, 8585 Stemmons Freeway, Dallas TX 75247. (214)643-1234. Contact: Bill Claypool. Advertising agency. Serves petroleum, aviation, financial, insurance and retail clients. Uses services of songwriters for jingles and background music in commercials. Pays by the job. Buys all rights.
How to Contact: Submit demo tape of previous work. Prefers reel-to-reel. SASE, but prefers to keep material on file.
Music: Radio spots and TV background.

*YECK BROTHERS GROUP, Box 225, Dayton OH 45401. (513)294-4000. Advertising agency. Serves retail, industrial and financial clients. Commissions 3-5 pieces/year. Pays $800-4,000/job. Buys all rights.
How to Contact: Submit demo tape of previously aired work. Prefers cassette or 7½ ips reel-to-reel with 6-8 songs. Does not return unsolicited material.
Music: Uses jingles and background music in commercials and audiovisual productions. "Styles vary. We provide a guideline sheet that specifies the types of products wanted. We don't buy stock tracks or rewrites of some other jingle from another market."

Audiovisual firms create many products for many different purposes. Some provide the music for advertising agencies who wish to do most of the work on an ad campaign themselves, but have a limited creative team or little experience in music production. Audiovisual firms also produce slide presentations, films and videos for sales meetings and other corporate gatherings. They also do films, videos and slide shows for education markets as well as for the entertainment field. Some produce feature motion pictures and television shows. How-to videos are increasing in popularity, are available on nearly every subject, and represent a market for clever songwriters to explore. Some audiovisual productions don't even use music—an attractive or enthusiastic voice simply narrates over the visuals. But many audiovisual presentations _do_ utilize music, always very creatively. Many audiovisual production houses have limited staffs and tight deadlines, and welcome ideas (and ultimately finished products) from outside songwriters. They are likely to be especially interested in your work if you can demonstrate production, arranging and/or performing abilities in addition to writing appropriate music.

All the audiovisual firms listed here have expressed an interest in receiving queries or submissions from outside writers. Sometimes when audiovisual producers need music for a production, they turn to stock music houses simply because of time and budget considerations. But when they are searching for something fresh, original and unique, a competent and savvy songwriter can be called in to provide exactly what is needed—and be paid well for his efforts. But the songwriter must realize that the visuals, not the music, are the AV producer's main concern. Music is used in the background to maintain interest, set the mood and complement the visuals. The key to submitting is to demonstrate your versatility in writing specialized background music. Listings for specific companies will tell what facet(s) of the audiovisual field they are involved in and what types of clients they serve.

The listings in this section include all kinds of companies, from commercial music production houses to motion picture production companies. Most pay by the job, but some pay by the hour and others may negotiate a contract that includes royalty payments. Be sure you understand upfront exactly what is expected of you (number of songs, type of music, length of presentation, etc.) and know exactly how much you will be paid.

You may be asked to sell all rights or one-time rights depending upon the particular job and needs of the client. All rights means the buyer can use your work any way he wants and for as long as he chooses without further payment to you. One-time rights means your material can only be used for one presentation, and all other uses must be renegotiated with you.

Additional names and addresses (but no marketing information) of audiovisual firms can be found in the _Audiovisual Marketplace_ (R.R. Bowker).

A.C.T. FILMS LTD., 111 Wardour St., London W1V 4AY England. (01)437-8506. Executive Director: Richard F. Gates. Motion picture production company. Clients include cinema, television companies and trade unions. Uses the services of music houses and independent songwriters for scoring of and background music for features and documentaries. Commissions 1-2 songwriters/year. Pays by the job or per individual contracts. Buys all rights.
How to Contact: Query with resume of credits. SAE and IRC. Reports in 1 month.

*THE AD TEAM, Box 12444, Fresno CA 93777. (209)442-3332. Executive Producer: Robby Roberson. Jingle/commercial music production house. Uses services of independent songwriters and lyricists for jingles. Pays $75-2,500/job. Buys all rights or negotiates on national accounts.
How to Contact: Submit demo tape of previously aired work. Prefers cassette and lyric sheet. Does

not return unsolicited material; prefers to keep on file. Reports in 3 weeks.
Music: Uses easy listening, up-tempo, pop and country music for TV commercials.

*AFTERGLOW IMAGES PRODUCTIONS, INC., Box 1524, Northbrook IL 60065. (312)295-5421. Producer: Robert Peacock. Audiovisual firm. Clients include "technical, health care, service companies, insurance companies, etc." Uses the services of independent songwriters/composers and music libraries for background music for industrials and documentaries and jingles for corporate meetings. Pays by the job. Buys all rights or one-time rights.
How to Contact: Submit demo tape of previous work "with prices/price range" or tape demonstrating composition skills. "Please, no calls—the work will speak for itself." Prefers cassete. Does not return unsolicited material; prefers to keep on file.
Music: Uses all kinds of music for educational films, slide, video and sales programs.

*ALLEGRO PRODUCTIONS, INC., 2875 S. Congress Ave., Delray Beach FL 33444. (305)265-1700. Executive Producer: Kyle Campbell. Video production house. Clients include corporate, commercial and educational. Uses the services of independent songwriters/composers and music libraries for jingles for radio and TV. Pays by the job. Rights purchased are negotiable.
How to Contact: Query with resume of credits or submit demo tape of previous work. Prefers ¼" or ½" ips reel-to-reel (or ¾" videocassette). SASE, but prefers to keep material on file. Reports in 2½ weeks.
Music: Uses all types of music for educational films, logo scores and commercial jingles.

*ALPINE FILM PRODUCTIONS, 1623 Race St., Denver CO 80206. (303)393-1189. Producer: Dee B. Dubin. Audiovisual firm and film/video production company. Clients include corporations, advertising agencies, and real estate developers. Uses the services of music houses and independent songwriters/composers for background music for corporate films and commercials for TV. Commissions 5 composers/year. Pays by the job. Rights purchased varies by job.
How to Contact: Submit demo tape of previous work or tape demonstrating composition skills. Prefers cassette (or ¾" or ½" videocassette). Does not return unsolicited material; prefers to keep on file.
Music: Uses all styles of music for various kinds of assignments.

*AMERICAN VIDEO WORKS, Box 333, Evanston IL 60204. (312)328-0400. Vice President: Mark Zorfas. Audiovisual firm, commercial music production house, motion picture production company, music/sound effect library and record company (Hybrid Records). Uses the services of music houses, independent songwriters/composers and lyricists for scoring, background music, jingles and commercials for radio and TV. Pays by the job. Buys all rights.
How to Contact: Submit demo tape of previous work. Prefers cassette (or VHS videocassete) with 3 pieces. SASE.
Music: Uses all styles of music.

AUDIO-VISUAL ASSOCIATES, 334 E. 31st St., Kansas City MO 64108. (816)931-4102. Contact: Carl James. Clients include industrial firms. Uses services of songwriters for thematic scores in films and filmstrips. Payment negotiable. Buys all rights.
How to Contact: Query with demo tape of previously aired work. Prefers reel-to-reel or cassette. Keeps tapes on file.
Music: Broad range of musical styles for industrial, sales training and promotional shows.

*AUDIOVISUAL DESIGN STUDIOS, INC., 1823 Silas Deane Hwy., Rocky Hill CT 06067. (203)529-2581. President: J.J. Wall. Audiovisual firm. Clients include publishers, business and industry. Uses the services of independent songwriters/composers and music houses for scoring of AV shows and background music for sound filmstrips; lyricists for writing lyrics. Commissions 100 + pieces and 3 lyricists/year. Pays $50 minimum/job. Buys all rights.
How to Contact: Arrange personal interview. Prefers cassette with 1 song on demo. SASE. Prefers to keep material on file. Reports as needed for projects.

BALL COMMUNICATIONS, INC., 1101 N. Fulton Ave., Evansville IN 47710. (812)428-2300. President/Creative Director: Martin A. Ball. Audiovisual and television production and meeting production firm. Clients include Fortune 1000 firms. Uses the services of lyricists and independent songwriters/composers for jingles, background music and theme songs. Commissions 4 songwriters and 3 lyricists/year. Pays $1,500-2,500/job. Buys all rights.
How to Contact: Prefers cassette, 7½ ips reel-to-reel (or ½" videocassette). Does not return unsolicited material; prefers to keep on file. Reports in 1 month.
Music: All types.

Close-up

Maureen Crowe
Supervising Music Consultant
"Fame" Television Production

"What surprises me most about songwriters is that I don't think they really listen, for the most part, to current trends. They should try to think about how their songs are fitting into the marketplace. It's just like any other business—you're creating a product. If nobody's wearing purple and you're making purple fabric, you're not going to sell."

As Supervising Music Consultant for "Fame" Television Production, Maureen Crowe selected all the songs that were used on the successful TV program. She feels it's fairly easy to research the type of music being used on television. "The best thing to do," she says, "is watch a lot of TV. Television tends to follow trends. If you listen to the radio and then you watch TV shows, you notice they lag behind. You have to become aware of what's being played on television, and know the difference between the songs they may use on 'The Cosby Show' and the songs they're going to use on 'Miami Vice.' " Then you can focus on where your style of songwriting fits in.

Writing for television is very different from trying to get a recording artist to cut one of your songs, according to Crowe. First, songwriters must be prepared to write on assignment in a short period of time. "It's very hard!" Crowe sympathizes. "The pressure's on." For some songwriters, the pressure provides motivation to keep writing consistently. Also, the songs "have to be much more focused. Everything is contingent on what's going on dramatically, visually. The songs have to say something personal, that's related to the plot, without saying it directly."

Another difference is in the length of a song. "Television is very condensed. It's not like the four-minute cuts on the radio. The song needs to have a quick payoff." Crowe says usually a two- to three-minute version of a song is used. And some songs are rejected simply because an edited version wouldn't do them justice.

Perhaps the most significant differences between television and records are how the songwriter gets paid, and how big a "hit" the song can become. Crowe feels "records are the number one goal for most songwriters. You want artists cutting your stuff. With records, you can hit big with just one song. Television is a secondary field, but it's lucrative. Songwriters are paid per minute, per station. Once you get in, you're going to start getting income from your songs. I think most songwriters see television as a way of helping to support their craft."

So how do you get in? "I think the best thing to do," Crowe suggests, "is write a letter to the producer of the show you think your song is appropriate for, telling them a little about what you've done so far and why you think the song is good for their show. Send them a tape and tell them who you could see singing the song. Give them enough information that they'll be interested, without telling them how to do their job."

Then the most important thing becomes the follow-up. "You can have a lucky shot, but you have to show that you can deliver material consistently. Understand your role of providing material, because when someone's looking for songs, they need songs right away! There are writers who consistently contributed material to 'Fame' over the years, and then they became much more successful in the record industry, signing songs to major artists."

—Julie Wesling Whaley

*NORMAN BEERGER PRODUCTIONS, 3217 S. Arville St., Las Vegas NV 89102. (702)876-2328. Owner: Norman Beerger. Audiovisual firm and wilderness video producer/distributor. Clients include Reader's Digest, National Wildlife Federation, consumers. Uses the services of music houses and independent songwriters/composers for background music for wilderness exploration videos. Pays 1¢/minute/cassette royalty. Buys non-exclusive rights.
How to Contact: Submit demo tape of previous work. Prefers cassette (or ¾" VHS videocassette). SASE, but prefers to keep material file. Reports in 1 month.
Music: Uses New Age, contemporary, synthesizer music for educational films.
Tips: "Submit demo tape. It will be returned."

SAMUEL R. BLATE ASSOCIATES, 10331 Watkins Mill Dr., Gaithersburg MD 20879-2935. (301)840-2248. President: Samuel R. Blate. Audiovisual firm. Uses the services of music houses, independent songwriters and lyricists for scoring and background music for slide/tape, filmstrip and video. Commissions 1 songwriter and 1 lyricist/year. Pays by the job. Buys all rights or one-time rights. "Rights purchased generally depend client demand—we usually try to buy one-time rights."
How to Contact: Query with resume of credits and sample tape. Prefers Dolby B or C cassette, 7.5 ips reel-to-reel or videocassette with 5-10 pieces. "Submit resume with tape. We generally file both against future needs unless the composer desires to have the tape returned. SASE required. Please *label* submissions. We respond on a needs and interests basis. When a project comes through, we review our tape files and select an artist whose work most closely matches the project's needs."
Music: "We use all styles of music for backgrounds for slide/tape, filmstrip, and video production. Songwriters are used for message songs linked to the production."
Tips: "Be the best that you can be and be persistent. Our evaluations are 95% based on tapes submitted. Previous track record is not very important."

CABSCOTT BROADCAST PRODUCTION, INC., 517 7th Ave., Lindenwold NJ 08021. (609)346-3400. President: Larry Scott. Audiovisual firm and audio video location and post production company. Clients include business, industry and broadcast outlets (local and network). Uses the services of independent songwriters and music houses for "jingles for commercial music, bids in spots and industrial presentations and AV, video and film; lyricists for lyrics for jingles." Commissions 12-20 composers and 2-3 lyricists/year. Pays by the job. Buys all rights.
How to Contact: Query with resume of credits, submit demo tape of previous work or submit videocassette. Prefers 7½ or 15 ips reel-to-reel, cassette, videocassette or 16mm or 35mm film with 3-10 songs. SASE, but prefers to keep material on file. Reports in 1 month maximum.
Music: Jazz, MOR and all styles of music for jingles, music beds and background music.

*CAEDMON, 1995 Broadway, New York NY 10023. (212)580-3400 or 1-800-223-0420. Editorial Assistant: Linda Jewell-Brettler. Spoken word (story) recording company. Clients include schools, libraries, retail stores and wholesalers. Uses the services of independent songwriters for background music for spoken-word recordings. Pays by the job. Buys one-time rights.
How to Contact: Write first to obtain permission to submit. Prefers cassette. SASE. Reports in 2 months.
Music: Uses background music for children's recordings and dramatic recordings.

*CALF AUDIO, 157 Gray Rd., Ithaca NY 14850. (607)272-8964. President: Haines B. Cole. Vice President: J. Todd Hutchinson. Producer/Engineer: Alfred B. Grunwell. Assistant Engineer: Margaret T. Baker. Professional audio analysis and design; 24 track recording studio; audiovisual firm and music/ sound effects library. Uses the services of music houses and independent songwriters/composers for background music, jingles and radio and TV commercials and audiovisual presentations. Pays per quote. Buys all rights.
How to Contact: Submit demo tape of previous work; write to arrange personal interview. Prefers cassette or 15 ips reel-to-reel with 3-5 pieces. Send "full documentation." Does not return unsolicited material; prefers to keep on file. Reports in 3 weeks.
Music: Uses contemporary pop for educational films, slide presentations and commercials.
Tips: "Assimilate but don't duplicate works from the past. Take direction well."

CANARY PRODUCTIONS, 145 Barcladen Rd., Rosemont PA 19010. (215)527-8812. President: Andy Mark. Music library. Uses the services of music houses and independent songwriters for background music for AV use, jingles for all purposes, and commercials for radio. Commissions 15 composers/year. Pays 30% royalty, flat rate, or on consignment per composition.
How to Contact: Prefers cassette with 5-10 pieces. SASE. Reports in 2 weeks.
Music: All styles. "We pay cash for produced tracks of all styles and lengths. Production value is imperative. No scratch tracks accepted."

ANTHONY CARDOZA ENTERPRISES, Box 4163, North Hollywood CA 91607. (818)985-5550. President: Anthony Cardoza. Motion picture producer. Uses lyricists, music houses and independent songwriters/composers for scores for theatrical films and TV. Commissions 1 composer and 1 lyricist/year. Pays by the job or by contract. Buys all rights.
How to Contact: Submit demo tape of previous work. Prefers cassette. Does not return material; prefers to keep on file.
Music: All types.
Tips: "Never give up!!! Keep your music updated with the times. Watch the trends of new films."

*CAVOX/TAPE-A-THON CORP., 13633 Crenshaw, Hawthorne CA 90250. (213)676-6752. President: Leon E. "Lee" Tate. Background music broadcast syndication service. Clients include commercial and industrial business, hotel and hospital, radio and cable TV stations. Uses the services of music houses and independent songwriters/composers for background music for business and industrial environments. Pays "per title". Buys one-time rights.
How to Contact: Submit demo tape of previous work or tape demonstrating composition skills. Prefers cassette or 7½ or 15 ips reel-to-reel (or VHS videocassette). Does not return unsolicited material; prefers to keep on file. Reports in 6 weeks.
Music: Uses easy listening, up-tempo and pop for commercial background music.
Tips: Send "finished, arranged, and orchestrated titles."

*CHANNELL ONE VIDEO, Box 1437, Seabrook NH 03874. (603)474-5046. President: Bill Channell. Audiovisual firm, motion picture production company and TV programmer. Clients include TV stations, broadcast and cable and corporate clients for TV ads and product videos. Uses music houses, independent songwriters/composers, lyricists and music libraries for scoring of TV programs; background music for TV ads, training, sales, industrial and sports videos; jingles for TV ads; and commercials for TV. Pays by the job. Buys all rights or one-time rights.
How to Contact: Query with resume of credits or submit demo tape of previous work or tape demonstrating composition skills. Prefers cassette (or ¾ or VHS videocassette). Does not return unsolicited material; prefers to keep on file. Reports in 3 weeks.
Music: Uses up-tempo music for all kinds of assignments.

*CHANNEL ONE VIDEO TAPE INC., 3341 NW 82nd Ave., Miami FL 33122. (305)592-1764. General Manager: Jay P. Van Dyke. Video production house. Clients include commercial, industrial, medical and network programs. Uses music library for commercials for TV and industrials, medical, programs. Pays by the job or "yearly fee." Buys all rights.
How to Contact: Submit demo tape of previous work. Prefers 7½ ips reel-to-reel. Does not return unsolicited material; prefers to keep on file. Reports if interested.
Music: Uses all styles of music for all kinds of assignments.

CHAPPLE FILMS, INC., Rt. 198, Chaplin CT 06235. (203)455-9779. President: Wendy Wood. Audiovisual firm and motion picture and video production company. Clients include government, educational and industrial firms. Use the services of music houses, independent songwriters and lyricists. Pay "depends on budget."
How to Contact: Submit demo tape of previous work. Prefers cassette or 7½ or 15 ips reel-to-reel. SASE.
Music: Instrumental and vocal.

CINE DESIGN FILMS, 255 Washington St., Denver CO 80203. (303)777-4222. Producer: Jon Husband. Motion picture production company. Clients include business, industry and documentaries. Uses the services of music houses and songwriters. Commissions 6 composers and 1 lyricist/year. Pays by the job. Buys all rights or one-time rights.
How to Contact: Query with resume of credits; submit demo tape of previous work. Prefers cassette with 5-15 songs. Does not return unsolicited material.
Music: "Our needs could be from a full score to a spot jingle—depending on our needs at the time."
Tips: "Keep in touch and be flexible."

CLASSIC VIDEO, INC., Suite 100, 2690 State Rd., Cuyahoga Falls OH 44223. (216)928-7773. Producer: Bob Anderson. Jingle/production house, video programming and commercial producer. Uses independent songwriters, lyricists and music houses for background music for commercials, jingles and music themes. Commissions 20-30 songwriters and 10-15 lyricists/year. Pays $200-1,500 job. Buys all rights.
How to Contact: Submit demo tape of previously aired work. Prefers cassette or 7½ ips reel-to-reel with various pieces and lyric or lead sheets. "Please include basic structure and references." Does not

return unsolicited material; prefers to keep on file.

Music: "High tech electronic sounds for music backgrounds for high tech industrials and commercials for radio/TV consumer products."

Tips: "Be flexible in musical style, rates and turn around time."

COMMUNICATION DESIGN ASSOCIATES, Suite 1250, 921 Walnut, Kansas City MO 64106. (816)472-5101. Producer: Bill Foard. Chief Engineer: Larry Johnson. Clients include business and promotional firms. Uses the services of independent songwriters, lyricists and music houses for music in radio and TV productions and jingles and commercials for radio and TV. Payment negotiable. Rights purchased vary.

How to Contact: Submit demo tape of previously aired work. Prefers cassette with 4-5 songs. SASE.

Music: "We most often use background music."

COMMUNICATIONS CONCEPTS INC., Box 661, Cape Canaveral FL 32920. (305)783-5232. Manager: Jim Lewis. Audiovisual firm. Clients include resorts, developments and high tech industries. Uses the services of music houses, independent songwriters, lyricists and music libraries and services for scoring of TV shows and AV presentations, background music for AV programs, jingles for commercials and AV programs, and commercials for radio and TV. Commissions 2-3 composers/year and 1-2 lyricists/year. Pays $50-5,000/job. Buys all rights or one-time rights.

How to Contact: Prefers cassette. Does not return unsolicited material; prefers to keep on file.

Music: Corporate, contemporary and commercial.

*CONTINENTAL PRODUCTIONS, Box 1219, Great Falls MT 59403. (406)761-8816. Production Sales/Marketing: Duke Brekhus. Video production house. Clients include advertising agencies, business, industry and government. Uses the services of independent songwriters/composers for TV commercials and non broadcast programs and jingles for TV commercials. Commissions 1-6 composers/year. Pays $85-500/job. Buys all rights or one-time rights.

How to Contact: Write or call first and obtain permission to submit. Prefers cassette (or ½" VHS videocassette). SASE, but prefers to keep on file. Reports in 2 weeks.

Music: Uses contemporary music beds and custom jingles for TV and non-broadcast video.

Tips: "Songwriters need to build a working relationship by providing quality product in short order at a good price."

CREATIVE SUPPORT SERVICES, 1950 Riverside Dr., Los Angeles CA 90039. (213)666-7968. Contact: Michael M. Fuller. Audiovisual firm, scoring service and music/sound effects library. Clients include audiovisual production companies, ad agencies and broadcasters. Uses the services of independent songwriters and musicians for scoring of multi-image shows and videos, background music for AVs and commercials for radio. Commissions 3-5 songwriters and 1-3 lyricists/year. Pays by the job or by royalty. Buys varying rights, "tailored to specific vendor."

How to Contact: Write or call first to arrange personal interview. Prefers cassette "chrome or metal only," 7½ ips reel-to-reel or Beta videocassette with 3 or more pieces. Does not return unsolicited material; prefers to keep on file. Reports in 1 month-1 year. "Will call if interested."

Music: Uses "industrial music predominantly but all other kinds or types to lesser degree."

Tips: "Target your market. Lower your monetary expectations. Remember the risks that have to be incurred to buy someone's music."

A.S. CSAKY COMMUNICATIONS, 420 Legato Terrace, Silver Spring MD 20901. (301)681-3333 or 681-3390. Producer/Creative Director: A.S. Csaky. Motion picture/video production and advertising company. Clients include associations, corporate, small and mid-sized businesses and the world-wide theatre audiences. Services include scoring and background music for motion pictures (theme songs) and TV spots, jingles and commercials for radio and TV. Commissions 3-6 composers and 2-4 lyricists/year. Pays $500-15,000/job; 3-30% royalty; $25-150/hour; or negotiable fee per contract and project. Buys all rights or special uses privileges.

How to Contact: "Query first with letter to see if we have immediate needs." Submit demo tape of previous work demonstrating composition skills. Prefers cassette, 7½ ips reel-to-reel (or ¾" or VHS videocassette) with 5-8 pieces. SASE. Reports in 2 months.

Music: Motion picture theme music, TV spots, a few jingles. Seeking unusual "music with feeling and themes—evocative pieces. Contemporary music styles—digitally recorded orchestral music with positive, colorful sounds; atmospheric, dramatic, msterious and rhthmic, with romance and sentiment. Send a little but your very best."

*CZAR PRODUCTIONS, 9 Princeton St., West Hartford CT 06110. (203)232-4701. Executive Producer: Gene Czarnecki. Audiovisual firm, motion picture and music video production company . Cli-

ents include advertising agencies industrials and commercial TV. Uses music houses, independent songwriters/composers and lyricists for scoring and background music for films and videos, jingles for ads, commercials for radio and TV, and feature films. Commissions 1-5 composers and 1-5 lyricists/year. Pays $100-1,000/job. Buys all rights or one-time rights.
How to Contact: Submit demo tape of previous work, tape demonstrating composition skills, manuscript showing music scoring skills, query with resume of credits or write to arrange personal interview. Prefers cassette or 7½ ips reel-to-reel (or ½" VHS hifi videocassette). SASE, but prefers to keep material on file. Reports in 1 month.
Music: Uses all styles of music for various assignments.

D.S.M. PRODUCERS, Suite #1204, 161 W. 54th St., New York NY 10019. (212)245-0006. Contact: Suzan Bader. Scoring service, music/sound effects library and record production. Clients include industrial (Motorola), music publishers (song demos), groups (recording) and commercials (radio and TV). Uses the services of songwriters, lyricists and music houses for scoring and background music for films, TV and industrials; jingles and commercials for TV and radio. Pays by royalty. Rights purchased "as per contract." Commissions 6-12 songwriters and 3 lyricsist/year.
How to Contact: Submit demo tape of previous work. Prefers cassette or videocassette with 1-4 songs. SASE. Reports in 3 weeks. "If we decide to keep material, we correspond with the composer to see if publishing rights are available. If not available, we will return tape with an SASE. If no SASE, we do not keep tapes."
Music: Mostly crossover (contemporary); also rock/pop and R&B/dance.

*DASHER COMMUNICATIONS, Suite 205, 605 Third St., San Francisco CA 94107. (415)543-7864. Executive Producer: Jennifer Kauffman. Audiovisual firm. Clients include Fortune 500 companies. Uses music houses and independent songwriters/composers for scoring of and background music for film and video. Commissions 2-3 composers/year. Pays by the job.
How to Contact: Submit demo tape of previous work or query with resume of credits. Prefers cassette. SASE, but prefers to keep material on file. Reports in 2 weeks.
Music: Uses classical, "walk in/walk out music," and jazz for film, video, multi-image projects, and slides.

*DD&B STUDIOS INC., 401 S. Woodward, Birmingham MI 48011. (313)642-0640. Director of Creative Services: Rick Stawinski. Audiovisual, film and commercial music production house. Clients include Fortune 500 businesses. Uses the services of music houses, independent songwriters/composers, lyricists and music copyists of industrial shows and soundtracks, for scoring jingles and commercials for radio and TV. Commissions 8-10 composers and 15-20 lyricists/year. Pays $1,000-3,000/job or applicable union scale. Buys all rights or one-time rights.
How to Contact: Submit demo tape of previous work. Prefers cassette or 15 ips reel-to-reel (or ¾" or VHS videocassette) with 1-3 pieces. Does not return unsolicited material; prefers to keep on file. Responds "when a project exists that could use the submitted talent."
Music: Uses rock, techno/pop and synthesized music for industrials and commercials.
Tips: "Be aware of what your competition is doing—be unique! Send updated demo tapes on a regular basis."

*DEVINE VIDEOWORKS CORP., 100 Cambridge Ave., Toronto, Ontario M4K 2L6 Canada. (416)465-4499. Director: David Devine. Audiovisual firm and motion picture production company. Clients include rock videos, TV commercials, TV shows, and corporate industrials. Uses the services of independent songwriters/composers for scoring of and backgrund music for commercials, industrials and TV programs, and jingles for TV and radio commercials. Pays $50-5,000/job. Buys all rights or "one territory at a time, contingent on sales."
How to Contact: Submit demo tape demonstrating compositon skills or tape of previous work. Prefers cassette (or VHS videocassette) with 4-5 pieces. SAE and IRC.
Music: Uses all styles of music for commercials and TV programs.
Tips: "Send the work. We'll listen. If it's unique and well crafted, we'll be in touch."

DISK PRODUCTIONS, 1100 Perkins Rd., Baton Rouge LA 70802. (504)343-5438. Director: Joey Decker. Jingle/production house. Clients include advertising agencies, slide production houses and radio stations. Uses independent songwriters, lyricists and music houses for jingles and background music for commercials and albums. Commissions 4 songwriters and 4 lyricists/year.
How to Contact: Prefers cassette or 7½ ips reel-to-reel (or ½" videocassette) and lead sheet. Does not return unsolicited material; prefers to keep on file. Reports "immediately if material looks promising."
Music: Needs all types of music for jingles, music beds or background music for TV and radio etc.
Tips: "Be willing to change direction at a moment's notice."

DMA PRODUCTIONS, Box 1302, Rockefeller Center, New York NY 10185. (718)961-9583. Vice President/Executive Producer; Frank Derrick III. Scoring service and music/sound effects library. Clients include advertising agencies, film and theatrical producers and broadcasting companies. Uses the services of independent songwriters, lyricists, staff writers and arrangers for scoring of music for all phases of the industry, background music for TV and films, jingles for radio and commercials for radio and TV. Pays by the job; 50% royalty. Buys all rights.
How to Contact: Query with resume of credits. Prefers cassette. "Please no tapes without request." SASE.
Music: "All types from early jazz to classical to top 40."

DUBOIS/RUDDY, 2145 Crooks, Troy MI 48084. (313)643-0320. Contact: Ms. C. Ruddy. Multi-image and animation production service. Clients include corporate communications. Uses services of music houses for background music, musical scores and jingles; lyricists for movie themes. Commissions 2-5 composers and lyricists/year. Pays by the job. Buys all rights.
How to Contact: Query with resume of credits, arrange personal interview, submit demo tape of previous work demonstrating composition skills. Prefers reel-to-reel, cassette or videocassette. SASE, but prefers to keep material on file. Reports in 1 month.
Music: "Original music and lyrics created for multi-image openings, closes, etc., or TV spots, film underscores, etc."
Tips: "Only interested in local suppliers."

*****EARTH RECORDS VIDEO CO.**, Rt. 3, Box 57, Troy AL 36081. (205)566-7932. Contact: Eddie Toney. Music video producer.
How to Contact: Write or call first to arrange personal interview. Prefers cassette (or videocassette). Does not return unsolicited material. Reports in 1 month.

EDUCATIONAL INSIGHTS, 19560 S. Rancho Way, Dominguez Hills CA 90220. (213)637-2131. Director of Development: Dennis J. Graham. Audiovisual firm. Clients include schools and parents of young children. Uses the services of music houses and independent songwriters for scoring of children's plays, learning programs and music education materials. Commissions 4 composers/year. Pays by the job or 5% royalty. Buys all rights.
How to Contact: Submit demo tape of previous work. Prefers cassette. SASE. Reports in 4 weeks.
Music: Needs "music for young children, especially educational in nature."

DON ELLIOTT PRODUCTIONS, 15 Bridge Rd., Weston CT 06883. (203)226-4209. (New York office: 67 Park Ave., New York NY 10016. (212)679-5670.)Vice President in Charge of New Material: Doriane Elliott. Scoring service. Clients include advertising agencies, CBS Records, Arista Records. Uses the services of independent songwriters and lyricists for scoring of films and albums; background music for commercials; and jingles from radio and TV. Commissions for jingles only. Payment and rights purchased depend on the job.
How to Contact: Submit demo tape of previous work or tape demonstrating composition skills. Prefers cassette. Does not return unsolicited material; prefers to keep on file. Reports in 2 weeks.
Music: Looking for music for jingles or original music. "Presently, we are leaning toward more new albums. We have a 24-track, fully equipped studio."

*****BERT ELLIOTT SOUND INC.**, #115, 2080 Peachtree Ct., Atlanta GA 30341. (404)452-1140. President: Bert Elliott. Commercial music production house, motion picture production company, music/sound effect library and original music composer. Uses background music for film and video, jingles for radio and commercials for radio and TV. Pays by the job. Hires in-house writers.
How to Contact: Submit demo tape of previous work, tape demonstrating composition skills, manuscript showing music scoring skills, query with resume of credits or write to arrange personal interview. Does not return unsolicited material; prefers to keep on file. Reports in 2 weeks.

*****EMCOM**, 4000 W. 76th St., Minneapolis MN 55435. (612)835-4001. Contact: Sarah Silverson. Commercial music production house. Clients include corporations, universities and museums. Uses the services of independent songwriters/composers for scoring of new product introductions, point of purchase and background music for corporate image.

ENTERPRISES UNLIMITED, 9F, 400 E. 59th St., New York NY 10022. (212)832-6659. Director: J.O. Walman. Audiovisual firm, motion picture production company and scoring service. Uses the services of music houses, independent songwriters and lyricists for scoring of films; background music for movies and TV; jingles for products and services; and commercials for radio and TV.
How to Contact: Query with resume of credits or call first to arrange personal interview. Prefers cas-

sette. Does not return unsolicited material; prefers to keep on file. Reports in 10 weeks.
Music: All types.

ENTERTAINMENT PRODUCTIONS, INC., Box 554, Malibu CA 90265. (213)456-3143. President: Edward Coe. Motion picture and television production company. Clients include motion picture and TV distributors. Uses the services of music houses and songwriters for scores, production numbers, background and theme music for films and TV and jingles for promotion of films. Commissions/year vary. Pays by the job or by royalty. Buys all rights.
How to Contact: Query with resume of credits. Demo should show flexibility of composition skills. "Demo records/tapes sent at own risk—returned if SASE included." Reports by letter in 1 month.
Tips: "Have resume on file. Develop self-contained capability."

EXPANDING IMAGES, 14 Hughes B105, Irvine CA 92718. (714)770-2342. President: Robert Denison. Audiovisual firm. Clients include industrial firms. Uses the services of music houses, independent songwriters and lyricists for background music for multi-media shows and commercials for TV. Pays by the job.
How to Contact: Prefers cassette. Does not return unsolicited material; prefers to keep on file.
Music: All types.

*THE FANTASTIC ANIMATION MACHINE, INC., 12 E. 46th St., New York NY 10017. (212)697-2525. Sales Representative: Cathlyn Cantone. Digital computer animation firm. Clients include commercial, corporate, networks and medical. Uses music houses for scoring of animation projects. Pays by the job.
How to Contact: Write or call first and obtain permission to submit. Prefers cassette. "Please call in advance. Our needs are rare, but we would be interested."
Music: Uses music for "commercials, corporate videos and company demo reel."

FILM AMERICA, INC., 3132 Randolph Rd. NE, Atlanta GA 30345. (404)261-3718. President: Avrum Fine. Motion picture editing house. Clients include advertising agencies, corporate audiovisual producers and film/tape producer. Uses the service of music houses and independent songwriters for scoring of industrial films/TV spots; lyricists for jingles for TV spots, commercials for TV and theater trailers. Commissions 3 composers and 3 lyricists/year. Pays by the job. Buys all rights.
How to Contact: Submit demo tape of previous work. Prefers cassette (or VHS videocassette). Does not return unsolicited material; prefers to keep on file. Reports in 4 weeks.
Music: "All contemporary idioms."

PAUL FRENCH AND PARTNERS, 503 Gabbettville Rd., LaGrange GA 30240. (404)882-5581. Contact: Ms. Gene Byrd. Audiovisual firm. Uses the services of music houses and songwriters for musical scores in films and original songs for themes; lyricists for writing lyrics for themes. Commissions 20 composers and 20 lyricists/year. Pays minimum $500/job. Buys all rights.
How to Contact: Submit demo tape of previous work. Prefers reel-to-reel with 3-8 songs. SASE. Reports in 2 weeks.

JAY GILBERT PRODUCTIONS, 3340 Erie Ave., Cincinnati OH 45208. (513)871-6900. Producer: Jay Gilbert. Commercial music composers and producers. Clients include advertising agencies, house agencies, AV production houses, retailers and businesses without agencies, TV, radio and cable stations. Primarily uses the services of performers, singers, and announcers. Commissions 1 composer/year and 1 lyricist/year. Pays $75-300 job. "Regular jingles are paid by the job; long scores are paid by the hour." Buys all rights or one-time rights.
How to Contact: Write first and obtain permission to submit. Then submit demo tape of previous work demonstrating composition skills. Prefers cassette. "Be concise but try to show the range of what you can do. Selections don't have to be in their entirety; they can make their point and fade out. Be clear about your role in the material, i.e., is this your writing, your arranging, etc." Does not return unsolicited material; prefers to keep on file. Reports in 3 weeks.
Music: All styles. "A good tape is your strongest calling card. Follow up as best you can without overdoing it."

GLYN/NET, INC., 356 W. 58th St., New York NY 10019-1804. (212)560-6980. Vice President Production: John Oppenhimer. Motion picture and video production company. Clients include major corporations. Uses the services of music houses, independent songwriters and lyricists for scoring of and background music for films and TV shows. Commissions 2-3 composers/year. Pays by the job. Buys all rights or one-time rights.

How to Contact: Prefers cassette (or ¾" videocassette). Does not return unsolicited material. Reports in 3 weeks.
Music: All types.

*GORILLA FILM & ENTERTAINMENT, INC., 2424 35th St., Long Island City NY 11103. Music Department: Suzy Noel. Scoring service and motion picture production company. Estab. 1986. Uses the services of music houses and independent songwriters/composers for music videos, scoring of motion pictures, and background music for commercials and industrials. Commissions 5 composers/year. Pays $1,000/job. Buys all rights or one-time rights.
How to Contact: Query with resume of credits; write first to arrange personal interview and obtain permission to submit. "No phone calls, please." Prefers cassette (or ¾" videocassette) with 4 pieces. Does not return unsolicited material; prefers to keep on file. Reports in 1 month.
Music: Uses all styles of music for industrials and commercials.
Tips: "We do review files when jobs come up. It won't help to continue submissions after initial contact."

*GROUP TWO, INC., One E. 24th St., Baltimore MD 21218. (301)467-9000. Audio Engineer: Robert Bragg. Audiovisual firm. Clients include corporate accounts, mostly Fortune 500. Uses the services of music houses and independent songwriters/composers for scoring of film, video and multi-image slide productions. Commissions 1-2 composers/year. Pays $500-2,000/job. Usually buys one-time rights.
How to Contact: Submit demo tape of previous work. Prefers 7½ ips reel-to-reel (or ¾" videocassette). "Keep it short." SASE, but prefers to keep material on file. Reports in 6 weeks.
Music: Uses all styles of music for multi-image slide or corporate film/video (3-8 minutes).
Tips: "Our need for original music is dictated by the particular jobs (and budget) we are working on. Patience is necessary for those jobs which may fit your skills."

LENNY HAMBRO PRODUCTIONS INC., 78 Windsor Dr., McKee City NJ 08232. (609)391-0358. President: Lenny Hambro. Arranger/composer: Lou Forestieri. Scoring service and music production. Clients include ad agencies and film houses. Uses the services of independent songwriters and lyricists for background music and scoring of commericals, films, industrials, etc. Buys all rights.
How to Contact: Submit tape demonstrating composition skills or manuscript showing music scoring skills; query with resume of credits; or write to arrange personal interview. Prefers cassette or 7½ ips reel-to-reel with 5-10 pieces. Does not return unsolicited material; prefers to keep on file. Reports in 2-6 weeks.
Music: "Send all styles to show versatility."

*HILLMANN & CARR INC., 2121 Wisconsin Ave. NW, Washington DC 20007. (202)342-0001. President: Alfred Hillmann. Vice President/Treasurer: Ms. Michal Carr. Audiovisual firm and motion picture production company. Clients include corporate, government, associations and museums. Uses the services of music houses and independent songwriters/composers for scoring of films, video productions, PSA's and commercials for radio and TV. Commissions 1-2 composers/year. Payment negotiable.
How to Contact: Query with resume of credits, or submit demo tape of previous work or tape demonstrating composition skills, or write to arrange personal interview. Prefers cassette or 7½ ips reel-to-reel (or ¾" VHS or Beta videocassette) with 5-10 pieces. Does not return unsolicited material; prefers to keep on file. Reports in 1 month.
Music: Uses contemporary classical, up-tempo and thematic music for documentary film and video productions, multi-media exposition productions, public service announcements.

*HOME, INC.,. 731 Harrison Ave., Boston MA 02118. (617)266-1386. Director: Alan Michel. Audiovisual firm and video production company. Clients include cable television, pilot programs and industrials. Uses the services of music houses and independent songwriters/composers for background music for videos and TV commercials. Pays $50-300/job. Buys one-time rights.
How to Contact: Query with resume of credits, or submit demo tape of previous work. Prefers cassette with 6 pieces. SASE, but prefers to keep material on file.
Music: Uses all styles of music for educational videos.

INDIANER MULTI-MEDIA, Suite 204, 16201 SW 95th Ave., Miami FL 33157. (305)235-6132. Vice President, Systems: David Gravel. President: Paul Indianer. Uses music houses for jingles and background music for sound filmstrips; lyricists for jingles. Commissions 50-60 pieces/year. Pays $50/finished minute. Buys all rights or one-time rights.
How to Contact: Query with resume of credits or submit demo tape showing flexibility of composition skills. Prefers 7½ ips reel-to-reel with 5 songs minimum. SASE. Reports in 3 weeks.
Music: Industrial up tempo and jingles.

*INNERQUEST COMMUNICATIONS CORP., 6383 Rose Ln., Carpinteria CA 93013. (805)684-9977. Producer: Don L. Higley. Motion picture production company and music/sound effect library. Estab. 1986. Uses the services of music houses, independent songwriters/composers and lyricists for scoring of and background music for television series, industrial productions and commercials for radio and TV. Pays by the job depending on budget. Buys all rights.
How to Contact: Query with resume of credits. Prefers cassette. Does not return unsolicited material; prefers to keep on file. Reports in 2 weeks.

INTERNATIONAL MEDIA SERVICES, INC., 718 Sherman Ave., Plainfield NJ 07060. (201)756-4060. President: Stuart Allen. Audiovisual firm, motion picture and television production company. Clients include schools, businesses, advertising, and entertainment industry. Uses the services of music houses, songwriters/composers and lyricists for scoring of corporate and broadcast programs, background music for television and film, jingles for cable TV and broadcast spots, and commercials for radio and TV. Commissions 30 composers and 25 lyricists/year. Pays "per contract or license." Buys all rights or one-time rights.
How to Contact: Query with resume of credits or arrange personal interview. 'We accept no unsolicited material, contact required first." Prefers 7½ ips reel-to-reel, cassette (or ¾" videocassette) with 4-10 songs. SASE.
Tips: "Stay with professional and high quality material. Be persistant. Have a good broadcast quality demo. Follow-up periodically."

JACOBY/STORM PRODUCTIONS, INC., 22 Crescent Rd., Westport CT 06880. (203)227-2220. President: Doris Storm. Clients include schools, publishers, business and industrial firms. Uses the services of music houses and songwriters for film scores, background music and an occasional theme song. Commissions 2-3 pieces/year. Payment negotiable. Buys all rights or one-time rights.
How to Contact: Write first with resume of credits, then submit demo tape of previously aired work. "Don't send any material without writing first." Prefers 7½ or 15 ips reel-to-reel. SASE. Reports in 2 weeks.
Music: Needs songs and background music for films geared to elementary or high school students; also music suitable for industrial and documentary films.

KIMBO EDUCATIONAL UNITED SOUND ARTS, INC., 10-16 N. 3rd Ave., Box 477, Long Branch NJ 07740. (201)229-4949. Producers: James Kimble or Amy Laufer. Audiovisual firm and manufacturer of educational material: records, cassettes and teacher manuals or guides. Clients include schools and stores selling teachers' supplies. Uses the services of music houses, songwriters, and educators for original songs for special education, early childhood, music classes, physical education and pre-school children; lyricists for lyrics to describe children's activities centering on development of motor skills, language, fitness or related educational skills. Commissions 12-15 pieces and 12-15 lyricists/year. Pays by the job or royalty. Buys all rights.
How to Contact: Submit demo tape of previous work, tape demonstrating composition skills, manuscript showing music scoring skills or lead sheet with lyrics. Prefers 7½ or 15 ips reel-to-reel or cassette with 1-12 songs. "Upon receipt of a demo tape and/or written material, each property is previewed by our production staff. The same chances exist for any individual if the material is of high quality and we feel it meets the educational goals we are seeking." Reports in 1 month. Free catalog available.
Music: "Contemporary sounds with limited instrumentation so as not to appear too sophisticated nor distracting for the young or special populations. Lyrics should be noncomplex and repetitive."

SID KLEINER MUSIC ENTERPRISES, 3701 25th Ave. SW, Naples FL 33964. (813)455-2693 or 455-2696. Managing Director: Sid Kleiner. Audiovisual firm. Serves the music industry. Uses the services of music houses, songwriters and inhouse writers for background music; lyricists for special material. Pays $25 minimum/job. Buys all rights.
How to Contact: Query with resume of credits or submit demo tape of previously aired work. Prefers cassette with 1-4 songs. SASE. Reports in 3-5 weeks.
Music: "We generally need soft background music, with some special lyrics to fit a particular project. We also assign country, pop, mystical and metaphysical."

*KTVU RETAIL SERVICES, Box 22222, Oakland CA 94623. (415)874-0228. Retail Marketing Director: Richard Hartwig. Retail TV commercial production firm. Uses the services of music houses, independent songwriters/composers and lyricists for commercials for radio and TV.
How to Contact: Submit demo tape of previous work. Prefers cassette or 7½ ips reel-to-reel with 6 pieces. Prefers to keep material on file.

*LA BOV AND BEYOND MUSIC PRODUCTION, Box 5533, Ft. Wayne IN 46805. (219)483-2369. Creative Director: Cheryl Franks. President: Barry La Bov. Scoring service and commercial music production house. Clients include advertising agencies, film production houses and A/V firms. Uses the services of independent songwriters/composers and lyricists for scoring of films, background music for films and audiovisual projects, jingles and commercials for radio and TV. Commissions 4-10 composers and 2-5 lyricists/year. Pays $100-200/job. Buys all rights.
How to Contact: Submit demo tape of previous work, tape showing composition skills or manuscript showing music scoring skills. Prefers cassette, 7½ or 15 ips reel-to-reel (or VHS videocassette) with 5-10 pieces. SASE, but prefers to keep material on file. Reports in 3 weeks. "We will call when tape has been received and evaluated."
Music: Uses all styles of music for all kinds of assignments from commercials to songs. "We look for positive, eager writers who strive to create unique, outstanding music."
Tips: "Try new approaches and work to keep a fresh sound. Be innovative, conceptually strong, and positive."

LANE & JOHNSON, 4466 Laclede Pl., St. Louis MO 63108. (314)533-0010. Creative Director: George Johnson. President: Carla Lane. Audiovisual firm, scoring service and music contractor. Clients include business, industry, government, agricultural conglomerates and hospitals. Uses services of songwriters and lyricists for music for conventions, industrial shows, films, video, etc. Payment negotiable. Rights purchased as requested by client.
How to Contact: Query with resume of credits; submit tape of previous work or tape demonstrating composition skills or manuscript showing music scoring skills. Prefers cassette with any number of songs. SASE. Reports in 2 weeks.
Music: Depends on client's needs.

*LEDFORD PRODUCTIONS, INC., Box 7363, Furnitureland Station, High Point NC 27264-7363. (919)431-1107. President: Hank Ledford. Audiovisual firm and advertising firm. Clients include banks, manufacturers of heavy duty equipment and luxury items and Fortune 500. Uses music houses for background music for video/slide shows and radio commercials. Commissions 25 pieces or songs/year. Pays by the job. Buys all rights or one-time rights.
How to Contact: Submit demo tape of previous work. Prefers cassette (or ¾" VHS videocassette). Does not return unsolicited material; prefers to keep on file.
Music: Uses music for videos, slide presentation-industrial/product introductions.

*BRIEN LEE & COMPANY, INC., 2025 N. Summit Ave., Milwaukee WI 53202. (414)277-7600. Executive Vice President: Robert Jagelski. Audiovisual firm. Clients include industrial, service and consumer companies Uses the services of independent songwriters/composers for background music for soundtracks on videos and TV commercials. Pays by the job. Buys all rights or negotiates rights.
How to Contact: Write first and obtain permission to submit. Prefers cassette or 7½ ips reel-to-reel (or ¾" videocassette) with 4-6 songs. "Please contact us first." Prefers to keep material on file.
Music: Uses easy listening, up-tempo, pop, jazz, high tech/high energy and classical for industrial videos, image pieces and commercials.

*WILLIAM V. LEVINE AND ASSOCIATES, INC., 31 E. 28th St., New York NY 07463. (212)683-7177. President: William V. Levine. Audiovisual firm. Clients include media, industrial and package goods. Uses the services of music houses and independent songwriters/composers for original music and lyrics for use as sales meeting themes. Pays by the job. Buys all rights.
How to Contact: Submit demo tape of previous work. Prefers cassette with 4-6 pieces. SASE.
Music: Uses up-tempo for slide presentations.

*LIGHT PRODUCTIONS, 1915 Webster, Birmingham MI 48008. (313)642-3502. Producer: Terry Luke. Audiovisual firm. Clients include corporations, industrial, churches and educational institutions. Uses the services of music houses and independent songwriters/composers for background music for TV commercials, slide presentations and training videos. Commissions 3-15 songwriters and 1-2 lyricists/year. Pays $100-3,000/job or $4-65/hour. Buys all rights or one-time rights.
How to Contact: Write or call first and obtain permission to submit; submit demo tape of previous work. Prefers cassette (or VHS videocassette). SASE, but prefers to keep material on file. Reports in 3 weeks.
Music: Uses up-tempo, rock, spiritual, easy listening and inspirational for slide presentations, training videos and artistic video-MTV.

LONGBRANCH STUDIO, 6314 E. 13th St., Tulsa OK 74112. (918)832-7640. Manager: Greg Gardner. Scoring service and music/sound effects library. Clients include schools, producers, industry, business and advertising agencies. Uses services of songwriters, lyricists and inhouse writers to provide ideas or concepts; lyricists to provide ideas, concepts or musical content. Commissions 2 lyricists/year. Pays royalty. Buys all rights or one-time rights.

How to Contact: Query with resume of credits and submit demo tape of previously aired work or submit demo tape showing flexibility of composition skills. Prefers 7 ½ or 15 ips reel-to-reel or cassette with 3-6 songs. SASE. Reports in 10 days.

Music: Needs vary with client's desires.

LUNA TECH, INC., 148 Moon Dr., Owens Cross Roads AL 35763. (205)725-4224. Chief Designer: Norman A. Plaisted. Fireworks company. Clients include theme parks, municipalities and industrial show producers. Uses music houses, independent songwriters and client music departments for scoring of music for fireworks displays. Commissions 1-2 composers/year. Pays $500-3,000/job. Buys all rights or one-time rights.

How to Contact: Query with resume of credits or submit demo tape of previous work. Prefers cassette (or VHS videocassette) with 1-5 pieces. Does not return unsolicited material; prefers to keep on file. Reports in 1 month; will call if interested.

Music: "Music for fireworks choreography: dynamic, jubilant, heraldic, bombastic, original."

LYONS INC., 715 Orange St., The Market Place, Wilmington DE 19801. (302)654-6146. Producer, Manager Audio/Visual Departments: James Heffernan. Advertising agency with in-house audiovisual and video production company. Clients include industrial, training and broadcast. Uses the services of music houses, songwriters; some in-house writing for background music (film, video, AV); and some jingle work (radio, TV); lyricists for industrial (live or canned) shows, or jingle lyrics. Commissions 10 composers and 1-2 lyricists/year. Pay "depends on budget and circumstances." Buys all rights, except demo and publicity use by songwriter.

How to Contact: Submit demo tape of previous work or tape demonstrating composition skills. Prefers cassette with 3 songs. SASE. Returns material only "if requested." Reports as needs arise.

Music: Synthesizer, rhythmic and orchestral.

Tips: "Learn to put visual suggestions into sound (think visually); and learn to take intense direction without letting your pride interfere."

LEE MAGID INC., Box 532, Malibu CA 90261. (213)858-7282. President: Lee Magid. Audiovisual firm, scoring service and motion picture production company. Clients include business, industry, theatrical and educational. Uses the services of songwriters, lyricists and composer/arrangers, for scoring of film and commercials for radio and TV. Commissions 10 composers and 10 lyricists/year. Buys all rights. Pays by the job or by royalty.

How to Contact: Send resume of credits or submit tape demonstrating composition skills. Prefers cassette (or videocassette) with maximum 3 songs (or 3 minutes). "I would make direct contact with songwriter/composer and designate preference and style." SASE. Reports in 1 month.

Music: Mostly pop, rock and R&B; also jazz and country. Vocals and/or instrumental.

Tips: "Use your instincts. Write songs for visual and musical memory effect. Try to become an innovator. Think commercial."

*MARIAH PRODUCTIONS, 545 8th Ave., New York NY 10018. (212)947-0090. Producer: Stephen Maynard. Audiovisual firm and motion picture production company. Uses the services of music houses and independent songwriters/composers and recording studios for background music for industrials. Pays by the job. Buys all rights.

How to Contact: Submit demo tape of previous work. "No phone calls, please." Prefers 7 ½ or 15 ips reel-to-reel. Does not return unsolicited materail; prefers to keep on file.

Music: Uses all types of music for "industrials in all media."

MARTIN/ARNOLD COLOR SYSTEMS, INC., 150 5th Ave., New York NY 10011. (212)675-7270. Contact: Martin Block. Audiovisual firm. Clients include schools, publishers, business and industry. Uses the services of independent songwriters/composers for background music for AV presentations. Pays by the job. Buys one-time rights.

How to Contact: Query with resume of credits or submit demo tape of previously aired work. Prefers cassette. SASE. Reports in 2 weeks

Music: Soft music, background.

*MEDIA GROUP TELEVISION, 7th Ave. and 23rd Sts., Moline IL 61265. (309)764-6411. Media Director: Charles Olmstead. Video production company. Clients include advertising agencies, industrial and religious. Uses services of music libraries for background music for industrials and commercials for radio and TV. Pays by the job. Buys all rights.

How to Contact: Submit demo tape of previous work. Prefers cassette with 5 pieces. Prefers to keep

material on file. Reports in 3 weeks.
Music: "Specifically looking for an up-tempo jingle to use in chiropractic commercials across the US."

WARREN MILLER ENTERPRISES, 505 Pier Ave., Hermosa Beach CA 90254. (213)376-2494. Sales/ Promotions: Daniel Segal. Clients include industrial, sports, resort and airline firms. Uses the services of independent songwriters/composers for scoring of and background music for sports action films and videos, and TV and radio commercials. Commissions 10 songwriters and 2 lyricists/year. Pays by the job. Buys all rights.
How to Contact: Submit demo tape of previously aired work. Prefers cassette or disc with 1-3 songs. SASE.
Music: Classical variations, New Age, adult contemporary, hard rock and new wave. "High energy music for action is our primary need."
Tips: "It is important to be in this area to score a film. The musician must work closely with the editor. Be adept at scoring several instruments."

ARTHUR MILLS ASSOCIATES, INC., (Nodus Productions), 47 W. 68th, New York NY 10023. (212)787-1192. President: Arthur R. Mills. Clients include TV networks, cable networks, advertising agencies, film companies and industrial firms. Uses services of music houses and songwriters for film scores and original material for performers, nightclubs, Broadway, legitimate shows and TV specials. Pays "participation in profits." Buys various rights.
How to Contact: Query with resume of credits; submit demo tape of previously aired work, compositions for particular client or demo tape showing flexibility of composition skills. Prefers cassette with 4-6 songs. SASE. Reports in 2 months.
Music: "Anything from classical music to rock. We especially need music that can be adapted to film scores, and material for cabaret and nightclub performers. We also need original songs for TV movies and specials, the legitimate theater, and industrial shows (live and film)."

MOTIVATION MEDIA, INC., 1245 Milwaukee Ave., Glenview IL 60025. (312)297-4740. Production Manager: Glen Peterson. Audiovisual firm, video, motion picture production company and business meeting planner. Clients include business and industry. Uses the services of songwriters and composers "mostly for business meetings and multi-image production;" lyricists for writing lyrics for business meeting themes, audience motivation songs and promotional music for new product introduction. Commissions 6-10 songwriters and 6-10 lyricists/year. Pays minimum $500/job. Buys all rights.
How to Contact: Query with resume of credits; or submit demo tape of previous work. Prefers cassette with 5-7 songs. Does not return unsolicited material.
Music: Uses "up-beat contemporary music that motivates an audience of sales people."
Tips: "Keep in touch—let us know what new and exciting assignments you have undertaken."

*MULTI IMAGE PRODUCTIONS, 8849 Complex Dr., San Diego CA 92123. (619)560-8383. Sound Editor/Engineer: Christopher Potter. Audiovisual firm and motion picture production company. Clients include business, corporate, industrial, commercial, military and cultural. Uses music houses, independent songwriters/composers/arrangers and lyricists for scoring of industrials, corporate films and videos; background music for AV, film, video and live shows; and jingles and commercials for radio and TV. Commissions 2-10 composers and 2-5 lyricists/year. Pays $500 + /job. Buys all rights.
How to Contact: Query with resume of credits or write to obtain permission to submit. Prefers 7½ or 15 ips reel-to-reel with 2-5 pieces. Does not return unsolicited material; prefers to keep on file. Reports in 6 weeks.
Music: Uses "comtemporary, pop, specialty, regional, ethnic, national and international" styles of music for background "scores written against script describing locales, action, etc. We try to stay clear of stereotypical 'canned' music and prefer a more commercial and dramatic (film-like) approach."
Tips: "We have established an ongoing relationship with a local music production/scoring house with whom songwriters would be in competition for every project; but an ability to score clean, full, broad, contemporary commercial and often 'film score' type music, in a vareity of styles would be a benefit."

*MUSIC MASTERS, 17 Ponca Trail, St. Louis MO 63122. (314)821-2741. Producer: Greg Trampe. Commercial music production house and music/sound effect library. Clients include multi-image and film producers, advertising agencies and large corporations. Uses the services of independent songwriters/composers and lyricists for background music for multi-image and film, and commercials for radio and TV. Commissions 8 composers and 20 lyricists/year. Pays $100-2,000/job. Buys all rights.
How to Contact: Query with resume of credits or write and obtain permission to submit. Prefers cassette or 7½ or 15 ips reel-to-reel (or Beta or VHS videocassette) with 3-6 pieces. SASE, but prefers to keep on file. Reports in 1 month.
Music: "We use all types of music for slide presentations (sales & motivational)."

Tips: "Resume should have at least 3 or 4 major credits of works completed within the past year. A good quality demo is a must."

*NASHVILLE INTERNATIONAL TELEVISION, 116 17th Ave. S., Nashville TN 37203. (615)254-3464. Executive Producer: Reggie M. Churchwell. "We produce television shows and specials." Uses the services of script and concept writers for themes and special concept songs. Pays by the job. Buys all rights.
How to Contact: Write or call first and obtain permission to submit. Prefers cassette with 1-2 pieces. SASE. Reports in 6 weeks.
Music: Uses all types of music for television shows and specials.

NETWORK PRODUCTION MUSIC, INC., 11021 Via Frontera, San Diego CA 92127. (619)451-6400. Producer/Engineer: S. John Archer. Music/sound effects library "with tie-in to New Age/jazz label." Clients include production houses, broadcast, film and TV. Uses the services of independent songwriters for scoring of production music. Commissions 10 composers/year. Pays by the job "within library. Artist deals possible."
How to Contact: Submit demo tape of previous work demonstrating composition skills. Prefers cassette, 7½ or 15 ips reel-to-reel with 3-5 pieces. Does not return material; prefers to keep on file.
Music: All styles.

OMNI COMMUNICATIONS, 101 E. Carmel Dr., Carmel IN 46032-2669. (317)844-6664. President: W. H. Long. Television production and audiovisual firm. Clients include major corporations. Uses the services of music houses and songwriters for scoring of films and television productions; and background music for voice overs; lyricists for original music and themes. Commissions varying number of composers and lyricists/year. Pays by the job. Buys all rights.
How to Contact: Query with resume of credits. Prefers reel-to-reel, cassette (or videocassette). Does not return unsolicited material. Reports in 2 weeks.
Music: Varies with each and every project; from classical, contemporary to commercial industrial.
Tips: "Submit good demo tape to command the attention of our producers."

*ON-Q PRODUCTIONS, INC., 618 Gutierrez St., Santa Barbara CA 93103. (805)963-1331. President: Vincent Quaranta. Audiovisual firm. Clients include corporate accounts/sales conventions. Uses the services of music houses, independent songwriters/composers and lyricists for scoring of and background music for media productions and TV commercials. Commissions 1-5 composers and 1-5 lyricists/year. Pays by the job. Buys all rights or one-time rights.
How to Contact: Submit demo tape of previous work. Prefers cassette or 15 ips reel-to-reel (or VHS videocassette). SASE, but prefers to keep material on file. Reports in 1 month.
Music: Uses up-tempo music for slide and video presentations.

PHILADELPHIA MUSIC WORKS, INC., Box 947, Bryn Mawr PA 19010. (215)825-5656. President: Andy Mark. Jingle producers/music library producers. Uses independent songwriters and music houses for background music for commercials and jingles. Commissions 200 songwriters/year. Pays $200/job. Buys all rights.
How to Contact: Call first and obtain permission to submit. Prefers cassette. "We are looking for quality jingle tracks already produced, as well as instrumental pieces between 2 and 3 minutes in length for use in AV music library." Does not return unsolicited material. Reports in 4 weeks.
Music: All types.
Tips: Looking for "knowledge of the jingle business and what works as background music for audiovisual presentations, such as slide shows, video training films, etc."

PHOTO COMMUNICATION SERVICES, INC., 6410 Knapp NE, Ada MI 49301. (616)676-1499; 676-1454. President: M. Jackson. Audiovisual firm and motion picture production company. Clients include commercial, industrial and non-profit. Uses services of music houses, independent songwriters, and lyricists for jingles and scoring of and background music for multi-image, film and video. Negotiates pay. Buys all rights, or one-time rights.
How to Contact: Submit demo tape of previous work, tape demonstrating composition skills or query with resume of credits. Prefers cassette, 15 ips reel-to-reel (or VHS videocassette). Does not return unsolicited material; prefers to keep on file. Reports in 6 weeks.
Music: Uses mostly industrial.

*PMS COMMUNICATIONS, 629 E. Keefe, Milwaukee WI 53212. (414)372-1832. Vice President: Michael Gagliano. Audiovisual firm. Clients include agricultrual and medical. Uses the services of music houses, independent songwriters/composers and lyricists for scoring of theme songs, background

music for AVs and radio and TV commercials. Pays by the job. Buys all rights.
How to Contact: Submit demo tape of previous work. Prefers cassette. Does not return unsolicited material; prefers to keep on file.
Music: Uses up-tempo and pop music for AVs.

POP INTERNATIONAL CORPORATION, Box 527, Closter NJ 07624. (201)768-2199. Producers: Arnold De Pasquale, G. Thomas Smith and Peter DeCaro. Motion picture production company. Clients include "political campaigns, commercial spots, business and industry concerns as a production service; feature films and documentaries as producers." Uses services of music houses and songwriters for "mood purposes only on documentary films. However, Pop International Productions does conceptualize major theatrical and/or album musical projects." Commissions commercial and soundtrack pieces for entertainment specials; commissions 2-3 lyricists/year. Pays $75-200/hour; minimum $500/job; 10% minimum royalty. Buys all rights and one-time rights.
How to Contact: Submit demo tape of previously aired work. Prefers cassette with 2-4 songs. "We review tapes on file, speak with agents and/or referrals, then interview writer. Once committee approves, we work *very* closely in pre-production." SASE. Reports in 3 weeks.
Music: Uses "mood music for documentaries, occasionally jingles for spots or promotional films or theme music/songs for dramatic projects (the latter by assignment only from producers or agencies). Some material is strictly mood, as in documentary work; some is informative as in promotional; some is motivating as in commercial; some is entertaining as in theatrical/TV."
Tips: "Be persistent and very patient. Try to get an agent, use demos and build a reputation for working very closely with scriptwriters/producers/directors."

PREMIER VIDEO, FILM AND RECORDING CORP., 3033 Locust St., St. Louis MO 63103. (314)531-3555. President: Wilson Dalzell. Secretary/Treasurer: Grace Dalzell. Audiovisual firm and motion picture production company. Uses the services of songwriters for jingles and scoring and original background music and lyrics to reinforce scripts. Commissions 6-10 pieces and 5-10 lyricists/year. Pays by the job. Buys all rights and "occasionally one-time rights with composer retaining title."
How to Contact: Query with resume of credits. Prefers 7½ or 15 ips reel-to-reel or cassette with any number of songs. SASE. Reports "as soon as possible."
Tips: "A limited need for music makes freelance writers a necessity. Be flexible. Have a simple precise portfolio. Be sure your resume is direct, to-the-point and includes an honest review of past efforts."

*PRESTIGE PRODUCTIONS, 813 SW 18th St., Ft. Lauderdale FL 33315. (305)463-7062. Director of Production: Werner H. Stemer. Audiovisual firm. Clients include hotel chains, travel operations, building developers and music video. Uses the services of independent songwriters/composers and lyricists for background music for commercial/industrial/travel video, jingles for TV spots and commercials. Commissions 4-6 composers/year. Pays by the job. Buys all rights.
How to Contact: Query with resume of credits or submit demo tape of previous work or manuscript showing music scoring skills. Prefers cassette (or VHS videocassette) with 4-8 pieces. "Enclose short description and critique of each submission." Does not return unsolicited material; prefers to keep on file. Reports in 6 weeks.
Music: Uses up-tempo, soft jazz, pop and classical-pop for travel video and TV commercials.

PROFESSIONAL MEDIA SERVICES, Suite 205, 18530 Beach Blvd., Huntington Beach CA 92648. (714)964-0542. Owner: Roy Moosa. Advertising production firm. Clients include "corporate promos and TV commercials." Uses the services of independent songwriters for scoring of commercials, corporate presentations, background music for training tapes, jingles for TV and commercials for radio and TV. Commissions 1 composer and 1 lyricist/year. Pays by the job. Buys all rights.
How to Contact: Query with resume of credits. Prefers cassette, reel-to-reel (or videocassette). Does not return unsolicited material; prefers to keep on file. Reports "as needed."
Music: "Upbeat background" music.
Tips: "Keep a video resume of your work."

PULLIN PRODUCTIONS LTD., 822 5th Ave. SW, Calgary, Alberta T2P 0N3 Canada. (403)234-7885. Production Manager: Chris Pullin. Clients include business and industry. Uses the services of music houses, songwriters and lyricists for "original songs and themes for multi-image, motion picture and multi-media." Commissions 4 composers and 2 lyricists/year. Pays minimum $500/job. Buys all rights.
How to Contact: Submit demo tape or videocassette of previous work. Prefers reel-to-reel with 4-10 songs but "any format is OK." Does not return unsolicited material. "Contact is made only if interested."
Music: Looking for "strong themes for any number of instruments/vocals (single instrument to full orchestra). Requirements for each job are very carefully specified."

BILL QUINN PRODUCTION, Bldg. N, 2517 Route 35, Manasquan NJ 08736. (201)223-9075. Account Executive: Bill Newman. Audiovisual firm and motion picture production company. Clients include corporate and production companies. Uses the services of independent songwriters and lyricists for scoring of original productions, background music for client accounts, commercials for radio and TV and video/film production. Pays by the job. Buys one-time rights.
How to Contact: Submit demo tape of previous work or query with resume of credits. Call first to arrange personal interview. Prefers cassette. Will return unsolicited material accompanied by an SASE but prefers to keep on file. Reports in 3 weeks.
Music: "Everything from MOR to rock to easy listening. Interested in doing business with people in New York and New Jersey area."

*RARIDEN RECORDS, 6579 Backlick Rd., Springfield VA 22150. (703)866-9090. A&R Director: Larney Carson. Music/sound effect library. Clients include U.S. Navy, universities, trade associations, large corporations and production houses. Uses the services of independent songwriters/composers for background music for training videos, documentaries, talk shows, PSAs and commercials for radio and TV. Commissions 10-15 songwriters/year. Pays 10-15% royalty. Buys all rights.
How to Contact: Submit demo tape of previous work. "We keep a portfolio of previously created work and match these pieces with demand for custom projects as they arise." Prefers cassette with no more than 3 pieces. "Please only music on the tapes. Keep explanations or identifications confined to paper." Does not return unsolicited material; prefers to keep on file. Reports in 1 month. "We send an individualized critique stressing positive aspects and shortcomings in regards to our application."
Music: Uses all styles of music for training videos, ads, PSAs, slides shows, etc.
Tips: "Submit the best quality demo possible within your budget. Be patient, our report will tell you if we feel your work is appropriate for our clients. If so, time is needed to find the correct project for your piece. We prefer fully produced broadcast quality recordings we can license without re-recording. We pay higher royalties for broacast-quality recordings."

RICHTER PRODUCTIONS, INC., 330 W. 42nd St., New York NY 10036. (212)947-1395. President: Robert Richter. Motion picture production company. Clients include public and commercial TV, government agencies and nonprofit organizations. Uses services of music houses, songwriters and composers/arrangers for film scores and background music. Commissions 2 pieces/year. Pays by the job. Buys all rights or one-time rights.
How to Contact: Submit demo and resume of previously aired work. Prefers cassette with 2-5 songs on demo. SASE. "Also, put name, return address and phone number on the tape itself." Reportinsggovernment agencies and nonprofit organizations. Uses services of music houses, songwriters and composers/arrangers for film scores and background music. Commissions 2 pieces/year. Pays by the job. Buys all rights or one-time rights.
How to Contact: Submit demo and resume of previously aired work. Prefers cassette with 2-5 songs on demo. SASE. "Also, put name, return address and phone number on the tape itself." Reporting time varies "according to our business rush."
Music: "We have varying needs—sometimes we need a musical score to which we cut the film; at other times, we need music for already edited film."

RIVIERA PRODUCTIONS, 31628 Saddletree Dr., Westlake Village CA 91361. (818)889-5778. Contact: Will Zens. Motion picture production company and music/sound effects library. Uses the services of music houses and independent songwriters for scoring of films and background music for films. Pay negotiable.
How to Contact: Submit demo tape of previous work or tape demonstrating composition skills. Prefers cassette with any number of pieces. SASE.
Music: Uses non-synthesized, non-rock music.

RTG MUSIC, 130 E. 6th St., Cincinnati OH 45202. (513)381-0506. Creative Director: John Henry. Music production company. Clients include advertising agencies, AV producers and large corporations. Uses the services of lyricists, composers, arrangers, musicians and singers for scoring of AV and film, jingles and commercials for radio and TV. Pays by the job. Buys all rights.
How to Contact: Write first to arrange personal interview. Submit demo tape of previous work, tape demonstrating composition skills, or submit manuscript showing music scoring skills. Prefers cassette (or ¾" videocassette). "Tapes cannot be returned." Prefers to keep material on file. Reports in 6 weeks.
Music: All styles.

*S.A. PRODUCTIONS, INC., 330 W. 58th St., New York NY 10019. (212)765-2669. President: Stan Applebaum. Scoring service, commercial music production house and music/sound effect library. Clients include motion picture production companies, advertising agency, Broadway, music publishing and industrials. Uses the services of independent songwriters/composers and lyricists for scoring, background music, and jingles for national radio and TV commercials and industrials, and orchestrating for Broadway. Commissions 5 composers/year. Pays by the job. Buys all rights, one-time rights or negotiates rights purchased.

How to Contact: Query with resume of credits, or submit demo tape of previous work or tape demonstrating composition skills or manuscript showing music scoring skills, or write to arrange personal interview. Prefers cassette or 15 or 7½ ips reel-to-reel with 5-10 pieces. SASE, but prefers to keep material on file. Reports in 1 month.

Music: Uses all styles of music for various kinds of assignments.

Tips: "Be certain that your melody is strong and memorable. Be certain that your lyrics have 'hooks.' Be certain that your chord progressions are not stale."

TAMARA SCOTT PRODUCTIONS, 19062 Two Bar Rd., Boulder Creek CA 95006. Production Manager: Tamara Scott. Audiovisual firm, scoring service, motion picture production company and music/sound effects library. Clients include industrial firms. Uses the services of music houses, independent songwriters, lyricists and musicians for background music and scoring of film; jingles and commercials for radio and TV; and multi-image productions. Commissions 6-10 composers and 6-10 lyricists/year. Pays $150-1,000/job or $25-35/hour. Buys all rights or one-time rights.

How to Contact: Submit tape demonstrating composition skills, or query with resume of credits. Prefers cassette, reel-to-reel (or videocassette). Does not return unsolicited material; prefers to keep on file.

Music: Commercial and all others.

*SEATTLE MOTION PICTURE SERVICE, 4717 Aurora N., Seattle WA 98013. Manager: Dick Pappas. Audiovisual firm, motion picture production company and music/sound effect library. Uses original music for scoring of films, background music for tapes and productions, jingles and commercials for radio and TV. Pays by the job, by royalty or per hour. Buys all rights or one-time rights.

How to Contact: Write or call first and obtain permission to submit. Accepts cassette or reel-to-reel (or videocassette). Does not return unsolicited material; prefers to keep on file. Reports in 3 weeks.

Music: Uses up-tempo and classical music for all kinds of assignments.

*TOM SELLERS PRODUCTIONS, Box 283, Wayne PA 19087. (215)561-0999. Music production house. "Always looking for writers for records and commercials."

How to Contact: Send cassette(s) with lyric sheet. SASE.

Music: Top 40/pop, R&B crossover, with contemporary sound.

SILVER BURDETT & GINN, 250 James St., CN 018, Morristown NJ 07960. (201)285-8002. Associate Music Editor: Donald Scafuri. Publisher of textbooks and records for kindergarten through 8th grade. "Our books and records are sold directly to schools and are evaluated and chosen for use according to the adoption procedures of a particular school district." Uses the services of music houses, songwriters and lyricists for original songs for children K-8; lyricists for translating foreign lyrics into a singable English version and "writing original lyrics to a folk tune or a melody composed by someone else." Commissions 0-20 lyricists and 0-20 pieces/year. Pays $55 for lyrics and arrangements; $150 for original compositions (reprint rights plus statutory record royalty). Buys one-time rights.

How to Contact: Submit lead sheets of previous work. Prefers cassette. SASE. Reports in 1 month. Free catalog available.

Music: "We seek virtually any kind of song that is suitable both in words and music for children to sing. We are particularly interested in songs that are contemporary pop or folk-like in style. We are also interested in choral compositions for upper grades."

Tips: "Become acquainted with teachers and students in elementary or junior high classrooms. Find out what music they are presently using and what they would like to use."

*ROBERT SKILES MUSICAL PRODUCTIONS, 14224 Hunters Pass, Austin TX 78734. (512)266-1857. Writer: Robert Skiles. Scoring service and commercial music production house. Clients include artists, advertising agencies and corporations. Uses the services of music houses, songwriters/composers, lyricists and copyists for scoring of soundtracks and children's theatre; background music for film, video, events, theatre and public service announcements; jingles for radio and TV commercials. Pays by the job or $30-50/hour. Buys all rights or one-time rights.

How to Contact: Query with resume of credits; or submit demo tape of previous work or tape demon-

 The asterisk before a listing indicates that the listing is new in this edition. New markets are often the most receptive to freelance submissions.

Close-up

Stan Applebaum
President
S.A. Productions

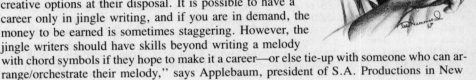

"Songwriters should try to write in all forms. It is essential if they hope to be 'on the cutting edge' of their craft. By working in all forms they also expand the number of creative options at their disposal. It is possible to have a career only in jingle writing, and if you are in demand, the money to be earned is sometimes staggering. However, the jingle writers should have skills beyond writing a melody with chord symbols if they hope to make it a career—or else tie-up with someone who can arrange/orchestrate their melody," says Applebaum, president of S.A. Productions in New York.

In addition to composing and arranging commercial jingles for national companies (General Electric, T.W.A., Sears), Applebaum has also arranged and orchestrated for the theatre (*Rag Dolly*, *House of Flowers*, *Bring Back Birdie*) and arranged the recent pop hit "Stand By Me" from the movie of the same name, as well as numerous No. 1 records for Neil Sedaka, Bobby Vinton and The Drifters.

Applebaum thinks a beginning songwriter might find it easier starting out in advertising "if he can first secure a position as a copywriter at an agency. In this way he might be able to 'sneak in' his own jingles and sustain himself while trying to crack the pop market."

Applebaum writes commercial/advertising music himself unless he is flooded with assignments and given impossible deadlines to meet. He then calls in a "versatile, experienced composer/orchestrator." He states, "I make it a practice to listen to a beginning songwriter's material." If he hears something outstanding he keeps the tape on file, otherwise, he returns the tape, if accompanied by a SASE.

Applebaum's advice to songwriters who want to learn more about jingle writing is to sit in front of a radio or television with a tape recorder and compile an hour's worth (or more) of spots and then analyze them, noticing in particular:
- The style and length of the melody
- The harmony and the rhythm
- The types of voices that sing the lyrics
- If the words are clear and if they fit the music

He suggests, "After you have studied these points, sit down and try to copy the music on manuscript paper. It is easier to learn and remember something when you see it in front of you. Now try to write something that 'looks and sounds like' what you've analyzed. It's not easy—but then again, nothing is that's going to prepare you for the [jingle] jungle."

—Cynthia Kephart

strating compositions skills or manuscript showing music scoring skills. Prefers cassette with 4-6 pieces. Does not return unsolicited material; prefers to keep on file.
Music: Uses pop, jazz and classical for educational films, slide presentations and commercials.

PHOEBE T. SNOW PRODUCTIONS, INC., 37 W. 26th St., New York NY 10010. (212)481-8001. Production Manager: Barbara J. Bagnold. Audiovisual firm. Clients include business and industry. Uses services of songwriters and lyricists for original music and songs for business shows. Commissions 1-5 songwriters for 10 pieces/year. Pays minimum $500/job. Buys all rights.
How to Contact: Query with resume of credits, then arrange personal interview. SASE. Reports in 1 month.
Music: "Need theme music for business shows."

*SONIC IMAGES PRODUCTIONS, INC., 4590 MacArthur Blvd. NW, Washington DC 20007. (202)333-1063. Vice President/Director of Video Services: Jolie Barbiere. Audiovisual firm, scoring services, commercial music production house, motion picture production company, music/sound effect library and CD-I development. Clients include independent producers, government, entertainment, associations, etc. Uses the services of music houses, independent songwriters/composers and lyricists for scoring of video and film productions; background music for art/experimental films and videos; jingles, public service announcements and radio and TV commercials. Commissions 2-4 composers and 1-2 lyricists/year. Pay varies. Buys all rights.
How to Contact: Submit demo tape of previous work or tape demonstrating composition skills. Prefers cassette (or ¾" VHS or Beta videocassette). "Include a resume." Does not return unsolicited material; prefers to keep on file. Reports if interested.
Music: Uses all commercial and classical styles of music for all kinds of assignments.
Tips: "We look for a clean professional product. Our clients demand it!"

*SOUND & VISION, 83 Leonard St., New York NY 10013. (212)219-3007. President: Tima Surmelioglu. Videopool/music and industrial video production company. Clients include record companies, corporations and video nightclub. Uses services of music houses for background music. Pays by the job. Buys all rights.
How to Contact: Submit tape demonstrating composition skills. Prefers cassette (or ¾" videocassette). SASE, but prefers to keep material on file. Reports in 1 month.
Music: Uses all styles of music for "ambient imagery tapes, industrial videotapes."

*SOUND TRACKS, 77 N. Washington St., Boston MA 02114. (617)226-8000. Chief Engineer: Thomas J. Love. Audiovisual firm and commercial music production house. Clients include commercial accounts and advertising agencies. Uses services of music houses for jingles for radio commercials. Commissions 20-25 composers and 15-20 lyricists/year. Pays 5% royalty. Buys all rights.
How to Contact: Write or call first to arrange personal interview. Prefers cassette. SASE, but prefers to keep material on file. Reports in 3 weeks.
Music: Uses classical, rock and up-beat music for commercials.

SOUND/VIDEO IMPRESSIONS, INC., 110 River Rd., Des Plaines IL 60016. (312)297-4360. Vice President: W.J. Holtane. Audiovisual, video production firm and recording studio. Uses the services of independent songwriters and music libraries for scoring of multi-image shows and commercials for radio and TV.

*SOUVENIRS OF HAWAII, Box 2457, Honolulu HI 96804. (808)847-4608. President: Donald P. McDiarmid III. Audiovisual firm, commercial music production house and music/sound effect library. Clients include resort retail gift shops. Buys all rights or one-time rights.
How to Contact: Submit demo tape of previous work. Prefers cassette. SASE.
Music: Uses Hawaiian music for Hawaiian videos, and phonograph records, etc.

*SPARTRONIX VIDEOSERVICES, 476 Lancaster Pike, Frazer PA 19355. (215)647-2800. President: Dick Spahr. Audiovisual firm and video production/post production house. Clients include primarily industrial and corporate accounts. Uses the services of music houses and independent songwriters/composers for scoring of sales, point of purchase displays, training programs and TV commercials. Commissions 10 composers/year. Negotiates pay. Buys all or one-time rights, depending on project.
How to Contact: Submit demo tape of previous work. Prefers cassette (or ¾" or VHS videocassette). SASE, but prefers to keep material on file. Reports in 2 weeks.
Music: Uses up-tempo, bright, hi-tech synth music for TV spots (broadcast and cable) and corporate and industrial, sales and training.

E.J. STEWART INC., 525 Mildred Ave., Primos PA 19018. (215)626-6500. General Manager: Robert Momyer. Audiovisual firm and video production company. Clients include broadcasting companies, cable TV, advertising agencies, schools, business, industry, government and the medical profession. Uses the services of music houses and songwriters for background music for commercials and programs. Commissions 50 pieces and 5 lyricists/year. Payment negotiable by the job. Buys all rights.
How to Contact: Query with resume of credits or submit demo tape of previous work. Prefers reel-to-reel or cassette with any number of songs. SASE. Reports "when needed."

STUDIO SONSCRIPT, 1242 Peel St., Montreal, Quebec H3B 2T6 Canada. (514)871-8608. President: Barry Lucking. Scoring service, music/sound effects library and sound recording studio. Clients include advertising agencies, radio, TV, video and audiovisual firms. Uses the services of music houses for scoring and background music for videos and AV presentations, and jingles for radio and TV commercials. Commissions 5 composers/year and 5 lyricists/year. Pays $5,000/job or 10% royalty. Buys all rights or one-time rights.
How to Contact: Submit demo tape of previous work. Prefers cassette. SAE and IRC. Reports in 6 weeks.
Music: Uses all types of music.

*SUEDE COMMUNICATION CENTER, 685 Main St., Hackonsack NJ 07601. (201)646-0416. President: Bob Suede. Audio-video production facility, scoring service, commercial music production house, motion picture production company, music/sound effect library and video recording studio. Clients include record companies, advertising agencies and corporations. Uses music houses, independent songwriters/composers and lyricists for scoring and background music for film, jingles and commercials for radio and TV. Pays by the job. Buys all rights or one-time rights.
How to Contact: Submit demo tape of previous work or tape demonstrating composition skills. Prefers cassette or 15 ips reel-to-reel (or ¾" videocassette) with 4 pieces. Does not return unsolicited material; prefers to keep on file.
Music: Uses easy listening, up-tempo and pop for all kinds of assignments.

SUNSET FILMS AND TELEVISION, 625 Market St., San Francisco CA 94105. (415)495-4555. Executive Producer: Paul Fillinger. Motion picture and video production company. Clients include business and industry. Uses the services of music houses and songwriters for background scores for films, video and TV shows ("How-to Series"). Commissions 5 pieces/year. Pays by the job. Buys all rights.
How to Contact: Query with resume of credits. "If you send tapes, they may not be returned quickly or at all."
Music: "Sponsored films use a bouncy, up-beat flavor; the emotional qualities are secondary most of the time although they're what make films tick. Most assignments are for non-feature, documentary style films or film/tape projects."
Tips: "Only contact us if you live in or visit the San Francisco Bay area. Have plenty of *variety* and sample tapes to prove it."

*SYSCON VIDEO, Suite G, 133 Gather Dr., Mt. Laurel NJ 08054. (609)234-5510. Producer/Director: Bob Knosde. Audiovisual firm. Clients include the armed forces and industrial firms. Uses music houses for background music for industrial videos. Pays $70 per needle drop. Buys one-time rights.
How to Contact: Submit demo tape of previous work, or tape demonstrating composition skills. Prefers cassette. Does not return unsolicited material; prefers to keep on file. Reports in 6 weeks.
Music: Uses synthesized up-tempo and pop (no lyric) for industrial training tapes. "Music needs very interesting intros. CDs are a plus."

*TALCO PRODUCTIONS, 279 E. 44th St., New York NY 10017. (212)697-4015. President: Al Lawrence. Audiovisual firm and motion picture production company. Clients include corporate, nonprofit and educational. Uses the services of music houses and independent songwriters/composers for scoring and background music for film and TV, and commercials for radio. Commissions 2 composers and 1 lyricist/year. Pays by the job. Buys all rights.
How to Contact: Query with resume of credits. Prefers cassette or 7½ ips reel-to-reel. SASE.
Music: Uses easy listening, up-tempo, pop, jazz, classical and rock for educational films and documentaries.

*TELECINE SERVICES & PRODUCTION LTD., 23/25 Seapoint Ave., Monkstown, Co. Dublin Ireland. 353-01-763188. Director: Anabella Nolan. Audiovisual firm and video production house. Clients include advertising and commercial business. Uses the services of songwriters and music houses for original songs for TV commercials and audiovisual and video programs; lyricists for writing lyrics for commercials and conference themes. Commissions 3 lyricists for 20 pieces/year. Pays $1,250 minimum/job. Buys all rights or rights within one country.

How to Contact: Query with resume of credits or submit tape demonstrating composition skills. Prefers 15 ips reel-to-reel or cassette with 3-10 songs. SAE and IRC. Reports in 1 month.

TELETECHNIQUES, INC., 1 W. 19th St., New York NY 10011. (212)206-1475. Contact: Michael Temmer. Scoring service. Clients include large corporations. Uses services of music houses, independient songwriters and lyricists for scoring of industrials, TV spots and films, background music, jingles and commercials for radio and TV. Pays negotiable royalty or various amount by the hour or by the job. Buys all rights or one-time rights.

How to Contact: Write first to arrange personal interview or write and obtain permission to submit. Prefers cassette. Does not return unsolicited material; prefers to keep on file.

Music: "Mostly background music for industrials and TV spots."

*TELEVISION ASSOCIATES, INC., 2410 Charleston Rd., Mt. View CA 94043. (415)967-6040. Producer/Director: Donna Bisbiglia. Video production house. Clients include hi-tech industrial and commercial accounts. Uses the services of music houses and independent songwriters/composers for scoring of documentaries, commercials for TV and opens and closes for industrial tapes. Pays by the job. Buys all rights.

How to Contact: Submit demo tape of previous work or tape demonstrating composition skills. Prefers cassette (or videocassette). Does not return unsolicited material; prefers to keep on file. Reports in 3 weeks.

Music: Uses various styles of music for video projects.

TOBY'S TUNES, INC., 2325 Girard Ave. S., Minneapolis MN 55405. (612)377-0690. Owner: Harley Toberman. Audiovisual firm. Clients include businesses such as 3M, Honeywell, Control Data and life insurance companies. Uses the services of independent songwriters for scoring of AV slide shows and commercials for radio and TV. Commissions 1 songwriter and 1 lyricist/year. Pays $2,000/job. Buys all rights.

How to Contact: Submit demo tape of previous work. Prefers cassette, 15 ips reel-to-reel (or ¾" videocassette) with 4 pieces. SASE. Reports in 2 weeks.

Music: "We prefer acoustic music for our business clients."

*TORODE DESIGN ASSOC., 2311 Lombard St., Philadelphia PA 19146. (215)732-6792. Audiovisual firm and marketing graphics company. Uses the services of music houses, independent songwriters/composers and libraries for scoring of AV/video, corporate and trade shows. Commissions 2-3 composers/year. Payment negotiated. Buys all rights or one-time rights.

How to Contact: Write first and obtain permission to submit. Prefers cassette. SASE, but prefers to keep material on file. Reports "when work materializes."

Music: Uses up-tempo and classical music for trade shows, slide presentations and training films.

TRANSLIGHT MEDIA ASSOCIATES, INC., 931 W. Liberty Dr., Wheaton IL 60187. (312)690-7780. Producer: John Lorimer. Audiovisual firm. Clients include industrial, religious and advertising firms. Uses the services of independent songwriters, lyricists and music houses for scoring of original audiovisual soundtracks for sales programs and business meetings and background music for audiovisual productions. Commissions 3 composers and 1 lyricist/year. Pays $2,500-10,000/job. Buys all rights. "Writer can use material for demonstration."

How to Contact: On initial contact prefers non-dolby cassette with 5-10 pieces. Does not return unsolicited material; prefers to keep on file. Reports "as suitable project develops. No phone calls please."

Music: "Background music for audiovisual programs. Strong themes with a contemporary feel. Programs generally 5-10 minutes in length."

Tips: "We prefer to work with local talent (Chicago market). When an appropriate project comes up, we review our files and select those most promising. We then contact those composers and invite them to make a more specific presentation."

*TRF PRODUCTION MUSIC LIBRARIES, 40 E. 49th St., New York NY 10017. (212)753-3234. President: Michael Nurko. Music/sound effect library. Uses services of independent songwriters/composers and lyricists for background music for all media, jingles and commercials for TV and radio. Pays by royalty.

How to Contact: Submit demo tape of previous work or tape demonstrating composition skills. Prefers cassette with 3-7 pieces. SASE.

Music: Uses all styles of music for assignments in all media.

TROMA, INC., 733 9th Ave., New York NY 10019. (212)757-4555. Director of Marketing: Stacey Adams. Motion picture production company and distributor. Clients include motion picture distributors and exhibitors. Uses music houses, independent songwriters and lyricists for scoring of motion pictures, background music for motion pictures, and commercials for radio and TV. Pays by the job. Buys all rights or one-time rights.
How to Contact: Submit demo tape of previous work demonstrating composition skills. Prefers cassette. SASE. Reports in 4 weeks.
Music: "We use all types and styles of popular music for our films."

U.S. GOVERNMENT, National Park Service, Division of Audiovisual Arts, Harpers Ferry Center, Harpers Ferry WV 25425. Chief Branch of Audio Production: Blair Hubbard. Clients include national parks, recreational areas and historic sites. Uses services of music houses and songwriters for thematic and background music for films and sound-slide and multimedia programs. Commissions 5 pieces/year. Payment negotiable. Buys all rights.
How to Contact: Query with resume of credits, submit demo tape of previously aired work or submit demo tape showing flexibility of composition skills. Prefers 7½ or 15 ips reel-to-reel with 3-10 songs. Does not return unsolicited material. "We maintain a permanent file." Reports "when we have specific needs." Free catalog.
Music: "Needs vary; usually background for a film or a sound-slide program for a national park, recreational or historic area. We are looking for high-quality work, preferably by previously-published writers."

*UNIVERSITY OF MICHIGAN MEDIA RESOURCES CENTER, 400 4th St., Ann Arbor MI 48103. (313)764-8228. Media Production Manager: Michael C. Berger. Instructional/educational production facility. Clients include university departments and nonprofit organizations. Uses the services of music houses and independent songwriters/composers for background music for educational/instructional productions. Commissions 3-5 composers/year. Pays $500-5,000/job. Buys all rights.
How to Contact: Submit demo tape of previous work or tape demonstrating composition skills. Prefers cassette or 7½ ips reel-to-reel (or ¾" videocassette) with 3-5 pieces. SASE, but prefers to keep material on file. Reports in 2 weeks.
Music: Uses all styles of music for educational, instructional and training slide/tape presentations and videos.

*VERITECH CORP., 37 Prospect St., E. Longmeadow MA 01028. (413)525-3368. Production Manager: Jeremy Cole. Video production/post production company. Serves industrial clients. Uses the services of music houses and independent songwriters/composers for scoring and background music for industrial videotapes, and commercials for TV. Pays by the job. Buys all rights or one-time rights.
How to Contact: Query with resume of credits, or submit demo tape of previous work or tape demonstrating composition skills. Prefers cassette or 7½ ips reel-to-reel (or ¾" videocassette). Does not return unsolicited material; prefers to keep on file.
Music: Uses mixed styles of music for industrial videotapes and commercials.

VIDEO COMMUNICATORS INTERNATIONAL, Suite 100, 2091 Business Center Dr., Irvine CA 92715. (714)752-5075. President: Christopher Harwood. Audiovisual firm, motion picture production company and video/TV production company. Clients include business, education, government, advertising agencies, broadcast and cable TV companies. Uses the services of music houses, independent songwriters, lyricists and independent musicians for scoring of program themes, background music for documentaries and TV series, themes for industrial videos and jingles for radio and TV commercials. Pays by the job. Buys all rights or one-time rights, "sometimes shares rights with composer."
How to Contact: Submit demo tape of previous work, or query with resume of credits. Prefers cassette (or ¾" videocassette). "Indicate in writing composer's/submitter's clear right to ownership and use." Does not return unsolicited material; prefers to keep on file. Reports in 3-4 weeks.
Music: Needs "contemporary music for program themes and/or scoring; rock/upbeat for commercials."
Tips: "Submit tape of completed material along with credits (if any). Stay in touch!"

VIDEO IMAGERY, 204 Calle De Anza, San Clemente CA 92672. (714)492-5082. Contact: Bob Fisher. Audiovisual firm. Clients include Apple Computer, AMF Inc., Potter & Brumfield and Scientific Drilling. Uses the services of music houses for background music for video productions. Pays by the job. Buys rights as required.
How to Contact: Submit tape demonstrating composition skills. Prefers cassette (or ½" VHS videocassette). Does not return unsolicited material; prefers to keep on file. Reports in 3 weeks.

*VIDEO MEDIA, 2727 W. Southern, Tempe AZ 85282. President: James W. Binkenberger. Audiovisual firm. Clients include corporate and hosptials. Uses the services of music houses and independent songwriters/composers for scoring of industrial films and commercials for TV. Pays by the job. Buys all rights or one-time rights.
How to Contact: Submit demo tape of previous work. Prefers cassette with 4-8 pieces. SASE, but prefers to keep material on file "if interested in material." Reports in 2 months.
Music: Uses easy listening, up-tempo, pop and jazz for educational films, slide presentations and commercials.

*VIDEO RESOURCES, Box 18642, Irvine CA 92713. Producer: Brad Hagen. Audiovisual firm. Serves corporate clients. Uses music houses for background music for video and film projects, jingles for spots, and commercials for TV. Commissions 0-1 composers and 0-1 lyricists/year. Pays by the job or per hour. Buys all rights or one-time rights.
How to Contact: Query with resume of credits or submit demo tape of previous work. Prefers cassette. SASE, but prefers to keep material on file.
Music: Uses all styles of music for educational films, slide presentations and commercials.

*VIDEOSMITH, INC., 3 Independence Way, Princeton NJ 08540. (609)987-9099. Manager: Patrick Crowley. Audiovisual firm and motion picture production company. Clients include corporations, independent producers and advertising agencies. Uses the services of independent songwriters/composers and music libraries for background music for videotape productions. Pays $500-1,200/job. Buys all rights.
How to Contact: Submit demo tape of previous work. Prefers cassette. Does not return unsolicited material.
Music: Uses various styles of music for background for marketing tapes, etc.

*VISION FILM GROUP, INC., 310-66 King St., Winnipeg, Manitoba R3B 1H6 Canada. (204)942-6215. President: Al Rosenberg. Audiovisual firm, motion picture and music video production company. Clients include industrial and entertainment. Uses the services of music houses, independent songwriters/composers and lyricists for background music for audiovisual and videos, and TV commercials. Commissions 5 composers and 5 lyricists/year. Pays $100-500/job. Buys all rights or one-time rights.
How to Contact: Submit demo tape of previous work, or tape demonstrating composition skills. Prefers cassete (or Beta videocassette). Does not return unsolicited material; prefers to keep on file. Reports in 2 weeks.
Music: Uses rock, contemporary, New Age, up-tempo, unpublished music for videos, marketing programs, audiovisual presentations and commercials.
Tips: "Currently looking for fresh material for a rock musical for TV and video—as well as touring."

*VISUAL COMMUNICATIONS GROUP, INC., 3300 Mitchell Ln., Boulder CO 80301. (303)443-6003. Facilities Manager: Joseph Garguild. Audiovisual firm. Clients include business and commercial/industrial clients with emphasis on high tech and bio medical fields. Uses the services of music houses, independent songwriters/composers and recording studios for scoring and background music for commercial/industrial sales videos, and commercials for TV; uses lyricists for jingles for TV. Pays $200-500/job or $20-35/hour. Buys all rights or one-time rights.
How to Contact: Call first and obtain permission to submit. Prefers cassette (or ¾" or ½" videocassette) with 4-7 pieces. "Please include as much information as possible: how it was used, cost, details of mix, etc." Does not return unsolicited material; prefers to keep on file. Reports in 1 month "if interested."
Music: Uses light classical, synthesizer and techno-pop for industrials and occassional spots.

WESTLAKE STUDIOS, #118, 31320 Via Colinas, Westlake Village CA 91362. (818)991-5452. Director, Project Development: Felix Girard. Audiovisual firm, motion picture production firm, scoring service and album/song producers. Clients include business, industry, entertainment, video and record companies. Uses the services of independent songwriters and lyricists for scoring of videos (entertainment and instructional), background music for industrials, jingles for radio and commercials. Commissions 6 composers and 3 lyricists/year. Pay negotiable by job. Buys all rights.
How to Contact: Call first and obtain permission to submit or query with resume of credits. Prefers cassette (or ½" VHS or ¾" videocassette). Does not return unsolicited material; prefers to keep on file. Reports in 4 weeks.
Music: MOR, country, pop mainstream and original compositions for video scores.
Tips: "Songwriters and lyricists must be able to work well with artists and business people."

*WESTON WOODS STUDIOS, Weston CT 06883. (203)226-3355 (outside CT, 800-243-5020). Production Manager: Paul R. Gagne. Audiovisual firm, motion production company and producer of films and audiovisual materials based on children's picture books. Clients include educational/institutional market and home market video. Uses services of independent songwriters/composers and copyists for scoring of motion pictures and filmstrips. Commissions 3-5 composers/year. Pays $500-4,000/job. Buys all rights.
How to Contact: Query with resume of credits; write to arrange personal interview; or submit demo tape of previous work or tape demonstrating composition skills. Prefers cassette or 7½ ips reel-to-reel (or ¾" or VHS videocassette) with 5-10 pieces. SASE, but prefers to keep material on file. Reports in 1 month.
Music: "Style depends on each project, but can be anything from classical/orchestral to contemporary jazz to traditional African drums."
Tips: "Our productions are *dramatic* adaptations of children's books. We therefore look for traditional dramatic film scoring, as opposed to incidental or background music. Stylistically, the music should not be condescending to children."

*WING PRODUCTIONS, 1600 Broadway, New York NY 10019. (212)265-5179. President: Jon Wing Lum. Clients include NBC and the New York State Education Department. Uses services of music houses, songwriters and lyricists for scores for film and tape, background music for sound filmstrips and original songs for themes. Commissions 20-40 lyricists for 20-40 pieces/year. Pays $500-5,000/job. Buys all rights.
How to Contact: Submit demo tape of previously aired work or tape showing flexibility of composition skills. Prefers 7½ or 15 ips reel-to-reel or cassette with 5 songs. SASE. Reporting time "depends on need." Free catalog.
Music: All types.

WREN MARKETING COMMUNICATIONS CO., 5 Independence Way, Princeton NJ 08540. (609)924-8085. Production Manager: Debbie Goodkin. Communications consulting firm. Clients include business and industry. Uses the services of music houses, songwriters/composers and lyricists for "background music for multi-media presentations (slide, film, video and live talent) also, original scores and songs for the same." Commissions 4-5 composers and 1-2 lyricists/year. Pays up to $2,500/job. Buys all rights.
How to Contact: Query with resume of credits, submit demo tape of previous work, or submit tape demonstrating composition skills. Prefers cassette (or videocassette) with minimum 5 songs. SASE, but prefers to keep material on file. Reports in 1 month.
Music: "We often look for a high-tech sound to use as background music in corporate presentations."
Tips: "Demonstrate experience in producing soundtracks for slide, film and video presentations."

ZAMACONA PRODUCTIONS, 3rd Fl., 350 Brannan, San Francisco CA 94107-1816. (415)495-3823. Producer: Frank Zamacona. TV production company. Serves industrial and broadcast clients. Uses the services of music houses and independent songwriters for scoring of public service announcements and background music for home video projects and industrial projects. Pays $450-2,000/job. Buys all rights or one-time rights.
How to Contact: Submit tape demonstrating composition skills. Prefers cassette (or ½" videocassette). SASE. Reports in 1 week or "when a budget and proposal is needed."
Music: "Melodic themes preferred. We also use abstract electronic music (computer science, technology)."
Tips: "Bay area location preferred."

ZM SQUARED, 903 Edgewood Lane, Box C-30, Cinnaminson NJ 08077. (609)786-0612. Clients include colleges, schools, businesses and audiovisual producers. Uses the services of songwriters "for themes for our no-needledrop music library and background for audiovisual presentations. We prefer to work with composer/arranger/performer and use primarily background music." Commissions 4-5 albums with 10 cuts each/year, and 1-2 lyricists/year. Pays 10-35% royalty. Buys all rights.
How to Contact: Submit demo tape of previous work. Prefers cassette with 4-6 songs. SASE. Reports in 3 weeks. Free catalog available.
Music: "We require a variety of background music—educational and industrial for general use with audiovisual programs."
Tips: "Know what we want and be able to produce what you write."

Play Producers and Publishers

Aficionados of musical theatre (and new and experimental theatre) are numerous and loyal. If you love musical theatre and have written musicals or have ideas for some, you should know that many theatres are established specifically to do musicals, or "plays with music." Some play producers devote their whole careers to developing new musicals and original performing arts pieces; others try to incorporate new works into a season of "standards" for their more conservative audiences.

Those theatres, producers and play publishers who have established reputations for quality musical theatre work receive hundreds of submissions each year from aspiring musical theatre writers. Obviously only a few new works are chosen for production and/or publication. You can increase in a number of ways the chances for your work being selected. First, familiarize yourself with the genre. Go to the theatre, order scripts from play publishers, and study them carefully. (You can write to play publishers requesting copies of their catalogs, and even order the scripts through the mail.) This will give you an idea of how song lyrics relate to the entire show, the number of songs used, and how and when songs are woven into the plot.

Second, learn what the individual play producers want and what type(s) of shows they have done recently. Study the listings, and write to theatres you are interested in, requesting a current program and any other helpful information they can send.

Third, keep your music theatre pieces simple. Shows with uncomplicated sets and small casts are a must for little theatres with limited facilities and funds. Even on Broadway, rising costs have forced producers and directors to seek material that can be produced inexpensively.

However, Broadway need not be—and should not be—your only goal. Many local groups—dinner theatres, children's theatres, high school and college groups, and community theatres—provide outlets for musicals. These groups are often open to original work from local playwrights, and are excellent testing grounds for your musical. They may not be able to pay well, or at all, but once your play has proven itself locally, you can send reviews of the performances along with a letter asking permission to submit your musical to producers in New York and elsewhere.

The following theatres, producers and play publishers give valuable information on what type of material they are interested in and how they wish to be contacted. Follow their submission instructions.

*ACADEMY OF PERFORMING ARTS, Box 1843, Orleans MA 02653. (617)255-9929. Artistic Director: Myles Corey. Play producer. Produces 3 plays and 4 musicals/year. "Winter audiences—retirement community; summer audience—resort community. Stage is ¾ thrust. House seats 172. There is a one row balcony." Pays by royalty. Submit complete manuscript, score and tape of songs. SASE.
Musical Theatre: "We have no limitations. Our shows range in style from 19th century operetta to modern rock musicals. Our shows have ranged in length from 1 hour to 2½ hours. Our casts limit is 35. We would be particularly interested in musicals with casts under 10 as we at times have difficulty finding these. No limitations on props or staging."
Productions:*Elizabeth The Queen*, by Maxwell Anderson, (historical drama); *Pirates of Penzance*, by Gilbert and Sullivan; and *A Christmas Carol*, by Charles Dickens.

ACT THEATRE/SONGWORKS, 100 W. Roy, Seattle WA 98119. Director of Songworks: David Koch. Play producer. Produces 5 plays/year (all musicals). Experimental plays, workshops, readings and staged readings are performed in a small space for a young professional audience (20-50 age range). Fee payments vary, some are by commission. Query with synopsis, character breakdown and set description. SASE. Reports in 8 weeks.

Musical Theatre: "Songworks is a development-oriented program. We are looking for writers with good crossover technique between pop music and musical theatre. We require a small cast, modern topics and the music and lyrics must be original. 90-120 minutes preferred. We will be working with a bare stage and limited lighting."

Productions: *18 Wheels*, by John Gray (truckers' musical); *Bridge to Terabithia*, by Scott Warrender (children's musical); and *Duffy and the Rhythm Dogs*, by Carl Sander/Chris Carlson (rock & roll musical).

Tips: "No retrospective reviews; we are looking for original 'musicals.' Don't get trapped into believing that there are rules you must follow to create a musical. Be adventurous, daring. Let me hear something *new*!"

ALLENBERRY PLAYHOUSE, Boiling Springs PA 17007. (717)258-6120. Contact: Managing Director. Play producer. Produces 9 plays (2 musicals)/year. Pays 3-5% royalty. Query with synopsis. SASE. Reports as soon as possible.

Musical Theatre: "Other than established material, we are looking for small cast, 4-10 characters, simply produced musicals—they should run between 2-2½ hours in length. Take into account that we are in a conservative, religiously oriented part of the country. Four letter words are fairly taboo, but then again, it depends on the four letter word! Stay away from what middle America finds objectionable: excessive dwelling on any violation of the Ten Commandments, slurs on the country (not necessarily the government), nudity, or esoteric subject matter."

Productions: *Annie*; *Pirates of Penzance*; and *The Music Man*.

AMAS REPERTORY THEATRE INC., 1 E. 104th St., New York NY 10029. (212)369-8000. Artistic Director: Rosetta Le Noire. Administrator/Business Manager: Gary Halcott. Development Director: Arnold Falleder. Play producer. Produces 3 original musicals/year. Also presents 2 children's theater productions and one summer tour. "AMAS is dedicated to bringing all people—regardless of race, creed, color or religion—together through the creative arts. In writing for AMAS, an author should keep this overall goal in mind." Does not pay for manuscripts but "provides a top quality New York showcase with a good record of commercial pick-ups." Query with synopsis or submit complete script with cassette of score (or partial score).

Musical Theatre: Musicals only. "All works to be performed by multi-racial casts. Musical biographies especially welcome. Cast size should be under 15 if possible, including doubling. Because of physical space, set requirements should be relatively simple. We do not want to see material with explicit sex or violence or very strong language. Prefer themes of love, joy and togetherness."

Productions: *Bubbling Brown Sugar*; *Bingo*, by Hy Gilbert, George Fischoff, & Ossie Davis (Negro baseball leagues); *Blackberries*, by Joseph George Caruso (minstrel shows/vaudeville); *Dazy*, by Phillip Rose; *Hot Sake*; and *Prime Time*, by Johnny Brandon.

Tips: "Concentrate on getting a good book. Most musicals die for lack of a book not because of poor music or lyrics. Also—get a good theatrical lawyer."

AMERICAN INDIAN COMMUNITY HOUSE, INC./NATIVE AMERICANS IN THE ARTS, 842 Broadway, New York NY 10003. (212)598-0100. Theater Program Director: Rosemary Richmond. Play producer and in-residence theater company. Produces minimum of 1 play/year. "Our work is presented at local area off and off-off Broadway theatres, with occasional tours to colleges and reservations and local area schools (elementary, junior high and high school)." Pays negotiable amount per performance. Query with synopsis, character breakdown and set description; or submit complete score and tape of song. SASE.

Musical Theatre: Seeking "American Indian subject material. Our first commitment is to support the development of American Indian composers and musicians. After that it would be American Indian subject material written by non-Indians and productions of the classics. We prefer contemporary material, possibly new music. Our plays, when not classics, are urban and contemporary in subject material. The music should reflect this. We are not interested in traditional Indian music (pow-wow songs etc.) unless done by Indians. We operate on a limited budget, so massive projects are out of the question. Maximum cast size would be 10, with 4 musicians accompanying."

Productions: *The Ecstasy of Rita Joe*, by George Ryga (urbanization of American Indians); *Grandma*, by Hanay Geiogamah (one-woman show/life, history of Indian woman); and *Midsummer Night's Dream*, by W. Shakespeare.

ARENA PLAYERS REPERTORY THEATRE, 296 Route 109, East Farmingdale NY 11735. (516)293-0674. Producer: Frederic De Feis. Play producer. Produces 30 plays/year. Plays performed in a "professional, arena-style repertory theater playing to a broad cross-section of teenagers to senior citizens, drawn from all over Long Island as well as Manhattan." Pays royalty averaging $600-1,200. Query with synopsis. SASE. Reports in 1 month.

Musical Theatre: "We are particularly interested in full-length intimate musicals which can be mounted with minimal orchestration and are well-suited to production in a small, arena-style theater."

Productions: *Umbrellas of Cherbourg*, by Demy; and *I Love My Wife*, by Michael Stewart and Cy Coleman.

ARENA STAGE, 6th and Maine Ave. SW, Washington DC 20024. (202)554-9066. Literary Manager: Ms. Lloyd Rose. Play producer. Produces 8 plays (1 musical)/year. "Our plays are produced for an educated, sophisticated urban audience interested in major social and moral issues. We have three theatres: an 800-seat in-the-round, a 500-seat thrust and a 180-seat cabaret." Pays negotiable royalty. Query with synopsis, character breakdown and cassette tape of songs. Include first 10 pages of book for a book show. SASE. Reports in 8 weeks.

Musical Theatre: Mini-operas and full-length musicals (especially book shows) for resident acting company of 18. "Serious subjects preferred. We do not want standard Broadway imitations, children's musicals or simple-minded reactionary works."

Productions: *Restoration*, by Edward Bond and Nick Bicăt (class struggle); *The Gospel At Colonus*, by Lee Brever and Bob Telson (Greek myth gospelized); and *Happy End*, by Brecht and Weill (Chicago myth).

Tips: "Music and lyrics must be of high quality and originality. The more resources required the more the project must justify their use. Take risks and have the talent to justify them. Make us pay attention."

ARKANSAS STATE UNIVERSITY-BEEBE CAMPUS, Box H, Beebe AR 72012. (501)882-6452. Director of Theater: L.R. Chudomelka. Play producer. Produces 6 plays (3 musicals)/year. Plays are performed in a "600 seat theater (proscenium) in a city of 4,000, 30 miles from metropolitan area of more than 200,000." Pays $35-100/performance. Submit complete manuscript and score. SASE. Reports in 2 weeks.

Musical Theatre: "Material should be within the ability of traditional community college with traditional and non-traditional students: simple dancing, innovative and traditional, not over-sophisticated (somewhat family oriented). Variety of music styles and balanced major role shows—no 'star' shows. Flexible cast size, props, staging, etc. We do not want extremes, unnecessary profanity or 'operatic' material."

Productions: *Something's Afoot*, by McDonald/Vos/Gerlach (mystery); *Happy Time*, by Nash/Kander/Ebb (family relations); and *Damn Yankees*, by Abbott/Wallop/Adler/Ross (baseball).

Tips: "Music should be singable and vary in style. Songs should be an intricate part of the show and not just put in for spectacle. Major roles should be balanced between 4 or 5 characters, rather than one-character shows with chorus."

ARROW ROCK LYCEUM THEATRE, Main St., Arrow Rock MO 65320. (816)837-3311. Artistic Director: Michael Bollinger. Play producer. Produces 7 plays (3-4 musicals)/year. "Lyceum is a not-for-profit regional theatre, and performs in her own theatre space seating 208." Royalties are paid and negotiated with each individual author/composer. Query with synopsis, character breakdown and set description. SASE. Reports in 5 months.

Musical Theatre: "We produce a varied and diverse season each year. Each season consists of 3-4 diverse musicals, 1 classic, 1 American drama, 1 comedy or mystery, and 1 wild card. All topics and styles are considered, as long as they are quality material. The theatre is not large, has little fly space, and generally operates in rotating repertory with several other plays. Twenty-five or fewer characters is better."

Productions: *Eleven-Zulu*, by Sean Clark (Vietnam War); *Cotton Patch Gospel*, by Chapin and others (Jesus Christ countryfied); and *Cabaret* by Masterhoff, Kander and Ebb (preNazi Germany).

ASOLO STATE THEATER, Drawer E, Sarasota FL 33578. (813)355-7115. Contact: Literary Manager. Play producer. Produces 8 plays (1 musical)/year. Plays are performed at the Asolo Theater (325-seat proscenium house) or by the Asolo Touring Theater (6-member company touring the Southeast). Pays 5% minimum royalty. "We no longer accept unsolicited manuscripts or tapes. Inquiries should be made in the form of a letter, a one-page synopsis and a self-addressed, stamped postcard." SASE.

Musical Theatre: "We want small non-chorus musicals only. They should be full-length, any subject, with not over 10 in the cast. There are no restrictions on production demands; however, musicals with excessive scenic requirements may be difficult to consider."

Productions: *Dames at Sea*, by Haimsohn/Miller/Wise; *The Drunkard*, by Herrod/Manilow; and *Man with a Load of Mischief*, by Clifton/Tarver.

Tips: "Musicals are produced infrequently here due to the 'classical' basis of Asolo's repertory and inability to 'job-in' musical-theater talent."

*ATTIC THEATRE, Box 02457, Detroit MI 48202. (313)875-8285. Artistic Director: Lavinia Moyer. Play producer. Produces 1-3 new musicals/year. Proscenium stage, 300 seat house. Pays by royalty. Query with synopsis, character breakdown and set description. SASE. Reports in 3 months.
Musical Theatre: Seeks "adult, minority-oriented musicals with small to medium cast (under 15) and small orchestration requirements (3-5 instrumentalists). Interested in Detroit music history—biographical topics." Will consider original music for scene transitions in a play being developed.
Productions: *Piaf*, by Pam Gems (life—biographical); *Vaudeville*, by Laurence Carr (1918 biographical); and *Ma Raineys Black Bottom*, by August Wilson (1927 biographical).

BAKER'S PLAYS, 100 Chauncy St., Boston MA 02111. (617)482-1280. Editor: John B. Welch. Play publisher. Publishes 18-28 plays (6-10 musicals)/year. Plays are used by children's theaters, junior and senior high schools, colleges and community theaters. Pays standard nonprofessional royalty/performance. Submit complete manuscript, score and cassette tape of songs. SASE. Reports in 3 months.
Musical Theatre: "We prefer large cast, contemporary musicals which are easy to stage and produce. We like children's musicals if the accompaniment is fairly simple. Plot your shows strongly, keep your scenery and staging simple, your musical numbers and choreography easily explained and blocked out. Originality and style are up to the author. We want innovative and tuneful shows but no X-rated material. We are very interested in the new writer and believe that, with revision and editorial help, he can achieve success in writing original musicals for the non-professional market."
Publications: *Great All American Backstage Musical*, by Tim Kelly and Jack Sharkey (spoof of Hollywood); *Cat in the Castle*, by Bill Solly (children's fantasy); and *O Happy Day*, by Jane Staab and Susan Kusoff (Christmas musical).
Tips: "Think about audience support and craft your work for that audience interest."

*THE BANFF CENTRE SCHOOL OF FINE ARTS, Box 1020, Banff, Alberta T0L 0C0 Canada. (403)762-6192. Artistic Director, Music Theatre: John Metcalf. Music theatre producer. Produces 3-6 new musicals/year. Provides workshops and training through participation in new musicals for serious actors/performers, composers and writers. Pays by royalty, per performance or "by commission contract." Query with synopsis, character breakdown, set description and sample of previous works; or submit complete manuscript, score and tape of songs. SAE and IRC. Reports in 6 weeks.
Musical Theatre: "Music theatre is the name most often given to the twentieth century movement which has worked to infuse a fresh immediacy into the singing theatre. Music theatre embodies economy of means, a wide approach, versatility of performers, variety of structural forms, and an awareness of other contemporary arts. Banff offers an integrated training program for singer-actors, composers, writers and others. Composers and writers work closely with performers to create new works for studio production." Uses "both children and adult music theatre works, written for voice and small ensemble." Would "most definitely" consider original music for use in a play being developed.
Productions: *Saint Carmen of the Main*, by Michel Tremblay, adapted for music theatre by Lee Devin with music by Sydney Hodkinson (Montreal's street life); *Jack and the Beanstalk*, by Vandervelde (Canadian premiere); and *Alice in Wonderland*, by Freedman (World premiere).
Tips: "Enquire, asking for program information for young composers and writers."

RICK BELZER/CANDLEWOOD PLAYHOUSE, Box 8209, New Fairfield CT 06812. (203)746-6557. Producer: Rick Belzer. Play producer. Produces 6-8 plays/year (all musicals). "Plays are performed at Candlewood Playhouse for an upper middle class audience." Pays by royalty, outright purchase or per performance. Submit complete manuscript, score and tape of songs. SASE.
Musical Theatre: Seeking "big musicals and children's musicals."
Productions: *King and I, Guys and Dolls, Fiddler on the Roof, Funny Girl,* and *Anything Goes*.

BERKSHIRE PUBLIC THEATRE, Box 860, 30 Union St., Pittsfield MA 01202. (413)445-4631. Artistic Director: Frank Bessell. Play producer. Produces 8 plays (2 musicals)/year. "Plays are performed in a 285-seat proscenium thrust theatre for a general audience of all ages with wide-ranging tastes." Pays negotiable royalty or negotiable amount per performance. Query first. SASE. Reports in 6 weeks.
Musical Theatre: Seeking musicals with "no more than 3 acts (2½ hours). We look for fresh musicals with something to say. Our company has a flexible vocal range. Cast size must be 2-50, no more, with a small orchestra (up to 8)." Would also consider original music "for a play being developed and possibly for existing works."
Productions: *Curse of the Starving Class*, by Sam Shepard (alcoholism, death of the West); *A Christmas Carol* (original adaption), by Charles Dickens (ghostly redemption of a miser); and *L'Histoire du Soldat*, by Igor Stravinsky (selling a soldier's soul to the devil).

Tips: "We are a small company. Patience is a must. Be yourself—open, honest. Experience is not necessary but is helpful. We don't have a lot of money but we are long on nurturing artists!"

*BIGFORK SUMMER PLAYHOUSE,Box 456, Bigfork MT 59911. (406)837-4886 (May through September); (406)837-6843 (winter). Producer: Donald E. Thomson. Produces 4 new musicals/year. Plays are performed for a "varied audience of all ages in a new 500-seat proscenium theater." Query first. SASE.
Musical Theatre: Seeks "all types of musicals—we are in the process of establishing an institute of musical theatre and will be looking for people interested in this endeavor. We work within a budget— normal company size limited to 20-25." Would also consider original music for use in a play being developed.
Productions: *Anything Goes*, by Cole Porter (musical comedy); *Cabaret*, by Joe Masteroff and John Kander (musical); and *Annie Get Your Gun*, by Irving Berlin (musical comedy).
Tips: "Musical comedies are needed today—producers are having to resort to "recycling" older established shows. All topics and areas are open to creative musicians."

BOARSHEAD: MICHIGAN PUBLIC THEATER, 425 S. Grand Ave., Lansing MI 48933. (517)484-7800. Artistic Director: John Peakes. Play producer. Produces 9 plays/year. Audiences are "mainly white upper-middle-class, college-educated, middle-aged." Theatre capacity is 249 with ¾ thrust stage. Pays 6-9% royalty or $65/peformance. Query with synopsis, character breakdown and set description. SASE.
Musical Theatre: Seeking musicals with "small cast, 2 acts or cabaret length, and limited orchestration. Can be political or social commentary. New experimental forms are fine. Intelligent, witty, sensitive, good plays are what we look for. Four to eight characters in cast is common—ideal cast size is 4-5. We work with an extremely tight budget." Does not wish to see "large casts, extensive set changes or orchestration."
Productions: *Homme*, by Samm-Art Williams; and *Musical Review*, by Jacques Brel.
Tips: "We are currently sponsoring *Winterfare*, our annual festival and showcase new work."

CALIFORNIA STATE COLLEGE, BAKERSFIELD, DEPARTMENT OF FINE ARTS, 9001 Stockdale Hwy., Bakersfield CA 93311. (805)833-3093. Assistant Professor of Theater: Jeffrey Mason. Associate Professor of Theater: Anita Mucha-DuPratt. Chairman, Fine Arts: Jerome Kleinsasser. Play producer. Produces 3 plays/year (musical occasionally). Plays performed in the 500-seat Dore Theatre to the college community and the community at large. Pays minimum $25/performance. Query. Does not return unsolicited material. Reports in 1 month.
Musical Theatre: Looking for "exciting plays with unit set and small casts."
Productions: *Antigone*; *Candida*; and *Measure For Measure*.

CAPITAL REPERTORY COMPANY, Box 399, Albany NY 12201-0399. (518)462-4531. Producing Director: Peter H. Clough. Produces 6 plays (1 musical)/year. Pays 5-7% royalty. Query with synopsis, character breakdown and set description. SASE. Reports in 10 weeks.
Musical Theatre: Seeking musicals that are "small in production scale with a meaningful and relevant theme and maximum of 12 characters." Would also consider original music for use in a play being developed.
Productions: *Emmett*, by Toni Morrison; *November*, by Don Nigro; and *Phantom of the Opera*, by Masterson/Bishop (musical horror).

WILLIAM CAREY COLLEGE DINNER THEATRE, William Carey College, Hattiesburg MS 39401. (601)582-5051, ext. 228. Managing Director: O.L. Quave. Play producer. Produces 2 plays (2 musicals)/year. "Our dinner theater operates only in summer and plays to family audiences." Payment negotiable. Submit complete manuscript and score. SASE. Reports as soon as possible.
Musical Theatre: "Plays should be simply-staged, have small casts (8-10), and be suitable for family viewing; two hours maximum length. Score should require piano only, or piano, electric piano, and drums."
Productions: *Ernest in Love*; *Rodgers and Hart: A Musical Celebration*; and *Side by Side*, by Sondheim.

CARROLL COLLEGE, Little Theatre, Helena MT 59625. (406)442-3450, ext. 308. Director of Theater: Jim Bartruff. Play producer. Produces 4-5 plays (1 musical)/year. "Our plays are produced in our Little Theatre for campus and community. The Little Theatre is a small proscenium house with flexible seating (90-120)." Pays $25-100/performance. Query or submit complete manuscript, score and tape of songs. SASE. Reports in 6 weeks.
Musical Theatre: "We consider all types of plays geared for small cast (8-12 people) and minimal set-

tings (unit preferred). Scoring should be for piano and percussion or an arrangement for guitar—keyboards—piano. Original material is preferred, but not readily available.''

Productions: *Good News*, by Schwab/De Sylva/Brown/Henderson (1920s campus life); *Joseph and the Amazing Technicolor Dreamcoat*, by Weber/Rice (Old Testament); and *A God in the Bush Is Worth Two in the Hand*, by Harper/Holmes (an original musical based on the life of Moses).

Tips: "Find a place, any place, to do it and get it done. Stay involved with the production. Don't be afraid to make changes if you need to. The best way to discover 'what works' is to get it done. There are literally thousands of little markets yearning for new and good material."

CENTENARY COLLEGE, THEATRE DEPARTMENT, Shreveport LA 71134-1188. (318)869-5011. Chairman: Robert R. Buseick. Play producer. Produces 6 plays (2 musicals)/year. Plays are presented in a 350-seat playhouse to college and community audiences. Submit manuscript and score. SASE. Reports in 1 month.

Productions: *Annie*; *Moliere*; *Baby*, *A Day in Hollywood/A Night in the Ukraine*; and *A Little Shop of Horrors*.

*CHARLOTTETOWN FESTIVAL,Box 848, Charlottetown, Prince Edward Island C1A 7L9 Canada. Artistic Director: Walter Learning. Play producer. Produces 4 plays, 4 musicals and 1-2 new musicals/ year. Plays are performed for "a large general audience in our 1100-seat festival theatre, 187-seat Mackenzie theatre, or 100-seat cabaret theatre." Pays 4-12% royalty. Submit complete manuscript, score and tape of songs. SAE and IRC. Reports in 4 months.

Productions: *Anne of Green Gables*, by Harron and Campbell (family); *Are You Lonesome Tonight*, by Alan Bleasdale (mature audiences); and *Babes, Bless Them All*, by Cliff Jones (general).

CHICAGO SHAKESPEARE COMPANY, 2647 N. Greenview, Chicago IL 60614. (312)871-8961. Artistic Director: Myron Freedman. Play producer. Produces 3 plays/year (no musicals). "We perform Shakespeare's plays year-round. During the summer we are touring outdoor theatres. We often need music for ambiance, transitions, songs within plays, etc." Pays per negotiable contract. Query first. Does not return unsolicited material.

Musical Theatre: "We seek music to complement our productions of Shakespeare. Occasionally we need melodies for his songs. We are very eclectic in our emphasis. The composer would work closely with the director in creating suitable music. Our emphasis on all production elements is minimal. We do not wish to see musicals."

Productions: *Midsummer Night's Dream, Measure for Measure, Twelfth Night*, and *A Winter's Tale*, all by William Shakespeare.

CIRCA' 21 DINNER PLAYHOUSE, Box 784, 1828 3rd Ave., Rock Island IL 61201. (309)786-2667. Producer: Dennis Hitchcock. Play producer. Produces 5 plays (3 musicals)/year. Plays produced for a general audience. Two children's works per year, concurrent with major productions. Pays by royalty. Query with synopis, character breakdown and set description or submit complete ms, score and tape of songs. SASE. Reports in 6 weeks.

Musical Theater: "We prefer 2-act children's musicals, 1½ hour limit with cast of no more than 8-12, piano and percussion accompaniment, and limited scenic requirements. Folk or fairy tale themes. Works that do not condescend to a young audience yet are appropriate for entire family. We're also seeking full-length, small cast musicals suitable for a broad audience." Would also consider original music for use in a play being developed.

Productions: *A Chorus Line*, by James Kirkwood/Marvin Hamlisch; *Oklahoma*, by Rogers and Hammerstein; *Mame*, by Jerry Herman; and *Hansel and Gretel*, with orignal music by John Luebker.

Tips: "Small, upbeat, tourable musicals (like *Pump Boys*) and bright musically-sharp children's productions (like *Prince Street Players*) work best. Keep an open mind. Stretch to encompass a musical variety—different keys, rhythms, musical ideas and textures."

CIRCLE IN THE SQUARE THEATRE, 1633 Broadway, New York NY 10019. (212)307-2700. Contact: Literary Advisor. Play producer. Produces 3 plays/year; occasionally produces a musical. Query with a letter and 1-page synopsis. Reports in 3-4 months.

Musical Theatre: "We are actively looking for original material."

Production: *Pal Joey*.

THE CLEVELAND PLAY HOUSE, Box 1989, 8500 Euclid Ave., Cleveland OH 44106. (216)795-7010, ext. 55. Dramaturg: Wayne Turney. Play producer. Produces 9 plays (2 musicals)/year. "Our audience is conservative but will definitely rise to an intellectual/musical challenge. We have three proscenium arch theatres: The Brooks—capacity 160; the Drury—capacity 499; and the Bolton—capacity 612. The two larger theatres have full flies and traps as well as orchestra pits. We negotiate with agent

and/or author for each production." Query with synopsis. SASE. Reports as soon as possible.
Musical Theatre: "We are completely flexible and have produced many classics as well as a number of new works. We do only full length work, and favor topics of 'universal' import—we don't go for the trendy. We are especially interested in smaller cast musicals (isn't everyone?) and women's roles. We can do most anything *if* the quality of the play warrants it."
Productions: *Canterbury Tales*, by Starkey/Coghill; *A Day in Hollywood/A Night in the Ukraine*, by Vosburgh/Lazarus (movies); and *The Robber Bridegroom*, by Uhry/Waldman (folk tale/love story).
Tips: Looking for "quality in everything from your writing to your typing. Also originality. There are so many classical musicals we long for something new. Give us the new and you've got it made."

*COCKPIT IN COURT SUMMER THEATRE, Essex Community College, Baltimore MD 21237. (301)522-1434. Managing Director: F. Scott Black. Play producer. Produces 8 plays (4 musicals)/year. "We operate four separate theaters on our campus. Broadway type musicals are performed in a well-equipped, beautiful theater. Cockpit, upstairs, is a cabaret theater. Classics are performed outdoors in the courtyard with stylized sets and full makeup. The children's theater, the Court Jesters, is located in the lecture hall of the administration building." Pays through rental and royalty agreement with firms who control rights. Submit complete manuscript and score. SASE. Reports in 1 month.
Musical Theatre: "Wholesome shows which are suitable for audiences of all ages. Musical score should be of top quality. We use a full orchestra in the pit. Large casts are OK. We like good leading and supporting roles. We prefer a cast of 20-30 for most of our summer musicals with some doubling. We use wagon sets, no turntables or revolving stages. We are also looking for small cabaret musicals or musical reviews."
Productions: *Hello Dolly*, *Chorus Line*, and *Edith Piaf*; and original musicals *Snow White* and *Tom Sawyer*.

THE COLONY/STUDIO THEATRE PLAYHOUSE, 1944 Riverside Dr., Los Angeles CA 90039. Literary Manager: Todd Nielsen. Play producer. Produces 10 plays (2 musicals)/year. Plays produced for "general audiences, mixed age range. Plays performed on thrust stage in 99-seat Equity waiver house." Pays $25-35 per performance. Query with synopsis, character breakdown and set description. SASE. Reports in 9 months.
Musical Theatre: Seeking "any topic. Set and cast requirements should not be great, same for number of musicians required. No overly vulgar or negative pieces of theatre work." Would also consider original music for use in a play being developed.
Productions: *The Robber Bridegroom*, by Alfred Uhry (folk tale musical); *Duck d'Amour*, by George Tibbles (French farce); and *Bearcat*, by Bob Wilson (comic-drama).
Tips: "We are seeking previously unproduced works for our New Play Festival."

*CORTLAND REPERTORY THEATRE, Box 783, Cortland NY 13045. (607)753-6161. Managing Director: Stella B. Syracuse. Play producer. Produces 5 plays (3 musicals)/year. "Our plays are performed in a rustic county park pavillion. Summer stock—light, gay musicals." Pays 6-10% royalty. Query with synopsis, character breakdown and set description. Does not return unsolicited material.
Musical Theatre: Seeks "primarily adult musicals that appeal to a summer audience. Mystery, fantasy and comedy are great elements. Small to medium cast, small staging, small instrument combo—we use no more than a pit band." Would consider original music for use in a play being developed.
Productions: *Summer Stock Murder*, by Kingsley Day (original murder/mystery musical); and *Westward Holmes*, by Sally Netzel/David Pursely (original period musical).
Tips: "A beginning writer must make contacts. We deal with people who we know or have been recommended. We have produced 3 new plays in the last 5 years and we are planning another. We know the quality of our writers because someone on our staff has worked with these writers previously."

CREATIVE HORIZONS, (formerly Musical Horizons), Suite 141, 19050 Colima Rd., Rowland Heights CA 91748. (818)965-6604. Creative Coordinators: Michael Ricciardi, David Holmes and Michele Bufone. Musical Director: Eric Schmidt. Play producer and publisher. "We are also a writers' organization in the process of developing a creative repertory company." Publishes/produces 3-4 musicals/year. "We are a growing organization of writers. We have been producing our own work in equity-waiver productions, community theaters and local high schools. We also have access to our own equity-waiver theater in Hollywood, and our literary agent provides needed industry contacts. We are always looking for new writers (composers and librettists), especially in the field of musical comedy, who would bring new vision to both musicals and straight plays. We are also looking for good tech people to create the costume, choreography, and lighting and sound guides we want to bring out with each show. We have a standard royalty schedule and at present work on 50/50 split. Arrangers are needed and are paid outright if no profit participation expected." Query with synopsis. Include tape of show's opening number, and "11 o'clock song (a song like 'Everything's Coming Up Roses' from *Gypsy*). If you submit a complete manuscript it should be in standard script format with all lyrics printed or within the scripts. When we ask for a script from a synopsis and tape, be sure to include a character description, a list of scenes, a complete tape of all musical numbers you have available. Simple piano OK. A set sketch would be most helpful. Be sure all work is copyrighted before submitting." SASE, but use a pre-printed reply form or postcard. Reports ASAP: synopsis with 3-song tape, usually within 1 month; complete manuscript with score, usually within 3 months. "We will be offering a catalog to schools and little theatres."

Musical Theatre: "Any audience-pleasing, well-plotted show with a good story line—anything creative without being vulgar. We prefer musicals in two acts, but would like to see musical one-acts, thematically related. Show ideas should be *universally* appealing, with characters the average theater-goer would care about; we don't want to see any unbelievable characters, stereotyped story lines or reworks of tired formulas. Be original. Work with a classic story in the public domain first to get your feet wet. Go from there to conceive new ideas. There *is* room in theater for original story lines. Also, keep it simple. Excessive sets, costumes, and scenery description don't make the show. Casts should be 5-21 people with good roles for both men and women. We look for musical biographies, fantasies and comedies and musical adventures like *Man of La Mancha*. We are all members of the Dramatists Guild of America and welcome other members."

Productions: *The Wizard of Oz* (original adaptation of classic story with new original score); *Skylark*, (a teenager growing up in Shakespeare's time); *A Moment With Mister "C"*, (Christmas musical fantasy); *Return of the Wizard of Oz* (sequel to the famous Oz story); and workshop productions of *King of the Colonies* (Louis XVI escape to America).

Tips: "Don't ever give up. Develop your craft every single day. Keep writer's notebooks. We want to work with new writers and possibly bring them directly into our organization working with us in a collaborative association. Please be certain you know what a musical is all about. Those who live in the California area might do well by writing us a letter about themselves, their skills, and their aspriations to write musicals. Pop songwriters are encouraged to send material, as these ideas can be developed into musicals as well."

THE CRICKET THEATRE, 9 W. 14th St., Minneapolis MN 55403. (612)871-3763. Artistic Director: William Partlan. Play producer. Produces 4 main stage shows, also Works-in-Progress shows. Pays negotiable royalty; or per diem, honorarium or commission. Submit one scene and cassette tape of songs. SASE. Reports in 6 months.

Musical Theatre: "We seek chamber musicals and cabaret with small cast and small orchestra—mainstream yet adventurous. New American playwrights and songwriters can use our Works-In-Progress program to develop new work."

Productions: *Billy Bishop Goes to War*, by John Gray with Eric Peterson (WWI Ace); *Tintypes* (immigrants in early 20th century US); and *Side by Side*, by Sondheim.

Tips: "Try to get a workshop of play done at the theatre you wish to work with."

CYPRESS COLLEGE THEATER ARTS DEPARTMENT, 9200 Valley View St., Cypress CA 90630. (714)826-4221. Contact: Theater Arts Department Chairman. Play producer. Produces 6-7 plays (2 musicals)/year. "Our audience at Cypress College is basically a middle-class, suburban audience. We have a continuing audience that we have built up over the years. Our plays now are produced in our Campus Theater (seating capacity 623) or workshop theater (maximum seating capacity 250)." Payment varies with each production. Submit complete manuscript, score and 7½ ips reel-to-reel tape of songs. SASE. Reports in 1 month.

Musical Theatre: "We must do large-cast shows, generally, because the shows are done as a class. Because we are on a slightly limited budget, we must look carefully at scenery requirements, costume requirements and props."

Productions: *Damn Yankees*; *A Funny Thing Happened on the Way to the Forum*; *The Cherry Orchard*; *Taming of the Shrew*; *Man for All Seasons*; and *Our Town*.

Tips: "Open show with a large group, energetic number. Intersperse dance (especially tap) throughout shows and end with a 'ripping' choral number."

DEPARTMENT OF THEATRE ARTS, SUNY—New Paltz, New Paltz NY 12561. (914)257-2081. Chairman: Joseph Paparone. Director of Production: Frank Kraat. Play producer. Produces 7 plays (3 musicals)/year. "Plays are performed on a college campus, with the audience comprised of community and student members." Pays according to individual arrangements. Submit complete manuscript, score and tape of songs. SASE. Reports in 4 weeks.

Musical Theatre: "All types of musicals are considered. Complete staging cannot cost over $8,000 by our requirements. Facilities are owned and operated by the state of New York." Would also consider original music for use in a play being developed.

Productions: *Swan Down Gloves*, by Bille Brown (English pantomine); *Jaques Brel*; *Rock'n'*, by D. George (rock musical); and *After Theatre, Theatre*, by B. Brumm and L. Yando (cabaret).

THE DRAMATIC PUBLISHING COMPANY, 311 Washington St., Woodstock IL 60098. (815)338-7170. Editor: Sally Fyfe. Play publisher. Publishes 35 plays (3-5 musicals)/year. Plays used by community theatres, little theatres, high schools, colleges, stock and professional theatres, churches and camps. Pays standard royalty. Submit complete manuscript, score and tape of songs. SASE. Reports in 5 months.
Musical Theatre: Seeking "children's musicals not over 1¼ hours, and adult musicals with 2 act format. No adaptations for which the rights to use the original work have not been cleared. If directed toward high school market, large casts with many female roles are preferred. For professional, stock, and community theatre small casts are better. Cost of producing a play is always a factor to consider in regard to costumes, scenery and special effects." Would also consider original music for use in a pre-existtng play "if we or the composer hold the rights to the non-musical work."
Publications: *A Tale of Two Cities*, by Peterson and Nestor (Dickens' story); *The Amazing Einstein*, by Tasca/Drachman/Tierney (life of Albert Einstein); *A Child's Christmas in Wales*, by Brooks and Mitchell (Dylan Thomas' story); and *Animal Farm*, by Hall/Mitchell/Peaslee (George Orwell's story).

EMPIRE STATE INSTITUTE FOR THE PERFORMING ARTS (ESIPA), Empire State Plaza, Albany NY 12223. (518)443-5222. Literary Manager: Barbara R. Maggio. Play producer. Produces approximately 6 plays (2 musicals)/year. Plays performed for student audiences grades K-12, family audiences and adult audiences. Two theatres: main theatre seats 950 with full stage, studio theatre seats 450 with smaller stage. Pay negotiable. Submit complete manuscript, score and tape of songs. SASE. Reports in 4 months.
Musical Theatre: Looking for "intelligent and well-written book with substance, a score that enhances and supplements the book and is musically well-crafted and theatrical. Length: up to 2 hours. Could be play with music, musical comedy, musical drama, or opera. Excellence and substance in material is essential. Cast could be up to 25; orchestra size up to 15. No incomplete scripts and scores."
Productions: *Raggedy Ann*, by William Gibson/Joe Raposo (musical play); *Wind in the Willows*, by Jakes/Stravelo (musical comedy); and *Prince & the Pauper*, by Vrecke/Leslie/Alexander (play with music).
Tips: "There is a great need for musicals that are well-written with intelligence and substance and suitable for young audiences."

*FLORIDA STUDIO THEATRE,1241 N. Palm Ave., Sarasota FL 33577. (813)366-9017. Director of New Play Development: Jeff Mousseau. Play producer. Produces 2 plays and 2 musicals/year. "Florida Studio Theatre is a professional, non-profit theatre. It seats 165 and has limited technical abilities. The audience is generally comprised of well-educated people over 50 years of age. FST subscribers expect innovative, contemporary theatre." Pays by royalty. "Workshop productions receive $200 honorarium." Query with synopsis, character breakdown and set description. SASE. Reports in 6 months.
Musical Theatre: "FST is looking for smaller cast musicals and cabaret musicals. We prefers innovative or off-beat shows. The stage is small. There is no pit. In the past we have had a 3 person musical combo. Send letter of inquiry first. A tape included with the script and score is helpful." Would also consider original music for use in pre-existing play. "Two of the straight plays we are putting on in the future will have original music underscoring."
Productions: *Billy Bishop Goes To War*, by John Gray, (WWI flying ace); *Little Shop of Horrors*, by Ashman/Menken, (plants take over the world); and *Ain't Misbehavin'*, by Fats Waller, (musical review).

FMT, Box 92127, Milwaukee WI 53202. (414)271-8484. Artistic Director: Michael Moynihan. Play producer. Produces 3-5 plays (3-4 musicals)/year. Plays are performed for family, juvenile and general audiences. All plays tour. Pays $200-1,200 outright purchase or $10/performance. Query first with synopsis, character breakdown, set description and tape of songs. SASE. Reports in 8 weeks.
Musical Theatre: "FMT develops new works and prefers to work in process rather than produce prewritten material." Will consider original music for use in a play being developed.
Productions: *The Cream City Semi-Circus*, and *Transformations* (company developed—various subject matter); and *The Snow Queen*, adapted from A.C. Andersen by M. Moynihan and A. Melchior (children's story).
Tips: "Writers should be interested in the company. See our work; volunteer your services. Create work that you care about (passionately)."

SAMUEL FRENCH, INC., 45 W. 25th St., New York NY 10010. (212)206-8990. Editor: Lawrence R. Harbison. Play publisher. Publishes about 80 scripts (8 musicals)/year. Plays used by community, stock and dinner theaters, regional repertories, and college and high school markets. Pays 10% royalty on play scripts sold, generally an advance against future royalties, and a per-performance royalty depending on various factors. "We take 10-20% agency fee. Submit only the libretto (book). If we like it, we may ask to hear music." SASE. Reports in 8 weeks minimum. If the work has been recommended for further consideration, the process may take considerably longer.

Musical Theatre: "We publish primarily New York-produced musicals, though we do occasionally bring out a show which has not had a New York City production. These are intended primarily, but not necessarily, for children's, community and dinner theaters. No religious material. We are particularly looking for small-cast, easy-to-produce musicals with good female roles. We are not interested in publishing big, splashy 'Broadway' musicals—unless they have been done on Broadway. Send us only the book of your musical. Musicals succeed or fail on the basis of their book, not their music. If we like the book, we may ask to hear a tape of the score."

Publications: *Nunsense*, by Dan Goggin; *Three Guys Naked from the Waist Down*, by Michael Rupert and Jerry Colker; and *Women in White*, by Jack Sharkey and Tim Kelly.

Tips: "Start small. Do a small-cast, easy-to-produce, inexpensive show. Then, once you have achieved a 'track record,' only then, try your Broadway musical. Never, ever, imitate what you think is 'commercial'—it never *will* be. Remember that musicals today are practically operas. In other words, they are mostly sung. Work with a director to develop concept."

THE GOODMAN THEATRE, 200 S. Columbus Dr., Chicago IL 60603. (312)443-3811. Artistic Director: Robert Falls. Occasionally produces musicals. Submit synopsis (summary, production demands, cast size, style, etc.) with SASE for consideration. No unsolicited manuscripts. Send to the Office of the Dramaturg, Tom Creamer.

GREEN MOUNTAIN GUILD, Box 548, Pittsfield VT 05762. (802)746-8320. Managing Director: Marjorie O'Neill-Butler. Play producer. Produces 18 plays (8-10 musicals)/year. Produces plays for a summer theater audience in Killington, Vermont. Pays $75 minimum/performance. Query with synopsis. Send script and cassette with music. SASE. Reports in 1 month.

Musical Theatre: "We are looking for musicals with a small cast, a good story line, well-developed characters, songs and music that come naturally out of the story and music that works with piano and drums only." No frivolous material. Prefers one-set shows.

Productions: *Jenny Lind*, by David Harlay (an original play); *Sweeney Todd*, by Stephen Sondheim; *Student Prince*, by Sigmund Romberg; *Naughty Marietta*, by Victor Herbert; and *Hello Dolly*, by Jerry Herman.

HERITAGE ARTISTS AT THE MUSIC HALL, Box 586, Cohoes NY 12047. (518)235-7909. Producing Director: Robert W. Tolan. Play producer. Produces 6-8 plays/year (all musicals). "We perform a subscription series of small and/or principal musicals in the 250-300 seat Cohoes Music Hall." Pays negotiable royalty per performance. Submit complete manuscript and tape of song. SASE. Reports in 8 weeks.

Musical Theatre: Seeking "adult themes, plays with music, review/cabaret shows and children's musicals." Requires "smaller casts." Would also consider original music for use in a play being developed.

Productions: *Baby*, by Pearson, Maltby, Shire (parenthood); *Billy Bishop Goes to War*, by John Gray, Eric Peterson (WWI air ace); and *The Wonder Years*, by David Levy, et.al. (baby boom).

HOWARD UNIVERSITY, Department of Drama/College of Fine Arts, Washington DC 20059. (202)636-7050. Chairperson: Dr. Carole W. Singleton. Play producer. Produces 5-6 plays (at least 1 musical)/year. "Plays are produced in a 300-seat theatre for a general audience, or in a 75-seat experimental space for student audiences." Pays $50-75/performance. Submit complete manuscript and cassette of songs. SASE. Reports in 4 months.

Productions: *Black Images/Black Reflections*, by Kelsey Collie; *The Whiz* by Charlie Smalls, choreographed by Lewis Johnson; *Black Birds*, by Howard Roberts; *The Fantastics*; *The Sound of Soul*, by Owen Dodson; *Raisin*; *The Me Nobody Knows*; and *Tambourines to Glory*, by Hughes.

ILLINOIS THEATRE CENTER, 400A Lakewood, Park Forest IL 60466. (312)481-3510. Artistic Director: Steve S. Billig. Play producer and resident theatre. Produces 8 plays (3 musicals)/year. "We are a subscription theatre—equity during season, non-equity during summer." Pays by royalty or per performance. "These are negotiable and vary with publisher." Query with synopsis, character breakdown and set description; or submit complete manuscript, score and tape of songs. SASE. Reports in 2 weeks.

Musical Theatre: Looking for "themes of family interest—humor preferable to drama—with small cast. No topical satire."

Productions: *Charlotte Sweet*, by Michael Colby (Victorian melodrama—all music); *Joseph and the Amazing Technicolor Dreamcoat*, by Weber & Rice (rock musical); and *Most Happy Fella*, by Frank Loesser (dramatic musical).

ILLUSTRATED STAGE COMPANY, 25 Van Ness Ave., San Francisco CA 94102. Executive Director: Barbara Malinowski. Play producer. Produces various number of plays and musicals/year. Plays performed for San Francisco Bay Area audiences. Pay varies. Query with synopsis, character breakdown, set description and tape of songs. SASE. Reports in 3 months.
Musical Theatre: Would consider original music for use in a play being developed.
Productions: *Dylan Thomas*, by Kevin Reilly (life of the poet); *Doo Wop*, (Black musical); and *Dan White Incident*, by Steve Dobbins (actual recreational of the Dan White case).

INDIANA REPERTORY THEATRE, 140 W. Washington, Indianapolis IN 46204. (317)635-5277. Artistic Associate: Janet Allen. Produces 10 full-length plays (10 cabarets)/year. Audiences are: "Mainstage (occasional full-length musical: conservative, middle-class audience, accustomed to classics; Upperstage: more liberal, younger audience, will accept a certain amount of experimentation and new forms; Cabaret: a regular audience which expects a 90-minute, musical format, comic piece. A certain amount of irreverence is expected, satire is welcome." Pays 5-6% royalty. Query with synopsis. SASE. Reports in 2-3 months.
Musical Theatre: "Our main forum for new musicals is our Cabaret Theatre. We rarely consider new musicals for either of our other 2 theatres. Our Cabaret Theatre runs all year, is a nightclub setting, and is set up for 90-minute performances, due to production schedule. Musicals can take the form of revue or plotted material, are often composer retrospective shows or modern comedy situations. All shows accompanied by piano only. Cast size cannot exceed 5 (4 is usual); *very* minimal staging (the stage is 8'x15'); simple props but no scenery except backdrop; costumes are emblematic—evening wear with added pieces is standard."
Productions: Upperstage—*Pump Boys and Dinettes*, by Tommy Thompson et al; Mainstage—*South Pacific*, by Rodgers and Hammerstein; *Tintypes*, by Mel Marvin (turn of the century nostalgia); *Murder in the Capitol*, by Tom Haas (40's mystery spoof); *Ho, Ho, Ho, The Christmas Show* (plotless seasonal collection) and *Annette Saves the World* (60s beach spoof), both by Paul Moser.

INTAR, INTERNATIONAL ARTS RELATIONS, INC., Box 788, New York NY 10108. (212)695-6134. Artistic Director: Max Ferra. Play producer. Produces 3 plays (1 musical)/year. Plays are performed in New York City. Pays $1,000-1,500. Query, submit complete manuscript and score, and/or send resume. SASE. Reports in 1 month.
Musical Theatre: "We are seeking material by Hispanics about Hispanics with a maximum cast of 10 and minimum 5 musicians." Length: 1-1½ hours.
Productions: *Lovers and Keepers*, book and lyrics by Maria Irene Forives, music by Tito Puente and Fernando Rivas; and *Santiago The Birdman*, book and lyrics by Alonso Alegria, music by Fernando Rivas.

JEWISH REPERTORY THEATRE, 344 E. 14th St., New York NY 10003. (212)674-7200. Associate Director: Edward M. Cohen. Play producer. Produces 5 plays (2 musicals)/year. Pays 4-6% royalty. Submit complete manuscript, score and tape of songs. SASE. Reports in 4 weeks.
Musical Theatre: Seeking "musicals in English relating to the Jewish experience. No more than 8 characters."
Productions: *Kumi—Leml* (musical farce); *The Special* (musical comedy); and *The Shop on Main Street* (drama).

*THE JULIAN THEATRE, 953 De Haro St., San Francisco CA 94107. (415)647-8098. Artistic Director: Richard Reineccius. Play producer. Produces 2 new plays and 1 new musical/year plus many more co-productions. "Our audience is very diverse in socio-economic and cultural backgrounds—mostly working and middle class—interracial audience. We are a 22-year-old community theatre." Pays by royalty or per performance. Query with synopsis, character breakdown and set description. SASE. Reports in 6 months.
Musical Theatre: "We prefer new musicals with strong socio-political, historical or literary relevance. Because of scarce funding, we like to work with smaller casts (12 or under), and simple set designs. We do mostly plays for adult audiences, but are interested in doing more plays for children as we did in our early years."
Produced: *Sinning In Sun City*, by Selaelo Maredi and Ed Bullins (entertainment industry in South Africa); *The Belles of the Barbary Coast*, by Damaris Price (early San Francisco love); and *Andrea's Got Two Boyfriends*, by David Willinger (the lives of 3 retarded adults and their social worker).

*LAMB'S PLAYERS THEATRE, Box 26, National City CA 92050. (619)474-3385. Literary Manager: Kerry Cederberg. Play producer. Produces 7 plays, 2 musicals and 1 new musical/year. Plays are performed for a "varied audience—often families and church groups—in a 175 seat theatre with arena stage." Pays outright purchase of $500-1,500 or $50 per performance. Query with synopsis, character

breakdown and set description. SASE. Reports in 4 months.
Musical Theatre: Seeks full length musicals, "open to any topics, but from a broad based Christian perspective—not necessarily 'religious'. We prefer small cast, versatile staging and a small musical ensemble. No gratuitous sex, nudity or foul language."
Productions: *Godspell, Cotton Patch Gospel*, and *Tintypes*.

LOS ANGELES (INNER CITY) CULTURAL CENTER, 1308 S. New Hampshire Ave., Los Angeles CA 90006. (213)387-1161. Contact: Executive Director. Produces 6-8 plays (3 musicals)/year. A "multiethnic, multi-cultural arts organization." Pays 6% royalty. Query with synopsis. Does not return unsolicited material. Reports in 3 months.
Musical Theatre: "Those with a point of view that lend themselves to utilizing people of all ethnic backgrounds."
Productions: *Wings and Things*, music and lyrics by Mickey Stevens, book by Lonnie Stevenson ("angel" can't get past the pearly gates and must return to earth to make up for past mistakes); and *What Is to Be Done?*, by C. Bernard Jackson (political musical exploring the catostrophic events in contemporary South Africa).

MANHATTAN THEATRE CLUB, 453 W. 16th St., New York NY 10011. (212)645-5590. Literary Manager: Tom Szentgyorgyi. Artistic Assistant: Jonathan Alper. Play producer. Produces 10 plays (1-2 musicals)/year. Plays are performed at the Manhattan Theatre Club before varied audiences. Pays negotiated fee. Query with synopsis, "5-10 page libretto and lyric sample." SASE. Reports in 6 months.
Musical Theatre: "Small cast, original work. *No* historical drama, verse drama or children's plays."
Productions: *Real Life Funnies*, by Alan Menken and Howard Ashman (topical New York City); *Livin' Dolls*, by Scott Wittman and Marc Shaiman; *Ain't Misbehavin'*, by Fats Waller and Richard Maltby; *On the Swing Shift*, by Michael Dansicker and Sarah Schlesinger; and *New Tunes*, by Jonathon Sheffer and Alan Paul (revue).

MERIWETHER PUBLISHING, LTD. (CONTEMPORARY DRAMA SERVICE), 885 Elkton Dr., Colorado Springs CO 80907. (303)594-4422. Editor/President: Arthur Zapel. Play publisher. Publishes 70 new plays (5-10 musicals)/year. "We publish musicals for church school elementary, middle grade and teens. We also publish musicals for high school secular use. Our musicals are performed in churches or high schools." Pays 10% royalty or $150-750 outright purchase. "Sometimes we pay a royalty to a limited maximum." Query with synopsis, character breakdown and set description or submit script with cassette tape of songs. SASE. Reports in 2 months.
Musical Theatre: "We are always looking for good church/school musicals for children. We prefer a length of 15-20 minutes, though occasionally we will publish a 3-act musical adaptation of a classic with large casts and sets. We like informal styles, with a touch of humor, that allow many children and/or adults to participate. Musical scripts with piano accompaniments and guitar chords are best. We especially welcome short musicals for church use during the holidays of Christmas and Easter. We have more need for the kind of simple musicals that elementary or junior high children can perform. We would like to know of musicians who could adapt one of our best selling plays to musical form. Also we need to know of arrangers and copyists."
Publications: *Bicycles Built for Two*, by Kehret and Wiggins (family love story); *S.H.S. Pinafore*, by W.S. Kilbourne (a modern adaptation of the Gilbert and Sullivan classic); and *Dave*, by Hank Beebe (adaptation of the David and Goliath story).
Tips: "Keep the music manageable for unprofessional performers. Keep music book costs to a minimum in terms of arrangements and copy or engraving expenses. We will look only at materials that are neatly presented and of professional quality. Anything not completely developed is returned immediately. If the musician can provide a camera-ready music score we are more inclined to publish the work. The competition with Broadway name musicals is great. New musicals must have competitive appeal."

*ALAN W. MIANULLI, Pennsylvania Centre Stage, 213 Arts Building, University Park PA 16802. (814)865-7366. Producing Director: Alan W. Mianulli. Play producer. Estab. 1986. Produces 2 plays and 2 musicals/year. "Plays are performed in a fully-equipped 430-seat proscenium theatre to an audience from the greater center region of Pennys.lvania." Pays by royalty. Query with synopsis, character breakdown and set description or submit complete manuscript, score and tape of songs. SASE. Reports in 10 weeks.
Musical Theatre: "Seeking new musicals with small casts (12), simple technical demands. Interested in pieces stressing social issues but non-sexual themes." Would also consider original music for use in a play being developed, "for underscoring, etc."
Productions: *Peter Pan*, (re-orchestrated standard version); *Anything Goes*, (a bi-racial production); and *Rainmaker*, (incorporating original music).
Tips: "Try to have your musical done in a workshop setting before submitting it to a producer."

*MICHIGAN STATE UNIVERSITY, DEPARTMENT OF THEATRE,, 149 Auditorium, East Lansing MI 48824. (517)353-5169. Director: Dr. Jon Baisch. Play producer. Produces 15 plays (4-6 large scale and 4-6 small revue musicals/year. "Our audiences are students, faculty, and members of the Lansing community. We use 8 theatres, ranging from 100 to 2,500 seats, including proscenium, platform, arena, and cabaret dinner theatre types. We stage everything from large-scale productions with orchestra and large casts to small-cast, intimate shows and cabaret entertainment." Performance rights negotiable. Query with synopsis and production specifications. SASE. Reports in 1 month.
Musical Theatre: "We are interested in all types of new musicals. However, we are espcially interested in small cast revues and book shows for cabaret and dinner theatre productions, and unusual material for our small arena and studio theatres."
Productions: *Godspell*; *Oliver*; and *Man of LaMancha*.
Tips: "Write a good, modern show. Either write a good story or find one to adapt. The public—much of it—still wants a story."

MID-PLAINS COMMUNITY COLLEGE, State Farm Rd., North Platte NE 69101. (308)532-8980. Chairman, Humanities Division and Theater Director: Colin Taylor. Play producer. Produces 3 plays (1 musical)/year. Plays performed "at the college auditorium (small house) and on tour to area schools." Pays $500 maximum royalty. Query with synopsis or submit complete manuscript and score. SASE. Reports in 1 month.
Musical Theatre: Needs musicals, prefers to work with a small cast, "flexible staging a necessity. Beginning singers need consideration. We cannot fly scenery, but use free-standing sets and projections in a 'theatre of light.' We work with a limited budget and unlimited imagination." Would also consider original music for use in a play being developed.
Productions: *Fiddler on the Roof*, (musical); *Grease*, (musical); *Antigone* (drama); and *Guys & Dolls* (musical).
Tips: "The ideal musical for us includes a balance of roles and a sensitivity to our Bible belt audience."

RALPH AND TEDI C. MILLER, Box 313, New Hope PA 18938. (215)862-2041. Owners: Ralph and Tedi C. Miller. Play producers. Produce 11 plays/year (all musicals). Plays are performed in Bucks County Playhouse, Falmouth Playhouse, Woodstock Playhouse or Pocono Playhouse. Range from 485-600 seat capacity. Three are seasonal theatres and one is year-round. Pay negotiable amount. Submit complete manuscript, score and tape of songs. SASE.
Musical Theatre: Seeking "all types of musicals including children's theatre, with average cast size of 20." Would possibly consider original music for use in a play being developed.
Productions: *The William*, by Jonathan Daly (handicaps).

*MUSICAL THEATRE WORKS, INC.,440 Lafayette Street, New York NY 10003. (212)677-0040. Associate Artistic Director: Mark Herko. Play producer of new musicals only. Produces 4 new musicals/ year plus 30 readings. "Readings are presented at our rehearsal studios on 440 Lafayette Street. Productions are mounted at CSC Rep Theatre on East 13th Street. No payment for production. Submit complete manuscript and tape of songs. SASE Reports in 3 months.
Musical Theatre: "We are seeking full-length book musicals which have never been produced. Ten to fourteen cast maximum. Productions are mounted with a minimum of sets, costumes and props. Only completed projects will be considered for development."
Productions: *A Romantic Detachment*, by J. Clifton and R. Treyz (Texas War of Independence); *Abyssinia*, by J. Racheff and T. Kociolek (black gospel musical); and *Starmites*, by B. Keating and S. Ross (outerspace science fiction rock musical).

MUSIC-THEATRE GROUP/LENOX ARTS CENTER, 735 Washington St., New York NY 10014. (212)924-3108. Managing Director: Diane Wondisford. Music-theatre producer. Produces 6 music-theatre pieces/year. Plays are performed "off-broadway in New York City; for summer audiences in Stockbridge, MA." Pays negotiable royalty or fees. Query with synopsis, character breakdown, set description and tape of music. SASE.
Musical Theatre: "We don't actually seek developed properties, but examples of people's work as an indication of their talent in the event that we might want to suggest them for a future collaboration. The music must be a driving element in the work. We generally require not more than 10-12 in cast and a small band of 4-5."
Productions: *The Garden of Earthly Delights* (based on Bosch's painting), by Martha Clarke, music by Richard Peaslee; *The Long Journey of Poppie Nongena*, by Elsa Joubert, music by Sophie Mgcina (South African apartheid); *The Mother of Us All*, by Virgil Thomson/Gertrude Stein (women's suffrage); *The Tennis Game*; *The Club*; *Nightclub Cantata*; *Dr. Selavy's Magic Theatre*; *Africanis Instructus*; *The Making of Americans*; *Vienna: Lusthaus*; and *The Hunger artists*.

*MUSKOKA FESTIVAL,Muskoka Foundation for the Arts, Box 1055, Gravenhurst Ontario P0C 1G0 Canada. (705)687-3303/8700. Artistic Director: Michael Ayoub. Play producer. Produces 4 plays, 3 musicals and 1 new musical/year. "Audience—adults, primarily summer cottagers, tourists. Children 5-10. Location—Muskoka, Ontario a major holiday/vacation/lakeland area." Pays 30% royalty or $100/performance. Query with synopsis, character breakdown and set description or submit complete manuscript, score and tape of songs. SASE. Reports in 5 months.
Musical Theatre: "Mainstage musicals—2 hour length with one intermission. We prefer comedy with underlying message but fun; revues or book musicals accepted. Children's musicals—target age 5-10, maximum length 1 hour with no intermission. Cast size 4-8. One set or easy turnaround for two/three sets as stages are small with no wings, no flies. All sets must also be suitable for touring: ease of set-up and strike. No more than three musicians." Would consider original music for a new musical version of existing play.
Productions: *Thin Ice*, by Jim Betts and Doug Ellis (Canadian hockey); *Paper Wheat*, a 25th Street Theatre Collective (prairie farmers); and *Return of the Curse of the Mummy's Revenge*, by Joey Miller and James Saar ("B" horror movies).
Tips: "Have patience, it's competitive. Think high quality fun!"

NEGRO ENSEMBLE COMPANY, Suite 409, 165 W. 46th St., New York NY 10036. (212)575-5860. Artistic Director: Douglas Turner Ward. Play producer. Produces 4 plays/year. Pays percentage of box office take. Submit complete manuscript and score. SASE. Returns material "only if writer insists, otherwise, play is kept on library file."
Musical Theatre: "Submit only plays that deal with black life and the black experience."
Production: *A Soldier's Play*, by Charles Fuller.

*THE NEW PLAYWRIGHT'S THEATRE, 1742 Church St. NW, Washington DC 20036. (202)232-1122 or 232-4527. Literary Manager: Kathryn C. Bryer. Play producer. "We do developmental work with playwrights." Produces 5 plays (1 musical)/year. For general audience with interest in new works. Payment individually negotiated, 6% royalty or 6% of gross receipts/performance. Submit synopsis, cassette and any 10 book pages. SASE. Reports in 4 months.
Musical Theatre: Seeks all types: revues, musical comedies and musical theater with strong story line. Does not want material that has had major, fully professional prior production. "We would like new themes and innovative approaches. No one acts, no children's musicals, no 'TV sitcoms,' nothing too elaborate. Instrumental forces should be chamber-size; no more than 12 musicians. Ten-twelve cast members at the most, with simple staging."
Productions: *Out of the Reach of Children*, by Cornelia Ravenal; *Nightmare!!*, by Zim Grundmann; and *Beautiful Lady*, by Elizabeth Swados.

*THE NEW ROSE THEATRE, 904 SW Main, Portland OR 97205. (503)222-2495. Artistic Director: Michael Griggs. Play producer. Produces 10-12 plays/year. "We perform classic plays for adults as well as for younger audiences—besides our 119 seat ¾ thrust theatre, we perform in a 300-400 seat flexible staging theatre and tour." Pays standard royalty or per performance. Query with synopsis, character breakdown and set description. Does not return unsolicited material. Reports in 6 months
Musical Theatre: "We really don't do musicals per se, but do consider using plays with music. We do classic plays, new adaptations and translations of such, and original music lends itself to these especially."
Productions: *Bad Marriages*, by James Bierman (Moliere adaptation); *Watch on the Rhine*, by Lillian Hellman; and *The House of Bernarda Alba*, by Lorca.

NEW TUNERS THEATRE,1225 W. Belmont, Chicago IL 60657. (312) 929-7367. Contact: Associate Producer. Play producer. Produces 3 musicals (2 new musicals)/year. "The theatre building where we work houses three 148-seat theatres." Pays 6-10% royalty. Query with synopsis, character breakdown and set description, or submit complete manuscript, score and tape of songs. "Either submission method is fine. Score is less necessary than tape." SASE. Reports in 6 months.
Musical Theatre: "We're interested in traditional forms of musical theatre as well as the more innovative styles. We have less interest in operetta and operatic works, but are willing to consider anything. We are far more interested in shows in which the songs move the plot along rather than comment thereon, i.e. musicals more than plays with music. We are also interested in seeing individual songs, primarily comedic, for possible inclusion in a 'new faces' type revue. We can't really consider any show with a cast exceeding 15. Fewer is better. Also, we're interested in using younger (35 and under) actors. We have very little wing space and no fly space, so scene shifts should be minimal. Still, we're very imaginative and authors should submit their work. We'll see what we can do."
Productions: *Two*, by Fredricka Weber (growing up); *Babes in Barns*, by John R. Carroll, Charlotte Samples and John Sparks ("Micky and Judy" spoof); *Nightengale*, by Charles Strouse (the fairy tale);

and *Doonesbury* by Trudeau and Swados (the comic strip).
Tips: "Familiarize yourself with the form. This is not to say that you have to write 'formula' musicals, whatever that might be; but by knowing some successful solutions to the problems, you might avoid some common mistakes."

NEW VOICES: A WRITER'S THEATRE, 551 Tremont St., Boston MA 02116. (617)357-5667. Artistic Director: Stanley Richardson. Play producer. Conducts 12-20 readings, 4-5 studio productions (1 musical)/year. "New Voices tends to produce mainly 'straight' plays, but will consider musicals as well." Pays by royalty for full productions, and a fee for readings or studio productions. Query with synopsis, character breakdown and set description. Submit through agent only. SASE. Reports in 4 months.
Musical Theatre: "We generally produce full-length plays that deal with public, social, moral, or political subjects. Casts should be fewer than 8 with one unit set." Would also consider original music for use in a play being developed.
Productions: *I Love You, I Love You Not*, by Wendy Kesselman (reading); and *The Professional Frenchman*, by Mac Wellman (reading).
Tips: "We tend to focus on non-musical plays. 'Plays with music' are more likely to suit our needs, rather than full-scale musicals."

NEW YORK KIDS ON STAGE, 1230 5th Ave., Rm. 209, New York NY 10029. (212)860-1848. Artistic Director: Jennifer Vermont-Davis. Play producer. Produces 15 plays (5 musicals)/year. "New York Kids on Stage is a free children's theatre program sponsored by the Department of Parks and Recreation. We do amateur productions spring, summer and fall for audiences of all ages, usually outdoors at park sites. We provide theatrical training for children in the New York area for free, and almost all the plays include music." Does not pay writers. Submit complete manuscript and cassette tape of songs. SASE. Reports in 1 month.
Musical Theatre: "We produce plays that children can do, preferably with music (although we've been known to add our own.) Any style or topic is fine, but we prefer plays that run about an hour or less. Try to avoid the subjects of sex, politics and religion if possible. Try to keep the plays relatively simple and very interesting and fun for 7-17 year olds. We need plays that will accomodate a large cast of kids (15-30) but require a minimum of props or complicated costumes. Our shows run the gamut from a rap opera to *The Little Prince*." Would consider original music for use in a play being developed.
Tips: "Don't underestimate what kids are capable of—it doesn't have to be smooth and sweet for us to like it."

*NEW YORK SHAKESPEARE FESTIVAL, 425 Lafayette St., New York NY 10003. (212)598-7100. Contact: Play/Musical Department. Play producer. Produces 12 plays (approximately 2 musicals)/year. Plays performed in New York City in any of six theaters, including the Delcorte Theatre in Central Park. Query with synopsis, character breakdown and set description. SASE. Reports in 12 weeks.
Musical Theatre: "High quality musicals are important. We would like to see more current isues addressed and would like to hear more contemporary sounding music used." No staging limitations "but financing a production is a consideration."
Productions: *La Boheme*, by Puccini (with Linda Ronstadt); *The Human Comedy*, by Galt MacDermot (William Saroyan novel); *A Chorus Line*, by Michael Bennett, et al. (dancers); and *Mystery of Edwin Drood*, by Rupert Holmes.
Tips: "We are not looking for 'songs'—we want musicals with strong books. New forms for opera and musicals are welcome."

*NICKERSON THEATRES, INC.,30 Accord Park Dr., Accord MA 02018. (617)871-2400. Artistic Director: Diane LaFond. Play producer. Produces 8 plays (2 musicals)/year. Plays are performed for a "general audience with average age of 35; we are 85% subscribed." Pays 6-10% royalty. Query with synopsis, character breakdown and set descriptions or submit complete manuscript, score and tape of songs. Does not return unsolicited material. Reports in 2 months.
Musical Theatre: "We are looking for new, fresh, creative, commercial types of work. We require small cast, one set, low budget musicals. No more than 5 musicians required to play score. There is no orchestra pit; auditorium only seats 360. We do not wish to see avant-garde or really offensive material." Would consider original music for use in play being developed.
Productions: *Tintypes*, by Mary Kyte (late 1800's revue); *I Do I Do*, by Jones and Schmid (late 1800's); and *All Night Strut*, by Fran Charnas (1930-40's revue).

NORTH CAROLINA CENTRAL UNIVERSITY, DEPARTMENT OF DRAMATIC ART, Box 19593, Durham NC 27707. (919)683-6242. Chairperson: Linda Kerr Norflett, Ph.D. Play producer. Produces 4 plays (1-2 musicals)/year. "North Carolina Central University is a traditionally black university but the theater program is racially mixed. We put great emphasis on producing new works by black play-

Close-up

Jo Ann Schmidman
Production Director
Omaha Magic Theatre

Schmidman as she appeared
in *Astro*Bride*, a musical she wrote

Nearly 20 years ago, far away from the lights of Broadway, Jo Ann Schmidman started the Magic Theatre in her home town of Omaha, Nebraska. After studying drama in Boston, Schmidman realized that "to learn about acting, one must act." So she began the Omaha Magic Theatre to have "a life in the theatre—a place to put the dreams and skills together—not just a career as a paid actor."

In its 18 years of operation, the theatre has developed more than 78 new plays and musicals. The works she presented were unknown and new to the area and Schmidman virtually had to build an audience from scratch. "At the beginning, there were actually more people in the cast than were in the audience! We sometimes had to lead people in by the hand, but if we got them to one show, they came back," says Schmidman. "We don't do standard musicals; we're only interested in the newest works." Schmidman describes the "musicals" as "plays with music—the music being an integral part of the play. Music is the heartbeat of the piece."

The Magic Theatre is made up of a creative team of composers and writers, the director, and the acting company. They normally don't do unsolicited works, but if they receive something of quality, they will work with the playwright to develop it. Schmidman suggests that a songwriter who wants to work as a part of a creative team "should express this interest to theatres or directors who are already working this way. The time commitment for this kind of team process is far more demanding than the "write/compose-and-mail-off" approach, but the rewards, including the potential for compounded visions on the part of all involved, are greater. To put together a creative team, you must pick up the phone and do it—phone artists whose work you admire and who admire your work."

Schmidman's theatre company supports itself by touring. Since 1974, they have toured throughout the United States. They also receive grants from organizations that understand the need of bringing experimental "new works" to the Midwest and making people more aware of certain social issues. Schmidman says the need is great for theatres specializing in "new musical works." Her advice to anyone thinking about opening one of his own is: "Just do it! Don't wait until the money comes. Start it in your garage if you have to, but just do it!"

—*Cynthia Kephart*

66 *If football, the church, and rock concerts can attract so dedicated an audience, what can theatre learn from these performance venues?* **99**

—Jo Ann Schmidman

wrights as well as other minorities." Pays by royalty. Query with synopsis or submit tape of songs with or without manuscript and score. SASE. Reports in 2 weeks.

Musical Theatre: "We are looking for black musicals, children's musicals and new musicals that are preferably non-racial or racial with clean humanistic themes, music and dance compilations (revue styles), musical dramas, and experimental performance pieces. Be as creative and experimental as your talent will allow and don't underestimate the power of metaphor. Keep staging simple, props at a minimum and cast size below 20." Does not want culturally limiting material.

Productions: *Bubbling Brown Sugar*, book by Rosette LeNoire (Harlem history); *Christmas Is Comin Uptown*, original text by Charles Dickens and music by Udell and Philips (black Christmas Carol); *I Believe In Make Believe*, (children's play with music); and *Purlie*, by Ossie Davis (black/white relations).

Tips: "See plays; study audience reactions; Write; send out material. We welcome originality in scripts and music."

NORTHLIGHT THEATRE, 2300 Green Bay Rd., Evanston IL 60201. (312)869-7732. Assistant Artistic Director: Jimmy Bickerstaff. Play producer. Produces 4-5 plays (0-1 musicals)/year. "Audience is age 35-55 average; upper mid-class, ⅔ suburban; most college or post-grad educated." Pays by royalty. Query with synopsis, character breakdown and set description. SASE. Reports in 4 weeks.

Musical Theatre: "Musicals/adaptations are generally developed in-house through collaboration of artists. Musicals here are small cast (fewer than 10) with minimum scenic and orchestral requirements. Must have depth of character and substance; broad universal human issues, as well as sophisticated level of artistic craftsmanship." Would also consider using orignal music, incidental music—usually pre-recorded, for use in a play being developed.

Productions: *City on the Make*, by Jeff Berkson, Denise De Clue, John Karraker (original musical about Chicago criminals and working class of 1940's—developed in-house); *Quilters*, by Molly Newman and Barbara Damashek (women settlers); *The Real Thing*, by Tom Stoppard; *Dealing*, by June Shellene and Richard Five (non-musical, world permiere); and *Benefactors*, by Michael Frayne.

OFF CENTER THEATRE, 436 W. 18th, New York NY 10011. (212)929-8299. Producer: Abigail Rosen. Play producer. Produces 6 plays (2 musicals)/year. The plays are performed "off-Broadway." Pays percentage of box office receipts after initial expenses have been recouped. Submit complete manuscript, score and tape of songs. SASE. Reports in 1 month.

Musical Theatre: Issue oriented, small cast.

Productions: *Just for Fun—The Music of Jerome Kern* (revue); *Biting the Apple*, by Tony McGrath and Stanley Seidman (revue); and *Hello, This Is Barbara, I'm Not in Right Now . . .* , by Barbara Schottenfeld (singles in New York City).

OLD GLOBE THEATRE, Box 2171, San Diego CA 92112. (619)231-1941. Associate Director: Robert Berlinger. Play producer. Produces 12 plays/year of which a varying number are musicals. "This is a regional theatre with three spaces: 500-seat proscenium, 225-seat arena, and large outdoor festival stage. We serve an audience base of over 225,000." Query with synopsis, character breakdown and set description. Does not return unsolicited material. Reports in 6 months.

Musical Theatre: "We look for skill first, subject matter second. No prescribed limitations though the playwright should be aware of the fiscal realities of producing musicals and should not be unrealistic. No unsolicited work."

Productions: *Into The Woods*, by James Lapine and Stephen Soundheim; *Kiss Me Kate*; *Pump Boys*; and *Dinettes*.

OLDCASTLE THEATRE COMPANY, Box 1555, Bennington VT 05201. (802)447-0564. Producing Director: Eric Peterson. Play producer. Produces 7 plays (1-2 musicals)/year. Produces plays for a "general audience at the Southern Vermont College Theatre." Pays negotiable royalty. Query with synopsis, character breakdown and set description. SASE. Reports in 2 months.

Musical Theatre: Seeking "small cast musicals and revues for general audiences. No elaborate staging." Would also consider orignal music for use in a play being developed.

*OMAHA MAGIC THEATRE, 1417 Farnam St., Omaha NE 68102. (402)346-1227. Production Director: Jo Ann Schmidman. Play producer. Produces 4-8 new musicals/year. Plays are performed in "an intimate, store-front theatre, with maximum seating of 93, for a cross-section of the community—not just traditional theatre-goers." Pay is negotiable. Query with synopsis, character breakdown and set description. SASE. Reports ASAP.

Musical Theatre: Performs "new, American, musical plays. We are especially interested in new approaches and the avant-garde."

Productions: *Family Talk*, by Megan Terry (interpersonal communication within the family); *Sea of Forms*, by M. Terry/J.A. Schmidman (a large-scale inter-disciplinary project combining sculpture and concert performance); and *Line of Least Existence*, by Rosalyn Drexler (a comedy likened to the Marx Brothers comedy).

PAPER MILL PLAYHOUSE, Brookside Dr., Milburn NJ 07041. (201)379-3636. Producer: Angelo Del Rossi. Contact: Maryan F. Stephens, Literary Advisor. Play producer. Produces 2 plays and 4 musicals/ year. "Audience based on 40,000 subscribers; plays performed in 1192-seat proscenium theatre." Pays by royalty or will option play under Dramatist Guild. "A synopsis of book plus tape of songs should be submitted first. Scores not necessary. Letter of introduction should accompany each submitted synopsis." SASE. Reports in 8 weeks.
Musical Theatre: Seeking "traditional Broadway sized musicals—either original or adaptations. One act plays are not considered. Developing works can be submitted to our musical workshop series. No cast size limitations—minimum of 5 characters usually to maximum size of 40-45." No nudity, profanity, etc.
Productions: *Damn Yankees*, by Adler and Ross, Abbott and Wallop; *Barnum*, by Coleman, Stewart and Bramble; *Naughty Marietta*, by Herbert and Young, adapted by Johanson; and *Annie Get Your Gun*, by Berlin, Fields and Fields. Staged readings/workshops: *Kingfish*, by Frankel and Franceschina; *Sayonara* by Luce, Fischoff and Gilbert; *Juba*, by Lamb and Walden; and *One More Song*, by Edwards and Citron.
Tips: "Works not yet ready for full production on main stage may be considered for playreading and musical workshop series."

THE PASSAGE THEATRE, Box 10730, Chicago IL 60610. (312)975-5939. Artistic Director: Scott Guy. Play producer. Produces 4 plays (1 musical)/year. Adult and children's theatre works are performed by both legitimate theatre and touring company. Pays negotiable fee or royalty. Query with synopsis, character breakdown and set description. SASE. Reports in 3 weeks.
Musical Theatre: Seeking "background or incidental music for classics, original scores and childrens music."
Productions: *Dr. Jekyll and Mr. Hyde*, by Stevenson; *Just So Stories*, by Kipling; *The Little Prince*, by Exupery; and *Thurber's Fables*, by Thurber.
Tips: "We're more interested in composers than lyricists. Classical training very beneficial. Artistic Director is also the head writer for an NBC TV series, which uses original music."

PENNSYLVANIA STAGE COMPANY, 837 Linden St., Allentown PA 18101. (215)434-6110. Artistic Associate/Literary Manager: Wendy Liscow. Play producer. Produces 7 plays (1-2 new musicals)/ season. "We are a LORT C theatre with a subscriber base of approximately 6,000 people. Plays are performed at the Pennsylvania Stage Company in the J.I. Rodale Theatre." Payment is negotiated on an individual basis. Query with synopsis, character breakdown, set description and a tape of the music. "Please do not send script first." SASE. Reports in 2 months.
Musical Theatre: "We are interested in full-length musicals which reflect the social, historical and political fabric of America. We have no special requirements for format, structure or musical involvement. We ask that once submission of a musical has been requested, that it be bound, legibly typed and include SASE. Cast limit of 18, but we prefer cast limit of 12. One set or unit set. Ours is a 274 seat house, there is no fly area, and a 23-foot proscenium opening."
Productions: *Just So*, by Mark St. Germain (based on Rudyard Kipling's *Justso Stories*); *Shim Sham*, by Johnny Brandon and Eric Blau (Buddy Bradley, an American tap and jazz choreographer); *Feathertop*, by Bruce Peyton and Skip Kennon (Nathaniel Hawthorne short story); *Song of Myself*, by Gayle Stahlhuth, Gregory Hurst and Arthur Harris.
Tips: "Consider the importance of what the musical is to say. Book and lyrics should have equal weight—lyrics should further the plot rather than arrest it."

PIONEER DRAMA SERVICE, Box 22555, Denver CO 80222. (303)759-4297. Assistant Editor: Patrick Rainville Dorn. Play publisher. Publishes 6-10 plays (3 musicals)/year. "Plays are performed by junior high and high school drama departments, church youth groups, college and university theatres, semi-professional and professional children's theatres, parks and recreation departments." Pays $100-250 outright purchase, 10% copy sales or 50% royalties. Query with synopsis, character breakdown and set description. SASE. "No unsolicited manuscripts." Reports in 6 weeks.
Musical Theatre: "We seek full length children's musicals, high school musicals and one act children's musicals to be performed by children, secondary school students, and/or adults. Prefer one set, two act structure with many female roles and very few solos—mostly chorus numbers. We mostly want musicals intended for the amateur youth market. We are not interested in profanity, themes with exclusively adult interest, sex, drinking, smoking etc."
Publications: *Luann*, by Eleanor and Ray Harder (comic strip adaptation); *Tied to the Tracks*, by Kelly, Kittelson, Christiansen (musical melodrama); and *Emperor's Nightingale*, by Shirley Barasch and Don DiFonso (children's musical).
Tips: "Describe show in terms of plot synopsis, number of male and female characters, number of sets

or set changes, approximate duration and production history. Give indication of writer's credits, especially other published works."

PLAYERS PRESS, INC., Box 1132, Studio City CA 91604. (818)789-4980. Associate Editor: Marjorie Clapper. Vice President: Joe W. Witt. Play publisher. Publishes 3-4 plays/year. Plays are used primarily by children but also by adults. Pays 25% royalty or negotiable outright purchase. Submit complete manuscript, score and tape of songs. SASE. Reports in 3 months.
Musical Theatre: "We will consider all submitted works. Presently children's musicals are in demand. When cast size can be flexible (describe how it can be done in your work) it sells better."
Publications: *Rumplestiltskin*, by William Alan Landes; and *Nessie*, by William Hezlep (both childrens plays).
Tips: "When submitting, it is best to send a clean, clear sounding tape with music. We do not publish a play or musical which has not been produced."

PLAYHOUSE ON THE SQUARE, 51 S. Cooper, Memphis TN 38104. (901)725-0776. Executive Producer: Jackie Nichols. Play producer. Produces 8 plays (3 musicals)/year. Plays are produced in a "260-seat proscenium resident theatre." Pays $25 per performance. Submit complete manuscript and score. SASE. Reports in 4 months.
Musical Theatre: Seeking "any subject matter—adult and children's material. Small cast preferred. Stage is 26' deep by 43' wide with no fly system." Would also consider original music for use in a play being developed.
Productions: *Gypsy*, by Stein and Laurents; *The Spider Web*, by Agatha Christie (mystery); and *A Midsummer Nights Dream*, by William Shakespeare.

PORTHOUSE THEATRE, Kent OH 44242. (216)672-2082. Producer: Dr. Marya Bednerik. Play producer. Produces various number of plays and at least 2 musicals/year. Plays are presented at Blossom Music Center for an adult audience. Pays by royalty or per performance. Submit complete manuscript and score. SASE. Reports in 3 months.
Musical Theatre: Looking for "new unproduced musicals for adults; no restrictions." Would also consider original music for use in a play being developed.
Productions: *Apples in Eden*, by Rose Goldenberg (Alcott family's utopia); and *Legend*, by John Cameron (death of vaudeville performers).
Tips: "Write well—with passion. Spark the imagination."

*RICHARD ROSE—AMERICAN STAGE FESTIVAL,Box 225, Milford NH 01853. (603)673-4005. Managing Director: Richard Rose. Play producer. Produces 2-3 plays, 1 musical, and 1-2 new musicals/year. Plays are produced in 500 seat proscenium stage for a general audience. Pays 8-10% royalty or outright purchase of $2,000. Submit complete manuscript, score and tape of songs. SASE.
Musical Theatre: Seeks all types of musicals. "Besides our adult audience we have an active children's theatre. We will not do a large chorus musical if cast size is over 18. We use orignal music in plays on a regular basis, as incidental music, pre-show and between acts, or as moments in and of themselves."
Productions:*Rhymes with Evil*, by Charles Traegan (psych thriller); *Peg O' My Heart*, by David Heneker (romantic musical); and *Sullivan And Gilbert*, by Ken Ludwig (comic musical).

SAN DIEGO REPERTORY THEATRE, 79 Horton Plaza, San Diego CA 92101. (619)231-3586. Literary Manager: Scott Feldsher. Play producer. Produces 8 plays (2 musicals)/year. "We have three stages: a 535-seat thrust stage; a 225-seat black box space, and a 212-seat proscenium stage. We are Equity-Lort D." Pays negotiable royalty. "For *music only*, we would negotiate." Query with synopsis, character breakdown and set description. SASE. Reports in 2 weeks (letter) or 6 months (manuscript).
Musical Theatre: "No large scale musicals. Any well-written musical; no specific topics. We prefer full-length work. Also interested in literary cabaret, micro-operas and work that integrates music with poetry or media. We like to explore music in its relationship to other performance textures, i.e., verbal, aural, movement, media."
Productions: *Tooth of Crime*, by Sam Shepard (a play with rock and roll music); *Rap Master Ronnie*, by E. Swados and G. Trudeau (satire of Reagan's reign with music); and *Little Shop Of Horrors*, by Howard Ashman and Alan Menken (adaptation of film by Roger Corman).

SHAWNEE THEATRE, 6904 S. Harvard, Chicago IL 60621. (812)384-3559. Executive Producer: Frank Hayashida. Play producer. Produces 8 plays (1 musical)/year. Plays are performed in a "300-seat theatre located in Bloomfield. It has continental seating; built in 1979." Pays $35-75 per performance. Query with synopsis, character breakdown and set description; or submit complete manuscript and score. SASE. Reports in 1 month.

Musical Theatre: Musicals "can be about most any topic. Material needs to be realistic yet not involved with unacceptable Christian morals. Plays can be for children (plays with some kind of moral lesson). We could consult and make suggestions, but prefer work to be of writer/artist. Cast can be 12-15 but solo parts should be limited to 3-4 characters." Does not wish to see "topics dealing with negative moral thinking or philosophies." Would also consider original music for use in play being developed.

Productions: *King and I*, *South Pacific*, and *Student Prince*.

Tips: "Keep writing and composing and experimenting; only by doing so will one improve."

*GEOFFREY SHERMAN/PRODUCING DIRECTOR,441 W. 26th St., New York NY 10001. (212)760-9836. Literary Manager: Steven Ramay. Play producer. Produces 5 plays/year. "We are an off-Broadway theatre, supported by subscribers and grants. We operate in a 137 seat house." Pays flat fee of $1,000 for run of show. Submit complete ms, score and tape of songs. SASE. Reports in 10 weeks.

Musical Theatre: "Our five play season is aimed exclusively for adult audiences and any sort of children's musicals or puppet shows would be inappropriate. Other than that, the only criteria we demand is excellence. We cannot handle a cast size larger than twelve. We have a large space that is flexible to a certain extent. We are also interested in developing works that we feel have potential."

Productions: *Moms*, by Alice Childress (Moms Mabley); *Crackwalker*, by Judith Thompson (Canadian drama); *No Way to Treat a Lady*, by Douglas Cohen, (musical of Goldman novel).

Tips: "The competition is overwhelming—we get 1,200 submissions a year. Dont be discouraged if things don't happen right away for you."

SHOWBOAT MAJESTIC, Foot of Broadway, Cincinnati OH 45202. (513)475-5803. Producer: Suellen Childs. Artistic Director: R. Terrell Finney. Play producer. Produces 5 plays (3 musicals)/year. Plays are produced on the Showboat Majestic, the last of the original floating theaters located on the Ohio River. Pays $150/performance. "Most musicals are rented through New York. We follow regular royalty rental plan from them." Query. SASE. Reports in 1 month.

Musical Theatre: "We are seeking original songs, musical comedies no longer than two hours with an intermission, revues and small cast shows." No avant-garde or experimental scripts. Cast should be less than 10.

Productions: *The Fantasticks*, by Schmidt and Jones; *Gold Dust*, by Wann; *I Do! I Do!*, by Schmidt and Jones; *Show Me Where the Good Times Are*; *Da* (Broadway); and *A Funny Thing Happened on the Way to the Forum*.

Tips: "Begin with an acknowledged good story line. Find a play in the public domain that could be turned into a musical."

SOHO REPERTORY THEATRE, 80 Varick St., New York City NY 10013. (212)925-2588. Artistic Director: Jerry Engelbach. Play producer. Produces 3 plays (1 new musical)/year. Plays performed in off-off-broadway, AEA Tier 4 code, 100-seat thrust-stage theatre with high ceilings. Pays $10-50/performance or 6% royalty for extended run. Query "with description (no synopsis) of the play and how it will work as a theatre piece." Does not return unsolicited material. Reports in 2 weeks on queries; 90 days on submitted material.

Musical Theatre: "The music must be *excellent*, the script literate, the piece as a whole conducive to inventive, 3-dimensional staging." Looking for "adult mentality, sophisticated wit, situations of interest to grown-up people, i.e., emphatically non-broadway oriented with maximum cast size of 12. Orchestration is limited by budget to 2-5 pieces, e.g., our successful musical *Mandrake* used piano and harp." Would also consider original music for use in play being developed. "We use incidental music all the time, sometimes performed live."

Productions: *Mandrake*, music by Anthony Bowles, book by Michael Alfreds (satire on political and sexual mores); *The Grub Street Opera*, by Henry Folding, new musical score by Anthony Bowles (18th century musical satire); and *Almos' A Man*, book, music and lyrics by Paris Barclay, based on a story by Richard Wright (black Depression musical).

Tips: "Be a superb musician and have a sense of humor. Send us only high-quality sophisticated music: no three-chord wonders or TV theme music."

SOUTH WESTERN COLLEGE, 900 Otay Lakes Rd., Chula Vista CA 92010. (619)421-6700. Artistic Director: W. Virchis. Play producer. Produces 5 plays (3 musicals)/year. Query with synopsis. SASE. Reports in 3 weeks.

 The asterisk before a listing indicates that the listing is new in this edition. New markets are often the most receptive to freelance submissions.

Productions: *Evita* (world college premiere); *Wiz* (black musical); *Jesus Christ Superstar* (rock opera); *Pancho Diablo* (Chicano); *Nine* (musical); and *Leader of the Pack* (musical).

SOUTHERN CONNECTICUT STATE UNIVERSITY, DEPARTMENT OF THEATRE, New Haven CT 06515. (203)397-4431. Chairman: Sigurd A. Jensen. Play producer. Produces 4-6 plays (1 musical)/year. Plays performed to general audiences and college students. Pays $25/performance or standard royalty. Submit cassette and/or manuscript. SASE. Reports ASAP—"depends on time of year."
Musical Theatre: "Should require small cast, props, staging, etc." Does not want "big, old-fashioned musicals."
Productions: *The Best Little Whorehouse In Texas*, and *Anything Goes*.

SPANISH THEATRE REPERTORY OF NEW YORK, 138 E. 27th St., New York NY 10027. (212)889-2850. Musical Director: Pablo Zinger. Play producer. Produces 6 plays (2 musicals)/year. Plays are performed at Gramercy Arts Theatre and Equitable Towers in New York and tour nationally and internationally. Payment negotiable. Submit complete manuscript, score and tape of songs. Does not return unsolicited material. Reports in 2 months.
Musical Theatre: Seeking "musicals in Spanish, dealing with Hispanic subjects and concerns. Legitimate and operatic voices available. Piano vocal and/or small ensemble preferred to full orchestra. Full length should be 1½ to 2 hours, with or without dialogue. Use of Hispanic musical idioms required. Cast of 6-15 with few or no props and little or no scenery."
Productions: *Luisa Fernanda*, by Moreno Torroba (serious Zarzuela); *Puerto Rico Sings*, (anthology); *Havanna Sings*, (anthology); and *La Zarzuela*, (anthology).

STAGE ONE, 721 W. Main St., Louisville KY 40202. (502)589-5946. Managing Director: Debra Hymes. Play producer. Produces 7 plays (1-3 musicals)/year. Plays are performed for school and family audience in 626-seat thrust style theatre. Pays 5% royalty; $25-75/performance, or by commission. Submit complete manuscript, score and the tape of songs. SASE. Reports in 12 weeks.
Musical Theatre: "We want classic children's tales in honest adaptations, or stories of interest to kids,. Length: 60-120 minutes, one or two act. Preferred cast size—12 or under." No "camp or fractured fairy-tales."
Productions: "Sample seasons in T.C.G. Theatre Profiles."

THEATER FOR THE NEW CITY, 155 1st Ave., New York NY 10003. (212)254-1109. Director: George Bartenieff. Play producer. Produces 40-50 plays (6 musicals)/year. Plays are performed for a mixed audience. "Some writers are commissioned; others share the box office take with actors." Submit complete manuscript with lyrics. SASE. Reports in 12-18 months.
Musical Theatre: No limitations on cast size, props, staging, etc. "No children's plays with bunny rabbit feel."
Productions: *The Conduct of Life*, by Maria Irene Fornes; *Hamletmachine*, by Heiner Mueller; and *The Age of Invention*, by Theodora Skipitares.

THEATRE FOR YOUNG AMERICA, 7204 W. 80th St., Overland Park KS 66204. (913)648-6400. Artistic Director: Gene Mackey. Play producer. Produces 8 plays (2-3 musicals)/year. For children, preschool to high school. Pays $10-25/performance. Query with synopsis. SASE. Reports in 1 month.
Musical Theatre: 1-1½ hour productions with small cast oriented to children and high-school youths. "A clear, strong, compelling story is important; a well known title is very important."
Productions: *Androcles and the Lion*, by Aurand Harris and Glen Mack; *The Hare and the Tortoise*, by Cheryl Benge and Gene Mackey (adapted from Aesop's fable); *Tom Sawyer*, by Michael Dansicker and Sarah Marie Schlesinger (adapted from Mark Twain's novel); and *Chicken Little*, by Gene Mackey (book), and Chery Benge (music).

THEATREVIRGINIA, Boulevard and Grove Ave., Richmond VA 23221. (804)257-0840. Literary Manager: Bo Wilson. Play producer. Produces 4-5 plays (1-2 musicals)/year. "Plays are performed in a 500-seat LORT-C house for the Richmond-area community." Payment subject to negotiation. "Please submit synopsis, sample of diaglogue, and sample of music (on cassette) along with a self-addressed, stamped letter-size envelope. If material seems to be of interest to us, we will reply with a solicitation for a complete manuscript and cassette. Response time for synopses is 2-4 weeks; response time for scripts once solicited is 3-5 months."
Musical Theatre: "We do not deal in one-acts or in children's material. We would like to see full length, adult musicals. There are no official limitations. We would be unlikely to use original music as incidental/underscoring for existing plays, but there is potential for adapting existing plays into musicals."

Productions: *West Side Story*, by Bernstein/Sondheim/Laurents (love story among gangs); *Man of La Mancha*, by Wasserman/Darion/Leigh (Don Quixote/oppression); *The Amen Corner*, by James Baldwin, (family struggle in gospel setting); and *A Wireless Christmas*, by Wilson/Burgler/Liebman (an original musical about a radio station at Christmas).

Tips: "Read plays. Study structure. Study character. Learn how to concisely articulate the nature of your work. A beginning musical playwright, wishing to work for our company should begin by writing a wonderful, theatrically viable piece of musical theatre. Then he should send us the material requested in our listing, and wait patiently."

THEATREWORKS/USA, 131 W. 86 St., New York NY 10024. (212)595-7500. Associate Artistic Director: Barbara Pasterrack. Play producer. Produces 2-4 plays/year (all musicals). "We play for young and family audiences in schools, community centers and theatres. Also, the Promenade Theatre in New York City." Pays 6% royalty "for writers, to be divided if more than one. Submit manuscript or outline and tape of songs." SASE. Reports in 6 months.

Musical Theatre: "Seeking all types of musicals for young and family audiences including fairytales, historical, fantasy, adaptations of classics and contemporary works—issue-oriented. Our shows are one hour in length. Cast size limited to 5 or 6. Shows tour; therefore all scenery, props, and costumes must be portable by van." No opera.

Productions: *Rapunzel*, by David Crane, Marta Kauffman, and Michael Skloff (musical version of fairytale); *When the Cookie Crumbles*, (musical revue on subject of divorce); *Play to Win*, by James De Jongh, Carles Cleveland and Jimi Foster (musical biography of Jackie Robinson); and *New Road to Freedom: Martin Luther King*, by Charles Strouse and Leslie Lee.

*TOUCHSTONE THEATRE,908 E. 5th St., Bethlehem PA 18015. (215)867-1689. Director: William George. Play producer. Produces 4 plays/year. Pays by contract. Query with synopsis, character breakdown and set description. SASE. Reports in 6 weeks.

Musical Theatre: Seeking all types of musicals with "not more than ten in the cast. Stage is 20 feet by 20 feet." Would consider original music for use in play being developed.

Productions: *Passage of Ah-Lot-So*, by Ensemble (Indian spiritual); *Soldier's Tale*, by Ramus/Stravinsky (devil vs soldier); and *Handful of Earth*, by Ensemble (heroes of Poland).

UPSTAIRS DINNER THEATRE, 221 S. 19 St., Omaha NE 68102. (402)344-3858. Producer: Deborah Denenberg. Play producer. Produces 6 plays (3 musicals)/year. Plays are performed for a "midwest middle class audience interested in Broadway type of musical comedy. We have not produced original musicals, but we keep an open mind." Pays $50-100 per performance. Submit complete manuscript and tape of songs. Does not return unsolicited material.

Musical Theatre: "One hour children's fairy tales with recognizable titles, Broadway style musical comedy or twelve-minute musical revues. Comedy or light entertainment preferred. No full-length revues."

Productions: *A Chorus Line*; *Annie Get Your Gun*; and *Catch Me If You Can*.

Tips: "Be persistent. If you are a musical comedy performer who can also write or direct, we would be interested in talking."

CEDRIC VENDYBACK, Brandon University, Brandon, Manitoba R7A 6A9 Canada. (204)727-9662. Professor: C. Vendyback. Play producer. Produces 2-6 plays/year. Rarely produces musicals. Audience is urban and rural, middle-class, faculty and students. Pays $25-75/performance. Query with synopsis. SAE and IRC. Reports in 1 month.

Musical Theatre: Prefers "one- to three-act; social comment, smallish cast. We also like simple props and staging. Nothing lavish, possibly revue style."

Productions: *The Crucible*, by Miller (social conscience); *The Love of Four Colonels*, by Ustinov (good vs. evil); and *The Pirates of Penzance*, by Gilbert & Sullivan.

Tips: "Study Rodgers and Hart for good melody and witty lyrics. Also study *The Music Man*, *Pal Joey*, *Guys and Dolls*, etc. Eschew *bleak* melodies and lyrics of recent times. Audiences are pining for and in need of warmth and quality."

*WABASH COLLEGE THEATER, Wabash College, Crawfordsville IN 47933. (317)362-0677. Chairman/Theater Department: James Fisher. Play producer. Produces 4 plays/year. "Musicals are produced occasionally as schedule and personnel permit. Audience is small college town and the male student body of the college. We have two theaters: a 370-seat intimate proscenium with lift for stage; and a black box, seating up to 150. Looking for plays with moderate size cast with more male than female roles." Pays by royalty or $35-100/performance. Query with synopsis or submit complete ms and score. SASE. Reports as soon as possible.

Musical Theatre: Any type. "We are open to any exciting piece. Plays require mostly male characters with small- to medium-size orchestra and up to 25-30 in cast." Would consider original music for use in a play being developed.

Productions: *Guys and Dolls*; *Cabaret*; *Fantasticks*; *Canterbury Tales*; *The Crimson Bird*, by Strawn and Enenbach (medieval French nightingale legend); and *S.H. Ades*, by Seward (ghosts and aspiring showbiz hopeful).

*WALNUT STREET THEATRE COMPANY, 9th & Walnut Sts., Philadelphia PA 19107. (215)574-3584. Literary Manager: Deborah Baer Quinn. Play producer. Produces 10 plays (2 musicals)/year. Plays produced on a mainstage with seating for 1,052 to a family audience; and in studio theatres with seating for 79-99 to adult audiences. Pays by royalty or outright purchase. Query with synopsis, character breakdown, set description, and ten pages. SASE. Reports in 5 months.
Musical Theatre: "Adult Musicals. Plays are for a subscription audience that comes to the theatre to be entertained. We seek musicals with lyrical non-operatic scores and a solid book as well as revues. We are looking for a small musical for springtime and one for a family audience at Christmas time. We would like to remain open on structure and subject matter and would expect a tape with the script. Cast size: around 30 equity members (10 for smaller musical); preferably one set with variations. No gratuitous violence, nudity or obscene language." Would consider original music for use in play being developed.
Productions: *Tintypes*, by Mel Marvin (American patriotism); *A Little Night Music*, by Hugh Wheeler/Stephen Sondheim (romance); and *Tomfoolery*, by Tom Leher (political satire on American politics and life).

WATERLOO COMMUNITY PLAYHOUSE, Box 433, Waterloo IA 50704. (319)235-0367. Managing Director: Charles Stilwill. Play producer. Produces 13 plays (1-4 musicals)/year. "Our audience prefers solid, wholesome entertainment, nothing risque or with strong language. We perform in Hope Martin Theatre, a 368-seat house." Pays $15-150/performance. Submit complete manuscript, score and cassette tape of songs. SASE.
Musical Theatre: "Casts may vary from as few as 6 people to 54. We are producing children's theater as well. We're *especially* interested in new adaptations of classic children stories."
Productions: *Once Upon a Mattress*; *Snoopy*; *Barnum*; and *A Christmas Carol*, by Patricia Stilwill and Gary Hansburger.
Tips: Looking for "new adaptations of classical children's stories or a good Christmas show."

WEBER-PRIANTI PRODUCTIONS, % Three Little Bakers Dinner Theatre, 3540 Foxcroft Dr., Wilmington DE 19808. (302)368-1616. Producers: Jim Weber and Gary Prianti. Play producer. Produces 5-6 plays/year (all musicals). Plays are performed on a large thrust stage at the dinner theatre for a general/family audience. Pays $25-50 per performance. Submit complete manuscript, score and tape of songs. SASE. Reports in 10 weeks.
Musical Theatre: Seeking musicals with "1940's big band themes, radio-type show themes, Christmas musicals, family-oriented musicals and burlesque/vaudeville-type revues. Each act must not exceed one hour (2 hours total running time). Would consider original music for use in a play being developed. Maximum cast size is 18-20 characters, including chorus." Does not want "anything that is not appropriate for the entire family."
Productions: *Evita*, by Andrew Lloyd Weber; *Fiddler On The Roof*; *Sound of Music*, and *Ain't Misbehavin'*.
Tips: "Our theatre is very commercial. There is no market for work that does not fulfill this requirement."

WHOLE THEATRE, INC., 544 Bloomfield Ave., Montclair NJ 07042. (201)744-2996. Producing Artistic Director: Olympia Dukakis. Play producer. Produces 5 plays/year. Payment varies. Query first. SASE. Reports in 10 weeks.
Musical Theatre: Looking for "musicals in which you care about the characters—otherwise no restrictions as to theme or style. Send just a brief plot and theme description plus number in cast, sets, etc., and any other technical considerations. Must be small cast (3-6) with one set or unit set."
Productions: *Pops*, by Romulus Lennig; *Seagull*, by Chekhov; *We Won't Pay, We Won't Pay*, by Dario Fo; *Billy Bishopg Goes to War*, by John Gray; and *Steal Away*, by Ramona King.

*JENNY WILEY THEATRE, Box 22, Prestonsburg KY 41653-0022. (606)886-9274 and 886-3691. General Manager: Jim Deaton. Play producer (Jenny Wiley Drama Association, Inc./JWDA). Produces 3 musicals plus 1 new musical/year. Plays are performed for "tourist audience, middle-upper income (20-25,000 average attendance in summer) in Jenny Wiley State Resort Park Amphitheatre." Pays outright purchase of $4-6,000; "additional payment in ensuing years of performance is variable." Query. SASE. Reports in 3 weeks.

Musical Theatre: Seeking "family oriented shows not exceeding 2 hours maximum performance time. The works should not call for more than 10-13 in the ensemble. Twentieth century setting works best, but historical works with music are strongly considered. Musicals should deal with Appalachia or Kentucky historical figures. Shows are produced outdoors—beware of flashy spectacle at outset of show (while it's still daylight). It must be, at its basis, family entertainment (avoid the *Oh! Calcuttas* of the world)." Would also consider original music for use in play being developed "either as performance music (score + vocal), as part of a musical theatre production, or as background (underscoring)."
Productions: *Jenny Wiley Story*, by Daniel A. Stein (historical with music); and *Cotton Patch Gospel*, by Tom Key and Harry Chapin (folk/bluegrass/gospel of Matthew). Also sponsors "Roadside Theatre," by various writers (primarily Ron Short), featuring plays about Appalachian heritage.
Tips: "Present a scenario/synopsis for consideration. If we are interested, we would give aid in developing it (and funding it if it falls under our funding resource availabilities). We would like to develop quality works with appropriate music that deal with historical themes or Appalachian tales."

THE WILL GEER THEATRICUM BOTANICUM, Box 1222, Topanga CA 90290. (213)455-2322. Artistic Director: Ellen Geer. Play producer. Produces 3 plays (1 musical)/year. Plays are performed in "large outdoor amphitheatre with 60'x 25' wooden stage. Rustic setting." Pays by royalty or per performance. Query with synopsis, character breakdown and set description. SASE. Reports ASAP "depending on time of year script is submitted. If done in September—1 month."
Musical Theatre: Seeking social or biographical works, children's works, full length or 1 act musicals with cast of up to 10 equity actors (the rest non-equity). Requires "low budget set and costumes. We emphasize paying performers." Would also consider original music for use in a play being developed. Does not wish to see "anything promoting avarice, greed, violence or apathy."
Productions: *Dory! A Musical portrait!* (adapted from writings of Dory Previn); *Women and Other People* (adapted women's writing and lyrics); *Americana* (adapted writings of great poets, politicians and characters in American history); and *Pie In The Sky*, lyrics and music by Peter Alsop.
Tips: "Reach us with idea and show enthusiasm for theatre."

WILMA THEATER, 2030 Sansom St., Philadelphia PA 19103. (215)963-0249. Artistic Director: Jiri Zizka. Play producer. Produces 4-5 plays (1-2 musicals)/year. Plays are performed for a "sophisticated, adventurous, off-beat and demanding audience," in a 100-seat theater. Pays 6-8% of gross income. Submit complete manuscript, score and tape of songs. SASE. Reports in 10 weeks.
Musical Theatre: Seeks "innovative staging, universal issues, political implications and inventive, witty approach to subject. We emphasize ensemble style, group choreography, actors and musicians overlapping, with new inventive approach to staging. Do not exceed 4-5 musicians, cast of 12, (ideally under 8), or stage space of 30x20." Also interested in plays with music and songs.
Productions: *Happy End*, by Brecht and Weill (social change); *Hairy Ape*, by O'Neil (search for self-identity); *The Insect Comedy* (humorous analogy between the world of insects and human beings); *Marat/Sade* (basic questions of human existence); and *Three Guys Naked From the Waist Down* (worship of success).

WISDOM BRIDGE THEATRE, 1559 W. Howard, Chicago IL 60626. (312)743-0486. Associate Artistic Director: Doug Finlayson. Play producer. Produces 4-6 plays (1 musical)/year. "Wisdom Bridge Theatre is 196-seat house on Chicago's north side. We have a subscriber base of 9,500 and present an eclectic season of classics, premieres and musicals." Negotiates pay. Query with synopsis, character breakdown and set description. SASE. Reports in 4 months.
Musical Theatre: "Wisdom Bridge Theatre is looking for musicals which break tradition with style and subject matter. Innovation is key to our concerns. Our main season tends to have plays with strong social and political conscience; musicals of this nature are welcome. A synopsis and brief character description should be sent first. If the material seems appropriate, we would like to see libretto and tape. Our theatre is very intimate and wing space is limited. However, if the piece is innovative, we will entertain any possibility." Does not wish to see "musicals written as pure entertainment."
Productions: *The Middle of Nowhere in the Middle of the Night*, based on music by Randy Newman (love, death, war); *'Night Mother*, by Marsha Norman (suicide; mother/daughter relations); and *Rat in the Skull*, by Ron Hutchison (Northern Ireland).

Last year we introduced a new section to *Songwriter's Market* devoted specifically to fine arts compositions. *All* of the markets listed requested to be included again in this year's edition, plus so many new markets have asked to be listed that the total number of listings has more than doubled. It is encouraging to learn that so many fine arts companies, ranging from small community groups to major symphony orchestras, are open to new talent and feel their audiences are progressive enough to support original music. While these companies may not be able to pay well, as most of them are not-for-profit, it is a special thrill for a composer to hear his work performed by an established orchestra in a hall filled with interested listeners. And having a composition performed for a live audience can help the composer perfect his writing craft by observing the listeners' reactions and evaluating how the piece sounds in context. It may lead to further performances of the piece by other groups, or a chance for the piece to be included in a concert with an influential guest conductor. It may even lead to further commissions when the orchestra or ensemble has a future need for original music.

All of the organizations in this section have indicated an interest in hearing new music. Their standards are very high—don't hurt your chances by sending anything but your best compositions. Be professional when you contact the music directors; keep in mind the typical fine arts audience they are selecting music for. Many of the markets indicate they would like to be contacted by mail, receiving a query or an excerpt of a finished work, before receiving a complete submission.

This section is devoted to a very different kind of music and selection procedure than the pop music industry professionals of Los Angeles, Nashville, and New York deal with. These markets are for composers of "classical," "serious," or "fine arts" music who do not wish to make "songs" out of their compositions, but want exposure for their music nonetheless.

Hopefully this section will continue to bring composers and fine arts performers together to premiere fresh, original music, and make that music accessible to new audiences. If you feel that one of the organizations listed would be interested in your compositions, read the listing thoroughly and follow the instructions carefully. More names and addresses (but no marketing information) of fine arts companies can be found in the annual *Musical America* directory (ABC Consumer Magazines).

*ASHEVILLE SYMPHONY ORCHESTRA, Box 2852, Asheville NC 28802. (704)254-7046. Music Director: Robert Hart Baker. Symphony orchestra, chamber ensembles, and youth orchestra. Performs 20 concerts/year including 2 new works. Members are professionals. Commissions 1 composer or new work/year. Concerts performed in Thomas Wolfe Auditorium which seats 2,400. Subscription audience size is approximately 1,900. Pays by outright purchase (up to $1,000 when commissioning) or via ASCAP or BMI. Submit complete score and tape of pieces. SASE. Reports in 10 weeks.
Music: Seeks "classical, pops orchestrestrations, full modern orchestral works, concertos and chamber music. Winds in triplicate maximum; not too many extreme high ranges or exotic time signatures/notation. Do not send unaccompanied choral works or songs for voice and piano only."
Productions: Douglas Owens' *Play Us A Tune* (cycle for mezzo and orchestra); Howard Hanger's *For Barbara* (for jazz ensemble and orchestra); and Robert Hart Baker's *Fantasie* (arrangement of Chopin work for orchestra).

*ATLANTA POPS ORCHESTRA, Box 723172, Atlanta GA 30339. (404)435-1222. Conductor: Albert Coleman. Symphony orchestra. Members are professionals. Performs 10-15 concerts/year.

ELAINE BOOKWALTER, Box 1941, Indianapolis IN 46206. (317)545-2151. Artistic Director: Elaine Bookwalter. Opera producer. Produces 2 operas/year. Operas performed for mixed audience of contemporary/traditional. Pays by royalty. Query by phone. Does not return unsolicited material. Reports in 6 weeks.

Music: Seeking "good children's" works and operas dealing with contemporary issues. Would consider original music for use in an opera being developed. Does not wish to see works that call for nudity.

Productions: *Hotel for Criminal*, by Silverman (lesbian vampire); *Elephant Steps*, by Silverman; *El Capitan*, by John Phillips Sousa and *Trial by Jury*, by Gilbert/Sullivan.

*CARSON-DOMINQUEZ HILLS SYMPHONY, % Music Dept. California State University, Dominquez Hills, Carson CA 90747. (213)516-3947. Music Director: Dr. Frances Steinen. Symphony orchestra. Members are professionals and amateurs. Performs 4-5 concerts/year including many new works. Concerts performed in University Theatre (485 seats), Community Center (1000 seats) and an annual July 4th "Pops" Concert in Olympic Velodrome (10,000 attendance). Pays $100-200 for outright purchase or $25-200/performance. Query first, then submit complete score and tape of pieces. SASE.

Music: "Especially interested in women composers or ethnic minorities." Seeks arrangements for July 4th concert and annual children's concerts. 60-65 performers maximum. Does not wish to see "highly esoteric contemporary music or music which requires numerous unusual instruments."

Productions: Zwillich's *Symphony No. 1.*

*CHAMBER ORCHESTRA OF ALBUQUERQUE,2730 San Pedro, NE, Suite H-23, Albuquerque NM 87110. (505)881-0844. Music Director/Conductor: David Oberg. Chamber orchestra. Members are professionals. Performs 16 concerts/year including 1 new work (includes subscription, pops, children's, senior's and tours). Concerts performed for subscription audiences or special concert (University of New Mexico Composer's Symposium, etc.) audiences. Hall seats 626. Pays via ASCAP, BMI and private arrangements.

How to Contact: Query first. SASE.

Music: "No specific restrictions. Instrumentation: strings (6/4/3/3/1); woodwinds in pairs; trumpets and horns in pairs; harp; harpsichord/piano; and timpani/percussion. The orchestra is fully professional with limited rehearsal time available."

Productions: Max Schubel's *Punch and Judy* (multi-media); and Gordon Getty's *Plump Jack (Scene Three)* (opera).

*DC COMMUNITY ORCHESTRA ASSOCIATION,3669 Upton St. N.W., Washington DC 20008. (202)966-0772. Music Director: Dingwall Fleary. Community orchestra. Members are amateurs. Performs 5 concerts/year. "The orchestra we sponsor performs in school, church and neighborhood auditoriums for general audiences, especially those who do not ordinarily have easy access to live performances."

How to Contact: Query first. SASE.

Music: "Chamber sized orchestra of standard instruments, brief to moderate length. Chorus and orchestra a possibility. 50 performers, moderate difficulty."

Productions: Mozart's *Symphony No. 40* (symphony); Copland's *Rodeo Suite* (ballet); and Webber's *Cats* (Broadway show).

*DESERT OPERA THEATRE,Box 465, Palmdale CA 93550. (805)273-8470/268-1417. General Director: Anita L. Baekey. Opera company. Members are both professionals and amateurs. Performs 3 concerts/year. "Audience is 4,000 annual— 50% opera veterans/50% neophytes." Pays by royalty or $500-1,000 outright purchase.

How to Contact: Submit complete score and tapes of piece(s). Does not return unsolicited material.

Music: Seeks "flowing musical line, captivating story line. Light operas—90 minute maximum. Children's opera—60 minute maximum. Orchestration—15 maximum. 12 voice, 4 part chorus maximum. Children's opera—level appropriate for children's participation in chorus, at least." Does not wish to see atonal music.

Productions: Romberg's *The Desert Song*, (operetta); Smetana's *The Bartered Bride* (opera); and Carol Bender's *The Climb of Your Life*,(children's opera).

*DIABLO VALLEY PHILHARMONIC,321 Golf Club Rd., Pleasant Hill CA 94523. (415)685-1230. Conductor: Fredric Johnson. Members are both professionals and amateurs. Performs 4-7 concerts/year including 1-2 new works. Commissions 1-2 composers, new works every few years. "Performances in Performing Arts Center, 400 + ; and at St. Francis Cathedral 1,000, usually packed." Pays $200-300/performance or by outright purchase.

How to Contact: Submit complete score and/or score and tapes of piece(s). SASE. Reports in 2 months.

Music: Seeks "wild, flamboyant, music 5-10 minutes, experimental is good. Also will consider something more traditional, melodic. If it's good it doesn't matter, although great length would be difficult

for our audience (and orchestra). No more than 40 strings—probably the problems connected with engaging extra musicians would be disuading. The orchestra should be fully utilized."
Productions: West Coast premier: Mario Lombardo's *Spectrum* (traditional, like Gershwin); Earle Brown's *Modules* (2 conductors); Schoenberg's *Survivor* (12 tone nar.); and Jay Stebley's *13 Times* (tone poem).

*EDMONTON SYMPHONY SOCIETY,10010-109 Street, Edmonton Alberta T5M 1J4 Canada. (403)428-1108. Music Director: Uri Mayer. Members are professionals. Performs 97 concerts/year including 3 new works. Series include: masters, pops, connoisseur, young people's, Sunday matinee, specials, cafe and educational. Hall seats 2,694.
How to Contact: Submit complete score.
Music: Seeks classical music, 10-20 minutes in length. Orchestra size: 3333, T311, 4231 plus strings.
Productions: Malcolm Forsyth's *African Ode*; Alfred Fisher's *Warrior*; and Pakhmutova's *Concerto for Trumpet* (all symphonic).

*ELGIN SYMPHONETTE,1700 Spartan Dr., Elgin IL 60123. (312)888-7389. Music Director: David Katz. Symphony, philharmonic, and youth orchestra. Members are professionals and amateurs. Performs 6 concerts/year including 3 new works. Commissions 1 composer or new work/year. "Concerts are performed for suburban audience of white and blue collar music lovers in one of two halls— one is a large church seating 800—the other is a small concert hall seating 450." Pays $100-300/performance, "depending on soloist, event, length."
How to Contact: Submit complete score and tapes of piece(s). SASE. Reports in 6 weeks.
Music: "Seeking works for chamber orchestra—to standard orchestra: 3222 4200 timpani, percussion, harp, strings. Accessible works of moderate difficulty, not longer than 10-15 minutes." Does not wish to see "specifically pops music; unless it's of classical orientation."
Production: Gwyn Walker's *Fanfare, Interlude, Finale* (3-movement orchestra work—midwest premier); Steven Bero's *Gymnopedie* (1 movement orchestra work—world premier); and David Katz's *Romances* (4 songs for voice and orchestra—midwest premier).
Tips: "Call me! I would be very interested in the right piece and right composer."

*FLORIDA SPACE COAST PHILHARMONIC, INC.,Box 3344, Cocoa FL 32924 or 2150 Lake Dr., Cocoa FL 32926. (305)632-7445. General Manager: Alyce Christ. Artistic Director and Conductor: Maria Tunicka. Philharmonic orchestra and chamber music ensemble. Estab. 1986. Members are professionals. Performs 14 concerts/year. Concerts are performed for "average audience—they like familiar works and pops. Concert halls range from 525 to 2,000 seats." Pays 10% royalty (rental); outright purchase of $2,000; $50-600/performance; or by private arrangement. Query first; submit complete score and tape of piece(s). SASE Reports ASAP; "our conductor tours frequently thus we have to keep material until she has a chance to see and hear it."
Music: Seeks "pops and serious music for full symphony orchestra, but not an overly large orchestra with unusual instrumentation. We use about 55 musicians because of hall limitations. Works should be medium difficulty—not too easy and not too difficult—and not more than 10 minutes long." Does not wish to see avante-garde music.
Tips: "If we would commission a work it would be to feature the space theme in our area."

*GEORGIA STATE UNIVERSITY ORCHESTRA,School of Music, University Plaza, Atlanta GA 30303. (404)658-3676. Conductor: Kirk Edward Smith. Symphony orchestra. Members are college students. Performs 3-5 concerts/year including at least 1 new work. Commissions at least 1 composer or new work/year. Concert hall seats 400. "Audience expects traditional standard orchestral literature as well as explorations into 20th century literature. We always include at least one 20th century or American composition per program." Does not pay "because we perform free concerts."
How to Contact: Query. SASE. Reports in 1 month.
Music: Seeks music of "all durations for string or full orchestra or wind and brasses alone. Contemporary techniques useful for good college orchestra. We must be able to successfully perform pieces after ten 2 hour rehearsals per program."
Productions: Thomas Albert's *Hymnpiece* (work for contemporary orchestra—local premier); Jeffrey Hoover's *Prometheus* (piece for winds, brass and percussion—world premier); and V. Thomson's *The Plow That Broke The Plains* (orchestra piece).

THE GOTHAM CITY OPERA, #N1707, 575 Main St., Roosevelt Island NY 10044-0145. Executive Director: Sandra Van Cleve. Opera company. Operas are performed for New York audience. Pays by outright purchase or per performance, depending on material. Submit complete ms, score and tape of songs. SASE. Reports in 1 month.
Music: "Emphasis is on musical style—nice melodies. Children's material is acceptable. We have limited staging and like to employ smaller casts (around 6-8 performers)."

*GREAT FALLS SYMPHONY ASSOCIATION,Box 1090, Great Falls MT 59403. (406)453-4102. Music Director and Conductor: Gordon J. Johnson. Symphony orchestra and chamber music ensemble. Members are professionals and amateurs. Performs 6 concerts (2 youth concerts)/year including 1 new work. Commissions 1 composer or new work/year. "Our audience is conservative. Newer music is welcome, however, might be more successful if it were programatic." Plays performed in Civic Center Auditorium seating 1,750. Pays $200-1,000/performance.
How to Contact: Submit complete score and tapes of pieces. SASE.
Music: "Compositions should be for full orchestra. Should be composed ideomatically for instruments avoiding extended techniques. Duration 10-20 minutes. Avoid diverse instruments as alto flute, Wagner tuben, saxophones, etc. Our orchestra carries 65 members most of whom are talented amatuers. We have a resident string quartet that serves as principals. Would enjoy seeing a piece for quartet solo and orchestra. Send letter with clean score and tape (tape optional). We will reply withing a few weeks."
Productions: Stewart Grant's *Prairies and Mountains* (symphonic portrait); and John Cubbage's *Homage to Bach* (symphonic).
Tips: "Music for orchestra and chorus is welcome. Cross cues will be helpful in places. Work should not require an undue amount of rehearsal time (remember that a concerto and symphony are probably on the program as well)."

*THE HOBOKEN CHAMBER ORCHESTRA, 5 Marine View Plaza, Hoboken NJ 07030. (201)653-1999. Music Director: Gary M. Schneider. Chamber orchestra. Members are professionals. Performs 6 concerts/year including 2 new works. Concerts are performed for broad audience base with an average of 400 per concert. Hall can hold 900 people. Pays by royalty via ASCAP and BMI.
How to Contact: Submit complete score and tape of pieces. SASE.
Music: "Any style will be considered. Piece should not exceed 15 minutes and must be able to be prepared in 3 rehearsals."
Productions: M. Kallstrom's *Rapid Clearing* (chamber orchestra piece); Ulysses Kay's *Pieta* (work for E.H. and strings); and Schneider's *Concerto for Jazz Clarinet and String Orchestra*.

*IDAHO STATE—CIVIC SYMPHONY,Box 8099, Pocatello ID 83209. (208)236-3479. Music Director/Conductor: Dr. Thom Ritter George. Symphony orchestra. Members are professionals and amateurs. Performs 12 concerts/year. "Audience varied, ranges from highly musically educated to little background in music, in general prefer music with which they have some familiarity. The symphony performs in Goranson Hall, on campus of Idaho State University—seats 444, good acoustics." Pays by outright purchase or per performance.
How to Contact: Query first. Does not return unsolicited material
Productions: Griffes' *Poem for Flute and Orchestra*; Edouard Lalo's *Symphonie Espagnole*; and Sibelius' *Symphony No. 2 in D Major, OP. 43*.

ILLWINDS CHAMBER ENSEMBLE, Box 188, Narrowsburg NY 12764. (914)252-3910. Director: Gloria R. Krause. Chamber music ensemble. Performs 6 concerts/year including 4 new works. Members are professionals. Commissions 1 composer or new work/year. "Our concerts are performed in churches and in outdoor parks (in summer) and art galleries. Audiences are varied depending on the area." Pays $120 per performance through grants like Meet The Composer and New York State Council on the Arts Decentralization Program.

*KINGSPORT SYMPHONY ORCHESTRA,509 Watauga, Kingsport TN 37660. (615)246-9351. Music Director: John Gordon Ross. Symphony orchestra, youth orchestra and community chorus. Members are professionals and amateurs. performs 6 concerts/year including some new works. "General audience, Robinson Auditorium (1950's middle-school with hard seats and very live acoustics, capacity 983)." Pays royalty.
How to Contact: Submit complete score and tapes of piece. SASE. Reports in 25 weeks.
Productions: Edmund Cionek's *Sinfonietta* (neo-classical).

KNOX-GALESBURG SYMPHONY, Box 31 Knox College, Galesburg IL 61401. (309)343-0112, ext. 208. Music Director: Bruce Polay. Symphony orchestra. Performs 7 concerts/year including 1-5 new works. Members are professionals and amateurs. Audience is "middle to upper middle class. We will focus on building the former once we move performances from the present hall (600) to a new building (1,000)." Pays per performance via ASCAP and BMI. Submit complete score and tape of pieces. Does not return unsolicited material.
Music: "Chamber works are welcome. Moderate difficulty for strings due to lack of rehearsal time."
Productions: Poulenc/Polay's *Sonata for Oboe*, Bruce Polay's *TBA*, and C. Julstrom's *Adagio for Or-*

chestra. (The first two were commissioned.)
Tips: Submit "good manuscript with sensible orchestration, sticking to a common instrumentation with moderate difficulty."

LEHIGH VALLEY CHAMBER ORCHESTRA, Box 2641, Lehigh Valley PA 18001. (215)770-9666. Music Director: Donald Spieth. Symphony orchestra. Performs 30 concerts/year including 2 new works. Members are professionals. Commissions 1-2 composers or new works/year. Orchestra has "1,000 subscribers for Friday/Saturday pairs of concerts. Also offers youth programs, pops, etc." Pays by royalty, outright purchase or per performance. Submit complete score and tape of pieces. Reports in 2 months.
Music: "Serious, classical compositions/pops for chamber orchestra (with percussion, optional harp and strings). A composer should not write specifically for us without an agreement."
Productions: Season programs include works by the masters and new works featuring virtuoso soloists on piano, violin, cello, oboe, and more.

LEXINGTON PHILHARMONIC SOCIETY, 161 N. Mill St., Arts Place, Lexington KY 40507. Music Director: George Zack. Symphony orchestra, philharmonic orchestra and chamber music ensemble. Performs 20-30 concerts/year including 15 new works. Members are professionals. Commissions 1 composer or new work/year. Series include "8 serious, classical subscription concerts (hall seats 1500); 3-5 outdoor pops concerts (from 1500 to 5000 tickets sold); 3-5 run-out concerts (½ serious/½ pops); and 8 children's concerts (hall seats 1500). Pays via ASCAP and BMI, rental purchase and private arrangements. Submit complete score and tape of pieces. SASE.
Music: Seeking "good current pops material and good serious classical works. No specific restrictions, but overly large orchestra requirements, unusual instruments, and extra rentals help limit our interest."
Productions: Sam Adler's *Concerto for Piano* (regional premiere); Joseph Baber's *Rumpelstiltskin Suite* (opera suite); and Col. R.H. Sturges's *Frankfort, KY* (song of regional interest).
Tips: "When working on large-format arrangement, use cross-cues so orchestra can be cut back if required. Submit good quality copy, scores and parts. Tape is helpful."

*****LONDON CHAMBER PLAYERS**,Box 84, London NW11 8AL England. Phone: (01)455-6799. Artistic Director: Mr. Adrian Sunshine. Chamber orchestra. Members are professionals. Performs varying number of concerts/year including "several" new works. Performs in "various halls internationally for audiences of general concert-goers and young people; also for television audiences." Pays by royalty, outright purchase or per performance. Query. Does not return unsolicited material.
Music: Music for "chamber orchestra, string orchestra, solo works with orchestra, and formations up to 30 musicians." Does not wish to see "aleatoric, avant-garde or electronic pieces."

*****LOS ANGELES REPERTOIRE ORCHESTRA (SYMPHONY)**,14209 Chandler Blvd., Van Nuys CA 91401. (818)781-8484. Musical Director/Conductor: Walter F. Moeck. Symphony orchestra. Estab. 1986. Members are professionals. "So far we are just a reading orchestra to keep musicians up on the repertoire, help young soloists and composers. So far, no salary is involved. This is sponsored by the L.A. Musicians Union—Local 47."
How to Contact: Query first. Submit complete score and tape of pieces after query. "We appreciate that the composer pay for the mailings to and from our destination."
Music: Seeks "classical symphonic music—semi classical and light symphonic music like *Rhapsody in Blue*—by an experienced composer for a regular size symphony orchestra." Does not wish to see "commercial and music that is overly dissonant and free of meter. Good symphonic commercial music would be accepted."
Productions: Eddy Hunton's *Clarinet Concerto* (concerto for strings and horn); and Ara Sevanian's *Concerto* (concerto for kanon).

*****McHENRY COUNTY YOUTH ORCHESTRA**, 46 South Walkup Ave., Crystal Lake IL 60014. (815)459-7664. Music Director: Kevin R. McKelvie. Youth orchestra. Members are amateurs; children and young people. 4 orchestras perform 5 concerts/year. "Our audiences consist mostly of parents and other family members. We are beginning to attract community music lovers."
How to Contact: Submit complete score and tape of pieces. SASE. Reports in 3 months.
Music: Seeks "Contemporary 'classical' music in a variety of easy and moderate difficulties. Shorter pieces (5 minutes) would be best suited to our educational goals and audience appreciation. We have four groups: beginning string orchestra, grades 3-6; intermediate full orchestra, grades 5-8; high school full orchestra, grades 8-12 (performs mostly standard literature); and advanced string ensemble, grades 8-12 (performs standard string orchestra literature). At present we have no access to harp, english horn and the more exotic percussins (celeste). If we were absolutely convinced of the piece most any instrument and/or player could be hire—depending on budget."

Productions: George Flynn's *Lost and Found* (full orchestra piece).
Tips: "Consult music director. We have a committment to performing contemporary music but have had difficulty locating music of appropriate difficulty and length."

*MONTGOMERY CHAMBER ORCHESTRA,Box 429, Gaithersburg MO 20877. (301)762-8580. Music Director/Conductor: Piotr Gajewski. Chamber orchestra. Members are professionals. Performs 8 concerts/year including 2-4 new works. "The orchestra's audience is growing quickly. During the present (86-87) season the orhestra has 500 subscribers. The orchestra's activities include concerts at the National Bureau of Standards and the Montgomery College." Pays royalty via ASCAP and BMI. Submit complete score and tape of pieces. Does not return unsolicited material.
Music: Seeking "generally short works (5-20 minutes) with emphasis on greater Washington, D.C. area composers. The orchestra is generally a standard classical orchestra. The pieces performed vary in difficulty (it is a strong, professional orchestra). However, as with all professional orchestras, rehearsal time is limited." Does not wish to see pop music.
Productions: Tom Ludwig's *Sinfonia #1* (world premier); Witold Lutoslawski's *Dance Preludes*; and Andreas Makris' *Anemvesis*.

*NATIONAL ARTS CHAMBER ORCHESTRA, Box 4068, Ann Arbor MI 48106-4068. (313)973-6285. Music Director: Kevin R. McMahon. Symphony orchestra. Members are professionals and college students. Performs 20 concerts/year including 6 new works. Commissions 6 composers or new works/year. Performs for "varied audiences in halls across the country." Commissions vary. "Send complete score and tape if the work isn't a world premiere." SASE. Reports in 6 weeks.
Music: Seeking "music of the higest order written with integrity. Works for anywhere from seven to sixty-five performers are most ideal for our organization. Best to leave out low brass, but this is not a full restriction. Length should be anywhere from three minutes to an hour."
Productions: David Gompper's *Nimbus II*, Jacob Chi's *Spring in Xin Jiang*, and Thomas Massella's *Serenade to Dreams*, all world premieres.

*OPERA HAMILTON,Box 2080, Station A, Hamilton, Ontario L8N 3Y7 Canada. (416)527-7027. Artistic Director: Daniel Lipton. Opera company. Members are professionals and amateurs. Performs 2 operas/year plus 1 gala concert. Concerts are performed in a "2,100 seat concert hall with excellent acoustics (Hamilton Place). Opera's audience is expandig all the time."
How to Contact: Submit complete score and tape of pieces. SAE and IRC.
Music: Seeking "short new operas—maximum 60 minutes in length. We wish to begin with small works (i.e. no more than 4-5 principals, if possible)."
Productions: Gala concert, including *Popera* (popular opera arias); Verdi's *Un Ballo In Maschera*; and Bizet's *Carmen*.

*OPERA PACIFIC,17712 Mitchell, Irvine CA 92714. (714)474-8000. Director: Dr. David DiChiera. Opera and musical theatre producers. Members are professionals. Pays by royalty.
How to Contact: Query first. Does not return unsolicited material.
Music: Seeks "opera, or opera styled musical scores."
Productions: Gershwin's *Porgy and Bess*; Bernstein and Sondheim's *West Side Story*; and Puccini's *La Boheme*.

*THE PHILHARMONIA OF MELBOURNE, 27 Wallis Ave., E. Ivanhoe, Melbourne, Victoria 3079 Australia. Contact: Rosia Choate. String chamber ensemble. Members are professionals. Performs 10 concerts/year including 1-2 new works. Commissions 1 composer or new work/year. Concerts are performed "in an art gallery (The Great Hall) for a typical Sunday art gallery audience." Pays $500-600 outright purchase. Query. Does not return unsolicited material.
Music: Looking for "Short pieces (20 minutes maximum but preferably shorter) for string orchestra (and harpsichord if desired). Twelve strings only. Concertos for one instrument a possibility. Our normal number of rehearsals per concert is three, therefore piece must not be too complex. We prefer music written in a conventional but contemporary style."
Productions: Melvynn's *Two-Viola Concerto*.

PHILHARMONIC ORCHESTRA OF INDIANAPOLIS, Box 503, Indianapolis IN 46206. (317)283-5242. Music Director: Orcenith G. Smith. Symphony orchestra. Performs 10 concerts/year including "very few" new works. Members are professionals and amateurs. Commissions 1 composer or new work/year. Concerts performed for the "general public and family members in the newly refurbished Caleb Mills Hall (seats 1200)." Pays by royalty or outright purchase. Query first. Does not return unsolicited material.
Music: Seeking pieces for full orchestra (with no more than 3 woodwinds and 4 percussionists), with

Close-up

Albert Coleman
Conductor
Atlanta Pops Orchestra

Albert Coleman was born in Paris, the son of a French father and Italian mother. Both of his parents were in show business, and he traveled the world with them (he escaped the Russian Revolution by riding on top of a train!). After studying at the Paris Conservatory of Music, he began his own music career, again touring the world. He began conducting in Shanghai, China and composing in Sydney, Australia. He tells one story of walking on the streets of Johannesburg at 6:00 in the morning, "walking toward rehearsal, a terrific melody came in my mind and all I had in my hand was a pencil—no paper, no nothing. There was nobody on the street that early, so I started writing on the walls. When I got to the theatre, I took some music paper and went back and copied what I had written!" For the last 43 years, Coleman has been directing the Atlanta Pops Orchestra. This diverse experience has allowed him to write and conduct every type of music from vaudeville to classical.

While his background is extraordinary, his advice to composers is very basic. "What a composer needs, in my opinion, is a good sense of who will perform the type of music he writes. That's the secret. If he composes classical, naturally he must approach a symphony orchestra. If it's semi-classical or even lighter, approach a pops orchestra. Or if it's still lighter, approach a dance band.

"And that's a big headache," he admits. "It's hard to find many orchestras that will play new things. For instance, I try to have at least 80% of my program music that people know, that they could whistle if they wanted to. Because that's what attracts my crowd."

Coleman says he does receive and listen to demo tapes. "Every now and then I hear something worthwhile and I try to perform it. Just last year there was a local arranger/composer who sent me a solo with flute and alto saxophone. It was absolutely beautiful, so right away I used it in one of my concerts."

Coleman reveals that good opportunities exist for composers and musicians who make orchestral arrangements. "For one thing, it is hard to get music, and in the pops field it's almost impossible. And if you want something in a Gershwin vein or Cole Porter or something like that, they don't even sell it anymore. They rent it. So it's quite expensive to get music. Therefore, if somebody comes up with an arrangement that sounds great, the conductor will grab it immediately."

Generally, Coleman says, there's no payment for first performances of arrangements or compositions. "It's a show piece for the composer and publicity, and then if he can get it recorded he cashes in from there on. For instance, I was conducting the Toronto Symphony as guest conductor one time, and a trumpet player came over to me and said, 'I heard the last record you made—I have a tune here you may like. It's a trumpet solo.' He gave it to me, and almost three years later I put it on one of my albums."

Coleman himself wrote a piece with a country music feeling and symphonic instrumentation. He called it "Sophisticated Hoe-down," and it was included on his RCA album *Country*

Concerts several years ago. "And I still get royalties on that," he says.

While enjoying a lengthy and diverse career, Coleman tries to encourage others. He has featured as many as 3 to 4 guest performers or composers in his pops concerts. "It helps me get a tremendous crowd and it helps the young people to be ambitious and move ahead." His encouraging words for composers: "If a composer feels he can write and he's good, he should just keep on going. Try to present the work to as many people as possible, and eventually it'll break through."

—*Julie Wesling Whaley*

---

moderate difficulty level and 8-12 minutes in length. Does not wish to see electronic music.
Productions: A. Paul Johnson's *Clarinet Concerto* (for chamber winds).

PLYMOUTH PHILHARMONIC ORCHESTRA, INC., Box 3174, Plymouth MA 02361. (818)781-8484. Music Director: Rudolf Schlegel. Symphony orchestra and chamber music ensembles. Performs 25 concerts/year including 2-3 new works. Members are professionals and semi-professional musicians. Commissions 1 composer or new work/year. Concerts performed for "varied audiences in a 1,500-seat hall. Chamber music performances in area schools." Pays per performance. Query first. SASE. Reports in 3 months.
Music: Seeking "high quality orchestral music that is readily accessible to audiences. Send a simple inquiry with a description of available works."
Productions: Jerome D. Cohen's *Invincible Bunbury* (march); Robert DiDomenica's *Dream Journeys* (tone poem); and Daniel Pinkham's *Symphony No. 3*.

PROFESSIONAL REPERTOIRE ORCHESTRA, 817 Vine St., Los Angeles CA 90038. (818)781-8484. Musical Director/Conductor: Walter F. Moeck. Symphony orchestra and brass chamber music ensemble. Estab. March, 1986. Members are professionals. "We are a new reading orchestra made up of the finest musicians. Currently sponsored by Musicians Local 47." Query first. Reports in 6 weeks.
Music: "Our 72-piece professional reading orchestra will try to read through all styles of symphonic music, but we prefer traditional music with standard instrumentation. Music should be of high quality and enjoyable for the average audience. Do not send ultra-modern music ('free' music without measures, etc.)."

RED RIVER LYRIC THEATRE, 5 Brenna Dr., Wichita Falls TX 76302. (817)761-3692. Musical Director: Mr. Jan L. McDaniel. Opera/music theater company. Performs 6 productions/year including 1 new work. Members are professionals and amateurs. "We have a 1500-seat theater (converted movie house) as well as a few other smaller performance halls. Our audience is quite conservative in its tastes, though avante-garde works requiring small forces are possible." Pays "per special agreement with each composer. We try to have the composer in residence for a short time if possible." Submit complete score and tape of pieces. SASE.
Music: "Operas and musicals only. New works should be short (one-act works are best) and should require as few principle roles as possible. Any use of the chorus should be SATB or SSA (no divisi) and as simple as is practical for the drama. A ten-piece (or fewer) instrumental ensemble is preferred. Of special interest to us are short operas whose themes or subjects would complement the one-act works of standard composers (e.g., an opera which could be paired with Mozart's *The Impressario*). The music should contain singable vocal lines. We are not interested in vocal music of an aleatory nature."
Productions: Menotti's *Amahl and the Night Visitors* (Christmas opera); Puccini's *Madama Butterfly* (opera); and Bock's *Fiddler on the Roof* (musical).
Tips: "Of greatest interest to us would be the possibility in having input in the shaping of a new work by means of a dialogue with the composer."

SAN FERNANDO VALLEY THEATRE OF PERFORMING ARTS, Box 300, Van Nuys CA 91408. (818)781-8484. Musical Director and Conductor: Walter Moeck. Symphony orchestra, chamber music ensemble. Performs 5-6 concerts/year including 3 new works. Members are professionals. "No regular concert hall yet. Concerts are performed in various auditoriums in the area for audiences of all ages." Query for more information. SASE. Reports in 2 weeks.
Music: "We are primarily interested in new music for our chamber ensembles. We have a woodwind ensemble and a large brass group—4 French horns, 4 trombones, tuba and timpani. No limitation on length of pieces or level of difficulty, but we prefer a style that is fairly conventional or conservative. Nothing really avant-garde or overly dissonant."

*THE TULSA PHILHARMONIC,2210 S. Main, Tulsa OK 74114. (918)584-2533. Music Director: Bernard Rubenstein. Symphony orchestra, chamber music ensemble, philharmonic orchestra, youth orchestra and pops orchestra. Members are professionals. Performs 30-40 concerts/year. "Our concert hall seats 2,400. We do nine classics programs and 5 pops, runouts, especially with pops, short tours, educational concerts, and several out door concerts." Pays by outright purchase or per performance.
How to Contact: Submit complete score and tape of pieces. SASE.
Music: "Our biggest need is for pops material. Budget limitations dictate the size of our ensemble. A piece using smaller instrumentation or with the possibility of cross-cuing or other reductions is more likely to be considered."
Productions: Previn/Stoppard's *Every Good Boy Deserves Favor* (orchestra with actors); Louis Ballard's *Fantasy Aborigine #4* (full orchestra); and Wilfred Josephs' *Bass Concerto*.

VALLEY YOUTH ORCHESTRA ASSOCIATION, 18111 Nordhoff St., Northridge CA 91330. (818)885-3074. Music Director: H. Wesley Kenney. Symphony orchestra, youth orchestra and chamber orchestra. Performs 8 concerts/year including 2 new works. Members are amateurs and students. "Audience is comprised of parents of members, many senior citizens, other students and professional people. Halls are either Liberty Hall (seats about 1400 with wide but shallow stage) or a campus theater (seats 400 with large stage)." Pays outright purchase of $100-200, $100-200/performance, or negotiated amount. Submit complete score (full score only) and tape of pieces. SASE. Reports in 3 weeks.
Music: "Pieces should be orchestrated for full orchestra on one of two levels. The Junior Orchestra (ages 11-14) has a brass section of 2 horns, 3 trumpets, and 1-3 trombones. Divisi in strings acceptable—up to 2 parts for each section except basses. Pieces should not be longer than 10 minutes, and livelier works are better. For the Senior Orchestra (ages 14-20) any length is acceptable, but level of difficulty should not be severe. The players can do quite a bit, but concentration and maturity are limited. Any style is acceptable, but we strive to perform serious music. Interest of music is extremely important, so something that can be comprehended in a fairly short period is important."
Productions: Junior Orchestra: R.V. Williams' *Folk Song Suite*; Schubert's *Unfinished Symphony*; and R. Rodgers' *Highlights from The Sound of Music*. Senior Orchestra: West Coast premier of Richard Adler's *The Lady Remembers* (multi-movement, full orchestra piece); and Grofe's *The Mississippi Suite* (descriptive suite for orchestra.
Tips: "Learn the limitations of the instruments, and rudiments of orchestral balance."

*THE VENTURA COUNTY SYMPHONY ASSOCIATION,Box 1085, Ventura CA 93002. (805)643-8646. Music Director: Frank A. Salazar. Symphony orchestra and youth orchestra. Members are professionals and amateurs. Performs 18 concerts/year including 20% new works. Commissions 1 composer or new work/year. "Our concert hall holds 1600 seats, of which 1300 are sold on a season subscription basis. Our concert attendees include individuals of all age levels, and professions. We have three community colleges which provide a student population as well." Pays standard royalty, by outright purchase or per performance.
How to Contact: Submit complete score and tape of pieces. Does not return unsolicited material.
Productions: Chesne's *Symphony #4* (four movements); Myrow's *Variations* (seven movements); and Thow's *Canto de Quetzal* (18 minutes).

WARREN CHAMBER ORCHESTRA, Box 48, Warren OH 44482. Music Director: George Zack. Chamber orchestra. Performs 7-10 concerts/year. "Concerts are performed for subscribers, including some children's concerts and pops." Commissions 1 composer or new work/year. Payment is negotiated in individual contract with each composer. Submit complete score and tape of pieces. SASE.
Music: "We appreciate good, current material that uses reduced orchestra to fit our size. Our restrictions are those of chamber instrumentation, with full string complement and winds and brass as needed. No limitations on difficulty."
Productions: Robert Rollin's *Concerto Pastorale* (premiere).
Tips: "Cross-cued parts for reduced orchestra are appreciated."

*WAYNE CHAMBER ORCHESTRA,300 Pompton Rd., Wayne NJ 07470. (201)595-2694. Manager: Sheri Newberger. Chamber orchestra. Estab. 1986. Members are professionals. Performs 3-4 concerts/year. Regional audience from North Jersey area. Attractive and modern concert hall seating 960 patrons.
How to Contact: Query first. SASE.
Music: "We are a forty member chamber orchestra. We play traditional music but put special emphasis on American music. Although we have not performed new works yet, we are only in our debut season and plan to expand in future seasons. We use highly skilled professional musicians. We cannot perform works needing a very large orchestra. Please include resume with letter."
Productions: "Our last concert included works by Schubert, Prokofiev, Copland, Cowell."

*WEST COAST CHAMBER ORCHESTRA,Suite 304, 615 SE Alder, Portland OR 97214. (503)236-5537. Music Director: Niel B. DePonte. Professional chamber orchestra. Members are professionals. Performs 5-10 concerts/year including 1 new work. Commissioned 2 composers or new works in last 5 seasons. "Our audience is aged 29-42, white, professional, new to classical music. Concerts performed in Arlene Schnitzer Concert Hall which seats 2,778." Pays negotiable commission.
How to Contact: Submit complete score and tape of pieces. SASE.
Music: Seeking " program works using 10-42 players plus conductor. Scoring for strings 2-2-2-2, 2-2, T-keyboard are standard. Always interested in concerto grosso format. Pieces that do not require extensive brass sections are preferred. Please, no pops literature."
Productions: Bryan Johanson's *Partita* (premier (9/4/87).
Tips: "Follow up submission of score and tape with a phone call directly to the music director. Do not waste time convincing the business manager that your piece should be programmed, because the music director does all of the programming."

*WESTCHESTER CONSERVATORY SYMPHONY ORCHESTRA,20 Soundview Ave., White Plains NY 10605. (914)761-3715. Music Director: Elliot Magaziner. Symphony orchestra. Members are professionals and amateurs. Performs 5 concerts/year including several new works. Pays per performance.
How to Contact: Query first. Does not return unsolicited material.
Productions: Seymour Garat's *Bigger and Better* (orchestra, dance and narration); Fred Katz's *Symphony for Jazz Band and Orchestra*; and Irwin Stahl's *Tango* (symphonic dance).

WESTLAKE SYMPHONY ORCHESTRA, 14209 Chandler Blvd., Van Nuys CA 91401. (818)781-8484. Musical Director and Conductor: Walter Moeck. Symphony orchestra. Members are professionals. "We are just getting started and no concert hall has been constructed yet. Concerts are performed in various auditoriums and large churches for a general audience." Query should be sent to Mr. Walter Moeck at Box 300, Van Nuys CA 92408. SASE. Reports in 2 weeks.
Music: Submit "conservative, conventional compositions for orchestra. We have 50 performers, limited strings." No limitation on length of piece or level of difficulty.
Productions: Wagner's *The Meistersinger Overture*; Debussy's *Setes* (from The Nocturnes); and *The Carmen Suite*.

*WILLMAR COMMUNITY ORCHESTRA,c/o Music Dept, Willmar Community College, Willmar MN 56201. (612) 231-5125. Director: Dr. Chet Sommers. Community orchestra and chorus. Members are professionals and amateurs. Performs 6-8 concerts/year. "We perform 2-3 orchestra concerts, 1-2 Oratorios, dinner music, etc." Pays by outright purchase or per performance.
Productions: Rutter's *Requiem*; and Handel's *Messiah*.

*YELLOWSTONE CHAMBER PLAYERS, 4111 June Dr., Billings MT 59106. (406)656-7978 or 248-2205. President: Mary La Monaca. Chamber music ensemble. Performs 6-10 concerts/year including 3 new works. Members are professionals. Commissioned 1 new work in 1986-87 season. "Audiences include colleges, churches and art museums as each concert is in a different location. We also do several out-of-town concerts in smaller, rural communities. We must raise grant money to cover commissions."
How to Contact: Submit complete score and tape of pieces. SASE. Reports in 2 months.
Music: "We are open to traditional as well as contemporary styles. Our group includes strings, piano, guitar, oboe, and flute. We usually use smaller groups of 3-5 performers from those instruments, though we have done some large ensemble pieces such as Ives' 'Unanswered Question' and the Block *Concerto for Chamber Orchestra*. Difficulty of a composition should be such that a good performance can be achieved in five or fewer rehearsals. Folk-based compositions for rural audiences are appropriate."
Productions: David Thomas' *Trio for Clarinet, Violins, Piano* (premiered spring 1987); Uri Barnea's *Sonata* (flute and piano); and Bartoh's *Contrasts* (violin, clarinet, piano).
Tips: "Include any documentation which would enhance audience accessibility."

*ZION CHAMBER ORCHESTRA,Dowie Memorial Drive, Zion IL 60099. (312)872-4803. Music Director: Timoth C. Hall. Chamber orchestra. Members are professionals and amateurs. Performs 12 concerts/year including occasional new works. Audience is "low-middle class—middle class mostly. 522 seat auditorium, modern, effective acoustically, but a little dry for music."
How to Contact: Subit complete score and tape of pieces. Does not return unsolicited material.
Music: "Instrumentation for chamber group—full complement of brass, winds, strings. Not interested in dissonance at this time. Prefers medium level difficulty."
Productions: D. Dickering's *Our Inurement* (serial. . .anti abortion); A. Koetz's *Sweet Hour of Prayer* (sacred, traditional); and Mendelsohn, Bach, Mozart, Brahms, Ives, Prokofiev, etc.

Services & Opportunities

Organizations

Being a member of a songwriter or music organization can be valuable in many ways. Most organizations are staffed with knowledgeable experts able to answer questions and distribute helpful information. Many organizations offer seminars, workshops and classes, further educating their members and sometimes giving members a chance to meet important industry professionals and have their songs critiqued by them. Most songwriting organizations also offer the opportunity to meet potential collaborators.

Many other services are available from organizations, such as newsletters, performance opportunities, discounts on items of interest to songwriters and musicians, and competitions and awards.

Songwriters from anywhere are eligible to join national organizations like the National Academy of Songwriters, The Songwriters Guild of America, the Nashville Songwriters Association International, the Country Music Association, the Black Music Association, the Gospel Music Association and the Dramatists Guild.

Many mid-sized cities have strong songwriter groups and encourage local affiliation. If you don't live in a town where a songwriting organization exists, you might consider starting one. There are probably more people in your community interested in the music industry than you realize. At the very least, you could discuss your experiences, share contacts, and critique each other's songs at your meetings until you build up a large enough membership to sponsor other activities.

In each of the following listings, organizations describe what they have to offer. Write to any that interest you for more information.

THE ACADEMY OF COUNTRY MUSIC, #915, 6255 Sunset Blvd., Box 508, Hollywood CA 90028. (213)462-2351. Executive Secretary: Fran Boyd. For "professional persons connected with the country music industry. For professional membership the person must be affiliated with the country music industry in some manner." Offers newsletter and showcases. "Purpose is to promote country music."

AMATEUR SONGWRITERS MUSIC TALENT, Box 255 Dept. SWM28, Cave City KY 42127. Contact: Wiley E. McCluskey, Jr. Estab. 1986. Members are songwriters, lyricists and composers of all ages, musicians, poets, comedians, commercial music writers, recording artists and anyone who wants to correspond with others in the music field. "We offer our members a chance to correspond with other composers and performers and make contacts in the music business. We offer our clients low priced, professional demo tape and master service. We also offer 3 or 4 yearly songwriters contests." Applications are accepted throughout the year. Other services include lectures, performance opportunities, instruction and newsletter. Membership is $37.50/year in U.S.; $40 (U.S. dollars) for Canadian and overseas members.

AMERICAN COUNCIL FOR THE ARTS, 570 7th Ave., New York NY 10018. (212)354-6655. Contact: Membership Dept. "We are the leading private national nonprofit organization that serves all the arts." Members are state, regional and community arts agencies, arts centers, performing arts organizations, museums, libraries, parks and recreation departments, professional arts managers and artists and individuals interested in supporting the arts. Services include advocacy for the arts at the federal level; arts management training conferences and seminars; *Horizon* magazine with five *Vantage Point* supplements featuring articles about major issues facing the arts today; *ACA Up Date*, a monthly up-to-the-minute news bulletin; ACA Books (publisher and distributor of books on the arts); a research library of 7,500 books and documents; and reference and information services. Memberships include individual memberships (from $25-100) and institutional memberships (from $150-250), depending on services and benefits desired.

AMERICAN FEDERATION OF MUSICIANS (AFM), Suite 600, 1501 Broadway, New York NY 10036. (212)869-1330. Membership available to all qualified musicians and vocalists in the United States and Canada. "The American Federation of Musicians of the United States and Canada is the largest entertainment union in the world and exists solely for the advancement of live music and the benefit of its 250,000 members. In addition to enhancing employment opportunities for members the AFM aids members in negotiating contracts; enforces employers' observance of working conditions and wage scales; processes traveling members' claims at no cost to members; protects musicians from unfavorable legislation at the federal, state and local levels; negotiates pension, welfare and retirement benefits; offers instrument insurance to members; offers free job referral service to members who are seeking employment with traveling groups; and keeps membership informed of happenings in the business through its publication *International Musician*. Members also receive numerous benefits provided by each local." Initiation fees and local dues vary; a small percentage of work dues are contributed by members. Write for further information or contact AFM local nearest you."

AMERICAN GUILD OF MUSIC, Box 3, Downers Grove IL 60515. (312)968-0173. Registered Agent: Elmer Herrick. For musicians and students. Members are music studio operators, teachers, and students interested in teaching and performing. Offers competitions, instruction, lectures, newsletter, performance opportunities and workshops. "Purpose is to improve teaching methods, promote interest in string instruments, accordion, etc."

AMERICAN MECHANICAL RIGHTS AGENCY (AMRA), 2112 Broadway, New York NY 10023. (212)877-4077. Executive Director: Robert Goldberg. Members include songwriters and music publishers from the US, Canada and 18 European countries. Applicants must have a record released in the US. Purpose is to collect mechanical, synchronization and background royalties.

AMERICAN MUSIC CENTER, INC., Suite 300, 250 W. 54th St., New York NY 10019. (212)247-3121. Executive Director: Nancy Clarke. For composers and performers. Members are American composers, performers, critics, publishers, and others interested in contemporary American music. Offers newsletter, circulating library of contemporary music scores, advice on opportunities for composers and new music performers; disseminates information on American music. Purpose is to encourage the creation, performance, publication, recognition of contemporary American music. Members receive the quarterly *AMC Newsletter*, professional "Opportunity Updates," eligibility for group health insurance, and the right to vote in AMC elections.

AMERICAN MUSICIANS UNION INC., 8 Tobin Ct., Dumont NJ 07628. (201)384-5378. President: Ben Intorre. Serves songwriters, musicians, vocalists and managers. Primary value is contact with other musicians. Membership made up of "people of all ages with interest in all types of music: rock, disco, classical, ethnic, western, etc. People from all locations are eligible; only requirement is that artist is performing or wishing to perform in music business." Offers newsletter, meetings, life insurance ($2,000 till age 65, lower coverage up to age 70), and free classified ads in "Quarternote" newspaper. "For a modest cost, songwriter can be in contact with an active group of other musicians, and benefit from exchange of ideas." Applications accepted throughout the year. Initiation fee is $10; annual dues are $27.

AMERICAN SOCIETY OF COMPOSERS, AUTHORS AND PUBLISHERS (ASCAP), 1 Lincoln Plaza, New York NY 10023. (212)595-3050. Director of Membership: Paul S. Adler. Membership Department Staff: Phyllis Fischler, Ellen Meltzer, Lisa Schmidt, Vivian Scott and Terry Bleckley. Members are songwriters, composers, lyricists and music publishers. Applicants must "have at least one song copyrighted for associate membership; have at least one song commercially available as sheet music, available on rental, commercially recorded, or performed in media licensed by the Society (e.g., performed in a nightclub or radio station) for full membership. ASCAP is a membership-owned, perform-

ing right licensing organization that licenses its members' nondramatic musical compositions for public performance and distributes the fees collected from such licensing to its members based on a scientific random sample survey of performances." Primary value is "as a clearinghouse, giving users a practical and economical bulk licensing system and its members a vehicle through which the many thousands of users can be licensed and the members paid royalties for the use of their material. All monies collected are distrbuted after deducting only the Society's cost of doing business."
Tips: "The Society sponsors a series of writers' workshops in Los Angeles, Nashville and New York open to members and nonmembers. Grants to composers available to members and nonmembers. Contact the public relations or membership departments in New York or the following branch offices: 6430 Sunset Blvd., Los Angeles CA 90028; 2 Music Square W., Nashville TN 37203; 52 Haymarket, London SW1Y4RP, England."

ARTS INTERNATIONAL, 1400 K St. NW, 650, Washington DC 20006. (202)789-0600. Washington Program Officer: Ramona K. Silipo. Serves songwriters and musicians as an "information clearinghouse on opportunities (grants, programs, tours, etc.) abroad." Members are from all arts disciplines: dance, theatre, music, literature and visual arts. Offers newsletter and consulting facilities (members receive one hour of consulting at no charge) and promotes international arts exchange. Songwriters benefit from organization most if they are interested in working abroad, having their music performed at international festivals, need to locate traveling funds, etc."

ARTS MIDWEST/REGIONAL JAZZ PROGRAM, Suite 310, 528 Hennepin Ave., Minneapolis MN 55403. (612)341-0755. Jazz Coordinator: Willard Jenkins, Jr. Serves composers, musicians, dancers, actors and visual artists. "Arts Midwest is a not-for-profit arts organization which fosters and promotes the development of the arts in the Midwest. We are a resource for musicians (songwriters), and other artists in the region which includes the states of Illinois, Indiana, Iowa, Michigan, Minnesota, North Dakota, Ohio, South Dakota, and Wisconsin. Arts Midwest generates opportunities for artists and arts organizations, extending, enriching and complementing the programs and services of the member state arts agencies. The Jazz Program is but one of the programs of Arts Midwest. Other programs include the Performing Arts Touring Program, the Visual Arts Program, Services Program, and computer services." Applications are accepted throughout the year; however, "there are specific deadline periods for several of our funding programs, including the Performing Arts Touring Program, Meet the Composer, Visual Arts Fellowships, etc." Offers members competitions, lectures, performance opportunities, fellowships, workshops, touring programs and newsletter.

***AUSTIN SONGWRITERS GROUP**, #34, 504 W. 24th St., Austin TX 78705. (512)478-2009. Coordinators: Tommy Pierce and Christine Albert. Estab. 1987. Serves songwriters and publishers. "Our membership consists of songwriters and publishers of all styles of music and covering a broad range of experience and professional status, from amateur to established. We only require that members be interested in the creative or business aspects of songwriting. Members are accepted from any geographical location. Purpose is to provide a forum for songwriter development in the areas of creativity and business." Offers educational programs; access to resources; interaction with state, national and international industry professionals; competitions; instruction; lectures; library; newsletter; performance opportunities; and workshops. Applications accepted year-round. $50 annual membership dues, includes a membership in the Texas Music Association.

BLACK MUSIC ASSOCIATION (BMA), 307 S. Broad St., Philadelphia PA 19107-5813. President: Lee Michaels. For songwriters, musicians and anyone interested in music, entertainment, and arts industries. Members are individuals, companies and organizations involved in the music industry. Offers lectures, newsletter, workshops, industry contact resource center, seminars, annual tribute to renowned music contributor and an annual conference. "Purpose is the dedication to the advancement, enrichment, encouragement and recognition of black music."

BROADCAST MUSIC, INC. (BMI), 320 W. 57th St., New York NY 10019. (212)586-2000; Suite 1527, 8730 Sunset Blvd, Los Angeles CA 90069; and 10 Music Square E., Nashville TN 37203. President: Frances W. Preston. Senior Vice President: Theodora Zavin. Vice President, California: Ron Anton. Vice President, Nashville: Roger Sovine. Performing rights organization. "Applicants must have written a musical composition, alone or in collaboration with other writers, which is commercially published, recorded or otherwise likely to be performed. Purpose: BMI licenses the nondramatic performing rights of musical compositions to users of music which include radio and TV stations, hotels, night clubs, universities, colleges and the many other places in the US where music is publicly performed."

CANADIAN ACADEMY OF RECORDING ARTS & SCIENCES (CARAS), 3rd Floor, 124 Merton St., Toronto, Ontario M4S 2Z2 Canada. (416)485-3135. Executive Director: Daisy C. Falle. Serves songwriters and musicians. Membership is open to all employees (including support staff) in broadcasting and record companies, as well as producers, personal managers, recording artists, recording engineers, arrangers, composers, music publishers, album designers, promoters, talent and booking agents, record retailers, rack jobbers, distributors, recording studios and other music industry related professions (on approval). Applicants must be affliliated with the recording industry. Offers newsletter, performance opportunities and social outings, Canadian artist record discount program, music film screenings and discount tickets to Juno awards show. "CARAS strives to foster the development of the Canadian music and recording industries and to contribute toward higher artistic standards." Applications accepted year-round. Membership fee is $45/year.

CANDIAN COUNTRY MUSIC ASSOCIATION,(formerly the Academy of Country Music Entertainment), 833 The Queensway, Toronto, Ontario M82 521 Canada. (416)252-1025. Executive Director: Jack Feeney. Members are songwriters, musicians, producers, radio station personnel, managers, booking agents and others. Offers newsletter, workshops, performance opportunities and annual awards. "Through our newsletters and conventions we offer a means of meeting and associating with artists and others in the industry. The ACME is a Federally chartered, non profit organization, dedicated to the promotion and development of Canadian Country Music throughout Canada and the world and to provide a unity of purpose for the Canadian Country Music industry. We are now involved with the *Music Copyright Action Group* and the main objective of the group is to get the government of Canada to revise the copyright act. We are similar to the CMA in the United States, with approximately 1,000 members (some from the US)." Send for application.

CANADIAN RECORDING INDUSTRY ASSOCIATION (CRIA), 89 Bloor St. E., Toronto, Ontario M4W 1A9 Canada. (416)967-7272. President: Brian Robertson. Membership open to major record companies, independent record labels and recording studios. Applications accepted year-round. "CRIA is the 'voice' of the recording industry in Canada. Its 40 members represent over 98% of the sound recordings manufactured and sold in this country. The association represents the industry on many levels including communication with government, international liaison with music and recording industry organizations around the world, the control of record and tape piracy and other legal matters, and the direction of industry marketing programs such as the certification of gold and platinum records."

CENTRAL OPERA SERVICE, Metropolitan Opera, Lincoln Center, New York NY 10023. (212)957-9871. Executive Director: Maria F. Rich. Members are songwriters, musicians and opera/music theatre producers. "Central Opera Service maintains an extensive library of reference books and domestic and foreign music periodicals, and the most comprehensive operatic archive in the United States. COS draws on these unique resources to supply information to its members." Offers quarterly COS Bulletin (which includes a section "Attention Composers and Librettists"), directories and conferences. Applications accepted year-round.

COMPOSERS, ARRANGERS AND SONGWRITERS OF KANSAS, 117 W. 8th St., Hays KS 67601. (913)625-9634. Administrator: Mark Meckel. Serves songwriters, musicians, arrangers and lyricists. Membership open to "anyone desiring information on the business of songwriting, copyrights or marketing—from professional musicians to housewives. Our purpose is to help members get songs placed with publishing and record companies." No eligibility requirements other than "a desire for a career in the music industry." Applications accepted year-round.

COMPOSERS GUILD, Box 586, 40 N. 100 West, Farmington UT 84025. (801)451-2275. President: Ruth Gatrell. For songwriters and composers. "We are a nonprofit organization working to help the composer/songwriter. Each year we sponsor classes, workshops, seminars, a composition contest, and a performance at the Composers Guild Spectacular."

CONNECTICUT SONGWRITERS ASSOCIATION, Box 4137, Wallingford CT 06492. (203)387-8081. Executive Director: Chick Westover. "We are an educational, nonprofit organization dedicated to improving the art and craft of original music. We offer a monthly newsletter (subscription rate is $15 per year/12 issues), monthly seminars and song critique sessions, performing opportunities at songwriter showcases, song screening service, song tape library, discounts, awards and social outings." No eligibility requirements. Ages range from 12 to 70. Applications accepted year-round. Annual membership categories are: Individual $40, Student and Senior Citizen $20, Organizations $60, Sustaining $100, Benefactor $250, Lifetime $500. ("All memberships include newsletter subscription and are tax deductible to the extent allowed by law.")
Tips: "Members can learn about the music business, improve their songcrafting skills, gain performing opportunities and make collaboration contacts."

COPYRIGHT MANAGEMENT, INC., Suite 701, 50 Music Square W., Nashville TN 37203. (615)327-1517. Vice President: Tim R. Smith. Serves publishers. Members are generally 18-65 years of age, with interests in music, film and art. Members must desire to publish their own songs and have active copyrights. "Copyright Management, Inc. encourages songwriters and publishers to be aware of the professional business procedures that affect their royalty earning potential. It is our policy to take issue with status quo record company and traditional licensing practices that compromise the copyright and result in income losses due to lack of information. We also act as consultants to publishers in copyright infringement suits. It should be stressed that only publishers with active catalogs are eligible for our services. However, songwriters may be interested in our seminars to become better educated about how the music business works." We offer Songwriter/Publisher Awareness Seminars—education, lectures and worldwide publishing administration and licensing." Applications are accepted throughout the year.

COUNTRY MUSIC ASSOCATION, INC. (CMA), Box 22299, Nashville TN 37202. (615)244-2840. Branch: Suite 3, 52 Haymarket, London SW1Y 4RP England. Membership falls within following categories: advertising agency, artist manager/agent, artist/musician, composer, broadcast personality, international, publication, publisher, radio, TV/video, record company, record merchandiser, talent buyer/promoter, and affiliated. Members must be directly and substantially involved in the country music industry. Offers monthly magazine, lists of industry contacts, special discounted insurance policies and rental car discount cards. Purpose is to promote country music. A new European office is in operation in London to work on expanding country music popularity throughout Europe.

COUNTRY MUSIC FOUNDATION OF COLORADO, Box 19435, Denver CO 80219. (303)936-7762. President: Gladys Hart. Serves songwriters and musicians, promoters, publishers and record companies to assist them in learning the proper method of presenting new material to the publisher. "The membership roster comes from the country music industry in general with special interest in the annual Colorado Country Music Festival. Our purpose is to promote country music in all facets of the industry. The association provides new artists with information on the basic fundamentals essential for career advancement. Songwriters Day will be scheduled to include songwriter/publisher meeting. The evening show will be dedicated to the presentation of new material by bands and artists. All performers appearing at the convention are required to be members." Offers lectures, newsletter, performance opportunities and an annual convention. Membership fees are: individual, $15; groups or bands, $25 per year, and include all meetings and voting privledges.
Tips: "The Songwriter Award has been added to the presentations at the Annual Colorado Country Music & Trade Convention and is voted on performance and recorded material."

COUNTRY MUSIC SHOWCASE INTERNATIONAL, INC., Box 368, Carlisle IA 50047. (515)989-3679. President: Harold L. Luick. Vice President: Barbara A. Lancaster. "We are non-profit, educational performing arts organization for the preservation and promotion of country music art forms. These art forms include but are not limited to traditional country, old-time string, mountain music, western swing, country/western, bluegrass, country gospel, country classic, cajun, hillbilly and modern country. The organization produces on a regular basis a stage show, 'Country Classic's USA,' which is available to community groups, civic organizations, and other non-profit organizations such as fairs and festivals that wish to raise funds or sponsor country music events of this type. Our members perform in these shows, and through constructive criticism and workshops we help and teach all performers the art of showmanship and musicianship. Workshops and seminars are also offered on songwriting and all phases of the music industry. The organization produces educational videos on all the above subjects and offers a nationally-distributed newspaper. We maintain that an entertainer, musician or songwriter should associate with the people who know more then they do, otherwise they cannot learn or improve themselves. We also believe 'a music form that forgets its past will never have a future worth remembering.' For free information and brochure on organization, send SASE."

THE DRAMATISTS GUILD, INC., 234 W. 44th St., New York NY 10036. (212)398-9366. Membership includes over 8,000 playwrights, composers, lyricists and librettists nationwide. "As the professional association of playwrights, composers, and lyricists, the Guild protects the rights of all theater writers, and improves the conditions under which they work. Additionally, the Guild encourages and nurtures the work of dramatists in the U.S. through its program of seminars and workshops. To be a member of The Dramatists Guild, you must have completed a dramatic work (a one-act or full-length play or component part- book, music or lyrics- of a musical) whether produced or not. The Guild offers many services and activities, including use of the Guild's contracts and a royalty collection service; The Hotline, a nationwide toll-free phone number for business or contract problems; an annual marketing directory with up-to-date information on grants, agents, producers, playwriting contests, conferences and workshops; two publications—*The Dramatists Guild Quarterly* and *The Dramatists Guild Newsletter*; access to group health insurance and access to Guild's reference library and newsroom."

GOSPEL MUSIC ASSOCIATION (GMA), 38 Music Square W., Nashville TN 37203. (615)242-0303. Executive Director: Donald W. Butler, Sr. For songwriters, broadcasters, musicians, merchandisers, promoters, performance licensing agencies, church staff musicians, talent agencies, record companies and publishers. Offers lectures, newsletter, workshops and awards programs.

INDIANAPOLIS SONGWRITERS, % Robert Najera, Box 176, McCordsville IN 46055. (317)335-2310. Founder: Robert Najera. Purpose is "to create an affiliation of serious minded songwriters, promote the artistic value of the musical composition, the business of music, and recognition for the songwriter and his craft." Sponsors quarterly newsletter, monthly meetings and monthly showcases.

*INTERNATIONAL FAN CLUB ORGANIZATION, Box 177, Wild Horse CO 80862. (303)962-3543. Co-Presidents: Loudilla Johnson, Loretta Johnson and Kay Johnson. For songwriters, musicians and performers and their fan club presidents. Members are fan club presidents and/or artists/songwriters etc. Applicants must be involved in the field of country music. An artist must have a fan club—"we assist them in setting up the fan club although we do not personally manage each individual operation for them." Purpose is to promote/publicize country music in an effort to spread good will, understanding and enjoyment of it around the world. "We hold an annual overseas showcase (London), plus dinner/show/business meetings/showcases in Nashville, annually in conjunction with Fan Fair. We believe fan clubs are a vital part of any entertainer's life." Offers competitions, instruction, newsletter, performance opportunities, social outings, workshops, business meetings, overseas tours and showcases.

KERRVILLE MUSIC FOUNDATION INC., Box 1466, Kerrville TX 78029-1466. (512)257-3600. Executive Director: Rod Kennedy. The Kerrville Music Foundation was "founded in 1975 for the promotion and preservation of both traditional and new American music and has awarded more than $20,000 to musicians over the last ten years through open competitions designed to encourage excellence in songwriting, banjo, harmonica and bluegrass bands. Six new folk award winners are annually invited to share 20 minutes of their songs at the Kerrville folk festival with one selected to perform on the main stage the next year."

THE LAS VEGAS SONGWRITERS ASSOCIATION, 1650 Cookson Ct., Las Vegas NV 89115. (702)452-0954. President: Joan Walker. Vice President: Sharon Cookson. "We are an educational, non profit organization dedicated to improving the art and craft of the songwriter. We are an association that works with writers to make them better crafted songwriters. We focus our attention on the writers and not the song. If the writers are good; then so will the songs be. We offer quarterly newsletters, monthly general information meetings, workshops three times a month, seminars held quarterly with professionals in the music business, and mail-in critiques for our out of state members. Dues are $20 per year. You must be 18 years or older. We have a junior chapter for 17 years and under, dues $10 per year."

THE LOS ANGELES SONGWRITERS SHOWCASE (LASS), Box 93759, Hollywood CA 90093. (213)654-1660. Co-Directors: Len H. Chandler Jr. and John Braheny. General Manager: Joy Wildin. "The Los Angeles Songwriters Showcase (LASS), is a nonprofit service organization for songwriters, founded in 1971 and sponsored by Broadcast Music, Inc. (BMI). LASS also provides counseling, conducts lectures, and interviews top music industry professionals at the Showcase. Additional features of the Wednesday night Showcase: Cassette Roulette in which a different publisher every week critiques songs submitted on cassette that night; and Pitch-A-Thon in which a different producer or record company executive screens songs for his/her current recording projects and/or acts for the label every week. The Showcase takes place every Wednesday night in front of an audience of songwriters and music industry; there is no prescreening necessary. LASS also produces an annual Songwriters Expo in October or November." General membership: $75/year. Professional membership: $100/year. Included in both "general" and "professional" membership benefits are: priorities to have tapes listened to first at Pitch-A-Thon sessions; discounts on numerous items such as blank tapes, books, demo production services, tapes of Songwriters Expo sessions and other seminars; discounts on admission to the weekly showcase; and a subscription to the LASS "Musepaper," a magazine for songwriters (also available to non-members for $12 bulk rate/$15 first class). Professional membership is available to general members by invitation or audition only and features special private pitch-a-thon sessions and referrals.
Tips: "Members may submit tapes to the weekly cassette roulette and pitch-a-thon sessions from anywhere in the world and be sent the recorded comments of the industry guests for that week. Most of the record companies, publishers and producers will not accept unsolicited material so our Wednesday night showcase is the best way to get your material heard by these music industry professionals."

*LOUISVILLE AREA SONGWRITERS' COOPERATIVE, Box 16, Pewee Valley KY 40056. President: Paul M. Moffettt. Estab. 1986. Serves songwriters and musicians of all ages, races and all music genres. "The Louisville Area Songwriters' Cooperative is a not-for-profit corporation dedicated to the development and promotion of songwriting. Membership is open to any person in the Louisville area who is interested in songwriting. We offer a songwriters' showcase on the first Saturday of each month, an open stage on Mondays at the *Rudyard Kipling*, a series of tapes of songs by members of the cooperative (much like a literary journal or small magazine), meetings, speakers, the LASC newsletter, a songwriting contest, referrral for collaboration, promotion and song plugging to local, regional and national recording artists." Applications accepted year-round. Dues are $10/year.

MIDWESTERN SONGWRITERS ASSOCIATION,91 Terrace Ave., Columbus OH 43212. (614)274-2169. Vice President: Albert Van Hoose. Serves songwriters. "Our purpose is to critique songs, inform songwriters of current information on songwriting, publishers 'want lists'. Ages vary from 19 to 74. Almost all live in Central Ohio area (some Northeast and Northwest of Ohio). Some professional songwriters-musicians. The only requirement is that they are interested in learning the craft of songwriting and in learning will share this knowledge with others." Offers competitions, instructions, lectures, library, newsletter, performance opportunities, social outings and critiquing. "Our main function is to help the beginning songwriter to perfect his art, and learn from the professional songwiter(s). We cover all aspects of songwriting in every field. Our group is a "family" organization with direction toward teaching and learning songwriting." Applications accepted year-round. "$20 membership fee. This entitles the member to have his or her songs critiqued, participate in Christmas party, summer picnic and other group activities; also to vote for officers. We welcome anyone and everyone. We encourage co-writing and group songwriting projects. Our group is educational and fun. We also critique songs sent to us by mail."

MISSOURI SONGWRITERS ASSOCIATION, INC., 693 Green Forest Dr., Fenton MO 63026. (314)343-4765. President: John G. Nolan, Jr. Serves songwriters and musicians. No eligibility requirements. Applications accepted year-round. "The MSA (a non-profit organization founded in 1979) is a tremendously valuable resource of songwriting and music business information outside of the major music capitols. Only with the emphasis on education can the understanding of craft and the utilization of skill be fully realized and in turn become the foundation for the ultimate success of MSA members. Songwriters gain support from their fellow members when they join the MSA and the organization provides 'strength in numbers' when approaching music industry professionals." As a means toward its goals the organization offers: "(1) an extremely informative quarterly newsletter; (2) seminars on such diverse topics as creativity, copyright law, brainstorming, publishing, recording the demo, craft and technique, songwriting business, collaborating, etc.; (3) workshops including song evaluation, establishing a relationship with publishers, Broadway and off-Broadway, hit song evaluations, the writer verses the writer/artist, Create-a-Song nights, the marriage of collaborators, the business side of songwriting, lyric craft, etc; (4) services such as collaborators referral, publisher contacts, consultation, recording discounts, musicians referral, library, etc." Tax deductible dues are $20/year.

MUSIC INDUSTRY EDUCATORS ASSOCIATION (MIEA), Suite 301, 1435 Bleury St., Montreal, Quebec H3A 2H7 Canada. Purpose is to establish and maintain standards of music industry education throughout the world; to encourage and facilitate interaction between the educational community and the music industry; to foster interaction among individuals involved with music industry education; to assist institutions involved in the development of programs in music industry education; and to promote music industry related research, scholarship and outstanding achievement. Offers quarterly newsletter, seminars and workshops, annual conventions in major recording center, e.g., Nashville. Membership: individual, $25/year; student, $5/year; pre-college or 2-year colleges, $50/year; 4-year and graduate colleges, $100/year; national or international commercial music industry, $250/year; regional commercial music industry, $150/year; and local commercial music industry, $75/year. Write for application and more information.

MUSICIANS CONTACT SERVICE, 6605 Sunset Blvd., Hollywood CA 90028. (213)467-2191. For musicians and bands seeking each other in the greater Southern California area. "Also for songwriters (composers and lyricists) seeking each other for collaboration only. An updated nationwide list of hundreds of songwriters seeking each other is provided for $20 for a one year listing."
Tips: "We are a very stable organization, having been in business at the same location for eighteen years. We are the only contact service anywhere for lyricists and composers seeking each other."

MUSICIANS' UNION, LOCAL 47, 817 N. Vine St., Hollywood CA 90038. (213)462-2161. President: Bernie Fleischer. Serves musicians as a contact with working recording artists. Members must be "professional musicians 16 years of age or older, with an interest in performing on television, recording, motion pictures, symphonies, night clubs and casuals." Offers competitions, instruction, lectures, newsletter and workshops. Applications accepted throughout the year.

NASHVILLE SONGWRITERS ASSOCIATION, INTERNATIONAL (NSAI), 803 18th Ave. S, Nashville TN 37203. (615)321-5004. Executive Director: Maggie Cavender. Serves songwriters. "Our purpose is to gain recognition for the songwriter, to serve any purpose toward this recognition and to pursue this on a worldwide basis." Applicants may apply for 2 memberships; "active membership is having had at least one song published with an affiliate of BMI, ASCAP or SESAC. An associate membership is for the yet-to-be-published writer and others interested in the songwriter." Offers newsletter, seminars, symposium, workshop, showcases and awards.

NATIONAL ACADEMY OF SONGWRITERS (NAS), Suite 780, 6381 Hollywood Blvd., Hollywood CA 90028. (213)463-7178. Executive Director: Kevin Odegard. A nonprofit organization dedicated to the education and protection of songwriters. Membership is general—$55/year; professional—$75/year. Offers song registration service, group legal, US copyright registration service, hotline, song critique, seminars, publishers' workshops, songwriters network and tipsheet in newsletter, courses on songwriting, songwriting business and theory, library, lead sheet service and more. "We offer services to all songwriter members, from street-level to superstar." NAS also operates songwriting competitions, such as American Song Festival.

THE NATIONAL ASSOCIATION OF COMPOSERS/USA, Box 49652, Barrington Station, Los Angeles CA 90049. (213)541-8213. President: Marshall Bialosky. Serves songwriters, musicians and classical composers. "We are of most value for the concert hall composer. Members are serious music composers of all ages and from all parts of the country, who have a serious interest in composing, performing, and listening to modern concert hall music. The main purpose of our organization is to perform, publish, broadcast and write news about composers of serious concert hall music—mostly chamber and solo pieces." Composers may achieve national notice of their work through our newsletter and concerts, and the fairly rare feeling of support in a non-commercial music enterprise dedicated to raising the musical and social position of the serious composer. Offers competitions, lectures, performance opportunities, library and newsletter. Applications accepted throughout the year.
Tips: "Ninety nine percent of the money earned in music is earned, or so it seems, by popular songwriters who might feel they owe the art of music something, and this is one way they might help support that art."

NATIONAL MUSIC PUBLISHERS' ASSOCIATION, INC., 18th fl., 205 E. 42nd St., New York NY 10017. (212)370-5330. President and Chief Executive Officer: Edward P. Murphy. Trade association for popular music publishers. Eligible members include "any person, firm, corporation or partnership actively engaged in the business of publishing music in the U.S.A. for a period of at least one year, whose musical publications have been used or distributed on a commercial scale or who assumes the financial risk involved in the normal publication of musical works." Offers newsletter, workshops, special reports and information.

NEW DRAMATISTS, 424 W. 44th St., New York NY 10036. (212)757-6960. Associate Literary Director: Liz Wright. Membership organization that works with development of plays/musicals. "We do not pay, but merely give readings and workshops of members' works. Writers should write to New Dramatists to get information to apply for membership. We do not accept for membership composers who have not also written the book."

NORTHERN CALIFORNIA SONGWRITERS ASSOCIATION, Suite 211, 855 Oak Grove Ave., Menlo Park CA 94025. (415)327-8296. Executive Director: Tobey Hall. Serves songwriters and musicians. "Our 1,000 members are lyricists and composers from ages 16-80, from beginners to professional songwriters. Our purpose is to provide the education and opportunities that will support our writers in creating and marketing outstanding songs. NCSA provides support and direction through local networking and input from Los Angeles and Nashville music industry leaders, as well as valuable marketing opportunities." No eligibility requirements. Offers annual Northern California Songwriting Conference, monthly visits from major publishers, songwriting classes, monthly seminars conducted by hit songwriters, a monthly newsletter, monthly performance opportunities and workshops. Applications accepted year-round. Dues: $35/year.
Tips: "NCSA's functions draw local talent and nationally recognized names together. This is a tremendous value to writers outside a major music center. We are developing a strong songwriting community in Northern California. We serve both the San Jose and San Francisco area and we have the support of some outstanding writers and publishers from both Los Angeles and Nashville. They provide us with invaluable direction and inspiration."

*NORTHWEST SONGWRITERS NETWORK, Box 27221, Lake City Station, Seattle WA 98125. (206)365-6617. Secretary-Treasurer: Doris Matthews. Estab. 1987. Serves songwriters, musicians and general public. Members are Northwest songwriters and those who are interested in songwriting in the Northwest. "We provide networking and support for Northwest songwriters, we promote original music from the Northwest, educate songwriters and the general public, and provide contacts, performance opportunities, educational and moral support." Offers instruction, networking, lectures, newsletter and workshops. Applications accepted throughout the year. Annual dues are $20.

*OHIO SONGWRITERS ASSOCIATION, 14614 Pearl Rd., Strongsville OH 44136. (216)572-1124. President: J.N.A. Wunderle. Serves songwriters, musicians and related craftspeople (arrangers, sound engineers, producers, vocalists, etc.). "Members of the OSA encompass young adults to senior citizens, at all ranges of musical and theoretical advancement, from professionals to amateurs who have written their first song and don't know what to do next. No special eligibility requirements." Purpose is "to preserve and promote the creation of original music through education and opportunity." Also offers competitions, lectures, library, newsletter, performance opportunities, social outings, workshops, reduced studio rates at a 16-track recording facility, and critiques at song showcases. Applications accepted year-round. Annual membership fee is $25.
Tips: "We provide learning opportunities specifically geared toward successful songwriting, and a network of related craftspeople through learning and social activities. Our seminars and workshops are open to the public but are offered at reduced rates to OSA members. Some of these seminars have included nationally known songwriters, representatives of ASCAP, professional studio engineers, etc., presenting information on music law, recording techniques and source licensing."

PACIFIC NORTHWEST SONGWRITERS ASSOCIATION, Box 98324, Seattle WA 98198. (206)824-1568. "We are a nonprofit association, dedicated to serving the songwriters of the Pacific Northwest. Our focus is on professional songwriting for today's commercial markets. We offer monthly workshops and newsletters. We welcome new members. Anyone interested in the PNWSA may send a request for more information and an SASE. If you have any questions, just give us a call." Membership dues are $25/year.

PERFORMING RIGHTS ORGANIZATION OF CANADA LIMITED (PROCAN), 41 Valleybrook Dr., Don Mills, Ontario M3B 2S6, Canada. (416)445-8700. Writer/Publisher: Mark Caporal. Publicity Manager: Nancy Gyokeres. Serves Canadian songwriters and publishers. Purpose is to collect music user licence fees and distribute performance royalties to songwriters and publishers. Offers competitions, magazine, workshops, advice and direction.

*PSA PACIFIC SONGWRITERS ASSOCIATION,944 Howe Street, Vancouver, British Columbia V6Z 1N9 Canada. (604)683-Song or 683-7664. President: Barry Payne. Serves songwriters and musicians. Membership includes 14-75 age group interested in popular songwriting. Offers competitions, field trips, instruction, lectures, library, newsletter, performance opportunities, social outings and workshops. Purpose is to promote the education of songwriting and business consultation in groups only, networking in meetings only. Applications accepted througout the year; although fiscal membership period begins and ends December 1st each year.

RADIO & TV REGISTRY, 314 W. 53rd St., New York NY 10019. (212)582-8800. Manager: Roland Young. Serves songwriters, musicians and announcers. Members are professional freelance musicians and songwriters. "Most jingles and record dates produced in New York City are booked through our office." Applicants must be union members. "We provide a telephone answering service geared to the needs of the music industry. We take 'work calls' for our members and relay messages to them." Applications accepted year-round.
Tips: "Most music contractors in New York City find it convenient to call us to leave a work call for musicians or songwriters." Musicians Roster and complete information available by calling the business office (212)246-7676.

*ROCKY MOUNTAIN SONGWRITERS AND MUSICIANS ASSOCIATION, 231 Harrison St., Denver CO 80206. (303)355-7426. President: Katherine Dines. Serves songwriters and musicians. "Our membership ranges from age 18 to 79. Requirements are only that our members demonstrate a keen interest in songwriting, music composition and/or performance. The purpose of this organization is to provide an outlet for all songwriters and musicians in all genres, and to become an eventual "umbrella" for the Rocky Mountain music scene. We strive to aid all songwriters and musicians to become better-functioning members of the musical community. We can provide discounts at various recording studios, music stores and performances; and a songwriter's and musician's network." Offers lectures, performance opportunities, library, social outings, newsletter and workshops. Applications accepted year-round.
Tips: "A songwriter should belong to our organization so that trips to Nashville, New York or Los Angeles become unneccessary. There is a definite Rocky Mountain sound that deserves to be heard."

*SAN FRANCISCO FOLK MUSIC CENTER, Fort Mason Center, San Francisco CA 94123. (415)441-8910. "We are a nonprofit volunteer corporation. Our purpose is the preservation and presentation of traditional and folk music and dance and contemporary music. We provide an avenue to present new songwriters." Offers performance opportunities, library, instruction, newsletter, workshops, dances, concerts, 2-day free folk festival, information source, record sales and Plowshares Coffeehouse. Applications accepted year-round. Membership fee is $10/year for individual membership; $25/year for family membership; $50/year for patron membership; $100/year for organization membership and $200 or more for sponsor membership.

SANTA BARBARA SONGWRITERS' GUILD, Box 2238, Santa Barbara CA 93120. (805)569-2533. President: Laurie Dana. "The Guild is a non-profit organization for aspiring songwriters, performers, those interested in the music industry, and anyone interested in original music. Our members are able to meet other songwriters, to learn more about the craft of songwriting, to get their songs heard, and to network. The Guild sponsors monthly cassette tape presentations to L.A. publishers, with the top four member songs awarded studio time and gift certificates. Also sponsored are workshops; plus classes and lectures on studio recording, synthesis, music business contracts and copyright law, record production, song marketing, music composition, lyric writing, vocal techniques; and a directory of local music services and organizations. Discounts available to members include the following: blank tapes, books that deal with a wide range of pertinent music industry information, studio time at local recording studios, equipment and supplies at local music stores, plus a mail-in tape service for out of town members." Membership is $35/year.

SESAC INC., 10 Columbus Circle, New York NY 10019. (212)586-3450; 55 Music Square E., Nashville TN 37203. Executive Vice President: Vincent Candilora. Vice Presidents: Dianne Petty and Jim Black, Nashville. Serves writers and publishers in all types of music who have their works performed by radio, television, nightclubs, cable TV, etc. Purpose of organization is to collect and distribute performance royalties to all active affiliates. "Prospective affiliates are requested to present a demo tape of their works which is reviewed by our Screening Committee." For possible affiliation, call Nashville or New York for appointment.

SONGWRITERS ASSOCIATION OF WASHINGTON, Suite 632, 1377 K St. NW, Washington DC 20005. (202)682-7361. "The Songwriters Association of Washington was established in 1979 as a nonprofit organization. Today we are a thriving group of over 400 amateur and professional songwriters, lyricists, musicians, recording technicians and music industry professionals, from across the country and overseas. We publish a monthly newsletter ("SAW Notes," which contains markets for demo tapes, free classifieds for members and articles of interest to songwriters), sponsor an annual song contest and present a yearly seminar at which our members can meet music professionals from all areas of the country." Applications accepted year-round.

THE SONGWRITERS GUILD OF AMERICA, Suite 317, 6430 Sunset Blvd., Hollywood CA 90028. (213)462-1108. Regional Director: B. Aaron Meza. Serves songwriters. Collects writers' royalties from publishers. "The Songwriters Guild is a protective and advisory agency for songwriters. The Guild represents authors and composers all over the world covering all phases of music: pop, R&B, rock, folk, country, jazz, theatre, classical, motion picture and television scores as well as commercials. A full member must be a published songwriter. An associate member is any unpublished songwriter with a desire to learn more about the business and craft of songwriting. The third class of membership comprises estates of deceased writers." Offers songwriting contract, instruction, lectures, newsletter, royalty collection service, collaboration service, group life and medical insurance, monthly ASK-A-PRO sessions and workshops. Applications are accepted throughout the year. Annual dues are $30 for associate members and $55-350 for full members, depending on royalties collected by the Guild."

THE SONGWRITERS GUILD OF AMERICA, Suite 306, 276 Fifth Ave., New York NY 10001. (212)686-6820. West Coast: 6430 Sunset Blvd., Hollywood CA 90028. (213)462-1108. Nashville: United Artists Tower, 50 Music Square West, Nashville TN 37203. (615)329-1782. Founded as the Songwriters' Protective Association in 1931, name changed to American Guild of Authors and Composers in 1958, and expanded to AGAC/The Songwriters Guild in 1982. Effective 1985, the organizational name is The Songwriters Guild of America. President: George David Weiss. Executive Director: Lewis M. Bachman. National Projects Director: Bob Leone. West Coast Regional Director: Aaron Meza. Nashville Regional Director: Kathy Hyland. "A full member must be a published songwriter. An associate member is any unpublished songwriter with a desire to learn more about the business and craft of songwriting. The third class of membership comprises estates of deceased writers. The Guild contract is conceded to be the best available in the industry, having the greatest number of built-in protections for the songwriter. The Guild's Royalty Collection Plan makes certain that prompt and accurate payments are made to writers. The ongoing Audit Program makes periodic checks of publishers' books. For the self-publisher, the Catalogue Administration Program (CAP) relieves a writer of the paperwork of publishing for a fee lower than the prevailing industry rates. The Copyright Renewal Service informs members a year in advance of a song's renewal date. Other services include workshops in New York and Los Angeles, free Ask-A-Pro rap sessions with industry pros (see Workshops), critique sessions, collaborator service and newsletters. In addition, the Guild reviews your songwriter contract on request (Guild or otherwise); fights to strenghten songwriters' rights and to increase writers' royalties by supporting legislation which directly affects copyright; offers a group medical and life insurance plan; issues news bulletins with essential information for songwriters; provides a songwriter collaboration service for younger writers; financially evaluates catalogues of copyrights in connection with possible sale and estate planning; operates an estates administration service; and maintains a non-profit educational foundation (The Songwriters Guild Foundation)."

*SONGWRITERS WORKSHOP OF CLEVELAND, National Academy of Songwriters Affiliate, Suite 4, 2277 Lancashire Rd., Cleveland Heights OH 44106. (216)932-9522. President: Pat Davidson. Estab. 1986. Serves songwriters. Members are songwriters of all ages, from beginners to professionals. "We are interested in connecting songwriters in Cleveland with major music markets and we offer a unique support system for songwriters. We provide information, education, protection, advice and contacts. We have our own MIDI recording studio which is available to members." Offers competitions, performance opportunities, library, instruction, newsletter, workshops, annual events, meetings with industry professionals. Write or call to request application. Applications accepted year-round.

SOUTHWEST VIRGINIA SONGWRITERS ASSOCIATION, Box 698, Salem VA 24153. President: Sidney V. Crosswhite. (703)380-2921. Vice President: Adrian Willis. (703)563-9238. Non-profit tax exempt organization which sponsors monthly newsletter, mail-in critique service for out-of-town members at no charge, and monthly meetings featuring song critiques, guest speakers and workshops. One-time initiation fee is $15. Dues are $12/year.

*TEXAS MUSIC ASSOCIATION, #34, 504 W. 24th St., Austin TX 78705. (512)447-2744. Contact: Betty Fields. Serves songwriters, musicians and all music industry-related services. Members include promoters, booking agencies, civic groups, consultants, facilities, financial institutions and investment brokers, graphic artists, record producers, radio, studios, etc. "The Texas Music Association (TMA) exists to promote and develop the Texas music industry through networking, communication, and education." Offers social outings, newsletter, workshops, annual statewide convention and monthly chapter meetings. Applications accepted year-round.

THEATRE COMMUNICATIONS GROUP, INC., 355 Lexington Ave., New York NY 10017. (212)697-5230. Serves composers, lyricists, librettists for the theater. "TCG has a constituency of non-profit professional theaters for which it is the national organization. It provides services in casting, personnel and management, as well as numerous publications and literary services, to organizations and individuals. TCG publishes a monthly magazine, *American Theatre*; *New Plays USA* (anthology series); *Artsearch* (biweekly newsletter), and provides employment information for theater artists, managers and technicians. The Literary Services Department annually publishes *Dramatists Sourcebook* and also operates *Plays in Process* (a script circulation service). Writers of musicals may benefit from this program if their works receive full production at a TCG constituent theater and have not been otherwise published. The Publications Department is responsible for *Theatre Profiles*, the biennial illustrated reference guide to America's nonprofit professional theatre, and *Theatre Directory*, the annual pocket-sized contact resource of theatres and related organizations. Criteria for membership in TCG include longevity of operation, professional orientation and standards, and size of operating budgets. Membership benefits include discounts on TCG publications and services; free subscriptions to *American Theatre*; invitations to TCG workshops and conferences; access to TCG personnel files and information services. While individuals cannot become members, TCG's many publications are available to all."

*TRIAD SONGWRITER'S ASSOCIATION, Box 24095, Winston-Salem NC 27104-4095. (919)727-8100. President: Martie C. Smith. Serves songwriters. "Members are songwriters from 5 years to 65 years old. Interests vary and musical interests include jazz, folk, pop, R&B, rock, country, classical, gospel, new age, etc. The songwriters' backgrounds and musical tastes differ, but blend together in an exciting way. Membership is available to anyone interested in learning more about songwriting—no restrictions. TSA supports the craft of songwriting through educational workshops and other workshops designed to improve the skills of songwriters and to stimulate their creative efforts. TSA offers a unique artistic outlet in the community which allows songwriters to grow and to expose their talents. Belonging to TSA helps give the songwriter a place and a voice in the community. Songwriters have an opportunity to meet other songwriters and learn valuable insights into the art of songwriting." Offers competitions, performance opportunities, social outings, newsletter, workshops, critiques and seminars. Applications accepted year-round. Membership fee is $16/year; $24/year for family membership; $12/year for student membership and $100 for lifetime membership.

VOLUNTEER LAWYERS FOR THE ARTS, 3rd Floor, 1285 Avenue of the Americas, New York NY 10019. (212)977-9270. Contact: Staff Attorney. Serves songwriters, musicians and all performing, visual, literary and fine arts artists. Offers legal assistance and representation to eligible individual artists and arts organizations who cannot afford private counsel. Also sells manuals and guides on arts-related issues. In addition, there are affiliates nationwide who assist local arts organizations and artists. Offers conferences, lectures, seminars and workshops.

WASHINGTON AREA MUSIC ASSOCIATION, INC., #1000, 1101 14th St. NW, Washington DC 20005. (202)371-0187 or 965-4428. President: John L. Simson, Esq. Serves songwriters, musicians and all persons interested in or involved in music business. Primary value is in "networking contacts, and meeting artists who might wish to use a song, meeting other songwriters for the purpose of collaboration, meeting local publishers. Our membership represents a wide ranging cross section of the community, primarily the professional songwriter or musician." Eligibility requirements include geographic location and payment of dues. Offers lectures, performance opportunities, social outings, newsletter, workshops, and awards shows (members are eligible to nominate and vote). "We promote regional music from the Washington area and help educate area musicians in legal and business issues; we promote charitable events in the D.C. area and create an archive of D.C. area music." Applications accepted throughout the year.

*WYOMING COUNTRY MUSIC FOUNDATION,Sussex Route, Kaycee WY 82639. (307)738-2303. President and Founder: Helen D. Ullery. Serves songwriters and musicians. Members include "youth, amateurs, professionals, country and gospel/country songwriters, musicians and vocalists. No eleigibility requirements. Our purpose is to promote country music and country music performers, showcase talent, educate members, and coordinate our annual festival each summer." Offers competitions, lectures, performance opportunioties, social outings, newsletter, workshops and annual songwriters contest. "Our songwriter contest is held each spring. Contest deadline is April 20, 1988. Entry is $10/song; 50% of entry fee goes back as prizes to winners. Final judging is done in Nashville." Membership fee is $25; festival registration is $25.

❝ *Security, for me, is an attitude that keeps me thinking positively through lean and fat times.* **❞**
—*Stan Applebaum, composer, arranger, producer*

Songwriting skills, like anything else, can be improved with continual practice. Workshops provide a valuable means for songwriters to have songs evaluated, hear suggestions for further improvement, and receive feedback and motivation from industry experts. Although many workshops are located in or near the major music centers of Los Angeles, Nashville, and New York, there are some organizations—such as The Songwriters Guild of America, the Nashville Songwriters Association International, and the National Academy of Songwriters—that offer traveling workshops. More and more small and mid-sized cities with strong songwriter organizations are running their own workshops, drawing on resources from within their own group or importing professionals from the music centers.

The following is a list of some of the more well-known national and regional workshops. Each listing includes type and length of workshop(s) offered, as well as costs and admission requirements. Write to any you are interested in for more information.

If you are unable to attend any of these established workshops, why not start one of your own? You may even ask some of the national songwriting organizations about the possibility of co-sponsorship.

ASCAP "WELCOMES SONGWRITERS" Series, % ASCAP, 2nd Floor, 6430 Sunset Blvd., Hollywood CA 90028. (213)466-7681. ASCAP Western Executive Director: Todd Brabec. Workshop Directors: Julie Horton, Loretta Munoz, Lyn Benjamin. Offers programs for songwriters: "ASCAP offers a tuition-free, 8-week workshop series during which songs are performed and evaluated by a well-known songwriter or publisher guest moderator. Song casting and placement are discussed. The various song markets are analyzed. Additional workshops include The Business and Creative Sides of Writing for Film and Television; Black Contemporary Music; and Symphonic Music. Class size: 25-40 students in each workshop. Length: approximately 2 hours. Workshop classes take place at ASCAP as well as at outside forums. A piano and stereo and cassette tape playback system are among the facilities. Applicants are selected based on material submitted on cassette by prospective members. All workshops and seminars are designed to improve the participants' creative skills as well as business knowledge. Feedback and instruction from professionals is stressed." Write or phone ASCAP for information.

BMI-LEHMAN ENGEL MUSICAL THEATRE WORKSHOP, 320 W. 57th St., New York NY 10019. (212)586-2000. Director of Musical Theatre: Allan Becker. Offers programs "only to *advanced* musical theatre composers, librettists and lyricists. The BMI-Lehman Engel Musical Theatre Workshops were formed in an effort to refresh and stimulate professional writers, as well as to encourage and develop new creative talent for the musical theatre." Workshops meet one afternoon a week for two hours and are held at BMI, New York. Applicants should send for application. Tape of 3 compositions required with application. No entry fee.

*BROADWAY TOMORROW PREVIEWS, % Broadway Tomorrow Musical Theatre, Suite 53, 191 Claremont Ave., New York NY 10027. Artistic Director: Elyse Curtis. Purpose is the enrichment of American theatre by nurturing *new musicals*. Offers series in which librettos are presented and marketing and producing seminars to equip writers in techniques of promoting their works. Program open to writers living in Metropolitan New York area or able to spend time in city. Submission is by audio cassette of music, (or script if submitting to reading series) synopsis, resume, reviews, if any, acknowledgement postcard and SASE. participating membership fee is $15 if work is accepted. Non-participant seminar fee is $15. Programs are presented in fall and spring with possibility of full production of work presented in concert.

C-SC OPERA WORKSHOP, Culver-Stockton College, Division of Fine Arts, Canton MO 63435. (314)288-5221. Director of Opera Workshop: Dr. Carol Fisher Mathieson. "C-SC Opera Workshop provides students with experience in chamber opera through study and performance. We do one-act, small-cast chamber operas which require no chorus." Workshops offered annually, lasting 1 month (usually in February or March) with 1-4 performances. Performers are usually college students (3-8 per workshop) and occasional guests. "The experimental theatre at Culver-Stockton College seats 50. It can be used as a thrust or round stage. There is no curtain nor is there fly space. Lighting is minimal. We will present the works of composers of chamber opera which are within the ability range of our students (undergraduate) and require a small cast with no chorus. Keyboard or small wind ensemble accompaniment is necessary. Ours is a small workshop which aims at introducing students to the art of chamber opera. Our students are undergraduates; Culver-Stockton College is a liberal arts college. If a work is useful to our workshop, it will also be marketable to other small colleges, undergraduate workshops at universities and some civic groups. We are a church-related school, affiliated with the Christian church (Disciples of Christ), and would provide a testing ground for works marketable to church dramatic groups, too."

GROVE SCHOOL OF MUSIC, 12754 Ventura Blvd., Studio City CA 91604. (818)904-9400. Contact: Mike Julian. Workshops are offered for guitarists, bassists, synthesists, recording engineers, drummers, keyboardists, vocalists, and brass and reed players. "Grove School of Music offers a wide range of workshops and classes in the craft and business of music such as Song and Lyric Evaluation workshops at various proficiency levels, Music and Midi classes, and demo and master production workshops. Our instructors are all working, well-respected professionals on the caliber of Doug Thiele, Jack Smalley or John D'Andrea. Details on classes, instructors and procedure are available through the admissions office in brochure form." Four 10-week terms/calendar year. Average class size is 15. Classes range from $80-200 covering five to ten 2-hour sessions. Some classes require texts or materials that are not included in the tuition fee. Complete classroom facilities. "We offer year long, full-time programs for arrangers/composers, vocalists, players, recording engineers and synthesizer programmers. We also offer the Composition and Musicianship Program (COMP) for students wishing a primary career as a songwriter and the related experience in record producing, the record industry and publishing. Students will obtain in-depth experience in all styles of song composition and learn concepts from both the lyrical and compositional aspects of songwriting. Many of our students have won song contests, accepted positions at major publishing companies or trade magazines and have begun teaching or other music-related careers. Many other students have had songs recorded by such disparate artists as the Surf Punks and Jefferson Starship." Applicants must be interviewed for placement prior to enrolling. Certain classes require auditions. Request current catalog by mail or telephone.

HAYSTACK PROGRAM IN THE ARTS, Portland State University, Box 1491, Portland OR 97207. (503)229-4812. Director: Steve Reischman. Offers programs for musicians during summer only. Workshops last 1-2 weeks and take place in Cannon Beach, Oregon during June, July and August. 20 songwriters/musicians participate in each workshop. Performers are amateur and professional instrumentalists, vocalists, bands, ensembles and vocal groups. Send for application or call 1-800-547-8887, ext. 4812. Tuition is $175 for one week, $250 for two-week courses. "Haystack is a summer-long program with short courses in writing, visual arts, and music. The program is planned around the theme of arts and the environment, giving recognition to the special qualities gained from total immersion in educational activity with interspersed recreation. If you want an opportunity for growth and challenge, a chance to explore a new facet of yourself, a place to enhance your skills, and time to mingle with instructors and participants, Haystack is the place for you! The city of Cannon Beach and nearby communities have a variety of housing facilities. The area also has limited camp sites and trailer spaces available. Upon registration, all participants receive a guide to Cannon Beach, a housing listing, and lists of supplies and facilities."

KERRVILLE FOLK FESTIVAL, Kerrville Festivals, Inc., Box 1466, Kerrville TX 78029. (512)257-3600. Founder/President: Rod Kennedy. Sponsors songwriters school, guitar school and new folk concert competition. Programs held in late spring, late summer and fall. Festivals last 8 days and are held outdoors at Quiet Valley Ranch. Around 110 acts participate. Performers are professional instrumentalists, songwriters and bands. Participants selected by auditioning in person or submitting demo tape, by invitation only. Send cassette, promotional material and list of upcoming appearances. "Songwriters/guitar schools are $90 and include breakfast, instructors, camping on ranch, fish fry and concert. Rustic facilities—no hookups. Food available at reasonable cost."

THE LEHMAN ENGEL MUSICAL THEATRE WORKSHOP, 508 Grace Ave., Los Angeles CA 90301. (213)672-3698. Co-Director: Lenning Davis, Jr. Held at Los Angeles Music Center (September through May), a series of workshops offered for development of musical theater authors and projects. Book writers, composers and lyricists are eligible. Send for brochure and application. Deadline is first week of August.

*MUSICAL THEATRE WORKSHOP, One Lincoln Plaza, New York NY 10023. (212)870-7545. Director of Musical Theatre Activities: Bernice Cohen. Offers programs for songwriters, musical playwrights, composers and lyricists in the fall lasting 10 weeks. Workshops are held in ASCAP building from October to January. Send cassette of 4 songs and resume. Application materials will be accepted from July 1-August 7.

NATIONAL ACADEMY OF SONGWRITERS (NAS) WORKSHOPS, Suite 780, 6381 Hollywood Blvd., Hollywood CA 90028. (213)463-7178. Staff Members: Kevin Odegard, Gloria Sklerov and Pete Luboff. "Offers programs for songwriters including Publishers' Evaluation Workshops, SONGTALK seminar series featuring top names in songwriting, lyric writing, demo production and more." Attendance: up to 30/workshop. Length: 2-4 hours/workshop. Membership is $55/year, professionals $75/year. Send for application. "NAS is a nonprofit membership organization dedicated to the protection and education of songwriters. NAS also provides a bimonthly newsletter containing tipsheet *Open Ears* and collaborators' network."

OPERA/MUSIC THEATER CONFERENCE, 234 West 44th St., New York NY 10036. (212)382-2790. Artistic Director: Paulette Haupt. Sponsored by the Eugene O'Neill Theater Center, "The Conference offers composers, lyricists and book writers the opportunity to develop new music theater works of all forms during a 2-5 week residency at the O'Neill Theater Center. Some works are given public staged readings; others are developed in private readings during the conference with artistic staff and dramaturgs. All works selected are developed over at least a 2-3 month period. A professional company of approximately 20 singer/actors provide the writers with daily musical and dramatic readings during the Conference period. Staged works are read with script in hand, with minimal lighting and no physical properties, to allow flexibility for day-to-day rewrites. The Conference is held in August of each year. Composers and writers selected receive room, board, transportation and a stipend." Send SASE for application.

*OPERA WORKSHOP, % School of Music—Northern Illinois University, Dekalb IL 60115. (815)753-1551. Co-Director: Lee Strawn. Promotes Broadway musicals, operettas operas performed in cabaret, scenes and full productions in either 1,000 seat proscenium theatre or 150 seat black box theatre. Send for application. 15-20 students selected by audition at the school semi-yearly or as arranged. Deadlines: Sept. 1-Jan. 15. Tuition charged for workshop.

PERFORMING ARTS RESIDENCIES, % Yellow Springs Institute for Contemporary Studies and the Arts, Art School Rd., Chester Springs PA 19425. (215)827-9111. Public Affairs Director: Stephen L. Lanier. "Annual artists' residency program for the development of new works (primary interest in New Music)." Fellowships awarded to professional artists only, for work to be developed in residency. Works must be new (not previously performed). Programs offered year-round; primary residency period May-October. Average residency lasts 7-14 days at Yellow Springs Institute. Up to 12 songwriters/musicians including ensembles participate in one event. Residency awarded to composers, professional instrumentalists, vocalists, ensembles, and performance artists. Participants selected by jury, based on application. Send for application; tape/score/proposal to be submitted with application. Closing date for application is in January. No entry fee. "Artists are provided with room, board, technical and promotional support, some transporation and stipend. Facility is 250-seat fully equipped experimental theater, earthwork, and 8 track recording studio. Artists residence is in 20 acres of a historic village."

FRANKS SILVERA WRITERS' WORKSHOP, 3rd Floor, 317 W. 125 St., New York NY 10027. (212)662-8463. Contact: Karen Baxter. "Our workshop is open to *all* writers who are prepared to have their work read by members of the actors' pool. Each year 30-40 plays are read. Third World and women writers are especially encouraged."

SONGCRAFT SEMINARS, 441 East 20th Street, New York NY 10010. (212)674-1143. Year-round classes for composers and lyricists conducted by songwriter/teacher Sheila Davis, award-winning author of *The Craft of Writing*. All seminars emphasize craftsmanship and teach principles that apply to every musical idiom—pop, theatre, or cabaret. Write or call for applications, starting dates, and location of classes.
Successful Lyric Writing: A ten-week course held four times a year at the New York headquarters of the Songwriters Guild of America (see their listing for details).
Successful Lyric Writing: A one-day MiniCourse. This is a 6-hour synthesis of the instructor's 10-week course, which illustrates the major theories of rhyme and rhythm and the top-ten principles of fine writing, presents a guideline to figurative language, and pinpoints the most common lyric writing pitfalls, giving techniques to avoid them. Attendees receive *Keynotes on Successful Lyric Writing*, a digest of the main points covered in the seminar. Held semi-annually at The New School in New York and colleges around the country. Tuition $75.
Mastering the Song Forms: A one-day MiniCourse, which gives a thorough grounding in the seven

major song forms that have dominated popular music from the 30s to the 80s. Designed to enrich composers with a deeper understanding of song structures and the element of strong melody writing, and to fortify lyricists with a new musical vocabulary. Attendees receive *Keynotes on Song Forms*, a synthesis of the seminar's highlights. Held semi-annually at The Singers Forum Foundation in New York and colleges around the country. Tuition $75.

Song by Song by Sondheim: A one-day MinCourse. This lecture/demonstration illuminates the elements of fine craftsmanship as exemplified in the lyrics and music of Stephen Sondheim. During the 6-hour session, significant Sondheim songs are played and analyzed from the standpoint of form, meter, literary devices, repetitive techniques, and thematic development. Attendees will be guided in applying these elements of fine writing to their own work. Held twice a year at the Singers Forum Foundation in New York. Tuition $75.

SONGWRITER SEMINARS AND WORKSHOPS, 928 Broadway, New York NY 10010. (212)505-7332. President: Ted Lehrman. Vice President: Libby Bush. Offers programs for songwriters: introduction to pop songwriting; advanced workshop; and at-home songwriter workshop. Cycles begin in September, February and June. Approximately 10 in each songwriter workshop. Each cycle lasts eight weeks. "Our programs stress the craft and business realities of *today's* pop music industry. We guide our members in the writing of the hit single song (both lyrics and music) for those recording artists who are open to outside material. We also share with them our considerable experience and expertise in the marketing of commercial pop music product. Our instructors, Ted Lehrman and Libby Bush, both members of ASCAP, have had between them more than 80 songs recorded and commercially released here and abroad. They continue to be highly active in writing and placing pop songs for publication. Industry guests (record producers, record company, A&R people, publishers etc.) frequently attend workshop sessions." Workshops: Pop Songwriting—Preparing for the Marketplace; Advanced Songwriter Seminar and Workshop—Ready for the Marketplace. Cost of 8 week workshops: $145-150. Cost of at-home songwriter workshop: $15/lyric; $20/song. Private song and career consultation sessions: $40/hour. Top 40 single stressed. Collaboration opportunities available. No housing provided. Interviews/auditions held for songwriters and singer/songwriters to determine which workshop would be most helpful. Call for free brochure and/or set up interview.

THE SONGWRITERS ADVOCATE (TSA), 47 Maplehurst Rd., Rochester NY 14617. (716)266-0679. Director: Jerry Englerth. "TSA is a non-profit educational organization that is striving to fulfill the needs of the songwriter. We offer two opportunities for songwriters including: 1) an evening school course pertaining to the craft and business, which covers copyright law, methods and procedures of songwriting, home and professional demo recording, publishing and co-publishing, song sharks, functions of ASCAP, BMI, SESAC, Songwriter's Guild etc.; 2) song evaluation workshops that afford songwriters the opportunty to bounce their songs off other songwriters and receive an objective critique and improve their craft. TSA evaluates tapes and lyric sheets via the mail. We do not measure success on a monetary scale, ever. It is the craft of songwriting that is the primary objective. If a songwriter can arm himself with knowledge about the craft and the business, it will increase his confidence and effectiveness in all his dealings. However, we feel the songwriter should be willing to pay for professional help that will ultimately improve his craft and attitude. And by all means, join and strongly support a songwriting organization. In addition, for those of you who wish to have a demo made, TSA will also be able to accommodate you." Price list is available upon request. Membership dues are $10/year. Must be member to receive discounts or services.

THE SONGWRITERS GUILD OF AMERICA, Suite 317, 6430 Sunset Blvd., Hollywood CA 90028. (213)462-1108. Regional Director: B. Aaron Meza.

Ask-A-Pro: "2-hour music business rap session to which all writers are welcome, held on the first Monday of each month at 7:00 pm. Features industry professionals fielding questions from songwriters." Each session lasts 2 hours. Free to all Guild members, $2 for non-members. Reservations necessary. Phone for more information.

Jack Segal's Songwriting Workshop: "designed to give the songwriter additional techniques to write for today's song market. Both lyrics and music will be treated in terms of contemporary content and form. Song evaluation at every meeting. Workshop activities will include: the basics—form; content; design; tools; collaboration; the demo; the lyric and lead sheet; and the music business. Offered year-round. 12-15/class. Each session lasts 2 hours. Cost: $100 to Guild members, $145 to nonmembers for a 10-week course. All applicants must submit a tape and Jack Segal will make final selections."

THE SONGWRITERS GUILD OF AMERICA, 276 Fifth Ave., New York NY 10001. (212)686-6820. National Projects Director: Bob Leone.

Ask-A Pro: "2-hour bi-weekly music business rap session to which all writers are welcome. It features industry professionals—publishers, producers, record company executives, artists—fielding questions from new songwriters." Offered year-round except summer. 25-30/meeting. Charge: free to members, $2 to nonmembers.

Song Critique: "Guild songwriters can play one song at the Guild's New York headquarters, 276 Fifth Ave., New York NY. These weekly 2 hour sessions start at 5 pm every Thursday night. Nonmembers are invited to attend for $2 and help provide feedback. The moderator of Song Critique is Guild Projects Director Bob Leone." Critique sessions are also held in Los Angeles (213)462-1108 and Nashville (615)329-1782.

Hit Songwriting Workshop: "This workshop is designed to introduce the songwriter to the basics of writing commercial songs, with focus on both lyrics and music. Pop, soul, rock, dance and country songwriting will be discussed. Areas to be covered include formats, titles, themes, hooks, concept records, melody writing and the making of demos." Offered year-round with 10 to 12 in each workshop. Instructor is Lou Stallman whose songs have been recorded by Aretha Franklin, Deniece Williams, Laura Nyro, The Supremes, Robert John and many more. Cost: $130 to Guild members, $175 for nonmembers to cover ten 2-hour sessions.

Pop Music Workshop: "This workshop is designed to stimulate and develop creative musical talent and to explore the art and craft of composing pop music, learning new skills, discovering innovative techniques and ideas, and gaining valuable business information vital to the advancement of your music career. The principle areas covered include: analysis of the pop song form; wedding music and lyrics; demo production; composing for alternative markets such as jingles and new age music. Much attention is given to song marketing, and the structure and operation of the music business. Students should play either guitar or keyboard, and a knowledge of basic music theory will be helpful but is not essential." Instructor is Guild Projects Director Bob Leone, a composer/keyboardist who has worked with Stevie Nicks, Patti Smith, Steve Van Zandt, RCA recording group Flame, and Pam Johnson.

Successful Lyric Writing: "Conducted by composer/lyricist Sheila Davis, author of *The Craft of Lyric Writing*. Two workshop levels—The Basics and Beyond the Basics. The Basics is a 10-week course giving a thorough grounding in the principles and techniques that result in successful lyric writing in any genre—from country to cabaret. Tuition $175, plus $5 materials fee to the instructor. Beyond the Basics is an ongoing 8-week workshop designed to foster the development of each writer's voice. Assignments are tailored to overcome individual writing problems and expand productivity, and guidance is given to bring the student closer to his/her marketplace. Tuition $175. Both classes limited to 10.

Artist Develpment Workshop: "Conducted by Bob Leone and Lou Stallman. This course is designed for those who are considering careers as recording artists. Live performance opportunities will be available, and much relevant information will be made available through the course instructors and through special guest speakers, including music attornies, personal managers, booking agents, representatives of the performing rights organizations, vocal coaches and fashion and cosmetic consultants. This 8-week course is available all-year-round at a cost of $130 to Guild members, $175 to non-members. Classes are limited to 10 students.

*SONGWRITER WORKSHOP OF CLEVELAND,Suite #4, 2777 Lancashire Rd., Cleveland Heights OH 44106. (216)932-9522. President: Pat Davidson. Estab. 1986. Workshops provide education on songwriting, the music industry, and demo production. Programs offered year-round. Workshops are offered 2nd and 4th week of every month on Saturday, from 2-6 p.m. Ten songwriters/musicians participate in each workshop. Instructors include Pat Davidson (music business and songwriting technique classes), and recording engineer/computer programmer Gary Lehecka (demo production technique classes). The last hour of each session is for song critique; participants are asked to bring demos and lyric sheets. "We think our workshops are motivational because our writers are more active after attending." Phone for further information.

*SUMMER MUSIC FROM COURTENAY/CYMC, %Comox Valley Music Society, Box 3056, Courtenay, British Columbia V9N 5N3 Canada. (604)338-7463. General Manager: Marcus Handman. Promotes "summer 'community of musicians'—classical, jazz, band, musical theatre." Festivals last from July 5 to Aug. 2 at G.P. Vanier Sec. School Campus/Sid Williams Theatre. 45 professional and 300 amateur songwriters/musicians participate. Performers are individual instrumentalists, bands, ensembles, vocal groups, orchestras and opera/musical theatre companies. Submit tape; performers selected by invitation only. Applicants should contact by letter by Jan. 1 for following summer. Facilities are "1 proscenium theatre, 1 school gym, outdoor facilities. Housing—amateurs in dorms, professionals in local housing."

Tips: "We are both a summer musical school (CYMC) and a professional concert festival. Students are able to perform in some concerts with professional musicians. There are two student concerts each summer. We are B.C.'s longest running concert festival, now in our 21st season."

Contests and Awards

Songwriting contests and musician competitions can be important ways of gaining exposure for your songs and your talents, even though they are not "markets" in the usual sense. The winners, of course, receive a monetary prize, recording deal, merchandise, or some kind of award. But all the participants have an opportunity to make valuable contacts. Some contests—like the Music City Song Festival—are judged by music publishers and other industry professionals, which guarantees that your song will be heard by at least one specialist. Sometimes music professionals will personally request to hear more material after the contest is over. Beneficial business relationships can sometimes result.

When participating in a competition, you are "selling" yourself and your work. Marketing techniques and professionalism should not be forgotten. Each contest you enter should be studied so you can best prepare your material for each award you seek.

Contests listed here encompass all types of music and all levels of composition expertise. Most of them are annual, but some organizations sponsor different events throughout the year. Read each listing carefully and write a letter to any that interest you, asking to be put on their list to receive information about upcoming competitions.

AMERICAN SONG CONTEST, Box 4388, Hollywood CA 90028. (213)463-7178. Contact: ASC Director. Presented by The National Academy of Songwriters. Deadline to be announced. Open to everyone. Nominal entry fee. For more information, send a self-addressed stamped envelope marked "American Song Contest Info Request."
Purpose: To draw national attention to the emergence of new music in our culture, and to give new songwriters the opportunity to have their work evaluated by professionals and presented to the industry and the general public as the best of America's new songs.
Requirements: "A song is defined as being words and music. Any new song is eligible if a recorded version has not been released for sale to the public before the winners are notified."
Categories: "There is both a song and a lyric competition. Song competition categories include: rock/new wave (rock-and-roll, country rock to heavy metal to the most urban new wave songs); gospel/inspirational (songs of a religious or spiritual nature); pop/adult contemporary (pop songs with a softer sound that might appeal to an older audience; includes crossover type songs that might be performed by Anne Murray, Kenny Rogers, Lionel Richie, Dan Fogelberg and Little River Band); country/folk (songs in the style of Johnny Cash, Tammy Wynette, Waylon Jennings, Dolly Parton, Oak Ridge Boys and the like, as well as folk songs, bluegrass songs and songs on traditional instruments such as autoharps, zithers and dulcimers); black-oriented (songs with funky rhythms and/or black dialect in the styles of Kool & The Gang, Shalamar and some Doobie Brothers; also includes blues and reggae, as well as songs in a jazz vocal style). Please refer to these descriptions, as any song may be entered in more than one category."
Awards: To be established.

*THE ANNUAL NATIONAL COMPETITION FOR NEW AMERICAN MUSICALS, The American Musical Theatre Festival, Box I, Carmel CA 93921. (408)625-9900. Dramaturg: Moss Hall. For songwriters, composers and musical playwrights. Annual award.
Purpose: "The objective of the award is to help NEW and emerging musical theatre composers and lyricists and provide them a safe harbor in which to develop their work."
Requirements: Request application form and write for additional information. Deadline: Nov. 2. Send samples of work to be judged with application: "two scenes from the musical, two songs with lyrics on a cassette tape and a synopsis of the musical.
Awards: Grand prize is $2,000 cash plus possible production. "Initial applicants are judged by a local panel of professionals in the field. Finalists are judged by a professional panel through the New York-based NATIONAL MUSIC THEATRE NETWORK. All finalists are given a free evaluation by the NMTN.

Tips: "Cassette tape should be of professional quality; two songs submitted should show the range of the songs in the show; synopsis should be clear and understandable. The Competition is in its 4th year. Our previous winners have been from Los Angeles, Chicago, New York City and Troy, Michigan."

*RUBY LLOYD APSEY PLAYWRITING COMPETITION, Dept. of Theatre and Dance, University of Alabama at Birmingham, Birmingham AL 35294. Director of Contest: Dr. Rick J. Plummer. For musical playwrights. Annual award.
Purpose: "To recognize talented new American playwrights and promote their work through production of their plays."
Requirements: Send for application. Send cassette tape of music. Deadline: January 1.
Awards: $500 and possible non-royalty production (with all expense paid week-residency). "Applicants judged by a panel composed of Theatre UAB and University drama literature faculty members and departmental dramaturg."
Tips: "Prefers small cast—small musical ensemble."

ASCAP FOUNDATION GRANTS TO YOUNG COMPOSERS, ASCAP Bldg., 1 Lincoln Plaza, New York NY 10023. (212)870-7588. Director of Grants: Frances Richard. For composers.
Purpose: To provide grants to young composers to encourage them to pursue their studies in music composition and develop their skills and talents.
Requirements: "Applicants must be citizens or permanent residents of the US who have not reached their 30th birthday by March 15. Applicants must submit professional recommendations; complete an application listing prior education, experience and background in the field of music; and submit 1 example of their composition. Music of any style or category will be considered. Submissions must be original, unpublished works that have not previously won awards or competitions." Deadline: March 15. Send for application; samples required. "Submit copies only. Score reproductions and/or manuscripts may be submitted on regular music paper or reproduced by an accepted reproduction process. Cassette tapes will be accepted also."
Awards: ASCAP Foundation awards grants of $500-2,500. Length: 1 year. Applications judged by screening-panel of musical authorities.

BMI AWARDS TO STUDENT COMPOSERS, 320 W. 57th St., New York NY 10019. (212)586-2000. Director: Barbara Petersen. For composers of "serious concert music." Annual. Purpose: "to pick outstanding young (25 or under) composers and make cash awards for furthering their musical education."
Requirements: Applicants must not have reached their 26th birthday by Dec. 31 of the year preceding the Feb. 10th contest deadline. "Serious concert music is preferred to popular songs, but all music is considered. All geographic locations of the world, but applicant must be a citizen or permanent resident of the western hemisphere enrolled in an accredited public, private or parochial secondary school, in an accredited college or conservatory of music, or engaged in private study with recognized music teachers." Deadline: Feb. 10. One entry per student. Send for free application and rules. Rights retained. Entries returned, include SASE.
Awards: BMI Awards to Student Composers: "prizes totaling $15,000 ranging from $500 to $2,500 may be given to winning students, by check, with certificate of honor." Contest judged by "outstanding composers, music publishers and musicologists."

THE CANADIAN SONGWRITING CONTEST, Bag Service, Bag #510, Postal Station G, Calgary, Alberta, T3A 3K7 Canada. (403)258-0892. Director: David Strattford. Gives awards/grants to songwriters and composers. Annual award. Purpose of award is "to stimulate the whole music industry from its source, the songwriter. We also try to help songwriters sell their songs all year long."
Requirements: Send completed entry blank with a cassette tape of the song and an entry fee for each song entered. Deadline: August 31st each year. Send for application.
Awards: Grand prize $5,000. Category prizes (six—rock, pop/top 40, MOR, folk, soul R&B, country) are $1,000 first prize, $200 second prize, $200 third prize, 10 honorable mentions in each category (a total of 78 prizes). "All entries are judged by industry officials (radio personalities, publishers, record company executives, artists, C.S.C. staff) for originality and commercial airplay potential. We are looking for hits."
Tips: "Do the best recording you can afford to do and make sure that the vocals are right up front (most recordings we receive do not have the vocals up front). Songs are not judged for production. This contest offers all entrants an opportunity to have their work heard by top music industry officials (with the hope that some will sell their songs as a result) while competing for thousands in cash prizes. We also offer songwriter workshops and recording sessions. Everything that this contest does is aimed at helping the songwriter sell his/her song, no matter where entrant lives. Be sure your introductions are as short as possible. Do not start your tape with an introduction or your name, address, phone number etc. Replay your tape before mailing it to insure that your song is on tape (we have received a number of blank tapes)."

If you would like an acknowledgement that we have received your entry, enclose a self addressed post card with the song title on it and a loose stamp. If you would like any information about the contest, please contact David Strattford (director of the contest) during office hours 10:00 a.m.—4:00 p.m. mountain time. If you call after hours and leave your name and number for us to call you back, we will do so if you leave your name, area code, phone number, and the best time to call. Note we will only return calls to out of town entrants if we can call collect. Good luck!!!"

*CAPAC COMPOSITION AWARDS,1240 Bay Street, Toronto, Ontario M5R 2C2 Canada. (416)924-4427. Administrator: Anita Provanznik. For composers. Annual award.
Purpose: "To encourage and support young Canadian composers in the development of their career in compositions."
Requirements: Send or call for application. Samples of work required with application. Deadline: September 30.
Awards: The Sir Ernest MacMillan Awards (for an orchestral composition for no less than 12 performers up to a full symphony orchestra), in the amount of $3,000; The William St. Clair Low Awards (for a chamber music composition written for a minimum of three performers up to a maximum of 12 performers), in the amount of $3,000; The Rodolphe Mathieu Awards (for solo or duet compositions written for one or two performers only), in the amount of $3,000; The Hugh Le Caine Awards (for compositions realized on tape with electronic means where the intended performance is through audio transmission), in the amount of $1,500; and The Godfrey Ridout Awards (for choral compositions written for mixed choir with no maximum number of voices, either a cappella or with accompaniment), in the amount of $1,500. Judged by jury of qualified professionals chosen by CAPAC.

COMPOSERS GUILD, 40 N. 100 W., Box 586, Farmington UT 84025. (801)451-2275. President: Ruth Gatrell. For songwriters and composers. "We are a nonprofit organization working to help the composer/songwriter. Each year we sponsor classes, workshops, seminars, a composition contest, and a performance in Composers Guild Spectacular."
Requirements: "Annual dues of $25 entitles members to reduced entry fee for contest plus invaluable information kit. Cassette demo and lead sheet required for *popular and jazz* entries only. No other restrictions." Deadline: August 31. Send for application.
Awards: $1,900 distributed among 8 categories: keyboard, popular, choral, vocal solo, arrangements, instrumental, jazz and children's music. The best-of-the-show (can be from any music category) is awarded $500. "Applicants judged by professional, usually head of university music department or firmly established producer of performed music."
Tips: "Be as professional as possible—clear, neat manuscript. Have music taped on cassette. Sloppy manuscripts will not be accepted by Composers Guild."

*DALTON LITTLE THEATRE/WORLD CARPETS NEW PLAY PROJECT, Box 841, Dalton GA 30722. (404)226-6618. Co-Ordinator: Bruce Mitchell. For musical playwrights. Annual award.
Purpose: "To produce on our stage a new American play or musical."
Requirements: "No more than 2 scripts per person. Submit from December through January 31."
Awards: "$400 plus travel to Dalton for opening weekend." Applications are by a committee.
Tips: "Submit legible copy. Musicals need music plus tape with songs performed."

*FS DRAMA AWARD, Box 5187, Bloomington IN 47402-5187; Box 606, Nashville IN 47448. President, Feedback Services: Mollie Ann Meserve. For musical and non-musical playwrights. Annual award.
Purpose: "To reward and promote excellence in dramatic writing. We wish only to reward talented playwrights for outstanding efforts. The award may be used toward any goal the receipent chooses."
Requirements: "Works must be previously unpublished and may not have been professionally produced. An entry fee of $10 must accompany each script entered." Deadline: October 31. Applicants should write for information or simply submit scripts with SASE and entry fee. "Only completed scripts are accepted. Scripts shoud be neatly typed (clear copies, no originals) and bound in secure folders. Professional script format is preferred but not required. Cassette tape of music must accompany musical entries."
Awards: FS Drama Award: $300, possible publication, plaque (four to five runners-up receive certificates, and all entrants receive a one-page critique. Also, all entries are considered for publication). Previous winners are welcome to submit new material to future FS Drama Award competitions. "Each entry receives two or three readings, and a one-page critique based on judges' reactions is prepared. Of four or five finalists, one winner is chosen. The critiques are returned to the entrants after the winner and runners-up are announced. Little Nashville Playwriting Award. "For unpublished works of full length plays, one-acts, translations, adaptations, children's plays and musicals. No limitations on subject matter or style, but authors or translations and adaptations of works not in public domain must provide per-

mission in writing from copyright holder. Deadline for postmark: Dec. 31. Prizes: $200 for winner; all entries considered for publication, staged readings. SASE required for return of script. Cassette.''
Tips: "We are interested in playwrights who understand and utilize the principles of their craft. Specifically, economy of words and clearly focused action tend to appeal. As far as subject matter and style are concerned, we have no limitations. Because we are publishers rather than producers, we do not have technical limitations of our own, but we do consider stageability as one criterion when judging the plays. In the past, we have not awarded the prize to a musical. The two main reasons for this: (1) songs that are repetitive or similar in rhythm, tempo, mood and word choices or seem derivaive of well-known music, and (2) characterization and clarity of action sacrificed to contrived music.''

*INDIE BULLETT-SONGWRITERS CONTEST,3318-E SSW Loop 323, Tyler TX 75701. For songwriters of country music. Annual award. Deadline for entry is June 30.
Requirements: Submit 1 country song in demo form on cassette with lyric sheet. Enclose SASE for acknowledgement of your entry. Send entry fee of $20 with your entry. Entries will be judged on lyric, tune and commercial value by Indie Bullet Staff to determine 20 finalists. The 20 finalists' demos will be copied on a master cassette (alphabetically by song title) and lyric sheets copied. The master cassette will be sent to all paid subscribers for voting of top songwriter song. Winner will be notified by Indie Bullet Magazine by certified mail within 30 days following voting deadline by subscribers.
Award: $500 cash award.

*INTERNATIONAL SOCIETY OF DRAMATISTS, Box 1310, Miami FL 33153. (305)756-8313. President: Andrew Delaplaine. For composers, musical playwrights and librettists. The purpose of these awards is to "reward excellence in the area of music theatre writing."
Adriatic Award: "Scripts may be unproduced or produced previously, but only *one* previous professional production is permitted. Staged readings, workshops, etc., are not counted against an entry." Deadline: November 1. Applicants should submit script with cassette tape of songs. $10,000 award granted annually.
Lincoln Memorial One-Act Contest: Open to "unproduced one-act music theatre work in any style, musical, opera, etc." Deadline: January 15. Applicants should submit script with cassette tape of songs. $250 award granted annually.
Perkins Playwriting Contest: Open to "unproduced musical or music theatre work, full-length, any style or subject." Deadline: December 6. Applicants should submit script with cassette tape of songs. $500 award granted annually.
Senior Award: Applicant "must be currently enrolled in college or university (graduate or undergraduate)." Open to "musical theatre work in any style, any length, and any dramatic medium." Deadline: May 1. Applicants should submit script with cassette tape of songs. $1,000 award granted annually.

*MID-SOUTH PLAYWRIGHTS CONTEST, 51 S. Cooper, Memphis TN 38104. (901)725-0776. Executive Director: Jackie Nichols. For musical playwrights. Annual award.
Requirements: Send script, tape, SASE. "Playwrights from the south will be given preference." Open to full-length, unproduced plays. Musicals must be fully arranged for the piano when received. Deadline: April 1.
Awards: Grants may be renewed. Applications judged by three readers.

MUSIC CITY SONG FESTIVAL, 5660 Nolensville Rd., Box 17999, Nashville TN 37217. (615)834-0027. Executive Director: Roy Sinkovich. Festival Coordinator: John A. Clark. "The 1988 Music City Song Festival will be the 9th annual song, vocal and lyric competition. The MCSF is the world's largest international competition for professionals and amateurs. The contest should begin in early 1988, with the entry deadline to be determined at a later date. We plan to announce our 1987 winners and kick off the 1988 MCSF with the distribution of our free, informative newspaper, *MCSF Soundmakers*. Readers can get on the newspaper mailing list by contacting MCSF at Box 17999, Nashville TN 37217 or (615)834-0027." Competition open to amateur and professional songwriters, vocalists and lyricists with categories of pop/top 40, MOR/easy listening, country, gospel, rock/R&B and novelty/miscellaneous. MCSF also offers a year-round evaluations servcice for songwriters and lyricists. Call or write for complete information.
Awards: Separate awards in all categories will be given for amateur and professional songwriting, lyric writing and amateur vocal performance. Prizes for a single award range from $50-5,000, with over $40,000 in cash, prizes and certificates to be awarded. Contest judged by active music industry professionals (publishers, association and record company executives, disc jockeys, promoters, recording artists and producers).
Tips: "Submit each song on a separate tape, but you may send all the tapes in one package and pay the entry fees with one check. A separate entry form must accompany each entry but the original blank form may be photocopied as many times as you wish. Written entries (lyric and lyric poem) should be type-

written or legibly handwritten on legal or letter sized paper and taped entries (amateur and professional song) should include a lyric sheet. All taped entries should present song so that words, music and vocalizaiton can be clearly heard and understood. Elaborateness of production is not a factor in the judging."

*NATIONAL INSTITUTE FOR MUSIC THEATER, Kennedy Center, Washington DC 20566. (202)965-2800. Program Director: Alexander L. Aldrich. For composers/lyricists/librettists of opera, musical comedy and experimental music theater.
Purpose: "To support outstanding artists in the early stages of their professional careers.
Requirements: Send for guidelines and deadline information. Further information will be given in *Opera News* and *Backstage*.
Awards: Monetary grants.
Tips: "When entering, give all information requested, write clearly and keep photocopies of everything."

NEW FOLK CONCERTS, Kerrville Music Foundation, Inc., Box 1466, Kerrville TX 78029. (512)257-3600. Contact: Rod Kennedy. Gives awards/grants to songwriters and composers. Annual award.
Requirements: Send two original, previously unpublished and unrecorded songs on cassette. Entry fee: $5 check or money order to Kerrville Music Foundation. Deadline: April.
Awards: "Six winners each receive $100 and are invited to the Kerrville Folk Festival the following weekend to perform a 20-minute set of their original material." Applications are judged on originality.
Tips: "Keep production simple."

OPERA-MUSICAL THEATER PROGRAM, National Endowment for the Arts, 1100 Pennsylvania Ave. NW, Washington DC 20506. (202)682-5447. Contact: Program Director or Assistant Director, Opera-Musical Theater Program. For composers, performing artists and/or musical playwrights. "The Opera-Musical Theater Program assists all forms of music theater generally involving voice, from experimental musical theater to operetta, from ethnic musical theater to classic musical comedy, from grand opera to still-developing forms. Grants are awarded to support professional opera-musical theater organizations that produce works of high artistic quality and of national or regional significance; regional touring; the creation, development, rehearsal, and production of new American works and/or the support of seldom-produced works; independent producers, artist-producers, and artistic associates; projects which contribute significantly to the development and future of the art; and national and regional service organizations."
Requirements: "Eligibility requirements and deadline dates vary from category to category. Applicants should send for guidelines and application. Samples of work are required with application. The grant is good up to one-year, then applicants/grantees must reapply. Upon receipt of the Opera-Musical Theater Program Guidelines, applicants must carefully review the sections labeled 'We Fund' and 'We Do Not Fund.' Applicants must then consult the general instructions for application procedures for their category. These instructions list what supporting material is required with the application. Applicants are advised not to send supporting materials separately from the applications. If an applicant has any questions or needs help in completing the application forms or other required materials, they should contact the Opera-Musical Theater Program staff. Late applications will be rejected. Incomplete applications are not likely to be funded. After the Opera-Musical Theater Program staff has checked the application for completeness, the appropriate Opera-Musical Theater Program Advisory Panel, a rotating committee of experts in the field, reviews them. Following panel review, the National Council on the Arts makes recommendations to the Chairman of the Arts Endowment for final decision."
Awards: Grants are awarded in six categories and may range from $5,000-300,000.

*PROCAN COMPOSERS' AWARDS, Sponsored by the Performing Rights Organization of Canada Limited, 41 Valleybrook Dr., Don Mills, Ontario M3B 2S6 Canada. (416)445-8700. Director, PR: Mrs. Nancy Gyokeres. For composers. Annual award.
Purpose: "To bring recognition to Canadian composers and publishers."
Requirements: Applicant must be Canadian citizen or landed immigrant. "Applicants must be affiliates of Performing Rights Organization of Canada Limited or not affiliated with a performing rights society." Deadline: spring. Send for application. Samples of work to be judged required with application. Send scores with or without tapes.
Awards: PROCAN Young Composers' Competition—$12,000 (Canadian) awarded annually. PROCAN Jazz Composers' Competition—$2,000 (Canadian) awarded annually. Applications judged by juries of composers.

*THE QUINTO MAGANINI AWARD IN COMPOSITION, % Norwalk Symphony Society, Inc., Box 174, Norwalk CT 06852. (203)454-2011. Contact: Dr. Richard Epstein. For composers.
Requirements: The competition is open to all American composers. Entries should be submitted

anonymously, with some identifying mark and appropriate return envelope and return postage. In an accompanying sealed envelope, composer should give name, address and brief resume. All entries to be postmarked no later than August 31. The composition is to be scored for standard symphonic orchestra, and should not exceed 15 minutes in length. Write for more information.

Awards: The recipient will receive a cash award of $2,000 and will have the composition performed in world premiere by the Norwalk Symphony Orchestra under the direction of Jesse Levine, Musical Director.

RICHARD RODGERS PRODUCTION AWARD, American Academy and Institute of Arts and Letters, 633 W. 155th St., New York NY 10032. (212)368-5900. Assistant to the Executive Director: Lydia Kaim. "The Richard Rodgers Production Award subsidizes a production by a nonprofit theater group in New York City of a work by composers and writers who are not already established in the field of musical theater. Development grants for staged readings may be given in lieu of the Production Award or in addition to it. The award is only for musicals—songs by themselves are not eligible." (Guidelines for this award may be obtained by sending an SASE to above address.)

SONGWRITERS ASSOCIATION OF WASHINGTON MID-ATLANTIC SONG CONTEST, Suite 632, 1377 K St. NW, Washington DC 20005. (202)682-7361. Contact: Director. Gives awards to songwriters and/or composers annually. "Contest is designed to afford *amateurs* the opportunity of receiving awards/exposure/feedback of critical nature in an environment of peer competition. Deadline is usually in the spring of the year. Applicants must send for application; rules and regulations explained—amateur status is most important requirement. Samples of work are required with application: cassette, entry form and 3 copies of lyrics.

Awards: "Awards usually include free recording time/tapes for First Prizes; Grand Prize has been recording time/air fare. Awards change each year." Awards must be used within one calendar year. "Applications are judged by a panel of three judges per category, for five levels. First level is Pass/Fail; 2nd is point-judged to determine Honorable Mention; 3rd is for top twenty entries; 4th is for top ten and determines First Place Winner; 5th is for the top winners in each category, arriving at the grand prize winner. Reduced entry fees are offered for SAW members. Membership also entitles one to a monthly newsletter and reduced rates for special events/seminars."

THE UNIVERSITY OF MICHIGAN MUSICAL THEATRE PROGRAM, The David B. Marshall Award, 911 N. University, Ann Arbor MI 48109. (313)763-5213. Contact: Associate Director. Musical theater contest. Gives 1 or more major award each year.

WORLD POPULAR SONG FESTIVAL, Yamaha Music Foundation, 3-24-22, Shimo Meguro, Meguro-ku, Tokyo, 153, Japan. Contact: Festival Committee.

Requirements: Entry must be an original song, which has never been published or performed in public before July 31, 1987. Application deadline is at end of June; Festival scheduled for end of October. For more information, please contact the Festival Committee by early June.

Awards: Awards include Grand Prize, Most Outstanding Performance Awards and Outstanding Song Awards. Cash award, certificate of honor and medallion are given to the winners.

Tips: "No matter which category has been entered, the deciding factors in selecting a winner are song quality and vocal interpretation."

*WYOMING COUNTRY MUSIC FOUNDATION ANNUAL SONGWRITING CONTEST, WCMF Sussex Route, Kaycee WY 82639. (307)738-2303 or 836-2015. Executive and Promotional Director: Helen Ullery or Floyd Haynes. For songwriters, composers and performers. Annual Award.

Purpose: "To promote and encourage upcoming talent both in songwriters and performing artists."

Requirements: Applicants can be from any geographical area. Deadline: April 20. Send for application (include SASE). Samples are not required.

Awards: Top ten country and gospel songs are sent to Nashville for judging.

Market conditions are constantly changing! If this is 1989 or later, buy the newest edition of Songwriter's Market at your favorite bookstore or order directly from Writer's Digest Books.

Publications of Interest

The importance of reading and researching cannot be overemphasized. Reading all kinds of materials is essential for creative, entrepreneurial people such as songwriters. Reading about music business is important—it only makes sense to research and learn as much as you can about the industry you want to be part of. Reading about other songwriters can be enlightening and encouraging. Reading inspirational materials can get you over an occasional "writer's block." And even reading novels and nonfiction can provide ideas for future song lyrics.

This section lists publications and is divided into two groups. The first lists periodicals that offer information about songwriting and the music industry in general. These publications contain articles about songwriters, publishers, record producers, trends in the industry, how-to pieces, information on new companies and tips on who in the industry may be looking for material.

Read what each editor has to say about the content of these periodicals. Some of them are of interest to musicians as well as songwriters, while others are aimed only at writers or people interested in a particular type of music (e.g., country, rock).

Most of the magazines listed can be purchased at newsstands. This gives you a chance to look them over before you subscribe, and decide if they will benefit you in your career. If you can't find a certain publication on the newsstand, write the publisher for more information. Ask if you can receive a complimentary issue, or even buy a single issue, of the newsletters or tip sheets before investing in a subscription.

The second part of this section lists books. Many of them answer questions about the process of writing songs, give detailed information about the industry itself, or tell interesting and inspiring stories about other songwriters who have "made it." If you can't find one of these books at your local library or bookstore, write the publisher whose name is given in the listing.

Periodicals

AMERICAN SONGWRITER, 5065 Lebanon Rd., Old Hickory TN 37138. (615)754-5200. Contact: Administrative Assistant. Bi-monthly magazine; 48-56 pages. "A magazine for and about songwriters and the songwriting industry. Major focus on country music. Designed for hobby as well as professional songwriters."

*AMI The Audio, Video, Music Guide,Suite 319., 2857 Derry Rd. E., Mississauga, Ontario L4T1A6 Canada. (416)671-3372. Publisher: Shelagh Rogers. Published twice annually. Price: $10 per book or subscription for one year is $18 for two issues. "AMI has over 80 categories neatly indexed into a high quality, convenient to use, perfect bound book. Our listings include names, addresses, phone numbers and many description lines on everything from radio staions to booking agencies and managers to concert halls. AMI has over 3,000 listings and is the most comprehensive source book available on Canada's audio, video, music and film industry."

BILLBOARD, (The International Newsweekly of Music and Home Entertainment), Billboard Publications, Inc., 1515 Broadway, New York NY 10036. (212)764-7300. Subscription address: Box 1413, Riverton NJ 08077. Senior Vice President: Ann Haire. Promotion Director: Greta Gentile. Weekly magazine; 100 pages. "*Billboard* documents the most recent developments in the international music and home entertainment business, every week." Includes record charts, industry information, and "the thousands of weekly events" that tell what is happening in the music and home entertainment business.

*CANADIAN BLUEGRASS REVIEW, Buttenham Enterprises, Box 143, Waterdown, Ontario L0R 2H0 Canada. (416)689-5861. Circulation Manager: Donna Butternham. Bimonthly magazine; 24 pages. "Promoting Canadian Bluegrass; the music, the musicians, the festivals, records, shows and book reviews."

THE CANADIAN COMPOSER/LE COMPOSITEUR CANADIEN, Creative Arts Company for Composers, Authors, and Publishers Association of Canada, Suite 303, 1240 Bay St., Toronto, Ontario M5R 2A7 Canada. Subscription Department. Editor: Richard Flohil. Published 10 times/year; 48 pages. "*The Canadian Composer* is a bilingual magazine for the members of CAPAC. Its articles are about members of the organization and aspects of the music business in Canada."

CANADIAN MUSICIAN, 832 Mt. Pleasant Rd., Toronto, Ontario M4P 2L3 Canada. (416)485-8284. Circulation Co-ordinator: Maria Ralley. Published 6 times per year; 75 pages. "Magazine for the contemporary amateur and professional musician. Emphasis is on popular music. *Canadian Musician* keeps songwriters up to date with the latest goings on in the Canadian music industry, with an emphasis on people, products, business, and featuring helpful columns for songwriters in each issue."

COUNTRY SONG ROUNDUP, Charlton Publications, Inc., Charlton Bldg., Derby CT 06418. Published monthly; 56 pages. An in-depth look at country music: the entertainers, songwriters and people behind the scenes. Contains lyrics to currently popular country songs and interviews with country artists, songwriters and disc jockeys.

THE DRAMATISTS GUILD QUARTERLY, 234 W. 44th St., New York NY 10036. Published quarterly; 64 pages. "The magazine is an intercom for the authors of stage musicals."

*HIT PARADER, Charlton Publications, Inc., Charlton Bldg., Derby CT 06418. Monthly magazine; 80 pages. Contains articles and interviews on rock music personalities, information about trends in the music industry and rock music in particular. Also rock song lyrics, record and book reviews, new product reviews, and reader mail.

*INDIE BULLET, Country Music Magazine/ISI Songwriter Newsletter, 3318-E SSW, Loop 323, Tyler TX 75701. (214)581-9945. Publisher/Editor: Roy L. Haws. Monthly; 68 pages. Estab. 1986. "Includes: interviews with superstars like Alabama, Johnny Cash, Jerry Lee Lewis, Merle Haggard and Willie Nelson. 'Hot' new act discoveries and artist spotlights of the future stars in country music. Guest articles and editorials pertaining to country music. Insider information in regard to 'What's really happening in country music today.' " Features a top 50 independent label country chart and includes names, addresses and phone numbers of labels in numbered positions.

MUSIC CITY NEWS, Suite 601, 50 Music Square W., Box 22975, Nashville TN 37202. Monthly country music publication focusing on the Nashville music scene; 40 pages. Circulation: 100,000. Host of the Music City News Country Awards and the National Songwriters Awards Show for songwriters, both nationwide television programs. Also publishes articles on Nashville songwriters. One songwriters special issue each year.

*MUSIC CITY TRAX FAX, (A songwriters guide to what's happening in Nashville), Quinton Q. Qualls, Jr., The Denny Music Group, 39 Music Sq. E., Nashville TN 37203. (615)256-3558. Editor/Publisher: Quinton Q. Qualls, Jr. Monthly magazine; 8 pages. Estab. 1986. "*Trax Fax* bridges the gap between the songwriter and the music industry here in Nashville by providing priveleged information to the songwriter. *Trax Fax* features key interviews with Nashville's top writers and producers plus the hottest tip information on who's recording, what they're looking for, and when they are recording. *Trax Fax* goes a step further by providing writers an outlet for their material. Any material we find acceptable will be pitched to the producer or artist by *Trax Fax's* professional songplugger."

MUSIC CONNECTION, Suite 201, 6640 Sunset Blvd., Hollywood CA 90028. (213)462-5772. Contact: Subscription Dept. Biweekly magazine; 48-62 pages. "*Music Connection Magazine* is a musicians'/songwriters' trade publication. Departments include a gig guide connecting musicians and songwriters with agents, producers, publishers and club owners; a free classified section; music personal ads; interviews with music industry executives and major artists; and articles on songwriting, publishing and the music business. We cover current news, stories and interviews with up-and-coming music business people as well as established industry executives and major artists." Subscription rate is $30 for one year/25 issues.

MUSIC MAKERS, The Sunday School Board of the Southern Baptist Convention, 127 9th Ave. N, Nashville TN 37234. (615)251-2000. Contact: Church Music Dept. Music Editor: Sheryl Davis Tallant. Quarterly magazine; 36 pages. Publishes "music for use by 1st, 2nd and 3rd graders in choir at church. Includes spiritual concept and musical concept songs, plus stories and musical activities."

*MUSIC OF THE SPHERES,Box 1751, Taos NM 87571. (505)758-0405. Editor: John Patrick Lamkin. Quarterly magazine; 55 pages. Estab. 1986. "A quarterly magazine of new age art and music. It has articles, interviews, news, resource information, etc. of interest to the artist, musician and lay person alike. It also has art, fiction and poetry."

MUSICIAN MAGAZINE, Billboard Publications, Inc., Box 701, Gloucester MA 01930. (617)281-3110. President: Gordon P. Baird. Executive Editor: Jonathan Baird. Monthly magazine; 100 pages. "*Musician* is a magazine for musicians and music afficionados in the rock, soul, and jazz fields. We provide an insightful look into the creative process through the artist's own words."

OPEN EARS, Compiled by Pat Luboff, Suite 780, 6381 Hollywood Blvd., Hollywood CA 90028. (213)463-7178. Contact: National Academy of Songwriters. Bi-monthly insert in the NAS *Songtalk Newsletter*; 4 pages (*Songtalk Newsletter* is 32 pages). "*Open Ears* is part of the *Songtalk Newsletter* published by the National Academy of Songwriters for NAS members. *Open Ears* is a tip sheet to let members know who is looking for material in the music industry. NAS membership is now $55/year."

SIGMA ALPHA IOTA QUARTERLY: PAN PIPES, Sigma Alpha Iota, National Music Fraternity, 2820 Webber St., Sarasota FL 33579. National Executive Offices: 4119 Rollins Ave., Des Moines, IA 50312. Editor: Margaret Maxwell. For musicians at undergraduate, graduate and professional levels. Magazine published 4 times/year (Fall, Winter, Spring and Summer); 24 pages except 48 page/Winter issue. "We cover articles with the emphasis on the American composer. The Winter issue is devoted to American Music and the American composers, with a section devoted to the latest publications of their music."

SING OUT! MAGAZINE, Box 1071, Easton PA 18044-1071. (215)253-8105. Contact: Subscription Department. Published quarterly; 108 pages. "*Sing Out!* is a folk music magazine dedicated to bringing its readers a diverse and entertaining selection of songs and information about traditional and contemporary folk music. We print about 20 songs and tunes in each issue, some are traditional, some are newly written; most are solicited, some are not. We print songs in lead sheet format: first verse and chorus with chords and complete lyrics. We publish many new songwriters. Best form of song submission is on cassette with lyric sheet."

SONG PLACEMENT GUIDE, Box 8827, Universal City CA 91608-0827. (213)850-3606. Contact: *Song Placement Guide*, Attention: M. Singer. Monthly newsletter; 2 pages. " A six-year old endorsed Los Angeles tipsheet for music publishers/songwriters. Includes monthly list of 14 contacts (producers, managers, A&R reps of recording acts), and 14-20 artists. In addition to inside information on who's looking for what material and where to submit, we provide an InnerView with an industry pro, or write a column to educate and inspire readers. Also small classified and news flash section."

*SONGWRITER MAGAZINE, International Songwriters Association Ltd., Limerick City, Ireland. (061)28837. Subscription Manager: William P. Miller. Estab. 1967. Quarterly magazine; number of pages varies. "A magazine for songwriters and music publishers, featuring exclusive interviews with top American and European writers and publishers, plus detailed listings of record labels, music publishers, and recording artists. Readers can avail of unlimited free advice, song assessment, song copyright and other services. Readers in 52 countries worldwide. Correspondence in English, French, Spanish and Italian."

TRUSTY TIPS FROM THE COLONEL, Trusty International, Rt. 1, Box 100, Nebo KY 42441. (502)249-3194. President: Elsie Childers. Monthly 1-page newsletter. "Producers and artists who need material contact us and we fill an 8½x11 sheet with names and addresses of people needing songs for recording sessions or shows and types of song material needed. Subscribers to our sheet have been placing their songs regularly through tips from our tip sheet. Sample copy for SASE and 25¢."

WASHINGTON INTERNATIONAL ARTS LETTER, Allied Business Consultants, Inc., Box 15240 or 325 Pennsylvania Ave. SE, Washington DC 20003. (202)328-1900. Founder: Daniel Millsaps, III. Publisher: Nancy A. Fandel. Magazine published 10 times/year; 8 pages. Individual rate $35/year; institution, $62/year. "WIAL concentrates on discovering new sources of funding for the arts and keeping up with policy changes in funding by governments, private foundations, and businesses which give out grants to institutions and individual creative and performing artists. In addition, we publish the Arts Patronage Series, which are directories where all information is under one cover and updated periodically. We are the major source of information about funding for the arts in the US. Songwriters and composers can get grants for their work through our information and keep informed about Congressional actions which affect their lives. Areas covered include vexatious problems of taxation, etc. as well as how to get money for projects."

YOUNG MUSICIANS, The Sunday School Board of the Southern Baptist Convention, 127 9th Ave. N., Nashville TN 37234. (615)251-2000. Contact: Church Music Dept. Music Editor: Sheryl Davis Tallant. Quarterly magazine; 52 pages. Publishes music for use by 4th, 5th and 6th graders in church choirs. Includes spiritual and musical concept songs and activities, plus music insert containing four or five anthems. "This is an excellent publication to which songwriters whose interests and skills lie in the area of composing for children may submit their original manuscripts."

Books

THE BILLBOARD BOOK OF NUMBER ONE HITS, by Fred Bronson. Published: 1985. 640 pages. Price: $14.95. "Fascinating trivia and complete chart information on every number one single from 1955 to 1985." Published by Watson-Guptill Publications, 1515 Broadway, New York NY 10036.

THE BILLBOARD BOOK OF TOP 40 HITS (1955 To The Present), by Joel Whitburn. Published: 1985. 528 pages. Price: $14.95. A definitive listing of all records making the Top 40 on *Billboard's* charts from 1955 to the present. Published by Watson-Guptill Publications, 1515 Broadway, New York NY 10036.

*THE CRAFT AND BUSINESS OF SONGWRITING, by John Braheny. Published by Writer's Digest Books, 1507 Dana Ave., Cincinnati OH 45207. 1-800-543-4644. Attention: Book Order. Published Fall 1987; 300 pages. Price: $19.95 hardcover. "A powerful, information-packed—and the most up-to-date—book about the songwriting industry that thoroughly covers all the creative and business aspects songwriters need to know to maximize their chances of success."

THE CRAFT OF LYRIC WRITING, by Sheila Davis. Published: 1985. 350 pages. Price: $18.95. Davis, a gold-record lyricist and member of the faculty of the New School illuminates the theory, principles and techniques that result in songs with timeless appeal. Drawing on the work of such illustrious lyricists of yesterday and today as Larry Hart, Ira Gershwin, Johnny Mercer, Rupert Holmes and Sting, Davis illustrates the song forms and analyzes the elements of craft that produce Grammy- and Oscar-winning songs. A reference work which defines and illustrates over 100 literary terms and devices. Published by Writer's Digest Books, 1507 Dana Ave., Cincinnati OH 45207.

THE ENCYCLOPEDIA OF THE MUSIC BUSINESS, Published: 1981. "A comprehensive reference work that explains in lucid terms all facets of the music industry including copyright law, music publishing, contracts, recording, production, manufacturing, radio, unions, trade associations, technology, piracy, and international practices. Over 450 entries cover in meticulous detail everything the songwriter needs to know to approach the music business intelligently and judiciously. Supplemented with photos, charts, diagrams and other illustrative material." Published by Harper & Row, 10 E. 53rd St., New York NY 10022.

*GETTING NOTICED, A Musician's Guide to Self-Promotion and Publicity, by James Gibson. Published by Writer's Digest Books, 1507 Dana Ave., Cincinnati OH 45207. 1-800-543-4644. Attention: Book Order. Published Fall 1987; 224 pages. Price: $12.95 paperback. "The first book written to help performing musicians create effective, yet inexpensive publicity materials, then use them to get noticed and make money with their music."

HOW TO OPEN DOORS IN THE MUSIC INDUSTRY—THE INDEPENDENT WAY, by Frank Fara/Patty Parker. Published: 1987. 110 pages. List price: $8.95; $10 mail order. Book written from the "viewpoint of an unpublished writer or writer/artist needing to know the ground rules for succeeding in today's marketplace. Topics covered include song pitching, record promotion, international music markets, importance of a studio producer, independent record labels and how they can promote artist masters, and how to find the right publisher or record label. Also, where to work from: home or a music center, and the most frequently asked questions and answers on royalties, production, record sales and publishing. Popular music myths dispelled." Published by Autumn Gold Publishing; distributed by Starfield Press, Box 3357, Shawnee KS 66203.

IF THEY ASK YOU, YOU CAN WRITE A SONG, by Al Kasha & Joel Hirschhorn. Published: 1979. 352 pages. Price: $12.95. The A-Zs of how to write songs from two Academy Award-winning songwriters. Published by Simon and Schuster, Inc., 1230 Avenue of the Americas, New York NY 10020.

INSIDE COUNTRY MUSIC, by Larry E. Wacholtz. Published: 1986. 256 pages. Price: $14.95. "A behind-the-scenes look at the Nashville music industry featuring interviews with top personalities and executives." Published by Watson-Guptill Publications, 1515 Broadway, New York NY 10036.

MAKING IT WITH MUSIC, by Kenny Rogers and Len Epand. Published: 1978. Price: $6.95. Practical information on forming a group and making it succeed: equipment, recording, touring, songwriting and taking care of your money. Published by Harper & Row, 10 E. 53rd St., New York NY 10022.

MORE ABOUT THIS BUSINESS OF MUSIC, by Sidney Shemel and M. William Krasilovsky. Published: 1982. 204 pages. Price: $14.95. A practical guide to five additional areas of the music industry not treated in *This Business of Music*: serious music, background music and transcriptions, tape and tape cartridges, production and sale of printed music, and live performances. Published by Billboard Publications, Inc., 1515 Broadway, New York NY 10036.

MUSIC DIRECTORY CANADA '88, available through Circulation Coordinaror: Maria Ralley. Published 1987; 500 pages. Price: $24.95. "Made up of 45 categories related to the music business in Canada, ranging from Acoustic Consultants, Artwork & Graphics, Consumer & Trade Shows, to Music Education, Music Writers, Photographers, Concert Venues, Nightclubs, and Music Television Programs. The directory is as easy to use as a dictionary. Categories and listings are alphabetically arranged, with Radio Stations and Recording Studios listed by province. The information contained in the listings is up-to-date and accurate, with specifics about each company, organization and artist." Edited by Ted Burley. Published by CM Books, 832 Mt. Pleasant Rd., Toronto, Ontario M4P 2L3 Canada. (416)485-1049.

*MUSICAL NOTES, by Carol Lucho-Burns. Published by Greenwood Press, 88 Post Rd., Greenwood CT 06881. (203)226-3571. Contact: Order Deptartment. Published June 1986; 560 pages. Price: $49.95. "A detailed reference work on the American musical theatre with in-depth synopsis, vocal types, orchestration requirements and artistic staff. Charts at the end include details of specific songs, awards, chronological list of productions. A must for musical directors at theatres, schools and involved in summer stock."

NOTES ON BROADWAY, by Al Kasha and Joel Hirschhorn. Published 1985; 352 pages. Price $22.95. "Songwriters Kasha and Hirschhorn interview 25 of Broadway's most well-known and admired song and music writers. Illustrated with 135 photographs from the songwriters' personal files, *Notes on Broadway* gives aspiring songwriters a glimpse into the makings of Broadway musicals. Readers learn how the composers find ideas for songs, where their greatest challenges lie, what makes a show a hit, and what they foresee in the future for musical Broadway. Fully indexed." Contact: Customer Service Department, Contemporary Books Inc., 180 N. Michigan Ave., Chicago IL 60601. (312)782-9181.

THE PLATINUM RAINBOW (How to Succeed in the Music Business Without Selling Your Soul). Updated 1982, 239 pages. Price: $9.95. "*The Platinum Rainbow*, by Grammy Award-winning record producer Bob Monaco and nationally syndicated music columnist James Riordan, gives you an inside look at the recording industry and tells you and how to think realistically in a business based on fantasy; how to promote yourself, how to get a manager, producer or agent; how to get free recording time, how to make a deal, how to recognize and record a hit song, how to be a session musician, how to kick your brother out of the band, how to put together the six key elements a record company looks for. There are quotes from some of the biggest names in pop music and a complete analysis of: The Song; The Studio; The Stage; Demo Or Master; Cutting A Record; Hooks And Arrangements; The Producer; The Engineer; The Budget; The Basic Track; Vocals; Overdubs; The Mix; The 24 Track Monster; Things You Can Hear But Can't See; The Deal; The Creative Businessman; The Music Attorney; The Manager, Agent, Promoter; The Artist As Vendor; Leverage, Clout And The Ladder; Getting A Job With A Record Company; Gigs; The Golden Reel To Reel And The Platinum Turntable; Staying Happy; Waiting To Be Discovered And Nine Other Popular Myths About The Music Business. Published by Swordsman Press, Suite 10, 15445 Ventura Blvd., Box 573, Sherman Oaks CA 1413.

SOME STRAIGHT TALK ABOUT THE MUSIC BUSINESS, by Mona Coxson. Published 1984; 200 pages. Price: $14.95. "The book's sixteen chapters show the musician how to make the right career choices, how to get started and progress, and how to reach goals and avoid pitfalls. Coxson, a freelance consultant writer and college music teacher, has taken nothing for granted and has outlined each step of the way so that every musician can avoid unnecessary mistakes." Published by C.M. Books. Contact: Maria Ralley, Circulation Coordinator, 832 Mt. Pleasant Rd., Toronto, Onatrio M4P 2L3 Canada. (416)485-1049.

THE SONGWRITER'S DEMO MANUAL AND SUCCESS GUIDE, by George Williams. Published 1984. 200 pages. Price: $12.95. "A practical guide to selling songs and landing a record contract. Teaches how to work in the studio to prepare songs for professional presentation. The author is a recording studio owner, jingle writer and producer with twenty years experience in the Los Angeles music business." Available from Music Business Books, Box 881, Virginia City NV 89440. (702)847-9053.

THE SONGWRITER'S GUIDE TO CHORDS AND PROGRESSIONS, by Joseph R. Lilore. Published: 1982. 48-page method/instruction book and 90 minute cassette. Price: $14.95. "Gives songwriters ideas for new and commercially proven chords and progressions. There are 58 individual song outlines with complete directions for creating thousands of songs in any style. The accompanying cassette allows songwriters to hear each new idea as it is introduced and help them compose anywhere, anytime." Available through Lionhead Publishing, Box 1272, Clifton NJ 07012 or at your local music store. Distributed by Warner Bros. Music, Inc. If0220.

THE SONGWRITER'S HANDBOOK, by Harvey Rachlin. Published: 1977. Starts with the basic components of a song and covers the entire spectrum of the profession—from the conception of an idea for a song to getting it recorded. Published by Funk & Wagnalls, 10 E. 53rd St., New York NY 10022.

THE SONGWRITER'S RHYMING DICTIONARY, by Sammy Cahn. Published: 1983. 224 pages. "Cahn gives his ingenious system for organizing end rhymes, and also insights from his own experience as a multi-award-winning legend among songwriters." Published by Facts on File Publications, 460 Park Ave. S., New York NY 10016.

SUCCESSFUL LYRIC WRITING, A STEP—BY-STEP COURSE AND WORKBOOK. Published: 1987. 250 pages. Price $15.95. Modelled after the author's noted 10-week course at the New York headquarters of The Songwriters Guild of America, this followup to *The Craft of Lyric Writing* presents the first complete textbook to writing professional lyrics for any genre—from country to cabaret. Davis guides the reader in taking each vital step from knowing to doing with 35 warmup exercises and 10 graduated assignments that develop writing skill as they reinforce theory. Features include: Special work pages for first-through-final drafts, a ten-point guideline to the use of figurative language, a primer on right-brain/left-brain writing, and a blueprint to form a songwriting workshop and conduct a professional critique. Published by Writer's Digest Books, 1507 Dana Ave., Cincinnati OH 45207.

THIS BUSINESS OF MUSIC, 5th Ed., by Sidney Shemel and M. William Krasilovsky. (Updated 1985). 640 pages. Price: $22.95. Edited by Paul Ackerman. "A practical guide to the music industry for publishers, songwriters, record companies, producers, artists and agents. A standard reference source to the business side of the music industry. Latest edition has information on the 1976 copyright changes and the emergence of video." Published by Billboard Publications, Inc., 1515 Broadway, New York NY 10036.

*WORDS TO RHYME WITH: A Rhyming Dictionary, by Willard Espy. Published 1986; 652 pages. Price $40. "The book includes 80,000 rhyming words, making it the most exhaustive and up-to-date resource yet published. Words are divided by sound into single, double and triple rhyme lists. Any songwriter would find this absolutely invaluable for writing lyrics. This author is one of the country's most popular wordsmiths, and has written such books as *Oh Thou Uncommon Noun*, *An Almanac of Words at Play*, and several works of non fiction." Published by Facts on File Publications, 460 Park Ave,. S., New York NY 10016.

*WRITTEN IN MY SOUL, Conversations with Rock's Great Songwriters, by Bill Flanagan. Revised edition published 1987 (paperback); 496 pages. Price $11.95. "Twenty-seven of rock's greatest songwriters—Dylan, Springsteen, Chuck Berry, Bono, Costello, Jagger, Knopfler, Sting, Townshend and others—talk about creating their music, in in-depth person interviews. Complete with photos. Bill Flanagan is executive editor of *Musician magazine*, and has written about popular music for the *Boston Globe*, *Chicago Tribune*, *Rolling Stone*. Published by Contemporary Books, Inc. 180 North Michigan Ave., Chicago IL 60601. (312)782-9181.

Appendix

The Business of Songwriting

Being creative is not enough to assure success as a songwriter. Understanding how the music industry works is a great advantage when you approach music executives who may themselves be more business-oriented than creative.

This section gives insights into the structure and operation of the music business as well as detailed information on demos, contracts, royalties, copyright and more.

The structure of the music business

Los Angeles, New York City and Nashville claim the largest concentrations of companies involved in the music business. There are, of course, companies in cities across the country which continue to make important contributions to today's music scene. But it's the decisions made in the three music centers that determine the direction the industry takes: which songs are published, which artists are signed to recording contracts and which records are released.

There are music centers outside the U.S. as well, like London and Toronto. Actually the United States represents less than half of the international music market. Most major record labels and distributing companies have important foreign affiliate offices. The potential success of foreign submissions should not be overlooked.

No matter which city you're dealing in, there are typical ways for a song to come to the attention of music professionals. Though you should employ whatever creative means you can to get your material heard, Chart 1 shows the usual routes a song can take to becoming published, recorded and released. Those routes include taking your songs to the A) artist, B) artist's manager, C) music publisher, D) independent record producer, or E) record company.

Choosing where to submit your songs depends on many things. No one fool-proof method for getting a song published or cut exists. Until you establish a relationship with specific professionals in the industry who appreciate your music and are willing to work with you on a regular basis, you should submit your material to as many appropriate contacts as you can find. If you know a recording artist (A) personally and have a song you think would suit him, approach the artist first. If he likes the song he will take it to his producer and, if the producer agrees, it will be scheduled for the artist's recording session.

If you don't know an artist personally, you might try to contact the artist's personal manager (B). You can also submit your songs to the independent record producer (D), or the A&R director of a record company (E). They are always looking for songs for the artists they produce. If they and their artists think your song is a hit, it will be recorded and released.

If the artist being produced is already signed to a recording contract, the song will be released on that record company's label. Many times, however, independent producers will pay for and produce a session by an artist who is not yet under contract to a recording company.

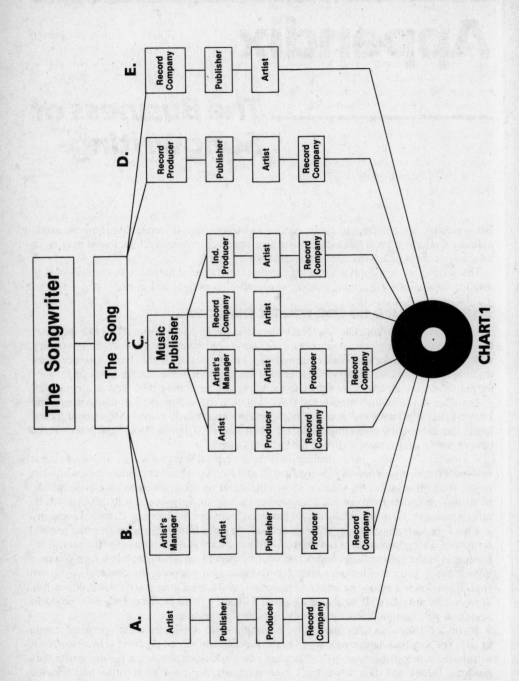

CHART 1

The producer then tries to sell the master tape of that session to the A&R directors of various recording companies. If he sells the master and negotiates a contract for the artist, the record is released on that label.

Songwriter's Market is the most comprehensive tool available for locating music professionals, but if you can't find the person or company you're looking for, there are other sources of information you can try. Check trade publications such as *Billboard* or *Cash Box*, available at most local libraries. These periodicals list new companies and the labels, producers and publishers for particular artists on the charts. There are several tip sheets available (see the Publications of Interest section) that name producers, managers and artists currently looking for new material. Album covers and record labels can be excellent sources of information. They give the name of the record company, producers, and usually the manager of the artist or group. Album liner notes can be revealing as well, telling how a song came to someone's attention or how a musical style evolved or what changes or new projects may lie ahead. Be creative in your research—any clue you uncover may help open some doors wide enough for you to get your foot in.

Whomever you approach in the music industry, somewhere along the line your song must be published. The advantage to approaching artists, producers, and record companies first, is that many of them have their own publishing companies. Since publishing means money if the song is successful and more money if it is recorded by other artists, a good song can have even greater appeal to artists, producers and record companies if the publishing is "open" (if the song has not yet been published).

There is much to be said, however, for taking your songs to a publisher (C) *first*. The publisher pitches your songs to artists, producers and A&R directors. Major publishers in music centers are regularly sent notification of who will be recording and when.

The greatest advantage, then, to approaching a music publisher first is his know-how and clout with the industry as a whole. You can concentrate on your business—writing songs—while the publisher works on getting cuts (recordings) of the songs you write. Some publishers do encourage their writers to do some pitching. That is not necessarily bad since it keeps the writer even closer to what's happening in the industry.

Any one (or a combination) of these ways of getting your song heard, published, recorded and released is the best way if it works for you. In this book are listed music publishers, record companies, record producers and managers with specifications on how to submit your material to each. The choice is yours.

Submitting your songs

Here are guidelines to help when submitting material to companies listed in this book:
- Read the listing and submit exactly what a company asks for and exactly how it asks that it be submitted.
- Listen to each demo before submitting to make sure the quality is satisfactory.
- Enclose a brief, neat cover letter of introduction. Indicate the types of songs you're submitting and recording artists you think they might suit. If you are a writer/artist looking for a record deal yourself, or pitching your demo for some reason other than for another artist to record your songs, you should say so in your letter. Be specific about your goals and intentions.
- Include typed or legibly printed lyric sheets. If requested, include a lead sheet. Place your name, address and phone number on each lead or lyric sheet.
- Neatly label each tape and tape box with your name, address, phone number and the names of songs on the tape in the sequence in which they appear.
- Keep a record of the date, the names of the songs and the company to which you are submitting.
- Include an SASE for the return of your material. Your return envelope to companies based in countries other than your own should contain an SAE and International Reply Coupons (IRC). Be certain the return envelope is large enough to accommodate your materials, and in-

clude sufficient postage for the weight of the package.
- Wrap and tie the package neatly and write or type the address and your return address so they are clearly visible. Your package is the first impression a company has of you and your songs, so neatness is very important.
- Mail First Class. Stamp or write "First Class Mail" on the package and on the SASE you enclose. Don't send by registered mail unless the listing specifically requests it. The recipient must interrupt his day to sign for it and many companies refuse all registered mail.

If you are writing to inquire about a company's current needs or to request permission to submit, your query letter should be neat (preferably typewritten), brief and pleasant. Explain the type of material you have and ask about their needs and current submissions policy.

To expedite a reply, you should enclose a self-addressed stamped postcard asking the information you need to know. Your typed questions (see Sample Reply Form) should be direct and easy for the receiver to answer. Don't forget to include a line for the respondent's name and title. Also remember to place the company's name and address in the upper left-hand space on the front of the postcard so you'll know which company it was you queried. Keep a record of queries, like tape submissions, for future reference.

Sample Reply Form

I would like to hear:

( ) "Name of Song" ( ) "Name of Song" ( ) "Name of Song"

I prefer:

( ) reel-to-reel ( ) cassette ( ) videocassette

( ) Beta ( ) VHS

With:

( ) lyric sheet ( ) lead sheet ( ) either ( ) both

( ) I am not looking for material at this time, try me later.

( ) I am not interested.

_____

Name   Title

Submitting in person

A trip to Los Angeles, New York or Nashville can give you an inside glimpse of the music business at work. If you've planned ahead, outlined your schedule, made appointments, and carefully prepared demos, you have only to reap the rewards of first-hand reaction to your material. Use the Geographic Index at the end of both the Music Publishers and Record Companies sections to contact, before you leave home, companies you'd like to visit.

Take several reel-to-reel and cassette copies and lyric sheets of each of your songs. More than one of the companies you visit may ask that you leave a copy with them. If the person who's reviewing material likes a song, he may want to play it for someone else. There's also a good chance the person you have the appointment with will have to cancel (expect that occasionally), but wants you to leave a copy of your songs so he can listen and contact you later. *Never* give someone the last or only copy of your material—if it is not returned to you, all the effort and money that went into your demo will be lost.

Many good songs have been rejected simply because they weren't deemed appropriate by one listener at one particular time, so don't take rejection personally. Realize that if one or two people didn't like your songs, they just could have been having a bad day. However, if there seems to be a consensus about your work, like the feel of the song wasn't quite right or a lyric needs work, you should probably give the advice some serious thought. Listen attentively to what the reviewers say and summarize their comments when you return home. That information will be invaluable as you continue to submit material to those people who now know you personally.

The money

The songwriter's payment comes in the form of royalty checks. Unless your contract stipulates you will receive a salary or advance on future royalties, you shouldn't expect your first money before three to six months after the song is released.

A look at the royalties chart (Chart 2) shows that the songwriter receives:
- Mechanical royalties from the sale of records and tapes.
- Performance royalties for airplay on radio and TV, plays on jukeboxes and live performances.
- Foreign royalties from foreign sub-publishers.
- Money for sheet music, choral arrangements and folio sales.

Mechanical royalties are due the songwriter and the publisher every time a recorded copy of your song is sold and not returned. You and the publisher split a portion of that revenue (50-50 is standard). At the time of this printing the statutory royalty (under the Compulsory License of the 1976 Copyright Act) is 5 cents for each record of a composition made and distributed. This rate is scheduled to increase biennially.

The money for mechanical royalties flows from retail record shops to the record company. The record company then pays the music publisher(s) 5¢ per song per record *sold*. You and the publisher split the 5¢ for your song less reasonable publisher's expenses. Reasonable publisher's expenses mean only the cost incurred for that particular song: phone calls, postage, etc.

The songwriter also shares 50-50 in any royalties the publisher receives from the sub-publisher who collects the publishing monies generated by your songs in the foreign music market.

The publisher pays you a share of the profit from the sale of sheet music, orchestrations, choral arrangements and folio sales. You earn a flat rate for each sheet of piano music sold and about 10-15% of the retail price of orchestrations, choral arrangements and folios. For more information see the Print Music Publishers section of this book.

Periodically (usually every six months) the publisher sends the songwriter a check that reflects his share of the mechanical royalties, foreign sub-publishing royalties, and sheet music, orchestrations, choral arrangements and folio sales.

Performance royalties are collected from radio and television stations, night clubs and jukeboxes by the performance rights organizations (ASCAP, BMI and SESAC). A published songwriter *must* belong to the same organization to which the publisher belongs. You'll notice that many publishers listed in this book have affiliate companies belonging to a different performance rights organization. That allows the publisher to deal with writers of more than one affiliation.

Each performance rights organization has its own unique method of determining how many times your song is performed during a given period. Their primary difference is *how* they make that determination. ASCAP monitors individual radio and television stations as well as concerts and clubs where music is performed. BMI uses logs sent them from radio and TV stations. SESAC uses the charts of the trade magazines (*Billboard* and *Cash Box*) to determine the popularity of individual songs. ASCAP charges a membership fee. BMI and SESAC do not.

The songwriter receives a statement of performances and a royalty check from his chosen performance rights organization quarterly. The amount earned depends on how many times the organization determined the song was performed.

ROYALTIES

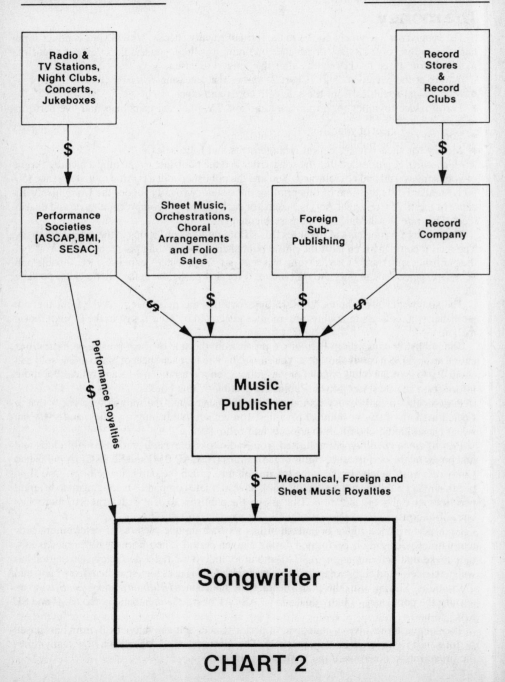

PERFORMANCE

MECHANICAL

Radio &
TV Stations,
Night Clubs,
Concerts,
Jukeboxes

Record
Stores
&
Record
Clubs

Performance
Societies
[ASCAP,BMI,
SESAC]

Sheet Music,
Orchestrations,
Choral
Arrangements
and Folio
Sales

Foreign
Sub-
Publishing

Record
Company

Performance Royalties

**Music
Publisher**

$ — Mechanical, Foreign and
Sheet Music Royalties

Songwriter

CHART 2

ASCAP, BMI and SESAC are highly professional and reputable friends of the songwriter. To look into the specific policies, procedures, benefits and requirements of each before joining, use the addresses given in our Organizations section to write them. Also, consult the chapter on these organizations in *This Business of Music* by Sidney Shemel and M. William Krasilovsky (Billboard Publications).

Copyright

One of the questions songwriters frequently ask is, "How do I protect my songs?" The answer is that since the new copyright law went into effect January 1, 1978, your songs are automatically copyrighted for life plus fifty years the moment you put them to paper or tape. To legally establish and protect your ownership of that copyright, however, you must register your songs. To register your song(s) send the following to the Register of Copyrights, Library of Congress, Washington DC 20559:

* a tape or lead sheet of your song(s). (Two copies must be deposited within three months of publication, but the publisher should help you with this when the time comes.)
* a government form PA, available on request from the Copyright Office or your local Federal Information Center.
* $10 registration fee for each song. It is possible to register a collection of songs at one time under a title such as "The John Doe Songbook" for one $10 fee. You will still have to register future songs separately.

It may take as long as four months before you receive your certificate of registration from the Copyright Office. However, since your songs are copyrighted from the moment of creation, you may use the copyright symbol immediately, affixing it to all written and taped copies of your songs. That is a "c" with a circle around it, followed by the date the song was written and your name (© 1988 by John Doe).

For more information, read Jay Collins' article on copyright in this appendix.

Record keeping

Your record keeping should include a list of income from royalty checks as well as expenses incurred as a result of your songwriting business: cost of tapes, demo sessions, office supplies, postage, traveling expenses, dues to songwriting organizations, class and workshop fees, and publications of interest. It's also advisable to open a checking account exclusively for your songwriting activities, not only to make record keeping easier, but to establish your identity as a business for tax purposes.

The royalties you receive will not reflect any tax or other mandatory deductions. It is the songwriter's responsibility to keep track of income and file the appropriate tax forms. Contact your local IRS office, or an accountant who serves music industry clients, for specific information.

Co-writing

A quick check of the charts in *Billboard* or *Cash Box* will show that collaboration is a very popular way of writing. Among the advantages are the instant feedback and criticism of your work. Another plus for collaboration is the talent that each songwriter brings to the task. And, each songwriter is actively pitching the song to industry contacts, increasing the song's exposure and chances for success.

Where do you find collaborators? Check the bulletin board at your local musician's union hall. If you don't see an advertisement that seems suitable for you, ask if you can post your own ad telling what type of writer you're looking for, what styles of music you're interested in, what experience you've had, what your goals are, etc. Other places to advertise are at music stores and college and university music departments, if they allow it.

Professional organizations like The National Academy of Songwriters in Los Angeles, The

Songwriters Guild in New York City and Los Angeles, and The Nashville Songwriters Association International (NSAI) in Nashville offer collaboration services. Check the Organizations section for addresses. Most local songwriter associations also provide names of potential collaborators. See if there's an organization in your area.

The rip offs

There are those who use the music business as a means to unfairly exploit others. Their offers are legal, but unethical; fairly typical, and easy to recognize. See Doug Thiele's article "Swimming Away from Songsharks" at the front of this book.

Alternatives

Alternatives a songwriter might consider other than the popular music market are advertising agencies, audiovisual firms, the theatre and writing songs for local and regional performers. Each is a specialized market requiring not only talent, but technical knowledge of that particular field.

The "total package" resulting from work in any of these alternative categories will most always result from the "team" efforts of several or many people other than yourself. Working with advertising agencies and audiovisual firms means not only getting involved with the company's production staff, but many times even with their clients. Likewise, the playwright may find himself working with the musical director, production staff and technical crew as his work is being staged. The personal manager and the artist (or group) will be part of that "team" when you're writing for local or regional performers.

Read the appropriate section introductions and Close-ups in this book for further information on these markets.

Use an up-to-date Market Directory!

Don't let your *Songwriter's Market* turn old on you.

You may be reluctant to give up this copy of *Songwriter's Market*. After all, you would never discard an old friend.

But resist the urge to hold onto an old *Songwriter's Market!* Like your first guitar or your favorite pair of jeans, the time will come when this copy of *Songwriter's Market* will have to be replaced.

In fact, if you're still using this *1988 Songwriter's Market* when the calendar reads 1989, your old friend isn't your best friend anymore. Many of the buyers listed here have moved or been promoted. Many of the addresses are now incorrect. Rates of pay have certainly changed, and even the record company's music needs are changed from last year.

You can't afford to use an out-of-date book to plan your marketing efforts. But there's an easy way for you to stay current—order the *1989 Songwriter's Market*. All you have to do is complete the attached post card and return it with your payment or charge card information. Best of all, we'll send you the 1989 edition at the 1988 price—just $16.95. The *1989 Songwriter's Market* will be published and ready for shipment in September 1988.

Make sure you have the most current marketing information—order the new edition of *Songwriter's Market* now.

(See other side for more books for songwriters)

To order, drop this postpaid card in the mail.

☐ YES! I want the most current edition of *Songwriter's Market*. Please send me the 1989 edition at the 1988 price—$16.95* (NOTE: *1989 Songwriter's Market* will be ready for shipment in September 1988.) #10004

☐ Also send me:

_____ (1148) The Craft of Lyric Writing, $18.95* (Available NOW)

_____ (10015) Successful Lyric Writing, $15.95* (Available October 1987)

_____ (10016) The Craft & Business of Songwriting, $19.95* (Available November 1987)

*Plus postage & handling: $2.00 for one book, 50¢ for each additional book. Ohio residents add 5½% sales tax.

☐ Payment enclosed (Slip this card and your payment into an envelope.)

☐ Charge my: ☐ Visa   ☐ MasterCard

Account #_____ Exp. Date_____

Signature_____

Name_____

Address_____

City_____ State_____ Zip_____

(This offer expires August 1, 1989.)

Writer's Digest Books

1507 Dana Avenue
Cincinnati, OH 45207

2478

More books for songwriters!

The Craft of Lyric Writing
by Sheila Davis
In this complete guide to writing words for and to music, successful lyricist, composer, and teacher Sheila Davis shows how to create lyrics with universal appeal, choose a song form, write strong openings, and avoid comon pitfalls.
350 pages/$18.95

NEW! Successful Lyric Writing: A Step-by-Step Course & Workbook
by Shelia Davis
A companion to *The Craft of Lyric Writing,* this hands-on course in writing professional lyrics includes warm-up exercises and specially-designed lyric writing assignments to stimulate your creativity and build writing skills.
224 pages/$15.95, paperback (Available October 1988)

NEW! The Craft & Business of Songwriting
by John Braheny
A powerful, information-packed book about the songwriting industry which thoroughly covers all the creative and business aspects you need to know to create and market artistically and commercially successful songs.
300 pages/$19.95

Use coupon on other side to order today!

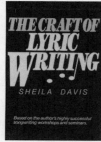

Copyright Protection

by Jay Collins, Ph.D.

Copyright is a protection provided by law for the works of authors. The current term of copyright is life of the last surviving author plus fifty years. Copyright ownership is immediate. As soon as the writer has fixed an original work of authorship in some tangible form it has statutory (federal) copyright protection and is owned by that author.

While copyright is a protection that is automatic, neophyte songwriters often confuse the protection itself with the copyright *notice* and the copyright *registration*. This article will follow the steps of writing and marketing a song, showing exactly when a song is considered created (and therefore protected), when it is necessary to provide notification of copyright ownership, and when the copyright must be officially registered with the U.S. Copyright Office.

Follow the song to the marketplace

- **Idea.** The songwriter gets an idea for a song. Ideas cannot be protected by copyright.
- **Title.** A title is decided upon. It also cannot be protected by copyright.
- **Song.** The song is developed by the writer who has both the music and words memorized. It is not yet protected by statutory copyright, even if the songwriter performs the song publicly.
- **Fixed.** The writer makes a tape recording of the song and/or writes it down in lead sheet form (including both music and words). When it has been fixed in one of these ways, the song is considered officially created and is protected by statutory copyright. Even if the songwriter has assistance in making a tape or lead sheet, he is considered the "author."

Exclusive rights

As the author of the song, the songwriter is the copyright owner and actually owns five exclusive rights at this point. They include the rights to:

1. Make copies or phonorecords
2. Make derivative works
3. Distribute copies or phonorecords
4. Perform publicly
5. Display publicly

The songwriter may at some point choose to authorize someone else to exercise one or more of those rights by granting a license. This is what happens when a songwriter signs a publishing contract, and that will be explained in more detail later. At this point in the songwriting process, it should be clear that the songwriter has created a song and owns these rights.

Since the song is now on a cassette and/or lead sheet (fixed), the songwriter will most probably want to pitch it to industry professionals. As you can see from the preceding list, it is your right as copyright owner to make copies or phonorecords of your song. Copies are material objects such as books, manuscripts, sheet music, film, videotape, or microfilm—materials from which a *work* can be perceived, reproduced, or otherwise communicated either directly or with the aid of a machine or device. Phonorecords are material objects such as audio tapes or phonograph disks (not including motion picture soundtracks or other audiovisual

Jay Collins is a professor of music business in the School of Business of Belmont College in Nashville, Tennessee. He is also President of the musicians' union in Nashville, Local 257 of the American Federation of Musicians. He has served as lecturer and consultant at songwriting workshops in various parts of the country.

works) from which the *sounds* can be perceived, reproduced or otherwise communicated either directly or with the aid of a machine or device. The phonorecord is the "container" that houses the sound recording. Before sending out any copies or phonorecords, you should provide *notice* of your copyright ownership. Notice for copies must include the symbol ©, the word "Copyright" or the abbreviation "Copr.," the year of first "publication" of the work, and the name of the copyright owner. Notice for phonorecords must include the symbol ℗, the year of first "publication" of the sound recording, and the name of the copyright owner.

Even though your song is protected by copyright automatically as soon as it is fixed, this notification proclaims your professionalism. It could also be very important later, if you ever needed legal proof that your material was stolen. You would have to show that the "thief" knew the song had been created by someone else (because copyright notification was clearly visible) and used the material anyway.

Proof

Even though a song has been fixed and notification of copyright ownership provided, it is still important for the writer to establish legal *proof* of ownership and the earliest possible date of the song's creation. There are several ways to achieve this—some methods are more effective than others, and you should be aware of all the options.

Poor man's copyright. This usually implies the mailing of a copy of the fixed version of the song to yourself in a sealed envelope or package that is kept unopened in a safe place in case the need for proof should ever arise. The postal date is relied upon in this instance for establishing the earliest possible date. This method has not proven to be reliable since a song thief could mail empty, unsealed envelopes to himself and later enclose songs that he might wish to "acquire" illegally.

Notarized copy. While this requires the preparation of written words and music, it is considered an effective way to establish the earliest possible date of the creation of the song. Take the song copy to a Notary Public and have it notarized. This will include the date and the signature of the Notary Public, and can also contain the writer's sworn statement that the song is his original work.

Registration service. Many songwriter organizations offer a service to their members, in which they will maintain a file of copies (or phonorecords) of songs, the name of the rightful author, and the date it was created (or at least the date it was first filed). The file for your song would be maintained for a specified length of time, for an agreed-upon fee.

Copyright registration. This is the best method of proof for establishing ownership of the song. Registration of copyright may occur at any time, but is *essential* before copyright infringement suits may be filed seeking statutory protection. Registration requires an application form (Form PA for copies or Form SR for sound recordings), a $10 fee, and one deposit copy. (Two deposit copies are required within three months of publication, should one of your registered songs later be published.)

To put it simply, registering your song with the U.S. Copyright Office gives you absolute legal proof of ownership of copyright and earliest possible date of creation. Your song will be assigned a registration number, different from any other registered song. You must have this legal proof if you ever wish to file suit for monetary damages.

Registration of a collection. It is also possible to register a collection of songs under one title (like "The John Q. Public Songbook") for one $10 registration fee. It provides the same excellent proof as registering songs independently and can save you money, but there are two slight drawbacks to this method. First, only the title of the *collection* will have a copyright registration number. If a publisher or someone happened to hear your song and be interested in it (and if your name were not on the demo or not known to the interested person for some reason), that person would not be able to locate you through the Copyright Office. He would not be able to find out who owned the copyright to that song, because the song title itself would not be registered.

Secondly, if a publisher wanted to sign a song that had been registered as a member of a collection, you would have to apply to the Copyright Office to change the registration on that one song (and transfer it to the publishing company's name). You would have to be careful not to give the publisher the copyright for your entire collection. Which brings us to the next step in the songwriting process.

Publication

Publication is the distribution of copies or phonorecords of a work to the public by sale or other transfer of ownership, or by rental, lease, or lending. The *offering* to distribute copies of phonorecords to a group of persons for purposes of further distribution, public performance or public display constitutes publication. Music publishers offer those services to a songwriter via a song contract.

The song contract is an assignment of exclusive rights to the publisher making the publisher eligible to function as the copyright owner by virtue of the contract provisions. What it means is that you are handing over your copyright to the publisher, and he will "administer" the copyright for the length of time you agree upon in your song contract.

If you had already registered the song in your name, the publisher would have to apply to the copyright office for a transfer of copyright registration. If you had registered the song as a member of a collection, the publisher would have to apply for a transfer of that song only, so that the copyright for that song would be registered in his name. While it sounds confusing, it is standard procedure. If a publisher is interested enough in one of your songs to offer you a contract, he will be interested in protecting the copyright, exercising professional caution in presenting the song to others in the industry, and prosecuting any infringement. If you had not previously registered the song, it would be necessary to do so at the time the song is published. The process would be a bit easier because the publisher could simply apply for registration in the publishing company's name.

It is possible for the copyright to revert back to the songwriter if certain terms of the song contract are not met by the publisher. [See Bob Leone's article on contracts in this Business Appendix.] It is also possible for a songwriter to recapture a song from the music publisher if proper notice is given not less than two years and not more than ten years of the termination date originally agreed upon in the song contract.

The importance of copyright

Of course, the process of songwriting goes on as the music publisher tries to secure commercial recordings of the song and find other uses for the song. The reason copyright is so important to the songwriter, is because it involves payment for his work. The songwriter's ultimate goal is to be paid a royalty for his original song (even though he may enjoy songwriting for artistic reasons). The songwriter's royalties are possible because of the rights obtained via copyright law.

It is important to realize that the U.S. Copyright Office is a record-keeping operation. It is not an enforcement agency. The responsibility for copyright enforcement is that of the copyright owner, who must sue for copyright infringement in order to collect for damages resulting from theft or illegal use of copyrighted songs. This does not mean beginning songwriters should feel paranoid about pitching songs in the industry ("I can't leave you a copy of my song to hear because I don't want to let any copies of it out of my posession"). Remember that song theft is rare, copyright protection is automatic, and legal proof of copyright is easy to obtain.

For free publications issued by the U.S. Copyright Office, write:

Information and Publications Section
LM-455, Copyright Office
Library of Congress
Washington DC 20559

Contracts

by Bob Leone

Maybe you never *really* thought it would happen. Oh, you knew it *could* happen, that some-day someone might like one or more of your songs enough to ask you to sign a contract. Now here you are, holding a contract in your hand, squinting at the percentages and dollar signs scattered throughout the lines of fine print. Your reaction, if you're like most never-before-published songwriters, is to panic. You ask yourself: Should I sign or shouldn't I? Is this a good contract or a bad one? Do I need an attorney?

The purpose of this article is to answer those questions and many others about contracts, to give you—the unpublished songwriter—all the information you need to make an informed decision when you're asked to sign a contract. The emphasis here will be on publishing con-tracts, in particular the "single song" contract, but other types of contracts with which a songwriter might be confronted will also be reviewed.

The "song sharks"

First of all, it is imperative that you be able to ascertain that you are dealing with a legiti-mate publisher, and not with what is unaffectionately referred to in the music business as a "song shark." As National Projects Director for The Songwriters Guild of America (SGA), I have heard from many unhappy, disillusioned songwriters who have paid hundreds, some-times thousands of dollars, to have lyrics reworded, melodies composed, and records made.

There are guidelines to help you determine the legitimacy of a publisher. The most impor-tant thing to remember is that no songwriter should ever have anything to do with a company that requires a fee to publish or record a song. Many of you, no doubt, have received literature through the mail, or have seen magazine ads offering to "set your poem to music" or "get your song recorded by a top artist."

The song shark never promises (not on paper, anyway) that your song will be played wide-ly, if at all. He has but one interest—to extract as much money from you, the writer, as he can. You won't find these companies listed on the *Billboard* or *Cash Box* charts as publishers of songs for top artists. Their track record is usually referred to only in one-sided, fast-moving conversations scattered with big names. Don't be intimidated by these name droppers. In-stead, ask for the names of songwriters and artists the publisher has actually done business with. Then check them out. (Read more about song sharks in the "Swimming Away from Songsharks" article in the front of this book.)

A legitimate publisher, producer, or record company, on the other hand, only takes a song in the expectation that it will make money for all concerned. This, of course, includes you, the writer.

The single song contract

What actually happens when you assign your song to a music publisher? It is important to realize that in signing a publishing contract you are not "selling" your song. Rather, you are assigning your rights to a particular song (or songs) to the publisher for a designated number of years. The contract, moreover, sets forth the royalties to be paid to you for various types of

Bob Leone *has been the National Projects Director for The Songwriters Guild of America since 1982. He is also a composer/keyboardist who has worked with such artists as Stevie Nicks, Patti Smith, Steve Van Zandt and Pam Johnson. He was principal writer and player for the RCA recording group Flame.*

song uses. (See the Copyright article in this Appendix for more information.)

An example of the "single song" contract is SGA's Popular Songwriters Contract. Prepared by SGA and its legal counsel, Linden and Deutsch, this contract represents what many music industry professionals believe to be the best minimum songwriter contract available.

SGA is not a union, but rather a voluntary association of songwriters (see their listings in the "Organizations" section of this book). Therefore, the SGA Contract is not a negotiated contract between publishers and the Guild. I strongly encourage all songwriters to request the Guild Contract whenever a publisher expresses an interest in their material. While not every publisher will grant you this contract, a large and ever-growing number of music publishers will do so if you request it. In those instances when a publisher refuses the Guild Contract (publishers have contracts of their own), the Guild will review and evaluate for its members, at no charge, whatever contract is offered by the publisher, and will advise how it measures up to the Guild Contract.

Songwriters who are not SGA members are strongly advised to retain an attorney who specializes in entertainment law to do a contract review before signing. Rates for such a service generally begin at around $100 per hour. If cost is a problem, contact Volunteer Lawyers for the Arts. (See their listing in the "Organizations" section of this book).

The basics

Those elements that a songwriter must consider when deciding whether a particular publishing contract should or should not be signed fall under at least one of three categories: basic, critical, and negotiable. The basic features of a contract include the name of the publisher, the name(s) of the writer(s), the title of the song to be assigned, and the date of the agreement. Also included among a contract's basic features is its purpose. It must be stated with clarity that the writer is assigning his song to the publisher for use throughout a specific territory (the United States, the world, or the universe, as the case may be) for a designated number of years. Also among the basic features is a statement by the writer to the effect that he or she is, in fact, the author of the song, that the song is original, and that rights to the song may be freely assigned to the publisher. While it is certainly expected that you will shop a song to more than one publisher at a time, you cannot assign exclusive rights to a song to more than one publisher at a time.

The critical and the negotiable

The critical aspects of a publishing contract are those which relate to payments, or royalties, to be made to the songwriter by the publisher for various types of uses of the song. These uses include commercial sound recordings; piano sheet music, song books and folios; arrangements (orchestral, vocal, band, and the like); concerts; synchronization with motion pictures; television, including pay-TV, cable, and video; radio broadcasting; and any uses not specifically set forth. The provisions for royalty payments, and the specific amounts for each of these song uses, must be set forth in the contract—and they are negotiable. This leads us to our third category of contract terms.

The negotiable elements of any contract are the most important ones. They are what make a contract great or horrendous, fair or unfair, acceptable or unacceptable. It is up to you to get the best deal that you can get, but remember that negotiation invariably means compromise. On the SGA contract, suggested royalty percentages are indicated. Anything less than these percentages are deemed by the Guild to be below generally accepted industry standards.

Another negotiable feature would be an advance on royalties. The amounts offered vary widely depending on your track record (chart success), or the impact the song has had on your publisher ("I haven't been able to get that hook out of my head!"). Generally, advances are in the $100 to $250 range. The publisher can recoup this sum by deducting the amount of the advance from your royalties, starting with the "mechanical" royalties. By definition, mechanical royalties are earned whenever records or tapes or print music are sold. If your publisher fails to obtain a release of a commercial sound recording of your song, or if he gets a release but it does not sell (and so fails to produce income), then you are not obliged to return the royalty advance. Under these circumstances, the advance is not recoupable.

Some publishers may attempt to deduct demo costs against future royalties, while others will take full responsibility for paying all demo costs.

The songwriter should receive no less than 50% of the gross receipts that the song earns in domestic royalties from mechanical reproductions, electronic transcriptions and synchronization licenses. The songwriter's 50% is called, quite appropriately, the "writer's share." The remaining 50% is referred to as the "publisher's share." When a publisher's share is 50%, it means that he has *all* the publishing, 100% of it.

In some instances, the songwriter may negotiate what is referred to as a "split publishing" deal. In such a situation, the publisher does not get all the publishing. Instead, he gets half the publishing, or 25% of the royalties, while the writer (if he is the sole writer) gets the remaining half of the publishing, in addition to his writer royalties—a total of 75% of the royalties earned by the song. Unless you have already had a hit song or two, do not expect a publisher to split publishing with you. Such a request from an unpublished songwriter almost inevitably gets rejected.

With respect to sheet music and arrangements, a good contract will provide for the writer to receive no less than 10% of the retail selling price. (See the "Print Music Publishers" section for more information.) In the SGA Contract, the greater the number of copies sold, the greater the songwriter's percentage, up to a maximum of 15% on copies in excess of 500,000.

Where your song is used in synchronization with sound motion pictures, your share should be equal to the publisher's share. The same is true when your song is being marketed in a country outside the United States.

A songwriter without a track record should not expect to get more, nor should he or she settle for less than what we have already outlined. As was previously mentioned, when you have achieved some chart success, you have earned the right to negotiate for larger percentages.

Be sure the contract is specific and clear with regard to how and when you will receive your royalty payments. Some publishers pay quarterly (four times a year, or once every three months), while others prefer to pay semi-annually (twice a year, or once every six months). Whatever the case, spell it out in the contract. Related to this is your right to inspect or audit your publisher's books. This right should exist for you or your accountant. The authority to audit your publisher's books is to be considered a critical feature of the contract, not a negotiable one. It should be part of any acceptable contract.

The performing rights organizations—ASCAP, BMI, and SESAC—pay the songwriter and publisher with separate checks. These performance royalties represent the money earned whenever a particular song or songs is played on radio, on television, or in concert. Both writer and publisher must belong to the same performing rights organization. SGA collects, on the writer's behalf, all royalties payable by the publisher according to the terms of the contract—which excludes performance royalties.

A good contract will also contain provisions that define whose responsibility it is to bring lawsuits against copyright infringers, and how the cost is to be handled. Furthermore, the contract should cover defending against lawsuits in the event that someone claims that your song infringes upon one of their copyrights. What this means, in essence, is that your song sounds an awful lot like someone else's.

Provision should also be made for arbitration in the event that a dispute develops between you and your publisher that the two of you simply cannot resolve.

A good contract places restrictions on the publisher's right to sell your song to another publisher. Unless a publisher's entire catalog of songs is being transferred or assigned to another publisher, the contract should provide for your prior written consent to the sale or transfer of your material to another publisher.

The final negotiable feature to be reviewed is the "reversion of rights" clause. Reversion means that for any one of a number of reasons specified in the contract, the contract is no longer binding and rights to the contracted song revert (return) to the songwriter. For example, if the contract stipulates that you or your accountant have the right to inspect your publisher's books (and, as pointed out earlier, it certainly should), and your publisher refuses to allow you to do so, then the contract is terminated and copyright ownership reverts to you. Another example: if your publisher transfers only your song, of all those in his catalog, to someone else without your permission, then again the contract terminates and you get back the rights to your song.

The most essential type of reversion is the one that occurs when a publisher fails to obtain a commercial sound recording of your song within a specified period of time. A song is not "published" merely because you have signed a contract assigning the rights to that song to a publisher. A song becomes a published song only when it is released on a commercial sound recording for sale to the general public. We recommend that a publisher be granted no more than one year to obtain a commercial sound recording of your song, after which time one of two things should happen. Either the song reverts to you, the writer; or, the publisher must pay you at least $250 for the right to extend this period.

As you can see, there are at least three negotiable features involved in any reversion of ownership for failure to publish; first, there is the initial time period; second, there is the amount of money to be paid to the writer for an extension of the initial period; and third, there is the amount of time stipulated for the extension (usually six months).

Something else to consider when negotiating a contract is how you feel about publisher rewriting. Unless you feel otherwise, specify that without your permission no changes can be made in your song (music, title, lyric, and so forth), or you may find yourself sharing royalties with someone you have never even met.

Lastly, under the Copyright Law, various uses of a song, such as sound recordings and arrangements, are considered "derivative works." Frequently, such derivative works have more of a monetary value than the original sheet music. Be sure to include a provision stipulating that when the contract terminates, the publisher loses all rights to such derivative works, as well as to the original version of the song.

Ultimately, you, the writer, must decide whether or not the contract offered to you is a fair and acceptable one. Do not make the mistake of thinking that any contract is better than no contract at all; if you do, you will very likely live to regret your decision. There are a lot of publishers out there, and they are all looking for material. After all, songs are the very lifeblood of the music industry. So shop around until you get a deal that meets at least your minimal expectations.

Other contracts

It should be noted that not all publishing contracts are of the "single song" variety. Some publishing companies will sign songwriters to exclusive contracts. In exchange for a weekly royalty advance, starting generally around $150, the rights to all the songs written by the writer within a specified time period (usually a year with a company option to renew for four more years) are assigned to that company. Exclusive contracts are usually offered only to songwriters who have shown genuine promise in the form of chart success.

Other types of contracts a songwriter might be asked to sign:

Artist/record company: The basic album deal (if such an animal really exists) is generally for a period of one year with a company option to renew the contract each year for a specified number of years (usually five). As a rule, you will be expected to record one album per year, but this can vary. The record company owns the masters that you record as an exclusive service for them. In return for this service, the artist can expect to receive an advance of several thousand dollars (or millions, depending on your "star status"), and a percentage of whatever money is earned from the sales of your records and tapes.

However, you will not receive any royalties until all of the money advanced to you has been recouped by the record company. Any money paid out to cover studio recording costs, producer fees, musician fees, touring (hotels, food, transportation, etc.) is paid by the artist from royalties.

Record company contracts are usually much more complex than publishing agreements, but look for many of the same rights that we discussed in relation to the latter: the right not to be assigned to another company without your written consent and the right to audit the company books are good examples. By all means, find yourself the very best entertainment lawyer available.

Artist/producer: This should involve a percentage, rather than a fee although, in some cases, both apply. Let me reiterate what I stated at the beginning of this article: *never* have anything to do with a company that charges a fee to publish or produce your songs. A typical production agreement allows a producer to produce your song, or a number of your songs, and to attempt to obtain a publishing or a recording contract, or both. Set forth in the contract is the period of time during which the producer does his shopping (one year is standard). As with publishers, the deal will be exclusive in that only he will be shopping your material during that time. If he gets you a deal, his share can be a piece of your publishing and record royalties and even a piece of your advance. It all depends, of course, on how the contract is negotiated.

Artist/manager: A standard management contract stipulates that, in exchange for personal career counseling, a personal manager takes a percentage of your earnings as an artist. The standard is 20%, but some managers take less, while others take more. Contracts usually run for one year.

Writer/writer: A collaboration agreement specifies each writer's share of royalties and control of copyright. Generally, each collaborator gets an equal share of royalties, and equal control of copyright, but provisions should be included to guide all parties involved in the event of the death of one of the writers.

International markets

You have probably noticed that a considerable number of foreign publishers and record companies appear in this edition of *Songwriter's Market*. You should be aware that the laws governing copyright, contracts, royalties, and so forth, can vary enormously from country to country. I will not discourage you from sending your material to these companies because many of them are highly competitive with regard to obtaining rights to songs written by American songwriters. And some of your material may actually be better suited to the European or Asian marketplace. If you consider signing a contract with an enthusiastic publisher from a country outside the United States, use the same criteria that we referred to earlier when making a decision as to the acceptability of the contract.

One final statement: never shop your songs until they have been copyrighted with the Register of Copyrights. Copyright forms can be obtained by writing to Register of Copyrights, Library of Congress, Washington DC 20559. Request "PA" forms.

Editor's Note: The Songwriters Guild of America will send the Popular Songwriters Contract to any interested songwriter upon request. Two copies of the contract will be sent at no charge. Additional copies cost 50¢ each.

Glossary

A&R Director. Record company executive in charge of the Artists and Repertoire Department who deals with new artists and songs and oversees coordinating the best material with a particular artist.

A/C. Adult contemporary.

ACM. Academy of Country Music.

Advance. Money paid to the songwriter or recording artist before regular royalty payments begin. Sometimes called "upfront" money, advances are deducted from royalties.

AFM. American Federation of Musicians. A union for musicians and arrangers.

AFTRA. American Federation of Television and Radio Artists.

AIMP. Association of Independent Music Publishers.

Airplay. The radio broadcast of a recording.

AOR. Album-oriented rock.

Arrangement. Adapting a composition for a performance or recording, with consideration for the melody, harmony, instrumentation, tempo, style, etc.

ASCAP. American Society of Composers, Authors and Publishers (a performing rights organization).

A-side. Side one of a single promoted by the record company to become a hit.

Assignment. Transfer of rights to a song from writer to publisher.

Audiovisual. Presentations using audio backup for visual material.

Bed. Prerecorded music used as background material in commercials.

Beta. ½" videocassette format.

BMA. Black Music Association.

BMI. Broadcast Music, Inc. (a performing rights organization).

B-side. Side two, or flip side, of a single promoted by a record company. Sometimes the B-side contains the same song as the A-side so there will be no confusion as to which song should receive airplay.

Booking agent. Solicits work and schedules performances for entertainers.

Business manager. Person who handles the financial aspects of artistic careers.

b/w. Backed with.

C&W. Country and western.

CAPAC. Composers, Authors & Publishers of Canada Ltd.

CARAS. Canadian Academy of Recording Arts and Sciences.

Catalog. The collected songs of one writer, or all songs handled by one publisher.

CCC. California Copyright Conference.

CD. Compact Disc.

Chart. The written arrangement of a song.

Charts. The weekly trade magazines' lists of the bestselling records.

CHR. Contemporary Hit Radio.

CIRPA. Canadian Independent Record Producers Association.

CMRRA. Canadian Musical Reproduction Rights Association.

CMA. Country Music Association.

CMPA. Church Music Publishers Association.

Collaborator. Person who works with another in a creative situation.

Compact disc. A small disk (about 4.7 inches in diameter) that is read by a laser beam in a CD player. On the disk, digitized music is housed in microscopic pits in an aluminum base.

Co-publish. Two or more parties own publishing rights to the same song.

Copyright. Legal protection given authors and composers for an original work.

Cover record. A new version of a previously recorded song.

CPM. Conference of Personal Managers.

CRIA. Canadian Recording Industry Association.

Crossover. A song that becomes popular in two or more musical styles (e.g. country and pop).

Cut. Any finished recording; a selection from an LP, or to record.

Demo. A recording of a song submitted as a demonstration of writer's or artist's skills.

Disc. A record.

Distributor. Sole marketing agent of a record in a particular area.

Donut. Jingle with singing at the beginning and end and only instrumental background in the middle.

Engineer. A specially trained individual who operates all studio recording equipment.

EP. Extended play record (usually 12") containing more selections than a standard single, but fewer than a standard LP.

Evergreen. Any song that remains popular year after year.

Exploit. To seek legitimate uses of a song for income.

FICAP. Federation of International Country Air Personalities.

Folio. A softcover collection of printed music prepared for sale.

GMA. Gospel Music Association.

Harry Fox Agency. Organization that collects mechanical royalties.

Hit. A song or record that achieves top 40 status.

Hook. A memorable "catch" phrase or melody line which is repeated in a song.

ILA. Independent Record Labels Association.

IMU. International Musicians Union.

ips. Inches per second; a speed designation for tape recording.

IRC. International Reply Coupon, available at most post offices and necessary for the return of materials sent out of the country.

IRMA. International Record Manufacturers Association.

Jingle. Usually a short verse set to music designed as a commercial message.

Label. Record company, or the "brand" name of the records it produces.

LASS. Los Angeles Songwriters Showcase.

Lead sheet. Written version (melody, chord symbols and lyric) of a song.

Leader. Plastic (non-recordable) tape at the beginning and between songs for ease in selection.

LP. Designation for long-playing record played at 33⅓ rpm.

Lyric sheet. A typed or written copy of a song's lyrics.

Market. A potential song or music buyer; also a demographic division of the record-buying public.

Master. Edited and mixed tape used in the production of records; a very high-quality recording.

MCA. Music Critics Association.

Mechanical right. The right to profit from the physical reproduction of a song.

Mechanical royalty. Money earned from record and tape sales.

MIEA. Music Industry Educators' Association.

Mix. To blend a multi-track recording into the desired balance of sound.

MOR. Middle of the road.

Ms. Manuscript.

Music jobber. A wholesale distributor of printed music.

Music publisher. A company that evaluates songs for commercial potential, finds artists to record them, finds other uses such as TV or film for the songs, collects income generated by the songs and protects copyrights from infringement.

NAIRD. National Association of Independent Record Distributors.

NARAS. National Academy of Recording Arts and Sciences.

NARM. National Association of Record Merchandisers.

NAS. National Academy of Songwriters, formerly Songwriters Resources and Services (SRS).

Needle-drop. Use of a prerecorded cut from a stock music house in an audiovisual soundtrack.

NMA. Nashville Music Assocation.

NMPA. National Music Publishers Association

NSAI. Nashville Songwriters Association International.

One-stop. A wholesale distributor of records (and sometimes videocasettes, blank tapes and record accessories), representing several manufacturers to record stores, retailers, and jukebox operators.

Payola. Dishonest payment to broadcasters in exchange for airplay.

Performing rights. A specific right granted by US copyright law that protects a composition from being publicly performed without the owner's permission.

Performing rights organization. An organization that collects income from the public performance of songs written by its members and then proportionally distributes this income to the individual copyright holder based on the number of performances of each song.

Personal manager. A person who represents artists, in numerous and varying ways, to develop and enhance their careers. Personal managers may negotiate contracts, hire and dismiss other agencies and personnel relating to the artist's career, screen offers and consult with prospective employers, review possible material, help with artist promotions, and perform many services.

Piracy. The unauthorized reproduction and selling of printed or recorded music.

Pitch. To attempt to sell a song by audition; the sales talk.

Playlist. List of songs that a radio station will play.

Plug. A favorable mention, broadcast or performance of a song. Also means to pitch a song.

Points. A negotiable percentage paid to producers and artists for records sold.

Press. To manufacture a record.

PROCAN. Performing Rights Organization of Canada Ltd.

Producer. Person who supervises every aspect of recording a song.

Product. Records, CDs and tapes available for sale.

Production company. Company that specializes in producing jingle packages for advertising agencies. May also refer to companies that specialize in audiovisual programs.

Professional manager. Member of a music publisher's staff who screens submitted material and tries to get the company's catalog of songs recorded.

Program director. Radio station employee who screens records and develops a playlist of songs that station will broadcast.

PRS. Performing Rights Society of England.

PSA. Public Service Announcement: a free broadcast "advertisement" for a non-profit service organization.

Public domain. Any composition with an expired, lapsed or invalid copyright.

Publish. To reproduce music in a saleable form and distribute to the public by sale or other transfer of ownership (rent, lease or lending).

Purchase license. Fee paid for music used from a stock music library.

Query. A letter of inquiry to a potential song buyer soliciting his interest.

R&B. Rhythm and blues.

Rack jobber. A wholesaler of records, tapes and accessories to retailers and mass-merchandisers not primarily in the record business (e.g. department stores).

Rate. The percentage of royalty as specified by contract.

Release. Any record issued by a record company.

Residuals. In advertising or television, payments to singers and musicians for subsequent use of music.

Rhythm machine. An electronic device that provides various tempos for use as background rhythm for other instruments or vocalists.

RIAA. Recording Industry Association of America.

Royalty. Percentage of money earned from the sale of records or use of a song.

SAE. Self-addressed envelope (with no postage attached).

SASE. Self-addressed stamped envelope.

Scratch track. Rough working tape demonstrating idea for a commercial.

Self-contained. A band or recording act that writes all their own material.

SESAC. A performing rights organization.

Shop. To pitch songs to a number of companies or publishers.

Showcase. A presentation of new artists or songs.

Single. 45 rpm record with only one song per side. A 12" single refers to a long version of one song on a 12" disc, usually used for dance music.

SIRMA. Small Independent Record Manufacturers Association.

Solicited. Songs or materials that have been requested.

Song shark. Person who deals with songwriters deceptively for his own profit.

The Songwriters Guild of America. Organization for songwriters, formerly called AGAC.

Soundtrack. The audio, including music and narration, of a film, videotape or audiovisual program.

Split publishing. To divide publishing rights between two or more publishers.

Staff writer. A salaried songwriter who writes exclusively for one publishing firm.

Standard. A song popular year after year; an evergreen.

Statutory royalty rate. The maximum payment for mechanical rights guaranteed by law that a record company must pay the songwriter and his publisher for each record or tape sold.

Stiff. The first recording of a song that commercially fails.

Subpublishing. Certain rights granted by a US publisher to a foreign publisher in exchange for promoting the US catalog in his territory.

Sweeten. To add new parts to existing recorded tracks to enhance the sound of a master recording.

Synchronization. Technique of timing a musical soundtrack to action on film or video.

Synchronization rights. Rights to use a composition in time-relation to action on film or video.

Tablature. A way of notating music for guitar, where six lines are used to represent the six strings of a guitar, rather than the traditional five lines of a music staff.

Take. Either an attempt to record a vocal or instrumental part, or an acceptable recording of a performance.

Track. Divisions of a recording tape (e.g., 24-track tape) that can be individually recorded in the studio, then mixed into a finished master.

Trades. Publications that cover the music industry.

U/C. Urban contemporary.

U-matic. ¾" professional videocassette format.

Unsolicited. Songs or materials that were not requested and are not expected.

VHS. ½" videocassette format.

Videocassette. Tape manufactured for video cassette recorder (VCR) that records and reproduces audiovisual programs.

Work. To pitch or shop a song.

Index

Anjoli Productions 277
Annual National Competition for New American Musicals, The 421
Another Ear Music 22, 123
Anthem Entertainment Group 23
Anthony Agency, Michael 277
Anti-Conscious Music 23
Antique Records 135
Apon Publishing Co. 23
Apon Record Company, Inc. 135, 213
Appropriate Productions 23, 213
April Recording Studios/Productions 214
Apsey Playwriting Competition, Ruby Lloyd 422
Arcade Music Co. 23
Arena Players Repertory Theatre 371
Arena Stage 372
Ariana Records 135
Ariola-Eurodisc GmbH 135
Aristo Music Associates, Inc. 277
Ark Record Co. 136
Arkansas State University—Beebe Campus 372
Arks Advertising and Marketing 329
Arminia Musikproduktion Erich Storz 136
Armstrong Advertising Agency, N. 329
Armstrong & Associates, Inc., Pat 277
Arpco Productions Ltd./Burnt Out Music (see Triple T/After Five 270)
Arrow Rock Lyceum Theatre 372
Ars Nova Management 23
Art Attack Records, Inc./Carte Blanche Records 136
Art Audio Publishing Company/Tight Hi-Fi Soul Music 24
Artasia Music Productions 214
Artel Videographics Corporation 329
Artists'/Heller Agency 278
Arts International 406
Arts Midwest/Regional Jazz Program 406
Arzee, Arcade and Clymax Records 214
Arzee Record Company 136
ASCAP Foundation Grants to Young Composers 422
ASCAP "Welcomes Songwriters" Series 416
Asheville Symphony Orchestra 394
Asolo State Theater 372
Associated Artists International (Holland) 24
Associated Artists Records International 136

Associated Music Productions 24
Astan Records 136, 214
Astrodisque Publishing 24
Atlanta Pops Orchestra 394
Atom Productions, Tom 214
Attic Publishing Group 24
Attic Records Ltd. 136
Attic Theatre 373
Attractions International 278
Audio Music Publishers 25
Audio-Visual Associates 346
Audiovisual Design Studios, Inc. 346
Austin Songwriters Group 406
Auteur Music 25
Avalon Records, Tapes, Compact Discs, Inc. 136
AVI Music Publishing Group (see Equinox Music, 48)
Avilo Music 25
Axbar Productions 25
Axbar Records 137
Azra Records 137
Aztec Productions 278
Azure Records 215

B
B. Sharp Music 25
B.C. Enterprises of Memphis Inc. 137
B.F.H.B. Audio Inc. 215
B.G. Productions 215
Baby Huey Music 26
Backstage Productions International 278
Bad Grammar Enterprises 215
Bad Grammar Music 26
Bagatelle Music Publishing Co. 26
Bagatelle Record Company 137
Bailey Entertainment Agency, Gary 278
Baker's Plays 373
Bal & Bal Music Publishing Co. 26
Bal Records 137, 215
Ball Communications, Inc. 346
Bam-Caruso Records 138
Banff Centre School of Fine Arts, The 373
Banjo Man Music, Inc. 26
Barkus Company, Inc., Ted 329
Barnard Management Services 278
Batzkall Productions, Inc., Bill 278
Bauers Music Productions, John 215
Bay Tone Music Publishing 26
Bay-Tone & Soul Set Records 138
BCP Strategy Creativity 329
Beals Advertising Agency 329
Bearsongs 27
Beau-Jim Agency, Inc., The 215

Beau-Jim Records, Inc. 138
Beautiful Day Music 27
Beckie Publishing Company, Inc. 27
Bee Bop Music 27
Bee Hive Jazz Records 138
Bee Ray Music 27
Beechwood Music 27
Beerger Productions, Norman 348
Bell Management, Willie 279
Bella Musica Tontraeger GmbH 138
Bellovin, Harvey 279
Belmont Records 138
Belzer/Candlewood Playhouse, Rick 373
Benedetti Music, Quint 27
Berandol Music Ltd. 27
Berandol Records 139
Berkshire Public Theatre 373
Bernard Enterprises, Inc., Hal 28, 216
Berns & Associates, Tom 330
Bernstein Music Publishing Co., M. 28
Bernstein Rein 330
Bernstein, Richard 216
Beth-Ridge Music Publishing Co. 28
Beverly Hills Music Publishing 139
Beverly Hills Music Publishing Division 28
BGM Records 139, 279
Big Bear Records 139, 216
Big Fish Music 28
Big "K" Music, Inc. 29
Big State Music Publishing 29
Big Wedge Music 29
Bigfork Summer Playhouse 374
Billboard 427
Billboard Book of Number One Hits, The 430
Billboard Book of Top 40 Hits, The 430
Billetdoux Music Publishing 29
Bing Advertising Co., Ralph 330
Birch Tree Group, Ltd. 123
Bird Booking Agency, J. 279
Birosik/Ready to Rock Productions, P.J. 216
Black Diamond Music Publishing & Production Group 216
Black Music Association 406
Black Stallion Country Publishing 29
Black Watch Productions 216
Black Watch Publishing Co. (see Post War Publishing Co. 91)
Blackheart Music 29
Blackwood Music Group, Mark 29, 217
Blade Agency 279
Blair Advertising, Inc. 330

Chacksfield Music/Eros Music, Frank 36
Chamber Orchestra of Albuquerque 395
Chameleon Music Group 147
Channel One Video Tape Inc. 349
Channell One Video 349
Chappell & Co. Pty Ltd. 36
Chapple Films, Inc. 349
Charles, Dick 282
Charlottetown Festival 375
Charta Records 147
Chartbound Music Publications Ltd. 36
Chase Music Productions, Co. 37
Chattahoochee Records 147
Cheavoria Music Co. 37
Chenoweth & Faulkner, Inc. 331
Cherie Music Co. 37
Cherry Lane Music Co., Inc. 124
Cherry Lane Music Publishing Co., Inc. 37
Chevis Publishing Corp 37
Chiat/Day Advertising 331
Chicago Shakespeare Company 375
Chip 'N' Dale Music Publishers, Inc. 37
Chris Music Publishing 38
Christian Image Agency 282
Chu Yeko Musical Foundation, The 38, 147
Ciano Publishing 38
Ciarus Music, Ltd. 147
Cicchetti, Lou 221
Cimirron/Rainbird Records, Inc. 147
Cine Design Films 349
Circa' 21 Dinner Playhouse 375
Circle in the Square Theatre 375
Circuit Rider Talent & Management Co. 282
Cisum Productions 221
City Publishing Co. 38
Clarus Music, Ltd. 38, 147
Classic Video, Inc. 349
Clay Pigeon Records 148
Clays Ferry Music Co. 39
Cleveland Play House, The 375
Clevere Musikverlag, R.D. 39
Clockwork Entertainment Management Agency 283
Cloudburst Records 148, 221
C-M-I Records/TTA Management 283
Coakley Heagerty 331
Coast Line Events/Shoreline Management 283
Coast to Coast Records 148
Cockpit in Court Summer Theatre 376
Cohn Music, Bruce 39
Collector Records 148, 221

Collins/Frantic Records, Michael 222
Colony/Studio Theatre Playhouse, The 376
Column One, Ltd., Music Group 39, 124
Comet Music Co. 39
Comma Records & Tapes 148
Communication Concept 283
Communications Concepts Inc 350
Communication Design Associates 350
Compo Record and Publishing Co. 148
Composers, Arrangers and Songwriters of Kansas 407
Composers Guild 407, 423
Compton Agency, Burt 283
Computer Music International Ltd. 39
Comstock Records Ltd. 148
Connecticut Songwriters Association 407
Contemporary Artist Management 283
Continental 222
Continental Communications Corp. 39
Continental Productions 350
Coons, Corker & Associates 332
Cooper Talent Agency, Robb 284
Copyright Management, Inc. 408
Cortland Repertory Theatre 376
Cosmotone Music 40
Cosmotone Records 149
Counterpart Creative Studios 149
Country Boys from Texas Music 40
Country Breeze Music 40
Country Charts 222
Country Classics Music Publishing Co. 40
Country International 149
Country Music Association, Inc. 408
Country Music Foundation of Colorado 408
Country Music Showcase International, Inc. 284, 408
Country Party Music 40
Country Showcase America 149
Country Song Roundup 428
Country Star Attractions 284
Country Star Internationals 149
Country Star Music 40
Country Star Productions 222
Courrier Records 150
Cousins Music 41
Covert Record Productions Inc. 222
Cowboy Junction Flea Market & Publishing Co. 41, 150, 222

Cowgirl Records 150
Craft and Business of Songwriting, The 430
Craft of Lyric Writing, The 430
Crash Productions 284
Creative Corps. 41
Creative Entertainment Corporation 41
Creative Horizons 376
Creative House Advertising 332
Creative Source Music 41
Creative Support Services 350
Creekside Music 42
Creole Music Ltd. 42, 124
Creole Records Ltd. 150
Creswell, Munsell, Fultz & Zirbel, Inc. 332
Cricket Theatre, The 377
Critique Records Inc. 150
Crosby Music Agency 284
Crosscurrents Management Group 285
Crusader Records and Tapes 223
Crystal Image Music 42
Crystal Ram Publishing 42
Csaky Communications, A.S. 350
CSB Kaminsky GmbH 43
CSB Records 151
C-SC Opera Workshop 416
CSK Management 285
Cude & Pickens Publishing 43
Curtiss Records 151
Cypress College Theater Arts Department 377
Czar Productions 350

D
D.S.M. Producers 43, 223, 351
Da Car Recording 151
Dalton Little Theatre/World Carpets New Play Project 423
Dalvanius 223
Dan The Man Productions 43, 151, 223
Dana Publishing Co. 43
Dark Cloud Music 43
DAS Communications, Ltd. 285
Dasher Communications 351
David City Publishing 43
David Music 44
Davike Music Co. 44, 124
Davis Advertising, Inc. 332
Davis, Mal 223
Dawn Productions 223, 285
Dawn Promotions and Agency, Ltd. 224
db Records 151
DC Community Orchestra Association 395
DD&B Studios Inc. 351
De Leeuw Ferguson Bashaw 332
De Miles Company, The Edward 285
De Walden Music International, Inc. 44

Other Books to Help You Make Money and the Most of Your Music Talent

The Craft & Business of Songwriting, by John Braheny—A powerful, information-packed (and the most up-to-date) book about the songwriting industry which thoroughly covers all the creative and business aspects that you need to know to maximize your chances of success. 300 pages/$19.95

The Craft of Lyric Writing, by Sheila Davis—Davis, a successful lyricist, composer, and teacher, shows how to create lyrics with universal appeal, choose a song form, write strong openings, and avoid common pitfalls. 350 pages/$18.95

Successful Lyric Writing: A Step-by-Step Course & Workbook, by Sheila Davis—A practical, self-contained lyric writing course, complete with exercises and lyric writing assignments designed to stimulate your creativity and build writing skills. 224 pages/$15.95, paperback

Getting Noticed: A Musician's Guide to Publicity & Self-Promotion, by James Gibson—Gibson helps performing musicians create effective, yet inexpensive publicity materials, then use them to *get noticed* and *make money* with their music. 224 pages/$12.95, paperback

How You Can Make $30,000 a Year as a Musician (Without a Record Contract), by James Gibson—Gibson shows you how to maximize your income by approaching music as a business and by sharing details on 100+ types of performing job opportunities. 197 pages/$9.95, paperback

Making Money Making Music (No Matter Where You Live), by James Dearing—Dearing shows you how to build a successful music career in any community—playing clubs, performing radio and TV jingles, operating a record studio, teaching, and selling lyrics through the mail. 305 pages/$12.95, paperback

A complete catalog of all Writer's Digest Books is available FREE by writing to the address shown below. To order books directly from the publisher, include $2.00 postage and handling for one book, 50¢ for each additional book. Allow 30 days for delivery.

Writer's Digest Books
1507 Dana Avenue
Cincinnati, Ohio 45207

Credit card orders call TOLL-FREE 1-800-543-4644 (Outside Ohio)
1-800-551-0884 (Ohio only)

Prices subject to change without notice

SERVICE AVAILABLE FROM WRITER'S DIGEST SCHOOL

Song Criticism Service: Songs are critiqued by a professional songwriter for $30/song. This is a thorough, objective critique of the strengths and weaknesses of your song, as well as an evaluation of its commercial potential. Your tape and lyric sheet will be returned, along with a 1- to 2-page personal letter from your critiquer. Maximum length: a 24-line lyric sheet or 10 minute tape. To use this service, please mail lyric sheet and/or cassette tape, along with check or money order and self-addressed stamped envelope to: Dept. SM, Writer's Digest Criticism Service, 1507 Dana Avenue, Cincinnati OH 45207. Or call 1-800-543-4958 for more information.

Demo Submission Checklist —————————

Before submitting your demos:

1. Create a clean, clear tape of your best songs

2. Record on one side of the tape only

3. Keep introductions short—no more than four bars in length

4. Re-wind the tape to the beginning

5. Prepare an attractive, professional-looking package

6. Include a typed cover letter, lyric sheet and cassette label

7. Only send a lead sheet, resume, photos, reviews or press clippings if requested